COMPLETE RELOADING GUIDE

JOHN E. TRAISTER
ROBERT J. TRAISTER

STOEGER PUBLISHING COMPANY

STOEGER PUBLISHING COMPANY
is a division of Benelli U.S.A.

Benelli U.S.A.
Vice President and General Manager:
Stephen Otway
Vice President of Brand Marketing and Communications:
Stephen McKelvain

Stoeger Publishing Company
President: Jeffrey K. Reh
Publisher: Jay Langston
Managing Editor: Harris J. Andrews
Design & Production Director: Cynthia T. Richardson
Photography Director: Alex Bowers
Imaging Specialist: William Graves
National Sales Manager: Jennifer Thomas
Special Accounts Manager: Julie Brownlee
Publishing Assistant: Christine Lawton
Administrative Assistant: Shannon McWilliams

© 1996, 2004
by John E. Traister and Robert J. Traister

All rights reserved. No part of this book may be reproduced or transmitted in any form or by any means, electronic or mechanical, including photocopying, recording, or by any information storage and retrieval system, without permission in writing from the Publisher.

Notice to the Reader: Publisher does not warrant or guarantee any of the products described herein or perform any independent analysis in connection with any of the product information contained herein. Publisher does not assume and expressly disclaims any obligation to obtain and include information other than that provided by the manufacturer.

The reader is expressly warned to consider and adopt all safety precautions that might be indicated by the activities described herein and to avoid all potential hazards. By following the instructions contained herein, the reader willingly assumes all risks in connection with such instructions.

The publisher makes no representations or warranties of any kind, including but not limited to, the warranties of fitness for a particular purpose or merchantability, nor are any such representations implied with respect to the material set forth herein, and the publisher takes no responsibility with respect to such material. The publisher shall not be liable for any special, consequential, or exemplary damages resulting, in whole or in part, from the reader's use of, or reliance upon, this material.

ISBN:0-88317-194-5 BK6194
Library of Congress Control number: 95-074754

Manufactured in the United States of America

Distributed to the book trade and to the sporting goods trade by:
Stoeger Industries, Stoeger Publishing Company
17603 Indian Head Highway, Suite 200
Accokeek, Maryland 20607-2501
www.stoegerbooks.com

Other Publications:
Shooter's Bible 2004 - 95th Edition
The World's Standard Firearms Reference Book
Gun Trader's Guide - 26th Edition
Complete Fully Illustrated Guide to Modern Firearms with Current Market Values
Elk Hunter's Bible
Shotgunning for Deer
Trailing the Hunter's Moon
Hunt Club Management Guide
The Turkey Hunter's Tool Kit: Shooting Savvy
Hunting Whitetails East & West
Archer's Bible
The Truth About Spring Turkey Hunting According to "Cuz"
The Whole Truth About Spring Turkey Hunting According to "Cuz"
Complete Book of Whitetail Hunting
Hunting and Shooting with the Modern Bow
The Ultimate in Rifle Accuracy
Advanced Black Powder Hunting
Hounds of the World
Labrador Retrievers
Hunting America's Wild Turkey
Taxidermy Guide
Cowboy Action Shooting
Great Shooters of the World
Sporting Collectibles
The Working Folding Knife
The Lore of Spices
Antique Guns
P-38 Automatic Pistol
The Walther Handgun Story
America's Great Gunmakers
Firearms Disassembly with Exploded Views
Rifle Guide
Gunsmithing at Home
Complete Guide to Modern Rifles
Complete Guide to Classic Rifles
FN Browning Armorer to the World
Modern Beretta Firearms
How to Buy & Sell Used Guns
Heckler & Koch: Armorers of the Free World
Spanish Handguns
The Handloader's Manual of Cartridge Conversions
Modern Sporting Rifle Cartridges
Complete Reloading Guide
Ultimate Bass Boats
Fishing Online: 1,000 Best Web Sites
Bassing Bible - 2004 Edition
The Flytier's Companion
Deceiving Trout
The Complete Book of Trout Fishing
The Complete Book of Flyfishing
Peter Dean's Guide to Fly-Tying
The Flytier's Manual
Flytier's Master Class
Handbook of Fly Tying
The Fly Fisherman's Entomological Pattern Book
The Legend of Harley-Davidson
The Legend of the Indian
Best of Harley-Davidson
Classic Bikes
Great Trucks
4X4 Vehicles
Fish & Shellfish Care & Cookery
Game Cookbook
Dress 'Em Out
Wild About Venison
Wild About Game Birds
Wild About Freshwater Fish
Wild About Waterfowl
The World's Best Catfish Cookbook

PREFACE

Perhaps the most eager firearm enthusiasts are the reloaders. Some refer to them as "handloaders," or just plain "loaders," but these people have probably done more for the development of the modern American rifle — and its cartridges — than any other single class of individual.

Reloading one's own ammunition may be classified as a hobby. However, it is a hobby that gives practical results. For those who shoot a lot, the cost of equipment and components is quickly recovered from savings derived over store-bought ammunition. If few shots are fired each year, the savings in reloading will probably not pay for the cost of equipment, but it produces results in other ways.

Reloading provides hunters with a means to load cartridges or shotshells for one gun that will serve the purpose of many guns. For example, let's assume that a hunter has one nice semiautomatic shotgun with a modified choke. He or she may have been thinking about having the gun modified to accept integral choke tubes — giving the convenience of switching chokes at will — merely by unscrewing one choke tube and screwing in another. However, the gun has been with the individual for many years, accruing more and more sentimental value with each hunting season. Does the owner really want to change the appearance of the gun — however slight — or worse, to take a chance on splitting the muzzle during the conversion? If the shotgun happens to be in the collector class, will the conversion lower its value as a collector's item?

The reloader can take this same shotgun, without any modifications whatsoever, and make it into a multipurpose shotgun for most of the owner's requirements. To obtain about a half degree of tighter choke, all that is required is to load the shells with a power-piston or a one-piece plastic wad that protects the shot as it travels down the barrel bore. The owner now has a shotgun with an improved-modified choke when using these loads. The gun may still not pattern tight enough for those ruffed grouse that get wilder as the season progresses and flush a good 35 yards out from the hunter and dogs or for shooting ducks over decoys. Switching to copper-plated shot in the owner's handloads should do the trick. The shotgun should now pattern close to a factory full choke using standard loads.

Reverting to the other end of the ladder, let's assume that the original modified choke is a little tight for those early-morning quail at the beginning of the season, when they hold well and seldom flush until the hunter walks up on them within 15 yards. The solution is simple! Merely insert cardboard dividers into the shot column while loading the shells, and the existing modified choke now becomes an "improved cylinder," when using these spreader reloads.

By the same token, centerfire rifle shooters have even greater latitude to diversify their rifle loads. Take, for example, the 90-year-old .30-06 cartridge. It's still one of the best ever developed for American hunting or combat. The reloader has the advantage of using bullet weights in this cartridge anywhere from 80 grains to 250 grains with all bullets striking a given point-of-aim at any given distance. Consequently, the reloading rifleman armed with such a weapon is equipped to tackle game from squirrel to brown bear. When loaded with solid bullets, this same rifle will do a fairly good job on Africa's tough-skin game like elephant, rhino, and Cape buffalo. It is not the ideal weapon for such work, nor is this cartridge recommended for such dangerous game, but in a pinch, it will get the job done if the right loads are used.

Despite modern technology, no two guns are alike. Pick two Sako Hunter rifles out of individual cartons, both the same caliber. Try these in a machine rest with standard factory ammunition, and some difference in accuracy will be noted.

Then experiment further. Try a few reloads. Use the same bullet, but raise or lower velocities. Use different kinds of powder. Soon a load will be found that will fit the individual rifle — one that will deliver much better accuracy than factory loads. Try this same load in the other rifle. While it may be better than the factory ammunition, it will probably not be as good as the first rifle for which the load was developed. This doesn't mean that the second Sako is not as accurate as the first. The load just has not been properly fitted to the second rifle.

Since the goal of all rifle loads should be accuracy, the serious reloader is in a position to obtain the best accuracy possible from any given rifle. Some shooters may seek power, but power without accuracy is next to useless, except perhaps for hunting dangerous game at extremely close range.

The benchrest clan is a group of shooters that spend much time and money trying to put several bullets through the same hole. These same people will quickly admit that while skill plays a big role in obtaining the smallest groups, the rifle and its fine-tuned reloads are more important. A serious benchrest shooter may experiment with hundreds of different loads before he or she finds the right one to fire the five shots at a match.

But don't expect perfect results the first time around. Just because this book, or any other book for that matter, recommends a given load, does not mean the load is going to give the same performance in every gun. This is another area where the reloader has the advantage — experimentation. A grain or two of powder, one way or the other, can make the difference between a poor, mediocre or excellent load. Consequently, the reloader should be encouraged to test each and every series of loads. (*See* Section V of this book.)

For target purposes, a reduced load is usually the best, and these loads can be obtained only by reloading. Factory ammunition loaded at maximum velocities is rarely as accurate as reloads loaded slightly under the maximum. Reduced loads also serve other purposes:

- Reduced loads are more economical.
- Firing reduced loads means a longer barrel life.
- More shots may be fired without tiring the shooter.

Perhaps it is desired to use a big-game rifle for varmint hunting. Factory ammunition for this rifle is more than likely loaded with tough bullets at moderate velocities to give good terminal performance on big game. Such bullets are subject to ricocheting when hitting rocks or even flat hard clay. When varmint hunting near populated areas, a ricochet could travel several hundred yards to cause damage to life and property. What is needed is a bullet that will explode readily on impact, loaded at the highest practical velocity in keeping with normal pressure levels. Develop the loads for accuracy and the rifle/load combination is all set to take care of all kinds of vermin.

Chapter 13 gives hundreds of loads for modern rifle cartridges to fit every purpose. The ultra high-velocity loads recommended for varmint hunting use bullets designed to blow up on impact. This means a clean kill, but what is more important, it eliminates ricochets.

The bullet diameter is another area of concern, especially when firing cast bullets. A variation of $\frac{1}{10,000}$ inch can make the difference between a load that gives fair accuracy and one that can drive tacks at 100 yards. The reloader with a bullet-casting outfit can obtain the exact size required by merely purchasing a smaller or larger bullet-sizing die. Then follow the instructions in Chapter 24 for perfect cast bullets that are designed to fit an individual rifle bore.

Perhaps the shooter has no interest in lead bullets. The velocities used in the shooter's rifles require jacketed bullets, yet none of the commercial varieties of bullets fit the shooter's needs exactly. Try swaging jacketed bullets as described in Chapter 25. Swaging dies can be made to any specification and can be designed to make almost any type of bullet imaginable.

Need to customize your handgun loads for taking care of snakes or collecting meat for the pot while big-game hunting? Chapter 11 sheds new light on shot loads in handguns.

Reloading should not be done in haste. Contrary to what some reloading manufacturers may advertise, the potential reloader must study the equipment, components and techniques carefully. Become thoroughly familiar with all necessary steps, and know the components used in individual loads. Powders, for example, have certain peculiar qualities. Use the powder designed for a particular type of cartridge and for given loads.

Develop practical loads. Until the reloader has gained plenty of experience and knowledge, he or she should be very conservative when experimenting with loads. Full-charge loads should not be attempted at first, nor should the reloader use powder and bullets not recommended for a given cartridge.

Always keep detailed records of reloading experiences, both pro and con. Even poor loads that develop during the testing should not be dismissed. Rather, record as much detail as possible. It may save making the same mistake later.

In summary, this book is a quick reference for those actively engaged in the field of reloading sporting ammunition of any type, a learning method for those starting this fascinating hobby and a refresher for those shooters with wide experience in the field.

The authors would like to thank the many manufacturers who generously contributed data, components, and illustrations for this book, and to those gun buffs, production personnel, and artists who so willingly and enthusiastically contributed their time and experience to this project. Without their help, there would be no book.

ACKNOWLEDGEMENT

The following list of contributors deserve a special bow of thanks for their untiring efforts in helping the authors in one way or another.

Randy Brooks
Barnes Bullets
P.O. Box 215
American Fork, UT 84003

Blount, Inc.
Sporting Equipment Division
2299 Snake River Avenue
Lewiston, ID 83501

CCI/Speer
P.O. Box 856
Lewiston, ID 83501

C. Keeler Chapman
Luray, VA 22835

Hercules Incorporated
Wilmington, DE 19894

Hodgdon
P.O. Box 2932
Shawnee Mission, KS 66201

Hornady Manufacturing Company
P.O. Box 1848
Grand Island, NE 68802

IMR Powder Company
Plattsburgh, NY 12901

John Karns
Martinsburg, WV 25401

Lyman Products Corporation
Route 147
Middlefield, CT 06455

Mayville Engineering Company, Inc.
715 South Street
Mayville, WI 53050

Nosler Bullets
Bend, OR 97709

Oehler Research, Inc.
P.O. Box 9135
Austin, TX 78766

Outers/Weaver
P.O. Box 39
Onalaska, WI 54650

RCBS
605 Oro Dam Blvd
Oroville, CA 95965

Sierra Bullets
1400 W. Henry Street
Sedalia, MO 65301

John B. Updike, III
Bentonville, VA 22610

Ruby R. Updike
Bentonville, VA 22610

ABOUT THE AUTHORS

John Traister has authored more than 100 different books, and continues to write at the rate of about three or four books per year. In 1978, he launched a gun-trading/gunsmithing business in his present home town of Bentonville, Virginia — and continued to write about the arms as well. Traister first found the need for reloading ammunition when he began collecting and shooting obsolete firearms for which no factory ammunition was available. Even a greater need arose when he began experimenting with wildcat cartridges and new cartridge designs. In lieu of a comprehensive reference such as ***Complete Reloading Guide***, Traister had to resort to notes and experimentation. Thus, it has taken over 30 years of planning, research, and experimentation to bring this comprehensive guide to its present form. Traister's research continues for the next enlarged, revised edition of this comprehensive reloading book.

Robert J. Traister began shooting at the age of 5 in Rockdale, Texas. His older brother, John, introduced him to the .22 rimfire and later to a 16-gauge shotgun (with a sizable portion of the shot removed to reduce recoil). In later years, he pursued careers in radio/television, computer programming, and writing, but he always found a way to combine these with his shooting and hunting interests. In recent years, he has been writing computer programs that directly address the shooting world and interfacing computer test equipment with the shooting bench. A Federally licensed gunsmith and gunbuilder, he has hunted bear in Canada, antelope in Wyoming, and elk in Colorado and Montana. Bob Traister has a particular appreciation of dangerous-game rifles and the "big" calibers designed for this pursuit. He has built several custom dangerous-game rifles that range from .378 Weatherby to the .510 Wells Magnum and .600 Nitro Express.

We respectfully dedicate this book to our uncle,

Charles Donovan Traister

1916 – 1996

who did much to get both of us started out right with firearms

CONTENTS

SECTION I
GENESES

Chapter 1

Introduction to Reloading

The subject of economy is a concern to many shooters. Authorities say that, to become thoroughly familiar with a rifle, hundreds of rounds should be fired through it yearly. With commercial centerfire ammunition costing anywhere from $.50 to $2 a round, this practice can become quite costly. Few people possess the means to do a fraction of the shooting they would really like to when using only factory loads. This is where reloading becomes relevant.

Upon firing a loaded cartridge, the case is almost as good as new and represents more than half the cost of the original cartridge. Primers, powder and bullets are easily replaced in the fired cases with a set of reloading tools, like those shown in Figure 1-1 on the next page. The cost of these components, even for the duplication of high-powered factory loads, is surprisingly low and represents a fraction of the price of the factory-loaded commercial cartridge. The smart reloader can save even more with reduced loads that are suited for smaller game and short-range target shooting.

If homespun cast bullets are used, centerfire cartridges can often be loaded at a cost close to that of .22 rimfire cartridges.

Reduced loads use only a small powder charge and, when used with cast bullets, thousands of rounds can be fired through any centerfire rifle without undue wear on the barrel. Full-powered, high-velocity loads, on the other hand, can wear out a barrel in fewer than 1,000 rounds if these high-powered rounds are fired rapidly.

It is recommended that shooters load for accuracy, using reduced loads for most shooting, and then use full-powered loads for hunting. Much money can be saved in ammunition costs, and the barrel will usually last longer. There is no need to load practice rounds at full power.

IMPROVED ACCURACY

As a rule, properly reloaded ammunition is more accurate than the average commercial cartridge. There are several reasons for this. Factory-loaded cartridges must be loaded to a definite standard; they must function properly in any arm chambered

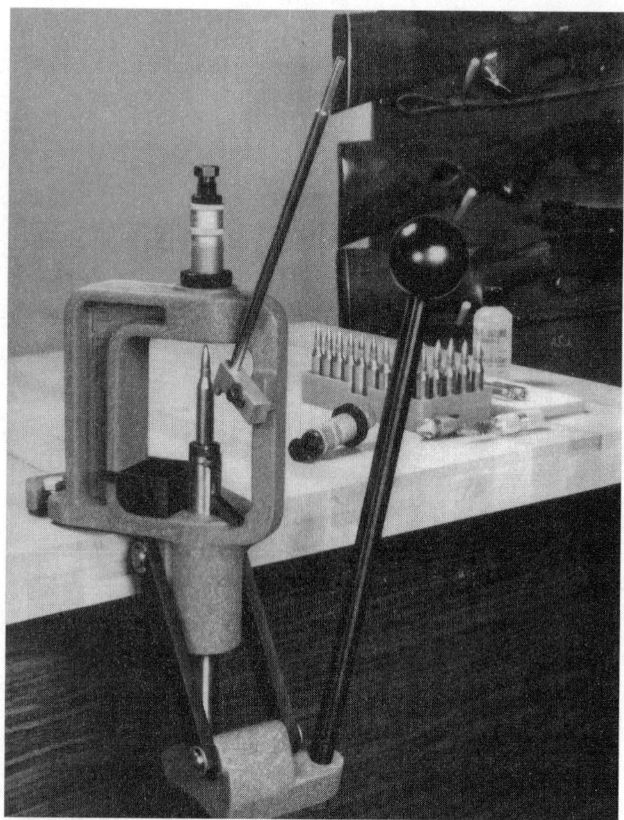

Figure 1-1: Basic reloading equipment . . . all you need to get started.

for a particular cartridge, whatever the model. The brass cartridge case must be small enough to freely enter the smallest chamber likely to be encountered. Factory-loaded cartridges must also be short enough to use in any action designed to receive the cartridge. Finally, factory-loaded cartridges must be loaded so they do not develop pressures that may prove dangerous in older firearms that are no longer made but are still used.

Handloaded cartridges adapted to an individual rifle or handgun are more accurate than average commercial cartridges because they were developed and reloaded for a particular firearm, not for just any gun of the same caliber. Cartridge cases once fired with full-power loads expand to fit exactly the chamber of the arm in which they were fired. A bullet carefully seated in an expanded case will be centered when placed in the chamber. This perfect centering increases accuracy. The overall length of the cartridge is also important. For best accuracy, the forward section of the bullet should nearly touch the rifling when the cartridge is chambered. Factory ammunition is of a standard length, but the reloaded ammunition may vary the depth of seating the bullet in the case to fit a particular rifle perfectly. In doing so, the shooter gets superior results.

When only factory ammunition is used, the greatest accuracy of a particular firearm is usually unknown to the user. The reason is that supposedly identical arms actually are not identical, and the bullet and powder charge that proves best in one will not be the most accurate in another. The handloader has a choice of bullets, powder and powder charges, as well as primers, etc. The handloader can then experiment with charges, powder and the like to develop cartridges that are more accurate in a certain firearm.

Every shooter is proud of a fine gun in his or her collection, but the pleasure derived from it depends largely upon its use. If the shooter does not reload, he or she has only commercial ammunition available. This centerfire ammunition, especially in calibers larger than .257, is designed primarily for big-game hunting. It is usually too powerful to use for smaller game. The recoil from it is usually excessive, and a good barrel will be worn out after firing 500 – 1,000 rounds. On the other hand, the handloader can take this same rifle, load it with reduced loads suitable for short-range work, load high-velocity loads with light bullets that will break up on impact rather than glance off rocks and other objects it might meet, and lower the recoil to a level in which more shots can be taken in any given period.

A shooter who reloads his or her own ammunition is not limited in the selection of components as is the person who is confined to using factory ammunition. The reloader has a large selection of bullets available, and an endless number of load combinations with each type. Many big-game rifles can be loaded with squib or reduced loads for small game, high-velocity light bullets that break up on impact for varmint hunting, or a full-charge load for the largest game animals — and all in the same rifle.

The reloader, however, must abide by certain ideas. A great deal of money can be spent on tools and components. The experienced reloader with the finest tools made can produce excellent ammunition. By the same token, the experienced reloader with the poorest tools on the market can also produce good ammunition. Some individuals, however, cannot adapt themselves for reloading. Reloading tool manufacturers cannot build the human element into the equipment. The practice takes knowledge of the techniques, concentration and patience. If any of these characteristics are lacking, the potential reloader should take steps to improve them or else take up another hobby.

In most cases, the beginner should buy only the minimum tools required to produce good reloads. Then as more knowledge is gained, the reloader will better understand the various features of all loading tools and he or she will then be more adept at making the correct selection. This is when more tools and equipment can be added to the loading bench. There is no perfect reloading tool on the market. In the better class of more expensive equipment, each model and style has certain features, advantages, and disadvantages over those of other models. It is up to the individual to make the final decision on the type and amount of equipment needed.

SAFETY

The question is often asked, "Is reloading dangerous?" If reasonable care is taken, it definitely is not. Few accidents occur during the process of reloading. Handloading ammunition does require care, but if the reloader reads a good handloading manual and the instructions that accompany the equipment before reloading, the practice is relatively safe . . . as safe as driving your car to the closest shopping mall, and probably safer than trying to cross any big-city street. Certain precautions, however, must be observed:

- Do not smoke while reloading.
- Wear eye protection.
- Do not manipulate reloading tools that would give a sharp or heavy blow to any primer. Primers normally will not explode from pressure alone. Handloaders should never attempt to prime cartridge cases that contain a powder charge. Prime only empty cases in good, clean condition.
- Before reloading, examine cartridge cases closely for defects. Give particular attention to the base of the case. Discard any cracked cases.
- When loading powder into cartridge cases, be extremely careful not to throw a double charge into the case. This is especially true when using fast-burning powder for reduced loads in rifle cases. A double charge can stretch the chamber and cause the rifle to explode. One good practice is to observe each case as the powder charge is thrown, noting the depth of a correct powder charge and comparing this to the others. If a charge does not look right, weigh it on an accurate powder scale just to be sure. Also, it is a good idea to check every tenth case when using a powder measure to make sure the measure is still throwing the correct charge.
- Always start a few grains under the maximum recommended charges and gradually work up, observing all signs of pressure during the process.

- Never exceed the maximum charges recommended by the reloading manuals.
- Do not continue to fire a lot of cartridges when signs of high pressure are present. Indications of excessive pressure are: undue recoil, difficult extraction of the fired case, and pierced primers or longitudinal streaks that appear on the body of the fired cartridge case.

Early in 1938, manufacturers of gun powders discontinued the release of reloading information. Several lawsuits were brought against the powder companies just prior to this time involving rifles being blown up using recommended loads by these manufacturers. The reason for these blowups apparently was due to reloaders using salvaged brass cases that had once been fired using mercuric primers. Even though the new Remington noncorrosive primers were used in the reloads, the cases that were once subjected to mercury were brittle and weak. Consequently, high pressures and cases previously fired with mercuric primers spells DANGER — resulting in many blown-up guns.

Mercuric primers have not been used for over 60 years, but every now and then a batch of these cases will turn up, especially when owners of obsolete firearms are searching for old brass to use in their rifles.

If there is any doubt about obsolete cartridge cases having been loaded with mercuric primers, do not use the cases. Cases for obsolete cartridges can normally be safely made using existing cases. *The Handloader's Manual of Cartridge Conversions* by John J. Donnelly, from Stoeger Publishing Company, is the most complete book available on the subject. Almost every obsolete cartridge case conceivable may be found in this book, and detailed instructions are given for making obsolete brass from existing cases.

Another problem facing reloaders is using obsolete reloading data. The reloading data published in the 1940s and 1950s were safe at the time of publication, but these same loads may cause higher-than-normal pressures if used with modern components, even with the same type of powder. For example, Lyman's 1948 *Ideal Hand Book* calls for a maximum load of 26.5 grains of No. 3031 powder behind a 117-grain jacketed bullet for the .25-35 Winchester cartridge. This load worked fine for years. Then about five years ago, I was testing a Winchester Model 94 carbine chambered for the .25-35, using this same load. On the first shot, I could feel the action "spring," and extraction was difficult. An examination of the case showed signs of abnormal pressure. At first, I thought my powder measure was off, so I pulled a few bullets and rechecked the charges before further firing. The powder charges were right on the button. I then reduced the load to 25 grains and gradually worked up, finding that 26 grains of 3031 was definitely maximum in this carbine — not 26.5 grains. I was using standard CCI large rifle primers.

I then searched through my assortment of old reloading components and found a partial box of 20-year-old Remington primers. These were tried in the same cases, with the same bullets and with the same powder. Pressures dropped at once, and the little carbine did, in fact, take the full 26.5-grain load with no signs of excessive pressure.

Further tests were made with other cartridges with similar results. Changes in primer composition are constantly being made by all primer manufacturers in an effort to provide a better product, and in most cases, a "hotter" primer means higher pressures. Therefore, use obsolete reloading data with caution. The new primers are better and hotter, resulting in higher pressures with loading data put out a couple of decades ago.

The original 4831 powder was discontinued several years ago, and was no longer available until Hodgdon came out with its new H4831. In the meantime, however, Du Pont introduced its IMR 4831, which caused higher pressures than the original. Many beginners and old-timers alike were

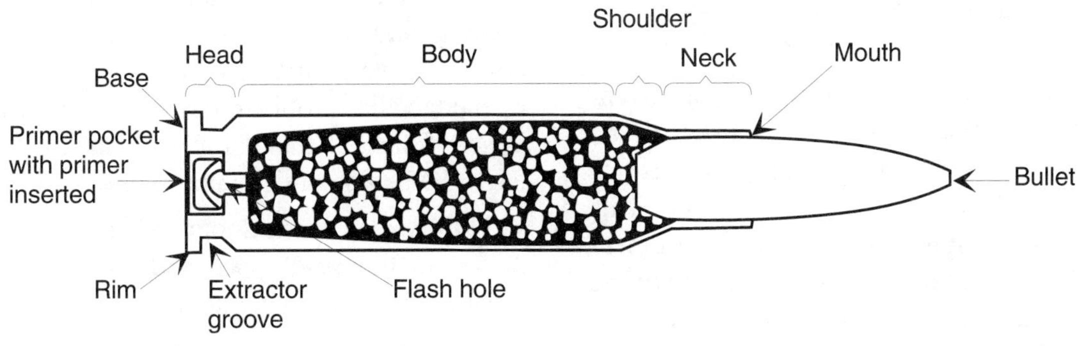

Figure 1-2: Cross-sectional view and nomenclature of a centerfire rifle cartridge.

experiencing sticking cases, blown primers, and similar signs of high pressures until the word finally got out that IMR 4831 was not like the original 4831 powder, and all loads must be reduced.

Never take any reloading data or instructions as gospel until you have investigated the information thoroughly. Typos are all too common, and the omission of a decimal point can mean disaster to the shooter.

Reloading manuals are compiled using tested loads and all data are checked and rechecked for accuracy. Every possible effort is made to print absolutely perfect data for the safety of the reloader. However, few manuals have been published without some errors.

Once the reloader has gained experience, he or she eventually acquires a special "reloader's sense" when reading loading data. If a load doesn't seem right, check the data with other manuals before proceeding. In fact, comparing loads for a specific cartridge, using several different manuals as references, is a good practice any time.

A PLACE TO RELOAD

Everyone who reloads centerfire ammunition for rifles, handguns or shotguns needs a special area to perform the various operations. When using hand reloading tools, the area can be the kitchen table, desk or even a footlocker. Many cartridges have been reloaded in camp, using the campfire as a source of heat for melting bullet-casting lead. However, the modern reloader — who uses a bench press — needs a sturdy bench to which the reloading tools are secured.

Reloading facilities will vary, but in general, a separate space should be provided that is out of the way of the usual household routine. It should be illuminated with approximately 100 to 150 foot-candles of well-diffused light; be provided with an adequate heating, cooling and ventilating system; and be of sufficient size to accommodate all the necessary reloading tools and components. If bullet casting is to be undertaken, steps must be taken to isolate the heat generated by bullet-casting furnaces from powder and primers, and also from any other combustible materials or components.

BASEMENT AREAS

Many reloading areas are located in the basement. This location has several advantages over other locations and the few drawbacks can usually be overcome. The chief advantages include:

- Easy to heat in winter.
- Cool in summer.
- It's out of the way of most family activities.

- It's quiet and can be made relatively soundproof from the living area.

The basement area also has several disadvantages, but as mentioned previously, most can be overcome. The majority of basement areas (as finished by the builder) are poorly illuminated. This gives a dark, dingy appearance. So, if the basement is the area chosen for the shop location, one of the first projects should be the installation of adequate lighting. Fluorescent lighting fixtures are ideal. However, if an acoustical T-bar ceiling is used, you may want to go with recessed fixtures — either incandescent or fluorescent.

One of the major disadvantages of a basement is dampness, which, of course, creates rust problems. To overcome this problem, epoxy waterproofing may be applied to basement walls from the inside and then foam insulation boards can be used to insulate basement walls and check dampness. A good dehumidifier is added insurance.

Flooding is another problem with some basements that can be a disaster. However, if the home owner grades all slopes away from basement walls, repairs all gutters and downspouts and installs a good sump pump, the chance of basement flooding is greatly reduced.

ATTIC AREAS

If dampness is a severe problem in the basement, the attic is another possibility. However, attics are usually hot in summer, cold in winter and short on head room, but improvements are possible.

First of all, fiberglass-insulation batts installed in the walls, roof and floor will help to keep a more controlled, comfortable temperature and muffle noises. An attic ventilating fan will reduce attic temperatures considerably as will the installation of several windows if there are none.

If the living area of the home is air-conditioned, it is usually possible to route ductwork to the attic area. This ductwork should be provided with a manual or automatic cutoff damper so that attic cooling may be turned ON and OFF at will; that is, an hour or so before using the attic, the damper is opened to allow cool air to flow into the attic space. When finished, the damper is shut off to save energy when the attic is not in use.

Tightly sealed attic doors will also help retain the noises in the attic space and cut down on dust escaping into the living area.

GARAGE AREAS

An enclosed garage is an excellent place to locate the reloading bench. Although garages are often drafty and hard to heat in winter, they can be made into excellent reloading shops that offer advantages over other areas in the home. First of all, a reloading bench in the garage allows the reloader to work into the wee hours of the morning without disturbing anyone in the home. You don't have to worry about fumes from lead-melting furnaces smelling up the home and, if you are faced with leaving a temporary mess, no one is going to care.

RELOADING BENCHES

The size of the available area will dictate the maximum dimensions of a reloading bench. In general, a reloading bench should be from 24″ to 30″ wide and at least 4′ long. Don't skimp on the length, however, because you will soon find that there is really no such thing as too much bench space.

The height of the workbench will vary depending on the height of the reloader. The average reloading-bench height is about 33½″, but they run anywhere from 30 to 35 inches. Above all, the bench must be sturdy and firm. You cannot produce the best reloads if the bench moves every time the press handle is pulled or a cartridge case is being trimmed to size. Therefore, the bench should be amply reinforced, and legs and top should be made of heavy timber.

An exploded view of one type of simple-to-construct reloading bench is shown in Figure 1-3. Although the bench legs are constructed of 2×4s, the plywood bracing makes it very sturdy.

Refer to the drawing (Figure 1-3) and note that the frame is made of 2×4s, solidly interlocked and

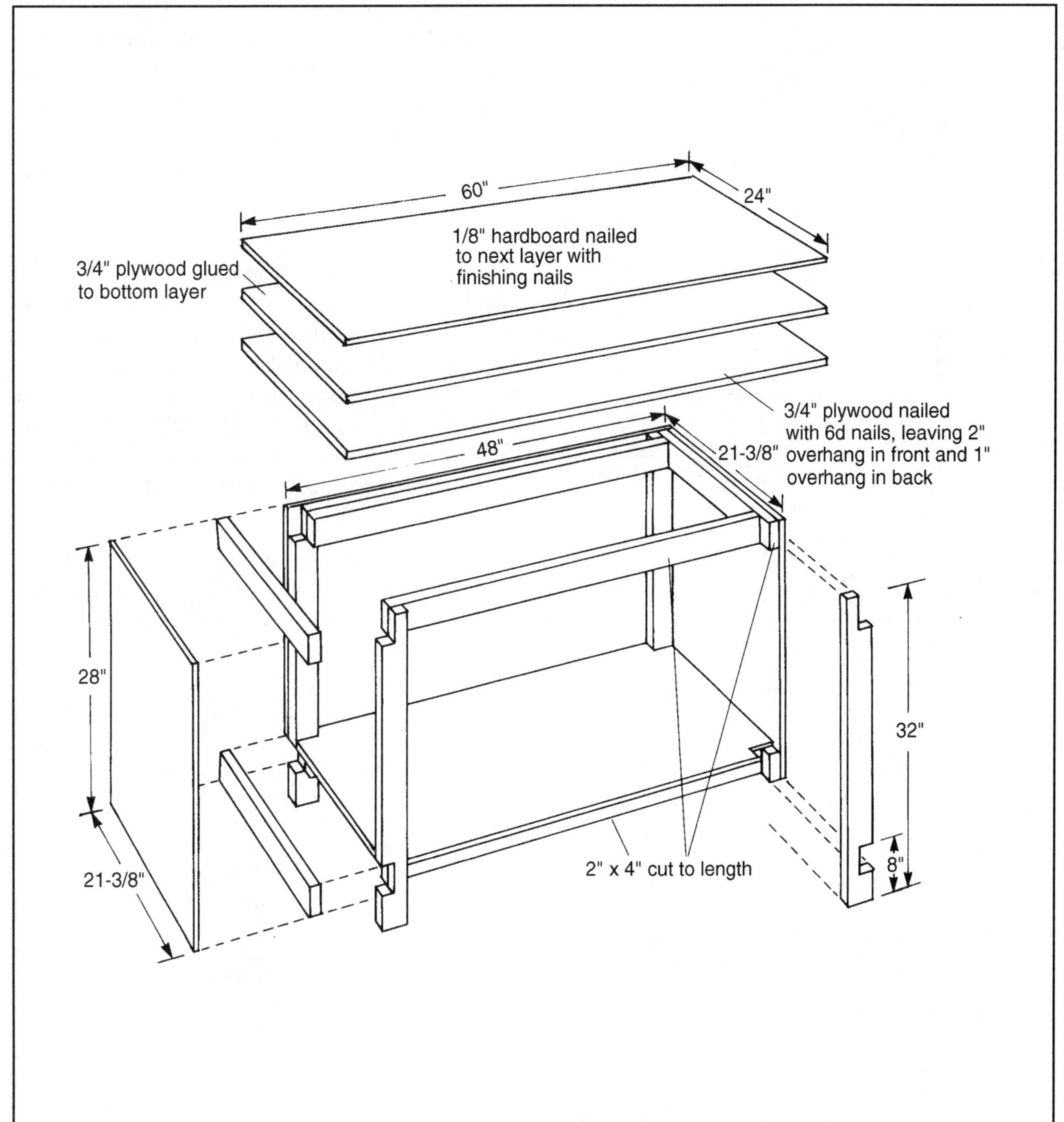

Figure 1-3: Exploded view of an inexpensive reloading bench that can be built with hand tools.

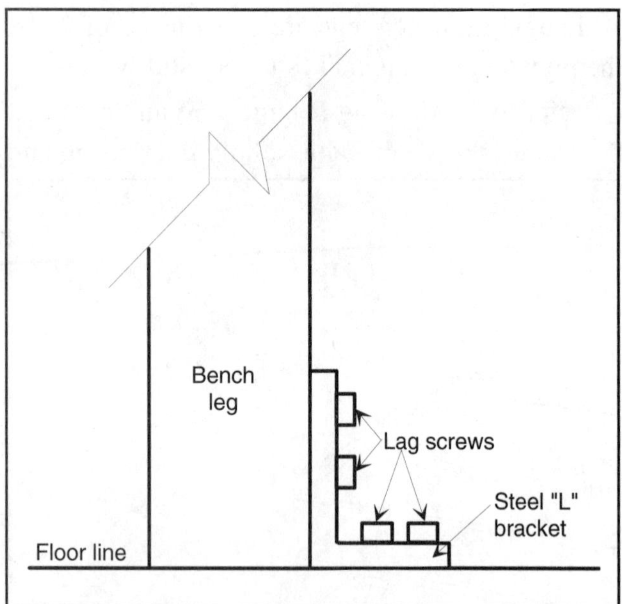

Figure 1-4: Securing bench legs to the floor with steel "L" brackets will increase the sturdiness of the bench.

secured with glue and ¼″ × 3″ flathead wood screws.

The top consists of two layers of ¾″ plywood with one layer of ⅛″ hardboard nailed to the top layer of plywood with finishing nails. The shelf also consists of ¾″ plywood (only one layer). For maximum rigidity, ⅜″ plywood is nailed to the backs and sides. With this arrangement, and with the legs anchored to the floor (see Figure 1-4), the bench will not budge under almost any treatment to which it is subjected.

To build this bench, lay out the diagram for the top pieces and shelf as shown in Figure 1-5. Use a straightedge and carpenter's square for the lines, and then cut out the various pieces with a hand or power saw.

Next cut all 2×4s, notching the legs as shown in the exploded view in Figure 1-3. Mark and drill screw holes as needed and then assemble the two end frames with glue and wood screws. Each member should be secured with two wood screws at each joint. You may want to countersink the screw holes for a neat appearance. Join the two end frames with the four long 2×4s, again using wood screws at all joints.

Insert the lower shelf as indicated after notching all four corners to fit the bench legs. Nail and glue

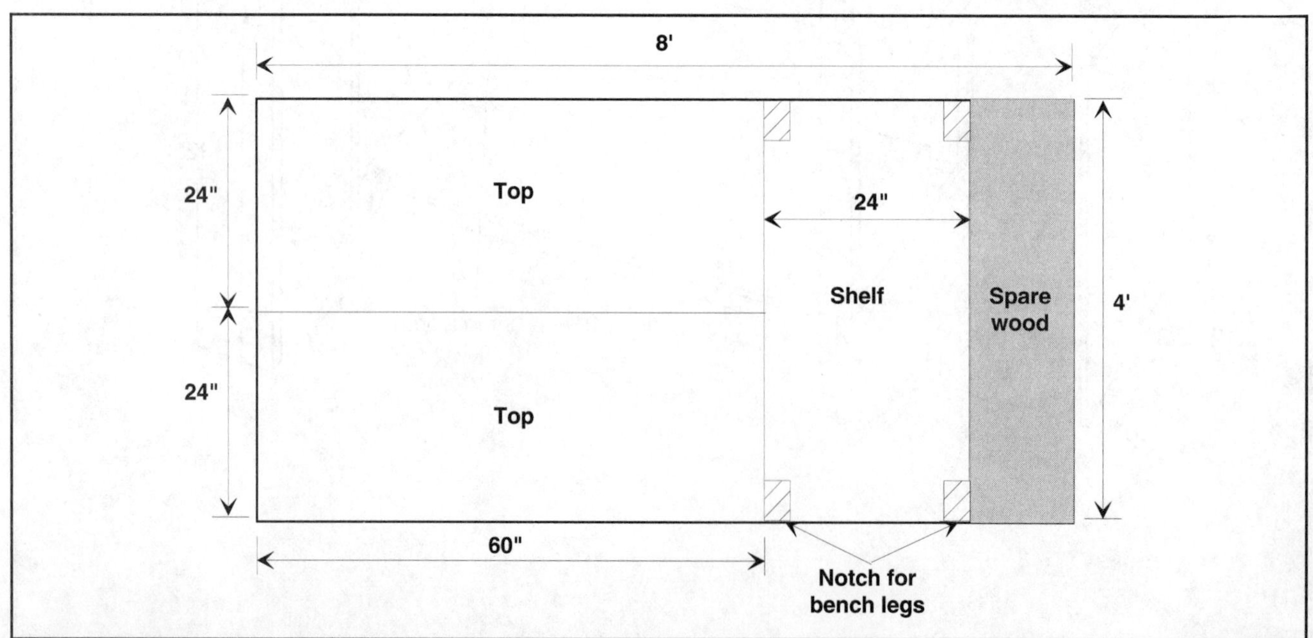

Figure 1-5: Layout of the ¾″ plywood for the bench tops and shelf.

them in place. At this point, the work should be taking the form of a reloading bench.

Continue by marking the cutting diagram on the 3/8″ plywood for the sides and back — again using a straightedge and carpenter's square. When they are cut out, nail and glue these panels to the sides and back as shown.

Now nail and glue the lower 3/4″ top panel to the top rails of the frame, followed by the next panel and the sheet of 1/8″ hardboard (nailed only). Keep all of these panels under pressure (using C-clamps) until the glue dries.

The top hardboard panel can be glued and not nailed for a better appearance, but when nailed only, the hardboard top may be removed in case it becomes stained, scratched or damaged.

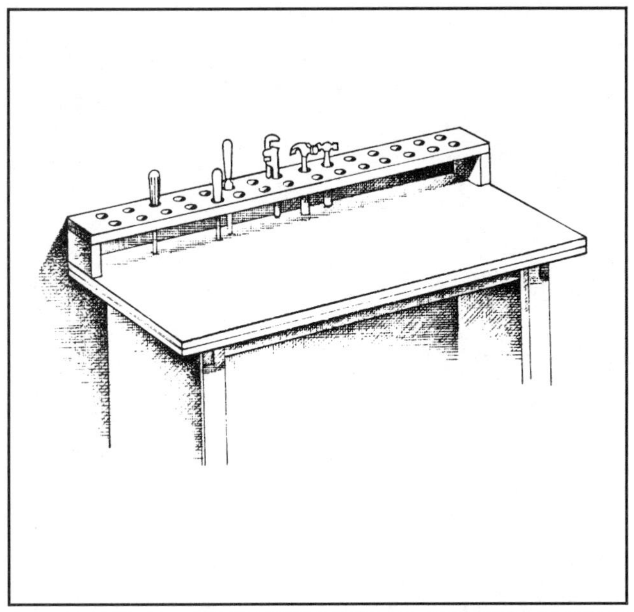

Figure 1-6: Reloading bench with simple tool rack installed.

A simple tool rack, such as the one shown in Figure 1-6, may be added to the top of the bench (at the rear) for a useful addition. This rack may be constructed of either 2×4s or 2×6s and drilled any way desired to accommodate tools, reloading dies, and similar items.

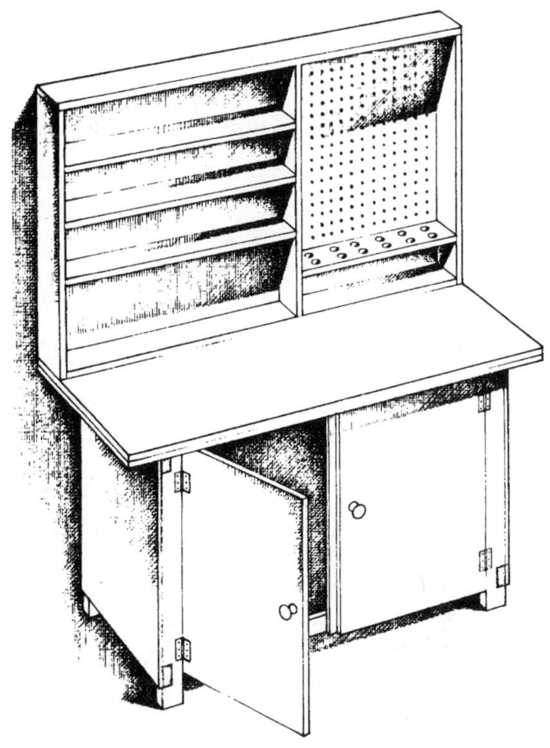

Figure 1-7: Shelving is often a handy addition to any bench.

If you want shelves over your bench, a shelving unit may be hung on a wall directly in back of the bench or mounted on the bench top. The top, sides, and shelves may be made from 3/4″ plywood or 1″ shelving boards of a width to suit any need. A pegboard area is also handy for tool hanging. The overall size of the unit, spacing of shelves, etc. can be varied to suit your needs (*see* Figure 1-7). The shelves are handy for storing cans of powder, while the pegboard can be equipped with pegboard hooks to hang tools and components.

CAUTION!

Ammunition reloading can be dangerous if done improperly and should not be attempted by persons not willing and able to read and follow instructions exactly. Older children should not be permitted to reload ammunition without strict parental supervision. Always wear safety glasses when reloading and shooting.

Chapter 2
Metallic Cartridge Cases

Cartridges went through several stages of development before becoming today's self-contained cartridge in which the projectile or small shot, powder and primer are all cased together.

Guns and ammunition are integral parts of shooting and can hardly be considered separately.

Until about 135 years ago, a cartridge was a lead ball or bullet plus a charge of powder wrapped in a paper case, called a *cartouche,* the French word for cartridge. These early cartridges, like the one shown in Figure 2-1, were usually carried in a cartridge pouch. To load them into a rifle or musket, the shooter would tear off the end containing the powder charge, dump the powder down the muzzle and, using the torn paper as a wad, ram the remainder with the bullet down the barrel with the ramrod. If the shooter was using a flintlock, he would pour a small amount of fine powder into the "pan." If he had a percussion gun, he would slip a cap on the nipple. In either case, he would be ready to fire when the hammer was thumbed back to full cock.

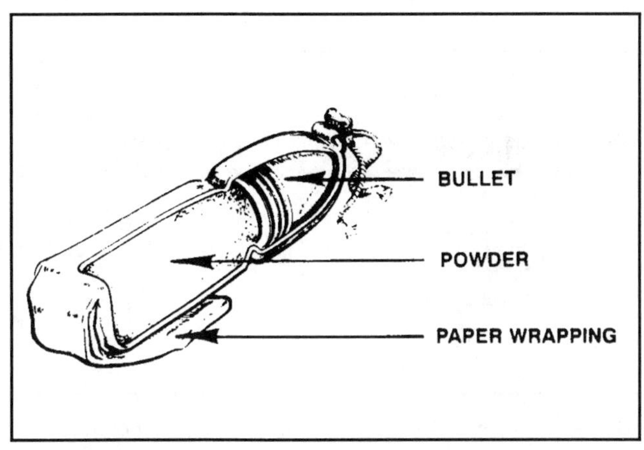

Figure 2-1: Muzzleloading *cartouche* for military rifle/musket.

Modern rifle and pistol cartridges have metallic cases and use either a rimfire or centerfire ignition system, depending on the type of priming.

Cartridges come in a variety of sizes and calibers. Usually, modern cartridges have descriptive names that were assigned by the original manufacturer. The caliber of the cartridge is indicated either by hundredths or thousandths of an inch in the United States and Canada, by thousandths of an inch in the United Kingdom, and by millimeters elsewhere. The caliber figure sometimes refers to the bore diameter between the lands of the rifling or between

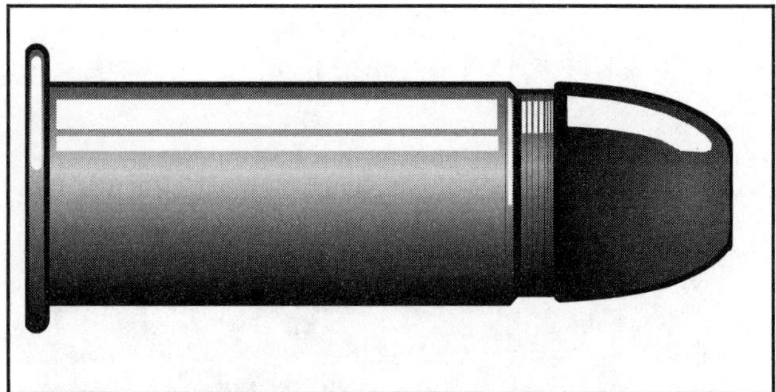

Figure 2-2: The .44 Henry was one of the first successful self-contained cartridges.

the grooves, and it sometimes refers to the diameter of the bullet.

One of the first self-contained cartridges to gain success was the .44 Henry rimfire cartridge, developed by B. Tyler Henry of New Haven, Connecticut. It was originally chambered for the Henry lever-action rifle, which was the forerunner of the first Winchester — the Winchester Model 1866 lever-action rifle. The bullet was roughly 0.44 inch in diameter.

Henry was a shop superintendent for the New Haven Arms Company in 1859 when he was given the task of redesigning their Volcanic rifle action. The new action had to be suitable for use with rimfire metallic cartridges. The first public record of Henry's direct participation in the design of the repeating action appears in U.S. Patent No. 30446, granted to Henry on October 16, 1860, for an "improvement in magazine firearms."

New features of the Henry rifle consisted principally of the addition of a two-prong firing pin, which struck on opposite sides of the flanged head of the rimfire cartridge, an extractor, and changes in the bolt and feeding mechanism. The system satisfactorily handled the loading and firing of the rimfire cartridge and the extraction and ejection of the empty, fired shell. The slotted tubular magazine under the barrel held fifteen .44-caliber rimfire cartridges. Henry later developed the .44 Henry flat cartridge, which was the answer to metallic cartridge arms. This cartridge was important to the development of firearms, especially repeating firearms. All successful guns on the market at the time, such as the Sharps, were single-shot weapons. Henry and Oliver Winchester wanted to develop a repeater, because they recognized the advantages of this type of weapon.

As a result, B. Tyler Henry completely revolutionized the firearms industry, and Henry rifles immediately became popular. The name Henry has been perpetuated in still another manner. If you buy a box of Winchester rimfire cartridges of any caliber, you will notice a trademark, a simple "H," stamped on the head of each case. This is Winchester's tribute to B. Tyler Henry. Since that first .44 Henry rimfire cartridge was produced, every Win-

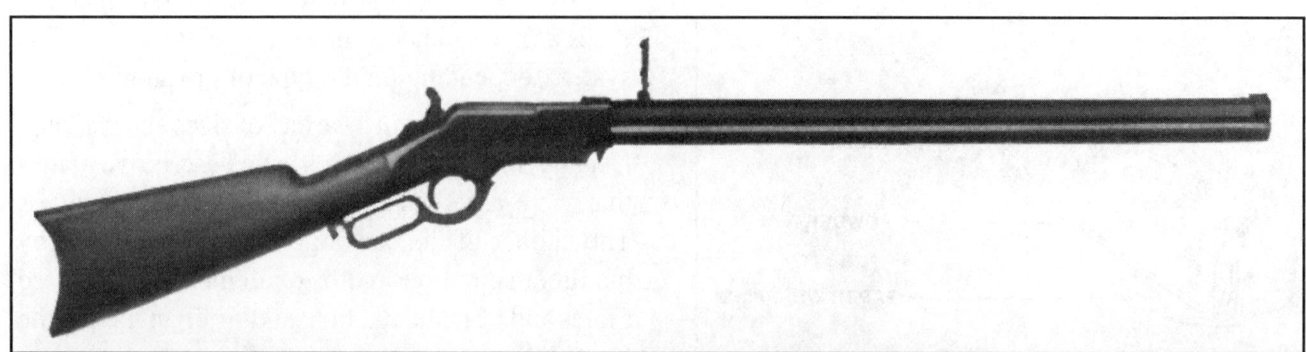

Figure 2-3: The Henry lever-action rifle was the forerunner of the first Winchester — the Winchester Model 1866 lever-action rifle.

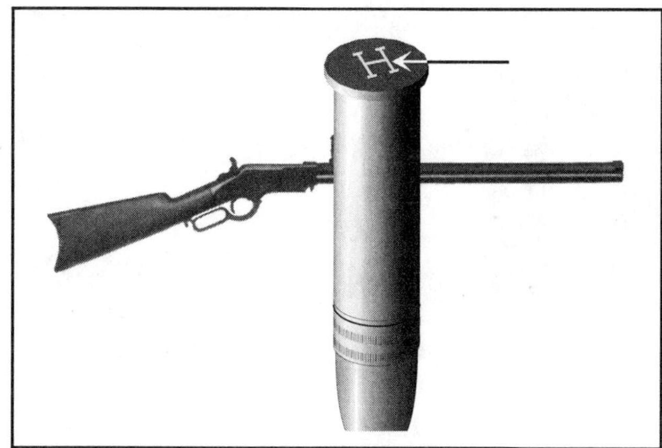

Figure 2-4: All Winchester rimfire cases are stamped with the letter "H" as a tribute to B. Tyler Henry.

chester rimfire has been identified with an "H." *See* Figure 2-4.

The main problems with the first rimfire cartridges were the weak cases and the relatively mild (low-powered) loads. The .44 rimfire had enough power to disable a human if hit, and perhaps to kill even a deer or black bear. However, for the larger game, such as elk, grizzly bear, moose, and the like, the rimfires left lots to be desired in a big-game rifle. Many western hunters, after putting a few of these low-powered .44-caliber slugs into a charging grizzly bear, were thankful for a nearby tree to climb. They were even more thankful that the grizzly could not climb!

A few years after the Winchester Repeating Arms Company brought out its new Model 1866 lever-action repeating rifle chambered for the .44 Henry cartridge, Colonel Henry Berdan devised a practical method of "drawing" brass — forming strong, seamless cases from solid metal. Brass proved to be almost the ideal material for cartridges. It was slightly elastic, expanding just enough under the pressure of the exploding powder to seal in the powder gases. Leaking gases had always been a problem previously.

Colonel Berdan soon joined forces with Marcellus Hartley of the Union Metallic Cartridge Company. Together they developed the centerfire cartridge. The modern cartridge was born along with the reloading era that continues today.

MAKING BRASS CARTRIDGE CASES

The method of drawing brass devised by Colonel Berdan is still in use today. Although the exact methods used will vary with the manufacturer, the operations shown in Figures 2-5 and 2-6 are basically the steps required to form modern brass cartridge cases. The quality of brass will vary, but the operations are practically the same.

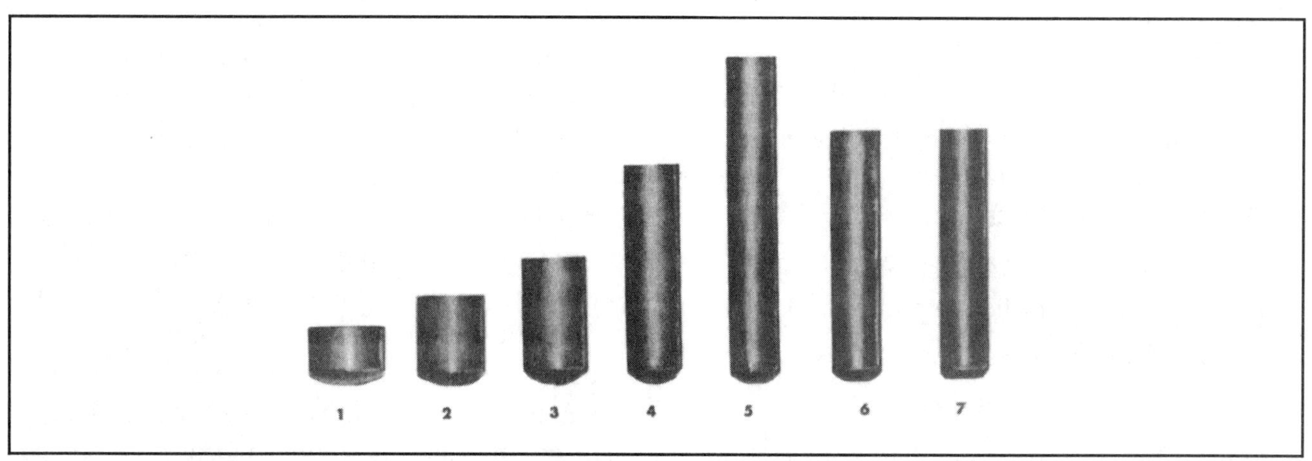

Figure 2-5: First operations required to form a brass centerfire cartridge.

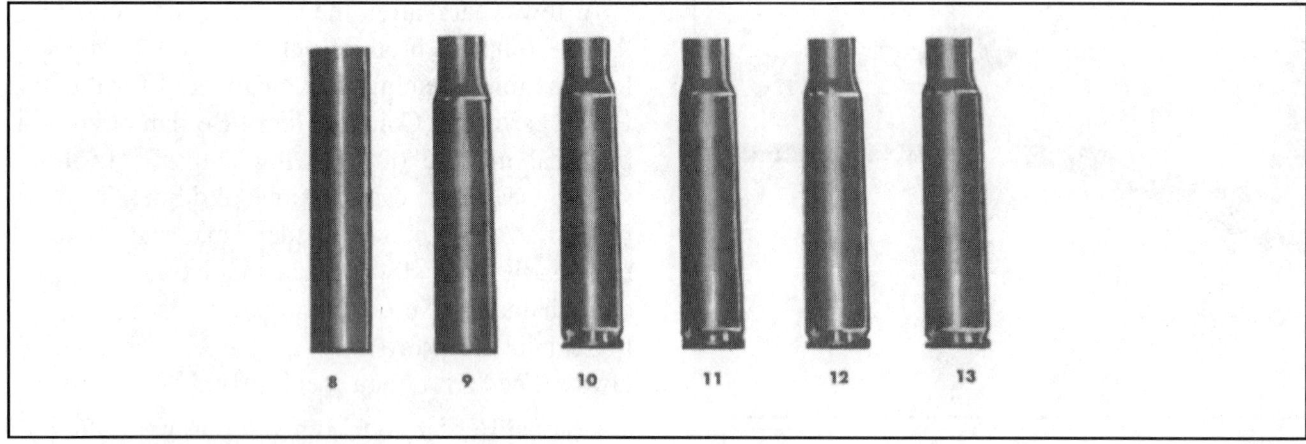

Figure 2-6: Final operations required to form a brass centerfire cartridge.

The steps for forming modern brass centerfire cartridges are (*see* Figure 2-5):

1. Cup for the case jacket is formed. The cup varies in size according to size of the cartridge case.
2. First draw.
3. Second draw.
4. Third draw.
5. Fourth draw.
6. Trim the case to its required length.
7. Form the primer pocket.

Refer to Figure 2-6, above, for the remaining steps.

8. Primer pocket is completely formed and the case is headstamped.
9. First necking operation.
10. Neck is trimmed and turned to size.
11. Flash hole is drilled in primer pocket.
12. Final annealing and sizing takes place.
13. Case is finished and polished.

Many annealing operations between drawing and forming of the cases are required during manufacture.

TURNING CARTRIDGE CASES

During World War II, when new brass cases were almost impossible to find, many gun buffs who had access to a metal-turning lathe, managed to turn (machine) brass cases from scrap brass. While these cases were extremely strong and lasted for many loadings, the thicker walls prevented getting full powder charges in them. Still, it was a logical way to beat the problem at the time. Accounts of the operations required to turn brass cases appeared in articles in *American Rifleman* magazines during the 1940s, but since there is no practical need for such brass at this time, exact manufacturing details are not given here.

In general, a brass cylinder was secured between lathe centers and turned to the appropriate outside dimensions. The inside of the case was then partially drilled with a twist drill and then turned to exact dimensions using an inside boring tool. The primer hole was turned using the same method. Drilling a flash hole completed the operation. Once lapped and polished, these cases functioned very well in rifles, even at the expense of having to use reduced loads. Brass shotshells were turned in a similar fashion. Such cases enabled hunters to keep meat on the table at a time when store-bought commodities were not only in short supply, but required ration stamps to be purchased.

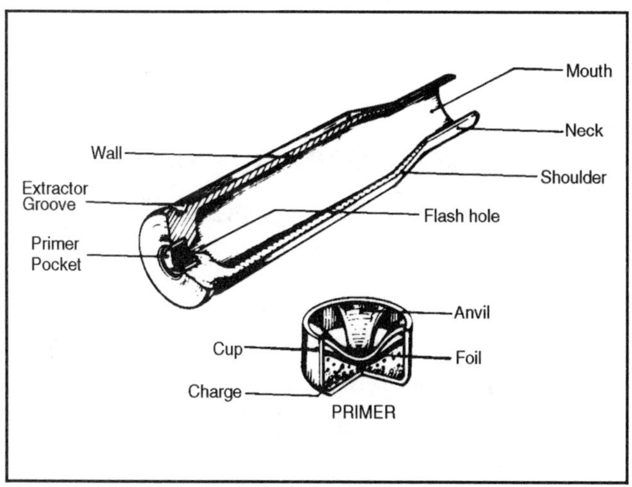

Figure 2-7: Sectional view of brass centerfire rifle case and primer.

TYPES OF CARTRIDGE CASES

Most centerfire rifle cartridge cases are of the bottleneck type; that is, the case itself is of appreciably greater diameter than the bullet, except near the case mouth where a shoulder slopes down to a neck in which the bullet is seated. This is done to provide room for adequate powder charges without unduly lengthening the cartridge, and so avoiding elongated and, therefore, heavier rifle actions, which would be impractical for most hunting purposes. Of course, there are exceptions: .444 Marlin, .45-70, and .458 Winchester, just to name a few.

Cartridge cases are generally made of brass. However, some military cases were constructed of steel during World War II. These steel cases were either lacquered or plated to prevent rust. Steel cases are not suitable for reloading as they are too hard to resize.

In general, there are five types of centerfire cartridge cases:

- Rimmed
- Semirimmed
- Rimless
- Belted
- Rebated

Rimmed cases were used on most of the early cartridges and several are still around today.

Semirimmed cases have a rim diameter slightly larger than the case body and also have an extractor groove cut under the rim — similar to the rimless cases. This design is seldom used. Cartridges utilizing the semirimmed design include the .225 Winchester and the .220 Swift.

The *rimless case* is the most popular. This design is used in the majority of modern centerfire rifle cartridges. Note in Figure 2-8 that an extractor groove is cut into the solid head.

Belted cases are commonly used for magnum cartridges such as the .300 Winchester, .375 H&H

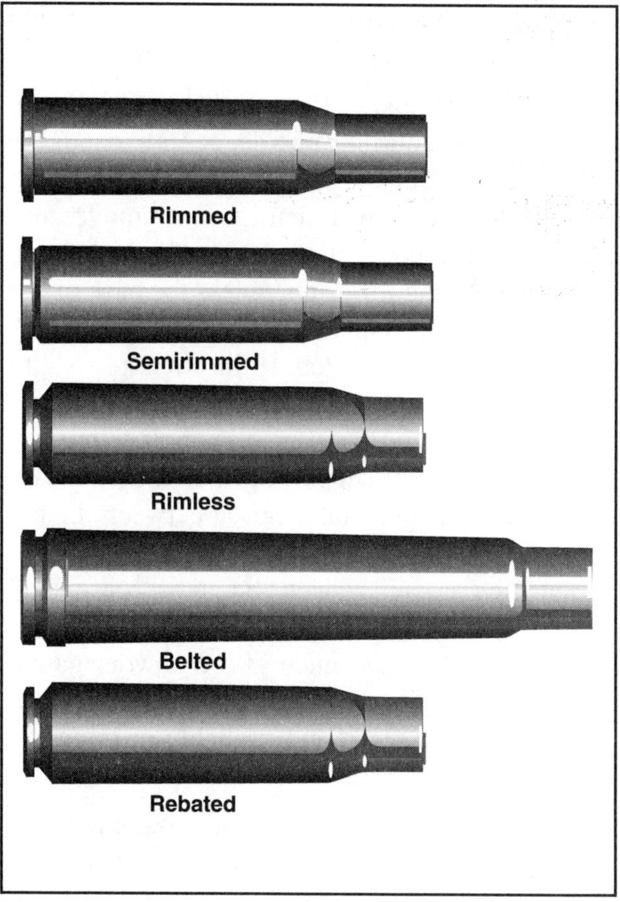

Figure 2-8: Types of cartridge cases.

Magnum, .458 Winchester, and all the Weatherby cartridges. A raised band is used around the base of the case ahead of the extractor groove.

The *rebated case* has a body diameter greater than the rim diameter and is a rare bird indeed. The only cartridges using this design that we know of now are the .284 Winchester and the .425 Westley Richards.

HEADSPACE

Headspace may be defined as the distance between the head of the cartridge in the chamber and the face of the bolt or breechblock. Headspace should be such that when a cartridge of maximum dimensions is positioned in the chamber, the bolt will close without effort and have almost a friction contact with the head of the cartridge case.

When a cartridge is fired, the terrific pressure generated by the burning powder gases expands the soft, thin brass of the case against the chamber walls, so tightly, in fact, that it cannot move until the pressure has been relieved by the bullet leaving the barrel. During this time, unless the base of the cartridge is firmly supported by the bolt or breechblock, the case will stretch. If the stretch is slight and within the tensile limit of the brass, nothing damaging occurs. However, if the bolt or breechblock is not firmly supporting the cartridge base and there is an appreciable space between, then a dangerous condition of excessive headspace exists. Under such circumstances, the brass case may stretch enough to rupture some distance back of the case mouth, allowing much of the powder gas to take the course of least resistance — going through the action, wrecking it and probably injuring the shooter in the process.

Excessive headspace, even if not to the point of being dangerous, can affect accuracy considerably.

Excessive headspace may develop from wear over a long period, or the condition may be due to the stretching of receiver walls from overloads in rifles having rear-locking breechblocks or bolts.

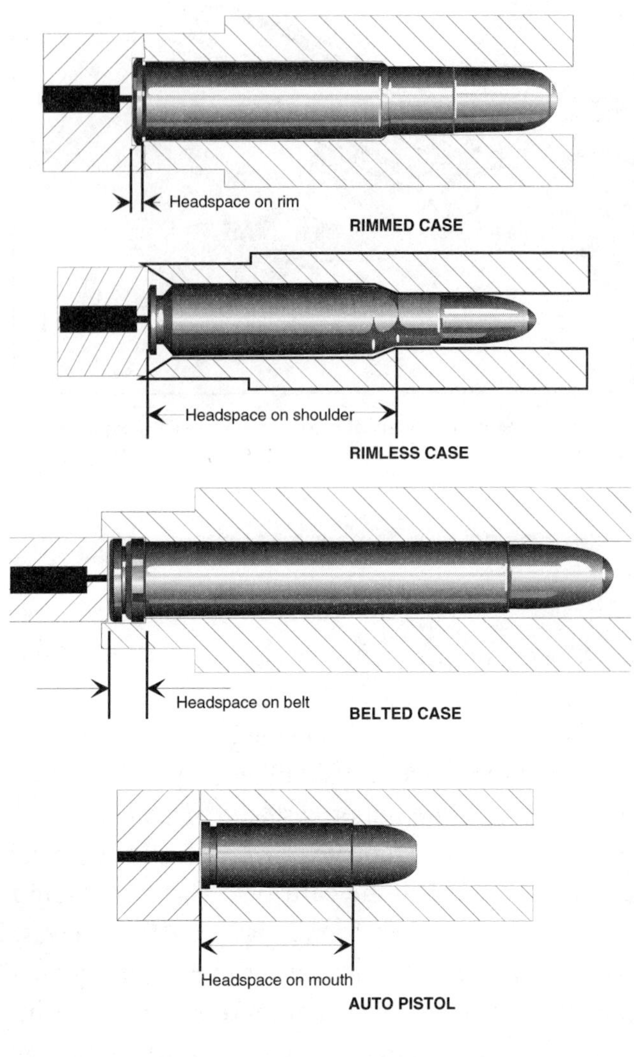

Figure 2-9: Four basic methods used for headspacing.

Improper loading methods can cause excessive headspace even though the rifle itself is okay. It is possible to create headspace in a rimless or rebated cartridge case by sizing the case far enough to set the shoulder back. If this condition exists, it usually can be remedied by backing off the sizing die about ¾ of a turn.

Semiautomatic pistol cases, such as the .45 ACP and the 9mm, which headspace on the case mouth, should not be trimmed excessively nor should the case be crimped on the bullet; doing so will, in effect, shorten the overall case length and create a headspace problem.

CASES FOR RELOADING

The majority of reloaders use once-fired factory cases for reloads. The average case can be reloaded many times, and it is not unusual to find reloaders who have reloaded a metallic case 20 times or more, provided no crimping is required. Those cases that require crimping, such as cartridges used in tubular magazines, and some pistol cartridges, have a somewhat shorter life. Another factor that shortens case life is loading maximum loads each time. In our experience, some cases loaded at maximum pressure and used in the springy lever-action rifles will last for only three reloadings. The crimp fold on shotshell hulls becomes frayed quickly, and few shotshell cases will last for more than four reloads.

The major ammunition manufacturers offer new unfired empty cartridge cases for reloading. There are also dozens of private firms that offer cases for obsolete and hard-to-find ammunition. Most of these are listed in Appendix I of this book. Obsolete cases may also be formed from existing brass. Again, see John J. Donnelly's book titled *The Handloader's Manual of Cartridge Conversions*, available from Stoeger Publishing Company, 5 Mansard Court, Wayne, NJ 07470. Call 1-800-631-0722 for current price.

Factory-new cartridge cases are packed either 20 or 50 to the box and are shipped unprimed. The following is a list of unprimed cartridge cases that are normally available from manufacturers. Others are available only on special order, and shipment may take as long as six months.

UNPRIMED RIFLE CASES

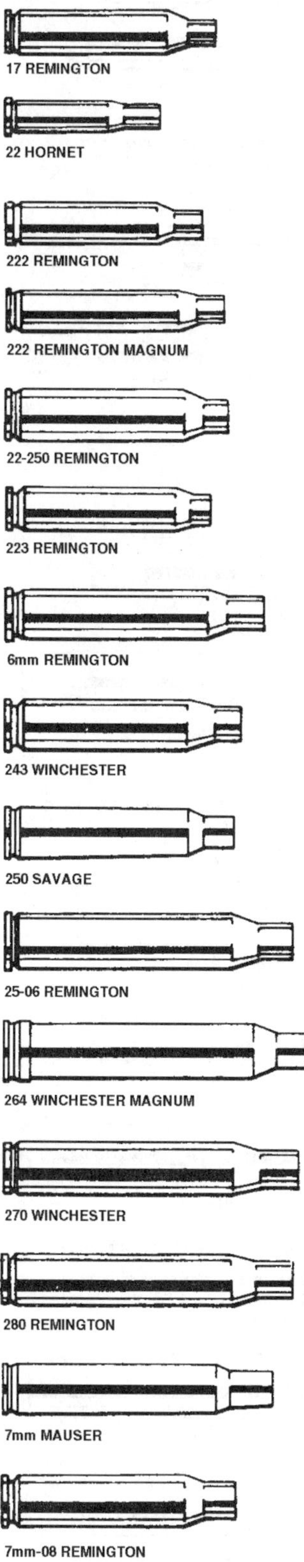

UNPRIMED RIFLE CASES

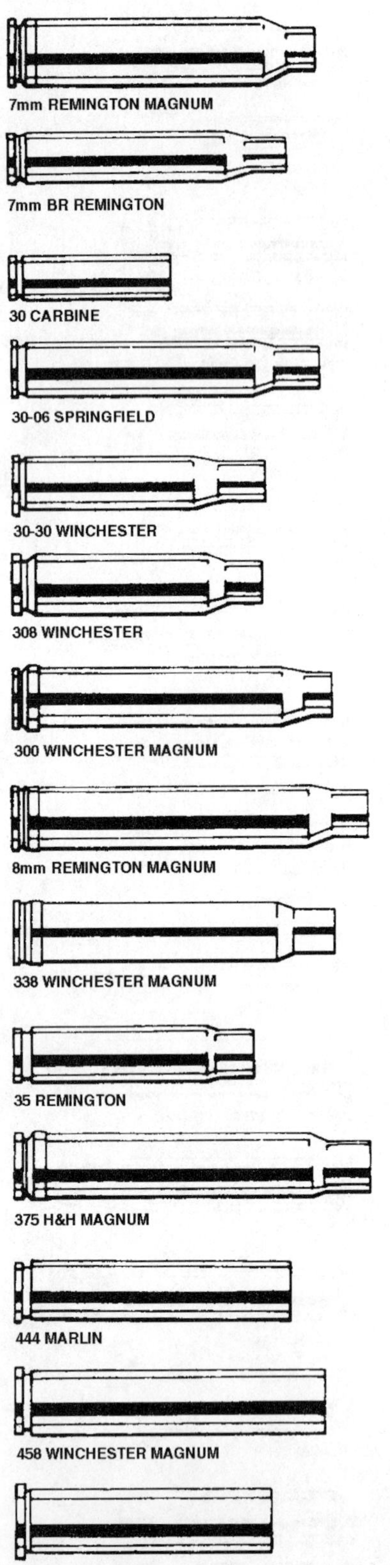

UNPRIMED PISTOL CASES

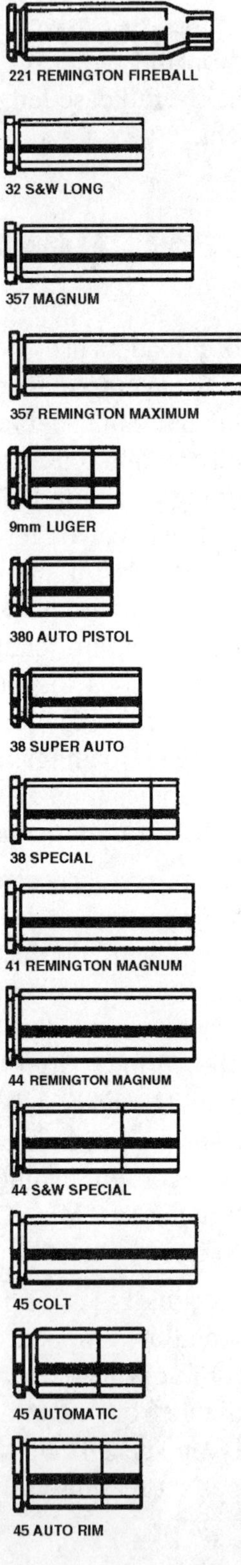

Chapter 3

Gunpowder: Black, Smokeless and Pyrodex

The reloader should never attempt to identify powder by appearance only. If you are not sure what it is, don't use it.

The origin of gunpowder is still uncertain, but its discovery is generally attributed to Roger Bacon, who recorded its formula in 1248.

In his later works, *Opus Tertium, De Secretis,* and *Opus Magnus* (published about 1270), there is little doubt that Roger Bacon was acquainted with explosive mixtures of sulfur, charcoal and niter (saltpeter). The substance was not, however, extensively developed until the invention of firearms more than a century later.

Berthold Schwartz, a monk of Freiburg, Germany, studied the writings of Bacon regarding explosives, and later did extensive experimenting with blackpowder. *See* Figure 3-1. He commonly is credited as its inventor, since he made the properties of gunpowder known and put it to practical use. The early uses of gunpowder, however, were confined to warfare; no use was made of it for hunting or other sporting purposes until several hundred years later.

Figure 3-1: Schwartz experimenting with gunpowder.

During the end of the 14th century, frequent references to gunpowder were made in literature, often in a way that proves the properties of gunpowder as a propellant were well known to most people. For example, Chaucer's reference in *The House of Fame* makes it apparent that a "pillet," which was fired out of the "gonne" by the explosion of the "pouder," was a single projectile.

Initially, gunpowder was manufactured by the crude method of pounding the ingredients together by hand. Edge runners, which greatly facilitated the milling process, were invented toward the end of the 16th century. During that century, the process of "corning," or "granulating," was introduced, assuring grains of equal size when grading the powder.

Bacon's notes on gunpowder call for several parts of saltpeter, five parts of sulfur and five hazel twigs. This "recipe" for blackpowder has been modified many times to reach today's proportions of 10% sulfur, 15% charcoal, and 75% saltpeter.

Even though smokeless powder began to replace blackpowder in the early 1890s, there was still a great demand for blackpowder through the first decade of the 20th century. Many blackpowder arms are still used for sporting purposes, requiring supplies and the proper ammunition. In many parts of the world, only blackpowder arms were allowed by law or were economically feasible. These markets required a constant supply of blackpowder. Today, however, these same blackpowder weapons have been replaced with Uzi machine pistols and other automatic assault-type weapons.

Recently, an increased interest in blackpowder arms has increased the demand for blackpowder over the amount required a few decades ago. For a while, Du Pont was the only active domestic manufacturer of blackpowder. The Du Pont Corporation withdrew from the blackpowder industry after a thunderous explosion destroyed the entire plant in the early 1970s. Du Pont's entire operation was sold to Gearhart-Owen, which is the only active domestic manufacturer of blackpowder today, Much blackpowder, however, is imported from Scotland and Canada.

THE MANUFACTURE OF BLACKPOWDER

In general, blackpowder is manufactured by mechanically mixing charcoal, saltpeter, and sulfur in the proper proportions in huge mixing drums. Water is added to form this mixture into a paste, which is finely ground and pressed into solid cakes. After drying, the cakes are granulated through the crushing process of riding the broken chunks of cake through assorted sets of grooved rollers. It is sifted at regular intervals and graduated on a basis of the size of the granulation. Designation of size of the powder for sporting firearms is by the "F" system, "F" referring to "fine," as in fine granulations. Sporting blackpowder is made in the following granulations:

- Fg
- FFg
- FFFg
- FFFFg
- FFFFFg

Fg being the coarsest type, while FFFFFg is the finest. The latter size, however, is seldom used.

Historically, additional extra-coarse grades that were used for mining and blasting with the coarsest type designated CCC, followed by C, F, FF, and FFF grades. The letter "C" apparently referred to "coarse." Other grades were designated for use in big-bore shotguns and military cannons; one such grade was designated "Grade A-1." An old Hazard Powder Co. advertisement appears in Figure 3-2, showing a comparison of several grades of blackpowder.

These various grades of blackpowder were graduated by straining them through a coarse screen that retained the larger lumps and allowed the rest to fall onto an even finer screen, and so on until the finest powder was graduated.

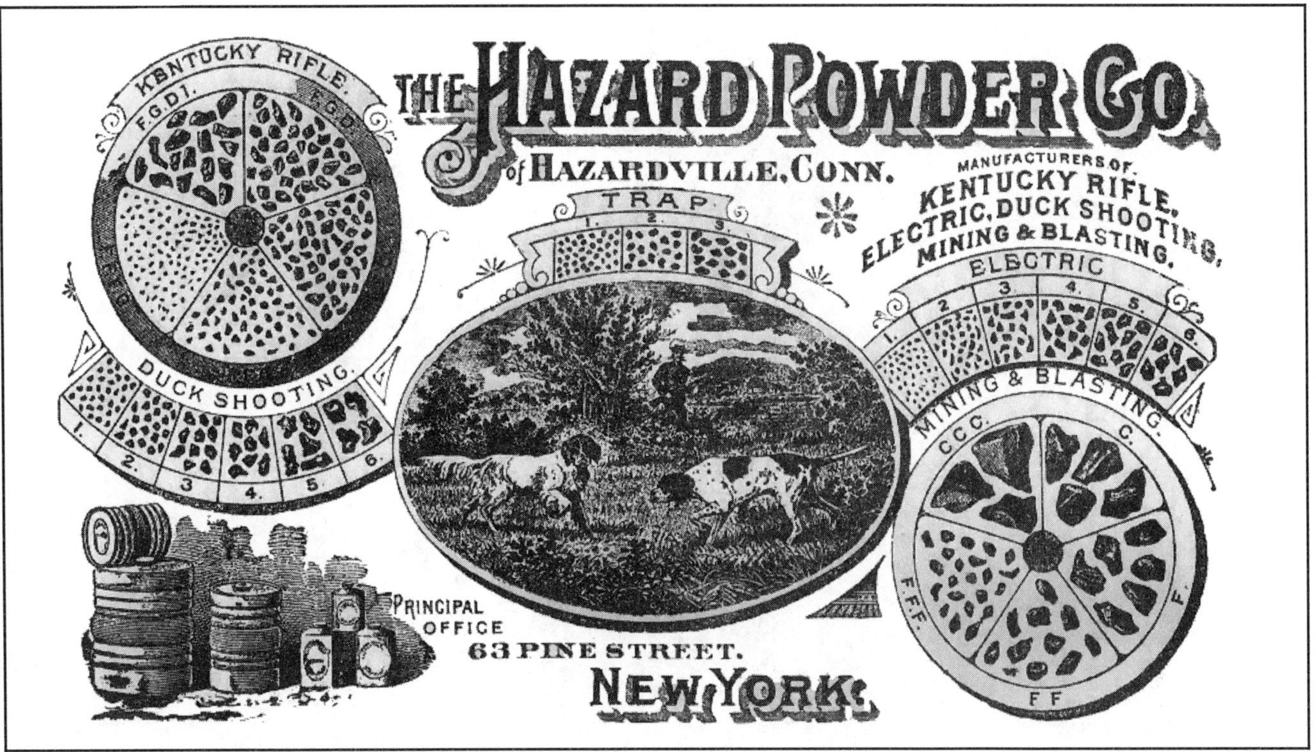

Figure 3-2: A page from an old blackpowder catalog comparing the different sizes of blackpowder, each of which has a specific purpose.

Before the sorting process, the powder was glazed and polished by mixing powdered graphite with the blackpowder and allowing this mixture to slowly revolve or tumble for several hours. During this process, the sharp, ragged edges of the broken blackpowder grains were rounded off through contact with each other, and the graphite adhered to create a shiny polish to the grains. Following this operation, they were given the final grading and blending and packed in canisters or kegs for the trade.

In general, blackpowder is a solid substance that, when burned, gives off gases having a much larger volume than the powder charge itself. When powder is ignited in the chamber of a firearm, the expanding gases build up pressure and, in seeking a means of escape, push the bullet or shot charge out of the barrel — the course of least resistance.

When a kernel or grain of powder is ignited, the outer surface burns first and, as the grain is consumed, the burning area constantly decreases until nothing is left. Therefore, the more surface that is exposed in the powder charge, the more rapidly the charge will burn. For example, look at Figure 3-3 on the next page. Let's assume that the largest cube is Fg blackpowder — the slowest burning of the lot. The total burning area of this cube is obviously six sides of the cube. If this cube is cut in half, it will burn quicker because two additional surfaces are now exposed. This represents FFg blackpowder. Further subdivisions of the powder grain will expose more area to the flame with a further increase in burning rate, representing FFFg and FFFFg powders, respectively. The total amount of gas given off by the divided grain is no greater than

WARNING

Do not use unidentified powder in reloads. If you are not sure of the powder type, do not use it.

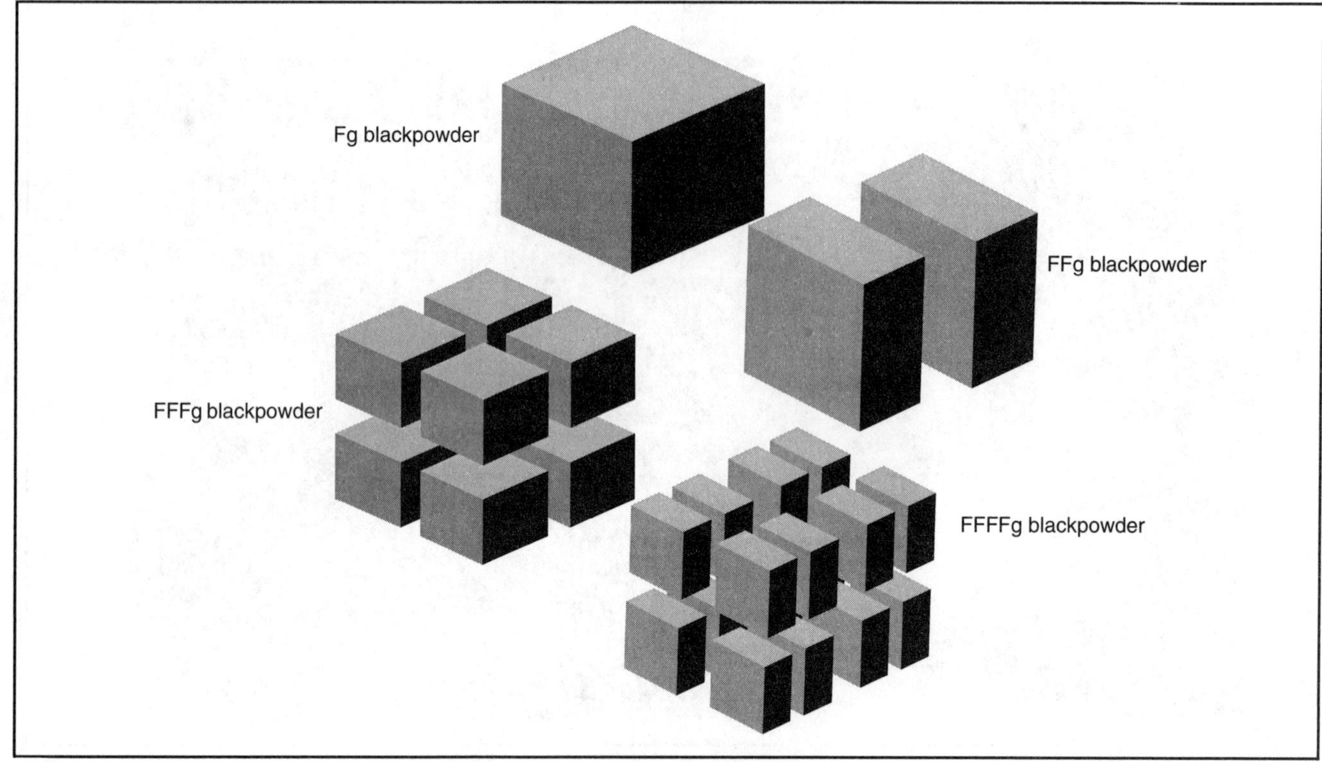

Figure 3-3: The burning area of powder grains increases as the grain size decreases.

the whole grain, but the time it takes for this conversion will be much shorter with the finer grains.

DEVELOPMENT OF SMOKELESS POWDER

The manufacture of smokeless powder in the United States began in 1890 by the E. C. Powder Company of Oakland, New Jersey. The U.S. Navy also began developments of smokeless powder in the same year.

In 1891, Du Pont built the guncotton plant at Carney's Point, New Jersey, where the manufacture of Du Pont smokeless shotgun powder began in 1893. In that same year, the California Powder Works at Santa Cruz went into production; so did the Leonard Powder Company at Bay Chester, New York. The products produced by these two latter manufacturing plants were found to be of sufficient merit to get a U. S. Army contract.

By 1898, Navy powder developments reached a stage sufficient to require a large manufacturing plant, which was established at Indian Head, Maryland.

Many smokeless powder manufacturing firms sprang up overnight, but most of them ran into financial difficulty — either because of plant explosions or poor business management — and were forced to close their doors. Only a handful remained in 1910.

The Hercules Powder Company was a Wilmington, Delaware corporation formed in 1912 when the Federal Courts dissolved the Du Pont trust. Its main plant, however, was located at Kenvil, New Jersey.

In recent times, the major American powder manufacturers remaining included Du Pont, Hodgdon, Hercules, and Gearhart-Owen. Du Pont powders, however, are now supplied by IMR Powder Company of Plattsburgh, New York.

There are also several foreign powder manufacturers that import their powders to the United States, where they are handled by domestic powder distributors. The types and characteristics of each are thoroughly discussed in this chapter. Reloading data, where available, are provided under the appropriate categories; that is, for handgun cartridges, rifles cartridges and shotshells.

PROPERTIES OF SMOKELESS GUNPOWDER

Smokeless powders, or propellants, are essentially mixtures of chemicals designed to burn under controlled conditions at the proper rate to propel a projectile (or projectiles) from a gun.

Smokeless powders are made in three forms:

- Thin, circular flakes or wafers
- Small cylinders (extruded or tubular)
- Small spheres (or ball powder)

Single-base smokeless powders derive their main source of energy from nitrocellulose. The energy released from *double-base* smokeless powders is derived from both nitrocellulose and nitroglycerin.

All smokeless powders are extremely flammable; by design, they are intended to burn rapidly and vigorously when ignited.

Oxygen from the air is not necessary for the combustion of smokeless powders since they contain sufficient built-in oxygen to burn completely, even in an enclosed space such as the chamber of a firearm.

In effect, ignition occurs when the powder granules are heated above their ignition temperature. This heating, resulting in ignition, can occur by exposing powder to one or more of the following conditions:

- A flame, such as a match or primer flash
- An electrical spark or the sparks from welding, grinding, etc.
- Heat from an electric hot plate or a fire directed against or near a closed container even if the powder itself is not exposed to the flame

When smokeless powder burns, a great deal of gas at high temperature is formed. If the powder is confined, this gas will create pressure in the surrounding structure. The rate of gas generation is such, however, that the pressure can be kept at a low level if sufficient space is available or if the gas can escape.

In this respect, smokeless powder differs from blasting agents or high explosives such as dynamite or blasting gelatin, although smokeless powder may contain chemical ingredients common to some of these products.

High explosives such as dynamite are made to detonate; that is, to change from solid state to gaseous state with an evolution of intense heat at such a rapid rate that shock waves are propagated through any medium in contact with them. Such shock waves exert pressure on anything they contact, and, as a matter of practical consideration, it is almost impossible to satisfactorily vent away the effects of a detonation involving any appreciable quantity of dynamite.

Smokeless powder differs considerably in its burning characteristics from common blackpowder. Blackpowder burns essentially at the same rate out in the open (unconfined) as when in a gun.

When ignited in an unconfined state, smokeless powder burns inefficiently with an orange-colored flame. It produces a considerable amount of light-brown, noxious-smelling smoke, and leaves a residue of ash and partially burned powder. The flame is hot enough to cause severe burns.

The opposite is true when it burns under pressure as in a cartridge fired in a gun. Then it produces very little smoke, a small glow, and leaves very little or no residue. The burning rate of smokeless powder increases with increased pressure.

When burning smokeless powder is confined, gas pressure will rise and eventually can cause the container to burst. Under such circumstances, the bursting of a strong container creates effects similar to an explosion.

POWDER DETERIORATION

Although modern smokeless powders are basically free from deterioration under proper storage conditions, safe practices require a recognition of the signs of deterioration and their possible effects.

Powder deterioration can be checked by opening the cap on the container and smelling the contents. Powder undergoing deterioration has an irritating acidic odor. (Don't confuse this with common solvent odors such as alcohol, ether and acetone.)

Check to make sure that powder is not exposed to extreme heat as this may cause deterioration. Such exposure produces an acidity that accelerates further reaction and has been known, because of the heat generated by the reaction, to cause spontaneous combustion.

Never salvage powder from old cartridges, and do not attempt to blend salvaged powder with new powder. Don't accumulate old powder stocks.

The best way to dispose of deteriorated smokeless powder is to burn it out in the open at an isolated location in small shallow piles (not over one inch deep). The quantity burned in any one pile should never exceed one pound. Use an ignition train of slow-burning combustible material so that you may retreat to a safe distance before powder is ignited.

STORAGE OF SMOKELESS POWDER

Smokeless powder is intended to function by burning, so it must be protected against accidental exposure to flame, sparks or high temperatures. For these reasons, it is desirable that storage enclosures be made of insulating materials to protect the powder from external heat sources. Once smokeless powder begins to burn, it will normally continue to burn (and generate gas pressure) until it is consumed.

Containers approved for use with smokeless powder should be constructed to open up at low internal pressures to avoid the effects normally produced by the rupture or bursting of a strong container. Storage containers for smokeless powder should be constructed in a similar manner; that is:

- Of fire-resistant and heat-insulating materials to protect contents from external heat.
- Sufficiently large to satisfactorily vent the gaseous products of combustion that would result if the quantity of smokeless powder within the enclosure were accidentally ignited.

If a small, tightly enclosed storage enclosure is loaded to capacity with containers of smokeless powder, the walls of the enclosure will expand or move outward to release the gas pressure — if the powder in storage is accidentally ignited. Under such conditions, the effects of the release of gas pressure are similar or identical to the effects produced by an explosion.

Therefore, only the smallest practical quantities of smokeless powder should be kept in storage, and then in strict compliance with all applicable regulations and recommendations of the National Fire Protection Association.

Store in a cool, dry place: Be sure the storage area selected is free from any possible sources of excess heat and is isolated from open flame, furnaces, hot water heaters, etc. Do not store smokeless powder where it will be exposed to the sun's rays. Avoid storage in areas where mechanical or electrical equipment is in operation. Restrict from the storage areas heat or sparks that may result from improper, defective or overloaded electrical circuits.

Never store smokeless powder in the same area with solvents, flammable gases or highly combustible materials.

Do not smoke in areas where powder is stored or used.

Do not subject the storage cabinets to close confinement. Storage cabinets should be constructed of insulating materials and with a weak wall, seams or joints to provide an easy means of self-venting.

Do not keep old or salvaged powders. Check old powders for deterioration regularly. Destroy deteriorated powders immediately.

CHARACTERISTICS OF SMOKELESS POWDER

Smokeless powders are greatly misunderstood even by the experienced reloader. Their rapidity of burning is very definitely controlled by the pressure developed. For example, if 50 grains of a certain type of smokeless powder are used in, say, a .30-06 case that is loaded with a 180-grain bullet, a certain amount of pressure will be developed; let's say 50,000 pounds per square inch (psi). This pressure will change when any of the following conditions exist:

- Increasing or decreasing the powder charge
- Changing the powder type (in most cases)
- Increasing or decreasing the bullet weight
- Changing the bullet type (in some cases)
- Increasing or decreasing the bullet (and case neck) diameter
- Increasing or decreasing the case capacity
- Increasing or decreasing the ambient temperature

As mentioned, smokeless powders are available in two basic types:

- Single base
- Double base

Single-base powders are made from a straight nitrocellulose composition, while double-base powders contain both nitrocellulose and a percentage of nitroglycerin.

Powders most commonly used by the reloader are available in three types:

- Extruded or tubular (Figure 3-4)
- Spherical or ball powder
- Flake

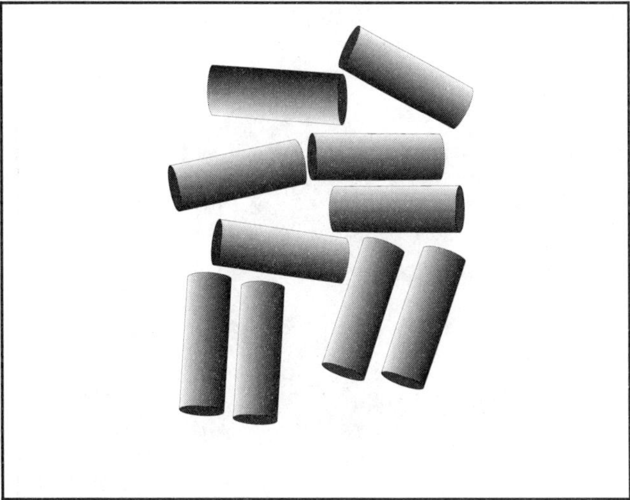

Figure 3-4: Extruded or tubular type powder.

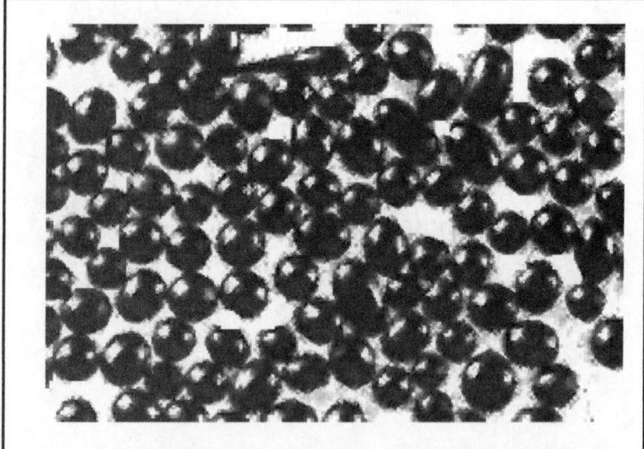

Figure 3-5: Spherical or ball powder.

Extruded powder is the most common type used in rifle cartridges, and it is usually single base. However, there are a few that are double base as described later in this chapter. Burning rate is controlled by composition, grain diameter and length, web thickness, and deterrent coating. Extruded powder can vary greatly in appearance and grain size.

Spherical powder (Figure 3-5) can look like tiny round balls or the grains can be flattened. The grains can vary in size, shape and color. The burning rate of spherical powders can range from a fast pistol powder to very slow-burning rifle powder. All spherical powder is double base, and burning rate is determined by chemical composition, grain size and deterrent coating. Spherical powder is harder to ignite than extruded powder and sometimes requires the use of magnum primers in certain loads for proper ignition.

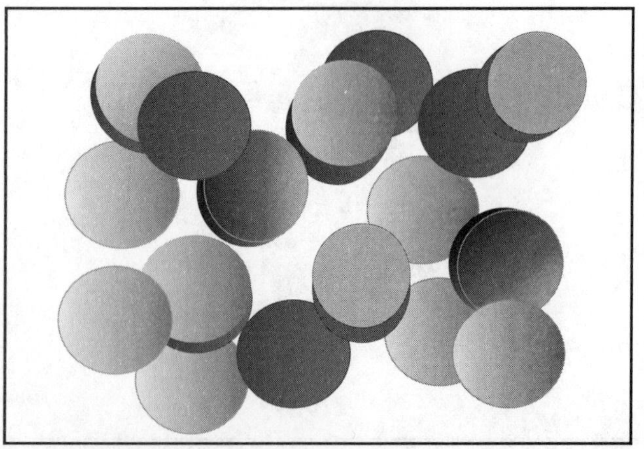

Figure 3-6: Flake powder.

Flake powder (Figure 3-6) is usually double base, fast burning, and is suitable for pistol, shotgun, and light low-velocity loads in rifles. Flake powders used at slower-burning rates suitable for moderate loads in rifles have also been used in Europe.

Bulk powders (Figure 3-7) were invented and used before the introduction of the dense smokeless types. A long chain of these was available at the beginning of the 20th century, and in most cases, blackpowder measures or scoops could be used with the bulk powder. In other words, say, 50 grains of bulk powder would give the approximate same ballistics and pressures as 50 grains of blackpowder.

Figure 3-7: Du Pont bulk shotgun powder.

The last surviving bulk powder was Du Pont's Bulk Shotgun Smokeless, which was discontinued nearly two decades ago. This bulk powder, however, remained on the market — with some improvements from time to time — for approximately 75 years. There is still lots of this powder around, and if found to be in good condition, it may be used with good results. Consequently, we have listed some shotshell loads in Section 4 using Du

Pont's bulk powder in case the reloader has a supply on hand.

EARLY SMOKELESS POWDERS

Dozens of gunpowder types have come and gone over the past 100 years. While many types are no longer available, a brief description of all powders is in order — both obsolete and those in current production. One reason is to have a complete reference under one cover to identify all powders and powder containers, the latter having reached collector status. Another reason is to identify the powders loaded in many of the antique, obsolete cartridges. Finally, it should be of interest to many readers to know what has gone before — the struggle over the past 100 years to obtain the fine quality of gunpowder in use today.

Listed below are obsolete powders, along with their dates of introduction, and the dates they were discontinued (when known). Some factory-recommended loads are listed, under the appropriate powder, for further reference.

Du Pont #1 Rifle Smokeless. Introduced 1894. Discontinued 1926: This was the first satisfactory smokeless powder and was intended for scoop measuring instead of weighing. No. 1 Rifle powder, of a pale grayish-yellow and irregular granulation, was sifted through a wire mesh, 16 to the inch, and caught on screens 26 to the inch. It was intended for low pressures and used in such cartridges as the .22 Single Shot Winchester, .22-15 and .22-16 Stevens, .25-20 Repeater and Single Shot, .25-25 Stevens, .32-20 Winchester, .32-40 Winchester, .38-55, and .38-56.

This powder was inclined to crumble under the pressure of the bullet. Therefore, the manufacturer recommended that the loaded cartridges be used *within a few days of loading.* This crumbling produced higher pressures than intended, and the more the powder crumbled, the higher the pressures became. One of the major reasons for its discontinuance was its tendency to soak in water, and thus become useless. This powder was designed to operate at pressures between 20,000 and 25,000 pounds.

Du Pont Smokeless Rifle #2. Introduced 1894. Discontinued 1926: This powder was identical with Smokeless Rifle #1 except for granulation. It was somewhat finer than #1 and was thus intended primarily for cartridges used both in rifles and revolvers interchangeably. A Du Pont booklet published in 1903 gave the loading in the table to follow. No velocities were given, but because of the nature of the powder, it may be assumed that these charges represented the standard blackpowder ballistics of that period; that is, for the same bullet weight and caliber, velocities and pressures obtained with blackpowder (bulk-for-bulk) were also obtained with Du Pont's Smokeless Rifle #2 powder. Consequently, blackpowder cups or scoops designed for the original cartridge could also be used with this smokeless powder.

Cartridge	Bullet Weight	Grains of No. 2 Rifle Powder
.45-35	255	10.0
.44-23 Russian	255	7.0
.44-40 Win.	200	17.0
.41 Colt	190	6.0
.38-40 Win.	180	16.0
.38 Long Colt	150	5.0
.38 S&W	147	4.5
.32 Long Colt	100	3.0
.32 S&W	87	3.0

Du Pont #2 powder was of very soft grain, requiring careful screening and elimination of dust prior to loading. When the dust was allowed to remain, it sometimes leaked into the primer pockets, resulting in blown primers. Pressures were also seriously increased because of this dusting and crumbling.

Du Pont Schuetzen. Introduced 1908. Discontinued 1923: Burning pressure 22,000 to 26,000 pounds. This was a true bulk-for-bulk smokeless rifle powder. In other words, charge cups for blackpowder could be used for an equal charge of Schuetzen, the same as in Du Pont #1. It was straight nitrocellulose and consisted of large grains of light red or pale orange color and irregular in shape. Schuetzen was designed for target shooting in the famous Schuetzen rifles, mostly the .32-40 or .38-55, although it has been used in various smaller bores such as .25-20 Single-Shot. It was long considered the most accurate smokeless powder ever manufactured, but was discontinued with the advent of improved, less hygroscopic powder.

Du Pont Bulk Shotgun. Introduced 1893: This was one of the first successful smokeless powders for use in shotguns. Not a true bulk-for-bulk but closely approaching it. While quite hygroscopic it was extremely successful in its field. In shot shells, it was the favorite with trap shooters because of its smooth recoil, even after more ballistically satisfactory shotgun powders had been developed. The recoil was easier on the shoulder than that developed by the dense powders exemplified in Infallible and Ballistite. It was designed to burn at around 9,000 pounds pressure and riflemen soon learned that it could be used in a variety of cartridges of many types, particularly for reduced loads much along the lines of the Schuetzen and Rifle Smokeless #1. It was coarse in granulation and quite friable.

Hercules E. C. Powder. Introduced 1894. Discontinued 1931: This powder was very similar in characteristics to Bulk Shotgun Powder, although slightly finer in granulation and colored a soft orange. This powder was also manufactured by Du Pont prior to the formation of Hercules.

Hercules Sharpshooter #1. Introduced in 1897. Discontinued about 195: Sharpshooter is the fastest-burning of the entire old line of Hercules nitroglycerine powders.

Du Pont Schultz Shotgun. Introduced 1898. Discontinued 1926: Schultz was another member of the Du Pont bulk shotgun family very similar to Bulk Shotgun. It has very clean, irregular egg-shaped granulation of a soft creamywhite color. Although designed for use in shotguns, it has been used by many handloaders with reasonable success for very light gallery charges, particularly with round balls, both in rifle and handgun cartridges. This powder, similar to other bulk shotgun types, produced excessive head pressure in metallic cartridges and reloaders had to use extreme caution to avoid overloads.

Hercules W.A. .30 Caliber. Introduced in 1898. Dicontinued in 1930: W.A. powder was not very flexible and burned best at pressures between 35,000 and 40,000 pounds. It burned more quickly than the later Hercules HiVel, but more slowly than either Shrpshooter or Lightning. It was very erosive on barrels — a fact that led this powder to its decline.

Hercules Lightning #1. Introduced 1899. Discontinued about 1950: This powder was first introduced by Laflin & Rand, then Du Pont, and finally Hercules in 1914.

Hercules Sharpshooter #2. Introduced in 1902. Discontinued in 1914: Originally introduced by Laflin & Rand-Du Pont and taken over by Hercules in 1913.

Hercules Lightning #2. Introduced 1903. Discontinued in 1929: This powder is almost identical to Lightning #1, but the grains are somewhat larger in diameter and considerably thinner.

Du Pont Gallery Rifle #75. Introduced 1904. Discontinued 1928: This powder was marketed under the name "Marksman." It was considered to be one of the most important rifle powders for reloaders for a long time. The powder was originally designed by Laflin & Rand.

Du Pont Empire Shotgun Powder. Introduced 1908. Discontinued 1914: Empire was a bulk smokeless shotgun powder originally designed by Curtis & Harvey of the Nobel-Du Pont organization in England. This was a very popular shotshell reloading powder in its day.

Du Pont 1908 Military (MR #19). Introduced 1908. Discontinued 1909: This was a nitroglycerine powder that had a very short life with Du Pont, but was resurrected by Hercules under the name of "HiVel." It was later replaced with HiVel #2.

Hercules HiVel #1. Introduced in 1908. Discontinued in 1915: This was originally a Du Pont powder and was known as "1908 Military" when manufactured by Du Pont. It was designed exclusively for use in the .30-06 cartrdige, but failed to give perfect satisfaction; hence its discontinuance shortly after the Hercules Powder Company was formed.

Hercules HiVel #2. Introduced in 1908. Discontinued in the 1960s: This is a double-base powder consisting of approximately 15% nitroglycerine. It is the slowest-burning of the Hercules double-base powders and became one of the most popular powders for reloading.

The HiVel series of Hercules powders continued on through HiVel #6, which was introduced in 1936 and discontinued at the beginning of World War II. HiVel #2, however, was the only HiVel number to be remanufactured after the war.

Du Pont MR #20. Introduced 1909. Discontinued 1927: This powder was mass-produced under various names such as Du Pont 1909 Military, Du Pont Military #20, and Government Pyro .30-caliber DG. This was the powder used in the original .30-06 government cartridge, and at the close of World War I, various American powder plants were turning out over one million pounds of this powder each day, seven days a week.

Du Pont MR #10. Introduced in 1910. Discontinued 1915: This powder was designed primarily for use in the infamous .280 Ross. In fact, the powder was marketed entirely for use in the .280 Ross and was not sufficiently flexible for reloading in other cartridges.

Du Pont Sporting Rifle #80. Introduced in 1913. Discontinued 1939: No. 80 was the last remaining American rifle powder in the so-called "bulk" class, although it was by no means a true bulk-for-bulk powder in which equal bulk charges of black and smokeless powders are used. No. 80 was designed to give its best results at a burning pressure of between 14,000 and 19,000 psi.

Du Pont #21. Introduced in 1913. Discontinued 1926: This powder consisted of tubular graphited grains of about .04 inch length and .03 inch diameter. No. 20 was designed as a companion to Du Point #20 for full-charge loads in such cartridges as the .25-35, .22 Savage Hi-Power, .30-30, and the .30 Remington.

Du Pont IMR #15. Introduced in 1914. Discontinued 1917: This powder was the first of the so-called IMR (Improved Military Rifle) series and was designed exclusively for full loads in military cartridges with full-metal jacketed bullets.

Hercules #308. Introduced 1915. Discontinued 1930: This powder is practically identical with Du Pont's #20 and with Pyro DG, and is merely the Hercules designation of the same powder. It was first manufactured by Hercules during World War I and marketed to reloaders in canister lots from 1915 to the time of its discontinuance.

Du Pont IMR #17. Introduced 1915. Discontinued 1925: This type of powder was a variation of Du Pont's #16 and was designed for wartime use in the British .303 Lee-Enfeld cartridge.

Du Pont IMR #18. Introduced in 1915. Discontinud 1930: This powder is similar to No. 15 except that the grain size was reduced to fit the smaller-capacity rifle cases.

Hercules #300. Introduced 1916. Discontinued 1932: This powder was almost identical to Du Pont's #15. It performed well in a wide variety of cartridges from the .22 Hi-Power to the .30-06. It was replaced by Hercules HiVel #2.

Du Pont IMR #16. Introduced in 1916. Discontinued in 1927: One of the more flexible of the IMR series at the time. This powder was adapted to more different sizes and shapes of cartridges along with a wider range of velocities and burning pressures than anything previously produced.

Du Pont IMR #13. Introduced in 1917. Discontinued about 1926: A slow-burning powder designed for such cartridges as the .256 Newton, 6.5mm Mannlicher, and similar bottleneck cartridges of the day.

Du Pont IMR #15½. Introduced 1919. Discontinued 1934: A replacement powder for Du Pont #15.

Du Pont IMR #17½. Introduced 1923. Discontinued 1933: This powder was one of the most popular Du Pont powders for reloaders. It is essentially the same as #16 with added tin. It was designed to replace #16.

Du Pont IMR #1147. Introduced in 1923. Discontinued 1935: This powder was introduced for use in cartridges in the .30-06 class, but was found useful in the .30-40 Krag and several metric cartridges from the 7mm Mauser to the 8mm Mannlicher. It was effectively replaced by IMR 4320.

Du Pont IMR #1204. Introduced in 1925. Discontinued 1935: This is the smallest granulation of any powder in the IMR series, and probably the smallest-grained perforated powder ever produced. It is credited with making the development of the .22 Hornet possible. No other powder during that period would produce the superlative accuracy obtained by Hornet bullets in the tiny case. Its successor is the modern IMR #4227 series.

Du Pont IMR #1185. Introduced in 1926. Discontinued 1938: This powder was designed primarily for Government use with the 173-grain bullet in the .30-06. It was never commercially available.

MODERN SMOKELESS POWDERS

ACCURATE ARMS RIFLE POWDER

Accurate Arms powders are relatively new when compared with the other manufacturers or distributors of gunpowder. These powders have established themselves among reloaders as reliable and stable, giving excellent results in the cartridges for which the various types were developed.

MR-223: A rifle powder designed for use in medium-capacity cases, it is best suited for the .223 Remington and .220 Swift.

MR-2460: This powder is designed for the precision rifle shooter. Reloaders claim excellent results in case capacities equal to about the .308 and .30-30 Winchester.

MR-2520: A spherical-type powder produced especially for the .30-06.

MR-3100: A fine extruded powder, suited for medium-capacity cases with heavy bullets.

MR-8700: Because of its slow-burning characteristics, this powder works well for the belted magnums and overbore capacity cases with heavy bullets.

ACCURATE ARMS PISTOL POWDER

No. 7: A spherical type powder expressly made for the 9mm Luger.

No. 9: A powder made for use in the .357, .41, and .44 Magnum. This type is also good for use in the .30 M1 carbine and .410 shotgun.

MP-5744: An extruded powder used for pistol silhouette cartridges and reduced loads with cast bullets.

HODGDON RIFLE POWDER

Hodgdon has been furnishing reloaders with powder since 1946 and gave a new light to shooting blackpower weapons with the introduction of their excellent Pyrodex® powder — a substitute for blackpowder.

H4198®: This is a specialized extruded powder that works extremely well in the 7.62 X 39 Russian. This propellant is also excellent for the .222 with 50 gr. bullets and some other calibers very different in nature including the .45-70 and the .444 Marlin.

H4198 also works well in some obsolete American rifle cartridges such as .32-40 Ballard and .40-70 Maynard. Hodgdon H4198 performs similar to most lots of IMR 4198.

H322®: This powder has won more benchrest matches than all other propellants combined. H322 is capable of amazing accuracy in all small and medium-capacity cases. It is outstanding in the .223 and .222 as well as the .22 and 6mm Pindle Palmisano cartridges. H322 is a very short grained extruded powder that flows through the measure as well as most spherical powders. H322 also works well in many TCU and IHMSA cartridges.

BL-C (2)®: This spherical powder is the propellant of choice for the .308 Winchester. It's actually military specification powder for the .308 (7.62 NATO). When it was first introduced, the benchrest shooters and other target shooters made it an immediate success and found that it gave excellent accuracy loads on both target and game. Known to the more experienced handloaders as "Ball C," BL-C (2) performs well in most cases smaller than .30-06.

H335®: This spherical powder is what the military uses for loading the .223 or 5.56 NATO. Like BL-C(2), H335 works very well in most cases from .30-06 down.

H4895®: This is one of the most versatile rifle powders available. This extruded powder is great for .17 Rem., .22-250, .308, and .458 Win. If you're a rifle shooter and don't want to store a lot of different rifle powder, this is the one for you. It is amazingly accurate in almost every cartridge listed. Its original use was in the .30-06 and it was the first powder Bruce Hodgdon sold to the loading public. Hodgdon H4895 performs similarly to most lots of IMR 4895.

H380®: H380 was an unnamed spherical rifle propellant when Bruce Hodgdon first laid his hands on it. After he shot a few rounds in his varminter (a wildcat at that time now known as the .22-250) and found it shot one hole groups with a 38 gr. charge behind a 52 gr. bullet, he named the powder after the charge weight, thus H380. H380 is also a fantastic propellant for the .220 Swift, .243, 6mm Rem., .257 Roberts, .30-06 and others.

H414®: This spherical powder has an extremely wide range of uses. From the .17 Remington to the .375 H & H, it will give excellent results. It delivers an incredibly consistent charge weight through any good powder measure. This propellant was designed to be the spherical equivalent of 4350. Although charge weights vary, it will produce very similar results when compared to the 4350 burning rate.

H4350: This is an extruded propellant that provides extremely consistent velocity, therefore accuracy. The 4350 burning rate has been known to rifle enthusiasts for decades. Hodgdon introduced its version in 1982. Great with the heavier bullets, from the .22-250 through the .375 H & H, it's the best choice for the .243 Winchester. H4350 performs similar to most lots of IMR 4350.

H450®: This relatively slow-burning spherical powder was designed to do the same kind of work that H4831 does. Success! H450 and 4831 do very close to the same thing in all rifle cartridges. H450 works similary, but may use different charge weights and could produce dramatically different results if instructions are not followed to the letter. This powder is also excellent in the .25-06, 7mm Mag., .30-06, .270 and .300 Win. and Wby. Mag.

H4831®: This extruded powder is a real stalwart of Hodgdon rifle powders. Hodgdon was the first supplier to introduce this popular burning rate in 1950. It's a relatively slow-burning propellant, so it does a great job with heavier bullet weights in the .25-06, .257 Wby, and .338 Win., as well as the cartridge listed in the description of H450.

H1000®: This extremely slow-burning extruded powder is perfect for the 7mm Rem. Mag. With a relatively narrow range of use, it also gives superior performance in the .270, .30-06, .300 Win. and Wby. Magnums. Many of the specialized 1000 yard cartridges such as the .30-338 give excellent results with H1000. A relatively new introduction to the Hodgdon line, this powder has received considerable notoriety among long-range shooters.

H870®: This spherical powder is great for heavy bullets in big, overbore magnum loads. H870 is also used by the boys who like to shoot .50-cal. BMG. The only surplus powder left in the canister line, H870 is inexpensive and can be used in many large-capacity cartridges where economy is a major consideration.

HODGDON SHOTSHELL AND PISTOL POWDERS

HP38: The fastest burning powder in the Hodgdon line. HP38 is a spherical powder that is great for low-velocity and midrange target loads in the .38 Special, .44 Special, 9mm and .45 ACP. This extremely high-energy powder provides economy in loading because of the slight charge weights it requires.

CLAYS®: A new powder developed for 12-gauge clay-target shooters. This extra-clean burning propellant is perfect for 1⅛- and 1-ounce. loads. Trap, skeet, and sporting clays' shooters will love it. Clays also performs well in many handgun applications. These include .38 Special, .40 S & W and .45 ACP.

INTERNATIONALCLAYS®: International was inspired by the new technology developed when Clays was designed. It is the answer for shotshell shooters who want reduced recoil in 12-and 20-gauge target loads.

UNIVERSALCLAYS®: This powder is an extremely small-grain extruded flake type. This small grain provides consistent charge weights through the powder measure. As the third member of the Clays technology powders, Universal is one of the most versatile of all Hodgdon's pistol/shotshell propellants. It loads nearly all of the straight-wall pistol cartridges as well as 12 gauge 1¼ oz. through 28 gauge ¾ oz. target loads. Pistolaro's and skeet shooters should love it.

HS6®: This is an excellent spherical propellant for all bullet weights in the 9mm. HS6 also performs well in most straight-wall pistol cartridges and is well suited for the .45 ACP. It's a dual-purpose powder many shotgunners prefer as well as pistol shooters. It propels 1¼ – 1½ ounce of shot in the 12-gauge and 1 ounce of shot in the 20-gauge quickly with minimum recoil. Perfect for upland game, rabbit and squirrel.

HS7®: HS7 is a spherical propellant that is an excellent heavy field load for game such as turkey and geese. HS7 has also received notoriety for its adaptability in steel shot loading. HS7 is used to load some pistol cartridges, including .357 Mag., .41 Mag., .44 Mag., and .45 Win. Mag.

H110®: This spherical powder is designed to develop high-operating pressures in the .357 and .44 Magnum. The high velocities developed with proper loading of this powder produce incredible accuracy down range. H110 is also recommended for the .30 carbine and the .410 bore.

H4227: This is an extruded powder that in many cartridges duplicates the performance of H110. As always, refer to good data when deciding on charge weights. The charge weights may vary slightly with significant difference in chamber pressure. The fastest burning of Hodgdon's extruded powders, H4227 is well adapted to the .22 Hornet and some specialized loading in the .45/70. Also excellent in magnum pistol cartridges. H4227 performs similarly to most lots of IMR 4227.

IMR POWDERS

The IMR Powder Company of Plattsburgh, New York now handles powders formerly supplied by Du Pont. This company offers IMR powders (the IMR stands for "Improved Military Rifle"), SR powders ("Sporting Rifle"), PB and "Hi-Skor."

IMR RIFLE POWDERS

IMR-4227: This is the fastest burning of the IMR series. It is well adapted to the .22 Hornet, light bullets in the .222 Remington and all bullets in the .357, .41, and .44 Magnum handguns. It is also popular for .410 shotgun loads.

IMR-4198: This powder has a medium burning rate and is popular for use in such cartridges as the .222 Remington. It is also adaptable to several medium-capacity cases such as the .30-30 Winchester and the .303 British.

IMR-3031: This was one of the first IMR powders, introduced in 1934. It gives excellent results in all medium-capacity cartridges and good accuracy in all.

IMR-4064: This powder was originally released in 1936 to replace Du Pont's #15½ powder. It performs best in large-capacity rifle cases. *See* section under "Early Smokeless Powders" in this chapter for further details.

IMR-4320: Slightly slower than IMR 4064 and performs well in cartridges from the .22-250 through the .30-06. It was introduced in 1935 to replace Du Pont's #1147 smokeless powder, and is still going strong today.

IMR-4350: This is the slowest of the IMR powders and is popular for heavy bullets in cases from the .243 Winchester up and for medium-weight bullets in the magnums.

VIHTAVUORI OY RIFLE POWDERS

Vihtavuori Oy (pronounced vee-ta-voo-ree) has been producing powder abroad for over 70 years. However, this powder has only recently been introduced to the United States and Canada. Besides furnishing powder that goes in Finland's Sako ammuntion, American manufacturers are also using this powder in some factory loads.

The N100 series are primarily rifle powders, with suitable burning speeds to optimize handloading from the tiny .17 Remington and .22 Hornet all the way to the large-magnum cartridges. There are 13 speeds in this series and include:

N110: This is a very fast-burning propellant that can be used in applications that previously used Hercules 2400, Hodgdon H110 or Winchester 296. Typical applications include: .22 Hornet, .25-20 Winchester, .357 S&W Magnum, .357 Maximum, .44 Magnum, and .45 Winchester Magnum.

N120: This speed needs higher pressure than N110 to optimize burning. Burning rate falls near the various 4227s. It works superbly with comparatively light bullets in 22 caliber cartridges. It is, by nature, a limited application propellant.

N125: This is a moderately fast propellant ideally suited to the 7.62 x 39mm Russian. It is another limited application propellant.

N130: Burning rate is between the IMR-4227 and the discontinued Winchester 680. This is the powder used in factory loaded .22 and 6mm PPC.

N132: A limited application type designed for 5.56mm tracer rounds.

N133: This speed is very close to IMR-4198 in quickness. Thus, it is ideal for the .222 Remington, .223 Remington, .45-70 Government and other applications where a relatively fast-burning rifle propellant is needed.

N134: Another special-purpose powder designed for 7.62 NATO tracer rounds.

N135: This is a moderate-burning propellant. It will fit applications similar to Hercules Reloder 12 and IMR-4895 or IMR-4064. Applications range from the .17 Remington to the .458 Winchester.

N140: This powder can usually be used in place of Hercules Reloder 15, IMR-4320, and Hodgdon H380. Applications include: .222 Remington Magnum, .22-250 Remington (factory powder), .30-30 Winchester, .308 Winchester, .30-06 Springfield, .375 H&H Magnum, and so on.

N150: This is a moderately slow powder that can help refine rifle cartridge ballistics when N140 is just a tad too fast and N160 is a tad too slow. Works well in many applications previously filled by 760, H414, and IMR-4350.

N160: A relatively slow powder ideally suited to many magnum and standard rounds requiring a slow propellant. It has characteristics that make it work well for applications previously using various 4350's, Hercules Reloder 19, and the various 4831's. For example, some ideal applications are: .243 Winchester, .25-06 Remington, .264 Winchester Magnum, .270 Winchester (factory load), 7mm Remington Magnum, .30-06 Springfield, .300 Winchester Magnum, .338 Winchester Magnum, .375 H&H Magnum, etc.

N165: A very slow-burning magnum propellant for use with heavy bullets. Applications begin with very heavy bullets in the .30-06 and include the .338 Winchester Magnum.

N170: This powder has the slowest speed in the series and is the slowest canister reloading powder generally available form any source.

VIHTAVUORI HANDGUN AND SHOTSHELL POWDERS

Handgun and shotshell powders include the N300 series of 28 propellants and one special speed. They are as follows:

N310: Very fast burning and competitive with Bullseye and Accurate No.2. It has applications in a very wide range from the .25 ACP to the 9mm Luger and on up to the .44 Magnum.

N312: This is a special powder used for loading blank cartridges. Not available in the U.S.

N318: This is their fastest burning shotgun powder having a flake shape. Not available in the U.S.

N320: A shotgun and handgun powder of comparatively fast burning rate. Useful in many popular cartridges. Currently available data includes 9mm Luger, .38 Special, .357 Magnum, .44 Magnum, .45 ACP and .45 (Long) Colt. Burning rate generally is perhaps a tad faster than 231 or generally about like Red Dot.

N324: Another shotshell powder not available in the U.S.

N325: A flake-grained shotgun powder with a burning rate about like "Hi-Skor" 700-X. Not yet available in the U.S.

N328: Still another flake-shape shotshell propel lant. Not available in the U.S.

N330: This is a handgun powder that has a burning rate similar to Green Dot, No. 5, or PB. Data is currently available only for 9mm Luger.

N331: Designed especially for the 9mm Luger with data available only for this cartridge. Somewhat similar in characteristics to Unique.

N338: This is a special powder for loading blanks and is also useful in shotshells.

N340: This powder has a wide application for the following handgun cartridges: .30 Luger, 9mm Luger, .38 S&W (Colt New Police), .38 Super Auto., .38 Special, .357 Magnum, .44 Magnum, .45 Auto., and .45 (Long) Colt.

N344: Still another shotgun powder of relatively slow-burning rate. Not available in the U.S.

N347: The slowest burning shotshell powder in flake form.

N350: This is the slowest burning propellant in the 300 series and has applications for both handgun and shotshell cartridges. Burning speed is about like Blue Dot, "Hi-Skor" 800-X or No. 7. Data is currently available for: 9mm Luger, .38 Super Auto., .38 Special, .357 Magnum, .44 Magnum, and .45 Auto.

3N37: This is a special powder designed for high-velocity rimfire cartridges and is not a true N300 series powder. Its burning speed is between N340 and N350, close to "Hi-Skor" 800-X. Therefore it has applications also in shotshell and handgun cartridges. Data is currently available for: 9mm Luger, .38 Super Auto., .38 Special, .357 Magnum, .357 Maximum, .44 Magnum, .45 Auto., and .45 Winchester Magnum.

Chapter 4
Primers

The primer is the initiator that changes the mechanical force of the firing pin into a chemical reaction that causes cartridge ignition.

There are four basic primers from which the metallic reloader must choose:

- Large rifle
- Small rifle
- Large pistol
- Small pistol

Both the large rifle and large pistol are approximately .210" in diameter. The small rifle and small pistol are approximately .175". Although the dimensions are the same, pistol and rifle primers *should not* be indiscriminately substituted. Rifle primers used in handgun cartridges can cause high pressure (due to the hotter priming mixture), and misfires might occur because of the thicker primer cups. Pistol primers used in rifle loads can cause perforated primers or inadequate ignition. Each individual primer has its own specific mixture, which varies in both formulation and quantity.

The primer is often referred to as a "spark plug." This can easily be misconstrued to imply that the primer merely "spits" a few sparks up through the flash hole and starts the propellant powder charge burning. *NOT SO!*

Actually, the primer shoots a white hot jet of flame through the flash hole and completely engulfs each individual granule of powder in a sea of gaseous energy. Anything less than this leaves ignition up to chance and affects accuracy.

Because of these performance requirements, Cascade Cartridge, Inc. (CCI), Lewiston, Idaho, developed a magnum primer in each of the four basic types. The CCI magnum primer is a premium primer that normally results in more uniform ignition and more stable velocities in all of your handloading. This improved uniformity is especially noticeable when 4831, 4064, 4350, all the ball powders, and other difficult-to-ignite powders are involved. The improvement becomes even more discernible when the firing is done under cold temperature conditions.

The pressure increase resulting from this new ignition efficiency is fairly insignificant unless you are loading maximum, then it is recommended that you decrease a grain or two and work up gradually. In some instances, where easy-to-ignite powders and small volume cases are involved, the increased uniformity of ignition is so slight that it is of little value to use a magnum primer; however, if it is felt that an accuracy problem exists — magnum primers may be the answer. Also, all loads for Weatherby cartridges recommend the use of Federal No. 215 Magnum primers. These primers were developed by Federal to Weatherby's specifications and may be identified by the green-colored rim of the primer. Other types of magnum primers can be identified only by the container markings.

All American primer manufacturers currently market flat-bottomed primers; therefore, only the flat primer plugs should be used. Check the primer-retaining sleeve (the device that holds the primer onto the primer plug) to make certain that it is free to slide down the plug.

The highly sophisticated quality-control system used in modern primer production along with proven manufacturing methods results in an extremely dependable product. In fact, the statistical probability of a legitimate primer misfire is no greater than approximately three times in 10 million!

To obtain the optimum in sensitivity and general uniformity, *primers must be seated all the way to the bottom of the cartridge primer pocket.* This is best accomplished by seating the primer firmly, turning the case 180° in the shell holder and then applying firm pressure again. This procedure assures that the anvil will physically contact the bottom of the pocket, thus forcing the anvil against the mixture, which assures anvil support and puts the mixture under "dry compression."

If a cartridge misfire is experienced — before putting the blame on the primer, make the following checks:

- Did the gun deliver an adequate firing-pin blow? Is the firing-pin indent well centered? Is the firing-pin tip spherical and not flat?
- Was the primer properly seated in the cartridge primer pocket? (All the way to the bottom?)

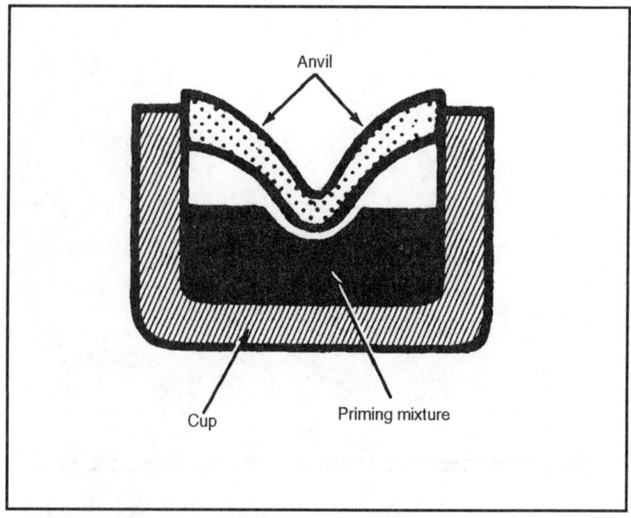

Figure 4-1: Cross-sectional view of a typical American boxer-type primer.

- Was the primer free from contamination, such as case-cleaning chemicals, case lubricants, solvents, oil, etc.?
- Is there powder in the case?
- Had the primer fired?

CAUTION

It is important that the new reloader realize that the primer is very powerful for its size and must be treated with respect. It is recommended that safety glasses be worn whenever primers are being handled. Always store primers in their original box, both for safety and identification. Storage life is almost indefinite under dry, cool conditions.

Live primers may safely be decapped — merely observe common-sense safety precautions. Seated and decapped primers are not recommended for reuse. *Never* seat a primer in a loaded round. Occasionally a reloader notices that the primer was not fully seated initially and attempts to reseat it more deeply — this is extremely hazardous.

The size of flash holes varies from .078" to .082" in diameter. Great variance from these dimensions seems to have little effect on pressure and velocity.

If the flash hole is large enough for the decapping pin, there is little cause for concern unless the ultimate in accuracy is your goal.

DEVELOPMENT OF THE MODERN CARTRIDGE PRIMER

The modern cartridge primer dates back to the research and invention of the Rev. Alexander John Forsyth (1768–1843), who in 1805 developed the mixture that made the old flintlock ignition system obsolete. Thus began the era of percussion ignition for muzzleloaders and, later, metallic cartridges. The mixture was fulminate of mercury, which could be detonated by a sharp blow and so used to ignite the powder charge of a gun. Forsyth called his 1805 mixture "detonating powder." From that date on, he and numerous others designed and patented ingenious devices for using it to ignite the powder in handguns, shoulder weapons, and cannons.

Although the properties of fulminates had been known prior to Forsyth's invention, apparently no one before Forsyth connected them with firearms. His method of applying them to a gun was crude but simple. First, he tapped the flash hole of a musket and inserted a small, hollow plug. Then he attached a rather clumsy gadget that served both as a magazine for the fulminate of mercury and as a striker to set it off. The hollow magazine end of the device held twenty charges of the fulminate. After the shooter had loaded his musket with powder and ball through the muzzle, he tilted the magazine so that a measured amount of the fulminate fell into the hollow plug. Then he reversed the device, bringing the cocked striker into place. When the trigger was pulled, the hammer fell on the plug and exploded the fulminate, which sent sparks through the flash hole and exploded the main powder charge.

Many people and nations take credit for the invention of the percussion cap, but all of our research points to Joshua Shaw, a British-born artist and sportsman who moved to Philadelphia in 1814 and lived there until his death in 1860. In 1814, Shaw made percussion caps with steel cups, changing to pewter in 1815 and to copper in 1816. From that time on, the percussion ignition system was on its way.

Shaw's percussion cap looked like the stovepipe hats of his day. Into the open end was poured fulminate of mercury, which was sealed in place with a foil disk. The cap was made to fit over a channeled nipple that had been inserted in the flash hole of the musket. When the shooter had loaded the gun with powder and ball, a cap was placed on the nipple, the hammer cocked, and the trigger pulled to fire the gun. Since the cap was not affected by dampness, the mechanism rarely malfunctioned as the flintlocks often did.

Between 1812 and 1825, 72 patents were issued to American inventors for various forms of primers. The Maynard tape primer was one of the most satisfactory, although it came at a time when the copper cap was thoroughly established. The famous Sharps rifles were made from 1848 to 1852 with a Maynard primer magazine on both military and hunting weapons.

Dr. Maynard took two narrow strips of varnished paper, placed fulminate of mercury "pills" at regular intervals between them, then sealed the strips together and wound them into a coil. *See* Figure 4-2. His product, which came to be known as the

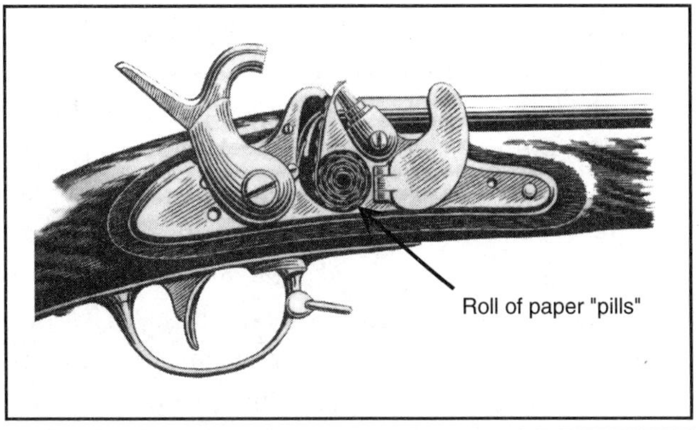

Figure 4-2: The Maynard percussion tapelock used "pills" of fulminate sealed in a roll of paper tape.

Maynard tapelock, was remarkably like the rolls of paper caps used in toy cap pistols that were popular with the kids of my generation.

Maynard designed an action to feed his tape into the flash plug. It consisted of a compartment to hold the coil of pills and a spring device that moved the caps upward when the trigger was pulled. There was always a fresh cap in place — the used one having been clipped off by the falling hammer.

CARTRIDGE GUNS

John H. Hall designed one of the first practical breechloading rifles. Although his invention was far from perfect, the Hall rifle proved superior to the muzzleloaders of the day. Captain Hall was appointed as assistant armorer at the Harpers Ferry Arsenal and given the job of producing these rifles for the government.

One of Hall's workers, Christian Sharps, had his own ideas of what a breechloading rifle should be. The guns he later designed and manufactured were prized by hunters and distinguished themselves above all others in the Civil War.

Although the Sharps was a single-shot rifle, a good rifleman could get off nine or more aimed shots a minute. The heavy blackpowder charge gave the .54-caliber, 475-grain lead bullet excellent striking power, and with considerable accuracy.

The government, however, was slow to adopt the Sharps rifle. Many Army staff personnel preferred careful aiming to rapidity of fire. But within a few years, the Civil War was to decide the issue in favor of the breechloader. When the war was over, a large number of the Sharps rifles — both military and hunting models — were carried into the West. There, in time, they gained their greatest fame in the hands of the buffalo hunters. These rifles became even more potent when new models, chambered for metallic cartridges, began to pour out of the Sharps factories. For nearly 40 years the Sharps rifles were considered to be the finest and most powerful rifles available for big-game hunting. The repeating rifles were not powerful enough for the largest game; that is, not until the development of the Winchester Model 1886 lever-action rifle, an invention and development of the famed John M. Browning.

CENTERFIRE CARTRIDGES

In 1869, Colonel Henry Berdan devised a practical method of "drawing" brass — forming strong, seamless cartridge cases from solid metal. Brass proved to be almost the ideal material for cartridges. It was slightly elastic, expanding just enough under an explosion to help seal in the powder gases, which had always been a problem with breechloaders.

Colonel Berdan soon joined forces with an inventive genius, Marcellus Hartley of the Union Metallic Cartridge Company. Together, they developed the centerfire cartridge as shown in Figure 4-3. In the center of a cartridge base was placed a tiny cup filled with the priming mixture. A piece of metal called the "anvil" was inserted near the priming mixture. When the firing pin drove the cup of

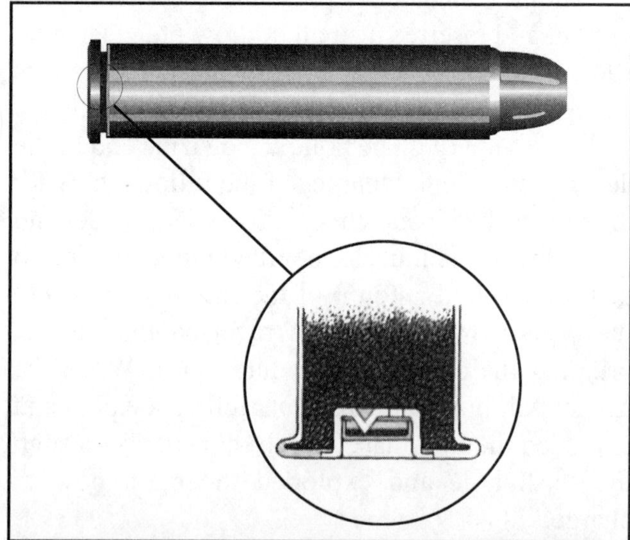

Figure 4-3: Cross-sectional view of the Berdan centerfire primer with anvil.

the primer against the anvil, it exploded to ignite the powder in the cartridge case. The modern centerfire cartridge had been born!

With the development of the metallic centerfire cartridge came the true beginning of the reloading era. All manufacturers of ammunition sold not only factory loads, but also all components from cartridge cases to primers and bullets. The first metallic cartridge cases were of the folded-head design, but the solid-head type followed shortly thereafter.

Since all metallic cartridges were loaded with blackpowder until the 1890s, primers had been a fulminate-of-mercury cap designed to ignite blackpowder efficiently. However, when smokeless powder was introduced, ignition problems were immediately noticed; blackpowder primers were insufficiently "hot" to ignite the new propellant. Consequently, ammunition manufacturers designed a new primer that was hot enough to ignite the new smokeless powders. But this new primer brought with it new problems for reloaders. Ammunition manufacturers began publishing warning messages on their ammunition boxes: "These shells cannot be reloaded." Circulars published by both Remington and Winchester stated:

> All smokeless powders are injurious to brass shells . . . Experiment shows that after the first firing with smokeless powder, the metal of the shell undergoes a slow but decided change, the exact nature of which the best experts have as yet failed to determine. No immediate deterioration attends the using of smokeless powder . . . If fired shells are allowed to set two or three days, clean or unclean, wet or dry, loaded or unloaded . . . the metal becomes brittle and rupture of the shells at the next discharge is probable. Various proportions and kinds of material used in the manufacture of the brass have been tried . . . Chemists have examined shells before and after firing to determine the exact corrosive effect of the gases . . . Experiments show that these problems are characteristic of all smokeless powders and are in no way due to the material used in the shells, the process of manufacture or the kind of gun used. . . .

One circular continued to quote reports of tests made at Frankford Arsenal in 1896. Then in 1897, the problem was solved! An extract from a report issued by the Chief of Ordnance, dated June 30, 1897, states the following: "The principal cause of brittleness in the present shell, which is made of brass composed of 70 copper and 30 zinc, has been traced to the action of the mercury in the primer composition reacting on the metal of the case, particularly on the zinc."

The first really successful smokeless-powder primer was developed at Frankford Arsenal in 1898 for use in the .30-40 Krag. This primer utilized a nonmercuric priming mixture and was widely copied by commercial ammunition makers. With the introduction of nonmercuric primers, reloaders were once again able to safely reload fired cases.

PRINCIPLES OF OPERATION

The moment the firing pin strikes the primer, the primer cup is driven toward the anvil. Almost instantly, the explosive mixture is violently compressed between the cup and anvil. The resulting explosion then ignites the main powder charge. This operation sounds simple, but the number of

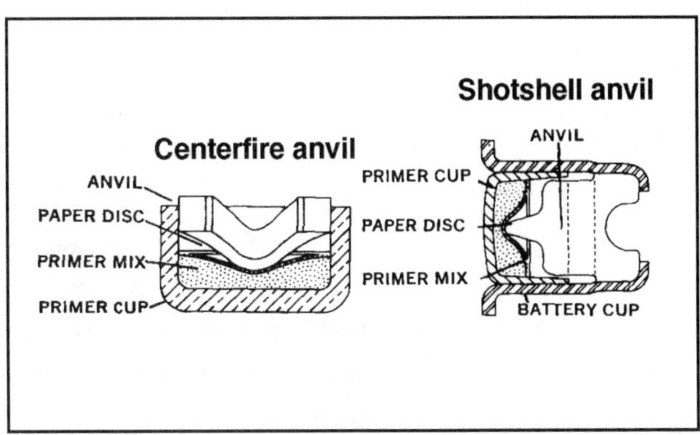

Figure 4-4: Cross-sectional views of centerfire rifle and shotshell primers.

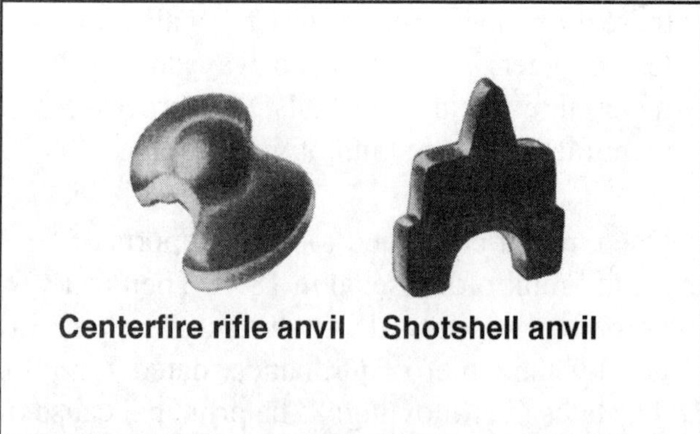

Figure 4-5: Even though the tiny anvils are produced by the millions, each is made, and must conform, to rigid specifications, to a minute fraction of an inch. Each is subject to close inspection.

factors needed to make sure that the primer goes off with the same results round-after-round is a little understood masterpiece of technology. There are a few significant differences between one primer and another, but what differences do exist have a subtle effect on the kind of consistent shooting that results in consistent accuracy.

The key to primer performance is sensitivity — making sure the primer consistently ignites with minimum striking force. The key to primer sensitivity is the explosive mixture. Lead styphnate now forms the explosive base for primers rather than the corrosive potassium chlorate-mercury fulminate mixtures used around the turn of the century. Using this lead styphnate base solves two previously-described problems:

- Residue from lead styphnate won't corrode the gun.
- There is no mercury to attack the brass.

Along with the basic explosives, oxidizers and sensitizers must be added. Oxidizers are added to help control the violence of the explosion and to increase the ignition power and efficiency of the priming mixture. Sensitizers are added to help make sure that misfires are virtually eliminated. A tiny drop of shellac is also added to the mixture as a protection from moisture.

In addition, the anvil has a great influence on primer sensitivity. Anvils for centerfire cartridges and shotshells are shown in Figure 4-5.

Regular primers and the hotter magnum primers are items that shooters and reloaders still argue about. A hot magnum primer may add a few feet per second to the velocity of the load, but in doing so, greater pressures will be generated which is not always a safe thing to let happen.

PRIMER SEATING

Primers should be seated a uniform distance below the head of the case for:

- Uniformity of performance
- Uniformity of firing-pin travel
- Safety

Any departure from this system will introduce variables in all three of the above categories, and variables should be avoided when reloading.

The improperly-seated primer in Figure 4-6 shows the primer cup resting on the primer well. Some primer cups measure .120 inch in height, and if seated with crowns .004 inch below the case head, the anvil would be forced through the crown, rendering the primer useless.

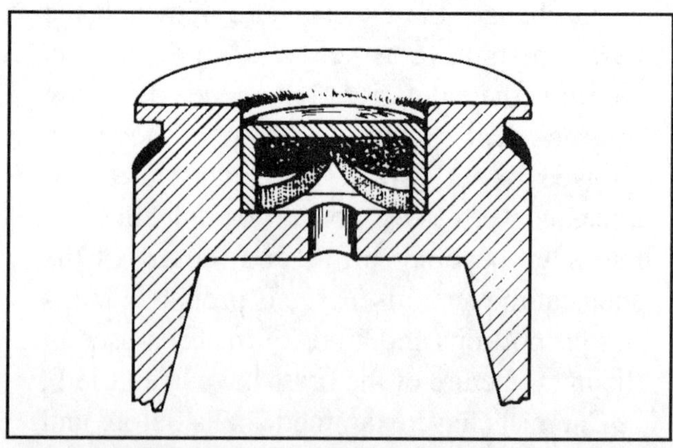

Figure 4-6: Improperly-seated primer showing the priming cup resting on the bottom of the primer well.

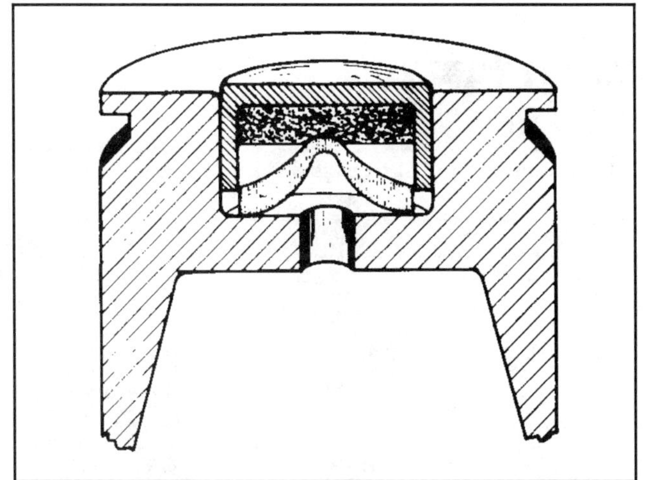

Figure 4-7: Improperly-seated primer showing the priming cup protruding above the case head.

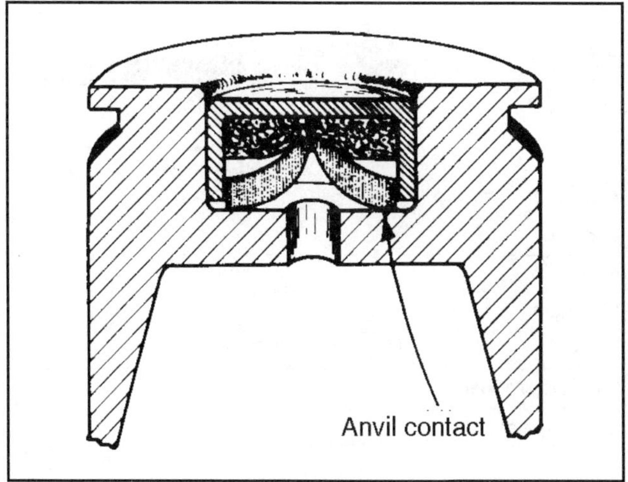

Figure 4-8: A properly-seated primer.

Another improperly-seated primer is shown in Figure 4-7. Here the primer is seated high, resulting in erratic performance. This arrangement is also dangerous and could explode in the chamber when the breechblock closes on it before being locked.

The primer shown in Figure 4-8 is properly seated. The primer crown is .004 inch below the head of the case, the anvils are on the bottom of the primer well, and the primer mixture is properly stressed by the anvil for best sensitivity. It is also a safe arrangement.

See the Primer Compatibility Table on the next page for the proper size primers to use in several popular cartridges.

PRIMER COMPATIBILITY TABLE

Primer Brand	Large Rifle	Small Rifle	Large Pistol	Small Pistol
CCI	200	400	300	500
Federal	210	200	150	100
Norma	large rifle	small rifle	large pistol	small pistol
Remington	9½	6½	2½	1½
RWS	large rifle	small rifle	large pistol	small pistol
Winchester-Western	8½ – 120	6½ – 116	7 – 111	1½ – 108
CCI Magnum	250	450	350	550
	FOR THESE CALIBERS	**FOR THESE CALIBERS**	**FOR THESE CALIBERS**	**FOR THESE CALIBERS**
	.219 Zipper .22 Savage HP .22-250 .220 Swift .224 Wby Mag .225 Win .240 Wby Mag .243 Win 6mm Rem .25 Rem .25-284 Win .25-35 .25-06 .250 Savage .257 Roberts .257 Wby Mag .6.5 Mann-Sch 6.5 Jap .264 Win Mag .270 Win .270 Wby Mag 7mm Wby Mag 7x57 Mauser .280 Rem .284 Win .30-30 WCF .30-40 Krag .30-06 .300 H&H .300 Savage .300 Wby Mag .300 Win Mag .308 Win .32 Win Spec .32-40 8x57 Mauser .33 Win .338 Win .348 Win .35 Rem and all larger calibers	.218 Bee .22 Hornet .22 K-Hornet .22 Rem Jet .221 Rem .222 Rem .222 Rem Mag .223 Rem .256 Win .25-20 .30 Carbine .32-20	.38-40 .41 Mag .44 Mag .44 Spec .44-40 .45 ACP .45 Auto Rim .45 Colt	.22 Rem Jet .256 Win .32-20 .357 Mag .38 S&W .38 Spec 9mm Luger

Chapter 5
Principles of Ballistics

***Ballistics* is a term used to describe the movement and property of the bullet or other projectile from the time it leaves the cartridge case until it reaches its destination.**

The Greeks called it "ballein" — meaning "to throw." An early Roman war machine, which hurled large objects, was called the "ballista." From these ancient words, the modern term *ballistics* was derived to indicate the science of moving projectiles.

As the study of ballistics progressed, the field of ballistics became divided into two groups:

- Interior
- Exterior

Interior ballistics pertains to performance inside the gun. *Exterior ballistics* deals with what happens to the projectile in its flight from gun muzzle to target and is of more interest to hunters, shooters, and reloaders because of its application to their problems. Interior ballistics is more the concern and interest of the ammunition manufacturer, but, is of importance when studying complete bullet performance. The reloader should be familiar with both.

INTERIOR BALLISTICS

The realm of interior ballistics extends — inside the barrel — from the *breech* (rear) to the *muzzle* (open end). The enlarged rear portion of the barrel accommodates the cartridge and is known as the *chamber.* Just in front of the chamber is a short conical section known as the *throat.* The area from the throat to the muzzle is called the *bore* of the gun.

The bore is either smooth or rifled. The shotgun is a smoothbore firearm. A rifled bore is so named because of the parallel *grooves*, from two to as many as twelve or more, which are cut spirally up the barrel to the muzzle. *See* Figure 5-1 on the next page.

These grooves are .002″ to .006″ in depth and are called *rifling*. The raised portion in the bore between two adjacent grooves is called a *land*. Rifle calibers are commonly designated by bore diameter, which is the inside diameter of the barrel before

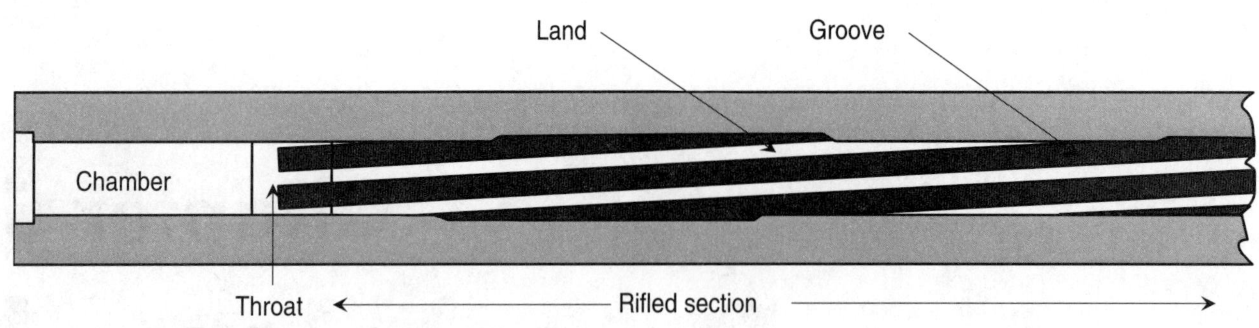

Figure 5-1: Longitudinal section of a rifle barrel.

the grooves are cut. Groove diameter, although seldom used, is measured from the bottom of one groove to the bottom of an opposite groove.

When the bullet enters the barrel, it engages the rifling and is forced into rotation. Without this rotation, any cylindrical bullet would tumble and have no accuracy upon leaving the muzzle. *See* Figure 5-2.

The rate of twist is usually expressed in the number of inches required for any single land or groove to make a complete turn. The longer the bullet in relation to its diameter, the faster it has to be spun. The rate of spin, or twist, in rifling varies

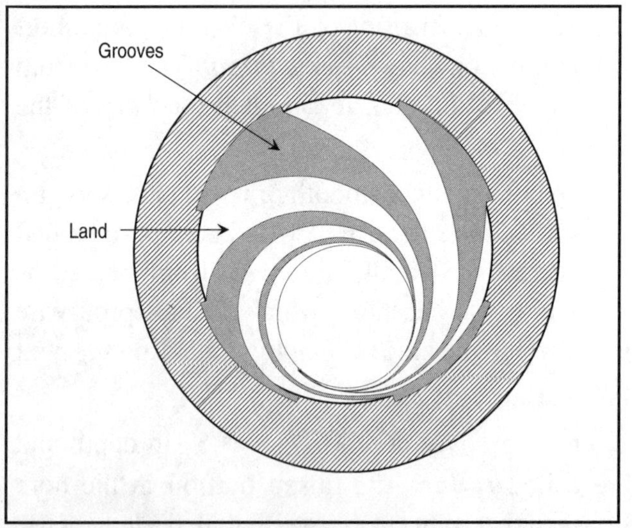

Figure 5-2: Rifling, consisting of lands and grooves, spins the fired bullet during its flight from the muzzle to the target. The spinning stabilizes the bullet in flight.

from as many as one turn every 6⅓″ to as few as one turn every 60″, depending on the velocity, diameter, and weight of the bullet. Because there is some leeway in the amount of spin a bullet needs to maintain its gyratory stability, different bullet weights may be fired successfully and accurately from the same rifle.

It all starts with the trigger. Depressing the trigger releases the firing pin, which strikes and detonates the primer. This primer detonation is much like an ordinary match that ignites when the tip is struck or scratched. The flash of the primer in turn ignites the powder, which is instantaneously converted into gas, causing very high pressure in all directions. The mouth of the cartridge case, where the base of the bullet is inserted, offers the least resistance to this exploding gas. Consequently, the bullet is forced out of the cartridge case into the bore of the rifle and continues to travel at high speed out of the muzzle.

Cartridge cases are controlled and gauged carefully during manufacturing to assure proper functioning in all standard chambers. A case must not only chamber easily and quickly, it must withstand a tremendous expanding pressure during firing and still be extracted with ease and certainty. To compensate for this, a metallic cartridge is slightly smaller in diameter than the chamber of the gun. Under pressure of the powder gas, obduration takes place, in which the case expands against the chamber wall, making a tight seal and preventing gas from escaping to the rear. At the same time, the cartridge case head is solidly supported in the breech mechanism to prevent separation of case and head from the inside pressure. As the bullet leaves the muzzle, the pressure in the bore and chamber drops and the cartridge case shrinks enough to allow extraction from the chamber.

One of the major problems in interior ballistics is uniform ignition of the powder by the primer. Only by close control of ignition can uniform pressure and muzzle velocities be maintained. All modern American primers are precisely engineered to perform efficiently with modern smokeless powder.

Routine ballistic and control tests conducted by various ammunition manufacturers include pressure-velocity measurements, barrel time (the time it takes a bullet to emerge form the muzzle after the firing pin falls), primer sensitivity tests, chamber gauging tests, and push-and-pull tests on the crimp of the bullet in the case.

Only by producing ammunition to exacting interior ballistic specifications is it possible to produce ammunition with uniform exterior ballistic performance.

BREECH PRESSURE

Questions are frequently asked concerning the amount of breech pressure, or chamber pressure, produced by a specific cartridge. This question cannot be answered with a single number of pounds per square inch (psi) since the pressure is never constant from the time the powder starts burning until the bullet leaves the barrel. For example, the maximum or peak pressure can be expressed as 50,000 psi, but this number is entirely misleading except to the experienced ballistician.

First, this peak pressure is an instantaneous peak, so its effects are completely different from the constant or slowly changing pressures of normal experience. Only an engineer experienced in interpreting the effect of this rapidly changing pressure can reliably apply these peak pressure measurements. Second, there are such a large number of conditions that affect this measurement that a simple number of psi is meaningless. Even an experienced ballistician cannot interpret such measurements unless the complete conditions are known.

While it becomes obvious that pressure results are almost meaningless to the lay person, they are of great importance to both gun and ammunition manufacturers.

Gun manufacturers correlate their gun designs with actual tests to make sure proper safety factors are built into their guns, while ammunition manufacturers control pressures within corresponding limits.

The psi rating is a measurement of the pressure that must be contained by the firearm breech, chamber walls, and barrel. This is the force that is applied outwardly from the chamber. The psi measurements and ratings for cartridges used in firearms are most often obtained by the use of a pressure barrel. There are two different methods that are associated with pressure barrels:

- Copper crusher method
- Piezoelectric transducer method

Both are invasive types; that is, both the chamber wall and the cartridge case are drilled for insertion of metering devices. The two methods are differentiated by the exact nature of sampling the pressure.

Copper Crusher Method

The oldest of the pressure barrel-metering techniques involves a mechanical metering device that subjects a small copper cylinder directly to the pressure of the expanding gases in the cartridge cases. A cross-sectional view of a pressure gun is shown in Figure 5-3. The chamber of the pressure barrel is drilled and tapped to accept the threads of a pressure gauge. Another hole is drilled in the cartridge case and aligned with the hole in the

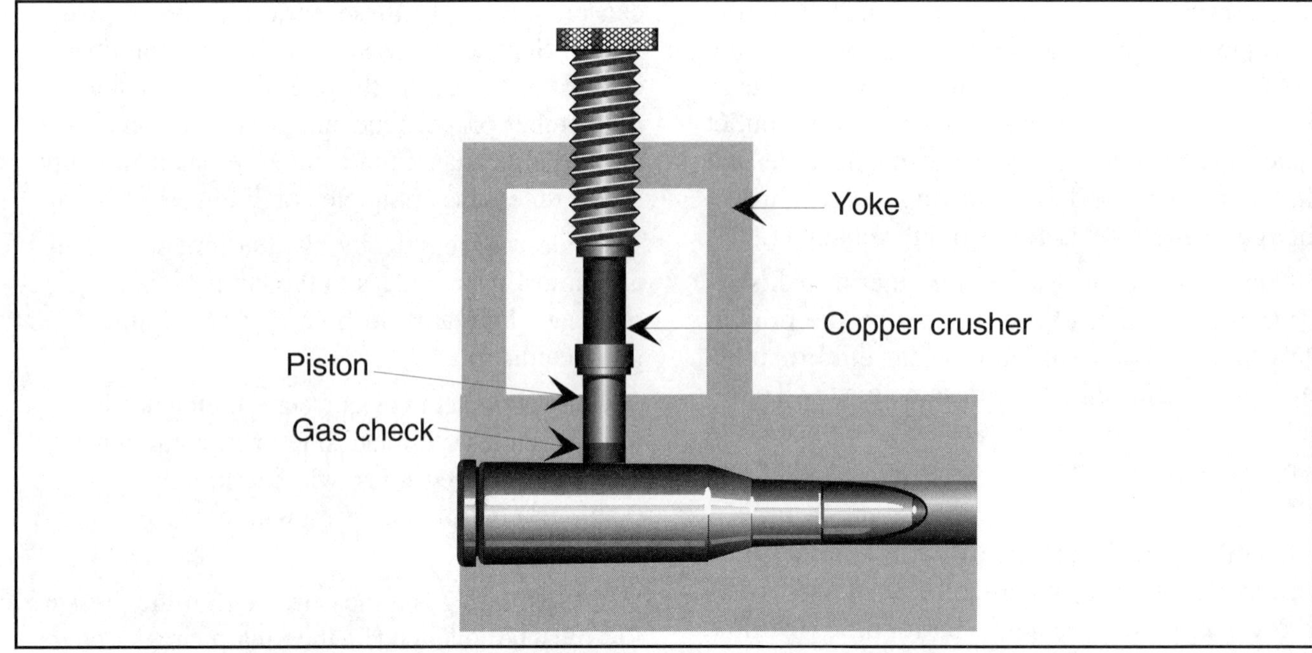

Figure 5-3: Cross-sectional view of a crusher-type pressure gun.

chamber. A mechanical piston-measuring device is inserted through these aligned holes. The piston contains a gas check at the point where it enters the cartridge case to prevent any of the expanding gas from escaping.

A small copper cylinder of specific construction and fixed dimensions is placed on top of the piston and held in place by a set screw. When the cartridge is fired, the expanding powder gases force the piston against the copper cylinder and crush it against the set screw. After firing, the compressed copper cylinder is removed and measured with a micrometer. The amount of compression is then compared to a chart that gives a fairly accurate reading of the internal average chamber pressure.

When a load of powder is ignited, a pressure curve is generated. The pressure builds from zero (prior to detonation) to a peak maximum and then drops to zero again as the bullet leaves the barrel. Due to the mechanical nature of the copper crusher method of pressure measurement, the peak pressure is not indicated. The peak occurs and then drops off so rapidly that the piston cannot move quickly enough or provide the force necessary to overcome the resistance of the copper cylinder.

The copper crusher method also leads to some safety concerns. The piston and copper cylinder could possibly become deadly projectiles, should the set screw fail. In this day and age, mechanical measurement of everything from automotive oil pressure to the temperature in homes and other buildings has been replaced with electronic methods. So it is with the measurement of firearm pressures. Although some manufacturers still stick with the tried-and-true methods of yesteryear, electronics are gradually gaining ground in all sorts of firearms tests.

The Piezoelectric Transducer Method

A more modern method of measuring internal pressure when a cartridge is fired, similar to the copper crusher method, is one in which the piston and copper cylinder are replaced by a solid-state transducer. A transducer is an electronic device that converts one form of energy into another. The best-known example of a transducer is the speaker in a stereo system. An electric current is fed to the speaker and is converted to sound. The reverse is true of a microphone, where sound is converted to an electric current. Both are transducers; each transforms one form of energy into another equivalent form.

The term *piezoelectric* simply describes the type of material used within the transducer to accomplish this transformation. In the case of one designed for measuring chamber pressure, a tiny wafer of quartz crystal is cut and ground to microscopically fine dimensions. This is very similar to a common microphone: a person's voice causes a slight pressure to be imposed on the microphone element, which actually flexes or moves in relationship to the sound waves produced by the voice. The microphone element (transducer) converts this movement into electric current that fluctuates in the same manner as the voice.

The transducer in a piezoelectric pressure barrel produces electric current when pressure is applied to its element. The higher the pressure, the larger the current. Instead of a copper cylinder, the electric output from the transducer is read on a simple meter. Rather than using a look-up chart, the meter can be directly calibrated in psi.

This is a simpler arrangement that does not use up copper cylinders and is a bit safer in that the transducer is simply screwed into the chamber hole and cartridge case. Due to the rapidity in which a transducer converts pressure to electricity, this method allows for far more accurate readings of pressure, because the transducer and meter can detect pressure speeds even greater than the expansion of gases in the cartridge. Therefore, the piezoelectric method of pressure testing is fully capable of reading the maximum peak pressure during any firing. Both methods are often used simultaneously, although the copper crusher method of pressure testing is still utilized in most ammunition and bullet-manufacturing plants.

Differences In The Two Methods

When chamber pressures are measured by the older copper crusher method and compared with readings obtained from the same pressure barrel using the piezoelectric transducer method, the latter method will usually present higher peak pressure readings. The two readings will almost never be the same — typically differing by several thousand psi. The reason for this lies in the fact that the copper crusher method is mechanical and doesn't really measure the absolute peak pressure. These high-pressure levels occur for such a brief period of time and then taper off, so the piston does not have time to react fully.

The piezoelectric transducer operates at a much higher sampling rate with no mechanics involved, so it truly does measure the absolute peak pressures. This is the major reason for the differences in the two readings.

The copper crusher method of chamber pressure determination has been used for over a century and on hundreds of thousands of different cartridges and loads. Therefore, a wealth of printed data has accumulated over this time. This means that the newer piezoelectric transducer readings can be compared directly with documented copper crusher measurements to arrive at meaningful data. For instance, if a pressure reading of 40,000 psi has been obtained via the copper crusher method for a particular load in a cartridge and the same load produces a reading of 48,000 psi using the piezoelectric transducer method, then the conversion factor between the two methods for this particular cartridge, powder charge, bullet, primer, case, etc. is obtained.

Despite its inability to measure peak pressure, the copper crusher method is still the standard by which all ammunition is tested, but the piezoelectric transducer method is being used more and more, so the amount of hard data available on these types of readings is growing. Eventually, the piezoelectric transducer method will probably replace the more awkward copper crusher method but not for quite a few years to come.

EFFECTS OF BARREL LENGTH ON VELOCITY

With the old blackpowder loads, long barrels were used to develop full velocity from the powder charge. But today, modern smokeless powders at higher pressures develop high velocity in shorter barrels.

Certain standard-length barrels — depending upon caliber — are used for velocity tests. Conditions vary widely with different cartridges and with the same cartridge in different guns. It is possible to set an exact figure for changes in velocity per inch of barrel length above or below standard. The correction may vary from 5 to as much as 25 feet per second (fps) per inch. A change of 25 fps per inch of barrel, above or below standard, will be approximately correct for rifles. For example, if the printed factory muzzle velocity for the .30-30 cartridge is 2220 fps, chances are the tests were made in a 30-inch barrel. When this cartridge is fired from a carbine with the 20-inch barrel, the approximate velocity may be calculated by the following equation:

Recorded velocity - (test barrel length – actual barrel length x 25 fps) = actual velocity

Therefore:

2220 - (30″ - 20″ x 25) = 1970 fps

Another way to find the actual velocity of a factory load used in a given barrel length is to use conversion factors. The manufacturer-published velocities of a given load are currently based on a barrel length of 26 inches, with some exceptions. To find the actual velocity in a given rifle, the following correction table may be used.

Barrel Length	Multiplication Factor
26″	1.000
25″	0.993
24″	0.985
23″	0.979
22″	0.969
21″	0.964
20″	0.954
19″	0.944
18″	0.939

For example, the factory-published velocity of a 139-grain bullet in a 6.5 x 54mm cartridge is 2580 feet per second. What is the velocity in an 18-inch carbine barrel?

Look at the above table and find the multiplication factor for an 18-inch barrel. This figure is 0.939. Multiply the factory-published velocity by this factor to obtain the approximate velocity in an 18-inch barrel.

2580 x 0.939 = 2422 fps

Therefore, the actual velocity in an 18-inch barrel is 2422 fps.

EXTERIOR BALLISTICS

Exterior ballistics, with its problems of air resistance, trajectory, wind drift, accuracy, and remaining energy, describes the behavior of the bullet after it leaves the muzzle of the gun.

The forward speed of a bullet, usually specified in feet per second (fps), is its velocity. It is perhaps the most interesting of all topics pertaining to exterior ballistics.

The faster a bullet covers the distance from gun to target, the less it drops and the flatter its path or trajectory. Shooters and manufacturers search for high velocity because a flat trajectory minimizes errors in range estimating and results in surer hits

Figure 5-4: Line-of-sight, range, and trajectory of bullet from muzzle to target.

at longer ranges. The need for high velocity is particularly apparent in long-range shooting.

The muzzle velocity is given in foot seconds, representing the number of feet the projectile would travel in one second if it continued at the same rate as when leaving the muzzle. Since the bullet is subject to two forces, air resistance and gravity, the speed of flight begins to drop at once. The speed with which the bullet continues to travel is dependent upon the weight and form of the bullet; also upon the wind.

Instantaneous muzzle velocity of any bullet cannot be measured accurately by any laboratory equipment. However, new scientific equipment, particularly the counter chronograph and photoelectric screen, makes it possible to measure velocities with great accuracy over ranges as short as six feet. Loss of velocity over these short ranges is small and, thus, muzzle velocity is closely computed.

The customary method of measuring bullet velocity is to time the bullet as it passes over a specific distance. By dividing this distance by the measured time, the average number of feet per second the bullet travels can be computed. This is the average velocity over the range on which the bullet was timed. By plotting velocities over a series of ranges, a curve can be established to estimate muzzle velocity.

The flight of the bullet from muzzle to point of impact is in the form of a curve, with the highest point about 54 percent of the way toward the target. *See* Figure 5-4. The greater the distance of the target the more the muzzle must be elevated to provide against a drop short of the target. Point blank range is that range at which the bullet travels practically flat and before any perceptible drop due to air resistance or gravitation has taken place and coincides with the line from muzzle to target.

Let's see what really happens after a bullet leaves the barrel. First, the bullet must be given a spin to keep it steady, like a spinning top, so it will stay on target. This is accomplished by the spiral lands of the rifling gripping the bullet. Long bullets require a more rapid spin than short bullets to stabilize. For this reason, the twist of the rifling varies according to caliber of the rifle — usually from one turn in 10″ to one turn in 14″. In most cases, a compromise is adopted that is satisfactory for the different weight bullets that are available in most calibers. If both the bullet base and the muzzle of the rifle are perfectly square, the bullet will leave the barrel without tipping, which is detrimental to good accuracy.

In many cases, however, the bullet is subjected to an uneven push from the escaping gases directly behind the bullet, which causes the bullet to wobble or yaw. The degree of swing from the perpendicular is referred to as the angle of yaw. The amount of yaw is directly influenced by the length of the bearing surface of the bullet against the barrel. The shorter this surface, the greater the angle of yaw. In either case, the bullet is immediately affected by two main forces — gravity and air resistance. Consequently, the instant the bullet leaves the muzzle, it immediately begins to lose speed and start to fall.

To better understand the effect of gravity and air resistance, let's assume that we have two rifles, one shooting a 150-grain bullet, the other a 180-grain bullet. Both are .30 caliber and both leave the muzzle at 3000 feet per second. Let's further assume that both are on a platform with their muzzles exactly 16.08 feet above the ground, and the axis of each barrel is exactly parallel to the ground, which in turn is perfectly level for a considerable distance away from the platform. Now, suppose both rifles are fired simultaneously, and that we let a bullet fall from our hand at exactly the same height, and at the exact same instant the two bullets leave the muzzle of the two rifles. What happens?

All three bullets will strike the ground at the same instant! The dropped bullet will land on the ground close to the platform; the 150-grain bullet at 2,186 feet away from the platform; the 180-grain bullet will strike at a distance 2,304 feet away from the platform. Although both fired bullets left the rifles at a rate of 3000 fps, neither bullet will achieve that distance. Air resistance will slow down their flight, so neither can go that far in the one second gravity will give them to fall 16.08 feet. The 150-grain bullet will be affected to the same extent as the 180-grain bullet by the heavy hand of gravity, but it will be affected by air resistance somewhat more than the 180-grain, since the 150-grain has more surface exposed in relation to its weight.

To get back to the platform, if we could actually see the flight of these two bullets, we would notice that they were following an ever-increasing curve until they hit the ground, as shown in Figure 5-5. That's because the bullet is both losing velocity and

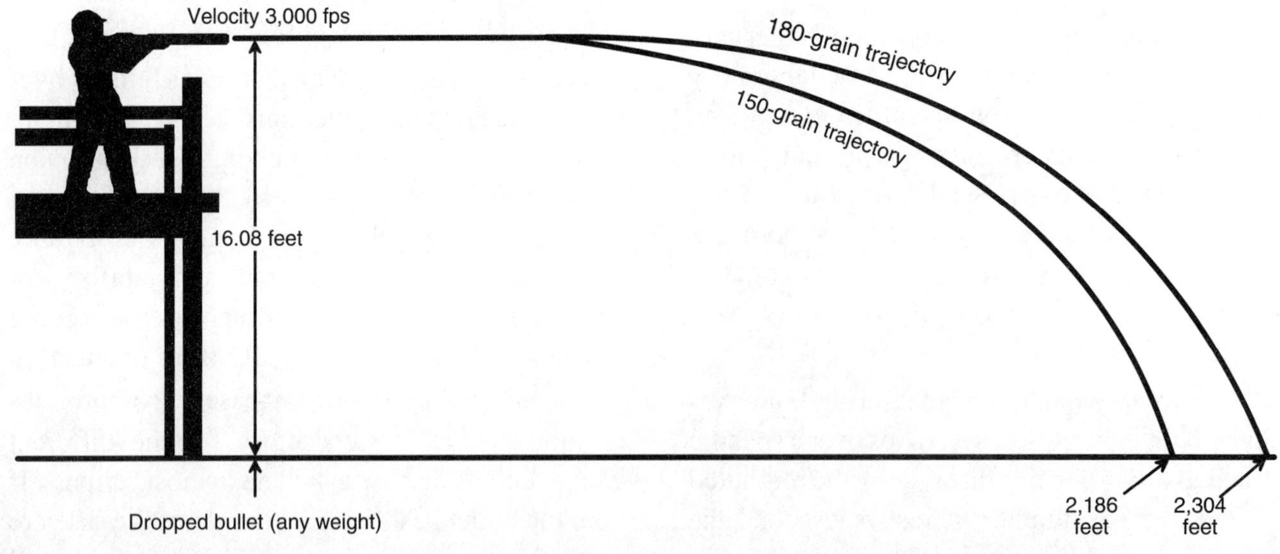

Figure 5-5: A dropped object falls 16.08 feet in one second. All fired bullets approximate this. The higher the velocity, the flatter the trajectory. But heavier bullets sustain their velocity longer than lighter ones.

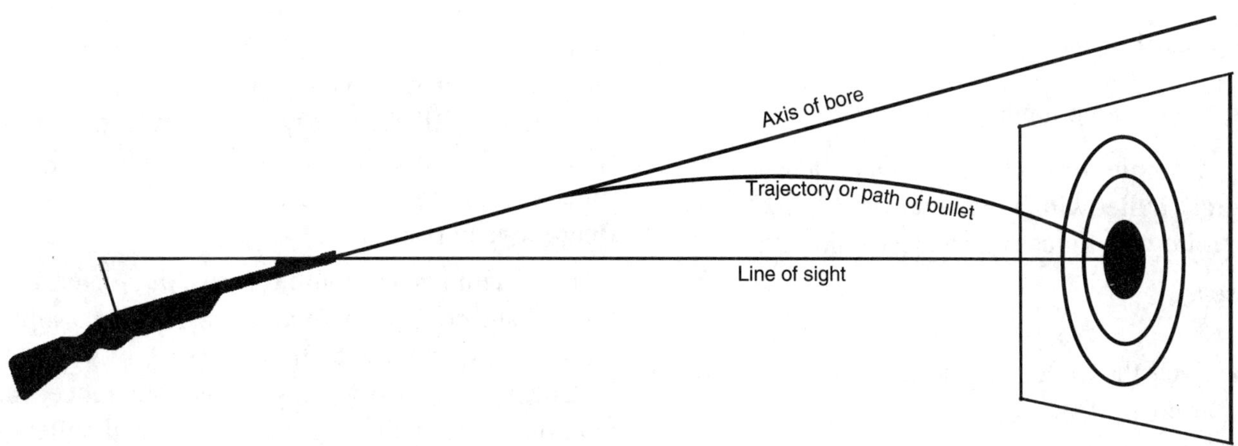

Figure 5-6: For the bullet to go farther, the barrel must be pointed upward so that the bullet is projected higher into the air, giving it more time to fall.

dropping at an ever increasing rate. Obviously, if we want the bullet to go further, we have to point the barrel upward and project the bullet higher into the air, giving it more time to fall.

Even though the line of sight is parallel to the ground, the bullet must rise above this line to reach the target. Figure 5-6 shows the relationship of the line of sight, axis of bore, and trajectory or path of the bullet. Note also that the bullet begins to fall the moment it leaves the muzzle, just as it did from the hypothetical 16.08-foot platform, and forms a curved path. The higher the velocity, the less curve there will be over a given distance. Because the trajectory is flatter, the rifle with higher velocity will demonstrate flatter shooting.

Most shots are seldom fired from exactly 16.08 feet above the ground. Shooters stand, kneel or perhaps lie prone on the ground, aiming at a target several yards away. Ignoring the human element, if a fairly high-velocity rifle is used, say, with a bullet traveling at 2400 fps, the bullet will hit the target anywhere from point-blank range to 200 yards or more if it is zeroed in; that is, sighted to hit where the shooter aims at a measured 150 yards. If the target is only 100 yards away, the hit will be a little high; at 150 yards, on the button; at 200 yards, a little low.

It follows that rifles with higher velocities and flatter trajectories can be zeroed in at 200 yards with good results at 250 to 300 yards. On the other hand, lower velocity rifles would be limited to a 100-yard range, and either the rear sight should be raised or a higher aim taken on a target beyond 150 yards.

SECTIONAL DENSITY

Sectional density is the weight of a bullet in relation to its diameter. It is determined by the bullet's weight (in pounds), divided by the square of its diameter (in inches). The resulting figure is used as a gauge to determine flight characteristics. To determine sectional density using most electronic calculators, perform the following steps:

- Enter bullet weight in grains
- Press Division key
- Enter 7000 to convert grains to pounds
- Enter bullet diameter
- Press Division key
- Enter bullet diameter again

- Press Equals key
- Answer in pounds per inch

For example, to find the sectional density of a 180-grain bullet with a diameter of .308 inch, key in the following values on an electronic calculator.

Steps

- Enter the bullet weight in grains
- Press Division key
- Enter 7000 to convert grains to pounds
- Press Division key
- Enter bullet diameter, 0.308
- Press Division key
- Enter bullet diameter, 0.308
- Press Equals key
- Answer in pounds per inch

The bullet in question has a sectional density of 0.271 pounds per inch.

BALLISTIC COEFFICIENT

The way in which a bullet behaves in flight is determined by its initial velocity, weather, altitude, wind conditions, and by its aerodynamic shape. The ballistic coefficient of a bullet, in general, is a description of how streamlined it is. Ballistic coefficients are given in decimal form as fractions of 1. The higher the ballistic coefficient, the more streamlined the bullet. Conversely, a bullet that is highly streamlined will fly through the air more efficiently than one that is not. The ballistic coefficient of any bullet is a very important factor for all reloaders, because this factor will be a large determinate of the bullet's uses, especially in regard to long-range performance.

Two methods are commonly used to determine the ballistic coefficient of a bullet. The more popular method was introduced in the 1930s by Wallace H. Coe and Edgar Beugless, ballistics engineers at Du Pont. This method compares an actual bullet to a point-shape chart, and when the closest possible match is made, the chart provides a point-shape factor — a number which is then divided into the bullet sectional density to give the ballistic coefficient.

The other method is direct measurement by means of firing tests. The test range must be instrumental so that both muzzle velocity and flight time over a known distance are measured for each shot fired. A computer program then derives the ballistic coefficient of each test bullet from these measurements.

For the average shooter, the best and easiest way to obtain the ballistic coefficient of a given bullet is from the bullet's manufacturer. Tables are available that give the sectional density, ballistic coefficient , etc., for nearly every bullet manufactured.

WIND DRIFT

Wind drift has a great bearing on the bullet's flight. A crosswind, particularly one at right angles to the bullet's flight, may push the bullet off target a noticeable amount at long ranges. At short ranges, the effect on high-velocity cartridges is small and need not be taken into account. However, wind drift will have little or no effect on a bullet that is traveling directly upwind or downwind.

In a crosswind of 10 miles per hour, a .22-caliber bullet, with a muzzle velocity of 1,335 fps, will be blown downwind 5 inches at 100 yards, and 17 inches at 200 yards. An identical wind will blow a .30-06, 180-grain soft-point bullet off its path 2½-inches at 300 yards. A 30-mile-an-hour wind will have three times this effect.

For all practical purposes, at normal shooting ranges up to 300 yards, even in fairly heavy winds, only a small allowance is necessary for wind drift. At 400 or 500 yards, and up to 1,000 yards — ranges ordinarily shot by target shooters — the wind drift must be carefully estimated. Wind estimating requires long practice and a great amount of skill and judgment on the part of the shooter because the wind is rarely constant.

ENERGY

Normally, energy is expressed in foot/pounds. By knowing the weight of the bullet and its velocity at the desired range, energy is easily computed. Here is the equation:

$$\frac{\textit{Velocity}^2 \times \textit{Bullet Weight (grains)}}{450{,}240} = \textit{Energy in ft/lbs}$$

The variables are velocity in feet per second and bullet weight in grains. The constant denominator is 450,250.

Bullet energy is of great interest to the hunter as well as the manufacturer, because of its close relationship to killing power, which in turn, is important to prevent the crippling of game. Killing power is not based on energy alone. The rate and method of application of energy to the animal is equally important. For example, a full metal case bullet may pass completely through an animal and travel on for some distance, while a soft-point bullet of the same velocity will expand and deliver its entire energy within the body of the animal.

KILLING POWER

A clean kill on all types of game is the desire of a true sportsperson. The hunter desires to prevent the suffering and mutilation of his prey. No one yardstick among present published information — which includes velocity, energy, bullet types and weights, and diameter — is available that can be used to measure killing power, although all of the above data has some influence in determining effective killing power. All other factors being equal, it is generally accepted that within the limits of proper cartridge use, a comparison of energies is a fair comparison of killing power.

When one cartridge uses a heavy bullet traveling at a slow speed and another has a light bullet that travels at high velocity, energy alone is not enough to make a fair comparison. For that reason, even though muzzle energies may be approximately equal, a lightweight, high-velocity bullet will tend to create a superficial wound on large game, whereas a slower and larger bullet will penetrate deeper and produce better killing power. Therefore, it is important that the proper bullet be selected.

RECOIL

Any gun that is fired has some recoil. This is true of the lightest rifles as well as the heaviest big-game guns. Bullet weight and velocity, the weight of the powder charge, and the weight of the gun affect the recoil. A lighter gun will have a heavier recoil than a heavier gun with the same cartridge.

Recoil begins the instant the bullet starts moving down the barrel. But due to the bullet's high velocity, the bullet is out of the barrel before the rifle actually moves. Consequently, the delayed action of recoil doesn't affect the shooter's aim. When the bullet and powder gases have left the muzzle, the rear of the rifle has received all the recoil velocity, although it has only moved a fraction of an inch at this time. The entire rifle, however, continues to move backward against the shooter's shoulder until all recoil energy has been absorbed.

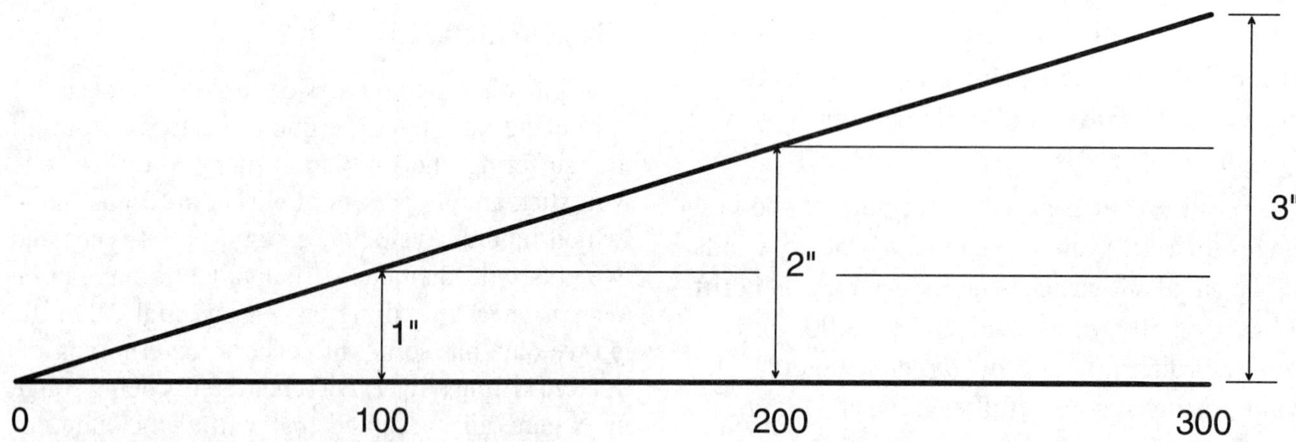

Figure 5-7: This diagram illustrates the effect of sight adjustment regarding range. The base line is calibrated to 300 yards with the angular line representing one minute-of-angle of sight adjustment.

Shooters are limited as to the bullet weight and velocity that can be built into a cartridge because of a shooter's choice of gun weight and ability to withstand recoil. Increasing either bullet weight or velocity or decreasing gun weight will increase recoil, and vice versa.

ACCURACY

No rifle will put all its bullets through exactly the same hole on the target. Instead, the bullets striking the target form a pattern known as a *group*. The size of a group is measured by the distance between the centers of the two shots that are farthest apart. Accuracy, therefore, is the measurement of this group.

A minute-of-angle is the term used in measuring bullet dispersion and is approximately 1″ at 100 yards. This is proportional to 2″ at 200 yards, 3″ at 300 yards, and so on, as shown in Figure 5-7. An ordinary sporting rifle is considered accurate for hunting purposes if it will shoot into three-minutes-of-angle.

Many special target rifles with the proper cartridges and also many hunting rifles and cartridges,

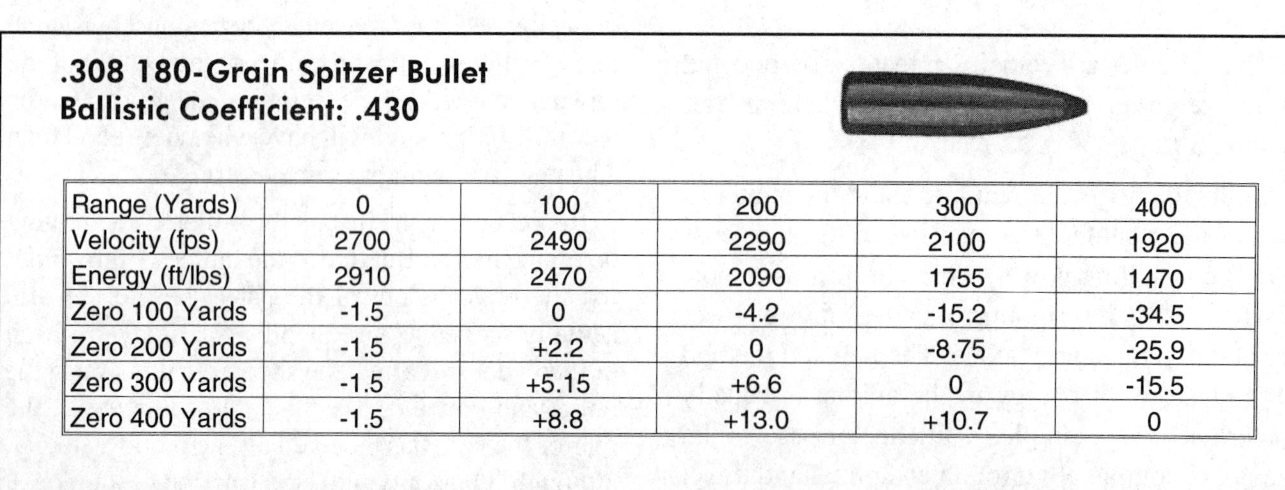

.308 180-Grain Spitzer Bullet
Ballistic Coefficient: .430

Range (Yards)	0	100	200	300	400
Velocity (fps)	2700	2490	2290	2100	1920
Energy (ft/lbs)	2910	2470	2090	1755	1470
Zero 100 Yards	-1.5	0	-4.2	-15.2	-34.5
Zero 200 Yards	-1.5	+2.2	0	-8.75	-25.9
Zero 300 Yards	-1.5	+5.15	+6.6	0	-15.5
Zero 400 Yards	-1.5	+8.8	+13.0	+10.7	0

Figure 5-8: Typical ballistic chart giving pertinent downrange information concerning the bullet performance.

.308 180-Grain Spitzer Bullet
Ballistic Coefficient: .430

Range (Yards)	0	100	200	300	400
Velocity (fps)	**2700**	**2490**	**2290**	**2100**	**1920**
Energy (ft/lbs)	2910	2470	2090	1755	1470
Zero 100 Yards	-1.5	0	-4.2	-15.2	-34.5
Zero 200 Yards	-1.5	+2.2	0	-8.75	-25.9
Zero 300 Yards	-1.5	+5.15	+6.6	0	-15.5
Zero 400 Yards	-1.5	+8.8	+13.0	+10.7	0

Figure 5-9: Typical ballistic chart highlighting range and velocity.

on the average, will shoot more accurately than the figures mentioned previously. In fact, most modern hunters will not use a rifle that does not shoot within one minute of angle. Some of the records that have been established with modern target equipment and ammunition are truly surprising.

INTRODUCTION TO BALLISTIC CHARTS

A typical ballistic chart is shown in Figure 5-8. This chart gives the bullet diameter (.308″ in this case), the bullet weight and type, along with the ballistic coefficient of the bullet. Complete information about bullet performance is also included; that is, velocity in fps, energy in ft/lbs, points of impact at various ranges, and the like. This particular chart gives bullet-performance information from the muzzle to 400 yards. Other charts may extend this range to 500 or even 600 yards, but are read in exactly the same manner as this one.

Figure 5-9 highlights the top two lines of this chart, which deal with velocities from zero to 400 yards. Referring to these two lines, note that the bullet starts out at a velocity of 2700 fps at the muzzle or zero yards. The velocity drops to 2490 fps at the 100-yard downrange point. This velocity is a result of two factors: the muzzle velocity and the ballistic coefficient of the bullet. If the muzzle velocity is lower than 2700 fps, then the velocity at 100 yards would be lower; if the ballistic coefficient is lower than .430 (the value in this chart), the velocity at 100 yards would also be lower.

Continuing with the chart in Figure 5-9, the velocity drops to 2290 fps at 200 yards, 2100 fps at 300 yards, and finally to 1920 fps at 400 yards.

The information given to this point does not tell much about the trajectory, but it does provide useful information about loss of velocity over the various ranges and allows reloaders to select bullets that offer the most ideal performance in terms of retained velocity over a given range. When these velocities are plugged into a computerized trajectory equation, all necessary information is obtained for graphing a trajectory curve. Fortunately, most ballistic charts provided by bullet manufacturers already have this information, so no mathematics is involved on the part of the reloader.

Let's expand the subsections of the basic chart as highlighted in Figure 5-10 on the next page. Here, the row that contains the energy information is matched with the downrange yardage and its related velocity — giving the remaining energy of a bullet of this weight and ballistic coefficient at

.308 180-Grain Spitzer Bullet
Ballistic Coefficient: .430

Range (Yards)	0	100	200	300	400
Velocity (fps)	2700	2490	2290	2100	1920
Energy (ft/lbs)	**2910**	**2470**	**2090**	**1755**	**1470**
Zero 100 Yards	-1.5	0	-4.2	-15.2	-34.5
Zero 200 Yards	-1.5	+2.2	0	-8.75	-25.9
Zero 300 Yards	-1.5	+5.15	+6.6	0	-15.5
Zero 400 Yards	-1.5	+8.8	+13.0	+10.7	0

Figure 5-10: Typical ballistic chart highlighting range and bullet energy.

various ranges. Let's assume that a bullet energy of 1500 ft/lbs is desirable for deer-size game. Referring to the chart, this bullet/load combination is adequate out to almost 400 yards. However, if larger game, such as moose or elk is hunted — requiring about 2000 ft/lbs of bullet energy for humane kills — then this bullet/load combination would be adequate out to just beyond 200 yards.

None of the chart information discussed thus far has reviewed the actual trajectory of the bullet. However, the remaining sections of the chart supply this information as shown in Figure 5-11 (see below) This is a convenient way to state trajectory of firearms sighted in at 100, 200, 300, and 400 yards. It indicates how high or low the bullet will strike a target at various ranges from 0 to 400 yards.

Starting with the first Zero column, note that a firearm sighted in to strike a target at 100 yards will be 1.5 inches below line of sight at the muzzle. This negative value occurs at the muzzle, because the sights of the firearm are located above the muzzle at an average height of 1.5 inches. Therefore, the

.308 180-Grain Spitzer Bullet
Ballistic Coefficient: .430

Range (Yards)	0	100	200	300	400
Velocity (fps)	2700	2490	2290	2100	1920
Energy (ft/lbs)	2910	2470	2090	1755	1470
Zero 100 Yards	**-1.5**	**0**	**-4.2**	**-15.2**	**-34.5**
Zero 200 Yards	**-1.5**	**+2.2**	**0**	**-8.75**	**-25.9**
Zero 300 Yards	**-1.5**	**+5.15**	**+6.6**	**0**	**-15.5**
Zero 400 Yards	**-1.5**	**+8.8**	**+13.0**	**+10.7**	**0**

Figure 5-11: Typical ballistic chart highlighting range and sighting information.

bullet is 1.5 inches below this line of sight when it leaves the barrel.

At 100 yards, the bullet is dead-on target, since this is the sighted-in distance. At the 200-yard point, the bullet has dropped a little over 4 inches. This is stated as a negative value, because it lies below the line of sight. At 300 yards, the bullet has dropped another 11 inches, and out at 400 yards almost an additional 20 inches over the 300-yard figure. Notice that as the bullet travels farther from the muzzle, it drops by a much larger percentage. This occurs because the bullet is constantly losing velocity as it travels farther downrange. The lower the velocity, the larger the drop.

If we assume deer-size game with a 5-inch-high or 5-inch-low error factor from line of sight, this would mean that the bullet rated by this chart at a muzzle velocity of 2700 fps and sighted in at 100 yards would be adequate for taking such game out to about 225 yards, when it would be 5 inches below line of sight. By "adequate" we mean that a hunter could aim at the center of the chest area of a deer at any range out to 225 yards (approximately) with killing results. The hunter would not have to aim low at 50 yards or high out to 225 yards, because the bullet stays within this 10-inch imaginary "kill" area over its entire trajectory to this range. This is known as the point-blank range (PBR), but it applies only to deer-size animals.

On small animals, the PBR would be less than 225 yards, because their effective kill zones would be smaller. PBR describes only the killing area of the target in regard to the bullet striking within this zone. This doesn't mean that any bullet that can stay within this zone is adequate for taking this size of game, only that it will strike within the broadside chest area of the animal if the shooter does his or her job. The energy of the bullet at the PBR is the deciding factor as to its ability to actually inflict lethal damage.

For this reason, we must also refer to the energy section of the ballistic chart in Figure 5-10. Here, we see that the bullet being rated has a retained energy level of a bit less than 2,090 ft/lbs Since 1000 to 1500 ft/lbs is considered adequate for deer-size animals, we know that the 225 yard PBR is a practical one.

However, if a hunter needs to be able to take game at ranges farther than 225 yards, it becomes necessary to sight the firearm in at a greater range. The 200 yard zero portion of the chart shows what happens to the trajectory when this is done.

The bullet is still 1.5 inches below line of sight at the muzzle and rises to 2.2 inches above line of sight at 100 yards. This is still easily within our plus or minus 5-inch point-blank range limit. At 200 yards, the bullet is right on the line of sight and drops to 8.75 inches below it at 300 yards. This effectively increases our PBR to about 250 yards with this bullet/velocity combination and the 200-yard sighting-in conditions, as the 300-yard drop point is over 3 inches below our optimum PBR.

Sighting in the firearm for 300 yards yields a rise above line of sight of 5.15 inches at 100 yards and 6.6 inches at 200 yards, while the bullet is on line at 300 yards. This tells us quite a lot. Still figuring on a plus or minus 5 inch rise or fall for the ideal PBR, the bullet/velocity combination is ideal only out to about 250 yards. Beyond this range, we cannot maintain the optimum results. To make this bullet an ideal performer out to 300 yards would require boosting its velocity by about 100 fps. If this bullet was chosen for use on deer out to 300 yards, 2700 fps muzzle velocity is not ideal. The velocity should be increased to 2800 fps if this can be done within safety limits. Then optimum trajectory performance could be maintained over the entire 300 yards. If not, switching to a bullet with a ballistic coefficient of .500 or more at 2700 fps would bring the trajectory specifications much closer to optimum.

The reloader has many choices to make when loading a cartridge for a specific purpose. It is first necessary to know the intended range over which the bullet will be used and the type of game it is intended to take. Armed with this information,

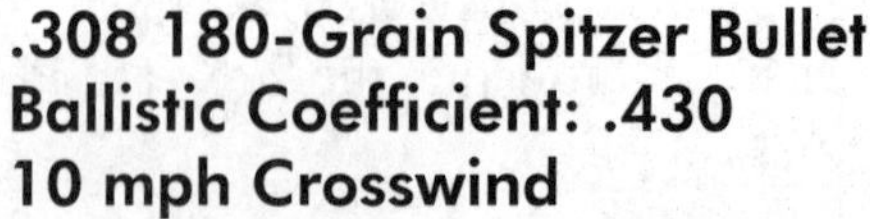

Range (Yards)	0	100	200	300	400
Velocity (fps)	2700	2490	2290	2100	1920
Wind Drift (inches)	0	0.7	3.3	7.8	14.5

Figure 5-12: Typical wind-drift chart.

ballistic charts may be referenced and the proper bullet/load combination obtained.

WIND DRIFT CHARTS

The ability of a bullet to hold its intended lateral course downrange is a factor of the speed of any crosswind, its initial speed, and ballistic coefficient. Charts are often provided by bullet manufacturers and by reloading component companies that will aid the reloader in calculating potential wind drift. Here, the weight of the bullet is not a factor in these calculations, as this is actually a factor in determining the ballistic coefficient. Therefore, all bullets with a ballistic coefficient of .450, for instance, will be affected in the same manner by crosswinds regardless of their calibers or weights. The determining factors in wind drift are ballistic coefficient and velocity only.

Most wind-drift charts assume a direct crosswind of 10 mph. However, it is possible to closely approximate direct crosswind if you know the velocity of the wind and its angle to the line of bullet flight. This is only necessary in long-range competition target shooting. In hunting situations, it is simply not practical to go through such gyrations. When hunting, you can estimate the crosswind velocity and then hold left or right accordingly if you know the approximate 10 mph wind drift in inches for a particular bullet and load.

Figure 5-12 shows a wind-drift chart for a bullet with a ballistic coefficient of .430. This is the same ballistic coefficient as the .308-caliber bullet represented in previous charts, but any bullet with the same ballistic coefficient and velocity applies equally.

From this chart, we see that as velocity falls off, wind drift increases. A 10 mph crosswind produces less than an inch of drift at 100 yards, and is less than 3.5 inches at 200 yards. The PBR discussed earlier may be thought of as a circle with a diameter of 10 inches for deer-size game. Therefore, the wind drift calculation should also abide by this plus or minus 5-inch factor. The wind-drift chart tells us that this bullet/velocity combination is good out to beyond 200 yards, assuming a 10-inch kill zone in calculating the PBR. At 300 yards, the drift has increased to almost 8 inches. Therefore, this chart, along with the previous ballistics charts, confirms that the bullet/velocity combination under discussion is adequate for deer-size game out to about 225-250 yards given normal wind conditions.

When crosswinds are blowing at speeds greater than 10 mph, the conversion factor from a 10-mph chart is an easy one. A 20-mph crosswind will cause the bullet to drift twice as far at any point downrange. Simply multiply the charted wind drift by the 2.0. For a 15-mph wind, multiply the drift in inches by 1.5.

SUMMARY

The reloader has many things to consider when determining the cartridge specifications prior to reloading. The purpose of the cartridge and the game it is intended to take will largely determine the bullet weight and caliber. The range over which the game is to be taken will be an equally large factor. Here is where ballistics charts are absolutely essential. If you know the caliber and general weight of the bullet, then these charts can help you decide the needed muzzle velocity and minimum ballistics coefficient rating necessary to get the job done.

No cartridge suits all general purposes, but the reloader has the advantage of being able to custom-design a cartridge for either a specific or wide range of purposes. By knowing how to read ballistics and wind-drift charts accurately, the ideal cartridge/bullet combination can be arrived at with little effort. It is only then that the reloader can go to the bench and assemble the components that should yield the desired results. It is important to range-test all loads to ensure that the bullets react to the specifications.

BALLISTIC CHARTS FOR FACTORY LOADS

All ammunition manufacturers provide ballistic charts for their loaded cartridges. Most of these charts include the following data:

- Name of cartridge and caliber
- Available bullet weights
- Muzzle velocity of each bullet type
- Remaining velocity at various ranges

Many ammunition manufacturers also provide the muzzle energy of each cartridge and the down-range bullet energies. Furthermore, trajectory data is provided in some instances.

The chart beginning on the next page is the most complete single ballistic chart in existence. It covers most of the sporting cartridges made in all parts of the world over the past 100 years or so.

In reviewing this chart, experienced shooters will note some duplications in loads. For example, the .236 Navy and the 6mm Lee Navy are identical cartridges. However, manufacturers called this cartridge by various names. Furthermore, the ballistics may also vary slightly among different manufacturers. Consequently, we have listed both names in different rows to aid in identifying the cartridge from headstamps that might appear on cartridge cases. Many of the cartridges listed are now obsolete and have fallen into the collector class.

Reloading information for the majority of the cartridges listed in this ballistics chart is covered in Section III of this book.

CENTERFIRE RIFLE BALLISTICS

Caliber	Bullet Wt. Grains	Bullet Type	Primer Type	Velocity — Feet Per Second Muzzle	100 Yards	200 Yards	300 Yards	400 Yards	500 Yards
.17 Rem.	25	Hollow Point Power Lokt	SRM	4040	3284	2644	2086	1606	1235
.218 Bee	46	Hollow Point	SRM	2760	2102	1550	1155	961	850
.219 Zipper	46	Soft Point	LR	3210	2740	—	—	—	—
5.6 x 35R Vierling	40	Lead		1950					
5.6 x 61mm Vom Hofe	77	Soft Point		3709	—	—	—	—	—
.22 Win. Single Shot	45	Lead		1300	—	—	—	—	—
.22 Hornet	45	Pointed Soft Point	SR	2690	2042	1502	1128	948	840
	45	Hollow Point	SR	2690	2042	1502	1128	948	841
.22 Maynard Extra Long	45	Lead		1125	—	—	—	—	—
.22-15-60 Stevens	60	Lead		1150	—	—	—	—	—
.22 Savage	70	Soft Point		2810	2400	2110	1840	—	—
.220 Swift	50	Pointed Soft Point	LR	3780	3168	2617	2135	1710	1357
.222 Rem.	50	Pointed Soft Point	SR	3140	2606	2123	1700	1350	1107
.222 Rem.	50	Hollow Point	SR	3140	2636	2182	1777	1432	1172
.222 Rem. Mag.	55	Pointed Soft Point	SR	3240	2748	2306	1906	1556	1272
.22 WCF	45	Lead		1340	1090	—	—	—	—
.223 Rem.	55	Pointed Soft Point	LR	3240	2747	2304	1905	1554	1270
	55	Hollow Point	LR	3240	2773	2352	1969	1627	1341
	55	Metal Case	LR	3240	2759	2326	1933	1587	1301
	60	Hollow Point Match	LR	3100	2712	2355	2026	1726	1463
.22-250 Rem.	55	Pointed Soft Point	LR	3680	3137	2656	2222	1832	1493
	55	Hollow Point	LR	3680	3680	2785	2400	2046	1725
.297/.230 Morris Short	37	Lead		875	720	—	—	—	—
	37	Lead Hollow Point		875	720	—	—	—	—
.297/.230 Morris Long	37	Lead		1200	920	760	—	—	—
	37	Lead Hollow Point		1200	920	760	—	—	—
.236 Lee Navy	112	Full-Metal Jacket		2560	2265	—	—	—	—
.240 Flanged Nitro-Express	100	Pointed Soft Point		2800	2440	2110	1800	—	—
	100	Copper-Pointed		2800	2570	2355	2145	—	—
.240 Belted Nitro-Express	100	Pointed Soft Point		2900	2530	2190	1875	—	—
	100	Copper-Pointed		2900	2665	2445	2235	—	—
.240 Holland, belted, rimless	100	Pointed Soft Point		3000	—	—	—	—	—
.242 Rimless Nitro-Express	100	Copper-Pointed		3000	2740	2490	2260	—	—
.242 Vickers	100	Pointed Soft Point		3000	2720	2345	2100	—	—

SR = Small Rifle   SRM = Small Rifle Magnum   LR = Large Rifle   LRM = Large Rifle Magnum

CENTERFIRE RIFLE BALLISTICS

Caliber	Bullet Wt. Grains	Bullet Type	Primer Type	Velocity — Feet Per Second Muzzle	100 Yards	200 Yards	300 Yards	400 Yards	500 Yards
.243 Win.	80	Soft Point & Hollow Point	LR	3350	2955	2593	2259	1951	1670
	100	Pointed Soft Point	LR	2960	2697	2449	2215	1993	1786
	105	Extended Range	LR	2920	2689	2470	2261	2062	1874
6mm Navy	112	Full-Metal Jacket		2530	2250	—	—	—	—
6mm Rem.	80	Pointed Soft Point	LR	3470	3064	2694	2352	2036	1747
	100	Pointed Soft Point	LR	3100	2829	2573	2332	2104	1889
	105	Extended Range	LR	3060	2822	2596	2381	2177	1982
6mm BR Rem.	100	Pointed Soft Point	SR	2550	2310	2083	1870	1671	1491
.244 Halger Mag.	87	Pointed Soft Point		3770					
.244 Rem.	75	Pointed Soft Point		3500	3070	2660	2290	—	—
	90	Pointed Soft Point		3200	2850	2530	2230	—	—
.297/.250 Rook	56	Lead		1150	940	805	—	—	—
.25-20 S.S.	86	Soft Point		1400	—	—	—	—	—
.25-20	60	Soft Point		2250	1660	1240	1030	—	—
	86	Soft Point		1460	1180	1030	940	—	—
.25 Rem.	87	Softnose		2700	—	—	—	—	—
	117	Soft Point		2320	1980	1700	1470	—	—
.25-35 Win.	87	Softnose	LR	2700	—	—	—	—	—
	117	Softnose		2300	1910	1600	1340	—	—
.25-36 Marlin	117	Softnose		1700	—	—	—	—	—
.250 Savage	87	Soft Point	LR	3030	2660	2330	2060	—	—
	100	Soft Point	LR	2820	2410	2070	1770	—	—
.257 Roberts	100	Hollow Point	LR	2900	2490	2140	1830	—	—
	117	Soft Point	LR	2650	2280	1950	1690	—	—
6.5 Mannlicher	160	Solid		2350	2120	1905	1700	—	—
	160	Softnose		2350	2045	1765	1520	—	—
6.5 Mannlicher Schoenauer	160	Solid		2300	2075	1860	1660	—	—
	160	Softnose		2300	2000	1725	1480	—	—
6.5 Mauser	155	Solid		2400	2160	1935	1725	—	—
	155	Softnose		2400	2095	1805	1555	—	—
.275 Nitro Express	160	Softnose Pointed		2700	2445	2205	1975	—	—
	160	Copper-Pointed		2700	2505	2320	2135	—	—
.270 Win.	100	Pointed Soft Point	LR	3320	2924	2551	2225	1916	1636
	130	Pointed Soft Point Core-Lokt	LR	3050	2776	2510	2259	2022	1801
	130	Bronze Point	LR	3060	2802	2559	2329	2110	1904
	150	Soft Point Core-Lokt	LR	2850	2504	2183	1886	1618	1385
	135	Extended Range	LR	3000	2780	2570	2369	2178	1995
	140	Extended Range Boat Tail	LR	2950	2749	2548	2355	2171	1995
7mm BR Rem.	140	Pointed Soft Point	SMR	2215	2012	1821	1643	1481	1336
7mm Mauser	173	Solid		2300	2095	1900	1720	—	—
	173	Softnose		2300	2015	1765	1530	—	—
	140	Copper-Pointed		2900	2705	2515	2335	—	—

CENTERFIRE RIFLE BALLISTICS

Caliber	Bullet Wt. Grains	Bullet Type	Primer Type	Velocity — Feet Per Second Muzzle	100 Yards	200 Yards	300 Yards	400 Yards	500 Yards
7mm-08 Rem.	140	Pointed Soft Point	LR	2860	2625	2402	2189	1988	1798
	120	Hollow Point	LR	3000	2725	2467	2223	1992	1778
	154	Extended Range	LR	2715	2510	2315	2128	1950	1781
.280 Rem.	140	Pointed Soft Point	LR	3000	2758	2528	2309	2102	1905
	150	Pointed Soft Point Core-Lokt	LR	2890	2624	2373	2135	1912	1705
	165	Soft Point Core-Lokt	LR	2820	2510	2220	1950	1701	1479
	120	Hollow Point	LR	3150	2866	2599	2348	2110	1887
	165	Extended Range	LR	2820	2623	2434	2253	2080	1915
.280 Flanged Nitro-Express	160	Hollow Point		2600	2300	2020	1760	—	—
	140	Hollow Point		2800	2425	2080	1755	—	—
	140	Copper-Pointed		2800	2570	2355	2145	—	—
	180	Solid		2400	2250	2100	1970	—	—
.280 Ross	160	Hollow Point		2700	2395	2110	1840	—	—
	140	Hollow Point		2900	2515	2165	1830	—	—
	140	Copper-Pointed		2900	2665	2445	2235	—	—
	180	Softpoint		2550	2395	2250	2105	—	—
	150	Softpoint		2800	2600	2405	2210	—	—
.280 Jeffery	140	Copper-Pointed		3000	2870	2735	2600	—	—
7mm Rem. Mag.	150	Pointed Soft Point Core-Lokt	LRM	3110	2830	2568	2320	2085	1866
	175	Pointed Soft Point Core-Lokt	LRM	2860	2645	2440	2244	2057	1879
	140	Pointed Soft Point	LRM	3175	2923	2684	2458	2243	2039
	165	Extended Range	LRM	2900	2699	2507	2324	2147	1979
7mm Wby. Mag.	140	Pointed Soft Point	LRM	3225	2970	2729	2501	2283	2077
	175	Pointed Soft Point Core-Lokt	LRM	2910	2693	2485	2288	2098	1918
	165	Extended Range	LRM	2950	2747	2553	2367	2189	2019
.300 Rook Rifle	80	Lead		1100	915	785	—	—	—
.300 Sherwood	140	Lead		1400	1195	1060	—	—	—
.30 Carbine	110	Soft Point	SR	1990	1567	1236	1035	923	842
.30 Rem.	170	Soft Point Core-Lokt	LR	2120	1822	1555	1328	1153	1036
	110	Softnose	LR	2550	—	—	—	—	—
	160	FMJ	LR	2020	—	—	—	—	—
	165	Softnose	LR	2250	—	—	—	—	—
	170	Sort Point	LR	2020	—	—	—	—	—
.30-30 Win. Accelerator	55	Soft Point	LR	3400	2693	2085	1570	1187	986
.30-30 Win.	150	Soft Point Core-Lokt	LR	2390	1973	1605	1303	1095	974
	170	Soft Point Core-Lokt	LR	2290	1895	1619	1381	1191	1051
	170	Hollow Point Core-Lokt	LR	2200	1895	1619	1381	1191	1061
	160	Extended Range	LR	2300	1997	1719	1473	1268	1116

CENTERFIRE RIFLE BALLISTICS

Caliber	Bullet Wt. Grains	Bullet Type	Primer Type	Velocity — Feet Per Second: Muzzle	100 Yards	200 Yards	300 Yards	400 Yards	500 Yards
.300 Savage	180	Soft Point Core-Lokt	LR	2350	2025	1728	1467	1252	1098
.300 Savage	150	Pointed Soft Point Core-Lokt	LR	2630	2354	2095	1853	1631	1432
.30-40 Krag	180	Sof tPoint	LR	2430	2213	2007	1813	1632	1468
	220	Soft Point	LR	2200	1990	1800	1630	—	—
.303 Savage	190	Soft Point	LR	1980	1680	1440	1250	—	—
.308 WIN. Accelerator	55	Pointed Soft Point	LR	3770	3215	2726	2286	1888	1541
.308 Win.	150	Pointed Soft Point Core-Lokt	LR	2820	2533	2263	2009	1774	1560
	I80	Soft Point Core-Lokt	LR	2620	2274	1955	1665	1414	1212
	180	Pointed Soft Point Core-Lokt	LR	2620	2393	2178	1974	1782	1604
	168	Boat Tail Hollow Point Match	LR	2680	2493	2314	2143	1979	1823
	166	Extended Range Boat Tail	LR	2700	2497	2303	2117	1941	1773
	178	Extended Range	LR	2620	2415	2220	2034	1857	1691
.30-03 Springfield	220	Soft Point	LR	1100	—	—	—	—	—
.30-06 Accelerator	55	Pointed Soft Point	LR	4080	3485	2965	2502	2083	1709
.30-06 Springfield	125	Pointed Soft Point	LR	3140	2780	2447	2138	1853	1595
	150	Pointed Soft Point Core-Lokt	LR	2910	2617	2342	2083	1843	1622
	150	Bronze Point	LR	2910	2656	2416	2189	1974	1773
	165	Pointed Soft Point Core-Lokt	LR	2800	2534	2283	2047	1825	1621
	180	Soft Point Core-Lokt	LR	2700	2348	2023	1727	1466	1251
	180	Pornted Soft Point Core-Lokt	LR	2700	2469	2250	2042	1846	1663
	180	Bronze Point	LR	2700	2485	2280	2084	1899	1725
	220	Soft Print Core-Lokt	LR	2410	2130	1870	1632	1422	1246
	168	Boat Tail H.P. Match	LR	2710	2522	2346	2169	2003	1845
	152	Extended Range	LR	2910	2654	2413	2184	1968	1765
	165	Extended Range Boat Tail	LR	2800	2592	2394	2204	2023	1852
	178	Extended Range	LR	2720	2511	2311	2121	1939	1768
.300 H&H Magnum	220	Solid		2300	2085	1880	1690	—	—
	220	Softnose		2300	2045	1810	1590	—	—
	180	Softnose		2750	2430	2130	1855	—	—
	180	Core-Lokt		2880	2640	2412	2196	1990	1798
	150	Softnose		3000	2660	2350	2055	—	—
.30 Flanged Nitro-Express	150	Softnose		2700	2385	2090	1815	—	—
.300 Win. Mag.	150	Pointed Soft Point Core-Lokt	LRM	3290	2951	2636	2342	2068	1813
	180	Pointed Soft Point Core-Lokt	LRM	2960	2745	2540	2344	2157	1979
	200	Swift A-Frame(TM) PSP	LRM	2825	2595	2376	2167	1970	1783
	178	Extended Range	LRM	2980	2769	2568	2375	2191	2015
	190	Extended Range Boat Tail	LRM	2885	2691	2506	2327	2156	1993

CENTERFIRE RIFLE BALLISTICS

Caliber	Bullet Wt. Grains	Bullet Type	Primer Type	Velocity — Feet Per Second: Muzzle	100 Yards	200 Yards	300 Yards	400 Yards	500 Yards
300 Wby. Mag.	180	Soft Point	LRM	3120	2866	2627	2400	2184	1979
	220	Soft Point Core-Lokt	LRM	2850	2541	2283	1984	1736	1512
	178	Extended Range	LRM	3120	2902	2696	2497	2308	2126
	190	Extend Range	LRM	3030	2930	2638	2455	2279	2110
.303 British	180	Softpoint	LR	2460	2124	1817	1542	1311	1137
.307 Win.	150	Soft Nose	LR	2760	2321	1924	1575	1289	1091
	180	Soft Nose	LR	2510	2179	1874	1599	1362	1177
7.62 × 39mm	125	Softpoint	LR	2365	2062	1783	1533	1320	1154
7.62mm Russian	145	Hollow Point	LR	2820	2560	2320	2090	—	—
32-20 Win.	80	Hollow Point	SR	2100	1430	1090	950	—	—
	100	Lead	SR	1210	1021	913	834	769	712
	100	Soft Point	SR	1210	1021	913	834	769	712
.32-40	165	Soft Point	LR	1440	1250	1100	1030	—	—
.32 Win. Special	170	Soft Point Core-Lokt	LR	2250	1921	1626	1372	1175	1044
.32 Win. SL	165	Soft Point	LR	1390	1180	1050	970	—	—
.32 Rem.	110	Softnose	LR	2550	—	—	—	—	—
	170	Softnose	LR	2110	—	—	—	—	—
8mm Mauser	170	Soft Point Core-Lokt	LR	2360	1969	1622	1333	1123	997
8 x 56mm	200	Soft Point	LR	2190	1880	1630	1430	—	—
8mm Lebel	170	Soft Point		2550	—	—	—	—	—
8mm Rem. Mag.	185	Soft Point Core-Lokt	LRM	3080	2761	2464	2186	1927	1688
.33 Win.	200	Soft Point	LR	2190	1860	1600	1390	—	—
.338 Win. Mag.	225	Pointed Soft Point	LRM	2780	2572	2374	2184	2003	1832
	250	Pointed Soft Point	LRM	2660	2455	2261	2075	1898	1731
	225	Swift A-Frame(TM) PSP	LRM	2785	2517	2266	2029	1808	1605
.340 Wby Mag.	200	Pointed Expanding	LRM	3260	3011	2775	2552	2339	2137
	210	Partition	LRM	3250	300	2763	2539	2325	2122
	250	Round Nose Expanding	LRM	3002	2672	2365	2079	1814	1574
	250	Partition	LRM	2980	2780	2588	2404	2228	2059
.348 Win.	150	Soft Point	LR	2890	2360	1860	1420	—	—
	200	Soft Point	LR	2530	2140	1820	1570	—	—
	250	Soft Point	LR	2350	1970	1660	1410	—	—
.35 Win. SL	180	Soft Point	LR	1400	1150	1030	940	—	—
.351 Win.	180	Softpoint	LR	1800	1395	1120	990	—	—
.35 Rem.	150	Pointed Core-Lokt	LR	2300	1874	15K	1218	1039	934
	200	Soft Point Core-Lokt	LR	2080	1698	1376	1140	1001	911
350 Rem Mag.	200	Soft Point Core-Lokt	LRM	2710	2410	2130	1870	1631	1421
.35 Whelen	200	Pointed Soft Point	LRM	2675	2378	2100	1842	1606	1399
	250	Soft Point	LRM	2400	2066	1761	1492	1269	1107
	250	Pointed Soft Point	LRM	2400	2197	2005	1823	1652	1496
.356 Win.	200	Soft Nose	LR	2460	2114	1797	1517	1284	1113
	250	Soft Nose	LR	2160	1911	1682	1476	1299	1158
.358 Win.	200	Soft Nose	LR	2490	2171	1876	1610	1379	1194
9mm Mannlicher	245	Solid & Softnose		2100	1805	1540	1320	—	—
9mm Mauser	245	Solid & Softpoint		2150	1850	1585	1340	—	—

CENTERFIRE RIFLE BALLISTICS

Caliber	Bullet Wt. Grains	Bullet Type	Primer Type	Velocity — Feet Per Second					
				Muzzle	100 Yards	200 Yards	300 Yards	400 Yards	500 Yards
.360 Nitro-Express	300	Solid & Softnose		1650	1490	1345	1225	—	—
.360 Nitro, Black Powder	190	Jacketed		1650	1285	1070	950	—	—
9.3mm Mauser	285	Solid		2250	1970	1720	1490	—	—
	285	Softnose		2250	1930	1645	1395	—	—
9.3 x 74R	258	H-Nantle		2460					
	285	Round Nose Softpoint		2280					
	285	Full Metal Jacket		2280					
	293	T.U.G.		2280					
.369 Nitro-Express	270	Softnose		2500	2135	1800	1505	—	—
9.5mm Mannlicher	270	Roundnose Softpoint		2150	1815	1515	1275		
	270	Solid		2150	1880	1635	1420		
.375 Win.	200	Soft Point	LR	2200	1841	1526	1268	1089	980
	250	Soft Point	LR	1900	1647	1424	1239	1103	1011
.375 Flanged Nitro-Express	270	Solid		2000	1780	1515	1320	—	—
	270	Soft Point		2000	1735	1405	1195	—	—
.375 Flanged Mag.	300	Solid		2400	2140	1895	1670	—	—
	300	Softnose		2400	2105	1825	1580	—	—
	270	Softnose		2600	2280	1980	1705	—	—
.375 Belted Nitro-Express	300	Solid		2500	2235	1980	1750	—	—
	300	Softnose		2500	2200	1915	1655	—	—
.375 H&H Mag.	270	Soft Point	LRM	2690	2420	2166	1928	1707	1507
	300	Swift A-Frame(TM) PSP	LRM	2530	2245	1979	1733	1512	1321
.378 Wby. Mag.	270	Pointed Expanding	LRM	3180	2976	2781	2594	2415	2243
	300	Round Nose Expanding	LRM	2925	2603	2303	2024	1764	1531
	200	Full Metal Jacket	LRM	2925	2580	2262	1972	1710	1482
.38 Long Rifle	124	Solid & Softnose		1050	885	755	—	—	—
.38-40	180	Soft Point	LR	1330	1070	960	850	—	—
.38-55	255	Soft Point	LR	1320	1160	1050	1000	—	—
.40-60 Win.	210	Lead	LR	1560	—	—	—	—	—
.40-65 Win.	260	Soft Point	LR	1420	—	—	—	—	—
.40-72	330	Soft Point	LR	1410	—	—	—	—	—
.40-82	260	Soft Point	LR	1530	—	—	—	—	—
.400 Purdy	230	Solid & Softnose		2050	1620	1280	1075	—	—
.450/.400 Nitro-Express, 3″	400	Solid		2100	1880	1675	1490	—	—
	400	Softnose		2100	1845	1610	1405	—	—
.45/.400 Nitro-Express, 3¼″	400	Solid		2150	1925	1715	1530	—	—
	400	Softnose		2150	1890	1650	1440	—	—
.401 Win.	200	Solid & Softnose		2100	1575	1200	1010	—	—
.404 Nitro-Express	400	Solid & Softnose		2125	1885	1670	1475	—	—
.405 Win.	300	Softnose		2200	1860	1555	1305	—	—
.416 Rigby	410	Solid		2400	—	—	—	—	—
.416 Rem. Mag.	400	Solid	LRM	2400	2042	1718	1436	1212	1062
.416 Rem. Mag.	400	Swift A-FramePSP	LRM	2400	2175	1962	1763	1579	1414
	350	Swift A-Frame(TM) PSP	LRM	2520	2270	2034	1814	1611	1429

CENTERFIRE RIFLE BALLISTICS

Caliber	Bullet Wt. Grains	Bullet Type	Primer Type	Velocity — Feet Per Second Muzzle	100 Yards	200 Yards	300 Yards	400 Yards	500 Yards
.416 Wby. Mag.	400	Swift A-Frame(TM)	LRM	2650	2411	2185	1971	1770	1585
	400	Round Nose Expanding	LRM	2700	2390	2101	1834	1591	1379
	400	Monolithic Solid	LRM	2700	2397	2115	1852	1613	1402
11mm Mauser	385	Jacketed Softnose		1360	1150	1030	—	—	—
	386	Lead		1425	1260	—	—	—	—
.425 Westley Richard	410	Solid		2400	—	—	—	—	—
.43 Egyptian	400	Lead	LR	1225	—	—	—	—	—
.43 Spanish-Rem.	375	Lead		1380	—	—	—	—	—
	390	Lead		1350	1200	—	—	—	—
.44-40 Win.	200	Soft Point	LR	1190	1006	900	822	756	699
.44 Marble Game Getter	115	Lead	LR	1200	—	—	—	—	—
.44 Rem. Mag.	240	Soft Point	LP	1760	1380	1114	970	878	806
	240	Semi-Jacketed Hollow Point	LP	1760	1380	1114	970	878	806
	210	Semi-Jacketed Hollow Point	LP	1920	1477	1155	982	880	802
.444 Marlin	240	Soft Point	LR	2350	1815	1377	1087	941	846
.45-60	300	Lead	LR	1320	—	—	—	—	—
.45-70 Govt.	405	Soft Point	LR	1330	1168	1055	977	918	869
	300	Jacketed Hollow Point	LR	1810	1497	1244	1073	969	895
.45-90	300	Soft Point	LR	1530	—	—	—	—	—
.450 Nitro-Express	480	Solid		2150	1900	1665	1460	—	—
.577/.450 Martini-Henry	325	Lead		1600	1295	1095	990	—	—
	370	Lead		1450	1255	1115	1030	—	—
	480	Lead		1350	1210	1110	—	—	—
.458 Win. Mag.	500	Metal Case	LRM	2040	1823	1623	1442	1237	1161
	510	Soft Point	LRM	2040	1770	1527	1319	1157	1046
.460 Wby. Mag.	500	Full Metal Jacket	LRM	2600	2330	2077	1839	1623	1426
	500	Round Nose Soft Point	LRM	2600	2310	2039	1787	1559	1359
.500/.465	480	Solid		2150	1900	1665	1460	—	—
.470 Nitro-Express	500	Solid		2150	1890	1650	1440	—	—
.475 Nirto-Express	480	Softnose		2175	2000	1830	1670	—	—
.475 No. 2 Nitro Express	480	Solid		2200	1925	1690	1455	—	—
.475 No. 2 Jeffery Nitro-Express	500	Solid		2150	1880	1635	1420	—	—
.50-110 Win.	300	Soft Point	LR	1600	—	—	—	—	—
.50-100 Win.	450	Soft Point	LR	1495	—	—	—	—	—
.500 Nitro-Express	570	Solid		2150	1890	1650	1440	—	—
.500 Nitro for Black Powder	440	Lead		1900	1570	1290	1105	—	—
.577 Snider	480	Lead		1250	1055	940	—	—	—
.577 Nitro-Express 3-inch	750	Solid		2050	1795	1570	1370	—	—
	750	Jacketed Softnose		2050	1795	1570	1370	—	—
.600 Nitro-Express	900	Solid		1850	1565	1320	1145	—	—
	900	Solid HV		1950	1650	1390	1190	—	—

Chapter 6

Reloading Tools and Accessories

Reloading ammunition is a pursuit that can range from simple to complex, depending upon the types of cartridges involved. If the reloader is dealing with standard ammunition types, where cases and bullets are available from manufacturers, there are few complexities. If it is necessary to form cases and/or swage bullets for wildcat or obsolete cartridges, then more work and equipment will be required.

The present-day reloader probably does not realize that there was a time in our history when reloading cartridges was not only common procedure among shooters, but one of prime necessity. Reloading tools were standard accessories that accompanied many rifle sales of the day. Reloading was created for one or more of the following reasons:

- To reduce the cost of shooting
- To produce a variety of loads for specific hunting and shooting situations
- Necessity

Early-day hunters, with a reloadable cartridge case, often found the source of re-supply many miles away . . . perhaps days, weeks, or even months. The early buffalo hunters, as well as the market hunters, were the first shooters who put reloading tools in big demand. In the same light, credit also goes to the early settlers, pioneers, ranchers, farmers, cowboys and soldiers. All played an important role in creating the demand which placed reloading tools on the everyday American scene.

At one time, reloading tools were furnished by Winchester, Sharps, Colt, Remington, Smith & Wesson, Whitney, Starr, Maynard, Evans, Browning, Savage, Manhattan, Stevens, Ballard, Massachusetts Arms Company and others, including the U.S. Government armories. In fact, almost every firearms company either made or furnished reloading tools to fit the rifles and cartridges sold by each. Firearm companies which did not make their own reloading tools resorted to other, more specialized, manufacturers. The Bridgeport Gun and Implement Company, for example, is still identifiable by its name or initials on many of the old tools and moulds. Another was the Ideal Manufacturing

Company, which originated under the patents of J. H. Barlow. After Marlin Firearms Company acquired this firm and ran it for several years, Marlin's name appeared on the tools. Today, this firm is known as the Lyman Products Corporation.

Reloading rifle and pistol cartridges is a multistage operation that begins with decapping (removing the spent primer), repriming, resizing, casemouth expansion, charging the case with powder and, finally, seating and crimping the new bullet. While this sounds complex, all of these operations are usually done using a number of components that have been assembled into a single reloading unit.

Figure 6-1: Reloading dies are the key tools to reloading and should be of the finest possible quality.

BASIC RELOADING TOOLS FOR RIFLE AND PISTOL AMMUNITION

While there are many types of tools and accessories that may become a part of the well-equipped reloading bench, a few are essential and make up the minimum complement required to produce ammunition that is safe, accurate and effective.

Every handloader will need reloading dies for each cartridge type and a reloading press to facilitate primer removal, case resizing and bullet seating/crimping. Reloading dies, as shown in Figure 6-1, are the key tools to reloading and should be of the finest possible quality. There are sub-components that are a part of the reloading press and there are a few other items such as a powder scale and a powder measure, but the reloading press is the central complex component in this operation, as it contains the reloading dies and usually the decapping/repriming elements, all assembled into one piece of machinery.

RELOADING PRESSES

Almost all reloading tools were hand implements a century ago, and this type remained popular with shooters until only a few decades ago. The Lyman Ideal No. 310 tool (and its earlier variations), for example, remained on the market for over 75 years. *See* Figure 6-2. These were fine inexpensive tools for the average shooter who loaded only a few boxes of ammunition each year.

When small handgun cases were reloaded, or only the case necks on rifle cases were resized, hand pressure was quite sufficient to perform the major reloading operations. In fact, these tools helped to coin the word "handloader."

Today, however, nearly all brass is full-length sized and this process usually requires more power than can be produced efficiently by the hands alone. The reloading press provides the leverage neces-

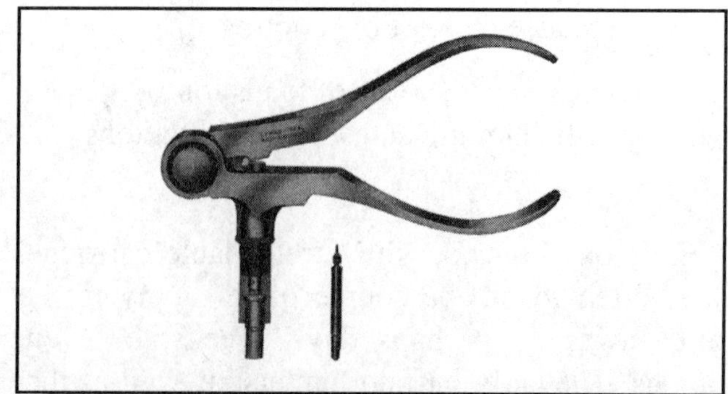

Figure 6-2: The most popular handloading tool ever developed — the Lyman No. 310.

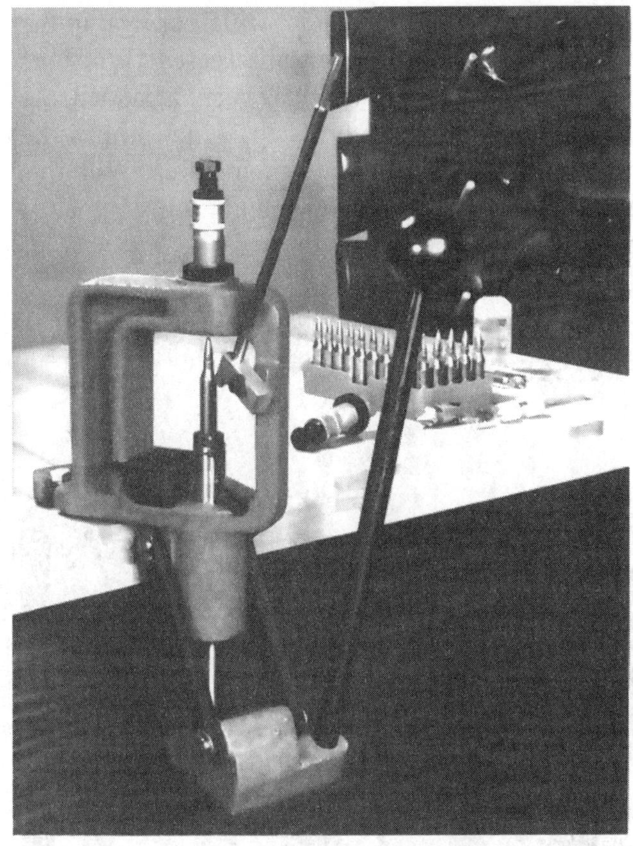

Figure 6-3: A single-stage press accommodates one die at a time.

sary for performing full-length resizing on all cases, and accomplishes the remaining loading operations with ease.

Basic reloading presses are available in several different styles. A single-stage press, for example, can accommodate only one reloading die at a time. Shown in Figure 6-3, a single die is threaded into the top of the press and the cartridge case is forced into this die when the handle is pulled. This provides the necessary leverage, especially for the resizing operation. The cartridge case is fitted into a shellholder that stabilizes it in the staging area. During the resizing operation, the resizing die is threaded into the top of the press. When the press handle is activated, the staging area rises and the cartridge is forced into the die, where it is decapped and resized.

When using a single-stage press, most reloaders will install the resizing die and then run all cartridges through this stage of the operation. The resizing die is then removed and replaced with the expansion die (for straight-walled cases only), and all cases are run through this stage. After a new primer has been seated and the case charged with powder, the seating/crimping die replaces the one that preceded it, and the bullet is seated in the case mouth, and crimped if necessary.

Reloading ammunition in single steps is far more practical with the single-stage die than attempting multi-step reloading with each single cartridge, where a new die would have to be installed after each operation. Much time would be wasted in constantly mounting and unmounting dies. The single-stage process is quite efficient, especially when a fair number of identical cartridges are to be reloaded in a single sitting. However, if one or two loadings of several different cartridges are to be performed, the single-stage press loses some of its appeal; that is, except for the Forster/Bonanza CO-AX Model B-2 loading press. This press was designed by C.E. Prudie of Bonanza Sports, Mfg. Co. many years ago, and is still one of the best single-stage presses on the market. It allows for instant snap-in and snap-out die changes and this press has three times the mechanical advantage of a typical "C" press. Changing dies in this single-stage press is as fast, if not faster, than revolving the turret to the next die on a turret press. The press is now manufactured by Forster Products. *See* Figure 6-4 on the next page.

A turret press is very similar to the single-stage design, with one big difference. A circular turret is mounted to the top of this press, and it will accommodate three or more dies at any one time. With this arrangement, all the dies necessary for reloading a single caliber can be mounted and adjusted at one time. Once the setup is complete, each cartridge can be taken through each stage of the reloading operation without having to constantly install a different die. After resizing/decapping is complete,

Figure 6-4: The Forster/Bonanza CO-AX Model B-2 reloading press remains one of the best single-stage presses on the market.

the turret is rotated one step, which brings up the expansion die (for straight-walled cases). When the mouth of the cartridge case has been expanded, the turret is rotated one more step, which brings the seating die in line with the staging area. With this arrangement, each cartridge can be fully reloaded before moving on to the next.

PRIMING SYSTEMS FOR RELOADING PRESSES

Figure 6-5: One type of integral priming attachment for reloading presses.

Several types of priming attachments are available for reloading presses. Figure 6-5, for example, shows a priming system that consists of a small cup mounted on the end of a spring-loaded plunger. With the cartridge in the staging area, the handle is pulled downward slightly to expose the priming cup. A primer is placed in this cup and the handle is lowered with enough force to firmly seat the primer in the cartridge. Pressure on the handle is then released to remove the primed cartridge.

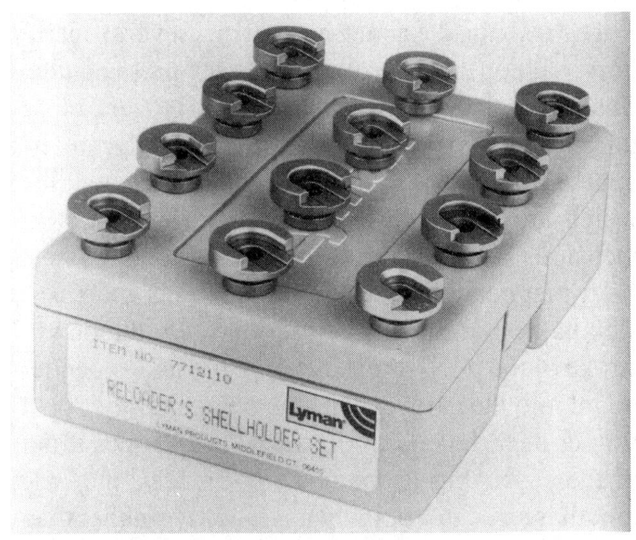

Figure 6-6: A collection of various sizes of shellholders to accomodate a wide range of cartridge types.

Most modern presses are designed so that they will accept an optional automatic primer-feed attachment. These devices consist of a hollow metal tube into which primers may be inserted in tandem. The tube is aligned to engage the primer cup in the priming system. This speeds the reloading process by avoiding insertion of the primers into this cup by hand. This arrangement also protects the primers from hand oil, which can cause misfires.

The cartridge case is attached to the press plunger by means of a hardened steel shellholder. Shellholders are available in various sizes to accommodate the full range of cartridges as shown in Figure 6-6. It is not necessary to purchase a new shellholder for each and every cartridge that is reloaded; one size accommodateS many different cartridges. For instance, a shellholder for a .300 Winchester Magnum will fit any of the standard belted magnums such as the .375 H&H, .300 H&H, .300 Wby, 7mm Remington, .350 Remington, etc.

The shellholder is attached to the end of the plunger via a friction-fit coupling that is standard. This means that most shellholders from any manufacturer will fit most presses, regardless of who makes them. The shellholder set shown in Figure 6-6 is manufactured by Lyman and consists of 12 shellholders. They are of industry standard design and will fit reloading presses of most manufacturers, as well as Lyman's. This selection has been carefully packaged to accommodate better than 70% of current pistol calibers and more than 80% of rifle calibers.

Most reloading presses set up their handles and plungers so that they magnify and accelerate the force applied by hand power. The press handle is forced downward using slow, steady pressure (as opposed to quickly ramming it down), so this force magnification is necessary for smooth, consistent forming of brass and seating of bullets.

RELOADING DIES

When a brass cartridge is fired in a rifle or handgun, it expands to the full dimensions of the chamber. Each cartridge that is ready for firing is actually a tiny bit smaller than the chamber. After firing, it is larger due to its expansion to chamber dimensions. The mouth of the cartridge has expanded to the point that a bullet will usually drop through the neck and into the powder chamber.

Dies, generally, must be purchased in sets of two or three for each caliber that is to be reloaded. Two-die sets are standard for bottleneck cartridges like the .30-06. Cases without a bottleneck (the .444 Marlin, for instance) will require a three-die set. The extra die is used to expand the case mouth slightly in order to properly seat the bullet. In bottleneck cartridges, the resizing die will expand the mouth automatically after resizing has taken place.

In order to prepare this fired case for reloading, it must be resized approximately to its original, pre-fired dimensions. Resizing may be thought of as squeezing or compressing the brass of the cartridge back to the dimensions necessary for it to properly fit in the chamber and to firmly seat the bullet. This is a fairly detailed and complex operation that is performed by a very simple-appearing device, the resizing die.

Figure 6-7: Resizing/decapping die on right; bullet-seating die on left.

There are two basic types of resizing dies: the full-length die which resizes the entire case; and the neck resizer that only reforms the neck to original dimensions so that it will properly seat the bullet. Using a neck resizing die, the body of the cartridge is left in its original expanded size. This type of die is thought by some to produce better accuracy in bolt-action rifles. Due to the camming effect of the bolt when seating the cartridge in the chamber, a case that has already been expanded to chamber size by a previous firing can be more tightly seated in the chamber. However, neck resizing is only practical when reloading a cartridge for the gun that fired it originally. It is not recommended that a neck-resized cartridge be used in a gun other than the one that originally fired it.

In addition, his type of resizing is not suitable for other actions, in which the camming effect is very weak. This applies especially to semiautomatic, pump, and lever actions. If a reloader is producing ammunition for rifles with these types of actions or for more than one bolt-action rifle of the same caliber, full-length resizing of all cases must be performed.

The resizing die actually performs several operations with one complete stroke of the press handle. The internal shape of the die is cut to very close tolerances in order to resize the cartridge to its approximate original (pre-firing) dimensions, which are just slightly under actual chamber dimensions. At the center of the die is a hardened steel shaft that contains a decapping pin and an expansion ball on at the end of the shaft. On the downstroke of the press, the decapping pin and expander travel into the cartridge. The pin engages the spent primer near the end of the stroke and forces it out of the case. During the resizing process, the case mouth is sized to a point that is slightly smaller than necessary to accommodate the bullet. However, on the upstroke of the press, this component expands the case mouth slightly, as the central shaft leaves the recesses of the cartridge case. This allows the bullet to be easily started into the case mouth during the seating/crimping stage of reloading.

This type of system won't work with straight-walled cases, so resizing dies for these kinds of cartridges only contain a decapping pin. The flaring of the case mouth is done via an expansion die, which inserts an expander into the case mouth as a separate operation. Examples of cartridges that require a three-die set are the .30 M1 Carbine, .375 Winchester, .444 Marlin, .45-70 Government, and the .458 Winchester. Also, the great majority of revolver/pistol cartridges are included in this group, as most are straight or taper-walled. When other rifle cartridges contain a shoulder, a two-die set should be used.

Resizing dies are the most tolerance-critical components in a reloading system. Every square millimeter of the internal chamber of a resizing die is critical, because the cartridge case must be sized to exact specifications. If the resizing is off by a few thousandths of an inch, accuracy problems will certainly result and safety can easily be undermined. The resizing die must be carefully adjusted after it is screwed into the press to make certain that the entire cartridge is properly resized. For cases that headspace on the shoulder, this alignment is even more critical. Forcing a cartridge too far into the resizing die can cause the shoulder to be set back, creating a potentially dangerous headspace condition. This does not apply to belted and rimmed cartridges, where headspace tolerance is determined by rim thickness or position along the case length.

Due to the close tolerances required, modern dies are manufactured from fine steel that has been heat-treated for extreme hardness. Additionally, the internal surfaces are usually polished to a mirror finish to avoid placing dents and irregularities into the brass cartridge case.

Since no two reloading presses are exactly alike, an adjustable collar is a part of all reloading dies. This collar allows the depth with which the die is inserted into the press to be adjusted. Once this alignment is complete, the collar is secured in place (usually via a hex screw lockup). This allows the dies to be removed from the press and reinstalled at a later time without going through the elaborate alignment procedure again. However, if these dies are to be used in different presses, they must be realigned to address the new press environment.

The final die that the cartridge case is run through after it has been resized, primed, and charged is the seating/crimping die. This die contains an internal shaft that engages the nose of the bullet, which has already been started (partially seated) by hand into the case mouth. As the cartridge is inserted further into the die, the shaft pushes the bullet deeper into the case. At the bottom of the press stroke, the cartridge mouth engages a ridge within the die, which bends the mouth edge inward to engage the bullet cannelure. The length of the shaft is adjustable via threads that engage the seating die. The farther into the die that this bolt is screwed, the deeper the bullet is seated. Adjusting this die requires getting the bolt down far enough to seat the bullet to the desired depth at the bottom of the stroke, where the crimping operation also takes place by another component within the die.

Some reloaders prefer not to crimp their cases due to the types of actions they are using and/or for accuracy concerns. This is no problem, as the die is simply seated less deeply into the reloading press so that the cartridge is not forced against the crimping collar at the bottom of the stroke. The seating shaft bolt is then adjusted to provide the required seating depth given this uncrimped arrangement. As with the resizing (and expansion) dies, a collar is provided to secure the press seating depth position so that this alignment is maintained, should the die be removed from the press for any reason. As with the resizing die, changing to a different press will require readjustment of the seating/crimping die.

RELOADING ACCESSORIES

Although the reloading press and dies make up the core tools needed to reload ammunition, many other components are desirable, if not mandatory, o have available at the modern reloading bench. Most of these complement the dies and press, preparing them for the reloading operation.

HAND-PRIMING TOOLS

While most modern presses offer a priming system, these must be laboriously loaded by hand even if an optional primer feed is purchased. The latter places the tube of primers on the press, but the priming operation is still far from automatic. Also, stacking a large number of primers in tandem in a metal tube is not the safest thing to do. Should one primer ignite due to some shock, the entire string of primers will go off spontaneously. Primers contain a highly volatile chemical mixture that produces a lot of power within a very small package. Should a string of 20 or 30 go off simultaneously, there is a real danger to life and limb. Having said this, we have never experienced such a mishap (or even heard of one) in thousands of hours of reloading. However, the possibility is always there and safer, faster ways of priming are available at minimal cost.

When a large number of cartridges are to be reloaded at one sitting, it is often more convenient to size and decap the cases and then prime each one using a hand-priming tool, such as the RCBS Prime Guard hand-priming tool shown in Figure 6-8. This device seats primers rapidly and makes the whole process much safer. A patented shielding mechanism separates the entire seating operation from the primer supply, virtually eliminating the possibility of primer detonation.

Figure 6-8: The RCBS Prime Guard hand-priming tool allows many cases to be quickly and safely primed.

Primers are carefully poured into the circular tray. A slight shake causes all of the primers to align themselves in the anvil-up position. Tilting the tool slightly causes a single primer to slide into the loading slot. Pressing the hand lever causes a small piston to move upward, carrying the primer into the pocket of the cartridge case mounted to the top of the tool. At this point, the cartridge has been fully primed and is quickly removed and replaced by another. One more press of the hand lever primes another case, and so on.

This type of system has many advantages, not the least of which is safety. The primers are not stacked in tandem, so the chances of detonation of many primers simultaneously is greatly diminished. From a practical standpoint, one great advantage of this system is that the primers need never be touched by human hands. Oils on human skin can absolutely ruin primers, although this spoilage often takes months. Loads containing contaminated primers may perform normally, at first. After a period of time, however, misfires may occur. This can be a lethal situation when dangerous game is the target, or very disheartening if the situation causes a prized trophy to get away.

Primers should never be handled without using rubber gloves and, preferably, not at all. Using the hand-priming tool, the primers are poured into a tray, entirely avoiding the possibility of primer contamination by human contact.

Hand-priming tools have been available for a number of years, but most of them required special shellholders designed for the particular brand of tool. Standard universal shellholders for reloading presses would not work. This is not the case with the RCBS unit that is designed to accept the universal shellholders. This means that the reloader does not have to duplicate every standard shellholder with a special one designed solely for the hand-priming tool. This is quite a monetary savings and important because there never was a legitimate reason why other hand-priming tools should have required special shellholders.

Since primers, generally, come in two standard sizes in the United States, small rifle/small pistol and large rifle/large pistol, two primer feeds are supplied with the Prime Guard tool. This means that the tool is complete in itself, and the reloader need buy nothing additional for proper operation. Simply supply the decapped, resized cases along with the primers and you're in business.

POWDER SCALES

No reloading bench is complete without a powder scale. This device allows powder to be accurately measured in units as small as .1 grain. Certainly, there was a time when cup-like volume measuring devices were in vogue, but precision reloading requires accurate measurements that can only be made with a finely-balanced scale. Although electronic scales are now available, the older mechanical types are still favored by the majority of reloaders. Figure 6-9 shows the Lyman Pro 1000 and Pro 505 series of powder scales, capable of measuring powder in weights up to 1005 grains and 505 grains, respectively. For most reloading operations, the 505 will be more than adequate.

Based on a lever/fulcrum arrangement whose ancestors date back to pre-biblical days, the quality of the measurements from such scales is based upon the mechanical rigidity and fine grading of the printed scale on the balance arm or beam and by the finely honed pivots or bearings that allow the beam to move up and down in relation to the weight placed at the end that holds the powder pan.

The scales are easily adjusted and calibrated by setting the movable weights on the beam to the zero

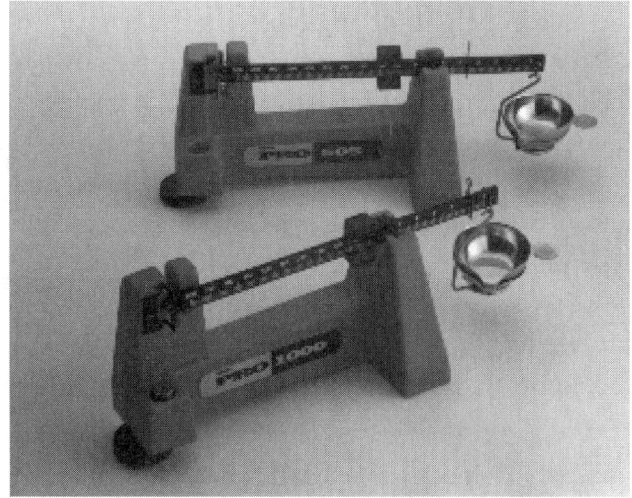

Figure 6-9: The Lyman series of powder scales span a wide range of uses and applications.

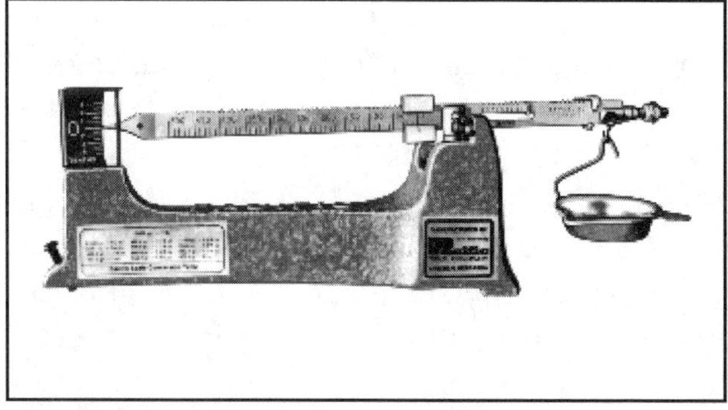

Figure 6-10: Regardless of the manufacturer, the lever/fulcrum method of measuring is the most common type of powder scale.

position with no powder in the scale pan. If the needle indicator on the left side of the beam aligns with the center line mounted on the left of the scales platform, then the scales are calibrated. If the pointer shows that it is out of alignment, an adjustment wheel on the lower left side of the scales is turned. This rebalances the entire scale and recalibrates the device when the pointer aligns with the center line on the platform. This takes only seconds.

Scales of this type have two counterweights, one for coarse adjustment and one for fine. If a particular load calls for 39.8 grains of powder, then the course adjustment weight would be set to 35 and the fine adjustment weight to 4.8. This means that the scales have been sct to balance at exactly 39.8 grains. Powder is poured into the holding pan until the beam pointer aligns with the centering mark on the scales' body. The pan may then be removed and the powder poured directly into the case mouth, often with the aid of a plastic funnel. It is generally a good idea to rebalance the scales at the beginning of a reloading operation and, perhaps, midway through the longer sessions.

A great deal of the precision of such scales is determined by the bearings. These should be kept free of dirt, dust, and oils. If they become fouled in any way, the accuracy of the scale will deteriorate rapidly. Should the scale be accidentally bumped or upset, it is necessary to go through the realignment procedure. Any physical disturbance has the capability of throwing the scale off by a large enough margin to dramatically affect accuracy and possibly create a safety hazard when maximum loads are being measured.

Scales are essential to reloading operations and must be checked often to make certain that they are holding their calibration. The bearings on the Lyman scales pictured are made from agate, but other types may use metal. Check often for signs of rust or other degradation. You cannot afford to have scales that provide other than readings that are accurate to .1 grain.

POWDER TRICKLERS

Today's handloads are very precise, wherein a tenth of a grain of powder can make a noticeable difference, especially when long-range or benchrest target shooting is involved. While scales have the capability of accuracy down to a tenth of a grain, it is difficult to pour powder into the scale pan in such small increments. When considering a load of 39.8 grains, it should be physically easy to pour powder from a canister up to 39 grains or so, but it is those last few fractions of a grain that create problems. Usually, you will pour a little too much, making it necessary to scrape a little powder out of the pan. This is bothersome and time-consuming, but there is a better way to dole out small increments of powder. This requires a tool called a "trickler."

The powder trickler is able to drop individual grains (the physical grain, not the weight measurement) of powder into the scale pan. Tricklers come in manual and electric models. Both contain a receptacle for the powder and a small spigot that is fed by a hollow tube that can be rotated. The tube extends through the powder compartment, and has a hole that picks up a few grains of powder. Threads inside the tube cause the powder grains to be directed out of the spigot during rotation. This provides a quick way of increasing the powder in the scale pan by very small increments until the exact amount is obtained. Manual models require that the internal "screw" be turned by hand. Electric models use a small motor controlled by a momentary switch to do the turning.

Figure 6-11: The Lyman Auto Trickler carefully dispenses powder a single grain at a time. An electric motor makes the operation more automatic.

Figure 6-11 shows the Lyman Auto Trickler, a motorized unit that allows reloaders to automatically trickle the last few grains of powder into the scale pan. It has built-in vertical and horizontal height adjustments that allow the spigot to be set to the correct height for any type of powder scale. A simple press of the power switch starts the powder feed operation. The powder reservoir is removable for easy cleaning. This is important because different types of powder will undoubtedly be poured into it from time-to-time, and every grain of one type of powder must be removed before another powder is used to provide adequate safety. This trickler handles all conventional ball-, stick-, and flake-powder types.

While it is possible to get by without a powder trickler, it is inconvenient and can lead to under- or overloaded charges. This is one accessory that will pay for itself in short order. Even the electric mod-

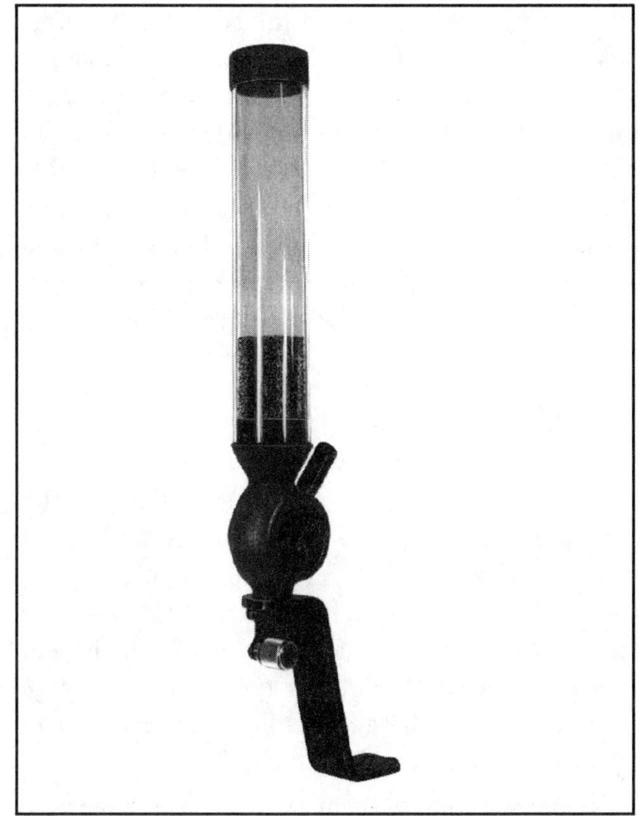

Figure 6-12: Typical powder measure.

els are priced within the reach of every reloader. The manual models, of course, are less expensive.

POWDER MEASURES

A powder measure, often called a *powder thrower*, does not take the place of a powder scale, but it can expedite certain reloading operations, especially when a large amount of cartridges are to be charged. Shown in Figure 6-12, the powder is poured into a reservoir or drum. Adjustments are then made with (usually) calibrated micrometer controls to allow a certain amount of powder to be dispensed each time the handle is pulled. Powder is dropped out of a tube at the bottom of the thrower directly into a cartridge case or into a powder-scale pan for weighing.

While great strides have been made in powder throwers, the calibration of these devices generally leaves a lot to be desired. The standard method of using them calls for making course adjustments to the micrometer controls, throwing a sample charge into a scale pan, and then measuring the charge. If the amount thrown is too little, the micrometer adjustment on the thrower is opened a little more, or if too much powder is being thrown, the micrometer controls are reduced a bit. Eventually, you should be able to get the amount you desire. However, it is a good idea to recheck the calibration occasionally during the reloading run.

Manufacturers often tout the accuracy of their throwers along with their ability to dispense all types of powders. Most powder measures do an excellent job of dispensing ball and flake powders, but many lack this same excellence when it comes to measuring stick powders like IMR or Hodgdon 4350, 4831, 4320 and the like. When using a powder measure with stick powder, the operator must get a "feel" for the pull and then ensure that the handle is operated uniformly each time.

Selecting one powder measure over another is about like selecting an automobile. One model may suit one reloader the best, while another swears by a different model. In testing practically all powder measures on the market, one author likes the Forster/Bonanza Bench Rest Powder Measure the best, and uses this measure — along with his obsolete Belding & Mull powder measure — for all his or her reloading needs.

Powder throwers have been responsible for more than a few reloading mishaps, due to the nature in which they are used. Primed cartridge cases are usually held beneath the powder dispenser and the charge is thrown directly into them. This is a quick, simple operation. However, if you don't keep adequate track of which cases have been charged and which haven't, it is easy to throw a second charge into an already-charged case. A double charge of powder is bound to have startling (and sometimes lethal) results when the cartridge is fired. The ease and simplicity provided by a powder thrower calls for more caution on the part of the reloader than

Figure 6-13: RCBS cartridge counter attached to the Uniflow powder measure to count the number of charges thrown.

might be required when working with the more laborious powder scales.

To safeguard against double charging, RCBS offers a cartridge counter that attaches directly to the RCBS Uniflow powder measure. The counter is incremented by one each time the drum dispenses a charge. This allows the reloader to know exactly how many charges have been thrown at the end of a reloading session. *See* Figure 6-13. As an example, assume that the counter registers 101. This means that 101 charges were thrown. Assume also that you count only 100 cartridges that have been reloaded. This would indicate that one of the reloads contains a double charge and all of them should be weighed in an attempt to find the culprit.

The counter is a good device to have if you reload a lot of ammunition in one sitting using the thrower, but it does not absolutely protect you from firing a double-charge load. While double-charges are a problem with powder throwers when used in a less than attentive manner, "uncharges" also occur. This means that a cartridge may be given no powder charge at all. The result here upon firing is usually a bullet stuck in the barrel of the firearm from the impetus provided by the detonated primer alone. If you have the misfortune to throw a double charge and an "uncharge" in a single reloading session, then the counter will accurately reflect the total number of cartridges reloaded. However, it won't tell you that one cartridge got a double charge while another got no charge at all. This points to the necessity of always being alert and attentive during every phase of a reloading session, whether you use a powder measure or not.

BULLET PULLERS

The discussion on powder measures and double charges leads naturally to a look at bullet pullers. Suppose you do throw a double charge and detect this condition by weighing the completed cartridges, looking for one that weighs more than the rest. How do you correct the problem? The answer is: you remove the bullet, empty the powder charge from the case, recharge it with the correct amount of powder and reseat the bullet.

Removing a bullet from a charged cartridge case is an operation that is best not tackled with pliers. Besides damaging the new bullet, you also take a chance on accidentally detonating the primer from the friction and pressure of the pliers. A cartridge loaded with smokeless powder whose primer detonates outside the confines of the chamber does not usually present any lethal danger, although a bad

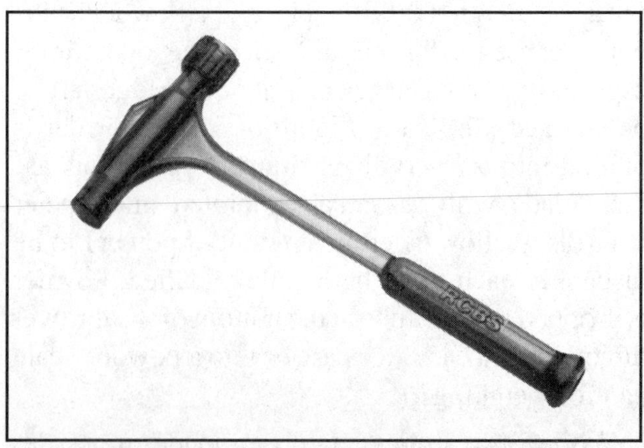

Figure 6-14: RCBS Pow'r Pull is a kinetic bullet puller that suspends the case in the hammer head and removes the bullet by impacting the head on a firm surface.

burn might result. However, it is a situation to be avoided at all costs.

The best way to remove a bullet from a charged case is by incorporating a tool known as a bullet puller. The type shown in Figure 6-14 is more accurately know as a kinetic bullet puller, and it looks very much like a hammer. It is even operated in the same manner. The RCBS Pow'r Pull illustrated has a 3-jaw chuck that grips the rim of the cartridge when the plastic cap is screwed into place. The cartridge is then suspended inside the head of the puller. By rapping the end of the puller on any solid surface (as you would a hammer), the bullet is propelled from the case along with the powder, which is collected in the portion of the head opposite the part that grips the rim of the case. Both the bullet and powder may be reused.

The head is constructed entirely of tough plastic, so there is no metal-to-metal contact. A soft cushion in the collection portion of the head protects the nose of the bullet from being damaged by the impact as it strikes the collector end of the head. This is an improvement over earlier models that did not contain the soft pad. Older models were famous for damaging the tips of spire point bullets, but inventive reloaders corrected the problem by stuffing a small amount of soft paper into the collection end. The built-in pad is a commercialization of this modification.

The puller will accommodate most cartridges, although the fit may be too tight for some of the large African magnums, such as the .470 Nitro Express. RCBS states that it is designed to handle cartridges in the .22- to .45-caliber range. Using it with rimfire cartridges is strictly forbidden. Since the bullet is held by its rim, the striking force is applied to the rim, which could cause rimfire cartridges to discharge.

When pulling bullets from any charged cartridge, caution is urged. Even if the primer should detonate, there shouldn't be any disastrous results, because the pressure will not be allowed to build to dangerous levels as would be the case in the confines of the firearm chamber. However, a discharge within the puller will often cause the unsupported primer to fly out of the head with enough velocity to penetrate human skin. A case was reported several years ago where a detonatation occurred within a kinetic puller, driving the primer into the reloader's eye. Fortunately, it struck the lower portion of the eyeball and did not cause blindness. This stresses the fact that, when dealing with a charged cartridge, caution is to be practiced at all times. Never look at the back of the puller (the primer end) when striking the head on a hard surface and always wear safety glasses when performing any reloading operations.

There are other types of bullet pullers, but the hammer type is and always has been the most popular, due to its very low cost and ease of operation. Collet-type bullet pullers (Figure 6-15) are seen from time-to-time and work within the reloading press. The collet is mounted in a die slot and firmly grips the bullet while the cartridge is seated in the shellholder. Lowering the press handle causes the case to pull away from the captive bullet. The reason for the low popularity of collet-type pullers is cost and complexity of use. Different collets must be purchased for each caliber, and the press setup is more time-consuming compared with the simplicity of the kinetic type.

Figure 6-15: Collet-type bullet pullers is another type of bullet puller that some reloaders prefer over the kinetic type.

CASE TRIMMERS

As high-pressure loads are fired again-and-again in a cartridge case, it begins to lengthen at the neck. If this condition is allowed to go too far, the neck exceeds the maximum length of the firearm chamber and the mouth can actually be crimped by the throat of the bore. This condition will occur only in bolt-action rifles where the camming effect of the bolt provides enough force to crimp the case mouth. In lever, pump, and automatic actions, the cartridge simply won't chamber.

An overlength cartridge that has its mouth crimped into the bullet causes chamber pressures to rise dramatically, because so much more pressure is required to free the bullet and send it down the barrel. For this reason, maximum length figures are available for every modern cartridge type.

The reloader should measure every resized cartridge case prior to reloading it. If the overall length exceeds the maximum allowable dimensions, then the neck will have to be trimmed. There are several ways that this can be accomplished. Special trim dies are available for each cartridge that causes the overly long mouth to protrude through the top of the die. This portion of the brass can then be removed with a file. This is laborious and leaves quite a bit of residue. It also tends to deform the case mouth, which must be set right again by running it through the resizer one more time.

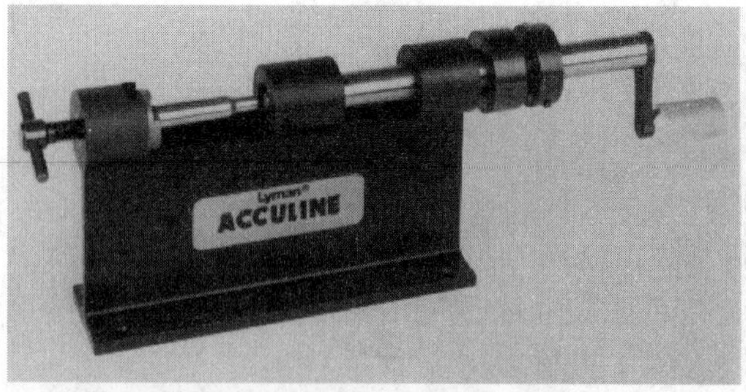

Figure 6-16: The Lyman Acculine case trimmer is representative of low-cost trimmers that do an excellent job with very little effort on the reloader's part.

Most reloaders will opt for a case trimmer, a handy little lathe-like device that mounts the cartridge case longitudinally so that a turning cutting edge can be applied to the mouth. Figure 6-16 shows a typical hand-operated trimmer, the Lyman Acculine. This trimmer uses standard reloader press shellholders to hold the rim of the cartridge in-line with the hand-operated trim shaft and cutter head. This trimmer is designed for the complete range of American calibers from .17 through .458.

To keep the mouth from collapsing or becoming distorted during the cutting process, the trimmer is designed with a hole through the center of the cutter head through which the shaft of a pilot is inserted. The *pilot* is a tapered, elongated ball whose maximum diameter is the same as that of the cartridge mouth. When inserted into the cartridge mouth during the trimming procedure, the pilot keeps the mouth circular and uniform. A pilot is necessary for every caliber size to be trimmed. Packs of pilots are available that typically cover all cartridges that fire .22, .24, .27, .284/7mm, .30, 9mm, .357, .44 and .45 caliber bullets. Here, we are interested only in the caliber of the bullet the cartridge fires. A .22-caliber pilot will address every .22-caliber cartridge such as .223, .22-250, .224 Weatherby Magnum, .220 Swift, etc. The same applies for all other calibers. Additional pilots may be ordered for other calibers.

The trimmer illustrated can be classified as an economy model, but it will adequately and efficiently trim all cases to the desired dimensions using hand-power alone. An adjustable collet is provided to allow each case to be trimmed to the desired length, once it is calibrated. The reloader slowly turns the trimmer handle, applying a small amount of force toward the case mouth until the collet prevents further trimming.

Figure 6-17 shows another trimmer, the RCBS Trim Pro. This is similar to the Lyman model just discussed, except it adds a bit of convenience. Instead of requiring the use of a reloading press standard shellholder, this model provides a lever-

Figure 6-17: The RCBS Trim Pro case trimmer is operated by hand and uses an adjustable collet to determine cutting depth.

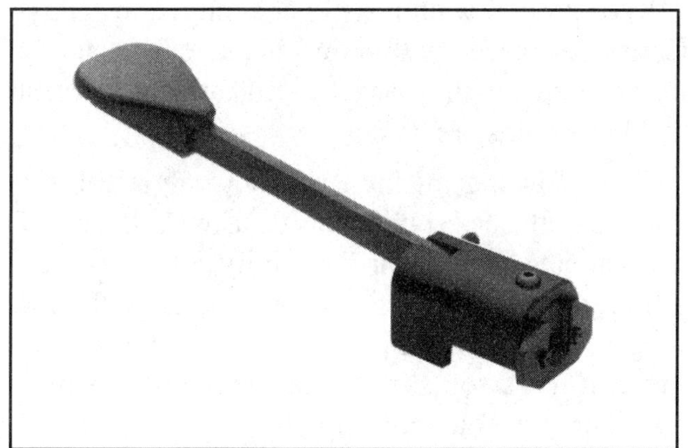

Figure 6-18: The RCBS case-trimmer handle is a lever-actuated shellholder that will accomodate nearly every cartridge head.

operated, universal shellholder. The reloader simply presses down on the handle (shown in more detail in Figure 6-18), inserts the cartridge and releases. The case is held tightly in place with its center line along the line of the cutter shaft. Standard pilots are necessary for each caliber trimmed and a conventional collet is used to control the depth of cut.

The RCBS Trim Pro can be upgraded to motorized control by adding the Power Trimmer unit shown with the original Trim Pro in Figure 6-19. This package contains a low-rpm motor, a spring-fed cutter arrangement, and a positive locking handle. It operates in the same manner as the manual

Figure 6-19: The RCBS Power Trimmer couples a low-rpm motor and spring-fed cutter.

unit, but the low-speed motor does most of the work when the engaging handle is depressed.

The Lyman-equivalent of the power trimmer is shown in Figure 6-20. This arrangement includes an on/off switch mounted to the base of the trimmer case. This model uses a universal chuck to hold the cartridge rim. The chuck is rotated to the open position and the cartridge is inserted. The chuck is

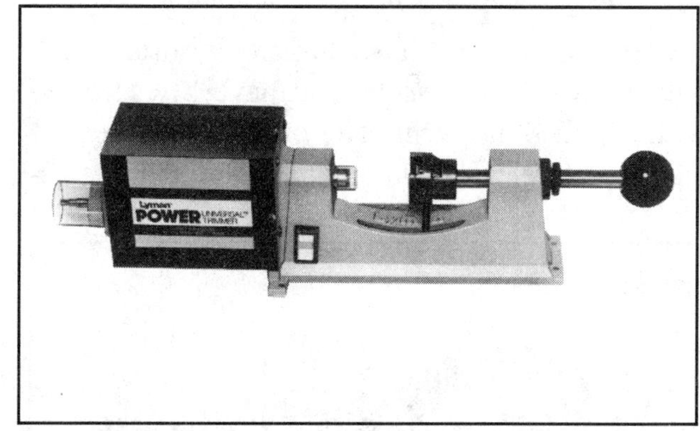

Figure 6-20: The Lyman Power Trimmer incorporates a low-speed motor with its Universal Trimmer, the latter normally powered by hand.

then rotated closed and the case is held firmly in alignment with the cutter. The cutting portion of this motorized arrangement is Lyman's Universal Trimmer. The low-end model is hand operated, but an attachment can be ordered to allow a standard variable-speed drill motor to be attached for motorized trimming.

Power trimmers are very useful for full-time reloading benches, where hundreds of cartridges may be reloaded each day. However, they may represent slight overkill for the occasional reloader, who may reload a maximum of ten or twenty cartridges during any one sitting. The reloader will have to be the final judge. If case trim work using the hand-powered models seems to be a burden, a motorized unit may be the answer to the problem.

CASE TUMBLERS

Before reloading previously-fired cartridge cases, each case should be wiped clean and inspected carefully for defects. When these cases are stained with powder residue, or corroded from storage, defects cannot be detected easily, and a thorough cleaning of the cases are in order. This operation can be done by hand, using one of the commercial case-polishing chemicals, but if many cases are in need of polishing, many reloaders equip their benches with a case tumbler.

In the meanest of terms, a tumbler is a drum filled with ground up corncobs that have been treated with a polishing agent. The drum is vibrated by means of an electric motor, and the mild abrasiveness of the corncob media combined with the polish removes dirt and other matter from both inside and outside of the cases.

Figure 6-21: The Lyman 1200 and 600 tumbler models demonstrate the variety of sizes available for tumblers designed for cleaning cartridge cases.

Figure 6-21 shows two examples of case tumblers, the Lyman 1200 and 600. The major difference between these two is the size of their holding drums. The 1200 can hold twice as many cartridges as the 600. Supposedly, the 1200 is capable of cleaning up to 1200 cartridges simultaneously. Of course, this will depend on the size of the cartridges, so the designation is only a relative term.

Tumblers contain an internal motor that causes the entire drum to vibrate rapidly. The vibrations cause the polishing media (usually ground up corncobs or ground walnut shells) to churn constantly. Cartridges placed within this media are constantly bombarded by the particles, and even the most stubborn stains are abraded off eventually.

The polishing medium will not only clean the outside of the case but the inside as well. It usually takes about an hour to arrive at fully polished cases, although those with stubborn stains will take longer. As the polishing medium is used more and more, it loses some of its cleaning ability, which also increases total polishing time.

When cartridges are removed from the tumbler, they must be carefully inspected to make certain that all of the cleaning medium has been removed. It's easy to pour the medium out of the cases, but a grain or two of ground-up corncob will often become wedged in the primer flash hole. If this goes undetected and a primer is eventually seated with the obstruction still in place, a misfire can occur. For this reason, primer pockets on each and every cartridge that comes out of the tumbler must be closely examined.

In recent years, tumblers have been designed with water tight lids to allow for the use of wet polishing media (Figure 6-22) as well as the more conventional dry corncob media. Some reloaders prefer the convenience of a wet cleaning medium because it is a softer cleaning process that cannot etch the cases. This requires a tumbler drum that

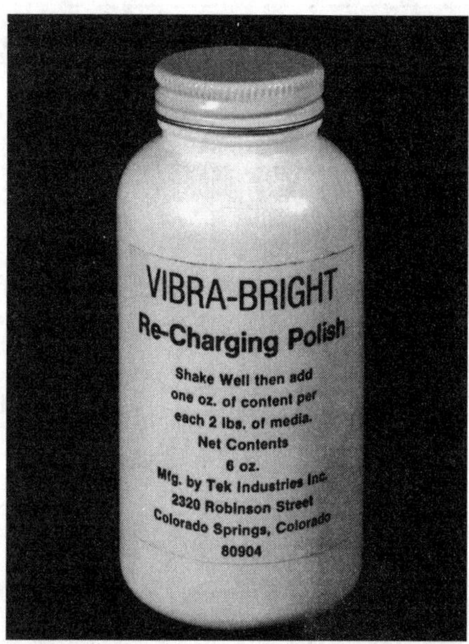

Figure 6-22: Liquid polishing media have become popular in recent years. These can be used as the sole polishing agent or for pre-cleaning/polishing prior to polishing using standard dry tumbler media.

can be sealed tightly enough to contain the liquid. If not, the vibrations will cause it to fly all over the reloading bench. If you have an older tumbler, check with the manufacturer to see if it is rated to contain liquid media.

From a practical standpoint, few reloaders will require a truly large tumbler. The 1200 model shown in Figure 6-21 is typical of the large tumblers that have application in the majority of reloading operations. However, even larger models that require far greater amounts of cleaning media are available, and they will clean thousands of cases at one time. One advantage of these large models, even in smaller reloading operations, is the fact that the cleaning medium does not have to be changed as often if only a small number of cases are cleaned at any one time.

Since there is a trend toward larger tumblers, some manufacturers are offering accessories that complement the large-volume reloader. Lyman supplies a product called "Brass Baggies" that allows reloaders to preset their cases by caliber or lot, tie them up in a baggie, and pop them directly into the tumbler. The mesh bags allow the cleaning media to get through to the cases, while keeping them separate from any other cases that may lay loose in the tumbler or be contained in separate mesh bags. After the tumbling operation is completed, the cases are clean and no separating is required.

Polishing media generally have a good life expectancy, but they won't last forever. As the medium ages beyond a certain point, you will notice that it takes longer and longer to get the cases completely clean. This is the time to replace the old medium. Polishing media are available from every manufacturer of tumblers, and it's a good idea to have a spare charge of it on hand at all times. Media are subject to water contamination, so the drum lid should be screwed down tightly even when the tumbler is not being used. Spare media charges should also be stored in watertight containers. These are a commercial product made specifically for reloaders, but many household containers should serve as well.

As discussed previously, tumblers clean brass cartridge cases by bombarding them repeatedly with a mild abrasive containing a polishing agent. Tumblers vibrate constantly, which sets up a churning action, causing the cases to constantly rise and then submerge within the cleaning medium. Due to the constant vibration within the tumbler drum, the reloader should never polish fully loaded cartridges. The main danger in doing this really doesn't involve accidental primer detonation, although this is always a possibility. The real danger comes from the potential of powder degradation.

Modern smokeless powders are treated with surface agents that retard burning. These agents largely determine the speed of the powder (how fast it burns). If a charged and loaded case is placed in a tumbler for a long period of time, the vibrations could cause the retardants to be flaked off the powder, effectively increasing its burning speed and causing chamber pressures to soar. The authors have never known this to actually happen even though a few reloaders still insist on cleaning the fully loaded cartridges. However, it is a potentially lethal possibility, so never put loaded cartridges into a vibrating tumbler.

SHOTSHELL RELOADING TOOLS

It is estimated that nearly one billion shotshells are loaded annually. The majority of these are target loads — designed for trap, skeet, and clay-target shooting. The remaining loads are for hunting or self-defense.

Competition shooters frequently fire from 50 to 100 shotshells daily for practice. If commercial shells are used, this means nearly $1000 per month in ammunition expense. The reloader can cut this amount tremendously.

The initial steps required to reload shotshells are quite similar to reloading centerfire cartridges for rifles and handguns; that is, the process involves resizing, priming, and charging the hull with powder. With shotshells, however, the reloader must contend with wad placement, shot pouring, and crimping.

The shotshell reloader deals with a much smaller range of case sizes (10-, 12-, 16-, 28-gauge and .410 bore), but these are broken down into different lengths and brass/base heights for most shells or "hulls" as they are usually called by reloaders.

For all of these reasons, the shotshell reloading press is usually a more complex unit than presses designed for reloading metallic cartridges. Means are provided for powder charging and shot pouring on the press itself.

SHOTSHELL RELOADING PRESSES

The MEC (Mayville Engineering Company, Inc.) 600 JR. Mark 5 is typical of single-stage shotshell presses that are currently available. It offers simplicity, but it doesn't sacrifice efficiency, and is a very convenient press to use. Every pull of

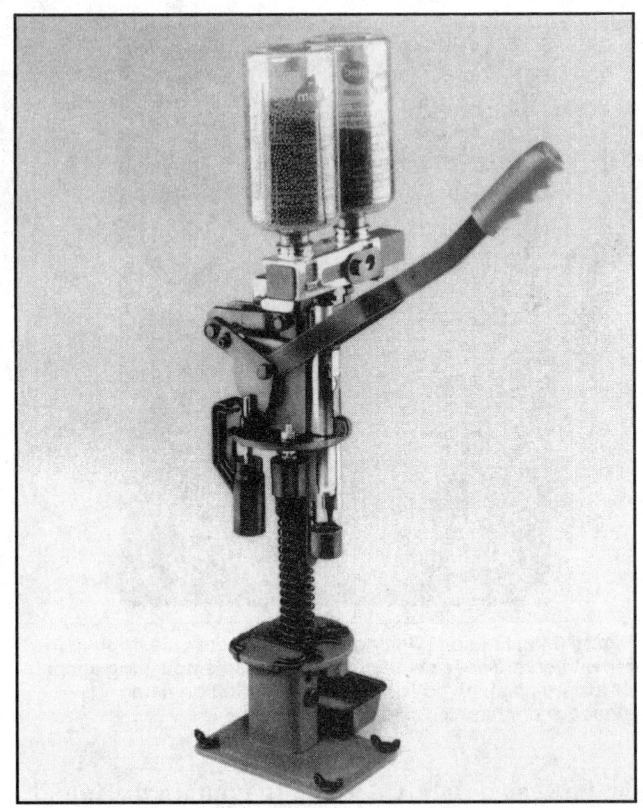

Figure 6-23: MEC 600 Jr., Mark 5 shotshell reloading press.

the handle completes one of the basic reloading steps, including depriming, priming, resizing the metal base, measuring the correct amount of powder, seating the wad column, pouring shot, and crimping. A description of the various components of this press follows.

A shot bottle and a powder bottle sit on top of this press. Shot and powder are fed through two parts of a charging bar, which is located just under these bottles. Moving the bar to the left charges the powder. Moving it to the right charges the shot.

A wad height indicator is provided at about eye level on this press to indicate improper wad placement. A wad pressure indicator provides a readout of the exact amount of pressure actually being applied to the wad column at the bottom of the handle stroke.

One main components of this press that processes the shotshell is the reconditioning die, the first die in the shotshell staging area that ejects the spent primer, irons the shell mouth, and resizes the metal base. These operations are completed with one stroke of the handle.

The next stage of processing locates the shell atop the repriming punch, where a new primer is seated as it is fed from the primer seating assembly.

Then the rammer tube is brought in line with the shotshell mouth. Powder and shot are dropped into the shell through the rammer tube, which is fed directly from the charging bar. Powder or shot drops from the bottles into this tube, depending on the position of the charging bar. This tube is also used to seat the wad column. The next staging area uses a wad feed attachment that permits accurate seating of the wad column.

A crimp starter stage initiates crimping of the shell mouth in an 8-point or 6-point star for plastic shells or a smooth cone (optional) for paper shells. The next step is the actual crimping station — a two-stage crimping apparatus that is completely adjustable for depth of crimp.

THE MEC 600 JR BASIC RELOADING PROCEDURE

All shells are processed in a clockwise rotation, and the operation is quite simple, once the press is set up.

The reloader takes the fired hull in his/her right hand and places it into the deprime/resize station. The left hand is used to press the handle to the bottom of its stroke. Resistance will be felt as the ring begins to resize the brass base and as the primer is being ejected. Resizing and depriming are completed when the handle is pressed to full stroke. The handle is then lifted and the shell is pushed from the resize ring. The shell is then removed from the deprime/resize station and placed onto the reprime punch. The reloader places a new primer into the staging pocket and strokes the handle again to complete the repriming operation.

At this point in the reloading procedure, the primed shell is placed in the charging station of the press (station #3). The handle is pushed downward only until the rammer tube enters the shell. The reloader then moves the charging bar to the left for powder charging, and the powder is metered into the shell.

Next, the handle is raised again and a wad is placed on the rammer tube. The handle is pressed for a full stroke, which seats the wad on the powder charge from the previous step. The handle is raised part way (with rammer tube still in shotshell mouth), and the charge bar is moved to the right. The shot drops into the shell.

The handle is then lifted to the top of the stroke, and the shell is placed into the crimp-start station. The handle is pressed to the bottom of the stroke. The handle is lifted again, the shell is placed in its final staging position, and the final crimping action is completed with another stroke.

Upon lifting the handle, the completely reloaded shotshell is released, and the procedure can start all over again for the next hull. Reloading a shotshell from start to finish is accomplished in seven steps using this press, which the reloader can use to load 6 to 10 boxes of shells per hour, once the process is mastered. The 600 JR. Mark 5 Model accommodates 10- through 28-gauge and .410-bore shells using separate die sets, and is designed for lead shot loading.

In order to load steel shot, an optional conversion kit is necessary. It consists of a shot bottle, drop tube, rammer tube, and charge bar all designed for steel shot only. (*See* Figure 6-24.)

The kit is user-installed on the press, replacing the lead counterparts. Once installation is complete, steel shot is loaded in exactly the same manner as lead shot, described above. This company also offers a single-stage press designed specifically for steel shot reloading, although it works equally well for lead shot.

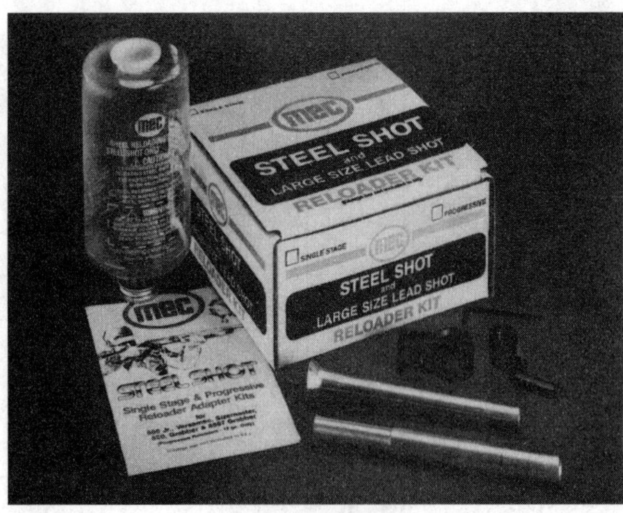

Figure 6-24: Conversion kit used when steel shot is loaded in the MEC press.

The MEC Steelmaster offers the same features as the Mark 5, handles brass or steel heads, and is available in 10 gauge, $3\frac{1}{2}$ inch and in 12 gauge for

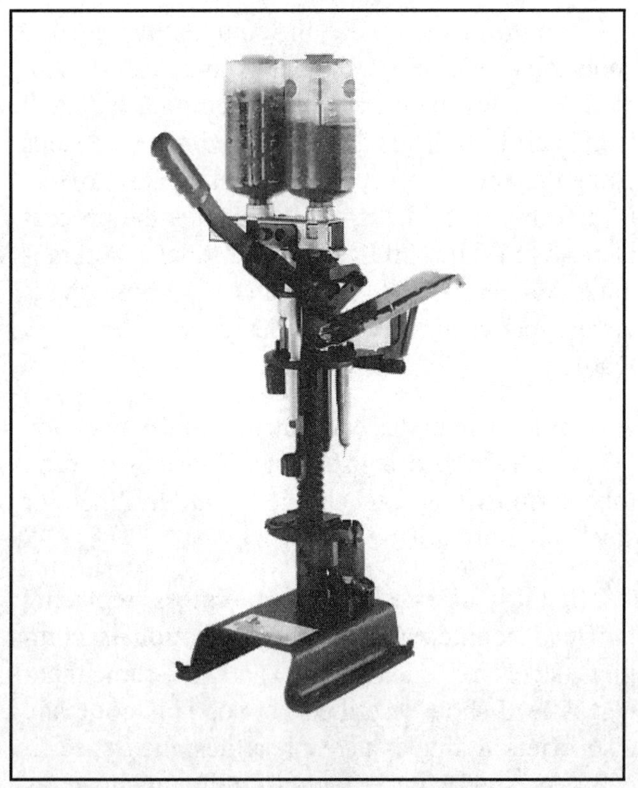

Figure 6-25: MEC Steelmaster shotshell reloading press.

$2\frac{3}{4}$-, 3- or $3\frac{1}{2}$-inch shells. This is not an adjustable press, in that no die sets are available. The press is ordered specifically for the gauge and length of shells to be reloaded. (*See* Figure 6-25.)

PROGRESSIVE PRESSES

The single-stage shotshell presses are all that will be required by most shotshell reloaders, as the capability of conveniently reloading up to 10 boxes of shells per hour is usually more than is needed on average. However, those reloaders who may do a considerable shotshell business with shooting clubs, game bird ranches, skeet and trap organizations may need more output. To efficiently produce up to 20 boxes of shells per hour, the reloader must resort to a progressive press.

A progressive press allows the shotshell to be completely reloaded without having to manually move it to the various staging areas. Additionally, most offer the capability of reloading 4 or more shells at a time. Each of the shells is at a different stage of reloading at any one time, but it can certainly be described as an "assembly-line" operation.

The MEC Model 8567 "Grabber" press is a progressive press available for gauges 12 – 28 and for .410-bore shotshells. Optional kits are needed to reload 3-inch magnum shells. This is a dedicated press, which means it must be purchased for a single gauge. No die sets are available.

This press has six stages of reloading, and a rotating carrier holds the shells in place for each of these stages. After one stage is complete, the carrier is rotated, which brings the shell or shells in line with the next stage.

Each reloading stage closely follows those described earlier for the single-stage press. They are:

Stage 1: Resize/deprime
Stage 2: Reprime/powder charging
Stage 3: Wad seating/shot charging
Stage 4: Crimp Start

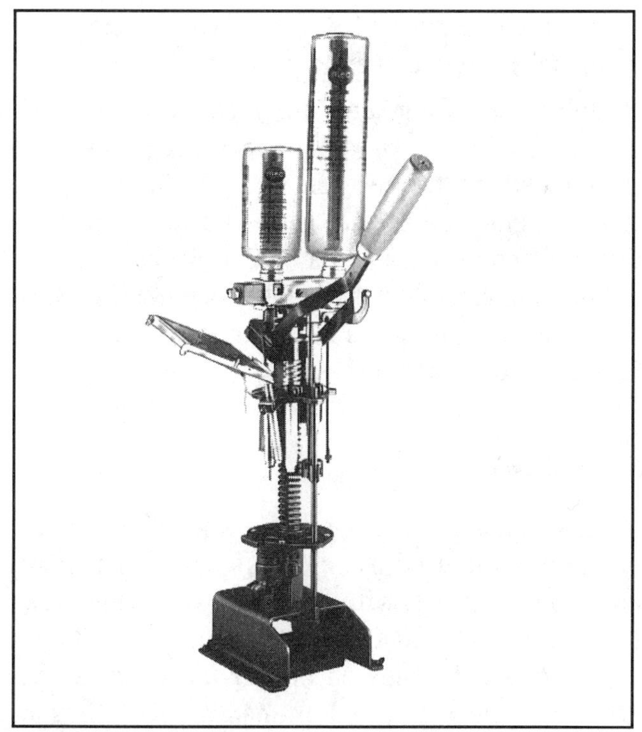

Figure 6-26: MEC 8567 Grabber.

Stage 5: Crimping
Stage 6: Shape and radius

As before, each stage of operation is completed with one full stroke of the handle. After each stroke, the carrier is rotated to the next stage.

For assembly-line loading, the first shell is placed at stage one, and the handle is pulled to resize the base and expel the spent primer. The carrier is then rotated to stage 2 for repriming and powder charging. Before this takes place, however, a second shell is placed at stage 1 again. Now, when the handle is pressed, the first shell is reprimed and charged with powder, while the second shell is resized and deprimed.

Turning the carrier once again moves the first shell to the wad seating/shot charging stage and the second shell to the repriming/powder charging stage. A third shell is placed at stage 1. On the throw of the lever, three shotshells receive their stage of processing. This process continues until all staging areas contain a shotshell (6). On the sixth throw of the handle, all of the operations described previously (stages 1-6) are accomplished on six different shells. A finished shotshell comes out one side, while an untreated shotshell is once again placed at stage 1.

This operation is not as easy as this description might indicate. It takes practice to fully utilize this or any other progressive press with highest efficiency. Practice will allow the reloader to develop the proper "feel" and rhythm necessary for a true assembly-line operation of this nature. However, once the process is learned, it becomes almost second nature, and a capable reloader can often turn out as many as 20 boxes of shells per hour using this press.

Progressive presses are quite complex. If they get out of adjustment due to improper use or poor maintenance, the assembly line can quickly become a "disassembly line." This is not something that you simply set and forget. All presses require a certain amount of maintenance for proper operation, but progressive presses require more attention to detail. Whereas a single-stage press may be made to work when slightly out of adjustment, a progressive press usually won't.

Fortunately, maintenance and adjustment are quite simple and can be performed according to a strict schedule based upon how much the press is used. A progressive press of this type is a finely-tuned machine, and should be treated as such.

Progressive presses require more mechanical advantage at the handle than single-stage presses, because multiple shotshells are at one stage in the reloading sequence during every handle stroke. This means that up to 6 times the force of a single-stage press may be required when the carrier is fully loaded. While the handle linkages do provide a good mechanical advantage, the reloader is bound to suffer from a sore arm after hours of reloading. To overcome this problem, hydraulic attachments for progressive presses have come about.

For an even more streamlined shotshell assembly operation, the Model 8567 or any MEC progressive shotshell press can be fitted with an add-on hydraulic system containing an electric motor that is operated via a foot pedal. This system is light, compact, and designed for long service under (sometimes) grueling conditions. The motor operates from 110-volt house current, and the pump that it drives supplies instant, constant pressure to drive the rams downward into the shotshell cases and back up again. Each time the foot pedal is pressed, one full stroke takes place. Every stroke of the hydraulically-driven piston is positive and performs all operations at the six reloading stations. When the carrier is fully loaded with six shotshell cases, each push of the pedal produces a finished shotshell. This can greatly speed up production while preventing fatigue.

The hydraulic shotshell presses certainly represent the "ne plus ultra" in reloading convenience and efficiency, but most reloaders will be as well served by the less expensive, manual versions. If your shotshell reloading operation requires thousands of reloadings each day, then a hydraulic press is the only practical way to go.

Unlike reloading tools for metallic cartridges, shotshell reloading is quite specialized and confined mostly to the press and its attachments. Many types of shotshell presses are dedicated, requiring that a different press be purchased for each gauge or bore reloaded. Shotshell presses are not inexpensive, but once the press has been purchased, very few accessories are necessary.

SUMMARY

This chapter has reviewed some of the more common tools used by reloaders. However, there are hundreds more, with new innovations and new modifications of old ideas showing up almost daily. The reloader depends on his/her tools for safety, efficiency and accuracy. Fortunately, all of this can be obtained at a fairly modest cost, as all of the tools discussed here are not essential for every reloading bench. Many reloaders buy a few new tools every year and eventually build up a well-complemented bench over time.

Chapter 7
Bullets for Reloaders

Reloaders have an almost endless assortment of bullets from which to choose. Each type has its own specific use, and knowing the characteristics of each bullet type will enable the reloader to select with authority.

Bullet styles, shapes and weight can vary considerably, even in the same caliber rifle or handgun. For example, Speer bullets for the .38 Special or .357 Magnum start out with a light, 110-grain hollow point, jump to a 125-grain bullet style in either softnose or hollow point, and continue on to 140 grains, 146 grains, 158 grains, and finally to a 160-grain half-jacket soft point. There are even more variations for .308 caliber rifles. Bullets are available from a 77-grain lightweight lead bullet used for squib loads on small game or for plinking, through at least a dozen bullet weights, to a 250-grain soft nose bullet that is suitable for the largest North American game.

Besides variations in bullet weight, an equal number of standard bullet designs are available:

- Flat nose
- Round nose
- Soft nose
- Spitzer-type soft point
- Hollow point
- Full-metal jacket
- Semi-wadcutter
- Flat-Base wadcutter
- Boattail

Other specialty bullets are available from custom bullet makers and from foreign ammunition manufacturers.

Lightweight bullets are used in rifles for either reduced loads for small game or high-velocity varmint loads, where bullet blow-up is wanted. Medium to heavy bullets are most often used on larger game, where deep penetration and controlled expansion are needed. Boattail bullets are usually at their best for long-range target or game shooting. Round or flat-nose bullets must be used in rifles with tubular magazines. Full-metal-jacket bullets

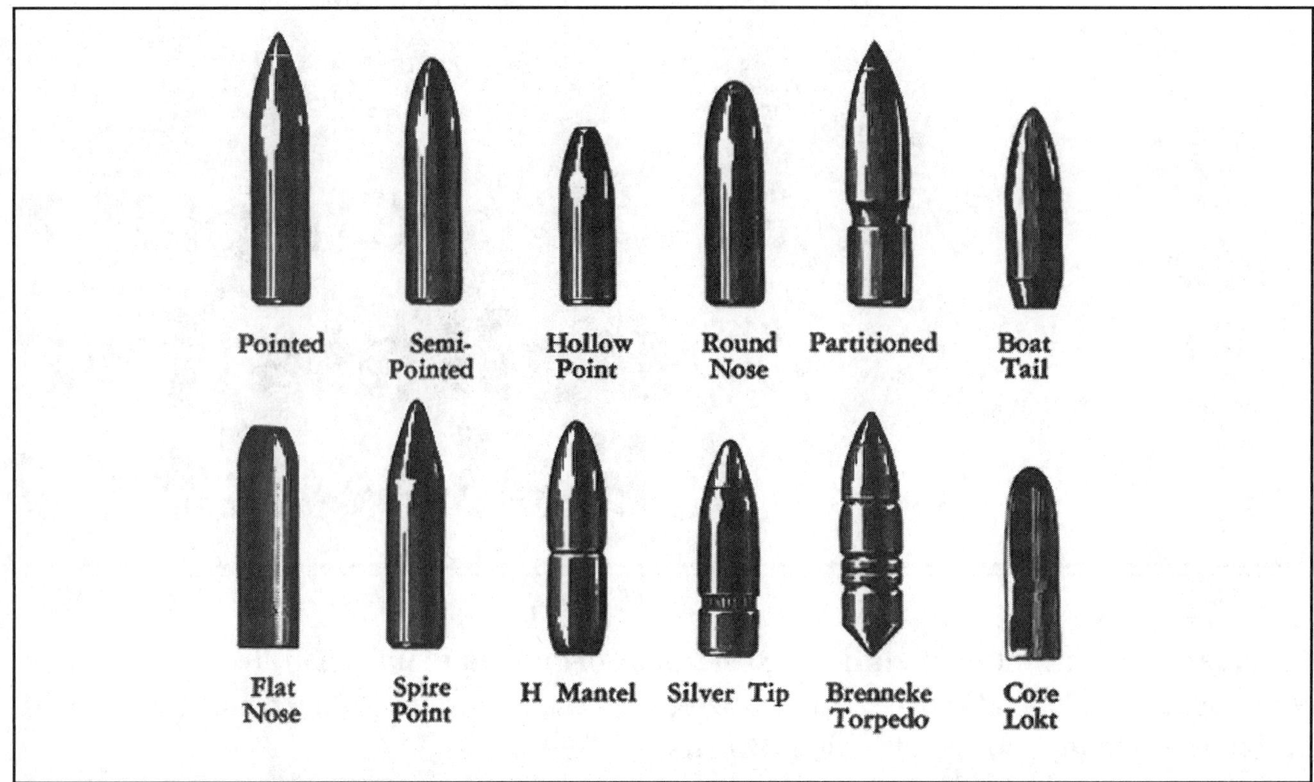

Figure 7-1: A few of the many styles of bullets available for reloading.

are used for both target shooting, combat, and for thick-skinned African game.

Several styles of bullets are shown in Figure 7-1. A brief description of each follows:

Pointed: The pointed or spitzer bullet has good wind-bucking abilities, but tends to deflect when it strikes brush.

Semi-Pointed: This type of bullet is probably the most popular of all for big-game hunting. It has good wind-bucking abilities, and tends to deflect less than pointed bullets when brush is struck.

Hollow Point: The cavity in the end of the bullet facilitates mushrooming and is considered very accurate. This type of bullet explodes readily at high velocities and is good for varmint hunting in populated areas.

Round Nose: Good brush-bucking capabilities. It expands well and offers adequate penetration on big game. It usually drifts badly in high winds.

Partitioned: The Nosler partition bullet has good penetration on game animals and good controlled expansion.

Boattail: Good for long-range shooting. Easy bullet to reload.

Flat Nose: This type is designed to be used in rifles with tubular magazines.

Spire Point: A version of the pointed bullet. Poor accuracy and mushrooming in many cases.

H Mantel: Designed to halt mushrooming when expansion reaches crimp.

Silver Tip: Made only by Winchester. Functions similarly to the semi-pointed soft-nose bullet.

Brenneke Torpedo: Good penetration and ballistic coefficient.

Core Lokt: Made only by Remington. Performance is similar to semi-pointed soft-nose bullets and has a record of high performance.

BARNES BULLETS

Caliber	Jacket Thickness	Sectional Density	Ballistic Coefficient
.17 CALIBER .172" Diameter			
25 Gr. Spitzer Soft Point	.030"	.121	.173
.22 CALIBER .224" Diameter			
60 Gr. Spitzer Soft Point	.030"	.171	.244
60 Gr. Spitzer FMJ	.030"	.171	.244
70 Gr. Semi-Spitzer Soft Point (.228 diameter also available)	.030"	.199	.284
6mm CALIBER .243" Diameter			
90 Gr. Spitzer Soft Point	.030"	.218	.311
105 Gr. Spitzer Soft Point	.030"	.266	.380
117 Gr. Round Nose Soft Point	.030"	.290	.322
.25 CALIBER .257" Diameter			
90 Gr. Spitzer Soft Point	.032"	.195	.279
90 Gr. Spitzer FMJ	.032"	.195	.279
125 Gr. Spitzer Soft Point	.032"	.270	.386
6.5mm CALIBER .264" Diameter			
130 Gr. Spitzer Soft Point	.032"	.266	.380
150 Gr. Spitzer Soft Point	.032"	.307	.439
165 Gr. Spitzer Soft Point	.032"	.338	.483
.270 CALIBER .277" Diameter			
130 Gr. Spitzer Soft Point	.032"	.242	.346
130 Gr. Spitzer FMJ	.032"	.242	.346
150 Gr. Spitzer Soft Point	.032"	.279	.399
160 Gr. Spitzer Soft Point	.032"	.298	.426
180 Gr. Round Nose Soft Point	.032"	.335	.372
7mm CALIBER .284" Diameter			
125 Gr. Spitzer Soft Point	.032"	.221	.316
140 Gr. Spitzer Soft Point	.032"	.248	.354
160 Gr. Spitzer Soft Point	.032"	.283	.404
175 Gr. Spitzer Soft Point	.032"	.319	.387
195 Gr. Semi-Spitzer Soft Point (.288 diameter also available)	.032"	.345	.493
.30 CALIBER .308" Diameter			
150 Gr. Spitzer Soft Point	.032"	.226	.323
165 Gr. Spitzer Soft Point	.032"	.247	.364
180 Gr. Spitzer Soft Point	.032"	.271	.387
200 Gr. Spitzer Soft Point	.032"	.301	.430

Caliber	Jacket Thickness	Sectional Density	Ballistic Coefficient
.30 CALIBER .308" Diameter			
225 Gr. Spitzer Soft Point	.032"	.339	.484
250 Gr. Round Nose Soft Point	.032"	.376	.417
250 Gr. Round Nose FMJ	.035"	.376	.417
8mm CALIBER .323" and .318" Diameter			
150 Gr. Spitzer Soft Point	.032"	.205	.293
180 Gr. Spitzer Soft Point	.032"	.246	.351
200 Gr. Spitzer Soft Point	.032"	.274	.391
225 Gr. Spitzer Soft Point	.049"	.308	.440
250 Gr. Semi-Spitzer Soft Point	.032"	.342	.489
.338 CALIBER .338" Diameter			
210 Gr. Spitzer Soft Point	.049"		
250 Gr. Spitzer Soft Point	.049"	.313	.447
300 Gr. Round Nose Soft Point	.049"	.375	.416
300 Gr. Round Nose FMJ (.333 diameter also available)	.049"	.375	.416
.348 WINCHESTER .348" Diameter			
250 Gr. Flat Nose Soft Point Cannelured	.032"	.295	.327
.35 CALIBER .358" Diameter			
200 Gr. Spitzer Soft Point	.032"	.223	.319
250 Gr. Spitzer Soft Point	.032"	.285	.407
275 Gr. Spitzer Soft Point	.049"	.307	.439
300 Gr. Round Nose Soft Point	.032"	.334	.371
300 Gr. Round Nose Soft Point	.049"	.334	.371
300 Gr. Round Nose FMJ	.049"	.334	.371
9.3mm CALIBER .366" Diameter			
250 Gr. Spitzer Soft Point	.032"	.267	.381
300 Gr. Spitzer Soft Point	.032"	.320	.457
.375 WINCHESTER .375" Diameter			
220 Gr. Flat Nose Soft Point Cannelured	.032"	—	—
255 Gr. Flat Nose Soft Point Cannelured	.032"	—	—

BARNES BULLETS

Caliber	Jacket Thickness	Sectional Density	Ballistic Coefficient
.38-55 .375" and .377" Diameter			
255 Gr. Flat Nose Soft Point-Cannelured	.032"		
.375 CALIBER .375" Diameter			
270 Gr. Spitzer Soft Point	.049"	.275	.404
300 Gr. Spitzer Soft Point	.049"	.305	.436
350 Gr. Round Nose	.049"	.356	.395
350 Gr. Round Nose FMJ	.049"	.356	.395
.401 WINCHESTER .406" Diameter			
250 Gr. Round Nose Soft Point	.032"	.217	.241
.411 CALIBER .411" Diameter			
300 Gr. Semi-Spitzer Soft Point	.032"	.254	.363
300 Gr. Semi-Spitzer Soft Point	.049"	.254	.363
400 Gr. Round Nose Soft Point	.032"	.338	.375
400 Gr. Round Nose Soft Point	.049"	.338	.375
400 Gr. Round Nose FMJ (.408 Diameter also available)	.049"	.338	.375
.416 CALIBER .416" Diameter			
300 Gr. Semi-Spitzer Soft Point	.032"	.284	.363
300 Gr. Semi-Spitzer Soft Point	.049"	.284	.363
400 Gr. Round Nose Soft Point	.032"	.330	.366
400 Gr. Round Nose Soft Point	.049"	.330	.366
400 Gr. Round Nose FMJ	.049"	.330	.366
.404 JEFFERY .423" Diameter			
400 Gr. Round Nose Soft Point	.032"	.319	.354
400 Gr. Round Nose Soft Point	.049"	.319	.354
400 Gr. Round Nose FMJ	.049"	.319	.354
.444 MARLIN/.44 MAGNUM .430" Diameter			
250 Gr. Flat Nose Soft Point Cannelured	.032"	.193	.214

Caliber	Jacket Thickness	Sectional Density	Ballistic Coefficient
.444 MARLIN/.44 MAGNUM (Cont.)			
300 Gr. Flat Nose Soft Point Cannelured	.032"	.232	.258
.425 WESTLEY RICHARDS .435" Diameter			
410 Gr. Round Nose Soft Point	.049"	.310	.344
410 Gr. Round Nose FMJ	.049"	.310	.344
.45-70 CALIBER .458" Diameter			
300 Gr. Semi-Spitzer Soft Point	.032"	.204	.291
300 Gr. Flat Nose Soft Point-Cannelured	.032"	.204	.227
400 Gr. Semi-Spitzer Soft Point	.032"	.272	.389
400 Gr. Flat Nose Soft Point-Cannelured	.032"	.272	.302
500 Gr. Semi-Spitzer Soft Point	.032"	.341	.487
500 Gr. Flat Nose Soft Point-Cannelured	.032"	.341	.379
.458 MAGNUM CALIBER .458" Diameter			
400 Gr. Semi-Spitzer Soft Point	.049"	.272	.389
400 Gr. Round Nose Soft Point	.049"	.272	.302
500 Gr. Semi-Spitzer Soft Point	.049"	.341	487
500 Gr. Round Nose Soft Point	.049"	.341	.379
500 Gr. Round Nose FMJ	.049"	341	379
600 Gr. Round Nose Soft Point	.049"	.409	.454
600 Gr. Round Nose FMJ (.455 diameter also available)	.049"	.409	.454
.465 NITRO .468" Diameter			
500 Gr. Round Nose Soft Point	.049"	.326	.362
500 Gr. Round Nose FMJ	.049"	.326	.362
.470 NITRO – .475 A&M .475"Diameter			
500 Gr. Round Nose Soft Point	.049"	.317	.352

BARNES BULLETS

	Jacket Thickness	Sectional Density	Ballistic Coefficient
.470 NITRO – .475 A&M .475"Diameter			
500 Gr. Round Nose FMJ	.049"	.317	.352
600 Gr. Round Nose Soft Point	.049"	.380	.422
600 Gr. Round Nose FMJ	.049"	.380	.422
.475 No. 2 JEFFREY .488" Diameter			
500 Gr. Round Nose Soft Point	.049"	.300	.333
500 Gr. Round Nose FMJ (.483 diameter also available)	.049"	.300	.333
.505 GIBBS .505" Diameter			
600 Gr. Round Nose Soft Point	.049"	.336	.436
600 Gr. Round Nose FMJ	.049"	.336	.436
700 Gr. Round Nose Soft Point	.049"	.392	—

	Jacket Thickness	Sectional Density	Ballistic Coefficient
700 Gr. Round Nose FMJ (.510 diameter also available)	.049"	.392	—
.50/110 WINCHESTER .510" Diameter			
300 Gr. Flat Nose Soft Point Cannelured	.032"	.165	.183
450 Gr. Flat Nose Soft Point-Cannelured	.032"	—	.274
.577 NITRO .585" Diameter			
750 Gr. Round Nose Soft Point	.049"	.313	.348
750 Gr. Round Nose FMJ	.049"	.313	.348
.600 NITRO .620" Diameter			
900 Gr. Round Nose Soft Point	049"	.334	.371
900 Gr. Round Nose FMJ	049"	334	371

HORNADY RIFLE BULLETS

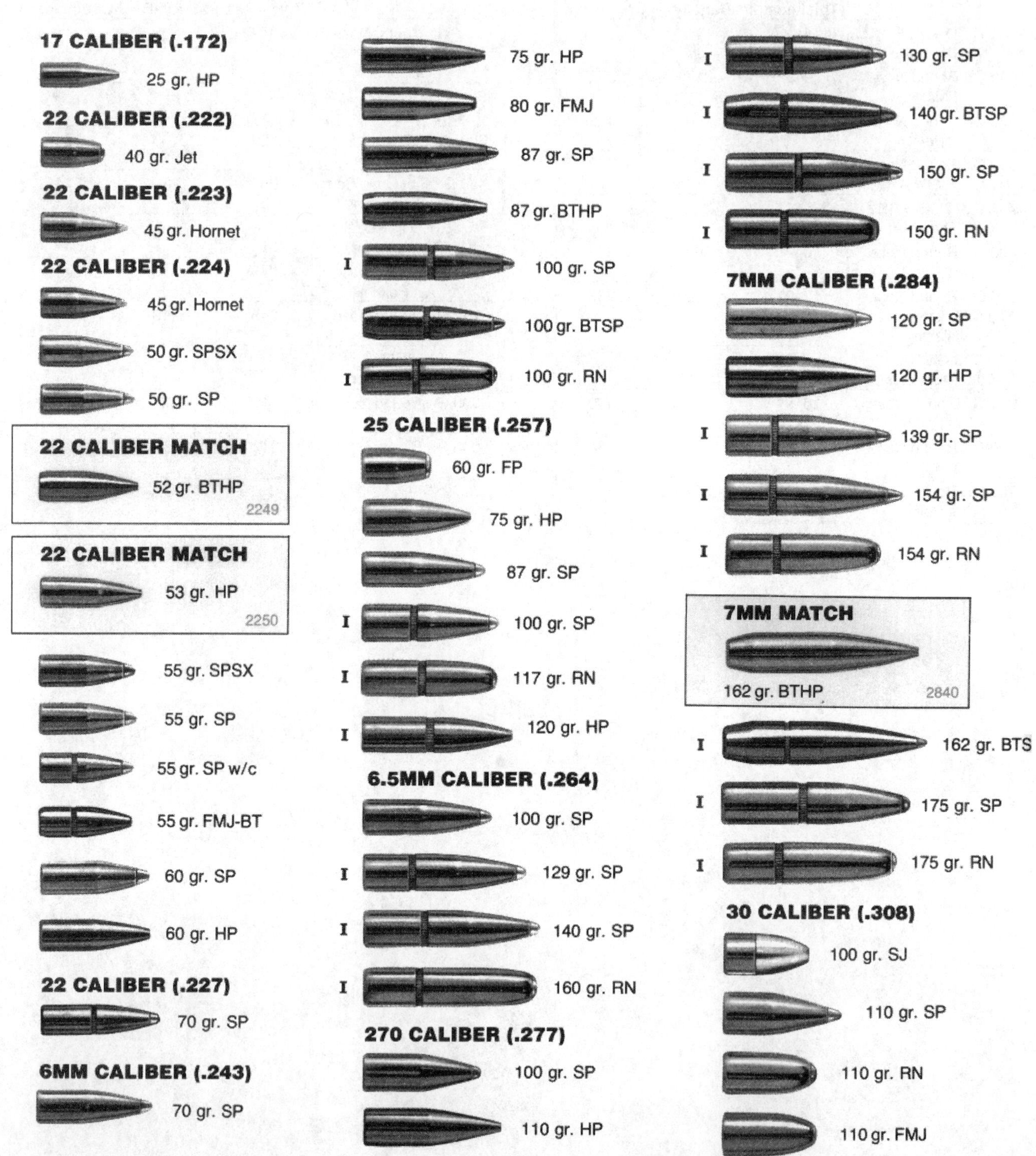

HORNADY RIFLE BULLETS

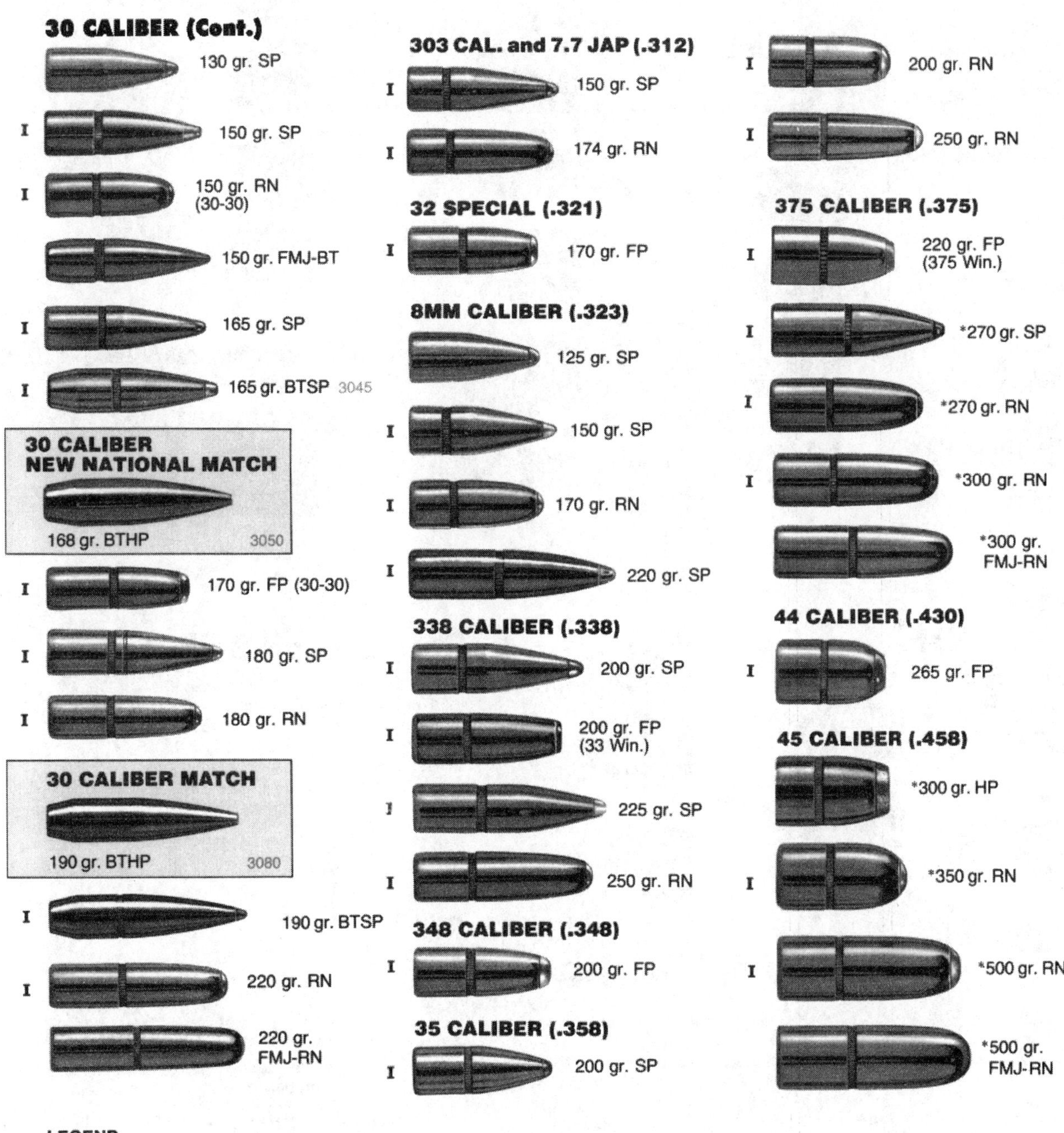

LEGEND

BBWC—Bevel Base Wadcutter
BT—Boat Tail
DEWC—Double End Wadcutter
FMJ—Full Metal Jacket
FP—Flat Point
HBWC—Hollow Base Wadcutter
HP—Hollow Point
JFP—Jacketed Flat Point
JHP—Jacketed Hollow Point
LRN—Lead Round Nose
RN—Round Nose
SJ—Short Jacket
SP—Spire Point
SWC—Semi-Wadcutter
SX—Super Explosive

Packed 50 per box.

HORNADY PISTOL BULLETS

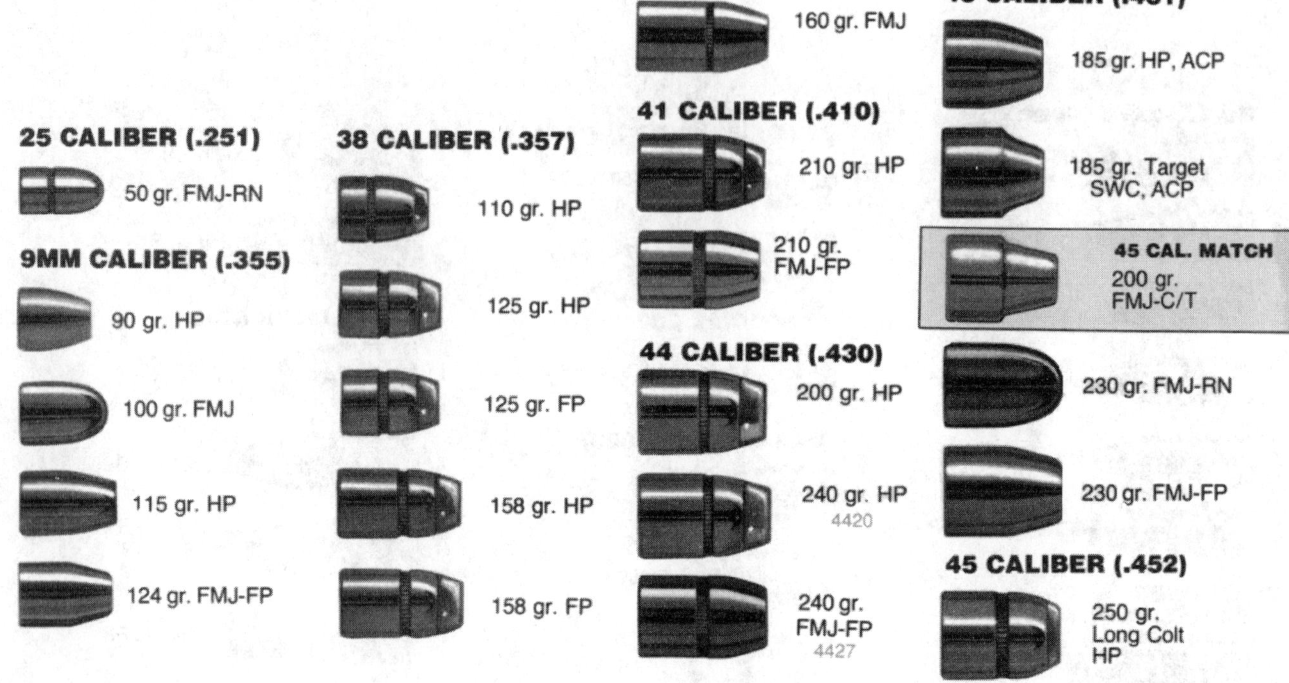

Lead Bullets

32 cal. (.314)

90 gr. SWC

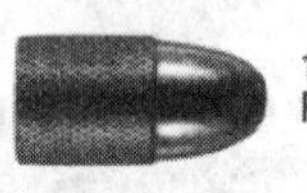

158 gr. RN

158 gr. SWC

38 cal. (.358)

148 gr. BBWC

148 gr. HBWC

148 gr. DEWC (Bulk only)

44 cal. (.430)

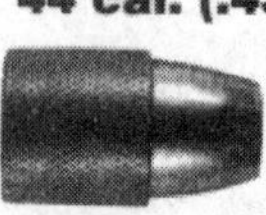

240 gr. SWC

45 cal. (.452)

200 gr. SWC

Hornady Bullets and Frontier Ammunition are available through your local sporting goods or firearms dealer.

Round Lead Balls

Hornady round balls for muzzleloading are swaged from pure lead. Swaging eliminates the sprue and guarantees uniformity from one ball to the next. Hornady round balls were widely used by the U.S. team at the International Muzzleloading Championships.

.350	**.440**	**.454**	**.530**
.375	**.445**	**.457**	**.535**
.433	**.451**	**.490**	**.570**

**Packed 50 per box. All others packed 100 per box.*

Crimp-On Gas Checks

For shooters who prefer to cast their own bullets, Hornady offers our effectively designed crimp-on gas check. When sized, the gas check crimps permanently to the bullet. It's become the most widely used gas check on the market today.

Before sizing on bullets

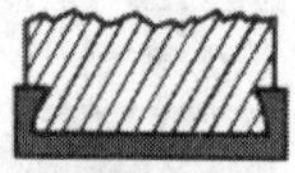

After sizing on bullets

22 cal.	**270 cal.**	**338 cal.**	**44 cal.**
6mm cal.	**7mm cal.**	**348 cal.**	**45 cal.**
25 cal.	**30 cal.**	**35 cal.**	
6.5mm cal.	**32 cal. (8mm)**	**375 cal.**	

NOSLER PARTITION BULLETS

Caliber	Diameter	Bullet Weight and Style	Sectional Density	Ballistic Coefficient	Part Number
6mm	.243″	95 Gr. Spitzer	.229	.372	16315
	.243″	100 Gr. Semi Spitzer	.242	.315	16316
.25	.257″	100 Gr. Spitzer	.216	.409	16317
	.257″	115 Gr. Spitzer	.249	.440	16318
	.257″	117 Gr. Semi Spitzer	.253	.334	16319
6.5mm	.264″	125 Gr. Spitzer	.256	.394	16320
	.264″	140 Gr. Spitzer	.287	.491	16321
.270	.277″	130 Gr. Spitzer	.242	.403	16322
	.277″	150 Gr. Spitzer	.280	.482	16323
	.277″	160 Gr. Semi Spitzer	.297	.435	16324
7mm	.284″	140 Gr. Spitzer	.248	.439	16325
	.284″	150 Gr. Spitzer	.265	.481	16326
	.284″	160 Gr. Spitzer	.283	.508	16327
	.284″	175 Gr. Semi Spitzer	.310	.484	16328
.30	.308″	150 Gr. Spitzer	.226	.370	16329
	.308″	165 Gr. Spitzer	.247	.422	16330
	.308″	180 Gr. Spitzer	.271	.456	16331
	.308″	180 Gr. Protected Point	.271	.355	25396
	.308″	200 Gr. Round Nose	.301	.358	16332
.338	.338″	210 Gr. Spitzer	.263	.386	16337
	.338″	250 Gr. Round Nose	.313	.364	16338

NOSLER SOLID BASE BULLETS

Caliber	Diameter		Bullet Weight and Style	Sectional Density	Ballistic Coefficient	Part Number
.22	.224"		50 Gr. Spitzer	.142	.244	26308
	.224"		50 Gr. Hollow Point	.142	.201	28467
	.224"		50 Gr. Hollow Point Match	.142	.201	28468
	.224"		52 Gr. Hollow Point	.150	.222	25856
	.224"		52 Gr. Hollow Point Match	.150	.222	25857
	.224"		55 Gr. Spitzer	.157	.282	16339
	.224"		60 Gr. Spitzer	.171	.290	30323
6mm	.243"		70 Gr. Hollow Point	.169	.257	26400
	.243"		70 Gr. Hollow Point Match	.169	.257	28469
	.243"		85 Gr. Spitzer	.206	.357	16341
	.243"		100 Gr. Spitzer	.242	.381	30390
.25	.257"		100 Gr. Spitzer	.216	.416	30402
	.257"		120 Gr. Spitzer	.260	.471	30404
6.5mm	.264"		120 Gr. Spitzer	.246	.422	31041
.270	.277"		100 Gr. Spitzer	.186	.315	30396
	.277"		130 Gr. Spitzer	.242	.404	30394
	.277"		150 Gr. Spitzer	.280	.513	30392
7mm	.284"		120 Gr. Spitzer	.213	.434	30343
	.284"		140 Gr. Spitzer	.248	.501	29599
	.284"		150 Gr. Spitzer	.265	.544	29600
.30	.308"		150 Gr. Flat Point	.226	.220	30406
	.308"		150 Gr. Spitzer	.226	.408	27583
	.308"		150 Gr. Hollow Point	.226	.381	28470
	.308"		150 Gr. Hollow Point Match	.226	.381	28471
	.308"		165 Gr. Spitzer	.247	.446	27585
	.308"		168 Gr. Hollow Point	.252	.443	28472
	.308"		168 Gr. Hollow Point Match	.252	.443	28473
	.308"		170 Gr. Flat Point	.256	.242	30408
	.308"		180 Gr. Spitzer	.271	.507	27587

SIERRA BULLETS

RIFLE BULLETS

.22 Caliber Hornet
(.223/5.66MM Diameter)

40 gr. Hornet
Varminter #1100

45 gr. Hornet
Varminter #1110

.22 Caliber Hornet
(.224/5.69MM Diameter)

40 gr. Hornet
Varminter #1200

45 gr. Hornet
Varminter #1210

.22 Caliber
(.224/5.69MM Diameter)

40 gr. HP
Varminter #1385

45 gr. SMP
Varminter #1300

45 gr. SPT
Varminter #1310

50 gr. SMP
Varminter #1320

50 gr. SPT
Varminter #1330

50 gr. Blitz
Varminter #1340

52 gr. HPBT
MatchKing #1410

53 gr. HP
MatchKing #1400

55 gr. Blitz
Varminter #1345

55 gr. SMP
Varminter #1350

55 gr. FMJBT
GameKing #1355

55 gr. SPT
Varminter #1360

55 gr. SBT
GameKing #1365

55 gr. HPBT
GameKing #1390

60 gr. HP
Varminter #1375

63 gr. SMP
Varminter #1370

69 gr. HPBT
MatchKing #1380
7"-10" TWST BBLS

6MM .243 Caliber
(.243/6.17MM Diameter)

60 gr. HP
Varminter #1500

70 gr. HPBT
MatchKing #1505

75 gr. HP
Varminter #1510

80 gr. Blitz
Varminter #1515

85 gr. SPT
Varminter #1520

85 gr. HPBT
GameKing #1530

90 gr. FMJBT
GameKing #1535

100 gr. SPT
Pro-Hunter #1540

100 gr. SMP
Pro-Hunter #1550

100 gr. SBT
GameKing #1560

107 gr. HPBT
MatchKing #1570
7"-8" TWST BBLS

.25 Caliber
(.257/6.53MM Diameter)

75 gr. HP
Varminter #1600

87 gr. SPT
Varminter #1610

90 gr. HPBT
GameKing #1615

100 gr. SPT
Pro-Hunter #1620

100 gr. SBT
GameKing #1625

117 gr. SBT
GameKing #1630

117 gr. SPT
Pro-Hunter #1640

120 gr. HPBT
GameKing #1650

6.5MM .264 Caliber
(.264/6.71MM Diameter)

85 gr. HP
Varminter #1700

100 gr. HP
Varminter #1710

120 gr. SPT
Pro-Hunter #1720

120 gr. HPBT
MatchKing #1725

6.5MM .264 Caliber (cont.)
(.264/6.71MM Diameter)

140 gr. SBT
GameKing #1730

140 gr. HPBT
MatchKing #1740

160 gr. SMP
Pro-Hunter #1750

.270 Caliber
(.277/7.04MM Diameter)

90 gr. HP
Varminter #1800

110 gr. SPT
Pro-Hunter #1810

130 gr. SBT
GameKing #1820

130 gr. SPT
Pro-Hunter #1830

135 gr. HPBT
MatchKing #1833

140 gr. HPBT
GameKing #1835

140 gr. SBT
GameKing #1845

150 gr. SBT
GameKing #1840

150 gr. RN
Pro-Hunter #1850

7MM .284 Caliber
(.284/7.21MM Diameter)

100 gr. HP
Varminter #1895

120 gr. SPT
Pro-Hunter #1900

140 gr. SBT
GameKing #1905

140 gr. SPT
Pro-Hunter #1910

150 gr. SBT
GameKing #1913

150 gr. HPBT
MatchKing #1915

160 gr. SBT
GameKing #1920

160 gr. HPBT
GameKing #1925

168 gr. HPBT
MatchKing #1930

170 gr. RN
Pro-Hunter #1950

175 gr. SBT
GameKing #1940

SIERRA BULLETS

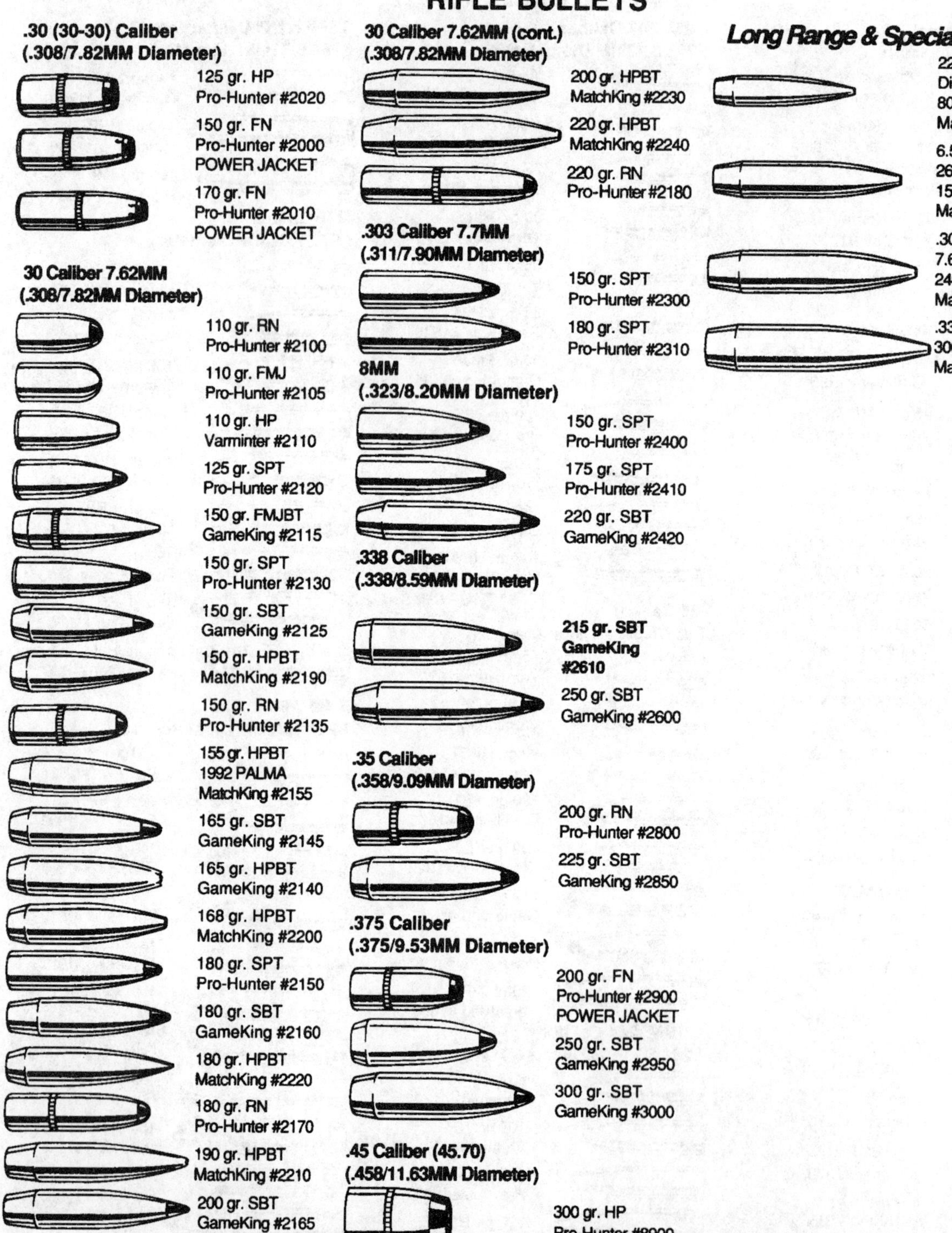

SIERRA BULLETS

HANDGUN BULLETS

Single Shot Pistol Bullets

6MM .243 Dia. 80 gr. SPT
Pro-Hunter #7150

7MM .284 Dia. 130 gr. SPT
Pro-Hunter #7250

.30 cal. .308 Dia. 135 gr. SPT
Pro-Hunter #7350

.25 Caliber
(.251/6.38MM Diameter)

50 gr. FMJ
Tournament Master #8000

.32 Caliber 7.65MM
(.312/7.92MM Diameter)

71 gr. FMJ
Tournament Master #8010

.32 Mag.
(.312/7.92MM Diameter)

90 gr. JHC
Sports Master #8030
POWER JACKET

9MM .355 Caliber
(.355/9.02MM Diameter)

90 gr. JHP
Sports Master #8100
POWER JACKET

95 gr. FMJ
Tournament Master #8105

115 gr. JHP
Sports Master #8110
POWER JACKET

115 gr. FMJ
Tournament Master #8115

125 gr. FMJ
Tournament Master #8120

130 gr. FMJ
Tournament Master #8345

9MM Makarov
(.363 Diameter)

95 gr. JHP
Makarov #8200

100 gr. FPJ
Makarov #8210

.38 Super
(.356 Diameter)

.38 SUPER 150 gr. FPJ
Tournament Master #8250

.38 Caliber
(.357/9.07MM Diameter)

110 gr. JHC Blitz
Sports Master #8300
POWER JACKET

125 gr. JSP
Sports Master #8310

25 gr. JHC
Sports Master #8320
POWER JACKET

140 gr. JHC
Sports Master #8325
POWER JACKET

158 gr. JSP
Sports Master #8340

158 gr. JHC
Sports Master #8360
POWER JACKET

170 gr. JHC
Sports Master #8365
POWER JACKET

170 gr. FMJ Match
Tournament Master #8350

180 gr. FPJ Match
Tournament Master #8370

10MM .400 Caliber
(.400/10.16MM Diameter)

150 gr. JHP
Sports Master #8430
POWER JACKET

165 gr. JHP
Sports Master #8445
POWER JACKET

180 gr. JHP
Sports Master #8460
POWER JACKET

190 gr. FPJ
Tournament Master #8480

.41 Caliber
(.410/10.41MM Diameter)

170 gr. JHC
Sports Master #8500
POWER JACKET

210 gr. JHC
Sports Master #8520
POWER JACKET

220 gr. FPJ Match
Tournament Master #8530

.44 Magnum
(.4295/10.91MM Diameter)

180 gr. JHC
Sports Master #8600
POWER JACKET

210 gr. JHC
Sports Master #8620
POWER JACKET

220 gr. FPJ Match
Tournament Master #8605

240 gr. JHC
Sports Master #8610
POWER JACKET

250 gr. FPJ Match
Tournament Master #8615

300 gr. JSP
Sports Master #8630

.45 Caliber
(.4515/11.47MM Diameter)

185 gr. JHP
Sports Master #8800
POWER JACKET

185 gr. FPJ Match
Tournament Master #8810

200 gr. FPJ Match
Tournament Master #8825

230 gr. FMJ Match
Tournament Master #8815

240 gr. JHC
Sports Master #8820
POWER JACKET

300 gr. JSP
Sports Master #8830

SPEER BULLETS

22 CALIBER (.223)

1005 40 Gr. Spire Point

1011 45 Gr. Spitzer

22 CALIBER (.224)

1017 40 Gr. Spire

1023 45 Gr. Spitzer

1029 50 Gr. Spitzer

1035 52 Gr. Hollow Point

1045 55 Gr. F M J

1047 55 Gr. Spitzer

1049 55 Gr. Spitzer

1053 70 Gr. Semi-Spitzer

6mm CALIBER (.243)

1205 75 Gr. Hollow Point

1211 80 Gr. Spitzer

1213 85 Gr. Boat Tail

1215 90 Gr. F M J

1217 90 Gr. Spitzer

1223 105 Gr. Round Nose

1229 105 Gr. Spitzer

25 CALIBER (.257)

1241 87 Gr. Spitzer

1405 100 Gr. spitzer

1407 100 Gr. Hollow Point

1410 120 Gr. Boat Tail

1411 120 Gr. Spitzer

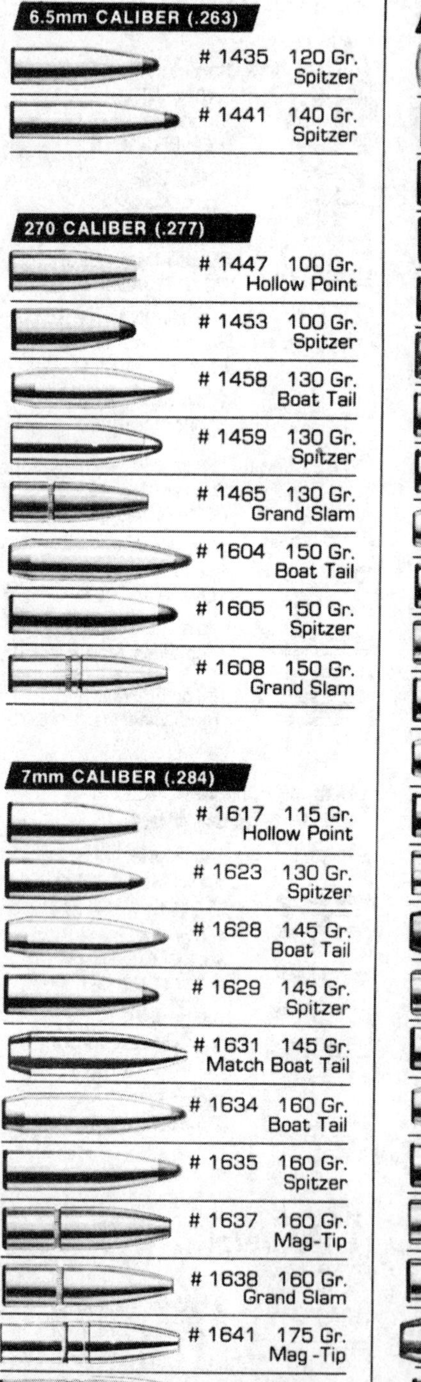

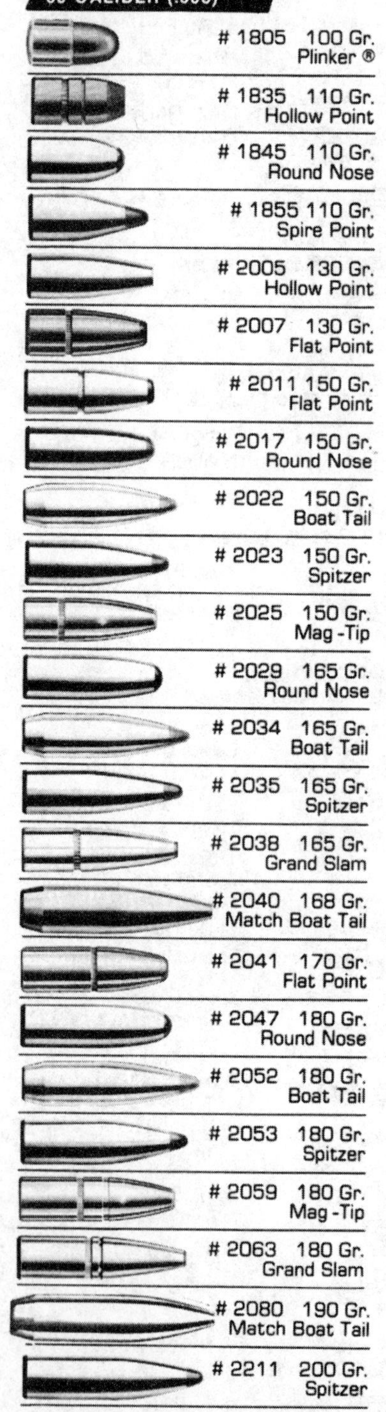

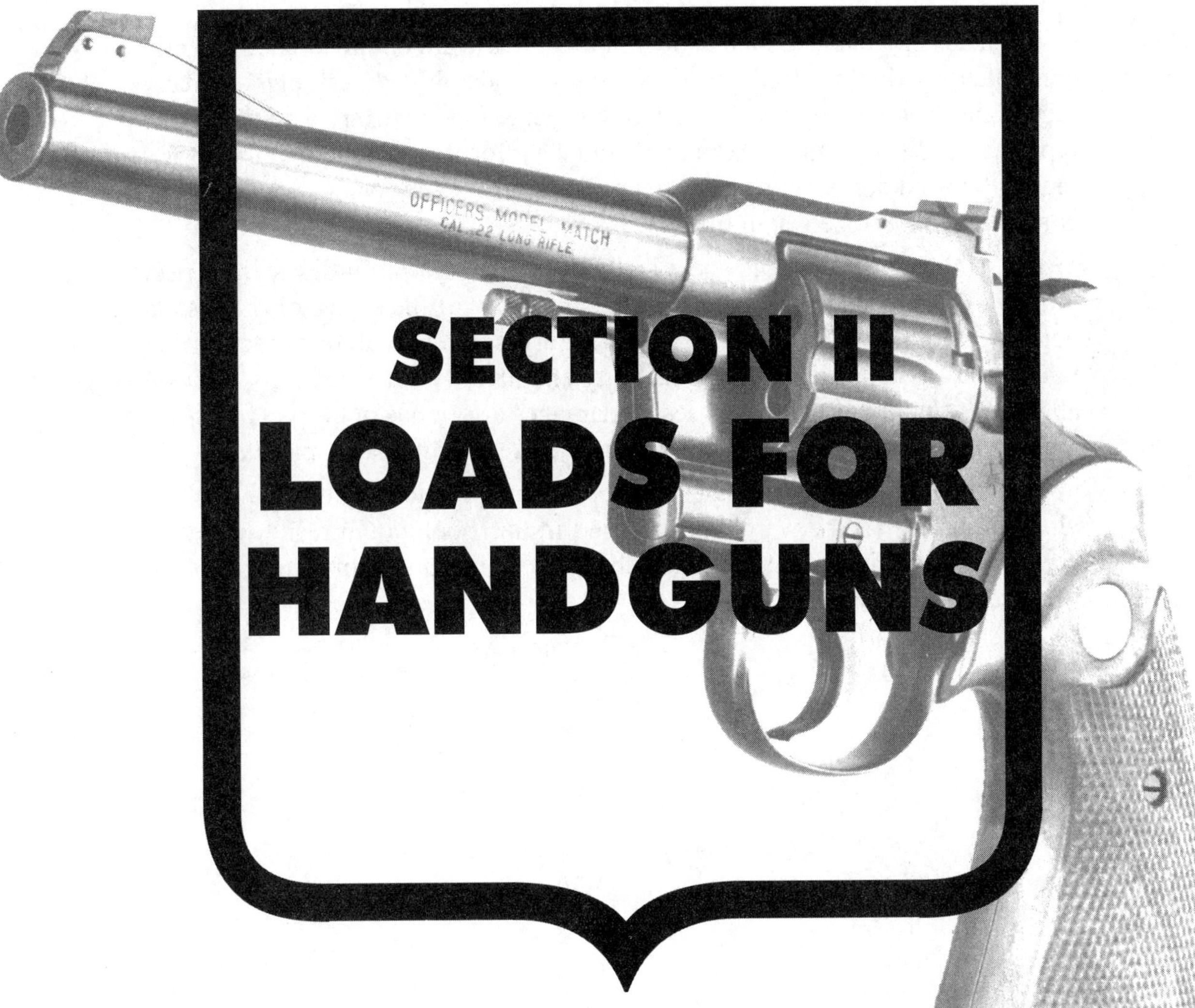

SECTION II
LOADS FOR HANDGUNS

WARNING

The loads and ballistic data shown in this book were obtained under strictly controlled conditions. Ballistic data vary considerably depending on many factors, including components used, how such components are assembled, the type and condition of the firearm used, and the reloading techniques. Therefore, the loads listed are not for inexperienced persons; safety precautions must be considered and utilized at all times.

The publisher and authors specifically disclaim any warranties with respect to any and all loads listed, the safety or suitability of the loads, or the results obtained with the listed loads. Readers and users of any load or product listed in this book assume all risk, responsibility and liability whatsoever for any and all injuries (including death), losses, or damages to persons or property (including consequential damages), arising from the use of any load or product.

The individual assumes the risk of safe loading practices. Failure to do so or violation of any of the warnings specified in this book could result in severe personal injury (including death) to the user or bystander or damage to the firearm.

Chapter 8

How To Reload Handgun Cartridges

Pistol or handgun cartridges are reloaded in almost the same manner as rifle ammunition, except that a three-die set and a slightly different technique are used to resize and expand straight-sided handgun cases.

With the three-die set, the first die is used only to resize the case. The second die expands the case to avoid unnecessary resizing of the case mouth after expansion. The third die seats and crimps the bullet. Decapping is performed by either the first or second die, depending on the manufacturer of the reloading dies.

Figure 8-1: A three-die set of reloading tools for straight-sided handgun ammunition.

Figure 8-2: All cases for use in semiautomatic pistols should be full-length resized to ensure proper feeding.

Bottleneck pistol cases, such as the .30 Mauser, require only a two-die set. A few pistol cartridges require a four-die set for best results.

RELOADING PROCEDURE

The exact steps required to reload handgun ammunition will vary with the type of reloading equipment. For example, if only a few rounds of ammunition will be loaded at any one time, or the reloader desires the reloading equipment to be portable for use in the field or on the range, then one of the inexpensive hand tools may be the type to choose. If several dozen cartridges are frequently loaded, then one of the more sophisticated tools should be considered. Local sporting goods or shooting-supply dealers and certain mail-order houses can supply the tools, plus all the components needed for reloading any type of ammunition. (Refer to Chapter 6 for a description of most available tools.)

Regardless of the equipment used, the following steps should always be performed when reloading pistol cartridges:

- Inspect cases
- Trim cases to correct length
- Lubricate cases
- Resize cases
- Decap cases
- Prime cases
- Charge cases with powder
- Seat the bullet in the case
- Inspect loaded cartridge

INSPECT CASES, TRIM, AND LUBRICATE

Cases that have been fired must be wiped clean with a cloth to prevent dirt scratches. Doing so will also extend the life of cases and reloading dies.

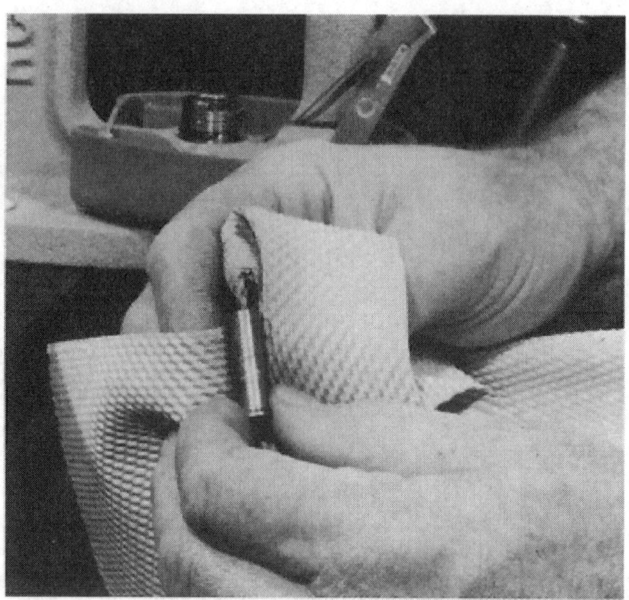

Figure 8-3: Wipe case clean to prevent dirt from scratching case, and insides of sizer die.

Inspect each cartridge case before loading to make sure that they are in good reloading condition. This same type of inspection should be performed each time the case is loaded.

Look for bent, dented or deformed cases, chewed-up rims, split necks, head separation, and enlarged primer pockets. Discard any unsuitable cases. It is also recommended that different brands of cases be separated and loaded in lots according to brand names. Also separate any military brass, such as the .45 ACP, and check for crimped-in primers.

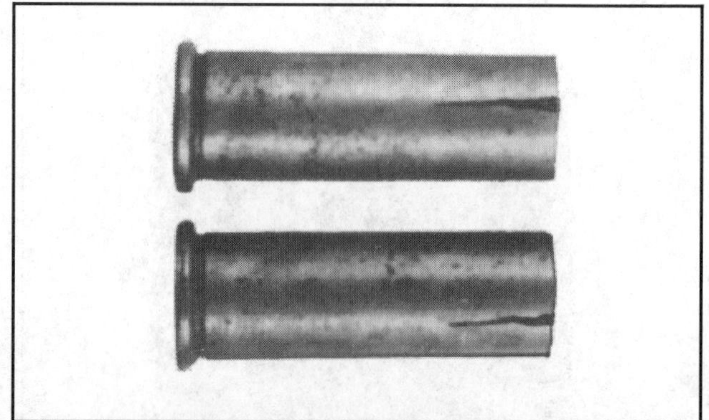

Figure 8-4: Splits may occur after several reloadings as a result of repeated crimping of the bullet. Even the tiniest crack is cause for rejection.

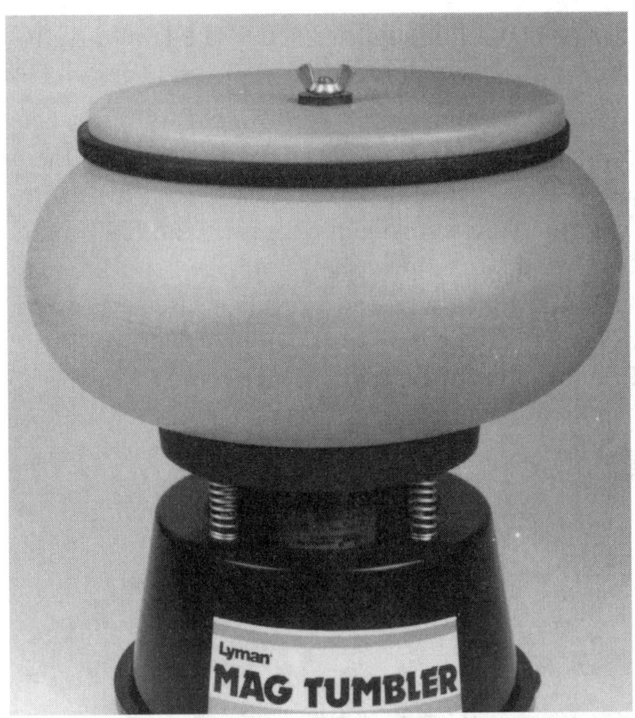

Figure 8-5: The Lyman Mag Tumbler will clean more than 1500 pistol cases in each cycle.

Once all cases are separated, some may need polishing. If so, there are two generally accepted methods:

- Chemical polishing
- Tumbler or vibration polishing

Chemical polishers are fine when only a few cases need polishing or when the reloader does not have the time to wait the several hours required to adequately polish cases in polishing tumblers or vibrating polishing apparatus.

When many cases require polishing, and when the reloader does not want to waste his or her time, yet can wait on the polishing job, cartridge tumblers — ranging in price from $60 to over $300 — are the way to go. See Figure 8-5. The least expensive tumblers will polish about 100 pistol cases in less than two hours, while more expensive models will handle 1500 or more cases during one polishing cycle. Furthermore, the polishing media may be reused on thousands of cases before it will have to be renewed or replaced. Load the tumbler with polishing media, dump in the cartridges, and flick on the switch. The tumbler will polish the cases unattended for the next hour or so, depending upon the condition of the cases.

It is good practice to once again inspect each cartridge case after it has been polished; this time with more scrutiny. Many defects will show up better after polishing than before. This time examine the inside of the case mouth, preferably under a magnifying glass. Such examinations will often disclose seams and scratches that may develop into cracks. It will also reveal uneven chamfering of the case mouth. Don't try to hurry during this final inspection. Do the job right, or don't waste any time on this second inspection.

On bottleneck cases, such as the .221 Remington Fire Ball, .256 Winchester Magnum, 7mm Nambu, 7mm BR Remington, 7.62mm Russian Tokarev, .30 Mauser, and others, the inspection should be extended to cover the shoulder of the cartridge; that is, where it starts to neck down. On rimless cartridges, this point controls the headspace, and care must be taken to see that the case is not damaged here. Faint cracks may be found at this point, and such cases should be discarded promptly. While minor gas leakage through cracked or punctured cases is not necessarily dangerous, it may be serious. Such leakage will eventually cause a rough chamber, sticking cases, and opens the door for rust and corrosion.

CASE TRIMMING

Each time a cartridge is fired, the brass stretches or flows forward a small amount, increasing the overall length of the case. Cartridge cases that are too long can cause excessive pressure, destroy accuracy and can be dangerous to the shooter and bystanders. To correct this problem, cases must be measured and trimmed before lubricating them.

The length of cartridge cases may be checked with calipers or other type of case-length gauge. The easiest way to trim cartridge cases is in a case

Figure 8-6: The Lyman Universal Trimmer.

trimmer such as Lyman's Universal Trimmer as shown in Figure 8-6. Operation of this tool only takes a few cranks of the handle, but if power is needed, Lyman now offers a "power pack" that converts the Universal Trimmer to power in only seconds. The power adapter is comprised of a specially designed trimmer shaft with a standard ¼-inch hex adapter designed to engage a standard electric drill head or power screwdriver. The power adapter comes with its own cutter and set of stop collars so the user can convert back and forth from power to hand trimming mode without changing caliber settings. See Figure 8-7.

If bullets are to be crimped, all of the cases must be the same length. If they are not, the longer cases will get too much crimp and the shorter ones not enough. Consequently, all short cases must be discarded and all others trimmed to the length of the shortest one remaining.

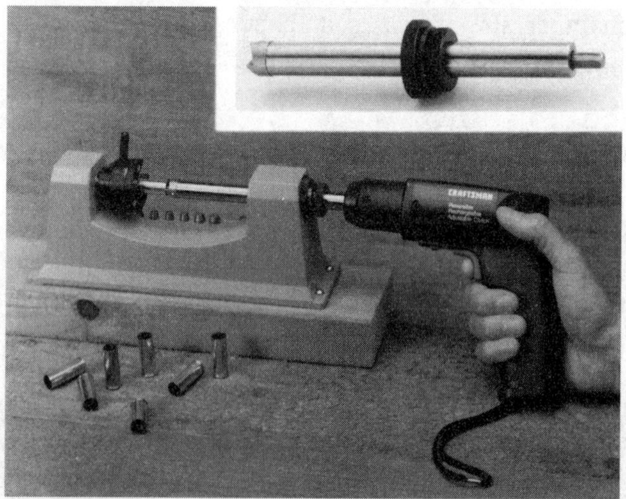

Figure 8-7: Lyman Universal Trimmer with power adapter attached.

Rather than using a case trimmer, as described previously, many reloaders prefer to trim their cases with a trim die. To use the RCBS trim die, for example, screw the die into the press until its mouth touches the extended shell holder when the press handle is all the way down. Insert a case in the shell holder and again pull the trim die all the way down. File the case off flush with the top of the die.

BEVEL AND DEBURR THE CASE

Figure 8-8: Simple beveling and deburring tool. This type is the most popular with reloaders.

For easier resizing and bullet seating, the mouths of all cases — new and old alike — should be chamfered (beveled). All trimmed cases should also be deburred. A bevel/deburring tool like the one shown in Figure 8-8 is ideal for these operations.

To use the bevel/deburring tool, insert the pointed end of the tool into the case mouth and twist it slightly. Do not make a knife edge, just enough to form a slight chamfer. To remove burrs left by trimming, place the other end of the tool over the case mouth and twist as shown in Figure 8-9 on the next page. The cases are now ready for lubricating.

LUBRICATE THE CASES

After the cases have been wiped clean, inspected for flaws, polished, trimmed, case mouths chamfered and deburred, they should be properly lubed before resizing to avoid needless wear on the die

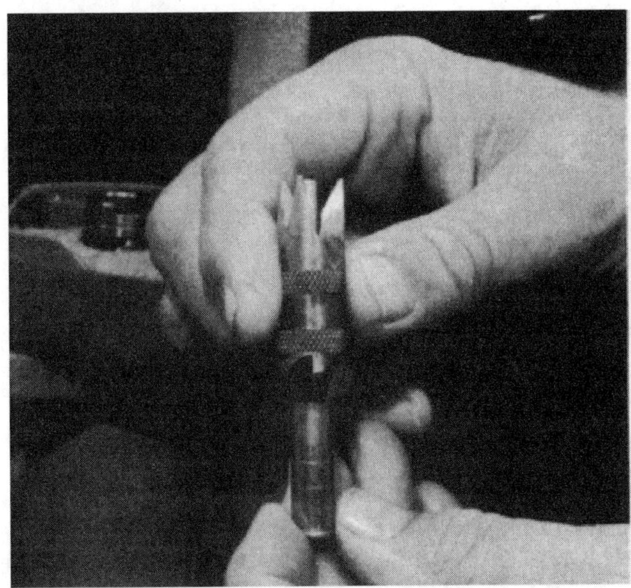

Figure 8-9: Using a deburring tool, remove any rough edges from inside and outside the brass case mouth.

and the cases. To do this, use a case-lube pad and rub a small amount of case lubricant into the pad. Don't have the pad overloaded, as too much lubrication can cause case dents during resizing when the oil is trapped between the outer case and die walls.

Next take a case-neck brush of the proper diameter, and brush out the inside of the case neck. This will remove grit and powder residue, making it easier to seat the new bullet. The case is now ready to be resized.

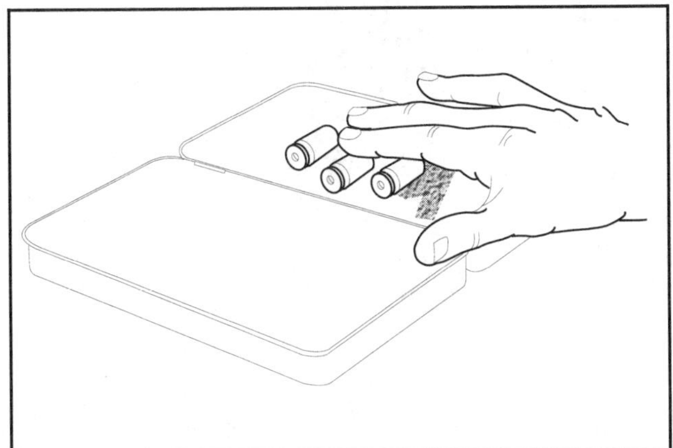

Figure 8-10: Lubricating the cases prior to resizing.

RESIZING

Opinions differ when it comes to resizing handgun cases. One group maintains that neck resizing is all that is necessary when the cartridges are loaded for the same handgun in which the cases were originally fired. This same group further claims that full-length resizing is necessary only when the cartridges are to be fired in a semiautomatic pistol or when the reloaded ammunition is to be used in a number of different guns of the same caliber.

While cases will generally last longer when only neck sized, most reloaders prefer to full-length resize their cases to their original dimensions. Full-length resizing better ensures that the cartridges will chamber properly and not stick in the chamber.

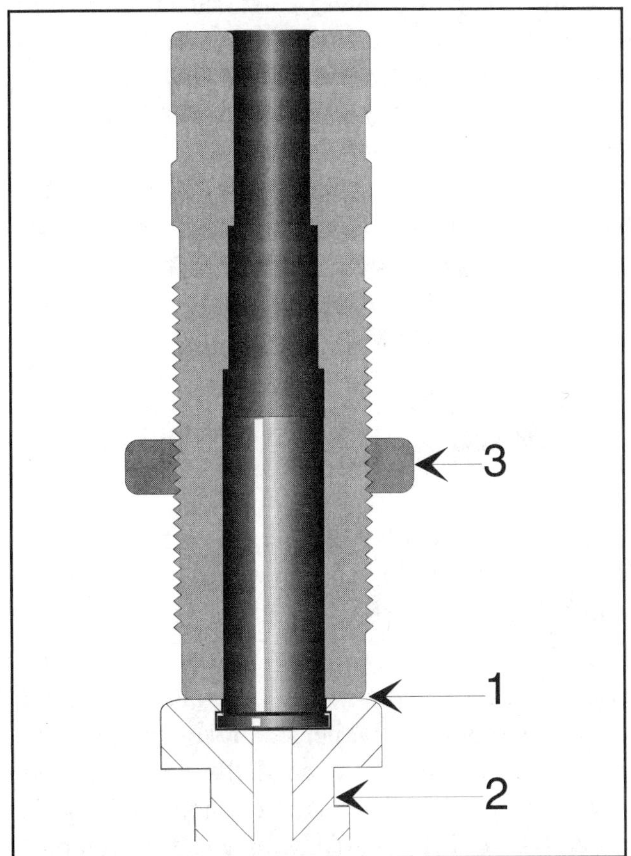

Figure 8-11: Sectional view of the pistol full-length resizing die.

To resize a cartridge case, make sure the correct shell holder is in place and firmly secured. Push the press handle all the way down to the end of its stroke. Screw the correct resizing die into the press until the bottom of the die (1) touches the shell holder (2). Now raise the press handle slightly and screw the resizing die down an additional ⅛-turn, or perhaps slightly less, and set the lock ring (3). The tools are now set to test the resizing of one cartridge case.

Place a lubricated case in the shell holder and run it up into the full-length resizing die. It should enter smoothly and without a great deal of force. If it doesn't, STOP! Do not use excessive force or the case may stick in the die. Check over the operation thoroughly before continuing. The case may not be properly lubricated, the wrong die may be used, or the die might be dirty on the inside.

If all goes well, withdraw the resized case from the die and examine it carefully. In doing so, you will notice that the neck is slightly smaller than the body. This is perfectly normal as the body does not need to be resized as much as the neck. Also try the case in the chamber in which the loaded cartridges will be used. If everything checks out okay, complete the resizing operation for all cases in the group; then move on to the next step — expanding and decapping the case.

EXPAND AND DECAP THE CASE

These steps involve removing the fired primer from the case and expand the case mouth to the diameter of the bullet to be seated.

During the resizing operation, the neck of the case is reduced to a diameter too small for the bullet to enter. Consequently, before proceeding, the inside of the neck must be expanded to a uniform and correct diameter. The neck-expanding plug is turned to two different diameters. The first step of the plug enlarges the inside of the case neck to a diameter approximately .001 inch smaller than the bullet diameter. This size ensures holding the bullet friction tight and keeps it from falling down into the case.

The larger diameter of the plug is approximately .001 inch larger than the bullet and expands only the very front portion of the neck. Doing so makes it easy to introduce the bullet into the cartridge neck without shaving or deforming the bullet and also to prevent damaging the case neck during the seating operation.

While performing the neck-expanding operation, the cartridge case is also decapped at the same time; that is, the fired primer is ejected out the bottom of the case by the force of the decapping rod as shown in Figure 8-12.

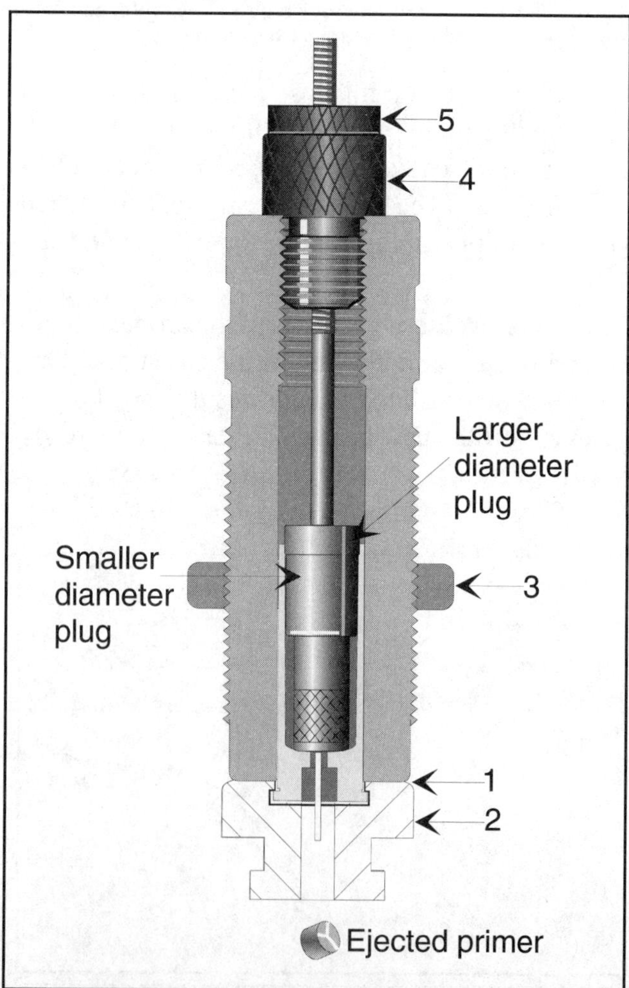

Figure 8-12: Expander-decapping die.

Refer again to Figure 8-12 during the set-up instructions. To set-up for the expanding and decapping operations, push the loading-press handle all the way down to the end of its stroke. Screw the expander-decapping die into the press until the bottom of the die (1) barely touches the shell holder (2) and then set the large lock ring (3). Also examine the decapping-rod pin. It must be perfectly straight and aligned with the primer hole in the case. Otherwise the pin will hit the base of the case and will either break or will not perform its intended operation.

The expander plug (4) must now be adjusted to expand the case neck and slightly flare the case mouth; the fired primer is also ejected — all in one operation.

Insert a case into the shell holder and slowly push the press handle down, forcing the case into the die. During this operation, a very slight resistance should be felt as the expanding plug enters the case mouth and the decapping rod engage the fired primer. If more resistance is felt, STOP! Something is wrong. Either the expanding plug is set too far down or the decapping-rod pin is out of alignment.

Return the handle to its upward position and remove the processed case from the shell holder. Examine the case mouth for flare and check to see that the fired primer has been ejected. If the plug does not enter the case far enough, the mouth will not be flared sufficiently to allow a bullet to be seated. If the plug goes too far into the case, the case mouth could be flared too much to enter the bullet-seating die.

Make any necessary adjustment by screwing the expander plug up or down. When correctly adjusted, lock the expander plug ring (5), and insert another case into the shell holder. As the case is run into the die, the fired primer will be knocked out, the case neck expanded, and the case mouth flared. Perform the expanding and decapping operations on all cases to be reloaded.

NOTE

Once the reloading dies have been set-up for loading a particular cartridge with a certain bullet and all lock rings have been "locked," no further adjustment is usually necessary. Carefully unscrew the dies from the reloading press and store them in their original containers. The next time the dies are used, they should be adjusted perfectly. However, always check one load before loading the whole batch.

CLEANING THE PRIMER POCKETS

There are a few primer-pocket cleaning brushes available to remove powder residue with merely a twist or two. The better ones come with both large and small interchangeable brushes. Since this operation takes only a minute or two, it is recommended that all primer pockets be cleaned before proceeding with the remaining reloading operations.

Primers are heavily crimped-in on most military cases which may cause ordinary decapping pins to bend or break. Heavy-duty punch-and-base sets are available from several tool manufacturers. In fact, many reloaders use these heavy-duty units for all of their reloading. See Figure 8-13.

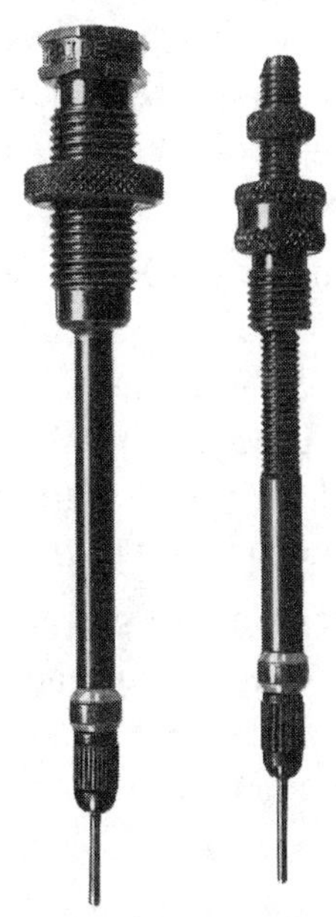

Figure 8-13: Heavy-duty replacement primer punches are available for removing heavily-crimped primers in military cases.

Once decapped, a primer-pocket reamer is used to remove the crimp from military cases. A slight twist on the top edge of the pocket is all that is necessary in most cases.

Match shooters sometimes take the time to chamfer the inside flash hole of match cases for round-to-round uniformity. These tools are used while the fired primer is still in place. The pointed end of the tool is inserted through the case neck until it goes into the flash hole. The tool is then rotated until it stops cutting.

This is also a good time to examine all primer pockets and flash holes for defects. Any deformed or damaged pockets mean immediately discarding the cartridges cases. Although saving money on ammunition is one reason for reloading, there is no reason to use less-than-perfect cases for all loads. To do otherwise is asking for trouble.

LOADING BLOCKS

If the reloader has not used reloading blocks to this point, now is the time to start. Reloading blocks help to separate the primed cases from the unprimed ones; the same is true for cases that have been filled with powder. More importantly, loading blocks prevent powder-filled cases from falling over and spilling out their contents.

Many reloaders use two different blocks for each reloading job. Resized and decapped cases are placed in one block. As the cases are primed, they are transferred to the other block. Then when it comes time to load the powder, the powder-filled cases are transferred back to the first block.

When only 20 or so cartridges are being loaded at one time, the same procedure may be used with one block; merely transfer the cases from one end of the block to the other as the various operations are completed.

Figure 8-14 shows a Pacific case-care kit which includes a plastic loading block, case lubrication, a lubrication pad, chamfering tool, case-mouth brushes, and primer-pocket cleaning brushes.

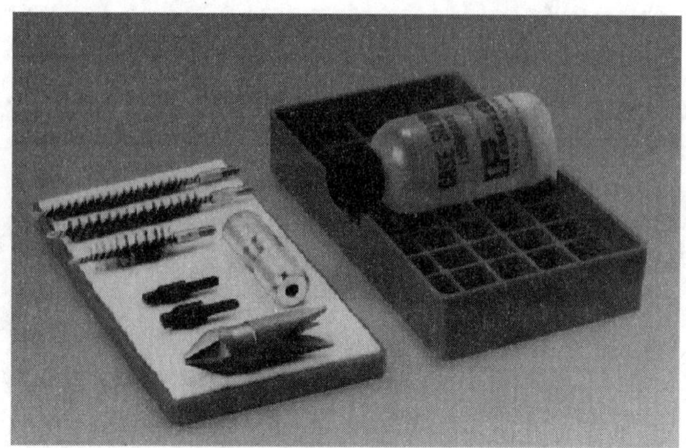

Figure 8-14: Pacific case-care kit includes a loading block.

PRIMING THE CASES

Most reloading presses have a built-in priming attachment and while the purpose of all is to insert a new primer into the case to be loaded, all operate in a slightly different way, depending upon the manufacturer.

The RCBS attachment in Figure 8-15, for example, is typical of those currently in use. Refer to this illustration as the steps are explained on the following page.

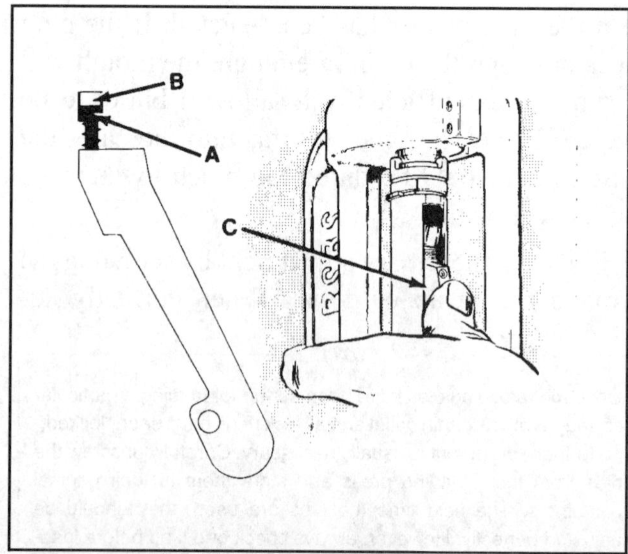

Figure 8-15: RCBS priming attachment.

- First, make sure the right size primer plug (A) and sleeve (B) are used and in position.
- Insert a primer (anvil up) in the primer-arm sleeve and push the primer arm into the shell holder slot (C).
- Gently raise the press handle and the case will be lowered onto the primer, seating it to the bottom of the primer pocket.

The primer should seat easily; if not, remove the case and inspect it carefully. The primer pocket is probably nicked or dented. If so, discard the case.

The primer should always be seated to the bottom of the pocket for uniform ignition. A little practice will enable the reloader to feel when it is in position. Never crush the primer with too much force, or allow it to protrude above the case head. A correctly-seated primer appears in Figure 8-16.

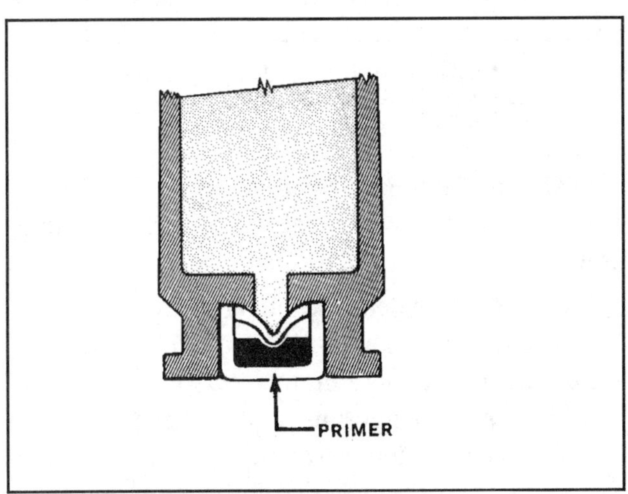

Figure 8-16: Correctly seated primer.

After the primer is correctly seated, lower the press handle enough to let the primer arm snap out of the slot. Don't lower the handle too far, especially if the decapping die is still in this press; doing so will punch out the new primer. Remove the primed case, and continue priming all cases in the batch.

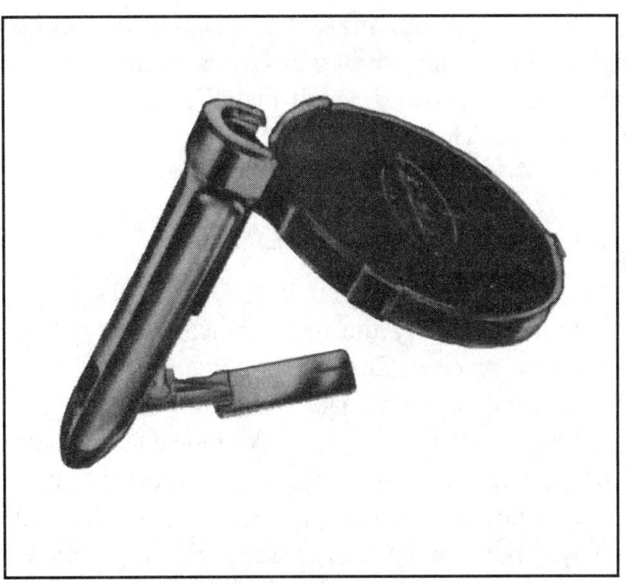

Figure 8-17: The Lee Auto-Prime is available from Lee Precision, Inc.

When only a few cases are to be loaded, the priming tool designed for the reloading press is normally the best. However, when many cases are to be primed, the authors have found that one of the separate hand-held tools is faster. The Lee Auto-Prime, for example, has been used on the authors' reloading benches for over 10 years and continues to be an invaluable tool. This little tool (Figure 8-17) automatically feeds and installs primers as fast as cases can be placed in the holder. Thumb pressure allows the reloader to feel primers being seated. The built-in primer flipper turns them right-side up. Merely dump the primers in the attached tray, shake a few times, and replace the tray cover. The tool is ready for operation.

RCBS also offers a hand-priming tool that features a patented shielding mechanism that separates the seating operation from the primer supply. This feature guards against accidental primer-tray detonation. This tool uses conventional RCBS shell holders.

CAUTION

Never seat a primer into a cartridge case already charged with powder!

The Forster/Bonanza B-2 CO-AX reloading press with its top priming device is another excellent choice for priming all metallic cartridges to factory specifications.

LOADING POWDER

This is probably the most critical stage of the reloading process. Consult the reloading tables in this book or other reloading manual to learn the right type and amount of powder to use for a given cartridge and bullet weight. Don't guess because the use of the wrong kind or quantity of powder will always give unsatisfactory results and may even be dangerous.

Increasing the powder charge will nearly always increase chamber pressure. The same is true when the weight of the bullet is increased with the same powder charge; the chamber pressure will again increase.

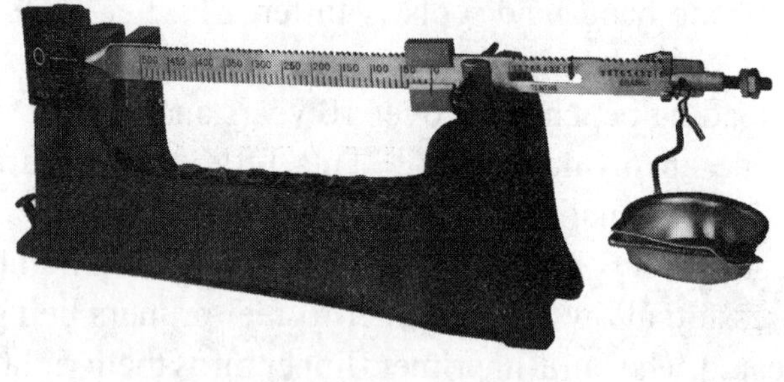

Figure 8-18: A powder scale is essential for any type of reloading.

No other phase of the reloading process will have a greater effect on the accuracy of reloaded cartridges than the care used to measure the powder charge. Consequently, a powder scale (Figure 8-18) is essential for measuring initial charges. When many cases are loaded at the same time, a powder measure (Figure 8-19) used in conjunction with a powder scale will throw faster charges and speed up the loading process. However, every 10 rounds

CAUTION

Never start with the maximum loads. A good rule-of-thumb is to start with the lowest suggested load and work up to the load that works best in an individual handgun. Begin at least two grains below maximum each time a load is being worked up.

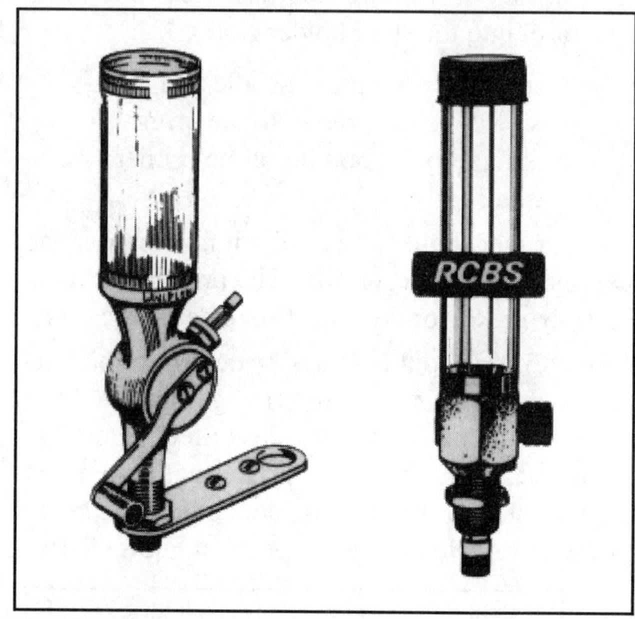

Figure 8-19: A powder measure used in conjunction with a powder scale will speed-up the reloading process.

or so should be checked with the powder scale to ensure that the powder measure is maintaining accurate charges.

Since most powders for handgun cartridges are quite dense, few handgun loads will fill up the entire cartridge case. For this reason, it is quite possible to get a dangerous double charge of powder if care is not taken. To avoid throwing a double charge into one case, place all unloaded cases in the loading block upside down (primer up) on one side of the loading block, or in a separate loading block as discussed previously. Then take a case out of the block, charge it, and put it back on the opposite side of the block or in a different reloading block; this time with the mouth of the case upward. Following this procedure will help ensure against putting two charges into one case.

After all cases have been charged with powder and are standing in the loading block upright, examine the level of powder in each case under a good light. If a case appears to have more powder in it than the others, remeasure the charge in this case just to be sure.

The actual placement of powder in handgun cartridge cases may be done in several different ways, but the way preferred by most reloaders is described as follows:

- Adjust the charge bar on the powder measure to throw the approximate size powder charge desired.
- Throw one charge and measure the charge with the powder scale.
- Make adjustments to the powder measure, checking each with the powder scale until the exact charge weight is obtained.
- Load five or six cases and again check the powder-measure charge with the powder scale. If the charge is accurate, load 10 more cases before checking the thrown charge with the powder scale.
- If a discrepancy is found, recheck all cases back to the last valid check.

Most powder measures are designed with a beveled mouth so that cartridge cases will fit tight against the measure spout. Therefore, once the correct setting has been obtained on the powder measure, all that is necessary is to take one of the uncharged cases (turned upside down in the loading block), place it under the measure spout, manipulate the measure handle to throw the charge, and then place the charged case in another loading block or on a different side in the original block, with the case mouth now in the upright position.

When individual charges are weighed with the powder scale and then transferred directly to the cartridge case, a powder funnel (Figure 8-20) is normally used to facilitate loading to keep from spilling any powder. These funnels are also handy when using some of the older powder measures and also for a number of other purposes.

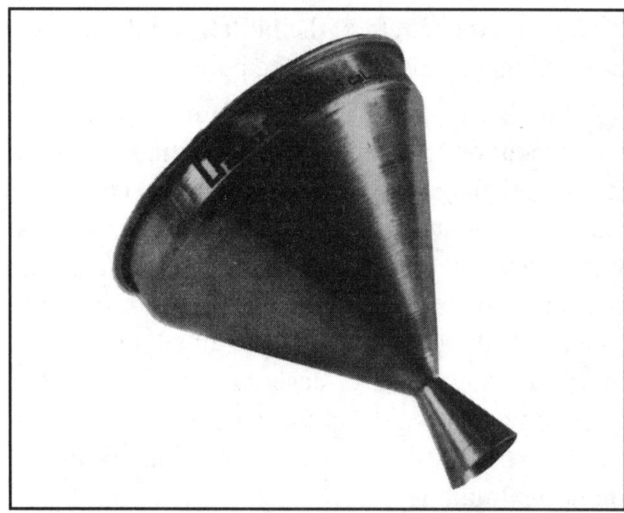

Figure 8-20: A powder funnel will find many uses on the reloading bench.

SEATING BULLETS

The last operation in the reloading cycle is to seat the bullets in the charged cases. Securing the seated bullets in place is normally done in one of two different ways:

- Friction fitted
- Crimped in place

Full-jacketed or swaged half-jacketed bullets can be held in place with a friction fit. Lead bullets, however, should be crimped into the case to hold them in place. In fact, many full-jacketed bullets for handguns have a crimping groove, and when such grooves are available, it is always best to crimp the bullets for added security.

Most reloading dies are designed to seat and crimp the bullet in one operation. Adjustments, however, are necessary to get the crimp exactly right. This adjustment is dependent upon the length of the case, the length of the bullet, and the appropriate crimping location on the bullet.

A number of years ago, one of the authors (we won't mention any names, but his initials are John Traister) managed to ruin several dozen cases because the seat and crimp die on his reloading press was frequently improperly adjusted. Finally, he took the time to read the manufacturer's instructions, and few cases have been ruined since. Another common cause of case damage (or insufficient crimp) during the crimping operation is failure to trim the cases to predetermined minimum/maximum lengths.

To adjust the seating and crimping die, refer to Figure 8-21 and follow these instructions:

- Push the press handle all the way down to the end of its stroke.
- Screw the seater die (2) into the press until it is about ⅛ inch above the shell holder (1).
- Unscrew the seater plug (3) out at least ¼ inch.
- A loaded factory cartridge or other cartridge with the bullet seated and crimped correctly should be inserted in the shell holder.
- Adjust the die until the cartridge makes contact with the crimping shoulder of the die.
- Bring down the seater plug until it bears against the nose of the bullet.
- Lock both the seater plug and die in place.

The above operations may be all that are required to properly seat the bullet. Remove the factory bullet and insert a charged case in the shell holder, and place a bullet in the case mouth. Then lower the press handle and run the case all the way into the seater die. Again raise the press handle, remove the case and check the seating depth of the bullet and also crimp at the case mouth (5). If an adjustment is needed, merely screw down the seater plug (3) and try seating another bullet.

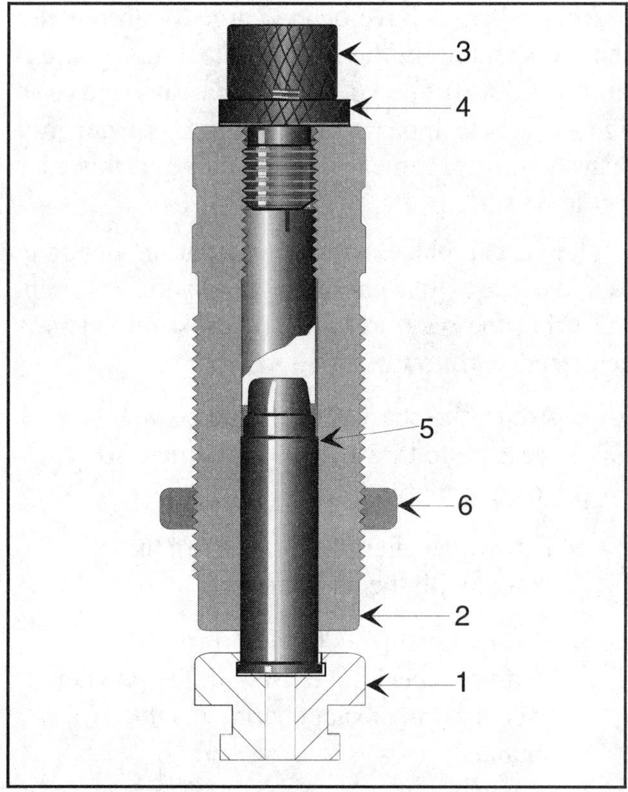

Figure 8-21: Cross-sectional view of seater die.

If the crimp needs adjusting, this is done by screwing the entire die in or out. However, if this adjustment is necessary, the seating plug will have to be readjusted afterwards.

If there is not enough crimp, unscrew the seater plug (3), backing it out at least ¼ inch so as not to touch the bullet. Insert a charged cartridge in the shell holder with its bullet in place, and run both into the seater die. Now screw the entire die down about ⅛ turn or until you feel the crimping edge touch the case mouth. Then pull the press handle down, forcing the case into the die, where the crimping shoulder (5) will force the case mouth into the bullet's crimping groove. Raise the press handle and check the crimp. Move the die up and down until the desired crimp is obtained. Then lock the ring (6) so these steps will not have to be repeated the next time reloading takes place.

Now that the crimp is perfectly adjusted, the seater plug (3) must be readjusted to obtain the correct bullet depth in the case. To accomplish this, insert a properly seated and crimped cartridge into the shell holder and run it all the way into the die. Screw the seater plug (3) downward until it touches the bullet, then set the seater-plug lock ring (4) to lock the die in this position.

NOTE

For a friction fit of jacketed bullets without crimping, adjust the bottom of the die to clear the shell holder by 1⁄16″ to 3⁄32″, then adjust the seating depth as before.

At this point, the cartridge should be tried in the handgun in which it will be used. Doing so may indicate some slight additional adjustment of the crimp or depth of bullet seating. Do they feed through semiautomatic actions okay? If loaded for revolvers, do the cartridges chamber easily?

The adjustments just described should enable the die to seat each bullet to the proper depth and crimp it. Finish loading the batch of cartridges in the group, and the lot is now ready for firing.

Chapter 9

Loads for Handgun Cartridges

Loads for handguns mean working with less case capacity than when loading for most centerfire rifle cartridges. Consequently, mere tenths of a grain of powder can make the difference between a good load and one that is dangerous. Approach the loading of handgun ammunition with these facts in mind.

The majority of handguns in use today will withstand only moderate pressure compared to pressures to which modern centerfire rifles are subjected. Any handgun load below maximum will perform satisfactorily in single-shot pistols or revolvers. On the other hand, loads for semiautomatic pistols must closely approximate the pressures of factory loads for the pistols to function properly. Low-pressure loads will not operate the action properly and the handgun will not stand high-pressure loads. Furthermore, jacketed bullets used in cartridges for semiautomatic pistols, such as the .25 ACP, .32 ACP, .45 ACP, etc. should not be crimped, or at most, a very light crimp. Most cartridges designed for semiautomatic pistols headspace on the case mouth and any major crimping will affect pressures, functioning of the action, etc. *See* Chapter 8.

The lengths of cartridges used in semiautomatic pistols are more critical than cartridges used in revolvers. Bullets should be seated to an overall cartridge length that will fit the magazine and feed through the action.

The loads to follow cover the entire range of handgun ammuntion from the .17 Bumble Bee to the .50 caliber Remington.

Figure 9-1: In most cases, loads in revolvers offer more versatility than loads for semiautomatic pistols.

.17 BUMBLE BEE

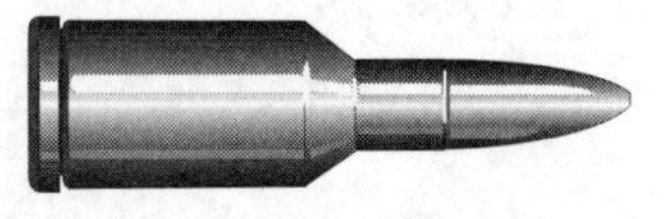

SPECIFICATIONS

Dia. of Rim — .408″
Dia. of Base — .350″
Dia. of Shoulder — .34″
Dia. of Neck — .197″
Length of Neck — .195
Angle of Shoulder — 27.73°
Dia. Jacketed Bullet — .172″
Dia. Cast Bullet — .172″
Length of Case — 0.92″
Max. Overall Length — 1.34″
Primer Size — Small Pistol
Water Capacity — 9.22grs.

25-grain Softpoint

POWDER MFGR.	POWDER TYPE	GRAINS	PRIMER TYPE	PRIMER MFGR.	VELOCITY	PRESSURE (C.U.P.)	REMARKS
Hodgdon	H4227	6.0	Small Pistol	Remington	2030	—	
Hodgdon	H4227	6.9	Small Pistol	Remington	2330	—	
Hodgdon	H110	6.0	Small Pistol	Remington	2240	—	
Hodgdon	H110	6.7	Small Pistol	Remington	2450	—	

.22 REMINGTON JET

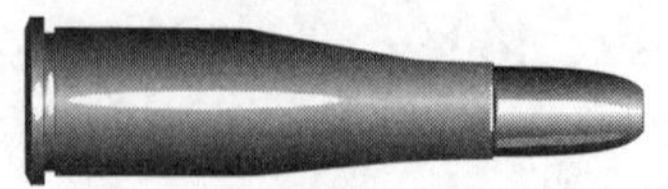

SPECIFICATIONS

Dia. of Rim — .440″
Dia. of Base — .380″
Dia. of Shoulder — .366″
Dia. of Neck — .248″
Length of Neck — .200″
Angle of Shoulder — 6.69°
Dia. Jacketed Bullet — .2225″
Dia. Cast Bullet — .224″
Length of Case — 1.28″
Max. Overall Length — 1.66″
Primer Size — Small Pistol
Water Capacity — 17.39 grs.

40-grain Softpoint

POWDER MFGR.	POWDER TYPE	GRAINS	PRIMER TYPE	PRIMER MFGR.	VELOCITY	PRESSURE (C.U.P.)	REMARKS
Hodgdon	H110	10.5	1½	Remington	2000	—	
Hodgdon	HS6	7.5	1½	Remington	1890	—	

.221 REMINGTON FIREBALL

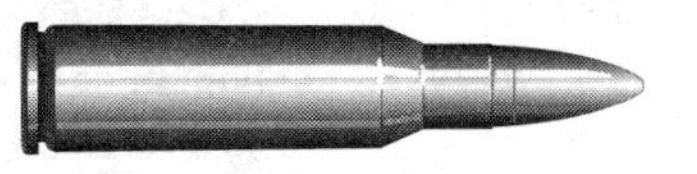

SPECIFICATIONS

Dia. of Rim — .378″	Dia. Jacketed Bullet — .224″
Dia. of Base — .377″	Dia. Cast Bullet — .226″
Dia. of Shoulder — ..361″	Length of Case — 1.40″
Dia. of Neck — .255″	Max. Overall Length — 1.84″
Length of Neck — .203″	Primer Size — Small Rifle
Angle of Shoulder — 23.19°	Water Capacity — 21.34 grs.

40-grain Softpoint

POWDER MFGR.	POWDER TYPE	GRAINS	PRIMER TYPE	PRIMER MFGR.	VELOCITY	PRESSURE (C.U.P.)	REMARKS
Hodgdon	H4227	16.5	7½	Remington	3000	—	
Hodgdon	H110	14.0	7½	Remington	2900	—	

50-grain Softpoint

POWDER MFGR.	POWDER TYPE	GRAINS	PRIMER TYPE	PRIMER MFGR.	VELOCITY	PRESSURE (C.U.P.)	REMARKS
Hodgdon	H4198	15.5	7½	Remington	2400	—	10.5-inch barrel
Hodgdon	H4198	16.0	7½	Remington	2500	—	↓
Hodgdon	H4227	15.0	7½	Remington	2575	—	
Hodgdon	H4227	15.5	7½	Remington	2650	—	
Hodgdon	H110	12.5	7½	Remington	2500	—	

60-grain Softpoint

POWDER MFGR.	POWDER TYPE	GRAINS	PRIMER TYPE	PRIMER MFGR.	VELOCITY	PRESSURE (C.U.P.)	REMARKS
Hodgdon	H4198	15.0	7½	Remington	2250	—	10.5-inch barrel
Hodgdon	H4198	15.5	7½	Remington	2400	—	↓
Hodgdon	H4227	14.0	7½	Remington	2325	—	
Hodgdon	H4227	14.5	7½	Remington	2400	—	

.25 ACP

SPECIFICATIONS

Dia. of Rim — .302″
Dia. of Base — .278″
Dia. of Shoulder — Straight
Dia. of Neck — .278″
Angle of Neck — Straight
Angle of Shoulder — Straight
Dia. Jacketed Bullet — .251″
Dia. Cast Bullet — .252″
Length of case — 0.615″
Max. Overall Length — 0.91″
Primer Size — Small Pistol
Water Capacity — 3.08 grs.

50-grain FMC

POWDER MFGR.	POWDER TYPE	GRAINS	PRIMER TYPE	PRIMER MFGR.	VELOCITY	PRESSURE (C.U.P.)	REMARKS
Hercules	Bullseye	0.8	1½	Remington	545	—	
Hercules	Bullseye	1.0	1½	Remington	675	10,500	
Hercules	Bullseye	1.3	1½	Remington	830	15,000	
Hercules	Herco	1.7	1½	Remington	735	15,600	
Hercules	Unique	1.7	1½	Remington	760	14,800	
Hodgdon	HP38	1.4	1½	Remington	848	—	Tested in 14″ barrel
Vihtavuori	No. 22	1.1	1½	Remington	804	18,800	P.S.I.

.256 WINCHESTER (Pistol)

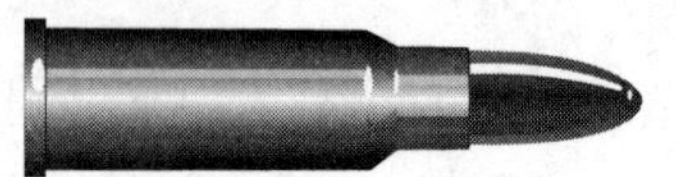

SPECIFICATIONS

Dia. of Rim — .440″
Dia. of Base — .380″
Dia. of Shoulder — .368″
Dia. of Neck — .285″
Neck length — .208″
Angle of Shoulder — 26.56°
Dia. Jacketed Bullet — .257″
Dia. Cast Bullet — .257″
Length of Case — 1.281″
Max. Overall Length — 1.78″
Primer Size — Small Pistol
Water Capacity — 20.49 grs.

60-grain Softpoint

POWDER MFGR.	POWDER TYPE	GRAINS	PRIMER TYPE	PRIMER MFGR.	VELOCITY	PRESSURE (C.U.P.)	REMARKS
Hodgdon	H4198	18.0		Remington	1704	—	10″ barrel
Hodgdon	H4227	15.0		Remington	2156	—	10″ barrel
Hodgdon	H110	15.0		Remington	2264	—	10″ barrel

.30 M1 CARBINE (PISTOL)

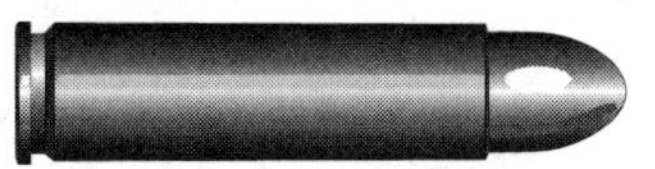

SPECIFICATIONS

Dia. of Rim — .360″
Dia. of Base — .356″
Dia. of Shoulder — Straight
Dia. of Neck — .336″
Length of Neck — Straight
Angle of Shoulder — Straight

Dia. Jacketed Bullet — .308″
Dia. Cast Bullet — .308″
Length of Case — 1.290″
Max. Overall Length — 1.680″
Primer Size — Small Rifle
Water Capacity — 18.050 grs.

100-grain Softpoint

POWDER MFGR.	POWDER TYPE	GRAINS	PRIMER TYPE	PRIMER MFGR.	VELOCITY	PRESSURE (C.U.P.)	REMARKS
Hodgdon	HS7	6.5	200	Federal	1050	—	
Hodgdon	HS6	5.7	200	Federal	900	—	
Hodgdon	Trap 100	2.9	200	Federal	825	—	
Hodgdon	HP38	2.9	200	Federal	790	—	
IMR	4227	14.5	200	Federal	1535	—	
IMR	4227	15.5	200	Federal	1700	—	Maximum
IMR	4198	14.0	200	Federal	1245	—	
IMR	4198	15.0	200	Federal	1360	—	Maximum

110-grain Softpoint

POWDER MFGR.	POWDER TYPE	GRAINS	PRIMER TYPE	PRIMER MFGR.	VELOCITY	PRESSURE (C.U.P.)	REMARKS
IMR	4227	12.0	200	Federal	1325	—	
IMR	4227	14.5	200	Federal	1575	—	Maximum
Hodgdon	H4227	12.0	200	Federal	1320	—	
Hodgdon	H4227	14.5	200	Federal	1570	—	Maximum

.30 LUGER

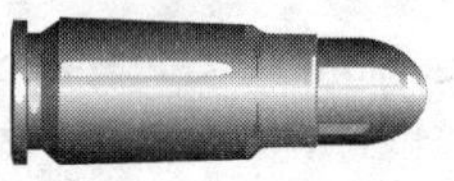

SPECIFICATIONS

Dia. of Rim — .391″
Dia. of Base — .388″
Dia. of Shoulder — .374″
Dia. of Neck — .322″
Length of Neck — .120″
Angle of Shoulder — 13°
Dia. Jacketed Bullet — .308″
Dia. Cast Bullet — .311″
Length of Case — .843″
Max. Overall Length — 1.15″
Primer Size — Small Pistol
Water Capacity — 16.0 grs.

93-grain FMJ

POWDER MFGR.	POWDER TYPE	GRAINS	PRIMER TYPE	PRIMER MFGR.	VELOCITY	PRESSURE (C.U.P.)	REMARKS
Hercules	Bullseye	3.5	1½	Remington	1025	—	
Hercules	Bullseye	4.0	1½	Remington	1175	29,000	
Hercules	Unique	4.7	1½	Remington	1250	—	Approximates factory load
Hodgdon	HP38	3.4	1½	Remington	950	—	
Hodgdon	Trap 100	3.3	1½	Remington	950	—	
VihtaVuori	N340	5.2	1½	Remington	1250	35,000	Approximates factory load

.32 ACP

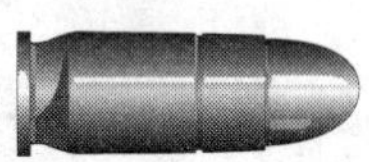

SPECIFICATIONS

Dia. of Rim — .354″
Dia. of Base — .336″
Dia. of Shoulder — Straight
Dia. of Neck — .336″
Angle of Neck — Straight
Angle of Shoulder — Straight
Dia. Jacketed Bullet — .309″
Dia. Cast Bullet — .312″
Length of Case — 0.68″
Max. Overall Length — 1.03″
Primer Size — Small Pistol
Water Capacity — 6.48 grs.

71-grain FMJ

POWDER MFGR.	POWDER TYPE	GRAINS	PRIMER TYPE	PRIMER MFGR.	VELOCITY	PRESSURE (C.U.P.)	REMARKS
Hercules	Bullseye	1.6	100	Federal	750	—	3-inch barrel
Hercules	Bullseye	2.1	100	Federal	890	—	3-inch barrel
Hercules	Red Dot	1.8	1½	Remington	755	—	3-inch barrel
Hodgdon	HP-38	1.6	1½	Remington	722	—	3-inch barrel
Hodgdon	HP-38	2.2	1½	Remington	904	—	3-inch barrel
Hercules	Unique	2.1	1½	Remington	614	—	3-inch barrel
Hercules	Unique	2.9	1½	Remington	903	—	3-inch barrel

.32 S&W

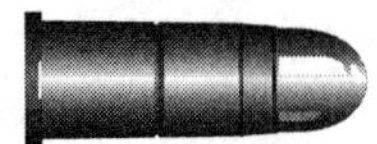

SPECIFICATIONS

Dia. of Rim — .375″
Dia. of Base — .335″
Dia. of Shoulder — Straight
Dia. of Neck — .334″
Length of Neck — .Straight
Angle of Shoulder — Straight
Dia. Jacketed Bullet — .312″
Dia. Cast Bullet — .314″
Length of Case — .605″
Max. Overall Length — .93″
Primer Size — Small Pistol
Water Capacity — 5.38 grs.

87-grain Lead

POWDER MFGR.	POWDER TYPE	GRAINS	PRIMER TYPE	PRIMER MFGR.	VELOCITY	PRESSURE (C.U.P.)	REMARKS
Hercules	Bullseye	1.4	1½	Remington	730	—	
Hercules	Unique	1.9	1½	Remington	830	—	
Hodgdon	HP38	1.1	1½	Remington	610	—	
Hodgdon	HP38	1.3	1½	Remington	675	—	
Hodgdon	Trap 100	1.0	1½	Remington	570	—	
Hodgdon	Trap 100	1.3	1½	Remington	665	—	

.32 S&W LONG (COLT NEW POLICE)

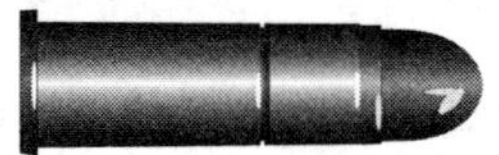

SPECIFICATIONS

Dia. of Rim — .375″
Dia. of Base — .335″
Dia. of Shoulder — Straight
Dia. of Neck — .334″
Length of Neck — .Straight
Angle of Shoulder — Straight
Dia. Jacketed Bullet — .312″
Dia. Cast Bullet — .314″
Length of Case — .92″
Max. Overall Length — 1.28″
Primer Size — Small Pistol
Water Capacity — 10.86 grs.

98-grain Lead

POWDER MFGR.	POWDER TYPE	GRAINS	PRIMER TYPE	PRIMER MFGR.	VELOCITY	PRESSURE (C.U.P.)	REMARKS
Hercules	Bullseye	1.6	1½	Remington	700	—	
Hercules	Unique	2.5	1½	Remington	725	—	
Hodgdon	HP38	2.2	1½	Remington	740	—	
Hodgdon	HP38	2.5		Remington	780	—	
Hodgdon	Trap 100	2.1	1½	Remington	735	—	
Hodgdon	Trap 100	2.4	1½	Remington	750	—	

.32 SHORT COLT

SPECIFICATIONS

Dia. of Rim — .374″
Dia. of Base — .318″
Dia. of Shoulder — Straight
Dia. of Neck — .313″
Length of Neck — Straight
Angle of Shoulder — Straight
Dia. Jacketed Bullet — .313″
Dia. Cast Bullet — .315″
Length of Case — 0.65″
Max. Overall Length — 1.01″
Primer Size — Small Pistol
Water Capacity — 6.78 grs.

80-grain Lead

POWDER MFGR.	POWDER TYPE	GRAINS	PRIMER TYPE	PRIMER MFGR.	VELOCITY	PRESSURE (C.U.P.)	REMARKS
Hercules	Bullseye	1.4	1½	Remington	790	—	
Hercules	Bullseye	1.8	1½	Remington	820	**8000**	
Black	FFFg	7.7	1½	Remington	820	8000	

.32 H&R MAGNUM

SPECIFICATIONS

Dia. of Rim — .375″
Dia. of Base — .337″
Dia. of Shoulder — Straight
Dia. of Neck — .334″
Length of Neck — Straight
Angle of Shoulder — Straight
Dia. Jacketed Bullet — .312″
Dia. Cast Bullet — .″
Length of Case — 1.075″
Max. Overall Length — 1.35″
Primer Size — Small Pistol
Water Capacity — grs.

85-grain Softnose

POWDER MFGR.	POWDER TYPE	GRAINS	PRIMER TYPE	PRIMER MFGR.	VELOCITY	PRESSURE (C.U.P.)	REMARKS
Hercules	Bullseye	3.4	1½	Remington	1020	**18.700**	
Hercules	Red Dot	3.4	1½	Remington	1030	**19,200**	
Hercules	Green Dot	3.5	1½	Remington	1035	19,500	
Hercules	Unique	4.1	1½	Remington	1050	18,700	
Hercules	Herco	4.6	1½	Remington	1060	18,900	
Hercules	Blue Dot	6.6	1½	Remington	1100	19,000	
Hodgdon	H4227	9.5	1½	Remington	1150	21,000	
Hodgdon	HS7	6.6	1½	Remington	1095	20,900	
Hodgdon	HS6	5.6	1½	Remington	1145	20,200	
Hodgdon	HP38	3.8	1½	Remington	1000	20,700	

.32-20 REVOLVER

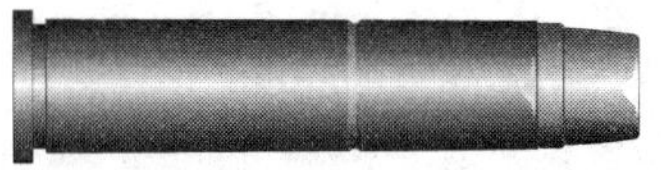

SPECIFICATIONS

Dia. of Rim — .374″	Dia. Jacketed Bullet — .313″
Dia. of Base — .318″	Dia. Cast Bullet — .315″
Dia. of Shoulder — Straight	Length of Case — 0.65″
Dia. of Neck — .313″	Max. Overall Length — 1.01″
Length of Neck — Straight	Primer Size — Small Pistol
Angle of Shoulder — Straight	Water Capacity — 6.78 grs.

85-grain Softpoint

POWDER MFGR.	POWDER TYPE	GRAINS	PRIMER TYPE	PRIMER MFGR.	VELOCITY	PRESSURE (C.U.P.)	REMARKS
Hercules	Bullseye	2.5	1½	Remington	850	—	
Hercules	Bullseye	3.5	1½	Remington	1050	**11,400**	
Hercules	Bullseye	4.1	1½	Remington	1180	—	
Hercules	Unique	5.8	1½	Remington	1220	—	
Hodgdon	HP38	4.5	1½	Remington	1050	—	

110-grain Softpoint

POWDER MFGR.	POWDER TYPE	GRAINS	PRIMER TYPE	PRIMER MFGR.	VELOCITY	PRESSURE (C.U.P.)	REMARKS
Hercules	Bullseye	2.0	1½	Remington	590	—	
Hercules	Bullseye	2.5	1½	Remington	715	**11,000**	
Hercules	Bullseye	3.0	1½	Remington	850	—	
Hercules	Unique	4.4	1½	Remington	925	—	
Hodgdon	HP38	4.0	1½	Remington	870	—	

.357 MAGNUM

SPECIFICATIONS

Dia. of Rim — .440″
Dia. of Base — .380″
Dia. of Shoulder — Straight
Dia. of Neck — .379″
Length of Neck — Straight
Angle of Shoulder — Straight
Dia. Jacketed Bullet — .357″
Dia. Cast Bullet — .359″
Length of Case — 1.29″
Max. Overall Length — 1.59″
Primer Size — Small Pistol
Water Capacity — 23.47 grs.

110-grain Jacketed Hollow Point

POWDER MFGR.	POWDER TYPE	GRAINS	PRIMER TYPE	PRIMER MFGR.	VELOCITY	PRESSURE (C.U.P.)	REMARKS
Hercules	Bullseye	8.5	1½	Remington	1605	34,900	
Hercules	Red Dot	8.5	1½	Remington	1615	39,600	
Hercules	Unique	10.0	1½	Remington	1655	34,900	
Hodgdon	HP38	7.9	1½	Remington	1415	27,600	
Hodgdon	H4227	19.5	1½	Remington	1815	34,200	
IMR	4227	21.0	1½	Remington	1510	35,600	Compressed Load

125-grain Jacketed Hollow Point

POWDER MFGR.	POWDER TYPE	GRAINS	PRIMER TYPE	PRIMER MFGR.	VELOCITY	PRESSURE (C.U.P.)	REMARKS
Hercules	Bullseye	8.3	1½	Remington	1515	39,200	
Hercules	Red Dot	7.8	1½	Remington	1465	40,000	
Hercules	Unique	9.3	1½	Remington	1515	39,500	
Hodgdon	HP38	7.0	1½	Remington	1265	27,200	
Hodgdon	H4227	17.8	1½	Remington	1685	34,600	
IMR	4227	18.5	1½	Remington	1325	35,400	Compressed Load

146-grain Jacketed Hollow Point

POWDER MFGR.	POWDER TYPE	GRAINS	PRIMER TYPE	PRIMER MFGR.	VELOCITY	PRESSURE (C.U.P.)	REMARKS
Hercules	Bullseye	7.4	1½	Remington	1390	39,900	
Hercules	Red Dot	6.3	1½	Remington	1275	37,500	
Hercules	Unique	8.0	1½	Remington	1380	37,200	
Hodgdon	HP38	5.9	1½	Remington	1130	27,100	
Hodgdon	H4227	15.0	1½	Remington	1380	34,100	
IMR	4227	14.9	1½	Remington	1100	35,400	

.357 MAGNUM (Cont.)

160-grain Jacketed

POWDER MFGR.	POWDER TYPE	GRAINS	PRIMER TYPE	PRIMER MFGR.	VELOCITY	PRESSURE (C.U.P.)	REMARKS
Hodgdon	HP38	3.4	1½	Remington	800	13,000	
Hodgdon	HP38	5.2	1½	Remington	1000	27,500	
Hodgdon	Trap 100	3.5	1½	Remington	850	15,000	
Hodgdon	Trap 100	5.3	1½	Remington	1050	29,600	
Hodgdon	H4227	12.5	1½	Remington	1175	26,000	
Hodgdon	H4227	14.0	1½	Remington	1400	34,000	
Hodgdon	HS7	9.0	1½	Remington	1150	21,000	
Hodgdon	HS7	9.8	1½	Remington	1300	29,000	
Hodgdon	H110	14.0	1½	Remington	1365	26,000	
Hodgdon	H110	14.3	1½	Remington	1450	35,000	

170-grain Jacketed

POWDER MFGR.	POWDER TYPE	GRAINS	PRIMER TYPE	PRIMER MFGR.	VELOCITY	PRESSURE (C.U.P.)	REMARKS
Hodgdon	Trap 100	4.2	1½	Remington	900	16,500	
Hodgdon	HS7	8.2	1½	Remington	990	24,000	
Hodgdon	H110	12.5	1½	Remington	1200	30,000	
Hodgdon	HP38	4.2	1½	Remington	900	17,000	
Hodgdon	H4227	12.5	1½	Remington	1200	30,000	

200-grain Lead

POWDER MFGR.	POWDER TYPE	GRAINS	PRIMER TYPE	PRIMER MFGR.	VELOCITY	PRESSURE (C.U.P.)	REMARKS
Hodgdon	HP38	3.4	1½	Remington	700	15,000	
Hodgdon	Trap 100	4.2	1½	Remington	725	18,500	
Hodgdon	HS6	5.2	1½	Remington	825	17,500	
Hodgdon	HS7	7.5	1½	Remington	1050	19,400	
Hodgdon	H110	9.5	1½	Remington	1100	27,000	
Hodgdon	H4227	10.5	1½	Remington	1075	28,000	

.357 MAXIMUM

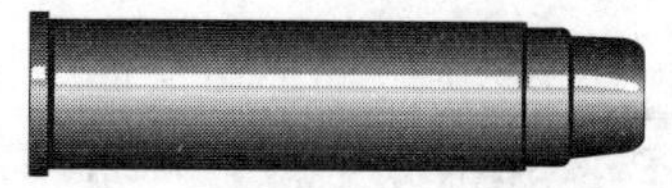

SPECIFICATIONS

Dia. of Rim — .440″
Dia. of Base — .379″
Dia. of Shoulder — Straight
Dia. of Neck — .378″
Length of Neck — Straight
Angle of Shoulder — Straight
Dia. Jacketed Bullet — .357″
Dia. Cast Bullet — .359″
Length of Case — 1.605″
Max. Overall Length — 1.99″
Primer Size — Small Pistol
Water Capacity — 31.08 grs.

158-grain Hollow Point

POWDER MFGR.	POWDER TYPE	GRAINS	PRIMER TYPE	PRIMER MFGR.	VELOCITY	PRESSURE (C.U.P.)	REMARKS
Hercules	2400	18.0	7½ BR	Remington	1790	40,400	12½" barrel
Hercules	Reloader 7	26.0	7½ BR	Remington	1845	33,600	12½" barrel

160-grain Softpoint

POWDER MFGR.	POWDER TYPE	GRAINS	PRIMER TYPE	PRIMER MFGR.	VELOCITY	PRESSURE (C.U.P.)	REMARKS
Hercules	2400	17.4	7½ BR	Remington	1775	41,200	12½" barrel
Hercules	Reloader 7	26.0	7½ BR	Remington	1830	32,700	12½" barrel
Hercules	Blue Dot	15.3	7½ BR	Remington	1760	40,700	12½" barrel

170-grain Softpoint

POWDER MFGR.	POWDER TYPE	GRAINS	PRIMER TYPE	PRIMER MFGR.	VELOCITY	PRESSURE (C.U.P.)	REMARKS
Hercules	2400	16.5	7½ BR	Remington	1670	40,500	12½" barrel
Hercules	Reloader 7	25.5	7½ BR	Remington	1840	40,100	12½" barrel
Hercules	Blue Dot	14.5	7½ BR	Remington	1675	41,300	12½" barrel

180-grain FMJ

POWDER MFGR.	POWDER TYPE	GRAINS	PRIMER TYPE	PRIMER MFGR.	VELOCITY	PRESSURE (C.U.P.)	REMARKS
Hercules	2400	16.8	7½ BR	Remington	1590	39,000	12½" barrel
Hercules	Reloader 7	25.0	7½ BR	Remington	1760	39,700	12½" barrel
Hercules	Blue Dot	14.9	7½ BR	Remington	1610	39,400	12½" barrel

.380 ACP

SPECIFICATIONS

Dia. of Rim — .374″
Dia. of Base — .373″
Dia. of Shoulder — Straight
Dia. of Neck — .372″
Angle of Neck — Straight
Angle of Shoulder — Straight

Dia. Jacketed Bullet — .355″
Dia. Cast Bullet — .357″
Length of Case — 0..68″
Max. Overall Length — 0.98″
Primer Size — Small Pistol
Water Capacity — 8.94 grs.

90-grain Softpoint

POWDER MFGR.	POWDER TYPE	GRAINS	PRIMER TYPE	PRIMER MFGR.	VELOCITY	PRESSURE (C.U.P.)	REMARKS
Hercules	Bullseye	2.5	1½	Remington	850	—	
Hercules	Red Dot	2.0	1½	Remington	700	—	
Hercules	Unique	3.7	1½	Remington	900	10,000	
Hodgdon	HS5	4.0	1½	Remington	895	12,600	
IMR	700X	2.0	1½	Remington	795	—	
IMR	SR-7625	2.5	1½	Remington	800	—	

.38 SUPER AUTO

SPECIFICATIONS

Dia. of Rim — .406″
Dia. of Base — .384″
Dia. of Shoulder — Straight
Dia. of Neck — .384″
Angle of Neck — Straight
Angle of Shoulder — Straight

Dia. Jacketed Bullet — .356″
Dia. Cast Bullet — .357″
Length of Case — 0..895″
Max. Overall Length — 1.28″
Primer Size — Small Pistol
Water Capacity — N/A

130-grain Softpoint

POWDER MFGR.	POWDER TYPE	GRAINS	PRIMER TYPE	PRIMER MFGR.	VELOCITY	PRESSURE (C.U.P.)	REMARKS
Hercules	Herco	5.3	1½	Remington	1025	22,000	
Hercules	Blue Dot	7.5	1½	Remington	1075	19,000	
Hercules	Unique	5.2	1½	Remington	1050	20,900	
Hodgdon	HS-7	7.9	1½	Remington	1000	17,600	
IMR	SR-4756	6.0	1½	Remington	1050	17,200	

.38 SPECIAL

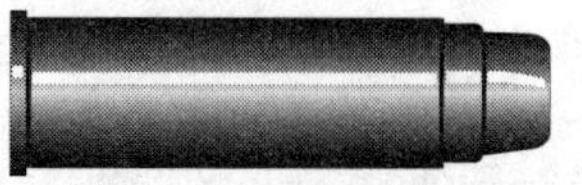

SPECIFICATIONS

Dia. of Rim — .440″
Dia. of Base — .379″
Dia. of Shoulder — Straight
Dia. of Neck — .379″
Length of Neck — Straight
Angle of Shoulder — Straight

Dia. Jacketed Bullet — .357″
Dia. Cast Bullet — .359″
Length of Case — 1.155″
Max. Overall Length — 1.48″
Primer Size — Small Pistol
Water Capacity — 20.25 grs.

110-grain Half-Jacket

POWDER MFGR.	POWDER TYPE	GRAINS	PRIMER TYPE	PRIMER MFGR.	VELOCITY	PRESSURE (C.U.P.)	REMARKS
Hercules	Bullseye	3.0	1½	Remington	880	—	
Hercules	Bullseye	3.5	1½	Remington	970	—	
Hercules	Bullseye	4.0	1½	Remington	975	—	
VihtaVuori	N320	5.8	1½	Remington	1147	16,000	
VihtaVuori	N340	7.3	1½	Remington	1242	16,000	
VihtaVuori	N350	8.5	1½	Remington	1258	16,000	
VihtaVuori	3N37	8.8	1½	Remington	1280	17,700	

140-grain Jacketed

POWDER MFGR.	POWDER TYPE	GRAINS	PRIMER TYPE	PRIMER MFGR.	VELOCITY	PRESSURE (C.U.P.)	REMARKS
Hercules	2400	8.7	1½	Remington	730	—	
Hercules	2400	9.5	1½	Remington	970	—	
Hercules	2400	11.1	1½	Remington	1170	—	
Hercules	Unique	4.3	1½	Remington	800	—	
Hercules	Unique	4.5	1½	Remington	930	—	
Hercules	Unique	5.0	1½	Remington	1050	—	
Hercules	Bullseye	2.4	1½	Remington	550	—	
Hercules	Bullseye	2.9	1½	Remington	645	—	
Hercules	Bullseye	3.4	1½	Remington	780	—	
Hodgdon	HS6	7.0	1½	Remington	969	15,800	
Hodgdon	HP38	4.0	1½	Remington	862	15,100	
Hodgdon	Universal	5.2	1½	Remington	939	15,400	
IMR	4227	10.3	1½	Remington	800	15,600	
VihtaVuori	N340	5.8	1½	Remington	959	16,000	
VihtaVuori	N350	6.8	1½	Remington	1004	16,000	
VihtaVuori	3N37	7.0	1½	Remington	1051	16,000	

.38 SPECIAL (Cont.)

146-grain Jacketed

POWDER MFGR.	POWDER TYPE	GRAINS	PRIMER TYPE	PRIMER MFGR.	VELOCITY	PRESSURE (C.U.P.)	REMARKS
Hercules	2400	9.0	1½	Remington	825	—	
Hercules	2400	10.0	1½	Remington	970	—	
Hercules	Unique	5.0	1½	Remington	900	—	
Hercules	Unique	5.5	1½	Remington	975	—	

160-grain Jacketed

POWDER MFGR.	POWDER TYPE	GRAINS	PRIMER TYPE	PRIMER MFGR.	VELOCITY	PRESSURE (C.U.P.)	REMARKS
Hercules	2400	9.0	1½	Remington	880	—	
Hercules	2400	10.0	1½	Remington	970	—	
Hercules	Unique	4.5	1½	Remington	800	—	
Hercules	Unique	5.0	1½	Remington	860	16,000	

.38 S&W

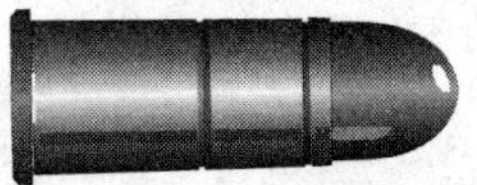

SPECIFICATIONS

Dia. of Rim — .433″
Dia. of Base — .387″
Dia. of Shoulder — Straight
Dia. of Neck — .386″
Length of Neck — Straight
Angle of Shoulder — Straight
Dia. Jacketed Bullet — .358″
Dia. Cast Bullet — .359″
Length of Case — .775″
Max. Overall Length — 1.20″
Primer Size — Small Pistol
Water Capacity — 11.24 grs.

135-grain Lead

POWDER MFGR.	POWDER TYPE	GRAINS	PRIMER TYPE	PRIMER MFGR.	VELOCITY	PRESSURE (C.U.P.)	REMARKS
Hercules	Bullseye	2.0	1½	Remington	615	—	
Hercules	Bullseye	2.5	1½	Remington	625	—	
Hercules	Bullseye	3.0	1½	Remington	840	—	Maximum
VihtaVuori	N340	3.5	1½	Remington	754	13,700	

.38 SHORT COLT

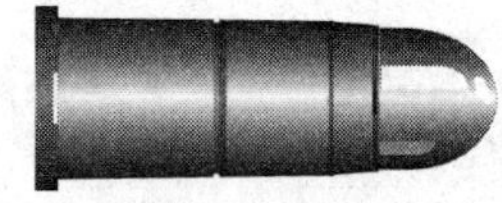

SPECIFICATIONS

Dia. of Rim — .433″
Dia. of Base — .378″
Dia. of Shoulder — Straight
Dia. of Neck — .377″
Length of Neck — Straight
Angle of Shoulder — Straight
Dia. Jacketed Bullet — .357″
Dia. Cast Bullet — .359″
Length of Case — .762″
Max. Overall Length — 1.07″
Primer Size — Small Pistol
Water Capacity — 10.94 grs.

130-grain Lead

POWDER MFGR.	POWDER TYPE	GRAINS	PRIMER TYPE	PRIMER MFGR.	VELOCITY	PRESSURE (C.U.P.)	REMARKS
Hercules	Bullseye	2.4	1½	Remington	745	—	
Black Powder	FFg	14.0	1½	Remington	765	—	

.38-40 REVOLVER

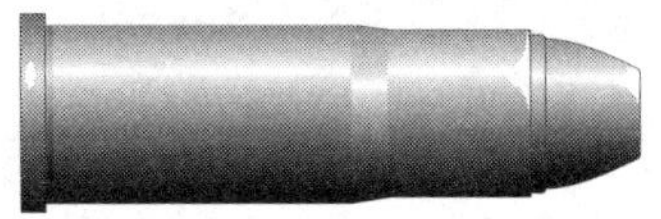

SPECIFICATIONS

Dia. of Rim — .525″
Dia. of Base — .470″
Dia. of Shoulder — .444
Dia. of Neck — .416″
Length of Neck — .153
Angle of Shoulder — 3.58°
Dia. Jacketed Bullet — .401″
Dia. Cast Bullet — .402″
Length of Case — 1.305″
Max. Overall Length — 1.59″
Primer Size — Large Pistol
Water Capacity — 38.15 grs.

130-grain Softpoint

POWDER MFGR.	POWDER TYPE	GRAINS	PRIMER TYPE	PRIMER MFGR.	VELOCITY	PRESSURE (C.U.P.)	REMARKS
Hercules	Bullseye	7.2	LP	Remington	1175	—	
Hercules	Unique	11.8	LP	Remington	1320	—	

158-grain Lead

POWDER MFGR.	POWDER TYPE	GRAINS	PRIMER TYPE	PRIMER MFGR.	VELOCITY	PRESSURE (C.U.P.)	REMARKS
Hercules	Bullseye	5.8	LP	Remington	1025	—	
Hercules	Unique	9.5	LP	Remington	1225	—	

174-grain Lead

POWDER MFGR.	POWDER TYPE	GRAINS	PRIMER TYPE	PRIMER MFGR.	VELOCITY	PRESSURE (C.U.P.)	REMARKS
Hercules	Bullseye	5.8	LP	Remington	975	—	
Hercules	Unique	9.5	LP	Remington	1100	—	

180-grain Lead

POWDER MFGR.	POWDER TYPE	GRAINS	PRIMER TYPE	PRIMER MFGR.	VELOCITY	PRESSURE (C.U.P.)	REMARKS
Hercules	Bullseye	5.5	LP	Remington	925	—	
Hercules	Bullseye	5.9	LP	Remington	1160	—	
Hercules	Unique	8.0	LP	Remington	930	—	
Hercules	Unique	9.6	LP	Remington	1100	—	

.40 S&W

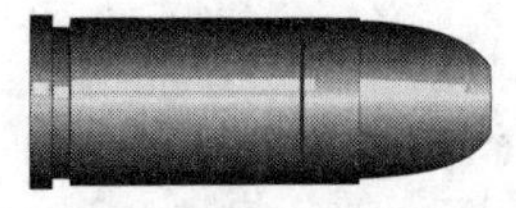

SPECIFICATIONS

Dia. of Rim — .424″
Dia. of Base — .424″
Dia. of Shoulder — Straight
Dia. of Neck — .423″
Length of Neck — Straight
Angle of Shoulder — Straight
Dia. Jacketed Bullet — .400″
Dia. Cast Bullet — .400″
Length of Case — .850″
Max. Overall Length — 1.135″
Primer Size — Small Pistol
Water Capacity —

180-grain Softpoint

POWDER MFGR.	POWDER TYPE	GRAINS	PRIMER TYPE	PRIMER MFGR.	VELOCITY	PRESSURE (C.U.P.)	REMARKS
IMR	Bullseye	4.0	WSP	Winchester	810	—	
IMR	Bullseye	4.5	WSP	Winchester	900	—	Maximum
Winchester	WSF	5.0	WSP	Winchester	850	—	
Winchester	WSF	6.0	WSP	Winchester	980	—	Maximum

200-grain Softpoint

POWDER MFGR.	POWDER TYPE	GRAINS	PRIMER TYPE	PRIMER MFGR.	VELOCITY	PRESSURE (C.U.P.)	REMARKS
IMR	Bullseye	3.5	WSP	Winchester	750	—	
IMR	Bullseye	4.2	WSP	Winchester	860	—	Maximum
Winchester	WSF	4.5	WSP	Winchester	750	—	
Winchester	WSF	5.0	WSP	Winchester	845	—	
Winchester	571	6.0	WSP	Winchester	700	—	
Winchester	571	7.0	WSP	Winchester	850	—	Near maximum

.41 LONG COLT

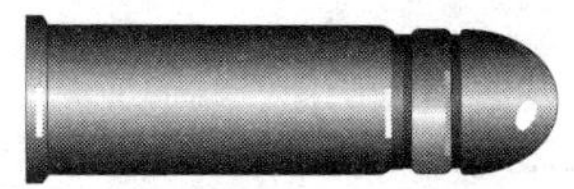

SPECIFICATIONS

Dia. of Rim — .435″
Dia. of Base — .408″
Dia. of Shoulder — Straight
Dia. of Neck — .404″
Length of Neck — Straight
Angle of Shoulder — Straight
Dia. Jacketed Bullet — .386″
Dia. Cast Bullet — .388″
Length of Case — 1.13″
Max. Overall Length — 1.39″
Primer Size — Small Pistol
Water Capacity — 23.53 grs.

196-grain Lead

POWDER MFGR.	POWDER TYPE	GRAINS	PRIMER TYPE	PRIMER MFGR.	VELOCITY	PRESSURE (C.U.P.)	REMARKS
Hercules	Bullseye	2.9	1½	Remington	700	—	
Hercules	Unique	4.9	1½	Remington	880	—	Maximum

200-grain Lead

POWDER MFGR.	POWDER TYPE	GRAINS	PRIMER TYPE	PRIMER MFGR.	VELOCITY	PRESSURE (C.U.P.)	REMARKS
Hercules	Bullseye	2.9	1½	Remington	700	—	
Hercules	Unique	4.9	1½	Remington	875	—	Maximum

.41 MAGNUM

SPECIFICATIONS

Dia. of Rim — .492″
Dia. of Base — .435″
Dia. of Shoulder — Straight
Dia. of Neck — .434″
Length of Neck — Straight
Angle of Shoulder — Straight
Dia. Jacketed Bullet — .410″
Dia. Cast Bullet — .411″
Length of Case — 1.29″
Max. Overall Length — 1.60″
Primer Size — Large Pistol
Water Capacity — 31.07 grs.

200-grain Hollow Point

POWDER MFGR.	POWDER TYPE	GRAINS	PRIMER TYPE	PRIMER MFGR.	VELOCITY	PRESSURE (C.U.P.)	REMARKS
Hercules	Bullseye	8.0	LP	Remington	1235	35,700	
Hercules	Unique	10.5	LP	Remington	1370	35,700	
Hercules	Red Dot	7.5	LP	Remington	1200	33,400	
Hercules	Green Dot	8.5	LP	Remington	1270	35,300	
Hercules	Herco	10.1	LP	Remington	1320	35,900	
Hodgdon	H4227	21.0	LP	Remington	1320	—	
Hodgdon	H110	21.0	LP	Remington	1450	—	
Hodgdon	HS7	13.5	LP	Remington	1220	—	
Hodgdon	HP38	6.9	LP	Remington	903	—	
IMR	IMR4227	20.5	LP	Remington	1395	30,000	

.41 MAGNUM (Cont.)

220-grain Softpoint

POWDER MFGR.	POWDER TYPE	GRAINS	PRIMER TYPE	PRIMER MFGR.	VELOCITY	PRESSURE (C.U.P.)	REMARKS
Hercules	Bullseye	7.5	LP	Remington	1150	35,800	
Hercules	Unique	9.5	LP	Remington	1235	35,200	
Hercules	Red Dot	7.5	LP	Remington	1145	35,900	
Hercules	Green Dot	8.0	LP	Remington	1155	35,700	
Hercules	Herco	9.3	LP	Remington	1220	35,800	
Hodgdon	H4227	20.0	LP	Remington	1290	—	
Hodgdon	H110	20.0	LP	Remington	1400	—	
Hodgdon	HS7	13.0	LP	Remington	1185	—	
Hodgdon	HP38	6.9	LP	Remington	890	—	
IMR	IMR4227	20.0	LP	Remington	1450	—	

250-grain Softpoint

POWDER MFGR.	POWDER TYPE	GRAINS	PRIMER TYPE	PRIMER MFGR.	VELOCITY	PRESSURE (C.U.P.)	REMARKS
Hodgdon	H4227	20.0	LP	Remington	1255	—	
Hodgdon	H110	20.5	LP	Remington	1340	—	

300-grain Softpoint

POWDER MFGR.	POWDER TYPE	GRAINS	PRIMER TYPE	PRIMER MFGR.	VELOCITY	PRESSURE (C.U.P.)	REMARKS
Hodgdon	H4227	18.5	LP	Remington	1000	—	
Hodgdon	H110	19.0	LP	Remington	1270	—	

.44 SPECIAL

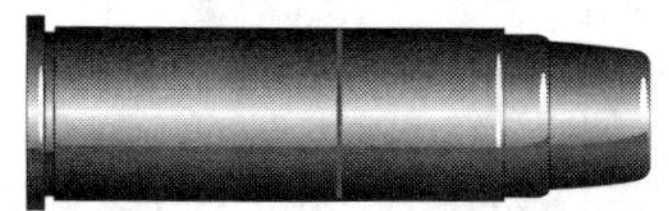

SPECIFICATIONS

Dia. of Rim — .514″
Dia. of Base — .457″
Dia. of Shoulder — Straight
Dia. of Neck — .456″
Length of Neck — Straight
Angle of Shoulder — Straight

Dia. Jacketed Bullet — .430″
Dia. Cast Bullet — .432″
Length of Case — 1.16″
Max. Overall Length — 1.50″
Primer Size — Large Pistol
Water Capacity — 29.61 grs.

180-grain Softpoint

POWDER MFGR.	POWDER TYPE	GRAINS	PRIMER TYPE	PRIMER MFGR.	VELOCITY	PRESSURE (C.U.P.)	REMARKS
Hercules	Bullseye	6.5	LP	Remington	910	12,000	
Hercules	Unique	9.5	LP	Remington	1010	12,600	
Hercules	Red Dot	7.0	LP	Remington	915	11,700	
Hercules	Green Dot	8.0	LP	Remington	975	12,800	
Hercules	Herco	10.0	LP	Remington	1050	12,600	
Hercules	Blue Dot	13.5	LP	Remington	1020	11,900	
Hercules	2400	16.0	LP	Remington	950	11,400	

246-grain Lead

POWDER MFGR.	POWDER TYPE	GRAINS	PRIMER TYPE	PRIMER MFGR.	VELOCITY	PRESSURE (C.U.P.)	REMARKS
Hercules	Bullseye	4.5	LP	Remington	765	11,700	
Hercules	Unique	6.5	LP	Remington	810	11,200	
Hercules	Red Dot	4.9	LP	Remington	775	11,500	
Hercules	Green Dot	6.5	LP	Remington	805	11,700	
Hercules	Herco	8.0	LP	Remington	825	12,000	
Hercules	Blue Dot	9.2	LP	Remington	845	12,300	
Hercules	2400	11.3	LP	Remington	805	11,500	

.44 MAGNUM

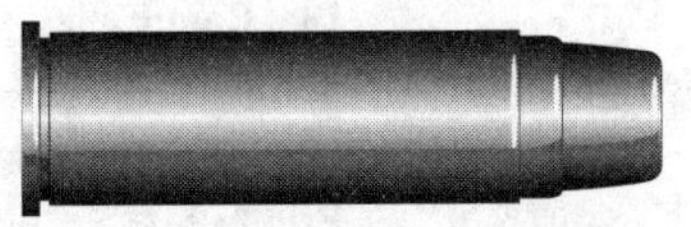

SPECIFICATIONS

Dia. of Rim — .514″
Dia. of Base — .457″
Dia. of Shoulder — Straight
Dia. of Neck — .456″
Length of Neck — Straight
Angle of Shoulder — Straight
Dia. Jacketed Bullet — .430″
Dia. Cast Bullet — .432″
Length of Case — 1.285″
Max. Overall Length — 1.61″
Primer Size — Large Pistol
Water Capacity — 33.94 grs.

180-grain Softpoint

POWDER MFGR.	POWDER TYPE	GRAINS	PRIMER TYPE	PRIMER MFGR.	VELOCITY	PRESSURE (C.U.P.)	REMARKS
Hercules	Bullseye	11.0	LP	Remington	1430	32,700	
Hercules	Unique	13.3	LP	Remington	1495	32,000	
Hercules	Red Dot	11.2	LP	Remington	1465	34,400	
Hercules	Green Dot	11.9	LP	Remington	1490	35,100	
Hercules	Herco	13.3	LP	Remington	1495	33,200	
Hercules	Blue Dot	17.4	LP	Remington	1585	33,500	
Hercules	2400	23.5	LP	Remington	1640	34,000	

265-grain Hollow Point

POWDER MFGR.	POWDER TYPE	GRAINS	PRIMER TYPE	PRIMER MFGR.	VELOCITY	PRESSURE (C.U.P.)	REMARKS
Hercules	Bullseye	10.4	LP	Remington	1235	35,800	
Hercules	Unique	11.2	LP	Remington	1245	34,200	
Hercules	Red Dot	10.0	LP	Remington	1200	35,300	
Hercules	Green Dot	10.7	LP	Remington	1245	35,300	
Hercules	Herco	11.7	LP	Remington	1265	35,600	
Hercules	Blue Dot	14.1	LP	Remington	1320	35,000	
Hercules	2400	18.7	LP	Remington	1350	35,000	

.44 AUTO MAG

SPECIFICATIONS

Dia. of Rim — .473″
Dia. of Base — .470″
Dia. of Shoulder — Straight
Dia. of Neck — .459″
Length of Neck — Straight
Angle of Shoulder — Straight
Dia. Jacketed Bullet — .430″
Dia. Cast Bullet — .431″
Length of Case — 1.298″
Max. Overall Length — 1.695″
Primer Size — Large Pistol M
Water Capacity — 34.96 grs.

200-grain Softpoint

POWDER MFGR.	POWDER TYPE	GRAINS	PRIMER TYPE	PRIMER MFGR.	VELOCITY	PRESSURE (C.U.P.)	REMARKS
IMR	2400	21.5	350	CCI	1360	—	
Hodgdon	H110	25.0	350	CCI	1450	—	
Hodgdon	H110	26.0	350	CCI	1500	—	Near Maximum
Winchester	296	25.0	350	CCI	1400	—	
Winchester	296	26.0	350	CCI	1500	—	Near Maximum

240-grain Softpoint

POWDER MFGR.	POWDER TYPE	GRAINS	PRIMER TYPE	PRIMER MFGR.	VELOCITY	PRESSURE (C.U.P.)	REMARKS
IMR	2400	19.5	350	CCI	1240	—	
IMR	2400	20.0	350	CCI	1300	—	Near Maximum
Hodgdon	H110	20.5	350	CCI	1265	—	
Hodgdon	H110	23.0	350	CCI	1400	—	Maximum
Winchester	296	22.0	350	CCI	1300	—	
Winchester	296	23.0	350	CCI	1350	—	Near Maximum

.45 ACP

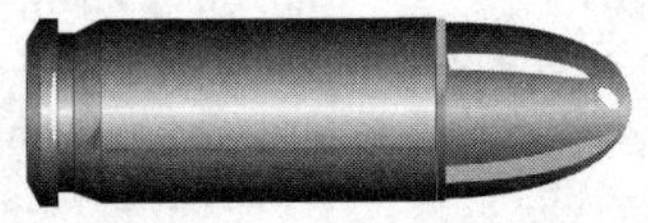

SPECIFICATIONS

Dia. of Rim — .479″
Dia. of Base — .474″
Dia. of Shoulder — Straight
Dia. of Neck — .473″
Length of Neck — Straight
Angle of Shoulder — Straight
Dia. Jacketed Bullet — .451″
Dia. Cast Bullet — .451″
Length of Case — .898″
Max. Overall Length — 1.24″
Primer Size — Large Pistol
Water Capacity — 22.87 grs.

185-grain Jacketed Hollow Point

POWDER MFGR.	POWDER TYPE	GRAINS	PRIMER TYPE	PRIMER MFGR.	VELOCITY	PRESSURE (C.U.P.)	REMARKS
Hercules	Bullseye	5.3	LP	CCI	920	15,900	
Hercules	Unique	7.0	LP	CCI	930	15,800	
Hercules	Red Dot	5.7	LP	CCI	975	16,200	
Hercules	Green Dot	6.5	LP	CCI	1030	16,200	
Hercules	Herco	7.0	LP	CCI	960	15,900	
Hercules	Blue Dot	9.5	LP	CCI	920	14,500	

200-grain Jacketed Hollow Point

POWDER MFGR.	POWDER TYPE	GRAINS	PRIMER TYPE	PRIMER MFGR.	VELOCITY	PRESSURE (C.U.P.)	REMARKS
Hercules	Bullseye	5.5	LP	CCI	930	16,100	
Hercules	Unique	6.8	LP	CCI	955	16,100	
Hercules	Red Dot	5.0	LP	CCI	880	15,700	
Hercules	Green Dot	5.6	LP	CCI	910	16,000	
Hercules	Herco	6.7	LP	CCI	930	16,000	
Hercules	Blue Dot	9.0	LP	CCI	890	15,200	

230-grain FMJ

POWDER MFGR.	POWDER TYPE	GRAINS	PRIMER TYPE	PRIMER MFGR.	VELOCITY	PRESSURE (C.U.P.)	REMARKS
Hercules	Bullseye	5.0	LP	CCI	905	16,200	
Hercules	Unique	6.0	LP	CCI	890	16,000	
Hercules	Red Dot	5.0	LP	CCI	910	16,200	
Hercules	Green Dot	5.4	LP	CCI	920	15,800	
Hercules	Herco	6.2	LP	CCI	890	16,200	
Hercules	Blue Dot	8.5	LP	CCI	900	16,200	
Hodgdon	HS6	8.2	LP	CCI	825	15,400	
Hodgdon	HP38	5.3	LP	CCI	835	16,800	
Hodgdon	Clays	4.0	LP	CCI	732	17,000	

.45 LONG COLT

SPECIFICATIONS

Dia. of Rim — .512″
Dia. of Base — .481″
Dia. of Shoulder — Straight
Dia. of Neck — .480″
Length of Neck — Straight
Angle of Shoulder — Straight
Dia. Jacketed Bullet — .452″
Dia. Cast Bullet — .454″
Length of Case — 1.198″
Max. Overall Length — 1.60″
Primer Size — Large Pistol
Water Capacity — 37.45 grs.

200-grain Jacketed Hollow Point

POWDER MFGR.	POWDER TYPE	GRAINS	PRIMER TYPE	PRIMER MFGR.	VELOCITY	PRESSURE (C.U.P.)	REMARKS
Hercules	Bullseye	6.0	LP	CCI	870	11,800	
Hercules	Unique	9.0	LP	CCI	895	11,600	
Hercules	Red Dot	7.0	LP	CCI	915	12,600	
Hercules	Green Dot	8.0	LP	CCI	940	12,500	
Hercules	Herco	9.5	LP	CCI	895	11,400	
Hercules	Blue Dot	13.0	LP	CCI	925	11,800	

250-grain Jacketed Hollow Point

POWDER MFGR.	POWDER TYPE	GRAINS	PRIMER TYPE	PRIMER MFGR.	VELOCITY	PRESSURE (C.U.P.)	REMARKS
Hercules	Bullseye	5.4	LP	CCI	805	11,800	
Hercules	Unique	8.0	LP	CCI	850	11,800	
Hercules	Red Dot	6.0	LP	CCI	830	12,000	
Hercules	Green Dot	6.8	LP	CCI	855	12,300	
Hercules	Herco	9.0	LP	CCI	910	12,600	
Hercules	Blue Dot	11.5	LP	CCI	890	12,200	

.45 WINCHESTER MAGNUM

SPECIFICATIONS

Dia. of Rim — .475″
Dia. of Base — .470″
Dia. of Shoulder — Straight
Dia. of Neck — .473″
Length of Neck — Straight
Angle of Shoulder — Straight
Dia. Jacketed Bullet — .451″
Dia. Cast Bullet — .453″
Length of Case — 1.198″
Max. Overall Length — 1.51″
Primer Size — Large Pistol
Water Capacity — 34.59 grs.

185-grain Softpoint

POWDER MFGR.	POWDER TYPE	GRAINS	PRIMER TYPE	PRIMER MFGR.	VELOCITY	PRESSURE (C.U.P.)	REMARKS
Hodgdon	HS7	19.0	LP	CCI	1490	38,400	5-inch barrel
Hodgdon	HS6	18.0	LP	CCI	1470	38,700	5-inch barrel
Hodgdon	HP38	11.6	LP	CCI	1360	37,000	5-inch barrel

200-grain Softpoint

POWDER MFGR.	POWDER TYPE	GRAINS	PRIMER TYPE	PRIMER MFGR.	VELOCITY	PRESSURE (C.U.P.)	REMARKS
Hodgdon	HS7	18.6	LP	CCI	1423	36,400	5-inch barrel
Hodgdon	HS6	17.5	LP	CCI	1410	37,000	5-inch barrel
Hodgdon	HP38	11.2	LP	CCI	1290	37,000	5-inch barrel

240-grain Softpoint

POWDER MFGR.	POWDER TYPE	GRAINS	PRIMER TYPE	PRIMER MFGR.	VELOCITY	PRESSURE (C.U.P.)	REMARKS
Hodgdon	H4227	25.0	LP	CCI	1260	33,000	5-inch barrel
Hodgdon	H110	27.0	LP	CCI	1410	37,400	5-inch barrel
Hodgdon	HP38	10.3	LP	CCI	1160	36,800	5-inch barrel

260-grain Softpoint

POWDER MFGR.	POWDER TYPE	GRAINS	PRIMER TYPE	PRIMER MFGR.	VELOCITY	PRESSURE (C.U.P.)	REMARKS
Hodgdon	H4227	23.0	LP	CCI	1210	35,400	5-inch barrel
Hodgdon	H110	25.0	LP	CCI	1340	37,400	5-inch barrel
Hodgdon	HS7	16.5	LP	CCI	1250	37,600	5-inch barrel
Hodgdon	HS6	15.0	LP	CCI	1220	37,000	5-inch barrel
Hodgdon	HP38	10.3	LP	CCI	1160	36,800	5-inch barrel

.50 REMINGTON

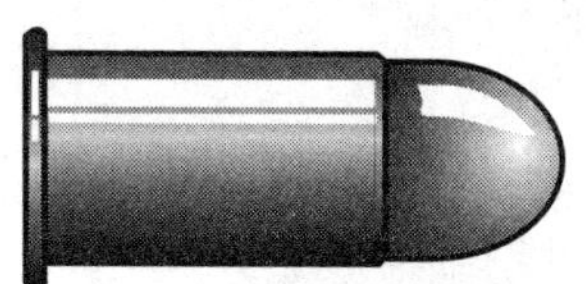

SPECIFICATIONS

Dia. of Rim — .665″
Dia. of Base — .565″
Dia. of Shoulder — Straight
Dia. of Neck — .532″
Length of Neck — Straight
Angle of Shoulder — Straight
Dia. Jacketed Bullet — .508″
Dia. Cast Bullet — .510″
Length of Case — 0.570″
Max. Overall Length — 1.24″
Primer Size — Large Pistol
Water Capacity — 13.87 grs.

265-grain Lead

POWDER MFGR.	POWDER TYPE	GRAINS	PRIMER TYPE	PRIMER MFGR.	VELOCITY	PRESSURE (C.U.P.)	REMARKS
Hercules	Unique	6.8	LP	CCI	730	—	
Black powder	FFg	25.0	LP	CCI	625	—	

300-grain Lead

POWDER MFGR.	POWDER TYPE	GRAINS	PRIMER TYPE	PRIMER MFGR.	VELOCITY	PRESSURE (C.U.P.)	REMARKS
Black powder	FFg	25.0	LP	CCI	600	—	

Chapter 10

Loads for Metric Handgun Cartridges

The United States is probably the only country in the world that has developed handguns and handgun ammunition for sporting purposes. Most, if not all, other countries have developed handgun/cartridge combinations for self-defense or military and police requirements. It is in this latter category that most metric cartridges fall.

Most countries, other than Britain and the United States, use the metric caliber designation for all rifle and handgun cartridges. There are a few exceptions, but for the most part, cartridge types and calibers are expressed in millimeters.

The United States broke tradition a few years ago with the introduction of the 9mm Winchester Magnum and the 10mm Auto. All other U.S. cartridges, however, use the decimal cartridge designation expressed in hundreds or thousands of an inch.

The smallest centerfire handgun cartridge of commercial manufacture was the 2.7mm Kolibri Auto. It was used in an ultra-small semiautomatic pistol introduced about 1914 and fired a 3-grain jacketed bullet at a velocity of around 700 fps. This miniature pistol cartridge was followed by the 3mm Kolibri and the 4.25mm Erika. All have been obsolete for many years and none had any practical purpose except, perhaps, for indoor target practice. Consequently, no loads were included for these miniature pistol cartridges.

The loading data in this chapter begins with the 5.5mm Velo Dog Revolver — a cartridge that was introduced about 1894. Many French, German, and Belgian revolvers were chambered for the 5.5mm Velo Dog, and apparently many of these found their way to the United States because the cartridge was offered commercially by Peters, Remington, and Winchester up until World War II.

One millimeter equals .03937 inch, or one inch equals 25.4 millimeters. Most inexpensive pocket calculators now have a function key that automatically converts from millimeters to inches, or vice versa. For manual calculations, use the following equations:

$$\text{Millimeters} \times .03937 = \text{caliber in inches}$$

$$\frac{\text{Inches}}{.03937} = \text{millimeters}$$

5.5mm VELO DOG REVOLVER

SPECIFICATIONS

Dia. of Rim — .308″	Dia. Jacketed Bullet — .225″
Dia. of Base — .253″	Dia. Cast Bullet — .227″
Dia. of Shoulder — Straight	Length of Case — 1.12″
Dia. of Neck — .248″	Max. Overall Length — 1.35″
Angle of Neck — Straight	Primer Size — Small Pistol
Angle of Shoulder — Straight	Water Capacity — 7.52 grs.

45-grain Softnose

POWDER MFGR.	POWDER TYPE	GRAINS	PRIMER TYPE	PRIMER MFGR.	VELOCITY	PRESSURE (C.U.P.)	REMARKS
Hercules	Unique	4.5	Small Pistol	Remington	595	—	

6.35mm AUTO PISTOL

SPECIFICATIONS

Dia. of Rim — .302″	Dia. Jacketed Bullet — .251″
Dia. of Base — .278″	Dia. Cast Bullet — .252″
Dia. of Shoulder — Straight	Length of case — 0.615″
Dia. of Neck — .278″	Max. Overall Length — 0.91″
Angle of Neck — Straight	Primer Size — Small Pistol
Angle of Shoulder — Straight	Water Capacity — 3.08 grs.

50-grain FMC

POWDER MFGR.	POWDER TYPE	GRAINS	PRIMER TYPE	PRIMER MFGR.	VELOCITY	PRESSURE (C.U.P.)	REMARKS
Hercules	Bullseye	0.8	1½	Remington	545	—	
Hercules	Bullseye	1.0	1½	Remington	675	10,500	
Hercules	Bullseye	1.3	1½	Remington	830	15,000	
Hercules	Herco	1.7	1½	Remington	735	15,600	
Hercules	Unique	1.7	1½	Remington	760	14,800	
Hodgdon	HP38	1.4	1½	Remington	848	—	Tested in 14″ barrel
Vihtavuori	No. 22	1.1	1½	Remington	804	18,800	P.S.I.

7mm BR REMINGTON

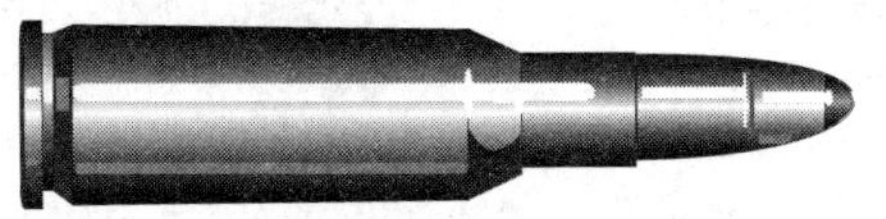

SPECIFICATIONS

Dia. of Rim — .473″
Dia. of Base — .470″
Dia. of Shoulder — .460
Dia. of Neck — .308″
Length of Neck — .314
Angle of Shoulder — 30.12°
Dia. Jacketed Bullet — .284″
Dia. Cast Bullet — .284″
Length of Case — 1.52″
Max. Overall Length — 2.33″
Primer Size — Small Rifle
Water Capacity — 38.8 grs.

139-grain Spire Point

POWDER MFGR.	POWDER TYPE	GRAINS	PRIMER TYPE	PRIMER MFGR.	VELOCITY	PRESSURE (C.U.P.)	REMARKS
IMR	IMR4198	24.0	SR	Remington	2165	50,400	
IMR	IMR3031	28.0	SR	Remington	2220	49,000	Compressed load
IMR	IMR4064	28.5	SR	Remington	2080	43,600	Compressed load
IMR	IMR4895	29.0	SR	Remington	2180	50,200	Compressed load

160-grain Spitzer Boattail

POWDER MFGR.	POWDER TYPE	GRAINS	PRIMER TYPE	PRIMER MFGR.	VELOCITY	PRESSURE (C.U.P.)	REMARKS
IMR	IMR4198	22.5	SR	Remington	2010	52,000	
IMR	IMR3031	26.0	SR	Remington	2000	42,600	Compressed load
IMR	IMR4064	26.0	SR	Remington	1900	41,000	Compressed load
IMR	IMR4895	26.5	SR	Remington	1980	46,100	Compressed load

162-grain Hollow Point Boattail

POWDER MFGR.	POWDER TYPE	GRAINS	PRIMER TYPE	PRIMER MFGR.	VELOCITY	PRESSURE (C.U.P.)	REMARKS
IMR	IMR4198	22.5	SR	Remington	2000	50,600	
IMR	IMR3031	26.0	SR	Remington	2015	44,000	Compressed load
IMR	IMR4064	26.0	SR	Remington	1870	38,600	Compressed load
IMR	IMR4895	27.0	SR	Remington	2015	48,000	Compressed load
Hodgdon	BL-C(2)	28.0	SR	Remington	1910	—	
Hodgdon	H335	27.0	SR	Remington	1890	—	
Hodgdon	H4895	27.0	SR	Remington	1975	—	
Hodgdon	H322	25.0	SR	Remington	1880	—	
Hodgdon	H4198	22.0	SR	Remington	1800	—	

7mm NAMBU

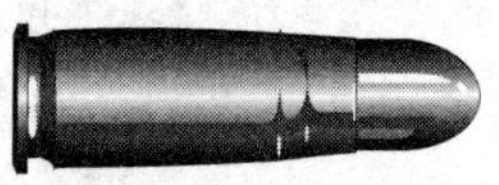

SPECIFICATIONS

Dia. of Rim — .360″
Dia. of Base — .351″
Dia. of Shoulder — .333″
Dia. of Neck — .296″
Angle of Neck — 13.5°
Length of Shoulder — .077″

Dia. Jacketed Bullet — .280″
Dia. Cast Bullet — .283″
Length of Case — .78″
Max. Overall Length — 1.06″
Primer Size — Small Pistol
Water Capacity — 9.98 grs.

60-grain Lead

POWDER MFGR.	POWDER TYPE	GRAINS	PRIMER TYPE	PRIMER MFGR.	VELOCITY	PRESSURE (C.U.P.)	REMARKS
Hercules	Bullseye	1.7	Small Pistol	Remington	995	—	
Hercules	Bullseye	1.8	Small Pistol	Remington	1035	—	

7.62mm RUSSIAN TOKAREV

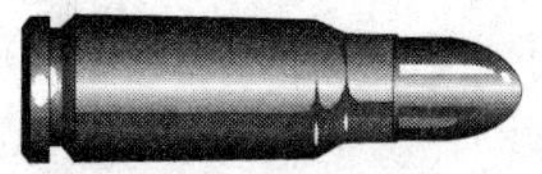

SPECIFICATIONS

Dia. of Rim — .390″
Dia. of Base — .380″
Dia. of Shoulder — .370″
Dia. of Neck — .33″
Length of Neck — .125″
Angle of Shoulder — 13.25°

Dia. Jacketed Bullet — .307″
Dia. Cast Bullet — .308″
Length of Case — .970″
Max. Overall Length — 1.35″
Primer Size — Small Pistol
Water Capacity — 15.98 grs.

86-grain Softnose

POWDER MFGR.	POWDER TYPE	GRAINS	PRIMER TYPE	PRIMER MFGR.	VELOCITY	PRESSURE (C.U.P.)	REMARKS
Hercules	Bullseye	4.9	Small Pistol	Remington	1375	—	Approximates factory ballistics
Hercules	Bullseye	4.7	Small Pistol	Remington	1345		Most accurate load tested

7.62mm RUSSIAN NAGANT

SPECIFICATIONS

Dia. of Rim — .388″
Dia. of Base — .335″
Dia. of Shoulder — Straight
Dia. of Neck — .288″
Angle of Neck — Straight
Angle of Shoulder — Straight
Dia. Jacketed Bullet — .295″
Dia. Cast Bullet — .296″
Length of Case — 1.53″
Max. Overall Length — ″
Primer Size — Small Pistol
Water Capacity — 25.24 grs.

100-grain Softnose

POWDER MFGR.	POWDER TYPE	GRAINS	PRIMER TYPE	PRIMER MFGR.	VELOCITY	PRESSURE (C.U.P.)	REMARKS
Hercules	Bullseye	3.6	Small Pistol	Remington	995	—	
Hercules	Bullseye	2.8	Small Pistol	Remington	745	—	Approximates factory load

7.63 MAUSER

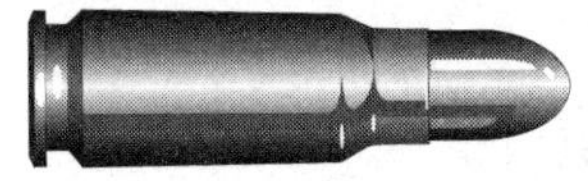

SPECIFICATIONS

Dia. of Rim — .390″
Dia. of Base — .381″
Dia. of Shoulder — .370″
Dia. of Neck — .332″
Length of Neck — .130″
Angle of Shoulder — 8.64°
Dia. Jacketed Bullet — .308″
Dia. Cast Bullet — .308″
Length of Case — .99″
Max. Overall Length — 1.36″
Primer Size — Small Pistol
Water Capacity — 16.3 grs.

80-grain Lead Alloy

POWDER MFGR.	POWDER TYPE	GRAINS	PRIMER TYPE	PRIMER MFGR.	VELOCITY	PRESSURE (C.U.P.)	REMARKS
Hercules	Bullseye	4.1	SP	Remington	1114	—	6-inch barrel
Hercules	Bullseye	4.8	SP	Remington	1230	—	6-inch barrel
Hercules	Unique	5.2	SP	Remington	1023	—	6-inch barrel
Hercules	Unique	6.5	SP	Remington	1128	—	6-inch barrel
Hercules	Red Dot	4.8	SP	Remington	1030	—	6-inch barrel
Hercules	Red Dot	6.5	SP	Remington	1134	—	6-inch barrel

7.63mm MANNLICHER

SPECIFICATIONS

Dia. of Rim — .334″
Dia. of Base — .332″
Dia. of Shoulder — Straight
Dia. of Neck — .331″
Length of Neck — Straight
Angle of Shoulder — Straight
Dia. Jacketed Bullet — .308″
Dia. Cast Bullet — .308″
Length of Case — .84″
Max. Overall Length — 1.12″
Primer Size — Small Pistol
Water Capacity — 9.34 grs.

86-grain Softnose

POWDER MFGR.	POWDER TYPE	GRAINS	PRIMER TYPE	PRIMER MFGR.	VELOCITY	PRESSURE (C.U.P.)	REMARKS
Hercules	Unique	3.1	Small Pistol	Remington	990	—	

7.65mm LUGER

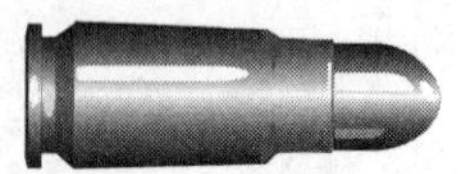

SPECIFICATIONS

Dia. of Rim — .391″
Dia. of Base — .388″
Dia. of Shoulder — .374″
Dia. of Neck — .322″
Length of Neck — .120″
Angle of Shoulder — 13°
Dia. Jacketed Bullet — .308″
Dia. Cast Bullet — .311″
Length of Case — .75″
Max. Overall Length — 1.15″
Primer Size — Small Pistol
Water Capacity — 16.0 grs.

93-grain FMC

POWDER MFGR.	POWDER TYPE	GRAINS	PRIMER TYPE	PRIMER MFGR.	VELOCITY	PRESSURE (C.U.P.)	REMARKS
Hercules	Bullseye	3.5	1½	Remington	1025	—	
Hercules	Bullseye	4.0	1½	Remington	1175	29,000	
Hercules	Unique	4.7	1½	Remington	1250	—	Approximates factory load
VihtaVuori	N340	5.2	1½	Remington	1250	35,000	Approximates factory load

7.65mm MAS

SPECIFICATIONS

Dia. of Rim — .337″
Dia. of Base — .337″
Dia. of Shoulder — Straight
Dia. of Neck — .336″
Length of Neck — Straight
Angle of Shoulder — Straight
Dia. Jacketed Bullet — .309″
Dia. Cast Bullet — .309″
Length of Case — 0.78″
Max. Overall Length — 1.19″
Primer Size — Small Pistol
Water Capacity — 8.20 grs.

86-grain FMJ

POWDER MFGR.	POWDER TYPE	GRAINS	PRIMER TYPE	PRIMER MFGR.	VELOCITY	PRESSURE (C.U.P.)	REMARKS
Hercules	Bullseye	2.3	Small Pistol	Remington	1100	—	Approximates factory load

7.65 BROWNING AUTOMATIC

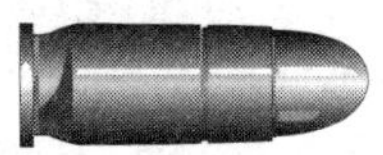

SPECIFICATIONS

Dia. of Rim — .354″
Dia. of Base — .336″
Dia. of Shoulder — Straight
Dia. of Neck — .336″
Length of Neck — Straight
Angle of Shoulder — Straight
Dia. Jacketed Bullet — .309″
Dia. Cast Bullet — .312″
Length of Case — 0.68″
Max. Overall Length — 1.03″
Primer Size — Small Pistol
Water Capacity — 6.48 grs.

71-grain FMC

POWDER MFGR.	POWDER TYPE	GRAINS	PRIMER TYPE	PRIMER MFGR.	VELOCITY	PRESSURE (C.U.P.)	REMARKS
Hercules	Bullseye	1.6	100	Federal	750	—	3-inch barrel
Hercules	Bullseye	2.1	100	Federal	890	—	3-inch barrel
Hercules	Red Dot	1.8	1½	Remington	755	—	3-inch barrel
Hodgdon	HP-38	1.6	1½	Remington	722	—	3-inch barrel
Hodgdon	HP-38	2.2	1½	Remington	904	—	3-inch barrel
Hercules	Unique	2.1	1½	Remington	614	—	3-inch barrel
Hercules	Unique	2.9	1½	Remington	903	—	3-inch barrel

7.5 SWISS ARMY

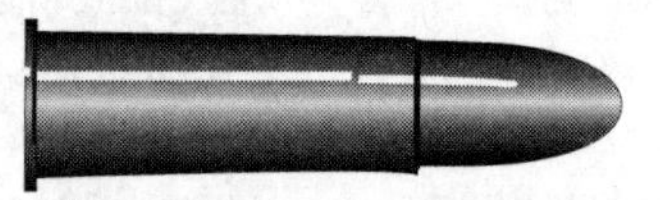

SPECIFICATIONS

Dia. of Rim — .407″
Dia. of Base — .345″
Dia. of Shoulder — Straight
Dia. of Neck — .335″
Length of Neck — Straight
Angle of Shoulder — Straight
Dia. Jacketed Bullet — .315″
Dia. Cast Bullet — .317″
Length of Case — 0.89″
Max. Overall Length — 1.29″
Primer Size — Small Pistol
Water Capacity — 11.35 grs.

110-grain Lead

POWDER MFGR.	POWDER TYPE	GRAINS	PRIMER TYPE	PRIMER MFGR.	VELOCITY	PRESSURE (C.U.P.)	REMARKS
Hercules	Bullseye	1.7	Small Pistol	Remington	685	—	Approximates factory load

7.5mm SWEDISH NAGANT

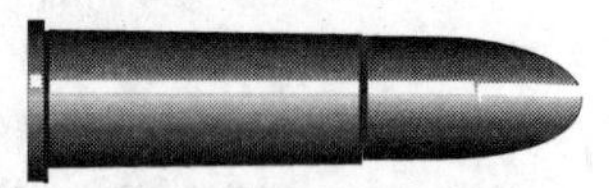

SPECIFICATIONS

Dia. of Rim — .406″
Dia. of Base — .350″
Dia. of Shoulder — Straight
Dia. of Neck — .328″
Length of Neck — Straight
Angle of Shoulder — Straight
Dia. Jacketed Bullet — .322″
Dia. Cast Bullet — .325″
Length of Case — 0.89″
Max. Overall Length — 1.35″
Primer Size — Small Pistol
Water Capacity — 12.97 grs.

105-grain Lead

POWDER MFGR.	POWDER TYPE	GRAINS	PRIMER TYPE	PRIMER MFGR.	VELOCITY	PRESSURE (C.U.P.)	REMARKS
Hercules	bullseye	1.9	Small Pistol	Remington	725	—	Approximates factory load

8mm NAMBU

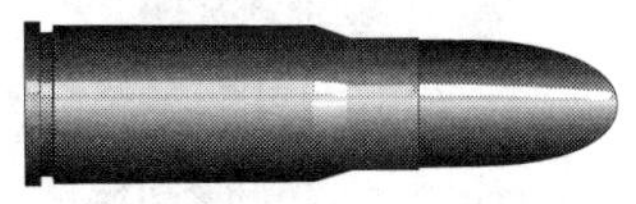

SPECIFICATIONS

Dia. of Rim — .413″
Dia. of Base — .408″
Dia. of Shoulder — .388″
Dia. of Neck — .338″
Length of Neck — Straight
Angle of Shoulder — Straight
Dia. Jacketed Bullet — .320″
Dia. Cast Bullet — .320″
Length of Case — 0.86″
Max. Overall Length — 1.25″
Primer Size — Small Pistol
Water Capacity — 14.6 grs.

86-grain Lead

POWDER MFGR.	POWDER TYPE	GRAINS	PRIMER TYPE	PRIMER MFGR.	VELOCITY	PRESSURE (C.U.P.)	REMARKS
Hercules	Unique	3.0	Small Pistol	Remington	960	—	Approximates factory load

8mm LEBEL

SPECIFICATIONS

Dia. of Rim — .401″
Dia. of Base — .384″
Dia. of Shoulder — Straight
Dia. of Neck — .350″
Angle of Neck — Straight
Angle of Shoulder — Straight
Dia. Jacketed Bullet — .323″
Dia. Cast Bullet — .323″
Length of Case — 1.07″
Max. Overall Length — 1.44″
Primer Size — Small Pistol
Water Capacity — grs.

115-grain Lead

POWDER MFGR.	POWDER TYPE	GRAINS	PRIMER TYPE	PRIMER MFGR.	VELOCITY	PRESSURE (C.U.P.)	REMARKS
Hercules	Bullseye	2.7	Small Pistol	Remington	625	—	Approximates factory load

8mm ROTH-STEYR

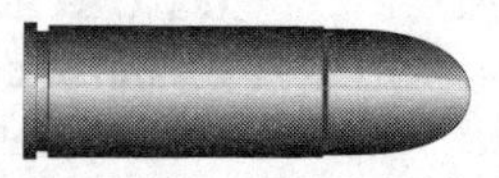

SPECIFICATIONS

Dia. of Rim — .356″
Dia. of Base — .355″
Dia. of Shoulder — Straight
Dia. of Neck — .353″
Length of Neck — Straight
Angle of Shoulder — Straight
Dia. Jacketed Bullet — .329″
Dia. Cast Bullet — .329″
Length of Case — 0.74″
Max. Overall Length — 1.14″
Primer Size — Small Pistol
Water Capacity — 8.71 grs.

116-grain FMJ

POWDER MFGR.	POWDER TYPE	GRAINS	PRIMER TYPE	PRIMER MFGR.	VELOCITY	PRESSURE (C.U.P.)	REMARKS
Hercules	Bullseye	3.2	Small Pistol	Remington	1065	—	Approximates factory load

9mm GLISENTI

SPECIFICATIONS

Dia. of Rim — .393″
Dia. of Base — .392″
Dia. of Shoulder — Straight
Dia. of Neck — .380″
Length of Neck — Straight
Angle of Shoulder — Straight
Dia. Jacketed Bullet — .355″
Dia. Cast Bullet — .356″
Length of Case — 0.75″
Max. Overall Length — 1.15″
Primer Size — Small Pistol
Water Capacity — 10.7 grs.

116-grain FMC

POWDER MFGR.	POWDER TYPE	GRAINS	PRIMER TYPE	PRIMER MFGR.	VELOCITY	PRESSURE (C.U.P.)	REMARKS
Hercules	Bullseye	3.9	Small Pistol	Remington	1045	—	Approximates factory load

9mm STEYR

SPECIFICATIONS

Dia. of Rim — .381″
Dia. of Base — .380″
Dia. of Shoulder — Straight
Dia. of Neck — .380″
Length of Neck — Straight
Angle of Shoulder — Straight
Dia. Jacketed Bullet — .355″
Dia. Cast Bullet — .357″
Length of Case — 0.90″
Max. Overall Length — 1.30″
Primer Size — Small Pistol
Water Capacity — 13.84 grs.

124-grain Softnose

POWDER MFGR.	POWDER TYPE	GRAINS	PRIMER TYPE	PRIMER MFGR.	VELOCITY	PRESSURE (C.U.P.)	REMARKS
Hercules	Unique	4.5	Small Pistol	Remington	595	—	

9mm LUGER

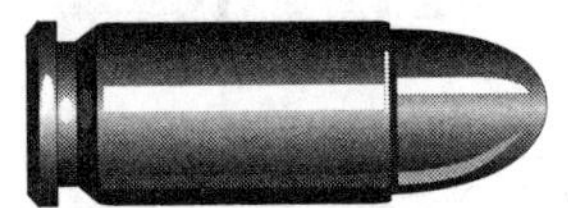

SPECIFICATIONS

Dia. of Rim — .393″
Dia. of Base — .392″
Dia. of Shoulder — Straight
Dia. of Neck — .380″
Length of Neck — Straight
Angle of Shoulder — Straight
Dia. Jacketed Bullet — .355″
Dia. Cast Bullet — .357″
Length of Case — 0.75″
Max. Overall Length — 1.15″
Primer Size — Small Pistol
Water Capacity — 10.80 grs.

88-grain Hollow Point

POWDER MFGR.	POWDER TYPE	GRAINS	PRIMER TYPE	PRIMER MFGR.	VELOCITY	PRESSURE (P.S.I.)	REMARKS
VihtaVuori	N310	4.9	500	CCI	1393	29,700	
VihtaVuori	N320	5.9	500	CCI	1450	29,000	
VihtaVuori	N330	7.0	500	CCI	1494	29,000	
VihtaVuori	N331	7.5	500	CCI	1469	29,000	
VihtaVuori	N340	7.2	500	CCI	1514	27,600	
VihtaVuori	3N37	8.2	500	CCI	1531	29,700	

9mm LUGER (Cont.)

90-grain Hollow Point

POWDER MFGR.	POWDER TYPE	GRAINS	PRIMER TYPE	PRIMER MFGR.	VELOCITY	PRESSURE (C.U.P.)	REMARKS
Hodgdon	HS6	7.9	Small Pistol	Remington	1475	—	
Hodgdon	Trap 100	5.8	Small Pistol	Remington	1425	—	
Hodgdon	HP38	5.8	Small Pistol	Remington	1430	—	

108-grain Soft Point

POWDER MFGR.	POWDER TYPE	GRAINS	PRIMER TYPE	PRIMER MFGR.	VELOCITY	PRESSURE (C.U.P.)	REMARKS
Hodgdon	HS6	7.1	Small Pistol	Remington	1275	—	
Hodgdon	Trap 100	5.0	Small Pistol	Remington	1145	—	
Hodgdon	HP38	5.3	Small Pistol	Remington	1160	—	

125-grain Soft Point

POWDER MFGR.	POWDER TYPE	GRAINS	PRIMER TYPE	PRIMER MFGR.	VELOCITY	PRESSURE (C.U.P.)	REMARKS
Hodgdon	HS6	6.6	Small Pistol	Remington	1145	—	
Hodgdon	Trap 100	4.3	Small Pistol	Remington	990	—	
Hodgdon	HP38	4.5	Small Pistol	Remington	990	—	

130-grain FMJ

POWDER MFGR.	POWDER TYPE	GRAINS	PRIMER TYPE	PRIMER MFGR.	VELOCITY	PRESSURE (C.U.P.)	REMARKS
Hodgdon	HS6	6.3	Small Pistol	Remington	1110	—	
Hodgdon	Trap 100	4.5	Small Pistol	Remington	1050	—	
Hodgdon	HP38	4.5	Small Pistol	Remington	1035	—	

9mm MAUSER

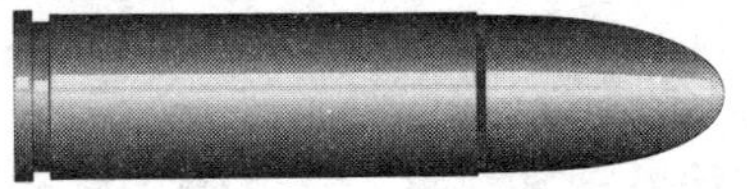

SPECIFICATIONS

Dia. of Rim — .390″	Dia. Jacketed Bullet — .355″
Dia. of Base — .389″	Dia. Cast Bullet — .355″
Dia. of Shoulder — Straight	Length of Case — 0.98″
Dia. of Neck — .376″	Max. Overall Length — 1.38″
Length of Neck — Straight	Primer Size — Small Pistol
Angle of Shoulder — Straight	Water Capacity — 16.49 grs.

130-grain Softnose

POWDER MFGR.	POWDER TYPE	GRAINS	PRIMER TYPE	PRIMER MFGR.	VELOCITY	PRESSURE (C.U.P.)	REMARKS
Hercules	Blue Dot	10.0	Small Pistol	Remington	1275	—	

9mm BROWNING AUTOMATIC

SPECIFICATIONS

Dia. of Rim — .374″	Dia. Jacketed Bullet — .355″
Dia. of Base — .373″	Dia. Cast Bullet — .357″
Dia. of Shoulder — Straight	Length of Case — 0.68″
Dia. of Neck — .372″	Max. Overall Length — 0.98″
Length of Neck — Straight	Primer Size — Small Pistol
Angle of Shoulder — Straight	Water Capacity — 8.94 grs.

90-grain FMC

POWDER MFGR.	POWDER TYPE	GRAINS	PRIMER TYPE	PRIMER MFGR.	VELOCITY	PRESSURE (C.U.P.)	REMARKS
Hercules	Herco	5.3	Small Pistol	Remington	1025	22,000	Maximum
Hercules	Blue Dot	7.5	Small Pistol	Remington	1075	19,000	
Hercules	Unique	5.2	Small Pistol	Remington	1050	20,900	

9mm BAYARD LONG

SPECIFICATIONS

Dia. of Rim — .392″
Dia. of Base — .390″
Dia. of Shoulder — Straight
Dia. of Neck — .375″
Length of Neck — Straight
Angle of Shoulder — Straight

Dia. Jacketed Bullet — .355″
Dia. Cast Bullet — .357″
Length of Case — 0.91″
Max. Overall Length — 1.32″
Primer Size — Small Pistol
Water Capacity — 14.91grs.

125-grain Lead

POWDER MFGR.	POWDER TYPE	GRAINS	PRIMER TYPE	PRIMER MFGR.	VELOCITY	PRESSURE (C.U.P.)	REMARKS
Hercules	Unique	6.5	Small Pistol	Remington	1150	—	

9mm RUSSIAN MAKAROV

SPECIFICATIONS

Dia. of Rim — .396″
Dia. of Base — .389″
Dia. of Shoulder — Straight
Dia. of Neck — .384″
Length of Neck — Straight
Angle of Shoulder — Straight

Dia. Jacketed Bullet — .363″
Dia. Cast Bullet — .363″
Length of Case — 0.71″
Max. Overall Length — 0.97″
Primer Size — Small Pistol
Water Capacity — 10.03 grs.

95-grain FMC

POWDER MFGR.	POWDER TYPE	GRAINS	PRIMER TYPE	PRIMER MFGR.	VELOCITY	PRESSURE (C.U.P.)	REMARKS
Hercules	Unique	4.5	Small Pistol	Remington	1050	—	

9mm WINCHESTER MAGNUM

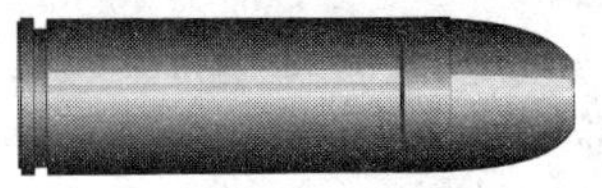

SPECIFICATIONS

Dia. of Rim — .394″
Dia. of Base — .392″
Dia. of Shoulder — Straight
Dia. of Neck — .379″
Length of Neck — Straight
Angle of Shoulder — Straight
Dia. Jacketed Bullet — .355″
Dia. Cast Bullet — .355″
Length of Case — 1.16″
Max. Overall Length — 1.55″
Primer Size — Small Pistol
Water Capacity — 20.72 grs.

115-grain Softnose

POWDER MFGR.	POWDER TYPE	GRAINS	PRIMER TYPE	PRIMER MFGR.	VELOCITY	PRESSURE (C.U.P.)	REMARKS
Hercules	Herco	7.0	1½	Remington	1200	—	

9x21mm

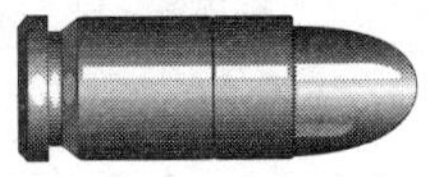

SPECIFICATIONS

Dia. of Rim — .367″
Dia. of Base — .385″
Dia. of Shoulder — Straight
Dia. of Neck — .378″
Length of Neck — Straight
Angle of Shoulder — Straight
Dia. Jacketed Bullet — .355″
Dia. Cast Bullet — .355″
Length of Case — 0.80″
Max. Overall Length — 1.05″
Primer Size — Small Pistol
Water Capacity — 11.72 grs.

100-grain Hollow Point

POWDER MFGR.	POWDER TYPE	GRAINS	PRIMER TYPE	PRIMER MFGR.	VELOCITY	PRESSURE (C.U.P.)	REMARKS
VihtaVuori	N340	7.6	No. 22	VihtaVuori	1550	36,300	
VihtaVuori	3N37	8.1	No. 22	VihtaVuori	1514	36,300	
VihtaVuori	N350	8.2	No. 22	VihtaVuori	1499	31,900	

10mm AUTOMATIC

SPECIFICATIONS

Dia. of Rim — .425″
Dia. of Base — .425″
Dia. of Shoulder — Straight
Dia. of Neck — .423″
Length of Neck — Straight
Angle of Shoulder — Straight
Dia. Jacketed Bullet — .40″
Dia. Cast Bullet — .40″
Length of Case — 0.992″
Max. Overall Length — 1.26″
Primer Size — Large Pistol
Water Capacity — 23.09 grs.

170-grain Hollow Point

POWDER MFGR.	POWDER TYPE	GRAINS	PRIMER TYPE	PRIMER MFGR.	VELOCITY	PRESSURE (C.U.P.)	REMARKS
VihtaVuori	N340	7.1	No. 22	VihtaVuori	1175	29,000	
VihtaVuori	N340	7.9	No. 22	VihtaVuori	1261	35,500	Maximum
VihtaVuori	3N37	8.0	No. 22	VihtaVuori	1172	27,600	
VihtaVuori	3N37	9.0	No. 22	VihtaVuori	1297	35,500	Maximum
VihtaVuori	N350	8.5	No. 22	VihtaVuori	1220	27,600	
VihtaVuori	N350	9.3	No. 22	VihtaVuori	1340	35,500	Maximum

180-grain Hollow Point

POWDER MFGR.	POWDER TYPE	GRAINS	PRIMER TYPE	PRIMER MFGR.	VELOCITY	PRESSURE (C.U.P.)	REMARKS
Winchester	231	5.0	No. 22	VihtaVuori	890	—	
Hercules	Unique	5.6	No. 22	VihtaVuori	900	—	
Hercules	Unique	6.1	No. 22	VihtaVuori	979	—	
Hercules	Blue Dot	8.5	No. 22	VihtaVuori	925	—	
VihtaVuori	N340	6.7	No. 22	VihtaVuori	1096	26,100	
VihtaVuori	3N37	7.8	No. 22	VihtaVuori	1132	26,100	
VihtaVuori	N350	8.4	No. 22	VihtaVuori	1211	26,100	

200-grain FMC

POWDER MFGR.	POWDER TYPE	GRAINS	PRIMER TYPE	PRIMER MFGR.	VELOCITY	PRESSURE (C.U.P.)	REMARKS
VihtaVuori	N340	5.8	No. 22	VihtaVuori	996	29,000	
VihtaVuori	N340	6.3	No. 22	VihtaVuori	1100	35,500	Maximum
VihtaVuori	3N37	7.0	No. 22	VihtaVuori	1059	29,000	
VihtaVuori	3N37	7.8	No. 22	VihtaVuori	1176	35,500	Maximum
VihtaVuori	N350	7.2	No. 22	VihtaVuori	1077	29,000	
VihtaVuori	N350	8.0	No. 22	VihtaVuori	1185	35,500	Maximum

Chapter 11

Shot Loads for Handguns

Hunters have always realized that the shotshell could be a very efficient small-game cartridge when used in handguns. It allowed the flexibility of hunting small game and game birds for the pot during big-game hunts, and also afforded snake protection in hunting areas where this problem existed.

The use of shot in pistols and revolvers is nothing new. Muzzleloading horse pistols were loaded with small rocks, nails, scraps of metal, and large shot over 200 years ago; and the records indicate that at close range such combinations were very effective. In more recent years, attempts have been made to shoot shot from revolvers — the results generally being far from encouraging.

There was a time when all of the American ammunition makers included shot loads in their line of ammunition for many rifle and revolver cartridges, particularly those having a straight case. These proved entirely unsatisfactory, as the rotation of the shot charge imparted by the rifling caused the individual pellets to fly off on an angle, thus creating a "cartwheel" effect and completely shattering the pattern. Tests made with these cartridges at 20 yards revealed a hollow-center pattern that would permit the total escape of game as large as a grouse. Accordingly, the ammunition makers abandoned most of these loads, and today, factory shot charges are available only in .22 Long Rifle, .22 WMR, .38 Special, 9mm, .44 magnum, .45 ACP and some Thompson/Center Hotshot loads.

Figure 11-1: A few of the many factory-loaded centerfire shot cartridges that were once available.

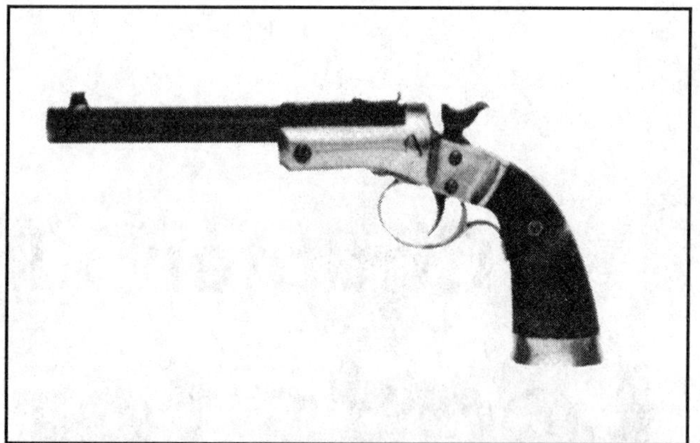

Figure 11-2: The Stevens Auto Shot No. 35 pistol was one of the most effective handguns adapted to firing shotshells. Its effectiveness closely resembled the .410 shotguns of the day.

Figure 11-3: The Thompson/Center Contender pistol, introduced in 1968, was the first efficient shot pistol since the Stevens Auto Shot No. 35.

One of the most effective pistols for firing shot loads is the Stevens Auto Shot No. 35 Pistol. About 2000 of these pistols were manufactured between 1929 and 1934 when manufacture was halted due to the passage of the National Firearms Act in 1934 restricted the use of shot cartridges in handguns with smoothbore barrels.

The Stevens Auto Shot No. 35 Single-Shot Pistol was chambered for the .410/2-inch shotshell and was available with either an 8-inch or 12¼-inch half-octagonal smoothbore barrel. An internal choke was used to control shot dispersion. This was a very effective small-game combination out to about 30 yards. Of course, this type of handgun is subject to the provisions (and restrictions) of the National Firearms Act and shooters should not attempt to acquire or dispose of specimens unless complying fully with those provisions. The No. 35 Single-Shot pistol was the last handgun manufactured by Stevens.

CONTENDER PISTOLS

The first Thompson/Center Contender shotshell barrel was offered on the 10-inch Octagon model and featured an external choke, which was actually a removable 2-inch extension in which the rifling had been "straightened out," doing away with the twist, so that the shot cup would stabilize in the barrel before exiting. This accomplished two things:

- The stabilizing choke allowed the shot cup to exit the barrel without spinning, which prevented the shot pattern from being propelled to the side when it exited. This feature produced a pattern similar to a shotgun.
- The choke is removable so that the rifling in the barrel could be used to stabilize a standard bullet fired in the same barrel. The pistol, therefore, served two purposes.

The 10-inch octagonal barrel with external choke was first offered in 1968, chambered in .45 Long Colt/.410, 2½-inch shotshell. Between 1968 to 1974, the barrel was also chambered in .44 Magnum, .45 Colt and .357 Magnum, and a line of shot cartridges, called T/C Hotshot, was developed to accompany the barrels.

The original .45/.410 barrel was discontinued in 1969, at the request of the BATF, due to their interpretation of the law concerning short-barreled shotguns. The other three chamberings were kept in the line until 1980, when the new 10-inch Bull Barrel with internal choke was introduced to replace the Octagon. In 1986, the BATF reversed

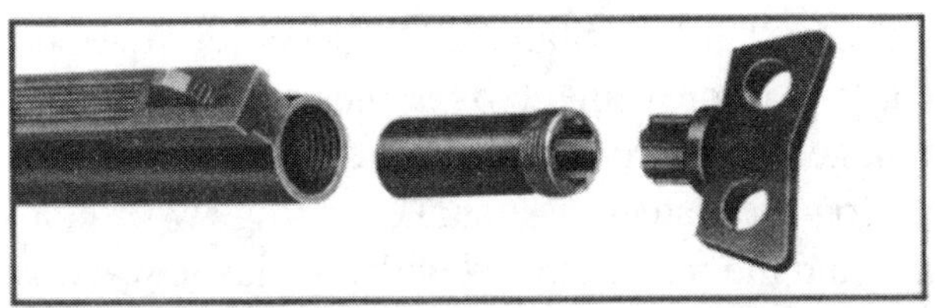

Figure 11-4: A 10-inch Bull Barrel with internal choke was introduced in 1980 to replace the Octagon barrel with its external choke. This type of barrel is offered in .357 Magnum, .44 Magnum, and .45 Colt.

Figure 11-5: The .44 T/C Hotshot load.

their finding on the .45/.410 chambering and, today, it is considered one of the best barrel combinations for the use of shot charges in handguns.

FACTORY SHOT LOADS

Winchester still loads a .22 Long Rifle cartridge with No. 12 shot. The metal case is extended and tapered and then crimped at the mouth to retain the shot. Upon firing, the crimp unfolds, allowing the shot to escape down the barrel and out the muzzle. Where it goes from there, few people know!

These .22 Long Rifle shot cartridges may have had some use in a choked smoothbore .22 caliber rifle barrel for short-range pest loads and for the once popular mini-skeet shoots; the latter called Mo-Skeet-O. However, when fired from a conventional rifled barrel, these loads are next to useless except for making noise.

Not long ago, a building supplier in Luray, Virginia obtained permission from the municipal offices to shoot pigeons in their warehouse. Since this warehouse was within the city limits, shooting was permitted only inside of the building. The owners did not want to damage their roof with larger shot loads, so .22 shot cartridges were chosen for the

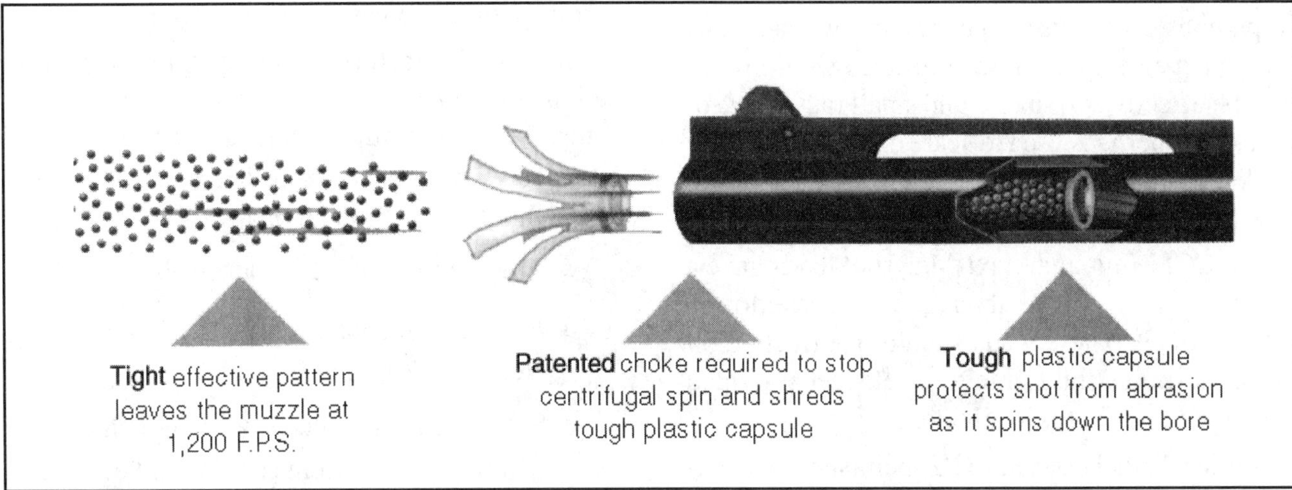

Figure 11-6: This is how the T/C Hotshot load works in a Contender barrel with internal choke.

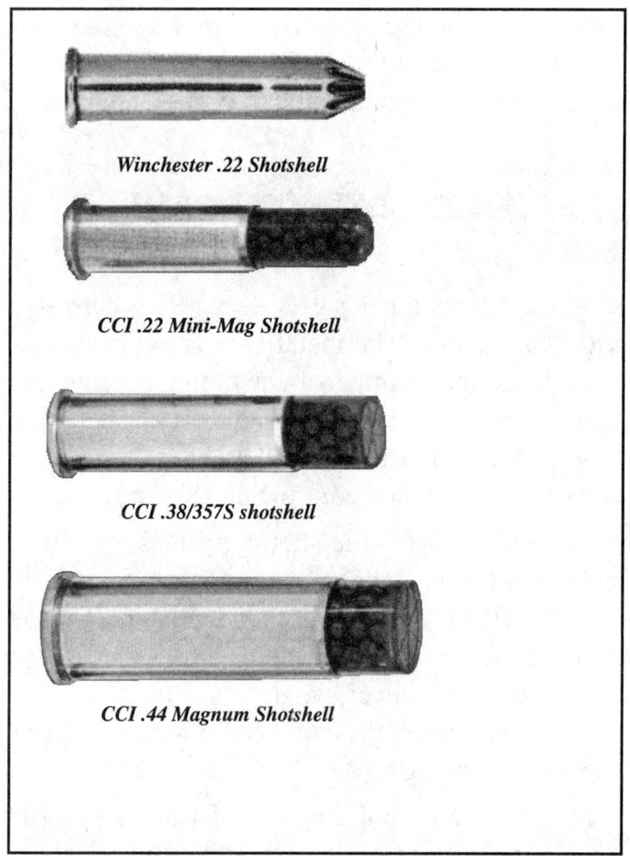

Winchester .22 Shotshell

CCI .22 Mini-Mag Shotshell

CCI .38/357S shotshell

CCI .44 Magnum Shotshell

Figure 11-7: Some of the available factory-loaded shotshells.

job. Three workers, armed with .22 rimfire rifles and a total of 50 cartridges between them, began banging away. An hour later, there were 50 fired cases on the concrete floor and a few feathers, but no pigeons! When used in handguns, worst results can be expected, but these cartridges would probably be effective on snakes and small rats at five or six feet, or perhaps used to scare chickens from the garden by the noise alone. I can think of no other uses for these cartridges at the moment.

The CCI Mini- and Maxi-Mag shot loads gave a little better performance than the Winchester loads, but not much. These loads should be effective on snakes at a maximum range of 10 feet provided more than one shot is available.

Neither Winchester nor CCI publishes any ballistic information on their .22 rimfire line of shotshells.

The CCI 38/357 Shotshell loaded with No. 9 shot is a big improvement over the rimfires. I have managed to bag two rattlesnakes and one rat with this load to date — the snakes taking two rounds each and the rat was killed with the plastic wad that hit him squarely on the side of the head at a range of about 10 feet.

I also shot a grouse with this load just outside the door of my camp near Sherman Mills, Maine. The range was about 15 feet and the load apparently did enough damage so the cock couldn't fly; rather, he took off running on the ground. I had to finish the job with a 16-gauge shotgun.

A .38 Special or .357 Magnum handgun loaded with these CCI shotshells is sufficient for killing snakes at short range and many fishermen carry this combination for this reason. In fact, if shotshells are used strictly for self-protection in snake-infested territory while fishing or camping, there is no practical purpose for reloading these cartridges. The factory cartridges will suffice nicely and the savings in reloads, if any, are not worth the trouble for the few rounds that will be used in the field.

The CCI 38/357 shot load has a muzzle velocity of 1150 fps, while the CCI 44 Magnum shot load has a muzzle velocity of 1200 fps. Since this latter load contains more No. 9 shot than the .38 load, its efficiency or effective range on snakes and small vermin should increase by about five feet.

The favorite factory handgun/shotshell combination among American sportsman for snake/pests control seems to be the American Derringer Model 1 loaded with 2½-inch .410 shotshells. The benefits of this combination are many:

- The shell has a full ½-ounce shot load.
- A variety of shot sizes are available: Nos. 4, 6, 7½, and 9.
- Since the shot contacts only ½-inch of rifling, the shot seems to pattern better than loads used in longer barrels causing contact with more rifling.

- A wider variety of reloading components are available for this shotshell; more than for conventional handgun cartridges.

Theoretically, the shot pattern in these handguns could be improved by installing a simple 1/4-inch "jug" choke in the end of the barrel as shown in Figure 11-8. According to the way I interpret the BATF's definition, a shotgun has a smoothbore barrel; one without rifling. Since the American Derringer Model 1 has rifling, a quarter-inch removed should not make any difference. In fact, I called a local BATF inspector about this modification. He told me that he would not have any problems with this modification, but final approval would have to come from headquarters. However, this inspector has since retired, and in recent months, the BATF is coming out with some strange interpretations of the firearms laws. Consequently, before performing such a modification, it would be advisable to check the current laws and get the blessings (in writing) from the BATF.

Still, these pistols are not ideal for taking small game. They are classified as "snake guns" for all practical purposes. They have an effective range from about 10 to 15 feet on snakes and small vermin, and when used with the three-ball .410 load, they are reasonably effective as a close-range self-defense weapon.

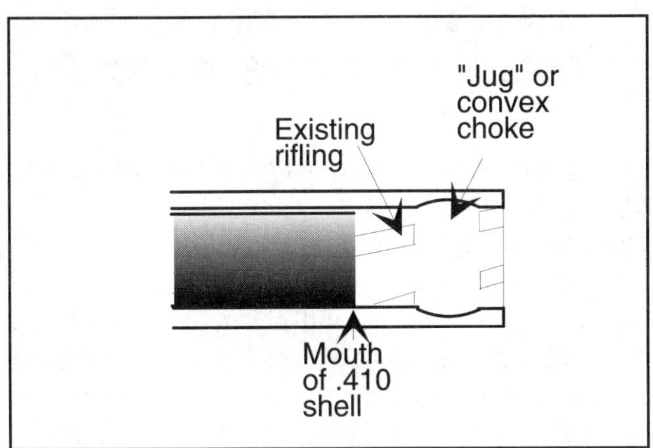

Figure 11-8: Choke installed at muzzle in .410 Derringer pistol.

THOMPSON/CENTER HOTSHOT LOADS

Thompson/Center single-shot pistols with choked barrels have already been discussed, but let's take a closer look at T/C's Hotshot loads.

The .357 Magnum Hotshot contains 1/2 ounce of shot — the same as the .410 2 1/2-inch load — and attains a muzzle velocity of 1200 fps. It is loaded with either No. 4, No. 6, No. 7 1/2 and No. 9 shot. This load, however, can be used only in the Contender pistol with a choke attachment, because the attachment is needed to shred the tough plastic shot capsule. We tried firing a few rounds through an unchoked barrel, and the entire capsule remained in tact and hit a cardboard target as a single unit about 30 yards down range. Furthermore, the length of this cartridge prohibits its use in conventional handguns.

The .44 Magnum Hotshot load contains 5/8 ounce of shot that leaves the muzzle at about 1200 fps. Again, the plastic capsule is too tough for use in conventional barrels; it is designed for use only in the T/C Contender pistol with a choke attachment designed to shred the shot capsule upon contact.

When used with the right combination, these T/C hotshot loads are hard to beat. They are much more than a "snake load." With a little practice, these loads will regularly bag small game (rabbits, quail, grouse, pheasants, etc.) out to about 20 yards.

RELOADING SHOT CARTRIDGES

Bud Dalrymple, of Scenic, South Dakota, started experimenting with shot loads in revolvers over 50 years ago. He preferred the single-action Colt with a 7 1/2-inch barrel chambered for either the .44 Special or .45 Long Colt cartridges.

When the barrels were bored out, a choke installed, and shot cartridges loaded with large shot, Mr. Dalrymple claimed his combination was quite effective out to 20 or 30 yards. His chokes were constricted from .010 inch to .012 inch for the smaller size shot and from .007 inch to .009 inch for the larger shot sizes (No. 4 and No. 2).

In loading shot in revolver cartridges without using the shot-filled capsules, one of the most important steps is the selection and assembly of the wads. These must make a gas-tight seal between the powder and the shot charge, both in the cylinder and in the barrel. To ensure this, the wad should be slightly larger in diameter than the largest part of the bore.

A stiff cardboard wad is first rammed down on the powder. A measured uniform pressure on this wad makes for regularity of combustion. This cardboard wad is followed by a thick greased felt wad and then by another stiff cardboard wad. See Figure 11-9.

The wad over the powder should be about 1⁄4 to 5⁄16 inch thick. Any attempt to make room for more shot by decreasing the amount of wadding leads to scattered and useless shot patterns.

The size of the shot to be used will depend upon the purpose of the load. If for medium-size game or self-defense, BB pellets are recommended. The .45 Long Colt will hold 16 BB pellets. At 20 yards, when used in a choked pistol barrel, much of this load will strike within a 20-inch circle and penetrate one inch of white pine. Actual tests with the .45 Long Colt loaded with BBs managed to place four pellets on a rabbit-size target at 20 yards, and the target was the actual aiming point. At half the distance, the results were discouraging; only six pellets hit target.

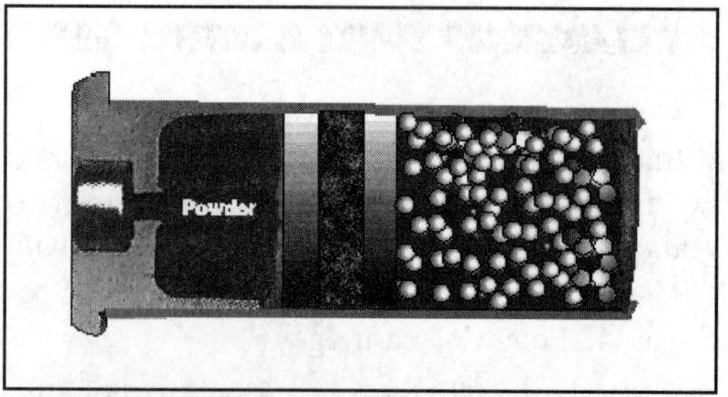

Figure 11-9: Cross-sectional view of a .45 Long Colt loaded with No. 12 (dust) shot. Some of the B-movie stars of the last generation used similar loads for trick aerial shots during personal appearances at rodeos and similar functions.

For general use on small game and snakes, No. 7½ shot works best. The .45 Long Colt will hold about 115 pellets (within the case itself) and will penetrate about 5⁄8 inch of white pine at 20 yards. The pattern, of course, depends on how the handgun barrel is constructed and choked.

When loading shot in .45 Colt cases, the shot should fill the case to within 1⁄16 inch of the case mouth. This leaves room for a stiff cardboard wad over the shot to hold it in position. Once the wad is in position, the case should be thoroughly crimped. In place of crimping, some shooters have used one of the "super glues" on the market to seal the wad in place, and to offer a high initial resistance to aid in powder burning.

Powder charges used in the .45 Long Colt with 115 No. 7½ shot pellets and with wadding as described previously are:

- 7½ grains Hercules Herco
- 7 grains Hercules Red Dot

LOADING SHOT LOADS WITH COMMERCIAL COMPONENTS

Any handloader can quickly and inexpensively make custom shotshell loads for .38 and .44 caliber handguns using the Speer shotshell cups — available from most shooting-supply outlets. These shot capsules consist of a small plastic cylinder and a removable plastic retainer cap. To load, remove the retainer cap, fill the capsule full with any size shot, and then replace the retainer cap. The loaded cap-

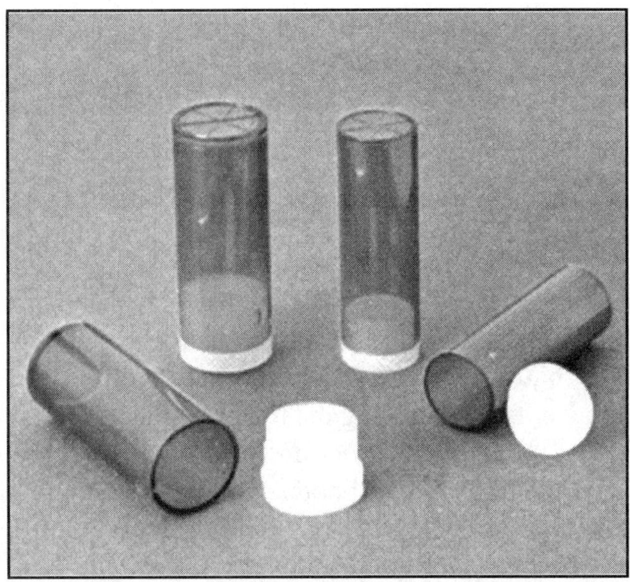

Figure 11-10: Speer shot cups are simple to use; merely fill the cup, insert the base plug, and then load similar to a regular bullet.

sule may then be loaded into the cartridge case similar to a solid projectile.

To use the Speer shot cups, remove the retaining cap and dip the cup into a container of the desired size shot, filling it slightly less than full to allow room for the retainer cap. Insert the retainer cap (base plug) into the filled capsule and push down until the shoulder of the base plug contacts the end of the capsule sleeve. Be careful in handling to avoid knocking the base plug loose and spilling the shot.

Perform resizing, decapping, priming, neck expansion, and charging with powder as for loading regular handgun cartridges (described in Chapter 8). Speer recommends a flat-nose punch in the seating die, but the semi-wadcutter punch works fine in most cases as very little pressure is required to seat the shot capsule. Seat the capsule in the loaded case with the base plug down to an overall length of:

- 1.5″ for .38 Special and .357 Magnum
- 1.6″ for .44 Special and .44 Magnum

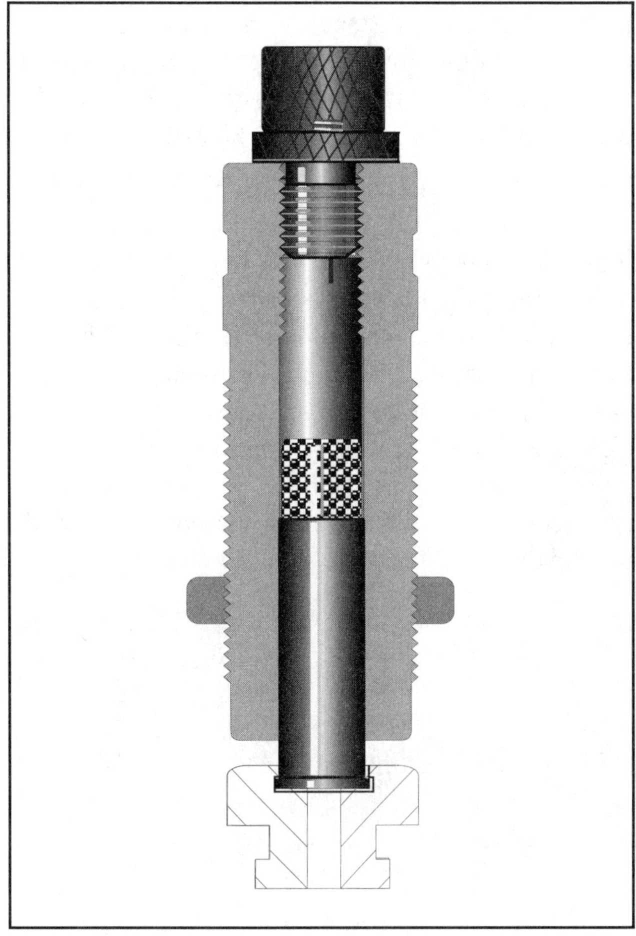

Figure 11-11: A flat-nose seating punch is recommended for seating the shot capsules into the cartridge case.

A slight crimp is required to lock the shot capsule in place. Otherwise, when one shot is fired, the capsules in the remaining cylinder chambers will move forward under recoil and possibly jam the action.

While Speer recommends No. 9 shot for all loadings, this may or may not be the best size to use. For example, in testing one Smith & Wesson Model 27 revolver with a 2½-inch barrel, using the factory 38/357 shot cartridges, it was difficult to get more than a few shot to hit the 8″ × 10″ test card at 15 yards; that is, 3 or 4 pellets. Yet, this same revolver, using handloaded shot capsules containing No. 4 shot threw a distinguishable “killing” pattern at the same distance. Further testing showed that by holding low, and slightly to the left, a relatively good pattern would be centered on the card with each shot. In another .38 caliber revolver with a 4-inch barrel, No. 7½ seemed to pattern best.

Determining the load that works the best in each individual handgun is a matter of experimentation — matching the load to the barrel. This is a balancing act at best, but the reloader can start with the following loads and make adjustments as necessary. Only a fraction of a grain can make the difference between a good load and a very poor one, so it is recommended that powder-charge adjustments be made in .2 grain increments — both up and down.

CALIBER	POWDER	GRAINS	VELOCITY
.38 Special	HP38	4.4	1040
.357 Mag.	HP38	4.0	1050
.44 Special	HP38	5.9	1050
.44 Mag.	HP38	6.5	1075
.44 Mag.	Bullseye	5.8	1123

CALIBER	POWDER	GRAINS	VELOCITY
.44 Mag.	Unique	7.0	1176
.44 Mag.	630	12.5	1075
.44 Mag.	231	7.0	1128

While the reloader has an excellent field for experimentation (loading shot loads in handgun cartridges), BATF restrictions regarding smoothbore barrels under 18 inches long, prohibit the reloader from obtaining the full potential with shot loads. Until such restrictions are lifted (which is very doubtful), most shooters will have to be content with "snake guns," or ultra-short shots on small game when using shot loads in their handguns.

The other alternative, as mentioned earlier, is one of the fine Thompson/Center Contender pistols with a choking device attached to the muzzle. However, some hunters find this model a little too bulky for carrying as a second firearm on hunts, fishing and camping trips. It isn't as compact as many would like it to be.

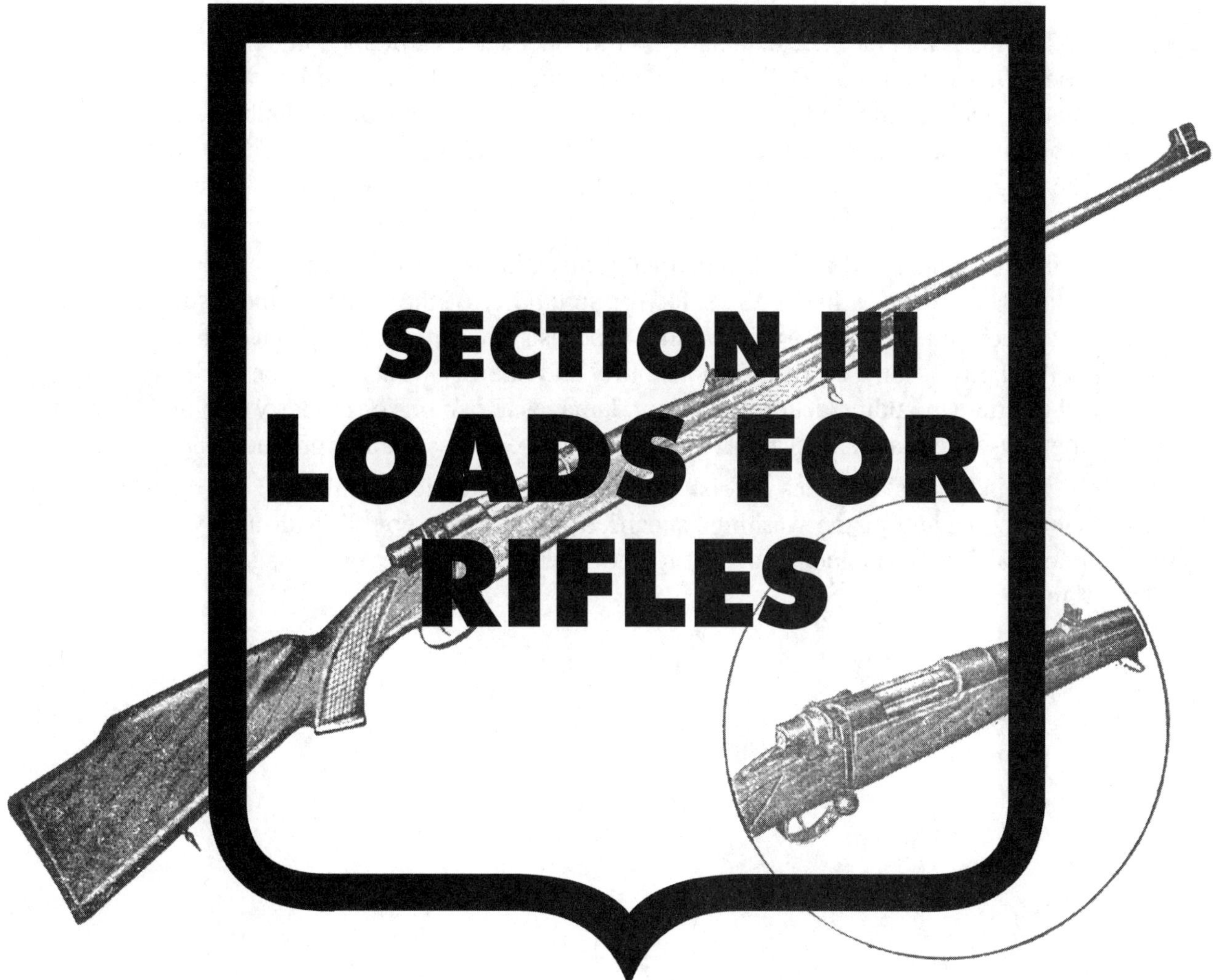

SECTION III LOADS FOR RIFLES

WARNING

The loads and ballistic data shown in this book were obtained under strictly controlled conditions. Ballistic data vary considerably depending on many factors, including components used, how such components are assembled, the type and condition of the firearm used, and the reloading techniques. Therefore, the loads listed are not for inexperienced persons; safety precautions must be considered and utilized at all times.

The publisher and authors specifically disclaim any warranties with respect to any and all loads listed, the safety or suitability of the loads, or the results obtained with the listed loads. Readers and users of any load or product listed in this book assume all risk, responsibility and liability whatsoever for any and all injuries (including death), losses, or damages to persons or property (including consequential damages), arising from the use of any load or product.

The individual assumes the risk of safe loading practices. Failure to do so or violation of any of the warnings specified in this book could result in severe personal injury (including death) to the user or bystander or damage to the firearm.

Chapter 12

How To Reload Rifle Cartridges

Reloading centerfire rifle cartridges involves the following basic steps:

- Clean and inspect the cases
- Lubricate the cases
- Resize and decap the cases
- Prime the cases
- Fill cases with proper amount and type of powder
- Seat the bullet and crimp if necessary

Note that these steps are very similar to the ones described for reloading handgun cartridges.

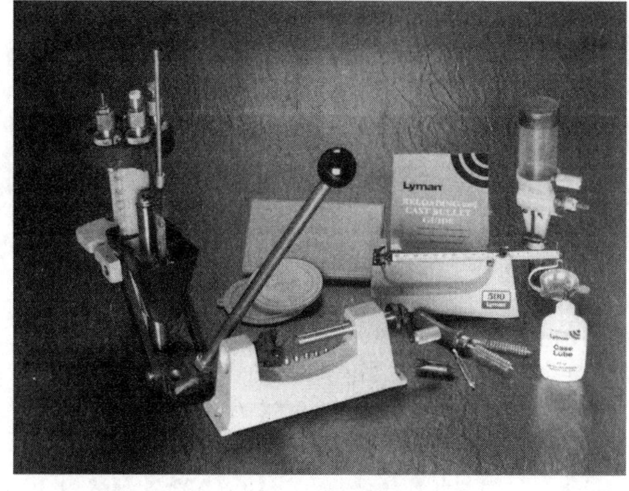

Figure 12-1: Basic set of reloading tools.

RELOADING EQUIPMENT

A basic set of reloading tools, as shown in Figure 12-1, is all that is required to produce quality reloads. The reloading dies are the key tools to reloading in this set and should be of the finest possible quality. Dies are designed to:

- Resize the fired case
- Eject the fired primer
- Seat the bullet

A two-die set is designed for reloading bottle-neck type cases only. One die is called a *sizer die*. It resizes the fired case to its approximate original dimensions, ejects the fired primer, and expands the neck of the case to receive the bullet. The second die, called the *seater die*, is used to seat the bullet and, when required or desired, to crimp the case neck around the bullet. Dies are screwed into the

Figure 12-2: The reloading press performs the major tasks when reloading rifle cartridges.

top of the reloading press, as illustrated in Figure 12-2.

When reloading straight-wall type rifle and pistol cases, a three-die set is normally used as shown in Figure 12-3. The first die is the sizer die and is used to resize the fired case down to its approximate original dimensions. The second die, the expander-decapping die, ejects the fired primer and slightly expands the case mouth to receive the bullet. In some brands of three-die sets, decapping is done in the sizer die. The third die, the seater die, seats and crimps the bullet.

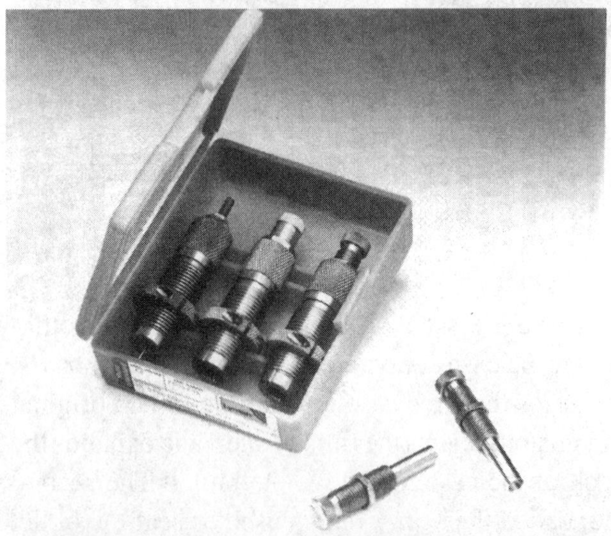

Figure 12-3: A three-die set is used for straight-wall type rifle cases.

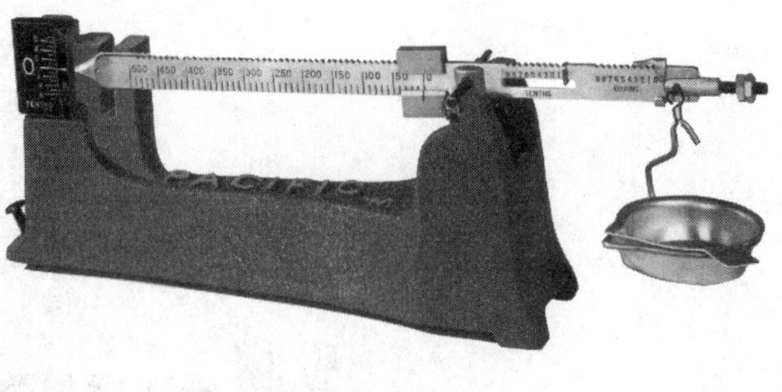

Figure 12-4: A good powder scale should be accurate, dependable, and easy to use.

Reloading Scale: The scale, shown in Figure 12-4, is used to accurately weigh powder charges. A good scale should be accurate, dependable, and easy to use. Inexpensive powder measures may be used if moderate and reduced loads are used. However, if the reloader is loading near maximum, a powder scale is recommended to ensure safety.

Powder Measure: With a good powder measure (Figure 12-5) it is necessary to weigh only the first

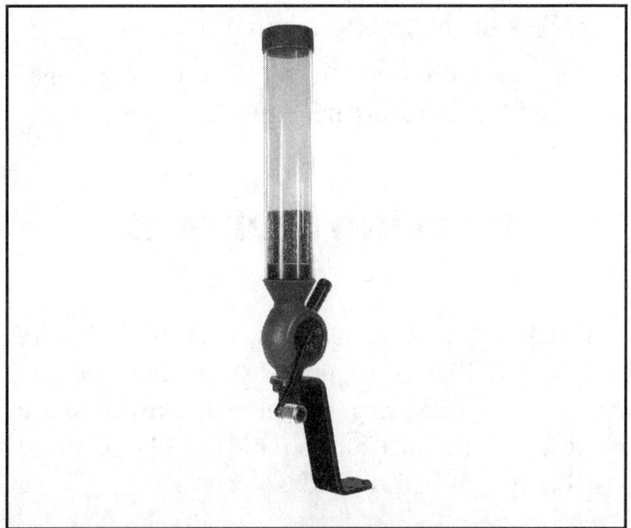

Figure 12-5: A powder measure will facilitate loading when many cartridges are involved.

Figure 12-6: A powder funnel is a handy device when loading cartridges directly from the powder pan to the case.

charge on the scale, thus eliminating the need to weigh powder for each case. The measure then performs two powder-charging tasks in one fast, simple operation: it throws consistently accurate charges, within a fraction of a grain, and swiftly dispenses powder directly into the cartridge case.

Powder Funnel: When powder charging involves just a few cases, powder can be poured from the powder pan through a plastic funnel (Figure 12-6) and into the cases without spilling.

Case Lube Kit: A good case lube kit will include a case lube pad, resizing lubricant (Figure 12-7), and a case neck brush for proper lubrication of cases before resizing.

Burring Tool: This tool removes burrs and bevels case mouths, inside and out, for ease of bullet seating.

Figure 12-7: A good case lubricant is absolutely necessary when resizing all cases.

Brass Cases, Primers, Powder, and Bullets: These components are necessary for reloading and are used in conjunction with the reloading tools.

A Place to Reload: The type of work bench for reloading will depend primarily upon the type of reloading press. Some presses put tremendous stress on the bench. Others, however, require no more than a sturdy table or a simple bench.

CLEAN AND INSPECT THE CASES

Cases that have been fired must be wiped clean with a cloth immediately to prevent dirt scratches. This will also extend the life of the cases and dies. Also, each case must be inspected for flaws before reloading. See Figure 12-8 on the next page.

In some instances, if cases have been in storage for a while or subjected to harsh climates, polishing may be required before a thorough inspection may be made, due to discoloration or corrosion. A case-cleaning compound may be used to quickly "polish" rifle cases, or else they may be polished using the tumbler process as described for reloading handgun cartridges in Chapter 8 — this latter process taking several hours to accomplish.

*Inspect Necks for Cracks and Splits:*The most common flaws in fired cases are cracked or split necks. Sometimes these flaws are hard to see with the naked eye, so the inside and the outside of case necks should be carefully examined with a magnifying glass. Even a tiny crack in the case neck means that the case won't hold a bullet tightly, and such cases must be discarded. Cases fired just once seldom show signs of neck splits, but after many firings they begin to appear. Much depends upon the age of the brass case, its heat treatment, the pressure in the chamber, and the chamber neck diameter of the gun in which the cases are fired.

Inspect for Head Separation: Another thing to look for is partial head separations, which usually occur about 1/4" above the case head. A head separation, though rare, is very dangerous. Unlike a cracked neck, which allows only powder gas to

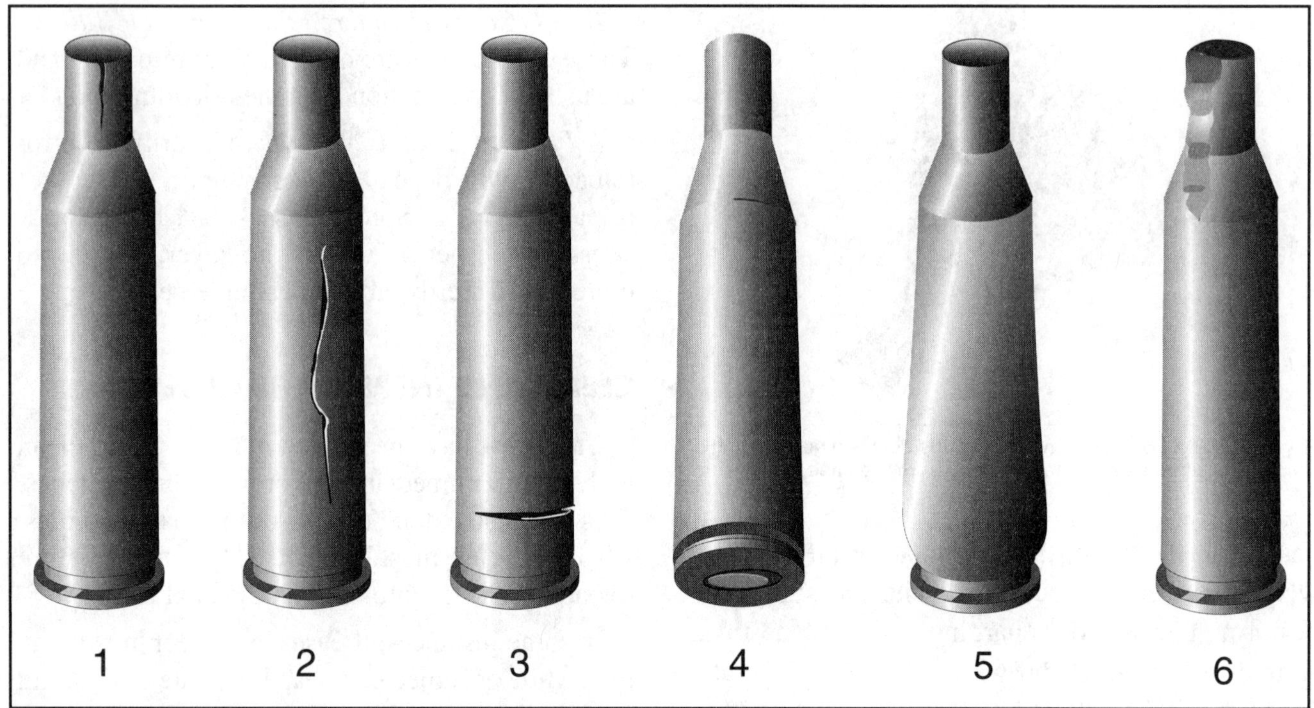

Figure 12-8: Items to look for when inspecting rifle cases prior to reloading: (1) split necks; (2) cracked cases; (3) head separation; (4) deformed or enlarged primer pockets; (5) excessive case bulges; (6) wrinkled cases.

escape at the front of the chamber, a separated head may let this gas leak out into the gun action, causing damage to the gun and possible injury to the shooter. A head separation may be due to extreme pressures, a defect in the gun, poor brass, or old brass that has been fired too often. It may also be due to a poorly made reloading press or die, or a misfit between the die and the gun chamber.

Inspect Overall Length: Besides freedom from flaws, cases should be inspected for overall length. If the case neck is too long, it will project into the throat of the barrel, squeezing the bullet between it and the rifling, causing a dangerous rise in pressure. Cases must be the same overall length to allow for bullet crimping.

Measuring Case Length: Case length gauges can be used for this, but the RCBS Trim Die performs two jobs: it can be used to check case length; and it provides an efficient way to trim those that are too long. To use the trim die, screw it into the press until the shell holder touches the bottom of the die when the ram is at the top of its stroke. Then place a case in the shell holder and run it into the die. If the case neck sticks out above the top of the die, file it off with a smooth-cut file.

Calipers (Figure 12-9) may also be used for measuring case lengths. All cases should be held within a few thousandths of an inch to obtain uniform reloads. If too long, the cases will not

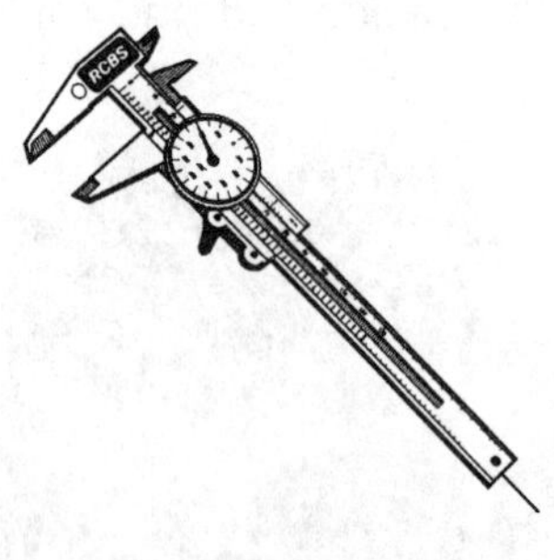

Figure 12-9: Any number of methods may be used to check the length of rifle cases, but many reloaders prefer inexpensive dial calipers for the measurement.

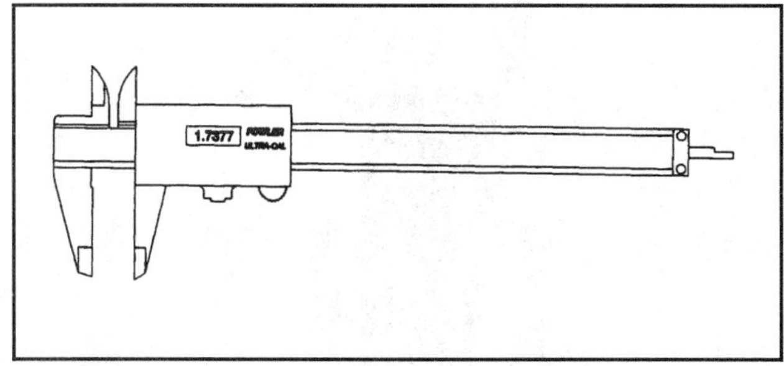

Figure 12-10: Electronic caliper.

chamber correctly and can cause excessive breech pressures. If too short, the bullet crimps will not be uniform.

Many reloaders are now using electronic calipers that offer the advantage of direct reading of each measurement, plus an automatic conversion button to change from English to metric. One such instrument is the Fowler Ultra-Cal electronic caliper shown in Figure 12-10. This instrument reads to .0005 inch or .01 mm easily, even in dim light, which ensures accuracy. The inch/metric reading feature permits immediate change to the standard preferred by the user. The floating zero feature allows one to "zero" instantly at any position, permitting the reading of deviations from the nominal size without performing any math.

Bevel and Deburr the Case: For easier resizing and bullet seating, the mouths of all cases should be chamfered (beveled). All trimmed cases should be deburred. To chamfer, insert the pointed end of a burring tool into the case mouth and twist slightly without making a knife-edge. To remove burrs left by trimming, place the other end of the tool over the case mouth and twist. See Figure 12-11. You are now ready to lubricate the case.

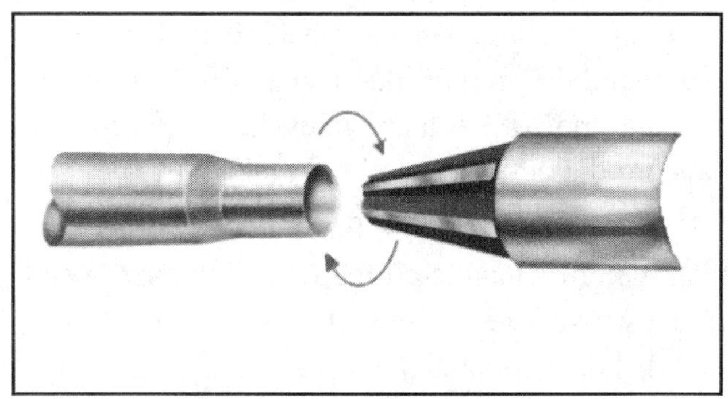

Figure 12-11: Chamfering the inside case mouth.

LUBRICATE THE CASE

Lubricating cases before reloading is a vitally important step that should never be overlooked if you want to avoid unnecessary resizing problems. Many reloaders neglect case lubrication, mainly because it is so simple, it doesn't seem important.

To lubricate cases properly, first start with a proper lubricant. Ordinary oils don't have enough body to stay on the case where needed; others have too much body or are too gummy. RCBS, Lyman and others have developed a special resizing lubricant for this purpose. A 2 oz. tube will lubricate hundreds of cases. To use, spread the lubricant evenly over the case-lube pad, then rub it in until the oil is no longer standing on the pad surface.

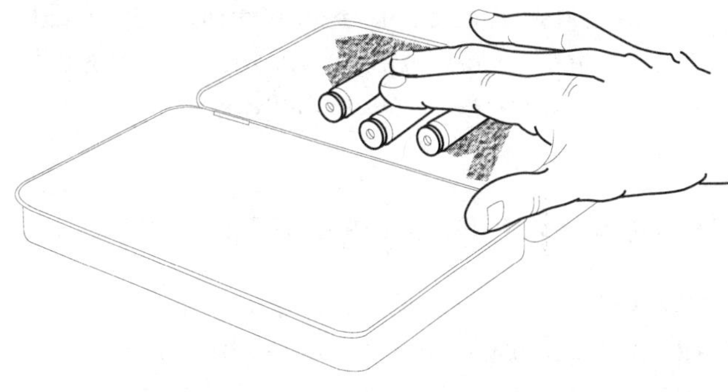

Figure 12-12: Lubricating the rifle cases.

Lubrication is needed mainly on the body of the case, about ½″ – ¾″ from the base, as shown in Figure 12-12. To lube a case, roll it lightly across the pad, using your fingers to lubricate the case neck with lubricant picked up from the pad. It is vitally important that you lubricate the case evenly, without lubricating the shoulder of the case. A properly lubed case should feel, but not look, oily. If you overlubricate the case, oil will be trapped between the case and reloading die, causing oil

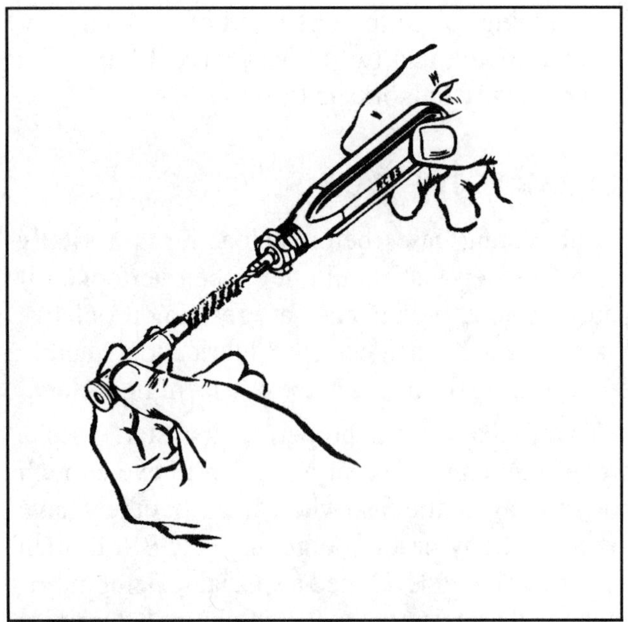

Figure 12-13: Lubricating the inside case neck.

dents when the case is sized. Under lubrication, however, may cause the base portion of the case to stick in the die. Stuck-case removers may be used to remove it. The use of properly lubricated, good brass cases can prevent such sticking.

LUBRICATE INSIDES OF CASE NECKS

The next step — seldom mentioned in reloading books and articles — is lubricating the inside of the case neck, as shown in Figure 12-13. This prevents the case from dragging in the die when the neck is expanded after sizing.

Equally important, lubricating the inside of the case neck removes the gritty primer and burned powder residue from the neck. The RCBS Case Neck Brush is ideal for lubricating the insides of the case necks. Roll the brush lightly across the lube pad so that it picks up only a trace of lubricant. After brushing out three or four necks, relubricate the brush. This helps to get rid of the grit and prevent getting too much lube inside the case neck. The case is now properly lubricated and ready to be resized and decapped.

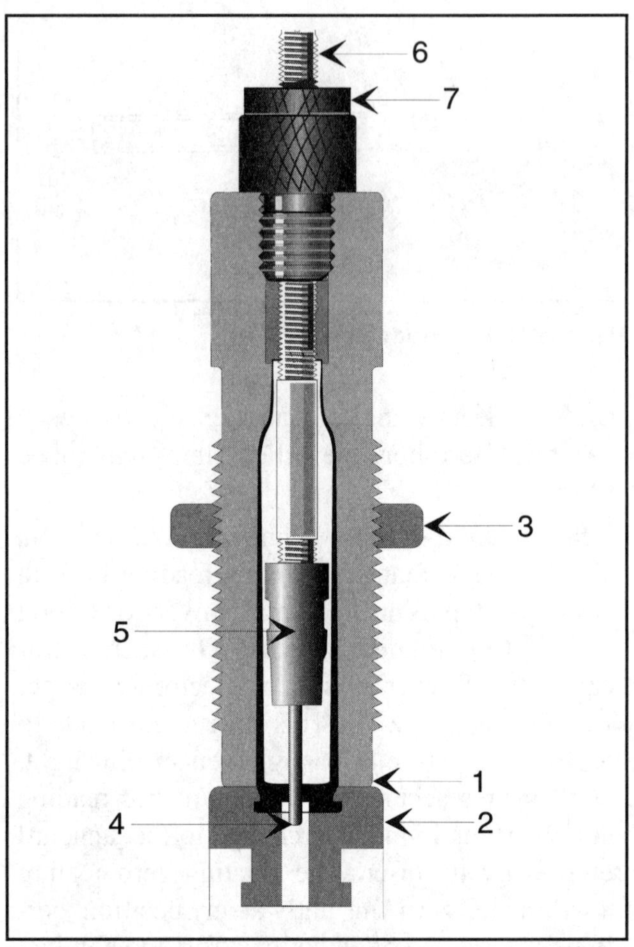

Figure 12-14: Resizing and decapping the case.

RESIZE AND DECAP THE CASE

When a cartridge is fired, the brass case containing the powder expands to the dimension of the rifle chamber. Before reloading, the fired case must be resized to its approximate original dimensions to make sure it fits the gun chamber. Also, because all rifle chambers are not identical, cases fired in one rifle may not fit another, unless it is resized to a standard diameter acceptable in all rifles.

Refer to Figure 12-14. For full-length resizing, push the press handle all the way down to the end of its stroke; then screw the sizer die into the threaded die station at the top of the press until the bottom of the die (1) firmly touches the shell holder (2). Now, raise the press handle very slightly, screw the sizer die down approximately one-eighth of a turn, and set the large lock ring (3). The bottom of the expander ball (5) should be $^3/_{16}''$ inside the die, and the decapping pin (4) should extend $^1/_8''$ out of the die just enough to knock the fired primer out of the case. If the pin extends too far out of the die, the expander ball will strike the inside bottom of the case and bend the rod. The decapping pin (4) and expander ball of the die shown (5) are adjusted by turning the expander-decapping rod (7), and locked in place by tightening the lock ring (7). Dies manufactured by others may adjust differently. Refer to the instructions that came with the dies that you use.

NOTE

Some groups of shooters maintain that neck resizing only is easier on the case, and that more accurate loads will result if the case is neck resized only. Some shooters, seeking the highest degree of accuracy, even go so far as to index their cartridges so they fall back into the chamber exactly as they were fired initially. Each individual reloader has the capabilities to determine which method is best. Testing your loads in your rifle is the answer.

When the sizer die is properly adjusted, insert a lubricated case into the shell holder and slowly push the press handle down. As the case is forced up into the die, the case will be resized and the fired primer will be knocked out.

PRIME THE CASE

If commercial cases rather than military cases are used, the case can be primed as it is withdrawn from the sizer die. Before doing this, make sure you have the correct size primer plug and sleeve in the primer arm.

With the case still in the sizer die insert a primer — anvil up — in the primer arm sleeve, then push the primer arm all the way into the slot of the shell holder arm. Now gently raise the press handle to lower the case onto the primer, seating it to the bottom of the primer pocket. See Figure 12-15. It should seat easily; if not, remove the case and see if the primer is nicked or dented. If so, discard the case. Primer pockets should be cleaned out regularly with a primer-pocket cleaner or a knife, being careful not to scratch the surface.

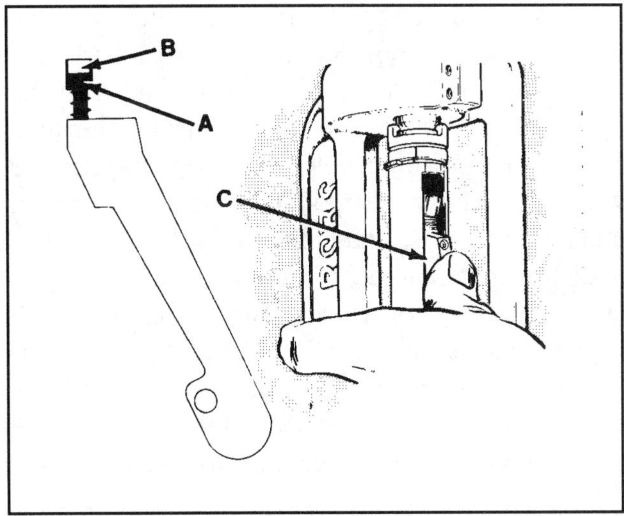

Figure 12-15: Seating the new primer.

After the primer is seated, lower the press handle just enough to let the primer arm snap out of the slot. If it is lowered too far, the decapping pin in the die will punch the new primer back out. Next raise the handle and remove the case from the shell holder. Do not leave a case fully inserted into a die for extended periods of time, since pressure may build up on the case sides, making it difficult to remove from the die. To prevent this, withdraw the case at least $^1/_2''$ out of the die.

Do not try to force a case that does not go into the die fairly easily. Excessive force may cause the case to stick in the die. This can be caused by a case that may not have been properly lubricated or by using the wrong die.

THE POWDER CHARGE

After priming, the case is ready for the powder. To determine the weight of the powder charge, consult reloading data such as found in Chapters 13, 14, 15, and 16 (for rifle cartridges) and use the recommended charges with caution. Start with the lowest suggested powder charge in the charts and work up. For example: load six rounds with the light charge; a couple with the medium charge; then if you want maximum velocity, load a couple more with the maximum charge. To identify each charge, mark the case base and bullet tips with nail polish, once for light charges, twice for medium charges, and three times for heavy charges. Test-fire each load in that order. Usually, a charge a bit under maximum will give nearly the same velocity as maximum, with considerably better case and barrel life, and perhaps better accuracy as well.

The weight of the bullet is just as important as the powder charge. The heavier the bullet, the more resistance there is to the expansion of the powder gases. Therefore, a maximum charge with a 150-grain bullet will be dangerously high with a 180-grain bullet. When loading to the limit, even such things as the bullet's core and jacket hardness, or the length of it that bears on the rifling make a difference — another reason for staying under the maximum.

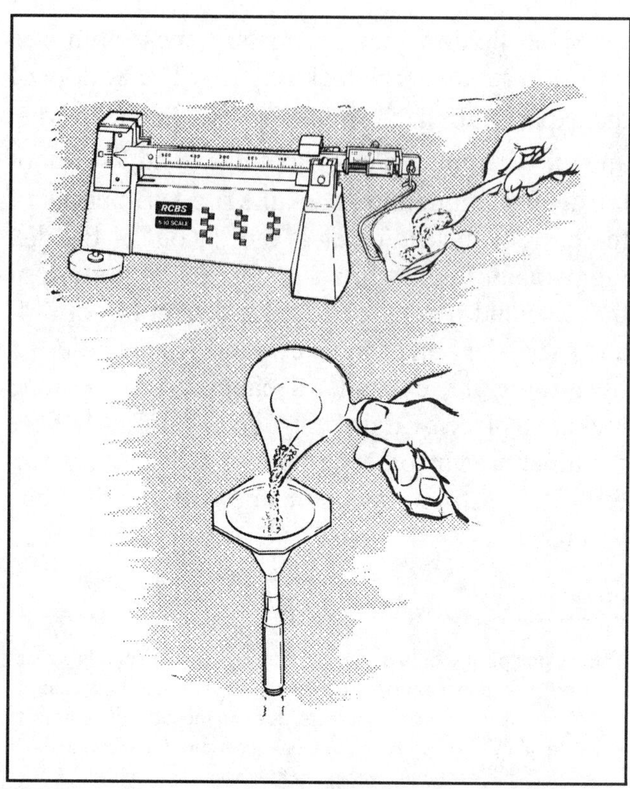

Figure 12-16: Using a powder scale and funnel to charge cases with powder.

LOADING THE POWDER CHARGE

The first step in loading the powder charge is to decide whether to throw your charges with a powder measure or to weigh them individually on a scale. This latter operation is shown in Figure 12-16. A measure is much faster and easier to use than a scale, but a scale is necessary to set the measure.

Use the instructions accompanying the powder measure to adjust the measure to throw the approximate powder charge required. Throw a sample charge in the powder-scale pan and weigh it. Make the necessary adjustments (up or down) to the powder measure and try another sample charge. Continue these steps until the charge is correct.

It is necessary to be systematic in charging cases to get only one charge of powder in each case. Most reloaders either make or buy a reloading block to hold and keep track of charged cases. Place uncharged cases on the left side of the block; then as they are charged with powder, put them in the holes on the right side of the block. After all of your cases are charged, look into each one to make sure that each case has only one powder charge.

SEAT THE BULLET

After the cases are charged, the bullets can be seated. To start this operation, unscrew the sizer die from the press and push the press handle down as far as it will go. Then screw the seater die into the press until it touches the shell holder. Now unscrew the die ¾ to a full turn and set the large lock ring. Test one round to make certain the bullet is seated in the cartridge case at the desired depth. If not, make the necessary adjustments before continuing. This will adjust the die to seat bullets without crimping them.

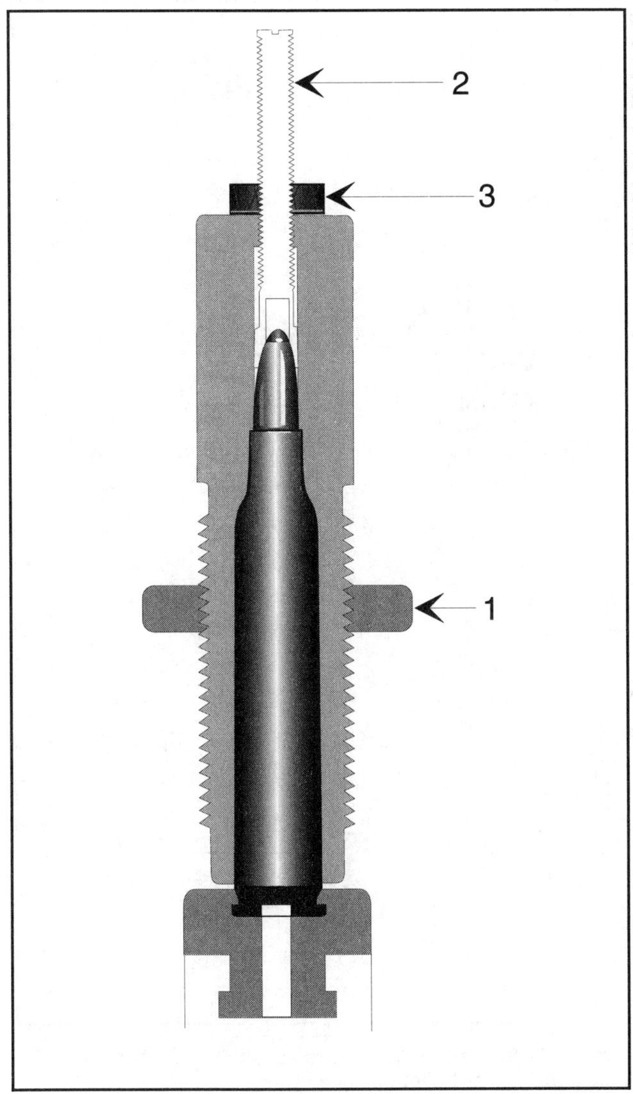

Figure 12-17: Seating die used to seat bullet in rifle case.

ADJUSTING FOR BULLET SEATING DEPTH

Once the bullet has been seated, the seating depth must be determined. See Figure 12-17. To determine the seating depth, first unscrew the seater plug (2) so it will not touch the bullet before the case is all the way into the die. Then insert a charged cartridge into the shell holder and place a bullet into the mouth of the case. Lower the press handle to run the case and bullet up into the die. Now screw the seater plug down until you feel it touch the bullet. Lower the case and screw the die in until the bullet is seated. If the bullet is not seated deeply enough, continue to screw down the seater plug until the desired depth is reached. Tighten the small lock ring (3).

If the bullet is not seated deeply enough, it can be adjusted. However, if it is seated too deeply on the first try, it may be hard to get back out of the case. If this happens, a bullet puller may be required to remove it. Always adjust the seater plug for minimum depth. It may help to remember that since the plug has 28 threads to the inch (on RCBS dies), screwing it down one turn will seat the bullet 1/28-inch deeper.

This raises the question of what seating depth is "right" for a particular bullet and cartridge. The rule-of-thumb is to seat the base of the bullet even with the bottom of the case neck. However, if custom bullets are used — ones that may be longer than standard — the bullets may have to be seated deeper into the case. The majority of the loads listed in this book gives the maximum overall length for each cartridge. This maximum length should not be exceeded.

On the other hand, if extremely short bullets are used in rifle cases, seating the bullet to the bottom of the case neck will be too much. For example, if a 77-grain lead bullet is used in, say, the .30-30 cartridge for a reduced small-game load, the bullet would almost be out of sight.

Another rule-of-thumb in these two instances would be to seat the bullet so that it does not exceed the maximum recommended length, feeds through the magazine easily, does not touch the barrel rifling (except in some rare cases) and looks like a loaded rifle cartridge.

BULLET CRIMPING

Jacketed bullets for most centerfire rifles do not need crimping except for cartridges used in tubular magazine rifles and the very heavy calibers from about .375 H&H magnum on up.

A bullet cannot be crimped satisfactorily unless the bullet has a crimping groove (cannelure). Cast bullets will always have this groove, but it is seldom found on jacketed bullets except those intended for tubular magazine rifles or heavy magnum rifles.

When bullets are intended to be crimped, all cases must be trimmed to exactly the same length; otherwise some cases will receive too much crimp and others not enough, or perhaps none at all. This means that the shortest case in the group must be found and then trim all others to match it.

To set the seating die for crimping, adjust the die just as before and refer to Figure 12-18. Unscrew the die out of the press about one turn so that the crimper in the die will not touch the case mouth (4 in Figure 12-18). Place a bullet in the charged case and run it into the die and back out again. Examine the seated depth of the bullet to make sure the case mouth comes to the middle of the crimping groove (cannelure) on the bullet. If not, make adjustments to the seater plug (2). When adjusted to seat the bullet properly, back out the seating plug one or two turns and then screw the entire die down gradually until it gives the desired crimp. Examine both the seating depth and crimp of the bullet carefully to see that both are exactly as wanted. If so, set the large lock ring (1).

The final step is to screw the seater plug (2) back down until the contact of the bullet is felt, then lock the large die ring (3). After this final adjustment, bullets may be seated and crimped in one operation.

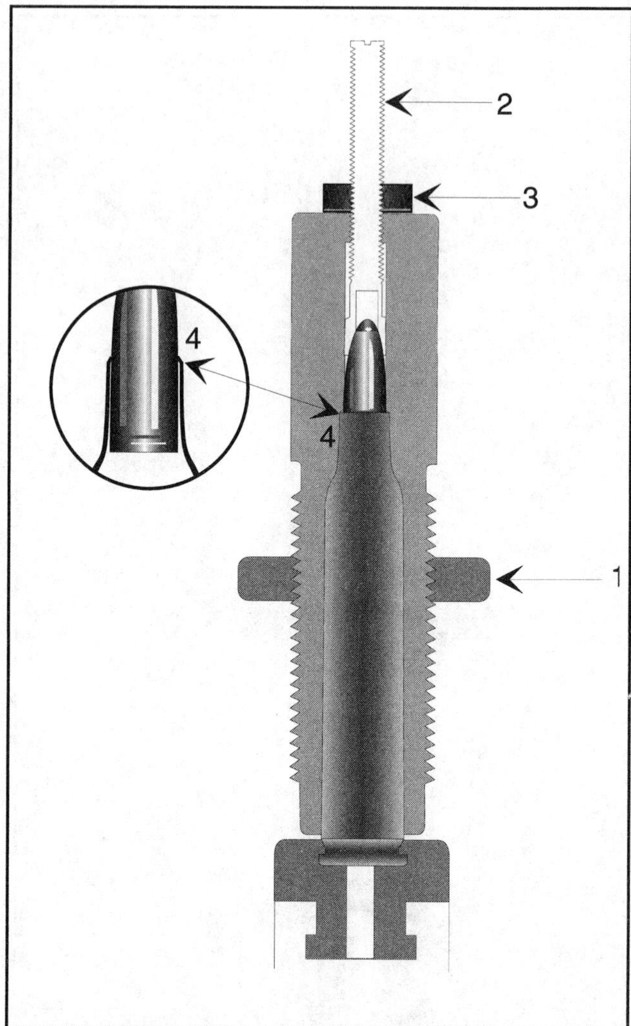

Figure 12-18: Seating die used to seat bullet in rifle case and also to crimp the bullet in place.

After seating (and crimping, if necessary) the trial bullet to the correct depth, the remaining cartridges may be loaded, using the same techniques described for the trial cartridge. They are then ready to fire.

Chapter 13

Loads for Modern Rifle Cartridges

Anyone who looks at a current ammunition catalog will be astonished at the vast array of different rifle cartridges available. If a complete list of all cartridges introduced since the invention of the metallic cartridge case were compiled, the reader would be absolutely amazed.

The birth of reloading began with the development of the centerfire metallic rifle cartridge in the 1800s. Almost immediately thereafter, reloading tools and cartridge components (powder, primers, and bullets) became readily available to shooters. In fact, in some rural areas, the components for "rolling your own" were more obtainable than the cartridges themselves. Gun manufacturers also began offering reloading tools to match cartridges used in their firearms. At one time, some gun manufacturers included a set of reloading tools packed in the same carton with the rifle.

Loads in this chapter are restricted to the most popular centerfire rifle cartridges with calibers designated in thousandths of an inch. Loads for metric cartridges are found in Chapter 14, while loads for obsoletecartridges are listed in Chapter 15. You will also find loads for a few wildcat cartridges in Chapter 16.

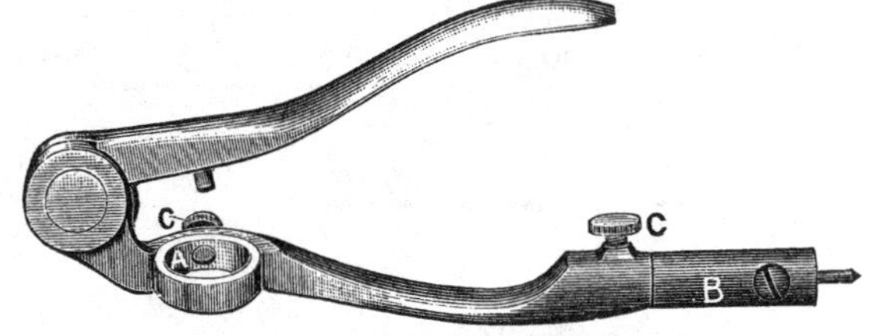

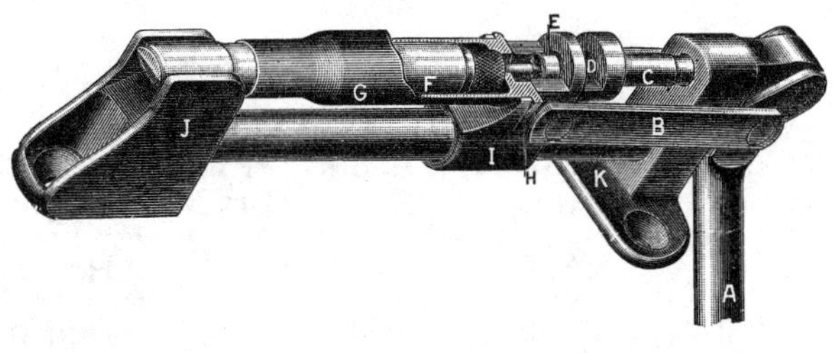

Figure 13-1: Early reloading tools that were produced at the beginning of the 20th century.

.17 REMINGTON

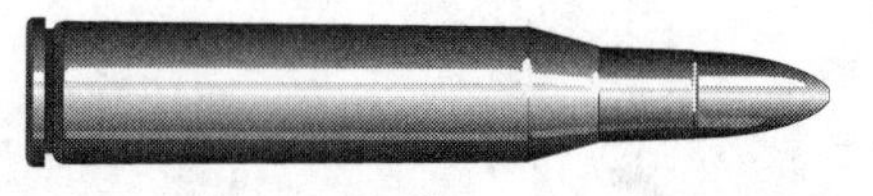

SPECIFICATIONS

Dia. of Rim — .378″
Dia. of Base — .377″
Dia. of Shoulder — .356″
Dia. of Neck — .199″
Length of Neck — .260″
Angle of Shoulder — 23°

Dia. Jacketed Bullet — .172″
Dia. Cast Bullet — .175″
Length of Case — 1.80″
Max. Overall Length — 2.17″
Primer Size — Small Rifle
Water Capacity — 27.23 grs.

25-grain Softnose

POWDER MFGR.	POWDER TYPE	GRAINS	PRIMER TYPE	PRIMER MFGR.	VELOCITY	PRESSURE (C.U.P.)	REMARKS
IMR	3031	22.5	7½	Remington	4000	52000	
IMR	4064	22.5	205	Federal	3850	—	
IMR	4198	19.0	205	Federal	3800	—	
IMR	4320	23.0	205	Federal	3700	—	
IMR	4320	25.0	7½	Remington	3975	51300	
IMR	4895	23.5	7½	Remington	3995	51400	
IMR	4350	24.5	7½	Remington	3570	39000	
IMR	4831	24.8	7½	Remington	3300	32500	
Winchester	748	22.0	7½	Remington	3750	—	
Winchester	760	26.8	7½	Remington	4000	—	
Winchester	785	27.5	7½	Remington	3700	—	
Hodgdon	H380	23.0	7½	Remington	3700	—	

.218 BEE

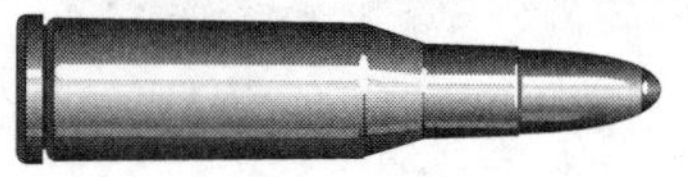

SPECIFICATIONS

Dia. of Rim — .408″
Dia. of Base — .349″
Dia. of Shoulder — .330″
Dia. of Neck — .242″
Length of Neck — .200″
Angle of Shoulder — 15°

Dia. Jacketed Bullet — .224″
Dia. Cast Bullet — .223″
Length of Case — 1.28″
Max. Overall Length — 1.63″
Primer Size — Small Rifle
Water Capacity — 17.07 grs.

50-grain Softnose

POWDER MFGR.	POWDER TYPE	GRAINS	PRIMER TYPE	PRIMER MFGR.	VELOCITY	PRESSURE (C.U.P.)	REMARKS
IMR	4198	14.0	7½	Remington	2460	—	
IMR	4198	13.8	7½	Remington	2422	—	
IMR	4198	13.5	7½	Remington	2350	—	
Hercules	2400	11.0	7½	Remington	2450	—	
Hercules	2400	10.8	7½	Remington	2340	—	

.22 HORNET

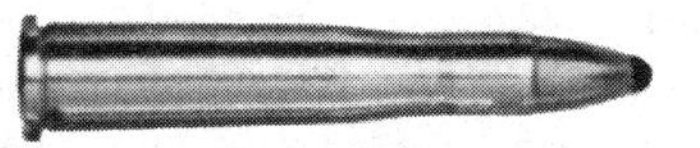

SPECIFICATIONS

Dia. of Rim — .350″
Dia. of Base — .299″
Dia. of Shoulder — .278″
Dia. of Neck — .244″
Length of Neck — .323″
Angle of Shoulder — 5.3°

Dia. Jacketed Bullet — .224″
Dia. Cast Bullet — .226″
Length of Case — 1.40″
Max. Overall Length — 1.80″
Primer Size — Small Rifle
Water Capacity — 13.27 grs.

45-grain Softnose

POWDER MFGR.	POWDER TYPE	GRAINS	PRIMER TYPE	PRIMER MFGR.	VELOCITY	PRESSURE (C.U.P.)	REMARKS
Hercules	2400	10.0	7½	Remington	2470	—	
Hercules	2400	9.0	7½	Remington	2290	—	
Hercules	2400	8.0	7½	Remington	1955	—	
IMR	4759	8.2	7½	Remington	2140	—	
IMR	4759	7.9	7½	Remington	2100	—	
IMR	4759	7.5	7½	Remington	1855	—	
Hodgdon	H4227	11.0	7½	Remington	2440	—	
Hodgdon	H4227	10.0	7½	Remington	2280	—	
Hodgdon	H4227	9.0	7½	Remington	2135	—	
Hodgdon	H414	44.0	7½	Remington	4100	—	

50-grain Softnose

POWDER MFGR.	POWDER TYPE	GRAINS	PRIMER TYPE	PRIMER MFGR.	VELOCITY	PRESSURE (C.U.P.)	REMARKS
Hercules	2400	9.5	7½	Remington	2315	—	
Hercules	2400	8.5	7½	Remington	2060	—	
Hercules	2400	7.5	7½	Remington	1815	—	
IMR	4759	8.2	7½	Remington	2025	—	
IMR	4759	7.8	7½	Remington	1925	—	
IMR	4759	7.3	7½	Remington	1835	—	
Hodgdon	H4227	10.5	7½	Remington	2375	—	
Hodgdon	H4227	9.8	7½	Remington	2255	—	
Hodgdon	H4227	9.0	7½	Remington	1835	—	

.220 SWIFT

SPECIFICATIONS

Dia. of Rim — .473″
Dia. of Base — .445″
Dia. of Shoulder — .402″
Dia. of Neck — .260″
Length of Neck — .300″
Angle of Shoulder — 21.20°
Dia. Jacketed Bullet — .224″
Dia. Cast Bullet — .224″
Length of Case — 2.205″
Max. Overall Length — 2.35″
Primer Size — Large Rifle
Water Capacity — 46.25 grs.

40-grain Softnose

POWDER MFGR.	POWDER TYPE	GRAINS	PRIMER TYPE	PRIMER MFGR.	VELOCITY	PRESSURE (C.U.P.)	REMARKS
IMR	3031	35.0	210	Federal	3850	—	
IMR	3031	37.5	210	Federal	4000	—	
IMR	4064	37.0	9½	Remington	3900	—	
IMR	4064	38.5	9½	Remington	4000	—	
IMR	4320	37.0	9½	Remington	3800	—	
IMR	4320	40.0	9½	Remington	4100	—	Caution: Max.
IMR	4895	35.0	9½	Remington	3700	—	
IMR	4895	38.0	9½	Remington	3995	50,800	
Hodgdon	H4895	39.0	9½	Remington	4010	—	
Hodgdon	H380	40.0	9½	Remington	3825	—	

45-grain Softnose

POWDER MFGR.	POWDER TYPE	GRAINS	PRIMER TYPE	PRIMER MFGR.	VELOCITY	PRESSURE (C.U.P.)	REMARKS
IMR	3031	35.0	210	Federal	3700	—	
IMR	3031	37.0	210	Federal	3950	52,000	
IMR	4064	36.0	9½	Remington	3600	—	
IMR	4064	38.0	9½	Remington	3900	—	
IMR	4320	36.0	9½	Remington	3650	—	
IMR	4320	38.0	9½	Remington	3900	50,100	
IMR	4895	36.0	9½	Remington	3700	—	
IMR	4895	38.0	9½	Remington	3950	52,000	
Hodgdon	H4895	39.0	9½	Remington	3900	51,400	
Hodgdon	H380	40.0	9½	Remington	3725	—	
Hodgdon	H380	43.0	210	Federal	4000	51,800	
Hodgdon	H414	42.0	9½	Remington	3925	49,000	
Hodgdon	H414	44.0	210	Federal	4100	—	

.222 REMINGTON

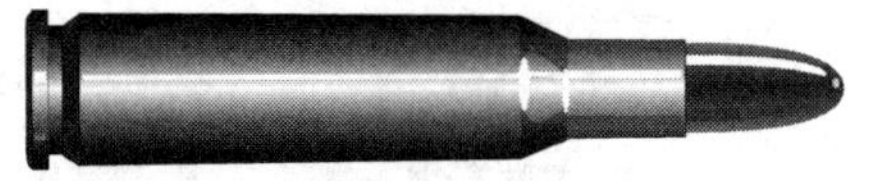

SPECIFICATIONS

Dia. of Rim — .378″
Dia. of Base — ..375″
Dia. of Shoulder — .357″
Dia. of Neck — .253″
Length of Neck — .313″
Angle of Shoulder — 22.14°

Dia. Jacketed Bullet — .224″
Dia. Cast Bullet — .224″
Length of Case — 1.700″
Max. Overall Length — 2.20″
Primer Size — Small Rifle
Water Capacity — 26.19 grs.

40-grain Softnose

POWDER MFGR.	POWDER TYPE	GRAINS	PRIMER TYPE	PRIMER MFGR.	VELOCITY	PRESSURE (C.U.P.)	REMARKS
IMR	3031	22.0	205	Federal	3300	—	
IMR	3031	24.0	7½	Remington	3350	47,000	
IMR	4064	22.0	7½	Remington	2900	27,000	
IMR	4064	24.0	7½	Remington	3250	44,000	
IMR	4320	24.0	7½	Remington	3175	39,000	
IMR	4895	22.0	7½	Remington	3000	27,900	
IMR	4895	24.0	7½	Remington	3300	46,000	
Hodgdon	H380	26.0	7½	Remington	3000	—	
Hodgdon	H4227	14.0	7½	Remington	3000	—	
Hodgdon	H335	22.0	210	Federal	2900	25,000	
Winchester	W748	27.0	7½	Remington	3400	—	

45-grain Softnose

POWDER MFGR.	POWDER TYPE	GRAINS	PRIMER TYPE	PRIMER MFGR.	VELOCITY	PRESSURE (C.U.P.)	REMARKS
IMR	3031	21.0	7½	Remington	3000	—	
IMR	3031	23.0	7½	Remington	3250	47500	
IMR	4064	23.5	7½	Remington	3050	33000	
IMR	4320	25.0	7½	Remington	3275	—	
IMR	4895	22.0	7½	Remington	3000	31000	
IMR	4895	24.5	7½	Remington	3225	—	
Hodgdon	H380	24.0	7½	Remington	2700	—	
Hodgdon	H380	26.0	7½	Remington	2800	—	
Hodgdon	H4198	19.0	7½	Remington	3175	—	
Hodgdon	H4198	20.0	210	Federal	3340	—	
Winchester	W748	23.0	7½	Remington	3050	—	

.222 REMINGTON (Cont.)

50-grain Softnose

POWDER MFGR.	POWDER TYPE	GRAINS	PRIMER TYPE	PRIMER MFGR.	VELOCITY	PRESSURE (C.U.P.)	REMARKS
IMR	3031	20.0	7½	Remington	2850	—	
IMR	3031	23.0	7½	Remington	3100	—	
IMR	4064	21.0	7½	Remington	2650	33,000	
IMR	4064	23.0	205	Federal	2800	37,000	
IMR	4320	23.0	7½	Remington	2700	33,500	
IMR	4320	25.5	7½	Remington	3000	41,500	
IMR	4895	22.0	7½	Remington	2800	32,800	
IMR	4895	24.0	7½	Remington	3075	—	
Hodgdon	H380	25.0	7½	Remington	2875	—	
Hodgdon	H335	23.0	7½	Remington	3075	46,000	
Hodgdon	H322	21.5	7½	Remington	3000	—	
Hodgdon	H4198	19.0	210	Federal	2040	44,000	
Winchester	W748	26.0	7½	Remington	3050	—	

55-grain Softnose

POWDER MFGR.	POWDER TYPE	GRAINS	PRIMER TYPE	PRIMER MFGR.	VELOCITY	PRESSURE (C.U.P.)	REMARKS
IMR	3031	23.0	7½	Remington	3000	40,200	
IMR	4064	22.5	205	Federal	2700	—	
IMR	4320	23.0	7½	Remington	2610	34500	
IMR	4320	25.0	7½	Remington	2900	—	
IMR	4895	21.0	7½	Remington	2700	—	
IMR	4895	23.0	7½	Remington	2850	—	
Hodgdon	H380	24.0	7½	Remington	2750	42,800	
Hodgdon	H335	21.0	7½	Remington	2750	44,600	
Hodgdon	H322	21.5	7½	Remington	3000	48,000	
Hodgdon	H4198	18.0	210	Federal	2900	44,000	

.222 REMINGTON MAGNUM

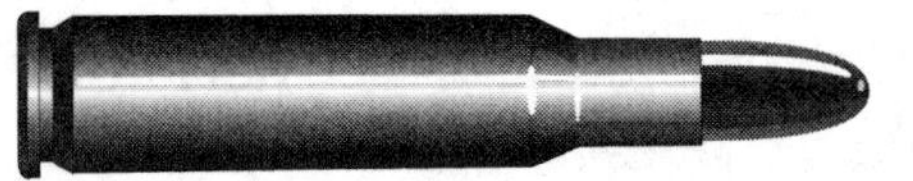

SPECIFICATIONS

Dia. of Rim — .378″	Dia. Jacketed Bullet — .224″
Dia. of Base — .375″	Dia. Cast Bullet — .224″
Dia. of Shoulder — .357″	Length of Case — 1.850″
Dia. of Neck — .253″	Max. Overall Length — 2.33″
Length of Neck — .235″	Primer Size — Small Rifle
Angle of Shoulder — 23.06°	Water Capacity — 29.84 grs.

40-grain Softpoint

POWDER MFGR.	POWDER TYPE	GRAINS	PRIMER TYPE	PRIMER MFGR.	VELOCITY	PRESSURE (C.U.P.)	REMARKS
IMR	3031	26.0	205	Federal	3500	—	
IMR	4064	26.5	7½	Remington	3300	40500	
IMR	4320	28.0	7½	Remington	3600	49000	
IMR	4895	26.0	7½	Remington	3400	—	
Hodgdon	BL-C(2)	28.0	7½	Remington	3450	—	
Hodgdon	H4895	28.0	7½	Remington	3350	—	
Hodgdon	H335	29.0	210	Federal	3650	45800	
Winchester	W748	28.5	7½	Remington	3700	—	

45-grain Softpoint

POWDER MFGR.	POWDER TYPE	GRAINS	PRIMER TYPE	PRIMER MFGR.	VELOCITY	PRESSURE (C.U.P.)	REMARKS
IMR	3031	26.0	205	Federal	3375	—	
IMR	4064	26.0	7½	Remington	3245	41600	
IMR	4320	26.0	7½	Remington	3325	35800	
IMR	4320	27.5	205	Federal	3465	47500	
IMR	4895	26.0	7½	Remington	3200	—	
IMR	4831	27.5	7½	Remington	2650	31000	
Hodgdon	BL-C(2)	26.5	7½	Remington	3375	—	
Hodgdon	BL-C(2)	25.0	7½	Remington	3050	—	
Hodgdon	H4895	27.0	7½	Remington	3350	37000	
Hodgdon	H335	27.0	210	Federal	3400	46800	
Winchester	W748	27.5	7½	Remington	3625	—	

.222 REMINGTON MAGNUM (Cont.)

50-grain Softpoint

POWDER MFGR.	POWDER TYPE	GRAINS	PRIMER TYPE	PRIMER MFGR.	VELOCITY	PRESSURE (C.U.P.)	REMARKS
IMR	3031	24.0	7½	Remington	3150	—	
IMR	3031	26.0	205	Federal	3300	48,600	
IMR	4064	25.5	7½	Remington	3300	—	
IMR	4320	24.0	7½	Remington	2925	—	
IMR	4320	25.5	205	Federal	3100	—	
IMR	4895	26.0	7½	Remington	3125	—	
IMR	4831	26.5	7½	Remington	2575	—	
Hodgdon	H4895	27.0	7½	Remington	3300	46,000	
Hodgdon	H335	27.5	210	Federal	3450	47,500	
Hodgdon	H322	25.0	7½	Remington	3300	48,000	
Winchester	W748	26.5	7½	Remington	3275	42,800	
Winchester	W760	30.5	205	Federal	3100	39,000	

55-grain Softpoint

POWDER MFGR.	POWDER TYPE	GRAINS	PRIMER TYPE	PRIMER MFGR.	VELOCITY	PRESSURE (C.U.P.)	REMARKS
IMR	3031	23.0	7½	Remington	3000	40,000	
IMR	3031	25.0	7½	Remington	3225	49,400	
IMR	4064	25.0	7½	Remington	3050	—	
IMR	4064	26.5	7½	Remington	3200	50,000	Caution: Maximum
IMR	4320	25.5	7½	Remington	2825	—	
IMR	4320	27.0	205	Federal	3100	50,200	Caution: Maximum
IMR	4895	26.0	7½	Remington	3065	—	
Hodgdon	H4895	27.0	7½	Remington	3200	47,600	
Hodgdon	H335	26.5	210	Federal	3295	43,200	
Hodgdon	H322	23.0	7½	Remington	2900	43,000	
Winchester	W760	29.0	205	Federal	3000	—	

.22-250 REMINGTON

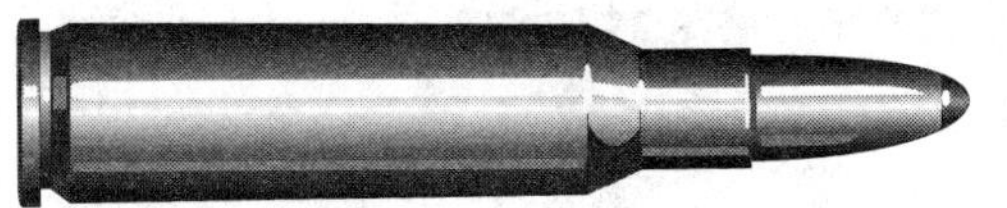

SPECIFICATIONS

Dia. of Rim — .472″
Dia. of Base — .468″
Dia. of Shoulder — .418″
Dia. of Neck — .253″
Length of Neck — .249″
Angle of Shoulder — 28°
Dia. Jacketed Bullet — .224″
Dia. Cast Bullet — .224″
Length of Case — 1.912″
Max. Overall Length — 2.35″
Primer Size — Large Rifle
Water Capacity — 44.62 grs.

40-grain Softnose

POWDER MFGR.	POWDER TYPE	GRAINS	PRIMER TYPE	PRIMER MFGR.	VELOCITY	PRESSURE (C.U.P.)	REMARKS
IMR	3031	31.0	210	Federal	3500	—	
IMR	3031	35.0	210	Federal	4000	—	Maximum
IMR	4064	36.0	9½	Remington	3700	43,200	
IMR	4064	38.5	9½	Remington	4000	50,400	
IMR	4320	35.0	9½	Remington	3700	43,500	
IMR	4320	37.0	9½	Remington	4000	51,000	
IMR	4895	35.0	9½	Remington	3750	45,000	
IMR	4895	36.5	9½	Remington	3995	49,000	
Hodgdon	H4895	34.0	9½	Remington	3750	—	
Hodgdon	H380	40.0	9½	Remington	3950	—	
Hodgdon	H414	38.5	9½	Remington	3750	—	
Hodgdon	H414	42.0	210	Federal	3975	—	

45-grain Softnose

POWDER MFGR.	POWDER TYPE	GRAINS	PRIMER TYPE	PRIMER MFGR.	VELOCITY	PRESSURE (C.U.P.)	REMARKS
IMR	3031	34.0	210	Federal	3800	49,200	
IMR	4064	34.0	9½	Remington	3475	41,200	
IMR	4064	37.5	9½	Remington	3950	51,800	
IMR	4320	34.5	9½	Remington	3500	42,000	
IMR	4320	37.0	9½	Remington	3800	49,800	
IMR	4895	34.0	9½	Remington	3500	40,100	
IMR	4895	36.0	9½	Remington	3875	48,500	
Hodgdon	H4895	34.0	9½	Remington	3700	47,500	
Hodgdon	H380	38.0	9½	Remington	3800	—	
Hodgdon	H414	41.0	9½	Remington	3920	—	

.22-250 REMINGTON (Cont.)

60-grain Softnose

POWDER MFGR.	POWDER TYPE	GRAINS	PRIMER TYPE	PRIMER MFGR.	VELOCITY	PRESSURE (C.U.P.)	REMARKS
IMR	4831	39.0	210	Federal	3300	—	
IMR	3031	32.0	210	Federal	3400	—	
IMR	4064	31.5	9½	Remington	3200	—	
IMR	4064	35.0	9½	Remington	3475	—	
IMR	4320	33.0	9½	Remington	3225	—	
IMR	4895	33.0	9½	Remington	3350	—	
Hodgdon	H380	35.0	210	Federal	3300	44,800	
Hodgdon	H414	35.0	9½	Remington	3300	44,100	

.223 REMINGTON

SPECIFICATIONS

Dia. of Rim — .378″
Dia. of Base — .377″
Dia. of Shoulder — .350″
Dia. of Neck — .253″
Length of Neck — .191″
Angle of Shoulder — 21.21°
Dia. Jacketed Bullet — .224″
Dia. Cast Bullet — .224″
Length of Case — 1.760″
Max. Overall Length — 2.30″
Primer Size — Small Rifle
Water Capacity — 28.12 grs.

40-grain Softnose

POWDER MFGR.	POWDER TYPE	GRAINS	PRIMER TYPE	PRIMER MFGR.	VELOCITY	PRESSURE (C.U.P.)	REMARKS
IMR	3031	23.0	205	Federal	3000	30800	
IMR	3031	24.0	205	Federal	3150	39500	
IMR	3031	25.0	205	Federal	3325	42000	
IMR	4064	25.0	7½	Remington	3050	34600	
IMR	4064	26.0	7½	Remington	3200	42000	
IMR	4320	25.0	7½	Remington	2975	30000	
IMR	4320	26.0	205	Federal	3100	34800	
IMR	4320	27.0	71/2	Remington	3200	40000	
IMR	4895	25.0	7½	Remington	3100	35200	
Hodgdon	BL-C(2)	24.0	7½	Remington	3080	—	
Hodgdon	BL-C(2)	26.5	205	Federal	3350	—	
Hodgdon	H335	26.0	210	Federal	3300	40800	
Winchester	W748	27.0	7½	Remington	3375	—	

.223 REMINGTON (Cont.)

45-grain Softnose

POWDER MFGR.	POWDER TYPE	GRAINS	PRIMER TYPE	PRIMER MFGR.	VELOCITY	PRESSURE (C.U.P.)	REMARKS
IMR	3031	24.0	205	Federal	3040	—	
IMR	3031	25.0	205	Federal	3275	42700	
IMR	4064	25.0	7½	Remington	3000	33000	
IMR	4064	26.0	7½	Remington	3150	41600	
IMR	4320	25.5	7½	Remington	3000	32800	
IMR	4320	26.5	7½	Remington	3200	37500	
IMR	4320	27.0	7½	Remington	3200	40000	
IMR	4895	24.5	7½	Remington	3000	30200	
IMR	4895	26.0	7½	Remington	3200	41500	
Hodgdon	BL-C(2)	26.0	7½	Remington	3100	35400	
Hodgdon	BL-C(2)	28.0	7½	Remington	3400	—	
Hodgdon	H335	26.0	210	Federal	3150	42800	
Winchester	W748	26.0	7½	Remington	3175	—	
Winchester	W748	27.0	7½	Remington	3300	—	
Winchester	W748	28.0	7½	Remington	3450	—	

50-grain Softnose

POWDER MFGR.	POWDER TYPE	GRAINS	PRIMER TYPE	PRIMER MFGR.	VELOCITY	PRESSURE (C.U.P.)	REMARKS
IMR	3031	24.0	205	Federal	3075	—	
IMR	3031	25.5	7½	Remington	3200	47000	
IMR	4064	24.0	7½	Remington	2900	32700	
IMR	4064	25.0	7½	Remington	3100	38900	
IMR	4064	26.0	7½	Remington	3160	47000	
IMR	4320	26.0	7½	Remington	3000	—	
IMR	4320	27.0	7½	Remington	3140	45600	
IMR	4320	27.5	7½	Remington	3200	50000	
IMR	4895	24.5	205	Federal	2900	—	
IMR	4895	26.5	7½	Remington	3200	48500	
Hodgdon	BL-C(2)	24.0	7½	Remington	2900	—	
Hodgdon	BL-C(2)	25.5	7½	Remington	3100	—	
Hodgdon	H380	26.5	7½	Remington	3000	—	
Hodgdon	H380	28.0	7½	Remington	3180	—	

.224 WEATHERBY

SPECIFICATIONS

Dia. of Rim — .430″
Dia. of Base — .415″
Dia. of Shoulder — .393″
Dia. of Neck — .248″
Length of Neck — .233″
Angle of Shoulder — 19.13°

Dia. Jacketed Bullet — .224″
Dia. Cast Bullet — .224″
Length of Case — 1.920″
Max. Overall Length — 2.38″
Primer Size — Large Rifle
Water Capacity — 39.19 grs.

45-grain Softnose

POWDER MFGR.	POWDER TYPE	GRAINS	PRIMER TYPE	PRIMER MFGR.	VELOCITY	PRESSURE (C.U.P.)	REMARKS
IMR	3031	26.0	210	Federal	3350	—	
IMR	3031	30.0	210	Federal	3600	—	
IMR	4064	29.5	210	Federal	3300	—	
IMR	4064	30.5	210	Federal	3500	—	
IMR	4320	31.5	210	Federal	3700	—	
IMR	4895	29.5	210	Federal	3400	—	
IMR	4895	31.0	210	Federal	3600	—	
Hodgdon	H4895	29.5	9½	Remington	3400	—	
Hodgdon	H4895	31.0	9½	Remington	3650	—	Near Maximum
Hodgdon	H380	32.5	9½	Remington	3500	—	
Hodgdon	H380	34.5	9½	Remington	3700	—	Near Maximum
Hodgdon	H414	35.0	9½	Remington	3500	—	
Hodgdon	H414	36.0	9½	Remington	3600	—	

50-grain Softnose

POWDER MFGR.	POWDER TYPE	GRAINS	PRIMER TYPE	PRIMER MFGR.	VELOCITY	PRESSURE (C.U.P.)	REMARKS
IMR	3031	29.0	210	Federal	3500	—	
IMR	3031	31.5	210	Federal	3800	—	
IMR	4064	30.5	210	Federal	3400	—	
IMR	4064	32.5	210	Federal	3800	—	
IMR	4320	32.5	210	Federal	3600	—	
IM$	4320	33.0	210	Federal	3700	—	
IMR	4895	29.5	210	Federal	3400	—	
IMR	4895	32.0	210	Federal	3700	—	
Hodgdon	H4895	29.5	9½	Remington	3400	—	
Hodgdon	H4895	31.0	9½	Remington	3600	—	
Hodgdon	H380	33.0	9½	Remington	3500	—,	

.224 WEATHERBY (Cont.)

55-grain Softnose

POWDER MFGR.	POWDER TYPE	GRAINS	PRIMER TYPE	PRIMER MFGR.	VELOCITY	PRESSURE (C.U.P.)	REMARKS
IMR	3031	29.0	210	Federal	3300	—	
IMR	3031	31.5	210	Federal	3700	—	Maximum
IMR	4064	30.0	210	Federal	3300	—	
IMR	4064	32.5	210	Federal	3600	—	Maximum
IMR	4320	30.5	210	Federal	3400	—	
IM$	4320	32.0	210	Federal	3600	—	Near Maximum
IMR	4895	30.0	210	Federal	3400	—	
IMR	4895	32.5	210	Federal	3700	—	Maximum
Hodgdon	H4895	30.0	210	Federal	3400	—	
Hodgdon	H4895	31.5	210	Federal	3600	—	Maximum
Hodgdon	H380	30.0	210	Federal	3150	—	
Hodgdon	H380	32.0	210	Federal	3450	—	Maximum
Winchester	W748	31.5	210	Federal	3300	—	
Winchester	W748	34.0	210	Federal	3600	—	Near Maximum
Winchester	W760	33.0	210	Federal	3200	—	
Winchester	W760	36.5	210	Federal	3650	—	

60-grain Softnose

POWDER MFGR.	POWDER TYPE	GRAINS	PRIMER TYPE	PRIMER MFGR.	VELOCITY	PRESSURE (C.U.P.)	REMARKS
IMR	3031	28.0	210	Federal	3200	—	
IMR	3031	30.5	210	Federal	3500	—	Maximum
IMR	4064	29.5	210	Federal	3200	—	
IMR	4064	31.5	210	Federal	3450	—	Near Maximum
IMR	4895	29.5	210	Federal	3300	—	
IMR	4895	31.5	210	Federal	3500	—	Near Maximum
Hodgdon	H335	30.0	210	Federal	3300	—	
Hodgdon	H335	31.5	210	federal	3500	—	Maximum
Winchester	W748	31.0	210	Federal	3200	—	
Winchester	W748	33.5	210	Federal	3500	—	Maximum
Winchester	W760	34.0	210	Federal	3200	—	
Winchester	W760	37.5	210	Federal	3500	—	Maximum

.240 WEATHERBY MAGNUM

SPECIFICATIONS

Dia. of Rim — .473″
Dia. of Base — .453″
Dia. of Shoulder — .432″
Dia. of Neck — .272″
Length of Neck — .308″
Angle of Shoulder — 21.8°
Dia. Jacketed Bullet — .243″
Dia. Cast Bullet — .244″
Length of Case — 2.50″
Max. Overall Length — 3.08″
Primer Size — Large Rifle
Water Capacity — 63.08 grs.

70-grain Softnose

POWDER MFGR.	POWDER TYPE	GRAINS	PRIMER TYPE	PRIMER MFGR.	VELOCITY	PRESSURE (C.U.P.)	REMARKS
IMR	4064	43.0	210	Federal	3400	—	
IMR	4064	48.0	210	Federal	3800	—	Maximum
IMR	4320	45.5	210	Federal	3450	—	
IMR	4320	49.0	210	Federal	3750	—	Near Maximum
IMR	4350	49.0	210	Federal	3400	—	
IMR	4350	52.5	210	Federal	3725	—	Near Maximum
IMR	4831	52.5	210	Federal	3525	—	
IMR	4831	56.0	210	Federal	3800	—	Near Maximum
Hodgdon	H414	49.5	210	Federal	3300	—	
Hodgdon	H414	53.0	210	Federal	3525	—	Maximum
Winchester	W760	48.0	210	Federal	3400	—	
Winchester	760	53.5	210	Federal	3800	—	Maximum

75-grain Softnose

POWDER MFGR.	POWDER TYPE	GRAINS	PRIMER TYPE	PRIMER MFGR.	VELOCITY	PRESSURE (C.U.P.)	REMARKS
IMR	4064	41.5	210	Federal	3200	—	
IMR	4064	47.0	210	Federal	3600	—	Maximum
IMR	4320	42.0	210	Federal	3210	—	
IMR	4320	49.0	210	Federal	3700	—	Maximum
IMR	4350	46.0	210	Federal	3225	—	
IMR	4350	51.5	210	Federal	3650	—	Near Maximum
IMR	4831	48.0	210	Federal	3200	—	
IMR	4831	55.0	210	Federal	3700	—	Maximum
Hodgdon	H450	50.0	210	Federal	3200	—	
Hodgdon	H450	57.0	210	Federal	3675	—	Maximum
Winchester	W760	47.5	210	Federal	3300	—	
Winchester	760	52.0	210	Federal	3650	—	Maximum

.243 WINCHESTER

SPECIFICATIONS

Dia. of Rim — .473″
Dia. of Base — .470″
Dia. of Shoulder — .455″
Dia. of Neck — .276″
Length of Neck — .240″
Angle of Shoulder — 19.55°
Dia. Jacketed Bullet — .243″
Dia. Cast Bullet — .243″
Length of Case — 2.045″
Max. Overall Length — 2.650″
Primer Size — Large Rifle
Water Capacity — 52.81 grs.

70-grain Softnose

POWDER MFGR.	POWDER TYPE	GRAINS	PRIMER TYPE	PRIMER MFGR.	VELOCITY	PRESSURE (C.U.P.)	REMARKS
IMR	3031	36.0	210	Federal	3100	43,400	
IMR	3031	40.5	210	Federal	3500	50,800	Maximum
IMR	4064	38.5	210	Federal	3150	43,900	
IMR	4064	42.0	210	Federal	3400	49,700	Maximum
IMR	4320	38.5	210	Federal	3100	42,100	
IMR	4320	42.5	210	Federal	3500	50,100	Maximum
Hodgdon	H414	43.0	210	Federal	3100	41,200	
Hodgdon	H414	47.5	210	Federal	3600	51,000	Maximum
Hodgdon	H4350	44.0	210	Federal	3000	40,100	
Hodgdon	H4350	47.5	210	Federal	3425	50,400	Maximum

75-grain Softnose

POWDER MFGR.	POWDER TYPE	GRAINS	PRIMER TYPE	PRIMER MFGR.	VELOCITY	PRESSURE (C.U.P.)	REMARKS
IMR	3031	36.0	210	Federal	3000	45,000	
IMR	3031	37.5	210	Federal	3175	49,800	Near Maximum
IMR	4064	38.0	210	Federal	3100	43,700	
IMR	4064	40.5	210	Federal	3300	50,000	Maximum
IMR	4320	39.0	210	Federal	3100	41,600	
IMR	4320	41.5	210	Federal	3350	49,000	Maximum
Hodgdon	H414	43.5	210	Federal	3100	42,100	
Hodgdon	H414	47.0	210	Federal	3500	50,900	Maximum
Hodgdon	H4350	45.0	210	Federal	3100	43,100	
Hodgdon	H4350	47.0	210	Federal	3300	50,400	Maximum

80-grain Softnose

POWDER MFGR.	POWDER TYPE	GRAINS	PRIMER TYPE	PRIMER MFGR.	VELOCITY	PRESSURE (C.U.P.)	REMARKS
IMR	3031	35.0	210	Federal	2900	42,100	
IMR	3031	36.5	210	Federal	3125	48,900	Near Maximum

.243 WINCHESTER (Cont.)

80-grain Softnose (Cont.)

POWDER MFGR.	POWDER TYPE	GRAINS	PRIMER TYPE	PRIMER MFGR.	VELOCITY	PRESSURE (C.U.P.)	REMARKS
IMR	4064	36.0	210	Federal	2900	42,300	
IMR	4064	39.5	210	Federal	3200	49,600	Maximum
IMR	4320	38.5	210	Federal	3100	45,300	
IMR	4320	40.5	210	Federal	3275	51,000	Maximum
Hodgdon	H414	42.0	210	Federal	3000	39,800	
Hodgdon	H414	46.0	210	Federal	3450	50,200	Maximum
Hodgdon	H4350	43.0	210	Federal	2900	42,100	
Hodgdon	H4350	45.5	210	Federal	3225	50,200	Maximum

87-grain Softnose

POWDER MFGR.	POWDER TYPE	GRAINS	PRIMER TYPE	PRIMER MFGR.	VELOCITY	PRESSURE (C.U.P.)	REMARKS
IMR	3031	34.0	210	Federal	2800	42,800	
IMR	3031	36.5	210	Federal	3000	49,900	Maximum
IMR	4064	36.5	210	Federal	2900	43,200	
IMR	4064	39.5	210	Federal	3100	50,300	Maximum
Hodgdon	H450	45.0	210	Federal	2900	41,000	
Hodgdon	H450	48.0	210	Federal	3200	50,400	Maximum
Hodgdon	H414	40.5	210	Federal	2800	42,100	
Hodgdon	H414	44.5	210	Federal	3200	50,700	Maximum

100-grain Softnose

POWDER MFGR.	POWDER TYPE	GRAINS	PRIMER TYPE	PRIMER MFGR.	VELOCITY	PRESSURE (C.U.P.)	REMARKS
IMR	4064	34.0	210	Federal	2700	43,800	
IMR	4064	36.0	210	Federal	2800	48,900	Near Maximum
IMR	4350	39.0	210	Federal	2700	43,900	
IMR	4350	42.0	210	Federal	3000	51,000	Maximum
Hodgdon	H450	43.0	210	Federal	2700	41,100	
Hodgdon	H450	45.5	210	Federal	3000	50,800	Maximum
Hodgdon	H414	39.5	210	Federal	2800	44,600	
Hodgdon	H414	41.5	210	Federal	2975	49,600	Maximum

.244 REMINGTON

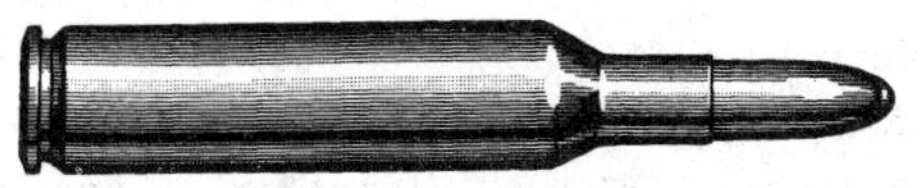

SPECIFICATIONS

Dia. of Rim — .472″	Dia. Jacketed Bullet — .243″
Dia. of Base — .471″	Dia. Cast Bullet — .245″
Dia. of Shoulder — .429″	Length of Case — 2.23″
Dia. of Neck — .276″	Max. Overall Length — 2.83″
Length of Neck — .240″	Primer Size — Large Rifle
Angle of Shoulder — 19.55°	Water Capacity — 54.43 grs.

70-grain Softnose

POWDER MFGR.	POWDER TYPE	GRAINS	PRIMER TYPE	PRIMER MFGR.	VELOCITY	PRESSURE (C.U.P.)	REMARKS
IMR	4350	49.0	210	Federal	3580	—	
IMR	4350	46.5	210	Federal	3350	—	
IMR	4350	44.0	210	Federal	3170	—	
IMR	4320	47.0	210	Federal	3455	—	
IMR	4320	43.5	210	Federal	3380	—	
IMR	4320	40.0	210	Federal	3200	—	
IMR	3031	42.0	210	Federal	3570	—	
IMR	3031	38.5	210	Federal	3340	—	
IMR	3031	44.0	210	Federal	3000	—	
IMR	4064	45.0	210	Federal	3190	—	

100-grain Softnose

POWDER MFGR.	POWDER TYPE	GRAINS	PRIMER TYPE	PRIMER MFGR.	VELOCITY	PRESSURE (C.U.P.)	REMARKS
IMR	3031	38.0	210	Federal	3020	—	
IMR	3031	35.0	210	Federal	2870	—	
IMR	4064	40.0	210	Federal	3135	—	
IMR	4064	38.0	210	Federal	3050	—	
IMR	4320	41.0	210	Federal	3165	—	
IMR	4320	39.5	210	Federal	3060	—	
IMR	4350	45.0	210	Federal	3220	—	
IMR	4350	43.0	210	Federal	3070	—	
IMR	4350	41.0	210	Federal	2950	—	

.250-3000 SAVAGE

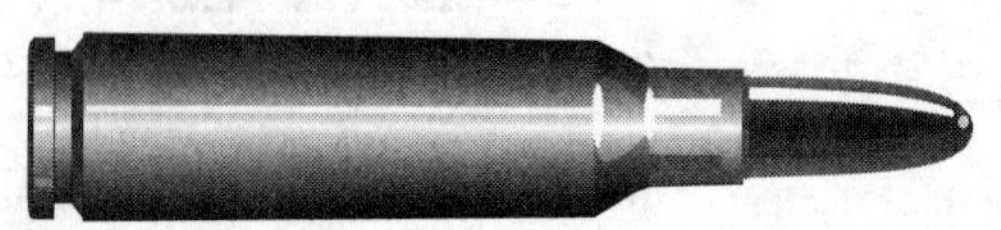

SPECIFICATIONS

Dia. of Rim — .473″
Dia. of Base — .468″
Dia. of Shoulder — .414″
Dia. of Neck — .285″
Length of Neck — .275″
Angle of Shoulder — 26.30°
Dia. Jacketed Bullet — .257″
Dia. Cast Bullet — .257″
Length of Case — 1.9120″
Max. Overall Length — 2.515″
Primer Size — Large Rifle
Water Capacity — 45.54 grs.

75-grain Softnose

POWDER MFGR.	POWDER TYPE	GRAINS	PRIMER TYPE	PRIMER MFGR.	VELOCITY	PRESSURE (C.U.P.)	REMARKS
IMR	3031	32.0	9½	Remington	3050	—	
IMR	3031	34.0	9½	Remington	3150	—	
IMR	4064	34.0	9½	Remington	3000	—	
IMR	4064	36.0	9½	Remington	3200	—	
IMR	4320	35.5	9½	Remington	3100	—	
IMR	4320	37.0	9½	Remington	3200	—	
IMR	4895	34.0	9½	Remington	3000	—	
IMR	4895	36.5	9½	Remington	3200	—	Maximum
IMR	4198	27.5	9½	Remington	2875	—	
IMR	4198	29.5	9½	Remington	3125	—	Maximum
Hodgdon	H322	31.5	9½	Remington	3100	—	
Hodgdon	H322	33.5	9½	Remington	3250	—	Near Maximum
Hodgdon	H335	34.0	9½	Remington	3000	—	
Hodgdon	H335	36.0	9½	Remington	3200	—	Near Maximum
Hodgdon	H414	42.0	9½	Remington	3200	—	
Hodgdon	H414	43.0	9½	Remington	3300	—	Near Maximum
Hercules	RL-7	30.5	9½	Remington	3000	—	
Hercules	RL-7	31.5	9½	Remington	3100	—	Near Maximum

87-grain Softnose

POWDER MFGR.	POWDER TYPE	GRAINS	PRIMER TYPE	PRIMER MFGR.	VELOCITY	PRESSURE (C.U.P.)	REMARKS
IMR	3031	30.0	9½	Remington	2800	—	
IMR	3031	32.5	9½	Remington	3000	—	
IMR	4064	32.0	9½	Remington	2900	—	
IMR	4064	34.0	9½	Remington	3100	—	
IMR	4320	33.0	9½	Remington	2800	—	

.250-3000 SAVAGE (Cont.)

100-grain Softnose

POWDER MFGR.	POWDER TYPE	GRAINS	PRIMER TYPE	PRIMER MFGR.	VELOCITY	PRESSURE (C.U.P.)	REMARKS
IMR	3031	29.5	210	Federal	2600	—	
IMR	3031	31.5	210	Federal	2800	—	
IMR	4064	30.0	210	Federal	2600	—	
IMR	4064	33.0	210	Federal	2800	—	Maximum
IMR	4320	31.5	9½	Remington	2600	—	
IMR	4320	34.5	9½	Remington	2850	—	Near Maximum
IMR	4350	34.0	210	Federal	2500	—	
IMR	4350	36.5	210	Federal	2700	—	
Hodgdon	H380	33.0	210	Federal	2600	—	
Hodgdon	H380	36.0	210	Federal	2800	—	Near Maximum
Hodgdon	H4895	32.0	210	Federal	2650	—	
Hodgdon	H4895	35.0	210	Federal	2950	—	Maximum
Hercules	RL-7	27.5	9½	Remington	2600	—	
Hercules	RL-7	29.0	9½	Remington	2700	—	Maximum

117-grain Softnose

POWDER MFGR.	POWDER TYPE	GRAINS	PRIMER TYPE	PRIMER MFGR.	VELOCITY	PRESSURE (C.U.P.)	REMARKS
IMR	3031	27.5	210	Federal	2400	—	
IMR	3031	30.5	210	Federal	2650	—	
IMR	4064	29.0	210	Federal	2600	—	
IMR	4064	32.5	210	Federal	2700	—	Maximum
IMR	4320	30.5	210	Federal	2400	—	
IMR	4320	34.0	210	Federal	2650	—	Near Maximum
IMR	4350	34.5	210	Federal	2400	—	
IMR	4350	36.5	210	Federal	2600	—	Maximum
Hodgdon	H380	31.5	210	Federal	2400	—	
Hodgdon	H380	33.5	210	Federal	2600	—	
Hodgdon	H4895	30.5	210	Federal	2500	—	
Hodgdon	H4895	33.0	210	Federal	2680	—	Near Maximum
Hodgdon	BL-C(2)	31.0	210	Federal	2500	—	
Hodgdon	BL-C(2)	33.0	210	Federal	2700	—	

.256 WINCHESTER

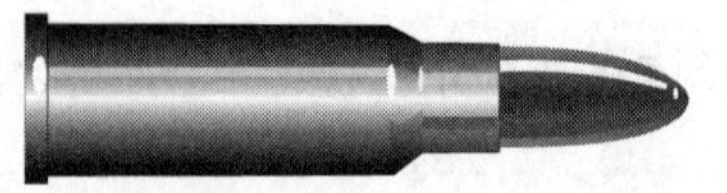

SPECIFICATIONS

Dia. of Rim — .440″
Dia. of Base — .380″
Dia. of Shoulder — .368″
Dia. of Neck — .285″
Neck length — .208″
Angle of Shoulder — 26.56°
Dia. Jacketed Bullet — .257″
Dia. Cast Bullet — .257″
Length of Case — 1.281″
Max. Overall Length — 1.78″
Primer Size — Small Pistol
Water Capacity — 20.49 grs.

60-grain Softnose

POWDER MFGR.	POWDER TYPE	GRAINS	PRIMER TYPE	PRIMER MFGR.	VELOCITY	PRESSURE (C.U.P.)	REMARKS
Hodgdon	H4198	17.0		Remington	2685	—	
Hodgdon	H4198	18.0		Remington	2790	—	
Hodgdon	H110	13.0		Remington	2600	—	
Hodgdon	H110	14.0		Remington	2725	—	

.25-20 WCF

SPECIFICATIONS

Dia. of Rim — .408″
Dia. of Base — .349″
Dia. of Shoulder — .334″
Dia. of Neck — .273″
Length of Neck — .345″
Angle of Shoulder — 13.10°
Dia. Jacketed Bullet — .257″
Dia. Cast Bullet — .259″
Length of Case — 1.330″
Max. Overall Length — 1.50″
Primer Size — Small Rifle
Water Capacity — 18.85 grs.

60-grain Softnose

POWDER MFGR.	POWDER TYPE	GRAINS	PRIMER TYPE	PRIMER MFGR.	VELOCITY	PRESSURE (C.U.P.)	REMARKS
IMR	4227	10.0	WSR	Winchester	2000	—	
IMR	4227	11.5	WSR	Winchester	2200	—	Maximum
Hodgdon	H110	8.0	WSR	Winchester	1900	—	
Hodgdon	H110	9.0	WSR	Winchester	2060	—	
Hodgdon	H4227	9.5	WSR	Winchester	2000	—	
Hodgdon	H4227	11.0	WSR	Winchester	2200	—	
Winchester	W296	8.0	WSR	Winchester	1900	—	
Winchester	W296	9.0	WSR	Winchester	2050	—	

.25-35 WCF

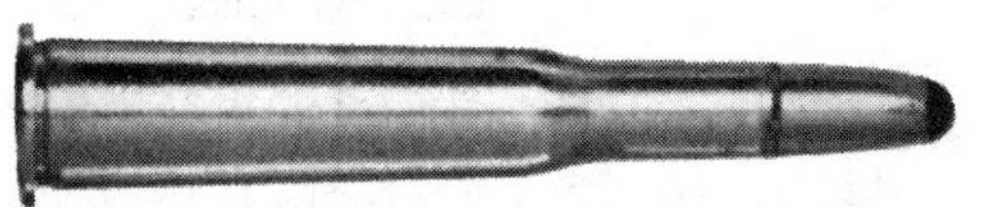

SPECIFICATIONS

Dia. of Rim — .506″
Dia. of Base — .422″
Dia. of Shoulder — .325″
Dia. of Neck — .281″
Length of Neck — .428″
Angle of Shoulder — 8.93°
Dia. Jacketed Bullet — .257″
Dia. Cast Bullet — .257″
Length of Case — 2.0430″
Max. Overall Length — 2.60″
Primer Size — Large Rifle
Water Capacity — 35.68 grs.

60-grain Softnose

POWDER MFGR.	POWDER TYPE	GRAINS	PRIMER TYPE	PRIMER MFGR.	VELOCITY	PRESSURE (C.U.P.)	REMARKS
IMR	3031	26.0	210	Federal	2500	—	
IMR	3031	28.0	210	Federal	2800	—	Maximum
IMR	4064	27.5	210	Federal	2500	—	
IMR	4064	30.5	210	Federal	2800	—	Maximum
IMR	4320	28.0	210	Federal	2500	—	
IMR	4320	32.0	210	Federal	2835	—	Maximum
Hodgdon	BL-C(2)	27.0	210	Federal	2500	—	
Hodgdon	BL-C(2)	30.0	210	Federal	2800	—	Maximum
Hodgdon	H4198	22.5	210	Federal	2500	—	
Hodgdon	H4198	23.5	210	Federal	2675	—	Near Maximum

117-grain Softnose

POWDER MFGR.	POWDER TYPE	GRAINS	PRIMER TYPE	PRIMER MFGR.	VELOCITY	PRESSURE (C.U.P.)	REMARKS
IMR	3031	22.5	210	Federal	2045	—	
IMR	3031	24.5	210	Federal	2200	—	Near Maximum
IMR	4064	21.5	210	Federal	1800	—	
IMR	4064	25.5	210	Federal	2265	—	Maximum
IMR	4320	24.5	210	Federal	2000	—	
IMR	4320	27.0	210	Federal	2250	—	Maximum
Hodgdon	H4198	19.0	210	Federal	1900	—	
Hodgdon	H4198	20.5	210	Federal	2100	—	Maximum

.25-06 REMINGTON

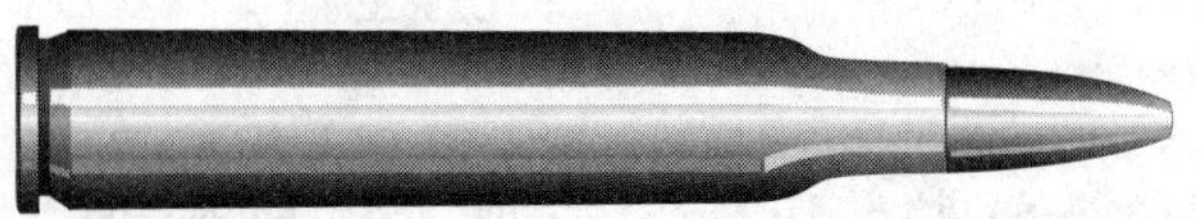

SPECIFICATIONS

Dia. of Rim — .473″
Dia. of Base — .470″
Dia. of Shoulder — .441″
Dia. of Neck — .290″
Length of Neck — .308″
Angle of Shoulder — 17.06°
Dia. Jacketed Bullet — .257″
Dia. Cast Bullet — .257″
Length of Case — 2.494″
Max. Overall Length — 3.250″
Primer Size — Large Rifle
Water Capacity — 65.03 grs.

75-grain Soft Point

POWDER MFGR.	POWDER TYPE	GRAINS	PRIMER TYPE	PRIMER MFGR.	VELOCITY	PRESSURE (C.U.P.)	REMARKS
IMR	4064	44.0	WLR	Winchester	3245	44,000	
IMR	4064	49.5	WLR	Winchester	3600	51,000	Near Maximum
IMR	4320	45.0	WLR	Winchester	3200	41,000	
IMR	4320	51.0	WLR	Winchester	3600	51,800	Maximum
IMR	4895	44.0	WLR	Winchester	3200	43,400	
IMR	4895	48.0	WLR	Winchester	3500	51,000	Maximum
IMR	4350	50.0	WLR	Winchester	3175	42,700	
IMR	4350	55.5	WLR	Winchester	3600	51,200	Maximum
IMR	4831	55.0	WLR	Winchester	3200	—	
IMR	4831	58.5	WLR	Winchester	3575	—	Near Maximum
Hodgdon	H380	45.5	WLR	Winchester	3250	—	
Hodgdon	H380	51.0	WLR	Winchester	3600	—	Maximum
Hodgdon	H450	52.0	WLR	Winchester	3000	—	
Hodgdon	H450	57.5	WLR	Winchester	3500	—	Near Maximum
Winchester	W760	50.5	WLR	Winchester	3275	42,800	
Winchester	W760	54.5	WLR	Winchester	3600	51,200	Maximum

87-grain Soft Point

POWDER MFGR.	POWDER TYPE	GRAINS	PRIMER TYPE	PRIMER MFGR.	VELOCITY	PRESSURE (C.U.P.)	REMARKS
IMR	4064	43.5	WLR	Winchester	3200	43,500	
IMR	4064	45.5	WLR	Winchester	3300	49,900	Near Maximum
IMR	4320	44.0	WLR	Winchester	3125	46,100	
IMR	4320	48.0	WLR	Winchester	3400	52,400	Maximum
IMR	4895	42.5	WLR	Winchester	3150	46,500	
IMR	4895	45.5	WLR	Winchester	3325	52,300	Maximum
IMR	4350	50.0	WLR	Winchester	3100	—	
IMR	4350	53.0	WLR	Winchester	3300	—	Near Maximum
Hodgdon	H380	45.0	WLR	Winchester	3200	46,700	
Hodgdon	H380	49.0	WLR	Winchester	3400	52,300	Maximum

.25-06 REMINGTON (Cont.)

100-grain Soft Point

POWDER MFGR.	POWDER TYPE	GRAINS	PRIMER TYPE	PRIMER MFGR.	VELOCITY	PRESSURE (C.U.P.)	REMARKS
IMR	4064	41.0	WLR	Winchester	2900	42,000	
IMR	4064	44.0	WLR	Winchester	3100	50,400	Maximum
IMR	4320	41.0	WLR	Winchester	2900	44,100	
IMR	4320	45.0	WLR	Winchester	3150	51,200	Maximum
IMR	4350	49.0	WLR	Winchester	3100	—	
IMR	4350	53.0	WLR	Winchester	3350	—	Maximum
Hodgdon	H380	43.5	210	Federal	2900	—	
Hodgdon	H380	45.0	210	Federal	3050	—	Near Maximum
Hodgdon	H4831	52.5	210	Federal	3000	—	
Hodgdon	H4831	55.0	210	Federal	3275	—	
Winchester	W760	44.0	210	Federal	2900	—	
Winchester	W760	45.0	210	Federal	3050	—	Near Maximum

117-grain Soft Point

POWDER MFGR.	POWDER TYPE	GRAINS	PRIMER TYPE	PRIMER MFGR.	VELOCITY	PRESSURE (C.U.P.)	REMARKS
IMR	4064	38.5	WLR	Winchester	2600	—	
IMR	4064	43.0	WLR	Winchester	2900	—	Near Maximum
IMR	4320	40.0	WLR	Winchester	2650	47700	
IMR	4320	43.0	WLR	Winchester	2825	52000	Maximum
IMR	4350	45.5	WLR	Winchester	2800	47000	
IMR	4350	48.0	WLR	Winchester	3000	52800	Maximum
Hodgdon	H450	46.5	WLR	Winchester	2650	—	
Hodgdon	H450	50.0	WLR	Winchester	3000	—	Near Maximum
Hodgdon	H4831	47.0	WLR	Winchester	2675	—	
Hodgdon	H4831	51.0	WLR	Winchester	3000	—	Maximum

.257 ROBERTS

SPECIFICATIONS

Dia. of Rim — .473″
Dia. of Base — .471″
Dia. of Shoulder — .429″
Dia. of Neck — .290″
Length of Neck — .321″
Angle of Shoulder — 20.69°

Dia. Jacketed Bullet — .257″
Dia. Cast Bullet — 259″
Length of Case — 2.233″
Max. Overall Length — 2.515″
Primer Size — Large Rifle
Water Capacity — 55.41 grs.

75-grain Soft Point

POWDER MFGR.	POWDER TYPE	GRAINS	PRIMER TYPE	PRIMER MFGR.	VELOCITY	PRESSURE (C.U.P.)	REMARKS
IMR	3031	38.0	210	Federal	3125	—	
IMR	3031	41.0	210	Federal	3400	—	Maximum
IMR	4064	40.5	210	Federal	3100	—	
IMR	4064	43.0	210	Federal	3300	—	Near Maximum
IMR	4320	42.5	210	Federal	3150	—	
IMR	4320	45.0	210	Federal	3300	—	Near Maximum
IMR	4895	40.0	210	Federal	3150	—	
IMR	4895	43.5	210	Federal	3400	—	Maximum
Hodgdon	H335	41.5	210	Federal	3100	—	
Hodgdon	H335	45.0	210	Federal	3500	—	Near Maximum
Hodgdon	H414	46.5	210	Federal	3200	—	

100-grain Soft Point

POWDER MFGR.	POWDER TYPE	GRAINS	PRIMER TYPE	PRIMER MFGR.	VELOCITY	PRESSURE (C.U.P.)	REMARKS
IMR	3031	33.0	210	Federal	2600	—	
IMR	3031	37.0	210	Federal	2900	—	
IMR	4064	36.0	210	Federal	2650	—	

117-grain Soft Point

POWDER MFGR.	POWDER TYPE	GRAINS	PRIMER TYPE	PRIMER MFGR.	VELOCITY	PRESSURE (C.U.P.)	REMARKS
IMR	3031	31.5	210	Federal	2500	—	
IMR	3031	33.5	210	Federal	2650	—	Near Maximum
IMR	4064	34.0	210	Federal	2500	—	
IMR	4064	36.0	210	Federal	2700	—	Near Maximum
IMR	4350	40.0	210	Federal	2600	—	
IMR	4350	42.0	210	Federal	2750	—	Near Maximum
Hodgdon	H380	37.0	210	Federal	2550	—	
Hodgdon	H380	39.5	210	Federal	2700	—	Maximum

.257 WEATHERBY MAGNUM

SPECIFICATIONS

Dia. of Rim — .530″	Dia. Jacketed Bullet — .257″
Dia. of Base — .511″	Dia. Cast Bullet — .259″
Dia. of Shoulder — .490″	Length of Case — 2.56″
Dia. of Neck — .282″	Max. Overall Length — 3.317″
Length of Neck — .308″	Primer Size — Large Rifle M
Angle of Shoulder — 25°	Water Capacity — 85.63 grs.

87-grain Soft Point

POWDER MFGR.	POWDER TYPE	GRAINS	PRIMER TYPE	PRIMER MFGR.	VELOCITY	PRESSURE (C.U.P.)	REMARKS
IMR	4320	61.0	215	Federal	3785	—	Maximum
IMR	4320	59.0	215	Federal	3680	—	
IMR	4320	57.0	215	Federal	3325	—	
IMR	4064	59.0	215	Federal	3720	—	Maximum
IMR	4064	57.0	215	Federal	3660	—	Near Maximum
IMR	4064	55.0	215	Federal	3530	—	
IMR	4350	68.0	215	Federal	3710	—	Maximum
IMR	4350	66.0	215	Federal	3700	—	
IMR	4350	64.0	215	Federal	3580	—	

100-grain Soft Point

POWDER MFGR.	POWDER TYPE	GRAINS	PRIMER TYPE	PRIMER MFGR.	VELOCITY	PRESSURE (C.U.P.)	REMARKS
IMR	4350	64.0	215	Federal	3500	—	Maximum
IMR	4350	62.0	215	Federal	3380	—	Near Maximum
IMR	4350	60.0	215	Federal	3190	—	
IMR	4064	55.0	215	Federal	3400	—	Maximum
IMR	4064	53.0	215	Federal	3280	—	
IMR	4064	51.0	215	Federal	3210	—	

117-grain Soft Point

POWDER MFGR.	POWDER TYPE	GRAINS	PRIMER TYPE	PRIMER MFGR.	VELOCITY	PRESSURE (C.U.P.)	REMARKS
IMR	4350	61.0	215	Federal	3200	—	Maximum
IMR	4350	59.0	215	Federal	3120	—	Near Maximum
IMR	4350	57.0	215	Federal	3000	—	
IMR	4064	52.0	215	Federal	3100	—	Maximum
IMR	4064	50.0	215	Federal	3020	—	
IMR	4064	48.0	215	Federal	2895	—	

.264 WINCHESTER MAGNUM

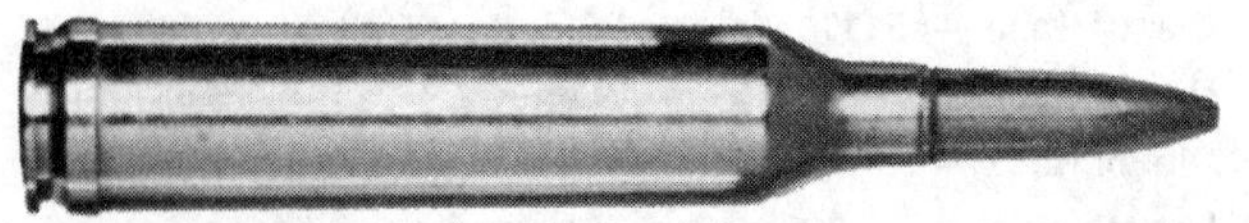

SPECIFICATIONS

Dia. of Rim — .532″
Dia. of Base — .513″
Dia. of Shoulder — .491″
Dia. of Neck — .298″
Length of Neck — .254″
Angle of Shoulder — 25.1°
Dia. Jacketed Bullet — .264″
Dia. Cast Bullet — .265″
Length of Case — 2.50″
Max. Overall Length — 3.35″
Primer Size — Large Rifle M
Water Capacity — 81.50 grs.

100-grain Softnose

POWDER MFGR.	POWDER TYPE	GRAINS	PRIMER TYPE	PRIMER MFGR.	VELOCITY	PRESSURE (C.U.P.)	REMARKS
IMR	3031	46.0	215	Federal	3100	—	
IMR	3031	50.0	215	Federal	3325	—	
IMR	4064	50.0	WLR	Winchester	3200	—	
IMR	4064	55.0	WLR	Winchester	3450	—	Near Maximum
IMR	4320	53.0	215	Federal	3300	—	
IMR	4320	55.5	215	Federal	3400	—	Near Maximum
IMR	4350	55.5	WLR	Winchester	3350	—	
IMR	4350	61.0	WLR	Winchester	3600	—	
IMR	4831	59.0	WLR	Winchester	3200	—	
IMR	4831	63.0	WLR	Winchester	3400	—	
IMR	7828	63.0	WLR	Winchester	3250	—	
IMR	7828	66.5	WLR	Winchester	3600	—	Near Maximum
Hodgdon	H4895	52.5	WLR	Winchester	3300	—	
Hodgdon	H4895	55.0	WLR	Winchester	3500	—	
Hodgdon	H380	54.0	WLR	Winchester	3300	—	
Hodgdon	H380	57.0	WLR	Winchester	3400	—	
Hodgdon	H450	62.0	WLR	Winchester	3250	—	
Hodgdon	H450	70.0	WLR	Winchester	3600	—	Maximum

129-grain Softnose

POWDER MFGR.	POWDER TYPE	GRAINS	PRIMER TYPE	PRIMER MFGR.	VELOCITY	PRESSURE (C.U.P.)	REMARKS
IMR	4064	50.0	WLR	Winchester	2900	—	
IMR	4064	55.0	WLR	Winchester	3100	—	Near Maximum
IMR	4320	51.5	WLR	Winchester	2900	—	
IMR	4320	56.0	WLR	Winchester	3175	—	
IMR	4350	52.5	WLR	Winchester	3000	—	
IMR	4350	55.5	WLR	Winchester	3150	—	
IMR	4831	57.5	WLR	Winchester	3000	—	
IMR	4831	60.0	WLR	Winchester	3100	—	

.264 WINCHESTER MAGNUM

129-grain Softnose (*Cont.*)

POWDER MFGR.	POWDER TYPE	GRAINS	PRIMER TYPE	PRIMER MFGR.	VELOCITY	PRESSURE (C.U.P.)	REMARKS
IMR	7828	60.0	WLR	Winchester	3000	—	
IMR	7828	64.0	WLR	Winchester	3200	—	Near Maximum
Hodgdon	H4895	52.5	WLR	Winchester	3000	—	
Hodgdon	H4895	55.0	WLR	Winchester	3100	—	
Hodgdon	H380	55.5	WLR	Winchester	2950	—	
Hodgdon	H380	58.5	WLR	Winchester	3100	—	
Hodgdon	H450	61.5	WLR	Winchester	3100	—	
Hodgdon	H450	63.5	WLR	Winchester	3200	—	Near Maximum

140-grain Softnose

POWDER MFGR.	POWDER TYPE	GRAINS	PRIMER TYPE	PRIMER MFGR.	VELOCITY	PRESSURE (C.U.P.)	REMARKS
IMR	4064	50.0	WLR	Winchester	2800	—	
IMR	4064	51.5	WLR	Winchester	2900	—	Near Maximum
IMR	4320	50.0	WLR	Winchester	2800	—	
IMR	4320	54.0	WLR	Winchester	2975	—	
IMR	4350	52.0	WLR	Winchester	2850	—	
IMR	4350	55.0	WLR	Winchester	3100	—	
IMR	4831	56.5	WLR	Winchester	2900	—	
IMR	4831	61.0	WLR	Winchester	3100	—	Near Maximum
IMR	7828	59.5	WLR	Winchester	2800	48,900	
IMR	7828	63.0	WLR	Winchester	3000	52,400	Maximum
Hodgdon	H4350	50.0	WLR	Winchester	2750	—	
Hodgdon	H4350	53.5	WLR	Winchester	3000	—	Maximum
Hodgdon	H4895	50.0	WLR	Winchester	2800	—	
Hodgdon	H4895	54.0	WLR	Winchester	3000	—	Maximum
Hodgdon	H380	51.0	210	Federal	2825	—	
Hodgdon	H380	54.5	210	Federal	3000	—	Near Maximum

160-grain Softnose

POWDER MFGR.	POWDER TYPE	GRAINS	PRIMER TYPE	PRIMER MFGR.	VELOCITY	PRESSURE (C.U.P.)	REMARKS
IMR	4064	46.0	WLR	Winchester	2500	—	
IMR	4064	50.0	WLR	Winchester	2700	—	Maximum
IMR	4320	47.0	WLR	Winchester	2500	—	
IMR	4320	53.0	WLR	Winchester	2800	—	Near Maximum

.270 WINCHESTER

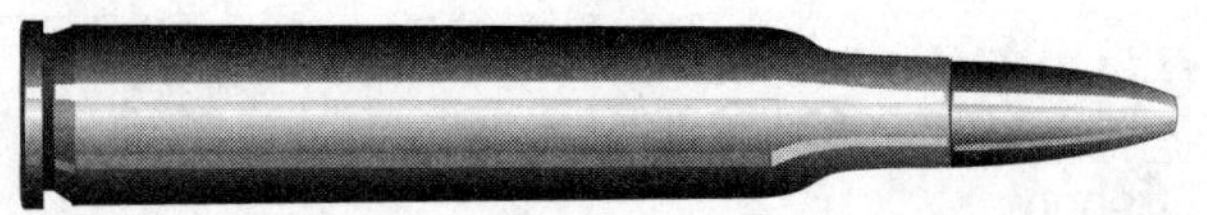

SPECIFICATIONS

Dia. of Rim — .473″
Dia. of Base — .470″
Dia. of Shoulder — .441″
Dia. of Neck — .308″
Length of Neck — .383″
Angle of Shoulder — 18°

Dia. Jacketed Bullet — .277″
Dia. Cast Bullet — .279″
Length of Case — 2.54″
Max. Overall Length — 3.35″
Primer Size — Large Rifle
Water Capacity — 67.4 grs.

100-grain Soft Point

POWDER MFGR.	POWDER TYPE	GRAINS	PRIMER TYPE	PRIMER MFGR.	VELOCITY	PRESSURE (C.U.P.)	REMARKS
IMR	4064	46.0	210	Federal	3000	41,300	
IMR	4064	51.5	210	Federal	3400	52,800	Maximum
IMR	4320	46.0	210	Federal	3000	40,100	
IMR	4320	51.5	210	Federal	3300	53,000	Maximum
IMR	4895	47.0	210	Federal	3150	46,000	
IMR	4895	50.0	210	Federal	3350	52,900	Maximum
IMR	4350	50.5	210	Federal	3040	43,000	
IMR	4350	57.0	210	Federal	3350	54,000	Maximum
Hodgdon	H380	48.0	210	Federal	3050	41,700	
Hodgdon	H380	54.0	210	Federal	3400	53,700	Maximum
Hodgdon	H450	56.0	210	Federal	3000	46,500	
Hodgdon	H450	62.0	210	Federal	3400	54,000	Maximum
Winchester	W760	52.5	210	Federal	3000	—	
Winchester	W760	56.5	210	Federal	3300	—	Maximum

110-grain Soft Point

POWDER MFGR.	POWDER TYPE	GRAINS	PRIMER TYPE	PRIMER MFGR.	VELOCITY	PRESSURE (C.U.P.)	REMARKS
IMR	4064	46.0	210	Federal	3000	41,300	
IMR	4064	50.0	210	Federal	3250	52,300	Maximum
IMR	4320	45.0	210	Federal	2800	39,700	
IMR	4320	50.0	210	Federal	3150	52,300	Maximum
IMR	4895	45.0	210	Federal	2850	41,900	
IMR	4895	48.0	210	Federal	3125	51,200	Near Maximum
IMR	4350	49.5	210	Federal	2800	39,800	
IMR	4350	56.0	210	Federal	3225	52,400	Maximum
Hodgdon	H380	48.0	210	Federal	3050	43,200	
Hodgdon	H380	52.0	210	Federal	3200	51,600	Near Maximum
Hodgdon	H450	56.0	210	Federal	2850	39,800	
Hodgdon	H450	60.0	210	Federal	3250	52,900	Maximum

.270 WINCHESTER (Cont.)

130-grain Soft Point

POWDER MFGR.	POWDER TYPE	GRAINS	PRIMER TYPE	PRIMER MFGR.	VELOCITY	PRESSURE (C.U.P.)	REMARKS
IMR	3031	42.0	210	Federal	2800	42,000	
IMR	3031	46.5	210	Federal	3100	53,100	Maximum
IMR	4064	44.0	210	Federal	2800	40,100	
IMR	4064	46.0	210	Federal	2950	50,100	Near Maximum
IMR	4320	44.5	210	Federal	2800	41,700	
IMR	4320	49.5	210	Federal	2985	52,400	Maximum
IMR	4895	42.5	210	Federal	2700	42,300	
IMR	4895	47.0	210	Federal	3000	—	Maximum
IMR	4350	49.0	210	Federal	2700	40,800	
IMR	4350	54.5	210	Federal	3000	53,400	Maximum
Hodgdon	H380	46.0	210	Federal	2800	—	
Hodgdon	H380	50.0	210	Federal	3100	—	
Hodgdon	H450	55.5	210	Federal	2800	—	
Hodgdon	H450	60.0	210	Federal	3150	—	Maximum
Winchester	W760	49.0	210	Federal	2795	—	
Winchester	W760	53.5	210	Federal	3000	—	Maximum

140-grain Soft Point

POWDER MFGR.	POWDER TYPE	GRAINS	PRIMER TYPE	PRIMER MFGR.	VELOCITY	PRESSURE (C.U.P.)	REMARKS
IMR	3031	41.0	210	Federal	2700	41,700	
IMR	3031	45.5	210	Federal	2950	50,600	Maximum
IMR	4064	41.5	210	Federal	2600	38,900	
IMR	4064	46.5	210	Federal	2900	52,000	Maximum
IMR	4320	42.5	210	Federal	2600	40,000	
IMR	4320	46.5	210	Federal	2900	52,600	Maximum
IMR	4350	47.5	210	Federal	2600	42,300	
IMR	4350	53.0	210	Federal	3000	51,900	Maximum
Hodgdon	H380	44.0	210	Federal	2600	41,000	
Hodgdon	H380	49.5	210	Federal	2900	53,100	
Hodgdon	H450	50.0	210	Federal	2600	37,800	
Hodgdon	H450	58.0	210	Federal	3000	51,300	Maximum - Compressed
Winchester	W760	48.0	210	Federal	2700	41,200	
Winchester	W760	52.0	210	Federal	2950	52,100	Maximum

.270 WEATHERBY MAGNUM

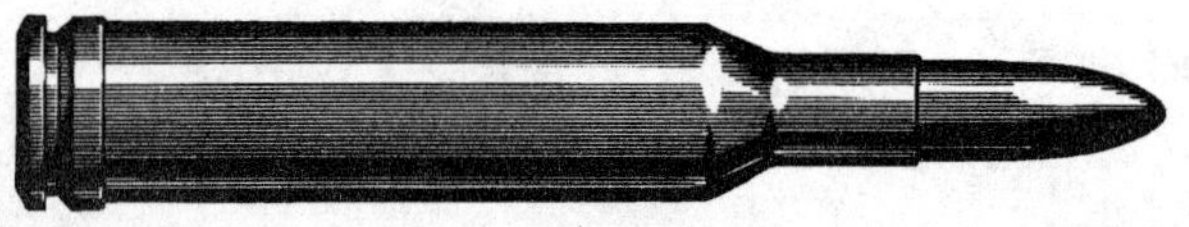

SPECIFICATIONS

Dia. of Rim — .530″
Dia. of Base — .511″
Dia. of Shoulder — .490″
Dia. of Neck — .301″
Length of Neck — .360″
Angle of Shoulder — 25°
Dia. Jacketed Bullet — .277″
Dia. Cast Bullet — .279″
Length of Case — 2.545″
Max. Overall Length — 3.28″
Primer Size — Large Rifle M
Water Capacity — 85.34 grs.

100-grain Soft Point

POWDER MFGR.	POWDER TYPE	GRAINS	PRIMER TYPE	PRIMER MFGR.	VELOCITY	PRESSURE (C.U.P.)	REMARKS
IMR	4064	56.0	215	Federal	3200	—	
IMR	4064	60.0	215	Federal	3500	—	Near Maximum
IMR	4320	58.0	215	Federal	3100	—	
IMR	4320	64.0	215	Federal	3500	—	Maximum
IMR	4831	66.0	215	Federal	3200	—	
IMR	4831	70.5	215	Federal	3500	—	Maximum
IMR	4350	63.5	215	Federal	3225	—	
IMR	4350	69.0	215	Federal	3550	—	Maximum
Hodgdon	H450	68.0	215	Federal	3000	—	
Hodgdon	H450	75.0	215	Federal	3400	—	Maximum
Hodgdon	H4831	72.0	215	Federal	3000	—	
Hodgdon	H4831	76.0	215	Federal	3300	—	Near Maximum
Winchester	785	69.0	215	Federal	3200	—	
Winchester	785	73.0	215	Federal	3400	—	Near Maximum

130-grain Soft Point

POWDER MFGR.	POWDER TYPE	GRAINS	PRIMER TYPE	PRIMER MFGR.	VELOCITY	PRESSURE (C.U.P.)	REMARKS
IMR	4064	52.5	215	Federal	2900	—	
IMR	4064	57.5	215	Federal	3200	—	Maximum
IMR	4320	54.5	215	Federal	2900	—	
IMR	4320	61.5	215	Federal	3300	—	Maximum
IMR	4831	62.5	215	Federal	3000	—	
IMR	4831	68.0	215	Federal	3300	—	Near Maximum
IMR	4350	60.5	215	Federal	3000	—	
IMR	4350	65.5	215	Federal	3275	—	Near Maximum
Hodgdon	H450	66.0	215	Federal	3000	—	
Hodgdon	H450	69.0	215	Federal	3150	—	Near Maximum
Hodgdon	H4831	66.0	215	Federal	3000	—	
Hodgdon	H4831	70.0	215	Federal	3225	—	Maximum

.270 WEATHERBY MAGNUM (Cont.)

140-grain Soft Point

POWDER MFGR.	POWDER TYPE	GRAINS	PRIMER TYPE	PRIMER MFGR.	VELOCITY	PRESSURE (C.U.P.)	REMARKS
IMR	4064	51.5	215	Federal	2800	—	
IMR	4064	57.0	215	Federal	3125	—	
IMR	4320	55.0	215	Federal	2900	—	
IMR	4320	60.5	215	Federal	3200	—	Maximum
IMR	4831	62.5	215	Federal	2900	—	
IMR	4831	66.0	215	Federal	3100	—	
IMR	4350	60.0	215	Federal	2900	—	
IMR	4350	65.0	215	Federal	3185	—	Maximum
Hodgdon	H450	65.0	215	Federal	2900	—	
Hodgdon	H450	68.0	215	Federal	3050	—	Near Maximum
Hodgdon	H4831	65.5	215	Federal	2925	—	
Hodgdon	H4831	68.5	215	Federal	3125	—	Maximum

150-grain Soft Point

POWDER MFGR.	POWDER TYPE	GRAINS	PRIMER TYPE	PRIMER MFGR.	VELOCITY	PRESSURE (C.U.P.)	REMARKS
IMR	4064	51.5	215	Federal	2725	—	
IMR	4064	56.0	215	Federal	2900	—	Maximum
IMR	4320	54.0	215	Federal	2800	—	
IMR	4320	57.5	215	Federal	3000	—	Maximum
IMR	4831	60.5	215	Federal	2800	—	
IMR	4831	67.5	215	Federal	3100	—	
IMR	4350	61.0	215	Federal	2800	—	
IMR	4350	65.5	215	Federal	3000	—	Maximum
Hodgdon	H450	63.5	215	Federal	2800	—	
Hodgdon	H450	68.0	215	Federal	2900	—	Maximum
Hodgdon	H4831	65.0	215	Federal	2850	—	
Hodgdon	H4831	68.0	215	Federal	3000	—	Maximum

.280 REMINGTON

SPECIFICATIONS

Dia. of Rim — .473″
Dia. of Base — .470″
Dia. of Shoulder — .441″
Dia. of Neck — .315″
Length of Neck — .341″
Angle of Shoulder — 17.5°

Dia. Jacketed Bullet — .284″
Dia. Cast Bullet — .286″
Length of Case — 2.545″
Max. Overall Length — 3.33″
Primer Size — Large Rifle
Water Capacity — 68.58 grs.

125-grain Soft Point

POWDER MFGR.	POWDER TYPE	GRAINS	PRIMER TYPE	PRIMER MFGR.	VELOCITY	PRESSURE (C.U.P.)	REMARKS
SR	4759	30.0	210	Federal	2445	49700	
IMR	4227	28.5	210	Federal	2375	48400	
IMR	4198	36.0	210	Federal	2680	50000	
IMR	3031	47.0	210	Federal	2975	48900	
IMR	4064	50.0	210	Federal	3055	49700	
IMR	4895	44.0	210	Federal	2845	49100	
IMR	4320	46.5	210	Federal	2880	49900	
IMR	4350	56.5	210	Federal	3055	48600	
IMR	4831	60.0	210	Federal	3115	50000	Compressed load

150-grain Soft Point

POWDER MFGR.	POWDER TYPE	GRAINS	PRIMER TYPE	PRIMER MFGR.	VELOCITY	PRESSURE (C.U.P.)	REMARKS
SR	4759	29.5	210	Federal	2200	50000	
IMR	4227	27.5	210	Federal	2115	49500	
IMR	4198	34.5	210	Federal	2375	49200	
IMR	3031	45.5	210	Federal	2745	48800	
IMR	4064	48.0	210	Federal	2810	50000	

165-grain Soft Point

POWDER MFGR.	POWDER TYPE	GRAINS	PRIMER TYPE	PRIMER MFGR.	VELOCITY	PRESSURE (C.U.P.)	REMARKS
SR	4759	29.0	210	Federal	2150	50000	
IMR	4227	27.0	210	Federal	2050	50000	
IMR	4198	33.5	210	Federal	2295	49400	
IMR	3031	44.5	210	Federal	2615	49700	
IMR	4064	46.5	210	Federal	2640	48800	
IMR	4895	42.0	210	Federal	2525	49400	
IMR	4320	44.0	210	Federal	2550	49900	

.284 WINCHESTER

SPECIFICATIONS

Dia. of Rim — .473″
Dia. of Base — .500″
Dia. of Shoulder — .475″
Dia. of Neck — .320″
Length of Neck — .285″
Angle of Shoulder — 35°
Dia. Jacketed Bullet — .284″
Dia. Cast Bullet — .286″
Length of Case — 2.2″
Max. Overall Length — 2.95″
Primer Size — Large Rifle
Water Capacity — 64.6 grs.

130-grain Softnose Spitzer

POWDER MFGR.	POWDER TYPE	GRAINS	PRIMER TYPE	PRIMER MFGR.	VELOCITY	PRESSURE (C.U.P.)	REMARKS
SR	4759	30.0	210	Federal	2425	51900	
IMR	4227	30.0	210	Federal	2460	52300	
IMR	4198	38.0	210	Federal	2775	52400	
IMR	3031	48.0	210	Federal	3055	54000	
IMR	4064	50.0	210	Federal	3085	50600	
IMR	4895	45.0	210	Federal	2905	52800	
IMR	4320	46.0	210	Federal	2890	52300	
IMR	4350	57.0	210	Federal	3130	53600	
IMR	4831	59.0	210	Federal	3100	50600	Compressed load

160-grain Softnose Spitzer

POWDER MFGR.	POWDER TYPE	GRAINS	PRIMER TYPE	PRIMER MFGR.	VELOCITY	PRESSURE (C.U.P.)	REMARKS
SR	4759	27.5	210	Federal	2105	51900	
IMR	4227	28.0	210	Federal	2170	52200	
IMR	4198	34.5	210	Federal	2440	52500	
IMR	3031	45.0	210	Federal	2660	52700	
IMR	4064	47.0	210	Federal	2760	53700	
IMR	4895	41.0	210	Federal	2584	53500	
IMR	4320	43.5	210	Federal	2635	52900	
IMR	4350	52.0	210	Federal	2720	53600	Compressed load
IMR	4831	52.0	210	Federal	2635	50600	Compressed load

.30 M1 CARBINE

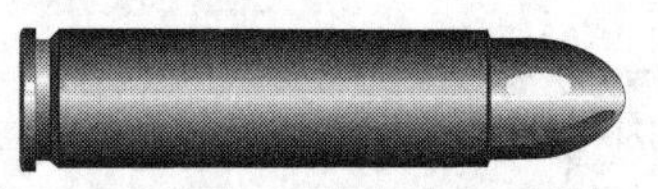

SPECIFICATIONS

Dia. of Rim — .360″
Dia. of Base — .356″
Dia. of Shoulder — Straight
Dia. of Neck — .336″
Length of Neck — Straight
Angle of Shoulder — Straight

Dia. Jacketed Bullet — .308″
Dia. Cast Bullet — .308″
Length of Case — 1.290″
Max. Overall Length — 1.680″
Primer Size — Small Rifle
Water Capacity — 18.050 grs.

100-grain Softnose

POWDER MFGR.	POWDER TYPE	GRAINS	PRIMER TYPE	PRIMER MFGR.	VELOCITY	PRESSURE (C.U.P.)	REMARKS
IMR	4227	14.5	200	Federal	1850	—	
IMR	4227	15.5	200	Federal	2050	—	Maximum
IMR	4198	14.0	200	Federal	1500	—	
IMR	4198	15.0	200	Federal	1640	—	Maximum

110-grain Softnose

POWDER MFGR.	POWDER TYPE	GRAINS	PRIMER TYPE	PRIMER MFGR.	VELOCITY	PRESSURE (C.U.P.)	REMARKS
IMR	4227	12.0	200	Federal	1600	—	
IMR	4227	14.5	200	Federal	1900	—	Maximum
Hodgdon	H4227	12.0	200	Federal	1600	—	
Hodgdon	H4227	14.5	200	Federal	1900	—	Maximum

.30-30 WCF

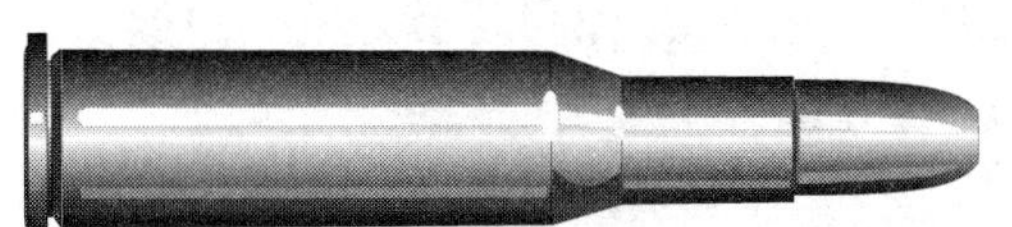

SPECIFICATIONS

Dia. of Rim — .506″
Dia. of Base — .421″
Dia. of Shoulder — .402″
Dia. of Neck — .330″
Length of Neck — .426″
Angle of Shoulder — 53.25°
Dia. Jacketed Bullet — .308″
Dia. Cast Bullet — .309″
Length of Case — 1.976″
Max. Overall Length — 2.55″
Primer Size — Large Rifle
Water Capacity — 44.50 grs.

110-grain Softnose

POWDER MFGR.	POWDER TYPE	GRAINS	PRIMER TYPE	PRIMER MFGR.	VELOCITY	PRESSURE (C.U.P.)	REMARKS
IMR	3031	31.5	210	Federal	2300	—	
IMR	3031	33.5	210	Federal	2400	—	Near Maximum
IMR	4064	31.0	WLR	Winchester	2170	—	
IMR	4064	35.5	WLR	Winchester	2500	—	Compressed
IMR	4198	26.5	WLR	Winchester	2300	—	
IMR	4198	29.0	WLR	Winchester	2600	—	
IMR	4320	33.0	210	Federal	2300	—	
IMR	4320	35.5	210	Federal	2400	—	
IMR	4320	36.5	210	Federal	2500	—	
Hodgdon	BL-C(2)	34.0	210	Federal	2300	—	
Hodgdon	BL-C(2)	36.5	210	Federal	2550	—	Near Maximum
Hodgdon	H322	32.5	210	Federal	2300	—	

150-grain Softnose

POWDER MFGR.	POWDER TYPE	GRAINS	PRIMER TYPE	PRIMER MFGR.	VELOCITY	PRESSURE (C.U.P.)	REMARKS
IMR	3031	30.5	210	Federal	2125	—	
IMR	3031	32.5	210	Federal	2275	—	Near Maximum
IMR	4064	32.5	210	Federal	2130	—	
IMR	4064	35.0	WLR	Winchester	2300	—	
IMR	4320	33.0	210	Federal	2100	—	
IMR	4320	34.0	210	Federal	2250	—	
Hodgdon	BL-C(2)	32.0	210	Federal	2100	—	
Hodgdon	BL-C(2)	34.5	210	Federal	2350	—	Near Maximum
Hodgdon	H322	30.0	210	Federal	2100	—	
Hodgdon	H322	32.0	210	Federal	2250	—	
Winchester	W748	33.0	210	Federal	2225	—	
Winchester	W748	35.0	210	Federal	2350	—	

.30-30 WCF (Cont.)

170-grain Softnose

POWDER MFGR.	POWDER TYPE	GRAINS	PRIMER TYPE	PRIMER MFGR.	VELOCITY	PRESSURE (C.U.P.)	REMARKS
IMR	3031	28.0	210	Federal	1900	—	
IMR	3031	30.5	210	Federal	2000	—	Near Maximum
IMR	4064	29.0	200	CCI	1850	—	
IMR	4064	31.0	200	CCI	2050	—	
IMR	4320	31.5	210	Federal	2000	—	
IMR	4320	33.5	210	Federal	2200	—	Near Maximum
Hodgdon	BL-C(2)	30.0	210	Federal	2000	—	
Hodgdon	BL-C(2)	33.0	210	Federal	2150	—	Near Maximum
Hodgdon	H322	27.5	200	CCI	1875	—	
Hodgdon	H322	29.0	200	CCI	2000	—	
Norma	201	27.0	200	CCI	1860	—	
Norma	201	29.5	200	CCI	2000	—	
Winchester	W748	31.5	210	Federal	1910	—	
Winchester	W748	34.5	210	Federal	2150	—	

190-grain Silvertip

POWDER MFGR.	POWDER TYPE	GRAINS	PRIMER TYPE	PRIMER MFGR.	VELOCITY	PRESSURE (C.U.P.)	REMARKS
IMR	4227	14.5	200	Federal	1850	—	
IMR	4227	15.5	200	Federal	2050	—	Maximum
IMR	4198	14.0	200	Federal	1500	—	
IMR	4198	15.0	200	Federal	1640	—	Maximum

.30-40 KRAG

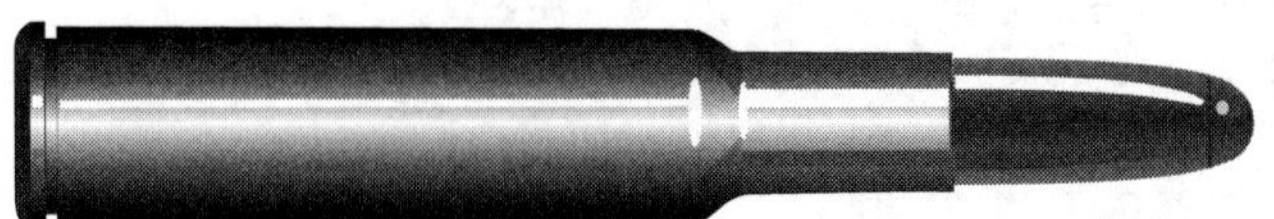

SPECIFICATIONS

Dia. of Rim — .545″
Dia. of Base — .457″
Dia. of Shoulder — .420″
Dia. of Neck — .337″
Length of Neck — .426″
Angle of Shoulder — 21°
Dia. Jacketed Bullet — .308″
Dia. Cast Bullet — .310″
Length of Case — 2.303″
Max. Overall Length — 3.09″
Primer Size — Large Rifle
Water Capacity — 56.4 grs.

110-grain Softnose

POWDER MFGR.	POWDER TYPE	GRAINS	PRIMER TYPE	PRIMER MFGR.	VELOCITY	PRESSURE (C.U.P.)	REMARKS
IMR	3031	40.5	210	Federal	2800	—	
IMR	3031	43.0	210	Federal	3000	—	Maximum
IMR	4064	44.0	210	Federal	2700	—	
IMR	4064	47.5	210	Federal	3000	—	Maximum
IMR	4320	43.0	210	Federal	2625	—	
IMR	4320	46.5	210	Federal	2900	—	Maximum
IMR	4895	43.5	210	Federal	2625	—	
IMR	4895	45.5	210	Federal	2800	—	Near Maximum
Hodgdon	H335	40.5	210	Federal	2600	—	
Hodgdon	H335	42.5	210	Federal	2800	—	Near Maximum
Hodgdon	H4895	44.0	210	Federal	2750	—	
Hodgdon	H4895	48.0	210	Federal	3000	—	Maximum
Winchester	W760	47.0	210	Federal	2750	—	
Winchester	W760	49.5	210	Federal	2800	—	Maximum

130-grain Softnose

POWDER MFGR.	POWDER TYPE	GRAINS	PRIMER TYPE	PRIMER MFGR.	VELOCITY	PRESSURE (C.U.P.)	REMARKS
IMR	3031	40.0	210	Federal	2550	—	
IMR	3031	42.5	210	Federal	2725	—	Maximum
IMR	4064	43.0	210	Federal	2450	—	
IMR	4064	46.0	210	Federal	2700	—	Maximum
IMR	4320	43.5	210	Federal	2450	—	
IMR	4320	47.0	210	Federal	2725	—	Maximum
Hodgdon	H380	44.0	210	Federal	2450	—	
Hodgdon	H380	47.0	210	Federal	2650	—	Maximum

.30-40 KRAG (Cont.)

150-grain Softnose

POWDER MFGR.	POWDER TYPE	GRAINS	PRIMER TYPE	PRIMER MFGR.	VELOCITY	PRESSURE (C.U.P.)	REMARKS
IMR	3031	36.5	210	Federal	2300	—	
IMR	3031	40.0	210	Federal	2550	—	Near Maximum
IMR	4064	42.0	210	Federal	2400	—	
IMR	4064	44.0	210	Federal	2600	—	Near Maximum
IMR	4320	41.5	210	Federal	2350	—	
IMR	4320	43.0	210	Federal	2500	—	Near Maximum
IMR	4831	47.5	210	Federal	2300	—	
IMR	4831	49.0	210	Federal	2400	—	Maximum
Hodgdon	H380	41.0	210	Federal	2350	—	
Hodgdon	H380	44.5	210	Federal	2500	—	Maximum
Hodgdon	H4895	39.0	210	Federal	2450	—	
Hodgdon	H4895	42.5	210	Federal	2600	—	Maximum

165-grain Softnose

POWDER MFGR.	POWDER TYPE	GRAINS	PRIMER TYPE	PRIMER MFGR.	VELOCITY	PRESSURE (C.U.P.)	REMARKS
IMR	3031	34.5	210	Federal	2200	—	
IMR	3031	37.5	210	Federal	2400	—	Maximum
IMR	4064	38.0	210	Federal	2200	—	
IMR	4064	42.0	210	Federal	2480	—	Maximum
IMR	4831	46.0	210	Federal	2125	—	
IMR	4831	49.0	210	Federal	2300	—	Maximum
Hodgdon	H380	38.0	210	Federal	2125	—	
Hodgdon	H380	42.5	210	Federal	2400	—	Maximum
Hodgdon	H4895	36.5	210	Federal	2150	—	
Hodgdon	H4895	40.5	210	Federal	2400	—	Maximum

180-grain Softnose

POWDER MFGR.	POWDER TYPE	GRAINS	PRIMER TYPE	PRIMER MFGR.	VELOCITY	PRESSURE (C.U.P.)	REMARKS
IMR	3031	34.5	210	Federal	2100	—	
IMR	3031	37.0	210	Federal	2275	—	Maximum
IMR	4064	36.0	210	Federal	2100	—	
IMR	4064	38.0	210	Federal	2210	—	Near Maximum
IMR	4831	45.0	210	Federal	2000	—	
IMR	4831	47.5	210	Federal	2200	—	Maximum

.30-40 KRAG (Cont.)

180-grain Softnose (*Cont.*)

POWDER MFGR.	POWDER TYPE	GRAINS	PRIMER TYPE	PRIMER MFGR.	VELOCITY	PRESSURE (C.U.P.)	REMARKS
Hodgdon	H380	37.5	210	Federal	2000	—	
Hodgdon	H380	40.5	210	Federal	2200	—	Maximum
Hodgdon	H322	33.0	210	Federal	2040	—	

220-grain Softnose

POWDER MFGR.	POWDER TYPE	GRAINS	PRIMER TYPE	PRIMER MFGR.	VELOCITY	PRESSURE (C.U.P.)	REMARKS
IMR	3031	30.5	210	Federal	1700	—	
IMR	3031	33.0	210	Federal	1900	—	Maximum
IMR	4064	33.5	210	Federal	1800	—	
IMR	4064	35.5	210	Federal	2000	—	Maximum
Hodgdon	H380	33.0	210	Federal	1700	—	
Hodgdon	H380	36.0	210	Federal	1900	—	Near Maximum
Hodgdon	H322	30.0	210	Federal	1850	—	
Hodgdon	H322	32.5	210	Federal	2000	—	Maximum

.303 BRITISH

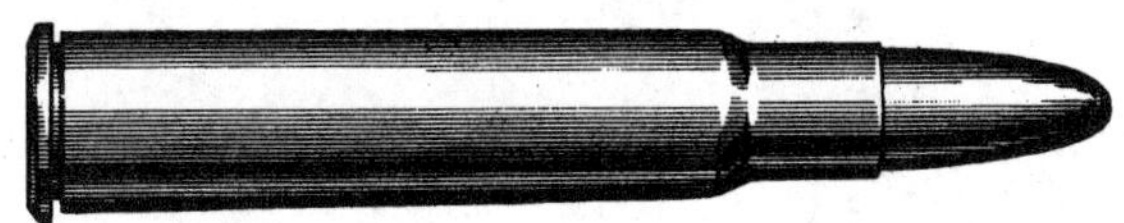

SPECIFICATIONS

Dia. of Rim — .540″
Dia. of Base — .456″
Dia. of Shoulder — .412″
Dia. of Neck — .339″
Length of Neck — .332″
Angle of Shoulder — 35.06°
Dia. Jacketed Bullet — .311″
Dia. Cast Bullet — 313″
Length of Case — 2.158″
Max. Overall Length — 3.08″
Primer Size — Large Rifle
Water Capacity — 54.70 grs.

150-grain Softnose

POWDER MFGR.	POWDER TYPE	GRAINS	PRIMER TYPE	PRIMER MFGR.	VELOCITY	PRESSURE (C.U.P.)	REMARKS
IMR	3031	35.0	210	Federal	2200	—	
IMR	3031	37.0	210	Federal	2400	—	
IMR	3031	41.0	210	Federal	2600	—	
IMR	4064	37.0	210	Federal	2200	—	
IMR	4064	40.0	210	Federal	2400	—	
IMR	4064	44.0	210	Federal	2700	—	Caution: Near Maximum
IMR	4320	44.0	210	Federal	2600	—	
Hodgdon	BL-C(2)	45.0	9½	Remington	2600	—	
Hodgdon	H4831	49.0	9½	Remington	2300	—	

.303 BRITISH (Cont.)

150-grain Softnose (*Cont.*)

POWDER MFGR.	POWDER TYPE	GRAINS	PRIMER TYPE	PRIMER MFGR.	VELOCITY	PRESSURE (C.U.P.)	REMARKS
Hodgdon	H450	50.0	210	Federal	2300	—	
Hodgdon	H380	41.0	210	Federal	2400	—	
Winchester	W760	47.0	9½	Remington	2400	—	
Winchester	760	50.0	210	Federal	2600	—	Caution: Maximum

180-grain Softnose

POWDER MFGR.	POWDER TYPE	GRAINS	PRIMER TYPE	PRIMER MFGR.	VELOCITY	PRESSURE (C.U.P.)	REMARKS
IMR	3031	36.0	210	Federal	2200	—	
IMR	3031	37.0	210	Federal	2250	—	
IMR	4064	36.5	210	Federal	2100	—	
IMR	4064	39.0	210	Federal	2300	—	
IMR	4064	40.0	210	Federal	2375	—	Caution: Near Maximum
Hodgdon	H4831	47.0	9½	Remington	2250	—	
Hodgdon	H450	50.0	210	Federal	2250	—	
Hodgdon	H380	39.0	210	Federal	2150	—	
Winchester	W760	40.0	210	Federal	2000	—	
Winchester	W760	43.5	210	Federal	2200	—	
Winchester	760	50.0	210	Federal	2600	—	Caution: Maximum

215-grain Softnose

POWDER MFGR.	POWDER TYPE	GRAINS	PRIMER TYPE	PRIMER MFGR.	VELOCITY	PRESSURE (C.U.P.)	REMARKS
IMR	3031	35.0	210	Federal	1950	—	
IMR	3031	39.0	210	Federal	2175	—	
IMR	4064	38.0	210	Federal	1970	—	
IMR	4064	42.0	210	Federal	2175	—	
IMR	4320	37.5	210	Federal	1975	—	
IMR	4320	42.5	210	Federal	2230	—	
Hercules	2400	12.0	9½	Remington	950	—	
Hercules	2400	13.0	210	Federal	1000	—	Practice load
Hercules	2400	14.5	210	Federal	1150	18,400	
Hercules	2400	18.5	210	Federal	1400	28,000	
Hercules	2400	20.0	210	Federal	1530	35,000	

.307 WINCHESTER

SPECIFICATIONS

Dia. of Rim — .506″	Dia. Jacketed Bullet — .308″
Dia. of Base — .471″	Dia. Cast Bullet — .308″
Dia. of Shoulder — .454″	Length of Case — 2.015″
Dia. of Neck — .334″	Max. Overall Length — 2.560″
Length of Neck — .303″	Primer Size — Large Rifle
Angle of Shoulder — 21.54°	Water Capacity — 56.69 grs.

110-grain Softnose

POWDER MFGR.	POWDER TYPE	GRAINS	PRIMER TYPE	PRIMER MFGR.	VELOCITY	PRESSURE (C.U.P.)	REMARKS
IMR	3031	41.5	9½	Remington	2700	—	
IMR	3031	43.5	9½	Remington	2845	—	Maximum
IMR	4064	45.0	9½	Remington	2750	—	
IMR	4064	48.0	9½	Remington	2950	—	Maximum
IMR	4320	44.5	9½	Remington	2650	—	
IMR	4320	47.5	210	Federal	2800	—	Near Maximum
IMR	4895	40.0	9½	Remington	2725	—	
IMR	4895	44.0	9½	Remington	2900	—	Near Maximum

150-grain Softnose

POWDER MFGR.	POWDER TYPE	GRAINS	PRIMER TYPE	PRIMER MFGR.	VELOCITY	PRESSURE (C.U.P.)	REMARKS
IMR	3031	38.0	9½	Remington	2350	—	
IMR	3031	43.0	9½	Remington	2700	—	Maximum
IMR	4064	42.5	9½	Remington	2550	—	
IMR	4064	45.0	9½	Remington	2750	—	Maximum
IMR	4320	43.0	9½	Remington	2500	—	
IMR	4320	45.0	210	Federal	2665	—	Maximum
IMR	4895	40.0	9½	Remington	2550	—	
IMR	4895	43.0	9½	Remington	2760	—	Maximum

170-grain Softnose

POWDER MFGR.	POWDER TYPE	GRAINS	PRIMER TYPE	PRIMER MFGR.	VELOCITY	PRESSURE (C.U.P.)	REMARKS
IMR	3031	36.5	9½	Remington	2325	—	
IMR	3031	39.0	9½	Remington	2500	—	Near Maximum
IMR	4064	39.5	9½	Remington	2400	—	
IMR	4064	41.5	9½	Remington	2625	—	Maximum
IMR	4320	39.5	9½	Remington	2360	—	

.308 WINCHESTER

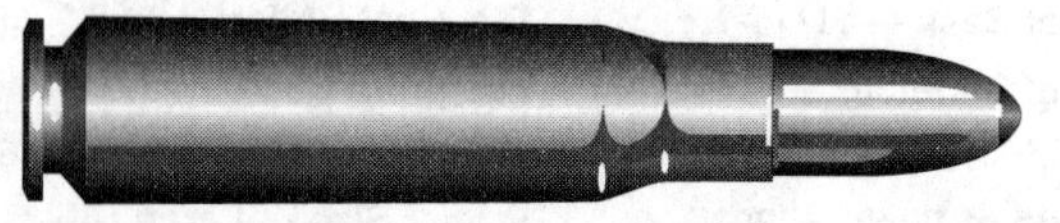

SPECIFICATIONS

Dia. of Rim — .473″
Dia. of Base — .470″
Dia. of Shoulder — .454″
Dia. of Neck — .343″
Length of Neck — .304″
Angle of Shoulder — 20.18°
Dia. Jacketed Bullet — .308″
Dia. Cast Bullet — .308″
Length of Case — 2.015″
Max. Overall Length — 2.800″
Primer Size — Large Rifle
Water Capacity — 53.53 grs.

110-grain Softnose

POWDER MFGR.	POWDER TYPE	GRAINS	PRIMER TYPE	PRIMER MFGR.	VELOCITY	PRESSURE (C.U.P.)	REMARKS
IMR	3031	40.0	9½	Remington	2625	31200	
IMR	3031	46.0	9½	Remington	3100	49800	Maximum
IMR	4064	45.5	9½	Remington	2900	37400	
IMR	4064	50.0	9½	Remington	3200	50200	Maximum
IMR	4320	45.5	9½	Remington	2800	39400	
IMR	4320	50.5	9½	Remington	3100	50600	Maximum
IMR	4895	44.0	9½	Remington	2900	40100	
IMR	4895	49.5	9½	Remington	3200	51800	Maximum
Hodgdon	H322	43.0	210	Federal	2950	41000	
Hodgdon	H322	46.5	210	Federal	3200	51000	Maximum
Hodgdon	H4895	45.0	210	Federal	2900	40900	
Hodgdon	H4895	48.5	210	Federal	3200	50000	Maximum
Winchester	W748	50.0	210	Federal	2965	43800	
Winchester	W748	53.0	210	Federal	3200	51200	Maximum

130-grain Softnose

POWDER MFGR.	POWDER TYPE	GRAINS	PRIMER TYPE	PRIMER MFGR.	VELOCITY	PRESSURE (C.U.P.)	REMARKS
IMR	3031	41.0	9½	Remington	2700	34500	
IMR	3031	44.0	9½	Remington	2900	49900	Maximum
IMR	4064	43.0	9½	Remington	2700	38300	
IMR	4064	47.0	9½	Remington	2975	50000	Maximum
IMR	4320	45.0	9½	Remington	2700	38100	
IMR	4320	49.5	9½	Remington	3000	50500	Maximum
IMR	4895	43.0	9½	Remington	2800	40900	
IMR	4895	46.0	9½	Remington	2985	51100	Maximum
Hodgdon	H322	40.0	210	Federal	2700	38600	
Hodgdon	H322	44.0	210	Federal	2900	51200	Maximum

.308 WINCHESTER (Cont.)

150-grain Softnose

POWDER MFGR.	POWDER TYPE	GRAINS	PRIMER TYPE	PRIMER MFGR.	VELOCITY	PRESSURE (C.U.P.)	REMARKS
IMR	3031	38.0	9½	Remington	2500	36000	
IMR	3031	41.5	9½	Remington	2725	49750	Near Maximum
IMR	4064	42.5	9½	Remington	2600	37600	
IMR	4064	45.0	9½	Remington	2800	49800	Maximum
IMR	4320	43.0	9½	Remington	2500	36500	
IMR	4320	48.0	9½	Remington	2800	51100	Maximum
IMR	4895	40.0	9½	Remington	2500	33000	
IMR	4895	43.0	9½	Remington	2700	49000	Maximum
Hodgdon	H322	37.5	210	Federal	2450	38900	
Hodgdon	H322	41.0	210	Federal	2650	49100	Maximum
Hodgdon	H4895	40.0	210	Federal	2500	40000	
Hodgdon	H4895	42.0	210	Federal	2635	49700	Near Maximum
Hodgdon	H414	48.0	210	Federal	2600	41300	
Hodgdon	H414	51.0	210	Federal	2725	49200	Near Maximum
Winchester	W748	45.0	210	Federal	2600	—	
Winchester	W748	48.5	210	Federal	2800	—	Maximum

165-grain Softnose

POWDER MFGR.	POWDER TYPE	GRAINS	PRIMER TYPE	PRIMER MFGR.	VELOCITY	PRESSURE (C.U.P.)	REMARKS
IMR	3031	36.5	9½	Remington	2300	34000	
IMR	3031	40.5	9½	Remington	2600	48700	Near Maximum
IMR	4064	39.5	9½	Remington	2400	33500	
IMR	4064	43.5	9½	Remington	2700	51000	Maximum
IMR	4320	42.0	9½	Remington	2450	—	
IMR	4320	45.0	9½	Remington	2600	—	Near Maximum
IMR	4895	38.5	9½	Remington	2400	—	
IMR	4895	41.5	9½	Remington	2600	—	Maximum
Hodgdon	H322	36.0	210	Federal	2350	—	
Hodgdon	H322	38.5	210	Federal	2510	—	Near Maximum
Hodgdon	H4895	38.0	210	Federal	2350	39000	
Hodgdon	H4895	41.0	210	Federal	2550	48600	Near Maximum
Hodgdon	H414	44.0	210	Federal	2300	38900	
Hodgdon	H414	47.5	210	Federal	2700	50000	Maximum

.30-06

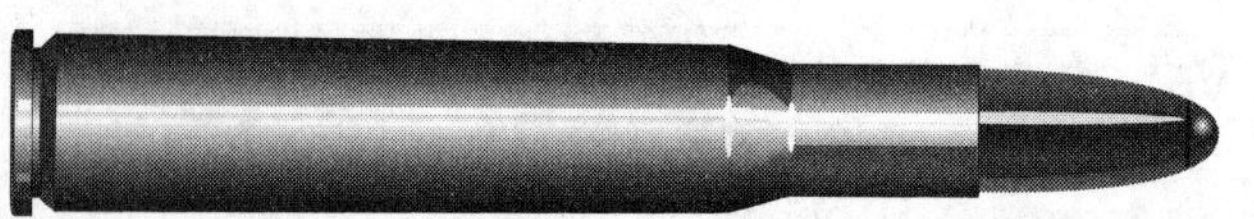

SPECIFICATIONS

Dia. of Rim — .473″
Dia. of Base — .470″
Dia. of Shoulder — .441″
Dia. of Neck — .339″
Length of Neck — .383″
Angle of Shoulder — 17.47°

Dia. Jacketed Bullet — .308″
Dia. Cast Bullet — .308″
Length of Case — 2.494″
Max. Overall Length — 3.340″
Primer Size — Large Rifle
Water Capacity — 68.01 grs.

110-grain Softnose

POWDER MFGR.	POWDER TYPE	GRAINS	PRIMER TYPE	PRIMER MFGR.	VELOCITY	PRESSURE (C.U.P.)	REMARKS
IMR	3031	49.5	210	Federal	3100	42000	
IMR	3031	53.0	210	Federal	3300	49000	
IMR	4064	53.0	210	Federal	3125	41800	
IMR	4064	56.0	210	Federal	3400	49000	Near Maximum
IMR	4320	54.0	210	Federal	3100	41700	
IMR	4320	56.0	210	Federal	3300	48600	Near Maximum
IMR	4895	51.0	210	Federal	3100	42300	
IMR	4895	53.5	210	Federal	3300	49500	Near Maximum

125-grain Softnose

POWDER MFGR.	POWDER TYPE	GRAINS	PRIMER TYPE	PRIMER MFGR.	VELOCITY	PRESSURE (C.U.P.)	REMARKS
IMR	3031	47.0	210	Federal	2900	45100	
IMR	3031	51.0	210	Federal	3100	49700	Maximum
IMR	4064	51.0	210	Federal	3000	46800	
IMR	4064	53.0	210	Federal	3100	49200	Near Maximum
IMR	4320	51.5	210	Federal	3000	45000	
IMR	4320	53.0	210	Federal	3100	49900	Maximum
IMR	4350	57.0	210	Federal	2950	42300	
IMR	4350	60.0	210	Federal	3100	50000	Maximum
IMR	4895	49.0	210	Federal	2900	46200	
IMR	4895	52.0	210	Federal	3100	49700	Maximum
Hodgdon	H335	50.0	210	Federal	2900	—	
Hodgdon	H335	53.5	210	Federal	3150	—	Near Maximum
Hodgdon	H4895	49.0	210	Federal	3000	—	
Hodgdon	H4895	50.5	210	Federal	3100	—	Near Maximum
Winchester	W748	51.0	210	Federal	2900	41200	
Winchester	W748	55.0	210	Federal	3100	48200	
Winchester	W760	58.0	210	Federal	3000	—	
Winchester	W760	60.5	210	Federal	3100	—	Near Maximum

.30-06 (Cont.)

150-grain Softnose

POWDER MFGR.	POWDER TYPE	GRAINS	PRIMER TYPE	PRIMER MFGR.	VELOCITY	PRESSURE (C.U.P.)	REMARKS
IMR	3031	44.0	210	Federal	2650	44600	
IMR	3031	51.0	210	Federal	3000	50000	Maximum
IMR	4064	46.0	210	Federal	2600	42300	
IMR	4064	51.0	210	Federal	2900	49700	Near Maximum
IMR	4320	46.5	210	Federal	2700	44000	
IMR	4320	50.0	210	Federal	2900	—	Maximum
IMR	4350	54.0	210	Federal	2700	41500	
IMR	4350	59.0	210	Federal	3080	48900	Near Maximum
IMR	4831	57.5	210	Federal	2750	—	
IMR	4831	60.0	210	Federal	2900	—	Maximum
Hodgdon	H380	48.0	210	Federal	2725	—	
Hodgdon	H380	51.5	210	Federal	2900	—	
Hodgdon	H4895	45.0	210	Federal	2700	46900	
Hodgdon	H4895	48.5	210	Federal	2925	49900	Maximum

165-grain Softnose

POWDER MFGR.	POWDER TYPE	GRAINS	PRIMER TYPE	PRIMER MFGR.	VELOCITY	PRESSURE (C.U.P.)	REMARKS
IMR	3031	42.0	210	Federal	2525	—	
IMR	3031	46.0	210	Federal	2700	49900	Near Maximum
IMR	4064	45.0	210	Federal	2500	40300	
IMR	4064	49.0	210	Federal	2700	49300	Near Maximum
IMR	4320	45.0	210	Federal	2500	42500	
IMR	4320	49.0	210	Federal	2775	49700	Maximum
IMR	4350	54.0	210	Federal	2680	42400	
IMR	4350	56.5	210	Federal	2800	49100	Near Maximum
IMR	4831	56.5	210	Federal	2600	39700	
IMR	4831	58.5	210	Federal	2820	48300	Near Maximum
Hodgdon	H414	54.0	210	Federal	2750	44800	
Hodgdon	H414	56.0	210	Federal	2900	49400	Maximum
Hodgdon	BL-C(2)	45.5	210	Federal	2600	44300	
Hodgdon	BL-C(2)	47.5	210	Federal	2725	49100	Near Maximum
Hodgdon	H380	47.5	210	Federal	2600	41000	
Hodgdon	H380	51.0	210	Federal	2775	48600	Near Maximum
Winchester	W748	45.5	210	Federal	2600	—	
Winchester	W748	49.5	210	Federal	2800	—	Maximum

.30-06 (Cont.)

180-grain Softnose

POWDER MFGR.	POWDER TYPE	GRAINS	PRIMER TYPE	PRIMER MFGR.	VELOCITY	PRESSURE (C.U.P.)	REMARKS
IMR	4064	45.0	210	Federal	2450	—	
IMR	4064	48.0	210	Federal	2650	—	Near Maximum
IMR	4320	45.0	210	Federal	2420	—	
IMR	4320	48.0	210	Federal	2600	—	Near Maximum
IMR	4350	53.5	210	Federal	2500	—	
IMR	4350	56.0	210	Federal	2800	—	Maximum
IMR	4831	54.0	210	Federal	2500	—	
IMR	4831	59.0	210	Federal	2800	—	Maximum
Hodgdon	H4350	53.5	210	Federal	2600	45000	
Hodgdon	H4350	55.5	210	Federal	2725	49000	Maximum
Hodgdon	H414	50.0	210	Federal	2500	39700	
Hodgdon	H414	54.0	210	Federal	2700	48200	Maximum
Hodgdon	BL-C(2)	44.0	210	Federal	2400	44500	
Hodgdon	BL-C(2)	47.0	210	Federal	2550	49400	Maximum
Winchester	W748	45.0	210	Federal	2500	—	
Winchester	W748	47.0	210	Federal	2600	—	Near Maximum
Winchester	W760	52.0	210	Federal	2600	—	
Winchester	W760	55.0	210	Federal	2700	—	Near Maximum

220-grain Softnose

POWDER MFGR.	POWDER TYPE	GRAINS	PRIMER TYPE	PRIMER MFGR.	VELOCITY	PRESSURE (C.U.P.)	REMARKS
IMR	4350	49.0	210	Federal	2300	—	
IMR	4350	52.5	210	Federal	2460	—	Maximum
IMR	4831	50.0	210	Federal	2300	—	
IMR	4831	54.0	210	Federal	2450	—	Maximum
Hodgdon	H4350	49.5	210	Federal	2300	—	
Hodgdon	H4350	51.5	210	Federal	2400	—	Maximum
Hodgdon	H414	47.5	210	Federal	2300	—	
Hodgdon	H414	50.0	210	Federal	2400	—	Near Maximum
Winchester	W760	48.0	210	Federal	2300	—	
Winchester	W760	50.0	210	Federal	2380	—	Maximum

.300 H&H MAGNUM

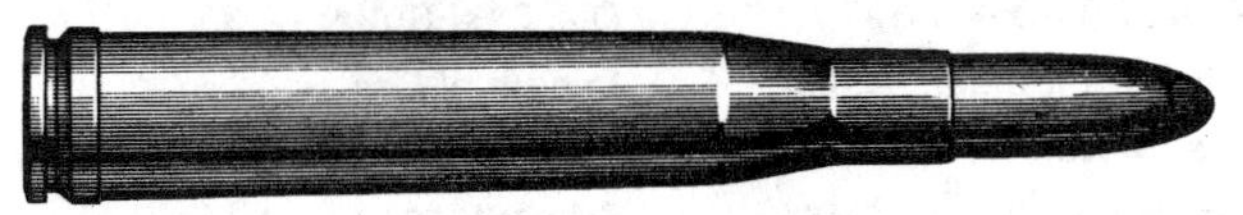

SPECIFICATIONS

Dia. of Rim — .532″
Dia. of Base — .513″
Dia. of Shoulder — .457″
Dia. of Neck — .339″
Length of Neck — .30″
Angle of Shoulder — 7.7°

Dia. Jacketed Bullet — .308″
Dia. Cast Bullet — .308″
Length of Case — 2.85″
Max. Overall Length — 3.65″
Primer Size — Large Rifle M
Water Capacity — 88.82 grs.

150-grain Softnose

POWDER MFGR.	POWDER TYPE	GRAINS	PRIMER TYPE	PRIMER MFGR.	VELOCITY	PRESSURE (C.U.P.)	REMARKS
IMR	4064	59.0	215	Federal	3010	—	
IMR	4064	61.0	215	Federal	3220	—	Maximum
IMR	4320	59.0	215	Federal	3040	—	
IMR	4320	66.0	215	Federal	3325	—	Maximum
IMR	4895	60.0	215	Federal	3120	—	
IMR	4895	66.0	215	Federal	3400	—	Near Maximum
IMR	3031	55.0	215	Federal	3000	—	
IMR	3031	61.0	215	Federal	3220	—	Maximum

180-grain Softnose

POWDER MFGR.	POWDER TYPE	GRAINS	PRIMER TYPE	PRIMER MFGR.	VELOCITY	PRESSURE (C.U.P.)	REMARKS
IMR	4064	54.0	215	Federal	2675	—	
IMR	4064	60.0	215	Federal	2950	—	Maximum
IMR	4320	55.0	215	Federal	2740	—	
IMR	4320	61.0	215	Federal	2950	—	Maximum
IMR	4895	53.0	215	Federal	2675	—	
IMR	4895	59.0	215	Federal	2925	—	Near Maximum
IMR	3031	50.0	215	Federal	2625	—	
IMR	3031	58.0	215	Federal	3000	—	Maximum

220-grain Softnose

POWDER MFGR.	POWDER TYPE	GRAINS	PRIMER TYPE	PRIMER MFGR.	VELOCITY	PRESSURE (C.U.P.)	REMARKS
IMR	4064	50.0	215	Federal	2375	—	
IMR	4064	56.0	215	Federal	2625	—	Maximum
IMR	4320	52.0	215	Federal	2450	—	
IMR	4320	58.0	215	Federal	2725	—	Maximum
IMR	4895	51.0	215	Federal	2425	—	
IMR	4895	57.0	215	Federal	2700	—	Near Maximum

.308 NORMA MAGNUM

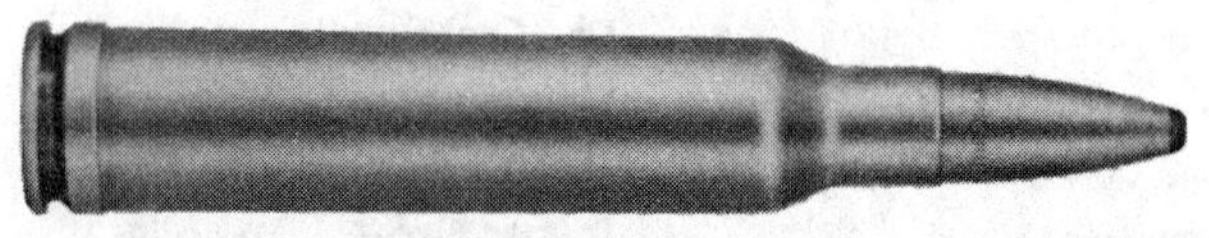

SPECIFICATIONS

Dia. of Rim — .532″
Dia. of Base — .513″
Dia. of Shoulder — .489″
Dia. of Neck — .339″
Length of Neck — .318″
Angle of Shoulder — 25.67°
Dia. Jacketed Bullet — .308″
Dia. Cast Bullet — .308″
Length of Case — 2.559″
Max. Overall Length — 3.30″
Primer Size — Large Rifle M
Water Capacity — 85.78 grs.

110-grain Softnose

POWDER MFGR.	POWDER TYPE	GRAINS	PRIMER TYPE	PRIMER MFGR.	VELOCITY	PRESSURE (C.U.P.)	REMARKS
IMR	3031	63.5	215	Federal	3500	—	
IMR	3031	66.5	215	Federal	3700	—	
IMR	4064	66.0	215	Federal	3500	—	
IMR	4064	70.0	215	Federal	3800	—	Maximum
IMR	4320	69.0	215	Federal	3550	—	
IMR	4320	73.0	215	Federal	3700	—	Near Maximum
IMR	4350	76.0	215	Federal	3500	—	
IMR	4350	79.5	215	Federal	3700	—	Near Maximum
Hodgdon	H380	69.0	215	Federal	3500	—	
Hodgdon	H380	73.0	215	Federal	3700	—	Maximum
Hodgdon	H414	68.0	215	Federal	3425	—	
Hodgdon	H414	74.0	215	Federal	3700	—	Maximum

125-grain Softnose

POWDER MFGR.	POWDER TYPE	GRAINS	PRIMER TYPE	PRIMER MFGR.	VELOCITY	PRESSURE (C.U.P.)	REMARKS
IMR	3031	58.0	215	Federal	3200	—	
IMR	3031	65.0	215	Federal	3500	—	Maximum
IMR	4064	62.0	215	Federal	3200	—	
IMR	4064	65.5	215	Federal	3500	—	Near Maximum
IMR	4320	64.5	215	Federal	3300	—	
IMR	4320	68.5	215	Federal	3500	—	Near Maximum
IMR	4350	72.0	215	Federal	3200	—	
IMR	4350	76.5	215	Federal	3400	—	Near Maximum
Hodgdon	H4895	62.0	215	Federal	3200	—	
Hodgdon	H4895	64.5	215	Federal	3400	—	Maximum
Hodgdon	H414	66.5	215	Federal	3200	—	
Hodgdon	H414	72.0	215	Federal	3450	—	Maximum

.300 WINCHESTER MAGNUM

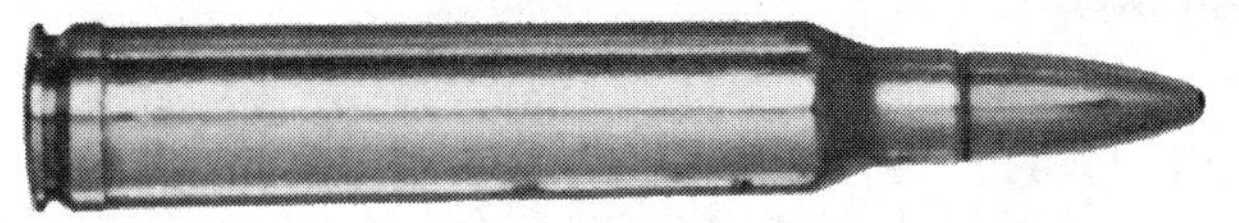

SPECIFICATIONS

Dia. of Rim — .532″
Dia. of Base — .513″
Dia. of Shoulder — .491″
Dia. of Neck — .339″
Length of Neck — .264″
Angle of Shoulder — 28.15°
Dia. Jacketed Bullet — .308″
Dia. Cast Bullet — .308″
Length of Case — 2.620″
Max. Overall Length — 3.340″
Primer Size — Large Rifle M
Water Capacity — 90.36 grs.

110-grain Softnose

POWDER MFGR.	POWDER TYPE	GRAINS	PRIMER TYPE	PRIMER MFGR.	VELOCITY	PRESSURE (C.U.P.)	REMARKS
IMR	4064	66.0	215	Federal	3300	—	
IMR	4064	70.0	215	Federal	3500	—	Maximum
IMR	4350	74.0	215	Federal	3350	—	
IMR	4350	79.0	215	Federal	3600	—	Maximum
IMR	4895	66.0	215	Federal	3400	—	
IMR	4895	68.5	215	Federal	3600	—	Near Maximum
Hodgdon	H4350	76.0	215	Federal	3350	—	
Hodgdon	H4350	79.0	215	Federal	3625	—	Maximum

130-grain Softnose

POWDER MFGR.	POWDER TYPE	GRAINS	PRIMER TYPE	PRIMER MFGR.	VELOCITY	PRESSURE (C.U.P.)	REMARKS
IMR	4064	60.5	215	Federal	3050	—	
IMR	4064	66.0	215	Federal	3300	—	Maximum
IMR	4350	67.0	215	Federal	3000	—	
IMR	4350	74.0	215	Federal	3300	—	Maximum
IMR	4831	70.0	215	Federal	3000	—	
IMR	4831	79.5	215	Federal	3400	—	Maximum
Hodgdon	H4350	68.5	215	Federal	3000	—	
Hodgdon	H4350	76.0	215	Federal	3400	—	Maximum

150-grain Softnose

POWDER MFGR.	POWDER TYPE	GRAINS	PRIMER TYPE	PRIMER MFGR.	VELOCITY	PRESSURE (C.U.P.)	REMARKS
IMR	4350	70.5	215	Federal	3050	—	
IMR	4350	74.0	215	Federal	3250	—	Maximum
IMR	4831	72.0	215	Federal	3000	—	
IMR	4831	77.0	215	Federal	3250	—	Maximum
Hodgdon	H4350	71.5	215	Federal	3100	—	
Hodgdon	H4350	74.0	215	Federal	3200	—	Maximum

.300 WINCHESTER MAGNUM (Cont.)

165-grain Softnose

POWDER MFGR.	POWDER TYPE	GRAINS	PRIMER TYPE	PRIMER MFGR.	VELOCITY	PRESSURE (C.U.P.)	REMARKS
IMR	4350	66.0	215	Federal	2800	—	
IMR	4350	73.0	215	Federal	3200	—	Maximum
IMR	4831	68.0	215	Federal	2800	—	
IMR	4831	72.5	215	Federal	3000	—	
Hodgdon	H4350	67.0	215	Federal	2800	—	
Hodgdon	H4350	71.0	215	Federal	3000	—	

180-grain Softnose

POWDER MFGR.	POWDER TYPE	GRAINS	PRIMER TYPE	PRIMER MFGR.	VELOCITY	PRESSURE (C.U.P.)	REMARKS
IMR	4350	63.0	215	Federal	2700	—	
IMR	4350	69.0	215	Federal	3000	—	Near Maximum
IMR	4831	67.5	215	Federal	2850	—	
IMR	4831	70.0	215	Federal	3000	—	
Hodgdon	H4350	66.0	215	Federal	2700	—	
Hodgdon	H4350	71.0	215	Federal	3000	—	Maximum

220-grain Softnose

POWDER MFGR.	POWDER TYPE	GRAINS	PRIMER TYPE	PRIMER MFGR.	VELOCITY	PRESSURE (C.U.P.)	REMARKS
IMR	4350	59.0	215	Federal	2450	—	
IMR	4350	65.0	215	Federal	2700	—	Maximum
IMR	4831	64.0	215	Federal	2500	—	
IMR	4831	68.0	215	Federal	2700	—	
Hodgdon	H4350	62.0	215	Federal	2500	—	
Hodgdon	H4350	65.5	215	Federal	2700	—	Maximum

.300 WEATHERBY MAGNUM

SPECIFICATIONS

Dia. of Rim — .530″
Dia. of Base — .511″
Dia. of Shoulder — .490″
Dia. of Neck — .332″
Length of Neck — .325″
Angle of Shoulder — N/A

Dia. Jacketed Bullet — .308″
Dia. Cast Bullet — .308″
Length of Case — 2.82″
Max. Overall Length — 3.56″
Primer Size — Large Rifle M
Water Capacity — 100.4 grs.

150-grain Softnose

POWDER MFGR.	POWDER TYPE	GRAINS	PRIMER TYPE	PRIMER MFGR.	VELOCITY	PRESSURE (C.U.P.)	REMARKS
IMR	4064	64.0	215	Federal	2865	—	
IMR	4064	70.0	215	Federal	3225	—	Near Maximum
IMR	4320	67.5	215	Federal	3080	—	
IMR	4320	73.0	215	Federal	3350	—	Maximum
IMR	4350	75.0	215	Federal	3060	—	
IMR	4350	81.0	215	Federal	3400	—	Maximum

180-grain Softnose

POWDER MFGR.	POWDER TYPE	GRAINS	PRIMER TYPE	PRIMER MFGR.	VELOCITY	PRESSURE (C.U.P.)	REMARKS
IMR	4064	61.0	215	Federal	2600	—	
IMR	4064	67.0	215	Federal	2950	—	Near Maximum
IMR	4320	62.5	215	Federal	2775	—	
IMR	4320	69.5	215	Federal	3050	—	Maximum
IMR	4350	71.0	215	Federal	2790	—	
IMR	4350	78.5	215	Federal	3200	—	Maximum

200-grain Softnose

POWDER MFGR.	POWDER TYPE	GRAINS	PRIMER TYPE	PRIMER MFGR.	VELOCITY	PRESSURE (C.U.P.)	REMARKS
IMR	4064	60.0	215	Federal	2575	—	
IMR	4064	65.0	215	Federal	2785	—	Near Maximum
IMR	4320	60.0	215	Federal	2640	—	
IMR	4320	67.0	215	Federal	2875	—	Maximum
IMR	4350	69.0	215	Federal	2675	—	
IMR	4350	75.5	215	Federal	3000	—	Maximum

.32-20 WCF

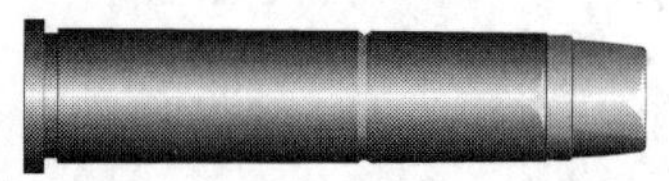

SPECIFICATIONS

Dia. of Rim — .408″
Dia. of Base — .353″
Dia. of Shoulder — .342″
Dia. of Neck — .326″
Length of Neck — .376″
Angle of Shoulder — 7.86°

Dia. Jacketed Bullet — .312″
Dia. Cast Bullet — .314″
Length of Case — 1.315″
Max. Overall Length — 1.59″
Primer Size — Small Rifle
Water Capacity — 21.89 grs.

87-grain Softnose

POWDER MFGR.	POWDER TYPE	GRAINS	PRIMER TYPE	PRIMER MFGR.	VELOCITY	PRESSURE (C.U.P.)	REMARKS
IMR	4227	14.0	WSR	Winchester	1800	—	
IMR	4227	16.5	WSR	Winchester	2200	—	Maximum
Winchester	W680	14.5	WSR	Winchester	1900	—	
Winchester	W680	17.5	WSR	Winchester	2200	—	

110-grain Softnose

POWDER MFGR.	POWDER TYPE	GRAINS	PRIMER TYPE	PRIMER MFGR.	VELOCITY	PRESSURE (C.U.P.)	REMARKS
IMR	4227	13.0	WSR	Winchester	1700	—	
IMR	4227	15.0	WSR	Winchester	1925	—	Near Maximum
Hodgdon	H110	12.0	WSR	Winchester	1720	—	
Hodgdon	H110	15.0	WSR	Winchester	2000	—	Near Maximum
Winchester	W680	14.0	WSR	Winchester	1700	—	
Winchester	W680	16.5	WSR	Winchester	2020	—	

.32 WINCHESTER SPECIAL

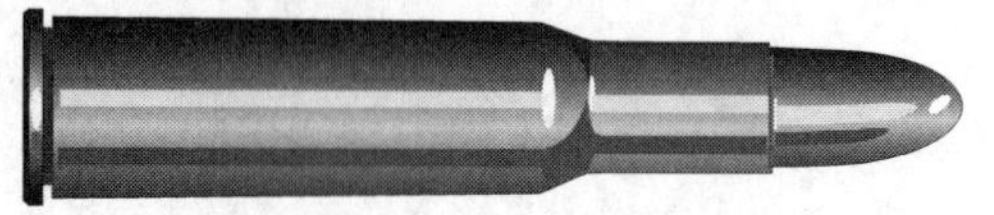

SPECIFICATIONS

Dia. of Rim — .506″
Dia. of Base — .422″
Dia. of Shoulder — .399″
Dia. of Neck — .339″
Length of Neck — .344″
Angle of Shoulder — 14.5°

Dia. Jacketed Bullet — .321″
Dia. Cast Bullet — 323″
Length of Case — 2.04″
Max. Overall Length — 2.55″
Primer Size — Large Rifle
Water Capacity — 45.0 grs.

170-grain Softnose

POWDER MFGR.	POWDER TYPE	GRAINS	PRIMER TYPE	PRIMER MFGR.	VELOCITY	PRESSURE (C.U.P.)	REMARKS
IMR	3031	33.0	210	Federal	2160	—	
IMR	3031	31.0	210	Federal	2080	—	
IMR	4320	36.5	210	Federal	2100	—	
IMR	4320	37.0	210	Federal	2120	—	
IMR	4320	35.0	210	Federal	2060	—	

.338 WINCHESTER MAGNUM

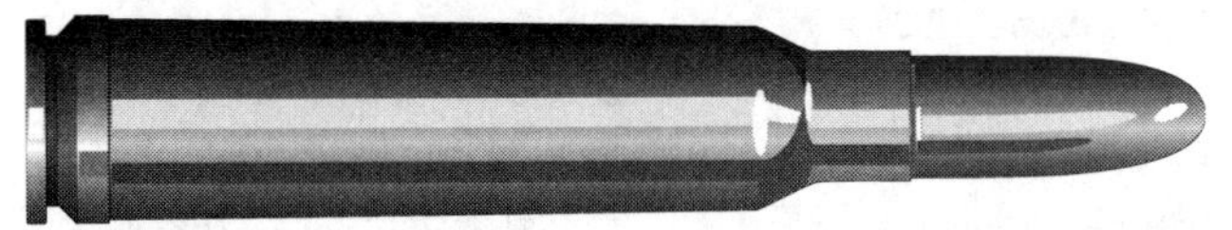

SPECIFICATIONS

Dia. of Rim — .532″
Dia. of Base — .513″
Dia. of Shoulder — .491″
Dia. of Neck — .369″
Length of Neck — .331″
Angle of Shoulder — 25.30°
Dia. Jacketed Bullet — .338″
Dia. Cast Bullet — .338″
Length of Case — 2.5″
Max. Overall Length — 3.34″
Primer Size — Large Rifle M
Water Capacity — 85.62 grs.

200-grain Softnose

POWDER MFGR.	POWDER TYPE	GRAINS	PRIMER TYPE	PRIMER MFGR.	VELOCITY	PRESSURE (C.U.P.)	REMARKS
IMR	3031	54.0	LRM	Winchester	2625	—	
IMR	3031	60.0	LRM	Winchester	2850	—	Maximum
IMR	4895	58.0	LRM	Winchester	2660	—	
IMR	4895	64.0	LRM	Winchester	2900	—	Maximum
IMR	4064	59.0	LRM	Winchester	2650	—	
IMR	4064	64.5	LRM	Winchester	2900	—	Maximum

250-grain Softnose

POWDER MFGR.	POWDER TYPE	GRAINS	PRIMER TYPE	PRIMER MFGR.	VELOCITY	PRESSURE (C.U.P.)	REMARKS
IMR	3031	50.0	LRM	Winchester	2275	—	
IMR	3031	56.0	LRM	Winchester	2470	—	Maximum
IMR	4895	55.0	LRM	Winchester	2350	—	
IMR	4895	61.0	LRM	Winchester	2600	—	Maximum
IMR	4064	56.0	LRM	Winchester	2350	—	
IMR	4064	61.5	LRM	Winchester	2575	—	Maximum

275-grain Softnose

POWDER MFGR.	POWDER TYPE	GRAINS	PRIMER TYPE	PRIMER MFGR.	VELOCITY	PRESSURE (C.U.P.)	REMARKS
IMR	3031	48.0	LRM	Winchester	2150	—	
IMR	3031	53.0	LRM	Winchester	2290	—	Maximum
IMR	4895	54.0	LRM	Winchester	2250	—	
IMR	4895	60.0	LRM	Winchester	2450	—	Maximum
IMR	4064	54.0	LRM	Winchester	2225	—	
IMR	4064	60.0	LRM	Winchester	2450	—	Maximum

.340 WEATHERBY MAGNUM

SPECIFICATIONS

Dia. of Rim — .532″
Dia. of Base — .513″
Dia. of Shoulder — .490″
Dia. of Neck — .361″
Length of Neck — .344″
Angle of Shoulder — N/A°
Dia. Jacketed Bullet — .338″
Dia. Cast Bullet — .338″
Length of Case — 2.820″
Max. Overall Length — 3.68″
Primer Size — Large Rifle M
Water Capacity — 102.05 grs.

200-grain Softnose

POWDER MFGR.	POWDER TYPE	GRAINS	PRIMER TYPE	PRIMER MFGR.	VELOCITY	PRESSURE (C.U.P.)	REMARKS
IMR	4064	67.5	215	Federal	2700	—	
IMR	4064	72.0	215	Federal	2925	—	Maximum
IMR	4320	66.0	215	Federal	2700	—	
IMR	4320	74.0	215	Federal	3000	—	
IMR	4350	76.5	215	Federal	2800	—	
IMR	4350	83.5	215	Federal	3150	—	Near Maximum
IMR	4831	79.5	215	Federal	2800	—	
IMR	4831	83.5	215	Federal	3000	—	
IMR	7828	87.0	215	Federal	2800	—	
IMR	7828	91.5	215	Federal	3000	—	Near Maximum
Hodgdon	H4831	84.5	215	Federal	2800	—	
Hodgdon	H4831	89.5	215	Federal	3050	—	Near Maximum
Hodgdon	H450	85.0	215	Federal	2810	—	
Hodgdon	H450	89.0	215	Federal	3000	—	Maximum
Hodgdon	H4350	77.0	215	Federal	2800	—	
Hodgdon	H4350	79.5	215	Federal	2960	—	Maximum
Winchester	W760	76.5	215	Federal	2800	—	
Winchester	W760	82.0	215	Federal	3150	—	Maximum

.340 WEATHERBY MAGNUM (Cont.)

225-grain Softnose

POWDER MFGR.	POWDER TYPE	GRAINS	PRIMER TYPE	PRIMER MFGR.	VELOCITY	PRESSURE (C.U.P.)	REMARKS
IMR	4320	66.0	215	Federal	2650	—	
IMR	4320	70.5	215	Federal	2800	—	Maximum
IMR	4350	75.0	215	Federal	2700	—	
IMR	4350	80.0	215	Federal	2950	—	
IMR	4831	79.0	215	Federal	2800	—	
IMR	4831	83.0	215	Federal	3000	—	Maximum
IMR	7828	89.0	215	Federal	2965	51000	Maximum
Hodgdon	H4831	78.5	215	Federal	2700	—	
Hodgdon	H4831	84.0	215	Federal	2950	—	Maximum
Hodgdon	H450	80.5	215	Federal	2700	—	
Hodgdon	H450	86.0	215	Federal	2925	—	
Hodgdon	H4350	75.5	215	Federal	2700	—	
Hodgdon	H4350	78.0	215	Federal	2800	—	

250-grain Softnose

POWDER MFGR.	POWDER TYPE	GRAINS	PRIMER TYPE	PRIMER MFGR.	VELOCITY	PRESSURE (C.U.P.)	REMARKS
IMR	4320	63.0	215	Federal	2450	—	
IMR	4320	70.0	215	Federal	2700	—	Maximum
IMR	4350	72.0	215	Federal	2550	—	
IMR	4350	79.0	215	Federal	2800	—	
IMR	4831	76.5	215	Federal	2600	—	
IMR	4831	80.5	215	Federal	2800	—	Maximum
IMR	7828	87.5	215	Federal	2860	53100	Maximum
Hodgdon	H4831	77.0	215	Federal	2500	—	
Hodgdon	H4831	82.5	215	Federal	2800	—	Maximum
Hodgdon	H450	78.0	215	Federal	2700	—	
Hodgdon	H450	82.5	215	Federal	2800	—	
Hodgdon	H4350	73.5	215	Federal	2600	—	
Hodgdon	H4350	75.5	215	Federal	2700	—	Near Maximum

275-grain Softnose

POWDER MFGR.	POWDER TYPE	GRAINS	PRIMER TYPE	PRIMER MFGR.	VELOCITY	PRESSURE (C.U.P.)	REMARKS
IMR	4350	69.5	215	Federal	2350	—	
IMR	4350	75.0	215	Federal	2600	—	Maximum

.348 WINCHESTER

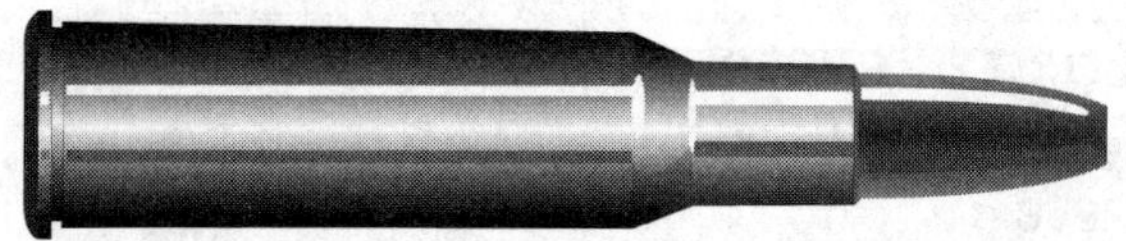

SPECIFICATIONS

Dia. of Rim — .610″
Dia. of Base — .553″
Dia. of Shoulder — .485″
Dia. of Neck — .375″
Length of Neck — .450″
Angle of Shoulder — 32.90°
Dia. Jacketed Bullet — .348″
Dia. Cast Bullet — .349″
Length of Case — 2.185″
Max. Overall Length — 2.83″
Primer Size — Large Rifle
Water Capacity — 77.54 grs.

150-grain Softnose

POWDER MFGR.	POWDER TYPE	GRAINS	PRIMER TYPE	PRIMER MFGR.	VELOCITY	PRESSURE (C.U.P.)	REMARKS
IMR	4320	47.0	9½	Remington	2225	—	
Hodgdon	H450	62.0	210	Federal	2300	—	
Hodgdon	H4831	67.0	210	Federal	2450	—	
Winchester	W760	56.0	210	Federal	2330	—	
Winchester	W760	59.0	210	Federal	2500	—	Maximum

200-grain Softnose

POWDER MFGR.	POWDER TYPE	GRAINS	PRIMER TYPE	PRIMER MFGR.	VELOCITY	PRESSURE (C.U.P.)	REMARKS
IMR	3031	43.5	9½	Remington	2200	—	
IMR	3031	45.5	9½	Remington	2300	—	
IMR	4064	45.0	210	Federal	2200	—	
IMR	4064	48.5	210	Federal	2300	—	
IMR	4320	47.0	9½	Remington	2225	—	
Hodgdon	H450	62.0	210	Federal	2300	—	
Hodgdon	H4831	67.0	210	Federal	2450	—	
Winchester	W760	56.0	210	Federal	2330	—	
Winchester	W760	59.0	210	Federal	2500	—	Maximum

250-grain Softnose

POWDER MFGR.	POWDER TYPE	GRAINS	PRIMER TYPE	PRIMER MFGR.	VELOCITY	PRESSURE (C.U.P.)	REMARKS
IMR	4895	46.5	9½	Remington	2160	—	
IMR	4064	49.0	9½	Remington	2270	—	
IMR	4350	54.5	210	Federal	2200	—	

.357 MAGNUM RIFLE

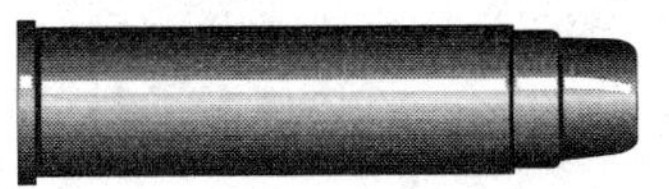

SPECIFICATIONS

Dia. of Rim — .440″
Dia. of Base — .380″
Dia. of Shoulder — Straight
Dia. of Neck — .379″
Length of Neck — Straight
Angle of Shoulder — Straight
Dia. Jacketed Bullet — .357″
Dia. Cast Bullet — .359″
Length of Case — 1.29″
Max. Overall Length — 1.59″
Primer Size — Small Pistol
Water Capacity — 23.47 grs.

140-grain Jacketed

POWDER MFGR.	POWDER TYPE	GRAINS	PRIMER TYPE	PRIMER MFGR.	VELOCITY	PRESSURE (C.U.P.)	REMARKS
Hodgdon	H4227	15.0	SPM	Remington	1570	—	
Hodgdon	H4227	16.0	SPM	Federal	1675	—	Maximum
Hodgdon	H110	16.5	SPM	Federal	1790	—	
Hodgdon	H110	17.0	SPM	Federal	1850	—	Maximum
Hodgdon	HP38	4.8	SPM	Federal	1020	—	
Hodgdon	HP38	6.5	SPM	Federal	1380		Maximum

150-grain Jacketed

POWDER MFGR.	POWDER TYPE	GRAINS	PRIMER TYPE	PRIMER MFGR.	VELOCITY	PRESSURE (C.U.P.)	REMARKS
Hodgdon	H4227	13.5	SPM	Remington	1430	—	
Hodgdon	H4227	15.5	SPM	Federal	1650	—	Maximum
Hodgdon	H110	15.0	SPM	Federal	1660	—	
Hodgdon	H110	17.0	SPM	Federal	1730	—	Maximum
Hodgdon	HP38	4.3	SPM	Federal	950	—	
Hodgdon	HP38	6.3	SPM	Federal	1350		Maximum

170-grain Jacketed

POWDER MFGR.	POWDER TYPE	GRAINS	PRIMER TYPE	PRIMER MFGR.	VELOCITY	PRESSURE (C.U.P.)	REMARKS
Hodgdon	H4227	12.0	SPM	Remington	1350	—	
Hodgdon	H4227	14.0	SPM	Federal	1500	—	Maximum
Hodgdon	H110	13.5	SPM	Federal	1490	—	
Hodgdon	H110	14.0	SPM	Federal	1580	—	Maximum
Hodgdon	HP38	4.0	SPM	Federal	870	—	

.35 REMINGTON

SPECIFICATIONS

Dia. of Rim — .460″
Dia. of Base — .458″
Dia. of Shoulder — .428″
Dia. of Neck — .384″
Length of Neck — .335″
Angle of Shoulder — 21.80°

Dia. Jacketed Bullet — .358″
Dia. Cast Bullet — .358″
Length of Case — 1.920″
Max. Overall Length — 2.500″
Primer Size — Large Rifle
Water Capacity — 51.76 grs.

180-grain Softnose

POWDER MFGR.	POWDER TYPE	GRAINS	PRIMER TYPE	PRIMER MFGR.	VELOCITY	PRESSURE (C.U.P.)	REMARKS
IMR	3031	34.0	9½	Remington	1950	—	
IMR	3031	37.0	9½	Remington	2000	—	
IMR	4064	37.5	210	Federal	1900	—	
IMR	4064	39.5	210	Federal	2100	—	
IMR	4320	39.0	9½	Remington	2100	—	
Hodgdon	H414	43.0	210	Federal	1950	—	
Hodgdon	H380	41.0	210	Federal	1900	—	
Hodgdon	H4895	37.0	210	Federal	1850	—	
Hodgdon	BL-C(2)	39.0	210	Federal	2000	—	
Hodgdon	H4198	32.0	210	Federal	2000	—	
Winchester	W748	41.0	210	Federal	2050	—	
Winchester	W760	45.0	210	Federal	2030	—	

200-grain Softnose

POWDER MFGR.	POWDER TYPE	GRAINS	PRIMER TYPE	PRIMER MFGR.	VELOCITY	PRESSURE (C.U.P.)	REMARKS
IMR	3031	32.0	9½	Remington	1775	—	
IMR	3031	34.5	9½	Remington	1900	—	
IMR	4064	36.0	9½	Remington	1850	—	
IMR	4064	38.5	210	Federal	2000	—	
IMR	4320	37.0	9½	Remington	1850	—	
IMR	4320	39.0	210	Federal	1975	—	
Hodgdon	H380	38.0	210	Federal	1800	—	
Hodgdon	H380	39.5	210	Federal	1920	—	
Hodgdon	BL-C(2)	36.0	210	Federal	1825	—	
Hodgdon	H4198	27.5	210	Federal	1800	—	
Hodgdon	H4895	36.0	210	Federal	1790	—	
Hodgdon	H4895	38.0	210	Federal	1965	—	
Winchester	W748	38.0	210	Federal	1900	—	

.35 WHELEN

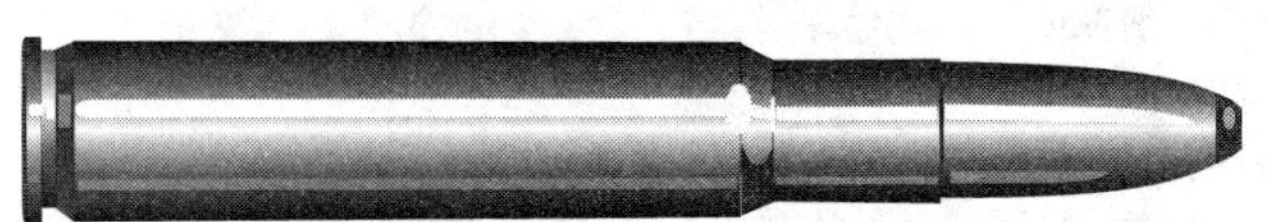

SPECIFICATIONS

Dia. of Rim — .473″
Dia. of Base — .470″
Dia. of Shoulder — .441″
Dia. of Neck — .385″
Length of Neck — .434″
Angle of Shoulder — 14.03°
Dia. Jacketed Bullet — .358″
Dia. Cast Bullet — .358″
Length of Case — 2.494″
Max. Overall Length — 3.30″
Primer Size — Large Rifle
Water Capacity — 72.63 grs.

200-grain Softnose

POWDER MFGR.	POWDER TYPE	GRAINS	PRIMER TYPE	PRIMER MFGR.	VELOCITY	PRESSURE (C.U.P.)	REMARKS
IMR	3031	49.0	210	Federal	2300	—	
IMR	3031	53.0	210	Federal	2600	—	
IMR	4064	51.5	210	Federal	2400	—	
IMR	4064	55.5	210	Federal	2610	—	
IMR	4320	55.0	210	Federal	2400	—	
IMR	4230	59.0	210	Federal	2700	—	
IMR	4198	44.0	210	Federal	2400	—	
IMR	4198	47.0	210	Federal	2620	—	
IMR	4895	52.0	210	Federal	2425	—	
IMR	4895	56.0	210	Federal	2640	—	Near Maximum
Hodgdon	H4198	42.5	210	Federal	2400	—	
Hodgdon	H4198	44.5	210	Federal	2500	—	
Hodgdon	BL-C(2)	51.5	210	Federal	2450	—	
Hodgdon	BL-C(2)	55.5	210	Federal	2700	—	Near maximum
Winchester	W748	56.5	210	Federal	2400	—	
Winchester	W748	59.0	210	Federal	2600	—	
Winchester	W760	60.5	210	Federal	2400	—	
Winchester	W760	63.0	210	Federal	2550	—	

250-grain Softnose

POWDER MFGR.	POWDER TYPE	GRAINS	PRIMER TYPE	PRIMER MFGR.	VELOCITY	PRESSURE (C.U.P.)	REMARKS
IMR	3031	47.0	210	Federal	2200	—	
IMR	3031	51.0	210	Federal	2400	—	Maximum
IMR	4064	48.5	210	Federal	2200	—	
IMR	4064	52.0	210	Federal	2400	—	Maximum
IMR	4320	50.0	210	Federal	2250	—	
IMR	4230	52.5	210	Federal	2400	—	
Hodgdon	H4895	49.0	210	Federal	2200	—	
Hodgdon	H4895	52.0	210	Federal	2400	—	Near Maximum

.356 WINCHESTER

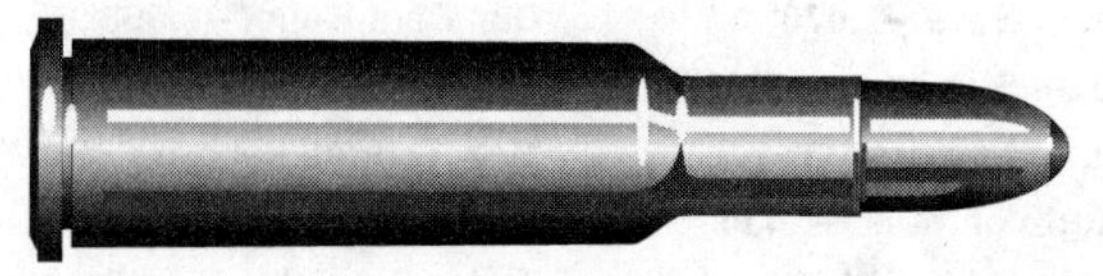

SPECIFICATIONS

Dia. of Rim — .506″
Dia. of Base — .471″
Dia. of Shoulder — .454″
Dia. of Neck — .388″
Length of Neck — .345″
Angle of Shoulder — 20.00°
Dia. Jacketed Bullet — .358″
Dia. Cast Bullet — .359″
Length of Case — 2.015″
Max. Overall Length — 2.560″
Primer Size — Large Rifle
Water Capacity — 57.0 grs.

180-grain Softnose

POWDER MFGR.	POWDER TYPE	GRAINS	PRIMER TYPE	PRIMER MFGR.	VELOCITY	PRESSURE (C.U.P.)	REMARKS
IMR	3031	43.5	9½	Remington	2325	—	
IMR	3031	46.5	9½	Remington	2450	—	Near Maximum
IMR	4064	46.5	9½	Remington	2300	—	
IMR	4064	49.0	9½	Remington	2450	—	Maximum
IMR	4320	47.0	9½	Remington	2325	—	
IMR	4320	49.0	9½	Remington	2450	—	Maximum
IMR	4198	38.5	210	Federal	2400	—	
IMR	4198	41.5	210	Federal	2500	—	Near Maximum
Hodgdon	H335	48.5	210	Federal	2300	—	
Hodgdon	H335	51.0	210	Federal	2460	—	Maximum
Hodgdon	H4198	40.0	210	Federal	2450	—	
Hodgdon	H4198	42.5	210	Federal	2550	—	Maximum

250-grain Softnose

POWDER MFGR.	POWDER TYPE	GRAINS	PRIMER TYPE	PRIMER MFGR.	VELOCITY	PRESSURE (C.U.P.)	REMARKS
IMR	3031	42.0	9½	Remington	2200	—	
IMR	3031	44.0	9½	Remington	2300	—	
IMR	4064	45.0	210	Federal	2140	—	
IMR	4064	48.0	210	Federal	2300	—	
IMR	4320	45.5	9½	Remington	2150	—	
IMR	4230	47.5	210	Federal	2250	—	
IMR	4198	37.5	210	Federal	2200	—	
IMR	4198	39.5	210	Federal	2360	—	
Hodgdon	H335	48.5	210	Federal	2210	—	
Hodgdon	H4198	40.0	210	Federal	2350	—	
Hodgdon	BL-C(2)	49.5	210	Federal	2200	—	
Winchester	W748	48.0	210	Federal	2000	—	

.358 WINCHESTER

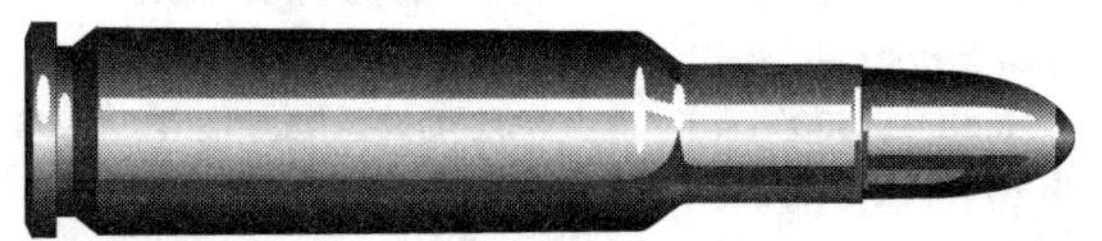

SPECIFICATIONS

Dia. of Rim — .473″
Dia. of Base — .470″
Dia. of Shoulder — .455″
Dia. of Neck — .388″
Length of Neck — .365″
Angle of Shoulder — 20.00°
Dia. Jacketed Bullet — .358″
Dia. Cast Bullet — .359″
Length of Case — 2.015″
Max. Overall Length — 2.560″
Primer Size — Large Rifle
Water Capacity — 57.5 grs.

150-grain Softnose

POWDER MFGR.	POWDER TYPE	GRAINS	PRIMER TYPE	PRIMER MFGR.	VELOCITY	PRESSURE (C.U.P.)	REMARKS
IMR	3031	45.0	9½	Remington	2500	—	
IMR	3031	50.0	9½	Remington	2800	—	
IMR	4064	46.0	210	Federal	2275	—	
IMR	4064	51.0	210	Federal	2575	—	
IMR	4320	49.5	9½	Remington	2540	—	
IMR	4230	54.5	210	Federal	2700	—	
IMR	4895	47.5	210	Federal	2500	—	
IMR	4895	52.5	210	Federal	2800	—	
Hodgdon	H335	51.5	210	Federal	2700	—	
Hodgdon	H380	50.0	210	Federal	2350	—	
Hodgdon	H380	54.0	210	Federal	2500	—	
Hercules	Rx7	40.0	210	Federal	2625	—	

200-grain Softnose

POWDER MFGR.	POWDER TYPE	GRAINS	PRIMER TYPE	PRIMER MFGR.	VELOCITY	PRESSURE (C.U.P.)	REMARKS
IMR	3031	43.0	9½	Remington	2325	—	
IMR	3031	44.0	9½	Remington	2350	—	
IMR	4064	45.0	210	Federal	2140	—	
IMR	4064	48.0	210	Federal	2300	—	
IMR	4320	45.5	9½	Remington	2150	—	
IMR	4230	47.5	210	Federal	2250	—	
IMR	4198	37.5	210	Federal	2200	—	
IMR	4198	39.5	210	Federal	2360	—	
Hodgdon	H335	48.5	210	Federal	2210	—	
Hodgdon	H4198	40.0	210	Federal	2350	—	
Hodgdon	BL-C(2)	49.5	210	Federal	2200	—	
Winchester	W748	48.0	210	Federal	2000	—	
Winchester	W748	50.0	210	Federal	2260	—	

.350 REMINGTON MAGNUM

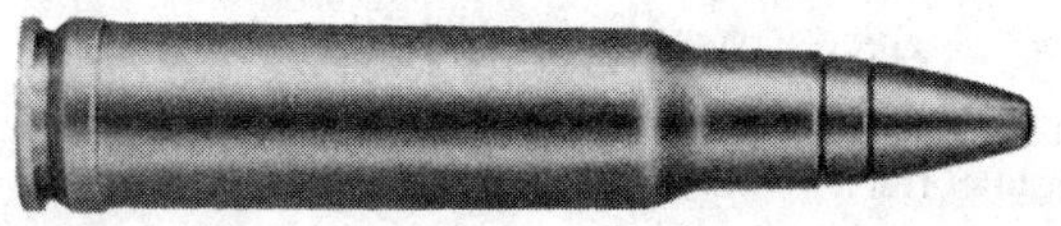

SPECIFICATIONS

Dia. of Rim — .532″
Dia. of Base — .513″
Dia. of Shoulder — .496″
Dia. of Neck — .388″
Length of Neck — .355″
Angle of Shoulder — 20.42°
Dia. Jacketed Bullet — .358″
Dia. Cast Bullet — .358″
Length of Case — 2.170″
Max. Overall Length — 2.93″
Primer Size — Large Rifle M
Water Capacity — 73.74 grs.

200-grain Softnose

POWDER MFGR.	POWDER TYPE	GRAINS	PRIMER TYPE	PRIMER MFGR.	VELOCITY	PRESSURE (C.U.P.)	REMARKS
IMR	3031	50.0	210	Federal	2400	—	
IMR	3031	53.5	210	Federal	2600	—	Near Maximum
IMR	4064	52.0	210	Federal	2400	—	
IMR	4064	55.0	210	Federal	2600	—	
IMR	4320	53.0	210	Federal	2300	—	
IMR	4320	58.5	210	Federal	2600	—	
Hodgdon	H4198	43.0	210	Federal	2300	—	
Hodgdon	H4198	45.5	210	Federal	2450	—	
Hodgdon	H4895	51.0	210	Federal	2300	—	
Hodgdon	H4895	56.0	210	Federal	2550	—	
Hodgdon	BL-C(2)	55.0	210	Federal	2600	—	
Hodgdon	BL-C(2)	58.0	210	Federal	2750	—	
Winchester	W760	61.5	210	Federal	2400	—	
Winchester	W760	64.5	210	Federal	2600	—	Maximum

250-grain Softnose

POWDER MFGR.	POWDER TYPE	GRAINS	PRIMER TYPE	PRIMER MFGR.	VELOCITY	PRESSURE (C.U.P.)	REMARKS
IMR	3031	45.5	210	Federal	2100	—	
IMR	3031	51.0	210	Federal	2400	—	Near Maximum
IMR	4064	48.0	210	Federal	2100	—	
IMR	4064	52.5	210	Federal	2300	—	Near Maximum
IMR	4320	51.0	210	Federal	2200	—	
IMR	4320	55.0	210	Federal	2400	—	Maximum
IMR	4895	50.0	210	Federal	2150	—	
IMR	4895	54.0	210	Federal	2350	—	
Hodgdon	H4198	40.0	210	Federal	2100	38000	
Hodgdon	H4198	42.0	210	Federal	2200	49800	
Hodgdon	H4895	49.0	210	Federal	2150	39700	
Hodgdon	H4895	51.0	210	Federal	2300	50000	

.358 NORMA MAGNUM

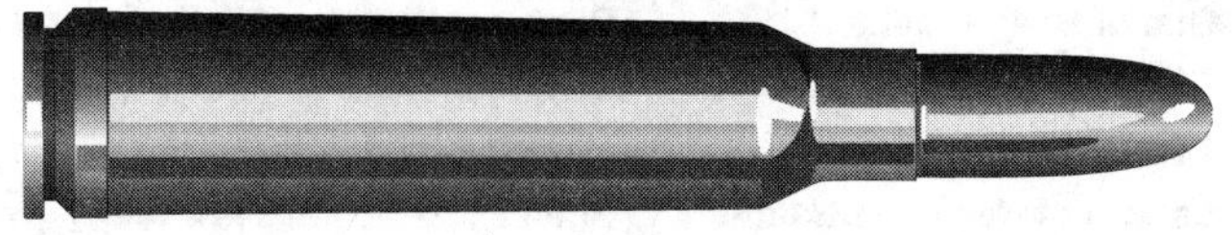

SPECIFICATIONS

Dia. of Rim — .532″
Dia. of Base — .513″
Dia. of Shoulder — .489″
Dia. of Neck — .388″
Length of Neck — .328″
Angle of Shoulder — 25.47°
Dia. Jacketed Bullet — .358″
Dia. Cast Bullet — .358″
Length of Case — 2.519″
Max. Overall Length — 3.30″
Primer Size — Large Rifle M
Water Capacity — 87.57 grs.

200-grain Softnose

POWDER MFGR.	POWDER TYPE	GRAINS	PRIMER TYPE	PRIMER MFGR.	VELOCITY	PRESSURE (C.U.P.)	REMARKS
IMR	3031	56.5	215	Federal	2600	—	
IMR	3031	60.5	215	Federal	2800	—	
IMR	4064	60.0	215	Federal	2600	—	
IMR	4064	66.0	215	Federal	2900	—	
IMR	4320	61.0	215	Federal	2600	—	
IMR	4320	68.0	215	Federal	2920	—	
IMR	4350	68.5	215	Federal	2600	—	
IMR	4350	74.5	215	Federal	2900	—	
Hodgdon	H380	64.0	215	Federal	2700	—	
Hodgdon	H380	67.5	215	Federal	2900	—	
Hodgdon	H4895	58.0	215	Federal	2600	—	
Hodgdon	H4895	63.5	215	Federal	2800	—	
Hodgdon	H4350	71.0	WLR	Winchester	2625	—	
Hodgdon	H4350	77.0	WLR	Winchester	2900	—	

250-grain Softnose

POWDER MFGR.	POWDER TYPE	GRAINS	PRIMER TYPE	PRIMER MFGR.	VELOCITY	PRESSURE (C.U.P.)	REMARKS
IMR	3031	56.5	215	Federal	2400	—	
IMR	3031	62.0	215	Federal	2700	—	Near Maximum
IMR	4064	61.5	215	Federal	2500	—	
IMR	4064	64.5	215	Federal	2650	—	Near Maximum
IMR	4320	61.5	215	Federal	2500	—	
IMR	4320	68.0	215	Federal	2800	—	Maximum
IMR	4350	70.0	215	Federal	2600	—	
IMR	4350	74.0	215	Federal	2775	—	
Hodgdon	H380	64.5	215	Federal	2450	—	
Hodgdon	H380	66.0	215	Federal	2550	—	
Hodgdon	H4895	62.0	215	Federal	2500	—	

.375 WINCHESTER

SPECIFICATIONS

Dia. of Rim — .506″
Dia. of Base — .420″
Dia. of Shoulder — Straight
Dia. of Neck — .400″
Length of Neck — Straight
Angle of Shoulder — Straight
Dia. Jacketed Bullet — .375″
Dia. Cast Bullet —.377″
Length of Case — 2.020″
Max. Overall Length — 2.560″
Primer Size — Large Rifle
Water Capacity — N/A

220-grain Softnose

POWDER MFGR.	POWDER TYPE	GRAINS	PRIMER TYPE	PRIMER MFGR.	VELOCITY	PRESSURE (C.U.P.)	REMARKS
IMR	3031	36.0	210	Federal	1950	—	
IMR	4064	36.0	210	Federal	1700	—	
IMR	4064	37.5	210	Federal	1800	—	
IMR	4064	38.5	210	Federal	1900	—	Maximum
IMR	4198	28.5	WLR	Winchester	1825	—	
IMR	4198	32.0	WLR	Winchester	2000	—	Maximum
IMR	4895	37.0	210	Federal	1800	—	
IMR	4895	39.0	210	Federal	1900	—	Caution
Hodgdon	BL-C(2)	39.5	9½	Remington	1750	—	
Hodgdon	BL-C(2)	42.0	9½	Remington	1900	—	Maximum
Hodgdon	H322	36.0	WLR	Winchester	1900	—	
Hodgdon	H322	38.5	WLR	Winchester	2000	—	Maximum
Hodgdon	H4198	29.5	210	Federal	1875	—	
Hodgdon	H4198	31.0	210	Federal	2000	—	Maximum
Winchester	W748	39.0	210	Federal	1700	—	
Winchester	W748	41.5	210	Federal	1900	—	Near Maximum
Norma	N200	31.5	210	Federal	1800	—	
Norma	N200	35.5	210	Federal	2100	—	Caution: Maximum

250-grain Softnose

POWDER MFGR.	POWDER TYPE	GRAINS	PRIMER TYPE	PRIMER MFGR.	VELOCITY	PRESSURE (C.U.P.)	REMARKS
Hodgdon	H4895	35.0	210	Federal	1730	—	
Hodgdon	H4895	37.0	210	Federal	1845	—	
Hodgdon	BL-C(2)	38.0	210	Federal	1690	—	
Hodgdon	H335	38.0	210	Federal	1700	—	
Hodgdon	H332	34.0	210	Federal	1730	—	
Hodgdon	H4198	28.0	210	Federal	1740	—	
Hodgdon	H4198	30.0	210	Federal	1860	—	

.375 H&H MAGNUM

SPECIFICATIONS

Dia. of Rim — .532″
Dia. of Base — .513″
Dia. of Shoulder — .460″
Dia. of Neck — .405″
Length of Neck — .300″
Angle of Shoulder — 7.95°
Dia. Jacketed Bullet — .375″
Dia. Cast Bullet — .377″
Length of Case — 2.850″
Max. Overall Length — 3.60″
Primer Size — Large Rifle (M)
Water Capacity — 96.37 grs.

235-grain Softnose

POWDER MFGR.	POWDER TYPE	GRAINS	PRIMER TYPE	PRIMER MFGR.	VELOCITY	PRESSURE (C.U.P.)	REMARKS
IMR	3031	66.5	215	Federal	2500	—	
IMR	3031	73.0	215	Federal	2800	—	
IMR	4064	70.0	215	Federal	2600	—	
IMR	4064	74.0	215	Federal	2800	—	
IMR	4320	70.5	215	Federal	2600	—	
IMR	4320	74.5	215	Federal	2750	—	
IMR	4350	80.0	215	Federal	2600	—	
IMR	4350	84.0	215	Federal	2800	—	
IMR	4831	80.0	215	Federal	2600	—	
IMR	4831	84.0	215	Federal	2625	—	
Hodgdon	H4895	72.0	215	Federal	2725	—	
Hodgdon	H4831	86.0	215	Federal	2600	—	
Hodgdon	H450	87.0	215	Federal	2675	—	
Hodgdon	H4350	81.0	215	Federal	2650	—	
Winchester	W760	81.0	215	Federal	2600	—	

270-grain Softnose

POWDER MFGR.	POWDER TYPE	GRAINS	PRIMER TYPE	PRIMER MFGR.	VELOCITY	PRESSURE (C.U.P.)	REMARKS
IMR	3031	60.0	215	Federal	2400	—	
IMR	3031	65.0	215	Federal	2600	—	
IMR	4064	63.0	215	Federal	2300	—	
IMR	4064	68.0	215	Federal	2500	—	
IMR	4320	64.0	215	Federal	2400	—	
IMR	4320	66.0	215	Federal	2600	—	
IMR	4350	72.0	215	Federal	2500	—	
IMR	4350	77.5	215	Federal	2700	—	
IMR	4831	77.0	215	Federal	2500	—	
IMR	4831	82.5	215	Federal	2700	—	

.375 H&H MAGNUM (Cont.)

270-grain Softnose (Cont.)

POWDER MFGR.	POWDER TYPE	GRAINS	PRIMER TYPE	PRIMER MFGR.	VELOCITY	PRESSURE (C.U.P.)	REMARKS
Hodgdon	H4895	67.0	215	Federal	2525	—	
Hodgdon	H4831	82.0	215	Federal	2500	—	
Hodgdon	H450	84.0	215	Federal	2600	—	
Hodgdon	H4350	77.0	215	Federal	2625	—	
Winchester	W760	82.0	215	Federal	2500	—	

300-grain Softnose

POWDER MFGR.	POWDER TYPE	GRAINS	PRIMER TYPE	PRIMER MFGR.	VELOCITY	PRESSURE (C.U.P.)	REMARKS
IMR	3031	60.0	215	Federal	2300	—	
IMR	3031	65.0	215	Federal	2500	—	Near Maximum
IMR	4064	65.0	215	Federal	2400	—	
IMR	4064	67.5	215	Federal	2500	—	
IMR	4320	62.0	215	Federal	2300	—	
IMR	4320	65.0	215	Federal	2400	—	
IMR	4350	75.0	215	Federal	2400	—	
IMR	4350	77.5	215	Federal	2500	—	
IMR	4831	77.0	215	Federal	2400	—	
IMR	4831	79.5	215	Federal	2480	—	
Hodgdon	H4895	64.0	215	Federal	2340	—	
Hodgdon	H4831	82.0	215	Federal	2450	—	
Hodgdon	H450	83.0	215	Federal	2475	—	
Hodgdon	H4350	75.0	215	Federal	2450	—	
Winchester	W760	75.0	215	Federal	2450	—	
Winchester	W760	78.0	215	Federal	2500	—	

.378 WEATHERBY

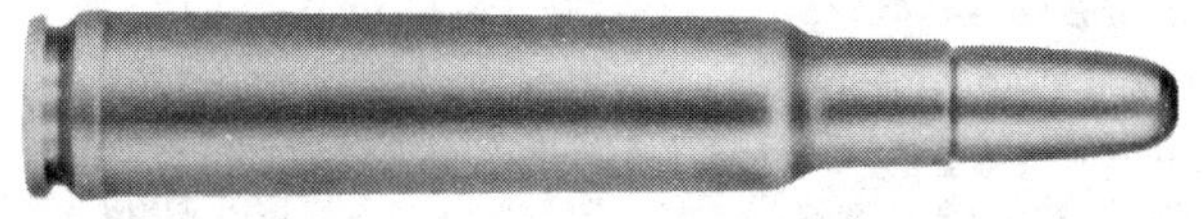

SPECIFICATIONS

Dia. of Rim — .582″
Dia. of Base — .582″
Dia. of Shoulder — .560″
Dia. of Neck — .398″
Length of Neck — .370″
Angle of Shoulder — N/A
Dia. Jacketed Bullet — .375″
Dia. Cast Bullet — .377″
Length of Case — 2.908″
Max. Overall Length — 3.65″
Primer Size — Large Rifle M
Water Capacity — 138.45 grs.

270-grain Softnose

POWDER MFGR.	POWDER TYPE	GRAINS	PRIMER TYPE	PRIMER MFGR.	VELOCITY	PRESSURE (C.U.P.)	REMARKS
IMR	3031	83.5	215	Federal	2825	—	
IMR	3031	86.5	215	Federal	2900	—	
IMR	4064	87.0	215	Federal	2900	—	
IMR	4064	90.0	215	Federal	3000	—	
IMR	4320	90.5	215	Federal	2900	—	
IMR	4320	96.5	215	Federal	3100	—	
IMR	4350	100.0	215	Federal	2800	—	
IMR	4350	105.0	215	Federal	3000	—	
Hodgdon	H4895	91.0	215	Federal	2925	—	
Hodgdon	H4895	95.0	215	Federal	3000	—	
Hodgdon	H4831	106	215	Federal	2875	—	
Hodgdon	H4831	112.5	215	Federal	3100	—	
Hodgdon	H450	110.0	215	Federal	3000	—	
Hodgdon	H4350	100.0	215	Federal	2800	—	

300-grain FMJ

POWDER MFGR.	POWDER TYPE	GRAINS	PRIMER TYPE	PRIMER MFGR.	VELOCITY	PRESSURE (C.U.P.)	REMARKS
IMR	3031	82.5	215	Federal	2725	—	
IMR	3031	85.5	215	Federal	2800	—	
IMR	4064	85.0	215	Federal	2700	—	
IMR	4064	88.5	215	Federal	2800	—	
IMR	4320	87.5	215	Federal	2700	—	
IMR	4320	93.5	215	Federal	2875	—	
IMR	4350	100.0	215	Federal	2750	—	
IMR	4350	103.0	215	Federal	2875	—	
Hodgdon	H4895	85.0	215	Federal	2700	—	
Hodgdon	H4895	89.0	215	Federal	2800	—	
Hodgdon	H450	106.0	215	Federal	2750	—	

.38-55

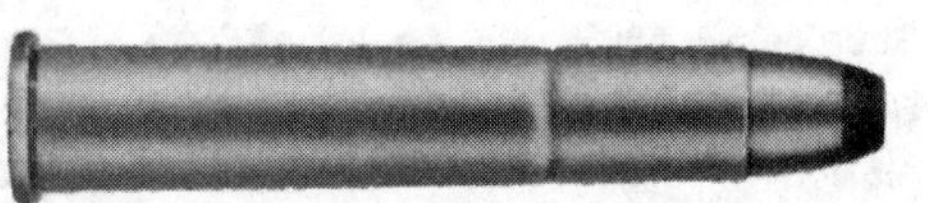

SPECIFICATIONS

Dia. of Rim — .506″
Dia. of Base — .421″
Dia. of Shoulder — N/A
Dia. of Neck — .393″
Length of Neck — N/A
Angle of Shoulder — N/A
Dia. Jacketed Bullet — .376″
Dia. Cast Bullet — .377″
Length of Case — 2.1285″
Max. Overall Length — 2.55″
Primer Size — Large Rifle
Water Capacity — 52.7 grs.

255-grain Softnose

POWDER MFGR.	POWDER TYPE	GRAINS	PRIMER TYPE	PRIMER MFGR.	VELOCITY	PRESSURE (C.U.P.)	REMARKS
Hodgdon	BL-C(2)	38.0	LR	Federal	1660	—	
Hodgdon	H336	37.0	LR	Federal	1680	—	
Hodgdon	H4895	35.0	LR	Federal	1730	—	
Hodgdon	H322	33.0	LR	Federal	1640	—	
Hodgdon	H4198	24.0	LR	Federal	1415	—	
IMR	4227	19.5	LR	Federal	1270	—	
IMR	4227	22.0	LR	Federal	1375	—	Maximum
IMR	4198	21.0	LR	Federal	1230	—	
IMR	4198	23.0	LR	Federal	1325	—	Maximum
IMR	3031	31.0	LR	Federal	1270	—	
IMR	3031	35.0	LR	Federal	1815	—	Caution! Hot!
Hercules	2400	17.0	LR	Federal	1225	—	Factory duplication
Hercules	2400	19.0	LR	Federal	1375	—	Maximum
Hercules	Rx7	27.0	LR	Federal	1220	—	
Hercules	Rx7	30.0	LR	Federal	1545	—	Maximum

CAUTION!

The loads listed on this page are for rifles with modern steel barrels, strong actions, and in good shooting condition. Such rifles include the Winchester Model 94 lever-action rifle and the Winchester Model 1885 single-shot rifle. Many blackpowder rifles were chambered for the 38-55 and may be unsafe with modern loads.

.416 REMINGTON

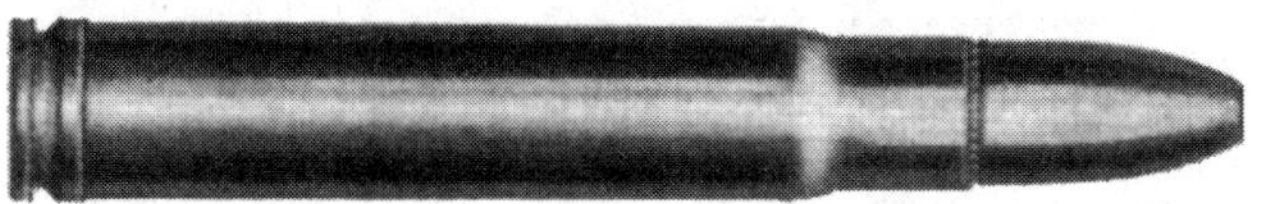

SPECIFICATIONS

Dia. of Rim — .532″
Dia. of Base — .513″
Dia. of Shoulder — .487″
Dia. of Neck — .447″
Length of Neck — .419″
Angle of Shoulder — 25.0°
Dia. Jacketed Bullet — .416″
Dia. Cast Bullet — .416″
Length of Case — 2.850″
Max. Overall Length — 3.600″
Primer Size — Large Rifle M
Water Capacity — 108.0 grs.

400-grain Softnose

POWDER MFGR.	POWDER TYPE	GRAINS	PRIMER TYPE	PRIMER MFGR.	VELOCITY	PRESSURE (C.U.P.)	REMARKS
IMR	4064	75.5	9½M	Remington	2350	45,,800	
IMR	4064	79.5	9½M	Remington	2450	52,000	Maximum
IMR	4320	71.0	9½M	Remington	2250	47,500	
IMR	4320	74.5	9½M	Remington	2350	52,000	Maximum
IMR	4350	82.0	9½M	Remington	2250	—	
IMR	4350	86.0	9½M	Remington	2350	—	Caution: Maximum
IMR	4895	73.0	9½M	Remington	2300	—	
IMR	4895	76.5	9½M	Remington	2420	—	Caution: Maximum
Hodgdon	H4350	85.0	9½M	Remington	2315	—	
Hodgdon	H4895	71.0	9½M	Remington	2250	—	
Winchester	W760	80.0	9½M	Remington	2200	44,800	

.416 RIGBY

SPECIFICATIONS

Dia. of Rim — .582″
Dia. of Base — .589″
Dia. of Shoulder — .539″
Dia. of Neck — .445″
Length of Neck — .460″
Angle of Shoulder — 19.88°
Dia. Jacketed Bullet — .416″
Dia. Cast Bullet — .416″
Length of Case — 2.900″
Max. Overall Length — 3.72″
Primer Size — Large Rifle (M)
Water Capacity — 132.56 grs.

400-grain FMJ

POWDER MFGR.	POWDER TYPE	GRAINS	PRIMER TYPE	PRIMER MFGR.	VELOCITY	PRESSURE (C.U.P.)	REMARKS
IMR	4350	89.0	215	Federal	2300	—	
IMR	4350	92.5	215	Federal	2400	—	Maximum
IMR	4831	90.5	215	Federal	2200	—	
IMR	4831	94.0	215	Federal	2400	—	Maximum
IMR	7828	95.0	215	Federal	2125	—	
IMR	7828	102.5	215	Federal	2350	—	Near Maximum

.416 RIGBY (Cont.)

400-grain Softnose

POWDER MFGR.	POWDER TYPE	GRAINS	PRIMER TYPE	PRIMER MFGR.	VELOCITY	PRESSURE (C.U.P.)	REMARKS
IMR	4350	89.0	215	Federal	2300	—	
IMR	4350	92.5	215	Federal	2400	—	Maximum
IMR	4831	90.5	215	Federal	2200	—	
IMR	4831	94.0	215	Federal	2400	—	Maximum
IMR	7828	95.0	215	Federal	2125	—	
IMR	7828	102.5	215	Federal	2350	—	Near Maximum
Hodgdon	H450	95.5	215	Federal	2250	—	
Hodgdon	H450	103.0	215	Federal	2400	—	Near Maximum
Hodgdon	H4350	92.0	215	Federal	2200	—	
Hodgdon	H4350	97.5	215	Federal	2400	—	Near Maximum
Hodgdon	H4831	99.0	215	Federal	2300	—	
Hodgdon	H4831	104.0	215	Federal	2400	—	Maximum

.416 WEATHERBY

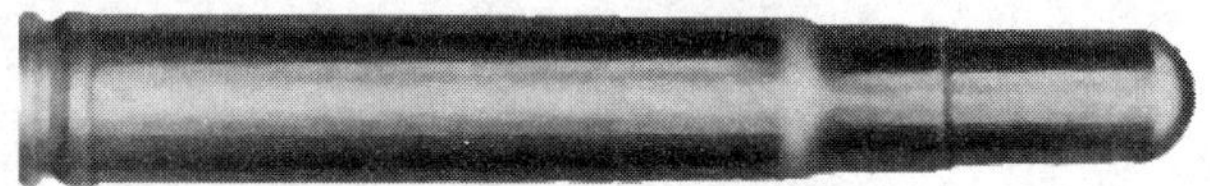

SPECIFICATIONS

Dia. of Rim — .582″
Dia. of Base — .582″
Dia. of Shoulder — .560″
Dia. of Neck — .444″
Length of Neck — .416″
Angle of Shoulder — N/A

Dia. Jacketed Bullet — .416″
Dia. Cast Bullet — .416″
Length of Case — 2.908″
Max. Overall Length — 3.70″
Primer Size — Large Rifle (M)
Water Capacity — 139.87 grs.

400-grain FMJ

POWDER MFGR.	POWDER TYPE	GRAINS	PRIMER TYPE	PRIMER MFGR.	VELOCITY	PRESSURE (C.U.P.)	REMARKS
IMR	4831	105.5	215	Federal	2550	—	
IMR	4831	110.0	215	Federal	2650	—	
IMR	7828	113.0	215	Federal	2475	—	
IMR	7828	118.0	215	Federal	2600	—	
Hodgdon	H450	114.0	215	Federal	2600	—	
Hodgdon	H450	120.0	215	Federal	2700	—	
Hodgdon	H4350	102.5	215	Federal	2400	—	
Hodgdon	H4350	110.0	215	Federal	2620	—	
Hodgdon	H1000	115.0	215	Federal	2300	—	
Hodgdon	H1000	119.5	215	Federal	2400	—	
Hercules	RL-22	112.0	215	Federal	2600	—	
Hercules	RL-22	115.5	215	Federal	2700	—	

.44-40 WCF

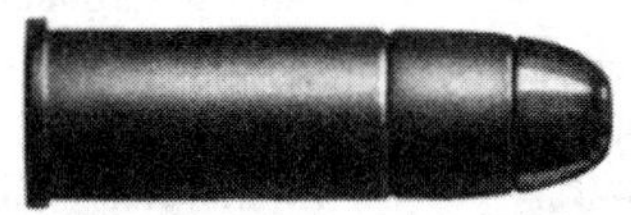

SPECIFICATIONS

Dia. of Rim — .525″
Dia. of Base — .471″
Dia. of Shoulder — .457″
Dia. of Neck — .248″
Neck Length — .10″
Angle of Shoulder — 4°

Dia. Jacketed Bullet — .427″
Dia. Cast Bullet — .428″
Length of Case — 1.305″
Max. Overall Length — 1.55″
Primer Size — Large Rifle
Water Capacity — 38.42 grs.

140-grain Hollow Point

POWDER MFGR.	POWDER TYPE	GRAINS	PRIMER TYPE	PRIMER MFGR.	VELOCITY	PRESSURE (C.U.P.)	REMARKS
Hercules	Unique	12.0	LR	Federal	1790	—	All loads for Winchester Model 92 or stronger rifles
Hercules	Unique	14.0	LR	Federal	2025	—	
Hercules	2400	30.0	LR	Federal	2425	—	
Hercules	2400	32.5	LR	Federal	2700	—	

200-grain Softnose

POWDER MFGR.	POWDER TYPE	GRAINS	PRIMER TYPE	PRIMER MFGR.	VELOCITY	PRESSURE (C.U.P.)	REMARKS
Hercules	Unique	11.3	LR	Federal	1520	—	All loads for Winchester Model 92 or stronger rifles
Hercules	2400	25.5	LR	Federal	1875	—	
Hercules	2400	27.0	LR	Federal	2125	—	
Hercules	4227	28.5	LR	Federal	1900	—	
Hercules	4759	17.0	LR	Federal	1600	—	
Hodgdon	H4227	18.0	LR	Federal	1550	—	
Hodgdon	H110	18.0	LR	Federal	1660	—	
Hodgdon	HS6	9.0	LR	Federal	1290	—	

.44 MAGNUM

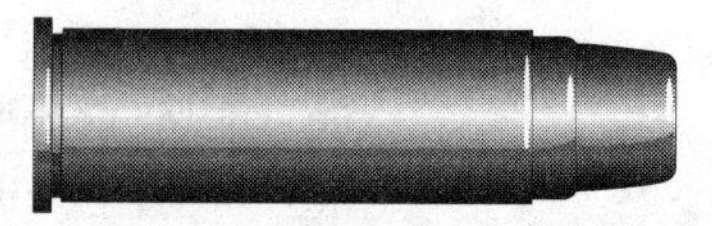

SPECIFICATIONS

Dia. of Rim — .514″
Dia. of Base — .457″
Dia. of Shoulder — Straight
Dia. of Neck — .456″
Length of Neck — N/A
Angle of Shoulder — N/A

Dia. Jacketed Bullet — .430″
Dia. Cast Bullet — .430″
Length of Case — 1.285″
Max. Overall Length — 1.610″
Primer Size — Large Pistol
Water Capacity — 33.94 grs.

200-grain Softnose

POWDER MFGR.	POWDER TYPE	GRAINS	PRIMER TYPE	PRIMER MFGR.	VELOCITY	PRESSURE (C.U.P.)	REMARKS
IMR	4227	23.0	WLP	Winchester	1660	—	
IMR	4227	27.0	WLP	Winchester	1850	—	Maximum
Hercules	2400	21.5	2½	Remington	1725	—	
Hercules	2400	23.0	2½	Remington	1850	—	Maximum
Hodgdon	H110	22.5	2½	Remington	1800	—	
Hodgdon	H110	26.0	2½	Remington	2000	—	Near Maximum
Winchester	W296	25.0	2½	Remington	1850	—	

240-grain Softnose

POWDER MFGR.	POWDER TYPE	GRAINS	PRIMER TYPE	PRIMER MFGR.	VELOCITY	PRESSURE (C.U.P.)	REMARKS
IMR	4227	23.0	WLP	Winchester	1580	—	
IMR	4227	24.5	WLP	Winchester	1700	—	Maximum
Hercules	2400	20.0	2½	Remington	1560	—	
Hercules	2400	23.0	2½	Remington	1800	—	Maximum
Hodgdon	H110	22.0	2½	Remington	1625	—	
Hodgdon	H110	24.5	2½	Remington	1850	—	Near Maximum
Winchester	W296	23.5	2½	Remington	1700	—	
Winchester	W296	24.5	2½	Remington	1800	—	Near Maximum

265-grain Softnose

POWDER MFGR.	POWDER TYPE	GRAINS	PRIMER TYPE	PRIMER MFGR.	VELOCITY	PRESSURE (C.U.P.)	REMARKS
IMR	4227	20.5	WLP	Winchester	1425	—	
IMR	4227	23.0	WLP	Winchester	1575	—	Near Maximum
Hercules	2400	17.5	WLP	Winchester	1420	—	
Hercules	2400	20.0	WLP	Winchester	1550	—	Near Maximum
Hodgdon	H110	18.5	2½	Remington	1450	—	
Hodgdon	H110	21.0	2½	Remington	1600	—	Near Maximum

.444 MARLIN

SPECIFICATIONS

Dia. of Rim — .514″
Dia. of Base — .470″
Dia. of Shoulder — Straight
Dia. of Neck — .453″
Length of Neck — N/A
Angle of Shoulder — N/A

Dia. Jacketed Bullet — .430″
Dia. Cast Bullet — .429″
Length of Case — 2.225″
Max. Overall Length — 2.60″
Primer Size — Large Rifle
Water Capacity — 69.54 grs.

240-grain Softnose

POWDER MFGR.	POWDER TYPE	GRAINS	PRIMER TYPE	PRIMER MFGR.	VELOCITY	PRESSURE (C.U.P.)	REMARKS
IMR	3031	49.0	210	Federal	1900	—	
IMR	3031	51.5	210	Federal	2040	—	
IMR	3031	54.5	210	Federal	2200	—	Near Maximum
IMR	4064	55.0	210	Federal	2100	—	
IMR	4064	56.0	210	Federal	2150	—	
IMR	4198	42.0	9½	Remington	2100	—	
IMR	4198	45.0	9½	Remington	2210	—	
IMR	4320	54.5	9½	Remington	2050	—	
IMR	4320	56.5	9½	Remington	2150	—	Near Maximum

265-grain Softnose

POWDER MFGR.	POWDER TYPE	GRAINS	PRIMER TYPE	PRIMER MFGR.	VELOCITY	PRESSURE (C.U.P.)	REMARKS
IMR	3031	46.0	210	Federal	1800	—	
IMR	3031	48.0	210	Federal	1900	—	
IMR	3031	51.0	210	Federal	2100	—	
IMR	4064	50.0	210	Federal	1900	—	
IMR	4064	53.5	210	Federal	2100	—	
IMR	4198	41.5	9½	Remington	2000	—	
IMR	4198	44.0	9½	Remington	2150	—	
IMR	4320	50.0	9½	Remington	1900	—	
IMR	4320	53.5	9½	Remington	2100	—	
IMR	4895	51.0	9½	Remington	1900	31600	
IMR	4895	54.5	9½	Remington	2075	—	
Hodgdon	H4198	40.5	9½	Remington	1950	—	
Hodgdon	H4198	47.0	9½	Remington	2200	—	Maximum
Hodgdon	H322	46.0	9½	Remington	1900	—	
Hodgdon	H322	50.0	9½	Remington	2100	—	

.45-70

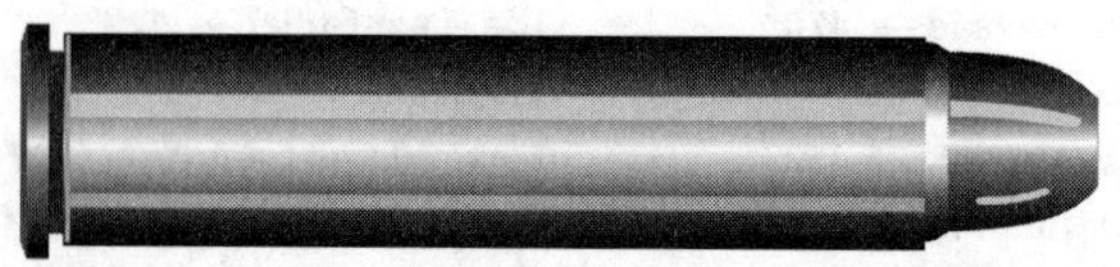

SPECIFICATIONS

Dia. of Rim — .608″
Dia. of Base — .505″
Dia. of Shoulder — Straight
Dia. of Neck — .480″
Angle of Neck — Straight
Angle of Shoulder — Straight
Dia. Jacketed Bullet — .458″
Dia. Cast Bullet — .460″
Length of Case — 2.1″
Max. Overall Length — 2.55″
Primer Size — Large Rifle
Water Capacity — 75.5 grs.

300-grain Jacketed

POWDER MFGR.	POWDER TYPE	GRAINS	PRIMER TYPE	PRIMER MFGR.	VELOCITY	PRESSURE (C.U.P.)	REMARKS
Hercules	Rx7	38.0	LR	Federal	1430	—	All loads for Winchester Model 1886 or stronger rifles
Hercules	Rx7	45.0	LR	Federal	1820	—	
Hercules	2400	30.0	LR	Federal	1660	—	
IMR	4227	32.0	LR	Federal	1600	—	
IMR	4227	37.0	LR	Federal	1850	—	
IMR	3031	43.0	LR	Federal	1560	—	
IMR	3031	50.0	LR	Federal	1830	—	

405-grain Jacketed

POWDER MFGR.	POWDER TYPE	GRAINS	PRIMER TYPE	PRIMER MFGR.	VELOCITY	PRESSURE (C.U.P.)	REMARKS
Hercules	Rx7	34.0	LR	Federal	1200	—	All loads for Winchester Model 1886 or stronger rifles
Hercules	Rx7	44.0	LR	Federal	1600	—	
Hercules	2400	27.0	LR	Federal	1350	—	
Hercules	2400	32.0	LR	Federal	1590	—	
IMR	4227	30.0	LR	Federal	1380	—	
IMR	4227	35.0	LR	Federal	1625	—	
IMR	3031	38.5	LR	Federal	1300	—	
IMR	3031	48.0	LR	Federal	1740	—	
IMR	4198	36.0	LR	Federal	1340	—	
IMR	4198	41.0	LR	Federal	1780	—	

.458 WINCHESTER

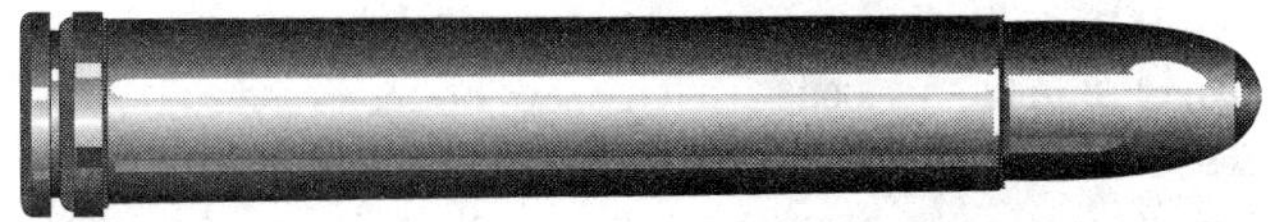

SPECIFICATIONS

Dia. of Rim — .532″
Dia. of Base — .513″
Dia. of Shoulder — Straight
Dia. of Neck — .481″
Length of Neck — Straight
Angle of Shoulder — Straight
Dia. Jacketed Bullet — .458″
Dia. Cast Bullet — .457″
Length of Case — 2.500″
Max. Overall Length — 3.30″
Primer Size — Large Rifle (M)
Water Capacity — 93.29 grs.

350-grain Softnose

POWDER MFGR.	POWDER TYPE	GRAINS	PRIMER TYPE	PRIMER MFGR.	VELOCITY	PRESSURE (C.U.P.)	REMARKS
IMR	3031	66.5	215	Federal	2100	—	
IMR	3031	70.5	215	Federal	2275	—	
IMR	3031	75.0	215	Federal	2400	—	
IMR	4064	74.0	215	Federal	2100	—	
IMR	4064	76.0	215	Federal	2200	—	
IMR	4198	66.0	215	Federal	2400	—	
IMR	4198	69.5	215	Federal	2475	—	
Hodgdon	H4198	64.0	9½M	Remington	2300	—	
Hodgdon	H4895	77.0	9½M	Remington	2250	—	
Norma	N200	66.0	215	Federal	2200	—	
Norma	N200	71.0	215	Federal	2400	—	
Norma	N201	72.0	215	Federal	2200	—	
Norma	N202	78.0	215	Federal	2200	—	
Winchester	W748	78.0	215	Federal	2300	—	

500-grain FMJ

POWDER MFGR.	POWDER TYPE	GRAINS	PRIMER TYPE	PRIMER MFGR.	VELOCITY	PRESSURE (C.U.P.)	REMARKS
IMR	3031	66.0	215	Federal	2000	—	
IMR	3031	70.5	WLR	Winchester	2100	—	
IMR	4064	74.0	WLR	Winchester	2050	—	
IMR	4198	63.5	WLR	Winchester	2050	—	
IMR	4198	65.0	WLR	Winchester	2100	—	
IMR	4320	72.0	215	Federal	2000	—	
IMR	4320	76.0	215	Federal	2150	—	
IMR	4895	72.0	WLR	Winchester	2100	53000	
Hodgdon	BLC-(2)	75.0	9½M	Remington	2000	—	
Hodgdon	H4198	60.0	9½M	Remington	1950	—	
Hodgdon	H4895	70.0	9½M	Remington	2050	—	

.460 WEATHERBY MAGNUM

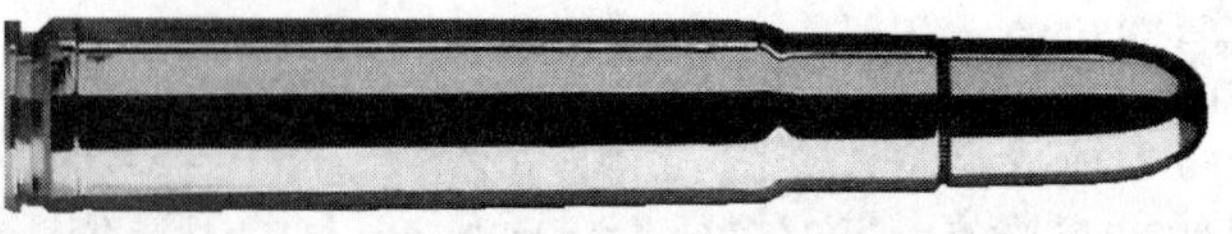

SPECIFICATIONS

Dia. of Rim — .582″
Dia. of Base — .582″
Dia. of Shoulder — .560″
Dia. of Neck — .481″
Length of Neck — .416″
Angle of Shoulder — N/A

Dia. Jacketed Bullet — .458″
Dia. Cast Bullet — .457″
Length of Case — 2.908″
Max. Overall Length — 3.70″
Primer Size — Large Rifle (M)
Water Capacity — 144.67 grs.

350-grain Softnose

POWDER MFGR.	POWDER TYPE	GRAINS	PRIMER TYPE	PRIMER MFGR.	VELOCITY	PRESSURE (C.U.P.)	REMARKS
IMR	3031	97.5	215	Federal	2700	—	
IMR	3031	100.5	215	Federal	2750	—	
IMR	3031	103.0	215	Federal	2825	—	
IMR	4064	98.5	215	Federal	2600	—	
IMR	4064	105.0	215	Federal	2700	—	
IM$	4064	110.0	215	Federal	2900	—	
IMR	4320	100.0	215	Federal	2500	—	
IMR	4320	110.0	215	Federal	2800	—	
IMR	4350	115.0	215	Federal	2625	—	
IMR	4350	120.0	215	Federal	2700	—	
Hodgdon	H4895	100.0	215	Federal	2500	—	
Hodgdon	H4895	109.0	215	Federal	2750	—	
Hodgdon	H4831	119.5	215	Federal	2450	—	
Hodgdon	H4831	124.5	215	Federal	2600	—	
Hodgdon	H4831	127.0	215	Federal	2650	—	
Hodgdon	H380	105.0	215	Federal	2600	—	
Hodgdon	H414	112.5	215	Federal	2500	—	
Hodgdon	H450	118.0	215	Federal	2500	—	
Hodgdon	H450	125.0	215	Federal	2600	—	
Hodgdon	H4350	115.5	215	Federal	2600	—	
Hodgdon	H4350	120.0	215	Federal	2700	—	
Winchester	W760	116.5	215	Federal	2700	—	
Winchester	W760	120.0	215	Federal	2850	—	

.460 WEATHERBY MAGNUM (Cont.)

400-grain Softnose

POWDER MFGR.	POWDER TYPE	GRAINS	PRIMER TYPE	PRIMER MFGR.	VELOCITY	PRESSURE (C.U.P.)	REMARKS
IMR	3031	96.5	215	Federal	2550	—	
IMR	3031	100.5	215	Federal	2650	—	
IMR	4064	101.0	215	Federal	2650	—	
IMR	4320	104.0	215	Federal	2500	—	
IMR	4320	108.0	215	Federal	2600	—	
IMR	4350	115.0	215	Federal	2550	—	
IMR	4350	119.0	215	Federal	2600	—	
Hodgdon	H4895	98.0	215	Federal	2400	—	
Hodgdon	H4895	105.0	215	Federal	2625	—	
Hodgdon	H4831	120.5	215	Federal	2400	—	
Hodgdon	H4831	126.5	215	Federal	2500	—	
Hodgdon	H380	107.0	215	Federal	2500	—	
Hodgdon	H414	115.0	215	Federal	2500	—	
Hodgdon	H450	124.0	215	Federal	2500	—	
Hodgdon	H4350	111.5	215	Federal	2500	—	
Hodgdon	H4350	117.0	215	Federal	2620	—	
Winchester	W760	114.5	215	Federal	2600	—	
Winchester	W760	118.0	215	Federal	2700	—	

500-grain FMJ

POWDER MFGR.	POWDER TYPE	GRAINS	PRIMER TYPE	PRIMER MFGR.	VELOCITY	PRESSURE (C.U.P.)	REMARKS
IMR	3031	95.0	215	Federal	2400	—	
IMR	3031	99.0	215	Federal	2475	—	
IMR	4064	100.0	215	Federal	2425	—	
IMR	4064	104.0	215	Federal	2500	—	
IMR	4320	102.5	215	Federal	2400	—	
IMR	4320	107.0	215	Federal	2500	—	
IMR	4350	108.0	215	Federal	2400	—	
IMR	4350	118.0	215	Federal	2600	—	
IMR	4831	114.0	215	Federal	2400	—	
IMR	4831	120.0	215	Federal	2500	—	
IMR	7828	117.0	215	Federal	2360	41900	
Hodgdon	H4895	99.0	215	Federal	2350	—	

.470 NITRO EXPRESS

SPECIFICATIONS

Dia. of Rim — .646″
Dia. of Base — .572″
Dia. of Shoulder — .528″
Dia. of Neck — .500″
Length of Neck — .790″
Angle of Shoulder — 4.15°

Dia. Jacketed Bullet — .483″
Dia. Cast Bullet — .483″
Length of Case — 3.250″
Max. Overall Length — 3.86″
Primer Size — Large Rifle
Water Capacity — 156.65 grs.

500-grain FMJ

POWDER MFGR.	POWDER TYPE	GRAINS	PRIMER TYPE	PRIMER MFGR.	VELOCITY	PRESSURE (C.U.P.)	REMARKS
IMR	3031	76.0	215	Federal	2145	—	

Chapter 14

Loads for Metric Rifle Cartridges

A metric cartridge designation "turned off" most American shooters before the 1950s. Until that time, a metric cartridge usually meant "war surplus" and no respectable American hunter was going to be seen with such a weapon. Today, however, the scene has changed. Metric cartridge designations are as popular, or perhaps more popular, than the English/American inch caliber designation.

In the United States, the great majority of cartridges, past and present, use descriptive designations based upon the inch as the unit of measure. European cartridges have traditionally used the millimeter for this same purpose. However, there is probably just as much confusion over exactly what these reference designations mean as there are for American cartridges. For instance, the American .30-06 means .30 caliber developed in 1906. However, the Winchester .30-30 means .30 caliber and 30 grains of powder. The .356 Winchester fires a bullet .358 in diameter, while the .340 Weatherby uses a .338 caliber bullet.

Using European metric designations, the first value specifies caliber in millimeters, and if there is a second designation such as 7 X 57, this latter value is often the cartridge length, also in millimeters. Should the European designation be followed by the letter 'R', this indicates a rimmed version of the cartridge, which is also available in a rimless style. For example, the 7 X 57R is the rimmed version of the 7 X 57mm Mauser. This form of cartridge designation is usually the case, but not always. For instance, The 7.62mm Russian Nagant pistol cartridge is also known as the 7.62 X 38 R and fires a bullet with a .295 inch diameter. The 7.5 X 53 Rubin fires a bullet with a diameter of .312 inch. So, like many American cartridges, European cartridge designations don't always specify exact bullet diameter or even cartridge case length. There is no, fixed standard applied to all cartridges, European or American.

The loads in this chapter assume use in properly-designed firearms of modern steel construction. Many of the older rifles designed to fire metric cartridges were manufactured for military use. Some of these exhibit varying degrees of sturdiness and dimensions, depending upon the date of manufacture and the success or failure of wartime efforts at the time of manufacture. For instance, some of the Japanese Arisaka rifles of World War II are extremely strong, but others, manufactured near the end of the war, are poorly made and may be unsafe. The same is true of other military rifles. Any firearm that falls in this category should be thoroughly inspected by a qualified gunsmith, and verified to be in good shooting condition, before firing. Check the headspace and bore diameter in all such arms.

6mm PPC

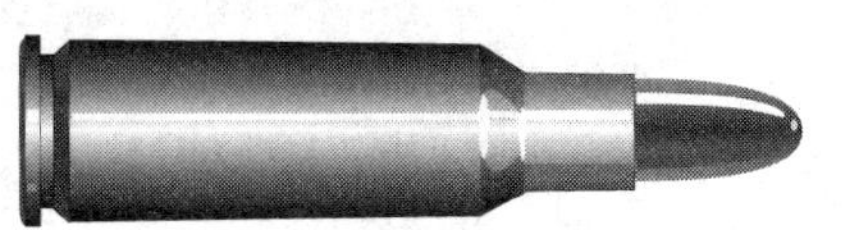

SPECIFICATIONS

Dia. of Rim — .445″
Dia. of Base — .440″
Dia. of Shoulder — .430″
Dia. of Neck — .265″
Length of Neck — .272″
Angle of Shoulder — 25.00°
Dia. Jacketed Bullet — .243″
Dia. Cast Bullet — .243″
Length of Case — 1.525″
Max. Overall Length — 2.10″
Primer Size — Small Rifle
Water Capacity — 33.80 grs.

70-grain Softnose

POWDER MFGR.	POWDER TYPE	GRAINS	PRIMER TYPE	PRIMER MFGR.	VELOCITY	PRESSURE (C.U.P.)	REMARKS
IMR	3031	24.0	7½	Remington	2800	43800	
IMR	3031	25.5	7½	Remington	3000	49900	
IMR	4064	27.0	7½	Remington	2800	42700	
IMR	4064	27.5	7½	Remington	2900	51000	
IMR	4198	22.0	205	Federal	2900	—	
IMR	4198	25.0	205	Federal	3175	—	Maximum
Hodgdon	H322	25.5	205	Federal	2900	—	
Hodgdon	H322	28.0	205	Federal	3150	—	Maximum
Hodgdon	H335	28.0	205	Federal	2950	—	
Hodgdon	H335	29.0	205	Federal	3050	—	
Winchester	W748	27.5	205	Federal	2750	—	
Winchester	W748	29.0	205	Federal	2900	—	Maximum
Hercules	RL-7	22.0	205	Federal	2900	—	
Hercules	RL-7	23.5	205	Federal	3075	—	Near Maximum

75-grain Softnose

POWDER MFGR.	POWDER TYPE	GRAINS	PRIMER TYPE	PRIMER MFGR.	VELOCITY	PRESSURE (C.U.P.)	REMARKS
IMR	3031	23.5	7½	Remington	2650	42500	
IMR	3031	25.0	7½	Remington	2900	51000	Near Maximum
IMR	4064	25.5	7½	Remington	2600	41800	
IMR	4064	27.0	7½	Remington	2800	49000	
IMR	4198	23.0	205	Federal	2900	—	
IMR	4198	24.0	205	Federal	3060	—	Near Maximum
Hodgdon	H322	26.0	205	Federal	2800	—	
Hodgdon	H322	27.5	205	Federal	3000	—	
Winchester	W748	28.5	205	Federal	2800	—	
Winchester	W748	29.5	205	Federal	2980	—	Maximum
Hercules	RL-7	23.0	205	Federal	2800	—	

6mm BR REMINGTON

SPECIFICATIONS

Dia. of Rim — .473″
Dia. of Base — .469″
Dia. of Shoulder — .458″
Dia. of Neck — .265″
Length of Neck — .270″
Angle of Shoulder — 29.58°
Dia. Jacketed Bullet — .243″
Dia. Cast Bullet — .243″
Length of Case — 1.520″
Max. Overall Length — 2.165″
Primer Size — Small Rifle (M)
Water Capacity — 37.91 grs.

75-grain Softnose

POWDER MFGR.	POWDER TYPE	GRAINS	PRIMER TYPE	PRIMER MFGR.	VELOCITY	PRESSURE (C.U.P.)	REMARKS
Hodgdon	H322	25.0	7½	Remington	2850	—	
Hodgdon	H322	26.5	7½	Remington	3000	—	Maximum
Winchester	W748	29.0	7½	Remington	2800	—	
Winchester	W748	33.0	7½	Remington	3200	—	Maximum
Hercules	RL-12	27.5	7½	Remington	2800	—	
Hercules	RL-12	29.5	7½	Remington	3000	—	Maximum

POWDER MFGR.	POWDER TYPE	GRAINS	PRIMER TYPE	PRIMER MFGR.	VELOCITY	PRESSURE (C.U.P.)	REMARKS
Hodgdon	H322	21.5	7½	Remington	2580	—	
Hodgdon	H322	24.0	7½	Remington	2750	—	Near Maximum
Winchester	W748	28.0	7½	Remington	2750	—	
Winchester	W748	31.5	7½	Remington	3100	—	Maximum
Hercules	RL-12	25.0	7½	Remington	2600	—	
Hercules	RL-12	28.5	7½	Remington	2900	—	Maximum

87-grain Softnose

POWDER MFGR.	POWDER TYPE	GRAINS	PRIMER TYPE	PRIMER MFGR.	VELOCITY	PRESSURE (C.U.P.)	REMARKS
Hodgdon	H322	21.5	7½	Remington	2475	—	
Hodgdon	H322	24.0	7½	Remington	2700	—	Near Maximum
Winchester	W748	28.0	7½	Remington	2700	—	
Winchester	W748	31.0	7½	Remington	3000	—	Maximum
Hercules	RL-12	25.0	7½	Remington	2500	—	
Hercules	RL-12	28.0	7½	Remington	2750	—	Maximum

6mm REMINGTON

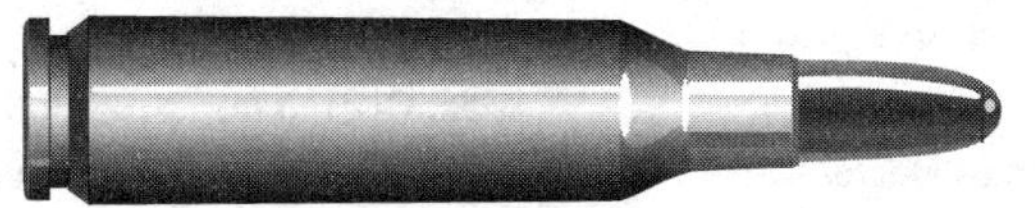

SPECIFICATIONS

Dia. of Rim — .472″
Dia. of Base — .471″
Dia. of Shoulder — .431″
Dia. of Neck — .276″
Length of Neck — .351″
Angle of Shoulder — 24°
Dia. Jacketed Bullet — .243″
Dia. Cast Bullet — .243″
Length of Case — 2.233″
Max. Overall Length — 2.84″
Primer Size — Large Rifle
Water Capacity — 54.57 grs.

70-grain Softnose

POWDER MFGR.	POWDER TYPE	GRAINS	PRIMER TYPE	PRIMER MFGR.	VELOCITY	PRESSURE (C.U.P.)	REMARKS
IMR	3031	37.0	9½	Remington	3100	—	
IMR	3031	41.0	9½	Remington	3450	—	Near Maximum
IMR	4064	38.0	9½	Remington	3100	—	
IMR	4064	42.5	9½	Remington	3500	—	Maximum
IMR	4320	40.0	9½	Remington	3125	—	
IMR	4320	44.5	9½	Remington	3500	—	Maximum
Hodgdon	H380	40.5	9½	Remington	3100	—	
Hodgdon	H380	45.0	9½	Remington	3470	—	Maximum

80-grain Softnose

POWDER MFGR.	POWDER TYPE	GRAINS	PRIMER TYPE	PRIMER MFGR.	VELOCITY	PRESSURE (C.U.P.)	REMARKS
IMR	3031	36.0	9½	Remington	2950	—	
IMR	3031	39.5	9½	Remington	3200	—	Maximum
IMR	4064	37.0	9½	Remington	2950	—	
IMR	4064	40.5	9½	Remington	3200	—	Maximum
IMR	4320	37.5	9½	Remington	2900	—	
IMR	4320	42.5	9½	Remington	3250	—	Maximum
Hodgdon	H4831	44.0	9½	Remington	2900	—	
Hodgdon	H4831	49.0	9½	Remington	3200	—	Maximum

100-grain Softnose

POWDER MFGR.	POWDER TYPE	GRAINS	PRIMER TYPE	PRIMER MFGR.	VELOCITY	PRESSURE (C.U.P.)	REMARKS
IMR	3031	32.0	9½	Remington	2650	—	
IMR	3031	35.5	9½	Remington	2850	—	Maximum
IMR	4064	33.5	9½	Remington	2650	—	
IMR	4064	37.0	9½	Remington	2900	—	Near Maximum

6.5 JAPANESE

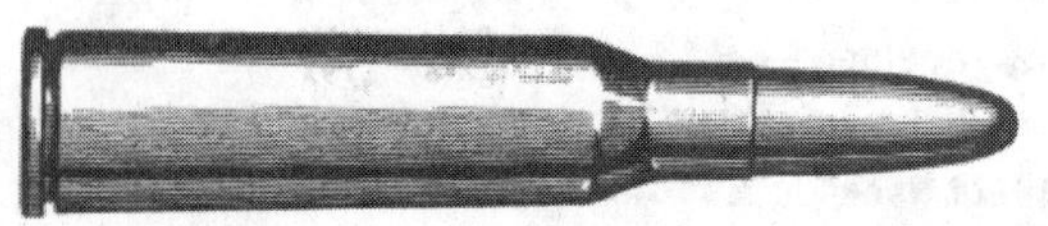

SPECIFICATIONS

Dia. of Rim — .466″
Dia. of Base — .447″
Dia. of Shoulder — .417″
Dia. of Neck — .288″
Length of Neck — .281″
Angle of Shoulder — 20.55°
Dia. Jacketed Bullet — .264″
Dia. Cast Bullet — .264″
Length of Case — 1.984″
Max. Overall Length — 2.85″
Primer Size — Large Rifle
Water Capacity — 41.67 grs.

100-grain Softnose

POWDER MFGR.	POWDER TYPE	GRAINS	PRIMER TYPE	PRIMER MFGR.	VELOCITY	PRESSURE (C.U.P.)	REMARKS
IMR	3031	30.5	210	Federal	2550	—	
IMR	3031	33.5	210	Federal	2825	—	Maximum
IMR	4064	32.0	210	Federal	2540	—	
IMR	4064	35.5	210	Federal	2875	—	Maximum
IMR	4320	32.0	210	Federal	2480	—	
IMR	4320	36.0	210	Federal	2850	—	Maximum

140-grain Softnose

POWDER MFGR.	POWDER TYPE	GRAINS	PRIMER TYPE	PRIMER MFGR.	VELOCITY	PRESSURE (C.U.P.)	REMARKS
IMR	3031	28.0	210	Federal	2150	—	
IMR	3031	31.0	210	Federal	2460	—	Maximum
IMR	4064	29.0	210	Federal	2125	—	
IMR	4064	33.0	210	Federal	2500	—	Caution
IMR	4320	29.5	210	Federal	2180	—	
IMR	4320	33.0	210	Federal	2425	—	Maximum

160-grain Softnose

POWDER MFGR.	POWDER TYPE	GRAINS	PRIMER TYPE	PRIMER MFGR.	VELOCITY	PRESSURE (C.U.P.)	REMARKS
IMR	3031	27.0	210	Federal	1900	—	
IMR	3031	30.5	210	Federal	2280	—	Maximum
IMR	4064	27.0	210	Federal	1930	—	
IMR	4064	33.0	210	Federal	2375	—	Maximum
IMR	4350	30.0	210	Federal	1910	—	
IMR	4350	35.5	210	Federal	2300	—	Maximum

6.5 X 55 mm SWEDISH

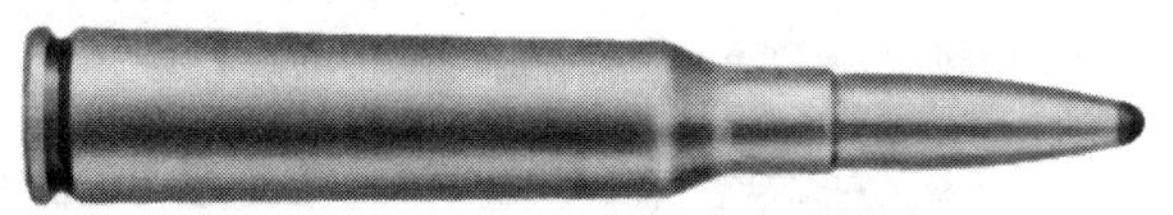

SPECIFICATIONS

Dia. of Rim — .476″
Dia. of Base — .476″
Dia. of Shoulder — .435″
Dia. of Neck — .297″
Length of Neck — .332″
Angle of Shoulder — 24.84°
Dia. Jacketed Bullet — .264″
Dia. Cast Bullet — .264″
Length of Case — 2.165″
Max. Overall Length — 3.03″
Primer Size — Large Rifle
Water Capacity — 55.04 grs.

100-grain Softnose

POWDER MFGR.	POWDER TYPE	GRAINS	PRIMER TYPE	PRIMER MFGR.	VELOCITY	PRESSURE (C.U.P.)	REMARKS
IMR	3031	34.0	9½	Remington	2500	—	
IMR	3031	38.0	9½	Remington	2750	—	Maximum
IMR	4064	37.0	9½	Remington	2550	—	
IMR	4064	40.5	9½	Remington	2765	—	Near Maximum
IMR	4320	37.0	9½	Remington	2525	—	
IMR	4320	41.5	9½	Remington	2810	—	Maximum
IMR	4350	43.5	9½	Remington	2540	—	
IMR	4350	48.0	9½	Remington	2800	—	Near Maximum

140-grain Softnose

POWDER MFGR.	POWDER TYPE	GRAINS	PRIMER TYPE	PRIMER MFGR.	VELOCITY	PRESSURE (C.U.P.)	REMARKS
IMR	3031	30.5	9½	Remington	2060	—	
IMR	3031	35.5	9½	Remington	2400	—	Maximum
IMR	4064	34.0	9½	Remington	2150	—	
IMR	4064	38.0	9½	Remington	2400	—	Maximum
IMR	4320	33.0	9½	Remington	2100	—	
IMR	4320	38.5	9½	Remington	22450	—	Near Maximum
IMR	4350	38.0	9½	Remington	2200	—	
IMR	4350	43.0	9½	Remington	2460	—	Near Maximum

160-grain Softnose

POWDER MFGR.	POWDER TYPE	GRAINS	PRIMER TYPE	PRIMER MFGR.	VELOCITY	PRESSURE (C.U.P.)	REMARKS
IMR	4350	36.0	9½	Remington	2000	—	
IMR	4350	42.0	9½	Remington	2300	—	Near Maximum
Hodgdon	H450	42.0	9½	Remington	2150	—	
Hodgdon	H450	45.0	9½	Remington	2345	—	Near Maximum

6.5 REMINGTON MAGNUM

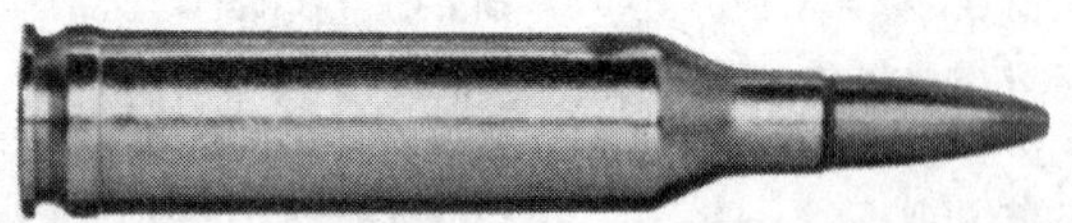

SPECIFICATIONS

Dia. of Rim — .532″
Dia. of Base — .513″
Dia. of Shoulder — .496″
Dia. of Neck — .298″
Length of Neck — .261″
Angle of Shoulder — 25.10°

Dia. Jacketed Bullet — .264″
Dia. Cast Bullet — .264″
Length of Case — 2.170″
Max. Overall Length — 3.05″
Primer Size — Large Rifle (M)
Water Capacity — 68.64 grs.

100-grain Softnose

POWDER MFGR.	POWDER TYPE	GRAINS	PRIMER TYPE	PRIMER MFGR.	VELOCITY	PRESSURE (C.U.P.)	REMARKS
IMR	3031	39.0	9½	Remington	2900	—	
IMR	3031	42.0	9½	Remington	3050	—	
IMR	4064	43.0	215	Federal	2900	—	
IMR	4064	45.0	215	Federal	3100	—	
IMR	4320	42.5	9½	Remington	2900	—	
IMR	4320	47.2	9½	Remington	3200	—	Near Maximum
IMR	4350	47.5	9½	Remington	2950	—	
IMR	4350	51.0	9½	Remington	3100	—	
Hodgdon	H4895	41.5	WLR	Winchester	2900	—	
Hodgdon	H4895	45.0	WLR	Winchester	3100	—	
Hodgdon	H380	47.0	WLR	Winchester	3000	—	
Hodgdon	H380	50.0	WLR	Winchester	3200	—	Near Maximum

129-grain Softnose

POWDER MFGR.	POWDER TYPE	GRAINS	PRIMER TYPE	PRIMER MFGR.	VELOCITY	PRESSURE (C.U.P.)	REMARKS
IMR	3031	39.0	9½	Remington	2710	—	
IMR	3031	43.0	9½	Remington	2900	—	Near Maximum
IMR	4064	40.0	9½	Remington	2650	—	
IMR	4064	44.0	9½	Remington	3045	—	
IMR	4320	42.0	9½	Remington	2710	—	
IMR	4320	45.5	9½	Remington	2950	—	
IMR	4350	46.0	9½	Remington	2750	—	
IMR	4350	49.0	9½	Remington	2925	—	
Hodgdon	H4895	40.5	WLR	Winchester	2700	—	
Hodgdon	H4895	44.5	WLR	Winchester	2950	—	
Hodgdon	H380	44.0	WLR	Winchester	2725	—	
Hodgdon	H380	47.0	WLR	Winchester	2900	—	

7 mm REMINGTON EXPRESS

SPECIFICATIONS

Dia. of Rim — .473″
Dia. of Base — .470″
Dia. of Shoulder — .441″
Dia. of Neck — .315″
Length of Neck — .341″
Angle of Shoulder — 17.5°
Dia. Jacketed Bullet — .284″
Dia. Cast Bullet — .286″
Length of Case — 2.545″
Max. Overall Length — 3.33″
Primer Size — Large Rifle
Water Capacity — 68.58 grs.

125-grain Softnose

POWDER MFGR.	POWDER TYPE	GRAINS	PRIMER TYPE	PRIMER MFGR.	VELOCITY	PRESSURE (C.U.P.)	REMARKS
SR	4759	30.0	210	Federal	2445	49700	
IMR	4227	28.5	210	Federal	2375	48400	
IMR	4198	36.0	210	Federal	2680	50000	
IMR	3031	47.0	210	Federal	2975	48900	
IMR	4064	50.0	210	Federal	3055	49700	
IMR	4895	44.0	210	Federal	2845	49100	
IMR	4320	46.5	210	Federal	2880	49900	
IMR	4350	56.5	210	Federal	3055	48600	
IMR	4831	60.0	210	Federal	3115	50000	Compressed load

150-grain Softnose

POWDER MFGR.	POWDER TYPE	GRAINS	PRIMER TYPE	PRIMER MFGR.	VELOCITY	PRESSURE (C.U.P.)	REMARKS
SR	4759	29.5	210	Federal	2200	50000	
IMR	4227	27.5	210	Federal	2115	49500	
IMR	4198	34.5	210	Federal	2375	49200	
IMR	3031	45.5	210	Federal	2745	48800	
IMR	4064	48.0	210	Federal	2810	50000	

165-grain Softnose

POWDER MFGR.	POWDER TYPE	GRAINS	PRIMER TYPE	PRIMER MFGR.	VELOCITY	PRESSURE (C.U.P.)	REMARKS
SR	4759	29.0	210	Federal	2150	50000	
IMR	4227	27.0	210	Federal	2050	50000	
IMR	4198	33.5	210	Federal	2295	49400	
IMR	3031	44.5	210	Federal	2615	49700	
IMR	4064	46.5	210	Federal	2640	48800	
IMR	4895	42.0	210	Federal	2525	49400	
IMR	4320	44.0	210	Federal	2550	49900	

7 x 57mm MAUSER

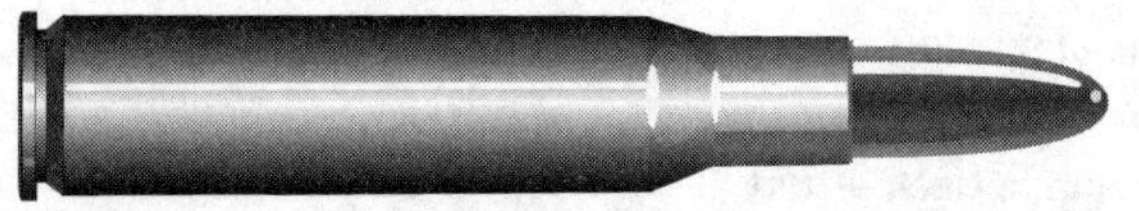

SPECIFICATIONS

Dia. of Rim — .473″
Dia. of Base — .471″
Dia. of Shoulder — .431″
Dia. of Neck — .321″
Length of Neck — .340″
Angle of Shoulder — 21.04°
Dia. Jacketed Bullet — .284″
Dia. Cast Bullet — .286″
Length of Case — 2.235″
Max. Overall Length — 3.02″
Primer Size — Large Rifle
Water Capacity — 55.55 grs.

139-grain Softnose

POWDER MFGR.	POWDER TYPE	GRAINS	PRIMER TYPE	PRIMER MFGR.	VELOCITY	PRESSURE (C.U.P.)	REMARKS
IMR	3031	40.0	210	Federal	2500	—	
IMR	3031	44.0	210	Federal	2800	—	Maximum
IMR	4064	42.0	210	Federal	2550	—	
IMR	4064	45.0	210	Federal	2800	—	Maximum
IMR	4320	41.5	210	Federal	2500	—	
IMR	4320	45.5	210	Federal	2800	—	Near Maximum
IMR	4350	47.0	210	Federal	2525	—	
IMR	4350	52.5	210	Federal	2900	—	Caution

154-grain Softnose

POWDER MFGR.	POWDER TYPE	GRAINS	PRIMER TYPE	PRIMER MFGR.	VELOCITY	PRESSURE (C.U.P.)	REMARKS
IMR	3031	37.5	210	Federal	2300	—	
IMR	3031	41.5	210	Federal	2600	—	Maximum
IMR	4064	38.5	210	Federal	2325	—	
IMR	4064	42.5	210	Federal	2600	—	Maximum
IMR	4320	40.0	210	Federal	2400	—	
IMR	4320	44.5	210	Federal	2700	—	Maximum
IMR	4350	42.5	210	Federal	2300	—	
IMR	4350	47.5	210	Federal	2600	—	Caution

175-grain Softnose

POWDER MFGR.	POWDER TYPE	GRAINS	PRIMER TYPE	PRIMER MFGR.	VELOCITY	PRESSURE (C.U.P.)	REMARKS
IMR	3031	36.5	210	Federal	2210	—	
IMR	3031	39.5	210	Federal	2400	—	Maximum
IMR	4064	38.0	210	Federal	2200	—	
IMR	4064	42.0	210	Federal	2500	—	Maximum
WIN	760	42.5	210	Federal	2250	—	
WIN	760	46.5	210	Federal	2500	—	Maximum

7mm X 08 REMINGTON

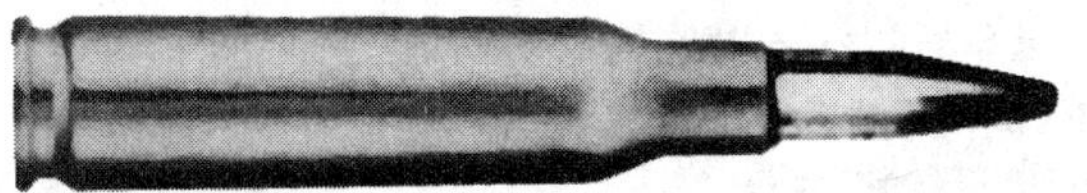

SPECIFICATIONS

Dia. of Rim — .473″
Dia. of Base — .470″
Dia. of Shoulder — .454″
Dia. of Neck — .315″
Length of Neck — .285″
Angle of Shoulder — 20.00°
Dia. Jacketed Bullet — .284″
Dia. Cast Bullet — .284″
Length of Case — 2.035″
Max. Overall Length — 2.850″
Primer Size — Large Rifle
Water Capacity — N/A

120-grain Softnose

POWDER MFGR.	POWDER TYPE	GRAINS	PRIMER TYPE	PRIMER MFGR.	VELOCITY	PRESSURE (C.U.P.)	REMARKS
IMR	4064	37.5	9½	Remington	2290	—	
IMR	4064	42.5	9½	Remington	2750	—	Maximum
IMR	4320	37.0	9½	Remington	2375	—	
IMR	4320	41.5	9½	Remington	2725	—	Maximum
Winchester	748	38.0	9½	Remington	2230	—	
Winchester	748	42.5	9½	Remington	2750	—	Near Maximum
Vihtavuori	N140	41.4	9½	Remington	2548	37,700	
Vihtavuori	N140	45.4	9½	Remington	2941	50,500	Maximum
Vihtavuori	N150	42.2	9½	Remington	2684	37,700	
Vihtavuori	N150	46.9	9½	Remington	2967	50,500	Maximum

140-grain Softnose

POWDER MFGR.	POWDER TYPE	GRAINS	PRIMER TYPE	PRIMER MFGR.	VELOCITY	PRESSURE (C.U.P.)	REMARKS
IMR	4064	36.0	9½	Remington	2210	—	
IMR	4064	39.5	9½	Remington	2515	—	Near Maximum
IMR	4320	35.0	9½	Remington	2230	—	
IMR	4320	39.5	9½	Remington	2560	—	Near Maximum
Winchester	748	35.0	9½	Remington	2250	—	
Winchester	748	39.5	9½	Remington	2470	—	Maximum
Vihtavuori	N140	38.5	9½	Remington	2407	37,700	
Vihtavuori	N140	42.7	9½	Remington	2857	50,500	Maximum
Vihtavuori	N150	39.2	9½	Remington	2419	39,900	
Vihtavuori	N150	43.6	9½	Remington	2852	50,500	Maximum

7mm REMINGTON MAGNUM

SPECIFICATIONS

Dia. of Rim — .532″
Dia. of Base — .513″
Dia. of Shoulder — .492″
Dia. of Neck — .369″
Length of Neck — .271″
Angle of Shoulder — 20.55°
Dia. Jacketed Bullet — .284″
Dia. Cast Bullet — .284″
Length of Case — 2.500″
Max. Overall Length — 3.30″
Primer Size — Large Rifle M
Water Capacity — 83.19 grs.

139-grain Softnose

POWDER MFGR.	POWDER TYPE	GRAINS	PRIMER TYPE	PRIMER MFGR.	VELOCITY	PRESSURE (C.U.P.)	REMARKS
IMR	4320	51.5	9½M	Remington	2860	—	
IMR	4320	55.0	9½M	Remington	3000	—	Maximum
IMR	4350	53.5	9½M	Remington	2845	—	
IMR	4350	60.0	9½M	Remington	3050	—	
IMR	4831	57.0	9½M	Remington	2800	—	
IMR	4831	64.5	9½M	Remington	3100	—	Maximum
Win	785	60.0	9½M	Remington	2850	—	
Win	785	65.0	9½M	Remington	3050	—	Maximum

154-grain Softnose

POWDER MFGR.	POWDER TYPE	GRAINS	PRIMER TYPE	PRIMER MFGR.	VELOCITY	PRESSURE (C.U.P.)	REMARKS
IMR	4350	54.0	9½M	Remington	2645	—	
IMR	4350	59.0	9½M	Remington	2900	—	Maximum
IMR	4831	58.0	9½M	Remington	2650	—	
IMR	4831	65.0	9½M	Remington	2960	—	Maximum
Hodgdon	870	73.5	9½M	Remington	2750	—	
Hodgdon	870	79.0	9½M	Remington	3100	49700	Maximum

175-grain Softnose

POWDER MFGR.	POWDER TYPE	GRAINS	PRIMER TYPE	PRIMER MFGR.	VELOCITY	PRESSURE (C.U.P.)	REMARKS
IMR	4350	50.0	9½M	Remington	2500	—	
IMR	4350	55.0	9½M	Remington	2650	—	Near Maximum
IMR	4831	52.5	9½M	Remington	2500	—	
IMR	4831	58.0	9½M	Remington	2700	—	Maximum
Hodgdon	870	70.0	9½M	Remington	2500	—	
Hodgdon	870	75.5	9½M	Remington	2800	—	Maximum

7mm WEATHERBY MAGNUM

SPECIFICATIONS

Dia. of Rim — .530″
Dia. of Base — .511″
Dia. of Shoulder — .490″
Dia. of Neck — .307″
Length of Neck — .350″
Angle of Shoulder — N/A°

Dia. Jacketed Bullet — .284″
Dia. Cast Bullet — .284″
Length of Case — 2.545″
Max. Overall Length — 3.30″
Primer Size — Large Rifle M
Water Capacity — 87.46 grs.

139-grain Softnose

POWDER MFGR.	POWDER TYPE	GRAINS	PRIMER TYPE	PRIMER MFGR.	VELOCITY	PRESSURE (C.U.P.)	REMARKS
IMR	4350	63.0	215	Federal	2900	—	
IMR	4350	68.5	215	Federal	3200	—	Near Maximum
IMR	4831	66.5	215	Federal	2900	—	
IMR	4831	69.5	215	Federal	3100	—	Maximum
Hodgdon	H4831	68.0	215	Federal	2950	—	
Hodgdon	H4831	73.0	215	Federal	3300	—	Caution

154-grain Softnose

POWDER MFGR.	POWDER TYPE	GRAINS	PRIMER TYPE	PRIMER MFGR.	VELOCITY	PRESSURE (C.U.P.)	REMARKS
IMR	4350	61.0	215	Federal	2750	—	
IMR	4350	67.5	215	Federal	3100	—	Near Maximum
Hodgdon	H4831	66.0	215	Federal	2800	—	
Hodgdon	H4831	71.5	215	Federal	3100	—	Maximum
Hodgdon	H450	67.5	215	Federal	2900	—	
Hodgdon	H450	72.0	215	Federal	3120	—	Near Maximum

175-grain Softnose

POWDER MFGR.	POWDER TYPE	GRAINS	PRIMER TYPE	PRIMER MFGR.	VELOCITY	PRESSURE (C.U.P.)	REMARKS
IMR	4350	60.0	215	Federal	2510	—	
IMR	4350	65.5	215	Federal	2850	—	
Hodgdon	H4831	62.0	215	Federal	2500	—	
Hodgdon	H4831	69.5	215	Federal	2900	—	Maximum
Hodgdon	H450	61.5	215	Federal	2480	—	
Hodgdon	H450	67.5	215	Federal	2800	—	Near Maximum

7 x 61mm SHARPE & HART

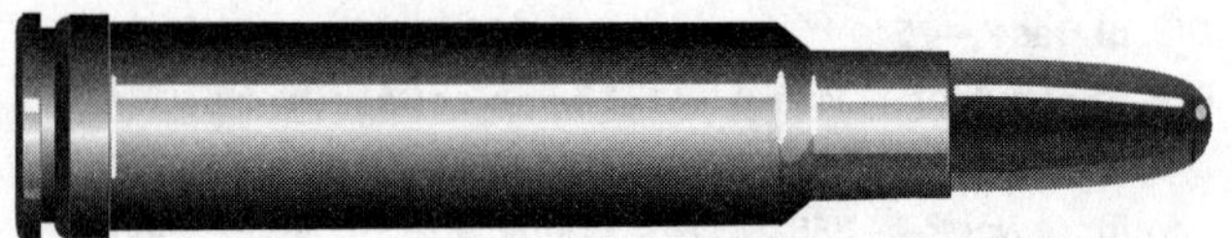

SPECIFICATIONS

Dia. of Rim — .532″
Dia. of Base — .513″
Dia. of Shoulder — .473″
Dia. of Neck — .313″
Length of Neck — .300″
Angle of Shoulder — 33.25°
Dia. Jacketed Bullet — .284″
Dia. Cast Bullet — .284″
Length of Case — 2.394″
Max. Overall Length — 3.30″
Primer Size — Large Rifle
Water Capacity — 77.40 grs.

139-grain Softnose

POWDER MFGR.	POWDER TYPE	GRAINS	PRIMER TYPE	PRIMER MFGR.	VELOCITY	PRESSURE (C.U.P.)	REMARKS
IMR	4064	50.0	9½	Remington	2750	—	
IMR	4064	55.5	9½	Remington	3135	—	Maximum
IMR	4320	49.0	9½	Remington	2810	—	
IMR	4320	56.0	9½	Remington	3080	—	
IMR	4350	56.0	9½	Remington	2800	—	
IMR	4350	62.0	9½	Remington	3100	—	
Hodgdon	H450	61.0	9½	Remington	2850	—	
Hodgdon	H450	66.5	9½	Remington	3140	—	Maximum

154-grain Softnose

POWDER MFGR.	POWDER TYPE	GRAINS	PRIMER TYPE	PRIMER MFGR.	VELOCITY	PRESSURE (C.U.P.)	REMARKS
IMR	4064	48.5	9½	Remington	2700	—	
IMR	4064	52.5	9½	Remington	3000	—	Maximum
IMR	4320	48.5	9½	Remington	2700	—	
IMR	4320	55.0	9½	Remington	3000	—	
IMR	4350	53.0	9½	Remington	2600	—	
IMR	4350	60.0	9½	Remington	3000	—	
Hodgdon	H450	57.0	9½	Remington	2680	—	
Hodgdon	H450	63.5	9½	Remington	3000	—	Maximum

175-grain Softnose

POWDER MFGR.	POWDER TYPE	GRAINS	PRIMER TYPE	PRIMER MFGR.	VELOCITY	PRESSURE (C.U.P.)	REMARKS
IMR	4064	45.5	9½	Remington	2450	—	
IMR	4064	51.0	9½	Remington	2700	—	Near Maximum
IMR	4320	47.0	9½	Remington	2500	—	
IMR	4320	54.0	9½	Remington	2800	—	Maximum

7.5 SWISS

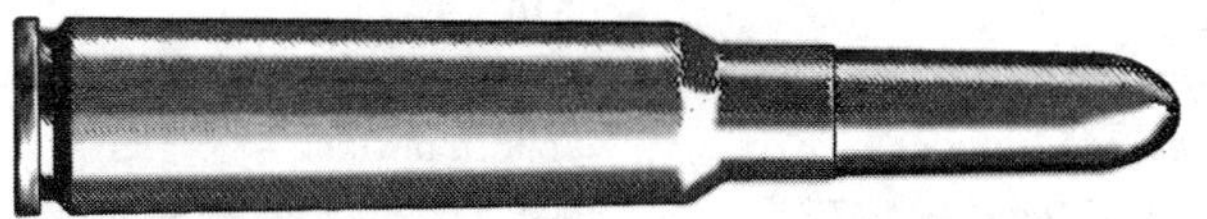

SPECIFICATIONS

Dia. of Rim — .495″
Dia. of Base — .493″
Dia. of Shoulder — .450″
Dia. of Neck — .337″
Length of Neck — .290″
Angle of Shoulder — 29.46°
Dia. Jacketed Bullet — .308″
Dia. Cast Bullet — .308″
Length of Case — 2.140″
Max. Overall Length — 3.03″
Primer Size — Large Rifle
Water Capacity — 62.89 grs.

150-grain Softnose

POWDER MFGR.	POWDER TYPE	GRAINS	PRIMER TYPE	PRIMER MFGR.	VELOCITY	PRESSURE (C.U.P.)	REMARKS
IMR	3031	38.0	217B	Berdan	2400	—	
IMR	3031	44.0	217B	Berdan	2650	—	Maximum
IMR	4064	40.0	217B	Berdan	2400	—	
IMR	4064	45.5	217B	Berdan	2640	—	Near Maximum
IMR	4320	41.0	217B	Berdan	2400	—	
IMR	4320	47.0	217B	Berdan	2700	—	Caution

180-grain Softnose

POWDER MFGR.	POWDER TYPE	GRAINS	PRIMER TYPE	PRIMER MFGR.	VELOCITY	PRESSURE (C.U.P.)	REMARKS
IMR	3031	36.0	217B	Berdan	2100	—	
IMR	3031	39.5	217B	Berdan	2300	—	Near Maximum
IMR	4064	36.5	217B	Berdan	2090	—	
IMR	4064	41.0	217B	Berdan	2280	—	Near Maximum
IMR	4350	41.0	217B	Berdan	2125	—	
IMR	4350	47.0	217B	Berdan	2445	—	Maximum

7.62 X 39 RUSSIAN

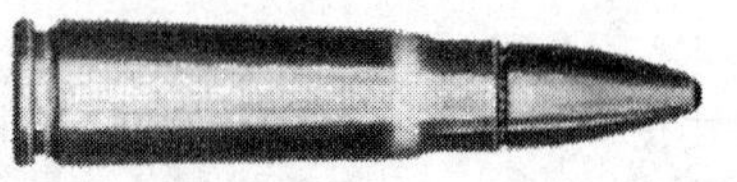

SPECIFICATIONS

Dia. of Rim — .447″

Dia. of Base — .443″

Dia. of Shoulder — .370″

Dia. of Neck — .337″

Length of Neck — .217″

Angle of Shoulder — 18.00°

Dia. Jacketed Bullet — .308 - .310″

Dia. Cast Bullet — .310″

Length of Case — 1.528″

Max. Overall Length — 2.190″

Primer Size — Small Rifle

Water Capacity — 33.98 grs.

125-grain Softnose

POWDER MFGR.	POWDER TYPE	GRAINS	PRIMER TYPE	PRIMER MFGR.	VELOCITY	PRESSURE (C.U.P.)	REMARKS
IMR	4198	22.5	WSM	Winchester	2100	—	
IMR	4198	23.5	WSM	Winchester	2290	—	Near Maximum
Hodgdon	H322	25.0	WSM	Winchester	2025	—	
Hodgdon	H322	28.0	WSM	Winchester	2300	—	Maximum
Hodgdon	H335	31.0	WSM	Winchester	2375	—	Maximum
Hodgdon	H4198	26.0	WSM	Winchester	2340	—	Near Maximum
Hodgdon	H4895	28.5	WSM	Winchester	2200	—	

7.62 X 54R RUSSIAN

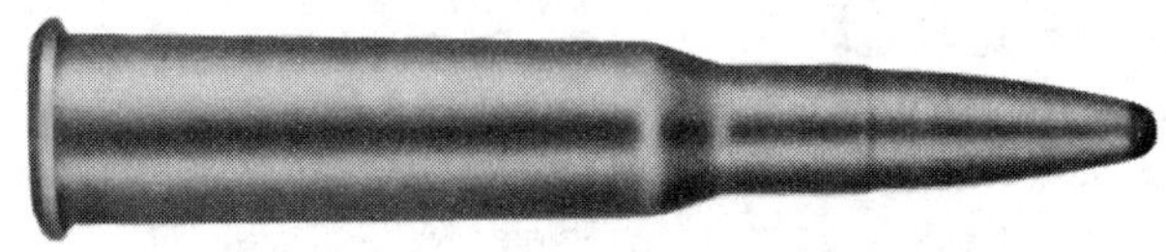

SPECIFICATIONS

Dia. of Rim — .570″
Dia. of Base — .489″
Dia. of Shoulder — .458″
Dia. of Neck — .336″
Length of Neck — .350″
Angle of Shoulder — 21.48°

Dia. Jacketed Bullet — .308″
Dia. Cast Bullet — .308″
Length of Case — 2.050″
Max. Overall Length — 3.035″
Primer Size — Large Rifle
Water Capacity — 58.91 grs.

150-grain Softnose

POWDER MFGR.	POWDER TYPE	GRAINS	PRIMER TYPE	PRIMER MFGR.	VELOCITY	PRESSURE (C.U.P.)	REMARKS
IMR	3031	40.5	9½	Remington	2500	—	
IMR	3031	45.0	9½	Remington	2710	—	Maximum
IMR	4064	44.0	9½	Remington	2500	—	
IMR	4064	49.0	9½	Remington	2750	—	Maximum
IMR	4320	44.0	9½	Remington	2450	—	
IMR	4320	50.0	9½	Remington	2800	—	Maximum
Hodgdon	H380	47.0	9½	Remington	2625	—	
Hodgdon	H380	52.0	9½	Remington	2800	—	Maximum

180-grain Softnose

POWDER MFGR.	POWDER TYPE	GRAINS	PRIMER TYPE	PRIMER MFGR.	VELOCITY	PRESSURE (C.U.P.)	REMARKS
IMR	3031	40.5	9½	Remington	2400	—	
IMR	3031	44.5	9½	Remington	2600	—	Maximum
IMR	4064	42.0	9½	Remington	2300	—	
IMR	4064	47.0	9½	Remington	2580	—	Maximum
IMR	4320	43.0	9½	Remington	2350	—	
IMR	4320	48.0	9½	Remington	2600	—	
Hodgdon	H380	44.5	9½	Remington	2400	—	
Hodgdon	H380	50.0	9½	Remington	2600	—	Near Maximum

7 .65 BELGIAN MAUSER

SPECIFICATIONS

Dia. of Rim — .470″
Dia. of Base — .468″
Dia. of Shoulder — .429″
Dia. of Neck — .338″
Length of Neck — .270″
Angle of Shoulder — 23.00°
Dia. Jacketed Bullet — .312″
Dia. Cast Bullet — .313″
Length of Case — 2.090″
Max. Overall Length — 2.95″
Primer Size — Large Rifle
Water Capacity — 57.11 grs.

150-grain Softnose

POWDER MFGR.	POWDER TYPE	GRAINS	PRIMER TYPE	PRIMER MFGR.	VELOCITY	PRESSURE (C.U.P.)	REMARKS
IMR	3031	37.0	210	Federal	2400	—	
IMR	3031	41.5	210	Federal	2700	—	
IMR	4064	40.0	210	Federal	2400	—	
IMR	4064	43.0	210	Federal	2600	—	
IMR	4064	41.0	210	Federal	2400	—	
IMR	4064	44.5	210	Federal	2700	—	
IMR	4320	42.0	210	Federal	2400	—	
IMR	4320	45.0	210	Federal	2625	—	
Hodgdon	BL-C(2)	40.0	9½	Remington	2400	—	
Hodgdon	H4350	49.0	9½	Remington	2625	—	
Hodgdon	H380	43.0	210	Federal	2400	—	
Hodgdon	H414	45.0	210	Federal	2500	—	
Norma	N204	48.0	210	Federal	2400	—	
Norma	N204	50.0	210	Federal	2500	—	

175-grain Softnose

POWDER MFGR.	POWDER TYPE	GRAINS	PRIMER TYPE	PRIMER MFGR.	VELOCITY	PRESSURE (C.U.P.)	REMARKS
IMR	3031	36.0	210	Federal	2100	—	
IMR	3031	40.5	210	Federal	2400	—	
IMR	4064	38.0	210	Federal	2200	—	
IMR	4064	40.5	210	Federal	2400	—	
IMR	4064	43.0	210	Federal	2550	—	
IMR	4320	39.0	210	Federal	2175	—	
IMR	4320	42.0	210	Federal	2425	—	
IMR	4320	44.5	210	Federal	2650	—	
Hodgdon	BL-C(2)	37.0	9½	Remington	2100	—	
Hodgdon	H4350	47.0	9½	Remington	2450	—	
Hodgdon	H380	42.0	210	Federal	2250	—	

7 .7 JAPANESE

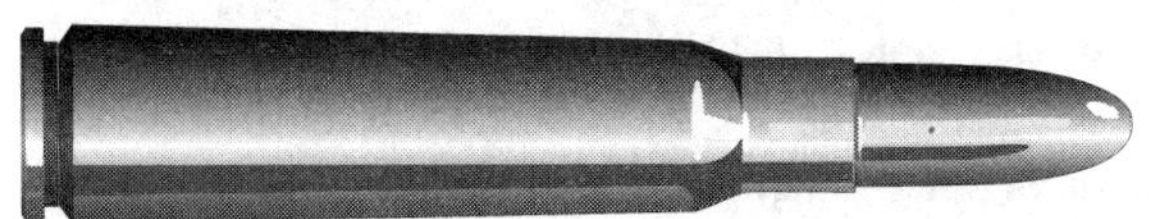

SPECIFICATIONS

Dia. of Rim — .471″
Dia. of Base — .471″
Dia. of Shoulder — .429″
Dia. of Neck — .337″
Length of Neck — .302″
Angle of Shoulder — 25.60°
Dia. Jacketed Bullet — .312″
Dia. Cast Bullet — .312″
Length of Case — 2.270″
Max. Overall Length — 3.15″
Primer Size — Large Rifle
Water Capacity — 63.29 grs.

150-grain Softnose

POWDER MFGR.	POWDER TYPE	GRAINS	PRIMER TYPE	PRIMER MFGR.	VELOCITY	PRESSURE (C.U.P.)	REMARKS
IMR	3031	36.0	210	Federal	2190	—	
IMR	3031	40.5	210	Federal	2540	—	Near Maximum
IMR	4064	38.0	210	Federal	2200	—	
IMR	4064	46.0	210	Federal	2580	—	Near Maximum
IMR	4350	48.0	210	Federal	2300	—	
IMR	4350	53.0	210	Federal	2600	—	Maximum

174-grain Softnose

POWDER MFGR.	POWDER TYPE	GRAINS	PRIMER TYPE	PRIMER MFGR.	VELOCITY	PRESSURE (C.U.P.)	REMARKS
IMR	3031	34.0	210	Federal	2000	—	
IMR	3031	38.0	210	Federal	2350	—	Maximum
IMR	4064	36.5	210	Federal	2040	—	
IMR	4064	41.0	210	Federal	2300	—	Near Maximum
IMR	4350	43.5	210	Federal	2050	—	
IMR	4350	47.0	210	Federal	2260	—	Maximum
Hodgdon	H4831	46.0	210	Federal	2000	—	
Hodgdon	H4831	51.5	210	Federal	2300	—	

8mm MAUSER

SPECIFICATIONS

Dia. of Rim — .473″
Dia. of Base — .469″
Dia. of Shoulder — .434″
Dia. of Neck — .349″
Length of Neck — .307″
Angle of Shoulder — 22.62°
Dia. Jacketed Bullet — .323″
Dia. Cast Bullet — .323″
Length of Case — 2.240″
Max. Overall Length — 3.00″
Primer Size — Large Rifle
Water Capacity — 62.68 grs.

150-grain Softnose

POWDER MFGR.	POWDER TYPE	GRAINS	PRIMER TYPE	PRIMER MFGR.	VELOCITY	PRESSURE (C.U.P.)	REMARKS
IMR	3031	43.0	9½	Remington	2500	—	
IMR	3031	48.5	9½	Remington	2840	—	Maximum
IMR	4064	45.0	9½	Remington	2525	—	
IMR	4064	50.0	9½	Remington	2850	—	Maximum
IMR	4320	46.0	9½	Remington	2475	—	
IMR	4320	53.0	9½	Remington	2850	—	Near Maximum
Hodgdon	H380	46.5	9½	Remington	2510	—	
Hodgdon	H380	54.5	9½	Remington	2840	—	Near Maximum

170-grain Softnose

POWDER MFGR.	POWDER TYPE	GRAINS	PRIMER TYPE	PRIMER MFGR.	VELOCITY	PRESSURE (C.U.P.)	REMARKS
IMR	3031	41.0	9½	Remington	2335	—	
IMR	3031	46.5	9½	Remington	2700	—	Maximum
IMR	4064	44.0	9½	Remington	2400	—	
IMR	4064	48.0	9½	Remington	2650	—	Near Maximum
IMR	4320	44.5	9½	Remington	2300	—	
IMR	4320	51.0	9½	Remington	2650	—	Near Maximum
Hodgdon	H4895	46.0	9½	Remington	2500	—	
Hodgdon	H4895	49.5	9½	Remington	2700	—	Caution

8mm REMINGTON MAGNUM

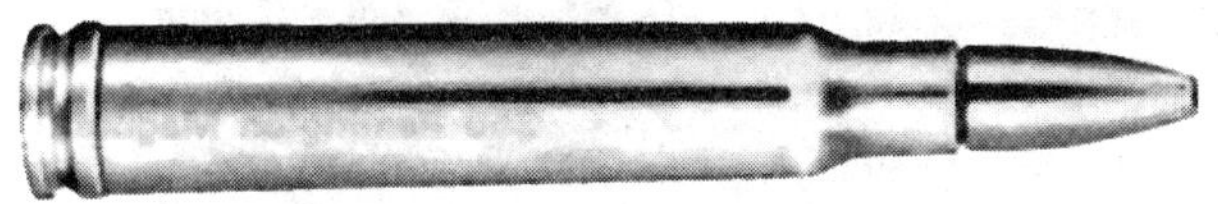

SPECIFICATIONS

Dia. of Rim — .532″
Dia. of Base — .513″
Dia. of Shoulder — .487″
Dia. of Neck — .354″
Length of Neck — .320″
Angle of Shoulder — 25.25°
Dia. Jacketed Bullet — .323″
Dia. Cast Bullet — .323″
Length of Case — 2.850″
Max. Overall Length — 3.60″
Primer Size — Large Rifle M
Water Capacity — 98.53 grs.

150-grain Softnose

POWDER MFGR.	POWDER TYPE	GRAINS	PRIMER TYPE	PRIMER MFGR.	VELOCITY	PRESSURE (C.U.P.)	REMARKS
IMR	4064	67.0	9½M	Remington	3050	—	
IMR	4064	74.0	9½M	Remington	3400	—	Maximum
IMR	4350	76.0	9½M	Remington	3125	—	
IMR	4350	79.5	9½M	Remington	3300	—	Maximum
IMR	4831	80.0	9½M	Remington	3100	—	
IMR	4831	84.0	9½M	Remington	3300	—	Near Maximum

220-grain Softnose

POWDER MFGR.	POWDER TYPE	GRAINS	PRIMER TYPE	PRIMER MFGR.	VELOCITY	PRESSURE (C.U.P.)	REMARKS
IMR	4320	61.0	9½M	Remington	2500	—	
IMR	4320	69.0	9½M	Remington	2810	—	Maximum
IMR	4350	65.0	9½M	Remington	2500	—	
IMR	4350	72.2	9½M	Remington	2750	—	Near Maximum
IMR	4831	72.0	9½M	Remington	2650	—	
IMR	4831	78.0	9½M	Remington	2910	—	Caution
Hodgdon	H450	75.0	9½M	Remington	2580	—	
Hodgdon	H450	81.0	9½M	Remington	2850	—	Maximum

9.3 X 74R

SPECIFICATIONS

Dia. of Rim — .524″
Dia. of Base — .465″
Dia. of Shoulder — .414″
Dia. of Neck — .387″
Length of Neck — .496″
Angle of Shoulder — 5.97°
Dia. Jacketed Bullet — .365″
Dia. Cast Bullet — .367″
Length of Case — 2.925″
Max. Overall Length — 3.47″
Primer Size — Large Rifle
Water Capacity — 84.3 grs.

193-grain Softnose

POWDER MFGR.	POWDER TYPE	GRAINS	PRIMER TYPE	PRIMER MFGR.	VELOCITY	PRESSURE (C.U.P.)	REMARKS
IMR	3031	59.5	9½	Remington	2670	—	Accurate load

250-grain Softnose

POWDER MFGR.	POWDER TYPE	GRAINS	PRIMER TYPE	PRIMER MFGR.	VELOCITY	PRESSURE (C.U.P.)	REMARKS
IMR	3031	35.0	9½	Remington	1525	—	Accurate load
IMR	3031	38.0	9½	Remington	1610	—	
IMR	3031	50.0	9½	Remington	2115	—	
IMR	3031	51.0	9½	Remington	2165	—	
IMR	4064	57.3	9½	Remington	2220	—	
Hercules	RL-7	36.5	9½	Remington	1735	—	
Hercules	RL-7	37.0	9½	Remington	1820	—	

286-grain Softnose

POWDER MFGR.	POWDER TYPE	GRAINS	PRIMER TYPE	PRIMER MFGR.	VELOCITY	PRESSURE (C.U.P.)	REMARKS
IMR	4064	57.3	9½	Remington	2220	—	

300-grain Softnose

POWDER MFGR.	POWDER TYPE	GRAINS	PRIMER TYPE	PRIMER MFGR.	VELOCITY	PRESSURE (C.U.P.)	REMARKS
IMR	4320	51.0	9½	Remington	2145	—	

Chapter 15
Loads for Obsolete Rifle Cartridges

There are literally thousands of rifles in good shooting condition throughout the world for which ammunition is no longer made. This chapter lists loads for some of the more popular obsolete cartridges.

The .22 Winchester centerfire cartridge was one of the first cartridges to meet a reloading die. It was originally designed and chambered for the Winchester Model 1885 single-shot rifle and remained a popular cartridge for American shooters for 40 years thereafter. The .22 WCF was also the predecessor of the famous .22 Hornet. Although loaded cartridges were discontinued just prior to World War II, brass cases are still available from some specialty reloading suppliers.

Loads for obsolete rifle cartridges in this chapter begin with the .22 WCF, and then on to the .219 Zipper, .22 Savage, .303 Savage, etc. and ending with the mighty .600 Nirto Express — the famous cartridge for African tough-skinned game that fires a 900-grain bullet at nearly 1900 fps.

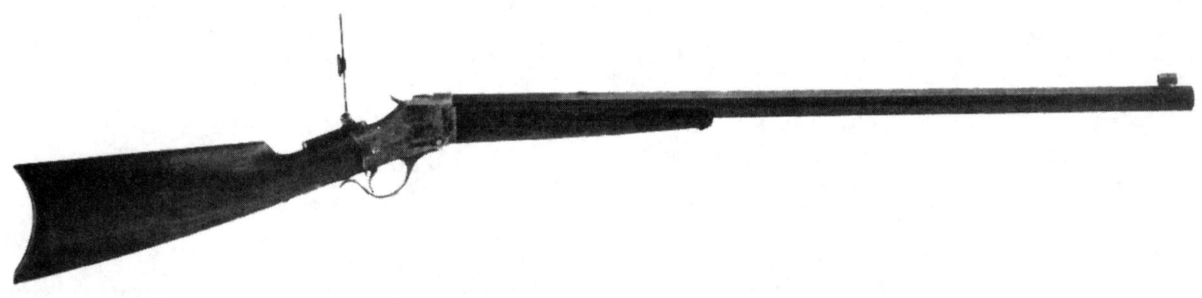

Figure 15-1: The Winchester Model 1885 single-shot rifle was chambered for the .22 WCF. The cartridge was the predecessor to the famous .22 Hornet which was introduced about 45 years later.

.22 WINCHESTER CENTERFIRE

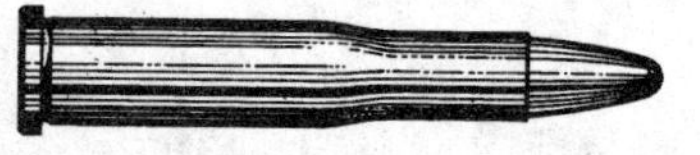

SPECIFICATIONS

Dia. of Rim — .342″	Dia. Jacketed Bullet — .228″
Dia. of Base — .295″	Dia. Cast Bullet — .228″
Dia. of Shoulder — .278″	Length of Case — 1.39″
Dia. of Neck — .241″	Max. Overall Length — 1.61″
Length of Neck — .383″	Primer Size — Small Rifle
Angle of Shoulder — 5.23°	Water Capacity — 14.28 grs.

46-grain Lead

POWDER MFGR.	POWDER TYPE	GRAINS	PRIMER TYPE	PRIMER MFGR.	VELOCITY	PRESSURE (C.U.P.)	REMARKS
Black	FFg	13.0	SR	CCI	1300	—	Factory load
Hercules	Unique	3.8	SR	CCI	1480	—	
Hercules	Unique	3.9	SR	CCI	1495	—	
Hercules	Unique	4.0	SR	CCI	1550	—	

.219 WINCHESTER ZIPPER

SPECIFICATIONS

Dia. of Rim — .506″	Dia. Jacketed Bullet — .224″
Dia. of Base — .422″	Dia. Cast Bullet — .226″
Dia. of Shoulder — .3649″	Length of Case — 1.84″
Dia. of Neck — .253″	Max. Overall Length — 2.40″
Length of Neck — .317″	Primer Size — Large Rifle
Angle of Shoulder — 28°	Water Capacity — 34.63 grs.

45-grain Soft Point

POWDER MFGR.	POWDER TYPE	GRAINS	PRIMER TYPE	PRIMER MFGR.	VELOCITY	PRESSURE (C.U.P.)	REMARKS
IMR	4759	15.0	9½	Remington	2440	—	
IMR	4759	17.0	9½	Remington	2602	—	
IMR	4759	19.0	9½	Remington	2868	—	Maximum
IMR	4320	25.0	9½	Remington	2885	—	
IMR	4320	27.0	9½	Remington	3022	—	
IMR	4320	29.0	9½	Remington	3261	—	Maximum
IMR	3031	23.0	9½	Remington	2955	—	
IMR	3031	25.0	9½	Remington	3115	—	
IMR	3031	27.0	9½	Remington	3287	—	Maximum

.22 SAVAGE

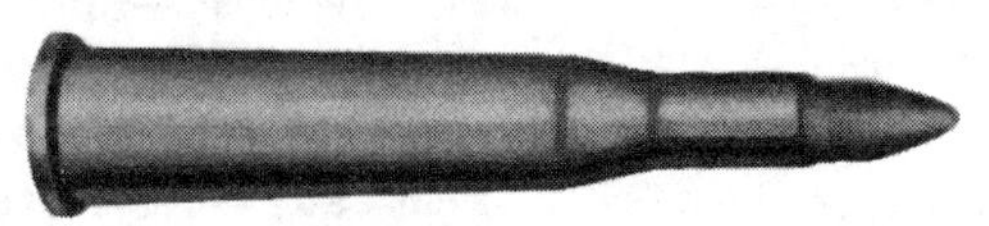

SPECIFICATIONS

Dia. of Rim — .492″
Dia. of Base — .418″
Dia. of Shoulder — .362″
Dia. of Neck — .252″
Length of Neck — .409″
Angle of Shoulder — 12.09°
Dia. Jacketed Bullet — .227″
Dia. Cast Bullet — .227″
Length of Case — 2.047″
Max. Overall Length — 2.51″
Primer Size — Large Rifle
Water Capacity — 36.70 grs.

40-grain Softnose

POWDER MFGR.	POWDER TYPE	GRAINS	PRIMER TYPE	PRIMER MFGR.	VELOCITY	PRESSURE (C.U.P.)	REMARKS
Hercules	2400	13.0	210	Federal	2775	—	
Hercules	2400	17.0	210	Federal	3100	—	

55-grain Softnose

POWDER MFGR.	POWDER TYPE	GRAINS	PRIMER TYPE	PRIMER MFGR.	VELOCITY	PRESSURE (C.U.P.)	REMARKS
Hercules	2400	15.0	210	Federal	2600	—	
Hercules	2400	15.9	210	Federal	2700	—	
IMR	3031	25.0	210	Federal	2850	—	
IMR	3031	28.7	210	Federal	3175	—	

70-grain Softnose

POWDER MFGR.	POWDER TYPE	GRAINS	PRIMER TYPE	PRIMER MFGR.	VELOCITY	PRESSURE (C.U.P.)	REMARKS
IMR	3031	24.5	210	Federal	2750	—	
IMR	3031	27.0	210	Federal	3000	—	
IMR	4198	21.0	210	Federal	2800	—	
IMR	4198	22.5	210	Federal	2950	—	
Norma	201	25.0	210	Federal	2800	—	
Norma	201	27.0	210	Federal	3000	—	
Norma	203	25.5	210	Federal	2825	—	
Norma	203	28.0	210	Federal	3050	—	

.303 SAVAGE

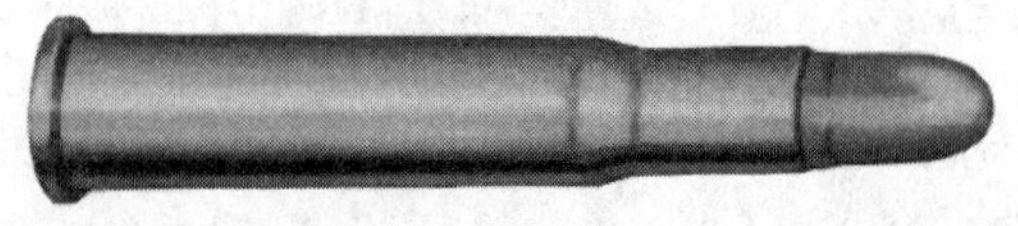

SPECIFICATIONS

Dia. of Rim — .505″
Dia. of Base — .442″
Dia. of Shoulder — .413″
Dia. of Neck — .333″
Length of Neck — .537″
Angle of Shoulder — 17.35°
Dia. Jacketed Bullet — .308″
Dia. Cast Bullet — .310″
Length of Case — 2.015″
Max. Overall Length — 2.52″
Primer Size — Large Rifle
Water Capacity — 46.58 grs.

150-Grain Softnose

POWDER MFGR.	POWDER TYPE	GRAINS	PRIMER TYPE	PRIMER MFGR.	VELOCITY	PRESSURE (C.U.P.)	REMARKS
IMR	4064	32.0	210	Federal	2200	—	
IMR	3031	32.0	210	Federal	2300	—	

170-Grain Softnose

POWDER MFGR.	POWDER TYPE	GRAINS	PRIMER TYPE	PRIMER MFGR.	VELOCITY	PRESSURE (C.U.P.)	REMARKS
IMR	4064	30.0	210	Federal	1925	—	
IMR	4064	32.0	210	Federal	2100	—	
IMR	3031	28.0	210	Federal	1950	—	
IMR	3031	30.0	210	Federal	2160	—	

190-Grain Softnose

POWDER MFGR.	POWDER TYPE	GRAINS	PRIMER TYPE	PRIMER MFGR.	VELOCITY	PRESSURE (C.U.P.)	REMARKS
Hercules	2400	18.0	210	Federal	1650	—	
Hercules	2400	18.5	210	Federal	1775	—	
IMR	4198	20.0	210	Federal	1500	—	
IMR	4198	26.0	210	Federal	1975	—	
IMR	3031	30.0	210	Federal	1850	—	
IMR	3031	30.5	210	Federal	1950	—	

.32-40

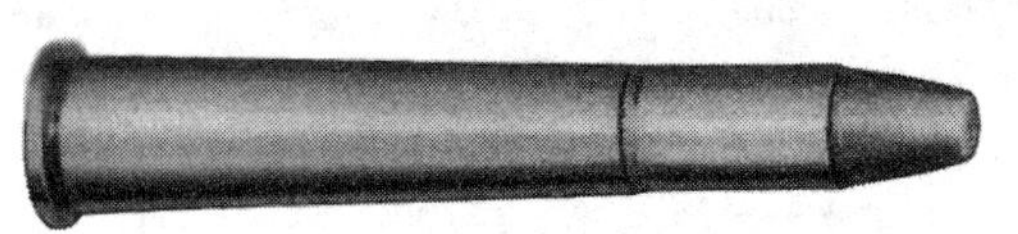

SPECIFICATIONS

Dia. of Rim — .506″
Dia. of Base — .424″
Dia. of Shoulder — N/A
Dia. of Neck — .339″
Length of Neck — .485″
Angle of Shoulder — 23.00°

Dia. Jacketed Bullet — .320″
Dia. Cast Bullet — .321″
Length of Case — 2.13″
Max. Overall Length — 2.5″
Primer Size — Large Rifle
Water Capacity — 45.25 grs.

170-grain Softnose

POWDER MFGR.	POWDER TYPE	GRAINS	PRIMER TYPE	PRIMER MFGR.	VELOCITY	PRESSURE (C.U.P.)	REMARKS
Hercules	2400	13.0	9½	Remington	1125	—	
Hercules	2400	14.0	9½	Remington	1300	—	
IMR	4227	14.0	9½	Remington	1050	—	
IMR	4198	19.0	9½	Remington	1295	—	
IMR	3031	26.0	9½	Remington	1545	—	
IMR	4895	28.0	9½	Remington	1700	—	
IMR	4064	23.5	9½	Remington	1525	—	

.32 REMINGTON

SPECIFICATIONS

Dia. of Rim — .421″
Dia. of Base — .421″
Dia. of Shoulder — .401″
Dia. of Neck — .344″
Length of Neck — .489″
Angle of Shoulder — 24.34°

Dia. Jacketed Bullet — .320″
Dia. Cast Bullet — .321″
Length of Case — 2.05″
Max. Overall Length — 2.53″
Primer Size — Large Rifle
Water Capacity — 46.45 grs.

170-grain Softnose

POWDER MFGR.	POWDER TYPE	GRAINS	PRIMER TYPE	PRIMER MFGR.	VELOCITY	PRESSURE (C.U.P.)	REMARKS
Hercules	Reloader 7	29.0	9½	Remington	2185	—	
IMR	4198	24.0	9½	Remington	1900	—	
IMR	3031	28.0	9½	Remington	1950	—	
IMR	4064	29.0	9½	Remington	2095	—	
IMR	4320	33.0	9½	Remington	1545	—	

.33 WINCHESTER

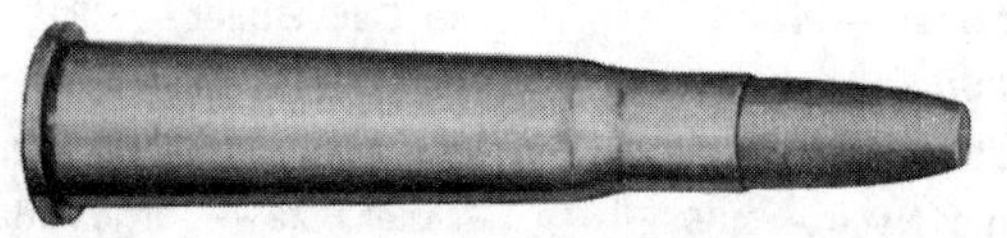

SPECIFICATIONS

Dia. of Rim — .610″
Dia. of Base — .508″
Dia. of Shoulder — N/A
Dia. of Neck — .366″
Length of Neck — .405″
Angle of Shoulder — 20.67°

Dia. Jacketed Bullet — .338″
Dia. Cast Bullet — .338″
Length of Case — 2.105″
Max. Overall Length — 2.70″
Primer Size — Large Rifle
Water Capacity — 62.6 grs.

200-grain Softnose

POWDER MFGR.	POWDER TYPE	GRAINS	PRIMER TYPE	PRIMER MFGR.	VELOCITY	PRESSURE (C.U.P.)	REMARKS
Hercules	2400	26.5	9½	Remington	2125	—	
IMR	4198	24.0	9½	Remington	1625	—	
IMR	4895	38.0	9½	Remington	2025	—	
IMR	3031	39.0	9½	Remington	2200	—	

.35 WINCHESTER

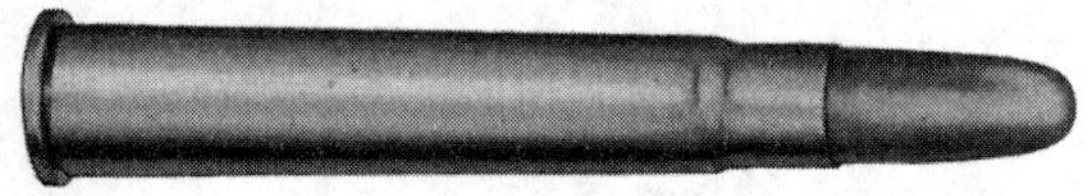

SPECIFICATIONS

Dia. of Rim — .543″
Dia. of Base — .461″
Dia. of Shoulder — .428″
Dia. of Neck — .383″
Length of Neck — .284″
Angle of Shoulder — 9.82°

Dia. Jacketed Bullet — .358″
Dia. Cast Bullet — .358″
Length of Case — 2.40″
Max. Overall Length — 3.16″
Primer Size — Large Rifle
Water Capacity — 68.7 grs.

250-grain Softnose

POWDER MFGR.	POWDER TYPE	GRAINS	PRIMER TYPE	PRIMER MFGR.	VELOCITY	PRESSURE (C.U.P.)	REMARKS
Hercules	2400	26.5	9½	Remington	1750	—	
IMR	4198	30.0	9½	Remington	1850	—	
IMR	4198	35.5	9½	Remington	2100	—	
IMR	3031	42.0	9½	Remington	2000	—	
IMR	3031	45.0	9½	Remington	2275	—	
IMR	4064	44.5	9½	Remington	1950	—	

.401 WINCHESTER

SPECIFICATIONS

Dia. of Rim — .457″
Dia. of Base — .429″
Dia. of Shoulder — Straight
Dia. of Neck — .428″
Length of Neck — Straight
Angle of Shoulder — Straight
Dia. Jacketed Bullet — .406″
Dia. Cast Bullet — .406″
Length of Case — 1.50″
Max. Overall Length — 2.00″
Primer Size — Large Rifle
Water Capacity — 37.2 grs.

200-grain Softnose

POWDER MFGR.	POWDER TYPE	GRAINS	PRIMER TYPE	PRIMER MFGR.	VELOCITY	PRESSURE (C.U.P.)	REMARKS
Hercules	2400	19.0	9½	Remington	1600	—	
Hercules	2400	23.5	9½	Remington	2000	—	
IMR	4227	29.0	9½	Remington	1950	—	
IMR	4227	29.9	9½	Remington	2100	—	

.405 WINCHESTER

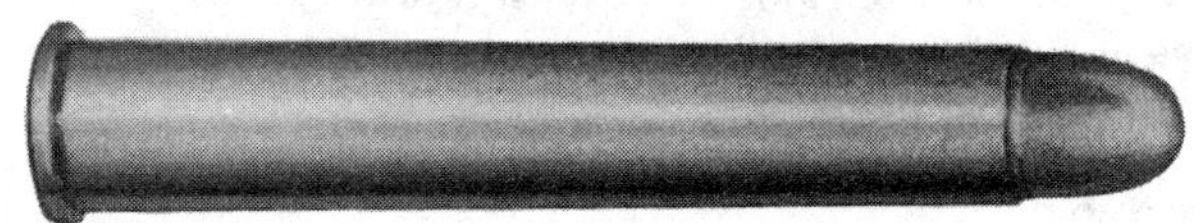

SPECIFICATIONS

Dia. of Rim — .543″
Dia. of Base — .461″
Dia. of Shoulder — Straight
Dia. of Neck — .436″
Length of Neck — Straight
Angle of Shoulder — Straight
Dia. Jacketed Bullet — .412″
Dia. Cast Bullet — .414″
Length of Case — 2.58″
Max. Overall Length — 3.18″
Primer Size — Large Rifle
Water Capacity — 76.9 grs.

300-grain Softnose

POWDER MFGR.	POWDER TYPE	GRAINS	PRIMER TYPE	PRIMER MFGR.	VELOCITY	PRESSURE (C.U.P.)	REMARKS
Hercules	2400	31.5	9½	Remington	1825	—	
Hercules	2400	33.5	9½	Remington	1930	—	
IMR	3031	45.0	9½	Remington	1740	—	
IMR	3031	55.9	9½	Remington	2245	—	
IMR	4320	51.8	9½	Remington	1900	—	
IMR	4320	60.5	9½	Remington	2200	—	

.40-82 WINCHESTER

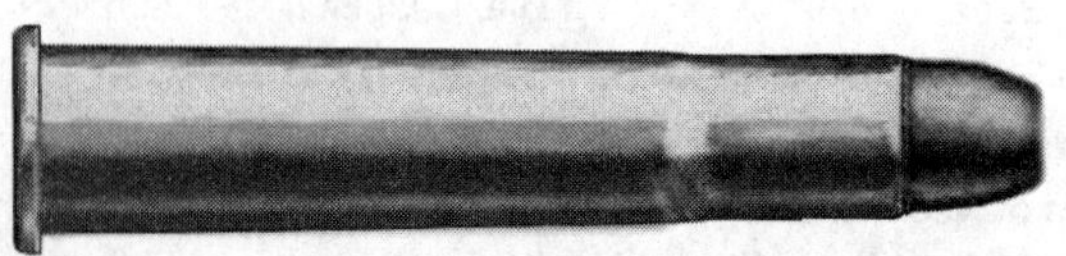

SPECIFICATIONS

Dia. of Rim — .604″
Dia. of Base — .502″
Dia. of Shoulder — .448″
Dia. of Neck — .428″
Length of Neck — .45″
Angle of Shoulder — 1.63²
Dia. Jacketed Bullet — .406″
Dia. Cast Bullet — .406″
Length of Case — 2.40″
Max. Overall Length — 2.77″
Primer Size — Large Rifle
Water Capacity — 79.4 grs.

260-grain Lead

POWDER MFGR.	POWDER TYPE	GRAINS	PRIMER TYPE	PRIMER MFGR.	VELOCITY	PRESSURE (C.U.P.)	REMARKS
Black	Fg	82.0	9½	Remington	1500	—	
IMR	4198	27.5.0	9½	Remington	1400	—	

.45-90 WINCHESTER

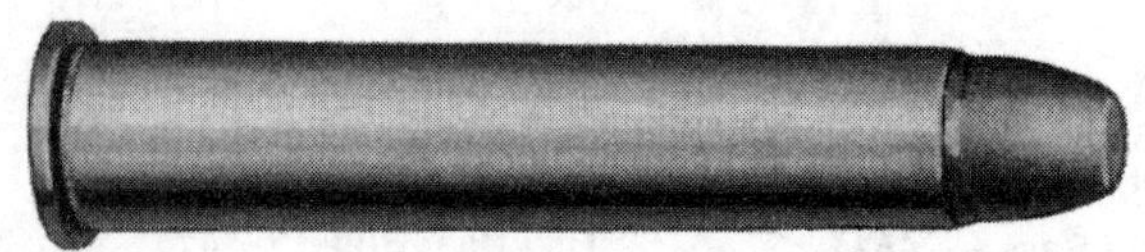

SPECIFICATIONS

Dia. of Rim — .597″
Dia. of Base — .501″
Dia. of Shoulder — Straight
Dia. of Neck — .477″
Length of Neck — Straight
Angle of Shoulder — Straight
Dia. Jacketed Bullet — .457″
Dia. Cast Bullet — .458″
Length of Case — 2.40″
Max. Overall Length — 2.88″
Primer Size — Large Rifle
Water Capacity — 87.7 grs.

300-grain Softnose

POWDER MFGR.	POWDER TYPE	GRAINS	PRIMER TYPE	PRIMER MFGR.	VELOCITY	PRESSURE (C.U.P.)	REMARKS
Hercules	2400	26.0	9½	Remington	1450	—	
Hercules	2400	31.0	9½	Remington	1675	—	
IMR	4198	42.0	9½	Remington	1600	—	
IMR	4895	50.0	9½	Remington	1575	—	
IMR	3031	50.0	9½	Remington	1600	—	

.50-110 WINCHESTER

SPECIFICATIONS

Dia. of Rim — .607″
Dia. of Base — .551″
Dia. of Shoulder — Straight
Dia. of Neck — .534″
Length of Neck — Straight
Angle of Shoulder — Straight
Dia. Jacketed Bullet — .512″
Dia. Cast Bullet — .512″
Length of Case — 2.40″
Max. Overall Length — 2.75″
Primer Size — Large Rifle
Water Capacity — 108.8 grs.

300-grain Softnose

POWDER MFGR.	POWDER TYPE	GRAINS	PRIMER TYPE	PRIMER MFGR.	VELOCITY	PRESSURE (C.U.P.)	REMARKS
IMR	4198	38.0	9½	Remington	1625	—	
Black	Fg	110.0	9½	Remington	1600	—	

.577 SNIDER

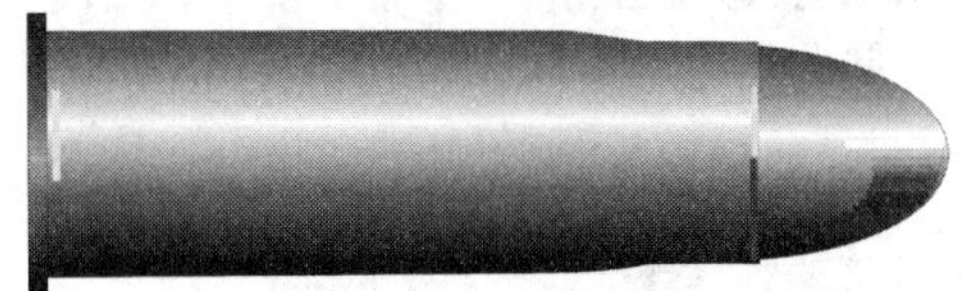

SPECIFICATIONS

Dia. of Rim — .747″
Dia. of Base — .660″
Dia. of Shoulder — Straight
Dia. of Neck — .199″
Length of Neck — Straight
Angle of Shoulder — Straight
Dia. Jacketed Bullet — .570″
Dia. Cast Bullet — .570″
Length of Case — 2.00″
Max. Overall Length — 2.45″
Primer Size — Large Rifle
Water Capacity — 144.55 grs.

450-grain Lead

POWDER MFGR.	POWDER TYPE	GRAINS	PRIMER TYPE	PRIMER MFGR.	VELOCITY	PRESSURE (C.U.P.)	REMARKS
IMR	4198	29.5	9½	Remington	1295	—	

.577 NITRO EXPRESS

SPECIFICATIONS

Dia. of Rim — .784″
Dia. of Base — .660″
Dia. of Shoulder — Straight
Dia. of Neck — .608″
Length of Neck — Straight
Angle of Shoulder — Straight
Dia. Jacketed Bullet — .585″
Dia. Cast Bullet — .587″
Length of Case — 3.00″
Max. Overall Length — 4.00″
Primer Size — Large Rifle
Water Capacity — 192.54 grs.

750-grain FMJ

POWDER MFGR.	POWDER TYPE	GRAINS	PRIMER TYPE	PRIMER MFGR.	VELOCITY	PRESSURE (C.U.P.)	REMARKS
IMR	3031	98.0	LR	CCI	1975	—	
IMR	3031	100.0	LR	CCI	1995	—	

.600 NITRO EXPRESS

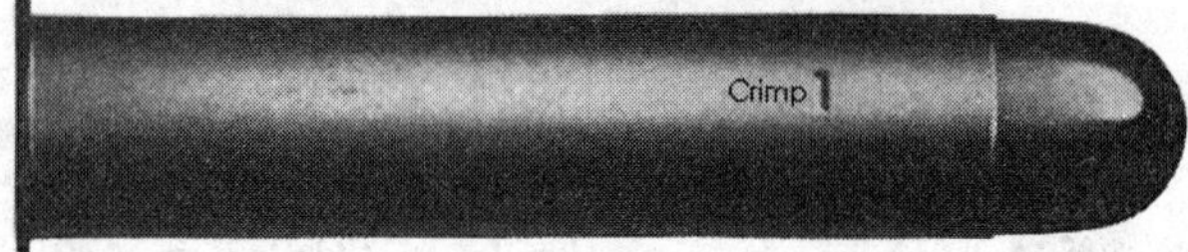

SPECIFICATIONS

Dia. of Rim — .802″
Dia. of Base — .698″
Dia. of Shoulder — Straight
Dia. of Neck — .649″
Length of Neck — Straight
Angle of Shoulder — Straight
Dia. Jacketed Bullet — .621″
Dia. Cast Bullet — .624″
Length of Case — 2.99″
Max. Overall Length — 3.60″
Primer Size — Large Rifle (M)
Water Capacity — 212.45 grs.

900-grain FMJ

POWDER MFGR.	POWDER TYPE	GRAINS	PRIMER TYPE	PRIMER MFGR.	VELOCITY	PRESSURE (C.U.P.)	REMARKS
IMR	3031	95.0	LR	CCI	1750	—	
IMR	3031	97.0	LR	CCI	1775	—	
IMR	3031	100.0	LR	CCI	1800	—	
IMR	3031	105.0	LR	CCI	1895	—	

Chapter 16

Loads for Wildcat Cartridges

A "wildcat cartridge" is simply a cartridge that is not — and never was — in regular factory production; one that can't be purchased through the usual outlets.

Wildcat cartridges are usually made from existing cartridge cases and are generally made to shoot existing bullets. Standard cases can be necked up to take a larger-diameter bullet, or they can be necked down to take a bullet of smaller diameter. The case can be shortened before it is necked up or down. The slope or angle of the shoulder can be changed either by running the case through a full-length sizing die or by "fire-forming" — firing the cartridge in an enlarged chamber so that the pliable brass will expand to fit the chamber and give a sharper shoulder for more powder capacity.

Wildcats have been with us almost as long as centerfire metallic cartridges have been in use. In this century, literally hundreds of wildcats have been designed. Some have become relatively popular, but the great majority of them are long since forgotten. Some wildcats have filled gaps for which no commercial cartridges existed. Many wildcats, however, simply do what factory cartridges do at much more expense and trouble. They seldom do better, and many times they often fail to do as well.

Some wildcats have been designed by intelligent ballisticians who had access to chronographs — and in some instances to pressure guns — and who knew what they were doing. Other wildcats, unfortunately, have been designed by hit-and-miss "experts" who worked without chronographs or pressure equipment and offered imaginary statistics when they publicized their creations. However, when commercial chronographs began to be priced within the reach of the average shooter, most of these erroneous claims were readily exposed.

The best of the wildcats have been useful cartridges with long lives. Some have become standard factory cartridges. One of the oldest of wildcats is the .25 Neidner Krag, a cartridge with about the same ballistics as the later .257 Roberts. It was developed by woodchuck hunters back before World War I. Another very early wildcat was the .30-35 which was the .30 WCF cartridge necked up to .358 caliber, around the turn of the century. This cartridge approached the ballistics of the later (and very popular) .35 Remington cartridge.

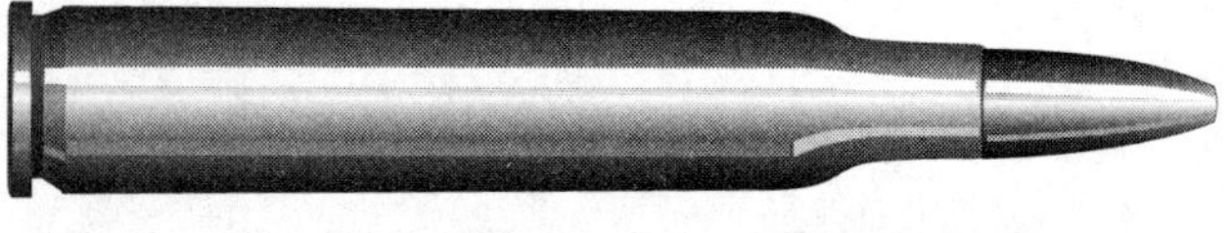

Figure 16-1: This cartridge has been known by several different names: the .25-06, .25 Neidner and the .25 Hi Power. Today, it is the standard .25-06 factory cartridge.

The cartridge which today is called the .25-06 Remington is another very old wildcat. It is simply the .30-06 case necked down to take a .25 caliber bullet. The same 17-degree, 30-minute shoulder slope is retained. At various times it has been called the .25 Neidner and the .25 Hi Power. Now it is well known as the .25-06 Remington — a standard factory cartridge. It came into its own after World War II, when such slow-burning powders as No. 4350 and No. 4831 became available.

A wildcat cartridge that has had an exceedingly interesting history is the one known as the .22-250. This is the .250-3000 Savage case necked down to accept a .22-caliber bullet, and given a 28-degree shoulder. This conversion of a .250- 3000 case was first done by Captain Grosvynor Wotkyns of California. He got very high velocity, flat trajectory, and good accuracy with .22-caliber jacketed bullets. He called his creation the Swift. He brought it to the attention of Winchester, and that company decided to bring out something similar and use the name Swift. However, instead of adopting the .250-3000 Savage case as a basis, Winchester used the old 6 mm Lee Navy case and necked it to .22 caliber. The .220 Swift gained some degree of popularity as it was the fastest commercial cartridge in existence for many years. The earlier version, the .250-3000 case necked to .22 caliber, became the most popular of wildcats.

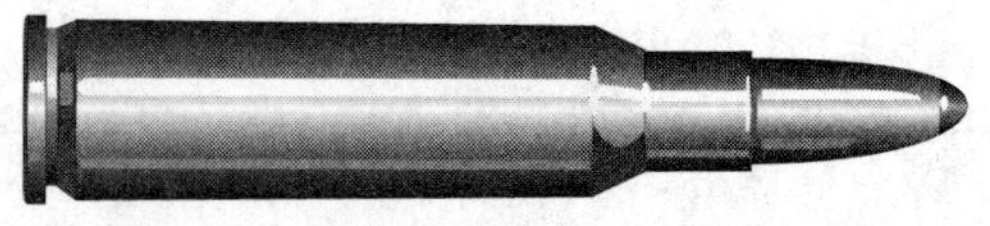

Figure 16-2: The .22-250 Remington, now a standard factory cartridge, is one of the most popular wildcat cartridges developed.

It was originally called the Varminter, but gunsmith Jerry Gebby trademarked the name, and most shooters called it the .22-250. As the popularity of the .220 Swift declined, that of the .22-250 increased. Actually, factory rifles were made for .22-250 before factory ammunition became available. Remington made rifles in .22-250. So did Browning. Then in the spring of 1965, the .22-250 ceased being a wildcat when Remington brought out the cartridge under the name .22-250 Remington.

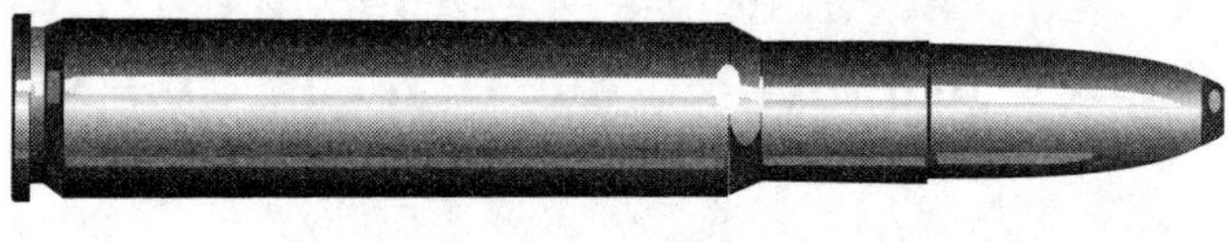

Figure 16-3: The very old and popular .35 Whelen wildcat has recently become a standard factory cartridge.

Another very old and popular wildcat has been the .35 Whelen. It was designed by James V. Howe, a gunsmith associated with Griffin & Howe and author of several gunsmithing books. This cartridge is named for the late Colonel Townsend Whelen. It is simply the .30-06 case necked up to .35 caliber and loaded with heavier bullets. The cartridge was relatively popular among those who thought they needed a heavier bullet than was furnished by the .30-06 for some of the larger African antelope and for the heaviest North American big game. When the .338 Winchester hit the marketplace, and with the .375 H&H Magnum already available, many experts thought that the .35 Whelen would rapidly lose its popularity. The opposite was true! Within the past ten years or so, Remington started chambering their rifles for the .35 Whelen and producing factory ammunition. Some other manufacturers have followed suit.

Wildcat cartridges were few as late as the mid-1920s. The age when wildcats became successful, particularly those of .22 caliber, began in the 1930s. The whole boom of hot .22 centerfire varmint cartridges was started by Captain Grosvynor Wotkyns. His first effort in this direction was with the old .22 Winchester centerfire case, which had previously been loaded with blackpowder. He loaded it with smokeless powder and the .22 caliber jacketed bullet of a foreign pistol cartridge known as the .22 Velo Dog. He achieved very fine accuracy and relatively flat trajectory with this combination. The cartridge was taken up by some of the technicians of the Springfield arsenal. Remington and Winchester still make this .22 Hornet cartridge.

The wildcat .22-3000 Lovell was the old .25-20 single-shot case necked to .22 caliber.

The factory cartridge named the .218 Bee was designed from a wildcat devised by gunsmith Emil Coshollek, but necked down from the .25-20 Repeater case.

The success of the various .22 centerfire factory and wildcat cartridges started a vast amount of experimenting. During the 1930s it was rare that at least one page in the American Rifleman wasn't taken up with wildcat developments. The .257 Roberts cartridge was developed by the late Ned Roberts, a gunsmith who was also an ardent woodchuck hunter. It is simply the 7 x 57mm Mauser case necked to .25 caliber.

In the 1930s, P. 0. Ackley, the renowned Salt Lake City gunsmith, was developing a series of wildcats with straight bodies and fairly sharp shoulders on belted cases. These cartridges were quite efficient and have subsequently influenced cartridge design. Ackley is also responsible for "improving" cartridges. By this is meant rechambering a rifle so that the cartridge will headspace with the beginning of the shoulder of the cartridge against the rear portion of the neck of the chamber. A cartridge fired in such a chamber expands to fit the chamber, forming a straight body and a sharp shoulder. Greater efficiency is claimed for such cases, but it is the feeling of many that they obtain their increased velocity only by using more powder to give higher pressures. However, the Improved .30-06, the Improved .30-30, and other cartridges have had quite a run with rifle fans.

Every time a new cartridge case comes along, the wildcatters go to work on it. They neck it down, neck it up, and blow it out. When the interesting .284 Winchester case came out, it had hardly hit the market before it was necked up to .30 caliber, and even .35 caliber; down to .24 caliber or .25 caliber.

When the .308 Winchester (7.62mm. NAT0) came out, it was necked down to .24 and .25 calibers. The .25 caliber version was a flop, but the .24 caliber version became the very popular .243 Winchester. The .244 (6 mm.) Remington cartridge was in fact the invention of Fred T. Huntington, the president of RCBS, a company which makes loading tools and dies. He called it the .244 Rockchucker and had necked down the 7mm. or .257 case to form this new case.

During the 1940s, Ralph Waldo Miller, a Southern California gunsmith, tried blowing out (fire-forming) .300 H & H Magnum cases to give a straight body, greater powder capacity, and a curiously shaped shoulder called the Venturi. This was called the .300 Miller Freebore, because Miller invented it and used long throats on his chambers to cut down on pressure. The cartridge was taken over by an astute promoter named E. Baden Powell, who called it the .300 P.M.V.F., which stood for Powell, Miller, Venturi, Freebore. Powell and Miller developed a whole string of cartridges using the Venturi shoulder, and marvelous things were claimed for them.

About the end of World War II, Roy E. Weatherby, an insurance salesman and rifle-lover, got interested in the P.M.V.F. series of cartridges. Instead of using the concave P.M.V.F. radius, he used the convex Weatherby radius, which is the trademark of his cartridges. Weatherby manufactured rifles for his cartridges, publicized them widely and intelligently, and has had considerable success. At

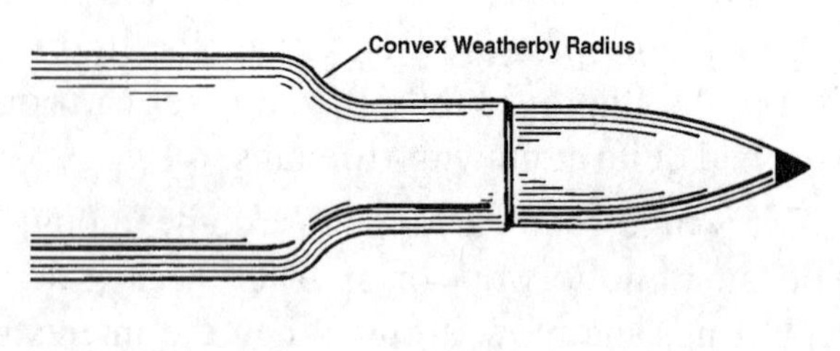

Figure 16-4: The convex Weatherby radius was developed by Roy Weatherby in the 1940s, and has become the trademark of Weatherby cartridges.

first he made his cartridges as any other wildcats are made. The .300 Weatherby cases were blown out from .300 H & H brass. The short Weatherby Magnums were made from .300 H & H cases shortened and blown out. Now, however, Weatherby rifles have been in regular factory production for decades, and Weatherby cartridges are distributed by Weatherby, Inc., in the United States.

These Weatherby cartridges, which started out as wildcats, have had a great influence on cartridge design in the United States. Weatherby was a thorn in the side of the major manufacturers. His spectacular rifles, his equally spectacular claims for killing power, and the talk about Weatherby rifles by hunters all over the world put the loading company designers on their mettle. Largely because of Weatherby, Winchester brought out the .264, the .338, and the .300 Winchester Magnum. Remington brought out the 7mm Remington Magnum. Norma brought out the .308 and .358 Norma. Various gunsmiths have brought out imitation Weatherby cartridges.

Wildcats are still being designed and publicized. "Wildcatitis," however, is not so virulent a disease as it has been. For one thing, there are more sophisticated gun enthusiasts than there were fifty years ago. When some inventor of a wildcat cartridge claims sensational accuracy, fantastic killing power, and trajectory as flat as a stretched string for 400 yards, the knowledgeable rifleman is wary. Today's shooters are better educated than their fathers were. If there is any doubt, the gun enthusiast will spend a few hundred dollars and chronograph his or her own loads.

Another reason that wildcats have fallen off in popularity is that most gaps in the cartridge list have been filled by good factory cartridges. At one time there were at least two dozen 7mm magnums on short magnum cases. Now there is no excuse whatsoever for any of these wildcats, because the niche has been filled by the fine 7mm Remington and Weatherby Magnum cartridges, and other cartridges as well. There was certainly some justification for Fred Huntington's .243 Rockchucker at one time, but now there is a .243 Winchester. Don Hopkins, Elmer Keith, and Charlie O'Neal necked down .30-06 brass for 7mm. bullets. The standard factory .280 Remington now sold is practically the same thing. These same rifle experimenters shortened, necked down, and reformed .300 H & H cases for the .333 Jeffery bullets imported from England. They called the cartridge the .333 OKH. If there was ever any need for this cartridge, it has long since evaporated, because the .338 Winchester fills the spot.

However, there always will be wildcats. Hobbyists and professional gunsmiths alike will experiment with new shoulder slopes, new cartridge shapes, new combinations of case, powder and bullet. On the whole, the wildcatters have served an exceedingly useful purpose. They have paved the way for many modern cartridge developments, and have served to keep the big loading companies on their toes. Anyone who doesn't believe this has only to look at the list of standard factory cartridges that once were wildcats. The number of these wildcats-turned-legit is truly astonishing.

.22 K-HORNET

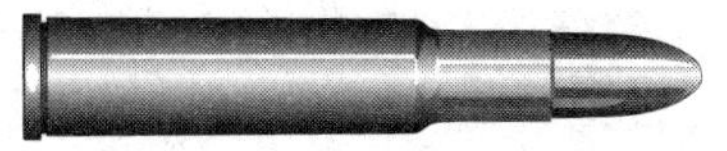

SPECIFICATIONS

Dia. of Rim — .345″
Dia. of Base — .294″
Dia. of Shoulder — 287″
Dia. of Neck — .240″
Length of Neck — .279″
Angle of Shoulder — 40°
Dia. Jacketed Bullet — .224″
Dia. Cast Bullet — .226″
Length of Case — 1.40″
Max. Overall Length — 1.75″
Primer Size — Small Rifle
Water Capacity — 14.8 grs.

45-Grain Softnose

POWDER MFGR.	POWDER TYPE	GRAINS	PRIMER TYPE	PRIMER MFGR.	VELOCITY	PRESSURE (C.U.P.)	REMARKS
IMR	4198	11.0	SR	Remington	2526	—	
IMR	4198	12.0	SR	Remington	2627	—	
IMR	4198	13.0	SR	Remington	2800	—	
IMR	4227	11.0	SR	Remington	2770	—	
IMR	4227	11.5	SR	Remington	2860	—	
IMR	4227	12.0	SR	Remington	2955	—	
Hercules	2400	10.0	SR	Remington	2810	—	
Hercules	2400	10.5	SR	Remington	2895	—	
Hercules	2400	11.0	SR	Remington	3010	—	

.219 IMPROVED ZIPPER

SPECIFICATIONS

Dia. of Rim — .505″
Dia. of Base — .422″
Dia. of Shoulder — 403″
Dia. of Neck — .253″
Length of Neck — .277″
Angle of Shoulder — 23.43°
Dia. Jacketed Bullet — .224″
Dia. Cast Bullet — .226″
Length of Case — 1.95″
Max. Overall Length — 2.39″
Primer Size — Large Rifle
Water Capacity — 39.8 grs.

45-Grain Softnose

POWDER MFGR.	POWDER TYPE	GRAINS	PRIMER TYPE	PRIMER MFGR.	VELOCITY	PRESSURE (C.U.P.)	REMARKS
IMR	4198	23.0	9½	Remington	3325	—	
IMR	4198	25.0	9½	Remington	3430	—	
IMR	4198	27.0	9½	Remington	3650	—	Maximum
IMR	4320	33.0	9½	Remington	3700	—	
IMR	4320	35.0	9½	Remington	3820	—	
IMR	3031	32.0	9½	Remington	3840	—	
IMR	4064	33.0	9½	Remington	3810	—	

.219 IMPROVED ZIPPER (Cont.)

50-Grain Softnose

POWDER MFGR.	POWDER TYPE	GRAINS	PRIMER TYPE	PRIMER MFGR.	VELOCITY	PRESSURE (C.U.P.)	REMARKS
IMR	4198	22.0	9½	Remington	3250	—	
IMR	4198	24.0	9½	Remington	3420	—	
IMR	4198	26.0	9½	Remington	3520	—	Maximum
IMR	4320	32.0	9½	Remington	3580	—	
IMR	4320	34.0	9½	Remington	3650	—	
IMR	4320	36.0	9½	Remington	3675	—	Maximum
IMR	3031	29.0	9½	Remington	3550	—	
IMR	3031	31.0	9½	Remington	3650	—	
IMR	3031	33.0	9½	Remington	3775	—	Maximum
IMR	4064	30.0	9½	Remington	3510	—	
IMR	4064	32.0	9½	Remington	3620	—	

55-Grain Softnose

POWDER MFGR.	POWDER TYPE	GRAINS	PRIMER TYPE	PRIMER MFGR.	VELOCITY	PRESSURE (C.U.P.)	REMARKS
IMR	4198	21.0	9½	Remington	3025	—	
IMR	4198	23.0	9½	Remington	3120	—	
IMR	4198	25.0	9½	Remington	3220	—	Maximum
IMR	4320	30.0	9½	Remington	3260	—	
IMR	4320	32.0	9½	Remington	3350	—	
IMR	4320	34.0	9½	Remington	3450	—	Maximum
IMR	3031	27.0	9½	Remington	3325	—	
IMR	3031	29.0	9½	Remington	3380	—	
IMR	3031	31.0	9½	Remington	3430	—	Maximum
IMR	4064	28.0	9½	Remington	3210	—	
IMR	4064	30.0	9½	Remington	3305	—	
IMR	4064	32.0	9½	Remington	3480	—	Maximum

.219 DONALDSON WASP

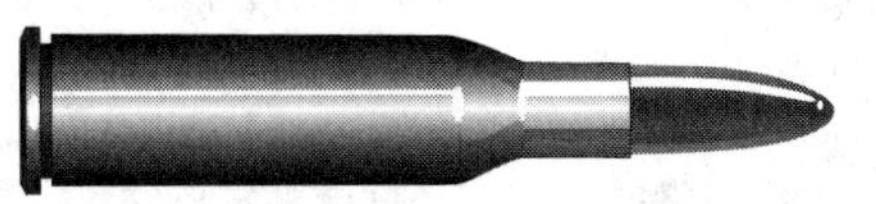

SPECIFICATIONS

Dia. of Rim — .497″
Dia. of Base — .422″
Dia. of Shoulder — .396″
Dia. of Neck — .253″
Length of Neck — .316″
Angle of Shoulder — 28°
Dia. Jacketed Bullet — .224″
Dia. Cast Bullet — .226″
Length of Case — 1.72″
Max. Overall Length — 2.21″
Primer Size — Large Rifle
Water Capacity — 36.85 grs.

45-grain Hollow Point

POWDER MFGR.	POWDER TYPE	GRAINS	PRIMER TYPE	PRIMER MFGR.	VELOCITY	PRESSURE (C.U.P.)	REMARKS
IMR	4198	21.0	9½	Remington	3250	—	
IMR	4198	22.5	9½	Remington	3420	—	
IMR	4198	24.0	9½	Remington	3520	—	Maximum
IMR	4320	28.0	9½	Remington	3300	—	
IMR	4320	30.0	9½	Remington	3290	—	
IMR	4320	31.0	9½	Remington	3475	—	Maximum
IMR	3031	24.0	9½	Remington	3290	—	
IMR	3031	26.0	9½	Remington	3415	—	
IMR	3031	28.0	9½	Remington	3500	—	Maximum
IMR	4064	26.0	9½	Remington	3160	—	
IMR	4064	28.0	9½	Remington	3320	—	
IMR	4064	30.0	9½	Remington	3480	—	Maximum

50-grain Hollow Point

POWDER MFGR.	POWDER TYPE	GRAINS	PRIMER TYPE	PRIMER MFGR.	VELOCITY	PRESSURE (C.U.P.)	REMARKS
IMR	4198	19.0	9½	Remington	3120	—	
IMR	4198	21.0	9½	Remington	3260	—	
IMR	4320	27.0	9½	Remington	3315	—	
IMR	4320	29.0	9½	Remington	3385	—	

55-grain Softpoint

POWDER MFGR.	POWDER TYPE	GRAINS	PRIMER TYPE	PRIMER MFGR.	VELOCITY	PRESSURE (C.U.P.)	REMARKS
IMR	4198	21.0	9½	Remington	3080	—	
IMR	4320	28.0	9½	Remington	3185	—	
IMR	3031	26.0	9½	Remington	3255	—	
IMR	4064	27.0	9½	Remington	3270	—	

.30-30 ACKLEY IMPROVED

SPECIFICATIONS

Dia. of Rim — .506″
Dia. of Base — .422″
Dia. of Shoulder — .404″
Dia. of Neck — .330″
Length of Neck — .340″
Angle of Shoulder — 27° 51′
Dia. Jacketed Bullet — .308″
Dia. Cast Bullet — .310″
Length of case — 2″
Max. overall length — 2.5″
Primer size — Large Rifle
Water Capacity — 46.6 grs.

110-grain Speer Varminter

POWDER MFGR.	POWDER TYPE	GRAINS	PRIMER TYPE	PRIMER MFGR.	VELOCITY	PRESSURE (C.U.P.)	REMARKS
Hercules	Reloader 7	32.5	9½	Remington	2554	—	
Hercules	Reloader 7	33.5	9½	Remington	2627	—	
Hercules	Reloader 7	34.5	9½	Remington	2695	—	
Hercules	Reloader 7	35.5	9½	Remington	2792	—	

150-grain Sierra Flat Nose

POWDER MFGR.	POWDER TYPE	GRAINS	PRIMER TYPE	PRIMER MFGR.	VELOCITY	PRESSURE (C.U.P.)	REMARKS
Hodgdon	4198	31.0	9½	Remington	2330	—	
Hodgdon	4198	31.5	9½	Remington	2420	—	
Hodgdon	4198	32.0	9½	Remington	2460	—	
Hodgdon	4198	32.5	9½	Remington	2557	—	

170-grain Flat Nose

POWDER MFGR.	POWDER TYPE	GRAINS	PRIMER TYPE	PRIMER MFGR.	VELOCITY	PRESSURE (C.U.P.)	REMARKS
Hodgdon	4198	29.0	9½	Remington	2190	—	
Hodgdon	4198	31.0	9½	Remington	2335	—	
Hodgdon	4198	31.5	9½	Remington	2353	—	
Hodgdon	4198	32.0	9½	Remington	2385	—	

180-grain Sierra Soft Point

POWDER MFGR.	POWDER TYPE	GRAINS	PRIMER TYPE	PRIMER MFGR.	VELOCITY	PRESSURE (C.U.P.)	REMARKS
IMR	3031	31.0	9½	Remington	1942	—	
IMR	3031	32.0	9½	Remington	2071	—	
IMR	3031	33.0	9½	Remington	2113	—	
IMR	3031	33.5	9½	Remington	2217	—	

.458 × 2 AMERICAN

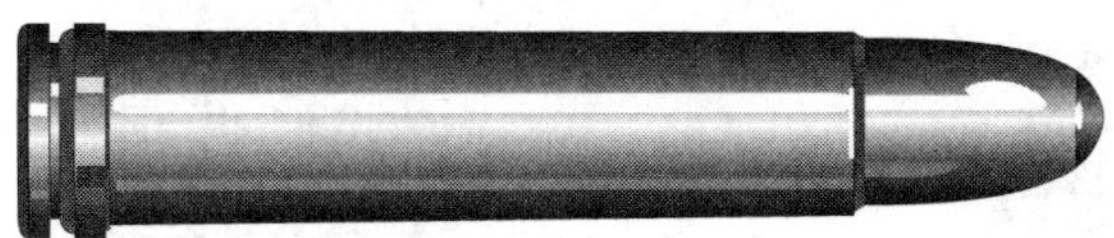

SPECIFICATIONS

Dia. of Rim — .532″
Dia. of Base — .513″
Dia. of Shoulder — N/A
Dia. of Neck — .478″
Length of Neck — N/A
Angle of Shoulder — N/A
Dia. Jacketed Bullet — .458″
Dia. Cast Bullet — .460″
Length of Case — 2.00″
Max. Overall Length — 2.60″
Primer Size — Large Rifle
Water Capacity — 72.98 grs.

300-grain Sierra Hollow Point

POWDER MFG.	POWDER TYPE	GRAINS	PRIMER TYPE	PRIMER MFG.	VELOCITY	PRESSURE (CUP)	REMARKS
Hercules	Reloader 7	50.0	9½	Remington	1842	—	1⅝″ group at 50 yds.
Hercules	Reloader 7	61.0	9½	Remington	2192	30,000	
IMR	4198	53.0	9½	Remington	1810	35,000	
IMR	3031	59.0	9½	Remington	1810	25,000	Mild load

350-grain Hornady Soft Point

POWDER MFG.	POWDER TYPE	GRAINS	PRIMER TYPE	PRIMER MFG.	VELOCITY	PRESSURE (CUP)	REMARKS
Hercules	Reloader 7	55.0	9½	Remington	2100	—	Good all-around short-range game load

400-grain Speer Soft Point

POWDER MFG.	POWDER TYPE	GRAINS	PRIMER TYPE	PRIMER MFG.	VELOCITY	PRESSURE (CUP)	REMARKS
Hercules	Reloader 7	50.0	9½	Remington	1740	—	Low chamber pressure
IMR	4198	47.0	9½	Remington	1782	—	Very accurate
IMR	4198	48.0	9½	Remington	1820	—	1⅛″ groups at 50 yds.
IMR	4198	49.0	9½	Remington	1896	—	Highly compressed

405-grain Remington Soft Point

POWDER MFG.	POWDER TYPE	GRAINS	PRIMER TYPE	PRIMER MFG.	VELOCITY	PRESSURE (CUP)	REMARKS
Hercules	Reloader 7	57.0	9½	Remington	2120	—	Most powerful load tested

510-grain Winchester Solid

POWDER MFG.	POWDER TYPE	GRAINS	PRIMER TYPE	PRIMER MFG.	VELOCITY	PRESSURE (CUP)	REMARKS
IMR	4895	55.0	9½	Remington	1730	—	2″ groups at 100 yds.
IMR	4895	57.0	9½	Remington	1770	—	Very heavy recoil

.450 ALASKAN

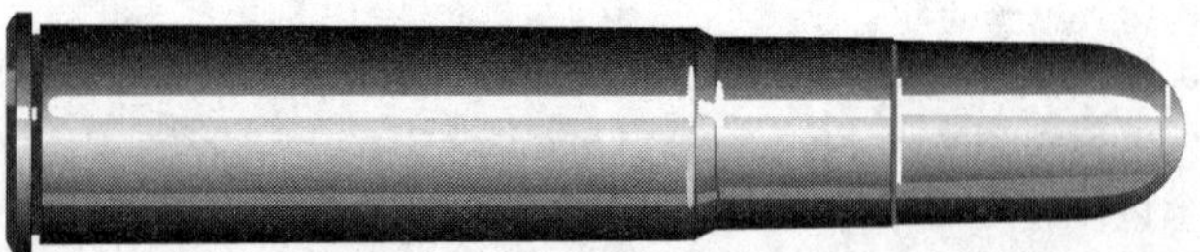

SPECIFICATIONS

Dia. of Rim — .610″	Dia. Jacketed Bullet — .458″
Dia. of Base — .553″	Dia. Cast Bullet — .460″
Dia. of Shoulder — .521″	Length of Case — 2.26″
Dia. of Neck — .480″	Max. Overall Length — 2.83″
Length of Neck — .430″	Primer Size — Large Rifle
Angle of Shoulder — 16.32°	Water Capacity — 97.1 grs.

Fire-Forming Load (no bullet in case)

POWDER MFGR.	POWDER TYPE	GRAINS	PRIMER TYPE	PRIMER MFGR.	VELOCITY	PRESSURE (C.U.P.)	REMARKS
Hercules	Bullseye	7.0	9½	Remington	—	—	Prime .348 Win. case, drop powder, fill remaining case with Cream of Wheat; hold in place with tissue paper. Fire in .450 chamber to form case.

400-grain Hollow Point

POWDER MFGR.	POWDER TYPE	GRAINS	PRIMER TYPE	PRIMER MFGR.	VELOCITY	PRESSURE (C.U.P.)	REMARKS
IMR	4064	67.0	9½	Remington	1990	—	
IMR	4064	68.0	9½	Remington	2025	—	
IMR	4064	69.0	9½	Remington	2100	—	
IMR	4064	70.0	9½	Remington	2150	—	

500-grain FMJ

POWDER MFGR.	POWDER TYPE	GRAINS	PRIMER TYPE	PRIMER MFGR.	VELOCITY	PRESSURE (C.U.P.)	REMARKS
IMR	4064	62.0	9½	Remington	1864	—	
IMR	4064	64.0	9½	Remington	1895	—	
IMR	4064	66.0	9½	Remington	1910	—	
IMR	4064	67.0	9½	Remington	1960	—	
IMR	4064	68.2	9½	Remington	2000	—	Caution!

CAUTION

When this cartridge is used in tubular-magazine rifles, like the Winchester Model 71, we have received reports of the roundnose bullet detnonating the primer of the cartridge ahead of it, due to the heavy recoil. Therefore, we recommend using only one cartridge in the magazine tube, and one in the chamber — giving the shooter two fast shots.

.510 WELLS MAGNUM

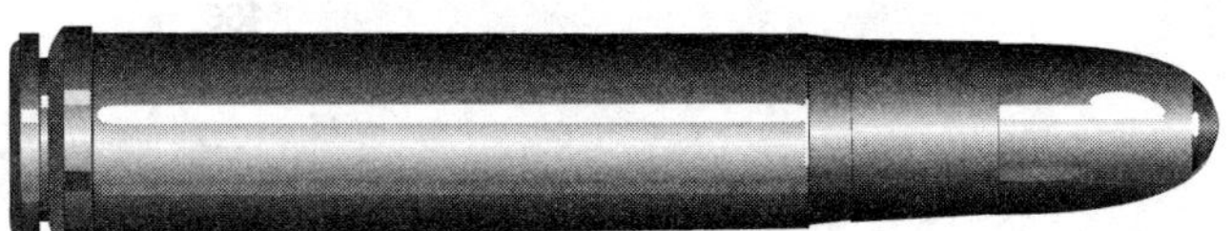

SPECIFICATIONS

Dia. of Rim — .582″
Dia. of Base — .582″
Dia. of Shoulder — 560″
Dia. of Neck — .534″
Length of Neck — .430″
Angle of Shoulder — 6.74°
Dia. Jacketed Bullet — .510″
Dia. Cast Bullet — .510″
Length of Case — 2.88″
Max. Overall Length — 3.70″
Primer Size — Large Rifle(M)
Water Capacity — 147.37 grs.

600-grain FMJ

POWDER MFGR.	POWDER TYPE	GRAINS	PRIMER TYPE	PRIMER MFGR.	VELOCITY	PRESSURE (C.U.P.)	REMARKS
IMR	4320	109.0	215	Federal	2210	—	
IMR	4320	114	215	Federal	2350	—	
IMR	4320	105	215	Federal	2150	—	
IMR	3031	100	215	Federal	2300	—	

Chapter 17
Shot Loads for Rifles

There was a time when most American ammunition makers offered shot loads for many of their rifle cartridges. These proved far from ideal. However, this is an excellent field for the reloader to experiment, and some shot loads in rifles may have some practical use.

When shot loads are used in rifle barrels, the rotation of the rifling sends the shot out the muzzle in a spiral motion and completely shatters any hope for a good pattern. *See* Figure 17-1. One local farmer tried firing some old factory-loaded .38-40 shot loads at unwanted chickens in his garden, at a range of about 15 yards, but failed to get any results other than the chickens flinching at the report of the rifle's muzzle blast.

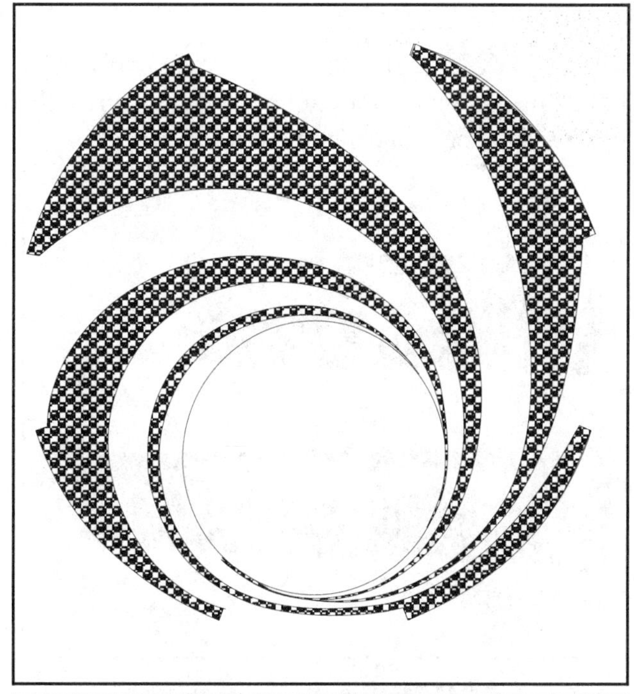

Figure 17-1: Rifled barrels tend to send shot in a spiral string that frequently by-passes the intended target.

In 1926, the Winchester Repeating Arms Co. manufactured shot cartridges for the following rifles:

- .22 rimfire BB shot: Lesmok powder used behind No. 12 soft lead shot.
- .22 rimfire Long shot: Lesmok powder used behind No. 12 soft lead shot.
- .22 rimfire Long shot: Smokeless powder used with No. 12 soft lead shot.

- .32 rimfire Long shot: Blackpowder used with No. 10 soft lead shot.
- 9mm Long shot: Smokeless powder used with No. 9 shot.
- .32-20 WCF: Blackpowder used with No. 10 soft lead shot.
- .38-40 WCF: Blackpowder used with No. 8 soft lead shot.
- .44-40 WCF: Blackpowder or smokeless powder used with No. 8 soft lead shot.
- .44 Game Getter: Blackpowder or smokeless powder loaded with No. 8 soft lead shot.
- .44 X.L.: Blackpowder or smokeless powder used with No. 8 chilled shot.

Most of the above loadings used a brass case with the neck extended to hold more shot. An over-shot wad was then crimped in place to seal the cartridge. *See* Figure 17-2.

The .44 X.L. (extra long), however, utilized a shot capsule, much the same as those currently supplied by Speer and Thompson/Center.

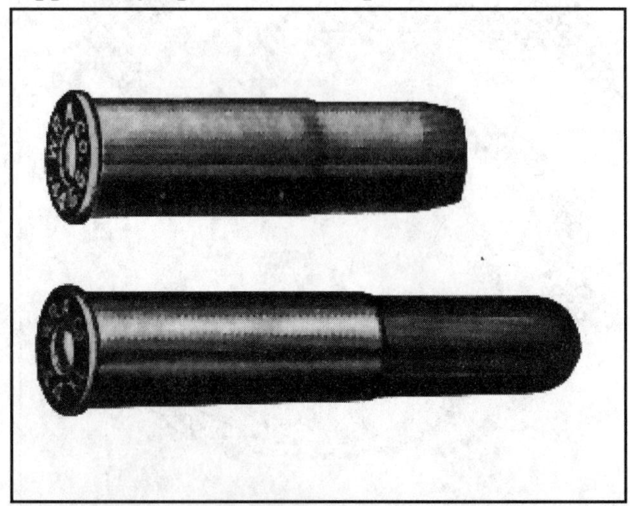

Figure 17-2: The .44 Game Getter (top) has an extended brass neck to hold more shot. The .44 X.L. (bottom) uses a shot capsule similar to Speer and Thompson/Center.

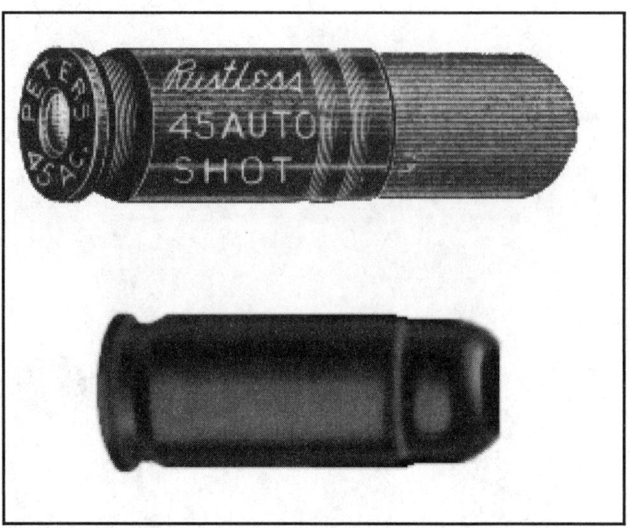

Figure 17-3: Original Peters .45 ACP shot cartridge (top). New Speer loading of the .45 ACP (bottom) is designed to function in semiautomatic handguns.

The Peters Cartridge Company once manufactured a shot load designed for the .45 ACP Thompson sub-machine gun as shown in Figure 17-3. This particular load was not designed for killing purposes. Rather, it was used in the machine gun to be fired over the heads of rioting mobs, giving the noise and psychological effect of regular ball cartridges, but created little or no damage at long range. This eliminated much of the danger to bystanders or distant windows.

The late Philip B. Sharp discussed this .45 ACP shot cartridge in the March-April 1933 issue of the *Journal of Criminal Law and Criminology* as follows:

"...This ammunition requires the use of a special 18-shot box magazine, and consists of a waxed paper bullet containing about 150 #8 chilled shot, propelled by what appears to be Ballistite shotgun powder. A perforated tip cup separates the shot charge from the powder and maintains the alignment in the bore until the charge leaves the muzzle."

Writing further in the December 1934 *American Rifleman*, and describing the use of this cartridge in the sub-machine gun, Mr. Sharpe writes: "The shot load spreads over the community and loses its initial power rapidly. It is designed primarily for riot work where the primary idea of the police is to force back the crowd. The rifling in the barrel scatters the shot so that it is impossible to pattern it at more than 15 or 20 feet when single shots are fired. If fired in bursts of from five to ten cartridges, however, the pattern shows extremely wide but reasonable dispersion of the charge."

Speer's relatively new 9mm shot load could be used by law-enforcement or military personnel for the same purpose in an Uzi or other automatic weapon.

MULTIBALL LOADS

One of the earliest forms of multiple-projectile firing in rifled barrels occurred over a century ago, using double-ball loads in muzzleloaders. Two round balls were loaded on top of a reduced charge of blackpowder. The results were less than encouraging. The spin of the rifling and the deformed balls (due to colliding with each other) caused both balls to fly considerably off the intended target path. Beyond 20 yards, the accuracy was so bad that any hit was uncertain.

John Wootters had much better luck with his "hockshop" load consisting of three soft lead balls at moderate velocity. Results were good up to about 25 yards, with all three balls in a 2½-inch circle. This load is described in his Stoeger book, *The Complete Book of Practical Handloading*.

Similar loads in a lever-action rifle chambered for the .444 Marlin gave equal or better results. The three spherical .429-inch lead balls consistently grouped within three inches of each other at exactly 30 yards. Furthermore, all three balls were within six inches of the aiming point with no sight adjustment from standard loads. This load would have practical use on running coyotes or similar size game out to about 35 yards. *See* Figure 17-4. This load should also prove useful on wild turkey, aiming dead center of the body at the same range.

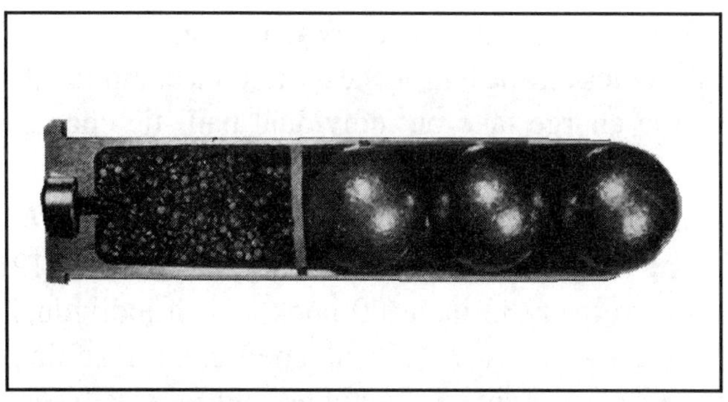

Figure 17-4: Three-ball shot load in .444 Marlin.

While developing this three-ball load for the .444 Marlin, I started out with 31 grains of H4198 powder, a stiff cardboard wad, and then the three soft lead balls of .429-inch diameter. A slight crimp at the mouth of the case held the balls secure.

Although the subject of shot loads in rifles is currently under discussion, two .410-grain rifled slugs used in one 12-gauge, 3-inch case has been loaded with excellent results for many years. A description of this load may be found in Chapter 22 of this book.

MULTIBULLET LOADS

Some experimental work took place in the 1950s utilizing two bullets loaded in the 7.62 Nato (.308 Winchester) cartridge with surprisingly good results. The intended purpose of this load was to have the first bullet strike dead-on target while the second bullet was to follow a three- to six-inch circular pattern around the first, caused by purposely swaging the second bullet's base at a slight angle.

CHARACTERISTICS OF SHOT LOADS

In general, a packet of shot projectiles cannot be treated in the same manner as a solid projectile in a rifled barrel. A bullet — being a single solid object — can withstand the lateral stresses placed on it by the rifling. A charge of shot, on the other hand, reacts like a single unit only while it is confined within the barrel. When the shot or packet of shot leaves the barrel, the individual components of the charge take on individual ballistic characteristics.

Shotshells of any type fire a group or package of round projectiles from as small as .05 inch (No. 12 shot) to over .33 inch (00 buck). Each individual shot has a very low ballistic coefficient, resulting in poor aerodynamic qualities and is greatly affected by air resistance. When used in a rifled barrel, any spin that is imparted on the shot package as a whole causes it to fly apart after it has left the confines of the barrel. The farther away from the muzzle, the greater the shot disperses. Consequently, any resemblance of a shot pattern is usually lost after 20 yards or so.

One of the most successful shot loads tested in a rifle barrel, without any choke or other barrel modification, was loaded in a custom-built Winchester Model 94 Big Bore lever-action rifle chambered for the .458 x 2 American wildcat cartridge. To hold the shot, a piece of plastic tubing with an outside diameter of .454 inch was used. A plastic cap, with an outside diameter of .457 inch, was inserted on the bottom of this tube (next to the powder), and the tube was then filled with $\frac{7}{8}$ ounce of copper-plated shot. The same type of retainer cap was also tried on the mouth of the tube, but this arrangement gave unsatisfactory results. In a last desperate attempt to find some suitable means of holding the shot in place, a stick of bullet lubrication happened to be lying on the bench; a part of this lubricant was melted to form a seal over the shot contained in the plastic tube. *See* Figure 17-5. The result: a very satisfactory pattern at 30 yards; not just with a few shots, but on every shot! At this range, there were spots where a quail, or perhaps a small squirrel might slip through, but not a goose, turkey, or similar size game. No testing was done at farther distances, but if meat was needed for the pot, shots would be attempted with this combination out to 40 or 45 yards.

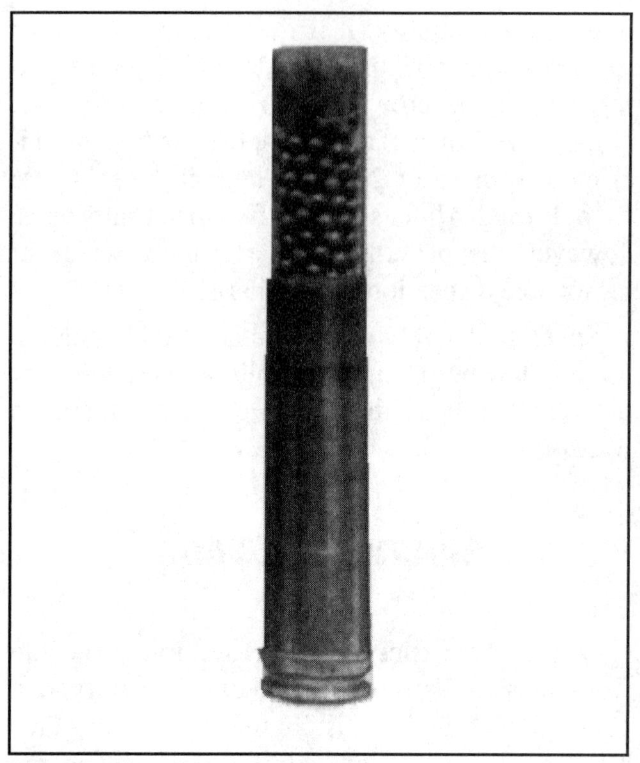

Figure 17-5: Custom shot load for the .458 x 2 American wildcat cartridge.

Of course, this load would not feed through the magazine. Rather, it had to be loaded directly into the chamber — firing as a single-shot.

Now before you go out and sell your 12-gauge shotgun in favor of this rifle load, we do not mean to imply that this is the ideal shot load for any situation. Rather, it is meant to be an auxiliary or supplemental load for the rifle. In many areas of the country, turkey season coincides with the deer season, and few hunters like to pass up a wild turkey. If a big gobbler is foraging in the direction of your tree stand, slipping in one of these shot loads may be the answer to a good Sunday dinner.

When hunting elk or other big game in wilderness areas, like the Scapegoat Wilderness area of Montana, where backpacking is almost essential to reach the better game areas, a few shot loads like the one just described can make the difference between a roasted blue grouse or a can of potted meat for dinner.

The shot cartridge in question was loaded with 20 grains of 2400 powder using standard large rifle primers — giving a muzzle velocity of 1175 fps.

This same load should give about equal results in a .45-70 rifle. In fact, any straight rifle case can be loaded in a similar fashion, adjusting the shot and powder charges accordingly. The following is a partial list:

- .38-55
- .375 Winchester
- .401 Winchester
- .405 Winchester
- .44-40 Winchester
- .44 Magnum (Rifle)
- .444 Marlin
- .45-70
- .45-90
- .458 Winchester

To work up loads for any of these cases, obtain plastic tubing that has an outside diameter about .001 inch smaller than the bore diameter of the rifle. Devise a means to hold the shot in the tube such as plastic retainer caps. Plastic tubing is available from several sources for use as tool-storage containers for drill bits, chamber reamers, etc. Again, experimentation is required to find the best shot load for any given firearm. On some loads, it may be necessary to partially score or slit the sides of the shot capsule (3 or 4) to allow the shot to disperse once it leaves the muzzle. Other loads may work fine without additional modification.

Once a suitable shot-containing capsule has been obtained, plan a mild starting load for testing. The main objective is to find a load that will pattern the shot best; we are not looking for power in shot loads, only good shot distribution at the maximum ranges possible. This usually means maximum velocities of 1200 fps.

The following are a few suggested starting loads for various cartridges:

CARTRIDGE	MAX. WEIGHT SHOT CHARGE	LOAD
.38-55	280 grains	15.0 grs. 2400
.375 Win.	280 grains	16.0 grs. 2400
.401 Win.	250 grains	16.5 grs. 2400
.405 Win.	300 grains	14.0 grs. Unique
.44-40 Win.	225 grains	20.0 grs. 2400
.44 Mag.	250 grains	4.8 grs. Bullseye
.444 Marlin	250 grains	30.0 grs. H4198
.45-70	400 grains	20.0 grs. 2400
.45-90	400 grains	14.0 grs. Unique
.458 Win.	500 grains	26.0 grs. 2400

Use only large rifle primers with the above loads; not magnum primers.

CAUTION!

One of the dangers of loading reduced shot loads, and also half-jacket bullets, is getting the velocity too low so that the heavier lead shot (or slug) goes out the muzzle leaving the shot-capsule base (or copper jacket) in the bore. Obviously, the next shot could cause trouble. Therefore, the object of a good shot load is one with enough velocity to not leave anything remaining in the bore, yet low enough so as not to give radical shot patterns.

Shot loads may also be loaded directly in the cartridge case using reduced powder charges, a combination of wads over the powder charge and then the remaining portion of the case filled with shot. A wad over the shot at the mouth of the case

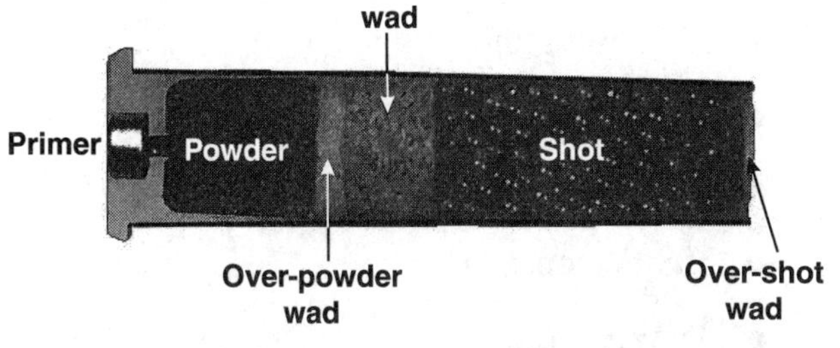

Figure 17-6: Cross-sectional view of shot-loaded rifle case.

retains the shot when the wad is crimped in place as shown in Figure 17-6.

These loads should be restricted to the large straight rifle cases with the .444 Marlin or .38-55 being about minimum size. Any smaller case won't hold enough shot to make the practice worthwhile.

LOADS FOR BOTTLENECK CASES

A family member once pulled the bullets on three .30-40 Krag cartridges, dumped out half the powder, inserted a stiff cardboard wad at the base of the neck — held in place with some type of wonder glue — before filling up the neck area of the case with copper-plated BB shot. Another thin cardboard wad was then glued in place at the case mouth to retain the shot. The purpose of this load was for use on wild turkey while deer hunting. All three of these cartridges were fired, but we didn't see any wild turkey on the table from this load.

The only means of obtaining shot loads in bottleneck rifle cartridges is the use of shot capsules. Ammunition manufacturers tried this at one time on many of their rifle cartridges, but soon gave up the practice as a lost cause.

The only practical purpose for shot loads in bottleneck rifle cartridges is for use on snakes at very close range while hunting, whereas the rifle bullet may richochet off rocks on the ground, or else the report of a full charge may scare game. Another reason that comes to mind is to scare chickens out of the garden without hurting them.

Speer 38/357 shot capsules can be loaded in the following bottleneck rifle cartridges:

- .35 Remington
- .35 Winchester
- .356 Winchester
- .358 Winchester
- .35 Whelen
- .350 Remington Magnum

The results and ranges will be almost identical to those described for the use of these capsules in revolvers (*See* Chapter 11); that is, 10 to 15 yards, maximum range. Velocities should be held to under 1300 fps to obtain any resemblance of a shot pattern. Furthermore, cartridges loaded with shot capsules should not be fed through the magazine of these rifles. Rather, they should be hand-fed into the chamber for each shot.

A COMPROMISE FOR SHOT LOADS IN RIFLES

Many times hunters of one species of game run into another that also happened to be in season, but their firearms were inadequate or just plain unsuitable.

Several years ago, I was hunting black bear in the George Washington National Forest, using a centerfire rifle. After walking a good 12 miles and spending almost the same number of hours in the woods, no bear was seen. However, that year happened to be the peak cycle for ruffed grouse in the area and they were thick as snowbirds. How I wished for a shotgun that day!

Figure 17-7: Sixteen-gauge side-by-side drilling with a 7 x 57R rifle barrel beneath.

The problem was eventually solved by purchasing a couple of nice German-made drillings: the first being a 16-gauge side-by-side double with a 9.3 x 74R rifle barrel beneath; the second was similar, except the rifle barrel was chambered for the 7 x 57R cartridge. A flick of a button on either immediately converted to the rifle barrel or vice versa.

However, long before I could afford the price for these two drillings, another route was taken. I had noticed Pete Dickey's article in the *American Rifleman* where he described procedures for converting a takedown rifle from a modern solid-frame Winchester Model 94 carbine. Prior to this time, I had also converted a Winchester Model 94, originally chambered for the .30-30 WCF cartridge, to shoot .410 shotshells. I then decided to combine Pete Dickey's idea with my own and make a handy takedown carbine with a two-barrel set: one to shoot the .444 Marlin rifle cartridge, and the other to handle .410 shotshells? I sent my solid frame .410 conversion to S&K Guns of Fargo, South Dakota along with a .44 caliber barrel blank. In approximately three weeks, the takedown conversion was returned. I now had a Winchester Model 94 carbine with an 18-inch .444 Marlin barrel, and a second 20-inch .410 barrel. Either barrel may be changed from one to the other in less than five minutes, and either barrel fits nicely in my pack basket so that one is on the gun while the other is in easy reach at all times.

But this is not the limit to rifle/shotgun combinations. If a bolt-action rifle is preferred, using a higher-velocity cartridge and perhaps a telescopic sight, a takedown version can be made by any competent gunsmith. A second shotgun barrel can also be made to fit the rifle so that either rifle or shot may be fired from the same action. A novelty? Sure, but a useful one at that.

The reloading gun buff has an endless variety of resources to choose from, and almost any rifle/shotgun combination imaginable can be produced with custom loads that fit the combination perfectly — another good reason for reloading!

SECTION IV
LOADS FOR SHOTSHELLS

WARNING

The loads and ballistic data shown in this book were obtained under strictly controlled conditions. Ballistic data vary considerably depending on many factors, including components used, how such components are assembled, the type and condition of the firearm used, and the reloading techniques. Therefore, the loads listed are not for inexperienced persons; safety precautions must be considered and utilized at all times.

The publisher and authors specifically disclaim any warranties with respect to any and all loads listed, the safety or suitability of the loads, or the results obtained with the listed loads. Readers and users of any load or product listed in this book assume all risk, responsibility and liability whatsoever for any and all injuries (including death), losses, or damages to persons or property (including consequential damages), arising from the use of any load or product.

The individual assumes the risk of safe loading practices. Failure to do so or violation of any of the warnings specified in this book could result in severe personal injury (including death) to the user or bystander or damage to the firearm.

Chapter 18

How To Reload Shotshells

Shotshell reloading, to many shooters, is not as popular or as interesting as loading for centerfire rifle and handgun cartridges. Even so, millions of shotshells are loaded annually in the United States, mostly for skeet, clay target and trap shooters, and also for shooters participating in turkey shoots using shotguns.

Hunters who can reload their own shotshells will take home more game with the least amount of trouble, using fewer firearms. For example, a person who has a 12-gauge shotgun with a modified choke can reload the shells and use the gun in different ways. By inserting a shot column (power piston), the hunter can tighten the choke to improved modified; using copper-plated shot will increase the choke another degree to about full choke. Just by reloading, the shooter has three different chokes for three types of hunting conditions. Add to this the interchangeable choke tubes on the newer shotguns, like the one in Figure 18-1, and the possibilities are endless.

On the other end of the spectrum, if the hunter wants a spreader load for upland game, where the average shot is less than 25 yards, a cardboard X-shaped wad can be inserted into the shot column

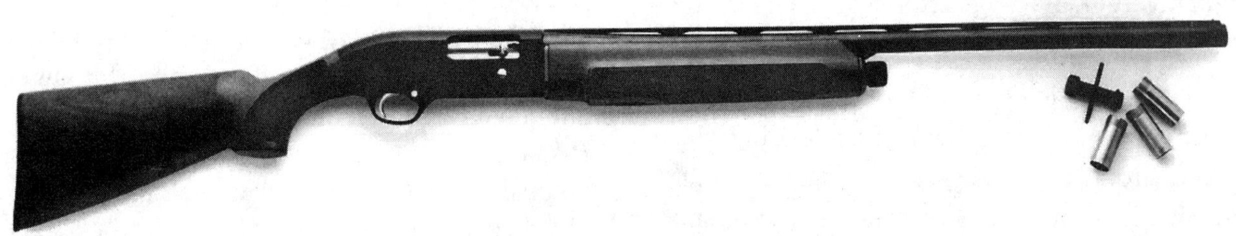

Figure 18-1: This Beretta features flush-mounted screw-in choke tubes and a magazine cutoff that allows feeding lighter or heavier loads into the breech without emptying the magazine.

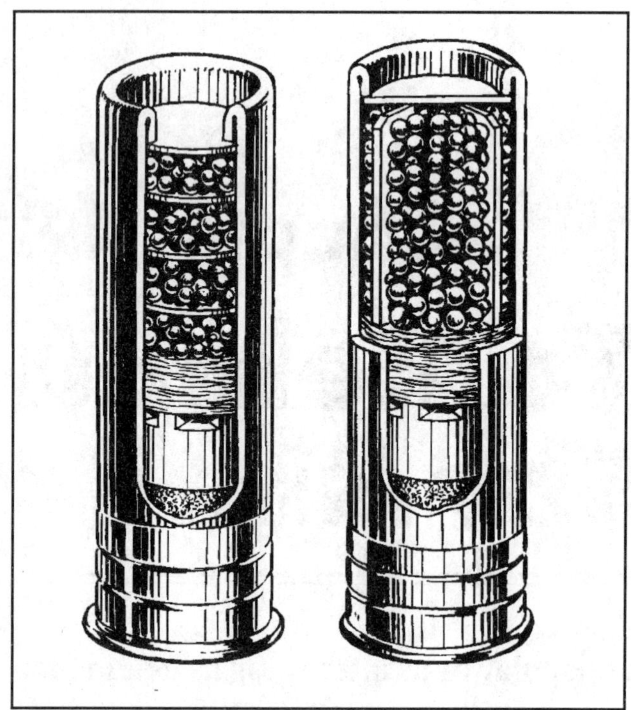

Figure 18-2: Spreader shotshell loads: thin cardboard wads divide the shot in the left shell while an X-shaped divider is used in the shell on the right.

to open the pattern up to improved cylinder. The same can be done by dividing the shot into three or four different compartments by inserting thin cardboard wads in the shot compartment. *See* Figure 18-2.

A shooter can reload for about one-third the cost of factory-bought shells. Skeet, trap, and competition shooters almost always reload their own shotshells. One reason is for the savings, but another is for the loads. Each shooter has a favorite combination that gives the best scores. These shooters would not think of using factory shotshells in competition.

Initially, shotshell reloading may seem simple when compared to rifle or handgun reloading, since the latter group has a wide variety of bullet weights, velocities, etc. But when you start studying shotshell reloading in detail, the number of different cases, shot columns, etc. can be confusing, and you may consider the practice anything but simple.

In shotshell reloading, you must first decide for what purpose the loads will be used, then use a good reference chart to select a trial load. Then, try different powders and loads until you find the one that patterns best in your shotgun.

Never exceed the factory recommendations, and if a load does not look right to you (even if it is printed in a reloading manual), always double check with another source before using the load.

SHOTGUN BASICS

Before practicing loading shotshells, let's look at the components that make up the various types of shotshells. Then you will be able to approach the practice of reloading with more authority.

As their name implies, shotguns are made to shoot shot. They are the only practical firearms for bird and waterfowl shooting. They are predominately used on small game, such as rabbits, and for trap, clay target and skeet shooting.

Like its muzzleloading predecessor, the shotgun has a smooth bore. Because its charge is a load of shot pellets, the shotgun bore is large in diameter. The size of the bore is designated by its gauge. Years ago, 4- and 8-gauge guns were fairly common. Today, however, only 10, 12, 20, 28 gauges and .410 bores are manufactured in the United States. The 16 gauge is still manufactured extensively in Europe and remains a favorite gauge for many shooters.

Gauges: The term *gauge* refers to the number of round lead balls required to make a pound. So, a 12-gauge shotgun has a bore the same diameter as a lead ball weighing $^1/_{12}$ of a pound. Although this antiquated means of measurement is no longer used in manufacturing, the term is still used in the marketplace because it describes the gun well. Actually, because of the choke, solid balls for 12-gauge guns weigh only 1 ounce, or 16 balls to the pound. The British, as well as many Americans, usually use the term *bore* instead of gauge.

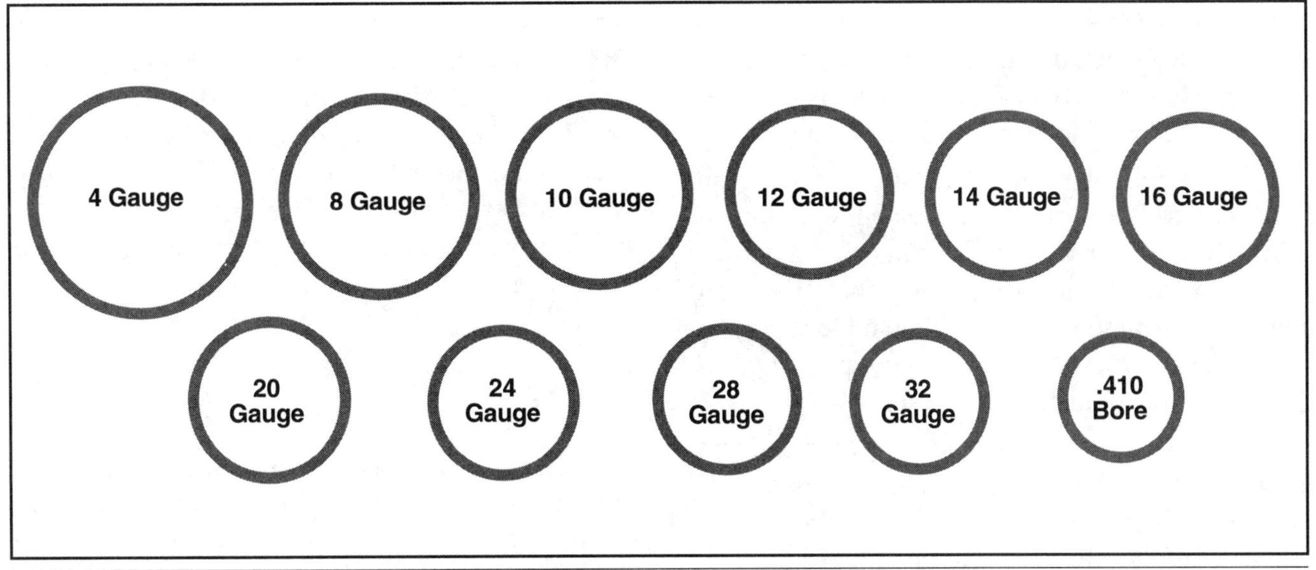

Figure 18-3: These circles represent the true size of cylinder bores of the shotgun gauges indicated.

The smaller the number, the larger the diameter of the bore. Twelve-gauge guns have larger-diameter barrels than 16-gauge guns; 16-gauge shotguns are larger than 20-gauge guns; and so on. Since the bore is larger, the 12 gauge can efficiently handle more shot than a 16 or 20 gauge.

The .410-bore shotgun has an actual barrel diameter of .410 inch. Because it was developed later than other shotguns, it escaped the older nomenclature. Actually, it's about 67 gauge. *See* Figure 18-3 for actual sizes of various shotgun bores. These true-cylinder-bore sizes represent the barrel diameter, but when the shotgun barrel has any choke, the diameter at the muzzle is somewhat smaller, depending on the amount and type of choke.

The chart to follow lists the standard factory shotshell loads available in 12, 16, and 20 gauges in 2¾-inch length. *Load* refers to the amount of shot in the shell.

Gauge	Magnum Loads
12	1½ oz.
16	1¼ oz.
20	1⅛ oz.

Gauge	Heavy Loads
12	1¼ oz.
16	1⅛ oz.
20	1 oz.

Gauge	Standard Loads
12	1⅛ oz.
16	1 oz.
20	⅞ oz.

There are also 3-inch shells with even more shot in them. Since more shot can be loaded in a 12-gauge shell than in a 16- or 20-gauge shell of the same length, the relationship doesn't change. The amount of shot in a charge greatly affects the efficiency of a shotgun. A small ⅛-ounce additional shot charge will make a big difference in the field for any type of shooting from clay targets to ducks and geese.

Barrels: A shotgun barrel must be long enough to allow complete combustion of the powder. Generally, combustion of smokeless powder occurs when the shot charge has traveled about 20 inches of barrel length.

Shotgun barrels start at a length of 18 inches (the minimum legal length) and can be found as long as 36 inches in some 10- and 12-gauge guns. Smaller gauges usually come in 26- or 28-inch lengths.

Short barrels give the advantage of faster gun handling, which is useful in upland shooting of quail, grouse, woodcock, and the like. Long barrels with more weight out front steady the swing and contribute to a more accurate aim and lead for the longer-range, more deliberate gun pointing required to shoot at ducks and geese.

All barrels have a chamber at the breech end that is larger than the barrel proper. The chamber holds the loaded shell and is long enough to allow the crimp to unfold. The cone is a funnel-like constriction between the chamber and the barrel bore. The rim of the shells fits into a groove at the rear of the chamber, which also has a cut large enough to house the extractor or ejector under the shell rim. *See* Figure 18-4.

Most shotguns made in the United States are chambered for 2¾-inch shells. This applies to 12-, 16-, and 20-gauge shotguns. Some 12- and 20-gauge guns are furnished with 3-inch chambers for use with extra-heavy, 3-inch magnum loads. There is also a 3½-inch 10-gauge shell. The .410-bore shotguns are usually chambered for 3-inch shells, although 2½-inch .410 shells are frequently used for skeet shooting.

Some shotguns, especially skeet and trap guns, have barrels fitted with a ventilated rib. The rib serves as a straightedge to assist in gun pointing, and is supported by stanchions, or stands, leaving an open space between the rib and barrel. The rib breaks up the heat mirage that shimmers up from a barrel hot from continuous firing. This heat mirage would otherwise distort the shooter's view of the target. Many skeet guns and some field guns have ventilated ribs.

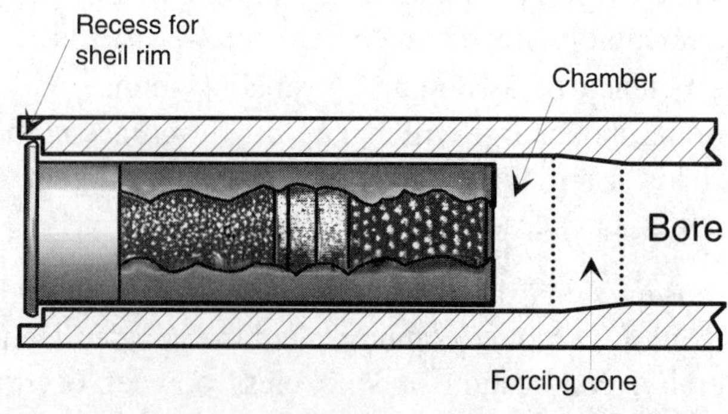

Figure 18-4: Chamber end of a shotgun barrel.

CHOKES

A choke is a constriction at the muzzle of a shotgun barrel. True cylinder bores (with no chokes) are confined to riot guns, barrels made especially for shooting rifled slugs, and some barrels designed strictly for skeet shooting. Shotguns are patterned by shooting at a large square of paper. The standard distance is 40 yards from the muzzle. A black bull's-eye is used as an aiming point.

After shooting, the target is inspected and a circle 30 inches in diameter is drawn around the greatest number of shot holes. This is done without reference to the bull's-eye, which may or may not be in the center of the resulting circle. The shot holes in the circle are then counted and compared to the number of shot known to be loaded in identical shotshells which have the same shot size and weight.

Chokes are made to certain constrictions to produce the following results:

- *Full Choke:* 65% – 70% minimum of charge in a 30-inch circle at 40 yards.
- *Improved Modified Choke:* 65% of charge in a 30-inch circle at 40 yards.
- *Modified Choke:* 50% – 65% of charge in a 30-inch circle at 40 yards.
- *Improved Cylinder Choke:* 35% – 50% of charge in a 30-inch circle at 40 yards.
- *Cylinder Bore:* 25% – 35% of charge in a 30-inch circle at 40 yards.

Full-choke barrels are limited to about .040-inch constriction. Tighter constrictions produce adverse effects. At one time, cylinder bores patterned poorly, with too few pellets in the center of the pattern and too many around the edges, in a sort of cartwheel effect. However, over the past couple of decades, steady improvements in shotshell loading have offset this tendency, and cylinder-bore patterns, which are the widest of all, now have good distribution. However, cylinder-bore patterns thin out rapidly, and their effective range does not extend much beyond 25 yards.

Full chokes narrow the degree of dispersion, concentrating the shot pattern, and are preferred for long ranges typical of shooting waterfowl, ducks, and geese. Improved cylinder chokes allow a wide dispersion and are therefore more suitable for closer shooting, such as quail, grouse and other upland game.

Modified chokes are very useful under certain conditions; they are actually a compromise between the others — an all-round boring often used with more success than the full choke.

Chokes which are an integral part of the gun are made either by cutting or swaging. Cut chokes are formed during reaming of the barrel, with the reaming tool carrying the shape, radius and dimensions of the constriction wanted. Swaged chokes are first formed on the barrel exterior by grinding less metal from the muzzle end, to a shape and dimension that forms an interior constriction when the muzzle is swaged in a heavy press. There are several adjustable chokes that screw into a threaded muzzle. Both types are sometimes coupled with recoil reducing attachments called compensators which allow powder gases to escape sideways from vents at the muzzle. The recoil is reduced to some extent, but the report is accentuated.

Shotgun Performance: Gauges, barrel lengths, and chokes all have a bearing on performance. Here are a few simple facts:

- Long barrels don't shoot harder.
- Barrel length has no effect on dispersion.
- Choke does affect dispersion.
- Gauge does not affect dispersion — the .410 bore is an exception.
- A 20 gauge does not "shoot harder" than a twelve.

A 12 bore full choke and a 20 bore full choke gun will throw the same spread of shot — that is, will have the same dispersion.

The 12 gauge will have more shot in its load than the 20 gauge; usually ¼ oz. or 24% more pellets. This means that 40 yards from the gun, the 12 gauge will put 25% more shot in a 30-inch circle than the 20 gauge.

To put it another way, a 12-gauge gun at 50 yards will put the same number of pellets in a 30-inch circle that a 20 gauge will at 40 yards.

The 16 gauge is right between the two. What the 20 gauge will do at 40 yards the 16 gauge will do at 45.

It follows then, that a 12 gauge magnum load of ¼ oz. shot will give about the same density at 60 yards as the 1¼ oz. load at 50 yards.

Carrying it further, a 12 gauge 3-inch Magnum load of 1⅞ oz. shot should duplicate our previous performance at 75 yards.

Conceivably, a seasoned gunner could connect with a fast flying mallard at this distance, but not one shooter in ten thousand has had the experience or opportunity to learn the long lead required.

Shotguns can be effective only up to the distance where the individual pellets have enough velocity to penetrate feathers and flesh and retain some shocking power.

Even large size shot lose velocity quickly, and this again, as well as skill, puts a limit on shotgun performance regardless of gauge or amount of shot.

Now if the 12 gauge consistently out performs them, why is there a need for the smaller 16 and 20 gauges; simply because they are lighter to carry, faster handling, more pleasant to shoot, and adequate for many uses. Most upland shooting is done under 40 yards, and the 20 gauge will provide effective patterns at that range, the 16 gauge even better, and the small .410 bore will perform quite effectively up to 30 yards if in modified choke or tighter.

Moreover, on upland shooting we use smaller shot in combination with an open choke, the smaller pellets filling up the wider pattern. This provides clean kills without tearing up game with concentrated heavy shot to the point where they are unfit for the table.

Small shot (7½, 8, 9) are ideal for close-up shooting on small birds, as they fill up the wide pattern thrown by improved cylinder choked guns. However, they lose velocity quickly and lack killing power at longer shotgun ranges. Heavy loads of larger size shot, in full-choked guns are required for the longer shotgun ranges and for larger species like ducks and geese. The chart in Figure 18-4 shows a comparison of the different shot sizes, while the table in Figure 18-5 gives the approximate number of shot pellets per ounce. The table in Figure 18-6 may be used as a shotshell selector for various applications.

Game	Type of Shell	Shot Size
Ducks	Magnum	4, 5, 6 Steel 2, 4, 6
Geese	Magnum	BB, 2, 4 Steel F, BB, 1, 2
Pheasants	Magnum	4, 5, 6, 7½
Ruffed Grouse and Hungarian Partridge	Field Load	6, 7½, 8, 9
Other Grouse and Chukar Partridge	Field Load	6, 7½, 8
Doves and Pigeons	Field Load	6, 7½, 8, 9
Rabbits	Field Load	4, 5, 6
Woodcock, Snipe, Rail	Field Load	7½, 8, 9
Squirrels	Field Load	4, 5, 6,
Wild Turkey	Magnum	4, 6
Crows	Magnum	5, 6, 7½,
Predators	Magnum	4 Buck, BB, 2

Figure 18-6: Shotshell selector.

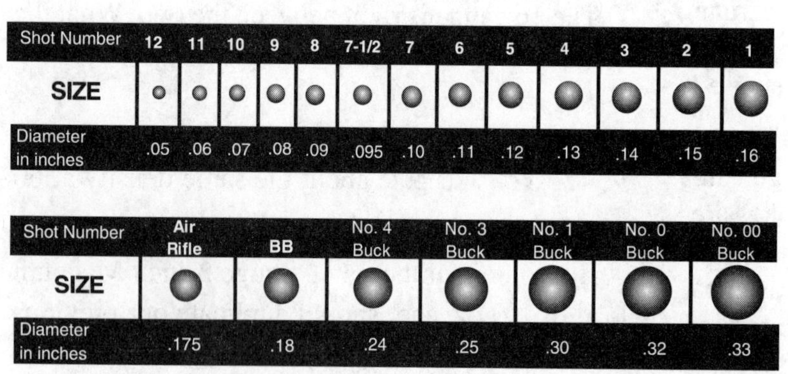

Figure 18-4: Comparison of shot sizes from No. 00 buck to No. 12.

LEAD				STEEL	
Size	Pellets	Size	Pellets	Size	Pellets
				F	40
BB	50	6	225	BB	72
2	87	7½	350	1	103
4	135	8	410	2	125
5	170	9	585	4	192
				6	315

Figure 18-5: The approximate number of shot pellets per ounce.

RANGE

Waterfowl hunting usually involves the longest distances for shotgun shooting. The practical range for taking ducks and geese is 35 to 50 yards. Individual pellets, however, often travel great distances. For safety, consider the following extreme ranges.

00 Buck	610 yards
No. 2 Shot	337 yards
No. 6 Shot	275 yards
No. 9 Shot	225 yards

DRAMS EQUIVALENT

This guide number, found on shotshell boxes, gives the weight of blackpowder used in the past to obtain established velocities for each load. Blackpowder is no longer used, so the figure does not represent the actual amount of modern smokeless powder used.

A dram, therefore, is a unit of measure. There are 16 drams (av.) in one ounce, or 256 in a pound. In the early days of blackpowder shotshells, the powder charge was measured in drams. Dram for dram, today's smokeless powder is more powerful. When loading a shell with smokeless powder, a smaller weight of powder is necessary to give the same muzzle velocity as would be obtained with blackpowder. For example, to load a 12 gauge shotshell to, say, 3¼ drams equivalent may require 23.5 grains of one type of modern smokeless powder, or perhaps 30 grains of another type of modern smokeless powder. In other words, the amount of modern smokeless powder to acquire a certain velocity of shot in shotshells can vary, depending upon the powder type. Consequently, the term "3 dram equivalent," "3¼ dram equivalent," etc. in describing a load means that the amount of smokeless powder used produces the same shot velocity as would 3, 3¼, etc. of blackpowder.

SHOTSHELL COMPONENTS

Figure 18-7 shows a sectional view of a typical shotshell and the various components used. The primer is secured in the head of the case. When struck by the shotgun's firing pin, it explodes to ignite the powder contained inside the shotshell case. The heat and gas produced by the burning powder forces the wad and shot out the end of the case, down the barrel, and out the muzzle. This is, in general, how a shotshell works. Now let's examine each of these components individually.

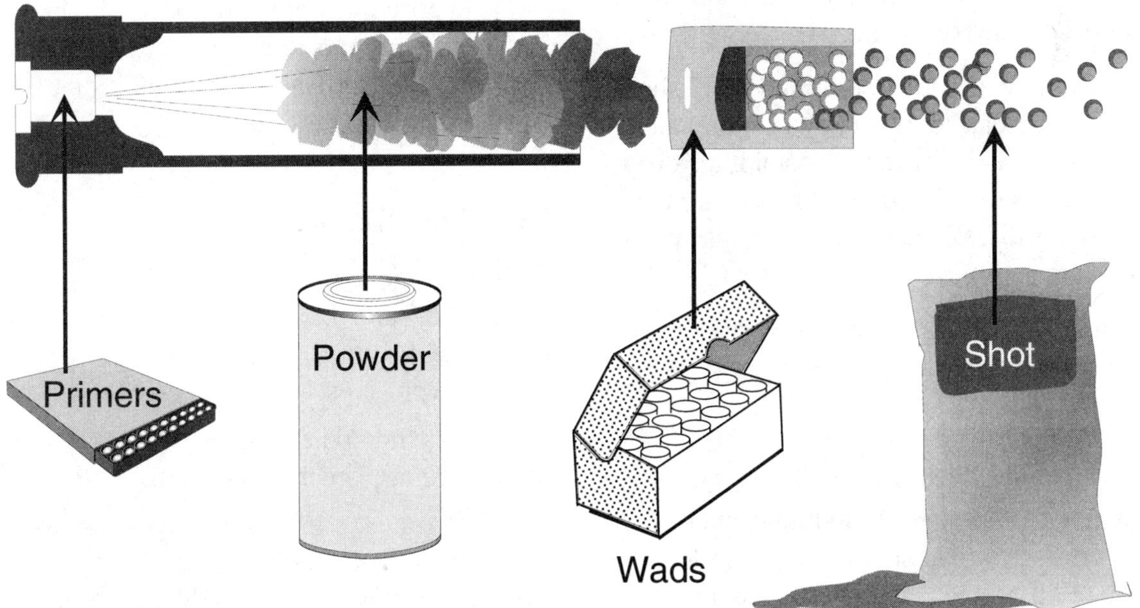

Figure 18-7: Sectional view of a modern shotshell showing the various components required to load a finished shell.

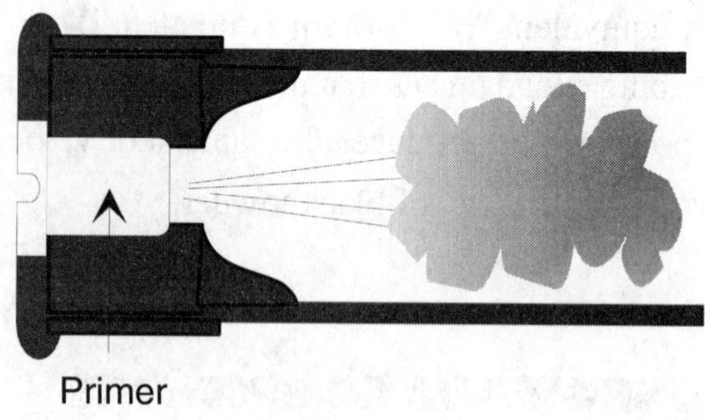

Figure 18-8: American battery-cup shotgun primer.

SHOTSHELL PRIMERS

The battery cup primer is the most common primer used for shotshells in the United States. It is larger than the common boxer-type primer used for centerfire rifle and handgun ammunition. *See* Figure 18-8.

Sporting ammunition primers contain carefully engineered mixtures of chemical ingredients. They are designed to explode and produce the heat, gas, and hot particles necessary to ignite propellant powders in sporting ammunition when the firing pin of the firearm strikes them.

Primers may explode if subjected to mishandling. Explosions can be caused by friction and by percussion, such as hammering, pounding, dropping, or bullet impact. Heating by fire, static electricity, sparks, and hot ashes may also cause primers to explode.

Properties of particular importance to the reloader are discussed below:

- If primers, loose or in bulk, have contact with each other, one exploding primer can cause a violent simultaneous explosion of all primers nearby. This could cause all of the primers to explode in one violent blast.
- Primers may "dust." Small particles of priming compound may separate from the primers in the form of dust, especially when they are subjected to shaking or jolting. Accumulation of this dust in primer feed tubes, loading machines, and loading areas is extremely hazardous, since it can cause explosions or fires.
- Primers exposed to water or any organic solvent, such as paint thinner, gasoline, kerosene, oil, grease, etc., may deteriorate, resulting in misfires or poor ignition.
- Modern sporting-ammunition primers will not absorb moisture under normal or even severe conditions of atmospheric humidity. Therefore, airtight containers offer no real advantage. The factory containers in which they are packaged need only normal conditions for storage. However, these containers should be kept dry and not exposed to high temperatures. If exposed to wet conditions or high temperatures, they may deteriorate, causing misfires or poor ignition of the propellant powder.

Handling Primers

Primers do explode. This is the purpose for which they have been designed. They demand the respect and careful handling due any device containing explosives.

Primers should never be handled, used, or stored in bulk, since primers in bulk can explode simultaneously.

The manufacturers of primers do not recommend using primer feeds for reloading shot without protection from possible explosion. Placing primers in tubes or columns, or using other bulk systems in which the explosion of one primer may cause the explosion of all primers, is a potentially hazardous condition. Manufacturers of primer handling systems are responsible for providing safety and protective features for their equipment. It is best to handle primers individually unless adequate safeguards are provided and used.

Be careful when handloading to avoid rough handling and undue force where a primer is involved, since the primer may fire. Any malfunction of equipment must be cleared with extreme caution. Avoid decapping shells or cases containing live primers.

When handling primers or when handloading, be careful to avoid buildup of static electricity. Loading equipment should be electrically grounded.

All loading equipment and adjacent areas must be kept clean and free of primer dust and powder accumulations. Work areas and loading equipment must be wiped clean with a damp cloth or sponge, which should be thoroughly rinsed after each use. Fired primers, primer cups, anvils, or other bits of hard, abrasive material are a hazard during loading operations, since contact with them may cause primers to fire.

Spilled primers should be picked up immediately, since they can explode if stepped on.

An absolute minimum of primers should be kept at the loading operation. Only one packing tray at a time should be removed from the primer storage.

When a priming operation is completed, any remaining primers should be returned to the package in which they were originally contained. These packages have a specific alloy designed to protect primers during shipment.

Primers should not be accessible to children, pets, or persons not recognizing them as potentially hazardous.

Never have an open flame, source of sparks, or hot particles in the vicinity of primers or any ammunition loading operation.

Do not smoke when handling primers.

You must wear safety glasses when performing any handloading operations. Additional protection such as face shields or machine guards are strongly recommended.

STORING PRIMERS

Storage cabinets containing only primers are recommended. These cabinets should be constructed of lumber at least 1" thick to delay or minimize the transmission of heat in the event of fire.

Keep your storage and working areas clean. Make sure the surrounding area is free of trash or other readily combustible materials.

Be sure the storage area is away from any source of excessive heat and is isolated from open flame, furnaces, water heaters, etc. Do not store primers where they will be exposed to direct sunlight. Avoid storage in areas where mechanical or electrical equipment is in operation.

Do not store primers in the same area with solvents, flammable gases, or highly combustible materials.

Store primers only in their original factory containers. Do not transfer the primers from this approved container into one which is not approved. The use of glass bottles, fruit jars, plastic or metal containers, or other bulk containers for primer storage is extremely hazardous.

Do not smoke in areas where primers are stored. Place "No Smoking" signs in these areas.

Do not store primers in any area where they might be exposed to gunfire, bullet impact, or ricochets.

Do not store primers with propellant powders or any other highly combustible materials.

Observe all regulations regarding quantity and methods of storing primers.

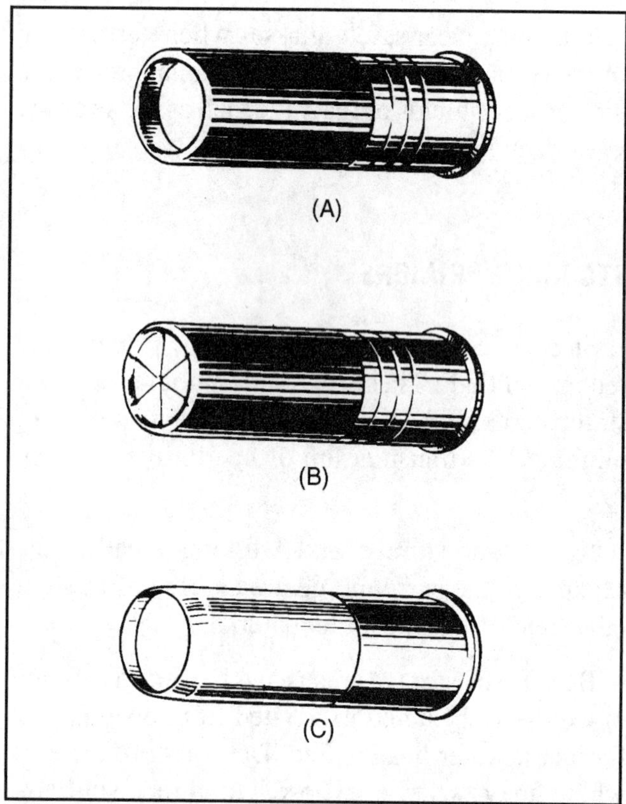

Figure 18-9: Three basic types of shotshell crimps used in the United States and abroad: (A) rolled crimp, (B) star crimp, and (C) cone crimp.

SHOTSHELL CASES

Shotshells have been made from a variety of materials since their introduction over 100 years ago. Brass shotshell cases were popular during the first 75 years of the shotshell's existence — especially for military and law enforcement use — since they could be reloaded an almost endless number of times. Furthermore, the less expensive rifle primers are used in brass cases rather than the battery-cup shotshell primers. However, American-made brass shotshells have not been on the market for at least 20 years, and all have now become collector's items, demanding prices starting at $1.00 per case. There are, however, some imported brass shotshells available from suppliers, but most (if not all) of these require the use of Berdan primers, which require special tools to remove. *See* Chapter 21 for more information on loading brass shotshells.

The most popular type of shotshell used in this country for the first half of this century was the paper case with a brass base. A *rolled crimp,* shown in Figure 18-9(A), was used until the 1950s. A rolled crimp consisted of a thin paper or cardboard over-shot disc placed over the shot charge; the end of the shotshell case was then rolled over to hold it in place.

Today, the *star crimp,* shown in Figure 18-9(B), is by far the most popular and widely used shotshell crimp except for slug and certain specialty loads. It lends an attractive appearance to a shotshell and is also easier to reload than the rolled crimp. About the same time as the star crimp was introduced, plastic shotshell cases were also introduced. Plastic cases remain the most popular at the present time.

Sometime between the rolled crimp and the star crimp, the now defunct Alcan company introduced a zinc shotgun shell case. These cases were die cast by Alcan and used a cone crimp, shown in Figure 18-9(C). The cone crimp consists of a thin cardboard disc placed over the shotshell with the end of the case tube slightly coned over to hold the over-shot wad in place. They did not prove to be very satisfactory. If dropped, they easily bent out of shape and would then jam the action.

SHOTSHELL WADS

Traditionally, shotshell wads have been made from felt, cork, cardboard, and more recently, plastic. When separate wads are used, the first wad, placed over the powder, is appropriately called the over-the-powder wad or nitro wad. They are made from cardboard or from plastic. These wads must never be lubricated, since the lubrication would deteriorate the powder charge. They must, however, form a perfect seal so that the wad seals in all the powder gases, forming a sealed gas chamber.

Figure 18-10: The plastic combination wad is now the most popular when large numbers of shells are to be loaded.

Most of the powder wads are shaped like a cup with its skirt or flange cupped downward over the powder charge. When the shell is fired, the resulting gas pressure spreads the skirt and seals the cup wad against the gun barrel. Consequently, the powder gases are completely imprisoned, keeping them from rushing into the shot column.

Next to the cup is the base wad, which functions similar to the over-the-powder wad. The upper-cupped base wad effectively seals off the powder gases from the base of the shell. No gases should be able to work into, or beyond, the layers of the base wad to cause head expansion or swelling.

The use of felt wads in shotloads provide a cushion platform for the shot pellets to impact against during the initial firing. This force is called setback and is one of the many factors that must be contained to create a good shot pattern at long ranges.

These days, most reloaded shotshells use a single plastic wad (sometimes called a power piston) that incorporates all the necessary wads into a single unit, plus the addition of a collar that protects the shot column. *See* Figure 18-10. This type of combination wad saves the reloader time and it serves the purpose of multiple wads and is good for average loads. However, the collapsible part of this wad is outside of the shot cup and really does not cushion the shot. Rather, it allows the wad to be used in a number of different loadings; that is, crushing the wad down farther in the case will enable more shot to be loaded. This type of wad is a good choice for high-speed loading machines producing many hundreds of loads per hour. The basic reasoning for the collapsible portion of the wad is to provide a decent basis for the crimp no matter what has been done to the load. How it shoots is considered secondary.

The individual reloader is not faced with the problem of having to produce hundreds of rounds per hour. Consequently, the reloader can go for quality in his or her loads.

Felt wads provide the best basis found to date for shot pellets to rest upon during the firing process. Pellets cannot penetrate the material nor can they stick into the felt. Release is immediate and clean. Consequently, it is recommended that felt wads be used in all quality loads. For speed, however, in progressive loading machines, the one-piece plastic wad is the only way to go.

LEAD AND STEEL SHOT

Lead and steel shot form the projectiles of the shotshell. Please read Chapter 26 in this book for a description of the various types of shot. Soft and hardened lead buckshot are also available. Solid shotgun slugs are also used as described in Chapter 22. The choice of lead shot and projectiles should always be given careful consideration if top-quality loads are desired.

POWDERS FOR SHOTSHELL RELOADING

Smokeless powders, or propellants, are essentially mixtures of chemicals designed to burn under controlled conditions at the proper rate to propel a projectile from a gun.

Smokeless powders are made in three forms and are available in various sizes of containers, as shown in the following table for Hercules smokeless powders:

POWDER	1-LB CANISTER	4-LB CANISTER	5-LB CANISTER	8-LB KEG	15-LB KEG
Bullseye	X	X	—	X	X
Red Dot	X	X	—	X	X
Green Dot	X	X	—	X	X
Unique	X	X	—	X	X
Herco	X	X	—	X	X
Blue Dot	X	—	X	—	—
2400	X	X	—	X	X
Reloader 7	X	—	—	—	—

The basic three forms of smokeless powder are:

- Thin, circular flakes or wafers.
- Small cylinders.
- Small spheres.

Single-base smokeless powders derive their main source of energy from nitrocellulose. The energy released from double-base smokeless powders is derived from both nitrocellulose and nitroglycerin.

All smokeless powders are extremely flammable; they are designed to burn rapidly and vigorously when ignited.

Oxygen from the air is not necessary for the combustion of smokeless powders since they contain sufficient built-in oxygen to burn completely, even in an enclosed space such as the chamber of a firearm.

In effect, ignition occurs when the powder granules are heated above their ignition temperature. This can occur by exposing powder to the following:

- A flame such as a match or primer flash.
- An electrical spark or the sparks from welding, grinding, etc.

Figure 18-11: Hercules Red Dot (left) is the preferred powder for light-to-medium shotshell loads. It is specifically designed for 12-gauge target loads. While Hercules Bullseye (right) was designed for pistol and revolver cartridges, it can also be used for 12-gauge, 1-oz. target loads.

- Heat from an electric hot plate or a fire directed against or near a closed container, even if the powder itself is not exposed to the flame.

When smokeless powders like the ones shown in Figure 18-11 burn, they form a great deal of gas. If the powder is confined, this gas will create pressure in the surrounding structure. The rate of gas generation is such, however, that the pressure can be kept at a low level if sufficient space is available or if the gas can escape.

In this respect, smokeless powder differs from blasting agents or high explosives such as dynamite or blasting gelatin, although smokeless powder may contain chemical ingredients common to some of these products. High explosives such as dynamite are made to detonate; that is, to change from solid state to gaseous state with evolution of intense heat at such a rapid rate that shock waves are produced.

Smokeless powder differs considerably in its burning characteristics from common blackpowder. Blackpowder burns essentially at the same rate out in the open (unconfined) as when confined.

When ignited in an unconfined state, smokeless powder burns inefficiently, with an orange flame. It produces a considerable amount of light-brown, noxious-smelling smoke. It leaves a residue of ash and partially burned powder. The flame is hot enough to cause severe burns.

The opposite is true when it burns under pressure, as in a cartridge fired in a gun. Then it produces very little smoke, a small glow, and leaves little or no residue. The burning rate of smokeless powder increases with increased pressure.

If burning smokeless powder is confined, gas pressure will rise and may eventually cause the container to burst. Under such circumstances, the bursting of a strong container is similar to an explosion.

RELOADING TOOLS AND PROCEDURES

Shotshell reloading tools are available in a variety of types from simple (and slow) hand reloading tools to highly sophisticated, progressive reloading machines that are capable of turning out hundreds of rounds per hour. Study the various descriptions of shotshell reloading tools in Chapter 6 and then select the type that you feel will suit your needs the best. Also request catalogs from the various manufacturers for a more-detailed description of their products, including retail prices.

The simplest shotshell reloading tool is one manufactured by Lee Manufacturing Company. It is fine for the reloader who loads only a few boxes of shells per year; it is also very inexpensive.

For those who do a great deal of reloading, a progressive reloading press is better — and still

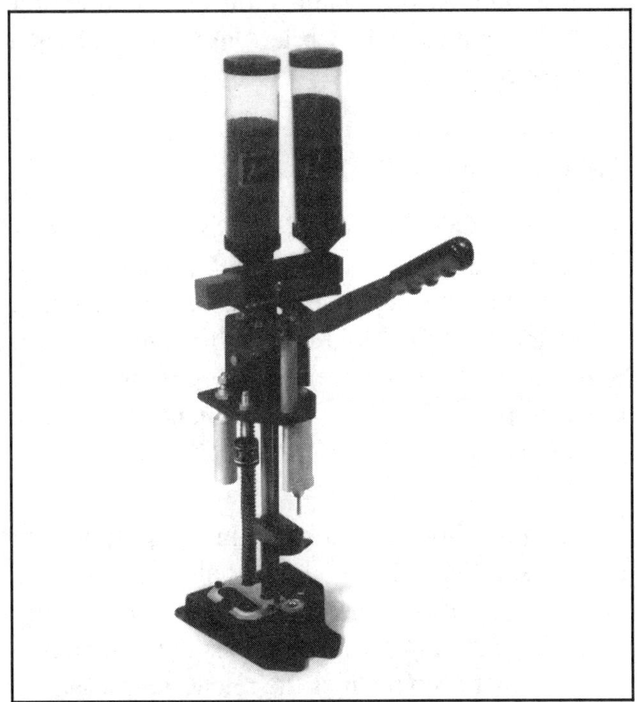

Figure 18-12: Typical shotshell loading press with integral dies, powder- and shot-charge bar, powder and shot containers.

relatively inexpensive. A typical tool is shown in Figure 18-12. The two plastic containers mounted on top of the tool are for holding powder and shot; powder is in one container and shot is in the other. Pushing the charge bar one way first drops a measured powder charge into the base of the shotshell. Once the wad is in place, pushing the bar in the opposite direction releases a measured charge of shot. Different sizes of interchangeable charge bars are available for different loads.

Reloading presses, like the one shown in Figure 18-12, have four or five stations that usually perform the following functions:

- Decapping and sizing station
- Recapping or priming station
- Wad-starting station
- Crimp-starting station
- Crimping and sizing station

Powder and shot are also dropped at one or two of these stations, depending upon the manufacturer of the reloading tool. A brief description of each function follows.

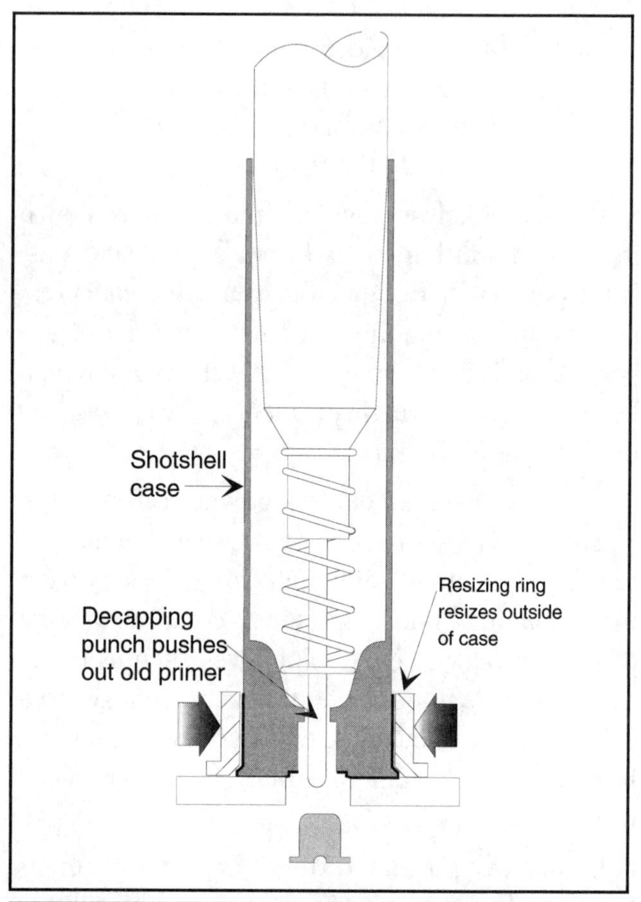

Figure 18-13: Station No. 1 on shotshell reloading presses decaps the old primer. On many presses, the hull is also resized in this position.

RESIZE AND DEPRIME

An empty shotshell case (hull) is placed in position 1, making sure the decapping punch is in the case mouth and the shell is reasonably centered under the size die. Hold the shell in this position with one hand while lowering the operating handle to the stop position with the other hand. Make sure the operating handle is not stopped by some obstacle during this operation.

On most shotshell presses, this first operation resizes and deprimes the hull as shown in Figure 18-13. Some presses, however, reserve the resizing until the last step. Always check the instruction material that accompanies the reloading press.

When the handle is raised, the hull (resized and deprimed) is removed from station No. 1 and is ready for the next operation.

PRIMING AND DROPPING POWDER

On some presses, it is necessary to place a new primer, striking end down, in the primer slot in station No. 2 as shown in Figure 18-14. Other tools, with an automatic primer feed, require the manipulation of a lever or button to place the primer in position. Place the hull in the circular recess at station No. 2, lined up directly over the primer. The downward pressure of the tool handle seats the new primer in the case; the pressure should be slight — just enough to fully seat the new primer; no more and no less.

On some brands of presses, the powder charge is dropped at station No. 2, after the primer is seated; that is, once the primer is fully seated, with the drop tube inside of the case, the charge bar is moved to

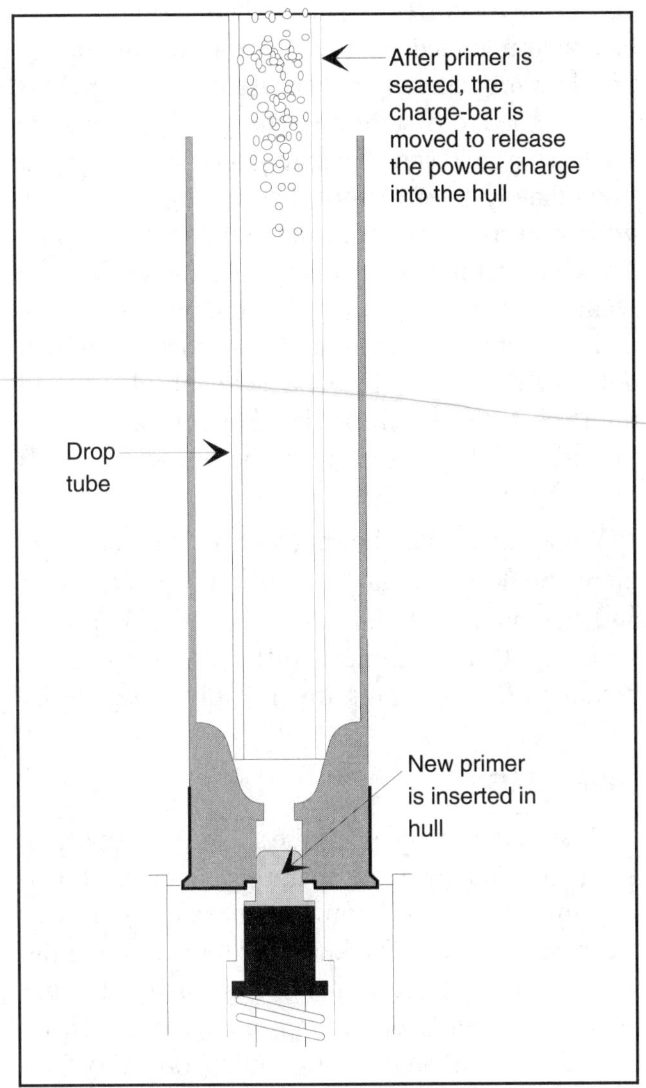

Figure 18-14: Station No. 2 on shotshell reloading presses primes the shotshell hull. On some presses, the powder charge is also dropped at this location.

drop the predetermined amount of powder into the primed hull. Most presses, however, reserve this operation for station No. 3. In either case, the primer must be installed first, and regardless of the station number, the next operation will be to drop the powder charge. Lower the operating handle to the full stop. While the handle is down, push the charge bar in the correct position to drop powder. The powder will then be released from the charge-bar bushing and fall through the drop tube into the primed shotshell hull.

SEATING WAD AND DROPPING SHOT

Raise the handle and place the wad(s) over the wad-seating stem/drop tube. Lower the handle, making sure the wad enters the wad guide. If the press is adjusted correctly, the handle will reach the full stop when the wad is seated. Lowering or raising the seating stem will increase or decrease wad seating depth and pressure. Most compression-formed wads for shotshells have the same wad column depth, so little adjustment is needed when changing wads. However, the seating depth and the seating pressure are two extremely important aspects to get reloads with consistent power and patterns. Some shotshell reloading presses, in fact, have a ting-gauge scale to indicate the amount of wad-seating pressure. Details of wad types and

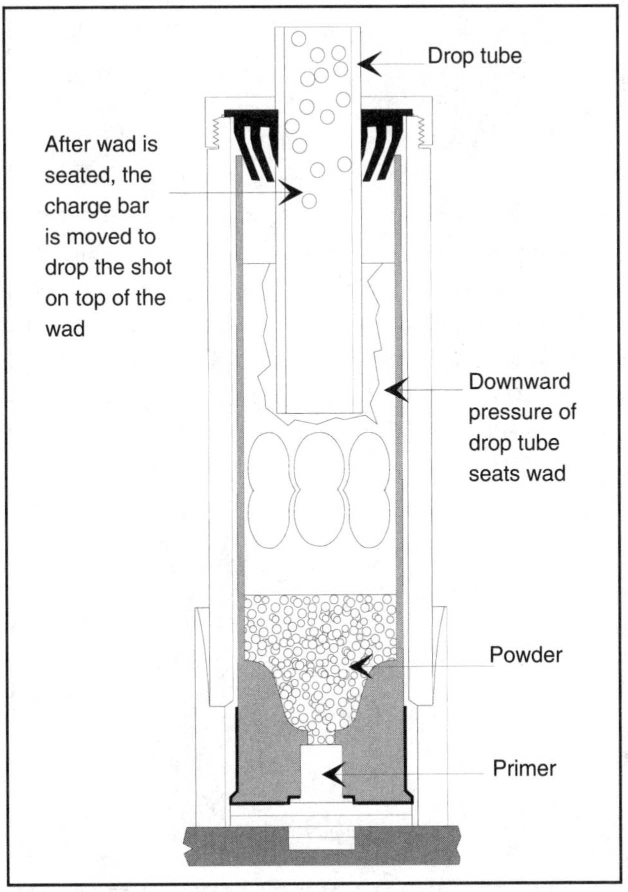

Figure 18-15: Station No. 3 is where the wad is seated and the shot charge dropped into the hull. Although station numbers vary with different brands of tools, this is the next operation after charging the hull with powder.

exact methods of seating are given in the chapters to follow on reloading various types of shotshells.

Now, before raising the operating handle, push the charge bar back in the opposite direction from throwing the powder. This releases the predetermined amount of shot from the bushing through the drop tube and into the shell which has the wad already in place.

Sometimes the shot will hang-up, preventing a full charge from being released. Consequently, it is good practice to visually inspect each case after the shot charge has been dropped. If the charge looks less than normal, dump the shot in the hull back into the storage tube on top of the press and put the case aside for correcting later when the entire batch has been reloaded. The reason for not solving the problem immediately is because most charge bars are designed to first throw a charge of powder, and then a charge of shot. To manipulate the charge bar immediately after the shot charge has been thrown, will throw a charge of powder into the shot column. Thus, correcting a short charge of shot will have to wait, or else use a pan to catch the powder charge and then the next motion of the charge bar will deliver shot. Most reloaders, however, like to wait until the entire batch of shotshells have been reloaded, and then take care of the one or two duds that may exist.

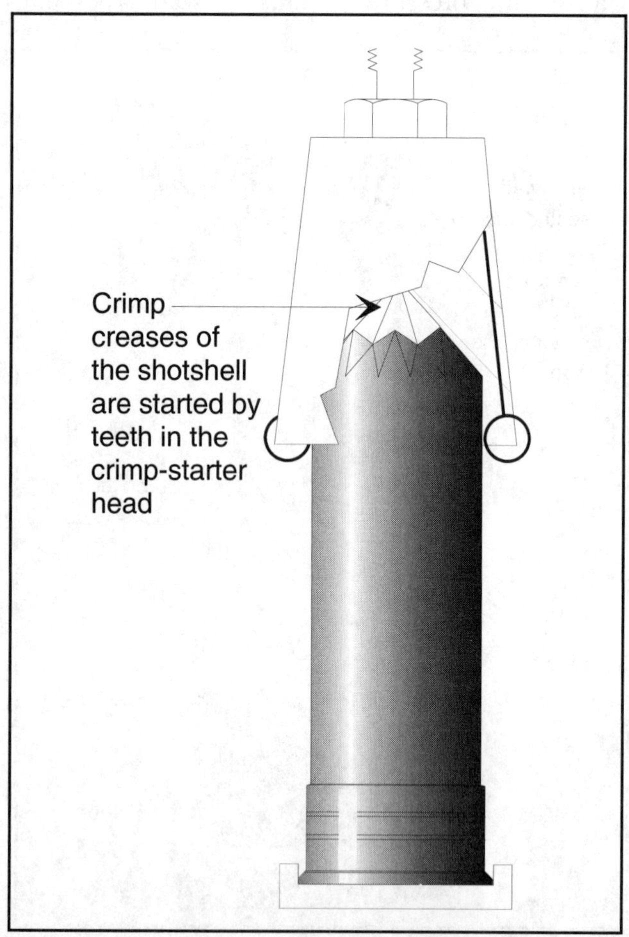

Figure 18-16: Station No. 4 is usually where the crimp is started. Always check the cases to make sure the proper crimp starter is being used.

When examining the shot dropped into the case, there should be about $\frac{1}{2}''$–$\frac{9}{16}''$ between the shot and the mouth of the case to allow for proper crimping. If measurements differ, the wrong combination of components are probably being used.

CRIMPING

To start the crimp, place the shot in the appropriate station and lower the operating handle as shown in Figure 18-16. The crimp starter easily aligns with the existing crimp. The knobs on the outside of the starter crimp die are to help in manually aligning the crimp when folded crimps are reloaded. However, depending on the brand and style of shotshell hull, the number or folds will vary. Some cases require eight fold; others require only six. Be sure that the crimp starter is equipped with the appropriate starting head for the case being loaded.

When loading older shotshell hulls or for loading some slugs in shotshells, a roll crimp is required and an altogether different procedure is required.

CAUTION

Do not try to load roll-type crimps in presses designed for the conventional star crimp. While not necessarily dangerous, the results will be poor. See Chapter 22 for details on crimping roll-type crimps.

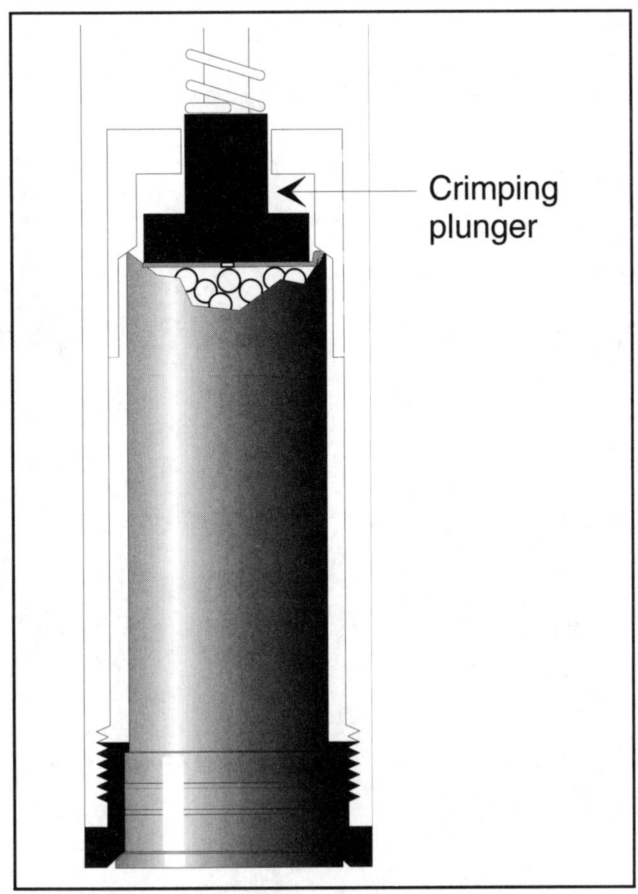

Figure 18-17: Make sure the operating handle is firmly depressed during the final crimping stage to properly seal and crimp the shotshell hull.

Crimping roll-type shells are discussed in Chapter 19.

Once the operating lever has been moved to the stop position in the crimp-starter station, move the hull to the next position. This next position final crimps the shell, and in some reloading presses, performs the resizing of the outer case.

During final crimping, make sure the operating handle is firmly depressed to obtain a good solid crimp on the shell as shown in Figure 18-17. To do otherwise means losing shot out the case mouth, and causing erratic shot patterns.

When completed, inspect each loaded shotshell to make certain the crimp is properly folded and gives a good, professional appearance. Any shells that fall short of this goal should be discarded. An improperly folded and sealed crimp not only looks bad, but feeding problems will often develop in repeating and semiautomatic shotguns. Furthermore, some shot frequently spills out to lodge in the action to cause jams and misfires.

The loading data contained in the next few chapters are designed for several practical uses from hunting to target. The reloader is cautioned against changing, or altering, the listed components and to use only the brands of cases listed. Shotshell ballistics and pressures can change drastically if cases, primers, wads, etc., are altered or substituted for those listed.

Chapter 19

Sporting Clays, Trap and Skeet Loads

The shotshell data in this chapter lists the cases and exact components used in each load. All loads have been carefully tested by powder manufacturers and verified by other shooters and technicians. The reloader is cautioned against altering, or substituting the components shown.

Shotshells classified as "target" loads fall into four basic categories:

- Trap
- Skeet
- Sporting Clays
- Live Bird

Trap shooting has been around for a long time. In fact, the sport goes back to at least 1831 when live pigeons were released from traps in Cincinnati, Ohio. Thus, the name "trap shooting." Passenger pigeons were used mostly, but quail were substituted from time to time. When the great slaughter of passenger pigeons got underway (about 1850), and the public outcry against shooting live pigeons became more pronounced, a substitute target was produced — the first being the glass ball, followed by many other types of targets until the clay target ("clay pigeon") eventually became standard.

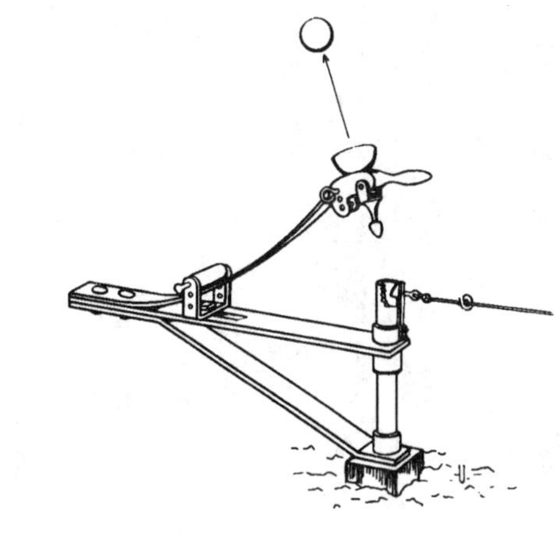

Figure 19-1: This ball-throwing device was one of the first devised to substitute glass balls for live birds.

Figure 19-1 shows an early ball-throwing device. It was made with flat leaf springs to which a holding cup and cocking handle were attached. Manual pressure was applied downward to seat the cocking plunger which was held in place by a manually-operated sear. After a glass ball was placed in the holding cup, the target could be released by pulling on the string or wire attached to the sear or locking catch. Spring pressure then caused the glass ball to be thrown up and forward.

For sporting clays enthusiasts, .410 and 28-gauge target loads are the most popular. Shells should be loaded with target-grade No. 8 shot for added long-range pellet energy and enhanced pattern performance. In 28-gauge, this means $\frac{3}{4}$ ounce shot with a muzzle velocity of about 1200 fps.

12 GAUGE TARGET — FEDERAL 2¾-INCH PAPER "CHAMPION"

PRIMER		IMR POWDER		WAD COLUMN		LEAD SHOT (Oz.)	MUZZLE VELOCITY	CHAMBER PRESSURE
MFR.	No.	DESIGNATION	GRAINS	MFG.	DESIGNATION			
Federal	209	"HI-SKOR" 700-X	17.5	Fed.	12S0	1	1145	7700
Federal	209	"HI-SKOR" 700-X	17.0	Win.	WAA12	1	1145	6800
Federal	209	"HI-SKOR" 700-X	18.5	Fed.	12S0	1	1200	8500
Federal	209	"HI-SKOR" 700-X	18.0	Win.	WAA12	1	1190	7400
Remington	209P	"HI-SKOR" 700-X	16.0	Fed.	12S3	1	1150	6600
Remington	209P	"HI-SKOR" 700-X	16.0	Activ	L29	1	1155	7800
Remington	209P	"HI-SKOR" 700-X	16.0	Win.	WAA12	1	1150	5800
Remington	209P	"HI-SKOR" 700-X	17.5	Fed.	12S3	1	1205	7900
Remington	209P	"HI-SKOR" 700-X	17.0	Activ	L29	1	1200	8500
Remington	209P	"HI-SKOR" 700-X	17.0	Win.	WAA12	1	1215	6900
Remington	209P	"HI-SKOR" 700-X	17.0	WTW.	WindJammer	1	1205	7000
Winchester	209	PB	22.0	Fed.	12S3	1	1150	5100
Winchester	209	PB	23.0	Rem.	R12L	1	1150	5000
Winchester	209	PB	23.5	Fed.	12S3	1	1206	5500
Winchester	209	PB	24.5	Rem.	R12L	1	1205	5400
Federal	209	SR 7625	24.5	Fed.	12S3	1	1150	4700
Federal	209	SR 7625	26.0	Rem.	R12L	1	1145	4200
Federal	209	SR 7625	25.5	Fed.	12S3	1	1200	5100
Federal	209	SR 7625	27.0	Rem.	R12L	1	1215	4700
Winchester	209	SR 7625	25.0	Fed.	12S3	1	1150	4400
Winchester	209	SR 7625	26.5	Rem.	R12L	1	1160	4200
Winchester	209	SR 7625	26.0	Fed.	12S3	1	1190	4800
Winchester	209	SR 7625	27.5	Rem.	R12L	1	1215	4700

12 GAUGE TARGET — FEDERAL 2¾-INCH PLASTIC "GOLD MEDAL"

PRIMER		IMR POWDER		WAD COLUMN		LEAD SHOT (Oz.)	MUZZLE VELOCITY	CHAMBER PRESSURE
MFR.	No.	DESIGNATION	GRAINS	MFG.	DESIGNATION			
Federal	209	"HI-SKOR" 700-X	17.0	Fed	12S0	1	1150	7100
Federal	209	"HI-SKOR" 700-X	17.0	Win.	WAA12	1	1150	6900
Federal	209	"HI-SKOR" 700-X	18.0	Fed.	12S0	1	1185	7800
Federal	209	"HI-SKOR" 700-X	18.0	Win.	WAA12M	1	1200	7600
Winchester	209	"HI-SKOR" 700-X	17.0	Fed.	12S0	1	1135	7000
Winchester	209	"HI-SKOR" 700-X	17.5	Win.	WAA12	1	1145	6200
Winchester	209	"HI-SKOR" 700-X	18.0	Fed.	12S0	1	1185	7700
Winchester	209	"HI-SKOR" 700-X	18.5	Win.	WAA12	1	1200	6900
Federal	209	PB	21.5	Fed.	12S3	1	1150	5400
Federal	209	PB	22.5	Rem.	R12L'	1	1150	5300
Winchester	209	PB	21.5	Fed.	12S3	1	1145	5200
Winchester	209	PB	22.5	Rem.	R12	1	1135	5100
Federal	209	PB	22.5	Fed.	12S3	1	1210	6000
Federal	209	PB	23.5	Rem.	R12L	1	1200	5600
Winchester	209	PB	22.5	Fed.	12S3	1	1190	5600
Winchester	209	PB	23.5	Rem.	R12L	1	1200	5600
Federal	209	SR 7625	24.5	Fed.	12S3	1	1140	5100
Federal	209	SR 7625	25.5	Rem.	R12L	1	1150	4900
CCI	209M	SR 7625	24.5	Fed.	12S3	1	1145	5000
CCI	209M	SR 7625	25.0	Rem.	R12L	1	1160	5000
Federal	209	SR 7625	26.0	Fed.	12S3	1	1205	5300
Federal	209	SR 7625	27.0	Rem.	R12L	1	1190	4900
CCI	209M	SR 7625	26.0	Fed.	12S3	1	1210	5400
CCI	209M	SR 7625	27.0	Rem.	R12L	1	1210	5000

12 GAUGE TARGET — WINCHESTER 2¾-INCH COMPRESSION-FORMED "DOUBLE A," "UPLAND" AND "SUPER-X"

PRIMER		IMR POWDER		WAD COLUMN		LEAD SHOT (Oz.)	MUZZLE VELOCITY	CHAMBER PRESSURE
MFR.	No.	DESIGNATION	GRAINS	MFG.	DESIGNATION			
Winchester	209	"HI-SKOR" 700-X	16.5	Win.	WAA12	1	1145	7700
Winchester	209	"HI-SK0R" 700-X	16.5	Fed.	12S0	1	1150	9000
Winchester	209	"HI-SKOR" 700-X	17.5	Win.	WAA12	1	1200	8500
Winchester	209	"HI-SKOR" 700-X	17.0	Fed.	12S0	1	1190	9700
Federal	209	"HI-SKOR" 700-X	16.0	Win.	WAA12FI	1	1155	8300

12 GAUGE TARGET — WINCHESTER 2¾-INCH COMPRESSION-FORMED "DOUBLE A," "UPLAND" AND "SUPER-X" (Cont.)

PRIMER		IMR POWDER		WAD COLUMN		LEAD SHOT (Oz.)	MUZZLE VELOCITY	CHAMBER PRESSURE
MFR.	No.	DESIGNATION	GRAINS	MFG.	DESIGNATION			
Federal	209	"HI-SKOR" 700-X	16.5	Fed.	12S0	1	1145	9300
Federal	209	"HI-SKOR" 700-X	17.0	Win.	WAA12	1	1210	9000
Federal	209	"HI-SKOR" 700-X	17.5	Fed.	12S0	1	1195	10100
Winchester	209	PB	21.5	Win.	WAA12	1	1140	5000
Federal	209	PB	20.5	Win.	WAA12	1	1160	6400
Winchester	209	PB	23.0	Win.	WAA12	1	1195	5500
Federal	209	PB	22.0	Win.	WAA12	1	1210	6700
Winchester	209	SR 7625	24.0	Win.	WAA12	1	1145	5000
Winchester	209	SR 7625	24.5	Rem.	RXPI2	1	1160	5100
Federal	209	SR 7625	21.5	Win.	WAA12	1	1140	6300
Federal	209	SR 7625	24.0	Rem.	RXP12	1	1140	4900
Winchester	209	SR 7625	26.0	Win.	WAA12	1	1210	5400
Winchester	209	SR 7625	26.0	Rem.	RXP12	1	1205	5400
Federal	209	SR 7625	23.0	Win.	WAA12	1	1205	7000

12 GAUGE TARGET — ACTIV 2¾-INCH TARGET

PRIMER		IMR POWDER		WAD COLUMN		LEAD SHOT (Oz.)	MUZZLE VELOCITY	CHAMBER PRESSURE
MFR.	No.	DESIGNATION	GRAINS	MFG.	DESIGNATION			
Federal	209	"HI-SKOR" 700-X	18.0	Activ	L-29	1	1155	6200
Remington	209P	"HI-SKOR" 700-X	17.0	Activ	L-29	1	1150	7100
Winchester	209	"HI-SKOR" 700-X	18.0	Activ	L-29	1	1155	6200
Federal	209	"HI-SKOR" 700-X	19.0	Activ	L-29	1	1205	7000
Remington	209P	"HI-SKOR" 700-X	18.0	Activ	L-29	1	1205	8000
Winchester	209	"HI-SKOR" 700-X	19.0	Activ	L-29	1	1200	6800
Federal	209	PB	23.0	Activ	T-28	1	1160	5400
Remington	209P	PB	22.0	Activ	T-28	1	1160	5800
Winchester	209	PB	23.5	Activ	T-28	1	1160	5100
Federal	209	PB	23.5	Activ	T-28	1	1200	6100
Remington	209P	PB	23.0	Activ	T-28	1	1215	6200
Winchester	209	PB	24.0	Activ	T-28	1	1195	5900
Federal	209	SR 7625	26.5	Activ	T-28	1	1160	4900
Remington	209P	SR 7625	26.5	Activ	T-28	1	1145	4800

12 GAUGE TARGET — PETERS 2¾-INCH TARGET LOAD

PRIMER		IMR POWDER		WAD COLUMN		LEAD SHOT (Oz.)	MUZZLE VELOCITY	CHAMBER PRESSURE
MFR.	No.	DESIGNATION	GRAINS	MFG.	DESIGNATION			
Remington	209P	"HI-SKOR" 700-X	16.0	Rem.	RXP12	1⅛	1140	7700
Remington	209P	"HI-SKOR" 700-X	16.5	Rem.	FIG 8	1⅛	1155	8000
Remington	209P	"HI-SXOR" 700-X	17.0	Activ	L-33	1⅛	1150	9200
Remington	209P	"HI-SKOR" 700-X	17.0	Lage	Uniwad	1⅛	1150	8200
Remington	209P	"HI-SKOR" 700-X	16.0	Pacific	Versalite	1⅛	1150	7800
Remington	209P	"HI-SKOR" 700-X	16.0	Win.	WAA12	1⅛	1145	8400
Remington	209P	"HI-SKOR" 700-X	17.5	Rem.	RXP12	1⅛	1200	8800
Remington	209P	"HI-SKOR" 700-X	17.5	Rem.	FIG 8	1⅛	1195	8700
Remington	209P	"HI-SKOR" 700-X	18.0	Activ	L-33	1⅛	1200	10200
Remington	209P	"HI-SKOR" 700-X	18.0	Lage	Uniwad	1⅛	1200	8700
Remington	209P	"HI-SKOR" 700-X	17.5	Pacific	Versalite	1⅛	1210	9000
Remington	209P	"HI-SKOR" 700-X	17.0	Win.	WAA12	1⅛	1205	10600
Remington	209P	"HI-SKOR" 700-X	17.0	WTW.	WindJammer	1⅛	1190	8300
Federal	209	"HI SKOR" 700-X	17.0	Rem.	RXP12	1⅛	1135	9200
Federal	209	"HI-SKOR" 700-X	17.5	Lage	Uniwad	1⅛	1145	9300
Federal	209	"HI-SKOR" 700-X	17.0	Pacific	Versalite	1⅛	1145	9500
Federal	209	"HI-SKOR" 700-X	17.0	Win.	WAA12	1⅛	1150	9600
Federal	209	"HI-SKOR" 700-X	18.5	Rem.	RXP12	1⅛	1200	10500
Federal	209	"HI-SKOR" 700-X	19.0	Lage	Uniwad	1⅛	1210	10900
Federal	209	"HI-SKOR" 700-X	18.0	Pacific	Versalite	1⅛	1195	10800
CCI	209	"HI-SKOR" 700-X	17.5	Rem.	RXP12	1⅛	1155	9200
CCI	209	"HI-SKOR" 700-X	17.S	Lage	Uniwad	1⅛	1140	9100
CCI	209	"HI-SKOR" 700-X	17.5	Pacific	Versalite	1⅛	1150	8500
CCI	209	"HI-SKOR" 700-X	17.0	Win	WAA12	1⅛	1135	8400
CCI	209	"HI-SKOR" 700-X	18.5	Rem.	RXP12	1⅛	1195	9700
CCI	209	"HI-SKOR" 700-X	19.0	Lage	Uniwad	1⅛	1205	10200
CCI	209	"HI-SKOR" 700-X	18.5	Pacific	Versalite	1⅛	1205	9700
CCI	209	"HI-SKOR" 700-X	18.5	Win.	WAA12	1⅛	1200	10100
Winchester	209	"HI-SKOR" 700-X	17.5	Rem.	RXP12	1⅛	1145	8700
Winchester	209	"HI-SKOR" 700-X	18.0	Lage	Uniwad	1⅛	1155	9300
Winchester	209	"HI-SKOR" 700-X	17.5	Pacific	Versalite	1⅛	1160	9100
Winchester	209	"HI-SKOR" 700-X	17.0	Win.	WAA12	1⅛	1140	9100
Winchester	209	"HI-SKOR" 700-X	18.5	Rem.	RXP12	1⅛	1195	9900

12 GAUGE TARGET — PETERS 2¾-INCH TARGET LOAD (Cont.)

PRIMER		IMR POWDER		WAD COLUMN		LEAD SHOT (Oz.)	MUZZLE VELOCITY	CHAMBER PRESSURE
MFR.	No.	DESIGNATION	GRAINS	MFG.	DESIGNATION			
Winchester	209	"HI-SKOR" 700-X	19.0	Lage	Uniwad	1⅛	1205	10600
Winchester	209	"HI-SKOR" 700-X	18.5	Pacific	Versalite	1⅛	1205	10100
Winchester	209	"HI-SKOR" 700-X	18.5	Win.	WAA12	1⅛	1205	10200
Remington	209P	"HI-SKOR" 800-X	21.5	Rem.	RXP12	1⅛	1155	6700
Remington	209P	"HI-SKOR" 800-X	22.0	Rem.	FIG 8	1⅛	1145	7800
Remington	209P	"HI-SKOR" 800-X	22.5	Activ	T-32	1⅛	1150	7400
Remington	209P	"HI-SKOR" 800-X	21.0	Fed.	12S4	1⅛	1160	7400
Remington	209P	"HI-SKOR" 800-X	22.0	Lage	Uniwad	1⅛	1140	6200
Remington	209P	"HI-SKOR" 800-X	21.5	Pacific	Versalite	1⅛	1140	6700
Remington	209P	"HI-SKOR" 800-X	21.5	Win.	WAA12	1⅛	1160	6700
Remington	209P	"HI-SKOR" 800-X	21.0	WTW.	WindJammer	1⅛	1140	6300
Remington	209P	"HI-SKOR" 800-X	23.0	Rem.	RXP12	1⅛	1205	6900
Remington	209P	"HI-SKOR" 800-X	23.5	Rem.	FIG 8	1⅛	1200	8400
Remington	209P	"HI-SKOR" 800-X	23.5	Activ	T-32	1⅛	1200	7900
Remington	209P	"HI-SKOR" 800-X	22.5	Fed.	12S4	1⅛	1205	7700
Remington	209P	"HI-SKOR" 800-X	23.5	Lage	Uniwad	1⅛	1200	7100
Remington	209P	"HI-SKOR" 800-X	22.5	Pacific	Versalite	1⅛	1205	7100
Remington	209P	"HI-SKOR" 800-X	22.5	Win.	WAA12	1⅛	1205	7200
Remington	209P	"HI-SKOR" 800-X	23.5	WTW.	WindJammer	1⅛	1215	6900
CCI	209	PB	20.5	Rem.	R12H	1⅛	1145	7200
CCI	209	PB	20.0	Win.	WAA12	1⅛	1140	7800
CCI	209	PB	20.0	Fed.	12S4	1⅛	1155	8300
CCI	209	PB	20.5	Lage	Uniwad	1⅛	1145	7500
CCI	209	PB	20.5	Pacific	Versalite	1⅛	1135	6600
CCI	209	PB	22.0	Rem.	R12H	1⅛	1195	7700
CCI	209	PB	21.5	Win.	WAA12	1⅛	1195	8200
CCI	209	PB	21.5	Fed.	12S4	1⅛	1210	9400
CCI	209	PB	22.0	Lage	Uniwad	1⅛	1215	8700
CCI	209	PB	22.0	Pacific	Versalite	1⅛	1200	7300
Federal	209	PB	20.0	Rem.	R12H	1⅛	1135	7400
Federal	209	PB	20.0	Win.	WAA12	1⅛	1155	8500
Federal	209	PB	19.5	Fed.	12S4	1⅛	1150	8700
Federal	209	PB	20.0	Lage	Uniwad	1⅛	1135	7900

12 GAUGE TARGET — PETERS 2¾-INCH TARGET LOAD (Cont.)

PRIMER		IMR POWDER		WAD COLUMN		LEAD SHOT (Oz.)	MUZZLE VELOCITY	CHAMBER PRESSURE
MFR.	No.	DESIGNATION	GRAINS	MFG.	DESIGNATION			
Federal	209	PB	20.0	Pacific	Versalite	1⅛	1145	7400
Federal	209	PB	22.0	Rem.	R12H	1⅛	1200	8200
Federal	209	PB	21.5	Win.	WAA12	1⅛	1200	8900
Federal	209	PB	21.0	Fed.	12S4	1⅛	1200	9700
Federal	209	PB	21.5	Lage	Uniwad	1⅛	1205	9000
Federal	209	PB	21.5	Pacific	Versalite	1⅛	1205	8400
Winchester	209	PB	20.5	Rem.	R12H	1⅛	1140	7200
Winchester	209	PB	20.0	Win.	WAA12	1⅛	1140	7500
Winchester	209	PB	20.0	Fed.	12S4	1⅛	1150	8500
Winchester	209	PB	20.5	Lage	Uniwad	1⅛	1140	7600
Winchester	209	PB	20.5	Pacific	Versalite	1⅛	1135	6600
Winchester	209	PB	22.0	Rem.	R12H	1⅛	1195	7800
Winchester	209	PB	21.5	Win.	WAA12	1⅛	1195	8100
Winchester	209	PB	21.5	Fed.	12S4	1⅛	1205	9400
Winchester	209	PB	22.0	Lage	Uniwad	1⅛	1210	8500
Winchester	209	PB	22.0	Pacific	Versalite	1⅛	1210	7800
CCI	209	SR 7625	22.5	Rem.	RXP12	1⅛	1135	6500
CCI	209	SR 7625	22.5	Win.	WAA12	1⅛	1150	6700
CCI	209	SR 7625	21.5	Fed.	12S4	1⅛	1145	7300
CCI	209	SR 7625	22.5	Lage	Uniwad	1⅛	1160	6900
CCI	209	SR 7625	22.5	Pacific	Versalite	1⅛	1140	6200
CCI	209	SR 7625	23.5	Rem.	RXP128	1⅛	1210	7800
CCI	209	SR 7625	24.0	Win.	WAA12	1⅛	1205	7400
CCI	209	SR 7625	23.0	Fed.	12S4	1⅛	1210	8400
CCI	209	SR 7625	24.0	Lage	Uniwad	1⅛	1205	7500
CCI	209	SR 7625	23.5	Pacific	Versalite	1⅛	1215	7400
Federal	209	SR 7625	22.5	Rem.	RXP12	1⅛	1145	6900
Federal	209	SR 7625	22.0	Win.	WAA12	1⅛	1145	7300
Federal	209	SR 7625	21.0	Fed.	12S4	1⅛	1150	7800
Federal	209	SR 7625	22.0	Lage	Uniwad	1⅛	1165	7500
Federal	209	SR 7625	22.0	Pacific	Versalite	1⅛	1160	6900
Federal	209	SR 7625	23.5	Rem.	RXP12	1⅛	1200	8000
Federal	209	SR 7625	23.5	Win.	WAA12	1⅛	1205	8000

12 GAUGE TARGET — PETERS 2¾-INCH TARGET LOAD (Cont.)

PRIMER		IMR POWDER		WAD COLUMN		LEAD SHOT (Oz.)	MUZZLE VELOCITY	CHAMBER PRESSURE
MFR.	No.	DESIGNATION	GRAINS	MFG.	DESIGNATION			
Federal	209	SR 7625	22.5	Fed.	12S4	1⅛	1205	8700
Federal	209	SR 7625	23.5	Lage	Uniwad	1⅛	1210	7900
Federal	209	SR 7625	23.0	Pacific	Versalite	1⅛	1205	7600
Winchester	209	SR 7625	23.0	Rem.	RXP12	1⅛	1150	6600
Winchester	209	SR 7625	23.0	Win.	WAA12	1⅛	1145	6500
Winchester	209	SR 7625	21.5	Fed.	12S4	1⅛	1140	7100
Winchester	209	SR 7625	22.5	Lage	Uniwad	1⅛	1155	6900
Winchester	209	SR 7625	23.0	Pacific	Versalite	1⅛	1150	6100

12 GAUGE TARGET — REMINGTON 2¾-INCH PREMIER (RTL)

PRIMER		IMR POWDER		WAD COLUMN		LEAD SHOT (Oz.)	MUZZLE VELOCITY	CHAMBER PRESSURE
MFR.	No.	DESIGNATION	GRAINS	MFG.	DESIGNATION			
Remington	209P	"HI-SKOR" 700-X	17.5	Rem.	FIG 8	1⅛	1145	9400
Remington	209P	"HI-SKOR" 700-X	17.5	Rem.	RXP12	1⅛	1145	9500
Remington	209P	"HI-SKOR" 700-X	17.5	Activ	T32	1⅛	1145	9400
Remington	209P	"HI-SKOR" 700-X	18.5	Fed.	12C1	1⅛	1150	9000
Remington	209P	"HI-SKOR" 700-X	17.5	Win.	WAA12	1⅛	1150	10000
Remington	209P	"HI-SKOR" 700-X	16.5	WTW.	WindJammer	1⅛	1145	8200
Remington	209P	"HI-SKOR" 700-X	19.0	Rem.	FIG 8	1⅛	1200	10400
Remington	209P	"HI-SKOR" 700-X	19.0	Rem.	RXP12	1⅛	1200	10300
Remington	209P	"HI-SKOR" 700-X	19.0	Activ	T32	1⅛	1200	10500
Remington	209P	"HI-SKOR" 700-X	19.5	Fed.	12C1	1⅛	1205	10400
Remington	209P	"HI-SKOR" 700 X	19.0	Win.	WAA12	1⅛	1205	10600
Remington	209P	"HI-SKOR" 700-X	17.5	WTW.	WindJammer	1⅛	1215	10000
Remington	209P	PB	21.5	Rem.	FIG 8	1⅛	1140	7500
Remington	209P	PB	21.5	Rem.	RXP12	1⅛	1140	7400
Remington	209P	PB	21.5	Activ	T32	1⅛	1150	7000
Remington	209P	PB	21.0	Fed.	12S4	1⅛	1145	7900
Remington	209P	PB	21.5	Win.	WAA12	1⅛	1150	7200
Remington	209P	PB	21.0	WTW.	WindJammer	1⅛	1155	7300
Remington	209P	PB	22.5	Rem.	FIG 8	1⅛	1190	8000
Remington	209P	PB	22.5	Rem.	RXP12	1⅛	1175	7700
Remington	209P	PB	23.0	Activ	T32	1⅛	1190	7500

12 GAUGE TARGET — REMINGTON 2¾-INCH PREMIER (RTL) (Cont.)

PRIMER		IMR POWDER		WAD COLUMN		LEAD SHOT (Oz.)	MUZZLE VELOCITY	CHAMBER PRESSURE
MFR.	No.	DESIGNATION	GRAINS	MFG.	DESIGNATION			
Remington	209P	PB	22.5	Fed.	12S4	1⅛	1205	8600
Remington	209P	PB	23.0	Win.	WAA12	1⅛	1195	7500
Remington	209P	PB	22.0	WTW.	WindJammer	1⅛	1190	7700
Remington	209P	SR 7625	25.0	Rem.	FIG 8	1⅛	1140	6900
Remington	209P	SR 7625	25.0	Rem.	RXP12	1⅛	1140	6700
Remington	209P	SR 7625	25.0	Activ	T32	1⅛	1140	6100
Remington	209P	SR 7625	24.0	Fed.	12S4	1⅛	1150	7100
Remington	209P	SR 7625	25.0	Win.	WAA12	1⅛	1150	6400
Remington	209P	SR 7625	24.0	WTW.	WindJammer	1⅛	1140	6100
Remington	209P	SR 7625	26.0	Rem.	FIG 8	1⅛	1200	7300
Remington	209P	SR 7625	26.0	Rem.	RXP12	1⅛	1195	7100
Remington	209P	SR 7625	26.0	Activ	T32	1⅛	1185	6600
Remington	209P	SR 7625	25.0	Fed.	12S4	1⅛	1195	7700
Remington	209P	SR 7625	26.0	Win.	WAA12	1⅛	1200	7100
Remington	209P	SR 7625	25.0	WTW.	WindJammer	1⅛	1190	6700
Remington	209	"HI-SKOR" 700-X	17.0	Rem.	FIG 8	1⅛	1140	9600
Remington	209	"HI-SKOR" 700-X	18.5	Rem.	FIG 8	1⅛	1190	10800
Federal	209	"HI-SKOR" 700-X	17.5	Rem.	FIG 8	1⅛	1145	9600
Federal	209	"HI-SKOR" 700-X	18.0	Fed.	12C1	1⅛	1145	9300
Federal	209	"HI-SKOR" 700-X	19.0	Rem.	FIG 8	1⅛	1200	10500
Federal	209	"HI-SKOR" 700-X	19.5	Fed.	12C1	1⅛	1210	10600
Winchester	209	"HI-SKOR" 700-X	17.5	Rem.	FIG 8	1⅛	1150	9500
Winchester	209	"HI-SKOR" 700-X	17.5	Win.	WAA12	1⅛	1145	9900
Winchester	209	"HI-SKOR" 700-X	19.0	Rem.	FIG 8	1⅛	1195	10500
Winchester	209	"HI-SKOR" 700-X	19.0	Win.	WAA12	1⅛	1205	10800
Remington	209	PB	20.5	Rem.	FIG 8	1⅛	1145	7900
Remington	209	PB	22.0	Rem.	FIG 8	1⅛	1205	8900
Federal	209	PB	21.0	Rem.	FIG 8	1⅛	1140	7700
Federal	209	PB	21.0	Fed.	12S4	1⅛	1155	8600
Federal	209	PB	22.5	Rem.	FIG 8	1⅛	1205	8700
Federal	209	PB	22.0	Fed.	12S4	1⅛	1200	9100
Winchester	209	PB	21.5	Rem.	FIG 8	1⅛	1145	7600
Winchester	209	PB	21.5	Win.	WAA12	1⅛	1150	7500

12 GAUGE TARGET — REMINGTON 2¾-INCH PREMIER (RTL) (Cont.)

PRIMER		IMR POWDER		WAD COLUMN		LEAD SHOT (Oz.)	MUZZLE VELOCITY	CHAMBER PRESSURE
MFR.	No.	DESIGNATION	GRAINS	MFG.	DESIGNATION			
Winchester	209	PB	22.5	Rem.	FIG 8	1⅛	1195	8600
Winchester	209	PB	23.0	Win.	WAA12	1⅛	1200	8000
Remington	209	SR 7625	24.0	Rem.	FIG 8	1⅛	1160	7600
Remington	209	SR 7625	24.5	Rem.	FIG 8	1⅛	1200	7800
Federal	209	SR 7625	24.0	Rem.	FIG 8	1⅛	1155	7100
Federal	209	SR 7625	23.5	Fed.	12S4	1⅛	1155	7500
Federal	209	SR 7625	25.0	Rem.	FIG 8	1⅛	1195	7300
Federal	209	SR 7625	24.5	Fed.	12S4	1⅛	1200	8000
Winchester	209	SR 7625	24.5	Rem.	FIG 8	1⅛	1140	6900
Winchester	209	SR 7625	24.5	Win.	WAA12	1⅛	1155	6900
Winchester	209	SR 7625	25.5	Rem.	FIG 8	1⅛	1200	7500
Winchester	209	SR 7625	26.0	Win.	WAA12	1⅛	1200	7500

12 GAUGE TARGET — FEDERAL 2¾-INCH PAPER "CHAMPION"

PRIMER		IMR POWDER		WAD COLUMN		LEAD SHOT (Oz.)	MUZZLE VELOCITY	CHAMBER PRESSURE
MFR.	No.	DESIGNATION	GRAINS	MFG.	DESIGNATION			
Federal	209	"Hi-SKOR" 700-X	18.0	Fed.	12C1	1⅛	1135	8300
Federal	209	"Hi-SKOR" 700-X	19.0	Rem.	R12L	1⅛	1150	7800
Federal	209	"Hi-SKOR" 700-X	18.0	Win.	WAA12	1⅛	1155	8400
Federal	209	"Hi-SKOR" 700-X	20.0	Fed.	.135 in. card + ⅜ in. + ⅜ in. FC	1⅛	1150	8000
Federal	209	"Hi-SKOR" 700-X	19.5	—	Action Spin	1⅛	1195	8900
Federal	209	"Hi-SKOR" 700-X	19.5	Fed.	12C1	1⅛	1200	9100
Federal	209	"Hi-SKOR" 700-X	20.5	Rem.	R12L	1⅛	1205	8500
Federal	209	"Hi-SKOR" 700-X	19.0	Win.	WAA12	1⅛	1200	9200
Federal	209	"Hi-SKOR" 700-X	21.0	Fed.	.135 in. card + ⅜ in. + ⅜ in. FC	1⅛	1195	8800
CCI	209	"Hi-SKOR" 700-X	18.5	Fed.	12C1	1⅛	1150	8500
CCI	209	"Hi-SKOR" 700-X	19.0	Rem.	R12L	1⅛	1130	6700
CCI	209	"Hi-SKOR" 700-X	18.0	Win.	WAA12P8	1⅛	1145	7500
CCI	209	"Hi-SKOR" 700-X	20.0	Fed.	12C1	1⅛	1210	9500
CCI	209	"Hi-SKOR" 700-X	20.5	Rem.	R12L	1⅛	1190	7600

12 GAUGE TARGET — FEDERAL 2¾-INCH PAPER "CHAMPION" (Cont.)

PRIMER		IMR POWDER		WAD COLUMN		LEAD SHOT (Oz.)	MUZZLE VELOCITY	CHAMBER PRESSURE
MFR.	No.	DESIGNATION	GRAINS	MFG.	DESIGNATION			
CCI	209	"Hi-SKOR" 700-X	19.5	Win.	WAA12P8	1⅛	1200	8500
Remington	209P	"Hi-SKOR" 700-X	17.0	Fed.	12C1	1⅛	1155	8100
Remington	209P	"Hi-SKOR" 700-X	17.5	Activ	L-33	1⅛	1150	8600
Remington	209P	"Hi-SKOR" 700-X	17.0	Rem.	R12L	1⅛	1145	7000
Remington	209P	"Hi-SKOR" 700-X	17.5	Win.	WAA12	1⅛	1150	7200
Remington	209P	"Hi-SKOR" 700-X	18.5	Fed.	12C1	1⅛	1210	8500
Remington	209P	"Hi-SKOR" 700-X	19.0	Activ	L-33	1⅛	1200	9000
Remington	209P	"Hi-SKOR" 700-X	18.5	Rem.	R12L	1⅛	1200	8100
Remington	209P	"Hi-SKOR" 700-X	18.0	Win.	WAA12	1⅛	1195	9300
Winchester	209	"Hi-SKOR" 700-X	19.0	Fed.	12C1	1⅛	1160	7500
Winchester	209	"Hi-SKOR" 700-X	19.0	Rem.	R12L	1⅛	1150	7400
Winchester	209	"Hi-SKOR" 700-X	18.5	Win.	WAA12	18	1150	7900
Winchester	209	"Hi-SKOR" 700X	20.0	Fed.	12C1	1⅛	1215	9400
Winchester	209	"Hi-SKOR" 700-X	20.5	Rem.	R12L	1⅛	1215	8400
Winchester	209	"Hi-SKOR" 700-X	20.0	Win.	WAA12	1⅛	1210	8200
Winchester	209	"HI-SKOR" 800-X	24.0	Fed.	12S3	1⅛	1215	7000
Winchester	209	"HI-SKOR" 800-X	24.5	Win.	WAA12	1⅛	1210	6600
Winchester	209	"HI-SKOR" 800-X	24.0	Rem.	RXP12	1⅛	1200	6200
Winchester	209	"HI-SKOR" 800-X	24.0	Pacific	Versalite	1⅛	1190	6300
Federal	209	PB	22.5	Rem.	R12H	1⅛	1155	6400
Federal	209	PB	22.5	Win.	WAA12	1⅛	1145	5800
Federal	209	PB	23.5	Fed.	12C1	1⅛	1190	6800
Federal	209	PB	24.0	Rem.	R12H	1⅛	1215	7000
Federal	209	PB	24.0	Win.	WAA12	1⅛	1200	6600
CCI	209	PB	23.0	Fed.	12C1	1⅛	1155	5900
CCI	209	PB	22.5	Rem.	R12HP8	1⅛	1140	5400
CCI	209	PB	22.5	Win.	WAA12P8	1⅛	1145	5800
CCI	209	PB	24.5	Fed.	12C1	1⅛	1195	6500
CCI	209	PB	24.0	Rem.	R12HP8	1⅛	1200	6200
CCI	209	PB	24.0	Win.	WAA12P8	1⅛	1195	6300
Winchester	209	PB	24.0	Fed.	12C1	1⅛	1135	5000
Winchester	209	PB	23.5	Rem.	R12H	1⅛	1155	5300
Winchester	209	PB	23.5	Win.	WAA12	1⅛	1140	5300

12 GAUGE TARGET — FEDERAL 2¾-INCH PAPER "CHAMPION" (Cont.)

PRIMER		IMR POWDER		WAD COLUMN		LEAD SHOT (Oz.)	MUZZLE VELOCITY	CHAMBER PRESSURE
MFR.	No.	DESIGNATION	GRAINS	MFG.	DESIGNATION			
Winchester	209	PB	25.5	Fed.	12C1	1⅛	1195	5800
Winchester	209	PB	25.0	Rem.	R12H	1⅛	1215	6000
Winchester	209	PB	25.0	Win.	WAA12	1⅛	1195	5900
Federal	209	SR 7625	25.0	Fed.	12C1	1⅛	1155	5500
Federal	209	SR 7625	25.0	Lage	Uniwad	1⅛	1160	5800
Federal	209	SR 7625	25.0	Win.	WAA12	1⅛	1150	5500
Federal	209	SR 7625	26.0	Fed.	12C1	1⅛	1210	6300
Federal	209	SR 7625	26.5	Lage	Uniwad	1⅛	1215	6500
Federal	209	SR 7625	26.5	Win.	WAA12	1⅛	1205	6000
CCI	209	SR 7625	25.5	Fed.	12C1	1⅛	1145	5200
CCI	209	SR 7625	25.5	Lage	Uniwad	1⅛	1150	5200
CCI	209	SR 7625	25.0	Win.	WAA12	1⅛	1165	5700
CCI	209	SR 7625	27.0	Fed.	12C1	1⅛	1195	5700
CCI	209	SR 7625	27.0	Lage	Uniwad	1⅛	1200	5700
CCI	209	SR 7625	26.5	Win.	WAA12	1⅛	1200	6100
Winchester	209	SR 7625	26.0	Fed.	12C1	1⅛	1150	5100
Winchester	209	SR 7625	26.5	Lage	Uniwad	1⅛	1135	4600
Winchester	209	SR 7625	26.0	Win.	WAA12	1⅛	1160	5200
Winchester	209	SR 7625	27.5	Fed.	12C1	1⅛	1215	5800
Winchester	209	SR 7625	28.0	Lage	Uniwad	1⅛	1190	5000

12 GAUGE TARGET — FEDERAL 2¾-INCH PLASTIC "GOLD MEDAL"

PRIMER		IMR POWDER		WAD COLUMN		LEAD SHOT (Oz.)	MUZZLE VELOCITY	CHAMBER PRESSURE
MFR.	No.	DESIGNATION	GRAINS	MFG.	DESIGNATION			
Federal	209	"HI-SKOR" 700-X	18.0	Fed.	12S3	1⅛	1145	7500
Federal	209	"HI-SKOR" 700-X	18.0	Rem.	R12L	1⅛	1140	7900
Federal	209	"HI-SKOR" 700-X	19.5	Fed.	12S3	1⅛	1215	8800
Federal	209	"HI-SKOR" 700-X	19.5	Rem.	R12L	1⅛	1195	8500
CCI	209	"HI-SKOR" 700-X	18.0	Fed.	12S3	1⅛	1145	7500
CCI	209	"HI-SKOR" 700-X	18.0	Rem.	R12L	1⅛	1130	7100

12 GAUGE TARGET — FEDERAL 2¾-INCH PLASTIC "GOLD MEDAL" (Cont.)

PRIMER		IMR POWDER		WAD COLUMN		LEAD SHOT (Oz.)	MUZZLE VELOCITY	CHAMBER PRESSURE
MFR.	No.	DESIGNATION	GRAINS	MFG.	DESIGNATION			
CCI	209	"HI-SKOR" 700-X	20.0	Rem.	R12L	1⅛	1205	8000
Remington	209P	"HI-SKOR" 700-X	16.5	Fed.	12S3	1⅛	1150	7900
Remington	209P	"HI-SKOR" 700-X	17.0	Activ	L-33	1⅛	1145	8500
Remington	209P	"HI-SKOR" 700-X	17.5	Rem.	R12L	1⅛	1160	8000
Remington	209P	"HI-SKOR" 700-X	18.5	Fed.	12S3	1⅛	1215	9100
Remington	209P	"HI-SKOR" 700-X	18.5	Activ	L-33	1⅛	1200	9300
Remington	209P	"HI-SKOR" 700-X	18.5	Rem.	R12L	1⅛	1220	8500
Remington	209P	"HI-SKOR" 700-X	18.5	WTW.	WindJammer	1⅛	1215	7300
Winchester	209	"HI-SKOR" 700-X	18.0	Fed.	12S3	1⅛	1150	7400
Winchester	209	"HI-SKOR" 700-X	18.0	Rem.	R12L	1⅛	1135	7400
Winchester	209	"HI-SKOR" 700-X	19.5	Fed.	12S3	1⅛	1205	8300
Winchester	209	"HI-SKOR" 700-X	19.5	Rem.	R12L	1⅛	1205	8300
Winchester	209	"HI-SKOR" 700-X	24.0	Win.	WAA12	1⅛	1205	6200
Winchester	209	"HI-SKOR" 700-X	24.5	Rem.	R12L	1⅛	1215	6200
Winchester	209	"HI-SKOR" 700-X	24.5	Pacific	Versalite	1⅛	1195	5700
Federal	209	PB	21.5	Fed.	12S4	1⅛	1150	6600
Federal	209	PB	22.5	Rem.	R12L	1⅛	1150	6100
Federal	209	PB	23.0	Fed.	12S4	1⅛	1215	7300
Federal	209	PB	24.0	Rem.	R12L	1⅛	1215	6800
CCI	209	PB	21.5	Fed.	12S4	1⅛	1150	6400
CCI	209	PB	23.0	Rem.	R12L	1⅛	1155	5500
CCI	209	PB	23.0	Fed.	12S4	1⅛	1205	6800
CCI	209	PB	24.5	Rem.	R12L	1⅛	1205	6000
Winchester	209	PB	21.5	Fed.	12S4	1⅛	1155	6400
Winchester	209	PB	22.5	Rem.	R12L	1⅛	1155	5800
Winchester	209	PB	23.0	Fed.	12S4	1⅛	1205	7300
Winchester	209	PB	24.0	Rem.	R12L	1⅛	1190	6100
Federal	209	SR 7625	25.5	Rem.	R12L	1⅛	1145	5400
Federal	209	SR 7625	26.0	Fed.	12S4	1⅛	1200	6400
Federal	209	SR 7625	27.0	Rem.	R12H	1⅛	1195	5700
CCI	209	SR 7625	24.5	Fed.	12S4	1⅛	1155	5800

12 GAUGE TARGET — FEDERAL 2¾-INCH PLASTIC "GOLD MEDAL" (Cont.)

PRIMER		IMR POWDER		WAD COLUMN		LEAD SHOT (Oz.)	MUZZLE VELOCITY	CHAMBER PRESSURE
MFR.	No.	DESIGNATION	GRAINS	MFG.	DESIGNATION			
CCI	209M	SR 7625	25.0	Rem.	R12L	1⅛	1135	5600
CCI	209M	SR 7625	26.0	Fed.	12S4	1⅛	1215	6600
CCI	209M	SR 7625	26.5	Rem.	R12H	1⅛	1200	6000
Winchester	209	SR 7625	25.0	Fed.	12S4	1⅛	1150	5800
Winchester	209	SR 7625	26.0	Rem.	R12L	1⅛	1135	5200
Winchester	209	SR 7625	26.5	Fed.	12S4	1⅛	1210	6400
Winchester	209	SR 7625	27.5	Rem.	R12H	1⅛	1200	5500

12 GAUGE TARGET — WINCHESTER 2¾-INCH COMPRESSION-FORMED "DOUBLE A," "UPLAND" AND "SUPER-X"

PRIMER		IMR POWDER		WAD COLUMN		LEAD SHOT (Oz.)	MUZZLE VELOCITY	CHAMBER PRESSURE
MFR.	No.	DESIGNATION	GRAINS	MFG.	DESIGNATION			
Winchester	209	"HI-SK0R" 700-X	17.5	Win.	WAA12	1⅛	1135	7900
Winchester	209	"HI-SK0R" 700-X	18.0	Fed.	12SI	1⅛	1150	8000
Winchester	209	"HI-SK0R" 700-X	18.5	Lage	Uniwad	1⅛	1145	8100
Winchester	209	"HI-SKOR" 700-X	17.5	Pacific	Versalite	1⅛	1145	8000
Winchester	209	"HI-SK0R" 700-X	18.0	Rem.	RXP12	1⅛	1155	8400
Winchester	209	"HI-SK0R" 700-X	19.0	Win.	WAA12	1⅛	1200	9200
Winchester	209	"HI-SKOR" 700-X	19.0	Fed.	12S1	1⅛	1190	8600
Winchester	209	"HI-SK0R" 700- X	19.5	Lage	Uniwad	1⅛	1205	9200
Winchester	209	"HI-SK0R" 700-X	19.0	Pacific	Versalite	1⅛	1205	9500
Winchester	209	"HI-SK0R" 700-X	19.0	Rem.	RXP12	1⅛	1190	8900
Federal	209	"HI-SK0R" 700-X	17.5	Win.	WAA12	1⅛	1150	9500
Federal	209	"HI-SK0R" 700-X	17.0	Fed.	12S1	1⅛	1135	8500
Federal	209	"HI-SKOR" 700-X	18.0	Lage	Uniwad	1⅛	1140	8900
Federal	209	"HI-SK0R" 700-X	17.0	Pacific	Versalite	1⅛	1140	9300
Federal	209	"HI-SK0R" 700-X	18.0	Rem.	RXP12	1⅛	1145	8500
Federal	209	"HI-SK0R" 700-X	19.0	Win.	WAA12	1⅛	1200	10100
Federal	209	"HI-SKOR" 700-X	18.5	Fed.	12S1	1⅛	1195	9800
Federal	209	"HI-SK0R" 700-X	19.5	Lage	Uniwad	1⅛	1200	10100
Federal	209	"HI-SK0R" 700-X	18.0	Pacific	Versalite	1⅛	1190	10300
Federal	209	"HI-SK0R" 700-X	19.0	Rem.	RXP12	1⅛	1190	9300

12 GAUGE TARGET — WINCHESTER 2¾-INCH COMPRESSION-FORMED "DOUBLE A," "UPLAND" AND "SUPER-X" (Cont.)

PRIMER		IMR POWDER		WAD COLUMN		LEAD SHOT (Oz.)	MUZZLE VELOCITY	CHAMBER PRESSURE
MFR.	No.	DESIGNATION	GRAINS	MFG.	DESIGNATION			
CCI	209	"HI-SKOR" 700-X	17.5	Win.	WAA12	1⅛	1145	8300
CCI	209	"HI-SKOR" 700-X	17.5	Fed.	12S1	1⅛	1155	8600
CCI	209	"HI-SKOR" 700-X	18.5	Lage	Uniwad	1⅛	1140	8100
CCI	209	"HI-SKOR" 700-X	18.0	Pacific	Versalite	1⅛	1145	8200
CCI	209	"HI-SKOR" 700-X	17.5	Rem.	RXP12	1⅛	1150	8300
CCI	209	"HI-SKOR" 700-X	19.0	Win.	WAA12	1⅛	1215	10200
CCI	209	"HI-SKOR" 700-X	19.0	Fed.	12S1	1⅛	1185	9100
CCI	209	"HI-SKOR" 700-X	19.5	Lage	Uniwad	1⅛	1190	9200
CCI	209	"HI-SKOR" 700-X	19.5	Pacific	Versalite	1⅛	1205	9100
CCI	209	"HI-SKOR" 700-X	19.0	Rem.	RXP12	1⅛	1195	9000
Remington	209P	"HI-SKOR" 700-X	16.0	Win.	WAA12	1⅛	1150	8300
Remington	209P	"HI-SKOR" 700-X	17.0	Activ	T-35	1⅛	1140	8700
Remington	209P	"HI-SKOR" 700-X	17.0	Fed.	12S1	1⅛	1150	8700
Remington	209P	"HI-SKOR" 700-X	16.5	Lage	Uniwad	1⅛	1140	7800
Remington	209P	"HI-SKOR" 700-X	16.5	Pacific	Versalite	1⅛	1155	8500
Remington	209P	"HI-SKOR" 700-X	16.5	Rem.	RXP12	1⅛	1145	7800
Remington	209P	"HI-SKOR" 700-X	17.0	Rem.	F1G 8	1⅛	1145	9400
Remington	209P	"HI-SKOR" 700-X	17.5	Win.	WAA12	1⅛	1200	8900
Remington	209P	"HI-SKOR" 700-X	18.5	Activ	T-35	1⅛	1190	9400
Remington	209P	"HI-SKOR" 700-X	18.0	Fed.	12S1	1⅛	1205	9200
Remington	209P	"HI-SKOR" 700-X	18.0	Lage	Uniwad	1⅛	1190	8900
Remington	209P	"HI-SKOR" 700-X	18.0	Pacific	Versalite	1⅛	1215	8700
Remington	209P	"HI-SKOR" 700-X	18.0	Rem.	RXP12	1⅛	1210	9700
Remington	209P	"HI-SKOR" 700-X	18.5	Rem.	FIG 8	1⅛	1195	10300
Winchester	209	"HI-SKOR" 800-X	22.0	Win.	WAA12	1⅛	1145	6700
Winchester	209	"HI-SKOR" 800-X	22.0	Rem.	RXP12	1⅛	1140	6300
Winchester	209	"HI-SKOR" 800-X	21.5	Fed.	12S4	1⅛	1140	7200
Winchester	209	"HI-SKOR" 800-X	21.5	Lage	Uniwad	1⅛	1130	6300
Winchester	209	"HI-SKOR" 800-X	22.0	Pacific	Versalite	1⅛	1145	6500
Winchester	209	"HI-SKOR" 800-X	22.5	WTW.	WindJammer	1⅛	1135	5500
Winchester	209	"HI-SKOR" 800-X	23.5	Win.	WAA12	1⅛	1205	7300

12 GAUGE TARGET — WINCHESTER 2¾-INCH COMPRESSION-FORMED "DOUBLE A," "UPLAND" AND "SUPER-X" (Cont.)

PRIMER		IMR POWDER		WAD COLUMN		LEAD SHOT (Oz.)	MUZZLE VELOCITY	CHAMBER PRESSURE
MFR.	No.	DESIGNATION	GRAINS	MFG.	DESIGNATION			
Winchester	209	"HI-SKOR" 800-X	23.5	Rem.	RXP12	1⅛	1200	6900
Winchester	209	"HI-SKOR" 800-X	23.0	Fed.	12S4	1⅛	1190	7700
Winchester	209	"HI-SKOR" 800-X	24.0	Lage	Uniwad	1⅛	1200	6900
Winchester	209	"HI-SKOR" 800-X	23.5	Pacific	Versalite	1⅛	1200	6900
Winchester	209	"HI-SKOR" 800-X	24.0	WTW.	WindJammer	1⅛	1210	6500
Winchester	209	PB	22.0	Win.	WAA12	1⅛	1145	6600
Winchester	209	PB	21.5	Fed.	12S4	1⅛	1150	7600
Winchester	209	PB	22.0	Lage	Uniwad	1⅛	1135	7000
Winchester	209	PB	22.0	Pacific	Versalite	1⅛	1155	6700
Winchester	209	PB	22.0	Rem.	RXP12	1⅛	1150	6100
Winchester	209	PB	23.5	Win.	WAA12	1⅛	1215	7300
Winchester	209	PB	22.5	Fed.	12S4	1⅛	1190	8400
Winchester	209	PB	23.5	Lage	Uniwad	1⅛	1195	7600
Winchester	209	PB	23.5	Pacific	Versalite	1⅛	1210	7600
Winchester	209	PB	23.0	Rem.	RXP12	1⅛	1195	7500
Federal	209	PB	21.0	Win.	WAA12	1⅛	1155	7600
Federal	209	PB	21.0	Fed.	12S4	1⅛	1140	7900
Federal	209	PB	21.0	Lage	Uniwad	1⅛	1135	7200
Federal	209	PB	21.0	Pacific	Versalite	1⅛	1150	6800
Federal	209	PB	20.0	Rem.	RXP12	1⅛	1135	6900
Federal	209	PB	22.0	Win.	WAA12	1⅛	1205	8400
Federal	209	PB	22.5	Fed.	12S4	1⅛	1200	8900
Federal	209	PB	22.5	Lage	Uniwad	1⅛	1195	7900
Federal	209	PB	22.5	Pacific	Versalite	1⅛	1215	7900
Federal	209	PB	22.0	Rem.	RXP12	1⅛	1205	8500
CCI	209	PB	21.5	Win.	WAA12	1⅛	1145	6400
CCI	209	PB	21.5	Fed.	12S4	1⅛	1155	7500
CCI	209	PB	22.0	Lage	Uniwad	1⅛	1135	6500
CCI	209	PB	22.0	Pacific	Versalite	1⅛	1160	6600
CCI	209	PB	21.5	Rem.	RXP12	1⅛	1150	6200

12 GAUGE TARGET — WINCHESTER 2¾-INCH COMPRESSION-FORMED "DOUBLE A," "UPLAND" AND "SUPER-X" (Cont.)

PRIMER		IMR POWDER		WAD COLUMN		LEAD SHOT (Oz.)	MUZZLE VELOCITY	CHAMBER PRESSURE
MFR.	No.	DESIGNATION	GRAINS	MFG.	DESIGNATION			
CCI	209	PB	23.0	Win.	WAA12	1⅛	1210	7500
CCI	209	PB	22.5	Fed.	12S4	1⅛	1190	8100
CCI	209	PB	23.5	Lage	Uniwad	1⅛	1195	7500
CCI	209	PB	23.5	Pacific	Versalite	1⅛	1210	7200
CCI	209	PB	22.5	Rem.	RXP12	1⅛	1195	7400
Winchester	209	SR 7625	24.0	Win.	WAA12	1⅛	1135	5800
Winchester	209	SR 7625	25.0	Lage	Uniwad	1⅛	1140	6300
Winchester	209	SR 7625	24.5	Pacific	Versalite	1⅛	1155	6400
Winchester	209	SR 7625	24.0	Rem.	RXP12	1⅛	1155	6000
Winchester	209	SR 7625	25.5	Win.	WAA12	1⅛	1200	6600
Winchester	209	SR 7625	26.0	Lage	Uniwad	1⅛	1195	6600
Winchester	209	SR 7625	26.0	Pacific	Versalite	1⅛	1200	6700
Winchester	209	SR 7625	25.0	Rem.	RXP12	1⅛	1195	6500
Federal	209	SR 7625	21.5	Win.	WAA12	1⅛	1135	7200
Federal	209	SR 7625	24.0	Lage	Uniwad	1⅛	1140	6600
Federal	209	SR 7625	24.0	Pacific	Versalite	1⅛	1145	6400
Federal	209	SR 7625	22.5	Rem.	RXP12	1⅛	1160	6900
Federal	209	SR 7625	23.0	Win.	WAA12	1⅛	1195	8200
Federal	209	SR 7625	25.5	Lage	Uniwad	1⅛	1190	7000
Federal	209	SR 7625	25.5	Pacific	Versalite	1⅛	1205	7000
Federal	209	SR 7625	23.5	Rem.	RXP12	1⅛	1195	7300
CCI	209	SR 7625	23.0	Win.	WAA12	1⅛	1145	6500
CCI	209	SR 7625	25.0	Lage	Uniwad	1⅛	1135	6000
CCI	209	SR 7625	24.5	Pacific	Versalite	1⅛	1150	6200
CCI	209	SR 7625	23.0	Rem.	RXP12	1⅛	1160	6100
CCI	209	SR 7625	24.5	Win.	WAA12	1⅛	1190	6900
CCI	209	SR 7625	26.0	Lage	Uniwad	1⅛	1190	6700
CCI	209	SR 7625	26.0	Pacific	Versalite	1⅛	1205	6600
CCI	209	SR 7625	24.5	Rem.	RXP12	1⅛	1210	6900

12 GAUGE TARGET — ACTIV 2¾-INCH TARGET

PRIMER		IMR POWDER		WAD COLUMN		LEAD SHOT (Oz.)	MUZZLE VELOCITY	CHAMBER PRESSURE
MFR.	No.	DESIGNATION	GRAINS	MFG.	DESIGNATION			
Federal	209	"HI-SKOR" 700-X	18.0	Activ	L-33	1⅛	1145	7700
Remington	209P	"HI-SKOR" 700-X	17.5	Activ	L-33	1⅛	1140	8500
Winchester	209	"HI SKOR" 700 X	18.5	Activ	L-33	1⅛	1140	7300
Federal	209	"HI-SKOR" 700-X	19.5	Activ	L-33	1⅛	1200	9100
Remington	209P	"HI-SKOR" 700-X	19.0	Activ	L-33	1⅛	1195	10000
Winchester	209	"HI-SKOR" 700-X	19.5	Activ	L-33	1⅛	1195	8000
Federal	209	PB	23.0	Activ	L-33	1⅛	1160	6500
Remington	209P	PB	22.0	Activ	L-33	1⅛	1155	6700
Winchester	209	PB	22.5	Activ	L-33	1⅛	1140	6100
Federal	209	PB	24.5	Activ	L-33	1⅛	1210	6900
Remington	209P	PB	23.0	Activ	L-33	1⅛	1200	7900
Winchester	209	PB	24.0	Activ	L-33	1⅛	1195	6500
Federal	209	SR 7625	26.0	Activ	L-33	1⅛	1155	5400
Winchester	209	SR 7625	26.5	Activ	L-33	1⅛	1155	5400
Federal	209	SR 7625	26.5	Activ	L-33	1⅛	1205	6000
Winchester	209	SR 7625	28.0	Activ	L-33	1⅛	1205	6000

12 GAUGE TARGET — FIOCCHI 2¾-INCH VIP AMERICAN TARGET

PRIMER		IMR POWDER		WAD COLUMN		LEAD SHOT (Oz.)	MUZZLE VELOCITY	CHAMBER PRESSURE
MFR.	No.	DESIGNATION	GRAINS	MFG.	DESIGNATION			
Fiocchi	209	"HI-SKOR" 700-X	17.0	Activ	T-32	1⅛	1155	9400
Fiocchi	209	"HI-SKOR" 700-X	17.0	Fed.	12C1	1⅛	1140	9800
Fiocchi	209	"HI-SKOR" 700-X	17.0	Rem.	RXP12	1⅛	1145	9700
Fiocchi	209	"HI-SKOR" 700-X	17.0	Rem.	FIG 8	1⅛	1140	8500
Fiocchi	209	"HI-SKOR" 700-X	17.0	Win.	WAA12	1⅛	1145	9400
Fiocchi	209	"HI-SKOR" 700-X	17.0	WTW.	WindJammwer	1⅛	1140	8400
Fiocchi	209	"HI-SKOR" 700-X	18.5	Activ	T-32	1⅛	1205	10000
Fiocchi	209	"HI-SKOR" 700-X	18.5	Fed.	12Cl	1⅛	1200	10800
Fiocchi	209	"HI-SKOR" 700-X	18.5	Rem.	RXPl2	1⅛	1205	10500
Fiocchi	209	"HI-SKOR" 700-X	18.5	Rem.	FIG 8	1⅛	1200	10300
Fiocchi	209	"HI-SKOR" 700-X	18.0	Win.	WAA12	1⅛	1190	10800

12 GAUGE TARGET — FIOCCHI 2¾-INCH VIP AMERICAN TARGET

PRIMER		IMR POWDER		WAD COLUMN		LEAD SHOT (Oz.)	MUZZLE VELOCITY	CHAMBER PRESSURE
MFR.	No.	DESIGNATION	GRAINS	MFG.	DESIGNATION			
Fiocchi	209	"HI-SKOR" 700-X	18.5	WTW.	WindJammer	1⅛	1200	9400
Remington	209P	"HI-SKOR" 700-X	17.5	Activ	T-32	1⅛	1155	9100
Remington	209P	"HI-SKOR" 700-X	17.5	Fed.	12Cl	1⅛	1140	8500
Remington	209P	"HI-SKOR" 700-X	18.0	Rem.	FIG 8	1⅛	1150	8200
Remington	209P	"HI-SKOR" 700-X	17.5	Rem.	RXPI2	1⅛	1145	8900
Remington	209P	"HI-SKOR" 700-X	17.5	Win.	WAA12	1⅛	1150	9700
Remington	209P	"HI-SKOR" 700-X	17.0	WTW.	WindJammer	1⅛	1140	8400
Remington	209P	"HI-SKOR" 700 X	19.0	Activ	T-32	1⅛	1210	9600
Remington	209P	"HI-SKOR" 700-X	19.0	Fed.	12Cl	1⅛	1210	10100
Remington	209P	"HI-SKOR" 700-X	19.0	Rem.	FIG 8	1⅛	1205	9100
Remington	209P	"HI-SKOR"700-X	19.0	Rem.	RXP12	1⅛	1195	9300
Remington	209P	"HI-SKOR" 700-X	19.5	Win.	WAA12	1⅛	1200	10000
Remington	209P	"HI-SKOR" 700-X	18.5	WTW.	WindJammer	1⅛	1205	9600

12 GAUGE TRAP — PETERS 2¾-INCH TARGET LOAD

PRIMER		IMR POWDER		WAD COLUMN		LEAD SHOT (Oz.)	MUZZLE VELOCITY	CHAMBER PRESSURE
MFR.	No.	DESIGNATION	GRAINS	MFG.	DESIGNATION			
Remington	209P	"HI-SKOR" 700-X	19.0	Rem.	RXP12	1⅛	1265	10000
Remington	209P	"HI-SKOR" 700-X	18.5	Rem.	FIG 8	1⅛	1235	9600
Remington	209P	"HI-SKOR" 700-X	18.0	Activ	T-32	1⅛	1250	10700
Remington	209P	"HI-SKOR" 700-X	19.0	Pacific	Versalite	1⅛	1265	10300
Winchester	209	"HI-SKOR" 700-X	19.5	Win.	WAA12	1⅛	1240	10900
Remington	209P	"HI-SKOR" 800-X	26.5	Rem.	RXP12	1⅛	1270	8800
Remington	209P	"HI-SKOR" 800-X	26.0	Rem.	FIG 8	1⅛	1270	9100
Remington	209P	"HI-SKOR" 800-X	24.0	Fed.	12S4	1⅛	1255	8200
Remington	209P	"HI-SKOR" 800-X	24.0	Win.	WAA12	1⅛	1250	7700
Federal	209	PB	23.0	Rem.	R12H	1⅛	1250	9300
Winchester	209	PB	23.0	Win.	WAA12	1⅛	1250	9400
Federal	209	PB	23.0	Lage	Uniwad	1⅛	1260	10000
Federal	209	PB	22.5	Pacific	Blue Verelite	1⅛	1245	9700

12 GAUGE TRAP — PETERS 2¾-INCH TARGET LOAD (Cont.)

PRIMER		IMR POWDER		WAD COLUMN		LEAD SHOT (Oz.)	MUZZLE VELOCITY	CHAMBER PRESSURE
MFR.	No.	DESIGNATION	GRAINS	MFG.	DESIGNATION			
Federal	209	SR 7625	25.0	Rem.	R12H	1⅛	1250	8300
Federal	209	SR 7625	24.0	Fed.	12S4	1⅛	1260	9600
Federal	209	SR 7625	25.0	Lage	Uniwad	1⅛	1250	8600
Winchester	209	SR 7625	25.0	Win.	WAA12	1⅛	1245	8100

12 GAUGE TRAP — FEDERAL 2¾-INCH PAPER "CHAMPION"

PRIMER		IMR POWDER		WAD COLUMN		LEAD SHOT (Oz.)	MUZZLE VELOCITY	CHAMBER PRESSURE
MFR.	No.	DESIGNATION	GRAINS	MFG.	DESIGNATION			
Federal	209	"HI-SKOR" 700-X	21.0	Rem.	R12H	1⅛	1250	10300
CCI	209	"HI-SKOR" 700-X	20.5	Fed.	12C1	1⅛	1245	10200
CCI	209	"HI-SKOR" 700-X	21.0	Win.	WAA12	1⅛	1270	10000
Remington	209P	"HI-SKOR" 700-X	20.0	Fed.	12C1	1⅛	1260	9700
Remington	209P	"HI-SKOR" 700-X	20.0	Activ	L-33	1⅛	1245	10100
Remington	209P	"HI-SKOR" 700-X	20.0	Rem.	R12H	1⅛	1260	9400
Winchester	209	"HI-SKOR" 700-X	21.0	Win.	WAA12	1⅛	1250	9300
Winchester	209	"HI-SKOR" 800-X	25.0	Fed.	12S3	1⅛	1250	7600
Winchester	209	"HI-SKOR" 800-X	25.5	Win.	WAA12	1⅛	1250	7100
Winchester	209	"HI-SKOR" 800-X	25.5	Rem.	R12L	1⅛	1255	6900
Federal	209	PB	25.0	Fed.	12C1	1⅛	1240	7400
Federal	209	PB	25.5	Win.	WAA12	1⅛	1250	7300
Winchester	209	PB	27.0	Fed.	12C1	1⅛	1260	6800
Winchester	209	PB	27.0	Win.	WAA12	1⅛	1260	6700
CCI	209	PB	26.0	Fed.	12C1	1⅛	1265	7100
CCI	209	PB	26.0	Win.	WAA12	1⅛	1255	7000
Federal	209	SR 7625	27.5	Fed.	12C1	1⅛	1260	6700
Federal	209	SR 7625	28.0	Lage	Uniwad	1⅛	1260	7000
Federal	209	SR 7625	28.0	Win.	WAA12	1⅛	1265	6500
Winchester	209	SR 7625	28.5	Fed.	12C1	1⅛	1260	6300
CCI	209	SR 7625	28.5	Lage	Uniwad	1⅛	1275	6900
CCI	209	SR 7625	28.0	Win.	WAA12	1⅛	1270	6700

12 GAUGE TRAP — FEDERAL 2¾-INCH PLASTIC "GOLD MEDAL"

PRIMER		IMR POWDER		WAD COLUMN		LEAD SHOT (Oz.)	MUZZLE VELOCITY	CHAMBER PRESSURE
MFR.	No.	DESIGNATION	GRAINS	MFG.	DESIGNATION			
Federal	209	"HI-SKOR" 700-X	21.0	Fed.	12S3	1⅛	1265	9700
Federal	209	"HI-SKOR" 700-X	21.0	Rem.	R12L	1⅛	1250	9200
Winchester	209	"HI-SKOR" 700-X	20.5	Fed.	12S3	1⅛	1245	9200
Winchester	209	"HI-SKOR" 700-X	21.0	Rem.	R12L	1⅛	1265	9700
Winchester	209	"HI-SKOR" 800-X	25.0	Fed.	12S3	1⅛	1245	6800
Winchester	209	"HI-SKOR" 800-X	25.5	Win.	WAA12	1⅛	1265	6600
Winchester	209	"HI SKOR" 800-X	25.5	Rem.	R12L	1⅛	1245	6400
Federal	209	PB	24.5	Fed.	12S4	1⅛	1250	7700
Federal	209	PB	25.5	Rem.	R12H	1⅛	1260	7200
Winchester	209	PB	24.5	Fed.	12S4	1⅛	1245	7500
Winchester	209	PB	26.0	Rem.	R12H	1⅛	1250	6800
Federal	209	SR 7625	27.5	Fed.	12S4	1⅛	1260	7200
Federal	209	SR 7625	28.0	Rem.	R12H	1⅛	1240	6000
CCI	209M	SR 7625	27.0	Fed.	12S4	1⅛	1250	6900
CCI	209M	SR 7625	28.0	Rem.	R12H	1⅛	1255	6200

12 GAUGE TRAP — WINCHESTER 2¾-INCH COMPRESSION-FORMED "DOUBLE A," "UPLAND" AND "SUPER-X"

PRIMER		IMR POWDER		WAD COLUMN		LEAD SHOT (Oz.)	MUZZLE VELOCITY	CHAMBER PRESSURE
MFR.	No.	DESIGNATION	GRAINS	MFG.	DESIGNATION			
Winchester	209	"HI-SKOR" 700-X	20.0	Win.	WAA12	1⅛	1245	10500
Winchester	209	"HI-SKOR" 700-X	20.5	Rem.	RXP12	1⅛	1245	10100
Winchester	209	"HI-SKOR" 700-X	21.0	Fed.	12S1	1⅛	1250	10000
Federal	209	"HI-SKOR" 700-X	20.0	Win.	WAA12	1⅛	1240	10600
Federal	209	"HI-SKOR" 700-X	20.5	Rem.	RXP12	1⅛	1245	10200
Federal	209	"HI-SKOR" 700-X	20.5	Fed.	12S1	1⅛	1245	10200
Winchester	209	"HI-SKOR" 800-X	25.0	Win.	WAA12	1⅛	1255	7800
Winchester	209	"HI-SKOR" 800-X	25.5	Rem.	RXP12	1⅛	1270	7600
Winchester	209	"HI-SKOR" 800-X	24.5	Fed.	12S4	1⅛	1250	8300
Winchester	209	"HI-SKOR" 800-X	25.5	Lage	Uniwad	1⅛	1255	7700
Winchester	209	"HI-SKOR" 800-X	25.0	Pacific	Versalite	1⅛	1270	7800

12 GAUGE TRAP — WINCHESTER 2¾-INCH COMPRESSION-FORMED "DOUBLE A," "UPLAND" AND "SUPER-X" (Cont.)

PRIMER		IMR POWDER		WAD COLUMN		LEAD SHOT (Oz.)	MUZZLE VELOCITY	CHAMBER PRESSURE
MFR.	No.	DESIGNATION	GRAINS	MFG.	DESIGNATION			
Winchester	209	"HI-SKOR" 800-X	25.5	WTW.	WindJammer	1⅛	1265	7100
Winchester	209	PB	25.0	Win.	WAA12F114	1⅛	1255	8500
Winchester	209	PB	24.5	Rem.	RXP12	1⅛	1245	8300
Winchester	209	PB	24.0	Fed.	12S4	1⅛	1250	9400
Federal	209	PB	24.5	Win.	WAA12F114	1⅛	1255	8700
Federal	209	PB	24.5	Rem.	RXP12	1⅛	1255	8800
Federal	209	PB	23.5	Fed.	12S4	1⅛	1245	9500
Winchester	209	SR 7625	27.0	Win.	WAA12F114	1⅛	1245	7600
Winchester	209	SR 7625	27.0	Rem.	R12H	1⅛	1260	7500
Winchester	209	SR 7625	26.0	Fed.	12S4	1⅛	1255	8400
Federal	209	SR 7625	26.5	Win.	WAA12F114	1⅛	1250	7700
Federal	209	SR 7625	26.5	Rem.	R12H	1⅛	1245	7700
Federal	209	SR 7625	25.5	Fed.	12S4	1⅛	1255	8400

20 GAUGE SKEET — REMINGTON 2¾-INCH "RXP"

PRIMER		IMR POWDER		WAD COLUMN		LEAD SHOT (Oz.)	MUZZLE VELOCITY	CHAMBER PRESSURE
MFR.	No.	DESIGNATION	GRAINS	MFG.	DESIGNATION			
CCI	209	PB	16.0	Rem.	RXP20	⅞	1200	10500
CCI	209	PB	16.5	Trico	No. 2	⅞	1200	10200
CCI	209	PB	16.0	Win.	WAA20	⅞	1200	10800
Federal	410	PB	Lage	lage	Uniwad	⅞	1210	10800
Winchester	209	SR 7625	17.0	Rem.	RXP20	⅞	1205	9600
CCI	209	SR 7625	16.5	Fed.	20S1	⅞	1210	10900
Federal	209	SR 7625	16.5	Trico	No. 2	⅞	1185	10500
Federal	209	SR 7625	16.0	Win.	WAA20	⅞	1200	10500
Federal	209	SR 7625	17.0	Lage	Uniwad	⅞	1190	10400
Winchester	209	SR 4756	20.0	Rem.	RXP20	⅞	1200	8600
Federal	209	SR 4756	18.5	Fed.	20S1	⅞	1210	10600
Federal	209	SR 4756	19.5	Trico	No. 2	⅞	1200	10100
Federal	209	SR 4756	19.0	Win.	WAA20	⅞	1215	10000
Federal	209	SR 4756	19.0	Lage	Uniwad	⅞	1200	9800

20 GAUGE SKEET — FEDERAL 2¾-INCH PAPER TARGET

PRIMER		IMR POWDER		WAD COLUMN		LEAD SHOT (Oz.)	MUZZLE VELOCITY	CHAMBER PRESSURE
MFR.	No.	DESIGNATION	GRAINS	MFG.	DESIGNATION			
Federal	209	“HI-SK0R” 700-X	14.5	Fed.	20S1	7/8	1190	10900
CCI	209	“HI-SKOR” 700-X	15.0	Trico	No. 2	7/8	1200	10700
Winchester	209	“HI-SKOR” 700-X	15.0	Win.	WAA20	7/8	1210	10500
Federal	209	“HI-SXOR” 800X	17.0	Fed.	20S1	7/8	1195	9300
Federal	209	“HI-SKOR” 800-X	17.0	Rem.	RXP20	7/8	1190	7800
Federal	209	“HI-SXOR” 800-X	17.5	Win.	WAA20	7/8	1210	8600
Federal	209	“HI-SKOR” 800-X	17.5	Lage	Uniwad	7/8	1195	8000
Federal	209	“HI-SXOR” 800-X	17.5	Pacific	Versalite	7/8	1205	8200
Federal	209	“HI-SXOR” 800-X	17.5	Trico	Precision 2	7/8	1210	9000
CCI	209M	“HI-SKOR” 800-X	17.0	Fed.	20S1	7/8	1190	8300
CCI	209M	“HI-SKOR” 800-X	17.5	Rem.	RXP20	7/8	1200	7900
CCI	209M	“HI-SKOR” 800-X	17.5	Win.	WAA20	7/8	1210	8500
CCI	209M	“HI-SKOR” 800-X	17.5	Lage	Uniwad	7/8	1190	8200
CCI	209M	“HI-SKOR” 800-X	17.5	Pacific	Versalite	7/8	1210	8200
CCI	209M	“HI-SKOR” 800-X	17.5	Trico	Precision 2	7/8	1205	8300
Federal	209	PB	17.5	Fed.	20S1	7/8	1205	9100
Federal	209	PB	17.5	Rem.	RXP20	7/8	1215	9000
Federal	209	PB	17.0	Trico	No. 2	7/8	1200	10700
Federal	209	PB	17.5	Win.	WAA20	7/8	1205	9000
Federal	209	PB	17.5	Lage	Uniwad	7/8	1205	10300
Federal	209	SR 7625	18.5	Fed.	20S1	7/8	1210	8700
Federal	209	SR 7625	18.5	Rem.	RXP20	7/8	1220	8500
Federal	209	SR 7625	18.0	Trico	No. 2	7/8	1195	8600
Federal	209	SR 7625	18.0	Win.	WAA20	7/8	1210	9100
Federal	209	SR 7625	18.5	Lage	Uniwad	7/8	1195	8800
Federal	209	SR 4756	20.5	Fed.	20S1	7/8	1200	8600
Federal	209	SR 4756	21.0	Rem.	RXP20	7/8	1210	8200
Federal	209	SR 4756	21.0	Trico	No. 2	7/8	1190	8100
Federal	209	SR 4756	21.0	Win.	WAA20	7/8	1215	8600
Federal	209	SR 4756	21.0	Lage	Uniwad	7/8	1190	8000

20 GAUGE SKEET — FEDERAL 2¾-INCH PLASTIC TARGET

PRIMER		IMR POWDER		WAD COLUMN		LEAD SHOT (Oz.)	MUZZLE VELOCITY	CHAMBER PRESSURE
MFR.	No.	DESIGNATION	GRAINS	MFG.	DESIGNATION			
Federal	209	"HI-SKOR" 700-X	15.0	Rem.	RXP20	7/8	1205	10200
Remington	209P	"HI-SKOR" 700-X	14.5	Activ	W-28	7/8	1200	10600
Remington	209P	"HI-SKOR" 700-X	15.0	Trico	No. 2	7/8	1215	10400
Remington	209P	"HI-SKOR" 700-X	15.0	WTW.	WindJammer	7/8	1205	9900
Federal	209	"HI-SKOR" 800-X	18.0	Fed.	20SI	7/8	1210	8600
Federal	209	"HI-SKOR" 800-X	18.0	Rem.	RXP20	7/8	1205	8000
Federal	209	"HI-SKOR" 800-X	18.0	Win.	WAA20	7/8	1200	7900
Federal	209	"HI-SKOR" 800-X	18.5	Lage	Uniwad	7/8	1215	8400
Federal	209	"HI-SKOR" 800-X	18.0	Pacific	Versalite	7/8	1205	8000
CCI	209M	"HI-SKOR" 800-X	18.5	Fed.	20SI	7/8	1215	8600
CCI	209M	"HI-SKOR" 800-X	18.5	Rem.	RXP20	7/8	1210	7700
CCI	209M	"HI-SKOR" 800 X	18.5	Win.	WAA20	7/8	1210	8200
CCI	209M	"HI-SKOR" 800 X	19.0	Lage	Uniwad	7/8	1210	7900
CCI	209M	"HI-SKOR" 800-X	18.5	Pacific	Versalite	7/8	1205	8000
Federal	209	PB	17.0	Rem.	RXP20	7/8	1205	9800
Winchester	209	PB	17.5	Trico	No. 2	7/8	1200	9400
Federal	209	SR 7625	17.5	Rem.	RXP20	7/8	1195	8400
Federal	209	SR 7625	18.5	Trico	No. 2	7/8	1205	8300
Federal	209	SR 4756	20.5	Rem.	SP20	7/8	1210	8300
Federal	209	SR 4756	21.5	Trico	No. 2	7/8	1215	8400

20 GAUGE TARGET — FEDERAL 2¾-INCH FIELD

PRIMER		IMR POWDER		WAD COLUMN		LEAD SHOT (Oz.)	MUZZLE VELOCITY	CHAMBER PRESSURE
MFR.	No.	DESIGNATION	GRAINS	MFG.	DESIGNATION			
Federal	410	"HI-SKOR" 700-X	15.5	Trico	No. 2	7/8	1205	10200
CCI	209	"HI-SKOR" 700-X	15.0	Trico	No. 2	7/8	1215	10700
Winchester	209	"HI-SKOR" 700-X	15.0	Lage	Uniwad	7/8	1200	10700
Federal	209	PB	18.0	Rem.	RXP20	7/8	1220	9000
Federal	209	PB	17.0	Trico	No. 2	7/8	1210	10300
Federal	209	PB	17.0	Lage	Uniwad	7/8	1195	9200
Federal	209	SR 7625	19.0	Rem.	RXP20	7/8	1220	7900
Federal	209	SR 7625	18.0	Trico	No. 2	7/8	1205	8900
Federal	209	SR 7625	18.5	Lage	Uniwad	7/8	1205	8300

20 GAUGE TARGET — FEDERAL 2¾-INCH FIELD (Cont.)

PRIMER		IMR POWDER		WAD COLUMN		LEAD SHOT (Oz.)	MUZZLE VELOCITY	CHAMBER PRESSURE
MFR.	No.	DESIGNATION	GRAINS	MFG.	DESIGNATION			
Federal	209	SR 4756	20.5	Rem.	RXP20	⅞	1190	8100
Federal	209	SR 4756	21.0	Trico	No. 2	⅞	1190	8100
Federal	209	SR 4756	21.0	Lage	Uniwad	⅞	1200	7700

20 GAUGE TARGET — WINCHESTER 2¾-INCH FIELD COMPRESSION-FORMED "DOUBLE A," "UPLAND" AND "SUPER-X"

PRIMER		IMR POWDER		WAD COLUMN		LEAD SHOT (Oz.)	MUZZLE VELOCITY	CHAMBER PRESSURE
MFR.	No.	DESIGNATION	GRAINS	MFG.	DESIGNATION			
Winchester	209	"HI-SKOR" 700-X	12.5	Win.	WAA20	⅞	1110	10800
Federal	209	"HI-SKOR" 700-X	11.7	Win.	WAA20	⅞	1080	10700
Winchester	209	"HI-SKOR" 800-X	17.0	Win.	WAA20	⅞	1210	9800
Winchester	209	"HI-SKOR" 800-X	17.0	Rem.	RXP20	⅞	1200	9500
Winchester	209	"HI-SKOR" 800-X	17.0	Fed.	20S1	⅞	1210	10600
Winchester	209	"HI-SKOR" 800-X	17.5	Lage	Uniwad	⅞	1215	9400
Winchester	209	"HI-SKOR" 800-X	17.0	Pacific	Versalite	⅞	1200	9300
Federal	209	"HI-SKOR" 800-X	16.5	Win.	WAA20	⅞	1200	9900
Federal	209	"HI-SKOR" 800-X	16.5	Rem.	RXP20	⅞	1195	9600
Federal	209	"HI-SKOR" 800-X	16.5	Fed.	20S1	⅞	1200	10800
Federal	209	"HI-SKOR" 800-X	17.0	Lage	Uniwad	⅞	1200	9800
Federal	209	"HI-SKOR" 800-X	16.5	Pacific	Versalite	⅞	1200	9900
Winchester	209	PB	16.0	Win.	WAA20	⅞	1180	10200
CCI	209	PB	16.0	Win.	WAA20	⅞	1185	10600
CCI	209	PB	16.5	Trico	No. 2	⅞	1205	10500
Federal	410	PB	16.5	Lage	Uniwad	⅞	1200	10700
Winchester	209	SR 7625	17.5	Win.	WAA20	⅞	1205	9300
Federal	410	SR 7625	17.5	Fed.	20S1	⅞	1200	9700
Winchester	209	SR 7625	17.5	Fed.	20S1	⅞	1210	10100
Winchester	209	SR 7625	17.5	Trico	No. 2	⅞	1210	9900
Federal	209	SR 7625	17.5	Lage	Uniwad	⅞	1215	10400
Federal	209	SR 4756	19.5	Win.	WAA20	⅞	1210	10100
Federal	209	SR 4756	19.5	Rem.	SP20	½	1215	9500

20 GAUGE TARGET — WINCHESTER 2¾-INCH FIELD COMPRESSION-FORMED "DOUBLE A," "UPLAND" AND "SUPER-X" (Cont.)

PRIMER		IMR POWDER		WAD COLUMN		LEAD SHOT (Oz.)	MUZZLE VELOCITY	CHAMBER PRESSURE
MFR.	No.	DESIGNATION	GRAINS	MFG.	DESIGNATION			
Federal	209	SR 4756	19.5	Trico	No. 2	7/8	1200	10000
Federal	209	SR 4756	19.0	Lage	Uniwad	7/8	1190	9600

20 GAUGE TARGET — Activ 2¾-INCH

PRIMER		IMR POWDER		WAD COLUMN		LEAD SHOT (Oz.)	MUZZLE VELOCITY	CHAMBER PRESSURE
MFR.	No.	DESIGNATION	GRAINS	MFG.	DESIGNATION			
Federal	209	"HI-SKOR" 800-X	17.0	Fed.	20S1	7/8	1190	8200
Remington	209P	"HI-SKOR" 800-X	17.5	Rem.	RXP20	7/8	1195	8000
Winchester	209	"HI-SKOR" 800-X	17.0	Win.	WAA20	7/8	1190	8000
Federal	209	SR 7625	18.5	Fed.	20S1	7/8	1225	9700
Remington	209P	SR 7625	19.5	Rem.	RXP20	7/8	1210	7800
Winchester	209	SR 7625	19.0	Win.	WAA20	7/8	1220	8200
Federal	209	SR 4756	20.5	Fed.	20S1	7/8	1210	9000
Remington	209P	SR 4756	21.0	Rem.	RXP20	7/8	1200	8100
Winchester	209	SR 4756	21.0	Win.	WAA20	7/8	1205	8000

28 GAUGE TARGET — REMINGTON 2¾-INCH SP EXPRESS

PRIMER		IMR POWDER		WAD COLUMN		LEAD SHOT (Oz.)	MUZZLE VELOCITY	CHAMBER PRESSURE
MFR.	No.	DESIGNATION	GRAINS	MFG.	DESIGNATION			
Remington	209P	"HI-SKOR" 800-X	15.0	Rem.	PT28	3/4	1200	9600
Remington	209P	"HI-SKOR" 800-X	15.0	Fed.	28S1	3/4	1220	9300
Remington	209P	"HI-SKOR" 800-X	15.0	Win.	WAA28	3/4	1215	9300
Remington	209P	"HI-SKOR" 800-X	17.0	Rem.	PT28	3/4	1305	11000
Remington	209P	"HI-SKOR" 800-X	16.5	Win.	WAA28	3/4	1295	10600
CCI	209M	"HI SKOR" 800-X	14.0	Rem.	SP28	3/4	1215	9400
CCI	209M	"HI SKOR" 800-X	14.0	Fed.	28S1	3/4	1195	9600
CCI	209M	"HI SKOR" 800-X	14.5	Win.	WAA28	3/4	1220	9400
CCI	209M	"HI-SKOR" 800-X	15.5	Rem.	SP28	3/4	1290	10700
CCI	209M	"HI-SKOR" 800-X	16.0	Win.	WAA28	3/4	1300	10800

28 GAUGE TARGET — REMINGTON 2¾-INCH SP EXPRESS (Cont.)

PRIMER		IMR POWDER		WAD COLUMN		LEAD SHOT (Oz.)	MUZZLE VELOCITY	CHAMBER PRESSURE
MFR.	No.	DESIGNATION	GRAINS	MFG.	DESIGNATION			
Federal	410	PB	14.5	Rem.	SP28	¾	1190	10800
Winchester	209	PB	14.0	Rem.	SP28	¾	1185	11100
Federal	209	SR 7625	14.0	Rem.	SP28	¾	1190	10300
Winchester	209	SR 7625	15.0	Rem.	SP28	¾	1200	9100
CCI	209	SR 4756	17.0	Rem	SP28	¾	1210	8700
Federal	209	SR 4756	16.0	Rem.	SP28	¾	1195	9800
Winchester	209	SR 4756	17.0	Rem.	SP28	¾	1205	8400

28 GAUGE TARGET — FEDERAL 2¾-INCH PLASTIC TARGET AND "HI-POWER"

PRIMER		IMR POWDER		WAD COLUMN		LEAD SHOT (Oz.)	MUZZLE VELOCITY	CHAMBER PRESSURE
MFR.	No.	DESIGNATION	GRAINS	MFG.	DESIGNATION			
Federal	209	"HI-SKOR" 800-X	14.5	Fed.	28S1	¾	1215	10300
Federal	209	"HI-SKOR" 800-X	14.0	Rem.	SP28	¾	1210	9600
Federal	209	"HI-SKOR" 800-X	14.5	Win.	WAA28	¾	1220	9600
Federal	410	"HI-SKOR" 800-X	16.0	Fed.	28S1	¾	1275	11200
Federal	209	"HI-SKOR" 800-X	15.5	Rem.	SP28	¾	1280	10700
Federal	209	"HI-SKOR" 800-X	16.0	Win.	WAA28	¾	1290	10700
CCI	209M	"HI-SKOR" 800-X	14.5	Fed.	28S1	¾	1205	9900
CCI	209M	"HI-SKOR" 800-X	14.5	Rem	SP28	¾	1210	8900
CCI	209M	"HI-SKOR" 800-X	14.5	Win.	WAA28	¾	1205	8800
CCI	209M	"HI-SKOR" 800-X	16.0	Fed.	28S1	¾	1280	10700
CCI	209M	"HI-SKOR" 800-X	16.0	Rem.	SP28	¾	1295	10600
CCI	209M	"HI-SKOR" 800-X	16.0	Win.	WAA28	¾	1290	10200
Federal	410	PB	14.0	Fed.	28S1	¾	1185	10900
CCI	209	PB	14.0	Fed.	28S1	¾	1195	11300
Federal	410	PB	14.0	Rem.	SP28	¾	1185	10000
CCI	209	PB	14.0	Rem.	SP28	¾	1200	10100
Federal	410	SR 7625	15.0	Fed.	28S1	¾	1200	10100
Winchester	209	SR 7625	15.0	Fed.	28S1	¾	1215	10700
Federal	209	SR 7625	14.5	Rem.	SP28	¾	1205	10400
Winchester	209	SR 7625	15.0	Rem.	SP28	¾	1195	9200

28 GAUGE TARGET — FEDERAL 2¾-INCH PLASTIC TARGET AND "HI-POWER" (Cont.)

PRIMER		IMR POWDER		WAD COLUMN		LEAD SHOT (Oz.)	MUZZLE VELOCITY	CHAMBER PRESSURE
MFR.	No.	DESIGNATION	GRAINS	MFG.	DESIGNATION			
Federal	209	SR 4756	16.0	Fed.	28S1	¾	1195	9900
CCI	209	SR 4756	17.0	Fed.	28S1	¾	1200	8700
Federal	209	SR 4756	16.5	Rem.	SP28	¾	1220	10400
Winchester	209	SR 4756	17.5	Rem.	SP28	¾	1200	8200

28 GAUGE TARGET — WINCHESTER 2¾-INCH FIELD COMPRESSION-FORMED "DOUBLE A," "UPLAND" AND "SUPER-X"

PRIMER		IMR POWDER		WAD COLUMN		LEAD SHOT (Oz.)	MUZZLE VELOCITY	CHAMBER PRESSURE
MFR.	No.	DESIGNATION	GRAINS	MFG.	DESIGNATION			
Winchester	209	"HI-SKOR" 800-X	14.0	Win.	WAA28	¾	1210	10800
CCI	209M	"HI-SKOR" 800-X	14.0	Win.	WAA28	¾	1210	10500
Remington	209P	"HI-SKOR" 800-X	15.5	Fed.	28S1	¾	1205	10400
Remington	209P	"HI-SKOR" 800-X	17.5	Win.	WAA28	¾	1290	9800

.410 BORE TARGET — REMINGTON 2½-INCH SP EXPRESS

PRIMER		IMR POWDER		WAD COLUMN		LEAD SHOT (Oz.)	MUZZLE VELOCITY	CHAMBER PRESSURE
MFR.	No.	DESIGNATION	GRAINS	MFG.	DESIGNATION			
Remington	209P	IMR 4227	18.5	Trico	Precision No. 4	½	1170	8300
Federal	209	IMR 4227	17.5	Trico	Precision No. 4	½	1210	11000
Winchester	209	IMR 4227	17.5	Trico	Precision No. 4	½	1170	10100
CCI	209	IMR 4227	17.5	Trico	No. 4	½	1140	8500
Federal	209	IMR 4227	15.5	Rem.	SP410	½	1105	10300
Federal	209	IMR 4227	15.5	Fed.	410SC	½	1105	10500

.410 BORE TARGET — FEDERAL 2½-INCH PLASTIC TARGET

PRIMER		IMR POWDER		WAD COLUMN		LEAD SHOT (Oz.)	MUZZLE VELOCITY	CHAMBER PRESSURE
MFR.	No.	DESIGNATION	GRAINS	MFG.	DESIGNATION			
Federal	209	IMR 4227	15.5	Fed.	410SC	½	1115	11200
Federal	209	IMR 4227	15.5	Rem	SP410	½	1115	11100
Federal	410	IMR 4227	17.5	Trico	No. 4	½	1155	9100
CCI	209	IMR 4227	17.5	Trico	No. 4	½	1165	9100
Remington	209P	IMR 4227	19.0	Trico	No. 4	½	1195	9000
Winchester	209	IMR 4227	17.5	Trico	No. 4	½	1180	10900

.410 BORE TARGET — WINCHESTER 2½-INCH COMPRESSED FORMED "DOUBLE A" AND "SUPER-X"

PRIMER		IMR POWDER		WAD COLUMN		LEAD SHOT (Oz.)	MUZZLE VELOCITY	CHAMBER PRESSURE
MFR.	No.	DESIGNATION	GRAINS	MFG.	DESIGNATION			
Winchester	209	IMR 4227	16.0	Trico	No. 4	½	1135	11100
CCI	209	IMR 4227	16.0	Trico	No. 4	½	1115	9700
Federal	410	IMR 4227	16.0	Trico	No. 4	½	1110	9600
Remington	209P	IMR 4227	16.5	Trico	No. 4	½	1135	9500

Chapter 20

Hunting Loads for Shotshells

Reloading shotshells for hunting purposes is not as popular as loading shotshells for sporting clays, skeet, and trap competition. Even so, hunters who can reload their own shotshells will take home more game using fewer firearms.

A shooter can reload for about one-third the cost of factory-bought ammo and each reloader has a favorite combination that gives the best results in the field for a particular situation or hunting conditions.

Another reason for reloading shotshells is for shotguns with shorter chambers. Many older shotguns and some models made abroad have shorter chambers than the modern lengths. Consequently, reloading the proper length shotshell for the chamber size enables these short-chamber shotguns to be fired safely.

When reloading shotshells for hunting purposes, you should first decide what the load will be used for, then use a good reference book or chart to select a trial load, such as the ones in this chapter. Then try different listed loads until you find the one that patterns best in your shotgun.

CAUTION

Shotshells have relatively low breech pressure when compared to modern, high-velocity rifle loads. Still, reloading can be dangerous if you do not take certain precautions. Most shotguns are not built to withstand pressures over 15,000 psi, whereas many modern rifles will handle breech pressures of 60,000 psi or more. You will be using fast-burning powder in shotshells, and just a grain or two too much can increase the breech pressure tremendously.

Never exceed the factory recommendations, and if a load does not look right to you (even if it is printed in a reloading manual), always double check with another source before using the load. Typos are not uncommon!

Before practicing loading shotshells, it is recommended that you review Chapter 18 in this book. Then you will be able to approach the practice of reloading with more authority.

10 GAUGE FIELD LOAD — REMINGTON 2⅞-INCH SP "EXPRESS"

PRIMER		IMR POWDER		WAD COLUMN		LEAD SHOT (Oz.)	MUZZLE VELOCITY	CHAMBER PRESSURE
MFR.	No.	DESIGNATION	GRAINS	MFG.	DESIGNATION			
CCI	157	"HI-SKOR" 700-X	22.5	Rem.	SP10	1⅜	1190	9700
CCI	157	PB	30.0	Rem.	SP10	1⅜	1310	10000
CCI	157	PB	31.0	Pacific	Versalite	1⅜	1310	9600
CCI	157	SR 7625	27.0	Rem.	SP10	1½	1120	7200
CCI	157	SR 7625	31.0	Pacific	Versalite	1½	1260	10000

10 GAUGE FIELD LOAD — REMINGTON 3½-INCH SP "EXPRESS"

PRIMER		IMR POWDER		WAD COLUMN		LEAD SHOT (Oz.)	MUZZLE VELOCITY	CHAMBER PRESSURE
MFR.	No.	DESIGNATION	GRAINS	MFG.	DESIGNATION			
Remington	209P	"HI-SKOR" 700-X	27.0	Rem.	SP10 + (4) 20 ga. .135 in. cards	1½	1195	9300
Remington	209P	"HI-SKOR" 700-X	26.5	Rem.	Versalite + (4) 20 ga. .135 in. cards	1½	1200	9600
CCI	157	"HI-SKOR" 700-X	29.0	Rem.	SP10 + (4) 20 ga. .135 in. card	1½	1250	9900
CCI	157	"HI-SKOR" 700-X	30.0	Pacific	Versalite + (4) 20 ga. .135 in. cards	1½	1255	9900
CCI	157	PB	37.0	Rem.	SP10 + (1) 20 ga. .135 in. card	1¾	1245	9700
CCI	157	PB	38.0	Pacific	Versalite + (1) 20 ga. .135 in. card	1¾	1260	9700
CCI	157	SR 7625	41.5	Rem.	SP10	2	1235	9600
CCI	157	SR 7625	43.0	Pacific	Versalite	2	1250	10000

10 GAUGE FIELD LOAD — FEDERAL 3½-INCH PLASTIC FIELD

PRIMER		IMR POWDER		WAD COLUMN		LEAD SHOT (Oz.)	MUZZLE VELOCITY	CHAMBER PRESSURE
MFR.	No.	DESIGNATION	GRAINS	MFG.	DESIGNATION			
Federal	209	"HI-SKOR" 700-X	29.5	Rem.	SP10 + (5) 20 ga. .135 in. cards	1½	1230	9900
Federal	209	"HI-SKOR" 800-X	35.0	Rem.	SP10 + (3) 20 ga. .135 in. cards	2	1205	9600
Winchester	209	"HI-SKOR" 800-X	34.5	Rem.	SP10 + (3) 20 ga. .135 in. cards	2	1190	9800
Winchester	209	"HI-SKOR" 800-X	32.5	BP	BPD + (2) 20 ga. ½ in. fiber	2	1195	9900
CCI	209M	"HI-SKOR" 800-X	32.5	BP	BPD + (2) 20 ga. ½ in. fiber	2	1200	9800
Federal	209	PB	37.5	Rem.	SP10 + (3) 20 ga. .135 in. cards	1⅝	1295	9800
Federal	209	SR 7625	41.0	Rem.	SP10 + (2) 20 ga. .135 in. cards	1⅞	1260	9700
Federal	209	SR 4756	40.5	Pacific	Versalite	2¼	1155	9900
CCI	209	SR 4756	42.5	Pacific	Versalite	2¼	1180	10000
Federal	209	SR 4756	37.5	Pacific	Versaute	2⅜	1150	9600
Winchester	209	SR 4756	38.5	Pacific	Versalite	2⅜	1155	9800

10 GAUGE FIELD LOAD — WINCHESTER 3½-INCH POLYFORMED PLASTIC

PRIMER		IMR POWDER		WAD COLUMN		LEAD SHOT (Oz.)	MUZZLE VELOCITY	CHAMBER PRESSURE
MFR.	No.	DESIGNATION	GRAINS	MFG.	DESIGNATION			
Winchester	209	"HI-SKOR" 700-X	29.0	Pacific	VERSALIIE + (4) 20 ga .135 b. cards	1½	1215	9900
Winchester	209	"HI-SKOR" 700-X	29.0	Rem.	SP10 + (4) 20 ga. .135 in. cards	1½	1215	9600
Winchester	209	"HI-SKOR" 800-X	34.5	BP	BPD + (1) 20 ga. ½ in. fiber + (1) .135 in. card	2	1205	10000
Winchester	209	"HI-SKOR" 800-X	36.5	Pacific	Versalite + (2) 20 ga .135 in. cards	2	1205	9600
Winchester	209	"HI-SKOR" 800-X	36.5	Rem.	SP10 + (1) .135 in. cards	2	1215	9700

10 GAUGE FIELD LOAD — WINCHESTER 3½-INCH POLYFORMED PLASTIC (Cont.)

PRIMER		IMR POWDER		WAD COLUMN		LEAD SHOT (Oz.)	MUZZLE VELOCITY	CHAMBER PRESSURE
MFR.	No.	DESIGNATION	GRAINS	MFG.	DESIGNATION			
CCI	209M	"HI-SKOR" 800-X	34.5	BP	BPD + (1) 20 ga. ½ in. fiber + (1) ·135 in. card	2	1200	9700
CCI	209M	"HI-SKOR" 800-X	37.5	Pacific	Versalite + (2) 20 ga. 135 in. cards	2	1215	9300
CCI	209M	"HI-SKOR" 800-X	37.0	Rem.	SP10 + (1) .135 in. card	2	1215	8700
Federal	209	PB	37.5	Pacific	Versalite+(1) 20 ga. .135 in. card	1⅞	1200	9700
Federal	209	PB	39.0	Rem.	SP10	1⅞	1220	10000
Federal	209	PB	35.0	Pacific	Versalite + (1) 20 ga. .135 in. card	2	1120	9900
Federal	209	PB	36.0	Rem.	SP10	2	1155	10000
Winchester	209	SR 7625	40.0	Pacific	Versalite	2	1210	9700
Winchester	209	SR 7625	41.0	Rem.	SP10	2	1230	10000
Winchester	209	SR 7625	39.5	Pacific	Versalite	2⅛	1165	9900
Winchester	209	SR 7625	38.5	Rem.	SP10	2⅛	1155	9900
Winchester	209	SR 4756	48.5	Rem.	SP10	2	1305	9900
Winchester	209	SR 4756	45.0	Rem.	SP10	2⅛	1240	9800

12 GAUGE BUCKSHOT — PETERS 2¾ TARGET LOAD

PRIMER		IMR POWDER		WAD COLUMN		BUCKSHOT		MUZZLE VELOCITY	CHAMBER PRESSURE
MFR.	No.	DESIGNATION	GRAINS	MFG.	DESIGNATION	SIZE	PELLETS		
Federal	209	"HI-SKOR" 700-X	19.0	Rem.	SP12	4	25	1200	10600
Federal	209	"HI-SKOR" 700-X	19.0	Win.	WAA12R	3	23	1220	10500
Federal	209	"HI-SKOR" 700-X	20.0	Win.	WAA12F114	1	12	1325	10600
Federal	209	"HI-SKOR" 700-X	19.0	Rem.	RP12	0	10	1235	10500
Federal	209	"HI-SKOR" 700-X	21.0	Rem.	SP12	00	8	1330	10700
Federal	209	"HI-SKOR" 700-X	24.5	Fed.	.200 in. Card + ½ in. + ¼ in. FC	000	6	1280	10900

12 GAUGE BUCKSHOT — PETERS 2¾ TARGET LOAD (Cont.)

PRIMER		IMR POWDER		WAD COLUMN		BUCKSHOT		MUZZLE VELOCITY	CHAMBER PRESSURE
MFR.	No.	DESIGNATION	GRAINS	MFG.	DESIGNATION	SIZE	PELLETS		
Federal	209	PB	24.5	Win.	WAA12R	4	25	1275	10600
Federal	209	PB	25.0	Win.	WAA12R	3	23	1310	10100
Federal	209	PB	26.0	Rem.	RP12	1	12	1425	10300
Federal	209	PB	25.5	Rem.	RP12	0	10	1335	10800
Federal	209	PB	27.5	Rem.	RP12	00	8	1425	10700
Federal	209	PB	33.0	Fed.	135 in. card + ⅜ in. FC	000	6	1405	10900
Federal	209	SR 7625	29.0	Win.	WAA12R	4	25	1365	10500
Federal	209	SR 7625	29.5	Win.	WAA12R	3	23	1410	10500
Federal	209	SR 7625	28.5	Rem.	RP12	1	12	1430	8500
Federal	209	SR 7625	30.0	Rem.	RP12	0	10	1430	10800
Federal	209	SR 7625	32.5	Rem.	RP12	00	8	1545	10900
Federal	209	SR 7625	39.0	Fed.	.135 in. card + ⅜ in. FC	000	6	1550	10800

12 GAUGE BUCKSHOT — REMINGTON 2¾ SP "EXPRESS" (with integral plastic wad) GREEN OR BLACK

PRIMER		IMR POWDER		WAD COLUMN		SUPER GREX GRAINS	BUCKSHOT		MUZZLE VELOCITY	CHAMBER PRESSURE
MFR.	No.	DESIGNATION	GRAINS	MFG.	DESIGNATION		SIZE	PELLETS		
Remington	209P	"HI-SKOR" 700-X	17.0	Rem.	RXP12	18	4	20	1200	8800
Remington	209P	"HI-SKOR" 700-X	17.0	Rem.	FIG 8	18	4	20	1205	8800
Remington	209P	"HI-SKOR" 700-X	17.0	Win.	WAA12F114	19	3	19	1195	9400
Remington	209P	"HI-SKOR" 700-X	16.5	Win.	WAA12F114	19	1	12	1185	10000
Remington	209P	"HI-SKOR" 700-X	17.5	Win.	WAA12	15	0	9	1205	9400
Remington	209P	"HI-SKOR" 700-X	17.0	Win.	WAA12F114	20	00	8	1185	9900
Federal	209	PB	22.5	Rem.	RP12	23	4	22	1250	9600
Federal	209	PB	23.0	Rem.	RP12	23	3	20	1285	10600
Federal	209	PB	22.5	Rem.	RP12	23	1	12	1270	10200
Federal	209	PB	21.0	Rem.	RP12	23	0	10	1170	9900

12 GAUGE BUCKSHOT — REMINGTON 2¾ SP "EXPRESS" (Cont.) (with integral plastic wad) GREEN OR BLACK

PRIMER		IMR POWDER		WAD COLUMN		SUPER GREX GRAINS	BUCKSHOT		MUZZLE VELOCITY	CHAMBER PRESSURE
MFR.	No.	DESIGNATION	GRAINS	MFG.	DESIGNATION		SIZE	PELLETS		
Federal	209	PB	23.5	Rem.	RP12	23	00	8	1310	10100
Federal	209	SR 7625	29.0	Rem.	RP12	20	4	21	1400	8800
Federal	209	SR 7625	29.5	Rem.	RP12	20	3	20	1400	9600
Federal	209	SR 7625	29.5	Rem.	RP12	20	1	12	1405	9500
Federal	209	SR 7625	28.0	Rem.	RP12	20	0	10	1320	9500
Federal	209	SR 7625	29.5	Rem.	RP12	20	00	8	1410	9000
Federal	209	SR 7625	24.0	BP	2 BPGS	30	000	8	1175	9300
Federal	209	SR 4756	28.0	BP	2 BPGS	25	4	27	1220	8500
Federal	209	SR 4756	28.0	BP	2 BPGS	25	3	25	1220	9000
Federal	209	SR 4756	28.0	BP	2 BPGS	25	1	1 5	1230	9400
Federal	209	SR 4756	27.5	BP	2 BPGS	25	0	12	1200	9800
Federal	209	SR 4756	28.5	BP	2 BPGS	25	00	10	1255	9400
Federal	209	SR 4756	28.0	BP	2 BPGS	25	000	8	1220	8500

12 GAUGE BUCKSHOT — FEDERAL 2¾ PLASTIC "HI-POWER"

PRIMER		IMR POWDER		WAD COLUMN		BUCKSHOT		MUZZLE VELOCITY	CHAMBER PRESSURE
MFR.	No.	DESIGNATION	GRAINS	MFG.	DESIGNATION	SIZE	PELLETS		
Federal	410	"HI-SKOR" 700-X	19.0	Fed.	12S3	4	27	1200	10900
Federal	209	"HI-SKOR" 700-X	19.5	Fed.	12S4	3	25	1190	10500
Federal	209	"HI-SKOR" 700-X	19.5	BP	4 BPGS	1	15	1200	10900
Federal	209	"HI-SKOR" 700-X	20.5	BP	4 BPGS	O	9	1345	10200
Federal	209	"HI-SKOR" 700-X	16.5	Fed.	12S4	00	8	1250	8100
Federal	209	"HI-SKOR" 700-X	18.0	Fed.	12S3	000	6	1255	7800
Federal	209	PB	25.0	Fed.	12S4	4	27	1275	10800

12 GAUGE BUCKSHOT — FEDERAL 2¾ PLASTIC "HI-POWER" (Cont.)

PRIMER		IMR POWDER		WAD COLUMN		BUCKSHOT		MUZZLE VELOCITY	CHAMBER PRESSURE
MFR.	No.	DESIGNATION	GRAINS	MFG.	DESIGNATION	SIZE	PELLETS		
Federal	209	PB	27.0	BP	4 BPGS	3	23	1375	10900
Federal	209	PB	26.5	BP	3 BPGS	1	15	1315	10800
Federal	209	PB	27.5	BP	4 BPGS	0	9	1410	9200
Federal	209	PB	26.0	Fed.	12C1	00	8	1355	8200
Federal	209	PB	28.0	Fed.	12S4	000	6	1425	8100
Federal	209	SR 7625	30.0	BP	4 BPGS	4	27	1315	8500
Federal	209	SR 7625	32.0	BP	4 BPGS	3	23	1375	8600
Federal	209	SR 7625	31.0	BP	4 BPGS	1	15	1355	9100
Federal	209	SR 7625	33.0	BP	4 BPGS	0	9	1445	7400
Federal	209	SR 7625	31.0	BP	4 BPGS	00	8	1440	7700
Federal	209	SR 7625	30.5	BP	4 BPGS	000	6	1405	6400
Federal	209	"HI-SKOR" 700-X	20.5	Rem.	SP12	4	24	1225	10800
Federal	209	"HI-SKOR" 700-X	20.5	Rem.	SP12	3	22	1235	10700
Federal	209	"HI-SKOR" 700-X	21.0	Fed.	12S4	1	12	1300	10900
Federal	209	"HI-SKOR" 700-X	20.5	Rem.	SP12	0	10	1230	10600
Federal	209	"HI-SKOR" 700-X	20.5	Fed.	12S4	00	8	1285	10700
Federal	209	"HI-SKOR" 700-X	23.0	BP	4 BPGS	000	6	1395	10600

12 GAUGE SLUG — FEDERAL 2¾ PAPER "CHAMPION" FOLD CRIMP

PRIMER		IMR POWDER		WAD COLUMN		SLUG MFR.	MUZZLE VELOCITY	CHAMBER PRESSURE
MFR.	No.	DESIGNATION	GRAINS	MFG.	DESIGNATION			
Federal	209	"HI-SKOR" 700-X	20.5	Fed.	.200 in. + .200 in. card	Brenneke	1230	10700
Federal	209	PB	27.5	Fed.	.200 in. + .045 in. card	Brenneke	1360	10800
Federal	209	SR 7625	32.5	Fed.	.200 in. + .045 in. card	Brenneke	1475	10,900
Federal	209	"HI-SKOR" 700-X	20.0	BP	2 BPGS	Brenneke	1250	10900
Federal	209	PB	26.0	BP	2 BPGS	Brenneke	1340	10100
Federal	209	SR 7625	31.0	BP	1 BPGS	Brenneke	1460	10700
Federal	209	SR 7625	37	BP	1 BPGS	Brenneke	1510	10100

12 GAUGE SLUG — FEDERAL 2¾ PLASTIC "HI-POWER"

PRIMER		IMR POWDER		WAD COLUMN		SLUG MFR.	MUZZLE VELOCITY	CHAMBER PRESSURE
MFR.	No.	DESIGNATION	GRAINS	MFG.	DESIGNATION			
Federal	209	"HI-SKOR" 700-X	20.5	Fed.	.200 in. + .200 in. card	Brenneke	1230	10700
Federal	209	PB	28.0	Fed.	.135 in. + .080 in. card	Brenneke	1340	10500
Federal	209	"HI-SKOR" 700-X	19.0	BP	2 BPGS.	Brenneke	1215	10300
Federal	209	PB	27.0	BP	1 BPG	Brenneke	1390	10600
Federal	209	SR 7625	31.0	BP	1 BPG	Brenneke	1460	10300
Federal	209	SR 4756	37.0	BP	1 BPG	Brenneke	1525	10700

12 GAUGE FIELD — PETERS 2¾ TARGET LOAD

PRIMER		IMR POWDER		WAD COLUMN		LEAD SHOT (Oz.)	MUZZLE VELOCITY	CHAMBER PRESSURE
MFR.	No.	DESIGNATION	GRAINS	MFG.	DESIGNATION			
Remington	209P	"HI-SKOR" 700-X	18.5	Rem.	RXP12	1	1285	9200
Remington	209P	"HI-SKOR" 700 X	18.0	Rem.	FIG 8	1	1285	10900
Remington	209P	"HI-SKOR" 700-X	19.5	Win.	WAA12	1	1280	9700
Federal	209	"HI-SKOR" 700 X	19.5	Rem.	RXP12	1	1285	10000
Federal	209	"HI-SKOR" 700-X	19.0	Pacific	Versalite	1	1290	10400
Remington	209P	"HI-SKOR" 800-X	24.0	Rem.	SP12	1¼	1225	8700
Remington	209P	"HI-SKOR" 800-X	24.5	Rem.	FIG 8	1¼	1220	8500
Remington	209P	"HI-SKOR" 800-X	24.0	ACTIV	T-32	1¼	1230	9100
Remington	209P	"HI-SKOR" 800-X	24.0	FED.	12S4	1¼	1230	9500
Remington	209P	"HHSKOR" 800-X	24.5	Lage	UMWAD	1¼	1220	8900
Remington	209P	"HI-SKOR" 800-X	24.0	Pacific	Versalite	1¼	1225	8900
Remington	209P	"HI-SKOR" 800-X	23.5	Win.	WAA12F114	1¼	1220	9400
Remington	209P	"HI-SKOR" 800-X	24.0	WTW.	WindJammer	1¼	1220	8700
Remington	209P	"HI-SKOR" 800-X	27.0	Rem.	SP12	1¼	1325	10300
Remington	209P	"HI-SKOR" 800-X	26.5	ACTIV	T-35	1¼	1325	10400
Remington	209P	"HI-SKOR" 800-X	27.0	Lage	Uniwad	1¼	1320	10600
Remington	209P	"HI-SKOR" 800-X	27.0	Win.	WAA12F114	1¼	1325	10900

12 GAUGE FIELD — PETERS 2¾ TARGET LOAD (Cont.)

PRIMER		IMR POWDER		WAD COLUMN		LEAD SHOT (Oz.)	MUZZLE VELOCITY	CHAMBER PRESSURE
MFR.	No.	DESIGNATION	GRAINS	MFG.	DESIGNATION			
Remington	209P	"HI-SKOR" 800-X	27.5	WTW.	WindJammer	1¼	1330	9600
CCI	209M	"HI-SKOR" 800 X	24.0	Rem.	SP12	1¼	1225	9600
CCI	209M	"HI-SKOR" 800-X	24.0	Fed.	12S4	1¼	1235	10500
CCI	209M	"HI-SKOR" 800-X	24.0	Win.	WAA12F114	1¼	1235	9700
CCI	209M	"HI-SKOR" 800-X	24.0	Lage	Uniwad	1¼	1215	9300
CCI	209M	"HI-SKOR" 800-X	24.0	Pacific	Versalite	1¼	1235	9900
CCI	209M	"HI-SKOR" 800-X	24.0	WTW.	WindJammer	1¼	1230	9000
CCI	209	"HI-SKOR" 800-X	24.5	Rem.	SP12	1⅜	1220	10600
CCI	209	"HI-SKOR" 800-X	24.5	Win.	WAA12R	1⅜	1220	10300
Federal	209	PB	23.5	Rem.	RXP12	1	1305	8100
Federal	209	PB	22.5	Fed.	12S3	1	1285	8900
Federal	209	PB	23.5	Lage	Uniwad	1	1295	8600
Federal	209	PB	23.0	Rem.	SP12	1¼	1220	10700
Winchester	209	PB	23.5	Rem.	SP12	1¼	1215	10100
Federal	209	SR 7625	25.5	Rem.	RXP12	1	1290	7400
Federal	209	SR 7625	25.0	Fed.	12S3	1	1295	7800
Federal	209	SR 7625	25.0	Pacific	Versalite	1	1280	6600
Federal	209	SR 7625	25.0	Rem.	SP12	1¼	1230	9700
Federal	209	SR 7625	24.5	Win.	WAA12F114	1¼	1225	10600
Federal	209	SR 7625	24.5	Lage	Uniwad	1¼	1215	10100
Winchester	209	SR 7625	28.5	Win.	WAA12R	1¼	1325	10800
Federal	209	SR 4756	27.5	Rem.	RP12	1¼	1220	9800
Federal	209	SR 4756	28.0	Lage	Uniwad	1¼	1230	10100
Federal	209	SR 4756	27.0	Pacific	Versalite	1¼	1215	10000
Federal	209	SR 4756	28.5	Win.	WAA12R	1¼	1230	9000
Winchester	209	SR4756	28.5	Rem.	RP12	1¼	1210	8600
Winchester	209	SR 4756	29.5	Win.	WAAI2R	1¼	1225	8400
Winchester	209	SR 4756	31.5	Rem.	RPI2	1¼	1325	10100
Winchester	209	SR 4756	32.0	Win.	WAA12R	1¼	1330	10100
CCI	209	SR 4756	31.5	Rem.	RP12	1¼	1320	10200

12 GAUGE FIELD LOAD — REMINGTON 2¾-INCH SP "EXPRESS"

PRIMER		IMR POWDER		WAD COLUMN		LEAD SHOT (Oz.)	MUZZLE VELOCITY	CHAMBER PRESSURE
MFR.	No.	DESIGNATION	GRAINS	MFG.	DESIGNATION			
Remington	209P	"HI-SKOR" 700-X	17.5	Rem.	RXP12	1⅛	1140	10000
Remington	209P	"HI-SKOR" 700-X	16.0	Rem.	FIG 8	1⅛	1145	10000
Remington	209P	"HI-SKOR" 700-X	17.0	ACTIV	T-32	1⅛	1155	8900
Remington	209P	"HI-SKOR" 800-X	24.5	Rem.	FIG 8	1⅛	1200	7700
Remington	209P	"HI-SKOR" 800-X	27.0	Rem.	FIG 8	1⅛	1300	8800
Remington	209P	"HI-SKOR" 800-X	30.0	Rem.	FIG 8	1⅛	1400	10400
Remington	209P	"HI-SKOR" 800-X	24.0	ACTIV	T-35	1⅛	1200	7800
Remington	209P	"HI-SKOR" 800-X	26.5	ACTIV	T-35	1⅛	1290	8900
Remington	209P	"HI-SKOR" 800-X	29.5	ACTIV	T-35	1⅛	1410	10800
Remington	209P	"HI-SKDR" 800-X	25.0	Rem.	SP12	1¼	1220	9300
Remington	209P	"HI-SKOR" 800-X	25.5	Rem.	RP12	1⅜	1215	10800
Remington	209P	"HI-SKDR" 800-X	25.5	ACTIV	T-35	1⅜	1210	10600
Remington	209P	"HI-SKOR" 800-X	25.5	Win.	WAA12R	1⅜	1220	10100
Remington	209P	"HI-SKDR" 800-X	24.0	Rem.	RP12	1½	1120	10700
Remington	209P	"HI-SKOR" 800-X	22.5	ACTIV	T-35	1½	1090	9700
CCI	209M	"HI-SKOR" 800-X	24.0	Lage	Uniwad	1⅛	1250	8200
CCI	209M	"HI-SKDR" 800-X	25.5	Lage	Uniwad	1⅛	1305	8700
CCI	209M	"HI-SKOR" 800-X	28.5	Lage	Uniwad	1⅛	1405	10400
CCI	209M	"HI-SKOR" 800-X	24.0	Lage	Uniwad	1¼	1225	9300
CCI	209M	"HI-SKOR" 800-X	27.5	Lage	Uniwad	1¼	1330	10900
CCI	209M	"HI-SKOR" 800-X	27.0	Rem.	SP12	1¼	1325	10600
CCI	209M	"HI-SKOR" 800-X	24.0	Lage	Uniwad	1⅜	1200	10800
CCI	209M	"HI-SKOR" 800-X	22.0	Win.	WAA12R	1½	1130	10800
CCI	209	PB	24.0	Rem.	RXP12	1	1285	7300
Federal	209	PB	23.0	Rem.	RXP12	1	1290	8300
CCI	209	PB	24.0	Win.	WAA12	1	1290	7400
Federal	209	PB	23.0	Win.	WAA12	1	1300	8700
CCI	209	PB	21.0	Rem.	RXP12	1⅛	1145	7100
CCI	209	PB	22.5	Rem.	RXP12	1⅛	1195	7500
CCI	209	PB	24.5	Rem.	R12H	1⅛	1260	8100
CCI	209	PB	23.0	Fed.	12S4	1⅛	1240	9000
CCI	209	PB	24.0	Rem.	RP12	1¼	1220	9900
Federal	209	PB	23.0	Rem.	RP12	1¼	1210	10800

12 GAUGE FIELD LOAD — REMINGTON 2¾-INCH SP "EXPRESS" (Cont.)

PRIMER		IMR POWDER		WAD COLUMN		LEAD SHOT (Oz.)	MUZZLE VELOCITY	CHAMBER PRESSURE
MFR.	No.	DESIGNATION	GRAINS	MFG.	DESIGNATION			
CCI	209	PB	24.5	Win.	WAA12R	1¼	1230	9600
Federal	209	PB	23.0	Win.	WAA12R	1¼	1210	10600
Federal	209	SR 7625	22.5	Fed.	12S4	1⅛	1195	8200
Federal	209	SR 7625	23.5	Win.	WAA12	1⅛	1205	8000
Federal	209	SR 7625	25.5	Rem.	R12H	1⅛	1250	7900
CCI	209	SR 7625	26.0	Rem.	RP12	1¼	1220	8200
Federal	209	SR 7625	25.0	Rem.	RP12	1¼	1215	8900
CCI	209	SR 7625	26.5	Win.	WAA12R	1¼	1225	8000
Federal	209	SR 7625	25.5	Win.	WAA12R	1¼	1225	8900
CCI	209	SR 7625	28.0	Rem.	RP12	1¼	1315	10500
CCI	209	SR 7625	29.5	Win.	WAA12R	1¼	1345	10600
Federal	209	SR 4756	28.5	Rem.	RP12	1¼	1220	9100
Winchester	209	SR 4756	29.5	Rem.	RP12	1¼	1215	8700
Federal	209	SR 4756	29.0	Win.	WAA12R	1¼	1215	8800
Winchester	209	SR 4756	30.5	Win.	WAA12R	1¼	1215	8300
Federal	209	SR 4756	31.5	Rem.	RP12	1¼	1330	10900
Winchester	209	SR 4756	33.0	Rem.	RP12	1¼	1340	10300
Federal	209	SR 4756	32.0	Win.	WAA12R	1¼	1325	10500
Winchester	209	SR 4756	33.5	Win.	WAA12R	1¼	1325	9800

12 GAUGE FIELD LOAD — REMINGTON 3-INCH SP "EXPRESS"

PRIMER		IMR POWDER		WAD COLUMN		LEAD SHOT (Oz.)	MUZZLE VELOCITY	CHAMBER PRESSURE
MFR.	No.	DESIGNATION	GRAINS	MFG.	DESIGNATION			
CCI	157	SR 4756	36.5	Rem.	SP12	1½	1330	10700
CCI	157	SR 4756	35.5	Win.	WAA12F114	1½	1305	10700
CCI	157	SR 4756	34.0	Rem.	RP12	1⅝	1235	10400
CCI	157	SR 4756	35.5	Win.	WAA12R	1⅝	1255	10500
CCI	157	SR 4756	31.5	Rem.	RP12	1¾	1150	10200
CCI	157	SR 4756	32.5	Win.	WAA12R	1¾	1170	10600

12 GAUGE FIELD LOAD — FEDERAL 2¾-INCH PAPER "CHAMPION"

PRIMER		IMR POWDER		WAD COLUMN		LEAD SHOT (Oz.)	MUZZLE VELOCITY	CHAMBER PRESSURE
MFR.	No.	DESIGNATION	GRAINS	MFG.	DESIGNATION			
Remington	209P	"HI-SKOR" 700-X	20.5	Fed.	12S3	1	1300	9600
Remington	209P	"HI-SKOR" 700-X	20.0	ACTIV	T-28	1	1295	8600
Remington	209P	"HI-SKOR" 700-X	20.0	Rem.	SP12	1¼	1195	10400
Winchester	209	"HI-SKOR" 700-X	21.0	Rem.	SP12	1¼	1215	10200
Federal	209	"HI-SKOR" 800-X	25.0	Fed.	12S4	1¼	1235	8700
Federal	209	"HI-SKOR" 800-X	25.5	Win.	WAA12F114	1¼	1215	8200
Federal	209	"HI-SKOR" 800-X	25.5	Rem.	R12H	1¼	1215	7800
Federal	209	"HI-SKOR" 800-X	25.5	Lage	Uniwad	1¼	1215	8000
Federal	209	"HI-SKOR" 800-X	28.0	Fed.	12S4	1¼	1325	10100
Federal	209	"HI-SKOR" 800-X	28.5	Win.	WAA12F114	1¼	1320	9700
Federal	209	"HI-SKOR" 800-X	29.0	Rem.	SP12	1¼	1325	9300
Federal	209	"HI-SKOR" 800-X	29.0	Lage	Uniwad	1¼	1330	9900
Federal	209	"HI-SKOR" 800-X	26.5	Fed.	12S4	1⅜	1255	10700
Federal	209	"HI-SKOR" 800-X	28.0	Rem.	SP12	1⅜	1270	10100
Federal	209	"HI-SKOR" 800-X	28.0	Win.	WAA12R	1⅜	1285	10100
CCI	209M	"HI-SKOR" 800-X	26.5	Fed.	12S4	1⅜	1260	10900
CCI	209M	"HI-SKOR" 800-X	27.5	Rem.	SP12	1⅜	1265	10200
CCI	209M	"HI-SKOR" 800-X	28.0	Win.	WAA12R	1⅜	1290	10300
Federal	209	"HI-SKOR" 800-X	27.0	Rem.	RP12	1½	1230	10600
Federal	209	"HI-SKOR" 800-X	27.5	Win.	WAA12R	1½	1260	10900
CCI	209M	"HI-SKOR" 800-X	27.0	Rem.	RP12	1½	1240	10600
CCI	209M	"HI-SKOR" 800-X	27.5	Win.	WAA12R	1½	1250	10900
Federal	209	PB	25.5	Fed.	12C1	1	1285	6900
Federal	209	PB	26.0	Rem.	R12L	1	1280	6500
Winchester	209	PB	26.5	Fed.	12C1	1	1285	6000
Winchester	209	PB	27.0	Rem.	R12L	1	1300	6300
Federal	209	PB	25.5	Rem.	RP12	1¼	1220	8200
Federal	209	PB	25.0	Win.	WAA12R	1¼	1220	9000
Winchester	209	PB	25.5	Rem.	RP12	1¼	1215	7900
Winchester	209	PB	26.0	Win.	WAA12R	1¼	1230	8400
Federal	209	PB	31.0	Fed.	.135 in. card + ¼ in. + 1¼ in. FC	1¼	1325	10900

12 GAUGE FIELD LOAD — FEDERAL 2¾-INCH PAPER "CHAMPION" (Cont.)

PRIMER		IMR POWDER		WAD COLUMN		LEAD SHOT (Oz.)	MUZZLE VELOCITY	CHAMBER PRESSURE
MFR.	No.	DESIGNATION	GRAINS	MFG.	DESIGNATION			
Federal	209	PB	26.5	Fed.	.080 in card + 1¼ in. FC + 12SC114	1⅜	1225	10800
Federal	209	SR 7625	28.0	Fed.	12C1	1	1270	5300
Federal	209	SR 7625	29.0	Rem.	R12L	1	1280	5100
Winchester	209	SR 7625	29.0	Fed.	12C1	1	1270	4900
Winchester	209	SR 7625	30.0	Rem.	R12L	1	1300	5200
Federal	209	SR 7625	27.0	Rem.	SP12	1¼	1225	7400
Federal	209	SR 7625	30.5	Rem.	RP12	1¼	1330	9300
Federal	209	SR 7625	31.0	Win.	WAA12R	1¼	1330	8600
Winchester	209	SR 7625	28.0	Win.	WAA12F114	1¼	1225	7300
Winchester	209	SR 7625	31.0	Rem.	RP12	1¼	1335	9000
Winchester	209	SR 7625	31.5	Win.	WAA12R	1¼	1325	8200
Federal	209	SR 7625	30.0	Rem.	RP12	1⅜	1290	10900
Federal	209	SR 7625	31.0	Win.	WAA12R	1⅜	1310	10500
Federal	209	SR 4756	30.5	Rem.	RP12	1¼	1215	7200
Federal	209	SR 4756	31.0	Win.	WAA12R	1¼	1225	6900
Winchester	209	SR 4756	32.0	Rem.	RP12	1¼	1225	6500
Winchester	209	SR 4756	33.5	Win.	WAA12R	1¼	1220	5800
Federal	209	SR 4756	34.0	Rem.	RP12	1¼	1325	8600
Federal	209	SR 4756	35.0	Win.	WAA12R	1¼	1335	8200
Winchester	209	SR 4756	34.5	Rem.	RP12	1¼	1325	8000
Winchester	209	SR 4756	35.5	Win.	WAA12R	1¼	1320	7800
Federal	209	SR 4756	36.0	Rem.	RP12	1⅜	1370	10900
Federal	209	SR 4756	36.0	Win.	WAA12R	1⅜	1370	10700
Federal	209	SR 4756	37.0	Fed.	.135 in. card + ⅜ in. FC	1½	1250	10900

12 GAUGE FIELD LOAD — FEDERAL 2¾-INCH PLASTIC "HI-POWER"

PRIMER		IMR POWDER		WAD COLUMN		LEAD SHOT (Oz.)	MUZZLE VELOCITY	CHAMBER PRESSURE
MFR.	No.	DESIGNATION	GRAINS	MFG.	DESIGNATION			
Federal	209	"HI-SKOR" 700-X	19.0	Fed.	12S3	1	1205	7200
Federal	209	"HI-SKOR" 700-X	21.0	Fed.	12S3	1	1295	8600
Federal	209	"HI-SKOR" 700-X	21.0	Rem.	R12L	1	1295	8400
Federal	209	"HI-SKOR" 700-X	18.0	Fed.	12S3	1⅛	1140	7800
Federal	209	"HI-SKOR" 700-X	19.5	Fed.	12S3	1⅛	1200	8800
Federal	209	"HI-SKOR" 700-X	21.0	Fed.	12S4	1⅛	1255	10300
Federal	410	"HI-SKOR" 700-X	21.5	Fed.	12S4	1¼	1210	9800
Federal	209	"HI-SKOR" 700-X	21.0	Rem.	SP12	1¼	1210	10400
Federal	209	PB	23.0	Fed.	12S3	1	1215	6200
Federal	209	PB	25.5	Fed.	12C1	1	1290	6600
Federal	209	PB	26.0	Rem.	R12L	1	1295	6600
Federal	209	PB	22.0	Fed.	12S4	1⅛	1150	6600
Federal	209	PB	23.0	Fed.	12S4	1⅛	1195	7300
Federal	209	PB	24.5	Fed.	12S4	1⅛	1250	8000
Federal	209	PB	25.5	Rem.	RP12	1¼	1230	8700
Federal	209	PB	25.5	Win.	WAA12R	1¼	1215	7800
Federal	209	PB	29.0	Rem.	RP12	1¼	1335	10900
Federal	209	PB	29.0	Win.	WAA12R	1¼	1330	10200
Federal	410	PB	30.0	Fed.	.080 in. card + ¼ in.FC+12SC112	1⅜	1295	10800
Federal	209	SR 7625	26.5	Fed.	12S3	1	1200	5400
Federal	209	SR 7625	29.0	Fed.	12C1	1	1285	5600
Federal	209	SR 7625	29.5	Rem.	R12L	1	1285	5600
Federal	209	SR 7625	24.5	Fed.	12S4	1⅛	1145	6000
Federal	209	SR 7625	25.5	Fed.	12S4	1⅛	1190	6400
Federal	209	SR 7625	27.0	Fed.	12S4	1⅛	1260	7100
Federal	209	SR 7625	27.5	Rem.	SP12	1¼	1225	7500
Federal	209	SR 7625	27.5	Win.	WAA12R	1¼	1215	7000
Federal	209	SR 7625	30.0	Rem.	RP12	1¼	1320	9200
Federal	209	SR 7625	31.0	Win.	WAA12R	1¼	1325	8600
Federal	209	SR 7625	30.5	Rem.	RP12	1⅜	1305	10300
Federal	209	SR 7625	32.0	Win.	WAA12R	1⅜	1340	10900
Federal	209	SR 7625	27.0	Win.	WAA12R	1½	1150	8900

12 GAUGE FIELD LOAD — FEDERAL 2¾-INCH PLASTIC "HI-POWER" (Cont.)

PRIMER		IMR POWDER		WAD COLUMN		LEAD SHOT (Oz.)	MUZZLE VELOCITY	CHAMBER PRESSURE
MFR.	No.	DESIGNATION	GRAINS	MFG.	DESIGNATION			
Federal	209	SR 4756	32.5	Rem.	SP12	1¼	1225	7000
Federal	209	SR 4756	33.0	Win.	WAA12R	1¼	1225	6700
Federal	209	SR 4756	36.0	Rem.	RP12	1¼	1330	8200
Federal	209	SR 4756	36.5	Win.	WAA12R	1¼	1330	7800
Federal	209	SR 4756	33.0	Rem.	RP12	1⅜	1255	8400
Federal	209	SR 4756	34.0	Win.	WAA12R	1⅜	1285	8600
Federal	209	SR 4756	30.0	Win.	WAA12R	1½	1160	8500

12 GAUGE FIELD LOAD — FEDERAL 2¾-INCH PLASTIC "GOLD MEDAL"

PRIMER		IMR POWDER		WAD COLUMN		LEAD SHOT (Oz.)	MUZZLE VELOCITY	CHAMBER PRESSURE
MFR.	No.	DESIGNATION	GRAINS	MFG.	DESIGNATION			
Federal	209	"HI-SKOR" 700-X	21.0	Fed.	12S3	1	1290	9100
Winchester	209	"HISKOR" 700-X	21.0	Fed.	12S3	1	1295	8400
Federal	209	"HI-SKOR" 700X	20.5	Fed.	12S4	1¼	1220	10900
Federal	209	"HI-SKOR" 700-X	21.0	Rem.	R12H	1¼	1225	10300
Winchester	209	"HI-SKOR" 700-X	20.5	Fed.	12S4	1¼	1215	10500
Winchester	209	"HI-SKOR" 700-X	21.0	Rem.	R12H	1¼	1225	9900
Federal	209	"HI-SKOR" 800-X	25.0	Fed.	12S3	1¼	1235	8300
Federal	209	"HI-SKOR" 800-X	25.0	Win.	WAA12F114	1¼	1225	7400
Federal	209	"HI-SKOR" 800-X	25.0	Rem.	R12H	1¼	1220	7900
Federal	209	"HI-SKOR" 800-X	25.5	Lage	Uniwad	1¼	1235	7900
Federal	209	"HI-SKOR" 800-X	27.5	Fed.	12S4	1¼	1325	9700
Federal	209	"HiSKOR" 800-X	28.0	Win.	WAA12F114	1¼	1330	8900
Federal	209	"HI-SKOR" 800-X	28.0	Rem.	R12H	1¼	1325	8900
Federal	209	"HI-SKOR" 800-X	28.0	Lage	Uniwad	1¼	1320	8900
Federal	209	"HHSKOR" 800-X	26.5	Fed.	12S4	1⅜	1280	10900
Federal	209	"HI-SKOR" 800-X	28.0	Rem.	SP12	1⅜	1310	10300
Federal	209	"HI-SKOR" 800-X	27.5	Win.	WAA12F114	1⅜	1310	10300
CCI	209M	"HI-SKOR" 800-X	26.5	Fed.	12S4	1⅜	1290	10600
CCI	209M	"HI-SKOR" 800-X	28.0	Rem.	SP12	1⅜	1305	10000
CCI	209M	"HI-SKOR" 800-X	27.5	Win.	WAA12F114	1⅜	1310	10200

12 GAUGE FIELD LOAD — FEDERAL 2¾-INCH PLASTIC "GOLD MEDAL" (Cont.)

PRIMER		IMR POWDER		WAD COLUMN		LEAD SHOT (Oz.)	MUZZLE VELOCITY	CHAMBER PRESSURE
MFR.	No.	DESIGNATION	GRAINS	MFG.	DESIGNATION			
Federal	209	"HI-SKOR" 800-X	27.5	Rem.	RP12	1½	1255	10900
Federal	209	"HI-SKOR" 800-X	27.0	Win.	WAA12R	1½	1270	10800
CCI	209M	"HI-SKOR" 800-X	27.5	Rem.	RP12	1½	1245	10800
CCI	209M	"HI-SKOR" 800X	27.0	Win.	WAA12R	1½	1265	10600
Federal	209	PB	24.5	Fed.	12S3	1	1295	6800
Winchester	209	PB	25.0	Fed.	12S3	1	1300	6700
Federal	209	PB	26.0	Rem.	SP12	1¼	1235	7800
Winchester	209	PB	26.0	Rem.	SP12	1¼	1235	7600
Federal	209	PB	29.0	Rem.	SP12	1¼	1335	10200
Winchester	209	PB	29.0	Rem.	SP12	1¼	1345	10400
Federal	209	SR 7625	28.5	Fed.	12S3	1	1305	6500
Federal	209	SR 7625	29.5	Rem.	R12L	1	1295	5800
Federal	209	SR 7625	28.5	Rem.	SP12	1¼	1230	6400
CCI	209M	SR 7625	28.0	Rem.	SP12	1¼	1225	6400
Federal	209	SR 7625	31.0	Rem.	SP12	1¼	1325	7700
CCI	209M	SR 7625	30.5	Rem.	SP12	1¼	1320	7600
Federal	209	SR 7625	31.5	Rem.	RP12	1⅜	1325	9800
Federal	209	SR 7625	31.5	Win.	WAA12R	1⅜	1305	9300
Federal	209	SR 4756	30.5	Rem.	SP12	1¼	1215	6300
CCI	209M	SR 4756	31.0	Rem.	SP12	1¼	1215	6300
Federal	209	SR 4756	34.0	Rem.	RP12	1¼	1325	7500
Federal	209	SR 4756	34.5	Win.	WAA12R	1¼	1325	7300
Federal	209	SR 4756	34.0	Rem.	RP12	1⅜	1340	9900
Federal	209	SR 4756	34.0	Win.	WAA12R	1⅜	1315	8600
Federal	209	SR 4756	32.0	BP	3 BPGS	1½	1245	9900

12 GAUGE FIELD LOAD — FEDERAL 3-INCH PLASTIC "HI-POWER"

PRIMER		IMR POWDER		WAD COLUMN		LEAD SHOT (Oz.)	MUZZLE VELOCITY	CHAMBER PRESSURE
MFR.	No.	DESIGNATION	GRAINS	MFG.	DESIGNATION			
Federal	209	"HI-SKOR" 700-X	24.0	Fed.	12S3	1¼	1275	10500
Federal	209	"HI-SKOR" 800-X	33.0	Fed.	12S3 + 20 ga.135 in. card	1¼	1420	9700
Federal	209	"HI-SKOR" 800-X	26.5	Fed.	12S3 + 20 ga. 135 in. card	1⅜	1200	7000
Federal	209	"HI-SKOR" 800-X	29.5	Fed.	12S3	1⅜	1295	8400
Federal	209	"Hi-SKOR" 800-X	32.0	Fed.	12S3	1⅜	1355	10000
Federal	209	"HI-SKOR" 800-X	27.5	Fed.	12S3	1½	1215	9400
Federal	209	"HI-SKOR" 800-X	30.0	Fed.	12S3	1½	1285	10700
Federal	209	"HI-SKOR" 800-X	28.0	Fed.	12S4	1⅝	1200	10700
Federal	209	"HI-SKOR" 800-X	25.5	Fed.	12S4	1¾	1105	10500
CCI	209M	"HI-SKOR" 800-X	30.0	Win.	WAA12	1½	1285	10600
CCI	209M	"HI-SKOR" 800-X	28.5	Lage	Uniwad	1⅝	1205	10000
CCI	209M	"HI-SKOR" 800-X	26.5	Lage	Uniwad	1¾	1120	10600
Federal	209	PB	31.0	Fed.	12S4	1¼	1365	10300
Winchester	209	PB	33.0	Win.	WAA12	1¼	1400	10400
Winchester	209	PB	29.0	Fed.	12S4	1⅜	1265	10500
Winchester	209	PB	30.0	Win.	WAA12	1⅜	1275	10500
Winchester	209	SR 7625	37.0	Fed.	12S4	1¼	1470	10900
Federal	209	SR 7625	37.0	Win.	WAA12	1¼	1440	9400
Federal	209	SR 7625	35.0	Fed.	12S4	1⅜	1375	10600
Federal	209	SR 7625	35.0	Rem.	R12H	1⅜	1370	10000
Federal	209	SR 7625	31.0	Fed.	12S4	1½	1235	10100
Winchester	209	SR 7625	33.0	Win.	WAA12F114	1½	1275	10400
Federal	209	SR 7625	32.0	Rem.	RP12	1⅝	1215	10500
Winchester	209	SR 7625	32.0	Win.	WAA12R	1⅝	1220	10500
Federal	209	SR 4756	42.0	Rem.	SP12	1⅜	1460	10400
Federal	209	SR 4756	43.0	Win.	WAA12R	1⅜	1480	10800
Federal	209	SR 4756	38.0	Rem.	SP12	1½	1350	10600
Federal	209	SR 4756	39.0	Win.	WAA12R	1½	1365	10700
Federal	209	SR 4756	36.0	Rem.	RP12	1⅝	1280	10900
Federal	209	SR 4756	36.0	Win.	WAA12R	1⅝	1275	10400
Federal	209	SR 4756	33.0	Rem.	RP12	1¾	1180	10800

12 GAUGE FIELD LOAD — WINCHESTER 2¾-INCH COMPRESSION-FORMED "DOUBLE A," "UPLAND" AND "SUPER-X"

PRIMER		IMR POWDER		WAD COLUMN		LEAD SHOT (Oz.)	MUZZLE VELOCITY	CHAMBER PRESSURE
MFR.	No.	DESIGNATION	GRAINS	MFG.	DESIGNATION			
Winchester	209	"HI-SKOR" 700-X	21.0	Fed.	12S1	1	1295	8800
Federal	209	"HI-SKDR" 700-X	20.5	Fed.	12S1	1	1285	8400
Winchester	209	"HI-SKOR" 800-X	25.0	Win.	WAA12F114	1¼	1225	8500
Winchester	209	"HI-SKOR" 800-X	25.0	Rem.	SP12	1¼	1230	8400
Winchester	209	"HI-SKOR" 800-X	24.5	Fed.	12S4	1¼	1215	9200
Winchester	209	"HI-SKOR" 800-X	25.0	Lage	Uniwad	1¼	1220	8400
Winchester	209	"HI-SKOR" 800-X	24.5	Pacific	Versalite	1¼	1215	8700
Winchester	209	"HI-SKOR" 800-X	25.0	WTW.	WindJammer	1¼	1215	7800
Federal	209	"HI-SKOR" 800-X	24.5	Win.	WAA12F114	1¼	1220	8900
Federal	209	"HI-SKOR" 800-X	24.5	Rem.	SP12	1¼	1220	8800
Federal	209	"HI-SKOR" 800-X	24.5	Fed.	12S4	1¼	1225	9900
Federal	209	"HI-SKOR" 800-X	25.0	Lage	Uniwad	1¼	1230	8600
Federal	209	"HI-SKOR" 800-X	24.5	Pacific	Versalite	1¼	1230	9400
Federal	209	"HI-SKOR" 800-X	24.5	WTW.	WindJammer	1¼	1210	8000
Winchester	209	"HI-SKOR" 800-X	27.5	Win.	WAA12F114	1¼	1320	10300
Winchester	209	"HI-SKOR" 800-X	28.0	Rem.	SP12	1¼	1330	10200
Winchester	209	"HI-SKOR" 800-X	28.0	Lage	Uniwad	1¼	1340	10500
Winchester	209	"HI-SKOR" 800-X	27.5	Pacific	Versalite	1¼	1325	10400
Winchester	209	"HI-SKOR" 800-X	28.5	WTW.	WindJammer	1¼	1335	9600
Federal	209	"HI-SKOR" 800-X	27.5	Win.	WAA12F114	1¼	1330	10900
Federal	209	"HI-SKOR" 800-X	28.0	Rem.	SP12	1¼	1335	10800
Federal	209	"HI-SKOR" 800-X	28.0	Lage	Uniwad	1¼	1330	10900
Federal	209	"HI-SKOR" 800-X	27.5	Pacific	Versalite	1¼	1325	10900
Federal	209	"HI-SKOR" 800-X	28.0	WTW.	WindJammer	1¼	1335	9700
Winchester	209	"HI-SKOR" 800-X	26.0	Rem.	SP12	1⅜	1235	10300
Winchester	209	"HI-SKOR" 800-X	26.0	Win.	WAA12R	1⅜	1250	10500
Federal	209	"HI-SKOR" 800-X	25.5	Rem.	SP12	1⅜	1205	10700
Federal	209	"HI-SKOR" 800-X	25.5	Win.	WAA12R	1⅜	1225	10300
Winchester	209	PB	25.5	Win.	WAA12	1	1290	6800
Federal	209	PB	24.0	Win.	WAA12	1	1285	7700
Winchester	209	PB	25.0	Win.	WAA12R	1¼	1220	8900
Winchester	209	PB	24.0	Rem.	RP12	1¼	1215	9800
Federal	209	PB	24.5	Win.	WAA12R	1¼	1220	9500

12 GAUGE FIELD LOAD — WINCHESTER 2¾-INCH COMPRESSION-FORMED "DOUBLE A," "UPLAND" AND "SUPER-X" (Cont.)

PRIMER		IMR POWDER		WAD COLUMN		LEAD SHOT (Oz.)	MUZZLE VELOCITY	CHAMBER PRESSURE
MFR.	No.	DESIGNATION	GRAINS	MFG.	DESIGNATION			
Winchester	209	SR 7625	28.0	Win.	WAA12	1	1285	6700
Federal	209	SR 7625	25.5	Win.	WAA12	1	1305	7800
Winchester	209	SR 7625	27.0	Win.	WAA12R	1¼	1215	7800
Winchester	209	SR 7625	26.5	Rem.	SP12	1¼	1215	8200
Federal	209	SR 7625	26.5	Win.	WAA12R	1¼	1225	8500
Federal	209	SR 7625	26.0	Rem.	SP12	1¼	1215	8600
Winchester	209	SR 7625	30.0	Win.	WAA12R	1¼	1335	10200
Winchester	209	SR 7625	29.0	Rem.	RP12	1¼	1330	10700
Federal	209	SR 7625	29.5	Win.	WAA12R	1¼	1330	10300
Federal	209	SR 7625	28.5	Rem.	RP12	1¼	1320	10800
Winchester	209	SR 4756	31.0	Win.	WAA12R	1¼	1210	7700
Winchester	209	SR 4756	30.5	Rem.	RP12	1¼	1215	8100
Federal	209	SR 4756	31.0	Win.	WAA12R	1¼	1225	7800
Federal	209	SR 4756	30.0	Rem.	RP12	1¼	1220	8400
Winchester	209	SR 4756	34.0	Win.	WAA12R	1¼	1330	9200
Winchester	209	SR 4756	33.5	Rem.	RP12	1¼	1335	9900
Federal	209	SR 4756	33.5	Win.	WAA12R	1¼	1320	9300
Federal	209	SR 4756	33.0	Rem.	RP12	1¼	1330	10000
Winchester	209	SR 4756	32.5	Win.	WAA12R	1⅜	1265	10000
Winchester	209	SR 4756	32.0	Rem.	RP12	1⅜	1260	10300
Federal	209	SR 4756	32.5	Win.	WAA12R	1⅜	1280	10400
Federal	209	SR 4756	32.0	Rem.	RP12	1⅜	1270	10700

12 GAUGE FIELD LOAD — WINCHESTER 3-INCH COMPRESSION-FORMED "SUPER-X"

PRIMER		IMR POWDER		WAD COLUMN		LEAD SHOT (Oz.)	MUZZLE VELOCITY	CHAMBER PRESSURE
MFR.	No.	DESIGNATION	GRAINS	MFG.	DESIGNATION			
Winchester	209	PB	29.0	Win.	WAA12	1¼	1325	9800
Winchester	209	PB	28.0	Rem.	RXP12	1¼	1310	10100
Federal	209	SR 7625	33.0	Win.	WAA12	1¼	1400	10400
Federal	209	SR 7625	32.0	Rem.	RXP12	1¼	1375	10300
Winchester	209	SR 7625	31.0	Win.	WAA12	1⅜	1290	10000
Federal	209	SR 7625	29.0	Fed.	12S4	1⅜	1260	10800
Federal	209	SR 7625	31.0	Rem.	RXP12	1⅜	1310	10700
Winchester	209	SR 7625	29.0	Win.	WAA12F114	1½	1205	10200
Winchester	209	SR 7625	29.0	Rem.	SP12	1½	1210	10000
Federal	209	SR 4756	36.0	Win.	WAA12F114	1⅜	1380	10800
Federal	209	SR 4756	36.0	Rem.	SP12	1⅜	1365	10600
Federal	209	SR 4756	33.0	Win.	WAA12R	1½	1255	10700
Federal	209	SR 4756	34.0	Rem.	SP12	1½	1290	10900
Federal	209	SR 4756	32.0	Win.	WAA12R	1⅝	1200	10400
Winchester	209	SR 4756	32.0	Rem.	RP12	1⅝	1200	10300
CCI	209	SR 4756	31.0	Win.	WAA12R	1¾	1140	10300
CCI	209	SR 4756	31.0	Rem.	RP12	1¾	1135	10000

12 GAUGE FIELD LOAD — ACTIV 2¾-INCH

PRIMER		IMR POWDER		WAD COLUMN		LEAD SHOT (Oz.)	MUZZLE VELOCITY	CHAMBER PRESSURE
MFR.	No.	DESIGNATION	GRAINS	MFG.	DESIGNATION			
Federal	209	"HI-SKOR" 800-X	29.0	Activ	T-32	1¼	1320	10000
Remington	209P	"HI-SKOR" 800-X	28.0	Activ	T-32	1¼	1290	10000
Winchester	209	"HI-SKOR" 800-X	28.5	Activ	T-32	1¼	1320	10200
Federal	209	PB	28.0	Activ	T-35	1¼	1330	10600
Remington	209P	PB	27.0	Activ	T-35	1¼	1315	10600
Winchester	209	PB	28.5	Activ	T-35	1¼	1330	10600
Federal	209	SR 7625	30.5	Activ	T-35	1¼	1330	8900
Winchester	209	SR 7625	31.0	Activ	T-35	1¼	1340	8800
Federal	209	SR 4756	34.5	Activ	T-35	1¼	1320	8200
Winchester	209	SR 4756	34.0	Activ	T-35	1¼	1320	7800

16 GAUGE FIELD LOAD — FEDERAL 2¾-INCH PLASTIC "HI-POWER"

PRIMER		IMR POWDER		WAD COLUMN		LEAD SHOT (Oz.)	MUZZLE VELOCITY	CHAMBER PRESSURE
MFR.	No.	DESIGNATION	GRAINS	MFG.	DESIGNATION			
Federal	209	"HI-SKOR" 700-X	15.5	Rem.	R16	1	1175	9700
Winchester	209	"HI-SKOR" 700-X	15.5	Rem.	R16	1	1160	9200
Federal	209	"HI-SKOR" 800-X	19.0	Rem.	R16	1	1170	7100
Federal	209	"HI-SKOR" 800-X	20.0	Rem.	R16	1	1215	7500
Federal	209	"HI-SKOR" 800-X	20.0	Rem.	SP16	1⅛	1185	8500
Federal	209	"HI-SKOR" 800-X	21.5	Rem.	SP16	1⅛	1230	9500
CCI	209M	"HI-SKOR" 800-X	19.0	Rem.	R16	1	1165	6700
CCI	209M	"HI-SKOR" 800-X	20.5	Rem.	R16	1	1230	7500
CCI	209M	"HI-SKOR" 800-X	20.5	Rem.	SP16	1⅛	1190	8100
CCI	209M	"HI-SKOR" 800-X	22.0	Rem.	SP16	1⅛	1245	8800
CCI	209M	"HI-SKOR" 800-X	23.5	Rem.	SP16	1⅛	1290	10000
Winchester	209	"HI-SKOR" 800-X	23.5	Rem.	SP16	1⅛	1305	10100
Federal	209	PB	18.0	Rem.	R16	1	1155	7700
Winchester	209	P8	18.5	Rem.	R16	1	1180	7600
Federal	209	PB	19.0	Rem.	SP16	1⅛	1170	10000
Winchester	209	PB	19.5	Rem.	SP16	1⅛	1180	10100
Federal	209	SR 7625	20.0	Rem.	R16	1	1160	6700
Winchester	209	SR 7625	20.5	Rem.	R16	1	1170	6700
Federal	209	SR 7625	21.0	Rem.	SP16	1⅛	1190	8900
Winchester	209	SR 7625	21.5	Rem.	SP16	1⅛	1185	8100
CCI	209	SR 7625	24.5	Rem.	SP16	1⅛	1295	9900
Federal	209	SR 4756	22.5	Rem.	R16	1	1160	6900
Winchester	209	SR 4756	23.5	Rem.	R16	1	1180	6800
Federal	209	SR 4756	23.5	Rem.	SP16	1⅛	1190	8300
Winchester	209	SR 4756	24.5	Rem.	SP16	1⅛	1190	7800

16 GAUGE FIELD LOAD — WINCHESTER 2¾-INCH COMPRESSED-FORMED "UPLAND" AND "SUPER-X"

PRIMER		IMR POWDER		WAD COLUMN		LEAD SHOT (Oz.)	MUZZLE VELOCITY	CHAMBER PRESSURE
MFR.	No.	DESIGNATION	GRAINS	MFG.	DESIGNATION			
Winchester	209	"HI-SKOR" 700-X	15.5	Rem.	R16	1	1175	10000
Remington	209P	"HI-SKOR" 700-X	15.0	Rem.	R16	1	1170	10300
Winchester	209	"HI-SKOR" 800-X	19.0	Rem.	R16	1	1155	7100
Winchester	209	"HI-SKOR" 800-X	20.5	Rem.	R16	1	1215	7900
Winchester	209	"HI-SKOR" 800X	20.0	Rem.	SP16	1⅛	1175	8800
Winchester	209	"HI-SKOR" 800-X	21.5	Rem.	SP16	1⅛	1235	9800
Federal	209	"HI-SKOR" 800-X	18.5	Rem.	R16	1	1160	7400
Federal	209	"HI-SKOR" 800-X	20.0	Rem.	R16	1	1215	8000
Federal	209	"HI-SKOR" 800-X	20.0	Rem.	SP16	1⅛	1185	9600
Federal	410	"HI-SKOR" 800-X	23.0	Rem.	SP16	1⅛	1285	10300
CCI	209M	"HI-SKOR" 800-X	21.5	Rem.	SP16	1⅛	1240	9600
Remington	209P	"HI-SKOR" 800-X	24.0	Rem.	SP16	1⅛	1290	8500
Winchester	209	PB	18.5	Rem.	R16	1	1175	8000
Winchester	209	SR 7625	20.0	Rem.	R16	1	1155	7000
Federal	209	SR 7625	19.5	Rem.	R16	1	1165	7400
Winchester	209	SR 7625	21.0	Rem.	SP16	1⅛	1200	9800
Federal	209	SR 7625	20.5	Rem.	SP16	1⅛	1195	10000
Winchester	209	SR 4756	23.0	Rem.	R16	1	1150	7000
Federal	209	SR 4756	22.5	Rem.	R16	1	1170	7400
Winchester	209	SR 4756	24.0	Rem.	SP16	1⅛	1190	9000
Federal	209	SR 4756	23.0	Rem.	SP16	1⅛	1185	9400

16 GAUGE FIELD LOAD — FEDERAL 2¾-INCH PLASTIC "HI-POWER"

PRIMER		HERCULES POWDER		WAD COLUMN		LEAD SHOT (Oz.)	MUZZLE VELOCITY	CHAMBER PRESSURE
MFR.	No.	DESIGNATION	GRAINS	MFG.	DESIGNATION			
Federal	209	Green Dot	17.5	Rem.	SP16	1⅛	1185	10600
Federal	209	Unique	18.5	Rem.	SP16	1⅛	1185	9800
Federal	209	Herco	20.0	Rem.	SP16	1⅛	1185	8200
Federal	209	Herco	22.0	Rem.	SP16	1⅛	1240	9300
Federal	209	Herco	23.0	Rem.	SP16	1⅛	1260	9900
Federal	209	Blue Dot	28.5	Rem.	SP16	1⅛	1260	9400
Federal	209	Blue Dot	30.0	Rem.	SP16	1¼	1265	10600

16 GAUGE FIELD LOAD — WINCHESTER 2¾-INCH PLASTIC UPLAND SHELLS

PRIMER		HERCULES POWDER		WAD COLUMN		LEAD SHOT (Oz.)	MUZZLE VELOCITY	CHAMBER PRESSURE
MFR.	No.	DESIGNATION	GRAINS	MFG.	DESIGNATION			
Winchester	209	Unique	18.5	Rem.	SP16	1⅛	1185	10100
Winchester	209	Herco	20.0	Rem.	SP16	1⅛	1185	8900
Winchester	209	Herco	21.5	Rem.	SP16	1⅛	1240	10900
Winchester	209	Blue Dot	28.0	Rem.	SP16	1⅛	1260	9600

16 GAUGE FIELD LOAD — REMINGTON - PETERS 2¾-INCH SP WITH PLASTIC BASE WAD

PRIMER		HERCULES POWDER		WAD COLUMN		LEAD SHOT (Oz.)	MUZZLE VELOCITY	CHAMBER PRESSURE
MFR.	No.	DESIGNATION	GRAINS	MFG.	DESIGNATION			
Winchester	209	Herco	19.5	Rem.	SP16	1⅛	1185	10900
Winchester	209	Blue Dot	26.5	Rem.	SP16	1⅛	1240	10600

20 GAUGE SLUG — FEDERAL 2¾-INCH PAPER TARGET

PRIMER		IMR POWDER		WAD COLUMN		SLUG MFR.	MUZZLE VELOCITY	CHAMBER PRESSURE
MFR.	No.	DESIGNATION	GRAINS	MFG.	DESIGNATION			
Federal	410	"HI-SKOR" 700-X	14.5	Fed.	(4) .135 in. cards	Brenneke	1120	10800
Federal	209	PB	17.0	Fed.	(3) .135 in. cards	Brenneke	1135	10400
CCI	209M	PB	17.5	Fed.	(3) .135 in. cards	Brenneke	1205	10600
Federal	209	SR 7625	20.0	Fed.	(3) .135 in. cards	Brenneke	1260	10600
CCI	209M	SR 7625	21.0	Fed.	(3) .135 in. cards	Brenneke	1285	10800
CCI	209M	SR 4756	25.5	Fed.	(2) .135 in. cards	Brenneke	1380	10600
Winchester	209	SR 4756	24.5	Fed.	(2) .135 in. cards	Brenneke	1340	10400

20 GAUGE SLUG — FEDERAL 2¾-INCH PLASTIC "HI-POWER"

PRIMER		IMR POWDER		WAD COLUMN		SLUG MFR.	MUZZLE VELOCITY	CHAMBER PRESSURE
MFR.	No.	DESIGNATION	GRAINS	MFG.	DESIGNATION			
Federal	209	"HI-SKOR" 700-X	14.0	Fed.	(4) .135 in. cards	Brenneke	1135	10800
CCI	209M	"HI-SKOR" 700-X	14.0	Fed.	(4) .135 in. cards	Brenneke	1135	10600
Federal	209	PB	17.5	Fed.	(3) .135 in. cards	Brenneke	1205	10700
CCI	209M	PB	18.0	Fed.	(3) .135 in. cards	Brenneke	1210	10500
Federal	209	SR 7625	20.5	Fed.	(3) .135 in. cards	Brenneke	1290	10900
CCI	209M	SR 7625	21.5	Fed.	(3) .135 in. cards	Brenneke	1325	10800
CCI	209M	SR 4756	25.5	Fed.	(2) .135 in. cards	Brenneke	1390	10700
Winchester	209	SR 4756	24.5	Fed.	(2) .135 in. cards	Brenneke	1360	10600

20 GAUGE BUCKSHOT — FEDERAL 2¾-INCH PLASTIC "HI-POWER"

PRIMER		HERCULES POWDER		WAD COLUMN		BUCKSHOT		MUZZLE VELOCITY	CHAMBER PRESSURE
MFR.	No.	DESIGNATION	GRAINS	MFG.	DESIGNATION	SIZE	PELLETS		
Federal	209	Herco	19.0	Rem.	SP20	4	18	1275	11000
Federal	209	Blue Dot	25.0	Rem.	SP20	4	18	1275	8300
Federal	209	Blue Dot	24.0	Rem.	SP20 with petals removed	3	24	1200	11200
Federal	209	Blue Dot	25.5	Rem.	SP20 with petals removed	1	12	1275	10100

20 GAUGE FIELD — REMINGTON 2¾-INCH "RXP"

PRIMER		IMR POWDER		WAD COLUMN		LEAD SHOT (Oz.)	MUZZLE VELOCITY	CHAMBER PRESSURE
MFR.	No.	DESIGNATION	GRAINS	MFG.	DESIGNATION			
Federal	209	"HI-SKOR" 700-X	12.1	Rem.	RXP20	7/8	1105	10900
Remington	209P	"HI-SKOR" 800-X	18.0	Rem.	RXP20	7/8	1205	9300
Remington	209P	"HI-SKOR" 800-X	17.5	Activ	W-32	7/8	1200	10100
Remington	209P	"HI-SKOR" 800-X	17.0	Fed.	20S1	7/8	1190	9600
Remington	209P	"HI-SKOR" 800-X	17.5	Lage	Uniwad	7/8	1200	9600.
Remington	209P	"HI-SKOR" 800-X	17.5	Pacific	Versalite	7/8	1210	9300.
Remington	209P	"HI-SKOR" 800-X	17.5	Win.	WAA20	7/8	1215	9200
Remington	209P	"HI-SKOR" 800-X	17.5	WTW	WindJammer	7/8	1210	9200
CCI	209M	"HI-SKOR" 800-X	17.0	Rem.	RXP20	7/8	1205	9100
CCI	209M	"HI-SKOR" 800-X	16.5	Fed.	20S1	7/8	1195	10400
CCI	209M	"HI-SKOR" 800-X	16.5	Win.	WAA20	7/8	1195	9500
CCI	209M	"HI-SKOR" 800-X	17.0	Lage	Uniwad	7/8	1210	9700
CCI	209M	"HI-SKOR" 800-X	16.5	Pacific	Versalite	7/8	1205	9600
Remington	209P	"HI-SKOR" 800-X	18.0	Rem.	RXP20	1	1160	9300
Remington	209P	"HI-SKOR" 800-X	18.5	Lage	Uniwad	1	1175	10200
Remington	209P	"HI-SKOR" 800-X	17.5	Win.	WA20F1	1	1150	9700
Remington	209P	"HI-SKOR" 800-X	18.5	WTW	WindJammer	1	1175	9700
Federal	410	SR 4756	19.0	Lage	Uniwad	1	1145	10500
CCI	209	SR 4756	20.5	Rem.	RP20	1	1165	9800
Winchester	209	SR 4756	20.0	Rem.	RP20	1	1165	10500
CCI	209	SR 4756	20.0	Trico	No.2	1	1145	10100
Federal	410	SR 4756	20.0	Trico	No.2	1	1170	10300
CCI	209	SR 4756	21.5	Rem.	RP20	1	1205	10300
Federal	410	SR 4756	21.5	Rem.	RP20	1	1205	10500

20 GAUGE FIELD — REMINGTON 2¾-INCH SP "EXPRESS"

PRIMER		IMR POWDER		WAD COLUMN		LEAD SHOT (Oz.)	MUZZLE VELOCITY	CHAMBER PRESSURE
MFR.	No.	DESIGNATION	GRAINS	MFG.	DESIGNATION			
Remington	209P	"HI-SKOR" 800-X	18.5	Rem.	RXP20	7/8	1200	8100
Remington	209P	"HI-SKOR" 800-X	17.5	Activ	W-32	7/8	1200	10700
Remington	209P	"HI-SKOR" 800-X	17.5	WTW.	WindJammer	7/8	1190	9200
Remington	209P	"HI-SKOR" 800-X	19.0	Rem.	RP20	1	1210	10600
Remington	209P	"HI-SKOR" 800-X	18.0	Rem.	RP20	1 1/8	1120	10700
CCI	209M	"HI-SKOR" 800-X	17.0	Win.	WAA20	7/8	1205	9000
CCI	209M	"HI-SKOR" 800-X	18.0	Lage	Uniwad	1	1210	10700
CCI	209M	"HI-SKOR" 800-X	17.0	Rem.	RP20	1 1/8	1130	10800
Federal	410	PB	16.0	Rem.	SP20	7/8	1185	10500
CCI	209	PB	16.0	Win.	WAA20F1	7/8	1190	10700
Federal	410	PB	17.0	Lage	Uniwad	7/8	1215	10400
Federal	209	SR 7625	17.0	Rem.	SP20	7/8	1215	10900
Federal	209	SR 7625	16.5	Win.	WAA20F1	7/8	1195	10700
Federal	209	SR 7625	17.0	Lage	Uniwad	7/8	1190	9700
Federal	209	SR 4756	19.0	Lage	Uniwad	7/8	1205	9600
Federal	209	SR 4756	18.0	Rem.	SP20	7/8	1210	10200
Winchester	209	SR 4756	18.5	Fed.	20S1	7/8	1200	10900
CCI	209	SR 4756	19.5	Rem.	RP20	1	1175	9900

20 GAUGE FIELD — REMINGTON 3-INCH SP "EXPRESS"

PRIMER		IMR POWDER		WAD COLUMN		LEAD SHOT (Oz.)	MUZZLE VELOCITY	CHAMBER PRESSURE
MFR.	No.	DESIGNATION	GRAINS	MFG.	DESIGNATION			
Remington	209P	"HI-SKOR" 800-X	22.0	Lage	Uniwad	7/8	1330	9200
Remington	209P	"HI-SKOR" 800-X	18.5	Rem.	RXP20	1	1205	9400
Remington	209P	"HI-SKOR" 800-X	18.5	Activ	W-28	1	1190	10800
Remington	209P	"HI-SKOR" 800-X	18.5	WTW.	WindJammer	1	1205	10300
CCI	209M	"HI-SKOR" 800-X	18.5	Win.	WAA20	1	1205	10700
Remington	209P	"HI-SKOR" 800-X	18.5	Rem.	RXP20	1 1/8	1110	9100
CCI	157	SR 7625	21.5	Rem.	RXP20	1	1225	9900
CCI	157	SR 7625	21.5	Fed.	20S1	1	1225	10300
CCI	157	SR 7625	21.5	Win.	WAA20	1	1235	10500

20 GAUGE FIELD — REMINGTON 3-INCH SP "EXPRESS" (Cont.)

PRIMER		IMR POWDER		WAD COLUMN		LEAD SHOT (Oz.)	MUZZLE VELOCITY	CHAMBER PRESSURE
MFR.	No.	DESIGNATION	GRAINS	MFG.	DESIGNATION			
CCI	157	SR 4756	28.5	Rem.	RP20	1	1375	10700
CCI	157	SR 4756	24.5	Rem.	RP20	1⅛	1205	10000
CCI	157	SR 4756	23.0	Lage	Uniwad	1⅛	1175	10000
CCI	157	IMR 4227	40.0	Lage	Uniwad (minus insert)	1¼	1115	7000

20 GAUGE FIELD — FEDERAL 2¾-INCH PAPER TARGET

PRIMER		IMR POWDER		WAD COLUMN		LEAD SHOT (Oz.)	MUZZLE VELOCITY	CHAMBER PRESSURE
MFR.	No.	DESIGNATION	GRAINS	MFG.	DESIGNATION			
Federal	209	"HI-SKOR" 800-X	17.5	Fed.	20S1	1	1175	10200
Federal	209	"HI-SKOR" 800-X	17.0	Rem.	SP20	1	1160	9500
Federal	209	"HI-SKOR" 800-X	17.0	Win.	WAA20F1	1	1160	9300
Federal	209	"HI-SKOR" 800-X	17.5	Lage	Uniwad	1	1165	9800
Federal	209	"HI-SKOR" 800-X	17.0	Trico	Precision 2	1	1160	9600
CCI	209M	"HI-SKOR" 800-X	17.5	Fed.	20S1	1	1175	10000
CCI	209M	"HI-SKOR" 800-X	17.0	Rem.	SP20	1	1160	9300
CCI	209M	"HI-SKOR" 800-X	17.5	Win.	WAA20F1	1	1170	9300
CCI	209M	"HI-SKOR" 800-X	18.0	Lage	Uniwad	1	1175	9500
CCI	209M	"HI-SKOR" 800-X	17.5	Trico	Precision 2	1	1160	9600
Remington	209P	"HI-SKOR" 800-X	20.0	Fed.	2051	1	1215	10500
Remington	209P	"HI-SKOR" 800-X	19.0	Activ	W-28	1	1200	10800
Remington	209P	"HI-SKOR" 800-X	20.0	WTW.	WindJammer	1	1210	9900
Federal	209	"HI-SKOR" 800-X	18.0	Rem.	SP20	1	1205	10400
Federal	209	"HI-SKOR" 800-X	18.5	Win.	WAA20F1	1	1215	10800
Federal	209	"HI-SKOR" 800-X	18.5	Lage	Uniwad	1	1210	10800
Federal	209	"HI-SKOR" 800-X	18.0	Trico	Precision 2	1	1200	10800
Winchester	209	PB	17.0	Rem.	SP20	1	1145	10900
CCI	209	PB	17.5	Win.	WAA20F1	1	1155	10500
Federal	209	SR 7625	17.5	Rem.	SP20	1	1155	10000
CCI	209	SR 7625	18.5	Trico	No. 2	1	1160	8900
CCI	209	SR 7625	18.5	Win.	WAA20F1	1	1165	9200
Winchester	209	SR 7625	19.0	Rem.	SP20	1	1200	10900

20 GAUGE FIELD — FEDERAL 2¾-INCH PAPER TARGET (Cont.)

PRIMER		IMR POWDER		WAD COLUMN		LEAD SHOT (Oz.)	MUZZLE VELOCITY	CHAMBER PRESSURE
MFR.	No.	DESIGNATION	GRAINS	MFG.	DESIGNATION			
CCI	209	SR 7625	19.5	Trico	No. 2	1	1210	10700
CCI	209	SR 7625	19.5	Win.	WAA20F1	1	1210	10700
Federal	410	SR 7625	20.5	Lage	Uniwad	1	1215	10700
Federal	209	SR 4756	20.5	Rem.	SP20	1	1175	9400
Federal	209	SR 4756	21.0	Trico	No. 2	1	1175	9800
Federal	209	SR 4756	20.5	Win.	WAA20F1	1	1165	9500
Federal	209	SR 4756	21.5	Rem.	SP20	1	1215	10500
Federal	209	SR 4756	22.0	Trico	No. 2	1	1215	10500
Winchester	209	SR 4756	22.0	Lage	Uniwad	1	1220	10600
Winchester	209	SR 4756	22.5	Win.	WAA20F1	1	1225	10000
Federal	410	SR 4756	22.5	Rem.	RP20	1⅛	1165	9600
Winchester	209	SR 4756	21.5	Rem.	RP20	1⅛	1155	10400

20 GAUGE FIELD — FEDERAL 2¾-INCH PLASTIC TARGET

PRIMER		IMR POWDER		WAD COLUMN		LEAD SHOT (Oz.)	MUZZLE VELOCITY	CHAMBER PRESSURE
MFR.	No.	DESIGNATION	GRAINS	MFG.	DESIGNATION			
Federal	209	"HI-SKOR" 800-X	17.5	Fed.	20S1	1	1160	9600
Federal	209	"HI-SKOR" 800-X	17.5	Rem.	SP20	1	1160	8900
Federal	209	"HI-SKOR" 800-X	17.5	Win.	WAA20F1	1	1160	8800
Federal	209	"HI-SKOR" 800-X	18.0	Lage	Uniwad	1	1165	9300
Federal	209	"HI-SKOR" 800-X	18.0	Pacific	Versalite	1	1165	9200
CCI	209M	"HI-SKOR" 800-X	18.0	Fed.	20S1	1	1175	9600
CCI	209M	"HI-SKOR" 800-X	18.0	Rem.	SP20	1	1165	8600
CCI	209M	"HI-SKOR" 800-X	18.0	Win.	WAA20F1	1	1175	8600
CCI	209M	"HI-SKOR" 800-X	18.5	Lage	Uniwad	1	1170	8500
CCI	209M	"HI-SK0R" 800-X	18.5	Pacific	Versalite	1	1180	9200
Federal	209	"HI-SKOR" 800-X	18.5	Fed.	20S1	1	1215	10500
Federal	209	"HI-SKOR" 800-X	19.0	Rem.	SP20	1	1220	9600
Federal	209	"HI-SKOR" 800-X	19.0	Win.	WAA20F1	1	1230	10000
Federal	209	"HI-SKOR" 800-X	19.0	Lage	Uniwad	1	1225	10200
Federal	209	"HI-SKOR" 800-X	19.0	Pacific	Versalite	1	1220	9900
Federal	209	"HI-SKOR" 800-X	19.0	Rem.	SP20	1⅛	1170	10700

20 GAUGE FIELD — FEDERAL 2¾-INCH PLASTIC TARGET (Cont.)

PRIMER		IMR POWDER		WAD COLUMN		LEAD SHOT (Oz.)	MUZZLE VELOCITY	CHAMBER PRESSURE
MFR.	No.	DESIGNATION	GRAINS	MFG.	DESIGNATION			
Winchester	209	"HI-SKOR" 800-X	19.0	Win.	WAA20F1	1⅛	1180	10700
Winchester	209	"HI-SKOR" 800-X	19.0	Lage	Uniwad	1⅛	1170	10600
CCI	209	PB	17.5	Rem.	SP20	1	1155	10600
CCI	209	PB	17.5	Trico	No. 2	1	1155	10800
Winchester	209	SR 7625	18.0	Rem.	SP20	1	1160	10200
Winchester	209	SR 7625	18.5	Trico	No. 2	1	1180	10600
CCI	209	SR 7625	19.5	Rem.	SP20	1	1205	10000
Federal	209	SR 4756	20.5	Rem.	SP20	1	1180	10100
Federal	209	SR 4756	21.0	Trico	No. 2	1	1175	10100
Federal	209	SR 4756	21.5	Rem.	RP20	1	1210	9900
Winchester	209	SR 4756	22.0	Rem.	RP20	1⅛	1180	10700

20 GAUGE FIELD — FEDERAL 2¾-INCH PLASTIC "HI-POWER"

PRIMER		IMR POWDER		WAD COLUMN		LEAD SHOT (Oz.)	MUZZLE VELOCITY	CHAMBER PRESSURE
MFR.	No.	DESIGNATION	GRAINS	MFG.	DESIGNATION			
Federal	410	PB	17.5	Rem.	SP20	1	1160	10300
CCI	209	PB	17.0	Trico	No. 2	1	1150	10500
Federal	410	PB	17.5	Lage	Uniwad	1	1170	10900
Federal	209	SR 7625	17.5	Rem.	SP20	1	1160	10000
Winchester	209	SR 7625	18.0	Trico	No. 2	1	1165	10100
Winchester	209	SR 7625	19.0	Rem.	SP20	1	1205	10500
CCI	209	SR 7625	19.5	Trico	No. 2	1	1225	10500
Federal	410	SR 7625	20.0	Lage	Uniwad	1	1205	9800
Federal	209	SR 4756	20.5	Rem.	SP20	1	1165	9300
Federal	209	SR 4756	20.5	Trico	No. 2	1	1170	9500
Winchester	209	SR 4756	21.5	Lage	Uniwad	1	1210	9900
Federal	209	SR 4756	21.5	Rem.	SP20	1	1220	10600
Federal	209	SR 4756	22.0	Trico	No. 2	1	1230	10300
Winchester	209	SR 4756	22.0	Rem.	RP20	1⅛	1185	10900

20 GAUGE FIELD — FEDERAL 3-INCH PLASTIC "HI-POWER"

PRIMER		IMR POWDER		WAD COLUMN		LEAD SHOT (Oz.)	MUZZLE VELOCITY	CHAMBER PRESSURE
MFR.	No.	DESIGNATION	GRAINS	MFG.	DESIGNATION			
Federal	209	"HI-SK0R" 800-X	20.5	Lage	Uniwad	1⅛	1200	10800
Federal	209	"HI-SKOR" 800-X	20.5	Fed.	20S1	1⅛	1205	10400
Federal	209	"HI-SKOR" 800-X	21.0	Rem.	RXP20	1⅛	1215	10700
Federal	209	"HI-SKOR" 800-X	19.0	Lage	Uniwad	1¼	1100	10900
Federal	209	"HI-SKOR" 800-X	19.5	Rem.	RXP20	1¼	1120	10400
Federal	209	SR 4756	24.0	Rem.	SP20	1⅛	1215	10900
Winchester	209	SR 4756	26.0	Rem.	SP20	1⅛	1270	10600
Federal	209	SR 4756	24.0	Trico	No. 2	1⅛	1200	10600
Federal	209	SR 4756	24.0	Win.	WAA20F1	1⅛	1215	10500
Federal	410	SR 4756	24.5	Lage	Uniwad	1⅛	1220	10500
Winchester	209	SR 4756	26.0	Win.	WAA20F1	1⅛	1265	10600
Federal	410	SR 4756	26.0	Rem.	RP20	1¼	1195	10600
Winchester	209	SR 4756	24.0	Rem.	RP20	1¼	1155	10400
Federal	209	IMR 4227	40.0	Rem.	RP20	1¼	1175	8700
Winchester	209	IMR 4227	40.0	Rem.	RP20	1¼	1150	7800
Federal	209	IMR 4227	42.0	Lage	Uniwad, (minus insert)	1¼	1190	7400

20 GAUGE FIELD LOAD — WINCHESTER 2¾-INCH PLASTIC UPLAND SHELLS

PRIMER		IMR POWDER		WAD COLUMN		LEAD SHOT (Oz.)	MUZZLE VELOCITY	CHAMBER PRESSURE
MFR.	No.	DESIGNATION	GRAINS	MFG.	DESIGNATION			
Winchester	209	"HI-SKOR" 800-X	16.5	Win.	WAA20F1	1	1160	10100
Winchester	209	"HI-SKOR" 800-X	17.0	Rem.	RXP20	1	1165	10300
Winchester	209	"HI-SKOR" 800-X	17.0	Lage	Uniwad	1	1165	9900
Winchester	209	"HI-SK0R" 800-X	17.0	Pacific	Versalite	1	1170	10300
Winchester	209	"HI-SKOR" 800-X	17.5	Win.	WAA20F1	1	1205	10700
Winchester	209	"HI-SKOR" 800-X	18.0	Lage	Uniwad	1	1205	10600
CCI	209M	"HI-SKOR" 800-X	18.0	Win.	WAA20F1	1	1215	10900
CCI	209M	"HI-SKOR" 800-X	18.0	Lage	Uniwad	1	1210	10700
Federal	209	"HI-SKOR" 800-X	16.5	Win.	WAA20F1	1	1165	10600
Federal	209	"HI-SKOR" 800-X	17.0	Rem.	RXP20	1	1175	10600
Federal	209	"HI-SKOR" 800-X	16.5	Lage	Uniwad	1	1155	10700

20 GAUGE FIELD LOAD — WINCHESTER 2¾-INCH PLASTIC UPLAND SHELLS (Cont.)

PRIMER		IMR POWDER		WAD COLUMN		LEAD SHOT (Oz.)	MUZZLE VELOCITY	CHAMBER PRESSURE
MFR.	No.	DESIGNATION	GRAINS	MFG.	DESIGNATION			
Federal	209	"HI-SKOR" 800-X	16.5	Pacific	Versalite	1	1155	10600
Remington	209P	"HI-SKOR" 800-X	20.0	Pacific	Versalite	1	1220	10900
Winchester	209	SR 4756	20.5	Rem.	RP20	1	1165	9400
Federal	209	SR 4756	19.5	Rem.	RP20	1	1165	10500
CCI	209	SR 4756	20.0	Trico	No. 2	1	1145	10100
Federal	410	SR 4756	20.5	Trico	No. 2	1	1170	10800
Winchester	209	SR 4756	21.5	Rem.	RP20	1	1215	10300
CCI	209	SR 4756	22.0	Rem.	RP20	1	1220	10300

20 GAUGE FIELD LOAD — WINCHESTER 3-INCH "SUPER-X"

PRIMER		IMR POWDER		WAD COLUMN		LEAD SHOT (Oz.)	MUZZLE VELOCITY	CHAMBER PRESSURE
MFR.	No.	DESIGNATION	GRAINS	MFG.	DESIGNATION			
Winchester	209	SR 4756	23.5	Win.	WAA20F1	1⅛	1185	10900
Federal	410	SR 4756	24.5	Win.	WAA20F1	1⅛	1200	10400
Winchester	209	SR 4756	23.5	Rem.	SP20	1⅛	1200	10900
Federal	410	SR 4756	25.0	Rem.	SP20	1⅛	t215	10900
Winchester	209	SR 4756	23.0	Trico	No. 2	1⅛	1170	10800
Federal	410	SR 4756	24.0	Trico	No. 2	1⅛	1190	10600
Federal	410	SR 4766	21.5	Lage	Uniwad	1⅛	1190	10900
Winchester	209	IMR 4227	39.0	Rem.	RP20	1¼	1135	9600
Federal	209	IMR 4227	39.0	Rem.	RP20	1¼	1185	10900
Federal	209	IMR 4227	40.0	Lage	Uniwad, (minus insert)	1¼	1180	8900

20 GAUGE FIELD LOAD — Activ 2¾-INCH

PRIMER		IMR POWDER		WAD COLUMN		LEAD SHOT (Oz.)	MUZZLE VELOCITY	CHAMBER PRESSURE
MFR.	No.	DESIGNATION	GRAINS	MFG.	DESIGNATION			
Federal	209	"HI-SXOR" 800-X	17.5	Win.	W-28	1	1195	10100
Remington	209P	"HI-SXOR" 800-X	18.0	Win.	W-28	1	1195	10700
Winchester	209	"HI-SKOR" 800-X	18.8	Win.	W-28	1	1210	10200
Winchester	209	SR 7625	19.5	Win.	WAA20	1	1205	10800
Federal	209	SR 4756	20.0	Fed.	20S1	1	1190	10900
Remington	209P	SR 4756	21.5	Rem.	SP20	1	1210	10500
Winchester	209	SR 4756	21.5	Win.	WAA20	1	1210	10200

28 GAUGE FIELD LOAD — WINCHESTER 2¾-INCH "SUPER-X"

PRIMER		IMR POWDER		WAD COLUMN		LEAD SHOT (Oz.)	MUZZLE VELOCITY	CHAMBER PRESSURE
MFR.	No.	DESIGNATION	GRAINS	MFG.	DESIGNATION			
CCI	209	"HI-SKOR" 700-X	10.8	Win.	WAA28	1¹⁄₁₆	1170	11400
Remington	209P	"HI-SKOR" 700-X	11.5	Win.	WAA28	1¹⁄₁₆	1190	10800
Winchester	209	PB	12.6	Win.	WAA28	1¹⁄₁₆	1190	11200
CCI	209	PB	12.3	Fed.	28S1	1¹⁄₁₆	1165	11200
Winchester	209	SR 7625	14.0	Win.	WAA28	1¹⁄₁₆	1225	10300
CCI	209	SR 7625	13.7	Fed.	28S1	1¹⁄₁₆	1210	11300
Federal	209	SR 7625	12.0	Win.	WAA28	¾	1100	10600
Winchester	209	SR 4756	15.0	Win.	WAA28	1¹⁄₁₆	1175	9000
Federal	209	SR 4756	15.0	Win.	WAA28	1¹⁄₁₆	1215	10600
Winchester	209	SR 4756	15.6	Fed.	28S1	1¹⁄₁₆	1225	11200
CCI	209	SR 4756	16.5	Fed.	28S1	1¹⁄₁₆	1265	11400

LOADING WITH STEEL SHOT

Hunting with steel shot is rapidly becoming the rule, rather than the exception. Today, steel-shot laws affect nearly every flyway in North America. That means changing loads and, more importantly, changing hunting habits.

> *WARNING!*
>
> Do not substitute steel shot in loading data specified for lead shot; the results may be dangerous.

Steel shot is 30% lighter than lead shot, but is loaded to shoot with increased initial velocity. This lighter pellet weight, however, means velocity will drop more rapidly. The result is that you need to change your forward lead when using steel shot.

At close ranges, you won't need to make any noticeable change in your shooting habits. However, at 40 yards, you will need to lead your target about 6 inches more than you would with lead shot.

Perhaps the best way to make the adjustment to steel shot is to make it act more like lead. Since steel is lighter than lead, you should select a shot that is two shot sizes larger than the lead shot you would normally use. That way, a pellet of No. 2 steel shot will have about the same velocity, deliver similar energy, and require about the same forward lead as No. 4 lead shot through the various ranges. Patterns stay dense because there are more pellets per ounce of steel than lead, and because steel pellets deform less, which means fewer stray out of the pattern. A shotshell, however, has a fixed amount of room for shot. And the larger steel shot takes up more of that room. So, if you really want pattern density of No. 2 shot to match more closely that of No. 4 lead, you must increase shot weight. The 12-gauge, 3½ magnum was designed to solve this problem. It delivers a bigger load of larger steel shot at extended ranges.

> *WARNING!*
>
> The potential for barrel damage is always present with steel shot, factory or handloaded. It will probably never occur. However for this reason, steel shot is not recommended for shooting in a valuable firearm.

Steel Shot Reloading Warnings

- Never substitute any powder or mix powders for the specific smokeless powder called for in any reloading manual.
- Never substitute any other wad for the specific ones listed in reloading manuals.
- Never load lead shot in loads listed for steel shot, or vice versa.
- Never load steel shot in any reloading press that has not been specifically retrofitted for the loading of steel shot.
- Never load any cartridge or shell without checking powder and shot charges with an accurate scale.
- Never smoke while reloading.
- Never allow children to reload and have access to the components.
- Never use steel shot loads that have become submerged in water, especially salt water.
- Never reload without wearing safety glasses.
- Never shoot steel-shot loads in your shotgun or screw-in choke system until you have checked with the gun's manufacturer to verify that it is okay to do so. Some firearm manufacturers void the warranty if steel shot is used.

The Mayville Engineering Company, Inc., 715 South Street, Mayville, WI 53050 has compiled a comprehensive manual on loading steel shot in shotshells for both 10- and 12-gauge hulls.

The MEC manual is so complete that there is very little that we could add in this book. Consequently, anyone who plans to reload steel shot in shotshells should obtain a copy of Mec's Steel Shot Reloading Manual and read every word before attempting to load your own shells.

We have, however, listed a few starter loads for steel shot on the next few pages to give reloaders an idea of what is involved. Both 10 and 12 gauges have been included.

10 GAUGE STEEL SHOT LOAD — REMINGTON 3½-INCH SP PLASTIC

PRIMER		POWDER		WAD COLUMN		STEEL SHOT (Oz.)	MUZZLE VELOCITY	CHAMBER PRESSURE
MFR.	No.	DESIGNATION	GRAINS	MFG.	DESIGNATION			
Winchester	209	571	43.0	MEC	105 + 1 card wad	1⅜	1375	10500
Winchester	209	IMR SR 4756	38.0	MEC	105 + 1 card wad	1⅜	1375	10400
Winchester	209	IMR SR 4756	37.0	MEC	105 + 1 card wad + 21 gr. plastic buffer	1⅜	1375	10400
Winchester	209	Hercules Blue dot	38.0	MEC	105	1½	1310	10500
Winchester	209	Hercules Blue dot	37.0	MEC	105 + 21 gr. plastic buffer	1½	1310	10500

NOTE: If the Remington SP plastic hull contains a 57-sized primer pocket, be certain to enlarge the primer pocket by seating a SPENT 209-sized primer, depriming and then repriming with a fresh 209-sized primer. Then tap hull upside down repeatedly to completely clear all dislodged base-wad particles from the primer flashhole. These operations must be done on the first reloading of the hull only.

12 GAUGE STEEL SHOT LOAD — FEDERAL 3½-INCH ONE-PIECE PLASTIC

WARNING! **Use 12-gauge 3½-inch loads only in shotguns originally chambered by the manufacturer for 3½-inch 12-gauge shotshells. Do not use these loads in any shotguns with shorter chambers or those shotguns that have been rechambered to accept 3½-inch ammunition.**

PRIMER		POWDER		WAD COLUMN		STEEL SHOT (Oz.)	MUZZLE VELOCITY	CHAMBER PRESSURE
MFR.	No.	DESIGNATION	GRAINS	MFG.	DESIGNATION			
Winchester	209	Hercules Blue Dot	42.0	MEC	1235 + 4 card filler wads or 1235 + 1 20 ga. ¼ in. fiber or felt wad + 1 card filler wad	1¼	1450	13200
Winchester	209	Hercules Blue Dot	38.0	MEC	1235 + 2 card filler wads	1⅜	1350	13100
Winchester	209	Hercules Blue Dot	35.5	MEC	1235	1½	1300	13800

12 GAUGE STEEL SHOT LOAD — FEDERAL 3-INCH ONE-PIECE PLASTIC

PRIMER		POWDER		WAD COLUMN		STEEL SHOT (Oz.)	MUZZLE VELOCITY	CHAMBER PRESSURE
MFR.	No.	DESIGNATION	GRAINS	MFG.	DESIGNATION			
Federal	209A	Hercules Blue Dot	32.5	MEC	312 + 1 card filler wad	1⅛	1375	11000
Winchester	209	IMR SR 4756	30.0	MEC	312 + 1 card filler wad	1⅛	1375	11500
Winchester	209	IMR SR 4756	28.0	MEC	312 + 18.0 gr. plastic buffer	1⅛	1330	11000
Winchester	209	IMR SR 4756	24.0	MEC	312	1¼	1260	10900
Winchester	209	IMR SR 4756	23.0	MEC	312 + 21.0 gr. plastic buffer	1¼	1220	11500
Federal	209A	Hercules Blue Dot	29.0	MEC	312	1¼	1260	11500
Federal	209A	Hercules Blue Dot	27.0	MEC	312 + 21.0 gr. plastic buffer	1¼	1220	11500
Federal	209A	Hercules 2400	40.0	MEC	312	1¼	1260	11500

12 GAUGE STEEL SHOT LOAD — FEDERAL 2¾-INCH "GOLD MEDAL"

PRIMER		POWDER		WAD COLUMN		STEEL SHOT (Oz.)	MUZZLE VELOCITY	CHAMBER PRESSURE
MFR.	No.	DESIGNATION	GRAINS	MFG.	DESIGNATION			
Federal	209A	IMR SR 7625	24.0	MEC	12 + two card filler wads	⅞	1375	8400
Federal	209A	IMR SR 7625	26.0	MEC	12 + two card filler wads	⅞	1425	9400
Winchester	209	IMR"HI-SKOR" 800-X	27.0	MEC	12 + two card filler wads	⅞	1425	11000
Winchester	209	IMR SR 4756	27.0	MEC	12 + one card filler wads	1	1375	10900
Winchester	209	IMR"HI-SKOR" 800-X	25.5	MEC	12 + one card filler wads	1	1375	10900
Federal	209A	Hercules Blue Dot	30.5	MEC	12 + one card filler wads	1	1375	11200
Winchester	209	Hodgdon 571	30.0	MEC	12	1⅛	1300	11000
CCI	209M	Hodgdon 571	29.0	MEC	12	1⅛	1300	11000
CCI	209M	Hodgdon HS-7	29.0	MEC	12	1⅛	1300	10950
Winchester	209	Hodgdon 571	29.0	MEC	12 + 18.0 gr. plastic buffer	1⅛	1290	10700
CCI	209M	IMR"HI-SKOR" 800-X	25.0	MEC	12	1⅛	1385	11500
Winchester	209	IMR SR 4756	25.0	MEC	12	1⅛	1365	11400

HUNTING LOADS FOR THE .410 BORE

The .410 bore shotgun is looked upon by many as next to useless for hunting purposes. However, from all indications, this little scattergun is on the rise.

The .410 bore shotgun is really measured in caliber, while the rest of the standard shotgun sizes are measured in gauge — gauge meaning the number of round lead balls to the pound that the bore will accept with a good fit. For example, it takes approximately 12 round lead balls the size of a 12-gauge shotgun bore to weigh one pound; it takes 16 balls in the 16-gauge shotgun to weigh a pound, and so on. However, the .410 designation is different; its bore is measured in thousandths of an inch (about .410 inch) just like a rifle barrel.

According to our research, the .410 shotgun was originally designated "12mm" — being a bigger brother to the 9mm short and long shotshells. The initial loading was 3⁄10-ounce shot in a short paper shell slightly less than two inches in length. A 1931 A. F. Stoeger catalog shows the 2-inch shell loaded in 4, 5, 6, 7½, and 9 shot sizes.

Some years ago, I purchased a Marble's Game Getter over/under from Turner Kirkland of Dixie Gun Works in Union City, Tennessee. This model had legal 18-inch barrels and was chambered for the .22 Long Rifle in the upper barrel, and .410 smoothbore in the lower; the lower barrel being chambered for 2-inch shells.

The only 2-inch .410 hulls that could be found were some old Winchester brass hulls that were picked up at a local antique shop. I then loaded a dozen of these with the original 3⁄10-ounce load, using No. 7½ shot. The results were miserable! Perhaps the choke was "shot out" of this particular firearm, but whatever reason, the famous gun writers of the past were correct in categorizing the early .410s as "playthings." My Marble's Game Getter

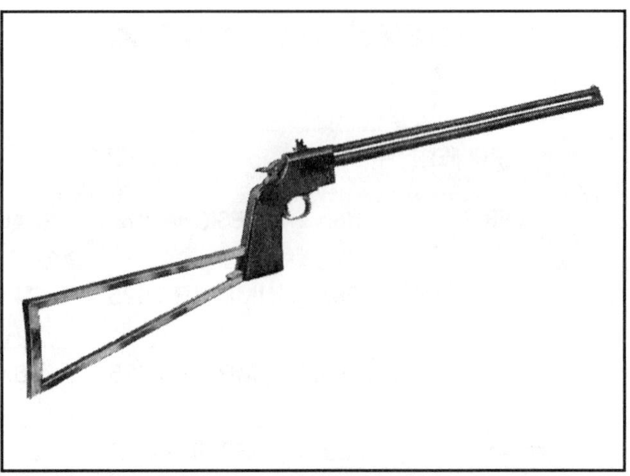

Figure 20-1: The author found the Marble's Game Getter with 2-inch .410 shells not much more than a sparrow or snake gun.

(Figure 20-1) was nothing more than a close-range sparrow and snake gun.

The .410 shell length was eventually increased to 2½ inches to hold 3⁄8 ounces of shot, and this greatly improved the gun's performance. The shell then moved out of the sparrow category and became an acceptable squirrel and rabbit gun. Due to its light recoil and muzzle blast, the .410 immediately became a favorite of women and youngsters.

Then in 1933, Winchester Repeating Arms Co. came out with a new slide-action repeating shotgun developed especially for the .410 shotshell. The gun, of course, was the famous Winchester Model 42 as shown in Figure 20-2. Along with this new gun came a new 3-inch .410 shell, holding ¾ ounce of shot, an amount equal to the 28-gauge shotshell. However, except for its class in skeet, most experts of the day still considered the .410 shotgun next to useless.

Actually, in the hands of an expert shotgunner, using No. 7½ shot, the .410 will regularly take quail, rabbit, ducks and grouse out to 30 or 35 yards.

Nearly all factory-built .410 shotguns are choked full, and according to some gun writers, this is a mistake for use in a starting gun for youngsters. "If the .410 was built with a modified choke," says one

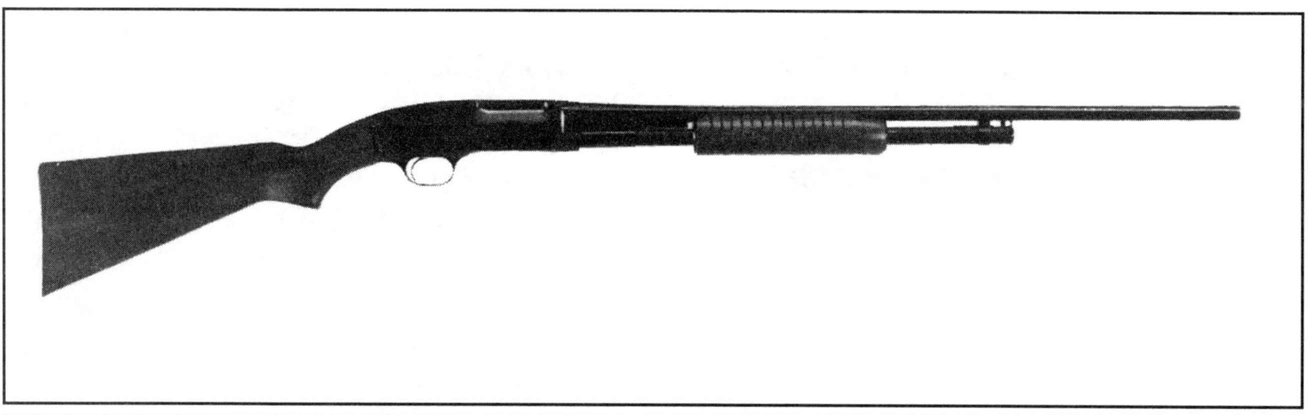

Figure 20-2: The Winchester Model 42 slide-action repeating shotgun was the first .410 chambered for the 3-inch shells.

expert, "more hits will be made." For hunting purposes, I disagree with the experts. I believe that all .410 shotguns that are used for hunting should be full choke, as the .410 shot charges are too light to permit much spread of the pattern and still retain a killing density.

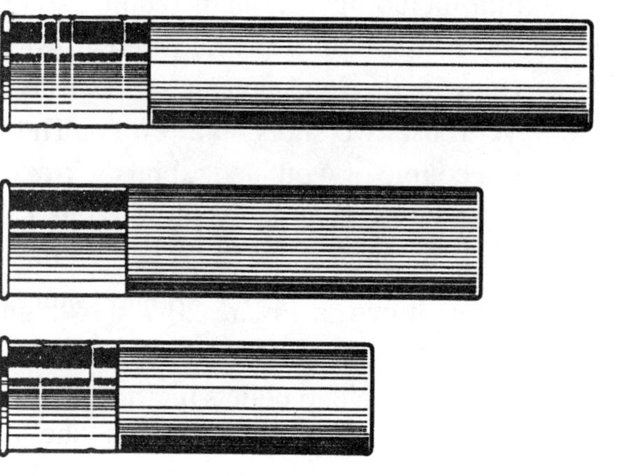

Figure 20-3: Comparison of the three standard sizes of .410 shells, from top to bottom: 3-, 2½-, and 2-inch shells.

Regarless of what some experts may write, the use of the .410 shotgun is on the rise. In fact, gun dealers in Maine have told me that it's hard to sell a shotgun larger than 28 gauge to the natives. The .410 remains the most popular gun for the woods loafers (in Maine) who use the gun on their trap line or to take a grouse for the pot. Although not recommended, the tiny .410 slug has also downed quite a few deer and black bear for these same people.

The chief advantages of the .410 shotgun is its mild recoil and low report; the .410 makes about a third less noise than the 12 gauge. With most areas in the United States becoming heavily populated, there will certainly be fewer complaints when firing the .410 over the larger gauges. With its lighter load

Figure 20-4: The Winchester Model 37 single-shot was chambered for all standard gauges, including the .410 bore. It remained in production until the 1960s.

of shot, small game will not be damaged as much either, giving a little more meat for the table.

TESTING THE .410 BORE

For use in testing loads for the .410 bore, we used two different shotguns:

- Savage Model 24 .22/.410 over/under with the lower barrel chambered for 3-inch shells and choked full.
- Custom-built Winchester Model 94 lever-action fitted with a .410 smoothbore barrel and choked extra-full — the final restriction being only .375 inch!

Before shooting for patterns with the .410 guns, we tested a 20-gauge Ithaca side-by-side double-barrel shotgun to obtain a reference point. This gun had accounted for all types of of small game, at least one white-tailed deer and one black bear over the past 50 years. It was indeed a "hunting shotgun."

The right barrel of the 20-gauge double had a modified choke while the left barrel was choked full. We patterned the right barrel at a little over 25 yards and obtained the shot pattern shown in Figure 20-5. Although all the hits on the quail target may not show up in the illustration, there were 11 hits — 7 of them being "killing" hits.

Before testing the .410s, we did not expect the patterns to be as good as a 20 gauge. However, we did want to see how close the .410s would be to the larger gauges in performance.

Testing 2½-Inch .410 Loads

The custom Winchester Model 94, chambered for 2½-inch .410 shells, was the first firearm tested. As mentioned previously, this gun had an ultra-tight full choke. Factory loads were used for all of the following tests.

No. 4 Shot, ½-Ounce Load: There are approximately 68 pellets in a ½-ounce .410 shot load. At 25 yards, 28 of these pellets landed on the 8½- by 11-inch paper target. *See* Figure 20-6. Four pellets hit the quail (two in the head) and 16 were inside the 7¾-inch ring. This is the exact load with which I shot the last two black mallard ducks — both at approximately 25 to 30 yards. They were jumped from a pond in back of my house, and the first was a clean kill, but the second required an extra shot. No, this load is not recommended for ducks, but if the situation arises, it will kill a duck or two for the pot if you hold your shots to under 35 yards.

No. 6 Shot, ½-Ounce Load: There are approximately 112 No. 6 pellets in a ½-ounce .410 shot load. This load has accounted for most small game in Virginia including cottontail rabbits, squirrels, and doves. To the best of my knowledge, all game that was hit with this load never got away wounded. I did have to use two shots on a few squirrels and finish off a couple of wounded rabbits with a stick, but over the years, I've had to do the same thing with 12 and 16 gauges.

The target shown in Figure 20-7 shows the results of No. 6 shot fired in the 2½-inch .410 factory load. Note that six No. 6 pellets hit the quail within the killing zone, and four others skimmed the edges. About 40 additional shot stayed within the 7¾-inch circle. Note also that this pattern closely resembled that fired from the 20-gauge double, shown in Figure 20-5. If any small game is hit solidly, few cripples will result out to 30 yards. Of couse, hitting the target is the major complaint with the small shotgun bores; there are not as many shot in the load and the shot-pattern diameter is smaller. Consequently, it is harder to hit a moving target with the smaller bores than with the larger ones. However, if a No. 6 shot pellet hits a rabbit in the head from a .410 bore shotgun, it will hit just as hard as that same No. 6 pellet from a 12 bore, as loads from both guns leave the muzzle at approximately 1200 fps.

Figure 20-5: Shot pattern from 20-gauge modified choke barrel at 30 paces, or a little more than 25 yards. The load was a Federal Hi-Power shell loaded with No. 6 shot.

Figure 20-6: Shot pattern from .410-gauge full-choke barrel at approximately 25 yards. A 2½-inch factory shell was used loaded with ½ ounce of No. 4 chilled shot.

Figure 20-7: Shot pattern from .410-gauge full-choke barrel at approximately 25 yards. A 2½-inch factory shell was used loaded with ½ ounce of No. 6 chilled shot.

Figure 20-8: Shot pattern from .410-gauge full-choke barrel at approximately 25 yards. A 2½-inch factory shell was used loaded with ½ ounce of No. 7½ chilled shot.

No. 7½ Shot, ½-Ounce Load: There are approximately 173 No. 7½ pellets in this .410 factory load. This is my choice for quail, doves, and similar size game when using the .410 shotgun. While I've taken squirrels with No. 7½ shot, the size is a little light for clean kills all the time. I've wound up using a second shot in some cases.

The test pattern using No. 7½ shot is shown in Figure 20-8. Note that 44 shot are in the 7¾-inch circle, with 8 shot pellets hitting the quail target in the "killing zone."

LOADS FOR THE 3-INCH .410 SHELL

When the 3-inch .410 shotshell was introduced in the early 1930s, all manufacturers issued warnings to the effect that they were NOT TO BE USED IN GUNS NOT CHAMBERED FOR 3-INCH SHELLS. Still, thousands of them were fired in standard 2½-inch chambers. To the best of my knowledge, the only adverse effects were feeding problems in repeating shotguns, and the ends of the shell, in most cases, were pinched off by the shot when the longer shells were fired in the shorter chambers. *See* Figure 20-9. There were a few reports of the cutoff shell section becoming lodged in the barrel, whereas the next shot would sometimes cause a bulge in the barrel and there was also the possibility of barrel fracture. Furthermore, any shell longer than the chamber in which it is fired is going to add to the breech pressure. Consequently, any or all of these adverse effects is enough reason ***NOT*** to fire 3-inch shells in the shorter .410 chambers.

If the reverse is tried, however, many skeet shooters claim that when 2½-inch shells are used in 3-inch chambers, the extra-length provides an air cushion for the shot, and better patterns develop for target shooting. But let's see what happened in our tests:

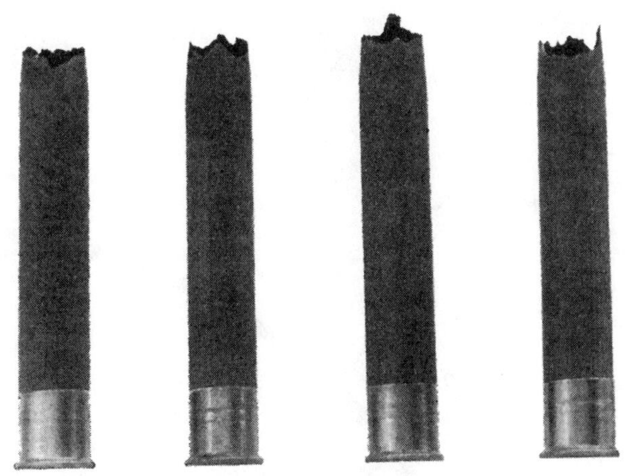

Figure 20-9: Pinched-off 3-inch .410 shells after firing in a 2½-inch chamber.

No. 7½ Shot, 3-Inch Shell: The pattern in Figure 20-10 shows a significant improvement over the 2½-inch load (Figure 20-8). Both loads use size 7½ shot, but the 3-inch shell pattern is much superior to pattern fired with 2½-inch loads. In fact, the .410 pattern in Figure 20-10 is superior to the 20-gauge pattern in Figure 20-5. Note that an astonishing 18 pellets the quail's body! In fact, in actual hunting conditions, there would not be much meat left after this many hits. There were also an additional 39 pellets inside of the 7¾-inch circle.

No. 7½ Shot, 2½-inch shell, fired in 3-inch chamber: The target in Figure 20-11 shows the results of a 2½-inch shell fired in a 3-inch chamber. When comparing this target to the one in Figure 20-10, note than only 7 pellets hit within the quail body. However, there are 49 additional pellets with the 7¾-inch circle — more than the 3-inch load in Figure 20-10. You will also note that the pattern fired from the 2½-inch shell is more evenly dispersed.

Figure 20-10: Shot pattern from .410-gauge full-choke barrel at approximately 25 yards. A 3-inch factory shell was used loaded with $^{11}/_{16}$ ounce of No. 7½ chilled shot.

Figure 20-11: No. 7½ shot in 2½-inch .410 shotshell fired in a 3-inch .410 chamber.

.410 Slug Loads

If you haven't guessed already, my .410 shotguns are used more than any other around my home. They have proven quite adequate for rattlesnakes, knocking down a crow that is set on eating baby rabbits, or even for a goundhog that wants to steal some tomatoes from my garden. I use the .410 for all of my squirrel hunting, and unless I'm on a real cottontail hunt wth beagles, I also use the little gun for rabbits.

I've never used the .410 slug loads on any game, but I always carry a few shells with me when I'm tramping through the woods . . . just in case.

Today, almost all ammunition manufacturers offer rifle slugs for the .410 bore — most chambered only for the 2½-inch shell. Brenneke, however, now offers a .410 slug in the 3-inch shell which should be good for coyotes and similar size game out to about 50 yards or so.

In actual tests using both standard and Brenneke slugs, any difference in accuracy at 50 yards was not detected. However, the Brenneke slug, due to its better sectional density, gives a little better down-range performance, including deeper penetration in soft pine.

Rifle sights installed on shotguns improve the accuracy of shooting slugs tremendously. Both of my .410 shotguns — the Winchester Model 94 and the Savage Model 24 — have open rear rifle sights, and I can always keep my shots in a 4-inch circle at 50 yards. A three-shot group fired at 50 yards is shown in Figure 20-12.

As mentioned previously, some residents of Silver Ridge Township in Aroostook County Maine find the .410 slug adequate for deer and black bear. I doubt that I'd ever take a .410 shotgun deer hunting, but if I were hungry enough, I'd certainly take a shot if the opportunity presented itself.

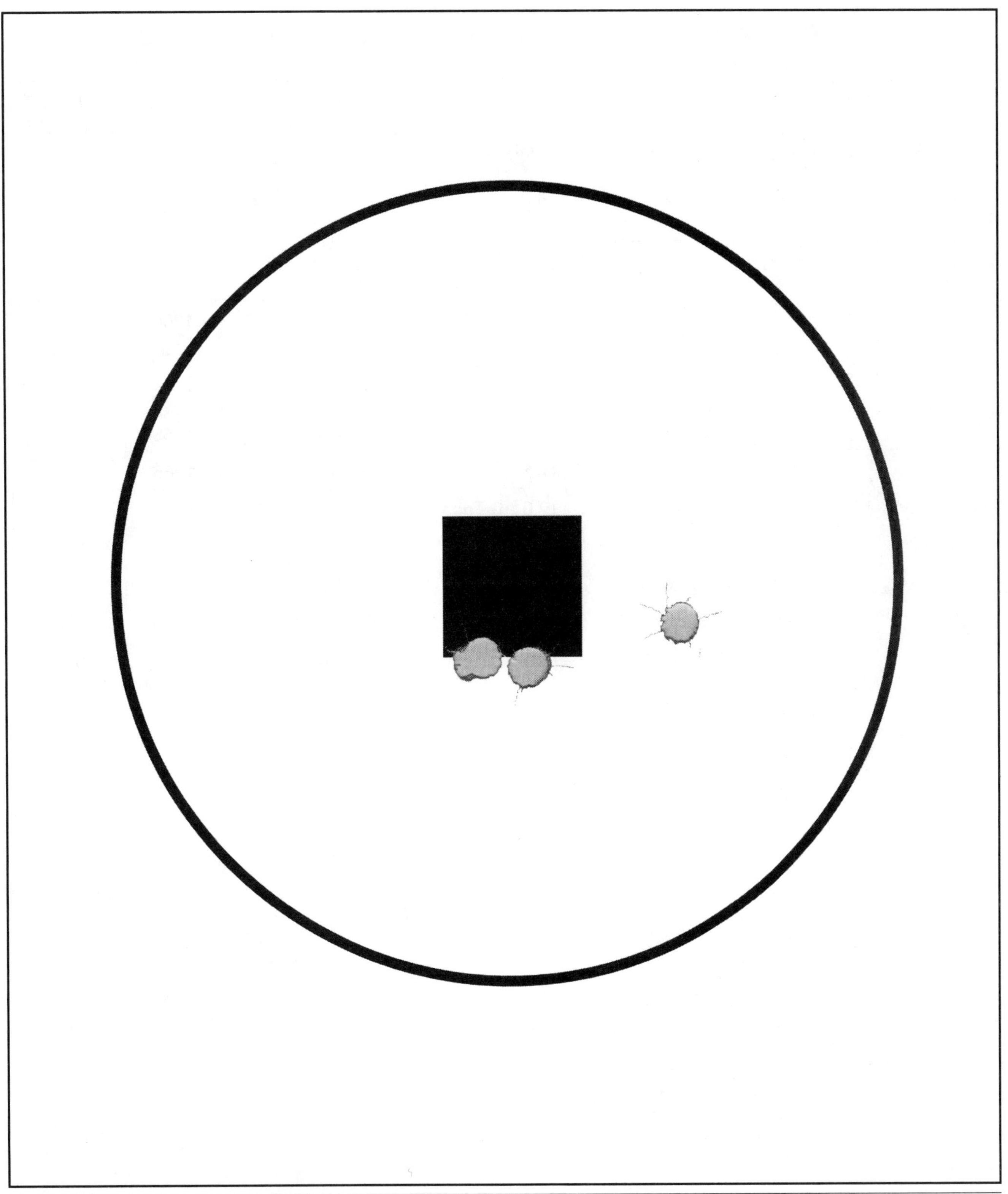

Figure 20-12: Three-shot group using Federal .410 hollow-point slugs. The second shot pulled to the right; probably because of the stiff trigger pull on the Savage Model 24.

.410 BORE FIELD LOAD — FEDERAL 2½-INCH PLASTIC

PRIMER		POWDER		WAD COLUMN		LEAD SHOT (Oz.)	MUZZLE VELOCITY	CHAMBER PRESSURE
MFR.	No.	DESIGNATION	GRAINS	MFG.	DESIGNATION			
Federal	209	Hercules 2400	13.5	Fed.	410SC	½	1200	11900
Federal	209	Hercules 2400	13.0	Rem.	SP410	½	1200	11500
Federal	209	Hercules 2400	13.0	Win.	WWAA41	½	1200	11300
Federal	410	Hercules 2400	13.5	Fed.	410SC	½	1200	12,000
Federal	209	IMR 4227	15.5	Fed.	410SC	½	1115	11200
Federal	209	IMR 4227	15.5	Rem	SP410	½	1115	11100
Federal	410	IMR 4227	17.5	Trico	No. 4	½	1155	9100
CCI	209	IMR 4227	17.5	Trico	No. 4	½	1165	9100
Remington	209P	IMR 4227	19.0	Trico	No. 4	½	1195	9000
Winchester	209	IMR 4227	17.5	Trico	No. 4	½	1180	10900
Federal	209	Hodgdon H-110	14.5	Win.	WWAA41	½	1160	10200
Federal	209	Hodgdon H-4227	17.0	Win.	WWAA41	½	1150	9800
Federal	209	Hodgdon H110	15.0	Rem.	SP410	½	1200	10600

.410 BORE FIELD LOAD — REMINGTON - PETERS 2½-INCH PLASTIC

PRIMER		POWDER		WAD COLUMN		LEAD SHOT (Oz.)	MUZZLE VELOCITY	CHAMBER PRESSURE
MFR.	No.	DESIGNATION	GRAINS	MFG.	DESIGNATION			
Remington	97	Hercules 2400	13.5	Fed.	410SC	½	1200	11400
Remington	97	Hercules 2400	13.0	Rem.	SP410	½	1200	11500
Remington	97	Hercules 2400	14.0	Win.	WWAA41	½	1200	11500
CCI	209	Hercules 2400	14.5	Rem.	SP410	½	1200	11500
CCI	209	Hercules 2400	14.0	Fed.	410SC	½	1200	10600
CCI	209	Hercules 2400	14.5	Win.	WWAA41	½	1200	10300
CCI	209M	Hercules 2400	13.5	Rem.	SP410	½	1200	11000
Remington	209P	IMR 4227	18.5	Trico	Precision No. 4	½	1170	8300
Federal	209	IMR 4227	17.5	Trico	Precision No. 4	½	1210	11000
Winchester	209	IMR 4227	17.5	Trico	Precision No. 4	½	1170	10100
CCI	209	IMR 4227	17.5	Trico	No. 4	½	1140	8500
Federal	209	IMR 4227	15.5	Rem.	SP410	½	1105	10300
Federal	209	IMR 4227	15.5	Fed.	410SC	½	1105	10500

.410 BORE FIELD LOAD — WINCHESTER - WESTERN 2½-INCH PLASTIC "AA" TYPE

PRIMER		POWDER		WAD COLUMN		LEAD SHOT (Oz.)	MUZZLE VELOCITY	CHAMBER PRESSURE
MFR.	No.	DESIGNATION	GRAINS	MFG.	DESIGNATION			
Winchester	209	IMR 4227	16.0	Trico	No. 4	½	1135	11100
CCI	209	IMR 4227	16.0	Trico	No. 4	½	1115	9700
Federal	410	IMR 4227	16.0	Trico	No. 4	½	1110	9600
Remington	209P	IMR 4227	16.5	Trico	No. 4	½	1135	9500
Winchester	209	Hercules 2400	13.0	Win.	WWAA41	½	1200	11700
CCI	209	Hercules 2400	13.0	Fed.	410SC	½	1200	12100
CCI	209	Hercules 2400	13.5	Rem.	SP410	½	1200	12000
Winchester	209	Hodgdon H-110	14.5	Win.	WWAA41	½	1180	10200
Winchester	209	Hodgdon H-110	15.0	Win.	WWAA41	½	1200	10800

.410 BORE SLUG LOAD — REMINGTON - PETERS 2½-INCH PLASTIC "SP" (Use only with Lyman Slug Molds Cast with No. 2 Alloy and Roll Crimp)

PRIMER		POWDER		WAD COLUMN		SLUG WT. (Grs..)	MUZZLE VELOCITY	CHAMBER PRESSURE
MFR.	No.	DESIGNATION	GRAINS	MFG.	DESIGNATION			
Remington	69	IMR 4227	20.0	Rem.	Three 3⁄16 in. felt and one .135 card	238	1320	—
Remington	69	IMR 4227	22.0	Rem.	Three 3⁄16 in. felt and one .135 card	238	1445	—
Remington	69	IMR 4227	23.0	Rem.	Three 3⁄16 in. felt and one .135 card	238	1565	—

.410 BORE FIELD LOAD — FEDERAL 3-INCH PLASTIC

PRIMER		POWDER		WAD COLUMN		LEAD SHOT (Oz.)	MUZZLE VELOCITY	CHAMBER PRESSURE
MFR.	No.	DESIGNATION	GRAINS	MFG.	DESIGNATION			
Federal	410	IMR 4227	17.5	Fed.	410SC	11⁄16	1125	11000
Winchester	209	IMR 4227	17.5	Fed.	410SC	11⁄16	1140	12400
Federal	410	IMR 4227	17.5	Rem.	SP4103	11⁄16	1125	10900
Federal	410	IMR 4227	19.5	Trico	No. 4	11⁄16	1215	11800
Federal	410	Hodgdon H-110	13.0	Rem.	Card plus ¼ in. felt	11⁄16	1000	10300
Federal	410	Hodgdon H-110	14.5	Rem.	SP4103	11⁄16	1050	11200
Federal	410	Hodgdon H-4227	16.0	Rem.	SP4103	11⁄16	1070	10000
Remington	69	IMR 4227	19.0	Rem.	One ¼ in. felt and two 3⁄16 in. felt	½	1190	—
Remington	69	IMR 4227	19.5	Rem.	One ¼ in. felt and two 3⁄16 in. felt	½	1270	—
Remington	69	IMR 4227	17.0	Rem.	One ¼ in. felt and two 3⁄16 in. felt	½	1115	—

DO NOT ATTEMPT TO USE 3-INCH SHELLS IN ANY GUN UNLESS THE GUN IS CLEARLY MARKED FOR SUCH USE

.410 BORE FIELD LOAD — REMINGTON - PETERS 3-INCH PLASTIC

PRIMER		POWDER		WAD COLUMN		LEAD SHOT (Oz.)	MUZZLE VELOCITY	CHAMBER PRESSURE
MFR.	No.	DESIGNATION	GRAINS	MFG.	DESIGNATION			
Remington	209P	IMR 4227	18.5	Rem.	SP410	1 1/16	1135	9800
Winchester	209	IMR 4227	17.5	Rem.	SP410	1 1/16	1135	11500
Remington	209P	IMR 4227	18.5	Fed.	410SC	1 1/16	1140	10300
Winchester	209	IMR 4227	17.5	Fed.	410SC	1 1/16	1140	12000
Remington	209P	IMR 4227	20.5	Trico	No. 4	1 1/16	1210	11100
Winchester	209	IMR 4227	19.0	Trico	No. 4	1 1/16	1180	11300
Remington	209P	Hodgdon H-110	14.5	Rem.	SP4103	1 1/16	1050	11200
Remington	209P	Hodgdon H-4227	16.0	Rem.	SP4103	1 1/16	1070	10000
Remington	97	Hercules 2400	14.5	Rem.	SP410	1 1/16	1135	13000
Remington	97	Hercules 2400	14.5	Fed.	410SC	1 1/16	1135	12600
Remington	97	Hercules 2400	14.5	Win.	WWAA41	1 1/16	1135	12300
Federal	410	Hercules 2400	14.0	Rem.	SP410	1 1/16	1135	12700
CCI	209M	Hercules 2400	14.5	Rem.	SP410	1 1/16	1135	12200

.410 BORE BLANK LOAD — REMINGTON - PETERS 3-INCH PLASTIC

PRIMER		POWDER		WAD COLUMN		LEAD SHOT (Oz.)	MUZZLE VELOCITY	CHAMBER PRESSURE
MFR.	No.	DESIGNATION	GRAINS	MFG.	DESIGNATION			
Remington	209P	Hodgdon Trap-100	10.0	Rem.	14 - .135 in. cards	—	—	—

.410 BORE FIELD LOAD — WINCHESTER - WESTERN 3-INCH PLASTIC "SUPER-X"

PRIMER		POWDER		WAD COLUMN		LEAD SHOT (Oz.)	MUZZLE VELOCITY	CHAMBER PRESSURE
MFR.	No.	DESIGNATION	GRAINS	MFG.	DESIGNATION			
Winchester	209	IMR 4227	17.5	Fed.	410SC	5/8	1160	12400
Remington	209P	IMR 4227	18.5	Fed.	410SC	5/8	1160	11300
Winchester	209	IMR 4227	17.4	Rem.	SP410	5/8	1160	12400
Remington	209P	IMR 4227	18.0	Rem.	SP410	5/8	1160	11000
Winchester	209	IMR 4227	18.8	Trico	No. 4	5/8	1220	12400
Remington	209P	IMR 4227	20.0	Trico	No. 4	5/8	1230	11900
Winchester	209	Hodgdon H-110	14.5	Win.	WWAA41	11/16	1058	1060

.410 BORE SLUG LOAD — REMINGTON - PETERS 3-INCH PLASTIC "SP" (Use only with Lyman Slug Molds Cast with No. 2 Alloy and Roll Crimp)

PRIMER		IMR POWDER		WAD COLUMN		SLUG WT. (Grs.)	MUZZLE VELOCITY	CHAMBER PRESSURE
MFR.	No.	DESIGNATION	GRAINS	MFG.	DESIGNATION			
Remington	69	IMR 4227	20.0	Rem.	Three 3/16 in. felt One 1/8 in. felt One .135 in. card	238	1335	—
Remington	69	IMR 4227	22.0	Rem.	Three 3/16 in. felt One 1/8 in. felt One .135 in. card	238	1465	—
Remington	69	IMR 4227	23.0	Rem.	Three 3/16 in. felt One 1/8 in. felt One .135 in. card	238	1535	—

Chapter 21

Loading Brass Shotshells

The metallic shotshell cartridge made its debut in the last half of the nineteenth century, but it did not have the same impact on the shotshell market as the metallic case had on the balance of the ammunition line. The paper-tube compound case was the primary shotshell product until it was displaced in the middle of the twentieth century by the poly-formed plastic hull.

The metallic shotshell was available from numerous manufacturers toward the end of the nineteenth century. Producers utilized a variety of materials to fabricate these cases including aluminum, brass, copper, steel and zinc. Of these, brass was the most commonly used. From their inception, the metallic shotshell evolved through many experimental stages which provided a tremendous array of case variations. The representative sampling of available cases shown in Figure 21-1 on the next page demonstrates the variety in both availability and design. Those illustrated represent only self-contained metallic shotshells in the self-primed cartridge category. Since we are considering these as candidates for reloading, no early pinfire cartridges or unusual configurations have been shown. Even with these acknowledged exclusions, the field of available candidates remains far too vast to consider in its entirety. To illustrate this point, metallic shotshells were produced in two separate series. Early production headstamps frequently identified the series with an "A" or "B" classification. The "A" series was designed for shotguns chambered to accept conventional paper shells. Headstamps with the "B" designation indicated ammunition designed for shotguns bored for metallic shells only. Eventually the "A" series became standard and later vintage headstamps display no series classifications.

In addition to the early dual "A-B" series classification, metallic shotshells were offered in a variety of bore sizes. This bore determination was frequently stated in terms of a gauge (a size classification derived from muzzleloading terminology defining a method of determining the size of a musket bore). These bore sizes ranged from 1 and 2 gauge down through 28 and 32 gauge and continued beyond the gauge derivation to the .410 and

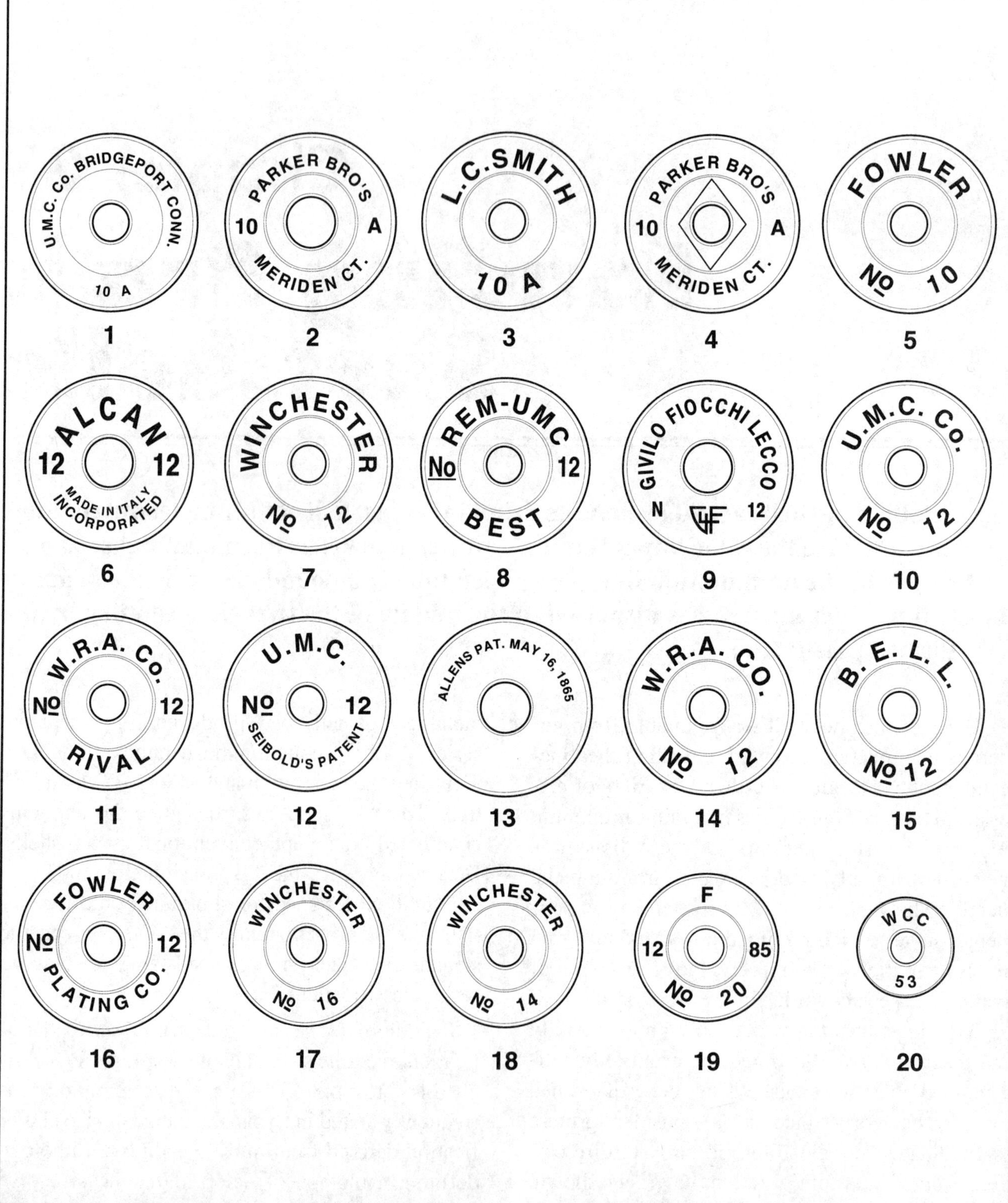

Figure 21-1: Various headstamps for brass shotshells made both in the United States and abroad.

9mm calibers. The extremely large bores, 1- and 2-gauge shells, were fired from punt guns mounted on a unipod secured to the bow of commercial fowling vessels. The remaining standard bore sizes for shoulder-mounted shotguns are given in the table to follow and illustrated in Figure 21-2.

Gauge	Diameter – Inches	Diameter – mm
4	.935	24.4
8	.835	21.8
10	.775	20.0
12	.729	18.6
14	.693	17.8
16	.662	16.8
20	.615	15.6
24	.579	14.7
25	.571	14.4
28	.550	14.0
30	.537	13.6
32	.526	13.2
40	.488	12.4
50	.453	11.4
.410	.410	10.5
9mm	.309	7.5

The practice of most commercial producers of metallic shotshells was to accept large special orders and to furnish that ammunition loaded to contracted specifications. This practice increased the growing number of case varieties even more. In addition to stipulating powder preferences and loading specifications — including special case lengths — these contract orders included personalized headstamps. Each stipulated variation created yet another version of the rapidly expanding assortment of metallic shotshells.

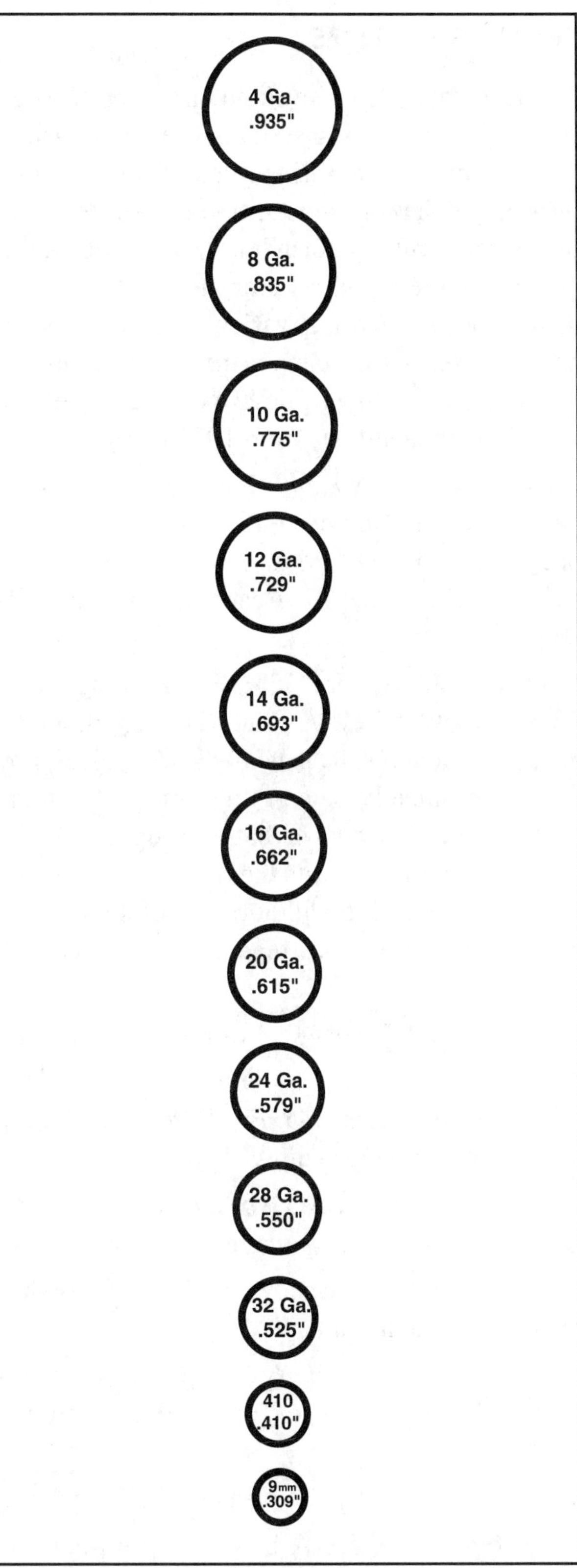

Figure 21-2: Standard bore sizes of shotguns for which brass shotshells were made (not to scale).

PRIMING SYSTEMS

The independent development of both foreign and domestic priming systems further contributed to the complexity of this problem. With developers pursuing their preferred ignition-system design and using a seemingly unending variety of Berdan, boxer or battery-cup style primers, it became evident that the growing variety of shotshells had become a serious problem to the entire ammunition industry. The following describes a variety of shotshell primers available from 1937 to 1953.

Alcan NM-NC No. 240: For Western, Winchester, and Federal empty tubes — all gauges. This primer is designed for low-cost shooting and is to be used with Super-M, Acapnia, Nike, and M-B powders.

Alcan NM-NC No. 225: For Remington and Peters empty tubes. A double-force primer that gives excellent results in heavy loads with all powders. A completely waterproof primer with a totally enclosed headed copper battery cup with inside primer cup and anvil with the flash hole sealed with plastic. The No. 225 will not deteriorate in storage even after long periods regardless of moisture or humidity.

Alcan NM-NC No. 645: Fits European manufacture 10, 12, 14, 16, 20, 24, and 28 gauge tubes.

Alcan NM-NC No. 545: Fits European manufacture 32 and 36 gauge empty shells.

Alcan Primer NM-NC No. DF: Fits 4 gauge, 6 gauge, and larger European manufacture.

Alcan NM-NC Berdan No. 645: For brass shells requiring Berdan primer.

Peters No. 2: A battery-cup primer for use in Peters "Victor," "Target" and "High Velocity" shells.

Peters No. 35: A plain primer for .410 gauge.

Remington No. 53: A battery-cup primer once used in 8-, 10-, 12-, 16- and 20-gauge shotshells (replaced by Remington No. 57).

Remington No. 57: Used in brass shotshells with a .224 inch primer-pocket diameter.

Remington No. 55: A battery-cup primer for 28-, 32- and 410-gauge shotshells with .207 pocket diameter.

Remington No. 2: A corrosive mercuric primer made for shotshells with .209 pocket diameter and will interchange with Winchester No. 2.

Western No. 209: A battery cup primer for Winchester and Western shells except 28 and .410 gauge.

Western No. 3: A battery cup primer for use in Western and Winchester 28 and .410 gauge shells.

Western No. 209: A battery cup primer for Winchester and Western shells of all gauges.

Winchester No. 33: For 28 and .410 gauge shells.

The following primers are in current production and should be considered for reloading brass shotshells. In many cases, the primer pockets of older brass shotshells will have to be modified.

Berdan Primers: The Berdan series of brass shotshells represented by Alcan, Fiocchi and CBC were designed to accept .254 diameter Berdan primers (in Alcan and Fiocchi originally designated "645B" indicating European "645mm diameter Berdan"). RWS produces this style primer in the required diameter and in two skirt heights (.09 and .133).

Battery-Cup Primers: The battery-cup series of brass shotshells represented by the redesigned Alcan whereas altered Berdan cases were modified to accept the new style priming system. The Alcan case was fitted with G57F primer (Alcan's version of the Remington-Peters 57). Current manufacturers including Activ, Federal, Fiocchi, Remington, Winchester and CCI have initiated some degree of standardization by reducing the number of available primer configurations to a basic 209 (standard) and a 209M (magnum). However, some special designations and individual manufacturer nomenclature still exist for target and small-bore primers including Winchester AATP and Fiocchi 615 and

616. This action eliminated previous primer designations including 57, 97, 109, 157 and 399 and resulted in the adoption of a standardized tapered battery cup design with a sealed flash hole. This new primer series is available from any of the above manufacturers and is adaptable to both cases.

The Boxer series brass shotshells are represented by both domestic and foreign manufacturers. The U.S. Ordnance Corps, 12 gauge, M19 shotshell and the three-inch aluminum .410 designated the M35 were both designed to accept a .211 diameter Boxer primer. B.E.L.L. brass, also designed to accept the Boxer priming system, represents foreign shotshell production extruded in China. Currently, all major primer manufacturers produce both "Large Rifle" (hotter and harder) and "Large Pistol" (milder and softer) primer components which are adaptable to this priming system.

AVAILABILITY OF BRASS SHOTSHELLS

Winchester and Remington ceased production of metallic shotshells on a regular basis a couple of decades ago. More recently, Alcan, Bell Extrusion Laboratories, Ltd. and Fiocchi have also stopped production. Therefore, the domestic supply of brass shotshells is limited to the early production sources. However, obsolete brass shotshells are generally available on a very limited basis. The most recent suppliers include:

Alcan: Alcan distributed two classes of brass shotshells produced by Fiocchi of Italy. The Berdan series was available in 12, 16, 20, 28 gauge 2½" length and .410 in 2" length all designed to accept .254 Berdan primers. The "Battery cup" series was available in 10 gauge 2⅞" length and 12 and 16 gauge 2½" length. Both were designed to accept Alcan G57F (Remington-Peters 57) primers.

Navy Arms: Navy Arms distributed Berdan series brass shotshells manufactured by CBC of Brazil in a variety of gauges which were designed to accept .254 diameter Berdan primers.

B.E.L.L. (Brass Extrusion Laboratories, Ltd.: This firm distributed Boxer series brass shotshells extruded in China which were designed to accept .211 diameter (Large Rifle or Large Pistol) primers.

Remington: Remington distributed commemorative brass shotshell ammunition in tins of twenty five in 1986-87. This brass was extruded by CBC for Remington as a commemorative promotion.

U.S. Ordnance Corps: This firm loaded an all-brass, No. 00 buckshot 12 gauge, M19 (combat and guard duty) shotshell and a three-inch aluminum .410 designated the M35 (used in 22/.410 survival gun) which was charged with smokeless powder and copper-coated No. 6 shot. Both metallic cases were procured commercially from manufacturers including, Remington and Winchester and both were designed to accept a .211 diameter Boxer primer.

Future sources for metallic shotshell components are developing on two fronts. Several domestic importers are actively seeking manufacturing sources. Products from both Brazil and China are under consideration to supply a domestic importation network. A third potential source presently exists in Australia. Bruce Bertram of Bertram Bullet Company has acquired two additional twenty ton brass extrusion presses to supplement his current operation. Sources supporting the current component production include Huntington Die Specialists and the Old Western Scrounger, both of California (projected availability of shotshell brass 1996).

CLASSIFICATION

To determine the usefulness of the available shells as potential reloading components, a system of classification, separation and evaluation must be established considering source, availability and design. Again, the reader is reminded that the sampling of illustrated metallic shotshell cases presented here represents only a very small percentage of the many variations that may be available for consideration. Also the general principles of evaluation which have been applied to this sampling are directed by degrees of probability and therefore, exceptions may exist. Although all the shells illustrated in this sampling may be reloaded, many require special components that have been out of production for a quarter century or more. Others may require case modification and all will certainly require special loading procedures. The following examples are intended to provide guidelines to help establish a system of evaluation suited for your particular reloading requirements.

CASE PREPARATION

After the basic selection process has been completed, the case preparation begins with cleaning. If you have been fortunate enough to secure a quantity of unprimed brass cases from one of the more recent suppliers such as Alcan, B.E.L.L. or Fiocchi, this step may be skipped. It is far more likely, however, that your collection of metallic shotshell cases will be comprised of uncleaned fired cases. If so, this phase of preparation is necessary to insure that all potentially harmful residues from black powder and mercuric primers will be removed from the fired cases. Unfortunately, both forms of residue also attack the brass case. Blackpowder draws and retains moisture which promotes corrosion. Fulminate of mercury used in the earlier priming compounds is a much greater threat because it penetrates the case and destroys the brass cohesion. This causes the brass to lose its elasticity and to become brittle which will cause the case to crack and fail prematurely. This problem is somewhat diminished by the straight wall configuration of the shotshell case which retains less mercury than a tapered or bottleneck case. With these diminished effects and the lower pressure range of the shotshell loads (usually below 10,000 psi) these cases might not be considered to be subject to catastrophic case failure. Do not allow this reasoning to lull you into a false sense of security. The primer pocket will retain sufficient amounts of mercury to cause the web of the case to become brittle. Therefore, if you even suspect that a case was loaded with a mercuric primer, set it aside and do not consider it as a reloading candidate.

Figure 21-3: Cut-away view of brass shotshells showing priming system.

CLEANING

The first phase of the cleaning process may involve washing the cases in a hot cleaning solution or abrasive cleaning in a tumbler, or possibly a combination of both. The condition of your cases will dictate what will be required. If the select group of cases contains uncleaned fired shells exhibiting a buildup of blackpowder residue, dry brushing the interior of the case will greatly enhance the cleaning process. A standard or spiral wound stainless steel brush chucked in a drill press or a flexible shaft motor tool will reduce the time required to complete the manual brushing method.

The recommended procedure for this first-time cleaning process will require removing fired primers to allow the primer pocket to be cleaned during this process (see the appropriate depriming method under reloading procedures). Several commercial cleaning solutions are available but chemicals should be used with caution. One early method involved two-solutions and a four-bath process with 2 ozs. of potassium bichromate and 2 ozs. of sulphuric acid diluted in a quart of water. The second solution was created by dissolving one-quarter pound of sodium cyanide in a quart of water. Two additional containers of clear water were required to rinse the cases after each chemical bath. This process requires acid resistant containers, protective clothing, goggles and gloves. These are rapid acting chemical solutions which are effective at cleaning brass cases but are equally efficient at dissolving the brass itself if emersed in the solution more than five seconds. This potentially hazardous situation is compounded by additional health concerns. If these acidic solutions are allowed to accidentally mix they produce poisonous fumes. Exercise extreme caution if you choose to use these or other potentially dangerous cleaning solutions. A less volatile acid bath may be mixed from common household products. A fifty-percent solution of vinegar and water will remove corrosion stains and verdigris from brass cases but will require an hour or more to act. It becomes quite apparent if this mild acidic solution is used to wash metallic cases because it produces a coral pink tint on many varieties of brass.

A safer and more cost effective method involves hot water and a mild soap or detergent solution. Using the appropriately sized brushes, the interior walls of the case and the primer pockets should be cleaned thoroughly. After scrubbing the cases inside and out, rinse them in clean boiling water. Drain the cases and individually shake off the excess water as you invert them on a paper or cloth to dry. The heat built up in the brass will promote evaporation and aid the drying process. To eliminate the possibility of corrosion forming as a result of the residual water evaporating too slowly, you may wish to further promote the drying process. This may be accomplished using a heat gun, dryer or a thermostatically controlled oven. Any drying process must be completed with controlled heat not exceeding 250 degrees. Drying cases may be addressed individually with a thermostatically controlled heat gun or hair dryer. But remember consistency and control must be maintained because the molecular structure of brass is altered at temperatures above 482 degrees.

The thermostatically controlled oven is a more consistent method of drying larger quantities of brass shells. Place a single layer of paper towels or newspaper on a cooking sheet or grill with the drip-dried cases arranged base down. Slide the sheet in on the center rack of the oven and maintain a temperature of 250 degrees. The drying process will be accelerated by increased circulation if the oven door is left open on the first open notch. With properly controlled heat, the absorbent layer of paper may slowly turn light brown as the moisture is dissipated. If the paper begins to scorch, reduce the heat range to complete the drying process.

You may wish to polish the washed and dried cases in a case tumbler prior to final inspection. This will remove any remaining grit or residue and expose any deterioration that may have occurred. As the polished cases are removed from the tumbler, inspect each case for flaws and defects. Examine the primer pocket and flash hole to determine that they are clear and free of residue. If additional attention is required, use a primer pocket cleaning tool and flash hole pick to correct the situation.

This group of cleaned cases is now ready for final inspection. Examine each shell individually and eliminate any that show signs of deterioration. If more than one headstamp is represented in the remaining group this final evaluation must be exacting with special consideration given to case dimensions including wall and web thickness, base design and case volume or capacity. If you do not have at your disposal precision measuring equipment, including micrometers and calipers, in order to make these critical measurements, do not combine dissimilar headstamps without consulting a qualified expert willing to made this determination for you.

CASE ADAPTATION AND ALTERATION

Having selected a group of shells that exhibit similar design characteristics and are adaptable to your reloading requirements, you must now established uniformity within that select group. This universal procedure should be applied to all acquired cases on a first time basis and thereafter only as required. The process involves restoring or correcting the case configuration and dimension by truing case rims and walls, trimming cracked or broken case mouths and confirming the primer pocket and flash hole dimensions to insure that they have not been previously altered.

Correct any case deformation that may exist. First, check the case head and rim. Since most metallic shotshells were developed on the balloon-head design which exhibits a relatively thin base with an extruded battery cup, they may be susceptible to bulged heads. This deformity may be the result of a case being fired in an older gun with excessive headspace or being forcefully driven from a hand resizing die during an earlier reloading procedure. If this situation exists, it may be easily detected if the base of the shell is placed on a flat machined surface. The second common deformity may occur if a case is dropped on a hard surface which may result in a bent rim. Either of these situations may be corrected by using an outside form die. This corrective procedure may be performed using an arbor press to apply the required pressure. An alternate tool that might be used for compression would be a standard bench vice with a four-inch throat adjustment. With the deformed case in the lightly lubricated form die, place the unit base down on the machined surface plate of the arbor press. Apply pressure to the top of the die to restore the case to its original configuration. The restored case generally slides effortlessly from the die. If required, you may use an inside plunger such as the primer seat swager or a dowel to facilitate case removal.

Second, check the mouth of the cases for distortion and cracks. Reshaping or truing may be accomplished by applying light pressure using a tapered case conditioner. If any cases show cracked or broken case mouths, trimming may be required. Consider your ammunition requirements and intended use to determine if all cases should be trimmed to a uniform length. The task of trimming may be addressed with a custom shell holder and piloted cutter used in conjunction with a drill press equipped with an adjustable depth gauge and positive stop. If you do not have access to the large piloted cutter required to trim shotshell, an alternate method of trimming may be implemented with a belt/disc sander fitted with an adjustable table. The disc sander used in conjunction with a V-block secured squarely to the adjustable table will allow you to trim cases to a predetermined length. Some commercially available power trimmers are adaptable to this task when used with special shell holders and custom pilots. Trim the case slowly to avoid loading the cutting tool and finish by deburring the case inside and out.

Third, resize all cases to ensure that they will chamber properly. This operation may be addressed with an independent sizing tool or with a custom resizing die. This "first time" resizing procedure should be completed using a resizing lubricant and case lube pad to ensure ease of operation and relieve stress on the case. In latter loading operations, an altered single-stage shotshell press may be adequate to address resizing requirements in sequence during the reloading process.

Fourth, check the primer pocket and flash hole using a primer pocket gauge and uniformer in conjunction with a flash hole gauge. Refer to the primer chart to determine the proper dimensions of your particular case. If the "No-Go" gauge enters the primer pocket, that case will present primer retention problems. To correct this, insert the primer seat swager into the suspect case and with its base on a solid flat surface use a light peening action to swage the primer seat. Check to see if the corrective action has closed the pocket sufficiently with the "No-Go" gauge. If not, repeat the action until the desired effect is obtained or discard the case. The flash hole gauge is now used to ensure that the orifice was not altered during the previous procedure. If corrective action is required, the flash hole may be opened with a No. 46 (.081) drill bit.

Fifth, consider the performance potential of the select group of case components as they relate to loading and powder specifications. If your case components are designed to accept the .254 Berdan primer and your intended load is in the heavy field category, the ignition requirements of the required powder may exceed the potential of the Berdan design. If this is the case, you may wish to consider case modification to resolve the problem by opening the primer pocket to accept a battery cup style primer. This process may be accomplished by reaming or drilling depending on the available facility. The reaming process is best accomplished using a lathe with a custom reamer chucked in the tail stock. With this custom ground step counterbore set to ream to a pre-determined depth, the procedure may be accomplished in one pass. Using a 15/64" counterbore to open the primer pocket in conjunction with a 5/16" piloted counterbore to cut the rim recess will require two separate setups. The drilling procedure is approached from inside the case using the detent in the top of the primer pocket to properly center the 15/64" drill bit. Invert the case and use a 90-degree countersink to cut the recess for the primer rim just deep enough to seat the primer flange flush with the base of the case. *See* Figure 21-4.

Sixth, if your loading procedure requires the case to be crimped, the life of the case may be greatly extended if the case mouths are annealed during initial preparation. When the case is in service repeat the process after each set of five reloading sessions. The annealing process (Figure 21-5) requires a heat source to rapidly heat the case mouth and a combined method to hold the case while heating and to cool the case quickly thereafter. One common heat source is Bernz-O-Matic propane torch. To contain and cool the cases you may use a three-inch deep baking pan containing two inches of cold water. Place this container on a turntable to allow it to rotate to promote an even controlled application of heat during the process. With a case placed base down in the center of the rotating pan, apply heat evenly. Read the color changes induced by the heat to determine the proper temperature. As

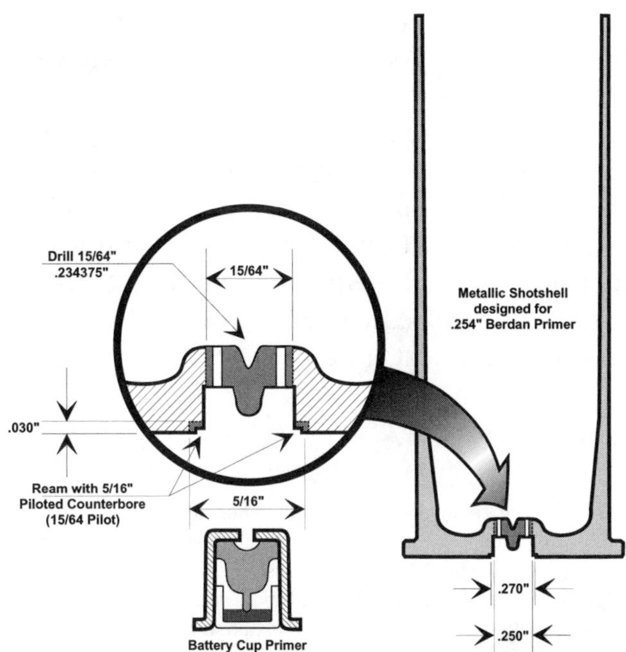

Figure 21-4: Modifying an obsolete primer pocket to accept a currently-manufactured shotshell primer.

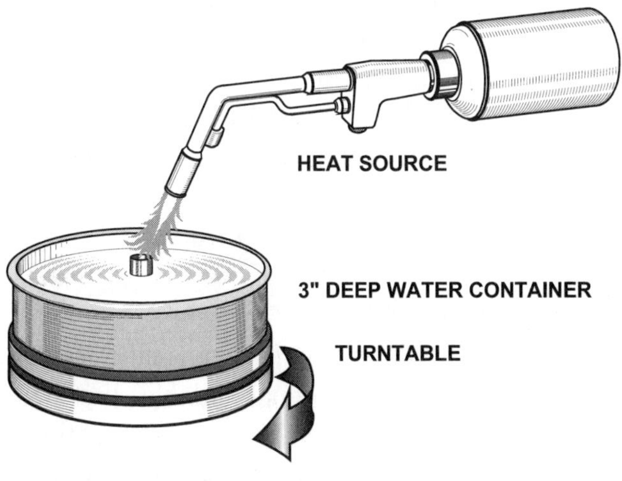

Figure 21-5: Annealing brass shotshells.

flame is applied the exposed brass will turn straw-brown then blue. As the blue color advances toward the protective water, the case mouth will begin to turn a dull red. Remove the heat source before the red color can intensify and advance down toward the water. The proper temperature has been reached and the case must be tipped over quickly to quench it in the cold water. Retrieve the annealed case and invert it on a padded surface to promote drying and proceed to the next case.

CAUTION!

Do not overheat the brass or allow it to become cherry red. The three color changes may occur in rapid progression but should be easily discernable. If the color succession is too rapid reduce the heat for better control. Avoid annealing too much of the case wall which could cause malfunctions and shorten case life. With the case submerged in water and no more than one-half inch of the case mouth exposed, the annealing will be confined to that area and this problem will be averted.

LOADING PROCEDURES

Your particular reloading specifications must be determined by your individual shooting requirements with special consideration given to type and vintage of the firearm involved. When reloading metallic shotshells, the additional variables that are involved concerning the case itself greatly influence and restrict the number of the adaptable components which are now available to complete the component chain. Determining the type and charge of powder with a given shot drop remains consistent with conventional loading data concerning breech pressure. However, the balance of the component chain must be made up from a relatively small number of adaptable choices. These remaining components including the primer, gas seal, filler and card wads, shot cup, crimp and/or sealer combine to produce additional variables that will affect the pressure curve. These determinations must be made with the absolute assurance and with the knowledge that the ballistic performance of the

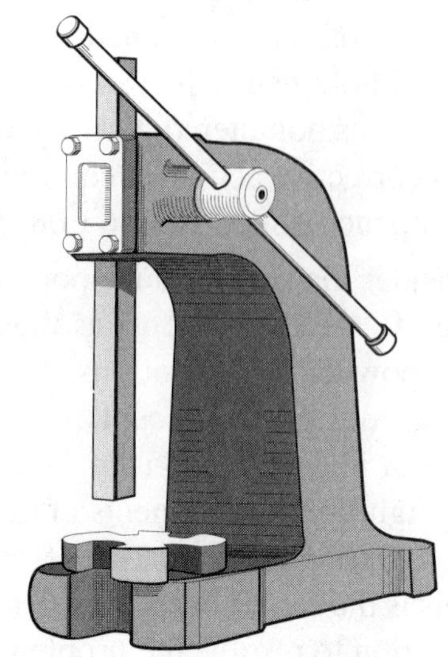

Figure 21-6: Arbor press used in conjunction with the appropriate dies to correct deformities in brass shotshells.

recommended ammunition is compatible with the qualified condition of the firearm involved.

Inspect all fired cases for signs of deterioration or defects and address those issues as required, eliminating cases that are beyond reconditioning. Correct any case deformation that may exist using a tapered case conditioner for distorted case mouths or an outside form die to correct bulged case heads or bent rims. These corrective procedures may be performed using an arbor press as shown in Figure 21-6.

Deprime all cases to expose the primer pocket during the cleaning process. A variety of case designs exist but considering only those with non-corrosive priming systems reduces the field to three basic designs. Each specific design requires different depriming procedures as outlined below.

The Berdan group as represented by Fiocchi is fitted with a .254 diameter Berdan primer. This style is best removed by externally piercing the primer cup and using leverage to lift it from the primer pocket.

The Boxer group as represented by REM-UMC and B.E.L.L. is fitted with a .210 diameter Boxer primer. Cases of this design may be deprimed through the flash hole. This procedure may be accomplished using hand tools or a modified single stage press.

The "Battery Cup" group, as represented by Alcan, and with modified Berdan cases fitted with 209-size battery cup style components, may be deprimed by using conventional methods, including the use of hand tools or a single-stage press.

Clean all cases as required with special attention given to the interior walls of the case and the primer pocket.

Trim any cases that show cracked or broken case mouths. Consider your ammunition requirements and intended use to determine if all cases should be trimmed to a uniform length. Finish by deburring the case inside and out.

Resize cases as required. This procedure may have been addressed during the depriming operation depending on the style of equipment used.

If applicable, check the primer pocket and flash hole using a primer pocket gauge and uniformer in conjunction with a flash hole gauge to ensure that these areas are the correct size, unobstructed and clean. If the primer pocket is found to be over-sized, insert the primer seat swager into the suspect case and with its base on a solid flat surface, use a light peening action to swage the pocket to the correct dimension. The flash hole gauge is now used to ensure that the orifice was not altered during the previous procedure. If corrective action is required the flash hole may be opened with a No. 46 (.081) drill bit. With the case properly prepared reprime with the appropriate style component. Refer to the primer chart to determine the proper dimensions of the required component. Repriming may be accomplished as an independent action in a hand priming tool, with an "O" frame ram press with custom shell holder or with a modified single-stage shotshell press.

Charging the cases with the selected powder drop may be accomplished using an appropriately sized powder dipper or powder bushing.

The flash hole of most metallic shotshells is an integral part of the one-piece component and may be singular in the Boxer style or multiple in those designed to accept the Berdan style primer. The larger gauge shells exhibit an extruded battery cup which extends into the shell's cavity with exposed and unsupported sidewalls. The battery cup of the smaller .410 is completely contained in that shell's base and therefore has supported sidewalls. Regardless of the fact that these cases more closely resemble modern rifle cartridges and therefore logically promote the reasoning that they are stronger than the paper tube or plastic hulls, resist the temptation to ignore the powder manufacturer's warning.

The procedure for seating wads will vary depending on the composition of the wad column. Early load recommendations from manufacturers required nitro cards and filler wads composed of compressed paper, cork and felt. Later component suppliers introduced plastic gas seals and combo wads in varying column heights. Then the plastic shot cup appeared and the current varieties of wads were developed combining the gas seal, shock absorbing cushion and shot cup concepts into one component. Using filler wads to develop a wad column with the proper height will be required if a crimp is used to retain it.

As with the powder drop, the shot may be dispensed by a dipper or bushing in either a "stage" or "series" process of loading. The volume of shot dispensed should also be verified by weight using a scale. Some experimentation with filler wads may be required to bring the shot column within an eighth inch of the case mouth to allow for proper crimping.

The crimp and top wad sealing process may vary according to your requirements and intended use. If the firearm is of the standing breech variety, single or double (side-by-side, over/under or combination), you may secure the shot with a .770 diameter overshot card sealed with several drops of top wad sealer. The crimp is not required if an adequate top wad seal is achieved to form both a moisture and retention seal. Application of the sealer is best accomplished using a clear squeeze bottle with a nozzle applicator to dispense the material in controlled measure. Strive to attain uniformity by applying the exact same amount of sealer to each case. This will maintain an established top wad resistance to ensure proper load performance. If using a repeating shotgun in the form of an automatic or slide action, a crimp will be required to ensure proper function. In this case, the proper wad column height must be established using filler wads to elevate the shot column to within one eighth of the case mouth. Insert the top wad and apply the crimp to retain the card wad. A lighter application of sealer may be used to support the wad and form a moisture barrier.

WAD COLUMN

Early load recommendations required over-powder wads (nitro cards), filler wads composed of compressed paper, cork or felt and over-shot wads. Manufacturers included Alcan, Herter's, Ljutic, Sullivan, Remington and Winchester. Most of the required components for metallic shotshells have been discontinued by those remaining manufacturers. As the component design evolved, suppliers introduced plastic gas seals, combo wads, plastic shot cups and the one-piece wad combining the gas seal, shock absorbing cushion and shot cup into one component. Alcan was the last supplier of the wad column components required in these early loading specifications on metallic shotshells. Adaptable components are available on a somewhat limited scale from current manufacturers. The principal supplier at this time is Ballistic Products. Available wads include:

- ½" Fiber Card Wads - 8-gauge thru .410-bore
- ½" Hard Card Wads - 12-gauge
- .125" Nitro Card Wads - 8-gauge thru .410-bore
- .030" Overshot Card Wads - 8-gauge thru .410-bore
- X-Spreader Wads - 8-gauge thru 20-gauge
- Poly-Wad Inserts - 10-gauge thru .28-gauge
- BP Shotcups - 12-gauge
- BPGS Plastic Gas Seal - 10- and 12-gauge
- CGS Plastic Gas Seal - 10- and 12-gauge
- OBGS Plastic Gas Seal - 12-, 16- and 20-gauge
- BPD-10 One-Piece Shotcup - 10-gauge
- BPD-10 Tuff One-Piece Shotcup - 10-gauge
- Teflon Wraps - 10- and 12-gauge
- Filler Wads ⅛" and ¼" (Cork, Felt and Fiber) - 12- and 20-gauge
- Remington SP10 - Power Piston 10-gauge thru .410-bore

Chapter 22

Solid Projectiles in Shotshells

Lead balls fired in smoothbore barrels have always been far from accurate. "Don't fire until you see the whites of their eyes" was shouted at Bunker Hill for a good reason. Hits beyond fifty yards became more and more unlikely as the range increased from shooter to target. Still, many hunters of the past who had to hunt big game with shotguns depended on "punkin balls," due to the notorious deer-crippling buckshot loads of the day.

In testing round lead balls in smoothbore barrels — from 12 to 20 gauge — it is difficult for me to keep five shots on a foot-square target at 50 yards, and this is from a bench rest. Sometimes two or three shots would stay within a 12-inch ring, but never five. Even those shots tested in shotguns equipped with rifle sights did not group much better. It became quite evident to me that the crys at Bunker Hill were not shouted without reason.

However, The Ideal Handbook — published by the Ideal Manufacturing Co., New Haven, Connecticut around the turn of this century — spoke very highly of round balls used in shotguns, especially when used in cylinder bore guns (no choke) and also when the lead balls were cast to match the individual shotgun bore, less .015 inch to allow for a linen patch.

This Ideal Handbook gives the correct diameter of standard shotgun gauges and bores (for the day) as follows:

Gauge or Bore	Diameter in thousandths of an inch	Diameter in Millimeters
8	.835	21.8
10	.775	20.0
12	.720	18.6
14	.693	17.8
16	.662	16.8
20	.615	15.6
25	.571	14.4
30	.537	13.6
32	.526	13.2
40	.488	12.4
50	.453	11.4

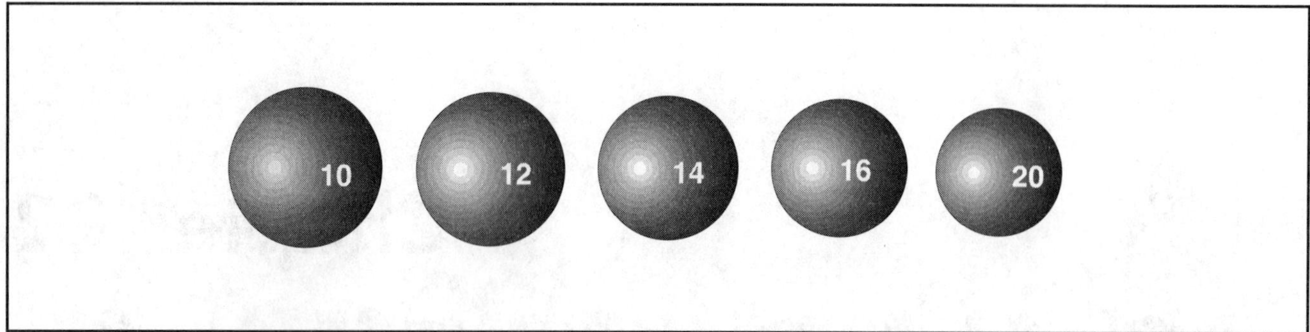

Figure 22-1: Types of lead-ball moulds made by the Ideal Manufacturing Co. around the turn of the century. These lead balls are approximately actual size.

The lead balls for the various gauges, however, as were cast in the Ideal moulds, were about .015 inch smaller in diameter than the figures designated in the previous table, allowing for the thickness of a patch.

The weight of round balls for use in smoothbore shotguns follows:

Gauge	Weight in Grains
10	630
12	510
14	465
16	390
20	300

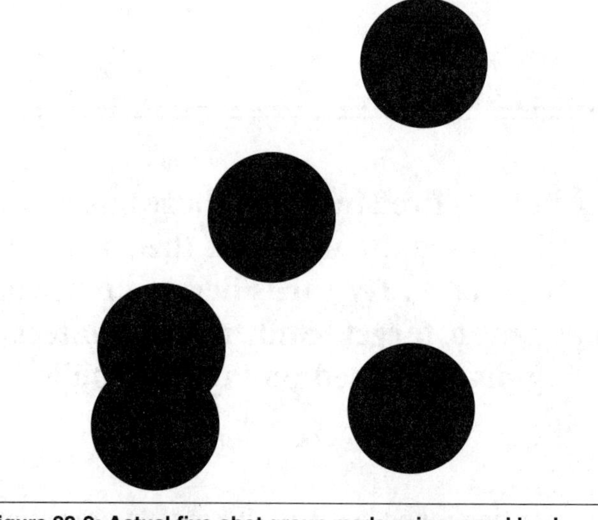

Figure 22-2: Actual five-shot group made using round lead balls in a 12-bore shotgun. Group is shown approximately actual size.

Round lead balls fired from smoothbore shotguns appear to group best when the lead ball is wrapped in a lubricated linen patch before placing the combination into the shell case. Recommended blackpowder loads for the 12 gauge include 4½ drams of FG or 3½ drams of FFG rifle powder — all fired from a true cylinder bore with no choke. With such combinations, the better shooters were able to obtain groups such as shown in Figure 22-2.

To attest to the value of solid lead balls in shotguns, John Taylor, the famed elephant hunter and author of *African Rifles and Cartridges*, found himself without cartridges for his double rifles back in the 1930s. A shipment of cartridges from England got lost and did not arrive for over 12 months. During this time, he was forced to use a 10-gauge caplock muzzleloading shotgun for his African hunts. His load was six drams of Curtis & Havey blackpowder behind a hardened spherical lead ball. Mr. Taylor's account of the gun's ability is as follows:

"Holding back the trigger of the gun, so that there would be no warning click, I drew the hammer of the muzzleloader to full cock. With a slow, steady, almost imperceptible movement I brought the gun up and then, as the big bull elephant reached the river bed and turned ever so slightly to his right front to make for the water, I squeezed the trigger. An orange-red flame leapt from the muzzle; a billowing cloud of light grey smoke . . . and the old bundook roared its song.

"It was a solid lung shot and the elephant lurched forward, flung his trunk up and back over his head, and surged forward into a run . . . .

". . . Sure enough, as I expected, he was flat out where the deep groan had come from (about 300 yards away) . . . .

". . . The two rhinos that I had shot earlier were found lying (dead) on the sand within about 60 yards of each other, and maybe 150 yards downstream of the water hole."

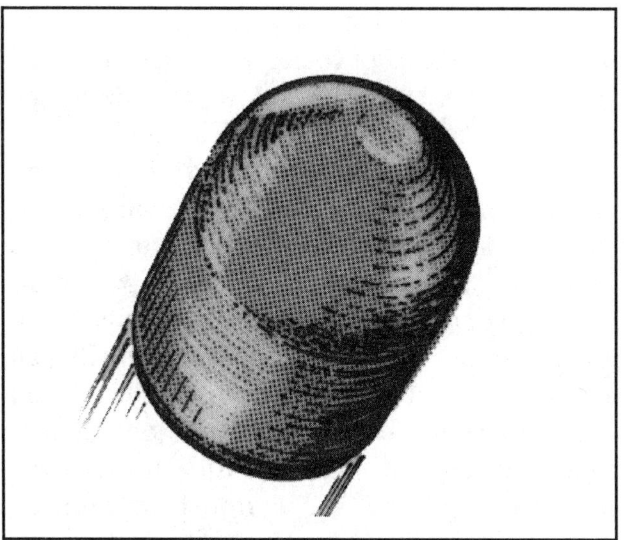

Figure 22-3: Karl Foster's original 20-gauge slug consisted of a conical projectile weighing about 300 grains.

FACTORY-LOADED PUNKIN BALLS

Prior to Winchester's introduction of the conical shotgun slug in 1936, all major ammunition manufacturers supplied factory-loaded single round-ball loads. Specifications of these loads are as follows:

Gauge	Powder Type	Drams	Powder Type	Grains	Weight of Ball in Ounces
12	Bulk	3	Dense	24	1
16	Bulk	2½	Dense	20	⅞
20	Bulk	2	Dense	16	⅝
410	Bulk	⅚	—	—	⅕

EVOLUTION OF THE MODERN SHOTGUN SLUG

Karl Foster started experiments in the late 1920s to improve the accuracy of ball loads used in shotguns. He first adopted a conical projectile weighing about 300 grains (in 20 gauge) and having a total length of ⅝″. He found the best diameter to be .590″ in his shotgun, as this slug diameter fitted the bore closely, giving a bearing on all sides of the slug; yet, the lead slug did not fit so tightly that it could not be pushed through the bore with a little hand pressure. Considerable time was spent on the slug design with the idea of having enough weight in the forward part of the slug to eliminate keyholing. This is like throwing a handful of sand in a paper bag and tossing it through the air. The weight of the sand will keep that portion of the bag in the forward position all the time.

His initial tests, however, proved discouraging. These slugs grouped only slightly better than the round balls. Experimental loads ranging from 18 to 27 grains of Du Pont bulk powder were tried to determine the one giving the most consistent results. After many tests, Mr. Foster did hit upon a load that showed a decided improvement — giving consistent groups at 50 yards.

During these tests, approximately one slug in five would keyhole, or show a strong tendency to do so. He also found that slugs hitting a target at 25 yards would keyhole about 50 percent of the time, while at 50 yards the number of keyholes was cut in half. At 100 yards (when it was possible to register a hit) none of the slugs showed any inclination of keyholing.

With the appearance of a fired rifle bullet in mind, and knowing, of course, the action of a rifled barrel on a bullet, rifling cuts were made on the plain slugs with a file. The keyholing immediately vanished. Groups were obtained which were well within 2 feet at 50 yards. With keyholing eliminated and fair accuracy obtained, a mould was made up to cast these slugs in a weight of 300 grains when using pure lead. It was intended to have the mould cast the rifling on the slugs, but the Lyman Gun Sight Corporation decided that while it could be done, it would be a very expensive job. Another manufacturer would not even consider it, saying the rifling would prevent the slug from being dropped from the mould. Mr. Foster finally decided to have a mould made up for the plain slug, and trust to luck and a little brains to develop a method of cutting the rifling after the slug was cast. These plain slugs, as cast, gave even better accuracy than his former handcut slugs with the filed rifling, although they would keyhole occasionally. The mould cast a perfect and uniformly balanced slug every time the lead was at the correct temperature.

The plain cast slugs were then rifled in a steel die. The first die was made out of a ⅛-inch piece of strap iron, drilled through with a ½-inch drill. This piece of iron was then put in a lathe and the drilled hole bored out to a diameter of .550". This left a sharp cutting edge for the rifling cutters, which were cut with a small sharp file. The piece was then ground smooth, hardened, and bolted to a 2-inch block of ¼-inch steel, which was then drilled out to allow the slug to pass through the die. *See* Figure 22-4. The slugs were pushed through the die with a bench vise, and resulted in a clean-cut rifled slug with hollow base sized to .593 inch. The grooves were cut to a depth of .020 inch. The base cavity, however, had to be filled in with paraffin to keep felt wads from being blown in the cavity when the shell was fired.

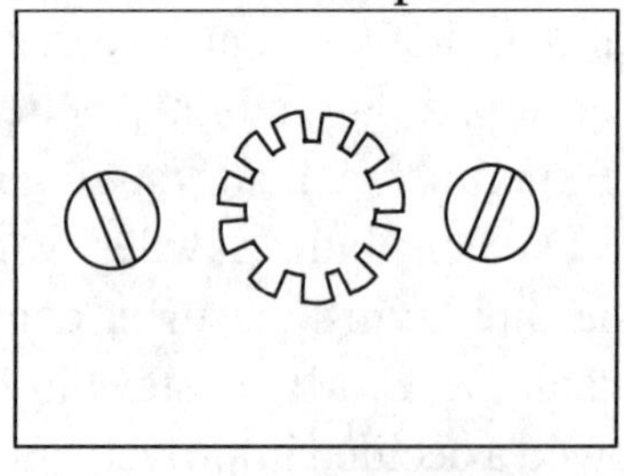

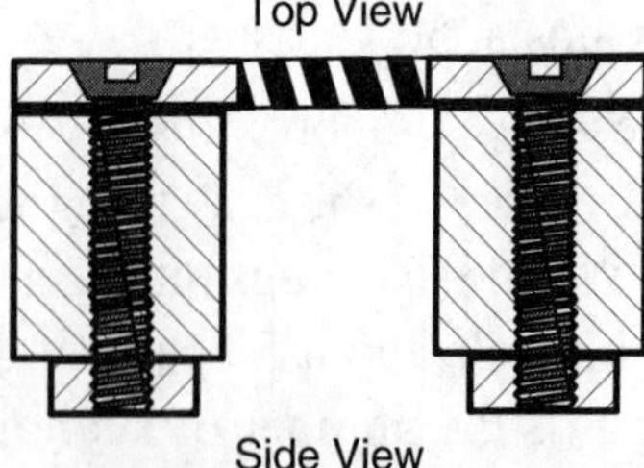

Figure 22-4: Top and side views of Karl Foster's homemade die used to cut rifling on his conical shotgun slug.

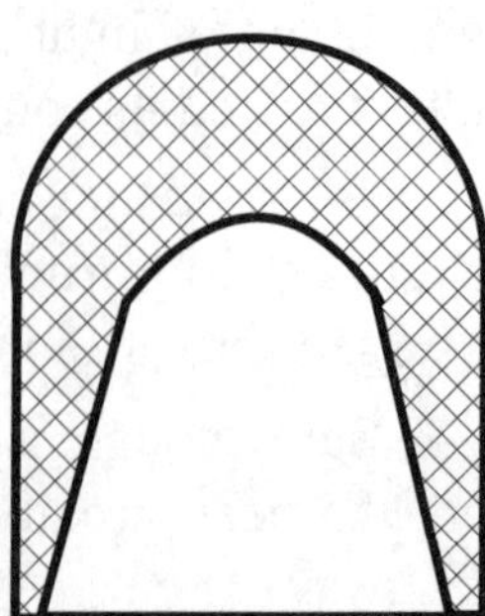

Figure 22-5: Side and cross-sectional view of Karl Foster's rifled slug for 20-gauge shotguns. The hollow base was filled with paraffin to prevent the wads from entering the hollow cavity.

Pure lead slugs mushroom upon impact similar to a soft-nose rifle bullet, and expand to about ¾ inch in soft pine wood. Mr. Foster recovered a slug of pure lead weighing 300 grains (original weight) from a 9-point, 180-pound buck, and found it had expanded to a diameter of ⅞ inch. This slug struck the buck as he was going away, passed through the neck and head from the rear, and was found in one piece back of the teeth in the lower jaw. This slug weighed approximately 270 grains when removed.

Further experiments showed that pure lead slugs have a penetration of about 4 inches in birch wood, while slugs made from lead/tin alloy penetrated to about 5 inches. Experimental slugs made from chilled shot were found too hard to mushroom much; and being brittle, would break up on impact.

Five-shot groups made with these early slug loads at 50 yards were as small as 5 inches. The best 10-shot group measured 10½ inches from outside the extreme holes. Both of these groups were made at 50 yards using a Winchester Model 12 slide-action shotgun with a matt ribbed, modified-choked barrel containing two Lyman bead sights.

Mr. Wallace Coxe, of the Burnside Laboratory, volunteered to offer ballistic tests on these loads, with the following results:

TESTS IN 20-GAUGE UNIVERSAL DU PONT RECEIVER NO. U384

Hollow-base rifled projectiles weighing 285.4 grains, base filled with paraffin; tests made with standard blend 105 of Du Pont smokeless shotgun powder in Climax shells.

Weight of Charge	Velocity at 25 feet Mean
25.0 grains	1,342
	1,325
	1,351
	1,302
	1,312
Average	1,327

Weight of Charge	Velocity at 25 feet Mean
27.0 grain	1,351
	1,351
	1,338
	1,364
	1,355
Average	1,352

Commenting upon the results of the tests, Mr. Coxe said, "You will note that the higher weight of charge developed a lower mean pressure. This seemed to be a more satisfactory charge in that the variations were reduced considerably, and that probably explains why the powder burned more efficiently."

Following the development of the 20-gauge slugs, a similar design was worked out for the 12- and 16-gauge sizes. Special moulds were obtained from the Lyman Gun Sight Corporation, and rifling dies were made for these gauges. It was decided to have the 12-gauge mould cast a slug weighing about 445 grains when cast in pure lead, with a diameter of about .700 inch. This diameter is practically the same as that of the 10-gauge single ball. By the use of different bullet metals the weights of the slug can be varied as much as 25 grains. The diameter can be varied as much as .030 inch by the rifling die. The 16-gauge slugs when cast of pure lead weighs 375 grains, or practically ⅞ ounce. The diameter of the cast 16-gauge slug is .640 inch, which can be given any desired variation by the rifling die. As to accuracy, there is no appreciable difference among the different weights of slugs provided the lot being tested is uniform. Pure lead was found to give the best results, having better expansion in barrels, and much quicker mushrooming.

In brief, target tests with 12-gauge slugs at 50, 100, and 300 yards, proved to be even better than the 20-gauge ones. Groups at 100 yards were held in a 20-inch circle. Ten-shot groups of 11inches at 50 yards were common. Three out of five shots at 300 yards hit a 4 × 5-foot target. The rifled slug was well on its way!

A comparison of velocities and energies of these slug loads with rifle ammunition may be of interest. The rifle cartridges chosen for comparison are among the old-timers, as their diameters more nearly approximate those of the shotgun slugs. It should be remembered that the 12-gauge slugs are of .70 caliber; the 16-gauge, of .64 caliber, while the 20-gauge is .59 caliber.

The Remington ballistic staff made thorough tests of the slugs for accuracy, velocity and pressure. Due to lack of time, the 12-gauge slugs received practically all the attention, a short test only being made of handloads in 20 gauge. Five of these 20-gauge slug loads were tested in the pressure gun and gave the very ordinary group of 8 inches at 40 yards. The load, using a 285.4-grain alloy slug, gave an average pressure reading of 8,520 psi, and the average velocity was 1,295 fps. The first 12-gauge slugs to be tried in the pressure gun consisted of a 445-grain pure lead slug, paraffind, and a charge of 25 grains of Infallible powder, using the 2¾-inch Nitro Club case and regular felt wadding. This group of five shots averaged 8,380 psi pressure, with an average velocity of 1,160 fps, and required an 18-inch circle to hold all shots at 40 yards. The next test was with the same slug and a charge of 26 grains of bulk powder. Average pressure was 8,970 psi, and average velocity 1,230 fps. This group was slightly smaller, measuring 16¾ inches. The third test was made with 27 grains of Infallible, with pressures running 9,160 psi, and velocity of 1,275 fps.

Of all the rifled slugs fired on the 100-yard range (including those fired entirely offhand), not one would have missed a deer. The slugs striking soft dirt mushroomed to about twice their normal diameter, the paraffin usually remaining with the slug. Fired against a heavy steel plate the slugs would indent it deeply, most of the body flying into small pieces while the nose remained in one piece, having turned completely inside out. Thinking that perhaps the idea of this rifled, hollow-base slug might be of some cash value, Karl Foster engaged the services of a patent attorney to investigate its possibilities. It was found that on self-rotating projectiles alone there have been issued approximately 200 patents. It is interesting to note that the principle of the rifled slug has been the subject of patents for at least 73 years — a silent tribute to the inventive genius of our grandfathers. A patent was issued in 1859 to a Mr. Holroyd, of Washington, D.C., covering this idea of self-rotating projectiles. This invention applied to projectiles for smoothbore cannons, and consisted of spiral vanes cast or cut on the sides of the projectile in such a way that the powder gases would act upon them and give the projectile the required spin. Another invention, patented in 1862, had to do with tubing spirally wound around the projectile, which derived its spin from the reaction of the air passing through the tubing. There was yet another patent, issued to a man in Kentucky in 1863, covering a cannon projectile rifled only on the rear portion, the grooves having an increasing, or "gain" twist. This projectile also embodied the hollow base of "minie" cavity at the rear, which caused the rifled portion of the projectile to expand under pressure of the powder gases and fill the bore. This expansion was also hastened in some cases by the addition of a wooden plug fitted in the base and acting as a wedge.

THE WINCHESTER SHOTGUN SLUG

The Winchester Repeating Arms Co. introduced a shotgun slug load to their regular line of ammunition in the mid-1930s. The development was in response for a more satisfactory shotgun projectile than the soft-lead time-honored "punkin ball."

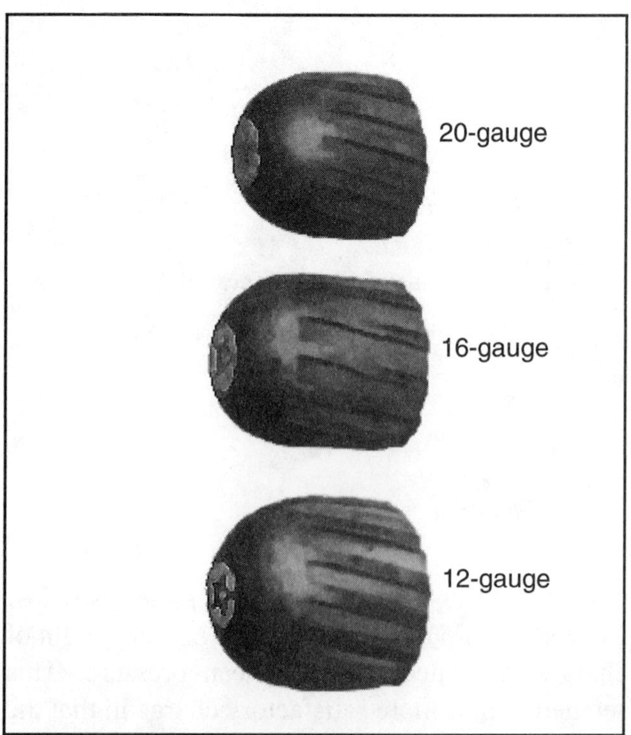

Figure 22-6: The initial Winchester rifled slugs had a star cast on the nose of each slug to distinguish these from their round-ball loads.

Winchester's product, due to uniform manufacturing methods, was an improvement over the custom-made rifled slugs of the day. Winchester did not use the rather flimsy felt wad in its loading, but used instead a gas-tight composition wad which held its shape back of the slug, and left the latter at the muzzle. By employing this wad, Winchester got excellent accuracy without the use of the paraffin filler as was required for the custom loads.

Groups of the Winchester slug loads in laboratory tests for accuracy averaged less than 5 inches at 50 yards, with occasional groups of 3 inches or better. This degree of accuracy is about on a par with what would be obtained with a good deer rifle if the regular sights were replaced with shotgun sights.

The Winchester-made slugs were marked on the nose with a star to distinguish the cartridges from ball loads, which they closely resemble when looking at the front of the shell. This star can also be identified by sense of touch, if there is no light. Unlike the ball loads, the slugs were not centered in the shells by perforated felt wads. They were self-centering, as they fit the bore more closely.

After the factory had proved to their entire satisfaction that the slugs were much superior to standard ball loads, accuracy tests were made in comparison with all other slug loads available, including the Brenneke slug of somewhat similar design. This imported slug failed to duplicate the accuracy of the rifled slug, and in addition, a large percentage of the shots were keyholes. The bare rifle slug, being inherently balanced, flies true; and in months of testing, Winchester reported no keyholing, nor any tendency to tip. Extensive tests were also made with different lead alloys, different diameters of slugs, various lengths, and at different velocities, to ensure the best accuracy, penetration, and expansion. Expansion and penetration tests were conducted on sides of beef and blocks of paraffin wax, which substances offered the nearest approach to animal tissues of the deer class, before most factories started using gelatin blocks.

BRENNEKE SLUGS — FACT OR FANCY?

While Karl Foster and Winchester were working on a conical shotgun slug in America, the munition factories across the Atlantic had their own ideas of what a solid projectile in smoothbores should do.

A. G. Parker & Co., Ltd. of Birmingham, England advertised a shotgun "bullet" called the Rotax. It was adapted to both cylinder and all choked guns and was advertised as being suitable for lion, tiger, leopard, bear, and all kinds of deer. The cylindrical hollow slug, with bearing lands to fit the bore, had a muzzle velocity of 1230 fps and a muzzle energy of 1690 foot-pounds.

This same British firm also made a shotgun "cartridge" called the Destructor. It contained 16 buckshot pellets placed in a lead jacket cast with bearing bands to ensure an accurate fit of the bore. These loads were available for 12-, 16-, and 20-gauge bores. Unlike the capsule loads of today, the lead jacket remained intact until a target was struck, and then everything opened up — being very destructive to what it hit.

The Rottweil Company of Hamburg, Germany, at about the same time, was also developing an improved shotgun slug that later became known as the Brenneke slug. The main theory behind this design was to attach the wads (as a group) to the lead projectile, thus giving better sectional density and a little more weight to the slug.

The first Brenneke design utilized a wadcutter-

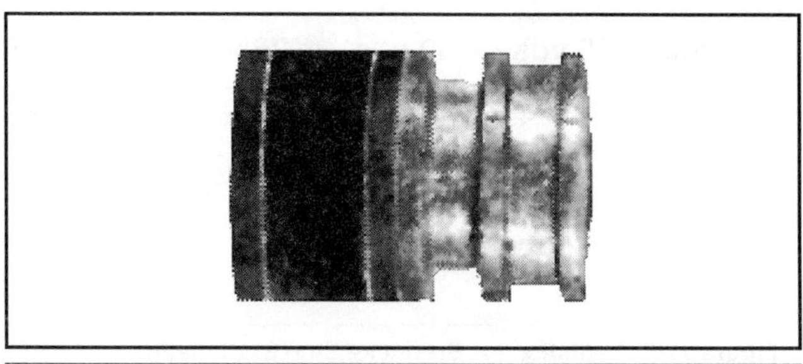

Figure 22-7: The original Brenneke slug had a flat nose, similar to our current wadcutter bullet.

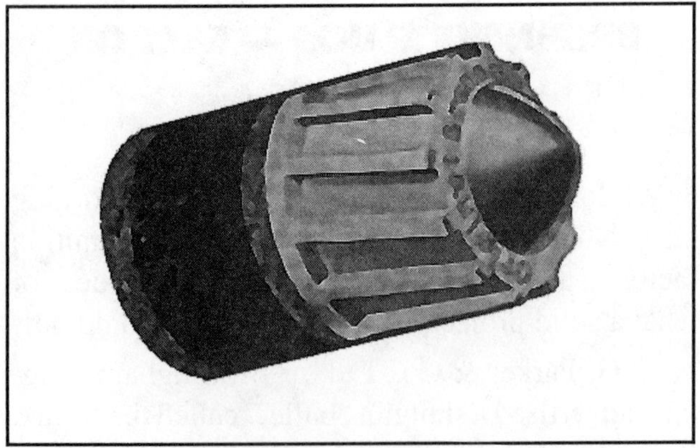

Figure 22-8: The final slug shape adopted for the Brenneke shotgun slug in the 1930s. The same basic shape remains today.

type shape as shown in Figure 22-7. However, this was soon replaced with the round-pointed projectile containing vanes, running longitudinally and set at an angle, with the intention of causing the slug to rotate in flight. This same design is in use today as shown in Figure 22-8.

During the 1930s, A. F. Stoeger began importing the much-publicized Brenneke slugs which had been used successfully on a variety of big game from deer, bear, wild boar and lion to tiger and water buffalo.

The manufacturer advertised this slug as being suitable for use in any standard shotgun regardless of boring — including full-choke guns.

The unique feature of the Brenneke is the union of wad and slug which, joined together, form one long projectile. Ballistic performance is vastly improved by this means because the sectional-density factor is virtually double that of most rifled slugs, or so claims the manufacturer.

The weight of the Brenneke slug is comparable to a standard field load of shot in the same gauge which is slightly heavier than most American-made slug loads. This additional weight, of course, is due to the wads being attached to the lead slug by means of a screw. The manufacturer claims groups of 2½ to 3½ inches at 50 yards are not uncommon, and keyholing is supposed to be impossible.

Penetration tests of the Brenneke slug indicated that it would average seven inches in solid white pine and over 27 inches in clay. Energy and shock-

Gauge	Weight of Slug (grains)	Length of barrel	Velocity (feet per second)					Energy (foot-pounds)				
			0	25 yds.	50 yds.	75 yds	100 yds	0	25 yds.	50 yds.	75 yds.	100 yds.

Height of Trajectory in inches when zeroed at a given range								
	Iron sights (distance in yds.) with line of sight 0.79 inch above centerline of barrel				Telescope sights (distance in yds.) with line of sight 1.959 inches above centerline of barrel			
Gauge	25 yds.	50 yds.	75 yds.	100 yds	25 yds.	50 yds.	75 yds.	100 yds.
12	+0.24 +0.75 +1.46	— +1.06 2.48	-1.62 — +3.74	-4.95 -2.79 —	-0.35 -0.08 +0.51	— +0.71 +1.93	-1.02 — +1.89	-3.85 -2.52 —

Figure 22-9: Ballistics for Brenneke Slug Shotshells.

58 A. F. STOEGER, INC., 507 FIFTH AVE., NEW YORK, N. Y.

Original Brenneke Shotgun Slugs

In response to the continued demand for a satisfactory shotgun slug, we have made arrangements to sell exclusively in the United States the world wide known Brenneke Slugs which are the finest made. Because of the excellent precision of these slugs, any shotgun, even those with heaviest choke bore, may be effectively used at ranges up to 100 yards against big game; up to 70 yards it is suitable for buffalo, bear, lion, tiger, etc. It may also be used in repeating and automatic shotguns.

In use for over 40 years. Suitable for use in any Nitro tested shotgun barrel with or without choke boring. Capable of best results. Universally recognized in all countries as the best shotgun slug in the world.

Suitable for all large game, elk, bear and dangerous game of all sorts. The Brenneke bullet is the very best replacement for the unsatisfactory single ball and buckshot loads. Especially suited for the upland hunter who is principally dependent upon his shotgun, to whom it offers the possibility of using his gun as an accurate double barrel rifle through use of the Brenneke Slugs. Because of this the double barrel shotgun may be considered the general all purpose hand weapon.

Highest accuracy is combined with satisfactory effect at a distance of 60 to 75 yards. The muzzle velocity and energy of the Brenneke Slug in 12 gauge is as follows:

Velocity 1485 foot seconds.
Energy 2712 foot pounds.
Breech pressure about 420 atmospheres.

The penetration is surprisingly great, 6 to 7 inches, in pine. Large game weighing up to 330 pounds is ordinarily shot through with normal angle shots. For very large or dangerous game the bullet with steel tip is recommended. With steel tip the penetration is increased to 12 inches in pine at 50 yards, and is adapted for the heaviest and most dangerous game including elephants.

The accompanying illustration was originally shot at 25, 50 and 80 meters at the German Proof House in Berlin with a double barrel shotgun and shows excellent precision. The rise or drop of the slug from line of sight as tested at the Proof House in 12 and 16 gauge is as follows, ⊙ representing the point blank sight setting:—

Distance	25 Meters or 27½ yards	50 Meters or 55 yards	75 Meters or 82½ yards	80 Meters or 88 yards
	⊙	—1″	—3¾″	—4¾″
	+⅝″	⊙	—2½″	—3¼″
	+1¼″	+1⅝″	⊙	—1¼″
	+1⅜″	+2″	+⅝″	⊙

Opinions of actual shooters: Phenomenal unequalled sledge-hammer effect; Performance such as few rifle bullets offer; Astonishing precision. Many hundreds of bear, elk, leopard, crocodile, lion and other large game have been dropped immediately by its terrific lightning-like performance.

In spite of the tremendous shocking power, the Brenneke slug is ideally suited for use against deer because its tremendous area and shocking power is vastly superior to that of almost any other available bullet, due to the fact that the bullet does not disintegrate in passing through the game and consequently does not spoil the trophy, still the game is dropped much faster than would be thought possible. Many experienced hunters advise us that the use of the Brenneke slug in double barrel shotguns for running game is always better and more successful than the use of any rifle or double rifle. The Brenneke slug may be shot from barrels even with heaviest choke bore without danger because the slug is especially constructed for use in barrels which have a choke as high as .047″ at the muzzle.

Official Proof House Group, 1⅜ x 1¾ inches (3½ x 4¼ Cm.) Shot at 66 yards

This 16 point elk was shot with Brenneke slug at a distance of 55 yards. The elk collapsed in its tracks without hearing the report of the gun

The felt wad screwed onto the bullet prevents "key-holing" and with the point always forward the accuracy is enhanced. The accuracy is about 3 inches at 50 yards and 6 inches at 100 yards. At 35 yards all shots can be placed in one regular hole.

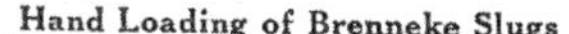

Hand Loading of Brenneke Slugs

The usual powder load used in regular shot shells is employed; the gas pressure is, however, lower than in normal shot shells, consequently 10% increased charges may be used to increase penetration. As will be seen from the illustrations the heavy wad is permanently attached by means of a screw, and consequently no other wad is to be used. The slug is loaded over the powder, and double crimped, once as in ordinary shells, a second time immediately above the top of the slug, as shown in illustration, to prevent slug from moving. A special crimper for these operations may be had from us

Price of crimper..............$1.75

Police, Guard & State Troopers

Police Departments, Guards, State Troopers, and other organizations entrusted with law enforcement will find the Brenneke Slugs ideal. For regular police work the Brenneke slug without point is preferable. Most organizations are equipped with pump action riot guns and for use against automobile bandits the Brenneke slug with steel tip is particularly recommended.

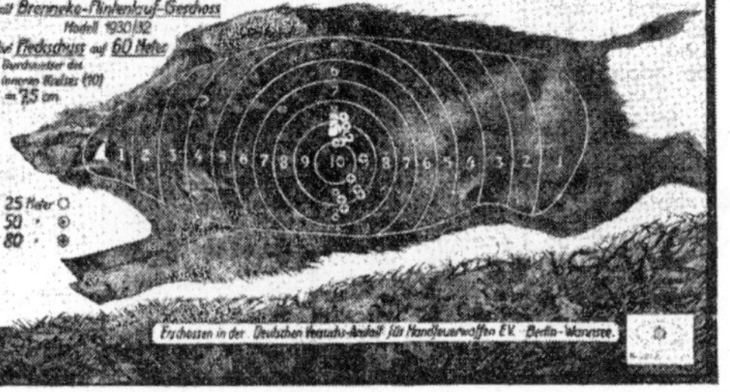

Official Proof House Target showing shots at 25 meters (27½ yards), 50 meters (55 yards), and 80 meters (88 yards)

Prices Per Box of 10

The Brenneke slugs, in their three types, are offered both as completely loaded shells and also as slugs only, suitable for hand loading.

We call attention to the fact that all loaded shells are loaded in the United States by one of the leading cartridge companies.

Brenneke Model 1930/32 with guide ribs, wad and hardened lead point.

	Slugs only	Loaded Shells
12 gauge	$1.50	$2.00
16 or 20 gauge	1.25	1.75

Brenneke Model 1930/32 with guide ribs, and wad but flat nose without point

	Slugs only	Loaded Shells
12 gauge only	$1.25	$1.75

Brenneke Model 1930/32 with guide ribs, attached wad and hardened steel point

	Slugs only	Loaded Shells
12 gauge	$2.25	$2.75
16 or 20 gauge	2.50	2.50

(All prices are in lots of ten pieces.)

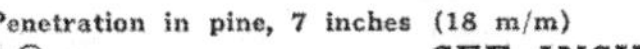

Penetration in pine, 7 inches (18 m/m)

Bear brought down with Brenneke slug

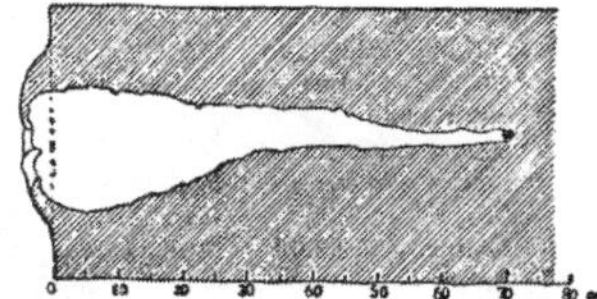

Penetration in clay, 27½ inches (70 m/m)

©

SEE INSIDE FRONT COVER "HOW TO ORDER"

Figure 22-10: Sample page from a 1930s A.F. Stoeger catalog advertising the then-new Brenneke shotgun slug.

Figure 22-11: Cut-away view of the loaded Brenneke shotgun shell.

ing power are unusually high as the ballistic table in Figure 22-9 shows.

The manufacturer suggests sighting-in the 12-gauge shotgun loads to shoot 2½ inches high at 50 yards. This will put the slug on center at 100 yards.

Stoeger was "a burr under the saddle" for American ammunition manufacturers. *See* Figure 22-10. The sales on Winchester's, Peters', and Remington's round-ball loads were satisfactory, and their attitude was, "if it ain't broke, don't fix it." However, the introduction of the Brenneke slug by A.F. Stoeger made all the American companies sit up and take notice. Winchester, for example, had been procrastinating over Karl Foster's idea for a conical-shaped shotgun slug. However, when A. F. Stoeger introduced the Brenneke slug to the American market, the procrastination stopped! They quickly brought out their rifled slugs as described previously. Other manufacturers followed suit, and

Figure 22-12: Reproduction showing the actual penetration of a Brenneke slug in a block of clay. Total penetration measured 27½ inches.

it was then a matter of politics to keep the American slug sales high.

All of the major shooting editors for the various outdoor magazines were wined and dined at the major manufacturers' game farms, with some good hunting and shooting to boot.

I'm sure it was quite difficult for Atkins, Cary, Sharpe, Keith, O'Connor, Page, Howe and Brown to recommend anything other than the American-made items after a weekend at Olin's game farm.

If there was any doubt, World War II put an end to it. The United States was at war with the country manufacturing the Brenneke shotgun slug, and none would be available to American shooters for another 10 years.

In actual tests using both standard and Brenneke slugs, any difference in accuracy at 50 yards was not detected. However, the Brenneke slug, due to its better sectional density, gives a little better down-range performance, including deeper penetration in soft pine.

Today, almost all ammunition manufacturers offer rifle slugs for the 12, 16, 20, and 410 gauges. Brenneke now offers a .410 slug in the 3-inch shell which should be good for coyotes and similar size game up to about 50 yards or so.

Rifle sights installed on shotguns improve the accuracy tremendously and some firearm manufacturers offer "buck" or "deer" barrels — especially designed for shooting rifled slugs and buckshot. There has also been some use of rifled shotgun barrels using both plain and rifled slugs with good results.

SABOT SLUGS FOR SHOTGUNS

Ballistic Research Industries developed an improved slug load for the 12-gauge shotgun almost 25 years ago that was based on the sabot principle. In general, the load uses a projectile, smaller in diameter than the bore, and is guided by means of

Figure 22-13: The sabot shotgun slug has been available to the shotgunner since 1971. It is one of the most popular slugs for the serious slug-slingers.

two split bushings which fall away as the projectile leaves the muzzle.

The sabot design has a circular cross-section throughout, with a wasp-waist behind the mid-point and a stabilizing section at the rear as shown in Figure 22-13. The diameter of the rear section is .50 inch, while the front section is slightly larger at .501 inch. A weight-reducing cavity drilled longitudinally in from the base is about .310 inch diameter to a depth of .275 inch. A solid plug of light-weight plastic is supplied to fill this cavity for resistance to accelerative forces.

The resulting slug has a sectional density of .251 — giving it an edge of superiority of approximately 134% over the typical factory-loaded shotgun slugs. This greatly enhances the slug's ability to retain velocity over extending ranges. In fact, tests indicate that the 12-gauge slug retained more energy at 300 yards than the .30-30 rifle cartridge at the same distance.

Accuracy tests indicate that the slug is capable of grouping within an 18-inch circle at 200 yards.

The factory loading starts the 440-grain slug at around 1500 pfs at the muzzle with approximately 2200 foot-pounds of energy. The Mark 9 slugs are for use only in cylinder to modified bores, while the Mark 7 is designed for use in full-choke barrels.

For reloading these slugs, virgin cases are recommended and a roll crimp should be used on the case mouth, using a roll-crimping head which may be rotated by hand or used in an electric drill.

A printed sheet of loading instructions is packed with the projectile sets.

LOADS FOR SOLID PROJECTILES

The tables in Chapter 20 lists recommended loads for round balls and conventional shotshell slugs. These loads were furnished by various powder manufacturers.

While each load listed has been tested for both accuracy and safety, individual guns vary and a different load may function better in another shotgun than those tested. Several factors are involved when loading slugs in shotshells, the same as when loading any other cartridge or shell. Some of the more important ones follow:

- The ambient temperature in which the shells will be fired.
- The size of the bore and the constriction at the muzzle (choke).

The modern reloader is set-up to experiment, and experimentation is half the fun of reloading, provided common sense is used at all times. Never exceed maximum loads, and always start a few grains under maximum and gradually work up to the heavier loads, observing signs of abnormal pressures at all times. To do otherwise, is taking an unnecessary risk.

SECTION V
PROJECTILES

Chapter 23

Bullet Design and Development

The majority of discussion and concern involved in reloading custom ammunition deals with powder, case construction, primer selection, and projectiles. The end product of these components is to propel the bullet to the target. In hunting situations, the performance of this bullet after it strikes the target (terminal performance) is the most important consideration of all. Everything that has gone before is useless if the bullet does not perform efficiently (and sufficiently) after it strikes the target. The most accurate, powerful load that can be constructed is useless if the bullet design does not permit proper terminal performance.

Within the last couple of decades, bullet construction and terminal performance have been emphasized more than in all of the years that have gone before. The reloading industry has seen the premium and super premium bullet touted, and reloaders have paid premium prices for these projectiles that are designed with terminal performance as their main criteria, while still retaining excellent ballistic and accuracy characteristics.

This chapter augments other chapters that have discussed bullet shape in regard to sectional density and ballistic coefficient; it concentrates mainly on bullet design and construction in regard to terminal performance. This is an area of reloading that can be equated in importance with all other aspects of this pursuit combined.

THE EVOLUTION OF THE MODERN BULLET

At the middle of the last century, most bullets were constructed entirely of lead or lead alloy. This metal is soft, easy to cast, and "upsets" or expands readily upon impact. Lead is also dense and offers the necessary weight in a small volume. Since the typical firearm of the last century fired large caliber bullets at relatively low velocities, the softest metal was essential to achieve the expansion necessary to dispatch game animals that ranged from squirrels all the way up to grizzly bear and moose. These same soft lead bullets also accounted for all African species of game.

During this era, the range between the lower performance and the higher performance American cartridges was not that great, so one basic bullet design material was considered adequate. If one cartridge fired a 400-grain, .45-caliber bullet at 1100 fps and another fired the same bullet at 1500 fps, the terminal performance of both types was similar. The lower velocity loading might not expand quite enough and the higher velocity loading might expand a little too much, but all in all the velocity difference between the two loadings was not of sufficient range to render the lead bullet design useless.

One must remember that at the middle of the 19th century, the shooting world was still in transition between muzzleloading and breechloading firearms. Bullets for muzzleloaders had to be slightly undersized, so that they could be forced down the muzzle end of the firearm and seated against the powder charge. If they had been designed full size, the force required to ram the bullet home would have rendered the entire firearm next to useless. The soft lead construction of these bullets caused the base to expand to full groove size upon firing, due to the sudden high pressure generated by the expanding powder gases. This was essential to accuracy, as the expanded base would then engage the rifling in the barrel and be imparted with stabilizing spin. With the coming of the breechloader, undersized bullets were no longer necessary or desirable.

Toward the latter part of the 19th century, experiments were conducted on various lead alloys, ranging from soft to hard, but all produce a bullet harder than one of pure lead. While following the accepted scientific methods of that era, these tests were largely inconclusive. By this time, the terminal performance of these bullets had become an important factor and marked the beginning of serious experiments to improve bullet design and construction to address this concern.

Plain lead bullets must be greased or lubricated either "inside" (the case) or "outside" (the case) to prevent leading or fouling of the rifle bore. Bullets lubricated inside the case neck are provided with grease retaining grooves or knurls that are filled before the bullet is loaded into the case. This lubrication is covered by the case after loading so that the lubrication does not pick up grit or other foreign matter.

Outside-lubricated bullets are greased after loading, and the bullet is generally completely covered with lubricant.

All factory bullet lubricants are combinations of waxes and greases that give maximum accuracy and prevent fouling or leading.

In an effort to control expansion of lead bullets, it was found that by partially encasing the lead projectile in a thin coating or gilding of a harder metal, the tendency for the bullet to set up upon impact was retarded. Expansion still occurred but in a slower manner that allowed for more penetration. A thin copper jacket was typically drawn over the undersized lead projectile for a distance of at least half its length. For more penetration, the jacket was extended to a point near the bullet nose. The combined diameter of the lead bullet and the copper jacket was sized to the exact dimensions of the rifle bore. The thin copper would still be cut by the rifling grooves to impart spin.

After the turn of the century, the jacket was refined by several manufacturers to be very thin near the nose of the bullet and thicken linearly toward the base. This further controlled expansion by allowing the lead nose to expand immediately upon impact and then more gradually as penetration continued. This resulted in a mushroom expansion pattern with the base of the bullet remaining largely intact and unchanged.

Non-expanding bullets were popular in Africa and in India, where large, dangerous game were the target. Usually called solids, they incorporated an undersized lead core completely encased in copper or nickel alloys from the nose back to the base. Such bullets were designed to penetrate, but not to expand. The lead core was retained to achieve the needed weight. British bullet makers were most successful at this type of construction, much more so than their European counterparts who attempted to corner the dangerous, thick-skin game bullet market. Many of the British designs used jackets that were very thick at the bullet nose and thinner toward the base. This prevented a tendency for such bullets to rupture upon impacting heavy bones. Riveting was another problem, where the projectile would collapse upon itself in accordion fashion. The British-invented tapered-jacket design helped to prevent this. Consequently, this design was quickly copied by most of the solid-bullet manufacturers.

The best solid bullets of this era could be fired into a large animal such as an elephant or rhinoceros and, upon recovery, would be almost unchanged from their unfired conditions, save for the rifling marks on the jacket. In some instances, these bullets were actually reloaded and used again for hunting purposes. In most cases, however, the bullets would bend or warp slightly upon impact.

Another problem associated with solid full-jacketed bullet designs was core separation. Since the jacket was installed over the nose toward the base, lead was exposed at the rear center of the bullet base where it was crimped. Upon impact, there was a tendency for the lead core to be partially or wholly ejected from the rear of the jacket. When this occurred during penetration, the jacket simply collapsed and further penetration was halted. This led to various designs for bonding the lead core to the jacket or stabilizing the core.

Modern bullets still use these basic design techniques, although there is far more control over jacket thickness, taper, and core bonding. There are also new materials and manufacturing processes available that allow bullets to be made without lead or to combine two expansion properties into a single bullet. The major considerations given to bullet selection include weight, shape, expansion control, sectional density, and the bullet's ballistic coefficient.

MODERN BULLETS

The samples shown in Figure 23-1 illustrate the wide variety of bullets made for rifle and handgun

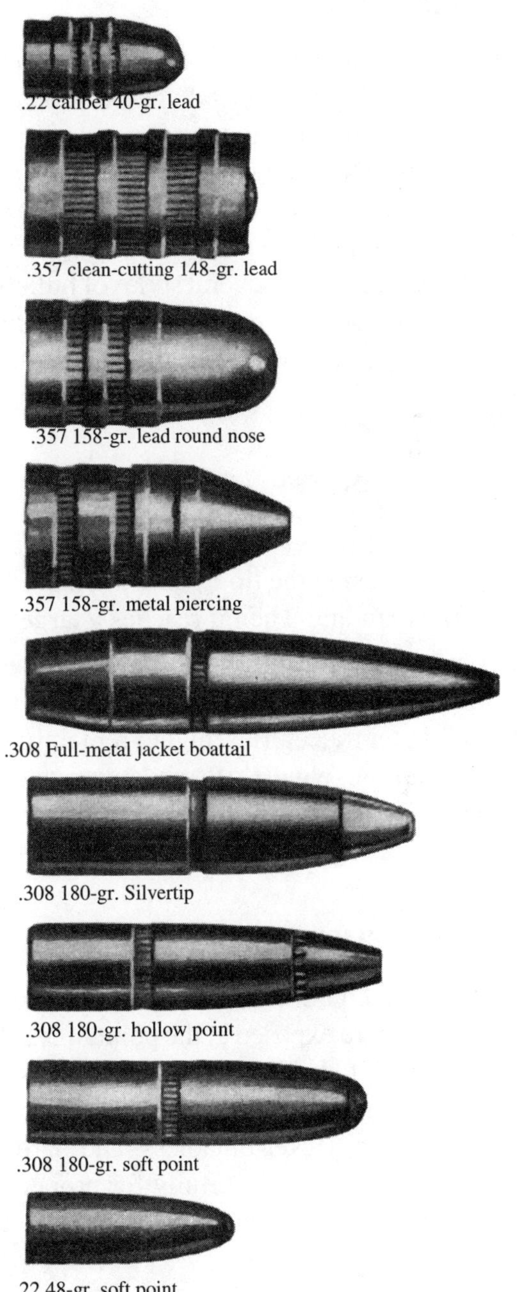

Figure 23-1: Several types of bullets available to shooters and reloaders.

ammunition. There are bullets for target shooting, big-game shooting, small-game hunting, self-defense, police work, and even for special gallery use. Each is discussed in the paragraphs that follow.

JACKETED BULLETS

A jacketed bullet has a lead core covered by an outside jacket of gilding metal. These jackets are especially alloyed for toughness and nonfouling characteristics. This prevents the bullet from deforming after firing and sends it out of the bore entirely free of unwanted fouling. The jackets and cores are assembled into several styles of bullets — full metal case, soft point, hollow point, etc. — each with a specific use for hunting and target purposes.

FULL-METAL JACKET

The full-metal jacket or case has a metal jacket completely enclosing the tip of the bullet, preventing it from expanding when it reaches a target.

The pointed or spitzer type of bullet is used in target shooting. The sharp profile gives less wind resistance, flatter trajectories, higher remaining velocities, minimum wind drift, and top accuracy. Round-nosed bullets with lower velocities are used for sure functioning in semiautomatic firearms.

SOFT-POINT BULLETS

When a jacketed bullet is closed at the base and has a part of its core exposed at the point, it is called a soft-point bullet. In factory-loaded bullets and those for use in reloading, the amount of lead exposed at the tip, jacket thickness, and hardness of the core are controlled carefully for proper performance within the velocity range of each cartridge.

When a soft-point bullet strikes game, the point expands and upsets or mushrooms. The energy of the bullet is expended quickly within the animal, creating shock and a large wound. In medium calibers, and at ordinary ranges, the soft-point is very effective on thin-skinned game. In heavy calibers, these bullets are designed for positive performance on larger game.

HOLLOW-POINT BULLETS

As Figure 23-2 shows, the hollow-point bullet has a cavity at the tip which gives it expansion characteristics different from the soft point. Hollow-point expansion is delayed, giving deep penetration. Its explosive opening action causes great tissue destruction. For positive stopping power of heavy, thick-skinned game, the hollow point has no equal for preference— particularly when the trophy is more valued than the meat and destruction of tissue is of little importance.

WAD-CUTTING BULLETS

These bullets were designed especially for target shooting, but in recent years, law enforcement agencies have found that these blunt, sharp-shouldered bullets tend to ricochet less than round-nosed bullets, and consequently are safer for use where a stray bullet may injure an innocent bystander. These bullets cut a clean hole through target paper and are therefore easier to spot and score.

METAL-PIERCING BULLETS

Developed especially for law enforcement officers, the metal-piercing bullets are used to stop criminals escaping in fast automobiles. The bullet's nose is conical in shape and is made of tough gilding metal. It punches its way through the steel body of the car and is carried on by the weight of the lead core or body of the bullet. This bullet does an effective job of stopping a criminal. *See* Figure 23-3 on page 464.

While all of these innovations added greatly to the terminal performance of bullets, there were still many problems. As more and more expansion control was built into bullet designs, the range of

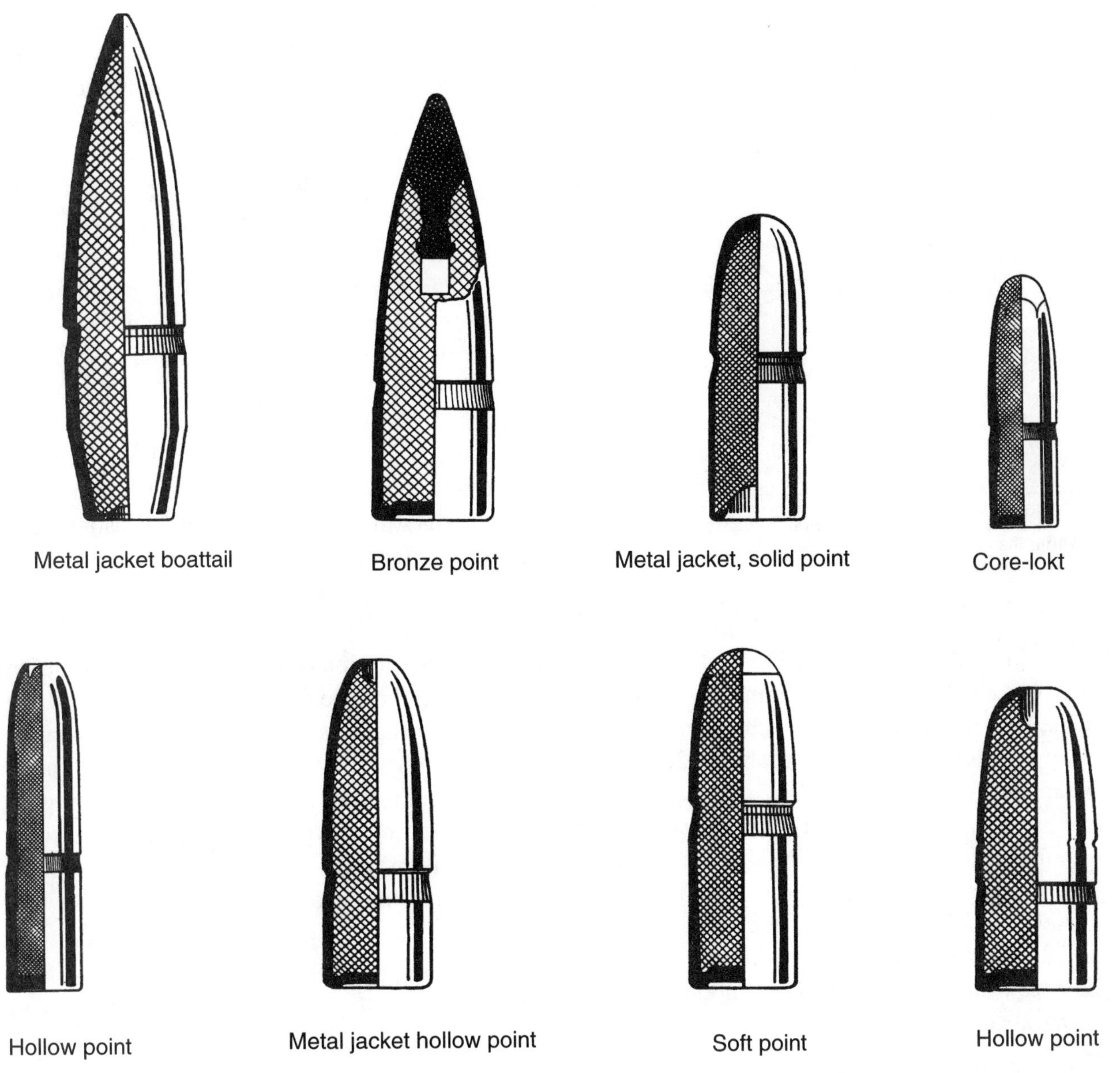

Figure 23-2: Various types of bullets offered by Remington.

velocities over which the expansion control would operate efficiently decreased. At slow velocities, jacketed bullets might not expand at all. At high velocities, all expansion control might be lost, resulting in fragmentation. Again, the reloader has greater control over the type of bullets used in each cartridge and loading.

THE GREAT COMPROMISE

Then, as now, any bullet design is a compromise. It is obvious that a bullet traveling at one velocity will behave differently upon impact than one traveling at a considerably higher or lower velocity.

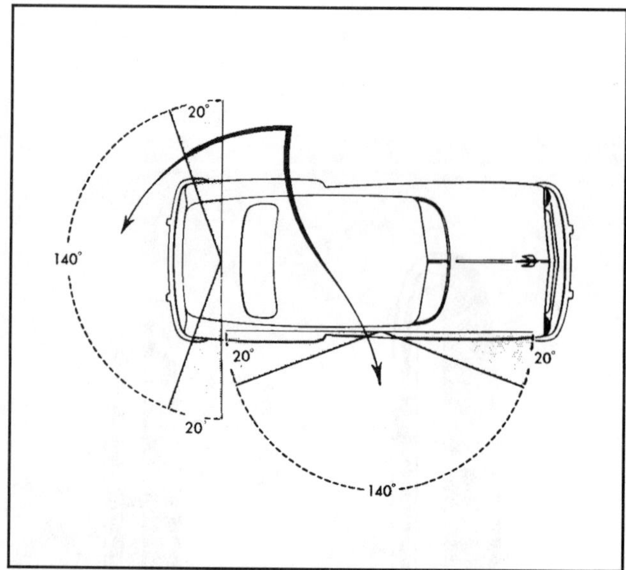

Figure 23-3: Bullet pierces car body when fired from any angle within the areas indicated.

Today's shooter has a vast selection of loadings and cartridges in any given caliber. For instance, the Remington .25-06 fires a 120-grain .257 caliber bullet at 3000 fps, while the much older 25-35 Winchester fires the same bullet at about 2200 fps. This is an 800 fps differential! Obviously, a bullet designed to expand properly at 3000 fps will not perform in the same manner at 2200 fps. The lower velocity loading may expand little or not at all. Conversely, a 120-grain bullet that expands properly at 2200 fps will probably expand too rapidly at 3000 fps. It may even fly to pieces upon impact and penetrate only superficially.

Bullet manufacturers address this problem by designing a compromise bullet. Given the velocities of the .25-06 and the .25-35, a compromise projectile would be designed to expand best at 2600 fps, the mid-range between the two velocities. This means that expansion should be a little less than optimum at the lower velocity and a little more than optimum at the higher velocity. However, "adequate" expansion is maintained over the entire range.

This comparison of the .25-35 and the .25-06 matches an old, almost obsolete cartridge with a modern one, so it might be more indicative of a typical use to compare the .25-06 velocity with that of the .257 Weatherby Magnum, which accelerates the 120-grain bullet to about 3200 fps. This is only 200 fps higher than the .25-06, so there need be little or no compromise in bullet design for either cartridge. Still, the bullet manufacturer wants one design to serve over a wide range of possible cartridges and loadings in order to decrease tooling expenses and realize the most monetary return for any one design. Even if we throw out the old .25-35, there is still the .250-3000 Savage, the .257 Roberts and a host of wildcats that can dramatically expand the velocity range of the .257-caliber bullet. A construction compromise for proper terminal performance is still necessary. For these reasons, many bullet manufacturers specify a *range* of velocities over which their various bullets are designed to function properly.

A further criterion is often placed on these bullets in regard to the type of animals being hunted. For instance, Hornady rates their 165-grain .30-caliber softpoint bullet at a velocity of 2500-3200 fps for medium and medium-heavy game. Medium game can be classified as typical whitetail and mule deer, while medium-heavy game includes black bear and larger North American deer.

Most manufacturers do or can supply information about muzzle velocity, range, and game types their various bullets are designed to address. Few, however, provide information on terminal velocity, the speed the bullet is traveling when it actually strikes the target. The muzzle-velocity rating, by itself, does not offer a great amount of data, because this velocity will be higher than the terminal velocity down range. However, when the muzzle velocity range of a bullet is considered along with the type of game the bullet is designed to take, a greater understanding of bullet performance downrange is garnered. It is the terminal (striking) velocity that determines the bullet performance. A varmint bullet is typically designed to perform properly at ranges between 100 and 300 yards. However, a

500-grain .458 bullet designed for hunting dangerous game is generally expected to perform properly at ranges of from 50 to a maximum of 125 yards. Obviously, the latter bullet will expand less than the design standard at 300 yards, because it will be traveling at a much reduced velocity. One would expect expansion to be much less at this extreme range with its inherent lower terminal velocity.

Since it is impossible for one bullet to offer the necessary terminal performance on all types of game animals when fired at widely-ranging velocities, manufacturer's specifications on bullets form a crucially important component of handloading. One must select a bullet that offers the proper terminal performance at the velocity that the handload will produce.

TYPES OF TERMINAL PERFORMANCE

There are three basic categories of terminal performance for bullets designed for hunting purposes:

- Explosive expansion
- Normal expansion
- No expansion

The first two expansion characteristics are very dependent upon the high and low terminal velocity range — the speed at which the bullet is traveling when it strikes the target. The non-expanding projectile is not affected by low terminal velocity but limited to the high terminal velocity rating at which it is designed to operate properly.

EXPLOSIVE EXPANSION

Explosive expansion is the design criterion that is placed on bullets used almost exclusively for varmint hunting, where the recovery of the animal or its hide is not a factor. Groundhogs and prairie dogs are good examples of this category. The idea here is to instantly kill the animal without regard to meat or hide damage.

Bullets designed for this type of hunting typically contain very thin jackets that fragment or fly apart when the target is struck. The entire bullet may even blow up on impact, but because of the small physical size of such animals, the killing potential is not diminished through less than adequate penetration of the fragments. Rarely do such bullet types fully penetrate the animal. Instead, a small entry hole is followed by the bullet fragmenting into many parts, each of which will usually penetrate at least to the center of the animal's body. Bullets that actually fragment radically (explode) create even more massive tissue destruction at the center of the animal's body.

Now, if such a bullet type were used on larger game, deer for instance, the terminal result would be the same, but owing to the larger size of the animal, penetration would not be to the center part of the body and a nasty flesh wound would occur. This could eventually lead to the death of the animal, but in all cases long suffering is the most predictable result.

Some categories of cartridges are commercially loaded only with bullets designed for explosive expansion. Examples of these are the .22-250 Remington and the .220 Swift. These are cartridges that are designed for varmint hunting only, therefore bullets that offer explosive expansion are the only types that are loaded. While it has been argued that either of these two can make excellent long range cartridges for small deer and antelope, they cannot be used for such purposes if they are firing bullets designed for explosive expansion on varmints. The argument is largely academic, because cartridges firing bullets of less than .23 caliber are generally illegal for taking big game in most states.

In summary, bullets designed for explosive expansion are used almost exclusively on animals in the small varmint class, where recovery of any part of the animal for any purpose is not a factor. These bullets expand violently and fragment on impact,

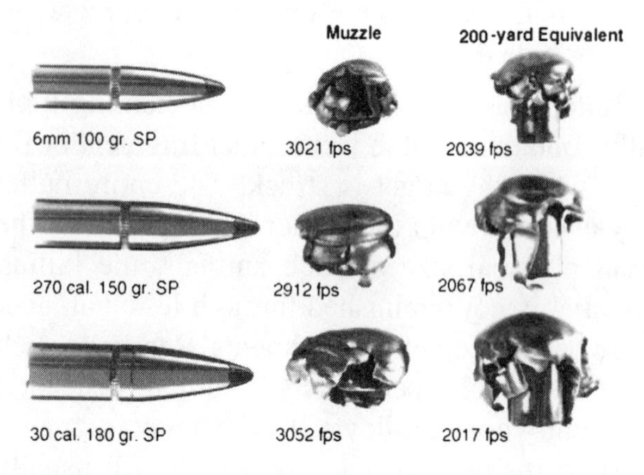

Figure 23-4: Expansion of three different types of bullets. The center bullets hit at 100 yards, while the ones in the right column show the expansion at 200 yards.

usually killing the animal instantly through massive tissue destruction. Bullets of this type are not limited to the smallest calibers (.22, .243, etc.), as rifles designed for medium and large game hunting can also be used for part-time varminting. Bullets in .243, .257, .264, .270, .284, and .30 caliber are available in explosive or rapid expansion types from many manufacturers. This means that the prudent reloader cannot assume that any bullet for a .30-caliber cartridge, for instance, is automatically suited for medium or large game.

It was stated earlier that the performance of non-expanding bullets (solids) is affected only by maximum and not by minimum velocity, because the bullet is not to expand at all. The lower the velocity upon impact, the more likely any bullet is to hold together. Conversely, one might think that bullets designed for explosive expansion would not contain a high-velocity limit, since the bullet is designed to fly apart anyway. This is an incorrect assumption.

There is a very definite high-velocity limit to all bullets, including those designed for explosive expansion. Whereas a bullet designed for normal expansion over a certain velocity range may explode upon impact at a much higher velocity, a bullet designed for explosive expansion over a certain velocity range may actually disintegrate before striking the target at a velocity higher than this range. The spin placed on a bullet by the rifling in the barrel exerts tremendous lateral stress on the projectile. Upon leaving the barrel at a velocity considerably higher than its design maximum, the fragile bullet can actual fly apart a few feet from the muzzle, rendering it absolutely useless. Most manufacturers offer varmint bullets designed for proper expansion when fired from older, lower velocity cartridges like the .22 Hornet. If such a bullet were used in a maximum .22-250 Remington loading, it is likely that it would disintegrate before striking the target, owing to the high velocity that lies far above its design maximum. The reloader must always consider the minimum and maximum velocity range for any type of bullet, no matter what the expansion characteristics of the projectile happen to be.

Another type of varmint bullet contains a solid copper jacket that is designed not to limit expansion entirely. This bullet type is used for taking small fur-bearing animals up to the size of coyotes, where it is necessary to do as little pelt damage as possible. Such bullets typically punch clear through the animal leaving a hole not appreciable larger than the caliber size. These bullets may not kill as instantly as those designed for explosive expansion, but they are more suited to preserving the pelt.

NORMAL EXPANSION

It is in this category that most hunting bullets designed for use in the United states are contained. The range of calibers for this type of bullet is the largest of the three basic categories, starting at .243 and moving up to .600. It is also this category that experiences the largest amount of failures.

Normal-expansion bullets are designed to expand to an ideal size of approximately twice the caliber upon impact, to retain a large percentage of their original weight, and to offer adequate penetration on the game for which they are designed.

Typically, these are soft-point designs, although some hollow points may be included. Standard grade soft-point bullets typically have a small amount of lead showing at the tip and contain a copper alloy jacket that is tapered in thickness from thin at the tip to thick at the base. This provides expansion control. *See* Figure 23-5.

"Normal expansion" is a question-begging term at best. Expansion will meet the design criteria only when such bullets leave the barrel at a velocity that is within the design range and when used on game animals for which they are intended. A bullet that is designed to expand normally on a whitetail deer may not expand at all on coyotes.

Again, we must consider the terminal velocity. A bullet designed to expand normally on a whitetail deer at a range of 150 yards may expand little or not at all at a range of 600 yards. At this extended range, the terminal velocity would be much lower, and probably below the normal performance range. This is true of any expanding type of bullet, and even those designed for explosive expansion may not expand much at extended ranges.

While range is a deciding criterion for bullet performance, this is just another way of stating relative velocity. All of this discussion points to terminal velocity. The higher the velocity at the muzzle, the higher the terminal velocity at any point downrange. The faster the bullet is moving on impact, the more it will expand, assuming all other factors (animal size, target area, etc.) remain constant.

It is in the category of normal-expansion bullets that muzzle velocity ranges provided by some bullet manufacturers must be taken with a grain of salt. If we assume the use of a 180-grain .30-caliber bullet intended for loads that develop between 2400 and 3200 fps, then a .300 Weatherby magnum loading will probably be somewhere near the high end of this range. Now, if this load is used to shoot a medium large animal at 25 yards, expansion will probably be destructive, maybe even explosive. The muzzle velocity range says little about terminal velocity, because such a load might be used out to 400 yards or more.

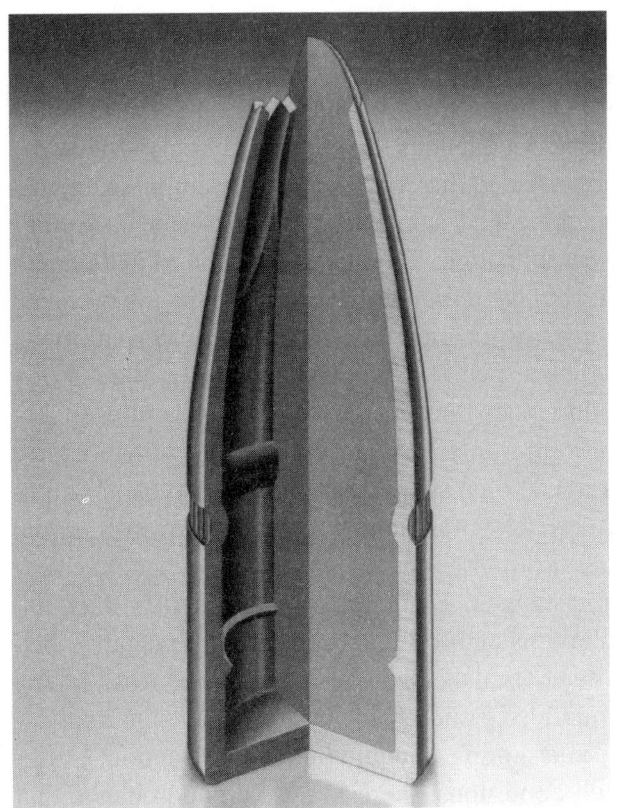

Figure 23-5: Cut-away view of a typical soft-point bullet.

Assuming a spire-pointed bullet design, this terminal velocity range would begin at approximately 100 yards when fired from a typical .300 Winchester Magnum and end near 250 yards. This assumes a muzzle velocity of approximately 3000 fps, a typical factory loading of the .300 Winchester. Using a .300 Weatherby Magnum, the ideal terminal velocity range would be entered at about 165 yards and would end at around 300 yards. These discussions involve "ideal" terminal velocity range, the range over which the most ideal expansion characteristics are likely to occur. We are also speaking here of standard (non-premium) lead core expanding bullets, typically designed for linear expansion characteristics. This is the type of bullet most frequently loaded in factory ammunition.

While it is always best to buy or load ammunition with ideal downrange terminal performance in mind, hunting situations cannot usually be this well regulated. Fortunately, ideal expansion is not necessary to adequately dispatch game animals. A bullet that expands too much will likely still do the job provided that it has struck the animal in a lethal location. The same applies to bullets that don't expand enough. The kill may not be as instantaneous, but the bullet will generally do its job if placed in a lethal location. Shooters are always cautioned to pick a specific place on the game animal's body and to place the shot carefully. This applies in any and all hunting situations. This is especially stressed when shots may lie beyond typical ranges of, say, 250-300 yards maximum. However, equal stress should be placed on shots that occur at very short ranges. Long range calibers like the .300 magnums call for equal shot placement care when fired at animals inside of 75 yards and less. Trying a quartering shot at these short ranges is inadvisable, assuming standard bullet construction. Under such conditions, there is a very good chance that the bullet will fragment and not penetrate adequately for a humane kill.

When using factory ammunition, the only control a hunter can have is to choose ranges carefully when in a shooting situation after being as fully informed as possible about bullet expansion potential. Unfortunately, this is next to impossible to obtain, because, by and large, a factory cartridge is considered a single component and information is not generally available about bullet muzzle velocity range, powder type, primer type, etc. All we usually know about factory ammunition is the weight and style of bullet and its factory-measured (or factory-published) muzzle and downrange velocities which are nearly always different from the shooter's rifle.

The reloader, however, may select the exact bullet anticipated for a particular application or hunt. Velocity can be adjusted to allow the terminal velocity to fall within the best estimate of distance over which shots may be taken; that is, within a reasonable variance. This allows for far more control and will result in better overall performance than is possible with factory loads.

NO EXPANSION

There are times when it is desirable for a bullet to not expand at all. In situations where very large or very tough animals such as elephant, rhinoceros, cape buffalo, etc. are involved, penetration is the key factor. Any expansion will automatically limit penetration. Non-expanding bullets are also erroneously known as solids, although most of the standard types are composed of a lead core and a copper jacket, just as are the expanding bullets.

Non-expanding bullets wrap the jacket from front to back so that the tip is completely encased. The jacket is then crimped into the lead core inside the base of the bullet, although more modern types may be completely encased from top to bottom. These bullet types typically exhibit thicker jackets at the tip with a slight diminishing of jacket thickness toward the base. The idea here is to protect the nose, the first part of the bullet to strike the target, in order to keep it from rupturing and expanding. Due to the stresses of concentric rotation as the bullet is being turned by the barrel rifling, lead cores will attain a softer state. At very high velocities, the lead may actually be molten or liquid. Any rupture in the metal jacket will allow the lead to flow out and expand.

There is a tradeoff here, as the thicker the bullet jacket is made, the less the overall weight of the bullet will be. Lead is heavier than copper, so more copper will result in less lead and less overall weight, given two bullets of the same dimensions.

The ideal non-expanding bullet can be fired through flesh and heavy bone and will still appear in like-new condition, save for the rifling cuts longitudinally on the jacket. However, non-expanding bullets can fail and fail disastrously. There are maximum velocity limitations and, when they are exceeded, the bullet may expand quite a lot, break up, or even disintegrate. There is no minimum velocity limit, as the slower the bullet is traveling when it strikes the target, the less chance there is for upset.

Non-expanding bullets of this type are rarely used in the United States. In fact, they are illegal for taking game animals in most states. Their use is almost wholly limited today to Africa and African dangerous game. They typically are of large caliber, .375 and more likely .416 to .600. The large-bore African guns typically fire projectiles at muzzle velocities of 2000 to 2200 fps, which helps to retard tendencies toward upset. Again, these bullets are designed to penetrate, hopefully pass completely through the animal. The large caliber of most of these bullets still allows for a sizable wound channel in spite of the lack of expansion.

If the nose of a non-expanding bullet with a lead core breaks upon impact, lead will flow and expansion will result, at the cost of penetration. Other type of failures include riveting, where the nose of the bullet simply collapses or flattens on impact. The jacket integrity may or may not be maintained. Such failures result in a very significant loss of penetration. Sometimes a non-expanding bullet will flatten laterally upon impact. This is often caused by the bullet being deflected by heavy bone and "keyholing", traveling sideways within the tissues or bone of the animal. Any bullet is designed for longitudinal (lengthwise) strength. When the attitude of the bullet changes to lateral, penetration is halted in a few inches and the bullet typically collapses laterally.

A very common failure of earlier non-expanding bullets was "core-backout". When the lead core is exposed inside the rear of the bullet, impact at the tip can cause the core to back out of the jacket. Usually, the core does not actually separate, but it can actually be seen extending for an eighth of an inch or so at the base. Such failures can also ultimately result in the nose collapsing upon itself for lack of internal support.

NOTE

A bullet designed for hunting does its work after it reaches the target. A bullet designed for target work does its work on the way to the target.

PREMIUM EXPANDING LEAD-CORE BULLETS

In the last decade and a half, many premium bullets have become available to the reloader. These bullets are designed to offer improved performance over those that are generally supplied in standard factory ammunition. In recent years, the factories have reacted to the demand for premium bullets by offering special loadings that use certain premium bullets, but handloaders have been able to take advantage of their improved performance characteristics for many years. Premium bullets cost more than standard designs, sometimes drastically more, especially when "super" premium bullets are involved. The "super" designation is applied to those bullets that are maintained to the closest manufacturing tolerances. These are largely hand-built designs. Premium bullets offer superior performance. But, what does this mean?

There are several areas in which premium bullets are touted as improvements over factory standard bullets. Some are said to be more accurate. Others claim to offer superior down range performance, and still others offer superior expansion characteristics. Some even offer several of these attributes.

ACCURACY

The accuracy of a bullet is largely determined by its consistency of concentricity. This simply means that the bullet's center of balance lies exactly along the center of the bore. A bullet with perfect concentricity characteristics will rotate without wobble when it is placed in-line with a rotating shaft that contacts the bullet at the center of its nose and the center of its base. When such a bullet travels up the barrel, it is imparted spin from the rifling. If the center of the bore and the center of the bullet do not align closely, wobble will be induced when the bullet leaves the muzzle. This will cause the bullet to yaw in flight and be pulled off the original target line.

Premium bullets may have no better concentricity than standard bullets, but they are usually manufactured to closer tolerances. There is no such thing as perfect concentricity, but all bullets, standard and premium, must fall within a certain tolerance range. The uniformity of premium bullets means that the tolerances are closer, so one premium bullet is more likely to behave like another premium bullet of the same type and manufacturer than are two non-premium designs. These closer tolerances can result in much-improved accuracy from premium bullets designed primarily for accuracy improvements.

TRAJECTORY PERFORMANCE

Premium bullets designed for superior trajectory performance generally offer a higher ballistic coefficient than standard loadings. Some of these are not premium bullets at all, especially those found in factory loadings. In such cases the "premium" bullet is manufactured to the same tolerances as standard bullets, but it is designed to be more aerodynamic, often assuming a boattail/spire-point configuration. Usually designed for long-range hunting, these bullets may have a slightly thinner jacket for better expansion at the lower downrange terminal velocities experienced at ranges exceeding 300 yards. These bullets may also weigh a bit more than standard bullets in the same weight range. The added weight can mean a longer bullet (for a better ballistic coefficient), and the boattail design means less barrel friction. The result is a heavier bullet with a high ballistic coefficient and sectional density that can be accelerated to a velocity commensurate with that of the lower weight standard bullet. Some of these designs are true premium bullets, offering the closer manufacturing tolerances most people expect of bullets in this category.

SUPERIOR EXPANSION CHARACTERISTICS

Most premium bullets are contained in this category. It should be obvious by now that standard lead-core expanding bullets (and even some non-expanding bullets) cannot be made (given present technology) to perform ideally over more than a narrow range of terminal velocities. This is a fact that most hunters who use factory ammunition and more than a few reloaders never consider. This is a limit that factory and custom ammunition share. However, custom-loaded ammunition can contain bullets specifically intended for a limited terminal velocity range. Generally, factory bullets are selected to give the best average performance over a much wider range, owing to the varied uses for which such ammunition is purchased. This means that, generally, the bullets contained in factory ammunition are a fairly drastic compromise. Custom loaded ammunition need not be.

Premium bullets with superior expansion characteristics often do not offer a single expansion rate as do most standard bullets. Rather, the expansion may be a two-part arrangement. This is the case with Nosler Partition Bullets, the premium bullet best known to reloaders and a bullet that is being used by more and more manufacturers in their premium loads. The Nosler Partition design offers two-part expansion via an arrangement of a two-part core as shown in Figure 23-6. The design begins with a single core, but the jacket is crimped into the core near the midpoint of the bullet. This process effectively locks the rear portion of the single core into the base of the bullet. The jacket is thinner near the bullet tip and thick at the base.

Upon impact, the front core section expands fairly rapidly, but the back section is designed to expand little or not at all. The rear section of the core behaves in much the same manner as a non-expanding bullet. Immediate expansion is obtained upon impact, but the stationary core in the rear allows for maximum penetration. Even if the front core section should separate from the jacket (and

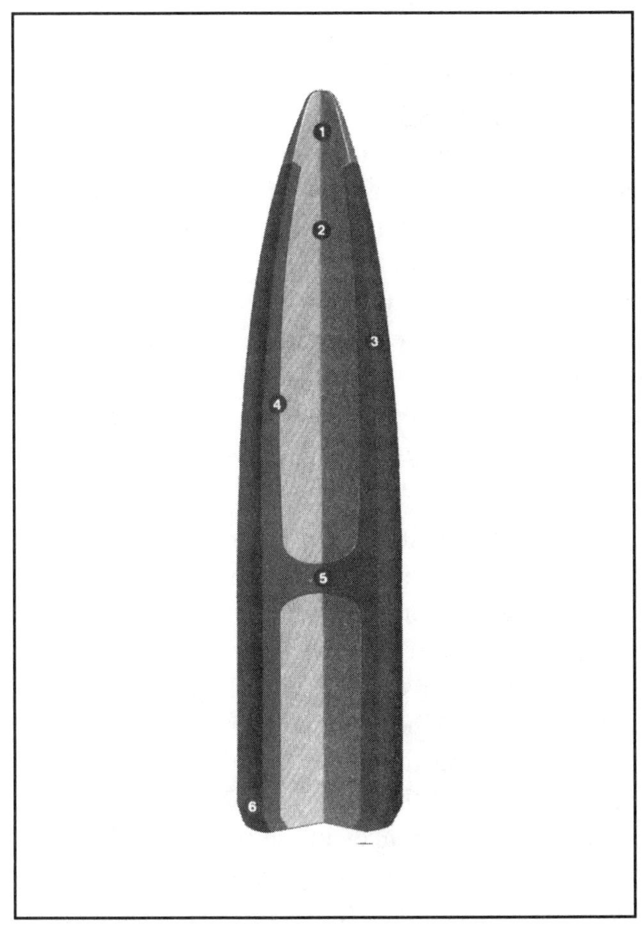

Figure 23-6: Cut-away view of a Nosler Partition bullet.

this can easily happen at high velocities), the rear section usually remains intact and continues to penetrate.

The end result of the Nosler design is a bullet that expands well and penetrates more like a non-expanding design. This means that the useful terminal velocity range is extended dramatically. I can remember extracting a 210-grain Nosler Partition .338-caliber bullet from the right hip of a bull elk, which had been shot at approximately 150 yards. The bullet was a perfect mushroom with excellent expansion of the front core section and jacket, while maintaining the integrity of the rear of the bullet. This bullet entered the elk in a front quartering shot through the left shoulder, took out the left lung, passed through the stomach and the intestines, and then lodged against the hide after passing through the pelvis. This speaks to the excellent expansion and penetration capabilities of this type of bullet design.

Other types of expanding premium bullets depend upon the taper thickness of the metal jacket along with the bonding of the lead core to the copper jacket. In standard bullet designs, the lead core is simply wrapped by the jacket. There is no bonding of the core to the jacket. However, bonded core bullets contain some mechanism for keeping the two different metals together. In the case of the Nosler Partition bullet, the bonding of the rear portion of the core is accomplished through a mechanical process of crimping the jacket to the core at the mid-way point. Other manufacturers use a conventional single core design but incorporate a heat treating process (sometimes called fusion bonding) to accomplish the bonding, along with a jacket taper of thin to very thick from nose to base.

All of these premium designs offer better expansion characteristics than their standard equivalents but only as long as they are fired within their acceptable range of velocities. Any of these designs can fragment or even disintegrate if their maximum velocity designs are exceeded drastically. I have seen Nosler Partition bullets blown to pieces after striking a close target at exceptional velocities that are often produced by some of the more radical wildcat cartridges. Premium bullets designed for superior expansion characteristics usually offer a dramatically extended terminal velocity range, but such range is not infinite.

One possible drawback to premium bullets designed for controlled expansion lies in the fact that some of them do not offer as high a ballistic coefficient as do some standard bullet designs. The best ballistic coefficients are derived from boattail designs, but the boattail bullet offers more opportunity for core separations than does the flat base design. For this reason, most premium bullets designed for superior expansion use the flat base design. They also may not offer tips that are as aerodynamic as bullets that exhibit standard expansion characteristics. This is not true in every case, but, as a rule, the highest ballistic coefficients are not found in premium bullets of this type. The lessened ballistic coefficient, however, will have marginal effects on downrange velocity performance, because the differences are not that great in most cases.

PREMIUM NON-EXPANDING BULLETS

As noted previously, non-expanding bullets are designed for one purpose: maximum penetration. These bullets must maintain their mechanical integrity after impact. They are not supposed to expand in any manner, and the perfect non-expanding bullet will retain its original shape and weight after striking the target. This bullet type is often called a "solid", but this is a misnomer, as most of the standard types are not solid, containing a lead core that is fully wrapped from nose to base by a tough copper jacket.

The premium non-expanding bullets of today are true solids. They do not contain a lead core at all but are manufactured as single units of a solid copper alloy.

The major difficulties encountered with the older type of non-expanding bullet are inherent in the two-piece design. A heavy lead core is surrounded by a light metal jacket. There are two types of metal used in the construction, and the lead core is considerably heavier and more "fluid" at velocity than the lightweight copper or copper alloy jacket. Lead is a convenient metal to use for the core of all bullets because of its high weight, low cost, and tendency to upset or expand more readily than other metals. The purpose of the lead core in the non-expanding bullet is to provide ample weight in a small mass. However, the inconsistencies between characteristics of the lead core and the copper jacket lead to problems, especially when dealing with non-expanding bullets. Such bullets are traditionally used on dangerous game, so a bullet failure can result in injury or death for the shooter when the dangerous animal is not put down quickly.

Core separation is a subject that has been mentioned several times in this chapter and is a major cause of poor penetration in both expanding and non-expanding bullets. The jacket is designed to control expansion of the lead core in an expanding bullet type. When the core sheds its jacket after impact, the light weight of the jacket causes it to stop penetrating almost instantly. The lead core expands dramatically when the controlling jacket is gone, so its progress is halted abruptly as well. The end result is poor penetration.

In a non-expanding bullet, the lead core can back out of the jacket even when the jacket does not burst. Since the non-expanding lead-core bullet is wrapped from nose to base by the copper jacket, the bullet base is usually crimped up into the base of the lead core. Upon striking flesh or heavy bone, the stresses placed on the bullet can cause this crimp to fail and the jacket and core to separate, owing to the differences in the weight of the two. If the nose of the non-expanding bullet should break open upon impact, the lead will expand outward and the end result is an expanding bullet. Again, penetration suffers greatly.

The premium solid bullet overcomes both of these failure types. This is a one-piece bullet made from a single metal. There is no core and no jacket, therefore a separation cannot occur. Certainly, solid bullets can become distorted if their maximum terminal velocities are exceeded, but there can be no core separation. Premium solid bullets are available from a small collection of manufacturers. The actual content of the copper alloys used for their construction is usually secret, and each company has its own "mixture." Barnes uses a copper/zinc alloy.

Lead has been traditionally used in non-expanding bullets mainly because it is cheap and packs a lot of weight into a small mass. This is just what is needed for bullet design. Premium solids do not use lead, so these bullets are typically a bit longer than their lead-core counterparts. A 500-grain, .45-caliber lead core bullet is shorter than a 500-grain, .45-caliber solid made from a copper alloy, because the alloy weighs less than lead. While measured in small fractions of an inch, the greater length of the premium solid has advantages and disadvantages.

The main disadvantage is that the extra length may necessitate seating the bullet deeper into the cartridge mouth so that the loaded cartridge can be accommodated by the rifle action and to maintain the proper leade length (the unrifled section of a barrel between the cartridge mouth and the point at which the rifling begins). If a long-loaded cartridge can be accommodated by the action and the nose of the bullet actually engages the rifling in the barrel, high pressures can result if the powder charge is not reduced appropriately.

One advantage of a longer bullet is that the ballistic coefficient is increased (assuming bullet shape remains the same). This means that the bullet is more aerodynamic and will possess better downrange velocity than will the same weight and caliber of bullet in a short design. However, this advantage is only of limited usefulness, since most solid bullets are used for dangerous African game that are usually taken at no more than 100 yards. This is not downrange enough to make much practical difference. These bullets contain round noses for maximum shock power upon impact and to better assure straight-line penetration. A small-diameter spire point design is inappropriate for most dangerous-game hunting, because the small-diameter point would be the weakest part of the bullet and is the part that receives the most abuse. Premium solids are available in spire point designs, but these are usually limited to small calibers and are designed for taking nondangerous fur-bearing animals with minimal pelt damage.

A major disadvantage of premium solids has nothing to do with their performance but involves their price. Premium and super premium solid bullets in the larger calibers can cost three to five dollars each. However, when such bullets are loaded for dangerous-game hunting, the safety of the hunter is at stake and the extra cost is warranted. Such bullets are expensive because of their non-standard construction and because only a small amount are sold, owing to their specialized uses.

PREMIUM CORELESS EXPANDING BULLETS

There is another category of expanding bullet that is so new that it merits a category all to itself. These are bullets that are of solid construction, containing no lead core, that are designed to expand. Perhaps "expand" is not the right word here as we think of lead core bullets expanding. In the latter, the lead "flows" outward, having assumed an almost liquid state due to the stresses of impact. This is a relatively linear expansion that results in a mushroom appearance in proper designs. Coreless expansion bullets are designed in a manner that causes the nose to evenly "peel" back in a number of predetermined sections.

The leader of premium bullets in this category is the Barnes X-Bullet. The Barnes design is a solid copper projectile with no separate jacket and no lead core. A cavity in the nose (resembling a hollow point design) causes the nose to peel back in four separate razor-edged petals upon impact. This is where the name for this design came from. When viewed head on, the appearance of these four petals form the letter X.

The Barnes X-Bullet has been tested by just about every gun writer in the country, and they all report excellent penetration, expansion (peeling), and accuracy. This is a tough bullet that offers excellent terminal properties even when pushed to velocities that cause premium lead-core bullets to fragment. It probably offers the widest terminal performance range of any expanding bullet currently offered. The bullet in unfired and in impacted form is shown in Figure 23-7 on the next page.

As with non-expanding solids, the Barnes X-Bullet is longer than equivalent lead-core designs

Figure 23-7: Barnes X-Bullet.

of the same weight and caliber. This results in improved ballistic coefficients (BC). Since the X-Bullet is manufactured for every caliber from .243 to .458, this can be a big advantage for long-range ballistic performance in typical sporting uses from varmint to big game hunting. Some of these bullets are even offered in boattail designs which increases the ballistic coefficient by approximately 10 percent. As an example, the 165-grain .30-caliber boattail X-Bullet has a ballistic coefficient of .505. This compares with a BC of approximately .460 common to lead-core boattail bullets of the same weight and caliber.

The X-Bullet has been available since 1989, and it would seem to be the wave of the immediate future, as other manufacturers are beginning to offer their own versions of bullets that can be classified as coreless expanding types.

The absence of a lead core in expanding bullets should be welcomed by most shooters, because as in the non-expanding solid designs, there is no chance of core separation. If the Barnes X-Bullet is any indication, the peeling of the petals seems to take place to a certain point and then stops. However, penetration still continues. In super high velocity loadings (intended for test purposes), one or more petals can break off, but the base of the bullet continues to penetrate.

It is arguably easier to make a more uniform solid bullet than a two-piece type. Referring to an earlier discussion in this chapter on bullet concentricity, manufacturing a bullet with its center of gravity along the longitudinal axis, a two-piece design must have a lead core that is concentrically balanced to which a copper jacket is applied. If the jacket is thicker at one circumferential point than at another, this will unbalance the entire package. So, a two-piece design must have a balanced lead core and a balanced copper jacket. In a one-piece design, we deal with only a single entity, so the double balancing act is avoided.

Shooting tests using the Barnes X-Bullet and other types of solid non-expanding bullets speak to the consistency of manufacture possible with solid designs. As a group, bullets exhibit greater accuracy (because of consistency) than the more conventional lead-core/copper-jacket designs.

Accuracy, consistency, higher ballistic coefficient, and rigidly controlled expansion over a much wider range of terminal velocities make the Barnes X-Bullet and those that are sure to follow reloading production that deserve serious consideration. The X-Bullet costs no more than lead-core premiums or about 40% more than standard lead-core bullets. This type of design may mark the eventual obsolescence of lead-core bullets, altogether.

JACKETED BULLET SHAPES

The shape of a bullet is another important consideration in choosing the proper types for various reloading applications.

Today's modern manufacturing techniques have drastically reduced the limitations various bullet types exhibited thirty years ago. However, many of the old limitations still persist in the minds of uninformed shooters. Thirty years ago, it was accurately assumed that round nose bullet designs offered better expansion than the spitzer or spire point design. Today, this is not true, as pointed bullets are manufactured to expand just as well as their round or flat nose counterparts. Before modern manufacturing techniques were developed, it was necessary to use heavy-for-caliber bullets to assure adequate penetration on large North American game. Lighter bullets would expand too much, resulting in inadequate penetration. This is no longer completely true, since even light-for-caliber bullets are designed for proper expansion control and maximum penetration. (Note: Heavy-for-caliber bullets will always have a higher sectional density than lighter bullets and will tend to penetrate more deeply, assuming proper expansion control.)

Another theory that has been largely proven untrue is that blunt or round nose bullets penetrate brush with less deflection than spire point bullets. This is coupled with the opinion that bullets traveling at relatively slow velocities are better in the brush than bullets fired at higher velocities. Various tests have shown that the shape of modern bullets has little to do with their ability to penetrate brush, and the same applies to velocity. Several years ago, a test was conducted on brush penetration capabilities of a large number of cartridges from .223 Remington to .458 Winchester. Surprisingly, the .223 Remington showed a slightly better ability to get its projectile through the test brush range with the least amount of deflection. However, the difference between the best performer in this test and the worst was not all that great. This means that a bullet that travels through brush is in danger of being deflected no matter what its shape, velocity, or caliber. Try to avoid shooting through brush if at all possible.

The modern reloader of jacketed rifle bullets has a small number of bullet shape designs to choose from. Most of the criteria regarding bullet shape deal with the nose configuration. Since modern manufacturing processes have rendered all bullet types suitable in the area of terminal performance (with the exception of some dangerous game bullet designs), the choice of bullet shape for a particular application can be based largely upon the downrange ballistic performance required or the specific type of rifle that is to be used.

Today, the reloader may choose from spire point or spitzer bullets, those that taper to an acute point; round nose designs that are more traditional and simply round off the nose of the bullet into a smooth oval; and flat nose bullets that are closely akin to round nose designs, but the nose offers a little more taper, which is suddenly chopped off to for a nose that is as flat as the bullet base.

Another category of bullet design describes the base, as opposed to the nose. Most bullets incorporate a flat base (the largest diameter is measured at the base), but there is also the boattail design, which tapers the base to a diameter that is less than the maximum bullet diameter. These are generally available only in bullets that have spire point noses.

TRADITIONAL ROUND NOSE

The round nose bullet design has been around since jacketed bullets were first developed. This bullet type exhibits an abrupt rounded nose as opposed to a smooth taper to a point. The round nose design maintains the true caliber diameter over a larger percentage of the bullet length, quickly tapering near the nose to a quick oval. For dangerous-game purposes, the round nose design is favored, because the bullet is more structurally rigid than are spire point designs. The nose measures out at a higher percentage of the base diameter than does a spire point, which tapers down to a small fraction of this diameter.

The ballistic coefficient of the round nose design is much lower than that of any spire point counterparts. For instance, a .30-caliber round nose bullet weighing 180 grains will typically have a ballistic coefficient about half that of an equivalent spire point.

Round nose bullets are most useful for short to moderate range shooting conditions, because their lower ballistic coefficient causes them to lose velocity and drop more rapidly downrange. It is felt that the round nose design offers more initial shocking power upon impacting a game animal because it presents a larger diameter at the nose than do spire point designs. For this and structural reasons, the majority of bullets designed for taking dangerous African large game, expanding and solid types, are of the round nose design.

Ballistic performance aside, the round nose bullet is often chosen for use in rifles with tubular magazines, which place the primer of one bullet against the nose of the one that follows it in the magazine. It is felt that a spire pointed design might dent the primer of the cartridge it is butted against in the magazine causing ignition.

SPITZER OR SPIRE POINT BULLETS

These are the sharp pointed bullet designs. The two types are treated as one, though from a technical standpoint, their tapers are slightly different. For practical application and the purposes of this discussion, they may be treated as one and the same.

This bullet type offers much better aerodynamic shape than the round nose and loses velocity less quickly. The finest long-range hunting bullets use this design, which typically offers twice the ballistic coefficient rating of equivalent round nose bullets. As was mentioned previously, spire point bullets are now designed to expand as well as round nose designs, something that was not the case thirty years ago.

There is a feeling that spire point bullets are more accurate than round nose types. This is not always true, but it is difficult to provide meaningful data in comparing the two, since they are designed for different downrange performance. Over a distance of 200 yards, the spire point shows no better accuracy than round nose bullets and either type can easily beat out the other over this range. When targets lie beyond 200 yards, the superior downrange performance of the spire point with its lower bullet drop becomes quickly apparent.

BOATTAIL BULLETS

This bullet differs from the conventional spitzer bullet only in the base configuration, which is tapered to a blunt end that is smaller than the maximum bullet diameter. The main purpose for this design is to increase the aerodynamic properties of the bullet. An approximate 10% to 15% increase in ballistic coefficient is gained by using a boattail over a flat base design, assuming that the rest of the bullet shape remains the same.

A nagging problem with boattail designs in earlier years was a greater tendency for them to shed their lead cores upon impact. It is more difficult to bond the core to the jacket in a boattail design, because there is less surface area at the base. Modern construction and bonding techniques, however, have overcome this problem to a large extent, so shooters may now have the best aerodynamic shape coupled with excellent terminal performance. Still, hunters who tackle the big North American bears and other dangerous game at longer ranges prefer the added core integrity of the flat base designs.

FLAT POINT BULLETS

The flat point bullet is made exclusively for rifles that have tubular magazines. Bullets of this design type offer about the same ballistic coefficient as round nose types. While the latter may also be used safely in tubular magazines, it is felt that the flat nose bullet may suffer less tip damage from being stacked vertically in the magazine.

VARIATIONS

There are other bullet types that fall loosely between any two of the types just discussed. Some specialty bullets may be of semi-spitzer types that have a long taper to a flat point. Many others may incorporate the same shape but the nose will be a hollow point design. Mistakenly, some reloaders think of a hollow point bullet as one of relatively low ballistic coefficient and designed for explosive expansion. This is not true of all hollow point designs. Many bullets manufactured for target/match shooting are of boattail hollow point design, and these offer some of the highest ballistic coefficients available, along with superb accuracy. However, the match bullet is not meant for hunting purposes and the hollow point serves a different purpose than the promotion of expansion.

There are many excellent hollow point hunting bullets intended for deer-size game. These do not expand explosively as some of the varmint hollow points do. In fact, they are constructed with a fairly tough copper jacket to promote controlled expansion. The hollow point initiates expansion when animal tissues are driven into the cavity and offers terminal performance similar to soft point expanding bullets. The hollow point design is just an alternate method of promoting expansion and is no better and no worse than any other type of controlled expansion bullet.

JACKETED PISTOL BULLETS

To this point, the discussions in this chapter have addressed rifle bullets for the most part. All of these apply equally to bullets in the specialty pistols that fire rifle cartridges. However, the traditional pistol calibers deserve further consideration, because the problems associated with terminal performance of their bullets are sometimes quite different from those in equivalent rifle cartridges.

To begin, pistol bullets from the .25 Automatic to the .44 Magnum and the .454 Casull are fired at relatively slow velocities when compared with rifles. The concern with such bullets is in getting them to expand enough. We don't need to worry so much about overexpansion in jacketed designs, and these discussions can be applied to the older rifle cartridges such as the .38-55, .25-20, etc. that may be used to fire modern projectiles at velocities that lie below the normal terminal velocity range.

Prior to the 1970s, when major concentration was first placed on handgun hunting, many bullets designed exclusively for handgun use were constructed entirely of lead or lead alloys. This was the best compromise that could be reached, but such bullets cause leading of the barrel and are rather fragile regarding handling deformation. Even then, some of these bullets did not expand well (or at all) at lower velocities. For instance, a .357-caliber bullet might expand too much when fired from a high-velocity .357 magnum loading and too little when fired from a low-velocity .38 Smith and Wesson loading.

As handgun velocities were increased due to new cartridge types combined with strong, new pistol designs, jacketed pistol bullets became practical and necessary. All along, the full-jacketed loadings were available for some calibers like .45 ACP and 9mm Luger. The latter two were relegated almost exclusively to semiautomatic pistols, which function more reliably with full-jacketed bullets. However, these bullet types do not expand and are not to be preferred for hunting situations nor even for certain defense applications.

At velocities below 800 fps, expansion of any lead core bullet type is a sometimes thing. Sometimes they expand a bit and sometimes not at all. For this reason, many of the jacketed pistol bullets were manufactured as hollow points. This design uses a cavity in the nose of the bullet and a channel to that cavity from the nose tip. This allows target matter to actually enter the inside of the bullet through the channel and cause the cavity to open due to the internal stresses, initiating a freer expansion. The hollow point construction serves as a catalyst to expansion. The size of the cavity and its channel determines the rate and amount of expansion, with the larger cavities/channels expanding more rapidly than the smaller ones. The hollow point approach works well but only over a fairly narrow range of terminal velocities. A hollow point design for a .357 magnum loading still might not expand at all in a .38 S & W.

The high-velocity loadings in the .357 magnum, .41 magnum, and .44 magnum present less expansion difficulties than older cartridges. Bullets designed for these cartridges generally expand well and nearly conventional jacketed softpoint designs are available, most of which are used in rifles designed to fire these cartridges, as well. Some of these are called half-jacket or partial-jacket designs, and enclose the lead core from the bullet base to near or just beyond the central half-way point on the core. This serves several purposes. The half jacket surrounds the lead core over the bullet length that engages the barrel rifling. This prevents severe leading. Also, the lead front half of the bullet expands rapidly and then is controlled when the jacket is engaged. The end result is a bullet that expands rapidly upon initial contact and then more slowly as the copper jacket is engaged. The half-jacket design is nothing new, as it was used in bullets for rifle cartridges like the .45-70 during the transition from all-lead to jacketed bullets.

The half-jacket pistol bullet came into its own when the higher powered cartridges became available. Whereas pistols had traditionally been relegated to defense, target, and small-game applications, the .357 and .44 magnums were considered adequate for taking deer and black bear. However, these larger animals required deeper penetration that simply could not be obtained from conventional all lead designs. The half-jacket, coupled with a hollow point nose in some instances, offered the expansion and penetration necessary to take the larger game, while providing the benefit of reduced barrel leading.

Depending on the expansion rate desired, pistol bullets are available in full-, standard-, and half-jacket designs and may also be constructed with a hollow point in the nose cavity. Also, jacket thickness can vary depending upon the intended use of the bullet, with the thinner jackets providing better expansion at lower velocities.

For defense purposes, bullet expansion is an especially critical factor, and it is almost always more desirable for the bullet not to penetrate fully through the human target. However, expansion in pistol bullets is a bit more complex than it is in many rifle applications. Standard pistol cartridges use relatively large-bore bullets that are light in weight for caliber and travel at low velocities. Due to the stubbiness of these bullets, the ballistic coefficient is low, as is the sectional density. The first rating affects downrange velocity and bullet drop, while the latter addresses penetration. Pistol bullets, in general, have rainbow trajectories and marginal penetration when compared with rifle bullets of the same caliber. Owing to their low ballistic coefficients, pistol bullets lose velocity rapidly and are useful over a relatively short range.

For instance, .44-caliber pistol bullets are generally available in weights ranging from 200 to 300 grains. The .45-caliber rifle bullet equivalents usually start at 300 grains to a maximum of 600 grains. The ballistic coefficient of the 200-grain .44 bullet is approximately .125, while the BC of the low-weight .45-caliber rifle bullet is on the order of .175. On the other end of the weight spectrum, the 300-grain .44-caliber pistol bullet has a typical BC of only .230, whereas the 600-grain .458-caliber rifle bullet comes in with a BC of approximately .450. Fired from a .44 Remington magnum at a typical velocity of 1500 fps and sighted in for 50 yards, the 200-grain bullet will drop about 6 inches at 100 yards. In short, the higher BC of the larger bullet improves the trajectory by about 75%, given the range and conditions in this example.

Since pistol bullets are usually light in weight for their caliber diameter, the sectional density(SD) is adversely affected. The 200-grain .44-caliber bullet has an SD of .185, but the 300-grain .45-caliber bullet has an SD of .204. On the top end of the weight spectrum, the 300-grain .44 bullet exhibits an SD of .232, while the 600-grain .45-caliber (rifle) bullet boasts a value of .409.

Trajectory and penetration aside, there is a much greater percentage of velocity loss in pistol cartridges than in rifle equivalents. The 200-grain .44 caliber bullet fired at 1500 fps will decrease to around 1300 fps at 50 yards and to 1125 fps at 100 yards. There are losses of approximately 13% and 25%, respectively. The 300-grain .458 bullet at 2000 fps will drop about 10% of its velocity at 50 yards and 20% at 100 yards. Pistol bullets shed a bit more velocity over short ranges (100 yards or less), owing to their lower BCs, but the big difference in downrange performance is attributable to the big difference in muzzle velocities between equivalent pistol and rifle calibers.

Pistol bullets must be of lower weight because of the limited powder space in cartridge cases that can be accommodated by their actions. This automatically means that the ballistic coefficient and the sectional density of such bullets is lower than in rifle equivalents.

All of this highlights the fact that pistol cartridges are short-range compromises at best, excluding the specialty pistols that fire rifle cartridges.

Chapter 24
Casting Lead Bullets

Although both lead and gunpowder were produced in America before the Revolution, most were imported. Both powder and lead came in bulk, requiring that the shooter cast his or her own bullets.

American-made flintlock rifles played an important role on the frontiers in the eighteenth century, and nearly all were supplied with bullet molds made by the gunmaker who made the rifle. These molds, however, often were lost or became worn — requiring that new molds be made.

American bullet molds were made of iron, brass, stone, and clay-lined wood. Since many of the smoothbore weapons for which bullets were made were not particularly accurate, small irregularities in the bullets were not important.

TYPES OF CAST BULLETS

Since the advent of powder and ball, there have been thousands of varieties of bullets, with many different shapes and sizes. Some bullets have flat bases, others have depressions of various depths and shapes, some were patched, and others have lubrication grooves. A few of the bullet molds available a few decades ago are shown in Figure 24-1 which begins on the next page. Since that time, however, some bullet casting molds have become almost extinct; only the most popular ones remain. Still, many are available to suit the shooter's every need.

Many of the Ideal and Lyman bullet designs shown in Figure 24-1 — although now obsolete — are still excellent designs. Consequently, they should not be overlooked by the reloader, especially those who intend to reload for some of the obsolete cartridges. The main problem is finding them. Try advertising in some of the monthly and bi-monthly shooting publications like *Gun List* and *Shotgun News*. Bullet molds will usually be in the table displays at gun shows, or you might come across some at flea markets and yard sales. Estate sales of known gun buffs is another possibility.

A complete list of firms producing or selling bullet molds may be found in the Appendix of this book. There are also many currently-manufactured bullet molds that are readily available and may be purchased at most shooting supply and sporting goods stores, or ordered directly from the manufacturer in many cases. The information contained in this chapter will help you select the equipment needed for bullet casting, and then guide you step-by-step through the general procedures.

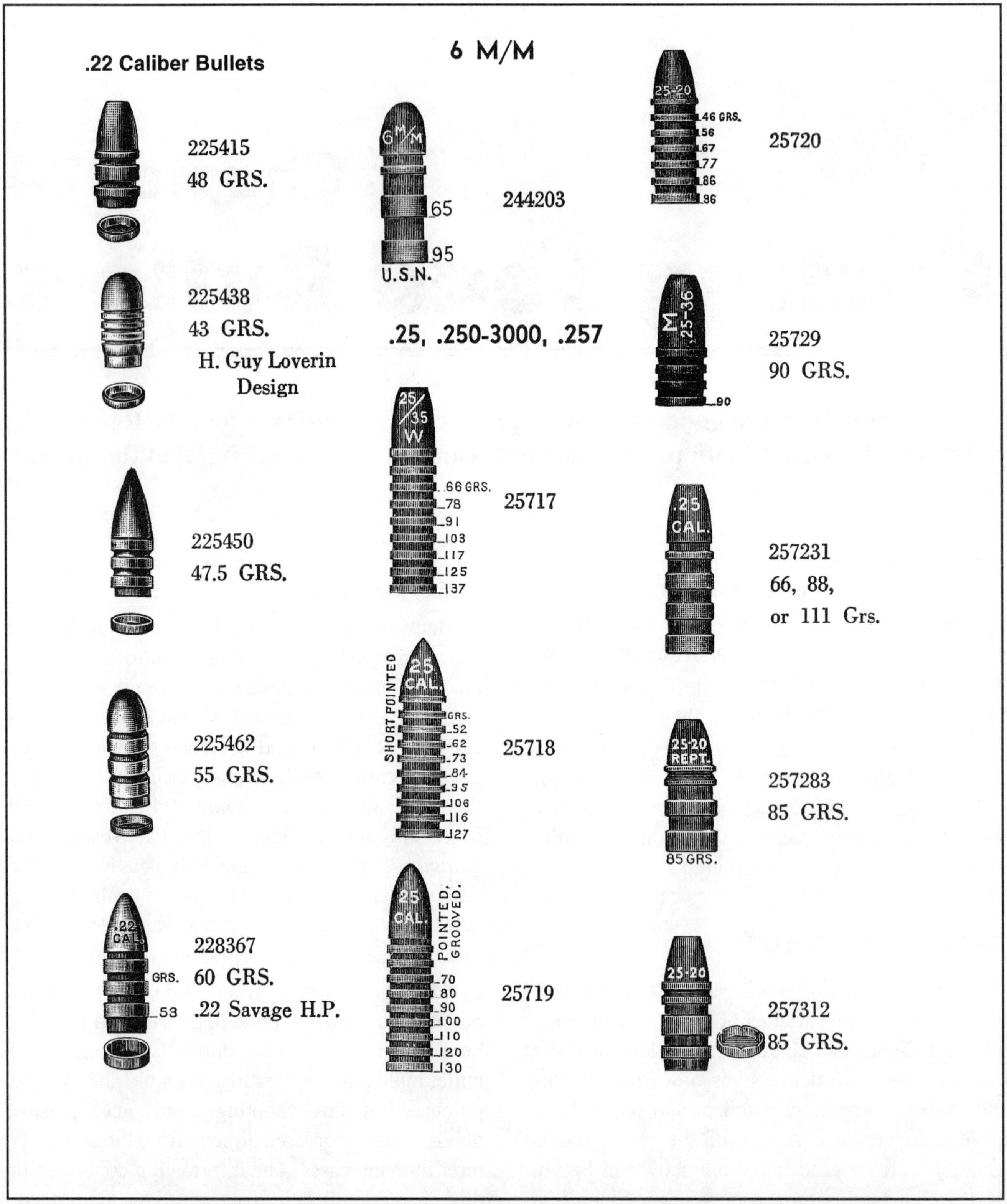

.22 Caliber Bullets
225415
48 GRS.
225438
43 GRS.
H. Guy Loverin Design
225450
47.5 GRS.
225462
55 GRS.
.22 CAL.
GRS.
53
228367
60 GRS.
.22 Savage H.P.
6 M/M
6 M/M
65
95
U.S.N.
244203
.25, .250-3000, .257
25/35 W
66 GRS.
78
91
103
117
125
137
25717
SHORT POINTED
25 CAL.
GRS.
52
62
73
84
95
106
116
127
25718
25 CAL.
POINTED. GROOVED.
70
80
90
100
110
120
130
25719
25-20
46 GRS.
56
67
77
86
96
25720
M 25-36
90
25729
90 GRS.
.25 CAL.
257231
66, 88,
or 111 Grs.
25-20 REPT.
85 GRS.
257283
85 GRS.
25-20
257312
85 GRS.

Figure 24-1: Several bullet molds once offered by Ideal and Lyman. Some are still made and are readily available to the reloader.

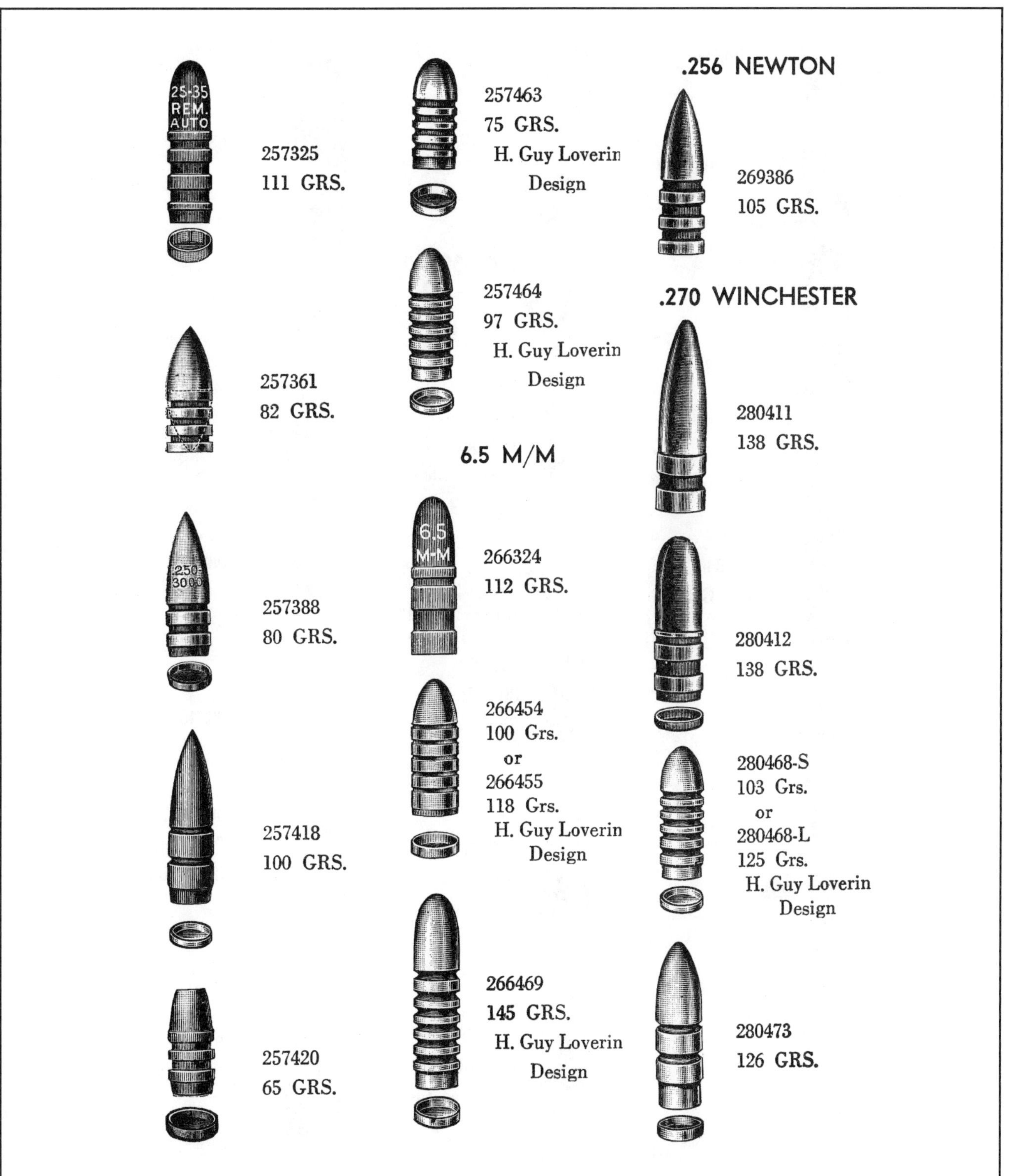

Figure 24-1: Several bullet molds once offered by Ideal and Lyman. (*Continued*)

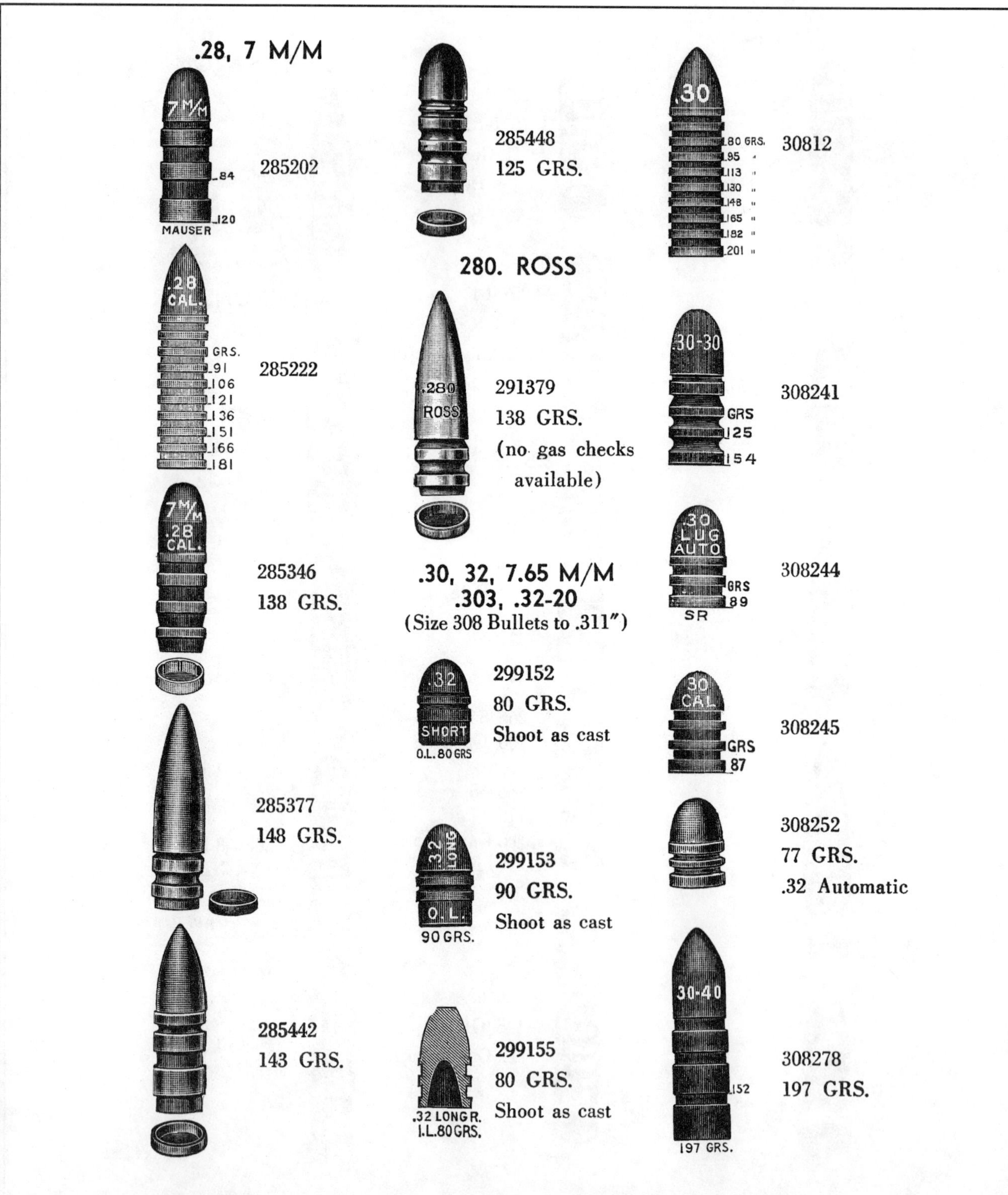

Figure 24-1: Several bullet molds once offered by Ideal and Lyman. (*Continued*)

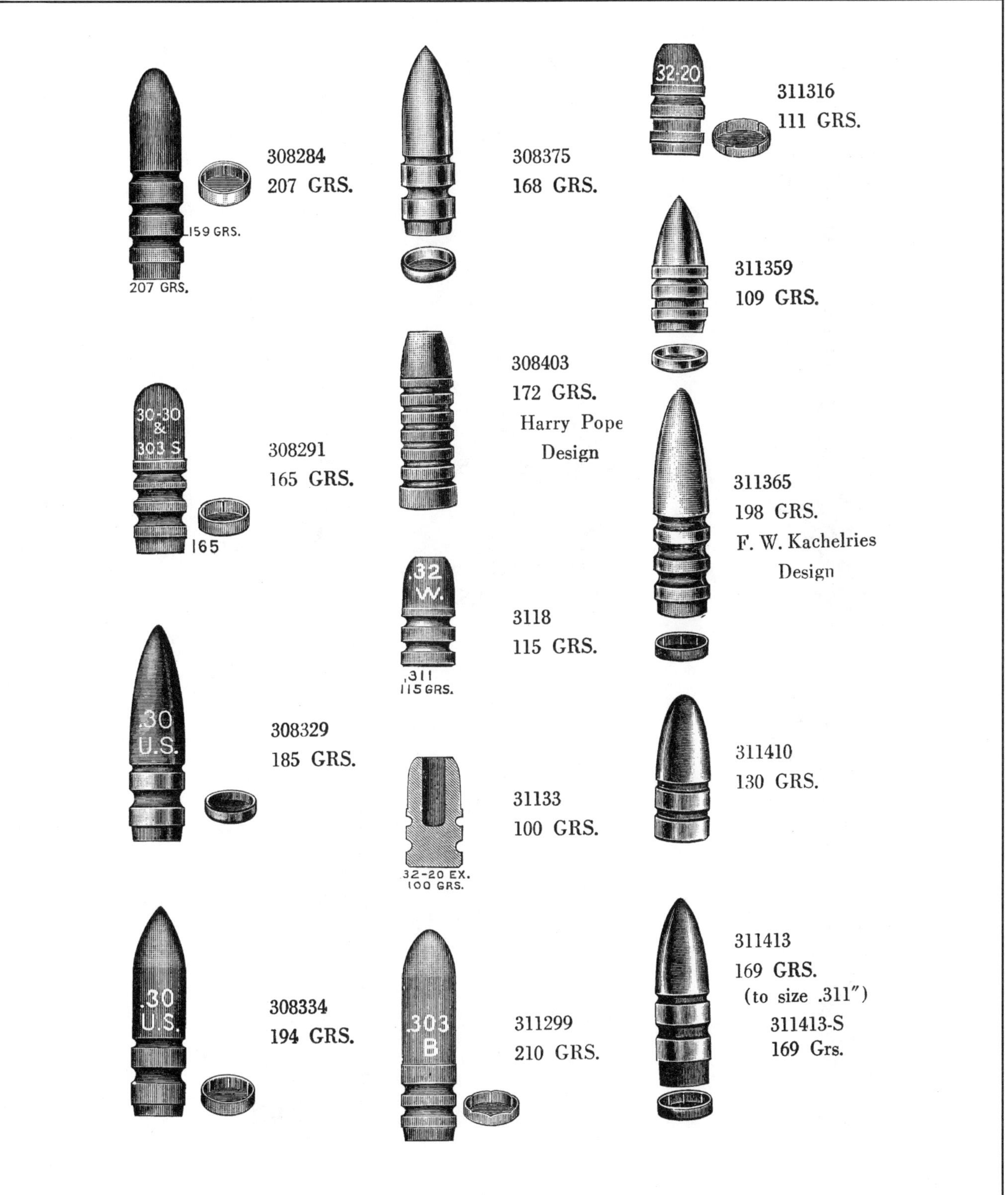

Figure 24-1: Several bullet molds once offered by Ideal and Lyman. (*Continued*)

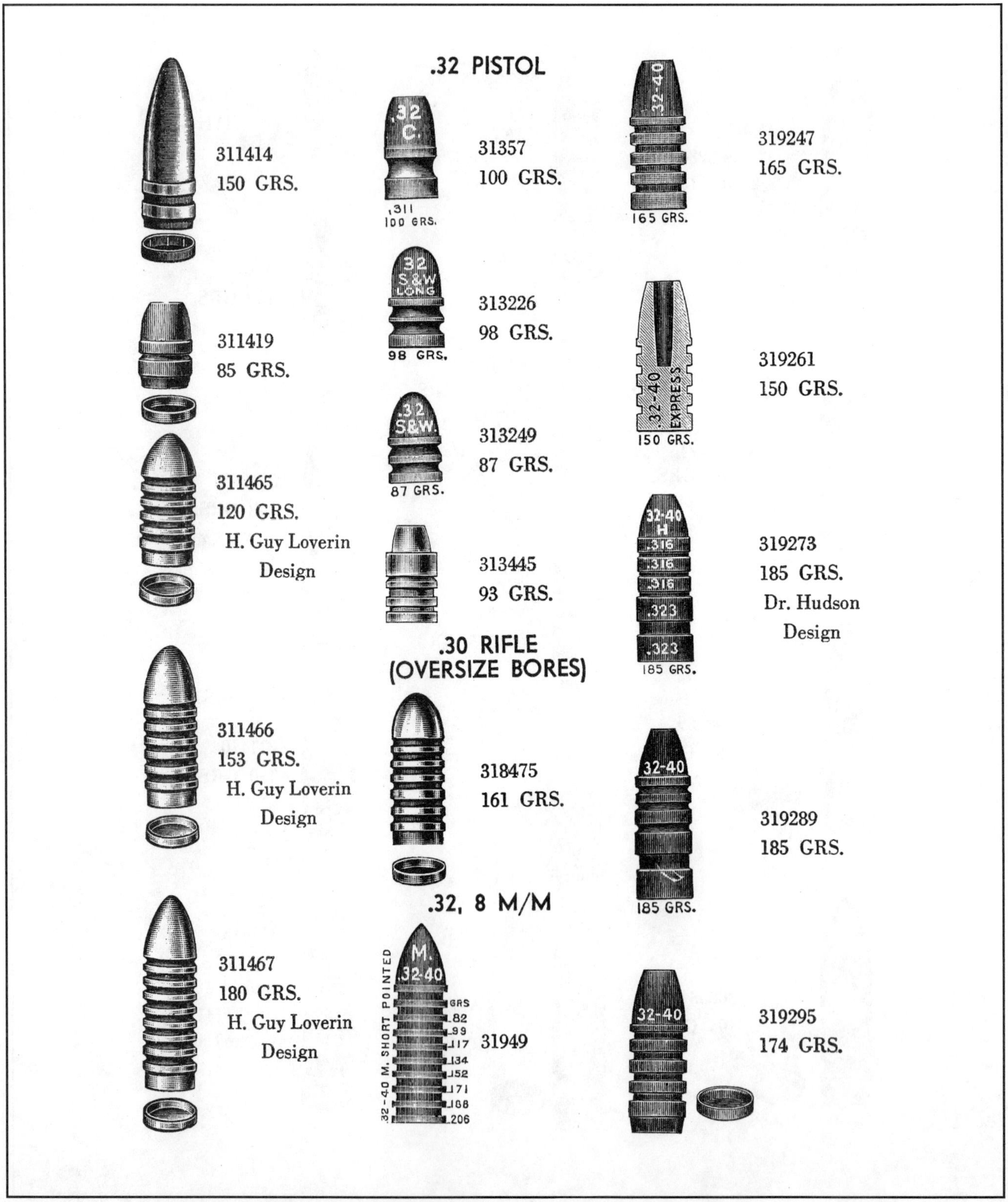

311414
150 GRS.
311419
85 GRS.
311465
120 GRS.
H. Guy Loverin Design
311466
153 GRS.
H. Guy Loverin Design
311467
180 GRS.
H. Guy Loverin Design
.32 PISTOL
.32 C.
.311
100 GRS.
31357
100 GRS.
32 S&W LONG
98 GRS.
313226
98 GRS.
.32 S&W.
87 GRS.
313249
87 GRS.
313445
93 GRS.
.30 RIFLE
(OVERSIZE BORES)
318475
161 GRS.
.32, 8 M/M
32-40 M. SHORT POINTED
M. 32-40
GRS
82
99
117
134
152
171
188
206
31949
32-40
165 GRS.
319247
165 GRS.
32-40 EXPRESS
150 GRS.
319261
150 GRS.
32-40 H
.316
.316
.316
.323
.323
185 GRS.
319273
185 GRS.
Dr. Hudson Design
32-40
185 GRS.
319289
185 GRS.
32-40
319295
174 GRS.

Figure 24-1: Several bullet molds once offered by Ideal and Lyman. (*Continued*)

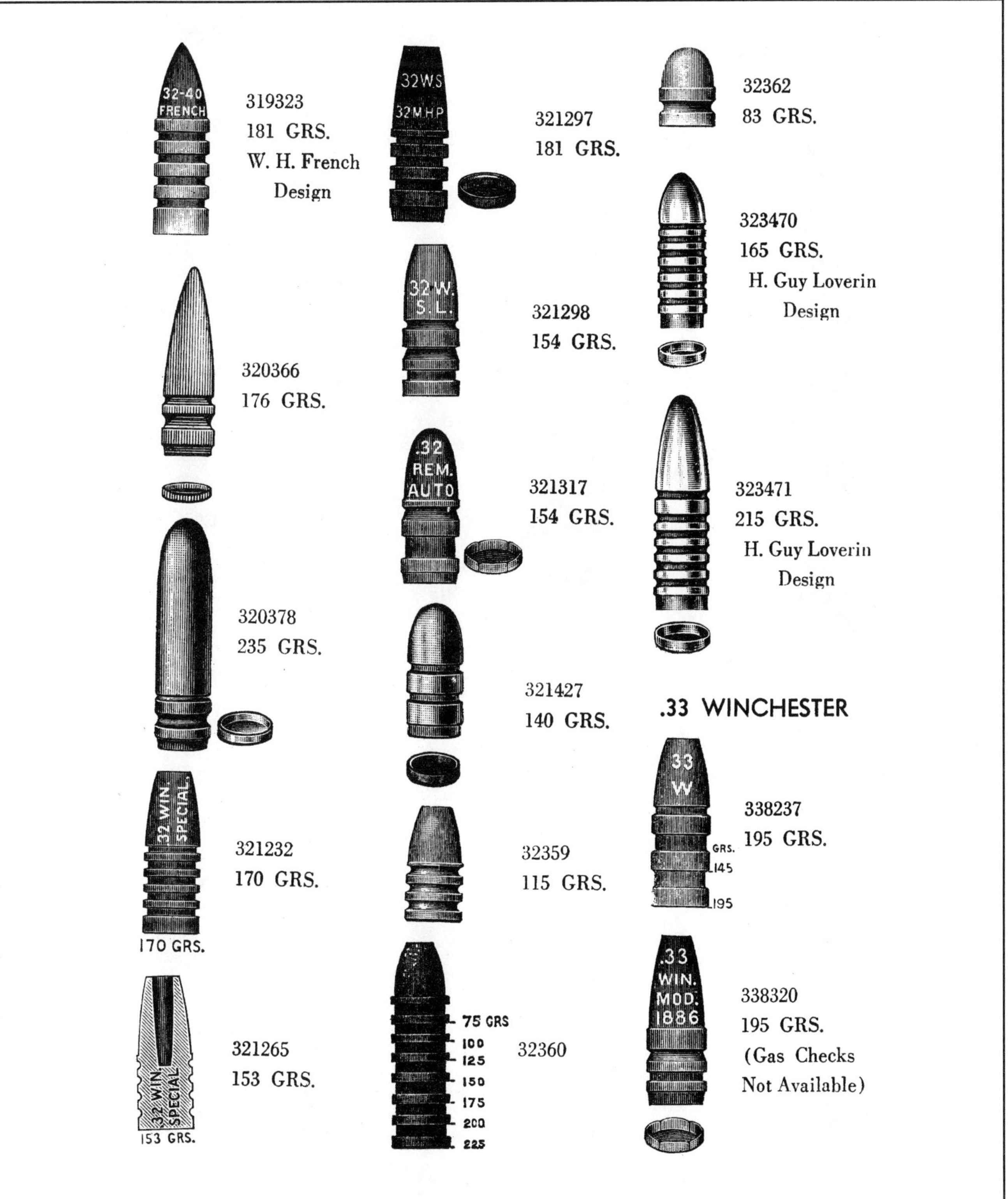

Figure 24-1: Several bullet molds once offered by Ideal and Lyman. (*Continued*)

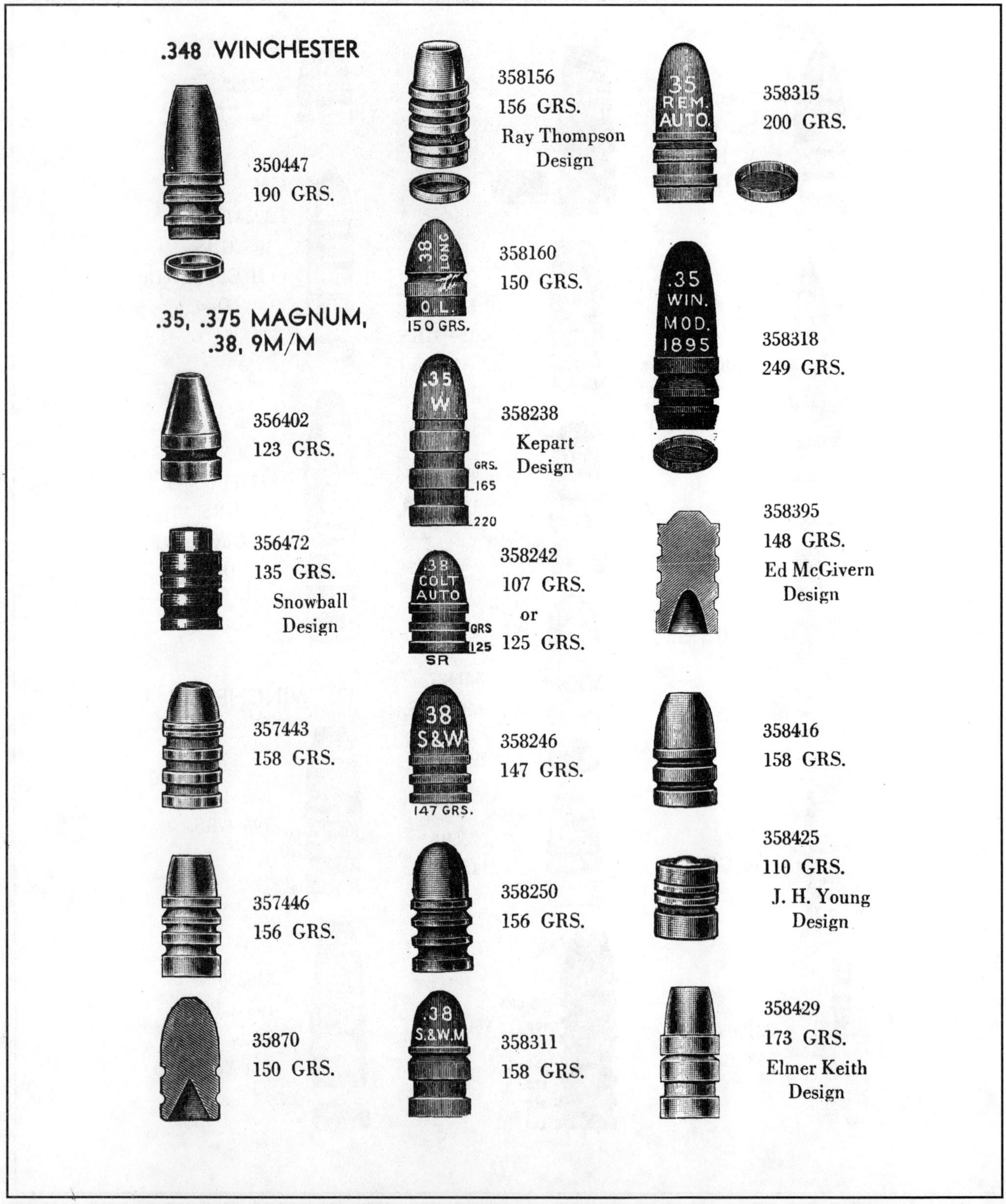
.348 WINCHESTER
350447
190 GRS.
.35, .375 MAGNUM, .38, 9M/M
356402
123 GRS.
356472
135 GRS.
Snowball Design
357443
158 GRS.
357446
156 GRS.
35870
150 GRS.
358156
156 GRS.
Ray Thompson Design
38 LONG
O.L.
150 GRS.
358160
150 GRS.
.35 W
GRS.
165
220
358238
Kepart Design
.38 COLT AUTO
GRS
125
SR
358242
107 GRS.
or
125 GRS.
38 S&W.
147 GRS.
358246
147 GRS.
358250
156 GRS.
.38 S.&W.M
358311
158 GRS.
35 REM. AUTO.
358315
200 GRS.
.35 WIN. MOD. 1895
358318
249 GRS.
358395
148 GRS.
Ed McGivern Design
358416
158 GRS.
358425
110 GRS.
J. H. Young Design
358429
173 GRS.
Elmer Keith Design

Figure 24-1: Several bullet molds once offered by Ideal and Lyman. (*Continued*)

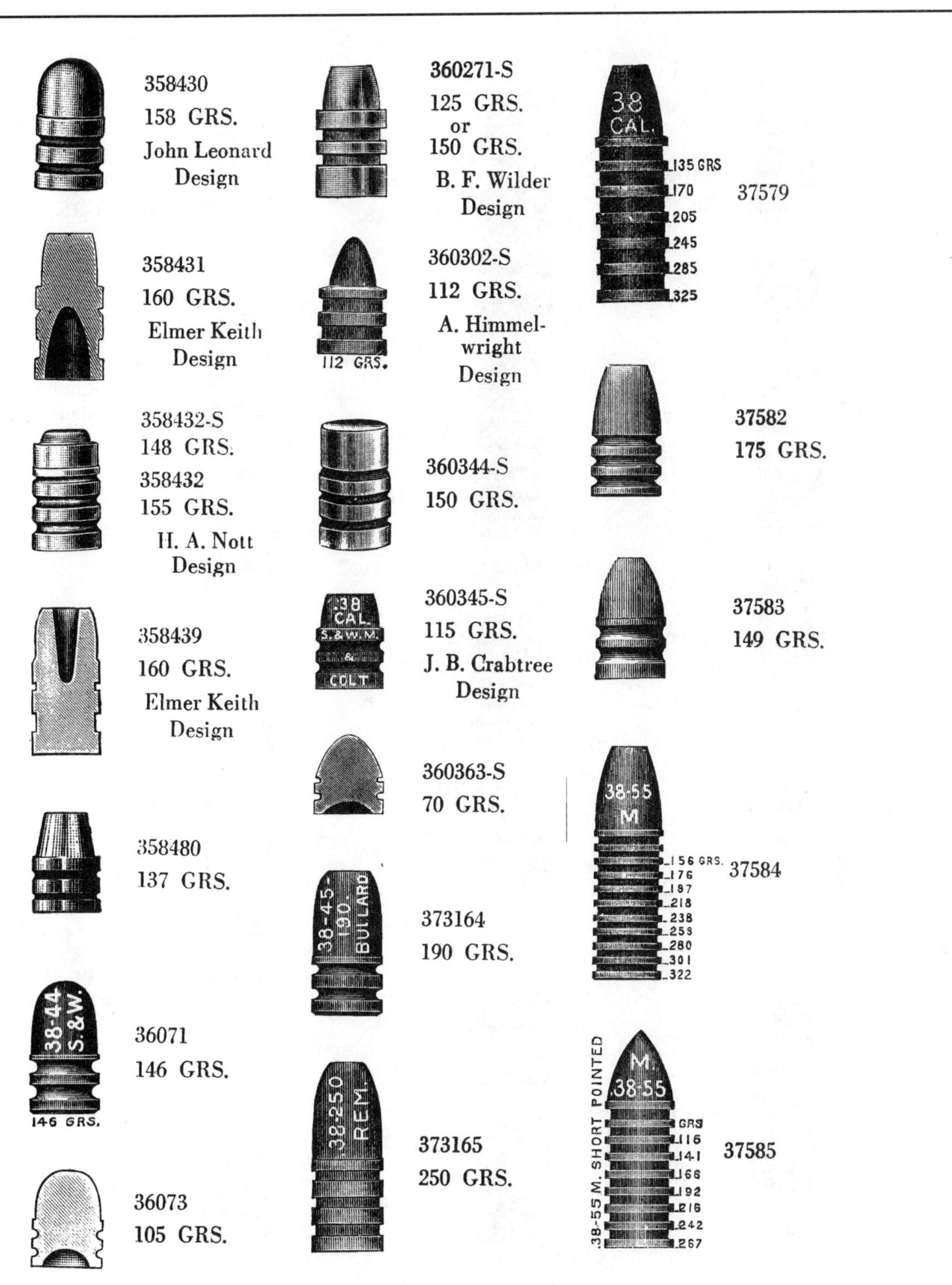

Figure 24-1: Several bullet molds once offered by Ideal and Lyman. (*Continued*)

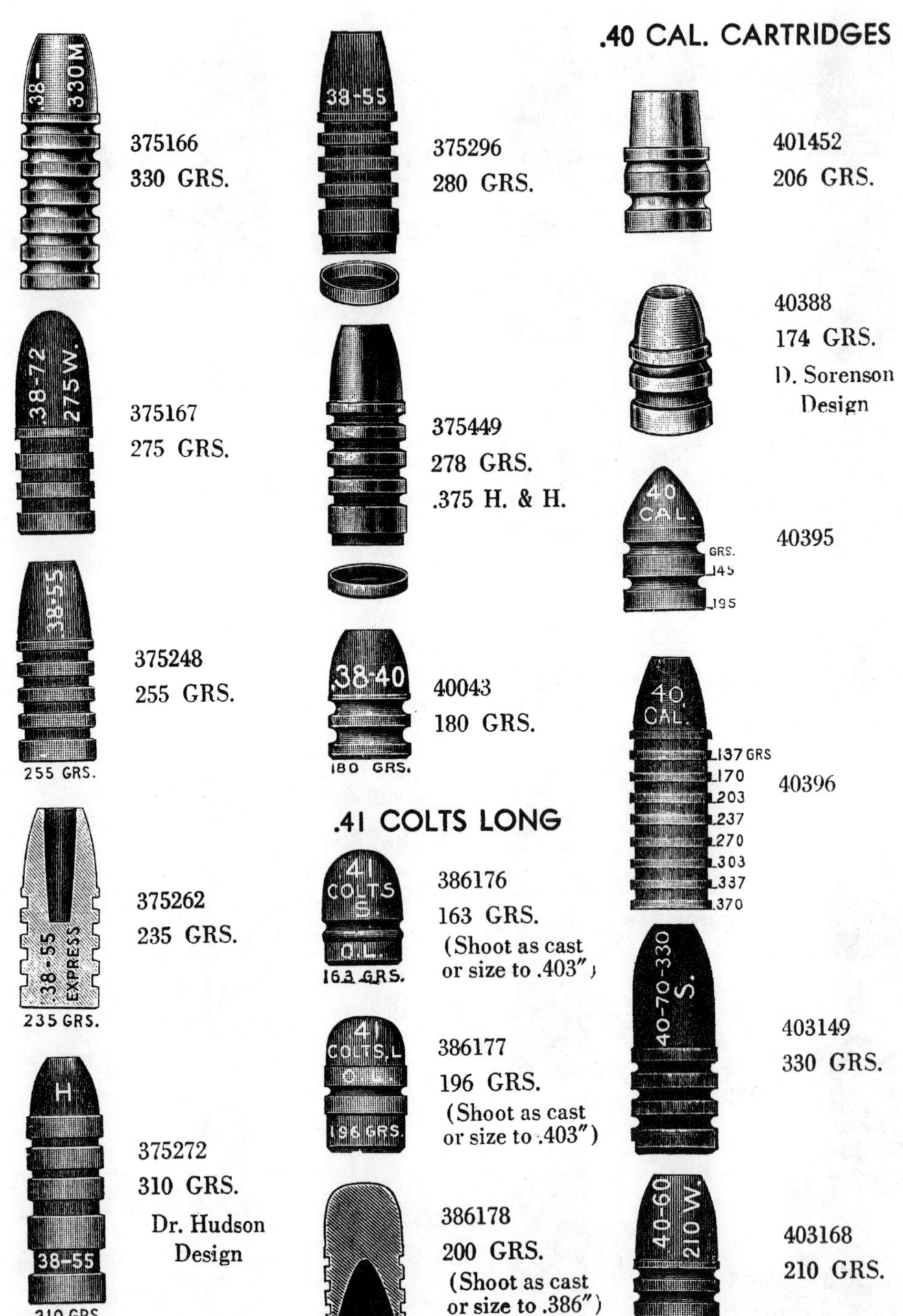

Figure 24-1: Several bullet molds once offered by Ideal and Lyman. (*Continued*)

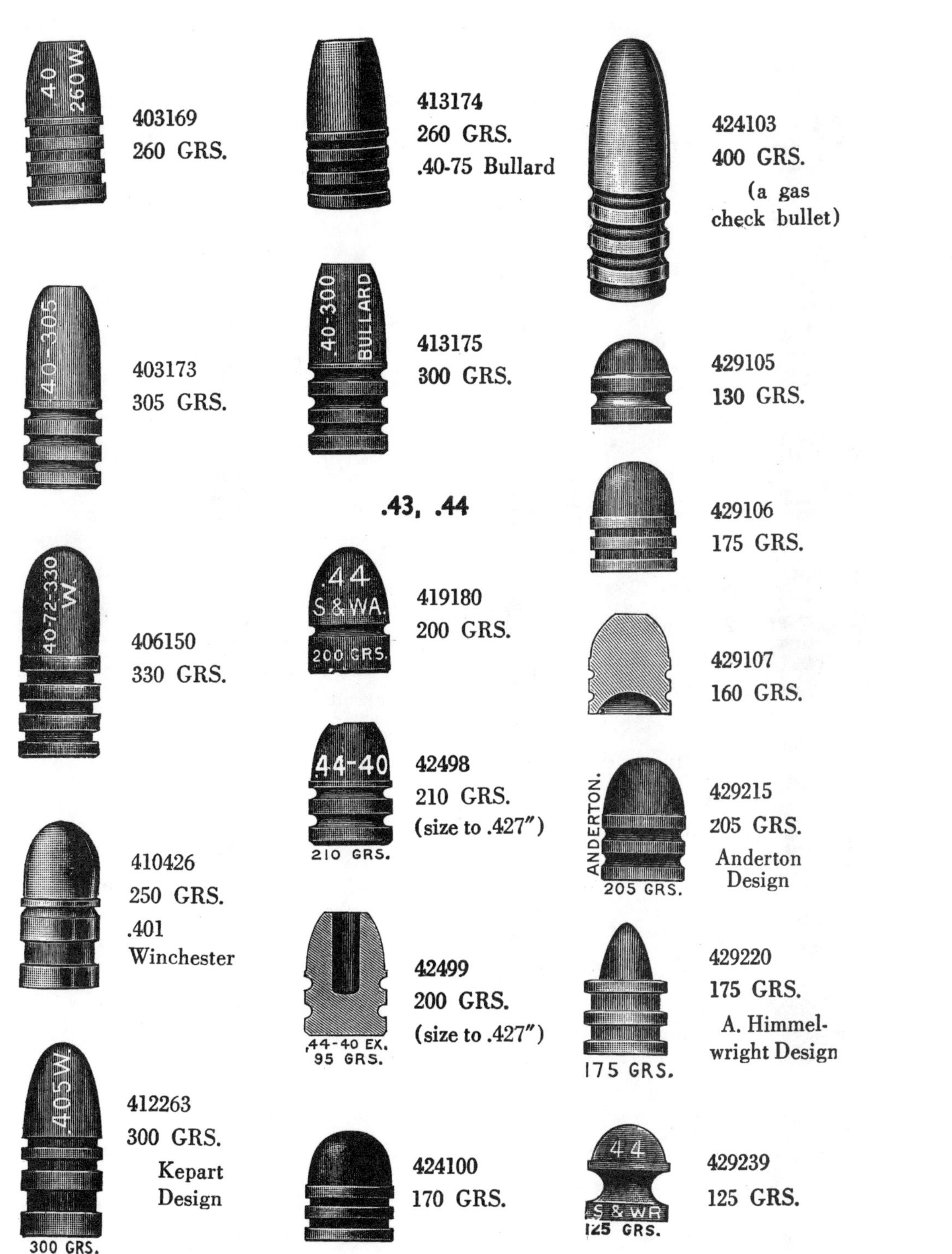

Figure 24-1: Several bullet molds once offered by Ideal and Lyman. (*Continued*)

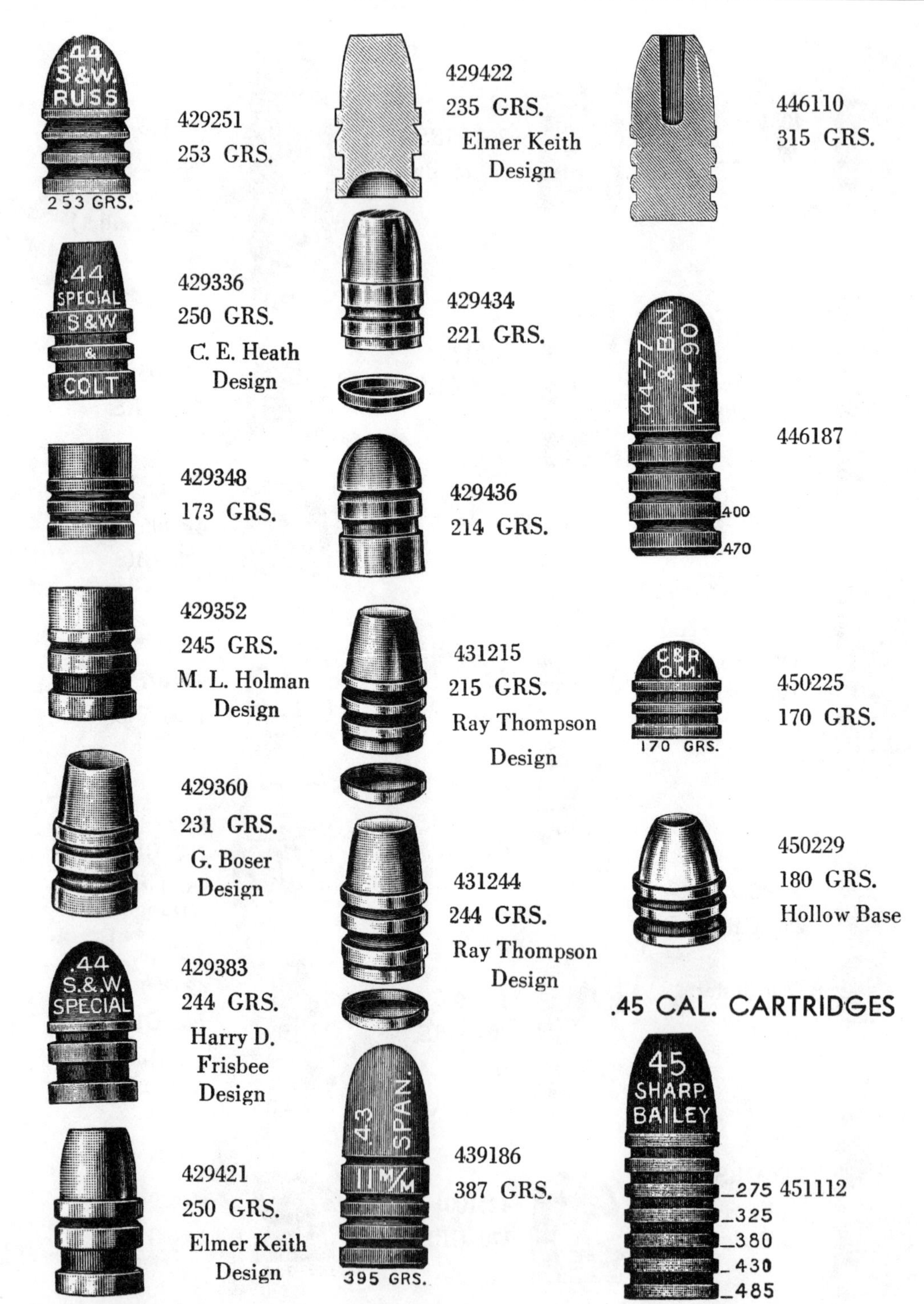

Figure 24-1: Several bullet molds once offered by Ideal and Lyman. (*Continued*)

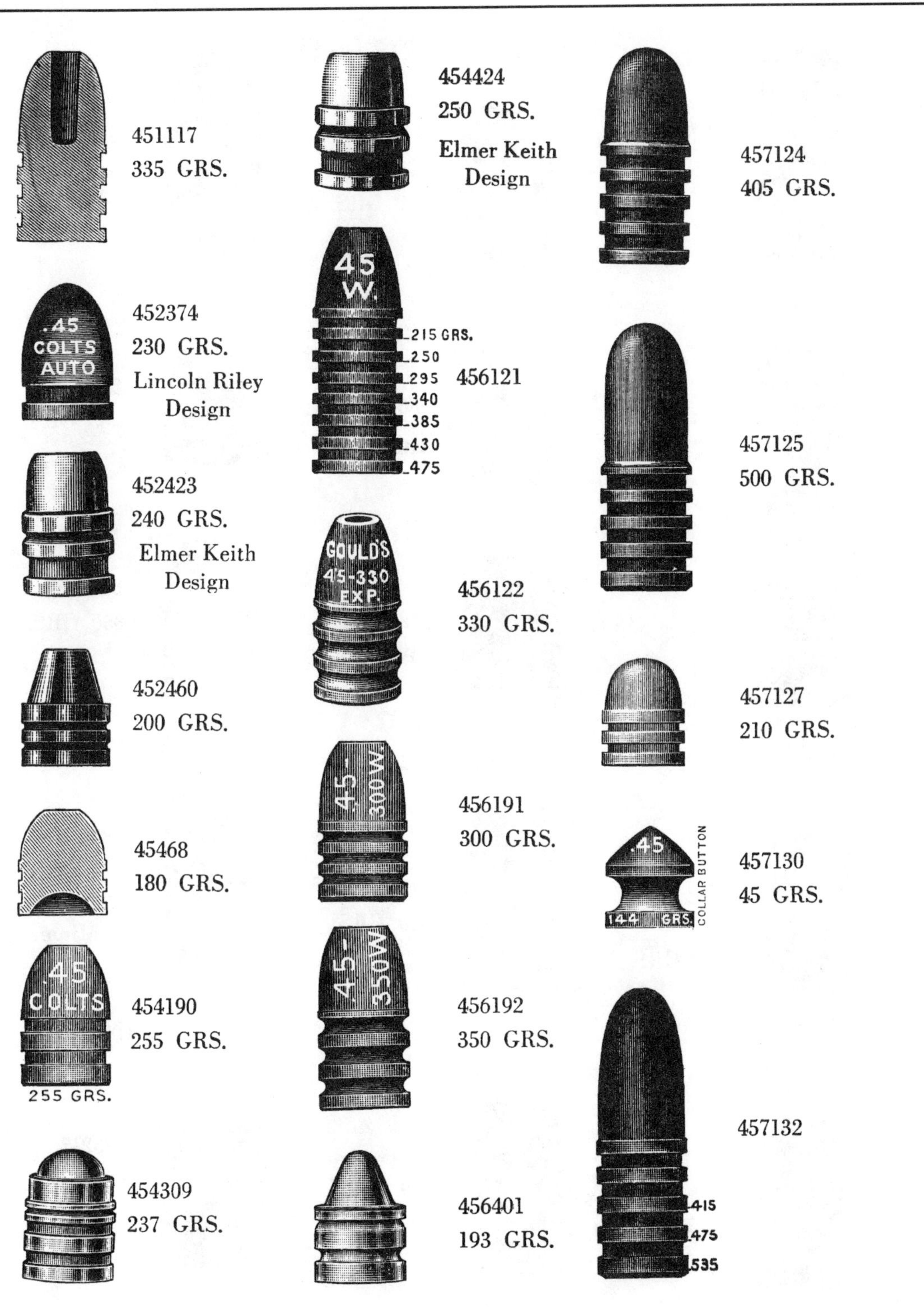

Figure 24-1: Several bullet molds once offered by Ideal and Lyman. (*Continued*)

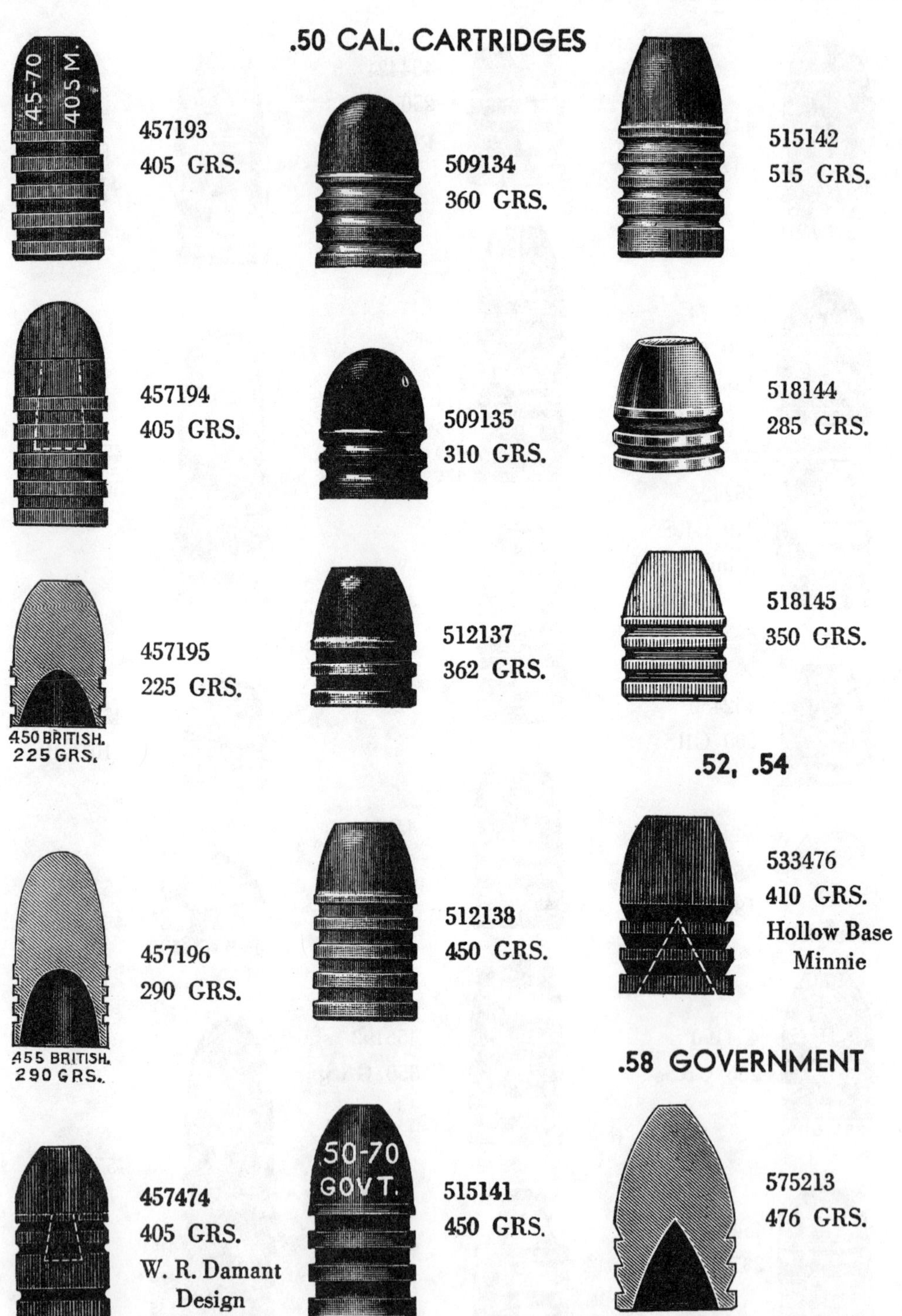

Figure 24-1: Several bullet molds once offered by Ideal and Lyman. (*Continued*)

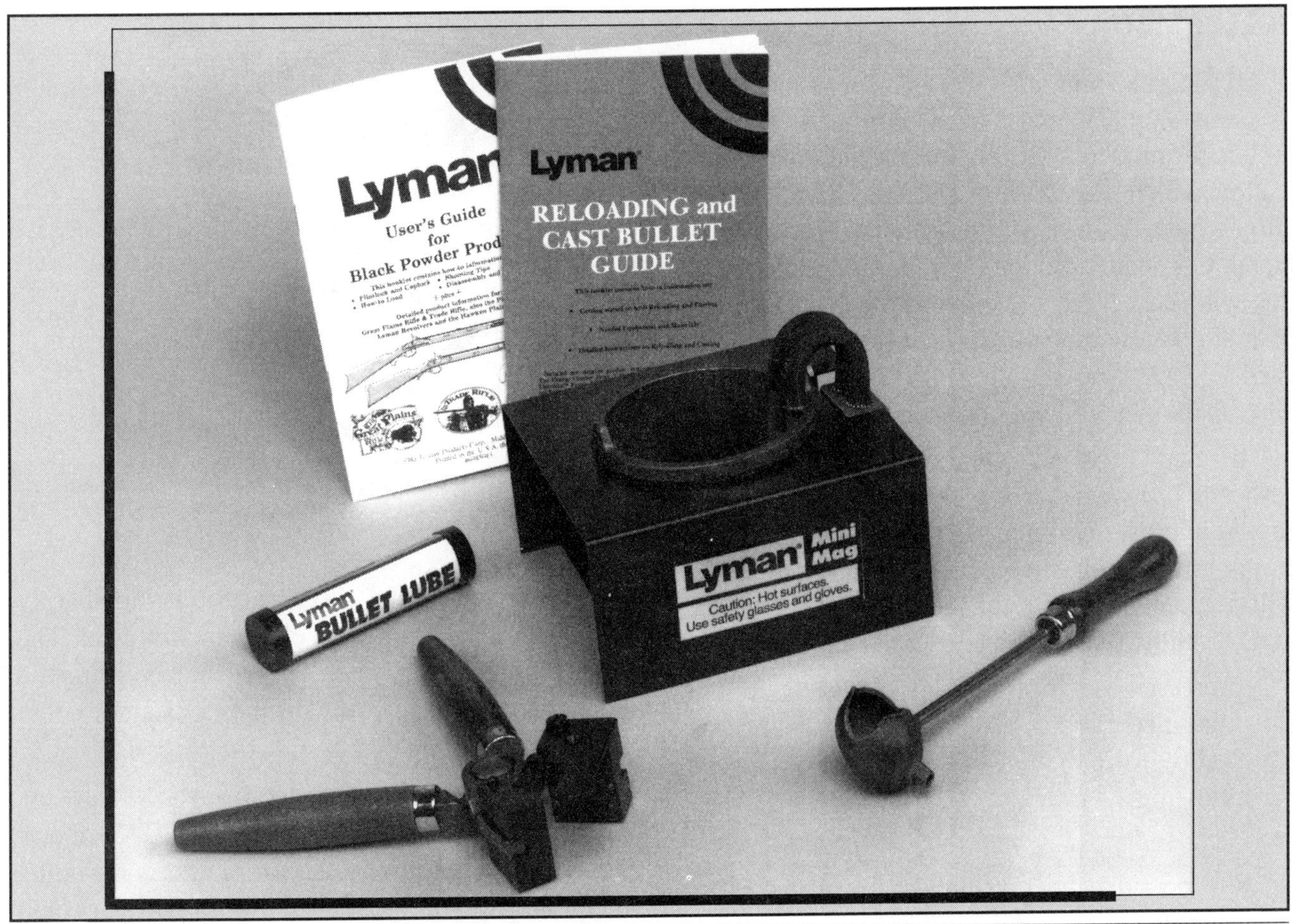

Figure 24-2: These are the minimum tools required for bullet casting. Anything less will give poor results.

BULLET CASTING TOOLS

Very few tools are needed for casting bullets. A simple ladle, a lead-melting pot, a bullet mold, and some bullet lube are all that is needed to get started. You can use a gas or an electric burner as a heat source, but a small electric furnace designed specifically for bullet casting is the best choice. The Lyman "starter" kit in Figure 24-2 is about the minimum amount of tools for casting lead bullets. Note the tube of bullet lube. For best accuracy and to keep the bullets from leading your rifle bore too quickly, you will need to size and lubricate the bullets.

Heed the following safety precautions when using heat to cast bullets:

- Wear heavy clothing and shoes that will protect you if you spill or splatter molten lead.
- Wear safety goggles or a face shield when working with molten lead.
- Wear heavy leather gloves when working with molten lead or when handling the bullet molds.
- Never allow liquids to come near the molten lead. A drop of liquid in the hot lead will cause a violent eruption, causing lead to splatter. Also guard against perspiration dropping into the molten lead.

BULLET METAL

All shotgun slugs and bullets for muzzleloading weapons should be cast from pure lead. To cast bullets for modern rifles, Lyman recommends No. 2 alloy, which shooters have used for decades. This alloy is quite hard, but not quite as hard as Linotype metal. Consequently, to obtain the highest velocities with cast bullets, Linotype metal, combined with the finest high-speed lubricants, should be used. For general shooting, however, the No. 2 alloy is the type of bullet metal recommended.

The metal required to make No. 2 alloy can be gathered from junkyard, gas stations, automotive supply houses, plumbing supply houses, hardware stores, and printing shops. Many of these materials will contain traces of other metals, but for bullet making, they may be considered pure.

Never use lead from auto or marine batteries, since the material can be harmful. Ten pounds of No. 2 alloy for bullet casting may be made using the following:

- 9 pounds wheel weights and 1 pound of 50/50 solder.
- 4 pounds Linotype, 1 pound 50/50 solder, and 5 pounds of pure lead.

MELTING BULLET METAL

One of the first requirements for working with bullet metal is a suitable heat source capable of heating the metal to about 750°to 800° Fahrenheit. If necessary, a simple cast iron pot to hold metal and almost any heat source (electric hotplate, camp stove, etc.) will suffice. An electric lead-melting pot is better, however. It is cleaner, safer, and more convenient. A lead-melting pot with an adjustable thermostat allows the best control of the melting temperature.

Regardless of the type of heat used, heat the metal for about 20 minutes until it becomes liquified and flows freely. As the metal melts, a gray scum will rise to the surface, contrasting sharply with the silver brightness of the molten lead. The scum contains tin which should not be removed because it is the most valuable component of bullet metal.

Figure 24-3: A lead-melting pot with an adjustable thermostat allows the best control of the melting temperature.

To combine this tin with the lead, a process known as fluxing must be performed. This operation is extremely important to obtain good bullet metal and should be done carefully. Drop a small bit of beeswax or bullet lubricant into the mixture so that a smoky gas rises from the top of the pot. This gas should immediately be ignited with a match to eliminate the smoke.

The fluxing procedure can also be performed by using a dry substance, such as the MARVELUX to eliminate smoke and greasy fumes and to obtain a good flux.

Whichever fluxing substance used, be sure to stir the mixture with a suitable instrument — like the lead dipper or clean iron rod, to mix air in with the molten mixture. Properly fluxed metal is almost mirror-bright and flecked with small black and brown particles which must be skimmed off and discarded.

After fluxing, when the metal is hot enough to pour easily through the dipper, it is ready for casting. Use a hardwood stick about 2″ in diameter and

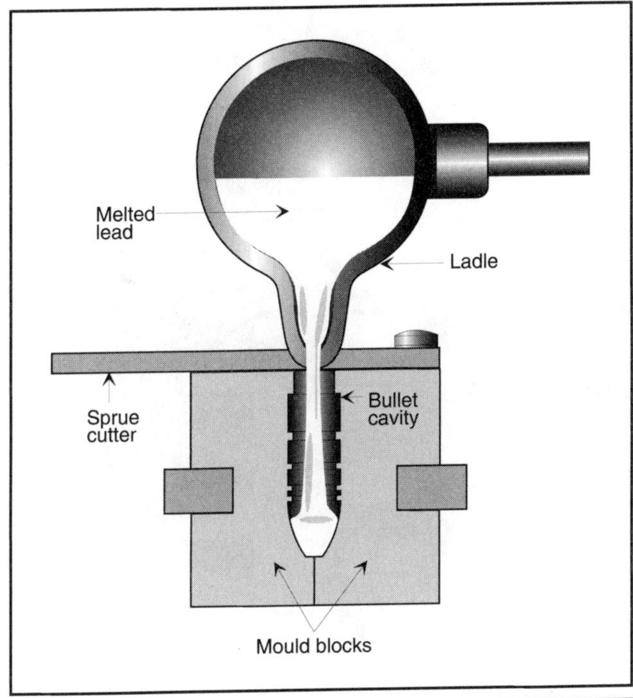

Figure 24-4: Sectional view of bullet mold and dipper during pouring operation.

about 10″ or 12″ long to open the bullet mold. Place a thick pad on the bench next to your lead melting pot or furnace. This will prevent the hot bullets from being damaged as they drop from the mold.

For best results, the bullet molds should be heated prior to pouring the lead. This may be accomplished by setting the mold on the edge of the furnace while the lead is melting.

If a melting pot and lead dipper is used, fill the dipper half-full of the molten bullet metal and place the spout of the dipper against the pouring hole. Holding the mold and dipper together, slowly turn them to a vertical position to fill the mold as shown in Figure 24-4.

The extra metal that runs over the top of the mold is called sprue. It will take only a few seconds for the sprue to harden, and when it does, use the hardwood stick to give the hinged sprue cutter on top of the mold a sharp tap. This will cut off the sprue evenly with the base of the bullet. Save the excess sprue to remelt later.

Now open the bullet mold and let the bullet fall out onto the thick pad on your bench. If the bullet does not fall out freely, use the hardwood stick to rap the hinge pivot sharply. Use only wood for this purpose and never strike the mold blocks. The first few bullets may be imperfect. However, as heat builds up in the mold blocks from casting one bullet after another, the quality of the bullets will improve. The mold-heating process can be sped up by setting the mold on the rim of the furnace or propping it against the top of the melting pot. Never put the mold into the molten lead; doing so can warp it, making it useless.

Wrinkled bullets, like the one shown in Figure 24-5B, indicate that the mold and/or metal is too cool. Frosted bullets (Figure 24-5C) indicate that the mold and/or metal is too hot. If either of these two conditions exist, adjust the heat accordingly. Good bullets (Figure 24-5A) should fill the mold and be clean and sharp. Imperfect bullets should be collected and, along with the sprue, returned to the pot for remelting.

Some bullet-casting furnaces have a bottom-pour spout, which eliminates the need for the dipper. Position the top of the bullet mold relatively snug onto the spout, lift the melting pot's valve handle for a second, and then release it. Once the

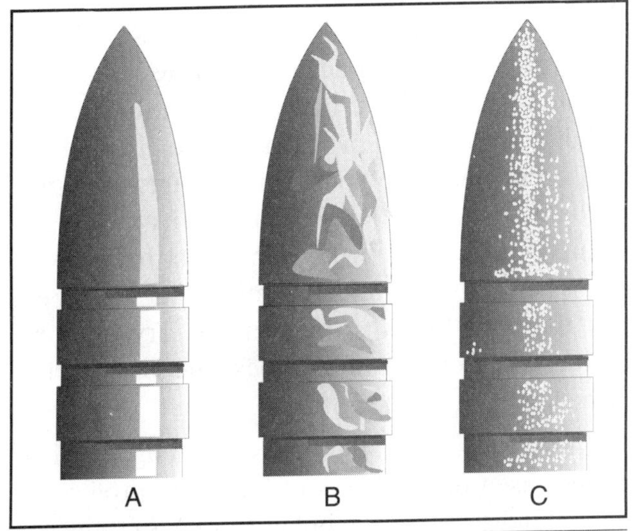

Figure 24-5: Different quality cast bullets.

mold is filled and the sprue has hardened, the remaining operations are the same as discussed previously.

SIZING AND LUBRICATION

For best accuracy and to ensure cleaner-shooting bullets, all cast bullets should be sized and lubricated. The equipment required for this operation can be inexpensive (in the case of Lee manufacturing equipment) to somewhat costly if you purchase a bench-mounted lubricator/sizer and related dies and punches. In general, the sizing process is a method of swaging cast bullets to a standard size that corresponds to or is slightly larger than the groove diameter of the rifle. Bullet sizing also ensures that the bearing bands of each bullet in the group are perfectly round.

The Lee lubricator/sizer kit, which costs less than $20, is a round, shallow pan into which the molded bullets are placed in an upright position. The bullet lubricant is melted into the band and forms a "lake" around each bullet. After the melted lubricant hardens, remove each bullet by running a sizing die over it. Each bullet will be pushed out of the die by the next one to be removed from the lubricant.

Sizing dies are made in a number of diameters for the same caliber bullets. Selecting the correct size requires that you accurately measure the dimensions of your rifle barrel, at both the muzzle and directly ahead of the chamber. To obtain these measurements, drive a pure lead slug into the barrel or chamber mouth, remove it, and then measure the results with a micrometer. Your cast bullet must never be smaller than this diameter, but it can be a few thousandths of an inch larger. Try different bullet sizes until you find the best one for your rifle or handgun.

Gas checks are little cups of gilding metal or copper used on the bases of bullets to protect the bases (and sides) of the bullet from gas cutting. In turn, the rifle bore is protected from exposure to tiny pieces of molten tin, which would be ironed into the bore walls as the bullet overtakes them.

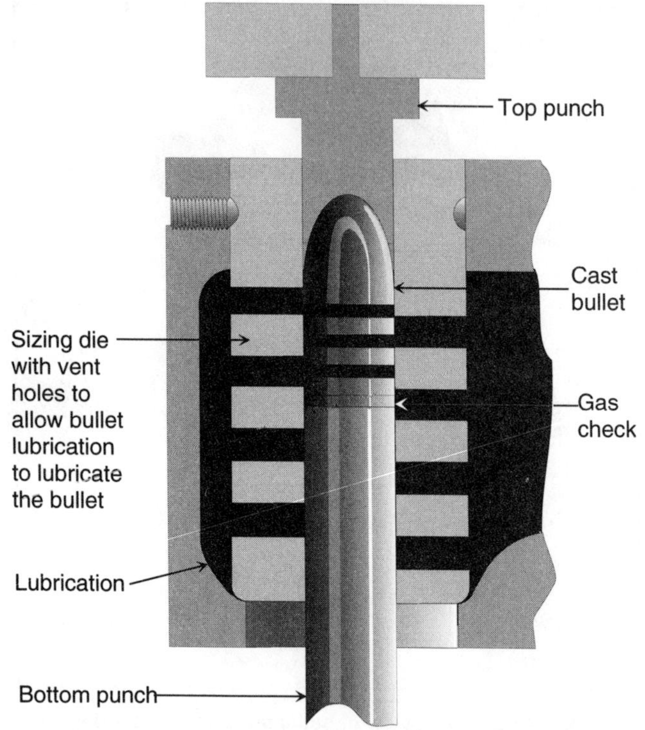

Figure 24-19: Cross-sectional view of a typical cast bullet sizing die.

Gas checks are normally applied as a part of the sizing and lubrication operation. It is important that the gas checks be squarely seated on the bullet. A crooked gas check will cause bullet inaccuracy.

To install the gas check, fit it on the bullet base as you are placing the bullet into the sizing die. The top punch will then push the bullet into the sizing die to swage it and the gas check to the proper diameter. Lubricant is applied to the bullet at the same time. On reversing the handle of the press, the bottom punch pushes the bullet back out the top of the sizing die to be grabbed with the fingers and set aside for later loading into your cases. The lubricant is forced into the sizing die by screw pressure, the same way hand-operated automotive grease guns work. *See* Figure 24-19.

Chapter 25

Bullet Swaging

Bullet swaging is the process of forming lead and copper alloy or pure copper jacket materials into finished bullets by using pressure. This differs from casting because no heat is required. The materials are made to flow under high pressure at room temperature into precise conformity with a highly finished, extremely strong die.

Corbin Manufacturing & Supply, Inc. of Phoenix, Oregon, is considered the authority on bullet swaging. Corbin furnishes dies, tools, and equipment for most swaging operations.

An ordinary reloading press can be used to supply the pressure for swaging several kinds of bullets. Some Corbin dies are made for use in standard reloading presses. Examples include the R.C.B.S. Rockchucker, the Pacific Multipower, and the C-H Champion. If the press accepts regular R.C.B.S. shell holders, and has standard reloading-die threads ($^7/_8$ inch × 14 threads per inch), the Corbin dies will fit the press.

Some types of presses, however, are more suitable than others for swaging. Turrets, lighter weight presses, and some special presses where the handle swings over the top are not suitable due to the way the dies operate. Great strength and power are not required for the Corbin dies that are available for reloading presses. All of the bullets that Corbin has for regular presses can be swaged with no more effort than resizing a case in a full-length resizing die.

Pressure is high because the dies are closed or semi-closed and the area of the punch is small. If you put 20 pounds of force on the press handle of a compound leverage press, and set the die high enough so that the press barely touches the end of the stroke when the punch touches the bullet, you can easily generate rifle chamber pressures with that die in some calibers. Brute force, however, is unnecessary and can be damaging.

Corbin dies for reloading presses are available in .224 and .243 rifle calibers and in the handgun sizes from .25 ACP to .38 Special. They also have jacket-making and bullet-reducing dies for reloading presses. A stronger Corbin press, the Mity-Mite System, shown in Figure 25-1 on the next page, is used to handle special jobs like rebated boattail bullets and big calibers. The Mity-Mite System is designed to withstand the heaviest requirements of bullet swaging. It features a special horizontal ram press, full floating alignment of the external punches using a universal floating punch holder, automatic bullet ejection, automatic retraction of the point-forming ejection pin, more than double

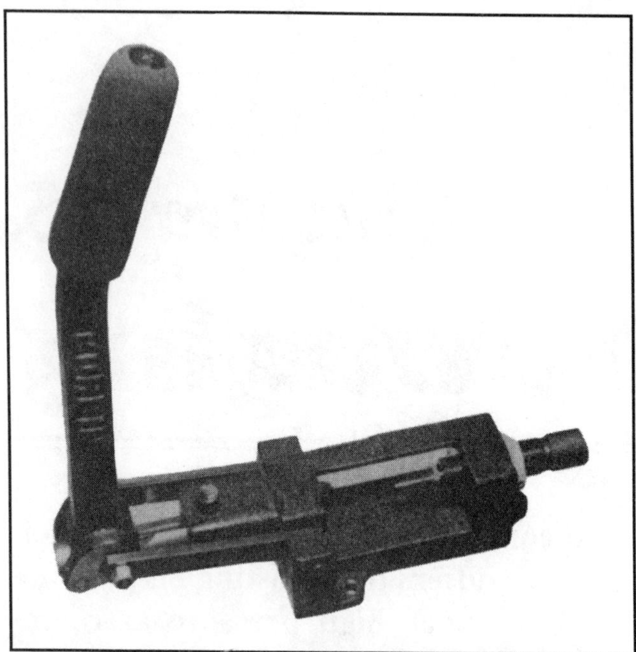

Figure 25-1: The Mity-Mite bullet-swaging press is a very accurate and extremely powerful press designed for swaging bullets only. Special dies and punches fit the ram and a floating alignment punch holder holds a punch in the press head. Automatic ejection occurs on the backstroke. This press was originally built by SAS dies in the 1950s, and a precision version is made today by Corbin for commercial and benchrest bullet swaging.

the power of a conventional reloading press, plus excellent "feel" that is not available with hydraulic presses. It is fast enough for commercial work, precise enough for target work, and is reasonably priced.

Figure 25-2: A set of Corbin swaging dies is a group of from two to five dies that together will form a completed bullet.

The dies and punches for the larger calibers only fit this press. They are easy to change from one caliber to another, and they come in sets. A set includes from two to five dies that together form a completed bullet. It includes the punches necessary for each die. *See* Figure 25-2.

The exact number of dies and punches needed for swaging depends on the caliber, bullet style, and jacket. Therefore, because of various price ranges, it isn't possible to predetermine the exact cost of equipment.

First, there is the jacket and the lead core. All-lead bullets can be swaged, but swaging gives you the choice of jacketed bullets also. Using pure lead in a variety of jacket styles and assemblies gives the density and high ballistic coefficient of pure lead, freedom from leading, control over expansion, and precision at high velocity.

Lead cores, which are swaged to form the heart of the bullet, can be cast from scrap lead in Corbin molds. This method is much faster than bullet casting, since Corbin molds eject upward and mount to the bench to be operated with one hand. This simultaneously produces four cores of any weight desired in one caliber, or rolls of precision-drawn lead wire can be cut with a die-type core cutter that measures out a precise length of core each time the handle is pulled.

Casting costs less than the lead wire method, but is usually more time-consuming. Cutting lead cores, although faster, is a little more expensive per bullet but still very reasonable compared to buying bullets.

Lead wire is sold in 175,000-grain spools. Divide by the bullet weight to see how many bullets can be obtained from one spool.

The lead wire used must be small enough to fit into the chosen bullet jacket. To make a core most accurate in weight, a core swage die, shown in Figure 25-3 on the next page, is used. It will accept either cast or cut lead cores, which should be 2-3 grains heavier than the weight of the bullet desired.

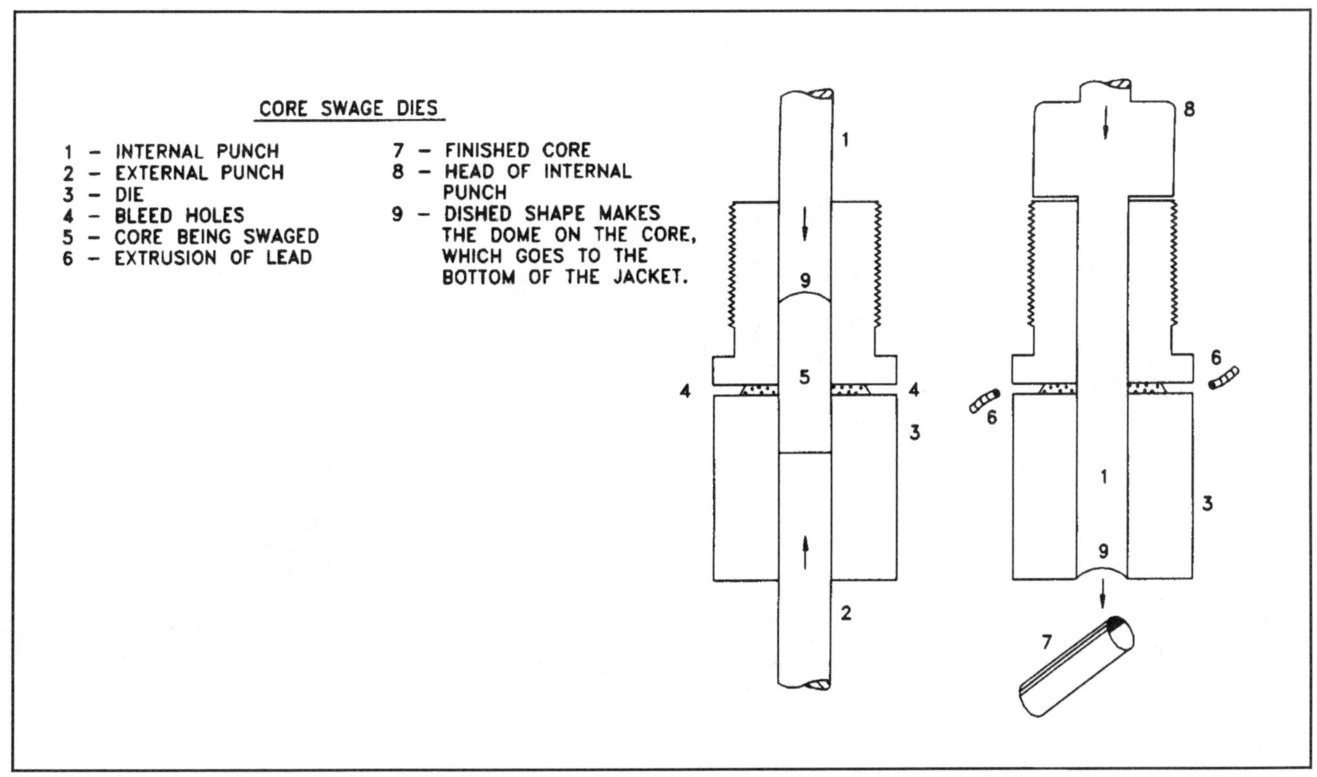

Figure 25-3: Core swage dies.

This allows for tolerance of weight. The die will swage these cores to a slightly shorter but larger diameter that is smooth and perfectly round, with correctly shaped ends.

The weight is adjusted by the core swage die. Small bleed holes surround the interior of the die and permit the tiny lead wires to be swaged from the surplus lead weight left in the core. Setting the press (adjusting the floating punch holder) so that when the ram moves all the way forward, the precise amount of volume is left between the external and internal punch within the die, gives the correct lead weight. It also automatically removes any variation in the core by swaging or pressing the excess lead into the bleed holes.

This near-perfect core is automatically ejected from the Mity-Mite die on the backstroke. Next, the core seating die, shown in Figure 25-4 on the next page, is used to insert the core into a jacket and to expand both upward to a precise diameter.

The core seating die is a straight, perfectly round, and highly polished cylinder. The internal punch usually presses on the bottom of the jacket, although for special jobs you can do this backwards. The external punch determines the kind of bullet that is made.

Bullet jackets vary in thickness, so a punch diameter that fits the jacket is needed. If it's too small, the lead will spurt out around the punch. If it's too large, the punch will plow up jacket material as it is pressed down. Jackets made of copper tubing are usually thick, requiring a small diameter punch. Those made of thin-walled rimfire cases, for making no-cost .224 or 6mm bullets, require a larger diameter punch.

To make semi-wadcutter pistol bullets, use a punch with a cavity machined into the end instead of a flat-tip punch to press the lead core. The lead core is made longer than the jacket so that when it is seated, it expands in the bullet jacket to touch the

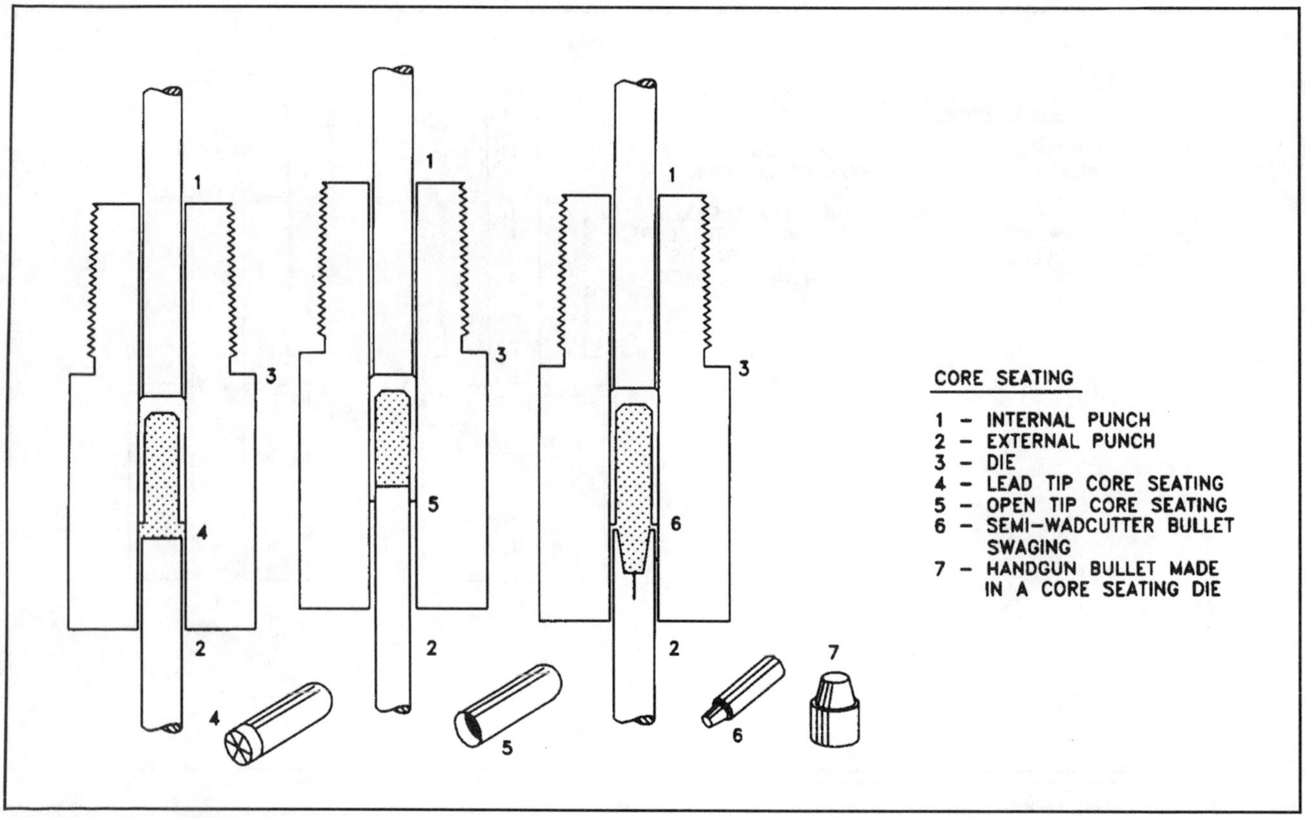

CORE SEATING

1 – INTERNAL PUNCH
2 – EXTERNAL PUNCH
3 – DIE
4 – LEAD TIP CORE SEATING
5 – OPEN TIP CORE SEATING
6 – SEMI-WADCUTTER BULLET SWAGING
7 – HANDGUN BULLET MADE IN A CORE SEATING DIE

Figure 25-4: Core-seating die.

die walls and fills up the cavity in the punch tip, taking the shape of the cavity. Semi-wadcutter jacketed bullets, as well as those of any other shape, can be made this way. *See* Figure 25-5.

When making a bullet in one die, enough lead must be available to ensure that the external punch doesn't press against the edge of the jacket. *See* Figure 25-6. If less than the correct amount of lead is used, the punch will press against the edge of the unfilled area of the jacket cavity, crushing the jacket. The jacket won't be able to jump over the edge of the punch and will start to curve inside the

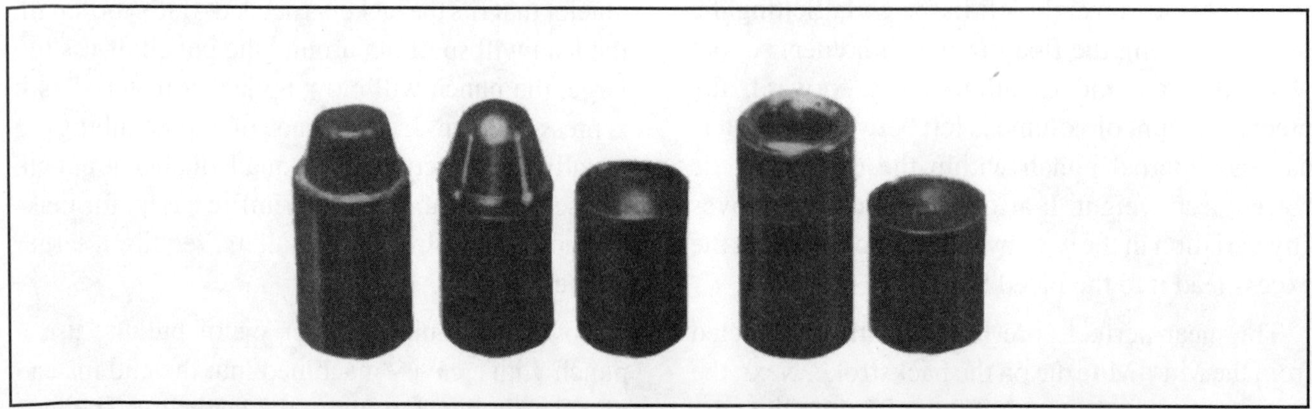

Figure 25-5: Straight-wall dies make bullets such as these, all of which have a small step between the cylinder portion and the actual ogive. These may be called semi-wadcutter styles. The actual nose shape is controlled by the cavity in the bottom punch, which can bear only against the lead core, not the jacket.

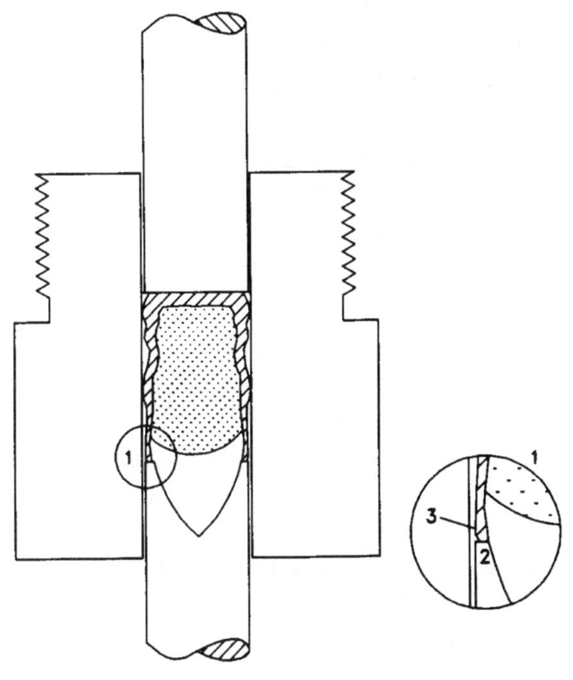

Figure 25-6: (1) Detail of improper core length for punch. Punch edge (2) is crushing jacket (3).

punch cavity. Jacketed bullets that are made in only one die are called short-jacket bullets.

To make any bullet with the jacket brought around the nose, like those shown in Figure 25-7, a matched set of two dies must be used. The core seating die is smaller than the point forming die, which is the next die in the set. This enables the slug to be ejected and to slip easily into the point forming the die's cavity. For example, to make a .357" bullet, use one core seating die for making semi-wadcutter bullets, and a slightly smaller die for seating cores to make a bullet with the jacket curved away from the full diameter.

The difference in die size for making handgun bullets is not enough to worry about. Approximately 0.0002"- 0.0005" is all the difference needed in a matched set of swage dies to allow proper operation of a core seat and point forming set. Therefore, using a core seating die for a semi-wadcutter nose shape with a step junction between the jacket end and the start of the nose is acceptable. For perfection in your handgun bullets, specify the core seater for making the final diameter of the bullet only, not for making rifle-style bullets with a point forming die at a later date.

Each step in swaging requires that the slug fit easily into the next die. A 0.2240" seated core and jacket cannot easily fit into a 0.2240" point forming die. Therefore, the point forming die should be 0.2242" in diameter, or the core seater should produce a 0.2238" seated core and jacket.

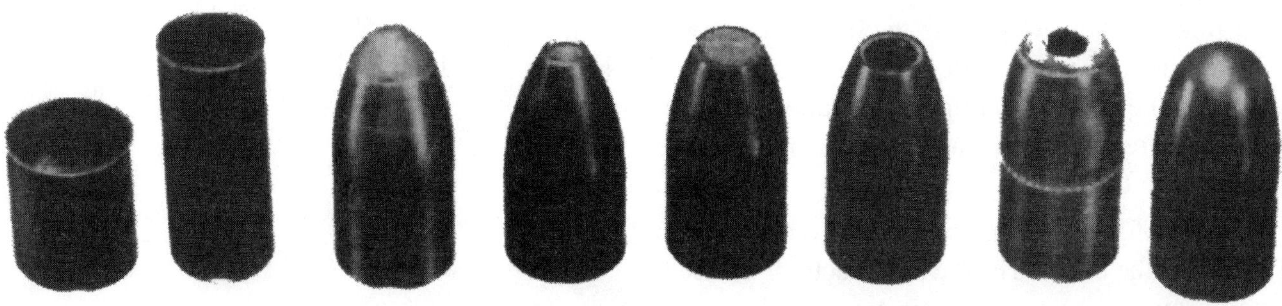

Figure 25-7: All of these bullets are made in two steps. First they must be formed in the core seating or straight-wall die, when they have a straight cylinder shape. Lead is normally left sticking out the end. Then, this slug is run lead-first into the ogive-wall die to form the rounded part.

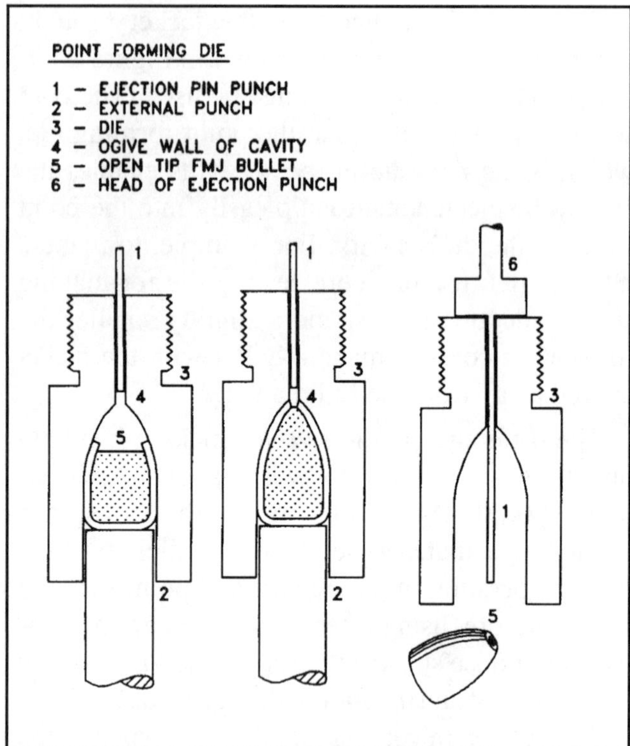

Figure 25-8: Point forming die. (1) Ejection pin punch. (2) External punch. (3) Die. (4) Ogive wall of cavity. (5) Open-tip FMC bullet. (6) Head of ejection pin.

The point forming die, shown in Figure 25-8, is the most costly die to make, and requires the highest skill in die making.

At the tip of this die is a tiny hole, just big enough for a tough spring steel ejection pin that is as long as the die. The pin is held back by a spring in regular reloading press dies, or by a tool steel pin in Corbin's Mity-Mite system. The ejection pin is held back from the die cavity while the bullet is being swaged, but upon ejection, it is driven down until it contacts the edge of the tip of the bullet jacket. More pressure makes the pin shove the bullet out of the die by its nose.

The size of the ejection pin depends on the size of the tip of the bullet. The die manufacturer needs this information because certain types of bullets and jackets have minimum size limits. If the bullet requires too much ejection pressure, an ejection pin with a very small diameter will bend and can't eject the bullet. Also, if you want a lead tip on the bullet, the dies must be designed accordingly.

Pressing the bullet out by its nose means that the flat end of the ejection pin will push a small flat area on the bullet tip. This is fine for most bullets, since the pin is typically about 0.081" or less in diameter. But to form a sharp spitzer lead tip or finish off the lead tip in another way, a die with a slightly larger diameter than the point forming die is needed. The larger diameter enables the bullet to be guided against a special internal punch having the desired shape lapped into its tip. This die, a lead-tip forming die, shown in Figure 25-9, requires so little pressure that the bullet diameter will not be changed. It is used only when a tiny flat area at the tip of the bullet is not required. This type of die is never used with open-tip bullets where the lead is seated completely with the jacket.

The lead-tip forming die comes with an internal punch only, since the same external punch is used to form the point. The point forming die has a punch that slips easily into its cavity. The bullet is formed with the open end of the jacket toward the top of the point forming die, except for full jacket, military-ball bullets.

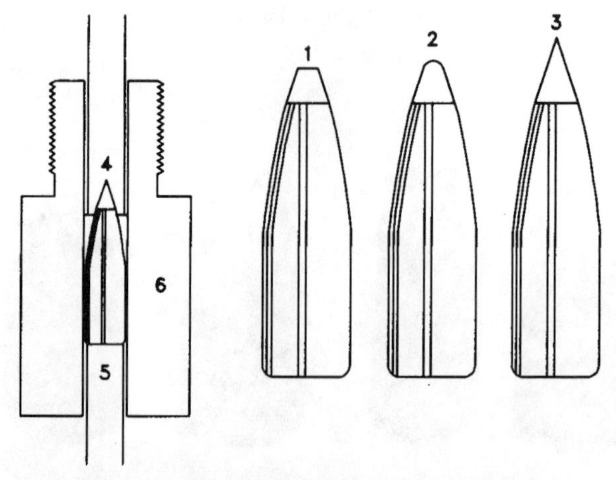

Figure 25-9: Lead-tip forming die. (1) Lead tip as it comes from the point-forming die. (2) Reshaped semi-spitzer tip. (3) Reshaped spitzer tip. (4) Internal punch. (5) External punch. (6) Die.

These are formed with the base of the jacket toward the closed end of the die.

All the bullets described so far have a flat base. To make a boattail bullet, the open and closed ends of the jacket must be curved. This presents a problem in a single die, because there is no way to get the bullet back out. However, the boattail can be formed while seating the core, using pressure of the lead to push the jacket out to meet the die.

A boattail die set differs from the standard flat-base die set, because it includes a boattail preforming die between the core seater and the core swager dies. The core seating punch goes into the jacket for open-tip bullets exactly as does a flat-base core-seating die. The internal punch precisely matches the base diameter of the boattail bullet and is exactly long enough to close the die where the base of the boattail bullet will be formed.

This punch runs forward to the die mouth to eject the bullet, which at this point is a straight-sided cylinder with a boattail on the closed end. The core is further seated and the boattail takes its final form in the second operation. The point forming die does its usual job, but the external punch is replaced with a punch having the boattail cavity machined into it.

Since these punches have a very thin edge to avoid putting a shoulder into the jacket, the true boattail uses very fragile punches. The slightest misalignment will damage the edges. The rebated boattail has many advantages over the true boattail. It has longer punch life, is very accurate, and is popular with long range centerfire shooters.

Jackets for swaged bullets are normally available for about half the cost of a complete bullet. In some of the larger rifle calibers, however, jackets are not available. In this case, dies are available to close the ends of ordinary copper tubing (type L, hard-drawn copper) and reduce it from standard fractional sizes to any proper diameter for swaging bullets. This is especially handy for bullets in

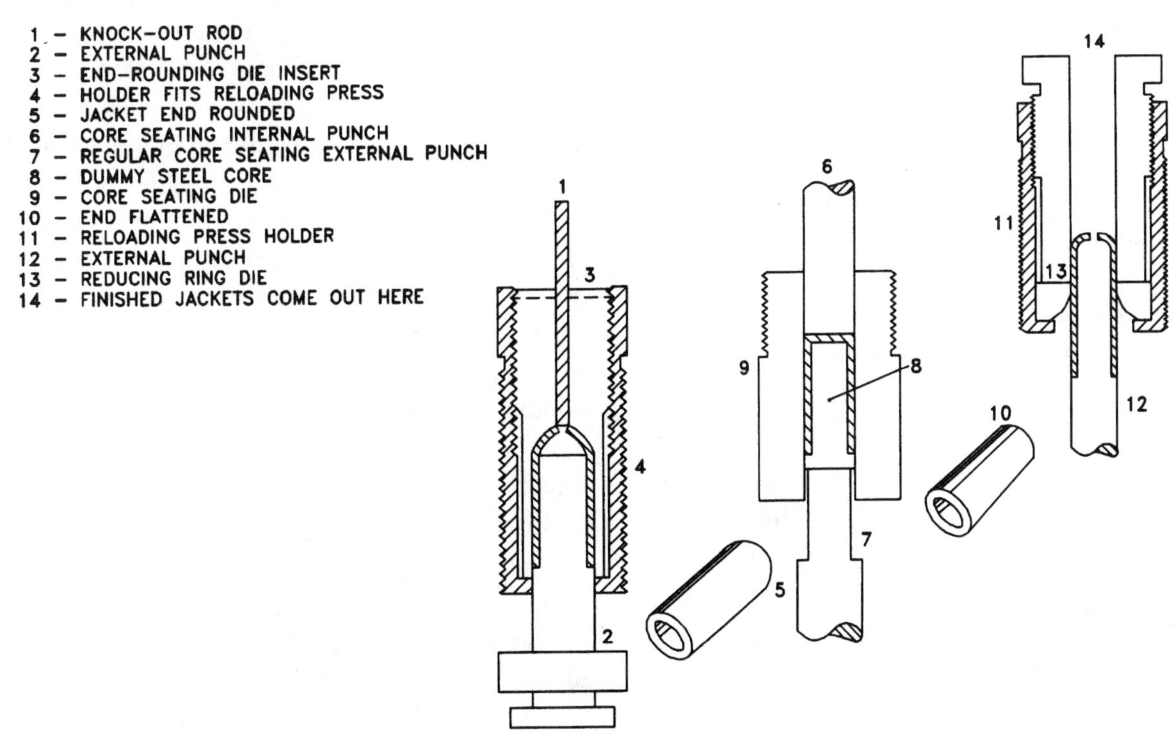

Figure 25-10: Copper tubing jacket-maker set.

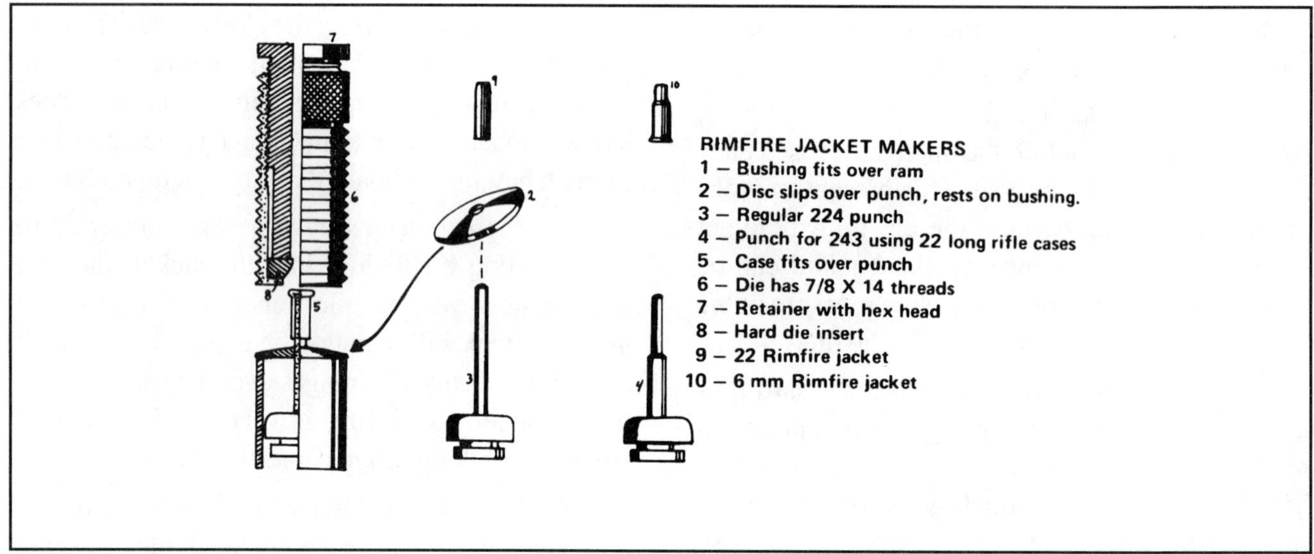

Figure 25-11: Rimfire jacket maker.

0.358", 0.375", 0.458", and larger diameters. A copper tubing jacket-maker set, shown in Figure 25-10, has an end-rounding die that puts a half-caliber round ball end on the piece of tubing cut to the desired length from the straight sections available. A dummy steel core is used inside this jacket in a regular core seating die to flatten and close the end. A draw die is then used to reduce the diameter to the size of the bullet.

Corbin's rimfire case jacket-maker dies, shown in Figure 25-11, can draw a .22 Long Rifle, Short, or CB Cap fired case into an excellent jacket for a .224 bullet. Corbin makes similar jacket makers for 6mm jackets from .22 Long Rifle cases, and also from .22 WMR cases.

To make rifle bullet jackets from fired rimfire cases, wash the cases in hot, soapy water. Dry them and press them partly through the ring die with the punch provided before ejecting them from the punch on the backstroke. A disc slips over the punch and a tube of steel contacts the disc on the down stroke of the press before the punch is installed. After the punch has been installed on a number of these cases, set the die lower and push them all the way through. This method requires very little effort.

After drawing the jackets, heat treat them for about 30 minutes at 500°F in a conventional kitchen oven, and allow to cool slowly overnight. This keeps them from wrinkling and folding when the bullet is swaged. Rimfire jackets are very explosive even at lower speeds, and are so explosive that they cannot be used at much higher than 3,200 fps without exploding in the air. They are ideal for varmint shooting, since they seldom cause a ricochet. The accuracy of these jackets is excellent, and because they are thin, they produce little friction. They are also easy on the rifling as long as the velocity is held to accurate limits. Fouling is almost nonexistent at 3,200 fps, but becomes worse at 3,500 fps and higher. Consequently, many shooters like to hold velocities to around 3300 fps, and certainly no higher than 3500 fps.

The advantage of using rimfire jackets is the low cost. If scrap lead is used, bullets can be made at almost no cost. Many shooters try swaging because of the lure of an unlimited supply of free bullets. The accuracy of these bullets and the satisfaction derived from swaging justifies the initial interest.

Chapter 26
Lead and Steel Shot

"Shotshells" or simply "shells" as they are known in the United States are termed "cartridges" in England. Shotshells have been made in brass, paper or plastic tubes —the latter encased within a brass head, which is flanged so it can be grasped by the gun's extractor. Inside the case is a base wad which, when the brass head is crimped, binds the tube, base wad and brass head together. This prevents the backward escape of powder gas through the shell. Both the brass head and base wad are perforated with a hole that accepts the primer and allows it to ignite the powder inside the case.

The shotshell, once primed, receives a powder charge over which are pressed one or more wads at considerable pressure. Many manufacturers and reloaders insert a cup and wad directly over the powder charge, which effectively prevents pattern-disrupting gas leakage into the shot column. A charge of shot is then placed over the wads and the unfilled end of the tube is crimped over the shot, making the shell ready for use. The three basic types of crimps are cone, rolled, and star — the latter being the most popular and widely used type of shotshell crimp.

Some earlier shotshells were loaded with round balls (often referred to as "punkin balls") for deer-size game. The rifled slug did not come into use until later in the 20th century. Winchester introduced their slugs in the 1930s.

MAKING SHOT FOR SHOTSHELLS

Lead is an ancient metal. It was first used in the year 3000 B.C. at the present site of the Dardanelles in a city called Abyeos. Lead was well known in biblical times and is mentioned in Exodus and many other places in the Old Testament.

In the days of the Pharaohs, lead was used to make solder and lead pipes, and to glaze pottery. The Egyptians made the first crude dropped lead, which was used as projectiles in slings.

Lead shot for muzzleloading shotguns and early shotshells was made by dropping molten lead from a shot tower. This method of manufacturing lead shot was invented in 1782 by William Watts, a plumber in Bristol, England. One night he dreamed that he was in a rainstorm and the raindrops were lead spheres. When he awoke in the morning, he was so impressed by his dream that he decided to try dropping melted lead from a great height to see if it formed a sphere in dropping. He poured molten lead through a sieve from the top of St. Mary's Redcliffe Church into some water below. The shot was indeed round. Watts sold the invention and became a wealthy man.

Shot towers dating back to the late 18th century have been recorded. One of the first to be built in America was constructed in Philadelphia in 1808. A few have been restored and are now managed by the National and State Park Services or the U.S. Department of Interior. One such shot tower is located in southwest Virginia and is still open for tours, although it is no longer in operation.

In general, there are two basic types of dropped shot. Early shot was made from pure lead and was therefore termed "soft shot," while most dropped shot made in the 20th century consisted of lead with antimony added to make it harder. This latter type is known as "chilled shot." Of course, many variations will be found. Tin is seldom used in dropped shot, since tin greatly lowers the melting point of lead, causing the shot to smear more easily in a hot shotgun barrel.

Dropped shot can only be made by pouring molten lead and antimony alloys through a sieve from a tower. The illustration on the opposite page (Figure 26-1) shows a cross-sectional view of a typical shot tower. Although industry took advantage of steam and electrical power in later years, the operational procedures remained the same and are described as follows:

Lead was first melted down and mixed on the first floor by means of a lead-melting furnace. The resulting mixture was cast into "pigs" which were then transferred to the top floor of the tower. Here the pigs were once again melted and the molten lead was channeled through a perforated pan or sieve. The size of the perforated openings in the sieve determined the shot size. This molten lead — heated to about 700°F.— then fell approximately 190 feet into a vat of water located in a pit beneath the first floor of the tower. As the lead fell toward the water, it formed into spheres. Air was sometimes blown up the tower to aid in forming large-shot. After the shot was dropped, it was sorted and tumbled in graphite. The graphite kept the shot from oxidizing and lubricates it slightly.

MACHINED SHOT

Machined shot is made by mixing a combination of lead and antimony in the proper proportions (usually 1 part antimony to 40 parts lead) and then running the mixture through a lead-wire extruding machine. The machine extrudes lead wire in the proper diameter by squeezing the lead billets. The lead is then fed into a shot-making machine where each machined shot is perfectly formed into a ball. This swaging or forming of the shot also hardened the lead, giving it a harder skin than conventional dropped shot. Furthermore, machined shot requires no graphite to keep it from oxidizing or for lubrication.

Shortly after World War II, some Belgian ammunition manufacturers began experimenting with machined shot for shotshells and offered loaded shells with both round and square shot — the latter being called Dispersante due to its square shape. Experiments proved that the round shot operated as good or better than the conventional dropped shot of the day, yet it was quicker and less expensive to manufacture. Consequently, many American ammunition manufacturers eventually changed to the new machining process and today almost all shot loaded in commercial ammunition is machined rather than dropped.

The square shot gives a very open pattern, similar to many American-made "spreader" loads; that is, when square shot is fired through a full-choke barrel, the shot pattern — out to about 30 yards — is similar to an improved cylinder or modified choke using conventional shot. Experiments have

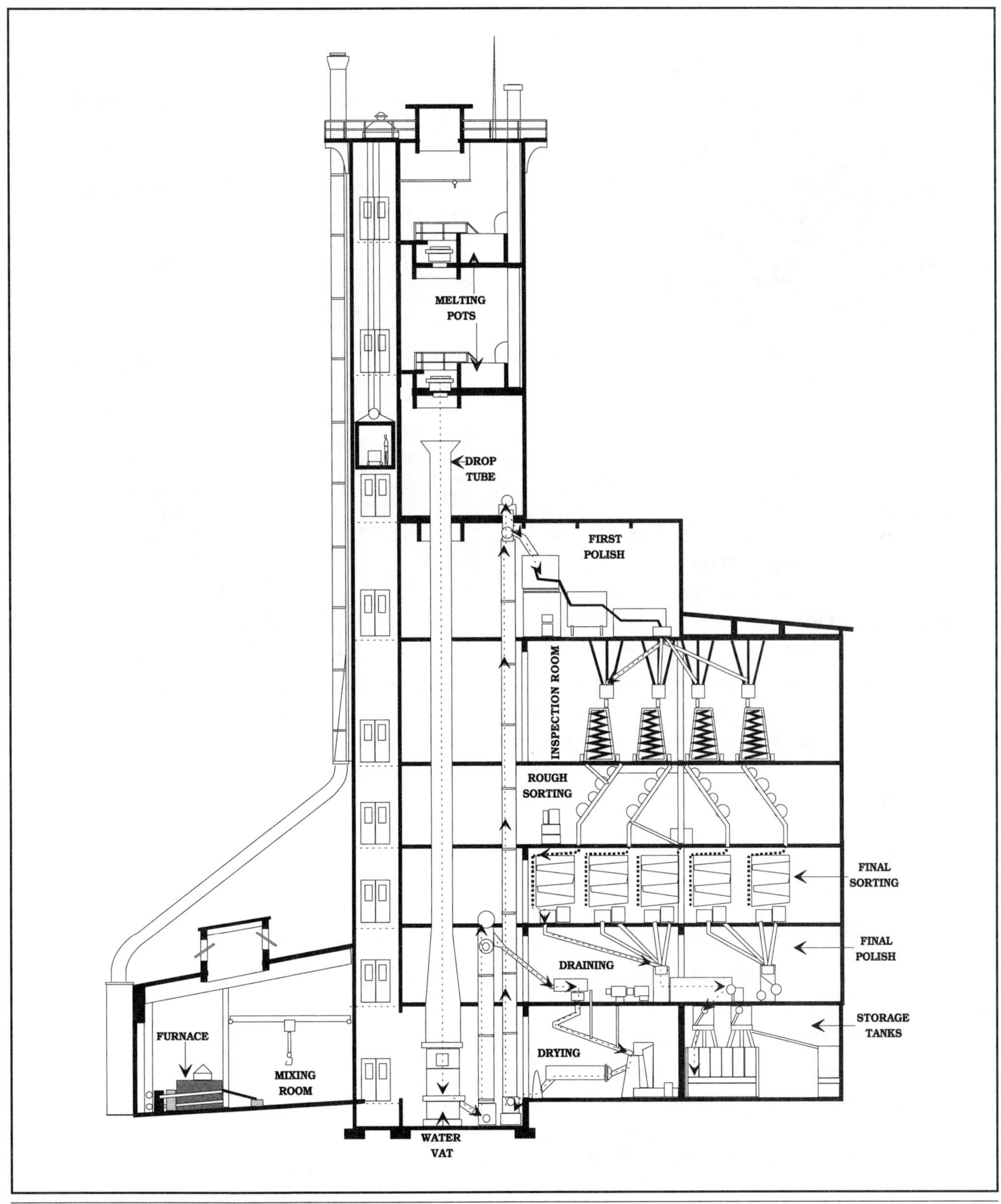

Figure 26-1: Cross-sectional view of typical shot tower.

Figure 26-2: Belgian-made square shot gives similar patterns as American spreader loads in shotshells.

shown that the smaller sizes (from about size 6 to 9) give the best results. *See* Figure 26-2. Beyond 30 yards, however, the shot patterns are too erratic to be consistently effective and the use of square shot is not recommended beyond this distance. Similar results should be obtained from cylindrical shot cut from lead wire.

Lead is ideal for shot, since it gives maximum striking power with the least surface for air to slow down the shot as it travels through the air. It is estimated that there are five tons of shot made for every ton of bullets made in the United States. Shot is usually sold in 25-pound bags as shown in Figure 26-3.

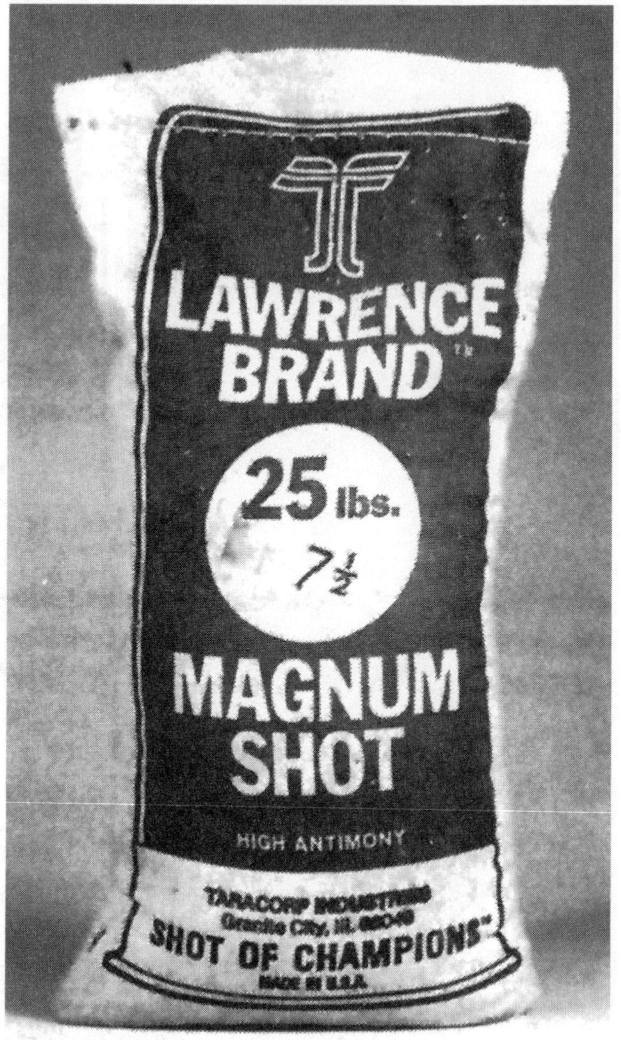

Figure 26-3: Shot is usually sold in 25-pound bags.

COMPOSITION OF LEAD SHOT

A large variety of shot sizes is available to shotshell loaders, along with many specialty shot types for almost every possible use.

See the chart in Figure 26-4 for various lead shot sizes. This chart enables one to accurately check sizes of lead shot from No. 12 through 000 Buck. Note that the diameter increases by .01″ for each number size from 2 through 12. Half sizes, such as No. 7½, increase by .005″ over the diameter of the full number (7) preceding them.

The tables beginning with Figure 26-5 on page 412 give specifications for the types of lead shot currently available from Taracorp Industries who manufactures Lawrence Brand Shot. Types include:

- Graphite-coated chill shot
- Graphite-coated drop shot
- Graphite-coated buck shot, both Western and American standard
- High-antimony magnum shot

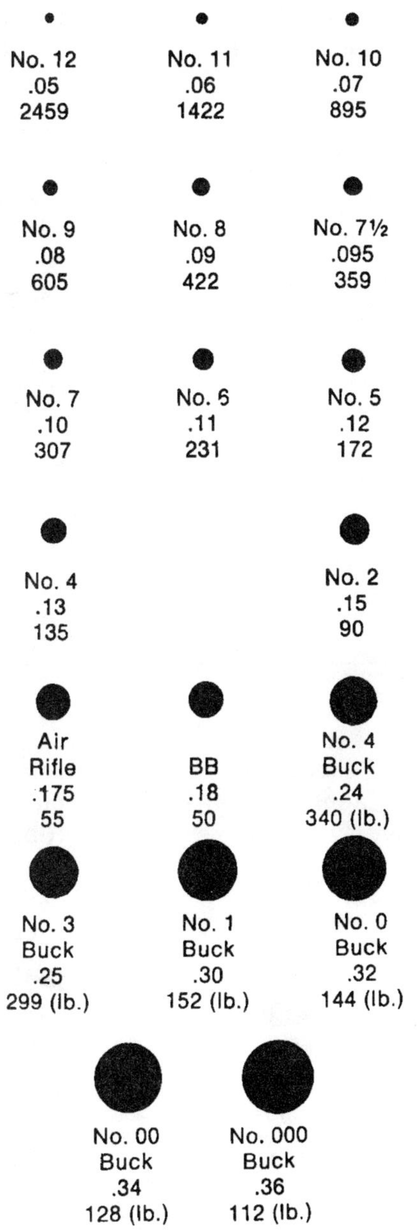

Figure 26-4: Check shot sizes by the circles.

- Copper-plated magnum shot
- Lead balls for muzzleloaders
- Western Brand high antimony shot for game and target shooters in Arizona, California, Idaho, Nevada, Oregon, Washington, and Hawaii only

The chilled, dropped, and buck shot consist of highly polished pellets that are uniformly round, accurately sized, and consistently dense. All are graphite coated.

High-antimony magnum shot matches the performance of premier factory-loaded ammunition, resulting in tight patterns, shorter shot strings, maximum density, and greater range. This shot is also graphite coated.

Copper-plated magnum shot retains more shot with less deformation, shorter shot strings, at maximum velocity and penetration. This type of shot gives uniformly superior patterns required for long-range hunting. This type is wax coated.

BUCKSHOT

Basically, buckshot loads may be categorized into two major types:

- Short-range loads
- Extended-range loads

Each size of buckshot — both copper-plated and conventional lead — has a particular usage. At close range, buckshot has a tremendous crushing effect. Professional hunters and guides have long used shotguns loaded with heavy buckshot loads as a backup weapon for their clients, and lions have been stopped in their tracks with a backup blast, in case the client's shot did not anchor the game, and the animal charged.

Shotguns loaded with buckshot are also ideal for hunting wild boar in heavy cover. When hunted with dogs, these hogs can become quite mean, and they are extremely difficult to stop in their tracks when charging, especially if they cannot be seen charging in thick cover. Buckshot is dandy for this situation. Most buckshot loads, however, are for longer range shooting, with the principal targets being deer, coyote, fox, wolf, and black bear.

Almost any buckshot load thrown together will serve as a short-range load. However, if the re-

Type of Shot	Shot Name or Number	Diameter (inches)	Pellets/Ounce (approximate)	Weight/ cu. ft. (lb.)
Graphite-Coated Lawrence Brand Chill Shot (American Standard)	Fine Dust	.03 and finer	-	445
	Dust	.04	4565	439
	No. 12	.05	2335	435
	No. 11	.06	1350	435
	No. 10	.07	850	434
	No. 9	.08 (skeet)	570	426
	No. 8	.09 (trap)	400	436
	No. 7½	.095 (game, trap)	340	
	No. 6	.11 (game)	220	436
	No. 5	.12 (game)	168	
	No. 4	.13 (game)	132	439
	No. 2	.15 (game)	86	

Figure 26-5: Specifications for Lawrence Brand chilled shot.

Type of Shot	Shot Name or Number	Diameter (inches)	Pellets/Ounce (approximate)	Weight/ cu. ft. (lb.)
Graphite-Coated Lawrence Brand Drop Shot (American Standard)	Fine Dust	.03 and finer	—	445
	Dust	.04	4565	439
	No. 12	.05	2335	435
	No. 11	.06	1350	435
	No. 10	.07	850	434
	No. 9	.08 (skeet)	570	426
	No. 8	.09 (trap)	400	436
	No. 7½	.095 (game, trap)	340	—
	No. 6	.11 (game)	220	436
	No. 5	.12 (game)	168	—
	No. 4	.13 (game)	132	439
	No. 2	.15 (game)	86	—
	No. B	.17 (game)	59	434
	Air Rifle	.175	55	—
	No. BB	.18 (game)	50	—
	No. BBB	.19 (game)	42	440

Figure 26-6: Specifications for Lawrence Brand drop shot.

Type of Shot	Shot Name or Number	Diameter (inches)	Balls/Pound (approximate)	Weight/ cu. ft. (lb.)
Graphite-Coated	No. 9	.25	299	426
Lawrence Brand	No. 8	.26	263	436
Compressed Buck-shot	No. 7½	.27	238	—
(Western Standard)	No. 7	.28	232	438
	No. 6	.29	186	435
	No. 5	.30	152	—
	No. 4	.32	144	439
	No. 3	.34	128	437
	No. 2	.36	112	—
	No. 1	.38	96	437

Figure 26-7: Specifications for Lawrence Brand Compressed Buckshot (Western Standard).

Type of Shot	Shot Name or Number	Diameter (inches)	Pellets/Ounce (approximate)	Weight/ cu. ft. (lb.)
Graphite-Coated	No. 4	.24	340	424
Lawrence Brand	No. 3	.25	299	426
Buckshot	No. 2	.27	238	428
(American Standard)	No. 1	.30	152	437
	No. 0	.32	144	437
	No. 00	.34	128	437
	No. 000	.36	112	437
	No. T	.20	544	426

Figure 26-8: Specifications for Lawrence Brand buckshot (American Standard).

Type of Shot	Caliber	Diameter (inches)	Balls (pound)	Weight/cu. ft.(lb.)
	.36	.36	112	437
Lawrence Brand	.44	.44	50	437
Lead Balls	.45	.45	48	437
(Pure Lead)	.50	.49	40	437
	.50	.50	38	437
	.54	.52	36	437
	No. 8	.09 (trap)	400	436

Figure 26-9: Specifications for Lawrence Brand lead balls for muzzleloaders.

Type of Shot	Shot Name or Number	Diameter (inches)	Pellets/Ounce (approximate)	Weight/ cu. ft. (lb.)
Graphite-Coated Lawrence Brand High Antimony Magnum Shot	No. 9	.08	585	426
	No. 8	.09	410	436
	No. 7½	.095	350	436
	No. 6	.11	225	435
	No. 5	.12	170	437
	No. 4	.13	135	439
	No. 2	.15	87	440
	No. BB	.18	50	442

Figure 26-10: Specifications for Lawrence Brand high-antimony magnum shot.

Type of Shot	Shot Name or Number	Diameter (inches)	Pellets/Ounce (approximate)	Weight/ cu. ft. (lb.)
Graphite-Coated Lawrence Brand Chill Shot (American Standard)	No. 9	.08	605	435
	No. 8	.09	422	435
	No. 7½	.095	359	435
	No. 6	.11	226	435
	No. 5	.12	172	437
	No. 4	.13	135	439
	No. 2	.15	88	440
	No. BB	.18	52	442

Figure 26-11: Specifications for Lawrence Brand magnum shot.

Type of Shot	Shot Name or Number	Diameter (inches)	Pellets/Ounce (approximate)	Weight/ cu. ft. (lb.)
Lawrence Western Brand High Antimony Shot (American Standard)	No. 9	.08	586	435
	No. 8	.09	413	435
	No. 7½	.095	350	435
	No. 6	.11	226	435
	No. 5	.12	174	437
	No. 4	.13	137	439

Figure 26-12: Specifications for Lawrence Western Brand high-antimony shot.

loader is seeking high performance at ranges up to 100 yards, then a lot of time and effort must go into each load, followed by much testing.

BUFFERING

Ballistic Products, Inc. of Long Lake, Minnesota offers a formulated buffering compound designed to handle heavy-weight buckshot pellets under severe stress. Using this compound in buckshot loads greatly increases their performance at longer ranges.

Ballistic Products, Inc. also offers at least two sizes of special buckshot:

- No. 4 which is .24″ diameter
- No. 00; .33″ diameter

Both are hard copper-plated pellets and both have given extremely good results at both target and in the field. Such pellets will also help increase the range of buckshot loads.

STACKING

Stacking of the larger buckshot sizes will usually extend the range of the loads. *See* Figure 26-13.

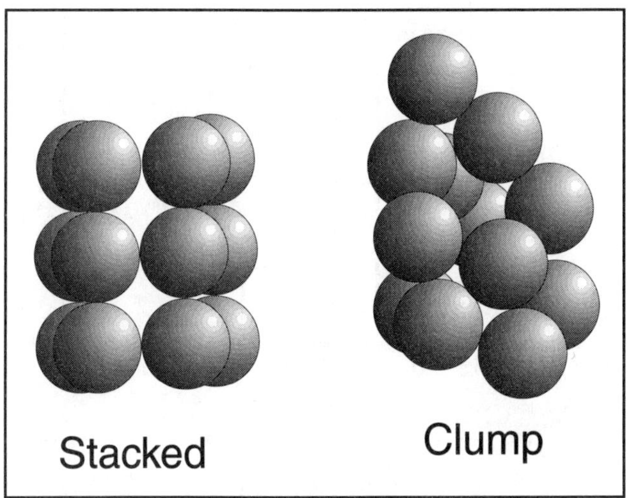

Figure 26-13: Stacked buckshot column and a clump of buckshot.

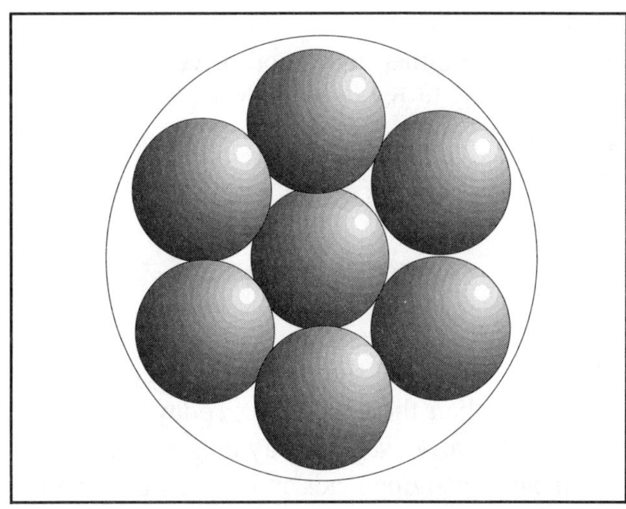

Figure 26-14: A seven-pellet layer of No. 4 buckshot.

However, stacking the shot seems to have little or no effect on the smaller shot sizes.

Stacking buckshot loads is greatly eased with the use of a "pellet packer" which may be made from a hardwood dowel to a diameter slightly smaller than the inside of the shotshell case (hull). It is used by the reloader to press the pellets in place.

To stack buckshot loads, the number of pellets in one layer must first be determined. Let's assume that No. 4 buckshot is being used and it has been determined that seven pellets will lie flat on one layer as shown in Figure 26-14. The reloader drops in seven pellets and then uses the pellet packer to press the pellets in place. Drop in another seven pellets and press with the pellet packer. Repeat these operations until the total pellet count is correct. This procedure will speed up loading and add to the quality of the load.

Some shot-size combinations will require more pressure than others, but no more than light pressure should ever be required.

It should be obvious that long-range quality buckshot loads for use in shotshells require much time and effort on the part of the reloader. To obtain the very best loads, it is also necessary to become heavily involved in a testing program to be sure of the expected shooting ability of the load and also the shotgun in which the load will be used. Buckshot loads are either very good or very bad; there are seldom any in-between loads. Consequently, if buckshot is to be used, always try for the best possible loads.

STEEL SHOT

Hunting with steel shot is rapidly becoming the rule, rather than the exception. Today, steel-shot laws affect nearly every flyway in North America. That means changing loads and, more importantly, changing hunting habits.

Steel shot is 30% lighter than lead shot, but is loaded to shoot with increased initial velocity. This lighter pellet weight, however, means velocity will drop more quickly. The result is that shooters must change their forward lead when using steel shot.

If you decide to adjust the way you lead your target, you'll have to consider steel shot's increased loss of velocity. At 20 yards, you won't need to make any noticeable change. Yet at 40 yards, you'll want to lead your target about 5 to 6 inches more than you would with lead shot.

Perhaps the best way to make the adjustment to steel shot is to make it act more like lead. Since steel is lighter than lead, a shot should be selected that is two shot sizes larger than the lead shot normally used. That way, a pellet of No. 2 steel shot will have about the same velocity, deliver similar energy, and require the same forward lead as No. 4 lead shot through the ranges. Patterns stay dense because there are more pellets per ounce of steel than lead, and because steel pellets deform less, which means fewer stray out of the pattern. A shotgun shell, however, has a fixed amount of room for shot. And the larger steel shot takes up more of that room. So if you really want pattern density of No. 2 steel to match more closely that of No. 4 lead, you must increase shot weight. The 12-gauge, 3½-inch magnum was designed to solve this problem. It delivers a greater load of larger steel shot at extended ranges. Comparisons between lead and steel shot at various ranges are shown in the charts and tables in Figure 26-15.

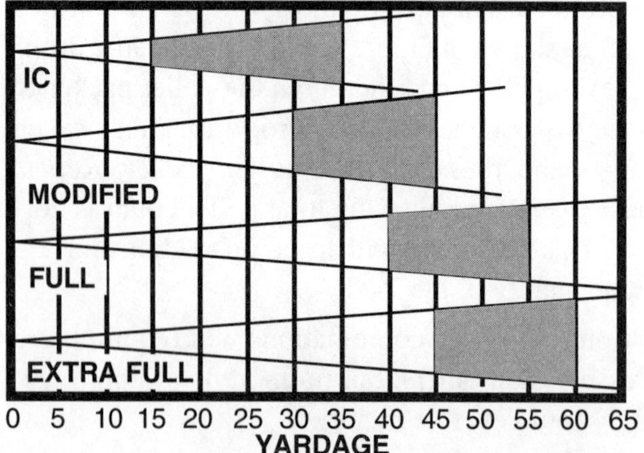

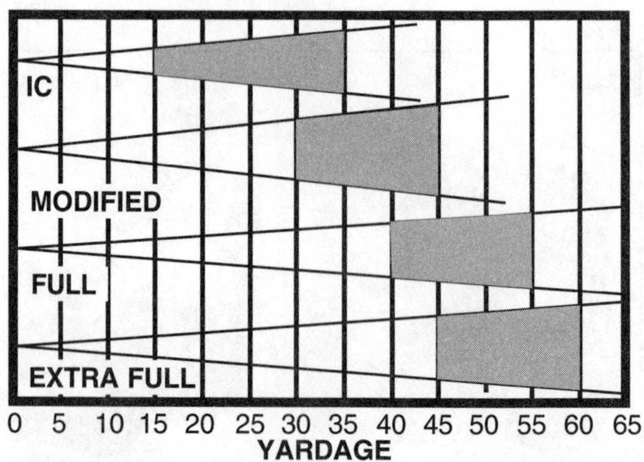

Figure 26-15: The effective range of conventional 12-gauge shotshells loaded with No. 4 lead shot is closely matched using No. 2 steel shot in 12-gauge, 3½-inch magnum loads.

SECTION VI
LOADS FOR MUZZLE-LOADERS

WARNING

The loads and ballistic data shown in this book were obtained under strictly controlled conditions. Ballistic data vary considerably depending on many factors, including components used, how such components are assembled, the type and condition of the firearm used, and the reloading techniques. Therefore, the loads listed are not for inexperienced persons; safety precautions must be considered and utilized at all times.

The publisher and authors specifically disclaim any warranties with respect to any and all loads listed, the safety or suitability of the loads, or the results obtained with the listed loads. Readers and users of any load or product listed in this book assume all risk, responsibility and liability whatsoever for any and all injuries (including death), losses, or damages to persons or property (including consequential damages), arising from the use of any load or product.

The individual assumes the risk of safe loading practices. Failure to do so or violation of any of the warnings specified in this book could result in severe personal injury (including death) to the user or bystander or damage to the firearm.

Chapter 27

Loads for Flintlock Rifles and Pistols

Francis Bannerman Sons of New York City was the largest supplier of authentic muzzleloading firearms during the first half of the twentieth century. Thousands of blackpowder firearms were sold to collectors and shooters alike.

A. F. Stoeger began importing authentic muzzleloading firearms before World War II and offered them for sale, mainly for decorative purposes. However, many of these weapons were in excellent condition, and many of them found their way to the shooting range, and even to the woods for bagging game.

Figure 27-1: One small section of firearms available from Francis Bannerman Sons during the 1930s. Over 2,000 blackpowder muzzleloaders were stocked at all times.

During the mid-1950s, a number of blackpowder buffs began importing replica arms from Europe. Although many take the credit for being the first, Turner Kirkland of Dixie Gun Works probably offered the first production replica in 1955. This was a typical Kentucky rifle manufactured to Kirkland's specifications in Belgium. Val Forgett of Navy Arms followed shortly thereafter with a basic Remington percussion revolver design manufactured in Italy.

Sale of these replica arms surpassed all expectations and quickly exceeded the supply.

Eventually, other models were introduced by the major importers, and soon several additional firms entered into the replica business. Custom shops also sprang up in the United States where higher quality blackpowder arms were produced on a limited basis, similar to the custom cartridge rifles made to individual specifications. It did not take long for replica arms to become big business nationwide, and even the major firearms manufacturers scrambled for a piece of the pie. Colt brought back into production several of the original Colt percussion designs; Harrington & Richardson came out with a replica model of the 1873 Springfield rifle chambered for the .45-70 cartridge; and

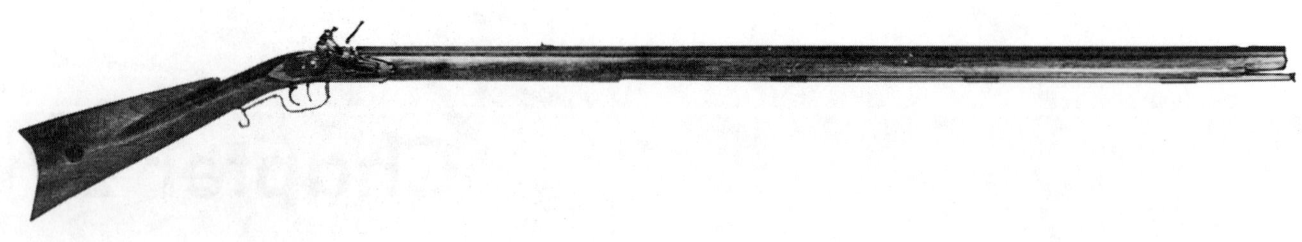

Figure 27-2: Turner Kirkland of Dixie Gun Works began importing flintlock replicas in the mid-1950s. This firm now carries dozens of blackpowder replicas and is probably the single largest distributor of blackpowder weapons and related products in the world.

Ruger introduced a blackpowder stainless steel percussion revolver. The trend continues today.

When re-enactments of major Civil War battles began in the early 1960s, the blackpowder industry blossomed even more. It was hard for suppliers of blackpowder to meet the demand. Blackpowder rifle and pistol matches sprang up all over the country and such events continue to grow at a rapid pace. Many states provide special hunting seasons for blackpowder or muzzleloading firearms. It looks like blackpowder firearms and shooting are here stay!

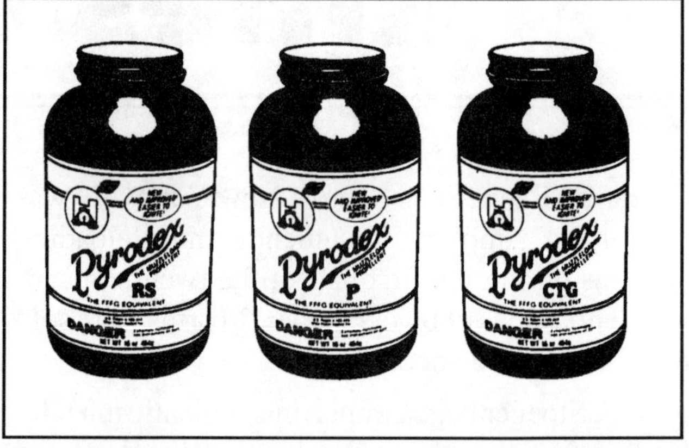

Figure 27-3: Hodgdon's Pyrodex is a replica blackpowder that looks like, smokes like, and smells like the real thing. However, it cannot be used in flintlocks because of its slow ignition characteristics.

PYRODEX®

The Hodgdon Powder Company of Shawnee Mission, Kansas, introduced a blackpowder substitute a few decades ago and called it Pyrodex. This propellant is designed for use in percussion and blackpowder cartridge arms found to be in good shootable condition by a competent gunsmith. Pyrodex, however, is not blackpowder. It is classified by the Bureau of Explosives as a flammable solid and can be shipped by most common carriers to licensed dealers. It is currently available at most shooting suppliers or sporting goods stores and comes in three grades:

- RS: rifle and shotgun
- P: pistol
- CTG: cartridge and shotshell

Pyrodex is intended to be used on a volume-to-volume basis the same as the appropriate granulation of blackpowder, and will give approximately the same velocity and pressure as black when used in this manner. For greater safety, Pyrodex is slightly harder to ignite than blackpowder, and so its use in flintlock rifles is not recommended. Even in percussion firearms, hot percussion caps and larger-than-normal nipple vent holes should be used for the best ignition. Furthermore, the ball or projectile must be seated firmly on the powder when loading. On the plus side, Pyrodex burns cleaner with less fouling than blackpowder, and pressure and velocity remain consistent shot after shot. *See* Chapter 3 for more details on Hodgdon Pyrodex powders.

BLACKPOWDER SAFETY PRECAUTIONS

- Never attempt to fire an old blackpowder weapon until it has been inspected by a competent gunsmith and found to be in good, sound, shootable condition.
- Never smoke while handling any type of powder.
- Store powder in its original container. Never put powder in a glass container. Store in a cool dry place.
- Never attempt to use any kind of smokeless powder in blackpowder firearms.
- Do not prime the pan of a flintlock before loading.
- Keep percussion caps away from powder.
- Do not put a cap on the nipple before loading a percussion arm.
- Do not use steel spoons, measures, or funnels with blackpowder or Pyrodex.
- Be sure to use the proper amount of powder for the caliber and bullet being used.
- Do not attempt extra-heavy loads in any blackpowder firearm.
- Keep firearms and all loading components away from children.
- Avoid distractions when loading to prevent double charging powder or projectiles, and to avoid leaving out the powder.
- Keep all loading components away from excessive heat or sparks.
- If a blackpowder firearm misfires, keep the muzzle pointed in a safe direction for at least 60 seconds. Sometimes a misfire can be a slow hangfire and the arm will discharge seconds later.
- Never load directly from a powder source; always use a separate powder measure.

SHOOTING THE FLINTLOCK

Please read the section on blackpowder and Pyrodex in Chapter 3 before attempting to shoot any blackpowder firearm.

The following items are necessary to shoot a flintlock rifle or pistol:

- A rifle or pistol in shootable condition as judged by a competent gunsmith.
- The proper granulation of blackpowder.
- A good sharp flint.
- A measuring device to hold the powder charge. This can be a powder horn or flask. Never load directly from the powder canister.
- Projectiles — either round balls or proper conical bullets of the correct diameter for the rifle or pistol bore.

Patch material is necessary for round balls used in rifles or single-shot pistols. The function of the cloth patch is primarily to provide a gas check for the ball. The patch should be of the proper thickness (.007 to .017 inch) and of strong material like pillow ticking. Patching cloth should be new material, washed in soap and water before using. Shallow-grooved barrels will use the thinner patching, while the ones with deep grooves will need the thick material. Precut patches are available commercially. Patches are not used with conical bullets or for round-ball loads in revolvers.

Patches should be lubricated before loading with a lubricant designed for the purpose.

While not absolutely necessary for firing flintlock rifles and pistols, the following accessories are quite helpful and are highly recommended:

- *Powder horn or flask:* These are used for portable storage of powder. They usually have a preset measuring device with them.
- *Long and short starter:* Used for starting a patched ball in the bore of a muzzleloading rifle.
- *Patch knife:* A sharp knife used to cut off excess patch material when loading using bulk patching material.
- *Vent pick:* A useful item for cleaning out the vent hole on flintlocks.
- *Loading block:* A block of wood with several holes drilled through it and used for holding patched balls. Very handy for fast reloading while hunting.
- *Accessory bag:* Handy for keeping needed items intact.
- *Patch worm:* Used on the ramrod to pull a patch that sticks in the barrel while cleaning.
- *Extra ramrod:* This comes in handy for cleaning the bore and serves as a spare in case the main ramrod is broken.
- *Bullet casting equipment:* For those who wish to cast their own round balls. Includes bullet mold, lead-melting furnace or lead pot, ladle, mallet, gloves, safety glasses, and lead. *See* Chapter 24.
- *Blackpowder cleaning solvent and gun oil:* A good blackpowder solvent for cleaning is necessary. A blackpowder arm must be cleaned and oiled after use or it will rust in short order.

Before firing a flintlock rifle or pistol, there are a few preliminary preparations that will make the process easier and safer.

Make sure the bore is completely empty and thoroughly clean. Run the ramrod completely down the bore until it contacts the breechplug. Make a mark on the ramrod even with the muzzle. This is the "empty" mark, and will allow shooters to see if their guns are loaded or not. When the rifle is being loaded for firing, and the ball has been properly seated, make a second mark on the ramrod. This is the "loaded" mark and will tell the shooter whether a proper load is in the barrel or an inadvertent double-charge.

When preparing for a hunt or shooting session, prelubricate a sufficient number of patches and fill a loading block with patched balls. This will save lots of time. Several extra sharp flints and a wire vent pick should be carried. Always check the powder charge on accurate scales when setting the powder measure. Then measure three or four charges to ensure that the measure is throwing consistent charges.

Always use a ball starter; this makes starting the ball down the bore easier and can also prevent a broken rod.

POWDER

Only blackpowder should be used in muzzleloading flintlock rifles and pistols. To experiment with any smokeless powder in these firearms is to be risking certain injury to oneself and bystanders, and destruction of the firearm.

Although Hodgdon Pyrodex is suitable for caplocks and blackpowder cartridges, its ignition is too slow for flintlocks. Consequently, only authentic blackpowder is suitable for use in these rifles.

In choosing the granulation of powder for a given caliber, it will be found that for most rifles up to .45 caliber, FFFg is generally used. Above .45 caliber, FFg is the accepted size. The following table lists recommended loads for flintlock rifles of various calibers. This table is NOT to be used for flintlock pistol loads; ONLY rifle. Furthermore, these loads are for use with round lead balls only. The use of conical bullets in these rifles will create heavy pressure beyond the safety limits of most flintlock barrels.

CALIBER	GRAINS OF BLACKPOWDER	GRANULATION OF POWDER
.32	25	FFFg
.34	30	FFFg
.36	38	FFFg
.38	40	FFFg
.40	45	FFFg
.42	50	FFFg
.44	60	FFFg
.46	68	FFg
.48	80	FFg
.50	90	FFg
.52	100	FFg
.54	115	FFg
.56	125	FFg

Blackpowder is regulated under Title XI, Organized Crime Control Act of 1970, and over 50 pounds of blackpowder is classified as a low explosive. To purchase 50 pounds or less in one's own state does not require a permit. However, Federal Form No. 4710 must be completed at the time of purchase.

The most-used brands of blackpowder at the present time include those manufactured by Curtis & Harvey and Gearhart-Owen. The Curtis & Harvey blackpowder has a coating that makes it dust-free and cleaner shooting. This coating also keeps the powder moisture-free longer so that it will not mat together while it is in storage over a long period of time. It is imported from Scotland and is available in Fg only.

Gearhart-Owen purchased the Du Pont facilities after the Du Pont plant experienced an explosion in 1970. The current powder is the same as the old Du Pont powders and is available in Fg, FFg, FFFg, and FFFFg. Size FFFFg is used for priming the pan of flintlocks, and FFFg for flintlock pistols and flintlock rifles up to .45 caliber or so, while FFg is recommended for rifles of .45 caliber or larger.

LEAD BALLS

Lead balls for flintlock rifles and pistols may be cast or purchased from bullet supply houses. The following table gives the weights of round lead balls of various diameters:

CALIBER	WEIGHT
.20	12.0 grains
.22	16.0 grains
.24	20.7 grains
.26	26.4 grains
.28	33.0 grains
.30	40.5 grains
.32	49.0 grains
.34	59.0 grains
.36	70.0 grains
.38	82.3 grains
.40	96.0 grains
.42	111.0 grains
.44	127.8 grains
.46	146.0 grains
.48	165.9 grains
.50	187.5 grains
.52	210.9 grains
.54	236.2 grains
.56	263.4 grains
.58	292.6 grains
.60	324.0 grains
.62	357.4 grains
.64	393.2 grains
.66	431.2 grains
.68	471.6 grains
.70	514.4 grains
.72	559.8 grains
.74	607.8 grains
.76	658.4 grains
.78	711.7 grains
.80	767.9 grains
.82	826.9 grains

Continued on next page

CALIBER	WEIGHT
.84	888.9 grains
.86	934.0 grains
.88	1022.1 grains
.90	1093.4 grains

ROUND BALL SIZES

In many cases, when an authentic flintlock was built, the gunsmith also made bullet molds to match the bore. In most cases, however, these molds have long been lost. Consequently, the ball size will have to be determined for each individual rifle or pistol. Since it is recommended that a competent gunsmith check all old firearms prior to shooting, this same gunsmith can check the bore size and make recommendations at the same time. Remember that the lead-ball diameter must be slightly smaller than the rifle bore to allow room for the cloth patch. If the bullet/patch is too tight, problems will develop.

The table to follow lists bore sizes for many of the replica firearms on the market, and also the recommended round ball sizes. For models not listed, check with the manufacturer for exact dimensions.

MANUFACTURER	MODEL	BALL DIAMETER	BORE DIAMETER
Centennial Arms	.44 Army Revolver	.451	(1)
Dixie (Barrels)	.40 Caliber	.390-.395	.400
Dixie (Barrels)	.45 Caliber	.440-.445	.450
Douglas (Barrels)	.32 Caliber	.315	.321
Douglas (Barrels)	.36 Caliber	.355	.363
Douglas (Barrels)	.40 Caliber	.395	.403
Douglas (Barrels)	.45 Caliber	.440-.445	.451
Douglas (Barrels)	.50 Caliber	.490-.495	.501
Hopkins & Allen	.36 Rifle	.340	.347
Hopkins & Allen	.36 Pistol	.340	.347
Hopkins & Allen	.45 Rifle	.435	.443
Hopkins & Allen	.45 Pistol	.435	.443
Hopkins & Allen	.58 Rifle	.575	.580
Navy Arms	.36 Colt Navy Revolver	.375-.380	(1)
Navy Arms	.36 Remington Revolver	.375-.380	(1)
Navy Arms	.44 Model 60 Army Revolver	.451-.455	(1)
Navy Arms	.44 Walker & Dragoon Revolver	.451-.455	(1)
Navy Arms	.44 Remington Army Revolver	.454	(1)
Navy Arms	.44 Revolving Carbine	.454	(1)
Navy Arms	.58 Zouave Rifle & Carbine	.575	.580
Navy Arms	.58 Mississippi Rifle	.575	.580
Navy Arms	.58 Harpers Ferry Rifle	.575	.580
Navy Arms	.54 Harpers Ferry Pistol	.555	.562
Numrich Arms (Barrels)	.31 Caliber	.290	.300-.301
Numrich Arms (Barrels)	.36 Caliber	.340	.350-.351
Numrich Arms (Barrels)	.45 Caliber	.435	.445-.446
Numrich Arms (Barrels)	.50 Caliber	.490-.495	.500-.501
Numrich Arms (Barrels)	.54 Caliber	.525	.530-.532
Numrich Arms (Barrels)	.58 Caliber	.570	.575-578
Other Dixie Guns	.40 Overcoat Pistol	.380	.390

Continued on next page

MANUFACTURER	MODEL	BALL DIAMETER	BORE DIAMETER
Other Dixie Guns	Flint Derringer	.410	.420
Other Dixie Guns	.40 Spanish Percussion Pistol	.400	.410
Other Dixie Guns	.40 Brass frame Derringer	.395	.410
Other Dixie Guns	.36 Target Pistol	.355	.360
Other Dixie Guns	.40 Philadelphia Derringer	.395	.410
Lyman	.44 Lyman Army Revolver	.451	(1)
Replica Arms	.45 Berdan Rifle	.445	.450
Replica Arms	.31 Wells Fargo Revolver	.320	(1)
Replica Arms	.36 Paterson Revolver	.380	(1)
Replica Arms	.38 Plainsman Rifle	.377	.380
Replica Arms	.44 Single-Shot Target	.424	—
Replica Arms	.44 Kentucky Pistol	.424	—
Sturm, Ruger	New Old Army .44 Revolver	.457	(1)
Thompson-Center	.36 Seneca	.350	—
Thompson-Center	.45 Hawken and Seneca	.440	—
Thompson-Center	.50 Hawken Rifle	.490	—
Thompson-Center	.54 Renegade	.530	—

NOTE

(1): In revolvers, chamber diameter, not bore size, controls ball diameter. Ball for rifles and pistols is patched to fit the bore.

LOADS FOR FLINTLOCK PISTOLS

CALIBER	POWDER TYPE	POWDER CHARGE
.30	FFFg	15 grains
.31	FFFg	15 grains
.32	FFFg	16 grains
.34	FFFg	17 grains
.36	FFFg	20 grains
.40	FFFg	25 grains
.44	FFFg	25 grains
.45	FFFg	25 grains
.54	FFFg	35 grains
.67	FFFg	35 grains

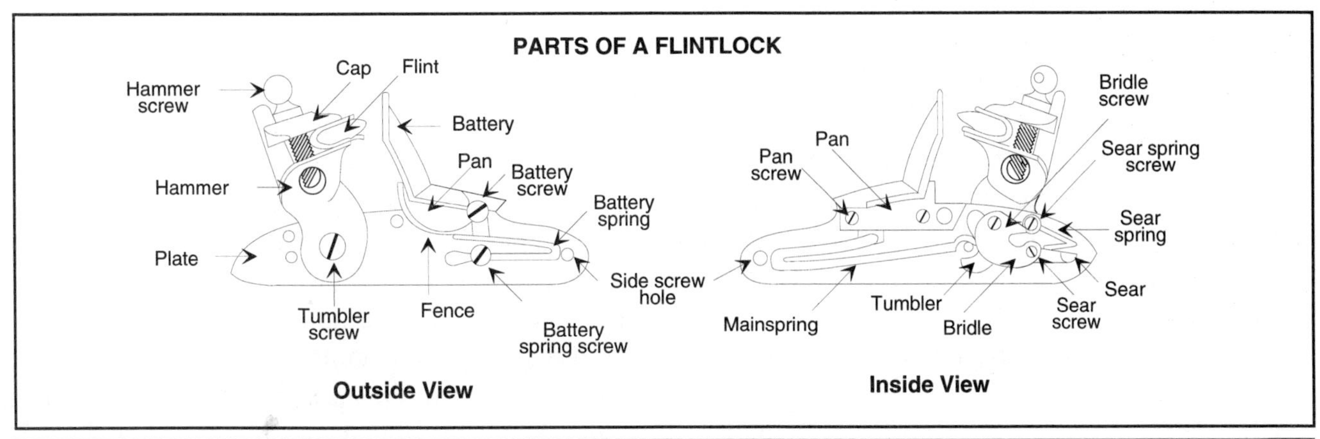

Figure 27-4: Parts of a flintlock.

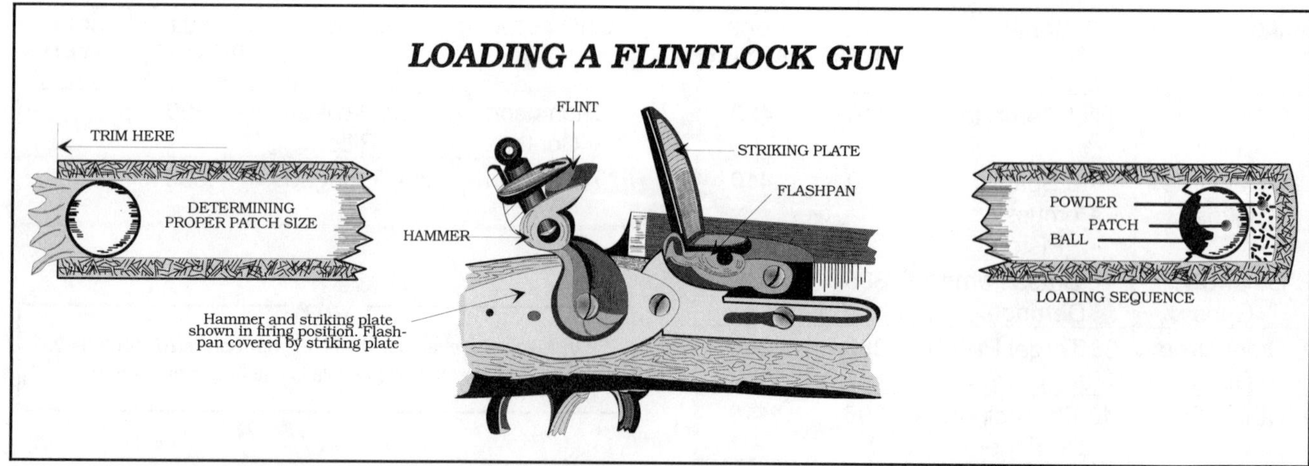

Figure 27-5: Loading a flintlock.

LOADING FLINTLOCKS

The drawing in Figure 27-4 shows the major parts of a typical flintlock. The left view is looking at the lock from the outside of the arm, while the right view shows the interior parts. In general, the movable hammer is the cocking piece and also contains a sharp flint, secured in place by the hammer screw. Once a powder charge, along with a patch and ball, have been loaded in the rifle bore, a priming charge of FFFFg blackpowder is placed in the pan. The hammer is cocked, and upon depressing the trigger, the sear releases the hammer under the pressure of the mainspring, causing the flint to strike the steel battery (striking plate), which sends sparks down into the pan to ignite the priming charge. This ignition, in turn, sends a flame through the vent hole to ignite the main powder charge inside the barrel. The burning powder produces an expanding gas that sends the patched ball down the bore and out the muzzle — on the way to the target. The basic firing principles of a flintlock are very similar to percussion arms, and even the modern metallic cartridge; that is, a primer ignites the main powder charge, which expands to force the bullet down the barrel and out the muzzle.

Now let's take the loading of a flintlock step-by-step and see how to get the best use out of these firearms.

DEGREASING

Before a flintlock rifle or pistol is fired, all oil and grease should be removed from the bore, the pan, the vent hole, and the front of the striking plate. We use AWA1,1,1, but any degreasing solution will work — even rubbing alcohol. Clean all of these areas thoroughly.

SELECTING FLINTS

There are several types and sizes of flints to choose from. All should be sharp and of the correct size. Furthermore, they must be secured tightly in the hammer. When the hammer is at half-cock, and the striker plate down over the pan, the end of the flint should be approximately ⅛ inch from the face of the striker plate. A flint that is too long will usually break on the first shot; one that is too short will fail to ignite the priming powder. With the bore and pan empty, use the thumb to lower the hammer and flint gently onto the striker plate; the end of the flint should hit the plate about ⅓ the way down from the top. This will ensure getting sufficient sparks into the pan upon firing.

The flint is mounted in the hammer locking jaws with the flint bevel usually on top, although the bevel-down position works better on some locks. Leather is frequently used to cushion the flint in the jaws. Tighten the hammer jaws as tightly as possible and then, with the pan and bore empty, spark the flint a few times to see that it is sparking properly.

POWDER AND PROJECTILES

Recommended powder charges for flintlock rifles and pistols are included in this chapter. If shooting a flintlock replica, recommended charges are usually included in a phamplet or brochure accompanying the rifle.

With the rifle in an upright position (butt on the ground) measure the required blackpowder charge and dump this into the bore. Never guess at the powder charge or pour it directly from the powder horn. Use a good powder measure for each charge. Bump the breech of the rifle a couple of times to seat the powder.

Pure lead round balls and 100% cotton patches should be used for best results. The diameter of the balls and the thickness of the patches are selected as described previously. The patch acts as a gas seal and when properly lubed, the ball/patch combination should push down the bore with little effort. *See* Figure 27-5. Use the ramrod to push the bullet/patch combination all the way down the bore and make sure that the ball is firmly seated on the powder. Do not, however, crush the powder during this process — just a firm seat. Doing otherwise can cause problems.

PRIMING

Once the main charge is loaded, use a vent pick to clear the vent hole before priming the pan. The vent hole should be cleaned after each firing to ensure proper ignition. Now pour some FFFFg (4F) priming powder into the pan. The pan should be about one-third full. Then rap the breech lightly to even the powder out. Be careful not to allow any of the priming powder to enter the vent hole. Check the flint, point the firearm in a safe direction, bring the hammer to full cock, aim, and fire. Keep your eyes on the sight and on the target. Do not watch the striker or pan during firing.

One of the best ways for the beginner to learn about firing blackpowder arms is to join a local muzzleloading gun club. Experienced blackpowder buffs will then be on hand to guide the beginner step-by-step through his or her first firing sessions, and to help overcome any problems that may occur.

CLEANING

At the end of each shooting session, fire out the final charge, and clean the rifle or pistol as soon as possible. Blackpowder is highly corrosive, and a fine barrel can be ruined overnight if it is not cleaned thoroughly.

The best way to learn more about shooting flintlock rifles and pistols as well as other muzzleloading firearms is to subscribe to one of the blackpowder magazines. *Muzzle Blasts*, published by the National Muzzleloading Rifle Association, is excellent. There are also other publications that may be found at your local news stand or library.

Chapter 28

Loads for Percussion Rifles and Pistols

Caplock or percussion muzzleloading rifles and pistols are the most popular and useful for modern applications. While still classified as "primitive" weapons for special hunting seasons in most states, modern caplocks have been refined to a point where they are as accurate and versatile as many short-range smokeless firearms.

Indeed, when modern caplock rifles are equipped with telescopic sights (often not permitted during primitive weapons hunting seasons), their accuracy often matches that of some modern smokeless firearms. With the growing popularity of sabots, modern muzzleloaders have formed their own niche in special hunting seasons established purely for muzzleloaders, or "smokepoles" as they are often called.

The flintlock (*see* Chapter 27) was an improvement over the lock systems that preceded it, and the caplock is a distinct improvement on the flintlock. The flintlock simply did not provide a fast and positive ignition system, and this became more troublesome as game became harder to find. The unsure ignition of the flintlock, especially in damp conditions, led to many total ignition failures. The lock time (the time it takes the load to discharge its projectile after the trigger is pulled) on flintlocks was and is horrible, to say the least. There is a measurable pause between the time the trigger is pulled and the full load is discharged, even when ignition is positive. This occurs because the flint must strike the frizzen, creating a shower of sparks, which ignite the priming charge in the pan. This priming charge burns through to the main charge, which is ignited and sends the projectile out of the barrel. The firing of a flintlock involves two, separate ignitions. The first occurs at the priming charge in the pan when the sparks from the flint/frizzen ignite it. The second ignition occurs when the pan charge burns through to the main charge.

Flint scraping against iron or steel could never be classified as a "positive" ignition system. Add to this the fact that the powder in the pan is partially exposed to the elements and ignition problems are further complicated, especially during periods of rain, snow, or even high humidity.

Owing to the shortcomings of the flintlock, research was undertaken to develop a new ignition system, one that was more positive and less affected by the weather. Experimentation took place in both Europe and America, and, after many unsuccessful attempts, the caplock or percussion lock was finally perfected in the early 1820s. Within 10 years, this new system was in widespread use.

Unlike the flintlock, the caplock consists of only three parts: hammer, nipple, and percussion cap. The hammer is the only moving portion of the lock, once the cap has been placed on the nipple. The cap is the single most important element of this ignition system and was a forerunner of today's modern primer. Originally, a dab of fulminate was sealed into each cap, and this ignition element was completely sealed from the weather. When the hammer struck the top of the cap, the fulminate ignited explosively and was channeled directly into the main powder charge at the base of the projectile. This was a closed ignition system. Once the cap was in place, there was no exposure of the powder charge to the air. As long as the flash channel from the nipple to the main charge was kept clear, very little could go wrong with the ignition sequence, assuming that the cap discharged properly.

Developed over 170 years ago, the basic caplock design has gone largely unchanged. Modern caplock rifles and pistols still use this same ignition system. When properly maintained, these systems rarely suffer a firing failure.

The popularity of the caplock lasted for only about 25 years. It was replaced by metallic cartridges, which offered an even more positive ignition system, one that was completely sealed from the weather. However, the caplock still prevails on modern muzzleloading rifles and pistols. While a limited number of flintlock designs are still available, the great majority of modern smokepoles are of the caplock design. In fact, the caplock was the best system ever devised for muzzleloading weapons. It was about as close as one could come to a metallic cartridge design while still requiring that powder and projectiles be loaded at the bore end.

MODERN CAPLOCK DESIGNS

The blackpowder shooter has a very large selection of weapons to choose from. This was not the case a decade or so ago, prior to the sudden boost in popularity of muzzleloaders for hunting and target shooting purposes.

The most popular model of the caplock rifle is still the Hawken style as shown in Figure 28-1.

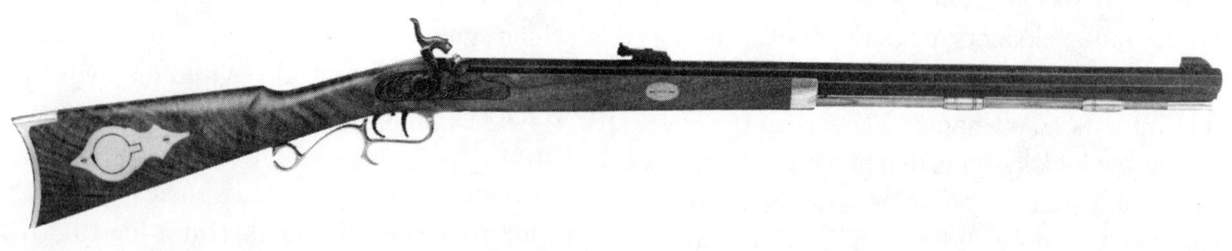

Figure 28-1: The Thompson/Center Hawken caplock rifle is a style that is preferred by many hunters who like its traditional appearance.

Figure 28-2: These Thompson/Center Renegade models closely resemble the higher-priced Hawken, but forego the bright trimwork. The Renegade may be more appropriate for hunting conditions, where glare from polished metal is undesirable. The left-hand model is shown at the center, while the model on the bottom is designed especially for the hunter and exchanges the double set trigger for a single adjustable model.

This is a traditional style that also offers some fancy niceties such as brass fittings at the buttplate, side compartment, and front of the forearm. While closely resembling weapons of 150 years or more ago, it is ultramodern, using the latest steel. This model is available from different manufacturers under different names, but it is most commonly known as a Hawken or Hawken-style.

The Thompson/Center Hawken is available in .45, .50, and .54 caliber and offers a double set trigger at the rear of the main trigger. By pulling the second trigger to the locked position, the main trigger becomes super sensitive. If a hair trigger is not desired, then the second trigger is left in the unset position and the main trigger functions with a much stiffer pull.

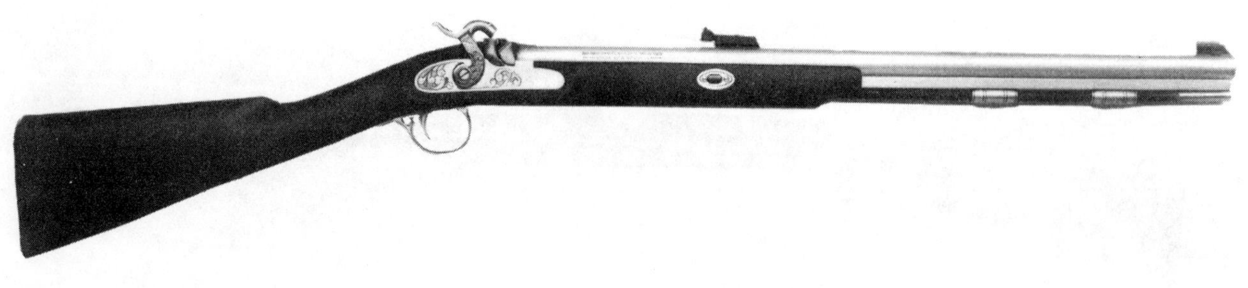

Figure 28-3: The Thompson/Center Grey Hawk combines traditional styling with stainless steel components and a Rynite synthetic stock.

For those blackpowder hunters who like the traditional design but don't desire the brass accoutrements that accompany the Hawken, the T/C Renegade in either .50 or .54 caliber offers the same basic features without the bright metallic trim.

As shown, the Renegade is available in several different models. There's even one for the left-handed blackpowder enthusiast. Functionally, the Renegade is closely equivalent to the Hawken.

For those hunters who desire a traditional style but also want the latest in steel technology, the stainless steel Grey Hawk model offers a traditional-styled caplock with components that are strictly out of the 1990s.

The Grey Hawk is equipped with a synthetic stock made from Rynite. This is a pure hunting model that does retain the traditional styling, but the concentration is really on durability and performance. It is available in .50 and .54 calibers.

The barrel lengths of the Hawken, Renegade, and Grey Hawk are 28, 26, and 24 inches respectively and each barrel has a rifling twist of 1 turn in 48 inches. This is the most ideal twist for firing the Thompson/Center Maxi-Balls as opposed to round balls. The minie or Maxi-Ball type of projectile has become a staple for caplock shooters, while the round ball is most popular with traditionalists who shoot flintlocks. However, either may be fired in most modern caplocks, although the 1-in-48 twist does not work as well with patched round balls. To address the round ball hunter, Thompson/Center and most other manufacturers offer replacement barrels or special models that are given a slower 1-in-66 twist. In the Thompson/Center Line, the Pennsylvania Hunter series of rifles and carbines is equipped with these slow-twist barrels designed to perform most ideally with patched round balls and less effectively with Maxi-Balls.

It will be noticed that as the models are farther and farther removed from the wholly traditional, the barrels get shorter. The Hawken model is a modern blackpowder weapon that follows traditional styling almost to the letter and it has a traditional-length barrel. The Renegade is a little less traditional, and its barrel is a little shorter. The Grey Hawk with the stainless steel construction and the Rynite stock is far less traditional, and it has a 24-inch barrel, equivalent in length to many standard smokeless powder rifles used for sporting purposes. This trend continues with the Thompson/Center White Mountain Carbine shown in Figure 28-4. This model still retains a lot of traditional styling, but it is equipped with a 21 inch barrel, making it a true carbine. Also available in .50 and .54 caliber, it weighs only 6.5 pounds (unloaded) and is fitted with minimal trim work and a single trigger.

The line of blackpowder rifles discussed to this point began with the ultratraditional (though mod-

Figure 28-4: The Thompson/Center White Mountain Carbine is equipped with a short 21-inch barrel that makes it handy to use in tight, brushy conditions.

ern) Hawken and ended with the White Mountain Carbine, far less traditional but still retaining an overall traditional appearance. This transition is indicative of what is happening in the overall caplock market. Caplock firearms are becoming less and less traditional and more and more in line with the principles that are applied to modern sporting rifles.

For Thompson/Center, the transition caplock between the traditional or semi-traditional and the ultramodern has to be the Scout carbine shown in Figure 28-5.

Also available in a rifle version with a 24-inch barrel, the carbine's 21 inch barrel makes it quite portable for brush work. It is also available in walnut and Rynite stocked versions. The main element of transition, however, is its ignition system. Instead of the traditional side-mounted hammer and nipple, the Scout model has an in-line ignition system. The nipple and ignition channel feed into the center of the barrel's breech through a ported opening that discharges any backward-flowing gases to the side. Since the ignition flame is applied at the center base of the load, it could be argued that overall ignition is more uniform.

The in-line ignition system also gets rid of the side-mounted lock hardware, creating cleaner lines that are less likely to snag on brush. The nipple lies just beneath the centrally-located hammer. To

Figure 28-5: The Thompson/Center Scout Carbine has an in-line ignition system and a 21-inch barrel.

Figure 28-6: The Thompson/Center Thunder Hawk Rifles offer modern stock configurations, in-line ignition systems, excellent balance, and can be easily fitted with telescopic sights as shown in Figure 28-7.

prime the carbine, the hammer is cocked, just as one might cock a Winchester Model 94 carbine and the cap is placed over the nipple. The hammer is then released to a half-cock position. To fire the carbine, the hammer is fully cocked, again, just as you would the Winchester Model 94.

The only traditional styling that is exhibited by this blackpowder carbine more closely mimics the breech-loading rifles and carbines of the 1800s. It resembles no muzzleloader of the past.

The Thompson/Center Scout, as was stated earlier, can be thought of as a transition firearm that bridges the gap between traditionally-styled muzzleloaders and those that are ultra-modern. The latter designs offer most of the attributes that hunters seek in a smokeless sporting rifle in regard to fit, reliability, and handling. The only difference is that these are loaded from the bore and the smokeless firearms are loaded from the breech.

Figures 28-6 and 28-7 show the Thompson/Center Thunder Hawk line of muzzleloaders. If not for the ramrod, these models could easily be mistaken for modern bolt-action sporters that fire smokeless loads in metallic cartridges.

Available in 24-inch rifle and 21-inch carbine configurations, the Thunder Hawk line is representative of the new types of muzzleloaders that are being offered by many companies. With weights of 6.75 and 7.0 pounds for the carbine and rifle, respectively, these firearms handle like the most modern of smokeless sporters on today's market. The short, one-piece breech and in-line ignition system provide especially fast lock times, enhancing accuracy, reliability, and utility. This model is

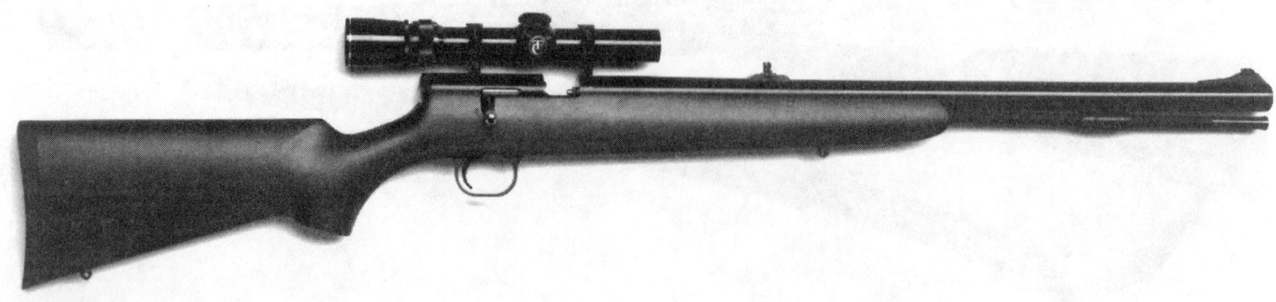

Figure 28-7: The Thompson/Center Thunder Hawk Rifle fitted with telescopic sight.

available in both Rynite and traditional walnut stocks and even in stainless steel configurations. When fitted with telescopic sights, this muzzleloader of modern design offers accuracy on a par with the better smokeless sporting rifles.

While the products of Thompson/Center Arms Company, Inc., probably the best known manufacturer of American-made muzzleloaders, have been featured in these descriptions, the evolution shown in the various models is indicative of what is taking place throughout the manufacturing world. The muzzleloader is no longer (necessarily) a throwback to earlier days but a modern firearm that can take its place alongside the newest centerfire rifles.

CAPLOCK PROJECTILES

Modern caplocks, for the most part, are designed with leanings toward firing conical bullets, often known as "minie" designs. These are traditional bullet-shaped projectiles that have a flat or hollow base and a tapered or rounded nose for more aerodynamic capability (i.e. a better ballistic coefficient). Figure 28-8 shows a Thompson/Center Maxi-Ball, which is fitted with grease grooves along its sides. These grooves are filled with bore lubricant prior to being loaded.

Typically, the minie-style bullets are of the same diameter as the rifling lands for a fairly tight fit. Upon firing, the projectile base flares a bit to provide a gas-tight seal (groove diameter) as it travels up and out of the barrel. Bore lubricant should be used liberally to entirely fill each groove.

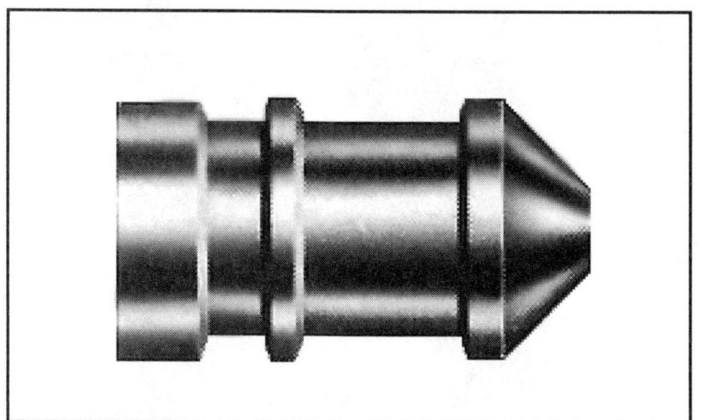

Figure 28-8: The Thompson/Center Maxi-Ball offers a higher ballistic coefficient than round balls for better accuracy and performance.

Alternative bullet designs have more shallow grease grooves, and often a hollow point to facilitate expansion. This type of design is often called a Hunter or Buffalo bullet and is quite popular among some hunters.

The other major type of projectile that is fired in caplock rifles and pistols is the traditional round ball, which is usually sized to 0.1 inch smaller than the barrel diameter. For instance, a .36-caliber rifle would use round balls with a .35-inch diameter. When the round ball is wrapped with a lubricated patch, the diameter increases to the size of the barrel lands.

In recent years, the use of saboted projectiles in muzzleloaders has become quite popular. Sabots are available from the major manufacturers and allow bullets designed for the .44 Magnum pistol and the .444 Marlin rifle to be fired from .50- and .54-caliber muzzleloaders. Some states do not allow the use of saboted loads for big game hunting during the muzzleloader season. Others allow sabots to be used but only with bullets made entirely of lead. Jacketed bullet designs are illegal in these states.

Thompson/Center has recently begun offering sabots that are designed to break into three separate pieces upon exiting the muzzle. Examples are shown in Figures 28-9 and 28-10 on the next page.

The three-piece design incorporates two sabot halves that are locked in place by a woven wool base that already contains bore lubricant. This design lubricates the barrel with each loading and also acts as an over-the-powder wad, which is touted to improve accuracy. Designed for jacketed or lead bullets (.429 to .430 caliber), the sabot separates into three pieces almost immediately upon leaving the muzzle. This provides a better transition into "free flight" for the now-stabilized bullet. Conventional one-piece sabots do not lose contact with the bullet as quickly, which diminishes accuracy. The

Figure 28-9: Basic components of the T/C Break-O-Way Sabot.

empty sabots are available from sporting goods dealers and also from mail-order suppliers. They may be purchased in bags of fifty or in preassembled packs of ten, each containing a 240-grain .44-caliber lead or jacketed bullet.

> *CAUTION!*
>
> Every year, some budding experimenter tells a tale of firing rocks, nails, pieces of tin cans, and other assorted memorabilia from a muzzleloader. This practice is, at the least, potentially damaging to the bore of the muzzleloader. In some instances, it can be highly dangerous. Only properly manufactured and sized projectiles designed specifically for muzzleloaders should be used.

BLACKPOWDER RELOADING MYTHS

As opposed to modern flintlock shooters, who tend to be traditionalists and very conservative regarding the authenticity of their weapons and loads, some users of modern caplocks assume many things that they should not. These assumptions often lead to some dangerous operations that can damage the weapon and the shooter alike. These discussions will, hopefully, cast the light of

Figure 28-10: Thompson/Center Break-O-Way sabots separate into three pieces after exiting the muzzle and are designed to accept jacketed or lead .44 (.429 - .430) caliber bullets.

reality on some of the more common improper practices.

As more and more modern gun enthusiasts return to the caplock muzzleloader for target and hunting purposes, the myths abound about this throwback to simpler times. We have all seen television movies where some grizzled trapper grabs a fist full of blackpowder from his bag, pours it down the barrel, quickly tamps home a round ball (or even a rock, nail, or some other unorthodox projectile), and then fires away at some marauding Indian, or in the Indian's case, at some land-grabbing white man. In one movie, some poor guy was completely impaled by the ramrod of a muzzleloading weapon when the gun had to be fired so quickly in self-defense that there was no time for its removal from the barrel.

Such questionable historicity has led many neophyte blackpowder enthusiasts to believe that, unlike smokeless powder weapons, a muzzleloader will tolerate just about anything. I even heard one practitioner state, "you can literally fill the entire barrel of a muzzleloader with blackpowder and touch it off without damaging the weapon. After all, blackpowder doesn't generate enough pressure to damage modern steel!" Wait a minute! The laws of physics just don't support this, and anyone who would try a stunt like this doesn't have any business whatsoever with any type of weapon, not even a longbow.

Blackpowder (and any blackpowder substitute) is a fuel that generates large quantities of gases when ignited. The expanding gas generates pressure, which must be contained within the barrel of the gun. If this pressure exceeds the tensile strength of the barrel, it is going to come apart. Also, if the shards of metal that fly back into the shooter's face and body exceed the tensile strength of human skin, flesh and bone, these body components are going to come apart as well.

While smokeless powder generates higher pressures than does blackpowder, these pressures are only generated when the smokeless charge is tightly contained in such a manner that the pressure can build. Pour a small quantity of smokeless powder in a heap on the ground and ignite it, and you will see that it burns robustly but not explosively. Do the same with blackpowder and it seems to burn even more robustly. This occurs because blackpowder will burn more progressively at lower pressures than does smokeless powder. This means that blackpowder becomes explosive when less tightly-contained than smokeless powder. In the authors' opinion, blackpowder is far more susceptible to accidental explosion from casual use than is smokeless powder. Many experienced reloaders tend to think of smokeless powder as a propellant, while considering blackpowder a true explosive!

If a muzzleloader is filled from breech to muzzle with blackpowder, it is obvious that, upon firing, the majority of the powder would be propelled out of the barrel unburned . . . in most instances. However, the proper set of circumstances could allow a much greater quantity to be ignited, drastically increasing pressure.

Even if most of the powder is blown out unburned, the weight of the additional powder represents a tremendous projectile weight. This alone would greatly increase the pressure at the breech end. Any way you look at it, such a stunt would be an extremely dangerous and absolutely foolish undertaking. The same would be true if smokeless powder were substituted for blackpowder. Never, never, never use smokeless powder in a blackpowder firearm and always abide by the manufacturer's ratings.

When loading a blackpowder weapon, it is essential that all loading data be followed to the letter. While it is true that a larger quantity of blackpowder is normally required to boost the pressure by a certain percentage than would be the case with smokeless powder, it is also true that the more powder that is burned, the higher the pressure.

Each year, blackpowder weapons are damaged (along with their shooters) by firing improper loads. As for modern steels being impervious to the pressures generated by blackpowder, this is pure hogwash. Modern muzzleloaders are designed to be safe within certain pressure limits, and these limits are far below the 50,000 psi level of most modern smokeless weapons. Manufacturer's provide loading data with each muzzleloader that they make and sell. Follow these instructions to the letter, starting with the minimum charge and working up to maximum, just as you would when developing loads for modern metallic cartridges.

It is sometimes difficult to identify high pressure signs in caplock firearms. With metallic cartridges, the case and primer are the main physical indicators of pressure. Since a caplock firearm does not contain these components, the high pressure signs are not as obvious unless catastrophic failure occurs. This is another reason for caution with all loads used for such firearms. One sign of high pressure that can be immediately evidenced is the hammer being forced back to the half-cocked or even the cocked position upon firing. This can be a sign that high pressure is being produced in sufficient quantity to eject some of the blast through the ignition channel and nipple, forcing the hammer back. However, this can also be caused by a defective nipple, one in which the opening has become enlarged. If hammer rebound is occurring and your load and projectile weight are within the manufacturer's specifications, then replacing the nipple will most likely rectify this situation.

Another myth that is prevalent involves "ramming" the projectile home. Certainly, a ramrod is used to force the projectile down the barrel so that it is firmly seated against the powder charge. However, the force needed to accomplish this has been greatly overemphasized. One of the authors was taught to ram the projectile down the barrel as far as he could possibly push it. Then, the ramrod was to be withdrawn and thrown down the barrel against the projectile several times. The loading process was complete when the ramrod would literally bounce out of the barrel from contacting the seated projectile.

The end result of this process was evidenced when this author found it necessary to pull a seated Maxi-Ball out of the barrel due to a contaminated powder charge. A worm screw was attached to the end of the ramrod, which was inserted into the barrel. After turning the ramrod several times to impale the bullet with the screw, the bullet was withdrawn.

Instead of a normal-appearing Maxi-Ball with a flat base and a tapered nose, what came out of the barrel was a slug that was perfectly flat on both ends. The tapered nose had been hammered flat by the ramrod pounding during the loading process. Now, muzzleloader projectiles, round ball or cylindrical, are not noted for high ballistic coefficients. However, this improper loading process had destroyed any ballistic advantages this projectile had. Why go to the expense of buying aerodynamic bullets if their shape is completely altered during the loading process? This author would have been better off shooting round balls!

The process of throwing the ramrod down the barrel several times after initial seating has been touted in order to assure that the projectile is actually seated against the powder charge without any air gap between the two. If an air gap exists, a hangfire may result, where the cap discharges and the main powder charge does not seem to. A few seconds or even up to a minute later, the firearm discharges. This is obviously a very dangerous situation, one that many blackpowder enthusiasts have experienced. It can also create extremely high pressures causing the barrel to be damaged.

By throwing the ramrod down the barrel several times, the projectile is certainly firmly seated, and even though the projectile is now deformed, there should be no hangfire. Therefore, safety is completely addressed. However, accuracy and efficiency suffer.

The reason a projectile will not firmly seat against the powder, assuming a correct barrel and bullet combination, is fouling. The more you shoot the caplock in one session, the more fouled the barrel becomes, especially around the area of the main charge. This is why over exertion on the ramrod is necessary. However, this situation can be remedied completely by running a dry patch down the barrel after each firing. This is more cumbersome, but it should be a part of the loading process for every blackpowder shooter.

A correct loading method also involves marking the ramrod to indicate a fully seated bullet. With a spotlessly clean barrel. The following is a summary of the procedure:

1. Load the charge and ram the projectile home with one smooth stroke. You should feel the bullet seat firmly against the main charge.

2. With a marking pen, piece of tape, or some other indicator, mark the ramrod at a point exactly even with the muzzle of the barrel.

3. After each shot, run a dry patch down the barrel to remove any loose fouling.

4. When reloading, force the projectile tight against the main charge again with one firm stroke, making certain that the index mark on the ramrod aligns with the muzzle of the barrel.

5. If the index mark is significantly out of alignment with the muzzle and the ramrod cannot be forced further into the barrel, then it will be necessary to gently drop the ramrod against the projectile to attain firm seating. However, this is a sign that fouling has increased to the point where a thorough barrel cleaning is necessary.

Again, the emphasis when ramming the bullet home is on a single smooth and forceful stroke. Ideally, the bullet should be seated to the same point and with the same force on each loading. This is equivalent to loading metallic cartridges with bullets that are seated to a predetermined depth and crimped to the same degree in each and every round. It is this consistency that results in the best accuracy whether it is applied to metallic cartridges or blackpowder firearms. Naturally, changing the quantity of powder or the projectile type will make it necessary to make a new index mark on the ramrod.

The authors also question the need for a "fouling shot" when using modern caplocks with modern projectiles. The fouling shot is a light powder charge that is touched off in a recently-cleaned barrel in order to dirty it up a bit. The idea here is that the shots that follow the first actual discharge will occur with a slightly fouled barrel, so better consistency is maintained if the first shot also meets with approximately the same degree of fouling. For hunting purposes, you are probably only going to get one shot at big game with your blackpowder firearm. If you practice the loading rules previously presented, then running the dry patch down the barrel after each shot will remove most of the loose fouling. The authors have tested firearms for accuracy using the fouling shot method and with perfectly clean barrels. No discernable difference was noted with firearms of .45 caliber and above when using either of the two methods. Fouling shots may apply more to the older blackpowder firearms that do not contain modern rifling or which may even be of smoothbore design.

POWDERS

Blackpowder or a blackpowder substitute such as Hodgdon Pyrodex is the only type of propellants that should be used in muzzleloading firearms. FFFg is the preferred rifle powder for calibers of .45 or less, while FFg is preferable when loading .45-caliber Maxi-Balls and in the larger bores up to .58 caliber. (*See* Chapter 3 for more details on powders.)

Pyrodex RS blackpowder substitute may be used in all modern caplock rifles due to the more positive ignition system. This powder is not recommended for flintlocks unless a small amount of blackpowder is used behind the Pyrodex load as a "getter" to initiate burning.

Pyrodex is designed to be substituted on a quantity-per-quantity basis with blackpowder. Pyrodex is bulkier than equivalent blackpowders, so a quantity of 120 grains of FFg blackpowder as poured from a cylindrical powder measure will contain about 96 grains (by weight) of Pyrodex. In other words, 120 grains of FFg blackpowder occupies the same volume as does 96 grains of Pyrodex. For blackpowder pistol loads, Pyrodex P may be directly substituted for equivalent pistol powders, again, on a quantity-per-quantity basis.

The authors prefer to weigh all loads, regardless of whether the propellent is black or smokeless powder. The weight conversion factor for FFg blackpowder to Pyrodex RS is .80. Multiply the blackpowder weight by .80 to derive the equivalent Pyrodex load weight. As an example, a blackpowder load has been worked up to include 100 grains of FFg behind a 370 grain projectile for a muzzle velocity of 1400 fps. The equivalent Pyrodex load for this same projectile would be 100 × .80 or 80 grains of Pyrodex RS. When 80 grains (by weight) of Pyrodex RS is substituted for the 100 grains of FFg, the muzzle velocity with the same 370-grain projectile should be closely equivalent to that of the same projectile backed by the 100 grains of FFg.

Blackpowder has been traditionally measured by volume, so Pyrodex has been manufactured to bulk the same as its blackpowder equivalent, although it weighs less. All loads in this chapter list powder quantities by weight. If you prefer to convert to bulk, then divide the weight of the Pyrodex powder by 0.80. This will give the proper bulk measurement. Make absolutely certain that you are totally aware of the units of measurement with which you are working. There is a great deal of difference between bulk and weight when comparing Pyrodex with blackpowder.

LOADS FOR BLACKPOWDER FIREARMS

The following loads were developed in modern caplock weapons using blackpowder and Pyrodex blackpowder-substitute. These loads are definitely not intended for antique muzzleloaders or for use in any blackpowder weapon not made from modern steels. All charges that use Pyrodex are measured by weight and NOT by volume.

.36 CALIBER RIFLE

65-grain Round Ball (.35 caliber)		
45 gr. FFFg	1850 fps	
55 gr. FFFg	2000 fps	
62 gr. FFFg	2100 fps	Maximum
35 gr. Pyrodex RS	1800 fps	
42 gr. Pyrodex RS	2050 fps	
50 gr. Pyrodex RS	2150 fps	Maximum

.45 CALIBER RIFLE

130-grain Round Ball (.44 caliber)		
58 gr. FFFg	1600 fps	
68 gr. FFFg	1700 fps	
77 gr. FFFg	1800 fps	
89 gr. FFFg	1900 fps	
46 gr. Pyrodex RS	1610 fps	
54 gr. Pyrodex RS	1730 fps	
62 gr. Pyrodex RS	1845 fps	

NOTE

All charges that use Pyrodex are measured by weight and NOT by volume.

.45 CALIBER RIFLE

240-grain T/C Maxi-Ball		
65 gr. FFg	1380 fps	
72 gr. FFg	1450 fps	
80 gr. FFg	1510 fps	Near Maximum
46 gr. Pyrodex RS	1322 fps	
55 gr. Pyrodex RS	1400 fps	
65 gr. Pyrodex RS	1500 fps	
75 gr. Pyrodex RS	1563 fps	Near Maximum

.50 CALIBER RIFLE

175-grain Round Ball (.49 caliber)		
70 gr. FFg	1545 fps	
80 gr. FFg	1700 fps	
90 gr. FFg	1810 fps	
100 gr. FFg	2000 fps	Maximum
55 gr. Pyrodex RS	1550 fps	
65 gr. Pyrodex RS	1750 fps	
75 gr. Pyrodex RS	1900 fps	Near Maximum
80 gr. Pyrodex RS	2000 fps	Maximum

370-grain T/C Maxi-Ball (.50 caliber)		
81 gr. FFg	1200 fps	
92 gr. FFg	1300 fps	
100 gr. FFg	1383 fps	
64 gr. Pyrodex RS	1243 fps	
74 gr. Pyrodex RS	1367 fps	
80 gr. Pyrodex RS	1426 fps	

.54 CALIBER RIFLE

230-grain Round Ball (.53 caliber)		
75 gr. FFg	1472 fps	
85 gr. FFg	1634 fps	
95 gr. FFg	1740 fps	
104 gr. FFg	1800 fps	
110 gr. FFg	1850 fps	
120 gr. FFg	1900 fps	

.54 CALIBER RIFLE (Cont.)

230-grain Round Ball (.53 caliber)		
60 gr. Pyrodex RS	1472 fps	
70 gr. Pyrodex RS	1638 fps	
80 gr. Pyrodex RS	1804 fps	
90 gr. Pyrodex RS	1875 fps	
95 gr. Pyrodex RS	1950 fps	

430-grain T/C Maxi-Ball (.54 caliber)		
100 gr. FFg	1234 fps	
110 gr. FFg	1325 fps	
120 gr. FFg	1413 fps	
80 gr. Pyrodex RS	1251 fps	
90 gr. Pyrodex RS	1358 fps	
96 gr. Pyrodex RS	1437 fps	

.58 CALIBER RIFLE

555-grain T/C Maxi-Ball (.58 caliber)		
80 gr. FFg	1093 fps*	
90 gr. FFg	1149 fps*	
100 gr. FFg	1221 fps*	
110 gr. FFg	1282 fps*	
120 gr. FFg	1331 fps*	

CAUTION!

The above loads are only for the Thompson/Center Big Boar, and other modern .58-caliber rifles of similar construction. Not for use in earlier .58 caliber rifles of less substantial construction.

*** Loads courtesy of Thompson/Center Arms, Inc.**

LOADS FOR CAP-AND-BALL BLACKPOWDER REVOLVERS

Blackpowder revolvers and pistols have not enjoyed the same popularity as muzzleloading rifles. The reason for this lies in the fact that blackpowder pistols may not be used for big-game hunting in any state. While they may be used for small-game hunting during regular (smokeless) hunting seasons, this has not been enough to peak the interest of the general shooting public.

Blackpowder rifles have surged in popularity due mainly to the extended big-game hunting seasons that have been opened only for such primitive firearms. Many hunters use blackpowder rifles, not for their historic value or even to be traditional, but to allow themselves more time pursuing big game. This is certainly the reason for the great influx of extremely modern blackpowder rifles, many of which resemble today's metallic-cartridge rifles and serve basically the same purpose.

No specific loads for cap-and-ball revolvers or other blackpowder pistols are provided in this book, because these firearms vary greatly in strength and construction. One revolver may have a maximum load rating that is drastically lower than another of the same caliber.

However, a general guide is provided in this section that will help reloaders choose loads for typical cap and ball revolvers of various calibers. The best source of reloading data for a specific pistol will be garnered directly from the manufacturer. Some revolvers whose construction has followed the most modern methods will withstand quite heavy loads. Some others that are manufactured in the "old style" with a main concentration on authenticity will max out at much lower charges. Some of the latter may not even use steel construction. Owing to this diversity, it is not possible to present a wide range of general loads for any particular caliber on a generic basis.

CAP-AND-BALL LOADS

Round Balls Only			
Caliber	Ball Diameter	FFFg (grains)	Velocity (fps)
.31	.32	12.0	520
.36	.375	22.0	725
.44	.451	32.0	750
.44 Ruger	.457	43.0	850

These are "typical" load weights recommended for modern cap-and-ball revolvers of steel construction. If there is any doubt as to the strength or workmanship of any revolver, or if it is of antique construction, in general, consult the manufacturer and/or a gunsmith before using ANY load.

Chapter 29

Loads for Muzzleloading Shotguns

When firearms with rifled barrels starting replacing the smoothbore musket and bores gradually became smaller in size, a special fowling gun was developed. This fowling piece came to be called a "shotgun" and was made with either single or double barrels.

Shotguns trace their descent from the ancient bell-mouth blunderbuss (Figure 29-1). The fowling piece that developed after that was simply a shorter, lighter version of the smoothbore musket.

The slow ignition of flintlock arms limited the success of hitting birds on the wing, and fowling pieces were seldom used until the introduction of the percussion cap. With its more rapid ignition, wing shooting became more practical.

Figure 29-1: CVA replica of ancient blunderbuss — the ancestor of the modern shotgun.

The average shooter of the 1800s found that the .69-caliber smoothbore musket, loaded with a charge of shot pellets, served well enough for sitting ducks. But rifled barrels were unsuited for shot loads. Consequently, a special smoothbore fowling piece was developed which was eventually called *shotgun*. This firearm rapidly acquired the characteristics that are found in the single-shot and side-by-side double-barreled shotguns of today. *See* Figure 29-2 on the next page.

Shortly after the introduction of the muzzleloading smoothbore fowling piece, choke boring was discovered. By constricting the bore at the muzzle, it was found that a gun would throw a narrower, denser pattern of shot, tremendously extending its effective range. While many replica muzzleloading shotgun barrels are choked, most authentic muzzleloading shotguns of the last century were cylinder

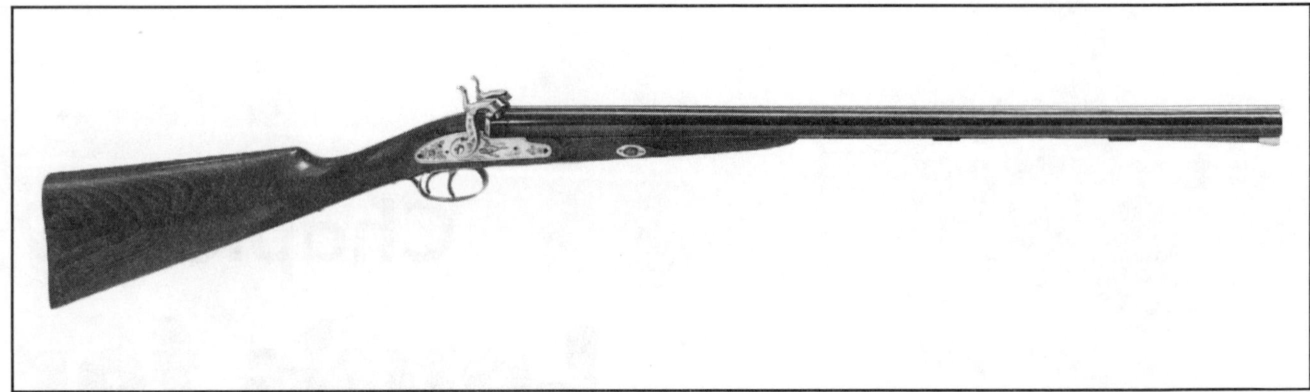

Figure 29-2: Muzzleloading shotguns of the last century quickly took on the characteristics that are still visible in modern single-shot and side-by-side double-barrel shotguns.

bored, so loads developed and the practical application of such weapons must be considered accordingly.

SHOTGUN CHOKES

Constricting the muzzle of a shotgun barrel to obtain denser shot patterns was invented by Henri Pellet of Liége, Belgium in 1861. This same basic choke design is still used by many shotgun manufacturers of today, especially on high-quality side-by-side and over/under double-barrel shotguns.

At about the time the choke appeared in Belgium, an American by the name of Fred Kimble also choked shotgun barrels, using a design very similar to the Belgian choke. With both choking systems, the barrel tapers to a parallel section known as a *Resserre* as shown in Figure 29-3.

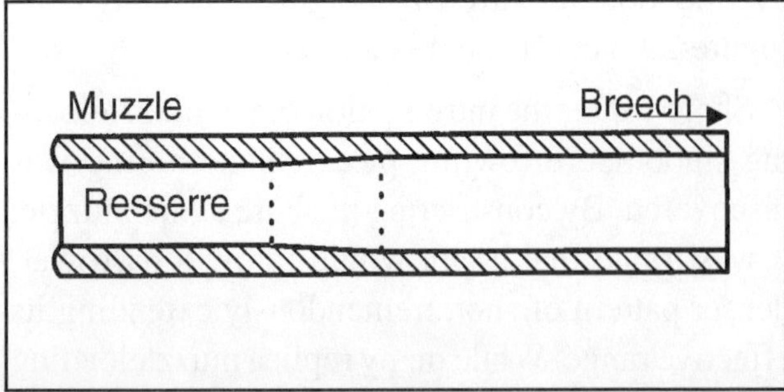

Figure 29-3: Cross-sectional view of Belgian choke, showing Resserre.

The straight-taper choke (Figure 29-4) originated in Germany and is currently used by several American shotgun manufacturers. Next to the Belgian choke, which usually gives more even patterns, the straight-taper choke is one of the better types of chokes. In actual tests, the straight-taper choke usually gives tighter patterns that the Belgian choke, but the patterns are not quite as even. Shooting-match buffs of today still use the older Winchester Models 12, 37, and 97 for most their shooting, and all utilize the straight-taper choke.

The swaged choke is installed by merely crimping the muzzle end of the shotgun barrel. This type of choke is frequently found on inexpensive single-shot guns.

For more information on shotgun chokes, *see* Section IV of this book — *Loading Shotshells*.

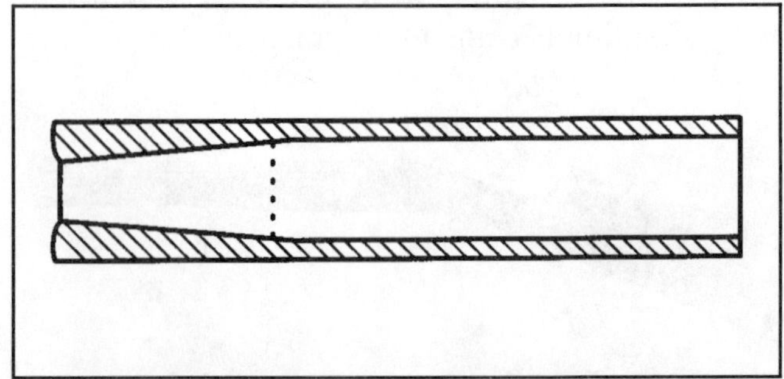

Figure 29-4: Cross-sectional view of straight-taper choke. This type of choke has been used by many American shotgun manufacturers.

LOADING THE MUZZLELOADING SHOTGUN

A muzzleloading shotgun is loaded almost identically to the more modern paper shotshell with a rolled crimp. The shotshell in Figure 29-5, for example, shows the primer, the powder, several layers of wads, the shot, and finally, an overshot wad and crimp to hold everything in place. Now refer to Figure 29-6 and note the similarities.

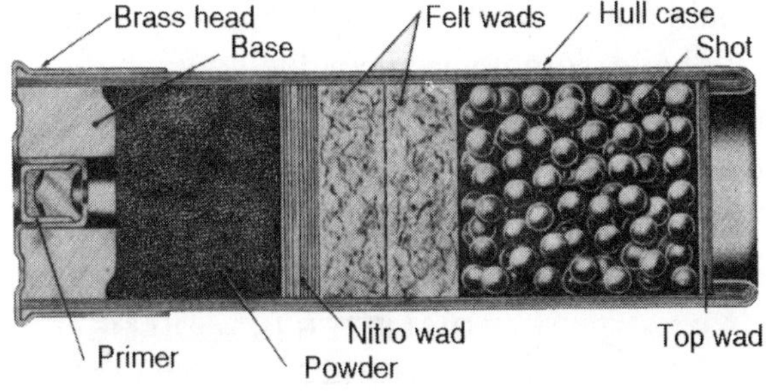

Figure 29-5: Cross-sectional view of a rolled-crimp shotshell.

In place of the battery-cup primer in a shotshell, a muzzleloading shotgun has either the priming charge of powder in the pan (for flintlocks) or a percussion cap placed on the nipple in the case of percussion shotguns. The remaining basic components are practically identical; that is, powder, wads, shot, and finally, another wad placed on top of everything to hold the charge in place for firing.

The shotshell is ignited, and consequently fired, when the firing pin strikes the battery-cup primer secured in the base of the shell. The battery-cup primer sends a hot spark to ignite the primary powder charge in the base of the shotshell. The burning of any powder in a confined area forms rapidly-expanding gases which, in turn, force the wads and shot out of the bore toward the target. The hammer containing the flint in flintlock fowling pieces strikes the striking plate which sends a spark to the priming pan containing the charge of priming powder. This powder ignites similar to the battery-cup primer and sends another flame through the vent hole to ignite the primary powder charge contained in the chamber of the muzzleloading barrel. The remaining sequence of combustion is almost identical to the shotshell.

The percussion shotgun operates in a similar fashion, except that the percussion cap takes the place of the flint, striking plate, and priming charge in the flintlock pan. When the hammer falls on a percussion cap, a hot spark or flame is sent through the nipple and vent hole to ignite the primary powder charge in the breech area of the muzzleloading barrel. Again, all reactions from this point on are very similar to the modern shotshell.

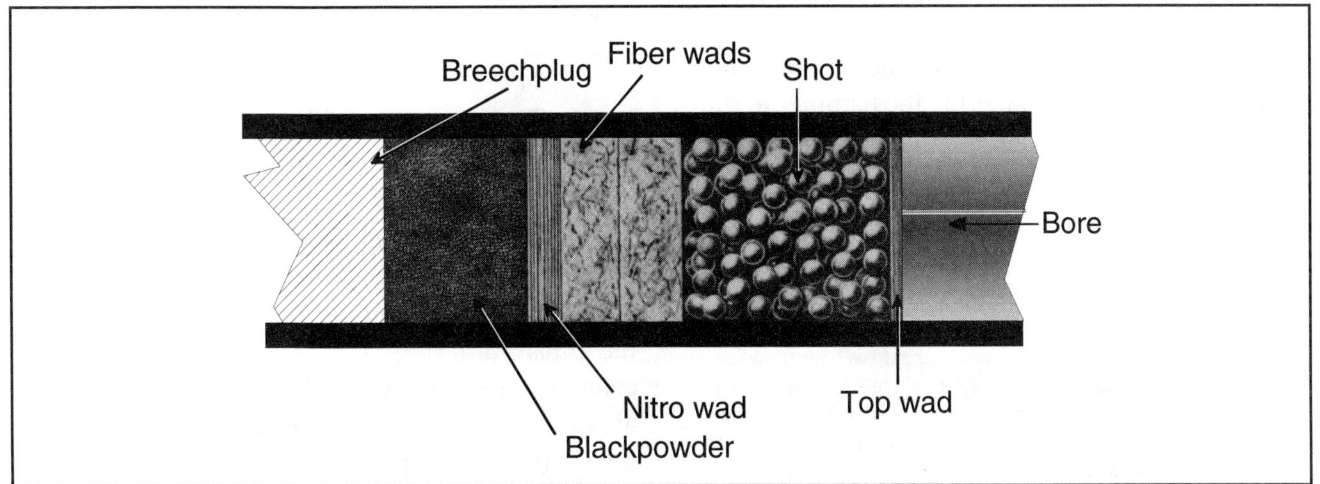

Figure 29-6: Cross-sectional view of the breech end of a muzzleloading shotgun.

To load a muzzleloading shotgun, make sure that the hammer or hammers are lowered on bare nipples (no caps) and the bore is clean and free. Then measure the required amount of blackpowder for a single barrel and pour in the powder. Next comes the wadding. In a pinch, this can be crumpled newspaper, but for best results, use an overpowder wad (nitro wad) of stiff cardboard about ⅛-inch thick, followed by one or two soft felt wads. The nitro wad should be slightly oversize to ensure a tight fit in the bore. Push the nitro wad firmly into the bore with the ramrod until it seats firmly on the powder charge — compressing the powder slightly. If two nitro wads are used, they should be loaded as a single unit.

The nitro wad is followed by a lightly-greased soft felt wad. The grease helps to keep fouling to the minimum and make cleaner shooting. Hodgdon "Spit Patch" works well for this application.

Pour a measured recommended amount of shot into the bore, followed by a thin top wad over the shot. This top or overshot wad should be relatively thin — just enough to hold the shot in place — and tamped down just enough to make the ramrod bounce when dropped into the bore. Too thick an overshot wad will result in erratic patterns. When loading double-barrel shotguns, however, the overshot wad should be a little tighter to make certain the firing of one barrel does not disrupt the charge in the other barrel.

Halfcock the hammer and cap the nipple. Point the gun in a safe direction, bring the hammer to full cock, and fire.

Muzzleloading experts claim that the powder, wad, and shot columns should be equal in length.

WARNING

Damascus barrels should be considered unsafe with any powder. Some shooters will disagree, but they should talk to a fellow who lives a cannon-shot away from us who is now walking around without the tops of four fingers — caused by a blow-up in his breechloading Damascus-barreled shotgun using ***blackpowder*** loads.

This may or may not be the case, depending on the individual gun.

To obtain the proper size wad for an individual gun, measure the inside bore diameter, then select a wad size that will not fall down the bore, but one that can easily be pushed down the bore with the ramrod without meeting too much resistance. An overtight wad will build up excessive pressure and also cause erratic shot patterns.

The following table lists the average bore sizes for various shotgun bores. These data, however, should not be taken as gospel. Each shotgun barrel will have some variance due to manufacturing methods, and it is always best to measure the bore of each individual shotgun before selecting wads.

GAUGE	BORE DIAMETER IN INCHES	BORE DIAMETER IN MILLIMETERS
2	1.325	33.0
4	1.052	27.0
8	0.835	21.2
10	0.775	19.6
12	0.729	18.4
14	0.963	17.6
16	0.662	16.8
20	0.615	15.6
24	0.579	14.6
28	0.550	13.8
32	0.526	13.2
34	0.515	13.0
36	0.506	12.8
.410	0.410	10.4

Older muzzleloading shotguns were sometimes made in other than standard gauges, such as 13, 33, 35, etc., depending upon the sizes of mandrels in the gunsmith's shop. Interpolation may be used to calculate sizes of shotgun bores that are not standard. For example, a shotgun bore measures, say, 0.637 inch. Comparing this measurement with those in the preceding table shows that this dimension lies between a 16- and 20-gauge bore. If pure

> *NOTE*
>
> One dram = 27.34 grains.

lead round balls were cast with a diameter of 0.637 inch, it would be found that approximately 18 of these lead balls would equal a pound in weight. Thus, a shotgun with a bore diameter of 0.637 inch would be an 18-gauge shotgun. But you don't have to go to the trouble of casting lead balls to find out the gauge. Merely measure the bore diameter to find the size wad required, and if the bore diameter falls somewhere between a 16- and 20-gauge bore, adjust your loads accordingly. For example, if the top load for a 16-gauge shotgun is 3⅛ drams of blackpowder, and the maximum recommended load for a 20-gauge shotgun is 2¾ drams of blackpowder, then a compromise for the 0.637-inch bore will be about 2.9 or 3 drams of blackpowder. Add the two dram weights and then divide by 2; that is, add the dram weight of the known gauge larger than the unknown gauge to the dram weight of the closest known gauge smaller than the unknown gauge, and then divide by 2. The equation is as follows:

$$\text{Powder charge for unknown bore} = \frac{\text{Charge weight of larger gauge} + \text{charge weight of smaller gauge}}{2}$$

Fortunately, blackpowder is more forgiving than smokeless powders, and a grain or two will not make a drastic difference in safety unless the shooter already happens to be well over the maximum recommended load; then, anything can happen when a couple of grains are added to the load.

The following blackpowder loads were developed for standard shotgun gauges and were found to be safe in guns in good condition. Always have older guns checked by a competent gunsmith before firing. Be especially cautious of older double-barrel shotguns with soft-soldered ribs.

4 GAUGE

POWDER TYPE	DRAMS	GRAINS	SHOT OUNCES	VELOCITY FPS	LOAD	REMARKS
Fg	8	218.7	3	950	Mild	
Fg	9	246.0	3	1016	Moderate	
Fg	10	273.4	3	1058	Heavy	

10 GAUGE

POWDER TYPE	DRAMS	GRAINS	SHOT OUNCES	VELOCITY FPS	LOAD	REMARKS
FFg	3¾	103.0	1¼	1060	Mild	
FFg	4	109.4	1½	1040	Moderate	
FFg	4½	123.0	1½	1075	Medium heavy	
Fg	5	136.7	1¾	1055	Heavy	

12 GAUGE

POWDER TYPE	DRAMS	GRAINS	SHOT OUNCES	VELOCITY FPS	LOAD	REMARKS
FFg	2¾	76.0	1⅛	1065	Mild	
FFg	3	82.0	1¼	1040	Moderate	Gave best pattern of the three
FFg	3¼	89.0	1¼	1055	Heavy	

14 GAUGE

POWDER TYPE	DRAMS	GRAINS	SHOT OUNCES	VELOCITY FPS	LOAD	REMARKS
FFg	2½	69.0	1	1030	Mild	
FFg	2¾	76.0	1	1070	Moderate	
FFg	3⅛	86.0	1⅛	1055	Heavy	

16 GAUGE

POWDER TYPE	DRAMS	GRAINS	SHOT OUNCES	VELOCITY FPS	LOAD	REMARKS
FFg	2¼	61.0	1	1000	Mild	
FFg	2½	69.0	1	1020	Moderate	
FFg	2¾	76.0	1	1035	Heavy	

20 GAUGE

POWDER TYPE	DRAMS	GRAINS	SHOT OUNCES	VELOCITY FPS	LOAD	REMARKS
FFg	2	55.0	¾	1000	Mild	
FFg	2¼	61.0	⅞	1015	Moderate	
FFg	2½	69.0	⅞	1025	Heavy	

28 GAUGE

POWDER TYPE	DRAMS	GRAINS	SHOT OUNCES	VELOCITY FPS	LOAD	REMARKS
FFg	1¾	48.0	⅝	1025	Mild	
FFg	2	55.0	⅝	1090	Moderate	
FFg	2	55.0	¾	1075	Heavy	

32 GAUGE

POWDER TYPE	DRAMS	GRAINS	SHOT OUNCES	VELOCITY FPS	LOAD	REMARKS
FFg	1½	41.0	½	1075	Mild	
FFg	1½	41.0	9⁄16	1050	Moderate	
FFg	1¾	48.0	⅝	1050	Heavy	

.410 BORE

POWDER TYPE	DRAMS	GRAINS	SHOT OUNCES	VELOCITY FPS	LOAD	REMARKS
FFg	1¼	34.0	½	1080	Mild	
FFg	1½	41.0	½	1125	Moderate	
FFg	1½	41.0	⅝	1100	Heavy	

SECTION VII
TESTING

Chapter 30

Range and Testing Facilities

All firearms are different. Even though two may be of the same model, same caliber, and even manufactured on the same day, they are still different in regard to chamber, breechface, and barrel dimensions. Therefore, all loads should be range-tested for accuracy, feeding, and safety prior to their use in the field.

If reasonable accuracy and performance are all that a shooter is seeking, then factory ammunition would suffice, and economy would be the only reason for reloading, or perhaps to satisfy the desire to "roll your own." However, most reloaders are going to want to squeeze the last ounce of accuracy and efficiency from their loads. The only way that this can be accomplished is by working up several loads for a particular firearm and extensively testing each on a firing/testing range.

THE BASIC RANGE

Basically, a firing range is a facility — either indoors or outdoors — that offers a clear area over which to fire at a target. Ideal testing conditions would further require the range to have a platform or bench, equipped with sandbag rests, on which the firearm can be conveniently placed for the firing sequence, a certain amount of clear area over which the projectiles are fired, and a safe target/backstop to determine point of impact and to stop the flight of the projectile. There are many other options that can add greatly to the utility of the firing range, but these are the essentials that must be established before options like ballistic chronographs, electronic targets, bullet traps, etc. should be incorporated.

THE CLEAR AREA

The clear area of a firing range is the space between the bench or shooting station and the target/backstop. This part of the range should be generally inaccessible, except from the shooting position. This means that it should be next to impossible — or highly inconvenient — for any person or animal to accidentally wander into the actual shooting path. This precaution goes without saying for most shooters, but many accidents have occurred to living things (including people) on ranges that were not properly set up with safety in mind.

Outdoor ranges may be able to take advantage of certain geographical features of the land on which the range is to be installed that precludes easy lateral access. Ideally, there should be only one entrance to the range and this one must provide egress only by means of the shooting position. Some communities, especially in the Western states, where out-of-state hunters provide significant local income, provide public shooting ranges. Invariably, the best of these are completely surrounded on all sides by a chain link fence. This provides maximum protection from the possibility of anyone straying onto the range. However, such accommodations are rarely practical for the average reloader. It may be practical to install a low wooden or steel wire "garden" fence paralleling the shooting station and the backdrop area. While not an impenetrable barrier, such a set up will serve to warn and deter human intervention and completely prohibit small animals from entering a danger area.

Many people think of the clear area as being a narrow expanse at least 100 yards long. While reloaders living on farms or in open rural areas may have the capability of building a range of this size, this will not be the case for most persons. Rather, a much shorter range is probably more practical and, through interpolation, can be used to determine bullet accuracy and performance out to several hundred yards. A range that offers a 25-yard clear area is adequate for testing most modern rifle ammunition. Due to the trajectory of modern loads and a general trend toward sighting-in big game rifles at 100 yards, many bullets will be dead on target at the 100-yard range and also at 25 yards.

Since a bullet begins dropping due to the force of gravity from the moment it leaves the rifle bore, the bore is aligned above the intended target point, causing it to rise above the target line to a certain point and then fall to the target line (hopefully, on impact), dropping below the target line past this point. By examining trajectory charts, it will be readily seen that there are two points along this line at which the projectile will be dead on target. The first point occurs somewhere around 25 yards and the second at the target proper. For this reason, a 25 yard range is considered adequate for testing most high-velocity rifle loads and for sighting them in at more distant ranges through interpolation.

Even if the first point of impact does not occur at exactly 25 yards, an examination of a trajectory chart, when the ballistic coefficient and muzzle velocity of the bullet are known, will yield the elevation figure (so many inches above or below target) that will allow a bullet to be sighted in at 100 or more yards. True, if you want to sight in a big-game rifle at 100 yards, the proof is in the pudding, and firing over a 100 yard range will yield proven results. However, sighting in the same load for 100 yards on a 25-yard range will work almost as well, so long as you are sure of the ballistic coefficient and muzzle velocity. The first can be derived from manufacturer's literature and the second from a chronograph.

The 25-yard rifle range is far more practical for the vast majority of reloaders who are not maintaining a commercial facility than is one of 100 yards. It makes it easier to provide security and there is less distance to walk (both ways) when retrieving targets. The authors have sighted in rifles for long range Western hunting on short ranges of the type described with excellent results.

The short range idea sounds fine for sighting in rifles, but what about accuracy determination? After all, it is easier to shoot accurately at 25 yards than it is at 100 yards. Again, interpolation is necessary. Bullet accuracy is determined in minutes-of-angle. A rifle whose projectiles deviate less than 1 inch in impacting a target at 100 yards is said to shoot to one minute-of-angle accuracy. Through interpolation, a rifle that shoots bullets that impact a target 25 yards distant with deviations of less than ¼ inch is shooting to the same minute-of-angle.

With hunting rifles, the minute-of-angle measurement has far less bearing that when discussing target rifles. Rarely can a hunter hold to such a close tolerance, which is only possible from a steady shooting bench. Practical interpolation of target impact points at 25 yards requires some "Tennessee Windage" and abiding by a loose rule of thumb. A firearm/load combination that shoots three bullets through a single hole at 25 yards will most-likely shoot a ragged hole or better at 100 yards. Likewise, if your rifle is shooting 2-inch groups at 25 yards, then it will probably shoot 8-inch groups at 100 yards. This comparison is general, as specifics can only be obtained by examining actual results fired at the longer range. However, when firing groups at 25 yards, they should be very tight. If they aren't (and the spread is due to the load and not to the human doing the firing), then this load is going to be disappointing at 100 or more yards. This is a common-sense approach, but it tests well under actual hunting/shooting conditions.

For pistol ranges, a 25-foot clear area should prove adequate for all but the specialty pistols that fire ammunition traditionally made for rifles. Pistols and revolvers are generally short-range firearms, so a long shooting range is not necessary. Some of the smaller defense pistols (.22, .25, .32, .380 automatics, for instance) are often sighted in at 15 feet. Even for specialty pistols used for hunting and target shooting, the 25 yard clear area discussed previously should be more than adequate.

All ranges must be planned with the first criterion being safety. A great mistake is made when safety is sacrificed in order to have a longer clear area for shooting. Even if you have the space to build a 100 yard range, don't even consider it if you can't be certain of maintaining absolute security over this distance. Longer shooting ranges also require much larger backstop areas, since the muzzle of the firearm may have to be angled higher above the target line than is the case with a shorter range. Longer ranges also require wider clear areas, because a bullet that is moving off-target will continue this angle of deviation the farther it gets from the muzzle. A bullet that is 6 inches left of the target at 25 yards will be on the order of 2 feet left of target at 100 yards. Overall, the security provisions and all physical tolerances will have to be at least four times more stringent at 100 yards than they are at 25 yards.

THE TARGET/BACKSTOP AREA

The target/backstop area is positioned at the far end of the clear shooting area. It is absolutely essential that a means be provided for stopping bullets that travel along the range, and it must be large enough, and of the proper composition, to stop accidental strays that may go far wide of the intended target line. Geographical features may make it easy to comply with this requirement. Ideally, your shooting range will be located so that a hill or steep bank can serve as the backstop. Never, never, never depend on a tree (large or otherwise) to serve as a backstop. One of the authors remembers a time from his youth when he was test firing a .45-70 Winchester Model 1886 at short range using a tree as a backstop. One of the loads completely penetrated the tree and traveled into a pasture containing a herd of cattle. Fortunately, the bullet missed the cows, but this was pure luck as it was certainly heading in their direction. As bad as wounding an animal is, if humans had been in that field, this memorable event might have been a truly tragic one.

The backstop area must be more than adequate to stop any and all projectiles. This relates to physical size and to density. The authors prefer a tall mound of soft earth as the most ideal natural backstop, and we're not speaking here of just any old hillside. Most naturally-laying soils contain a fair amount of rocks and solid clay. If either are struck by a bullet, there is a chance of a ricochet that could land 300 or more yards in any direction away from the target. While it may seem ridiculous to haul in a dumptruck load of fine topsoil for shooting purposes, if this prevents even one minor accident, it's well worth it.

An ideal backdrop area could consist of a heavy pine box, completely enclosed on all sides except the back, where it tightly abuts a large mound of soft dirt. Since ricochets can even occur when a bullet strikes hard dirt at the right angle, any such occurrence will probably deflect back, up or down, into the box, which also serves as a target platform. We realize that most shooters are accustomed to going to some out-of-the-way location, nailing a target to a tree or placing it against a hillside, and then firing away. Rarely does any harm result from this practice. However, when building a bona fide shooting range, you have a far greater responsibility, because you open yourself to all kinds of possible litigation should a mishap occur. This is not just casual shooting but a dedicated "structure" intended for the sole purpose of safely firing guns. The legal system in this country looks far differently at shooting structures than it does at casual field shooting.

The authors feel that some type of impenetrable natural barrier must exist at the end of the shooting range. However, this may not always be adequate to stop ricochets. In such instances, the reloader may wish to look into the possibility of purchasing or building a bullet trap.

Chapter 31

Velocity and Chronographs

Velocity is one of the most important single factors in measuring handloads. It is necessary to know the velocity at or near the muzzle in order to determine downrange trajectory (when velocity is coupled with the ballistic coefficient of the projectile), energy at any point downrange, wind drift and other external ballistics figures.

Reloading ammunition requires that it be tested for accuracy and efficiency. Accuracy testing does not often require a great deal of extra components, as a paper target placed at a given range will reveal most of the results in short order. Efficiency ratings concern the amount of powder used for the attained velocity. Velocity is one of the most important single factors in measuring handloads. It is necessary to know the velocity at or near the muzzle in order to determine downrange trajectory (when velocity is coupled with the ballistic coefficient of the projectile), energy at any point downrange, wind drift and other external ballistics figures.

The only practical way to measure projectile velocity is with a chronograph or *electronic ballistic chronograph*, as it is more accurately named. There were some mechanical contraptions devised in the past that crudely measured velocity by firing a projectile into a mass of known weight and determining how far it was moved by the force. This yielded the striking energy, from which the velocity could be derived by knowing the projectile weight. As one might expect, these mechanical devices were far from practical and even farther from being accurate.

A ballistic chronograph is little more than a high-speed stopwatch. A standard stopwatch is started by pressing a button and stopped by pressing the same button again. On the first push, the clock

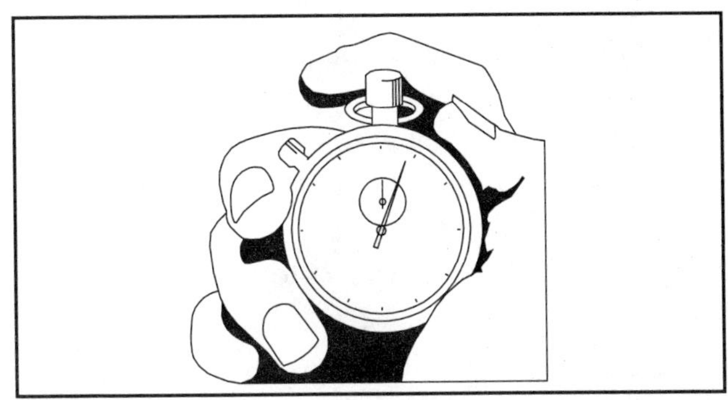

Figure 31-1: A ballistic chronograph may be compared to a stopwatch.

is started. On the second, it is stopped. The clock face reveals how much time passed during the interval.

An electronic chronograph doesn't measure intervals in seconds, but in microseconds (1 microsecond = $^1/_{1000000}$ of a second). The electronic clock is started and stopped by optical sensors/switches. Two sensors are placed just below the target line, so that the bullet will pass over each of them as it travels toward the target. Natural light from the sun keeps these electronic switches in the OFF position. However, when the projectile passes over the sensitive surface of the first electrode or skyscreen, it momentarily blocks this light and the sensor switches the clock ON. A split second later, the bullet passes over the second skyscreen, and it switches the chronograph OFF. There is a fixed distance between the two skyscreens, so the interval measured by this electronic clock gives the time it took the bullet to travel this distance.

If the travel distance is ten feet and the chronograph registers 1/300th of a second, then the velocity of the projectile is 300 × 10 or 3,000 fps. Fortunately, it is not necessary to perform mathematical computations to determine the velocity of the bullet, as modern chronographs handle the math electronically through digital circuitry — giving readouts in feet-per-second (fps).

Modern chronographs are very accurate — providing measurements that have error deviations of no more than approximately 10 fps for typical velocities. Technically, they do not measure muzzle velocity; rather, the velocity a few feet from the muzzle. If the last sensor is placed ten feet from the muzzle, then the reading, to be absolutely correct, is the velocity of the bullet at 10 feet. This is close enough to the actual velocity at the muzzle for almost all intents and purposes to be considered the actual muzzle velocity.

The first commercial ballistic chronographs that were marketed were quite expensive, but unlike most other types of products, anything that is electronic in nature usually drops in price over the years, as research and development costs are paid. Today, an inexpensive ballistic chronograph can be purchased for less than one hundred dollars. However, some more sophisticated models that have features to determine standard velocity deviation from a series of shots and hard copy printouts may run more on the order of $300 to $400.

The critical element in using a chronograph is to accurately position the skyscreens so that they are positively triggered by the projectile. Some models do better on overcast days than others. Some even employ an extra sensor and sun refractors for more positive triggering and internal accuracy testing. The clock mechanism, from the standpoint of practicality, is less important and critical to good measurements than are the skyscreen triggering units.

To aid chronograph users, most manufacturers now include cardboard or plastic targeting plates that attach to the top of each sensor. These give the shooter a target point at which to aim to better assure a positive triggering action from the projectile. They are normally calibrated for use with both scopes and iron sights, providing a different aiming point for each.

The less expensive chronographs are usually one-piece units that incorporate the sensors and the electronics in a single package. Those that cost a bit more separate the sensors from the electronic clock, connecting the two by means of a long cable. This keeps the electronics out of the shooting lane, so a mishap caused by aiming too close to the sensors will only result in the projectile damaging the skyscreens, which can be replaced inexpensively. The electronics remain undamaged.

CHRONOGRAPH RESULTS AND ACCURACY

A goal of any reloader is accuracy, and the first law of accuracy is shot-to-shot uniformity. When ammunition is uniform in characteristics, then it produces the best accuracy. It is obvious that one load that leaves the muzzle at 2750 fps is going to have a different point of impact on a downrange target than a load that leaves the muzzle at 2700 fps. Accuracy also depends heavily on the firearm and shooting technique, but ammunition characteristics must be uniform, or there is no basis for excellent accuracy.

One of the best ways to check for ammunition uniformity is with a ballistic chronograph. When measured velocities of a particular lot of ammunition are nearly identical, then ammunition uniformity has been obtained. The chronograph conveniently measures the velocity of each fired round, indicating the overall performance of the ammunition.

Ammunition uniformity occurs when the pressure generated by the primer/powder/case/bullet combination in one round in a lot is closely identical with that of another round in the same lot. Since it is very difficult (if not impossible) to measure chamber pressures in standard firearms, the ballistic chronograph serves as the most practical means of testing for uniformity.

CHRONOGRAPH TYPES

The reloader has many different brands of chronographs to choose from. However, most of these can be classified in two categories: Self-contained units, incorporating the electronic unit and the skyscreens in one compact package; and the two-piece units with the electronic processing/read-out section separate from the sensing electrodes. Each type has its advantages and disadvantages. Both types perform the same, basic function: measuring the velocity of projectiles.

THE SELF-CONTAINED CHRONOGRAPH

The self-contained, one-piece chronograph is a compact unit containing no external cables. The unit is normally mounted on a tripod, and projectiles are fired over the wire guides that are mounted on top. The front panel immediately displays the measured velocity after each shot.

Most units of this type are simple to use, inexpensive, and basic, making them ideal for field testing purposes, where a minimum of set-up complexities is desirable. Reloaders who are equipped with far more elaborate chronographs will often have one of these compact units on hand to be used in conditions where simplicity takes preference.

The Shooting Chrony, Inc. Model F-1 is accurate and very compact, folding into a unit that can easily be carried in one hand. To use it, all that is necessary is to unfold the package, mount it on a tripod (or even set it atop a fence post for field use), and turn the switch to the ON position. A 9-volt battery powers the unit for years of occasional use.

TWO-PIECE CHRONOGRAPHS

The two-piece chronograph types have a separate sensor and electronics unit. This means that the electronic readout unit may be placed at the shooting stand and the results seen immediately. Typically, these chronograph types provide a relatively long cable to connect the sensors to the electronic unit, so the more costly electronics portion of the chronograph are well out of the shooting line.

The Hornady Chronomax chronograph (Figure 31-2 on next page) consists of a miniature electronic readout unit and a unique sensor/stand arrangement. The skyscreen sensors are mounted on a hollow carrying tube, spaced two feet apart. The screens and the legs disassemble into individual components that are stored within the hollow tube. This results in a very compact two-piece package that is easy to set up, take down, and transport.

The electronics unit is powered by four AA batteries, which can last up to 72 hours of continuous use. High energy alkaline batteries are recommended for longest life. The readout is a liquid crystal display (LCD) that is easy to see and doesn't consume much energy from the batteries. How-

Figure 31-2: Hornady Chronomax chronograph.

ever, bright sunlight can sometimes hamper the view, and it's necessary for the shooter to shield the LCD screen from the bright sunlight or adjust the contrast in order to obtain a reading.

Set-up is straight-forward. Remove the individual components from the hollow tube, and attach the legs and screens. A single cable runs from the screens to the readout unit (which is small enough to fit in a coat pocket). A built-in easel is provided on the box to allow it to be positioned at an angle that makes it easy to read. The shooter may then fire as many shots as desired, without having to adjust or reset anything on the screens.

The electronic unit has only three buttons the shooter needs to bother with: POWER, RESET, and CONTRAST. The CONTRAST button helps in setting the digital readout display for the most clarity in varying light conditions.

The Chronomax has short sensor spacing (2 feet) but an extremely fast internal clock, so the readings are very accurate, and the range of velocities of this unit is excellent. Velocities of from 100 fps to 4999 fps are measured with a claimed deviation of only 1 fps. This means that it can be utilized for measuring the speed of arrows as well as bullets.

The LCD screen provides a readout of a continuous string of up to five shots. On the sixth shot, the first recorded velocity rolls off the screen display area. When the RESET button is pressed, the internal memory of the chronograph is cleared, and another string of shots may be fired and measured if desired.

One of the nicer features of this unit is the single cable connection between the skyscreens and the electronics unit. Many chronographs employ two, separate cables. The Chronomax really does have two sets of conductors, but they are contained in a single cable, which simply plugs into the readout unit at one end and the skyscreens at the other. This arrangement makes for far less clutter around the shooting area and simplifies initial set-up. Also, there are less wires to trip over when walking back and forth between the shooting position and the target.

THE OEHLER 35P CHRONOGRAPH

Oehler is probably the most-recognized name among chronograph manufacturers. Their chronographs are expandable and available with many options not found on less-expensive models. They are usually the standard by which all other ballistic chronographs are judged.

The Model 35, shown in Figure 31-3, is a basic battery-powered unit that can be expanded with various options. Used in this form, it is a basic chronograph that provides all of the usual chronograph features discussed previously. However, when attached to special screens or outfitted with a miniature printer, this model can be expanded to directly address a wide range of sophisticated tasks. The Model 35 electronically records strings of up to 20 shots that can be recalled whenever the shooter desires. They can even be edited.

This chronograph may be used with many different skyscreen combinations. Spacing between the

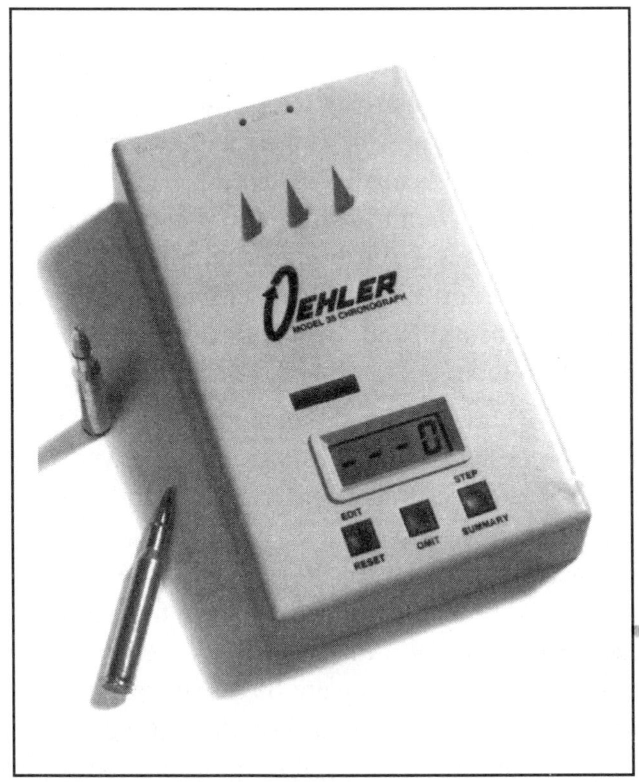

Figure 31-3: Oehler Model 35 chronograph.

sensors can be 1, 2, 4, or 8 feet. Accuracy of the measured velocities varies according to spacing between skyscreens and the actual velocities recorded. The wider sensor spacings provide the best accuracy. The following table lists the accuracy specifications for the Oehler Model 35 at various velocities and screen spacings.

Accuracy Specifications
Oehler Model 35 Chronograph

Screen Spacing	1 Foot	2 Feet	4 Feet	8 Feet
Velocity				
1000 fps	5 fps	3 fps	1 fps	1 fps
2000 fps	10 fps	5 fps	3 fps	2 fps
3000 fps	16 fps	8 fps	4 fps	2 fps
4000 fps	21 fps	10 fps	5 fps	3 fps

Given screen spacing of exactly 8 feet, the maximum deviation at projectile velocities of from 1000 to 4000 fps is only 3 fps. This is an error factor of less than one tenth of one percent at the highest velocity and 1 percent maximum at 1000 fps.

The Model 35 has many built-in features that make velocity testing a bit easier, especially when many shots are fired and measurements recorded. It has an editing feature where a suspicious reading can be removed from the recorded string of shots, so that it won't affect combinational readings that are also provided by this chronograph.

When a shot sequence is completed, the user can ask for a summary, which will result in a display of the highest velocity in the string, lowest velocity, extreme velocity spread, average velocity and standard deviation.

When a long string of shots is to be fired, these measurements are often recorded by the reloader for future reference. This means carrying a pencil and legal pad along to the shooting bench and laboriously recording the various data. However, The Oehler Model 35 may be equipped with an optional printer that produces a hardcopy printout of all data automatically. When the Model 35 is ordered with this printer already attached, it is designated as the Model 35P as shown in Figure 31-4 on the next page.

The printer prints in real ink on standard 2.25 inch plain paper (as opposed to the thermal printers that require expensive heat-sensitive paper). It prints velocity, shot number, and all statistical summaries.

The Model 35 (and 35P) also includes a special feature called *Proof Channel*. This is an internal arrangement of two clocks that can indicate bad readings by testing one clock's measurement against that of the other. It's almost like having two chronographs combined in one unit. To use the Proof Channel feature, a three-sensor skyscreen arrangement is required. A full discussion of the Oehler Proof Channel is presented later in this chapter.

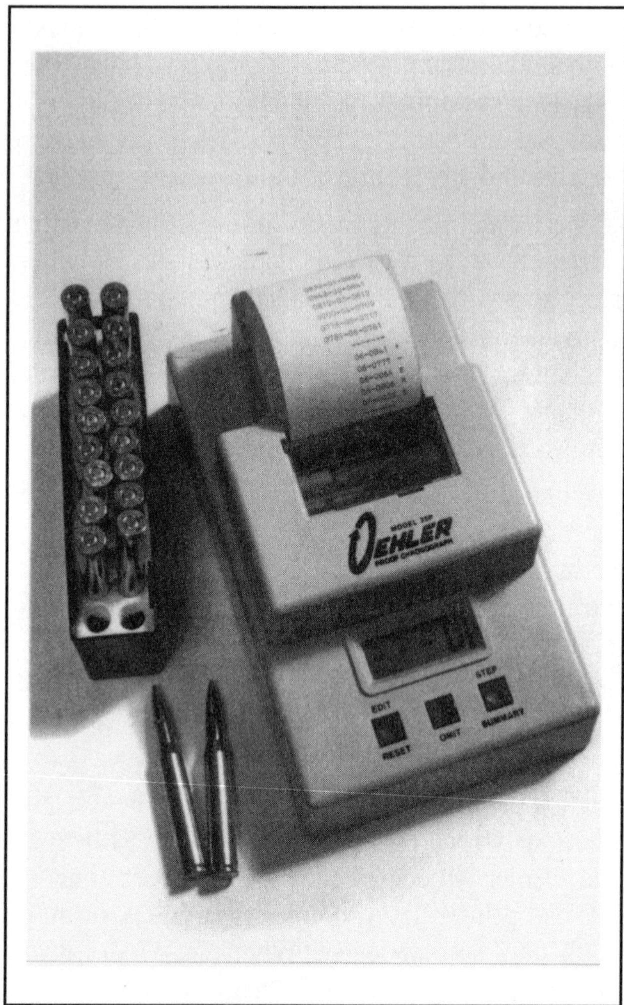

Figure 31-4: Oehler Model 35P chronograph.

The basic Model 35 with two skyscreen sensors and a mounting rail retails for approximately $195.00. Upgrading the basic model with the printer costs another $150. The Model 35P, with the built-in printer, retails for about $345.

GENERAL USE OF CHRONOGRAPHS

Chronographs are used to measure the velocity of fired projectiles. However, this basic measurement can be used to test many other aspects of ammunition and firearm performance.

Chronograph skyscreens are placed within the test range firing line, usually near the muzzle of the firearm. They should not be placed closer than about 10 feet from the muzzle of any high-powered rifle, as the muzzle blast can destroy the sensor cases and apparatus as well as the sensors themselves. Ten feet is a good distance because it is far enough away from the muzzle to prevent damage and close enough to it to measure what is, for all practical purposes, muzzle velocity. At 10 feet, the projectile has slowed very little from its actual muzzle velocity.

From a purely technical standpoint, the measurement recorded by any chronograph is the velocity of the projectile at a distance from the muzzle where the second sensor is located. If the first skyscreen is placed exactly 10 feet from the muzzle and the second is 8 feet beyond that, then the velocity recorded is that at a distance of 18 feet from the muzzle. Again, this may not be true muzzle velocity, but projectile deceleration at this short distance from the muzzle is negligible in all but the most exacting scientific tests.

SETTING UP FOR MAXIMUM ACCURACY

When discussing chronographs, there are two areas of velocity inaccuracy that concern the reloader. These areas relate to error factors and can be described as internal and external.

The internal error factor of a chronograph is determined by the electronic clock that serves as the master timer for the shooting sequence. Like any clock, this one has internal inaccuracies, but these are rarely any factor at all in practical chronograph uses. Generally, the higher the internal clock speed, the better the accuracy.

There is nothing that can be done about internal error factors, but the area of external error factors is one over which the reloader has direct control. This is also the area where big inaccuracies can creep into your chronograph readings. The factors that influence these errors are the EXACT distance between the skyscreens, ambient light conditions, bullet reflectivity, and bullet travel over the skyscreens.

SKYSCREEN PLACEMENT

The most accurate velocity measurements will be obtained when the chronograph skyscreens are placed as far apart as the specific chronograph design allows. Most one-piece chronographs do not allow for multiple skyscreen separation distances, but many of the two-piece units do. These latter types require that the skyscreens be separated by one of several distances. For instance, the Oehler Model 35 can operate at separations of 1, 2, 4, or 8 feet. Given this range, the 8-foot separation will yield the highest accuracy.

These are fixed distance separations, and the electronics unit is set to measure interval between these distances. If the distance is off by a small amount, then the accuracy of the reading is also off. For instance, if you set the Model 35 for a sensor separation of 8 feet and actually separate the sensors by 7 feet, then the velocity readings obtained will be flawed, giving measurements that are higher than the actual velocities. By the same token, if the skyscreen separation is more than 8 feet, then the readings will be lower than the true velocities.

It is absolutely essential that skyscreen separation be exactly what is called for. Even a quarter-inch error in the separation of these sensors can create a significant error factor, especially when small separations are used. When initially setting up your skyscreens, use a tape measure to obtain the exact separation required. This will assure the most accurate readings possible.

AMBIENT LIGHT CONDITIONS

Chronographs work best under good lighting conditions. This means a clear sky is preferable to a cloudy one. The skyscreens are light activated. The electronics unit calibrates itself based on the amount of ambient light detected by the sensors. When the projectile passes over the sensors, this light level is greatly reduced for an instant, due to the shadow created as the bullet temporarily blocks the light.

Most modern skyscreen arrangements are equipped with diffusers that help to prevent bright spots from direct sunlight that can sometimes play havoc with chronograph readings. The diffusers help to evenly distribute the ambient light over the entire sensor area. Some skyscreens can even be fitted with special overhead lights (attached to the diffuser area of each sensor) to allow them to be used when there is not enough ambient light to allow positive triggering.

BULLET REFLECTIVITY

When the bullet passes over a skyscreen, it creates a shadow, blocking light from the sensor. This causes the first sensor to start the electronic clock. When the bullet passes over the second sensor, the shadow causes it to stop the clock. However, copper-clad bullets can also reflect light when their surfaces are clean and shiny. Given particular light angles, these projectiles can sometimes direct light to the sensors instead of blocking it, causing false triggering of the chronograph.

For the most reliable triggering action, bullets fired over chronograph sensors should be darkened. The easiest way to accomplish this is to "smoke" the bullet surface by holding it over a lighted match. Don't heat the bullet (especially if it is sitting atop a charged case). Simply allow the smoke from the burning match to contact the bullet surface and darken it. You may also resort to shoe polish or other darkening agents.

The possibility of a bullet reflecting light onto the sensors is slim, but it can occur, especially on very sunny days. However, if false triggering does occur when making chronograph tests, darkening the bullet may correct this problem, and it takes only a few seconds to perform this operation with a match.

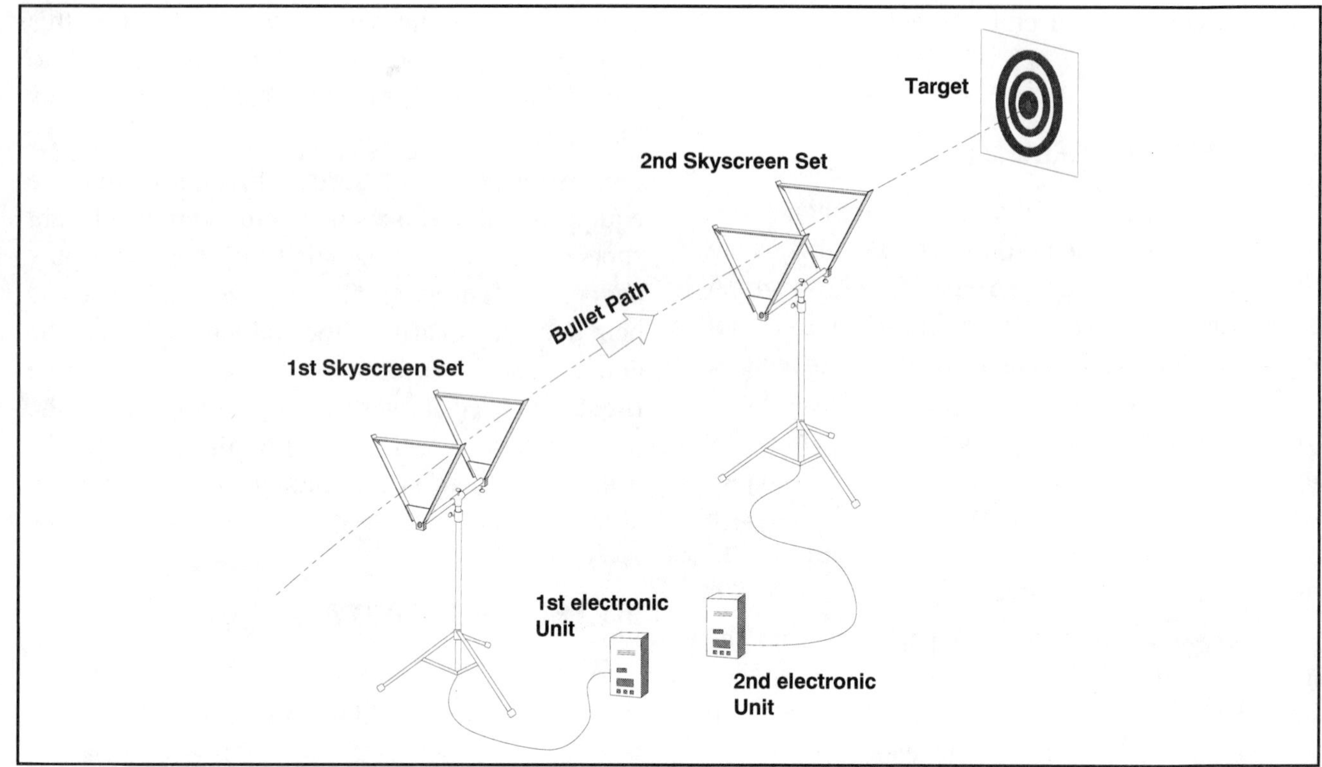

Figure 31-5: Using two sets of chronographs and screens to test measurement accuracy.

BULLET TRAVEL OVER THE SKYSCREENS

The most accurate chronograph readings will be obtained when the projectile passes directly over the center of the sensors. Modern skyscreens are usually equipped with some sort of aiming aids. These often take the form of twin rods that form a "V", with its vertex at the center of the skyscreen. Other forms include rectangular inserts that fit above the sensors with a vertical elliptical aiming slot. The latter may have markings for scope and iron-sight aiming points.

While fired projectiles that do not exactly center the sensor field will usually provide positive triggering and good readings, the most accurate readings are obtained when the bullet passes directly over the centers of both skyscreens and not more than about a foot above them.

Since chronograph tests are not usually conducted until after a load has been "shot in" and the firearm sights aligned for on-target performance, it is an easy task to aim directly over the electrodes. Some shooters feel that they have to aim so that the bullet passes very close to the surface of the skyscreen sensors. This is an incorrect assumption. As a matter of fact, the closer the bullet comes to the surface of the sensor, the smaller the shadow size. This can be demonstrated by placing a sheet of white paper on a table and holding your hand between this paper and an overhead light source. You will see that the closer your hand is held to the paper, the smaller the shadow becomes. The same principle applies to bullets passing over the sensors. Shooting very close to the sensors is less effective than aiming considerably above them but well within the confines of the aiming rods or templates, and you always take a chance on shooting through the sensors should you get a bit sloppy in your aiming.

When the skyscreens are set up, it is necessary to make sure that the first and last sensor are totally aligned with the downrange target. The ideal arrangement has the muzzle, first sensor, second sensor, and target point all in perfect alignment so that firing a bullet over the middle of the first sensor also causes it to fly over the middle of the second and into the target.

TESTING ACCURACY

Modern chronographs are accurate, dependable devices for measuring the velocity of projectiles. However, external conditions, such as changing ambient light levels, insects flying over the sensors, static electricity, electrical interference from motors, alternators, radio transmitters, and dozens of other interference sources can affect the accuracy of readings. Occasionally, the chronograph will give a reading that seems to be totally out of line, especially when compared with previous readings of the same cartridge/load combination. This may require you to shoot this load again and monitor the results.

The only way to test the accuracy of a chronograph reading for a certain load is to have another chronograph with its skyscreens in the shooting line. The two sets of skyscreens would be placed in tandem along the target line. When the shot is fired, the projectile passes over two sets of these sensors, and the velocity can be read on each electronic unit. This arrangement is shown in Figure 31-5 on the preceding page.

Admittedly, this is not a terribly practical arrangement for the average reloader, but it does work, although it rarely justifies the expense and trouble. However, this principle has been carried over into one chronograph that actually provides an automatic means of testing for accuracy in measurements.

The Oehler Model 35 (and 35P) chronograph is used just like any other chronograph when a standard two-sensor skyscreen arrangement is connected to its electronic unit. However, Oehler also offers a three-sensor skyscreen set that mates with their chronographs to provide a feature Oehler calls Proof Channel.

The Proof Channel uses three skyscreen sensors and two internal timers to make two velocity measurements on each shot fired. This does not require a second chronograph. All that is necessary is one Model 35 and the three-sensor skyscreen set.

Most skyscreens will function under perfect ambient lighting conditions, but they all can fail when ambient light conditions are bad. You expect skyscreens to fail when it gets dark, but there is a large twilight zone between perfect conditions and obvious dark. Frankly, it is better to have no chronograph reading at all than to have one that is incorrect. Using Oehler's Proof Channel feature, you get more positive assurance that your readings are correct.

Oehler likens its Proof Channel feature with comparing your checkbook's balance to the bank balance. If the balances agree, they are correct. If they differ by a few pennies, then you usually assume that the bank is right and you have made a minor, relatively unimportant error. If there is a huge difference, then you don't trust either balance until you can find the reason for the problem.

The Oehler Skyscreen III has been available since 1984, with many refinements being made over the years. This system produces fewer false triggers from static electricity and electrical interference. It comes equipped with a two-foot mounting rail, but better accuracy will be obtained by using the optional four-foot rail. Eight feet of separation between screens is even better, especially when applied to high-velocity firings. For use with the Oehler Proof Channel, three Skyscreen III sensors are mounted on a single rail as shown in Figure 31-6 on the next page.

The Proof Channel feature is built in to all Oehler Model 35 chronographs. It works by integrating the equivalent of four skyscreens and two electronic units into an arrangement of three skyscreens and one, multi-timing electronic unit. To understand the concept, it is necessary to remember that the

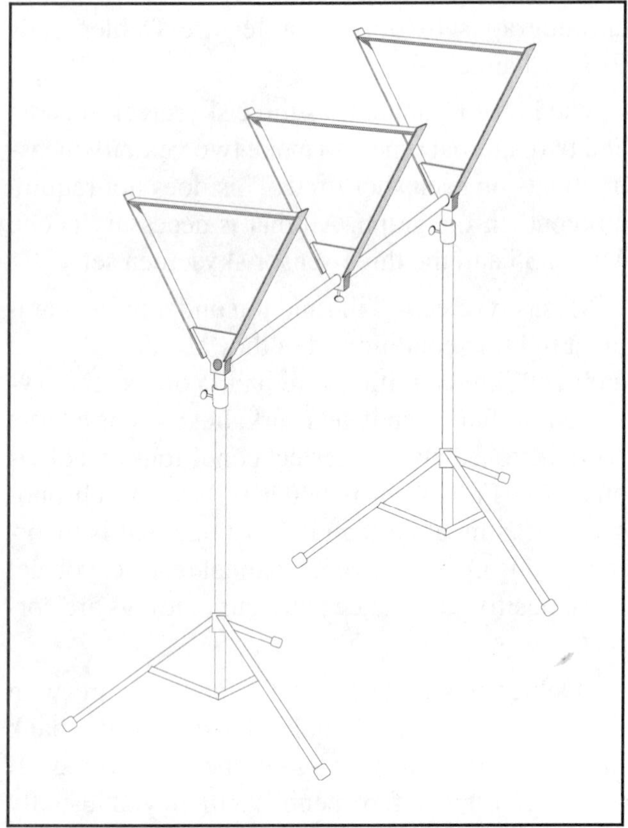

Figure 31-6: Oehler Skyscreen III.

Model 35 has two, internal timing circuits that are separate from each other.

When the shot is fired, it passes over the first skyscreen. This starts both internal clocks. When the bullet passes over the middle skyscreen, this stops one clock (the proof clock). However, the bullet is still traveling along its path, and when it passes over the third skyscreen, the other clock (primary clock) is stopped. The first clock is calibrated for the distance between the first and second skyscreens. The second clock is calibrated for the distance between the first and third skyscreens.

The two velocities will not be exactly identical because of the different distances of travel involved, but the Model 35 processes the two figures and decides if they are suspect. If so, the LCD display on the electronic unit begins flashing, indicating a suspect reading. Units equipped with the optional printer will add an asterisk (*) next to the hardcopy reading. Differences that trigger an alert vary depending upon velocity and skyscreen separation. The following chart shows the differences that trigger alerts for typical velocities and screen spacings.

Screen Spacing	1 Foot	2 Feet	4 Feet	8 Feet
Velocity				
1000 fps	42 fps	21 fps	10 fps	5 fps
2000 fps	83 fps	42 fps	21 fps	10 fps
3000 fps	125 fps	63 fps	31 fps	16 fps
4000 fps	166 fps	83 fps	42 fps	21 fps

In all cases, the second skyscreen will be placed exactly midway between the first and third sensors. As was mentioned previously, the spacing is critical and should not be off even as much as a quarter-inch. Use a tape measure to get it right!

The Model 35P (with the printer attachment) will print out the proof velocity, the shot number, and the primary velocity side-by-side. The following chart shows a typical printout.

3272-01-3268

3234-02-3235

3256-03-3256

3259-04-3257

3302-05-3259 *

The first figure is the proof velocity, the second is the shot number, and the third is the primary velocity. Assuming that there are no indications of a problem (flashing LCD display or printed asterisk), then the primary velocity is the most accurate reading. Notice that shot number 5 has an asterisk next to its figures, which deviate far more than the norm provided by the previous four shots. This means that the last shot should be retested, as the readings may be incorrect.

OTHER USES FOR CHRONOGRAPHS

While the basic purpose of a chronograph is to measure muzzle velocity (more accurately, velocity in close proximity to the muzzle), there are other uses that it can address. There is no reason why a chronograph cannot be used to measure downrange velocities, although the sighting becomes more critical.

For instance, instead of placing the skyscreens near the muzzle, place them just in front of the target. The reading will then state the velocity of the projectile at the target. There is no reason why the target can't be a hundred or more yards away from the muzzle, but again, your sighting must be dead-on to prevent the possibility of shooting through the sensors. Still, with modern scope sights, it shouldn't be too difficult to place a bullet through the sensor field at 100 yards. It will be harder to center the bullet over each sensor, so the readings may not be quite as accurate as those obtained near the muzzle. However, this is not a major problem.

When locating the skyscreens downrange, it will probably be necessary to also locate the electronic unit downrange as well, as cables cannot be extended for hundreds of yards without losing triggering ability and sensitivity.

When a velocity reading is taken at the muzzle and another at the target, the two can be compared to ballistics charts in order to approximate the ballistic coefficient of the bullet. Many types of factory ammunition do not have published ballistic coefficients of their bullets. The downrange chronograph will allow these figures to be found. Likewise, bullet energy can be calculated from downrange velocity measurements. Downrange use of chronographs is recommended only for two-piece units that separate the skyscreens from the electronics.

As was mentioned previously, most chronographs can also be used to measure the velocity of arrows fired over the sensors. However, these same units may have difficulty in reading the velocities of subsonic firearm loads. When the muzzle velocity of a bullet is below the speed of sound, the muzzle blast wave reaches the skyscreen before the projectile. This blast wave can be likened to a lens traveling through the air at the speed of sound. The resulting light diffraction can falsely trigger the skyscreens.

When the false trigger occurs only at the first skyscreen, this will result in velocities that are abnormally low. When both screens are prematurely triggered by the blast wave, then the resulting velocity measurement will be that of the speed of sound and not the projectile speed.

The speed of sound is approximately 1060 fps plus the current temperature. This means that a reading of 1,135 fps on a 75 degree day (1060 + 75) should be suspect. Using the Oehler Model 35 with the Proof Channel feature presents other interesting possibilities when firing subsonic projectiles, as only the first and second (proof) screen may be triggered by the blast wave, while the projectile triggers the third screen. This will result in an abnormally low primary velocity reading and the proof velocity to read the speed of sound.

There are several ways around this. The easiest method is to move the skyscreens farther from the muzzle to a point where the blast wave has died away (20 feet or so). The second method requires the installation of a barrier between the first sensor and the muzzle. A square piece of plywood with a slotted or circular cutout to allow for passage of the projectile should alleviate any tendency toward false triggering by the blast wave.

With archery chronographing, there is no blast wave, so this is no problem. The same applies to measuring the velocities of projectiles fired from air rifles. For archery work, blunted point arrows provide the most positive triggering. Needle-like field points and broadheads can give erratic results.

When chronographs are used to measure the velocity of shotshell loads, the front pellets in the shot string trigger the skyscreens. This results in velocity readings that are, typically, as much as 5% higher than factory-measured velocities, which are based on the speed of the center of the shot column. Chronographing shotshell loads can be done, but testing is not recommended for the average reloader. It is necessary to place the skyscreens very close to the shotgun barrel, typically four feet or less in order to catch the shot load prior to its spreading out. This brings a great deal of muzzle blast to bear on the sensors. Shotshell velocity readings should never be attempted with one-piece chronographs, as the muzzle blast can damage the in-line electronics units irreparably.

SUMMARY

A reloading tool kit without a chronograph is incomplete. Chronographs are absolutely essential for working up custom loads that address specific purposes. Certainly, velocity figures can be garnered from loading charts, but these apply only to the cartridges fired from a particular weapon. Using a different firearm will produce different pressures and velocities from the same cartridge. The only way to know for sure what a particular load is doing is to chronograph the projectile.

Chronograph work is relatively safe, so long as all of the safety precautions for range work are followed. The most persistent danger is to the skyscreens and chronograph when reloaders become too adamant about obtaining the actual muzzle velocity and place the units too close to the muzzle. This often results in skyscreens being blown completely off of their mounting brackets, causing severe damage to one-piece chronographs that are in the firing line.

A chronograph is a precision instrument that deserves to be treated gently. By keeping the sensors at a reasonable distance (about 10 feet) from the muzzle for most centerfire firearms, this protection is reasonably assured; that is, muzzle blast usually will not damage the sensors at this distance.

By charting chronograph measurements and keeping them in an appropriate file, you can refer to them months or years later and allow these readings to guide a current loading assignment. A reloader's collection of chronograph measurements becomes a valuable commodity as it builds in size and versatility.

Chapter 32

Testing Chamber Pressure

When a cartridge is fired, great pressure is necessary to push the bullet out the barrel. This pressure is applied outwardly from the chamber and must be contained by the firearm breech, chamber walls, and barrel.

When a load has been worked up in a rifle, shotgun, or handgun, it should be range-tested for accuracy, feeding, and safety before the load is used in the field or for official target work.

SIGNS OF PRESSURE

There are certain signs that indicate signs of high pressure. If these signs are detected early, problems may be avoided. This is why all reloads should be loaded a few grains under the published maximum and gradually worked up — a tenth of a grain at a time. At the first sign of any high pressures, STOP, and back off a few tenths of a grain. If the reloader starts with the maximum load, he or she may not be around to observe any signs! The rifle could explode on the first shot!

When testing reloads, the first thing to watch for is difficult extraction — provided, of course, that the rifle extracts factory loads with ease. Other signs of abnormal breech pressure is leaking primers, indicated by a sooty black area around the edge of the pocket; or primers that have blown out in the middle where the firing pin hit them. Look too, for a ridge or crater around the firing pin indent, or flowing of the primer out over the base of the case. Flattened primers are another indication of too much pressure. *See* Figure 32-1.

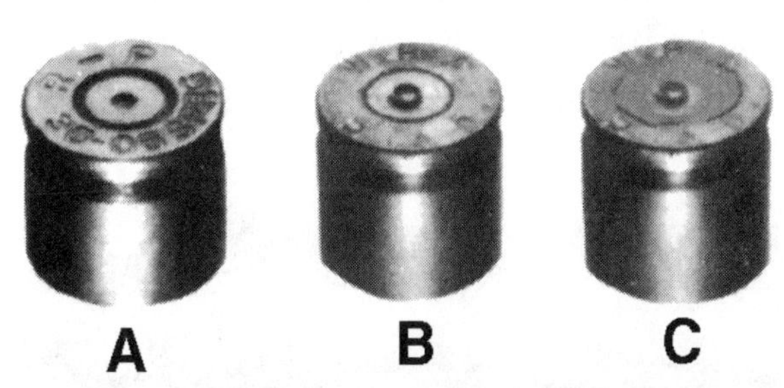

Figure 32-1: Case A shows primer of a case fired with normal pressures; Cases B and C were fired with heavier loads. Note how primer B flowed up into a ridge or crater, around the firing-pin indentation and out over the base of the case. This condition is even more evident in primer C.

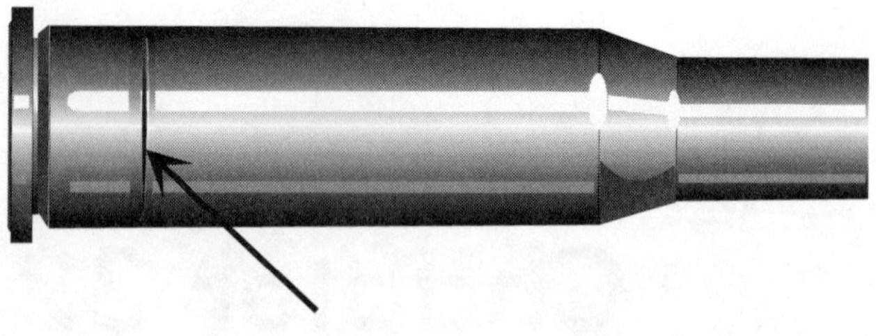

Figure 32-2: A partial head separation is easy to spot.

The cartridge case should be examined for a swelled base, or partial head separation. The latter situation is easily spotted; the metal will be cracked, usually just ahead of the base, and darkened by the escape of powder gas as shown in Figure 32-2.

A case on the verge of separation, however, is not so easy to see, but it can be detected if a careful examination of the case is made under magnification. Look for a stretched shiny area, perhaps 1/32″ wide, where the case is ready to rupture. See Figure 32-3. Do not confuse this marking with the normal ring left around the case by a sizer die. A stretching ring is irregular in shape, and may appear anywhere from just forward of the head to about halfway between the head and shoulder.

Unfortunately, the advice given in the above paragraphs is not always valid. All of these warning signs can appear at normal pressures, due to defects in the gun or defects in the brass. For these reasons, it is a good idea to compare fired reloads with fired factory rounds, used in the same rifle, before deciding that pressure is excessive.

When working up maximum loads, load five cartridges with a powder charge about 3.0 grains below the maximum listing. Fire one round, and extract the fired case. Examine it for all pressure signs described previously. If everything checks out okay, fire another round and examine this in the same way. If everything is still okay, fire the remaining three cartridges for accuracy, using a benchrest and the techniques described in Chapter 30. Record all characteristics of this load—especially the accuracy test.

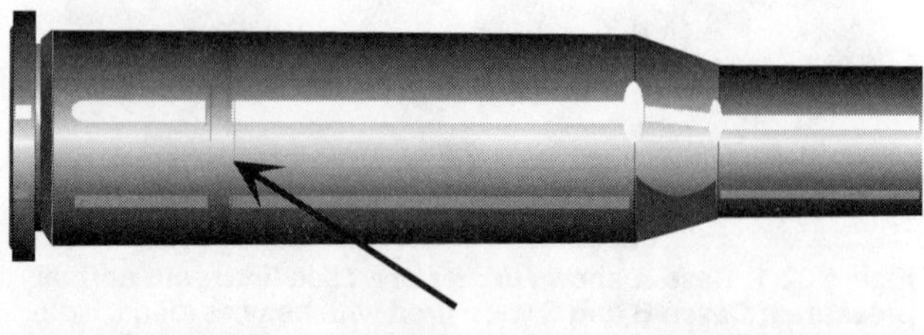

Figure 32-3: A case that is on the verge of rupturing requires a closer examination — preferably under magnification.

If all rounds fired thus far pass inspection, and these loads have been loaded 3.0 grains below the published maximum, increase the powder charge by 0.5 grain and load five more cartridges. Test these five rounds as before. Continue this procedure until loads have been loaded and fired up to 1.0 grain below maximum; that is, unless signs of high pressure appear. At this point, it is good practice to increase the powder charge by only 0.1 grain, until the maximum load has been reached or else signs of abnormal pressure appear. In the event that high-pressure signs appear, back off at least 0.5 grain and do not exceed this load. If the published maximum load appears to operate okay without signs of abnormal pressure, it may be reasonably assumed that the load is safe in the rifle in which it was fired.

EXAMINE TEST DATA

Once all loads have been fired, and all check out okay, study the recorded test data carefully. In 98% of all cases, the shooter should be striving for accuracy, not power alone. Power has no significance if the target is not hit. For example, if the most accurate load happens to be, say, 0.5 grain below maximum, this is the load that should be used. That little additional power gain in the full maximum load is not worth the sacrifice for accuracy.

WARNING!

Never exceed maximum published loads, even if there are no signs of high pressure.

PRESSURE VARIATIONS

Many factors can change the ballistic performance of a load, which in turn, will directly affect the chamber pressure. For example, the internal dimensions of a firearm can vary considerably, even between two guns of the same make and model. Pressures can vary to extremes as different firearms are used. Each change in brand and even within different lots of a specific brand component can cause notable ballistic changes. Changes in ambient temperature is still another factor that will cause a variation in chamber pressure.

Pressure is thought of in terms of reloading safety. Statements of concern like "I've got pressure signs here!" are evidence to this fact. In the language of reloading, "pressure signs" are usually indications of excess pressure, and this is what is to be avoided. The safe handloader is an excellent observer. He or she notices every element of reloading and the field testing process that must follow. Such tests are conducted to determine factors such as muzzle velocity, accuracy, bullet drop, etc. However, pressure should also be measured, even roughly, during these tests by observing pressure signs that manifest themselves on the cartridge case and in the primer.

Chamber pressure is measured in pounds-per-square-inch (psi), and it is probably the most difficult component of the firing process to monitor directly and accurately, due to the expense of equipment involved for such purposes. Most reloaders do not have the electronic or mechanical equipment needed to perform accurate pressure measurements. Fortunately, direct monitoring is rarely necessary for the average reloader, and relative measurements suffice.

GUNNERY VS. ROCKETRY

A firearm propels its projectiles by burning fuel and so does a rocket. Some persons confuse rocketry with gunnery, and while both depend on fuel energy for propulsion purposes, they are radically different areas of study. A rocket carries its own fuel source, therefore it can lift off at a slow speed and then increase that speed as it gets farther from the launching point. It can even be slowed down again by controlling the burn rate of its fuel. As the rocket burns more fuel, it becomes lighter, since that fuel weight is part of the overall weight of the payload being propelled. This means that a rocket may be able to travel much faster late in the flight, due to the decreased weight factor.

Like rocketry, gunnery depends on fuel energy, but this is about as far as similarities go. Gunnery principles call for the fuel to be completely expended (used up) at the time and point of launch. The projectile is given initial momentum by the burst of pressure created by the fuel energy, and that's the end of that. From launch point on, the gunnery projectile is on its own. It can gain no further momentum. In fact, all it can do is lose momentum (due to the force of gravity), because it carries no means of propulsion of its own.

Since a bullet, unlike a rocket, must obtain all of the needed momentum in one burst, the pressure generated by the fuel must be tremendous. It only needs to last a moment, but it's a notably intense moment.

Up to a certain point, higher pressures will impart higher velocities, so there is a direct relationship between gunnery pressures and bullet velocity. Low pressure results in low velocity; medium pressure in medium velocity; and high pressure in high velocity, assuming all other factors remain the same.

GENERATING PRESSURE

Modern pistol/rifle cartridges and shotshells use smokeless powder as a fuel. When the powder is ignited by the primer flash it burns so quickly that it is consumed in a split second. As the powder burns, gases are expelled and expand outward in all directions at a speed approaching 7000 fps.

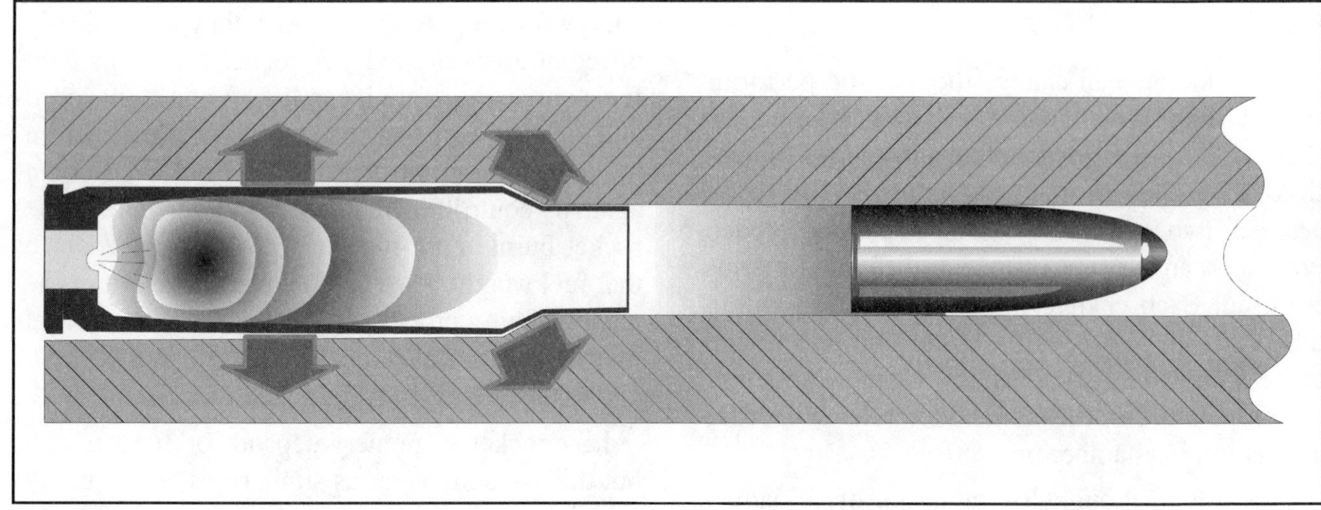

Figure 32-4: When powder in a cartridge case is ignited, gases are expelled and expand outwardly in all directions, at a speed approaching 7000 fps.

If you ignite a small amount of smokeless powder piled on the ground in the open air, you won't see anything highly dramatic. The result will look similar to that of small fireworks being set off. There is no loud explosion, only a fairly rapid, sparkling flame.

However, when this powder is confined to a very small enclosed area like the environment found in a cartridge case chambered in a firearm, and the ignition is violent like that produced by a typical primer, an entirely different set of events are set into motion. The powder burns much more rapidly because of the enclosed area, the contained pressure and heat, and because the gases are initially contained providing more heat and causing more rapid burning. In a split second, the great majority of the powder is turned into gas. The pressure from this rapid expansion is tremendous and would quickly build to a point where the entire firearm would be disintegrated, were it not for the "safety valve" that every firearm should contain: the open area of the barrel.

The bullet seated in the cartridge mouth is the weakest link in this pressure chain. It works like a blowout valve, popping out of the case mouth and traveling up the bore, propelled by the still-expanding gases that follow it all the way to the muzzle.

At the muzzle, the gases are expelled forcefully into the air, where they immediately dissipate. By this point, however, the gas has done its job, and the bullet is well on the way to the target.

THE PRESSURE WAVE

Effects of firearm chamber pressure may be described in terms of a "pressure wave." While the expansion of powder gases takes place in a moment, it does not happen instantaneously. During the split-second of expansion, many, many events occur. These events are all a part of the pressure wave.

The wave begins at zero pressure (prior to ignition), builds quickly to a peak pressure value and then tapers off more slowly to a zero value again, when all gases have exited the chamber and barrel. The speed at which the wave climbs to peak and then tapers off to zero again, is the wave shape, and this will be determined by the burning rate or "speed" of the powder. A slow powder takes longer to build to peak. A fast pistol or shotgun powder gets there more rapidly.

Some powders produce a relatively low-value peak, but maintain a longer average pressure value. Others achieve a very high-peak pressure at the

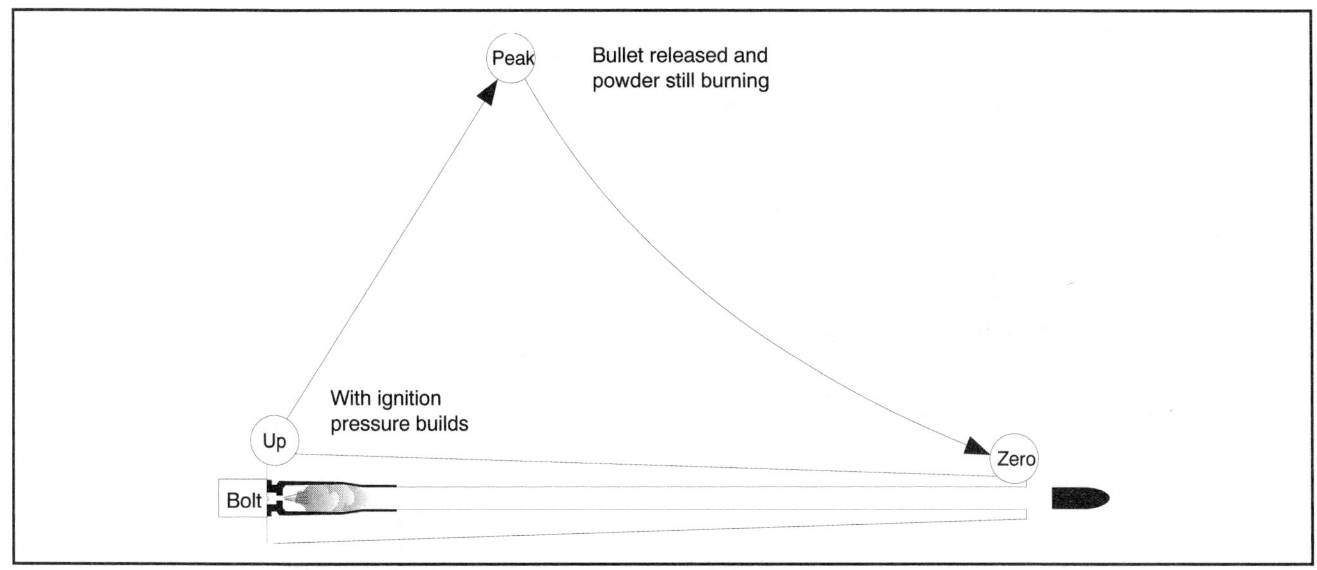

Figure 32-5: Pressure builds up to a peak and then drops off to zero as the bullet leaves the barrel.

expense of a shorter average pressure duration. Different cartridges perform best with powders of different burning rates, due to their physical nature. It is for this reason that so many different types of powders are available to the modern reloader. Each cartridge, primer, and bullet combination requires a different pressure wave than another combination does in order to perform most efficiently.

PRESSURE EFFECTS ON THE CARTRIDGE CASE

As the expanding powder gases produce the pressure wave, a series of mechanical events take place within the chamber and to the firearm action in the chamber area. The powder gases expand in all directions, but the force applied to the cartridge case and chamber are not equal in all places.

If a cartridge case were a perfect globe (and the chamber as well), then equal force would be applied to all areas of that globe. However, a modern cartridge has more length than diameter. Think of blowing up a balloon. Even though the internal pressure can be measured at any point within that balloon, the force applied to the balloon walls is different at different areas, and it does not assume the shape of a perfect globe. Rather, it is generally circular but has considerable elongation as well. A balloon that is longer than it is wide in the deflated state will assume a similar inflated shape proportionally. And so it is with a cartridge and its chamber in a firearm.

The largest surface areas of the case are along its length from base to neck. These areas are less mechanically stable than the base, which is of much smaller diameter. For this reason, the walls of the cartridge case are pushed outwardly and tightly against the chamber wall. There is also a backward thrust component that drives the cartridge base against the bolt face. The amount of rearward thrust depends upon the internal force of the powder gas expansion and even more on the actual shape of the cartridge case.

Cartridge cases that have a great deal of taper (the .300 H&H Magnum and the .32-40 Winchester immediately come to mind) tend to exert more force on the bolt face than do those cases with straight walls or mild tapers. This is really a funnel effect, where the taper of the chamber tends to squeeze the case backward during the pressure wave cycle. Improved cartridges (those based on standard cases with considerable taper), which remove most of the taper by fire forming, will have less backward thrust as will any cartridge case with relatively straight walls. However, should any case be covered with a layer of oil or other lubricant, this can dramatically increase rearward thrust, because the expanding case walls do not adhere as tightly to the chamber.

After the pressure wave has been totally depleted, the soft brass cartridge case is slightly larger than when in the pre-fired condition. It now more closely matches the exact dimensions of the chamber. However, the case is still loose enough to be easily extracted, assuming normal pressure levels. Brass, like all solid materials, has a certain amount of tensile strength. A proper load will not generate enough pressure to exceed the tensile strength of the case. This means that the case expands outward when the pressure is generated, but it springs back when the pressure wave subsides.

When the tensile strength of the case is exceeded by pressures that are too high, the brass does not spring back, and it remains tightly adhered to the chamber wall, just as it was during the peak of the pressure wave. It is at this point that some cases have to be driven from the chamber by inserting a steel rod down through the muzzle of the barrel into its mouth and tapped (sometimes, banged!) with a hammer.

PRESSURE EFFECTS ON THE FIREARM CHAMBER AND ACTION

The description of the effects of pressure on the cartridge case is easily applied to the firearm chamber as well. The amount of force that is applied to the cartridge case at any point is the same force that is applied to the chamber at that same point.

Many persons think that the chamber and action are designed to form an immovable barrier to the escape of powder gases. This is only partially correct. The steel that is used in modern firearms does form a barrier, but it is not immovable, even when pressures are normal. Like the cartridge case, the chamber and the action area surrounding the chamber expand outward due to the applied internal force. While the expansion is very small in human terms, it is a physical occurrence that can be measured easily by a sensor called a "strain gauge."

The tensile strength of modern steels is very great, so normal firearm pressures can be safely contained. Proper loads do not exceed the tensile strength of the action, so it springs back to its original shape when the pressure wave drops to zero. Unlike the brass cartridge case that has to be resized after each firing, the tensile strength of gun steels is such that they spring back to their original dimensions after firing.

When the tensile strength of the chamber and action is exceeded, interesting events can occur. The chamber can be expanded to an oversized condition that is irreversible. The receiver ring may be expanded to a point that the barrel will wobble where it meets the action. The ring can even be blown completely off the firearm, and the barrel may follow. These are some of the lesser things that can and do happen when safe pressures are exceeded.

Having discussed the effects of pressure on the chamber and the action in general, there is another very important component in the action that contains the internal pressure. The breechblock or bolt face in a firearm receives the brunt of any rearward thrust produced by firing a cartridge.

When the cartridge is fired, a portion of the internal pressure generated by the expanding gases

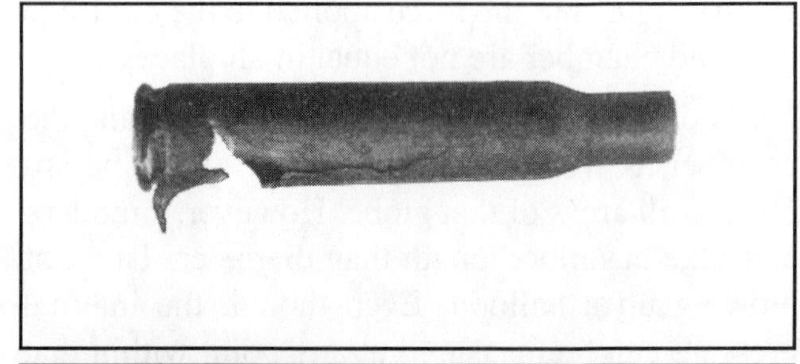

Figure 32-6: Ruptured cartridge case caused by a combination of excessive headspace and pressure.

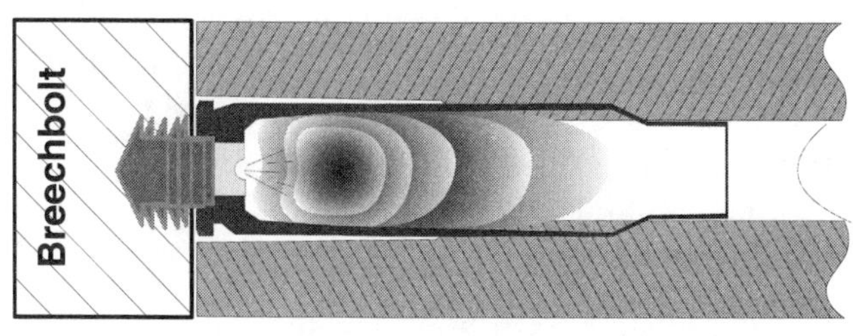

Figure 32-7: Tapered cartridges normally exert more back thrust on the locking bolt than cartridges with relatively straight cases.

causes it to slam backward against the bolt face. It is the bolt (or the breechblock) that seals the chamber from the shooter's end and keeps the cartridge case from flying back at the shooter. As was mentioned earlier in this chapter, the amount of thrust produced during firing is dependent upon the cartridge type, shape, specific load, and other factors.

It was once believed that a bolt failure, such as a broken locking lug, would cause the bolt to fly back into the shooter's face with enough momentum to completely penetrate the human head! The late P.O. Ackley challenged this notion, saying that bolt thrust in modern firearms, firing modern straight-body cartridges, was not all that great. To prove his point, he removed the locking bar from a Winchester Model 94 in .30-30 caliber. This meant that the only thing holding the bolt against the base of the cartridge during firing was the hammer. Since the hammer is designed to be cocked by hand, it doesn't take a great deal of pressure to force it back.

However, when the weapon was fired, nothing disastrous occurred. The cartridge behaved normally, and the bullet traveled on to the target. A close examination of the fired cases showed that the primers protruded from the case excessively. This was caused by the bolt being shoved back a bit to the rearward thrust, just enough to cause the primers to partially back out of their pockets but not enough for them to completely exit the case.

This discussion is not meant to undermine any safety precautions, only to point out an interesting experiment that seems to refute some of the stories told about firearm mishaps. The amount of rearward thrust can vary tremendously, even in the same gun firing the same load, especially when the chamber is oily. Even when firing from a dry chamber, certain loads create more thrust.

While testing .356 Winchester loads in a Model 94 Big Bore, signs of considerable backthrust were experienced. The lever handle could be felt to spring downward during firing and then up again, occurring so quickly that it had to be felt rather than seen. This probably occurred because the backward thrust on the bolt face caused the locking lugs to spring back a bit. Factory ammunition was being used at the time, and no signs of excessive pressure were indicated on the fired cases. It seems as though this particular lot of .356 ammunition was generating more back thrust than other lots.

When loads are fired that produce excessively high chamber pressures, the cartridge base is slammed against the bolt face with tremendous force. The impact can be so great that the base is stamped with the irregularities of the bolt face. The brass at the base can even flow into the extractor port. For all intents and purposes, the base will be a mirror image of the bolt face when pressure levels are this high, and the bolt probably won't even budge until it is hammered open. More serious situations can sometimes cause the bolt face to crack.

Another event that might occur is "setback", where the bolt lugs actually tear into or compress metal in the lug recesses of the action. This causes the headspace to increase, as the bolt face no longer seats as deeply into the chamber. While anything can happen during a high-pressure mishap, the authors have observed that it is more likely for the receiver ring to be blown off of most modern rifles than it is for the bolt or breechblock to let go.

CONDITIONS THAT CAUSE HIGH PRESSURE

The pressure generated by a particular reload is not fixed for all guns that fire it. The tolerance of any individual firearm will greatly affect chamber pressure. It is for this reason that a specific cartridge/powder/primer/bullet combination will behave differently in different firearms. One load that behaves normally in one gun may generate high pressures in another. Conversely, a load that develops a certain velocity in one firearm may produce much less velocity in a second. In this case, lower pressures are produced in the second gun, causing the bullet to depart the muzzle at a lower velocity.

The condition of the gun's throat, bore and groove diameter of the barrel, exact chamber dimensions, headspace, and other factors all have an impact on the actual pressure that is generated.

Changing any cartridge component will have an affect on pressure. Changing from one brand of case to another (or even from one lot to another within the same brand of case) can have a dramatic pressure effect. Case volume will vary slightly from brand-to-brand and from lot-to-lot.

The burning rate of different lots of powder may also be different. This means that if you have developed a safe load for a particular firearm using IMR 4320 powder (for instance) and, six months later, you decide to make that load again, using a different can of the same powder, the results may be quite different. This latest can of powder may have a slightly higher or slower burning rate, and pressure is immediately impacted. The differences may not matter a lot if a particular load is not near maximum. However, a maximum load may be well over maximum if a new lot of the same powder is used. For this reason, whenever you switch to a new can of powder, you must start well below maximum charges and work the load up again, just as you did when developing this particular load originally.

Changing from one brand or type of primer to another can cause pressures to rise or fall by large amounts. Don't ever make the mistake of developing a near-maximum load and then switching primers, without first going back to a lesser load and working up to near-maximum again. Many firearms have been ruined through not abiding by this rule of reloading.

A cartridge case that is too long can dramatically raise chamber pressure. When the case is chambered in a bolt action rifle, the camming effect of the bolt will cause the case mouth (which now exceeds the length of the chamber) to be crimped into the bullet within the freebore area of the firearm. This grips the bullet tightly, preventing it from disengaging the case as easily. The result is soaring chamber pressures, because the bullet that serves as a pressure-release safety valve when it discharges, needs far more than normal force to move it.

Bullet shape, size, and weight are an element in chamber pressure. Don't assume that a load comprised of one type of bullet will generate the same pressures if another bullet of the same weight and diameter but of a different style is used. A roundnose bullet will usually generate slightly higher chamber pressures than a spitzer design of the same weight. Generally, more surface area of a roundnose design engages the barrel rifling than does a spitzer, which tapers quickly to a sharp point. Since more of the surface area of a roundnose bullet engages the rifling lands, the resistance is higher and so is the chamber pressure.

The overall length of the reloaded cartridge is another factor that can affect pressure. Most bullets are loaded so that they fall just short of engaging the lands of the barrel when chambered. However, if a load is developed with this length arrangement and, later, the same load is used with the bullet seated farther out from the case, high pressure may result. If the bullet is seated far enough out to engage the lands, then the resistance to leaving the case is increased and higher pressure will be generated. It is certainly safe to load bullets far enough out of the case to engage the rifling, but loads must be worked up with this condition in mind. Most of these loads will use a bit less powder than those with bullets seated so as not to engage the lands.

Seating the bullet too deeply in the case can also cause pressure variations. When a bullet is seated very deeply in the case, pressure can rise, due to the effective lessening of case capacity.

One of the most critical components that affects pressure in any firearm is the bore and chamber dimensions. In comparison with the chamber for which a specific load was developed, a chamber that is slightly oversized will generate lower pressures using the same load. One that is undersized will produce higher pressures. Modern firearms have close tolerances for chamber and bore dimensions, so they shouldn't be a factor when firing reloads that do not approach maximum. However, older firearms, military weapons and those made in some foreign countries may have substantially different chamber and bore dimensions. Such firearms should be slugged prior to developing handloads. Then gradually work up from a low-pressure starting point.

RELATIVE PRESSURE READINGS

Obtaining absolute pressure readings is beyond the scope of most reloaders. These require invasive techniques using a pressure barrel with a copper crusher metering system or the new piezoelectric transducers, both of which were discussed in an earlier chapter.

Relative pressure readings are more easily (and inexpensively) obtained. Such readings are had simply by examining the fired case. The pressure signs to look for such as flattened primers, sticky ejection, etc. have already been discussed. These signs don't provide a precise measurement of pressure, but they do indicate over-pressure conditions. One other method involves measurement of the head of the fired case with a micrometer. Any load that causes a measurable increase in the diameter of the cartridge head (taken at or very near the base) is an indication of high pressure. Even the slightest increase in head diameter should be a warning sign. Most micrometers are accurate to about .001 inch, so head expansion of .001 or more certainly indicates excessive pressure, and the load should be reduced immediately.

THE OEHLER MODEL 43 PERSONAL BALLISTICS LAB

Oehler (pronounced A-lore) Research in Austin, Texas is best known among reloaders as makers of excellent chronographs for measurement of bullet velocity. However, this company, headed by Dr. Ken Oehler, also makes some sophisticated computer-interface equipment and software that can allow accurate relative chamber pressure readings to be obtained from most sporting arms without resorting to invasive procedures.

The Model 43, without the many options, sells for about $600 and, when interfaced with any IBM-compatible microcomputer is able to measure relative chamber pressures using a device known as a strain gauge that attaches to the outside of the chamber area of the firearm being tested. No holes are drilled in the barrel, and the relative pressures are indicated in pounds-per-square-inch. These are relative pressure readings, but they can compare favorably with those obtained by the invasive techniques discussed earlier when calibrated against known loads. More importantly, they provide accurate data on how a certain load is performing in the actual weapon in which it is fired. By now, it should be perfectly clear that pressure produced by a certain load in one firearm will produce different pressures in another. The Oehler Model 43, for the first time, allows a reloader to test chamber pressures in sporting (as opposed to laboratory) firearms.

Adding all of the options to this electronic device will boost the total price to over $1500 (not including the computer), but such a system will allow measurements of the following — all from a single location and without the reloader even getting out of his or her chair.

- Muzzle Velocity
- Proof Velocity
- Peak Pressure
- Pressure Rise Time
- Pressure Curve
- Area Under Curve
- Time of Flight
- Velocity at Target
- Ballistic Coefficient
- Group at Target

However, the basic Model 43 (about $600) and a strain gauge are all that is needed to measure relative pressures. This assumes that you already have a microcomputer running MS-DOS. The Model 43, for all of its capability, is an insignificant appearing device that's less than a foot wide and 1.5 inches high. It is designed to act as a small platform for a laptop computer, although a full-size PC will work just as well. In layman's terms, this "box" converts the electrical signals received from the strain gauge attached to the firearm into digital pulses that the microcomputer can process.

It was stated earlier in this chapter that the chamber area of the firearm action swells or springs outward in reaction to the pressure generated by the expanding gases whenever a cartridge is fired. As long as the tensile strength of the action is not exceeded, this is a normal occurrence. A strain gauge takes advantage of this physical event and responds to that swelling. When the gauge is attached to sensitive instrumentation (the Model 43), the actual chamber-area expansion can be accurately measured, and pressure readings extrapolated.

The strain gauge (also gage) is simply a flat coil of wire. The proximity of one loop of the coil to all others sets up specific electrical performance when a signal is passed through it. The flat coil is flexible and the interval between coil segments will increase as the surface on which it is mounted (the firearm chamber area) expands. This changes the reactance of the coil (its resistance at certain frequencies), and this is measured via the Model 43 computer interface. The computer software processes the change in the signal and outputs direct relative pressure readings based upon these changes.

The strain gauge is a tiny delicate sensor. Once it is attached to the external chamber area of the firearm, it cannot be removed without the strain gauge's destruction. However, it may be left permanently in place in many types of firearms without detracting from its shooting ability in any way.

Using the Oehler Model 43 system, the strain gauge is attached to the firearm by first degreasing the mounting area. A prepping conditioner is also applied to this area and, later, a neutralizer. The strain gauges supplied with this system have a bonding compound on one side that is activated by a catalyst. This is the side that is placed against the surface of the firearm. The gauge is mounted on a small length of cellophane tape (bonding side up), and it is initially applied to the chamber area. The tape is then partially removed, and the catalyst is applied to the strain gauge. The tape is then reap-

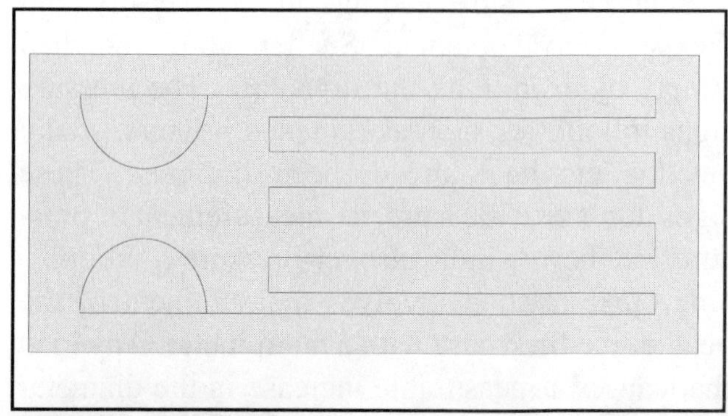

Figure 32-8: The strain gauge is simply a flat coil of wire embedded on cellophane tape.

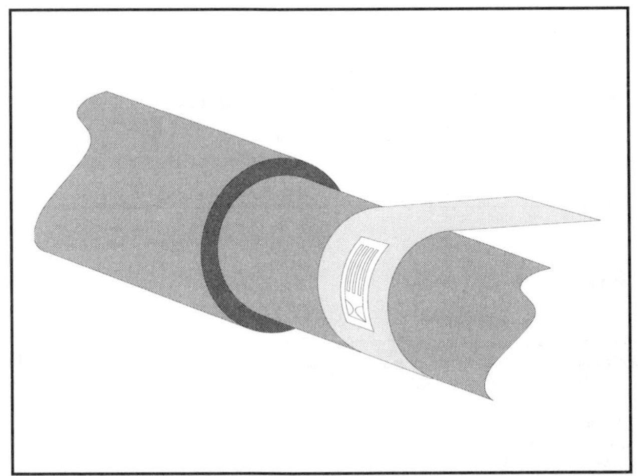

Figure 32-9: Locating strain gauge on barrel.

plied to the firearm, causing the strain gauge to be bonded in place. After the bonding compound has set up, the tape is removed and the gauge stays permanently in place. Two copper solder tabs on the gauge allow the small cable to the Model 43 unit to be connected.

The exact placement of the strain gauge will depend upon the type of firearm for which pressure measurements are to be conducted. Selecting the proper location will be quite simple when using break-open actions, such as those found on Thompson-Center Contender pistols and single-shot shotguns. Semiautomatic pistols will present very difficult mounting scenarios, and bolt-action rifles won't be a cinch either. However, when the gauge is in place, it shouldn't have to be removed again. It may remain a permanent part of the firearm, if desired. If not, it can be removed, but the gauge is destroyed in the process.

The strain gauge must be placed over the chamber area of any firearm. With single-barrel shotguns, the gauge should be mounted about 1 inch from the breech. For bolt-action rifles, it is necessary to first chamber an empty case, then insert a cleaning rod down the barrel until it bottoms out in the base of the case. The cleaning rod is marked with a small piece of tape at the point where it exits the muzzle. The cleaning rod is then removed, and the case is held next to its unmarked end. The strain gauge mounting position will be halfway between the receiver and the case shoulder. This area is marked on the rod, which is then held next to the gun barrel, with the tape marking the muzzle point aligned with the muzzle. The second mark made on the rod indicates the exact strain gauge mounting position on the barrel. Oehler offers a strain gauge startup kit that includes five gauges and all of the chemicals needed for attachment. It also includes the necessary tools like a soldering iron, solder, tape, tweezers, etc. The reloader need buy nothing else.

Proper placement and installation of the strain gauge is essential to obtaining accurate pressure readings. On bolt-action rifles, the gauge is best placed on the underside of the chamber area of the barrel. The barreled-action can then be remounted in the stock for normal use. The wire leads may be unsoldered from the gauge after all testing is done, or they may be coiled in place for future use.

The Oehler Model 43 system is an excellent alternative to invasive pressure testing methods that are just too expensive, especially when several different cartridges are to be tested. However, the Model 43 is not something you buy and simply use immediately. It is a complex system that requires proper setup. The user must have knowledge of the equipment and familiarity with microcomputers. To this end, Oehler Research offers a ballistic measurement workshop, a four-day event geared for reloaders. The first half of the workshop is an introduction to and demonstration of pressure measurement techniques. The second half is devoted entirely to the use of the Model 43. Cost is around $1000.

Once the system is set up, test firing may begin. Many users of this system incorporate a laptop, battery-operated computer that can sit on the shooting bench atop the Model 43 system unit. The sample output page shows complete documentation of a test firing of a Remington .30-06 using 150 grain factory loads using the complete Model 43 system with all equipment in place for measuring pressure as well as velocity, ballistic coefficient, time-of-flight, etc. The summary report is in four sections. The first details the test setup. This is data that is directly input by the user. The second section headed Shot Data lists the data for five test shots.

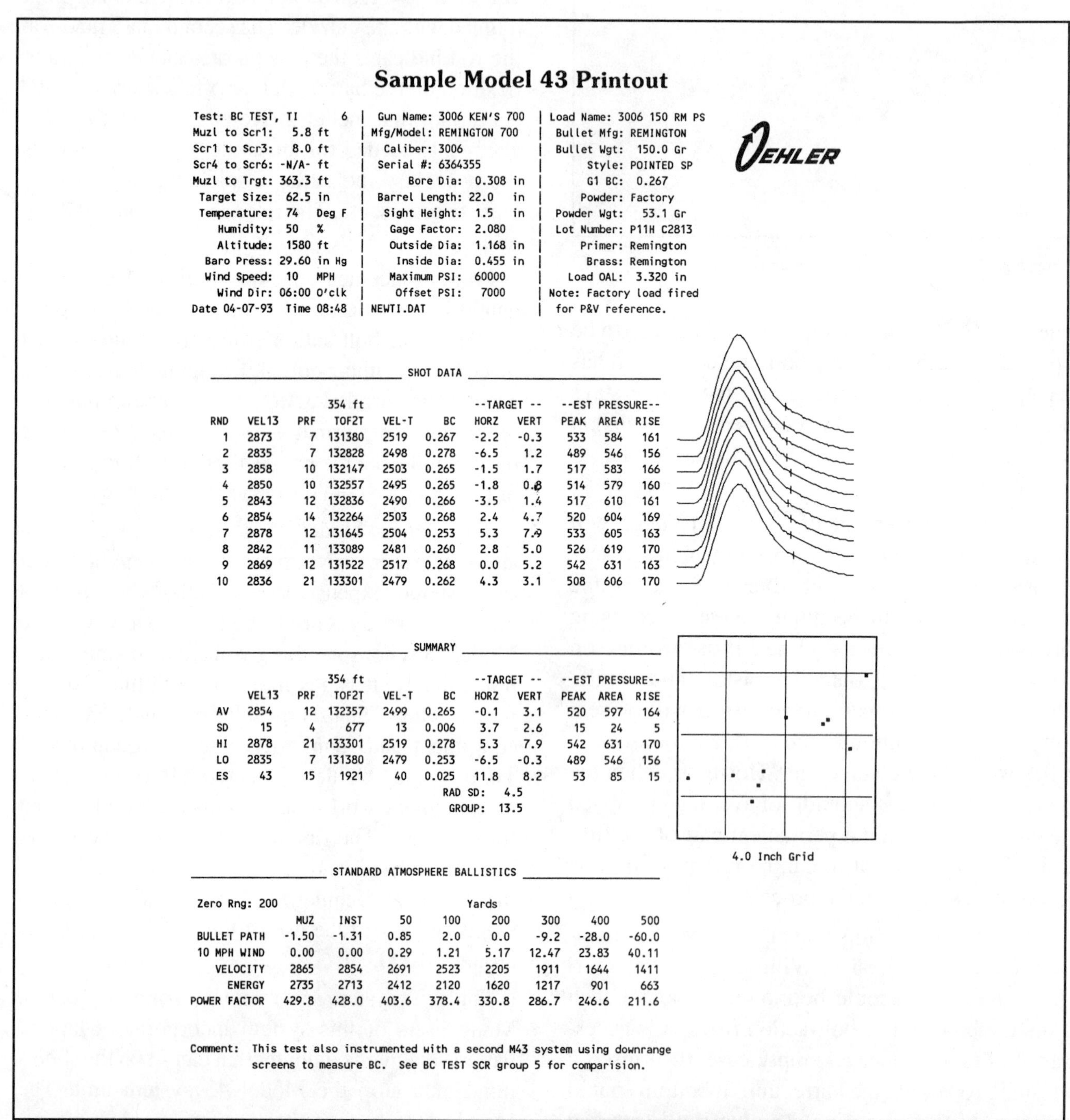

Sample Model 43 Printout

Test: BC TEST, TI 6	Gun Name: 3006 KEN'S 700	Load Name: 3006 150 RM PS
Muzl to Scr1: 5.8 ft	Mfg/Model: REMINGTON 700	Bullet Mfg: REMINGTON
Scr1 to Scr3: 8.0 ft	Caliber: 3006	Bullet Wgt: 150.0 Gr
Scr4 to Scr6: -N/A- ft	Serial #: 6364355	Style: POINTED SP
Muzl to Trgt: 363.3 ft	Bore Dia: 0.308 in	G1 BC: 0.267
Target Size: 62.5 in	Barrel Length: 22.0 in	Powder: Factory
Temperature: 74 Deg F	Sight Height: 1.5 in	Powder Wgt: 53.1 Gr
Humidity: 50 %	Gage Factor: 2.080	Lot Number: P11H C2813
Altitude: 1580 ft	Outside Dia: 1.168 in	Primer: Remington
Baro Press: 29.60 in Hg	Inside Dia: 0.455 in	Brass: Remington
Wind Speed: 10 MPH	Maximum PSI: 60000	Load OAL: 3.320 in
Wind Dir: 06:00 O'clk	Offset PSI: 7000	Note: Factory load fired
Date 04-07-93 Time 08:48	NEWTI.DAT	for P&V reference.

SHOT DATA

			354 ft			--TARGET	--	--EST	PRESSURE--	
RND	VEL13	PRF	TOF2T	VEL-T	BC	HORZ	VERT	PEAK	AREA	RISE
1	2873	7	131380	2519	0.267	-2.2	-0.3	533	584	161
2	2835	7	132828	2498	0.278	-6.5	1.2	489	546	156
3	2858	10	132147	2503	0.265	-1.5	1.7	517	583	166
4	2850	10	132557	2495	0.265	-1.8	0.8	514	579	160
5	2843	12	132836	2490	0.266	-3.5	1.4	517	610	161
6	2854	14	132264	2503	0.268	2.4	4.7	520	604	169
7	2878	12	131645	2504	0.253	5.3	7.9	533	605	163
8	2842	11	133089	2481	0.260	2.8	5.0	526	619	170
9	2869	12	131522	2517	0.268	0.0	5.2	542	631	163
10	2836	21	133301	2479	0.262	4.3	3.1	508	606	170

SUMMARY

			354 ft			--TARGET	--	--EST	PRESSURE--	
	VEL13	PRF	TOF2T	VEL-T	BC	HORZ	VERT	PEAK	AREA	RISE
AV	2854	12	132357	2499	0.265	-0.1	3.1	520	597	164
SD	15	4	677	13	0.006	3.7	2.6	15	24	5
HI	2878	21	133301	2519	0.278	5.3	7.9	542	631	170
LO	2835	7	131380	2479	0.253	-6.5	-0.3	489	546	156
ES	43	15	1921	40	0.025	11.8	8.2	53	85	15

RAD SD: 4.5
GROUP: 13.5

STANDARD ATMOSPHERE BALLISTICS

Zero Rng: 200

			Yards						
	MUZ	INST	50	100	200	300	400	500
BULLET PATH	-1.50	-1.31	0.85	2.0	0.0	-9.2	-28.0	-60.0
10 MPH WIND	0.00	0.00	0.29	1.21	5.17	12.47	23.83	40.11
VELOCITY	2865	2854	2691	2523	2205	1911	1644	1411
ENERGY	2735	2713	2412	2120	1620	1217	901	663
POWER FACTOR	429.8	428.0	403.6	378.4	330.8	286.7	246.6	211.6

Comment: This test also instrumented with a second M43 system using downrange screens to measure BC. See BC TEST SCR group 5 for comparision.

Figure 32-10: Typical Oehler data sheet.

The headings for the Shot Data Segment of this report are defined as follows:

- RND - The round number of the shot within the test group.
- VEL13 - The velocity measured from Screen 1 to Screen 3 in the Oehler multi-screen chronograph setup.
- PRF - The velocity proof number. This is a calibrating value that indicates whether or not the first part of the multi-screen chronograph system is properly calibrated.
- TOF25 - Time-of-flight measured in microseconds.
- VEL46 - Downrange velocity at target.
- PRF - The velocity proof number for the downrange chronograph sensors.
- BC - The ballistic coefficient interpolated from the muzzle chronograph readings and the downrange readings.
- PEAK - The estimated peak chamber pressure.
- AREA - The area-under-pressure curve.
- RISE - The time in microseconds from the 25% point to the 75% point of the pressure curve.

The pressure curve graph to the right of the Shot Data area shows the curve of the pressure from low to high and back to low again. One curve is provided for each shot, they are presented side-by-side for comparison.

The next chart area provides a summary of all previous information, averaging the test shot data taken from the previous report section. The last section charts the average ballistics of the shots fired, giving bullet drop, energy, wind drift, and energy out to 500 yards.

This is a comprehensive report and, perhaps, much more than most reloaders will deem needful. However, the system is expandable. You can purchase the basic Model 43 unit to do pressure testing only. Later, if the need arises, optional components can be connected to this system to provide some or all of the report capabilities outlined.

PRESSURE DANGERS

When chamber pressures are allowed to rise above the tensile strength of the firearm action, the action can fail. The extent of this failure will involve the hardness of the action, the actual amount of pressure, the type of action, and many other factors. The minimum physical damage to the firearm that can be expected during a damaging high pressure event of this sort is chamber expansion and/or locking lug setback. As was mentioned previously, the receiver ring may be literally blown away from the rest of the action in more damaging events.

Should the weaker brass case head fail, gases escape back into the action at tremendous force. In bolt-action rifles, well designed bolts will vent the gas downward through the magazine box and away from the shooter. However, this is no minor occurrence. The vented gas usually expands the action bolt rails and splinters the stock, as well as destroying the magazine box. A case head failure often results in damage to the firearm that is not repairable.

In very severe cases, the action simply flies to pieces, often creating a potentially lethal situation for the shooter. Barrels have been completely blown off of guns as the action gives way. Many shooters have experienced such cataclysmic events and lived to tell the tale. Some have escaped with only minor burns. Others have not been so lucky.

It has been stated by more conservative gunwriters that pressure should always be respected. Let's go one step farther, and state that high pressure should be feared! Fear automatically commands respect, and fear of the possible results of excessive pressure in firearms is a reasonable attitude for every reloader to have. Reloading is an inherently safe pursuit, but it is very unforgiving of errors. When reloading ammunition for yourself or for others, mistakes must not be made!

By following standard reloading procedures, there is no reason why a reloader should ever become involved in a disastrous high-pressure event. These safety rules demand that all loads be worked up individually, starting with a powder charge that is well below the published maximum. Remember, all firearms are different. A maximum load for one may be above maximum for another of the same caliber. Reloaders should begin with a minimum published load and then work up from there, increasing the charge in fractions of a grain. After each firing, the case should be examined for high pressure signs. When found, the load should be reduced by at least .5 grain. In no case, should the maximum published load be exceeded.

UNDERLOADING DANGERS

When it is stated that reloading safety steps should be followed to the letter, it means just this. Don't assume anything. If a published load calls for a minimum of 48 grains of a certain type of powder for a particular bullet/primer/case configuration and a maximum of 54 grains, then neither end of this scale should be exceeded. This means that you should not load less than 48 grains of powder or more that 54 grains.

Novice reloaders, without a sound grounding in the techniques, often assume (incorrectly) that, since it is the powder charge that creates the pressure, you're always safe with less powder. This is not correct for many reasons.

First of all, a less-than-minimum powder charge, especially in low-velocity loads, may not generate enough pressure to drive the bullet completely out of the barrel. If an initial load causes the bullet to become lodged at some point in the barrel and this condition is not discovered, then the next load may cause the barrel or receiver to burst. Minimum loads are published, in part, to prevent this, but they also represent the minimum useful load that can be produced, given a specific cartridge/powder/bullet combination.

While one would assume that if a load calling for a minimum of 48 grains of a certain powder type produces safe pressure levels, then a load of a lesser amount of the same powder must generate even lower pressure. Scientific studies certainly back up this principle. However, experience dictates otherwise. There have been instances where reduced charges somehow have caused pressures to soar enormously, so much so that the firearm was practically disintegrated. Why does this occur? No one really knows for sure!

The reduced load/high pressure syndrome has been a very controversial mystery with the firearms/reloading profession for well over a quarter of a century. It cannot be duplicated in laboratories (at least, not with any certainty), and there is no proven scientific explanation as to why it occurs. However, guns have been destroyed and people injured from these events.

Damaging pressures from significantly reduced loads seem to occur in large-capacity (magnum) cases with slow-burning powders, such as IMR or Hodgdon 4350, 4831, etc. The tendency seems to worsen with cartridges that have case capacities that are considerably over-bore capacity. The first persons to report these events were, typically, developing loads with these slow powders, and once a full load was obtained, tried half loads to see how they performed. As an example, assume that a load is worked up for a particular cartridge that ended with a maximum load of 58 grains of IMR 4831 powder. The half-load would consist of 29 grains of the same powder with all other components remaining the same.

It is half-loads such as these that have been known to completely destroy guns. They may work perfectly 99 times, with the cases giving no high pressure signs, whatsoever. Then, suddenly, on the 100th attempt, the firearm blows up!

There have been many explanations offered as to why this even can and does occur. No one of them has been fully embraced by the reloading community at large. However, the reloading community has, generally, accepted the fact that this phenomenon does occur (for whatever reason), and greatly-reduced loads of slow-burning powder are a potential danger that must be avoided.

Some experts feel that the high pressure is created due to a detonation effect that occurs when the powder is allowed to collect around the base of the bullet at the cartridge mouth. This situation would occur if the gun is fired with the muzzle pointing downward. Others feel that the small amount of powder (in comparison with the total case capacity) presents more of its surface area to the primer flash, which causes the powder coating on the surface of each granule to be burnt away by the initial, lower-intensity portion of the primer flash. This coating is what determines the burning rate of the powder. With the coating removed, the effective burning rate is greatly increased, so when the main portion of the primer flash arrives a split-second later, it ignites a powder that has a much faster burning rate with its retardant coating gone. The result is naturally, a high-pressure event.

These are just a few of the explanations. There are many others. However, knowing the reason behind this phenomenon is not all that important to the reloader. It is only important to know that high pressure can result from underloading, especially with slow powders in large-capacity cases. Another powder that can give underloading problems is some fast-burning pistol powders and some should not be reduced more than 3 percent. Therefore, the published minimum powder charges for these loads and cartridge types must never, never be reduced.

SUMMARY

The accurate measurement of chamber pressures in firearms forms the more esoteric element of reloading. Fortunately, most reloaders need only look for signs of excess pressures, as the exact measurement of pressure in psi is usually not practical from a cost standpoint. Then too, any pressure measurement of any load applies only to that load used in the test environment. When the load is used in another firearm, the pressure generated will be different because of the different dimensions of the chamber and the barrel.

Reloaders are always cautioned to work their loads up in small steps, starting with a minimum charge; that is, several tenths of a grain below the recommend maximum. Furthermore, maximum published loads should never be exceeded, even when no obvious high pressure signs are indicated by the fired cases.

Chapter 33
Measuring Recoil

To every action, there is always an equal and opposite reaction. This is Newton's third law of motion and it is why all firearms react when fired, however slight or great. This reaction is called *recoil.*

Recoil or gun "kick" can be a nuisance. It can take the joy out of shooting, inflict acute *flinchitis* and scare shooters into misses. But knowing what causes recoil and how to control it can go a long way in lickin' the kickin' problem.

Recoil can be accurately measured, as it is a product of the weight of the gun, projectile and powder charge, combined with the bullet's acceleration. If one of these components changes and all others remain the same, then the recoil energy will be changed as well. Increasing the weight of the bullet will increase the recoil if all other values remain the same. Decreasing the weight of the firearm creates an automatic increase in recoil. Therefore, recoil for an individual gun changes when any of the following conditions are changed:

- The weight of the firearm
- The bullet's rate of acceleration
- The rate of the powder and gas acceleration
- The jet push at the muzzle

The accurate measurement of recoil may be done in several different ways. One fairly conventional method is attaching the firearm to a movable cradle of known weight which, in turn, is equipped with heavy metal wheels and rides on a track similar to a railroad track. The gun is discharged, and the distance the gun's recoil causes the cradle to move backwards is converted to recoil energy which is measured in foot-pounds.

However, such measurements, while interesting, say little about the "felt" recoil experienced by the shooter. Before moving further into the technical aspects of recoil measurement, it is appropriate to fully discuss the human response and psychological reaction to what is probably the most feared area of shooting.

Whether they admit it or not, most persons who fire high-powered rifles, shotguns, and pistols give more than a passing thought to recoil. Recoil is more devastating to some shooters than to others, but most experts contend that the recoil effect on humans is more a matter of conditioning than physical in nature.

Another psychological aspect to recoil that makes it unpleasant, is the muzzle blast that accompanies it. Your reverie is suddenly destroyed by a loud thunderclap and an immediate, sharp pushing sensation. Either is completely manageable by the human psyche on its own, but the combination tends to overload the senses, magnifying the complex event. The muzzle blast makes the recoil seem more intense, and/or the recoil makes the blast seem much louder.

UNDERSTANDING THE COMPLEXITIES OF RECOIL

Most shooters consider recoil to be a straight, backward thrust. If it were this simple, then its effects would not be so hard to measure. The fact is that recoil from most modern rifles and shotguns is far more complex than a straight-line push. Recoil thrust will be impressed on the center of balance and this is where a major measurement problem lies. The center of balance of a single rifle can be easily determined. However, when the firearm is held to the shoulder and balanced by the shooter's hand on the forearm, the center of balance of the free rifle and the center of balance of the rifle/shooter combination are two different points entirely. Recoil is not impressed on the center of balance of the human body. If this were the case, the butt of the rifle would necessarily be placed somewhere on the human mid-section. Instead, the rifle butt is placed off-center on one shoulder.

When the firearm discharges, the thrust is generally backward, but it also has considerable vertical and horizontal thrust components as well. Under heavy recoil, the muzzle climbs (sometimes viciously), the human body rocks backward. This backward motion causes the human body to also bend backward at the waist, which further increases the vertical climb of the barrel. Further thrust after the maximum point of bending will cause the shooter to rock back on his or her heels. Again, the vertical climb is accentuated.

Horizontal movement of the firearm is often the single most uncomfortable element of recoil. Proper firing form calls for the shooter's cheek, shoulder, arms, and hands to be a "welded" single unit with the rifle. If this form is not followed, especially if the cheek is held away from the stock, it is common for the shooter to be smacked in the jaw by the stock of the recoiling rifle. The horizontal or lateral thrust factor of the firearm, coupled with the rearward and upward thrust factors create a twisting motion or circular thrust factor. Depending on the center of balance of the firearm and the shooter/firearm combination, this circular thrust can be clockwise or counterclockwise. For a right-handed shooter, clockwise thrust moves away from the right side of the face, while counterclockwise thrust moves into it. This order is reversed for left-handed shooters.

Pistol (handgun) recoil abides by the same principles as that from rifles and shotguns, but the effects are more acute because the center of balance lies farther away from the center of balance of the human body. Since pistols are dramatically shorter than rifles and shotguns, there is less distance from the free pistol center of gravity and its farthest points from this center than in longarms. This accentuates the vertical and circular thrust factors, coupled with the fact that the primary recoil anchoring point, the pistol/human center of gravity, is about 2.5 feet in front of the human body (in the hands) instead of at the shoulder.

Shooting form is stressed in recoil management because of the complex movements involved in a single recoil thrust wave. It is definitely not a straight-line push but a complex assortment of horizontal, vertical, and circular velocities, as experienced by the human body. Add sound or muzzle blast to these, and the problems increase for the shooter.

RECOIL REDUCTION BY MECHANICAL MEANS

Given a specific bullet weight, powder weight, muzzle velocity, and gun weight, there is little that can be done about the energy of recoil thrust. However, there are ways in which this thrust can be better directed or smoothed to make it more comfortable. When a specific load is fired from a firearm of a certain weight, then a specific amount of recoil energy is generated, period. It is how this recoil is impressed upon the body that determines its effect on the human shooter. This might be called the recoil comfort level.

While different persons have different tolerances to the effects of recoil, there are several factors that can allow "felt" recoil levels to be more comfortable for all shooters. Felt recoil can be likened to wind chill. A temperature of 40 degrees driven by a 40 mph wind will feel well below freezing to human skin. However, the temperature is still 40 degrees and water will not freeze. Humans may but water will not.

We have all heard someone say "my rifle kicks more than any other rifle in this caliber that I ever shot." If this rifle weighs no more than other rifles of the same caliber and is firing the same loads, then the recoil energy must be the same. So, why does this rifle kick more?

A more accurate statement would be that this particular rifle produces more "felt" recoil than any other. The reasons for this (assuming weight and load factors are the same) must be in the way that the firearm impresses that recoil on the shooter, what we like to call the shooter/firearm interface.

It is a fact that some rifles simply "fit" a shooter better than others. Generally, the better the fit, the lesser the felt recoil. Fit is usually based primarily in the gun stock. The angle of the comb, the width of the forearm, the drop, the presence or absence of a cheekpiece, the height and taper of the cheekpiece, and the surface area of the buttplate are all factors that impact felt recoil and are a part of the stock.

When a rifle is quickly placed on the shoulder, it should be perfectly aligned with the shooter. If not, the shooter must do some minor or major repositioning of his or her body in relation to the firearm. These adjustments may be made subconsciously, but they are made. For instance, if the drop of the stock (its downward angle from the receiver) is too great, then it is necessary for the shooter to lift his or her head slightly to align the eyes with the sights. Upon firing, the recoil can drive into the cheek, which has not been solidly held to the stock when firing. If the drop is too low, then the cheek must be pressed hard into the stock to attain sight/eye alignment. This added pressure causes the circular thrust to be more strongly felt.

A portion of recoil is absorbed in the hands and arms when firing longarms. For right-handed shooters, the left hand and arm play an important role in controlling recoil. For left-handed shooters, it's the right hand and arm. It is for this reason that stock forearm shape and diameter are so important. If you can't get a good, solid grip in a heavy recoiling longarm, then less recoil will be absorbed by this hand and arm. Also, the recoil thrust is less balanced, being pushed to the opposite side. A stock with a forearm that is too big or too small for your hands will most likely cause felt recoil to be stronger.

A very important factor in reducing felt recoil is the recoil pad and its surface area. The softness of the pad and its physical size where it meets the shoulder can make a very big difference in the human comfort level. Recoil pads range everywhere from a steel buttplate to special soft rubber compounds. Most found on retail rifles are made from a relatively hard rubber. By replacing the harder pads with the newer "soft" pads, perceived recoil is lessened. There is less shoulder "sting" caused by a hard surface being driven into the shoulder. The soft pads compress more and flatten out a bit upon recoil to cover more surface area of the human shoulder.

Modern rifles tend toward the lightweight, and this means smaller, narrower stocks. This is great for weight reduction, but it does nothing to lessen felt recoil. Since lightweight firearms produce more recoil anyway, there is a two-fisted increase in recoil. The surface area of the recoil pad or butt of the stock plays an important role in how recoil is felt. It can be compared with catching a heavy medicine ball on the tips of the fingers and the hands, instead of grabbing it with your arms and body. An even more graphic image is pressing a brick on your arm with a force of five pounds and comparing that with placing a sharp knife on the arm with the same force. The narrower surface area causes the problem, because a smaller portion of the human body acts as the initial impact point.

Recoil pads with ample surface area reduce felt recoil. To get around the small butts of modern stocks, some modern pads are even flared slightly at the shoulder end to increase their surface areas.

Stock composition is another factor of recoil. Wooden stocks are still the most plentiful, but each year, more and more composite stocks are available, either as user-installed add-ons or already fitted to certain models from the major manufacturers. Most of these artificial stocks reduce the amount of felt recoil, because they are not as stiff and firm as wooden stocks. When the firearm recoils, most composite stocks will compress more than wooden ones, so some of the recoil energy is absorbed in this compression. However, most composite stocks weigh less than their wooden counterparts, so the initial reduction in felt recoil is sometimes countered by an increase in actual recoil. Nevertheless, most shooters maintain that firearms mounted to composite stocks have slightly less recoil than those that use wood.

Several companies make cylindrical mechanical devices called "recoil compensators" that are fitted into rifle and shotgun stocks by removing the recoil pad, drilling a hole 1.5 inches in diameter and 6 to 8 inches deep and then inserting the compensator. *See* Figure 33-1. Some compensators are spring loaded. Others contain a mercury core. They are designed to change the center of gravity of the longarm after the recoil thrust has begun. Rather than lessening recoil, this type of compensator is positioned so that it modifies the circular recoil thrust energy. They can sometimes be successfully used to prevent a particular gun from slamming into the cheekbone by directing the circular thrust in the other direction.

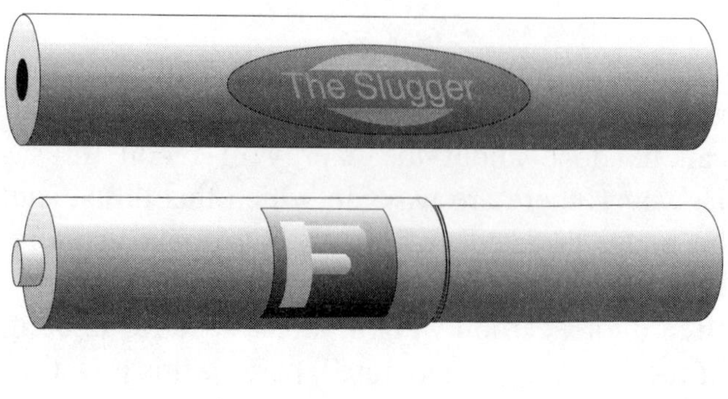

Figure 33-1: C&H mercury recoil suppresser (top); Hiram's Bear Trap recoil reducer (bottom).

Felt recoil is reduced by redirecting a component of the complex thrust wave or by absorbing that component. Fitted stocks, composite stocks, larger recoil-pad surface areas and recoil compensators all do this to larger or smaller degrees. However, there is one device that works at the other end of the gun, at the muzzle. When discharging a firearm, two basic components are driven from the muzzle: the bullet and the expanding gases that propel it.

The velocity and direction of powder gases play a role in actual recoil. By modifying the direction of these gases, an actual reduction in recoil at the butt end of the gun can be realized. Powder gas redirection is accomplished by a device called a "muzzle brake" that (as its name implies) is in-

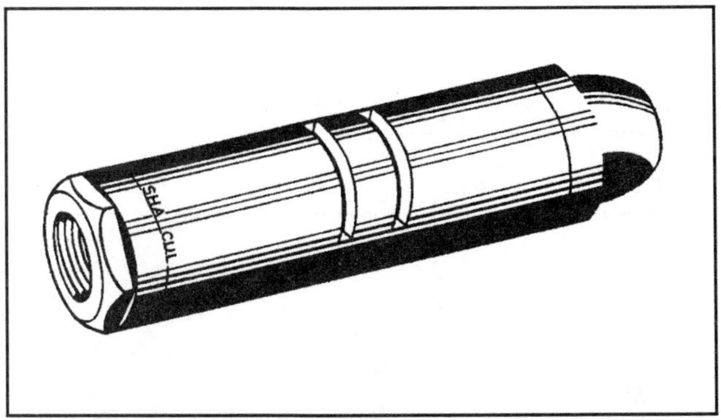

Figure 33-2: Several types of muzzle brakes have appeared on the market in the past 50 years. All, however, operate on practically the same principle.

stalled on the muzzle of the firearm. *See* Figure 33-2.

The brake is an extension of the barrel with an inside diameter large enough to allow the bullet to pass through unhindered. Unlike a closed barrel, however, the muzzle brake contains holes along its body to allow powder gases to escape in directions that are angled away from the line of the muzzle.

The muzzle brake's holes are drilled at precise angles. The greater the angle is away from the line of the muzzle, the greater the recoil reduction. Some brakes even angle the powder gases more than 90 degrees from the bore line, which produces forward thrust in a manner that is similar to thrust reversers on a jet aircraft. The forward thrust at the muzzle end reduces the rearward thrust at the butt end by a like amount. Other types of muzzle brakes never exceed the 90 degree angle, and these reduce recoil by a lesser amount.

The number of venting holes, their position along the brake and their angle or angles of gas deflection will vary from manufacturer-to-manufacturer. Their ability to reduce recoil is dependent upon the amount of powder gas produced by the fired cartridge as well as by their mechanical design. Some, quite frankly, are worthless and do almost nothing. Others are more effective, with many giving slightly less than 25% reduction in overall recoil, this being the absolute maximum with current technology. When the muzzle brake is used in combination with recoil-reducing stocks and recoil pads, this reduction may increase as much as 50%.

Muzzle brakes have a serious drawback, in that they greatly increase the muzzle blast that is heard by the shooter. Since muzzle blast is a factor in how most humans perceive recoil, this increase can sometimes offset any reduction in actual recoil. Hearing protection is absolutely essential in order to prevent immediate and permanent hearing loss from the high decibel level of blast sound produced by firearms fitted with muzzle brakes.

CALCULATING RECOIL

Most of the previous discussions on recoil reduction involve gunsmithing/stockbuilding practices. Is there anything the reloader can do to reduce recoil through custom loads designed to address this purpose? The answer is a definite YES, but before this issue can be tackled, it is first necessary to understand the role that cartridge and ballistic components like powder weight, bullet weight, and muzzle velocity play in producing recoil. By obtaining a working knowledge of recoil makeup and measurement, the reloader can then determine how a certain load should be constructed to best address the issue of recoil comfort for the shooter.

Since recoil is a physical result that is described by the law of the Conservation of Momentum, it can be scientifically calculated. Prior to the age of electronic calculators and microcomputers, this was an involved process. Today, it is much simpler.

In technical terms, firearm recoil is the equal and opposite reaction to the momentum of the bullet and powder charge. Determining free recoil energy in foot-pounds requires first arriving at recoil velocity, which is easily accomplished with a microcomputer or even a hand calculator using the equation in Figure 33-3 on the next page.

All of the weights are given in pounds and velocity is in feet-per-second. The 4700 value is a

$$\text{Recoil Velocity} = \frac{\text{Bullet Weight} \times \text{Bullet Velocity} + 4700 \times \text{Powder Weight}}{\text{Gun Weight}}$$

Figure 33-3: Equation for calculating recoil velocity.

powder gas expansion average constant. Powder gases accelerate from modern firearms at an average velocity of 4700 fps.

It is relatively simple to obtain all of these figures. The weight of the gun, bullet and powder charge is obtained by using scales, although the powder charge and bullet weight will, most often, be expressed in grains and must be converted to pounds by dividing by 7000 (7000 grains = 1 pound).

Once the free recoil velocity is obtained, it is worked through another equation that determines free recoil energy. It is this energy that we feel when firing a gun. With all of the substitutions made, the final equation for calculating free recoil energy is shown in Figure 33-4.

Reloaders with microcomputers may wish to use the following BASIC program, which will allow them to input the various figures in convenient units and obtain a readout of free recoil energy.

```
10 REM CALCULATE FREE RECOIL
ENERGY IN FOOT-POUNDS
20 INPUT "BULLET WEIGHT IN
GRAINS: ";BW : BW = BW/7000
30 INPUT "MUZZLE VELOCITY IN
FPS: ";MV
40 INPUT "POWDER WEIGHT IN
GRAINS: ";PW : PW = PW/7000
50 INPUT "GUN WEIGHT IN
POUNDS: ";GW
60 RE = (((BW * MV) + (4700 *
PW))^2) / (64.348 * GW)
70 PRINT:PRINT "RECOIL ENERGY
IN FOOT-POUNDS =";RE
```

This equation/program will reveal that a typical .30-06 rifle, firing a 180 grain bullet from a charge of 55 grains of powder at 2700 fps and weighing seven and a half pounds, produces free recoil energy of 23.44 foot-pounds. These values closely reflect factory loads and typical gun weights for rifles that fire this caliber. Now, what would be the result if the weight of the rifle were increased by one pound (to 8.5 pounds) and all other factors remain the same? The formula reveals that the free recoil energy would drop by over 10% to approximately 20.68 foot-pounds.

If any value that is worked through this formula is changed, so will the free recoil energy. Increasing gun weight will always decrease recoil energy, assuming all other values remain constant. Increasing powder charge, bullet weight, and/or velocity will always increase recoil. However, suppose we

$$\text{Recoil Energy} = \frac{(\text{Bullet Weight} \times \text{Bullet Velocity} + 4700 \times \text{Powder Weight})^2}{64.348 \times \text{Gun Weight}}$$

Figure 33-4: Equation for calculating recoil energy.

reduce the bullet weight, increase bullet velocity and increase powder charge? Here is where the formula worked into the computer program really pays off in convenience. The decrease in bullet weight will decrease recoil, but increasing the powder charge and the velocity will increase recoil. One factor pulls against the other two.

Assume we load the .30-06 case with 60 grains of powder and a 130 grain bullet for a muzzle velocity of 3200 fps. Comparing this with the 180 grain loading previously discussed, we know that the lower bullet weight will result in less recoil in comparison with the 180 grain bullet. However, the powder charge has been increased by five grains and the muzzle velocity by 500 fps. Will the extra five grains of powder and the greatly increased muzzle velocity offset the lower bullet weight?

By working all of these factors through the formula, the free recoil energy for this latter combination is calculated at 20.60 foot-pounds, assuming a 7.5 pound rifle. This means that there has been a better than 10% reduction in recoil over the 180 grain loading. As a matter of fact, the 130 grain loading in a 7.5 pound rifle produces about the same amount of recoil energy as does an 8.5 pound rifle firing the original 180 grain loading. This indicates that bullet weight is a very significant factor in recoil energy production, more so than is the powder charge and the velocity in comparison.

By dropping the velocity of the original 180 grain loading to about 2500 fps using 51 grains of powder in a 7.5 pound rifle yields recoil of about 20 foot-pounds. Alternately, using a 165 grain bullet at 2700 fps from 53 grains of powder also gives us about 20 foot-pounds.

However, the weight of the rifle is the single most predominant factor in recoil energy. To consider an extreme example, let's study the .460 Weatherby Magnum. It fires a 500 grain bullet at a velocity of approximately 2600 fps from a powder charge of about 112 grains, typically from an 11 pound rifle. When worked through the formula, the free recoil energy is just over 96 foot-pounds or about four times that of the 7.5 pound .30-06 firing a 180 grain bullet! Guns on the order of the .460 Weatherby must be heavy in order to make the recoil manageable. What would happen if the weight of the Weatherby .460 were increased by a few pounds or (unthinkably) decreased by a few? The formula reveals the answer to these questions.

When the .460 Weatherby rifle is increased in weight to 13 pounds, the free recoil energy drops to about 81 foot-pounds. This marks a reduction of 15 pounds of energy just less than 15%. When the rifle weight is reduced to only 9 pounds, the recoil energy climbs to nearly 118 foot-pounds, an increase of just under 20%. It now has the recoil of about five .30-06 rifles firing 180 grain loads at 2700 fps!

RELOADS FOR RECOIL REDUCTION

Now that a working understanding of recoil and the role the various cartridge components play in producing it, some thought can be given to producing reloads for a recoil-sensitive shooter, even if it is yourself.

Problem:

You must build some .338 Winchester Magnum reloads for a Western elk hunt, where shooting ranges will vary from 100 to 300 yards. However, the hunter is recoil sensitive, so these loads must address the problem. From interviewing the hunter, you discover that he can currently tolerate the recoil from his 7.5 pound .270 Winchester, firing 150 grain handloads at 2800 fps. Your client doesn't want much more recoil than that. His .338 rifle weighs 9 pounds with scope attached.

This problem is not as hypothetical as it is practical, as this fictitious client is very typical of the Eastern whitetail hunter who travels West for a first elk hunt. Perhaps, a .30-06 would be a bit more appropriate for him, but he has chosen a .338 Winchester. Can you help him?

The first thing to do is to calculate the current recoil level that this hunter feels he can comfortably tolerate at present. By working the .270 Winchester 150 grain load at 2800 fps through the formula, you will find that the free recoil energy produced in a 7.5 pound rifle is about 19 foot-pounds. Now, add a margin of 20% to that figure as an absolute comfort limit. This means that your job is to build a handload that will produce no more than approximately 23 foot-pounds of recoil from his 9 pound .338, while still maintaining the trajectory and energy figures necessary to humanely take an elk out to 300 yards. Figure a minimum retained energy level of 1500 foot-pounds for a clean kill and a kill zone deviation of 8 inches (in regard to point-blank range).

This is not an easy task, as you are sure to discover if you work a typical 225 grain .338 factory load in a 9 pound rifle with an average muzzle velocity of 2850 fps from a powder charge of approximately 70 grains. The free recoil formula will tell you that such a combination produces 33 foot-pounds of recoil energy. This is 50% more recoil than your client feels he can tolerate!

Since the caliber and weight of the rifle are fixed, these are not a variable. The only way that recoil can be adjusted is by loading ammunition that will bring about the needed reduction in recoil.

Being a reloader, you know that a 225 grain bullet of .338 caliber is adequate for elk, but you can save a little weight by going to a 200 grain premium bullet, such as the Barnes X-Bullet shown in Figure 35-5. Since it is a premium, solid copper-alloy bullet with controlled expansion, this should make up for the weight reduction. (The Nosler 210 Partition bullet wouldn't be a bad choice either, but it weighs an extra 10 grains.) The X-Bullet also has a high ballistic coefficient (over .450) for its weight and caliber, so this would give it superior down-range performance. The sectional density would be a bit low, but the added velocity should make up for this.

Figure 33-5: Barnes X-Bullet.

If we assume a load consisting of about 69 grains of IMR 4350 powder, the 200 grain bullet should leave the muzzle at about 2800 fps. This should be adequate for elk up to 300 yards, maximum. However, what will it generate in recoil?

Again the equation is used, and we find that such a load would generate just over 27.5 foot-pounds of recoil energy. This is some five pounds better than the factory load, but it is still a bit too brisk.

Since powder weight contributes to recoil energy just as bullet weight does, a logical choice would be to use a different type of powder, a faster powder that would generate the needed velocity with less weight. If the IMR 4350 is replaced by IMR 4064, the same velocity can be generated with about 60 grains of powder. How does this stack up when run through the equation?

Now we're getting somewhere. Calculated recoil energy is now just over 24 foot-pounds! This should be close enough to the ideal of no more than 20% higher than the .270 loading in the 7.5 pound rifle used as the basis for determining comfortable recoil. However, a perfectionist might reduce the powder charge by a grain or two (and the velocity along with it) to arrive at exactly 23 foot-pounds of calculated recoil energy.

The reloader must still determine energy levels and bullet drop downrange. By examining the appropriate ballistics charts, it will be immediately evident that this bullet should have over 2000 foot-pounds of energy at 300 yards. Furthermore, if the gun is sighted in at 300 yards, the bullet will be a maximum of only 5.5 inches high at any point out to that distance. However, most hunters would probably sight in the rifle for exactly 225 yards.

There you have it: A custom load for a recoil-sensitive hunter. The custom reloader, by being familiar with the component causes of recoil, has been able to design a load that exactly meets his or her client's needs, or for that matter, for his or her own needs. This problem has caused the reloader to dig deeply into his or her knowledge of ballistics and recoil principles, and then adding the principles of recoil dynamics, measurement and calculation. The problem was solved by a well-rounded grounding in the many components that encompass the pursuit of reloading. This type of research greatly enhances the pleasures derived from reloading for many shooters.

Appendix I
Sources of Supplies

Bullets

Hawk Inc.
P.O. Box 1689
Glenrock, WY 82637
Ph: 307-436-5561

Hornady Manufacturing Company
P.O. Box 1848
Grand Island, NB 68802-1848
Ph: 308-382-1390
Fax: 308-382-5761

Houston Cartridge Company
1526 Helen Drive
Spring, Texas 77386
Ph: 1-800-776-6717

North American Bonded Bullet Company
P.O. Box 797
Mundelein, IL 60060
Ph: 708-949-9569
Fax: 708-949-9570

Nosler Bullets, Inc.
P.O. Box 671
Bend, OR 97709
Ph: 503-382-3921
Fax: 503-388-4667

Old West Shooter's Supply
P.O. Box 4035
Rapid City, SD 57709-4035
Ph: 1-800-782-5889
Fax: 605-341-3785

Precision Ammunition & Shooting Supplies, Inc.
2402 Broadmoor Dil-101
Bryan, TX 77802
Ph: 409-774-4480
Fax: 409-774-1293

R & R Bullet
909 Hospt. Drive
Crawford, NE 69339
Ph: 1-800-865-1312
Fax: 308-665-1372

Sierra Bullets
P.O. Box 818
1400 West Henry St.
Sedalia, MO 65301
Ph: 816-827-6300
Fax: 816-827-6300

Speer
Blount, Inc.
P.O. Box 856
Lewiston, ID 83501
Ph: 208-746-2351
Fax: 208-746-2915

Cases

Grayback Wildcat
5306 Bryant Avenue
Klamath Falls, OR 97603
Ph: 541-884-1072

Houston Cartridge Company
1526 Helen Drive
Spring, TX 77386
Ph: 1-800-776-6717

Old West Shooter's Supply
P.O. Box 4035
Rapid City, SD 57709-4035
Ph: 1-800-782-5889
Fax: 605-341-3785

Precision Ammunition & Shooting Supplies
2402 Broadmoor Dil-101
Bryan, TX 77802
Ph: 409-774-4480
Fax: 409-774-1293

Precision Reloading, Inc.
P.O. Box 122
Stafford Springs, CT 06076-0122
Ph: 203-684-5680
Fax: 203-684-6788

Gunpowder

Accurate Arms Company, Inc.
Rt. 1 Box 167
McEwen, TN 37101
Ph: 615-729-4207

Ammo Junction
104 Pine Street
Narrows, VA 24124
540-726-7243

Hercules Inc.
Hercules Plaza
Wilmington, DE 19894
Ph: 302-594-5000
Fax: 302-594-5305

Hodgdon Powder Company, Inc.
6231 Robinson
P.O. Box 2932
Shawnee Mission, KS 66201
Ph: 913-362-9455
Fax: 913-362-1307

IMR Powder Company
R.D. 5, Box 247E
Plattsburgh, NY 12901
Ph: 518-561-9530

Kaltron-Pettibone
1241 Ellis Street
Bensenville, IL 60106

Lead Shot

J.F. Littleton
275 Pinedale Avenue
Oroville, CA 95966
Ph: 916-533-6084

Miscellaneous

GAR
590 McBride Avenue
West Paterson, NJ 07424
Ph: 201-754-1114

Hawk International
P.O. Box 219
Gary, SD 57237
1-800-429-5333
Fax: 605-272-5502

Keith's House of Guns
260 N. 50 W.
P.O. Box 207
Oak City, UT 84649
Ph: 1-800-846-2067

Lock, Stock & Barrel Shooting Supply
West Hwy. 20
Drawer B
Valentine, NE 69201
Ph: 1-800-228-7925

Whitman's Lube Sticks
1811 West 13th Avenue
Denver, CO 80204
Ph: 303-595-9636
Fax: 303-595-4413

Maine Cartridge Company, Inc.
Rt. 1 Box 381
Passadumkeag, ME 04475
Ph: 207-732-4979

Mason's Shooting Products
611 S. Hansell St.
Thomasville, GA 31792
Ph: 912-228-7369

The Reloading Center
16230 Parthenia Street
North Hills, CA 91343
Ph: 818-892-4654

Widener's Reloading & Shooting Supply, Inc.
P.O. Box 3009 CRS
Johnson City, TN 37602
Ph: 1-800-615-3006
Fax: 423-282-6651

Tools

Forster/Bonanza
Forster Products
82 East Lanark Avenue
Lanark, IL 61046
Ph: 815-493-6360
Fax: 815-493-2371

Hornady Manufacturing Company
P.O. Box 1848
Grand Island, NB 68802-1848
Ph: 308-382-1390
Fax: 308-382-5761

Huntington
P.O Box 991
601 Oro Dam Blvd.
Oroville, CA 95966
Ph: 916-534-1210
Fax: 916-534-1212

Lyman Products Corp.
Route 147
Middlefield, CT 06455
Ph: 203-349-3421
Fax: 203-349-3586

MEC Inc.
c/o Mayville Engineering Co.
715 South St.
Mayville, WI 53050
Ph: 414-387-4500
Fax: 414-387-2682

MTM Molded Products
P.O. Box 14117
Dayton, OH 45413
Ph: 513-890-7461
Fax: 513-890-1747

RCBS
Blount, Inc.
P.O. Box 856
Lewiston, ID 83501
Ph: 208-746-2351
Fax: 208-746-2915

Redding Reloading Equipment
1089 Starr Road
Cortland, NY 13045
Ph: 607-753-3331
Fax: 303-756-2338

Thompson/Center Arms
Farmington Road
P.O. Box 5002
Rochester, NH 03867
Ph: 603-332-2394
Fax: 603-332-5133

Appendix II
Bibliography

ABC'S of Reloading, 4th ed.
288 pages. Grennell. DBI Books.

Cartridges of the World. 6th ed.
Barnes. 448 pages. DBI Books.

Cast Bullets
144 pages. Harrison. Available from Brownells.

Cast Bullets, Supplement to
28 illustrated articles. Available from Brownells.

Complete Guide to Handloading
516 pages plus. Sharpe. Out of print.

Handbook for Shooters & Reloaders - Vols. I & II
576 and 495 pages, respectively. Ackley. Available from Brownells.

Handloader's Log and Refill (with charts)
Available from Brownells.

Hodgdon Data Manual No. 25
542 pages. Hodgdon Powder Co.

Hornaday Handbook. Volume 3
665 pages. Hornaday Manufacturing Co.

Lyman Cast Bullet Handbook. 3rd ed.
419 pages. Lyman Products Corp.

Lyman 46th Edition Handbook
8,000 loads plus. Lyman Products Corp.

Lyman Shotshell Reloading Handbook, 4th ed.
1995. Lyman products Corp.

Nosler Reloading Manual Number Three
582 pages. Nosler Bullets, Inc.

NRA Handloading
Available from Brownells.

Pet Loads, 3rd ed.
636 pages. Waters. Available from Brownells.

Pet Loads Supplements, 4 booklets
Available from Brownells.

Reloading for Shotgunners, 2nd ed.
256 pages. Anderson. Available from Brownells.

Sierra Reloading Manual, 3rd ed.
Separate companion volumes for rifle, handgun. Sierra Bullets.

Speer Reloading Manual No. 1
Blount, Inc.

The Art of Bullet Casting
264 pages. Wolfe. Available from Brownells.

The Handloader's Manual of Cartridge Conversions
1054 pages. Donnelly. Available from Stoeger Publishing Co.

The Home Guide to Cartridge Conversion, 2nd ed.
404 pages. Nonte. Available from Brownells.

Index

— I —

— J —

— K —

— L —

— M —

— N —

— O —

— P —

LUCÍA ASHTA

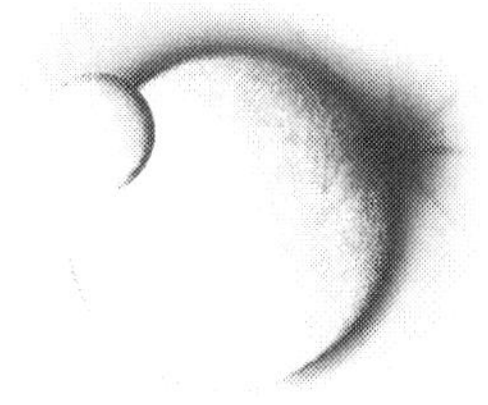

PLANET ORIGINS

Copyright 2017 Lucía Ashta.

All rights reserved.

Published by Awaken to Peace Press.

This book is a work of fiction.

Cover design by Lou Harper.

Edited by Ellen Campbell.

Also edited by Elsa Crites.

ISBN 978-1-5441540-2-2
April 2017

Learn about Lucía's books at LuciaAshta.com.

For the real Ilara,
who revels in her true nature

The most terrible of limitations are those we impose upon ourselves. Free your mind, and you free yourself.

1

Planet Origins Year 3,069 of the Andaron Dynasty rule

THE THREAT OF DEATH STARES EVERYONE IN THE face at one time or another, though it doesn't usually come from an eyeball. This one eyeball was swiveling furiously, reminding me of the many reasons I didn't normally let the King see me.

Even if he hadn't noticed me, I'd seen the King many times, always from afar; I allowed the masses to conceal me with their fervor. In the current political environment, the King—always guarded—made regular public appearances. It was important that the people of Planet Origins—Planet O for short—remember that he was still in control. It was likewise important for the King to remember that the people of Planet O wanted him as their king as they'd wanted his ancestors before him.

I lied and told myself that this latest near death experience might have gifted the King with uncommon patience and understanding. His legendary sharp mind and quick instincts to punish might have dulled since the attack that left him temporarily bedridden. Comforted by these lies, I took one step forward, out of the shadows that clung to the walls of the royal infirmary.

That one gray eye honed in on me in the same devastating way as an asteroid on a direct trajectory guarantees inevitable destruction. It undressed me, doing away with all pretense as quickly as a man could undress a woman with his sight. Already, my comforts were revealing themselves for the falsehoods they really were.

With my next step toward the King's prostrate form, I could feel his eye on me as if it were a hand, attempting to throttle me for a sin worse than any against his empire. I would have turned around right then, no matter what I'd resolved to do, but I couldn't. Retreat wasn't an option. Not when this was about her. I couldn't turn away from her.

I stepped directly into the light that filtered from the glass bed the King lay on. I bowed from a respectable distance. "Good morning, your Majesty." My voice squeaked at the start.

"You may rise," a voice said from the corner. I swiveled. The King's presence was imposing, even in his debilitated condition. I hadn't noticed the man whose job appeared to be to interpret the King's subtle gestures and thus to conserve his energy for healing. Ordinarily, I observed every detail of my surroundings. I tried to shake off the realization that I wasn't as sharp as usual.

At close range, the King pinned me with both cold, gray eyes, not just the one. Together, their impact doubled, and it was easy to believe that this man had ruled Planet Origins for nearly a millennium.

Those two eyes narrowed with obvious impatience. I didn't need anyone to interpret that look. I hurried to speak. I was lucky to have been granted an audience in the first place. If I hadn't said those two words—Princess Ilara—I would never have made it past the King's antechambers. I'd invoked her to gain access. After all, this was about her, as it had been for years.

"Your Majesty, I'm here about Princess Ilara," I said, never taking my eyes from those that held mine. Before a man like this, one could not show weakness. My entire plan depended on this man trusting me, and the King didn't trust anyone.

"So I've been told," the King croaked. I hoped I hid my reaction to the King's audible frailty in time and averted my eyes for a moment. But when I looked up again, I knew that I hadn't. Anger flared in the King's eyes.

"You are Lord Brachius' son." The statement was both factual and accusatory.

I didn't bother drawing up tall. I took no pride in being a potential tyrant's son. "I am. And there is nothing I can do to change that, regrettably."

Curiosity flashed across eyes that had grown still though I didn't presume to be safe in their stare. Animals of prey watched their target with deceptive calm before they ripped the throats out of victims that couldn't run fast enough to escape the unavoidable.

In this room with softly glowing yellow lights, a glass bed, and nothing more, I had nowhere to run. "I understand the risk I took in coming to see you. But I had to. You see, I know that Princess Ilara lives," I whispered so that only the King could hear.

One of the King's raspy breaths cut short in his chest, the sudden silence echoing in the sterile room. He flicked a nervous glance at his servant. When the King returned his gaze to me, rage brewed. I took a small step back before noticing what I'd done. I couldn't give up any progress. My visit today was too important. The King was a wild beast that had been civilized. To rule Planet O the way he had all these years, he had to be a bit like the hairy mowabs of the deserted wildernesses: fierce. Everyone on Planet O knew not to mess with the mowabs.

This king was groomed and polished, his gray beard trimmed into precision despite his convalescence. But the mowab in him still reared forth. "Lord Tanus, do not play with me."

I nodded without wanting to.

"You will find yourself in a game of cat and mouse, with me the cat."

Obviously, I thought. There wasn't a trace of mouse in the King of Planet Origins.

"If you've come here thinking you would take advantage of a flailing king, you were mistaken." The King's words could cut metal. The servant stepped out of the shadows in concern. He was there to ensure that the King rested when he should. Upon his recovery and his broad shoulders depended the future well-being of a planet.

And upon my shoulders rested the well-being of a princess. I took that responsibility as seriously as the King took his responsibility to rule. The King cut the servant short with one look, and the shadows swallowed the servant once more.

The King would do as he chose during his recovery, and he would do what he wanted with me as well. All it would take was a flick of a finger and I would be taken to the holds beneath the palace, where my screams of protest couldn't travel high enough to disturb the royal court.

King Oderon ruled with an iron fist. He showed compassion when necessary to appease his people. But this wasn't often. I'd heard nearly every rumor about him. I feared that most of them were true.

"Has your father sent you here?"

If I answered yes, I would be guilty of treason. My father had been suspected of betraying the Crown many times before. I presumed that he was trying to accomplish it once more right now.

"He did not. He doesn't know that I'm here, your Majesty."

The King's eyes roved, taking in my tall frame, sweeping all the places one could hide a weapon. Then he nodded. Continue.

"Milord, do not hold the son accountable for the sins of his father. He and I are nothing alike." I had to tread carefully here. I didn't care for the man my father had become, but neither did I wish to fill the role of his official accuser. My father lived despite the attacks against the King because no links survived between the assassination attempts and him. He was cunning and meticulous.

The King waited. Obviously, there was more. With a

slight nod of his head, he gave me leave to speak of his daughter, but quietly. No one—not even the servant in the corner—needed to hear what I had to say.

"I know that your daughter lives. And I know that she was sent off planet." I whispered. The surprise in the King's face confirmed that he'd heard.

"And what," the King hissed back, "makes you think this?"

"I know this because I feel her alive." I let my statement sink in. "At first, I didn't understand how she could have lived. Everything that I suspected went contrary to what was being said." There was no accusation there. No pointing fingers. The King did what he had to do to protect his family. I would have done the same.

"But then I began to look for her, to follow leads and dead ends, until finally, I discovered what I think now must be the truth. I broke into my father's facility to confirm it."

Neither astonishment nor alarm flared in King Oderon's eyes. What I saw was much worse: It was a promise, a promise that the King would use his last strength to fulfill. He would kill anyone that betrayed his daughter.

I had nothing of which to be ashamed. I forced myself to meet the King's challenge. I needed the King to understand. I couldn't get to Ilara without his help. And if he were to die before sharing this secret, I would never find her. She would be lost to me forever, and that was much worse than anything the King could do to me.

"Does Lord Brachius know?" The King waited for my answer, prepared to identify the truth or the lie within it.

I shook my head, brown hair cascading across my forehead. "No. And he'll never know. I'll take the secret of Princess Ilara's survival to my grave with me, if I must."

The King nodded. He could recognize a duty to protect a loved one. "And why is it that the Princess is so important to you? Is it that you are a loyal subject with interest in defending the royal family?"

I took a deep breath and made the right choice: Truth, blunt truth. "No. I don't particularly care who rules as long as he rules fairly. I know that I don't want my father to rule because he wouldn't rule fairly."

The King nodded curtly. There were certain types of men that respected the truth more than the content of what was said; the King was such a man. "Then, what is your interest in the Princess?"

The King still hadn't confirmed my theory. My next words were the best chance I had at getting through to a father who happened to be a king. "I love her. I've loved her for years."

I forced myself not to shrink from the King, even though I'd just revealed that the Princess and I had sneaked and hidden our relationship from him, the most powerful man on the entire planet, with a reach that extended much farther than one planet's orbit.

"And she loves me."

2

THE MOMENTS THAT TICKED BY DID SO SLOWLY. I experienced each one as a spasm in my chest. The divide between life and death—and how swiftly the King could bring about either—was louder than anything else in the room. The glass bed emitted a constant stream of healing rays for the King, without sound or other evidence of the work it did. The attendant was invisible as he was expected to be.

Yet my fear was palpable, thrumming audibly in a loop between my ears. I'd prepared so exhaustively to face the King that it seemed impossible that he could crush hope from me so easily. I'd known what King Oderon was like. Everyone knew. His reputation for ruthlessness and strength was how he'd maintained his rule without opposition for so long. Until my father.

And I'd just admitted to an illicit love affair between his only living child and myself.

A bead of salt water, a traitor to my resolve, erupted on

my temple. It began its descent down my face. I didn't move to brush it away. I didn't want to call the cat's attention to evidence of the mouse's weakness.

The King's mouth rose on one side, and I realized he'd spotted it. Even infirm, atop a healing bed, he wasn't just a cat but a lion. If he'd been standing, he might have rushed and pinned me to a wall—if kings did things like that. Or maybe he would have had one of his servants do it for him and then come around for the kill.

"So you and my daughter love each other? Well isn't that nice?" The edge in his voice revealed that he didn't think it one bit nice. Without thinking, I bent my head to my shoulder to wipe the dripping sweat against my coat. The King's half smile expanded into a sneer.

"And what makes you think that is permissible?" The words dripped with venom. Nothing of importance happened in his kingdom without his knowledge; it wasn't supposed to, at least. Now, another attack on the throne had taken place, one that had almost cost him his life. And worse, his daughter had been illicitly consorting with the heir of his enemy.

I gulped but plowed forward. It was now or never. And never could arrive all too swiftly. A signal from the King would be all it took. "It wasn't what we intended. It wasn't planned." The words many terrified men had uttered to furious potential fathers-in-law across the worlds. Some things didn't change no matter where you lived or what air you breathed. "We would have never chosen each other and the accompanying complications that come from who we are. But..."

"But what? Do not make your king wait!"

His voice thundered, and without looking up from the terrifying eyes that still seized mine, I felt the attendant stiffen across the room. "Pardon me, your Majesty, it's just that, well..." At the bulging of his eyes I nearly tripped over my tongue to complete my sentence. "We fell in love with each other."

I waited, but nothing came. Still, the tension in my shoulders didn't ease. I didn't know that love—true love—was one thing King Oderon did value. I didn't realize that his marriage to the recently deceased Queen had been more than an obligation to the royal bloodlines.

For the first time since I entered the room, the King brought his eyes to rest on something other than me. He stared at the ceiling. I swept the backs of my hands against my sideburns and then wiped them along my pants. When the King still hadn't returned his attention to me, I looked to the ceiling.

The ceiling was designed to mimic the sky. It was as if there were no ceiling at all. Stars, planets, and clouds swirled above us, suggesting that troubles even as great as mine were insignificant.

The King startled me away from the view when he finally spoke. "How can I be certain that what you tell me is the truth?" He wouldn't ask me that question if he didn't believe me already, at least some. I allowed real hope to flutter to life for the first time since I crossed the threshold into the golden yellow light of this room.

Flattery wouldn't work. I couldn't praise his ability to discern the truth. The King had a reputation for smelling out deviousness before it could begin to stink. I possessed nothing tangible to prove my love for Ilara and hers for me. We'd had to be careful. We understood better than most how easy it would be for our affair to be discovered if we left a trail. More than one scandal had initiated with love letters that the lovers assumed would never be discovered.

I did, however, have a way to access incontrovertible proof. I wished so desperately that there were another way. But there was none. The only chance to save Ilara's life lay in giving myself entirely to the lion, like sacrificial prey.

There was only one part of me that I'd been able to keep from the prying eyes of my father all these many years. It was this part that made me who I was. I shared it with no one. Had I been forced to share it with anyone, I'd have chosen Ilara.

There was no point in delaying the awful. I took a small step forward. The attendant reemerged from the shadows, alarm on his otherwise blank face. Without looking at the attendant, the King raised a hand to stay him. However, I wouldn't draw closer. Already, it was unprecedented that I should be allowed to be so close to him without his guards surrounding us.

I'd said the magic words. The King was in too tenuous of a position to turn away his curiosity at what the son of his sworn enemy would have to say about his daughter, the one that no one was supposed to know was still alive.

"I can prove that what I say is true, that Ilara—Princess Ilara—and I love each other. I can also prove that my intentions are good. That I mean only to help her."

"Go on."

"I can share my memories with you."

Something akin to respect flashed across the King's face for a moment before he stashed it away. It took one level of courage to fight in battles or to face a king with a reputation for dealing death daily. It took an entirely different level of courage to reveal what one is really made of, to show the tender parts of a man that only he—and perhaps a special woman—should ever truly know. It was the ultimate sacrifice. I would be giving a man everything he would ever need to destroy me—as if this particular man needed any more.

The King deliberated but only for a second. He waved his hand. The attendant moved to his side as quickly as he could while still retaining the composure that was required of him. The servant dipped his head in a bow. "How may I be of service, my Liege?"

"Summon the royal physicians immediately. Tell them to bring whatever is needed for a brain merge."

The attendant struggled between the appropriate measure of composure and alarm. Brain merges were rare for a reason. When a person chose to open his brain to another, he was at his mercy. The voyeur would look or take and even destroy. The King could do whatever he wanted with me. He could leave me a drooling puddle instead of the man I now was, and there'd be nothing I'd be able to do to prevent it. During a brain merge, physical movements were disengaged so that the brain wasn't distracted by anything other than its most essential bodily functions.

"Will that be all, Milord?"

"For now."

The attendant bowed again and scooted elegantly back to

his side of the room, where he waved a hand across the far end wall to reveal a communications panel.

Of course. My every step was being watched, guards likely perched at the ready to rush the room were I to advance on the King. The King hadn't made as many allowances for my visit as I'd thought. He was protected even in his state of relative physical vulnerability. He'd just not wanted anyone close enough to listen to any conversation about the Princess of which he couldn't predict the content beforehand.

Moments before the doors swept open, the King asked, "And why do you trust me?"

"Your Majesty, forgive my candor, but I don't. However, I know of no other way to gain your trust. And it is only with your trust that I stand any chance of helping the woman I love. I've exhausted all other avenues. This is the only way I see to move forward."

Once I'd offered myself up to the greatest risk I could take, my shoulders relaxed, and the sweat stopped flowing. It was as if, after the worst was done, there was nothing to worry about. Apprehension wouldn't influence the King's decision. Whatever else I did now, he would do as he wished with me.

The King would have access to all of my memories, not just those that contained his daughter. He would come out of the brain merge knowing precisely what kind of man I was and the kind of man I longed to be. He would know every one of my dark secrets if he chose to look for them.

"I see," was all he had to say before the magnitude of my sacrifice.

The doors to the chamber slid open in near silence. Two men entered with a tray hovering behind them. I stepped to the side so that one man could approach the King. This physician was less fidgety than the other, trying to subdue his nerves. "Your Majesty, are you certain that you are strong enough to attempt a brain merge? Perhaps it might be advisable to wait a few more days until Milord has recovered more of his strength. The attack occurred only yesterday."

"I'm well aware of when the attack occurred, Lord Broon. My faculties are in good order and your input, unnecessary."

"Of course, Milord, I didn't mean to imply otherwise. Forgive me if I didn't choose my words wisely." Lord Broon was well schooled in how to deal with royalty. "I was merely concerned for his Majesty's well-being."

"The only assistance I require is for you to facilitate a brain merge between me and this man."

Both physicians studied me just long enough to tuck away their surprise. As much as I tried to disassociate myself from my father, it was likely that they realized who I was.

"I do not wish to assume, your Majesty. Would you like the brain merge to go one way?"

"Of course."

Of course. There was no way this lion of a king would allow me or anyone else into his thoughts. Undoubtedly, that full mane of shiny silver hair hid a great many dark and terrible secrets. He must trust Lord Broon. Once both parties were under a brain merge, only a person on the outside could interrupt it—and control it. Lord Broon could, theoretically, open the pathways so that I could review the King's memories. But Lord Broon would never do that. Why should he want me to possess such information? A man such as Lord Broon valued his life.

"Very well." The physician motioned to his colleague to bring the tray closer. "You," to the attendant, "have a table brought in."

The King wanted this done now. I did too. Better to have it over and done with than to dread what would inevitably arrive. I couldn't retract my offer.

I removed my jacket and laid it on the pristine floor, beneath a sky suddenly colored orange by a setting sun that would deliver only temporary darkness before the second sun rose.

3

For such a significant procedure, the set-up was quick. There wasn't enough time for me to fully come to terms with what I was about to do. Like a man who recognized that death was imminent, I felt as if I desperately wanted more time, although it wouldn't change anything.

I'd anticipated that it might come to this. My arms master, Dolpheus, and I had explored multiple scenarios, and more often than not, they ended in this. Yet it was one thing to discuss a potential outcome. It was quite another to suddenly find yourself prone on a glass bed next to the mighty King Oderon, of whom myriad legends existed.

Physician Broon looked down at me with a clinical gaze that unnerved me further. The procedure hadn't even begun and already I felt entirely too exposed and vulnerable. Every one of my muscles, trained for combat since I could first walk, clenched and released repeatedly in a useless cycle.

Where I'd been hot just minutes before, now I was cold, as if my body were already dead and I were looking down at myself from above, watching Lord Broon examine me with clinical detachment. A quick shiver bolted through my shoulders. Lord Broon noticed it but didn't ask if I was cold.

He finished placing the last of the strands against my temple, and there was nothing left to be done. I wanted to turn my head from side to side, to see what I looked like with all these filaments attached to me, but I couldn't. Any movement would pull them free of the clips that clung to my hair to hold the strands against my scalp. I'd already been warned. The filaments were extremely delicate. Composed of crystal dust that held together through its own internal magnetism—each fragment of crystal was designed to join with its greater whole—any abrupt movement would cause the pieces to break apart.

Despite their fragility, there was nothing better for mind merging. The King of Planet O had the best technology power could coerce or buy. The fragments of crystal were only barely solid, energy condensed into form, each speck linked to the next by nothing greater than its desire to do so. It was the perfect conduit for thought—a kind of energy.

Physician Broon didn't attach the other end of the crystal strands to the King's head. Rather, he placed them atop his scalp, gently, and directed him to be still. To me, he said that all I needed to do was to intend to run my thoughts through the crystal particles and into the King's mind. Once my thoughts started to flow into his brain, the strands would harden and fix in their position.

Lord Broon informed the King—not me—that thought would travel across the lines between us fluidly. The monarch would be able to experience my memories as his own. There would be nothing that I could conceal. Nothing that I could explain away.

"Are you ready, my Liege?" Lord Broon asked.

"Yes. Proceed."

I received no final warnings although I imagined the disclaimers attached to this procedure had risks worth mentioning. No more words were uttered. None for my benefit. No sympathy or encouragement offered to settle my nerves. No smiles that indicated that anyone admired the backbone it took to do this.

The process began without notice. I hadn't meant to begin just yet, but a part of me—the morbidly curious part, I supposed—rushed ahead and yanked me in. And now I couldn't come out of it until the royal physician, a man I didn't know, decided it was over.

I could feel—perhaps even hear—the crystal dust coming to life. The strands grew rigid, the specks holding onto one another eagerly, as if they were long-lost friends or lovers. The seven crystal strands that attached to my head fixed to my skin like suction cups, pulling on my hair as the crystal strands adjusted from their initial limp positioning. Once the energy of my thoughts began to run through the crystal particles, they responded, uniting into a rigid mass capable of transmitting thoughts at a speed as great as that of light.

At the start of the mind merge, I felt the King's body jolt next to mine, just once; perhaps he was as surprised as I was that the process had already begun. It would continue to transmit the energy in the direction I sent it until Lord Broon interrupted it.

That was the most dangerous part, Broon had said,

although to me it all seemed dangerous. The person to interrupt the flow of thought and energy had to know what he was doing. There were all sorts of things that could go wrong if the flow were interrupted abruptly. When two brains merged, a powerful link, albeit a temporary one, was formed between them. If the two brains were torn apart prematurely, both brains could be left believing they were incomplete and incapable of functioning without the other.

It wasn't just my brain, but also the King's, that would be harmed. This one fact was the only reassurance that allowed me to relax at all. Lord Broon would do everything he could to protect the King. Therefore, my chances of surviving this procedure increased monumentally.

Through my peripheral vision and a tangle of erect strands, I saw the King's body visibly relax. And then there was nothing more. After that, I was incapable of keeping track of anything around me. The swirl of thoughts that encompassed an entire lifetime made it impossible to focus on the input my brain attempted to process from any of my other senses. I could still see, smell, hear, feel, and taste, but I had no idea what I was sensing.

It was an overwhelming jumble. Had I been a manmade system of operation, I would have crashed and refused to reboot ever again. Flashes of events in my life, of people that meant something to me, flew across my awareness so quickly that I couldn't absorb what I saw. Events and people distorted into a wave of colors, sounds and emotions so consuming that I had to direct what little ability to focus I had left to keeping nausea from overpowering me. I couldn't sit up to vomit. And if my movement tore the crystal strands from my head, throwing up all over myself would be the least of my problems.

I thought I closed my eyes in an attempt to shut out the stimuli, but I couldn't be sure that I had. Regardless, it didn't work. Nothing could push away the flood of private snippets of my life, the ones I'd hoped to reserve for myself. But I couldn't resist sharing them. It felt like the violation that it was; it didn't matter that I'd volunteered for this.

I ground my teeth against the worst ride of my life. People complained that traveling to other worlds and galaxies was barely worth it because of the intensity of the trip. It made you feel as though your insides were being torn from your body before being reinserted again. I'd done it before, and it did feel that bad.

This was worse. I clenched my hands into fists, ready to take on an opponent. But this was an invisible one that I'd brought on myself. I was facing a lion, and I felt infinitely smaller than a mouse. All that I was and ever hoped to be was divided into fragments so small as to be dust.

I'd entered the King's chamber partially to prove myself a man worthy of loving his daughter. He'd crushed me into powder.

It went on for what seemed like forever. My eyes rolled into the back of my head. My nails cut into the skin of my palms. Every muscle in my body tensed until it readied to explode. I was trapped in this reality that had become too brutal.

I couldn't breathe. I thought I'd die right then and be saved from this King and even the Princess, from my father and everything else.

Then, after one more excruciating and terrible moment, it was over.

I hadn't heard Lord Broon's movements, the ones that carefully and very slowly detached one crystal strand at a time, beginning with those linked to the King's head. I hadn't realized that my thoughts no longer flowed into the brain of another person, because once Broon fully disconnected the King, my thoughts collected feverishly in what now seemed like too shallow a well for them. They had nowhere to go, so they swirled and concentrated like water in a clogged drain.

The exact second when I was certain that all crystal cables were free from my head, I bolted upright. Then I vomited all over my lap.

4

As soon as I was capable of a modicum of thought, I reflected how regrettable it was that I'd gone through such a harrowing experience with no one that cared whether I lived or died. It's not that I expected Lord Broon to rub my back as a mother would her child, yet it did seem unnecessarily callous not even to offer me something with which to clean up.

I was sitting in a pool of my own vomit. It collected in eddies around the sides of my body, made interesting by the otherwise pristine glass it swirled across. Even with as wealthy as my father had become in recent decades, I'd never seen so much glass in one room. The beds alone must have cost the kingdom a small fortune.

Although I wasn't exactly having the most useful or organized thoughts, coherence was beginning to show promise of its eventual return. I noticed that my boots needed shining. That the vomit had spread along the glass to my back and was already soaking through my pants. I realized that I couldn't smell the rancid scent that all vomit carried and wondered hazily if that meant that my sense of smell hadn't yet returned.

I could see, but I looked at nothing in particular. I stared off into the open space of the room and the warm yellow glow that didn't cast shadows in its diffuse glow. The attendant wasn't at his station against the far wall anymore.

I considered if I should attempt to move since it seemed that no one was going to help me down from the table. I wondered if I was allowed to, now that the crystal dust strands had ben removed. But Physician Broon wasn't in front of me, and I couldn't swivel my head. My skull felt like it was being squeezed by a vise, and altogether too much screaming silence filled the space within it. I couldn't remember when, or if, I'd ever heard such thick silence before.

I sat, slouched, defeated-looking and unaware of whether I was actually defeated or not. Eventually, my muscles fully relaxed. Then I was putty. With nothing and no one to lean on, I vaguely thought I might melt to join my stomach acids, then cool into the form of the glass bed, as if I'd filled a mold. I felt formless. A beating heart, a throbbing head, and the all-encompassing silence.

I thought I could sit there forever. Getting up on my own didn't seem like an option. But when vomit soaked through the fibers of my pants, it became too much. I was feeling humiliated enough without vomit soaking my most private parts.

I'd revealed every piece of myself to a man I didn't trust, to a man that already possessed more than most other humans alive, and I hadn't wanted to be the one to give him even more. I'd opened myself up like a virgin maiden pressured into her first sexual encounter, and I hadn't received even a thank you or a pat on the rump.

I decided to get up. Fuck anyone else in the room. They didn't want to help me? Fine. They could just go ahead and be that way. I'd do my best to trail throw-up all the way to the exit.

I was firm in my resolve. I'd get out of here before I had to look any of these assholes in the face. They thought it was no big deal to do a mind merge with the mighty King Oderon? To hell with them.

After I made my decision, it took me a lot longer to get my body to respond to my mind's promptings. *Come on. Get up*. But it didn't work. When I finally was able to move, I realized it was a bad idea even before my foot made it all the way to the floor. However, I couldn't stop in time. My thoughts were moving as if through slop. I couldn't intercept my earlier messages to my body.

Comprehending that standing wasn't going to happen as I'd imagined didn't stop my toe from reaching the pristine floor. It didn't stop me from scooting to the edge of the bed and swinging my other leg over its side or from pressing off with my hands, launching myself into the seemingly inevitable course into which I was propelling myself. And it didn't stop me from mopping the floor with the puddled mess that I was, crashing to the ground heavily as metal.

I lay there, unable to ponder the turn my existence had taken this morning, when I caught a flash of frenzied movement over by the King.

Then I closed my eyes for what I hoped would be forever.

5

I DON'T KNOW HOW LONG I WAS OUT, BUT IT MUST have been a while because when I woke my eyes were crusty and my mouth sour. I blinked a few times and took in a subtly lit room that wasn't the royal infirmary. I shifted and every one of my muscles screamed in protest. At least they moved the way I wanted.

I looked down at myself. While I slept, my dignity had been restored. I was in fresh clothing that wasn't my own. I was so relieved that I hadn't been left on the floor, soiled and crumpled, that I didn't much care who'd been given the task of undressing and cleaning me.

I heard the soft whoosh that signaled a door opening and attempted to sit up. I did more groaning than sitting, and suddenly Dolpheus was at my side helping me. "Take it easy, Milord," my arms master said while he spread a strong arm behind my back to prop me up. "You've been through quite an ordeal."

Dolpheus and I had grown up together. We were born in

the same year, raised in the same household. He was the son of my father's manservant. My father outwardly discouraged our friendship for a long time. But once King Oderon had my grandmother killed, he poured his despair, his ambition, and his desire for revenge into his work. Soon thereafter, I transitioned into an afterthought. My father was too consumed by more important things to care about the division of classes.

Dolpheus became my closest friend. I wouldn't stand to hear him referred to as a manservant, so I donned him with the title of Arms Master. It wasn't in my power to confer any greater title upon him. Only a king may do that. Arms Master was a mostly irrelevant title, considering that I was neither at war nor anticipating attack, but it accomplished what I'd hoped it would. It afforded him respect from strangers that didn't know him enough to understand that he deserved deference independent of any title.

Whenever I left my father's lands, Dolpheus almost always accompanied me. And he only called me by my titles when others were in a position to overhear us. Calling me "milord" was a clear signal, even to my recovering mind, that I needed to be careful with my words. Within the walls of the royal palace, there was no such thing as true privacy. Ilara had discovered a listening device in her private chambers. If the King would stoop to spying on his daughter, he'd have no qualms about eavesdropping on anyone else.

"Thank you, Dolpheus." I leaned into his arm and rubbed my hands across my face. "How long have I been out?"

"It's been several days, Milord."

I turned my head sharply to look at my friend and instantly regretted it. "Several days? And my head still hurts this much?" I moved my hands to the back of my skull. "Ah." I winced.

"It hurts in the back?"

"It hurts everywhere."

"I can't believe you did a mind merge with King Oderon." Dolpheus spoke more softly now.

So did I. "We knew it might come to that."

"Still." He whistled in uncommonly subdued fashion. When the façade of obedience fell away later in private, I knew he'd have much more colorful things to say about it. He'd tried to dissuade me from doing a mind merge in our previous discussions by referring to it as a mind fuck that didn't go too well for the one getting fucked. There was a part of me that wished I'd listened. I did feel like I'd gotten fucked and badly, with all the soreness and none of the fun.

"Are you all right?" Dolpheus' astute eyes were studying me.

"I think so. Every part of me hurts right now, but I don't think any permanent damage was done."

"Although if permanent damage was done, you might not know it, right? A damaged mind might be unable to send messages of a change in its functioning."

I sighed. Sometimes I wasn't in the mood to hear Dolpheus express his high intelligence. Like right now. He and I had gone over this many times before coming to the royal palace. The risks of a mind merge were high, but there was no other good alternative to win the King's trust, and there was no other way to save Ilara than by gaining it. In fact, I'd found no other way.

Ilara and I knew how to prevent others from discovering our whereabouts. We'd purposefully made sure that no record of our togetherness existed. Besides, even if I'd been in possession of visual evidence of our relationship—an image of a shared kiss perhaps—it would be insufficient to prove our love for each other. Nor would it have been enough to prove my intentions to the King. Nothing short of allowing my lover's father to view my memories and thoughts could convince him to confide in me.

Without his trust, I couldn't find Ilara. He was the only one I was certain must possess information regarding his daughter's whereabouts. He had to know. A man like King Oderon wouldn't send his daughter to another planet without having some way of recalling her to him. No father would want to send his daughter off without any chance of ever seeing her again, this father especially.

My father's assassins killed the Queen, an attack that instigated the King to hurl my lover across space to some forsaken planet. Ilara was all the King had left now. There was no way that he'd agree to losing her forever when he was freshly mourning his wife, a wife that he'd apparently loved.

"Help me down from here," I said.

"Are you certain that's a good idea, Milord?" Dolpheus was speaking for our invisible audience again, his voice loud enough to carry throughout the small, sterile room. "Are you sure that you'll be stable on your feet, Lord Tanus?"

"No, I'm not certain at all," I grumbled. "But get me up anyway, will you?"

"Yes, Milord."

With Dolpheus' help, I stood, half leaning against him and half against the hovering bed behind me. There was no part of me that stood on its own, but at least I was erect. After the vulnerability I'd experienced from the mind merge, standing upright like a man made me feel better, even if in actuality I was doing none of the standing.

I pushed off the bed a little and nearly collapsed into my friend. "Get me home please, Dolpheus." I leaned all of my weight on him; I knew he could take it. Ordinarily, he was my match in strength.

"Uh, I'm not sure that we're allowed, Milord."

I snapped around to look at him faster than I should have. I studied his eyes that would tell me what his words couldn't. I found trepidation there.

"The mind merge was very difficult for our Liege Lord the King. He's only just woken. He slept nearly as long as you did. The royal physician has been most concerned. He couldn't wake the King once the mind merge was interrupted."

I stared back at my friend.

"Now that he's woken, it seems that he's stable and improving quickly. Remember, he's also still recovering from the latest assassination attempt."

How could I forget? It had been a very long time since my father had made anything easier for me. In fact, he was quite skilled at making everything as difficult for me as possible. Yet complicating my life was only an unintended side effect of his ambitions. I didn't want to imagine what my life would be like if my father were intentionally trying to harm me. He was a man of vast resources and questionable conscience.

I was silent for a moment while I processed the effect of the mind merge on the King. Of course, I hadn't realized what must have been going on around me in the royal infirmary. I couldn't hear a thing at the time, my hearing muted as if explosives had just detonated near me. It was no wonder that no one seemed bothered with me or my sickness. The King came first. He would always come first.

"Why aren't we allowed to leave?"

"I don't know. I think it was just easier to order us to stay, in case the King wanted us here when he woke. You know no one wants to do anything that would displease the King."

I nodded. The pain that burst in my head as I did was less than it had been before. I had the beast of all hangovers.

"Now that the King is awake, perhaps someone can ask for his permission to leave. If he doesn't need us, we can go home."

Again, I nodded. "Will you go request his permission while I wait here?" Now that I was on my feet, I didn't think I could make it too far.

"Yes, Milord."

"And help me back up on the bed."

Dolpheus did. It was just as painful to lay back down as it had been to get up in the first place. I could have given Dolpheus instructions on what to say to the King's attendants. However, Dolpheus knew the workings of the court and the current political environment as well as I did, and I made sure that I was an expert in them.

Instead, I closed my eyes to push out the pounding and hoped not to hear another sound for a while after the door to the infirmary swished open and shut.

6

It took Dolpheus some time—how long, I have no idea—to return. Still, he could have stayed away all day and I wouldn't have minded. My recovery was progressing, but it was doing so with agonizing slowness. When the door swished open, my head still throbbed and my insides seemed hollow.

I forced my eyes open only to squint in the dim light. I didn't care for the way Dolpheus was looking at me, like I was some kind of invalid.

"You don't look so good," he said.

"Yeah? Well neither do you. Your nose is particularly bulbous in this lighting."

Dolpheus chuckled. He and I both knew he was handsome. A steady history of women—the lower-class women in the open, the upper class ones in secret—luring him into dalliances was proof enough.

"We're free to leave for now."

"The King gave his permission?"

"No. He's awake but quite weak. Lord Drakos didn't want to bother the King with it. He gave his permission for us to leave, although we might be called back to court later if the King desires it."

Lord Drakos was the King's minister. While the King had his hand in every significant matter that concerned the rule of Planet O, he was forced to delegate less substantive issues, even if he didn't want to. There were only thirty-three hours in a day, even for a king, and Planet O was big and complex, with the outlying territories beyond the city still dangerous and largely resistant to regulation.

"All right. Then help me up."

This time, Dolpheus moved me more slowly. "I haven't seen you this beat up since our last pass through the Koal Desert."

I groaned, both from my upward motion and the memory of how bad it had been on the journey through the Koal Desert, searching for Ilara. "I seem to remember that even your pretty face was bruised and swollen then."

He smiled. Only a man with the spirit of a warrior could look back upon such a gruesome fight with any kind of pleasure. "Those mowabs were fierce."

"Aye. As were their riders." Many of those who rejected the rule of the Crown absconded to the Koal Desert. There, the rebels were largely left to their own ways. The Desert was harsh and unforgiving and the rate of survival low. If other rebels didn't kill you, the wicked sand storms would. "If I recall, the worst of your injuries was caused by a woman."

Dolpheus grinned. "That's right." He liked his women

feisty. "Your Il—" He caught himself just in time. "Your lady's as fierce a warrior as that woman was."

I smiled. "Yes. Yes, she is." I liked my women feisty too.

"Can you stand on your own?"

I pushed away from the bed against which I'd been leaning. When I began to waver, Dolpheus' hand shot out to grab me. "I think it best if you lean on me."

I didn't bother nodding my agreement. I wasn't making it anywhere without his assistance.

It took longer than it should have to cross the small room to the doorway. It looked just like the other four walls until we approached it. Then it slid open quietly to allow us exit to a wide, monotonous hallway. I knew the uninterrupted walls to either side of us must conceal many more rooms like the one that had just contained me.

The more we walked, the more my legs began to cooperate. By the time we reached the public areas of the palace, the queasiness had subsided some. Soon, I recognized the path Dolpheus was leading me on. He'd chosen not only the shortest route out of the place, but also the one that was least trafficked, at least by those of influence within the court. The regulars of the court didn't frequent this part of the palace. They came to be seen by others that mattered to them, and none of the servants that hurried across these corridors and vast spaces counted.

Still, as people began to pass us by, I did my best to walk on my own. I couldn't separate from Dolpheus entirely, but I did work to appear more independent than I was just then. It wasn't vanity—though I wasn't wholly free of that infirmity—it was something rather more important.

On Planet O, the greatest currency, even greater than glass, was power. The yielding of influence was far more valuable than anything else. I didn't yet know what would unfold—because I refused to accept an outcome that didn't involve Ilara's return. My father was working hard to change the tides of power. The future of King Oderon's rule was uncertain, which meant that everything was uncertain. It was now more than ever that I needed to preserve my reputation for strength.

Several passersby spared us glances. Perhaps a few even recognized me. However, most were in a hurry to get on with their duties. And after what seemed like far too long to traverse the palace, even for as grand as it was, one of the exits loomed large before us. I didn't speak of my relief to my friend. He knew it. I glued my eyes to the exit, willing my feet to continue just a bit longer. We were almost at the gate. Its glass sparkled away one of the sun's rays, making it seem like the magical doorway that it truly would be for me right now.

One of the guards had already honed in on us, anticipating our arrival. He turned his face to us, head on, waiting.

"Lord Tanus," he acknowledged once we finally reached him. I suppressed a sigh. It seemed that everyone at the palace knew who I was, despite my intentions otherwise. My father's notoriety haunted me wherever I went. Maybe I should have been the one considering going off planet, instead of bringing Ilara back to this world.

But then, this world was hers if it was anybody's. She loved Planet O like no one else I'd ever known. She'd told me more than once, when we lay in a naked embrace, sweaty limbs entwined, that she felt its pulse within her blood. She dismissed any suggestion I had of escaping this place so we could be together freely. She'd said that she had a responsibility to Planet O and all life upon it. Planet O spoke to her. When the time came, she'd know what to do—or so she said.

The guard swept his gaze up and down me and then across Dolpheus. Then he stepped toward us with a wand in his hand. Again, he swept the wand up and down me and then across Dolpheus. I always thought this process redundant. We'd been searched upon our entry, when detection of any sort of harmful device or weapon was appropriate. It didn't seem to matter much if someone exited with a weapon. Yet I knew better than to complain.

"Your hand please, Lord Tanus." I extended my hand to the guard's waiting wand. After he scanned it, "Your hand please, sir." Dolpheus gave the guard his hand.

We waited. "You are cleared to exit," the guard said.

"Thank you," Dolpheus said for me. He knew me so well that he realized that I'd begun to tremble inside even though no one else could see it.

The second we passed through the exit, he tightened his grip on my arm. But we didn't make it ten steps down the walkway before the guard chased after us.

7

I FROZE AT THE SOUND OF MY NAME, BUT I DIDN'T turn.

I'd almost been free of the royal palace and the consequent necessity of pretense. I breathed to steel myself. I called on patience I didn't possess. Then I leaned heavily on Dolpheus' arm as, finally, I turned.

"Yes? What is it?" I was both surprised and impressed with the composure I heard in my voice.

"His Majesty the King requests your presence, Lord Tanus," the guard said, curious as to what the King would want with the son of the man who'd just tried to kill him.

For a moment I didn't respond. The guard's eyebrows rose slightly, though he contained his questions. No one hesitated when the King called—at least, no one was supposed to.

Dolpheus nudged me. His elbow poked my ribs in a way that the guard didn't see, but I was certain to feel.

"Very well." I imbued pleasantry into my voice, hoping

to make up for my hesitation. Rumors spread quickly across Planet O, even eventually sprawling across the expanse of deserts. But nowhere did rumors travel more rapidly than at the royal court, where idle courtiers fed on them like the beasts of the wilds. They sniffed out a rumor as a mowab smelled weakness and blood.

“I have instructions that you’re to follow me.”

I smiled an awkward smile that strove to conceal the pain that pulsed through me. The guard turned and began to walk, reentering the palace. After ten paces, he stopped, just within the gate.

“Identification please.”

“You’re kidding, right?” Dolpheus said. The words he chose were much kinder than the ones running through my mind.

“I’m not. It’s my duty to check everyone’s identification as they enter and exit the royal palace.”

When neither one of us moved to proffer the requested identification, the guard threw his shoulders back to show us the full broadness of his chest, even though he was several inches shorter than either of us. “It’s the law, Lord Tanus. You must produce your identification to enter. And the King has requested your presence.”

Still hanging onto Dolpheus’ arm, I leaned around the guard. I thought to seek reason in the second guard on duty at the gate. Surely, the other man had noticed that we just showed our identification less than a minute before. Certainly, I thought, the other guard couldn’t be such an idiot as this man was. But if the second guard noticed me looking at him, he didn’t let on.

The smaller guard shot a look over his shoulder, into the royal palace. He didn't want to be late to respond to the King's summons. Regardless, when he turned back to face us, it was clear that he was prepared to wait as long as it took.

I was in no mood for a standoff. I offered my hand. On the way out, he'd held onto my wrist to steady my hand while he scanned my palm. Now, he hovered the wand above my palm. I noticed that the hand that held the wand wasn't steady.

After he scanned me, he stared at the readout on the wand, waiting. My nostrils flared even though I didn't mean them to. A second passed. Two. Three. "All clear," he said when the results came in.

I didn't say a word.

"Now you, Sir."

Dolpheus extended his arm, careful to keep his hold on me. To the guard, he would have seemed like an amiable gentleman. But I knew him better. He was as irritated as I was. His breathing was tense while we waited for the wand to spit out the exact same results it had moments before.

"Very well. You're all clear. Follow me now." And the guard set off at a clipped but efficient pace.

I did my best to keep up, but I only made it a hundred feet or so across the impeccable, reflective floor of the palace's interior before Dolpheus spoke up. "Guard!" he called. "Milord Tanus has only recently awakened from a debilitating procedure."

I froze in mid-stride, every muscle in my body stiff.

Dolpheus knew me well enough to understand why I didn't show weakness. Not now, not ever.

"Sir?" the guard said, backtracking toward us, not sure which one of us to look at.

"Do you know that the great King also took part in this debilitating procedure? And that he too only just woke from it after days of unconsciousness because of it?"

"No, Sir. I didn't know this." The guard snuck a glance at me. Sweat beaded across my hairline from the effort of keeping myself upright, even as I thought, *Not bad, Dolpheus.* It was hard to appear weak when he compared me to the mighty King Oderon.

"A procedure such as this requires a long recovery. Yet Milord has been unable to rest. He intended on doing so at his estate. As it's forbidden to transport within the palace grounds, he must walk when otherwise he shouldn't. So you will walk slowly as Milord uses his strength to walk when no ordinary man would."

The guard's eyes flicked between Dolpheus and me nervously. "Of course, Sir, Milord. I was unaware. My apologies."

I nodded graciously, my face expressionless while the world spun behind my eyes.

This was why Dolpheus was my closest friend. I leaned into him more than I had before, now that he'd explained my behavior away. The guard proceeded at an exaggeratedly slow pace, but I wasn't about to complain. At this rate, it would take us forever—much longer than the King was accustomed to waiting—to reach the King's chambers. He should have sent a hovering glass bed—the ones reserved for the ailing—to retrieve me. But he hadn't, and I probably wouldn't have accepted the ride, anyway. It was one thing to show some weakness while I dragged myself across the sleek floor. It was quite another to lay prone on a stretcher for all to witness.

By the time I reached the hall before the King's chambers, a film of sweat coated my entire body beneath my clothing, and my hands and forehead were clammy. I'd given up thinking I would faint halfway there. Somehow, when I thought I couldn't take one step more, my foot moved forward.

The first of the whispers that King Oderon and Lord Tanus had engaged in a mind merge had already reached the eager ears of the courtiers. The guard didn't select the most discreet route across the palace as Dolpheus had. He led us straight through the heart of the wasps' nest. I watched the wasps through glazed eyes, as if I were watching the scene play out from far above, an observer and not part of it.

The courtiers, in their elaborate costumes and gaudy colors, parted for us, opening up a trench in the midst of the artificial politeness of a barely disguised war zone. These were the most ambitious and vicious of people on Planet O, far more so than the rebels of the Koal desert, who mostly defended their right to be free from control and who did so openly and unapologetically. Still, the courtiers weren't nearly as ruthless as King Oderon. Or my father.

Not a single courtier bothered to disguise his stare. Not one of the ladies averted her gaze from my form, or from that of Dolpheus, although that probably had little to do with the rumors of the mind merge and more to do with the rumors that surrounded his lovemaking abilities.

I was the only son and heir to a fortune and an empire of which most, if not all, of these people were customers. Splicing was costly. Only the richest of the rich could afford the procedure. And only the greediest of all Oers would want to safeguard their lives against accident or illness. Only they believed it necessary to forestall their appointments with death. They didn't take any chances with their natural lives and the thousand or more years they spanned. They paid my father to eliminate chances, and my father hoarded every single grain of sand he demanded from them in exchange for an insurance policy against severe injury or death.

I called my father an extortionist. These same sniveling courtiers called him a genius, even as he plotted to kill their king. Their loyalties lay where it was to their greatest advantage. If one of my father's plotted coups were successful, they would congregate in the hall beyond my father's chambers just as they did the King's.

Now, they assembled in this great hall out of concern for the King's health. But it would be a fool who believed their ruse. And I knew King Oderon to be no fool. The courtiers were a necessity that any king had to tolerate. The King might rule all of Planet O, but the courtiers owned much of it. Their wealth lay in land and men. To remain king, a man needed the support of all the land owners and soldiers he could contrive.

As Dolpheus pushed on, following the guard to the shiny wall that demarcated the entrance to the King's private chambers, the whispers picked up behind us. By the time a door revealed itself from the sheer surface ahead of us, the whispers grew louder, so as to barely be whispers at all. The guard ushered us in, but didn't follow. When the door closed behind us, it shut out the din of eager malice.

The dim room behind the doors was still and quiet, and I thought I would like to collapse right there, in the middle of the floor. But instead, I released the vise-like grip I had on Dolpheus' arm and attempted to distance myself from him to stand on my own.

I couldn't. The moment I stood apart from him, I wobbled and a wave of nausea swelled within me. So I stood as tall as I could, with both arms at my side, and leaned into Dolpheus' frame, much like a toppling tree that very much wished it wouldn't topple.

Two guards stood at either side of the opposite wall. These guards weren't like those that checked identification at the palace's entrances. These were dedicated soldiers. These were the men to whom the King entrusted his life. They measured a person's strengths and weaknesses at first sight. Men such as these respected strength; it was the only real currency in which they dealt.

It was unfortunate that I wasn't my usual self. I had far too little left of what these soldiers valued. Still, there was nothing I could do about it. No one denied the King a request for an appearance. We'd already taken far longer than I would have wanted to respond to his summons. I needed the King on my side. Ilara needed her father on my side.

"Step forward to be admitted to see the King," one of the

guards said. I stumbled more than stepped, but I responded right away, eyeing the sword that hung from this one's belt. "Lord Tanus, you must step farther away from your Arms Master."

"Milord is un—" Dolpheus began, but I cut him short with a wave of my hand.

"It's all right, Dolpheus." I moved away from my support, and sweat streamed down the small of my back from the effort of holding myself upright. The guard unholstered a wand that hung from the other side of his belt and waved it across my body. He did the same to Dolpheus, then put the wand away.

I didn't know how much longer I could stand as the guard patted me down. Hands swept quickly and roughly across my damp clothing. I received a wondering glance and a nod at the same time. He moved on to Dolpheus.

Satisfied we didn't pose an immediate threat to the King —and his assurance was likely enhanced by the fact that I looked as if I would collapse at any moment—he returned to his station at one side of the door.

Another guard spoke. "You may proceed." A door materialized from the wall behind them and drew open with a soft whoosh that sounded much like the breath of a sleeping dragon.

Reasonably, I wanted all my strength with me before I stepped into the lair of any dragon. I wouldn't have it. I'd have to face the dragon with what little I had and wish for the best. Ilara's return to the home that meant so much to her depended on that one wish and the drops of strength I had left.

8

ONCE DOLPHEUS AND I ENTERED THE KING'S private chambers, the King asked Lord Broon to leave. The royal physician looked as if he considered this a terrible idea, but didn't question his liege. He bowed and left, with a long dubious look at Dolpheus and me.

When the door swept closed behind Broon, the silence was deafening.

We waited. Protocol was clear. No one spoke to the King unless he addressed you first. He sat in bed, propped upon a pile of luxurious pillows. His silver hair and beard were impeccable, his posture composed, but his gray eyes gave him away. They were tired, and their exhaustion reached beyond the mind merge.

In short time, the King had lost a woman to whom he'd been married for hundreds of years, and who was loved by her people. He'd lost a daughter to secret banishment, under the ruse of her death. He sat on an uncertain throne. If he died—and it was the only way to depose him—he might be the last of the Andaron line to rule. The Andaron dynasty had fought hard for peace for Planet Origins. It had been a bloody and merciless start, but peace had reigned for millennia since.

"Come closer." Like his eyes, the King's voice was tired, though he also knew better than to reveal too much of his weakness. If a show of debility was dangerous for me, it was even more so for him.

Sharp gray eyes studied us; I was certain they didn't miss a single thing. The silence pounded through my ears. My vision clouded over in waves. I didn't know how much longer I could stand on my own, without Dolpheus' support. There was no worse time to feel such weakness than right now before a legendary king.

The King addressed Dolpheus. "Draw up a seat for your friend and then leave us."

Dolpheus raised an eyebrow ever so slightly at the word "friend" but moved to do as the King asked. He set a seat before me and locked eyes with me before moving toward the door. Even before a royal command, my friend made it clear where his loyalties lay. I nodded in a way that I hoped was imperceptible to the King, and Dolpheus left us.

"Sit. You look as if you'll collapse at any second." I never thought I would sit before King Oderon, but I hurried to. I sat with a straight back even though I wanted nothing more than to melt into the upholstery. A drop of sweat trailed across my forehead. I didn't dare swat at it.

I waited again, acutely aware of how that gray gaze attempted to penetrate me. I wished I could swat it away too. Wasn't it enough for this King that I'd bared all my thoughts to him? Did he have to continue poking and prodding?

When the King finally spoke, relief washed over me. I didn't care much what he said anymore though I knew I should. I just wanted these very long last few days to be over. I wanted to be free of the palace, free of the reach of the King and everyone else. I wanted Ilara, the woman, not the princess. I didn't want all of this. I didn't want any of this.

"I saw enough in your memories of Dolpheus to know that he can be trusted. In fact, I wish I had a friend such as he. Yet I cannot speak of my daughter in front of him. I hadn't thought that I'd speak of her to you—ever—but I see now that I must."

At his words and the suggestion of trust, my shoulders relaxed although I hadn't known I was tensing them. Everything hinged on the King's next words. The well-being of my heart, the woman I loved, and perhaps an entire planet waited with me, to see what this man with a kingdom in his hand would say.

"That was my first mind merge. Did you know that?"

"No, your Majesty. I didn't."

"Well, it isn't a very common procedure. And with good reason. There has never been anyone brave enough—or foolish enough—to suggest one to me, before you. I saw everything I wanted to see—and things that no father wants ever to see. There was nothing that was hidden from me. Nothing."

I forced myself to meet the King's stare as he emphasized his last word. I'd faltered some in my initial meeting with the monarch; the man was larger than life and I'd known all that I was putting on the line in coming to see him. But since then I'd settled into the idea. I'd already taken the plunge. The worst of it was done.

There was little I could do now to influence the King's decision. All I could do—all I wanted to do—was to be myself. And I was a strong man. I might have felt like collapsing, but that was only my body threatening to give out. I—the real me—was going nowhere. It was my heart that was leading me to Ilara. It was my heart that was prepared to fight for her. And there wasn't a hint of weakness within my heart.

So what if, within my memories, he'd seen Ilara and I make love? I understood that was what he was referring to, that no father wanted to see his little girl with legs spread in passion and a man atop her. Ilara and I'd made loud, passionate love, and we'd done so often. But I wouldn't shrink away from what this father was extending as a form of judgment. I was finished shrinking away from things for now—and maybe for good. I thought perhaps that some of my usual strength was even returning to my body.

Again, the piercing gray stare. This time, I stared back with just as much resolve. After a few moments, the King looked away, into the shadowy recesses of the room, dimmed to promote the King's healing. "You took a big risk in coming to see me."

"Yes, your Majesty."

Again, the stare. Again, the heavy silence with the unfair advantage that this man knew me in a way I couldn't possibly know him.

"I'm glad that you did."

My heartbeat sped up for an instant. It was hope that dared to flutter within my chest cavity until I forced it down, wary. I knew better than to assume things would be easy. Nothing in my life had been easy, not since my mother left.

The King nodded. His shiny silver hair slid around his head while I watched, mesmerized, dazed, suddenly aware that I wasn't as present as I'd thought I was. *My brain is still not at its full strength since the mind merge*, I reminded myself. I had to remain alert.

"You took a great risk indeed. But I understand why you did. It was the only way to gain my trust." He paused, studying me again. I forced myself to keep my awareness within the room. I'd worked too hard and for too long to let it all go to waste. But have you ever tried to focus your mind when it didn't want to focus? It took more will to concentrate than it did to raise a sword in combat.

"You've gained my trust." The King's voice was soft. These were words he rarely spoke. The king of an entire planet had few people he could truly trust.

My breath hitched in my chest before rolling along. I stilled even further in anticipation of what would come next.

"It's difficult to accept that you and Ilara loved each other for so many years, and that she didn't trust me with this information."

Once more, the silence. The King let his words hang in the air before moving on, giving them the full impact he wished for them. "I understand why she made this choice, although I regret it. And you were both right. I wouldn't have trusted you. I wouldn't have approved of the match. Before the mind merge, I saw you as the son of a man who's determined to destroy my family and my kingdom. The son of a traitor and a schemer who's more dangerous than the Vikus vipers."

"And now? How do you see me now, your Majesty?"

Another pause. This man had the theatrics of royalty mastered. "I see you as a man I'd like to have as a son. I see you as a man worthy of being at my daughter's side."

This. This was more than I'd hoped for. I dared not speak for fear that I might have misheard.

"I see that I can trust you with her safety. You're a good soldier."

I raised my eyebrows. Had he looked at absolutely everything in my life? Was there nothing that he'd left to me? Couldn't he have left me something?

"It isn't just the mind merge, Tanus. I'm not isolated from rumors at the palace. As little as I enjoy the gossip, I'd be a fool not to pay attention to it. Within the exaggerations, more often than not, there's a seed of truth, a seed of what's to come. If I pay attention to the seed, I can often truncate the plant before it grows tall.

"I know that you are adept with a sword and other weapons. I know that you've trained since you first could walk and that there are few other horsemen as good as you on Planet O. I also know that your father hasn't asked for your help in his attacks against me because he doesn't trust you."

Were there rumors circulating that I didn't support my

father? Those were almost as dangerous as a rumor of lack of support for the King. I'd learned to be cautious with my father, and much of that meant doing nothing to give him cause to notice me.

"*That* I learned from the mind merge," King Oderon said. It seemed that this man didn't need to be connected to my mind through crystal dust to read my thoughts.

"My father wasn't always a man as terrible as he is now. There was a time, when I was a boy, that he was kind. At least, that's how I remember him."

The King didn't speak. My father had once been a captain of his armies, perhaps my father and the King had even been friends at one time.

King Oderon waited for me to continue. This man wouldn't be satisfied until he drained every last drop of information from me.

I raised my head in a hint of defiance, but kept it in check. I hadn't forgotten for a second with whom I was speaking. "He changed when you ordered his mother killed."

"When I ordered his mother killed?"

"Yes, your Majesty." The King might have said that I had his trust, but I wasn't stupid enough to say another word about the death of my grandmother, a woman that I didn't remember.

The gray eyes became steelier. They held mine for a long time before shifting to stare off into the distance. There was something there, but the King gave me no indication of what it might be. Finally, he spoke. "What are your plans for Ilara?"

"I'm not sure I understand exactly what you mean, your Majesty."

"You searched for my daughter everywhere on Planet O."

I nodded.

"You searched within the palace—which shows me that the palace isn't as secure as I believed it."

I thought that the fact that my father had almost managed to have him killed this time, and did kill the queen last time, would have been proof enough of this.

"You searched within the royal city. You even looked for her in the Koal desert where few dare to go."

"Yes, your Majesty. I searched for years."

"But you came up with nothing."

"Yes, your Majesty. Not even a rumor that she might still be alive."

"Yet you continued your search for her. You didn't give up."

I waited until the King met my eyes straight on, across the rest of the bed and the several feet of open space that separated us. "I will never give up on her."

"Yes. Yes, I see that. And what made you think to go to your father's laboratory? How did you think to search for a trace of her there?"

"It was the only other place I could think of to look for her. I'd looked everywhere I could think of—no matter how remote—on this planet. No rumor of her whereabouts reached me. No sightings of her. Nothing about her seemed to continue on Planet O. That left only one possibility."

"Because you knew she was alive."

"Yes. Because I knew she was alive. I can still feel her. I

knew the assassins hadn't killed her. They couldn't have, even if you sentenced them to death for her murder."

A glint of defiance crossed the King's eyes, although he hadn't had to justify his actions to anyone for a very long time. "It was the only way to keep her safe. It was the only way to cement the idea that the assassins killed her. Either way, they earned a death sentence. Entering the palace as they did, with the intentions they had, when the royal family slept—or was supposed to be sleeping." He gave me a meaningful look.

Ilara hadn't been at the palace as she should have been when the assassins slipped through its defenses. She'd been with me, in my chambers, where no one but Dolpheus knew we were together. She'd rocked her hips above mine, our bodies slicked with the heat of passion, even as the assassins killed one of her ladies and tore the sheets back from her bed.

"I would have done the same thing," I said. Compassion had its place. But in times such as these, when it was war even within a time of peace, a man had to do what he had to do. Sometimes, it was just that simple, and just that cruel. "If you hadn't ordered the assassins executed on the spot, they might have spoken. They might have said that they hadn't killed Ilara, and that would have been enough to encourage whoever sent the assassins to continue looking for her. That person would have hunted for her to wipe out the royal line of Andaron, so that it ends with you."

It was fucked up. The main threat to the woman I loved was my own father. As much as I'd hesitated and deliberated about sharing what I had with the King, I wished to share it with my father even less. At least the King cared for Ilara. My father would kill her, even if he knew what she meant to me. My father's ambitions surpassed any sense of decency. He'd become a different man altogether once the King killed his mother for treason. It had only gotten worse once my mother left my father for another man.

"In a way, I suppose I owe you thanks for my daughter's life. If she hadn't been with you, the assassins would have found her vulnerable in her bed, and they would have killed her. However, given the circumstances, I will not thank you, you understand."

I supposed I did. There weren't many fathers willing to thank a man for penetrating their daughters.

"Who have you told that you believe the Princess lives?"

"No one but Dolpheus, your Majesty. And as you saw, Dolpheus can be trusted. He would rather die than betray me. And he would betray me if he betrayed Ilara. He knows that."

The King's words came slower now, the pauses longer. He was thinking, reviewing the many possibilities of my unexpected involvement in Ilara's life. His gray eyes were as astute as ever, though they wandered the room distractedly, landing on me only occasionally now. "If I were to tell you of Ilara's location, what would you do with the information?"

My heart started beating faster. I was closer to Ilara now than I'd been in three long years. "I'd bring her back here, of course."

"No. I won't allow you to do that. She'd be in immediate danger the moment of her return. That's the whole reason I sent her away in the first place. To protect her from your father and his... ambitions."

"But your Majesty, she must return here. This is her home. She loves Planet Origins like no one else I've met."

The King sighed. He knew what I said was true. Ilara wouldn't be happy anywhere else. Planet O was an important part of who she was. She wouldn't want to become anyone else than the person she was destined to be. She was a princess of the Andaron dynasty, born to rule all of Planet O at the time of her appointment on King Oderon's death.

"No one would know she was here, your Majesty. I'd make sure of it."

He chuckled without mirth. "How do you expect to smuggle the most recognizable woman on the entire planet back here without anyone discovering her? Even if you managed this remarkable feat, how would you keep anyone from recognizing her once she was here? You can't expect that she would live here for long without someone discovering her presence."

"It's true, your Majesty. It's not possible to bring Ilara back in the open. However, I could sneak into my father's laboratory once more. I could bring Ilara back without a trace and without anyone finding out."

"And once you got her back here? Then what?"

"Well, unfortunately, there's no other woman that looks like her. A disguise would be nearly impossible."

"Yes. It would. Which is why your plan won't work. Only members of the Andaron line have ever been born with her eyes. Even someone who's never seen the Princess before will notice her eyes and know she's of the royal line. The eye color is legendary."

"I'm the first to admit this is a problem. However, I can work around it. With your permission, I can alter the identification records. Associate her palm and features with another person, a fictitious one, so that at least the security system you have in place across the planet won't pick her up."

"That still doesn't solve the problem of people recognizing her face."

"You're right, it doesn't. But it's a good start. Until we figure out something better, she could stay with me at one of the remote estates my father has given me to manage. He doesn't want to be bothered with these faraway locations now that all of his attention goes to the splicing. Dolpheus could accompany us there. He too is a good soldier. No one needs to be there but us. The servants could be managed so as not to be around when she is."

The King seemed to be considering it. I pressed on.

"It's not an ideal situation, I admit that. But it would work. My being at one of the remote estates for the long term won't arouse suspicion. My father barely notices me anymore, as consumed with splicing as he's become. And it will be natural for Dolpheus to accompany me."

Moments passed, marked only by more pregnant silence. I would have continued to speak, but the truth was that I hadn't fully developed a plan. I didn't really know what I'd do with Ilara once I got her back. I'd been so focused on getting her here, that it was hard to see past the step that had seemed so monumental before I came to the palace to face the King.

It would be tricky to keep her return to Planet O concealed. But I was certain she had to return, so I'd find a way. I had to. I knew Ilara almost as well as I knew myself, and I believed she'd agree with me. Even though we'd never spoken of it, I was following her unspoken wishes.

"I know that I can work it out. I can find a way."

"Really?" King Oderon cocked his head cynically.

"Yes, your Majesty. I understand that I don't have a perfected plan yet. But I wasn't sure if you'd be willing to trust me with Ilara's location. Without it, there was nothing more I could do."

"I've no doubt that you would have found a way to obtain this information without my cooperation." The cynicism was gone. It was, simply, the truth. I had no idea how else I could have procured the location, but the King was right: I would have found a way. In general, I didn't give up easily. When it came to Ilara, it was an absolute. I didn't give up. Ever. The mind merge had revealed every bit of me to him.

"I would have tried." Each moment, it grew easier to forget about my weakness. I began also to forget that I was speaking with the mighty and fearsome King Oderon. I was beginning to remember who *I* was.

The King nodded. There was no recrimination for the ways I might have gone about procuring information concerning Ilara's location, even if they likely would have involved some deceit toward him. He and I were similar in one way: We did what we needed to do to protect the people we loved. And neither one of us saw a single thing wrong with this.

"You do know where the Princess is, your Majesty?"

"Yes. I do know. In fact, I'm the only person that knows. There's no one left alive that does."

I wanted to know more. There was obviously more. But I didn't have the advantage of having studied the King's brain. I had to tread with some caution at least. The rumors of his fierce retribution were enough to remind me to choose my words more wisely than I usually did.

"And you will trust me with this fact?"

"Under ordinary circumstances, I wouldn't trust you with this information, not even now that I've seen enough of your thoughts and memories to know that my daughter wasn't foolish in placing her trust in you. However, the more people that know any one fact, the higher the chances are that this fact will be divulged."

This was true. And it was why I trusted no one but Dolpheus with my affair with Ilara.

"Yet these are not ordinary circumstances. They ceased to be so a long time ago when your father began his splicing business."

A spark struck somewhere in my brain. I hadn't linked the two events together. But now that the King mentioned it, I realized it was true. My father changed the most, to become who he was now, almost entirely unlike the person he used to be, when he discovered the mechanics for splicing, not when the King ordered his mother killed, and not when my mother left us.

"I'll recover from this latest attack. I'll fortify my

defenses so that no assassins can ever touch me or my family again. I'll continue to rule as I have."

King Oderon let the big *however* hang in the room like a fog thick enough to conceal hidden dangers. *However*, if anything were to happen to him, the Andaron dynasty would die with him unless Ilara were here to claim the throne. Without Ilara to claim her right to rule, my father would. And that would be the end of Planet Origins as either one of us knew it, and King Oderon had known it for much longer than I.

Without Ilara back on planet, the home she loved so much might cease to exist.

9

I WAS CERTAIN THAT THE KING HAD ALREADY MADE the decision to allow me to bring Ilara back to Planet O. It was how I'd found the patience to bear the King's theatrics even in my weakened and exhausted state. I was wholly unprepared to have him withdraw his permission.

"But Your Majesty, she has to come here."

"No." The silver head swiveled obstinately. "No, she doesn't. I've thought about it more and I've changed my mind. As is my prerogative." He let the reminder of the power he held over me smother me like a blanket. "The reason I sent her away in the first place was to protect her."

We'd already been over this. Or so I thought. "Yes, but Ilara won't be happy unless she's home. Home for her is here. There's no other place for her."

"I can appreciate your sentimentality, as I'm certain my daughter would. She always found impractical ways to look at the practical. However, returning her to the planet now, at this time of heightened threat, would be to endanger her greatly. I got very lucky this last time. It was an extremely close one. If not for your… liaison… she'd be dead. I can't chance it another time."

"Your Majesty, under no circumstances would I suggest bringing Ilara back here and into danger if I didn't think it imperative. But there are good reasons, other than her preference, why—"

"There is no reason you could give me that would be sufficient to warrant putting my only daughter and surviving heir in peril."

"And if it concerns the best interest of all of Planet Origins? The well-being of its people? What if her return is the only way to ensure that the Andaron rule continues?"

The King was a stubborn man. But no man could put his stubbornness before reason and rule for long. The decisions of a monarch lasted far longer than his emotional outlook on a subject. King Oderon waited, and I took it as permission to make my argument.

I spoke with measure, choosing each word mindfully. I remembered that this was the same king that had executed my grandmother without a trial. His declaration of treason was sufficient to end her life. He could end mine just as abruptly. "As I'm certain you'll agree, Your Majesty, it's of utmost importance that your rule continue. If someone were to manage to depose you, Planet O would fall into chaos, and the old battles that were waged for centuries will have been for naught. Under your rule, the royal city has maintained peace for a very long time, far longer than I've been alive to remember." I omitted the constant, bloody fighting that occurred nearly continuously outside the city's walls.

"The Princess doesn't need to be here for my rule and the royal city's peace to proceed."

"Your Majesty, I believe that she does." I paused to gauge whether or not my comment made him angry. I couldn't tell. I continued. "The people—your subjects—love you. They want your rule to go on. Things may not be perfect on Planet O, but the people understand the regulations and how everything works, and they know that so long as they keep to the limits defined by those regulations, they can expect safety for themselves and their families.

"But Oers are nervous, my Liege. They wonder what will happen to the city they love. They've seen the royal palace vulnerable, when we'd all believed it to be impenetrable. First the queen they adored was murdered. Then, they believe, the princess. And their king was attacked and is still recovering.

"These acts don't reassure the people. They terrify them. They very nearly worshiped the Queen, and she was taken from them. They also love the Princess, and they believe her dead as well. They fear what will happen if someone manages to get to you, a king of legendary prowess. What will happen? There's no one to continue the rule of the Andaron dynasty as far as they know. The instability of rule right now is a constant worry to them. All they've known is the order you and your ancestors have brought to this city, once you drove out the Harals.

"They see you, their mighty king, suddenly exposed, and no one to take your place if something should happen to you. They hear rumors of my father and his splicing empire that only accommodates the rich. My father doesn't care for the masses, your people, and they understand that. Your lack of an apparent heir makes your rule more susceptible."

I met those sharp gray eyes to assess his reaction. I still couldn't tell what he was thinking although I could be certain that he was. "The only way to fortify the throne—your throne—is to bring Ilara back."

"We already discussed that no one could discover that she's on the planet because it would endanger her life."

"I know."

The King waited for more. But I just didn't have it. The plan, if it could be called that at this stage, had holes as big as craters. I didn't know how I would bring her back, keep her safe, and all the while make her survival known to fortify the throne.

However, I'd said it before: I wouldn't give up. I wasn't a quitter. I didn't have a sliver of quitting in my body. "I'll find the way. I'll find a way that makes it all work."

"You sound confident."

"I am."

"Why?"

I debated for a beat, then continued. I was already all in. There was no pulling back now. "Your Majesty, you saw everything there is to see about me. You know why."

The King smiled a smile that was so charged with conflicting emotions that it resembled a grimace. "You really think you can find the way to do it?"

"I do. Without a doubt." I realized how bold it was of me to say this as I truly had no idea how I'd accomplish this monumental feat.

The King, infallible in the people's eyes, changed his mind. "All right. All right then. I'll allow you to try."

"Thank you, your Majesty." I smiled a better smile than he had. "Where is she?"

"I'll tell you that after you've convinced me that your plan will work. When you find a way to keep her safe upon her return to O, I'll tell you where she is."

My smile fell. "I understand, your Majesty. I'll get to work on it right away." I scooted forward on my seat to stand.

"Before you go, there's something else. Something you must do for me in exchange for the information of Ilara's whereabouts."

I didn't move a muscle, perched at the tip of my seat.

"You must give me information about your father."

"Your Majesty..."

"This isn't a request, it's an order. Do you understand?"

I sighed softly, keeping inside most of what I wanted to release. "My Liege, my father doesn't trust me. You said so yourself. You saw it in my memories. He won't reveal anything to me. He doesn't speak of his business in front of me. Much less does he mention any of his... plans. We cross paths when we must. But we don't lead shared lives as many fathers and sons do. I'm not privy to any secrets that might help you."

"You snuck into his splicing lab."

Dread flared in my belly. This wouldn't lead anywhere good. I knew it already. Reluctantly, I nodded. "Once, your Majesty."

"And you plan on doing it again to retrieve Ilara? If I choose to tell you where she is."

So we were back to *ifs*. "Yes. That was my idea."

"Then you can sneak into his lab to find information that you'll bring directly to me."

"His lab is very well protected. You must know this. It's as well protected as the palace. I could be detected. If I were caught, then I wouldn't be able to go back to use the lab to return Ilara."

"It's a worthwhile risk. For the good of the kingdom, of the people, as you've said."

I willed my emotions not to show on my face.

"You'll go to your father's lab. If I decide that you've brought me worthwhile information, I'll tell you where Ilara is."

"And what kind of information am I looking for?"

"You'll know when you see it."

My father revealed next to nothing about the splicing process. He enchanted his customers with promises of a second (or a third, or a fourth, or more) chance at life. They cared little about how he accomplished it other than to ask if it would hurt. The procedure was painless. The customer was asleep during the entire operation. He'd be induced into sleep, and when he woke, he'd have the most expensive insurance policy there ever was, but also the one with the greatest guarantee.

Not even I knew much about how my father managed to splice a person to replicate him exactly. A customer's splice looked identical to him, and behaved exactly like him as well once the customer's brain and the splice's were linked.

My father didn't tell me much, that was true. But I was curious. I always had been. Knowledge was power. Courtiers and the other influence wielders of O bartered sand and power to achieve their desires. But few went to the true source of power.

Still, despite years of eavesdropping, snooping, and investigating, I didn't understand the fundamental process of splicing. I didn't know if I'd find the answers I'd looked for all this time—and now the King was forcing me to find—in my father's laboratory. My father was careful to the point of paranoia. The only reason I'd found a trace of Ilara's exit off planet was because he hadn't been involved. He would have never left a trace of the voyage of any splice. I was certain of it.

"I'll do my best." What else could I say? "Is that all, your Majesty?"

"For now. Go home and get some rest. You look awful. You can't even be thinking about bringing my daughter anywhere like this. You couldn't defend a bee."

I liked it better when I'd gone all of my adult life without drawing the attention of the King. I nodded and bowed deferentially as was expected of me. I neither fell over nor vomited, and the clanging in my head receded as soon as I lifted my head back up. Progress.

I approached the wall where I knew the door to be. It opened when I reached it. Dolpheus was waiting just outside, next to the four guards who stood in the same positions as before I entered the King's inner chamber.

"Did you make any progress?" Dolpheus whispered as he joined me, offering me an arm to lean on.

"That depends on what you mean by progress," I growled and took his arm.

The next door opened. Right away, the sickly sweet scent of the courtiers enveloped us. I held my head high, focused on no one in particular, and forced myself to put one foot in front of the other, as fast as my body could manage it.

We got past the wasps before Dolpheus made me stop to rest.

The way out for the final time that day seemed to take even longer than it had the first two tries. The Suxle Sun was setting as the guard who'd already examined our palms before did so once more, for good measure.

10

THE LONGEST PART OF OUR JOURNEY WAS traversing the palace's interior, dodging people, who bustled back and forth, transferring supplies in and out of the palace.

The laws, which forbade transporting within the palace walls, ended precisely a foot behind where we stood. Finally, I could get to a place where I could focus on my recovery with relative ease. The chills and sickness that came with transporting when one began learning the process were a concern of the past.

I closed my eyes to push away the sounds everywhere around us. A constant chatter flowed along with the foot traffic that crossed the bridge, which stretched solidly across the chasm that plummeted below it. Friends and companion animals called out to each other across the way. This was where the people of O were their true selves, before they had to abide by palace etiquette.

Transporting required complete focus of the mind. If you

were distracted at the moment of transport, either it wouldn't work, or worse—you could end up some place entirely different than you'd intended. On Planet O, landing in the wrong place could be fatal.

I was a seasoned expert in transporting. There were few that had done it as often as I, other than Dolpheus. Not many thought the effort worth the trouble unless they were using transporting to traverse long distances. But what most Oers didn't realize was that transporting could become nearly effortless once you became skilled enough at it. Few were willing to endure the ill ease that accompanied early experiments with it.

As a boy, the mysteries and bad reputation of transporting had been sufficient to lure me to it. Already, Dolpheus and I were training as soldiers. What could be better to a soldier than the ability to materialize nearly anywhere he wanted? And what could better fulfill the sense of mischief of a boy than the ability to disappear and reappear anywhere across the planet?

Transporting could become painless for those who began to practice it early enough, before the body finished defining itself, and before too many of the fears and superstitions of transporting could influence the mind.

I waited until the moment was precisely right. I'd done this so many times that I recognized the moment as soon as it arrived. It came when I no longer heard what was going on around me after I reined in my senses, and I contained myself within my body.

I reached for thoughts of home—and no other ones—and

held onto them tightly while I allowed any notion of my physical body to dissolve.

Most people couldn't fathom that they might not exist in a physical body. Yet for me, it was easy. Once you transported enough times, you realized how simple it was for your body to dissolve into particles of energy, the same ones that composed everything else that considered Planet O its home.

Dolpheus was behind me, waiting to begin his transport only long enough to ensure that the particles of my body didn't become entangled with his.

I appeared in my rooms at the far end of my father's estate, in a building entirely apart from the one he inhabited. As I transported, I imagined myself seated in my chair in the center of the inner lair of my suites, where no one but Dolpheus—and Ilara—ever came. When I materialized, I did so in bits and pieces, as if I were a light on a slow-paced dimmer switch that grew brighter and more defined with each moment.

It was of utmost importance then that I hold the image of my body as I was accustomed to it. If I were to think of anything else, my body might complete its coalescing with a bit of someone or something else. At the very least, something would be out of place.

Just as I knew what the right moment felt like to initiate transport, I'd also learned to distinguish that sense that I was whole once more. I relaxed into the chair and propped my feet up on the stool in front of it, careful not to disturb Dolpheus, who'd only just arrived. I could still see through him.

As soon as Dolpheus was fully back, he stalked across the room to claim the seat next to me. He placed his forearms on his knees and leaned forward, not even a dark hair out of place. "Well? What happened? Did the King tell you where to find Ilara?"

I groaned as loudly as I'd wanted to while in the King's chambers.

"It's that bad?"

"Yeah. It's that bad. He's agreed to tell me of Ilara's whereabouts. Well, potentially agreed. The mind merge was successful. He now knows he can trust me. He knows that you can be trusted, too. He knows that my love for Ilara, and hers for me, is true."

"That doesn't sound bad..."

"That's not the bad part. Parts really. Bad parts. There are lots of bad parts."

Dolpheus groaned.

"For the King to tell me where Ilara is, I have to come up with a plan that will convince him that I can keep her safe from attack, while also revealing to the public that she's alive."

"But that's not possible. The only way to keep her safe is to conceal her identity. We've discussed this a hundred times."

"I know."

"So why on O does the King want her identity revealed?"

"Because knowing that she'd inherit the throne will solidify the people's support of the rule of the Andaron line."

"Well, that stinks."

"Yeah. It does. I have no idea how we'll pull it off."

"Your father will try to kill her the second he learns that she's alive."

"He will."

"You were right," Dolpheus said. "This is bad."

"That's not the worst of it."

"How could it get any worse than coming up with a plan to do the impossible?"

"The mighty King Oderon has ordered me to spy on my father."

"What?"

"He wants me to break into the lab again and bring him information. If he deems the information of sufficient worth, then he'll tell me where Ilara is, assuming that I have some miracle plan to place her in the public eye while keeping her alive."

"So the King is making espionage a condition of his daughter's return? So much for appearing to be an ideal father."

"Neither one of us ever thought he was one. I believe he truly loves Ilara. But he is, first and foremost, the king of an entire planet. You know the rumors that surround his rule as well as I. He didn't get to where he is now by being gentle and understanding."

"But you could be killed breaking into your father's lab! Where will that get him as far as Ilara goes?"

"I doubt the King would care if I died breaking into my father's lab. He behaved as if he accepted my relationship with Ilara. But it could have been an act to manipulate me. In fact, it's likely."

Dolpheus rubbed a hand across his face.

"The King didn't tell me how he managed to get Ilara off planet to begin with. The most secure way of doing so was through my father's lab. But maybe he has another way. I don't know. He made an obscure comment about him being the only one left that knew where Ilara was, implying that there had been at least one other person."

"If there was somebody else, it was probably the person the King commissioned to move her off planet. She couldn't have done it on her own since transporting only works on planet. The King must have had help. Then he probably killed whoever did his dirty work, to keep the secret of the Princess safe. Just as your father will kill you if he finds you meddling at his lab. He won't care that you're his son. The King has given us impossible odds to beat."

"Nearly impossible odds. Since when is anything impossible to the two of us?"

"Since right now."

"Come on. You don't believe that."

My friend rubbed his hand across his handsome face some more. "No, I guess I don't. But I have no idea how we're going to do this."

"Nor do I."

"Fuck."

"Yeah. Fuck."

At least we were in agreement.

11

UNDER ORDINARY CIRCUMSTANCES, I WASN'T THE most patient of men. Now that my instincts had been confirmed, and Ilara was indeed alive, the previous three years of searching I'd had to endure festered inside me until I was ready to explode. I didn't want to wait a single moment longer to bring her back to Origins.

It was the time when most Oers slept, except for those that got stuck with the undesirable shift. The Suxle sun had set hours ago. But I left the blackout drapes wide open, allowing in the light of the Auxle sun. There would be no sleep for us tonight. At least, it wasn't likely. Not at this rate.

Dolpheus looked disheveled and discouraged. "There's no way to do it. Even if you disable the royal recognition programs so that Ilara's presence doesn't trigger the system, someone, somewhere, will identify her. It would only be a matter of time. Her eyes are unlike anybody else's. She's the only person whose eyes reflect the shifts in the cosmos, and you know that."

I loved her eyes. When I stared into them, I felt the whole universe pull me into them, as if they were a portal and I the traveler. With her, life was ecstatic. And it all began with those eyes that anyone who saw would recognize.

"I could hide her away here."

"Forever? For the thousand plus years she might live?"

It sounded like a nice plan. But no, obviously I couldn't.

"And that doesn't take into account that you'd tell Oers she's alive. You know Oers. They've never been big on faith. They'll want to see her to believe it."

"If it weren't for her eyes, we could show her, then hide her again."

"If your father saw you with her, he'd know that all he'd have to do would be to trail you to find her."

"Father can't trail us. You know that." Father had limited imagination. He liked rules and technology. He liked the science that allowed him to splice human beings and control the resulting splices. He liked to discover ways to control what was never meant to be controlled.

"You know better than to underestimate your father. He's infiltrated the royal palace. Twice. And that's supposed to be impossible."

"He didn't do it personally."

Dolpheus cocked a dark eyebrow. He was right, of course. I knew better than to nitpick with semantics. My father was a powerhouse. I should never underestimate him.

"Other than her eyes, Ilara could, theoretically, blend in," I said.

"Yeah. Right."

"Seriously. If we could somehow conceal her eyes"—because I'd never suggest changing them—"then she might be able to travel across O without being recognized."

"You're fooling yourself. There isn't a more beautiful woman on this planet."

"True. But there are other beautiful women here. You've bedded most of them. If we were to hide enough of Ilara, she could disappear into the background a bit."

Dolpheus barked in laughter. "Ilara. Disappear. Right."

"Maybe we could put a veil on her."

"That covers her face as well as her eyes? And who wears veils anymore? She'd stick out just as much because of her veil as she would without it."

"The Devoteds still wear veils."

"The Devoteds avoid the royal city as if it were diseased. They dislike its greed and corruption, and its loose morals. They're only spotted rarely at the periphery of the city. They hardly ever leave their marharas."

"Well, now that's a possibility."

"What? To put Ilara in a marhara?" Again, another laugh. "Ilara? A Devoted?"

I shrugged. "These are desperate times, Olph."

"You want to put the most sensual woman either one of us has ever met in a marhara?" Dolpheus had met a lot of women, his point was a good one. His cynicism alone proved it. "Even covered from head to toe in a veil, Ilara'd still walk the way she walks, and she'd still talk the way she talks. Or do you have some plan to disguise the sway of her hips and the sultriness of her voice too?"

I sighed. "Okay. You're right. That won't work. Still, if we found a way to cover her eyes, she could come into the city under a Devoted veil, only when it's necessary. We could tell her not to speak, just as the Devoteds who take a vow of silence. People would wonder what she was doing so far from the marharas, but they wouldn't know she was the dead Princess."

"Except that we're supposed to reveal that she's not dead, but alive. Once the people know she's alive, don't you think they'll suspect any woman that seems out of place? Especially if we show her to the people, and then somehow abscond with her without your father or anyone else following us. Oers will be looking for her."

"Unless we tell them that it's their duty to protect her from the would-be assassins that want her dead. If she makes a quick public appearance where she asks her people not to look for her so that she can remain safe, the people will listen. They'll be reassured in the monarchy knowing their princess is alive. And they'll want to defend her. If the part they can take in her defense is to allow her to disappear, they'll do it."

"You're right. They will. That would work. We could find a way to make an appearance with her and then disappear without being followed. Although neither you nor I should be there with her. It would be too dangerous. If your father discovers you're involved, he'll eventually find Ilara, no matter what we do."

"We could figure it out. I'm sure the King would allow

us use of his personal guards. They looked like badasses."

Dolpheus nodded. "They could protect the Princess. Your father wouldn't dare attack her under the direct watch of hardened soldiers like them."

I sighed. The circumstances were far from ideal. "I know we've been over this before, but do you really think it's absolutely necessary that she appear in person? Perhaps Oers could be persuaded to be satisfied with a remote transmission. She could refer to the attack so that her people would be certain it was a recent transmission."

"You know how easy it is to tamper with transmissions. It wouldn't be solid proof of her survival. It would help, but it wouldn't be enough. In the end, she'd always need to make an appearance at some point."

"So we're back to how do we hide Ilara after she makes an appearance in person?" I sighed again, a tired sigh. "I wish there were some way to cover her eyes."

"But there isn't."

"No. There isn't." I'd never minded it before, not once since my mother first taught me as a child that the eyes were the way to see a being's eternal existence. They couldn't be covered, by anything, not even for a minute. It would extinguish the light that dwelled within. It would suffocate the being inside. Through the eyes, a person could reveal all of who she was, and all of who she wasn't.

"So we're back to having no real plan."

"Pretty much."

"Fuck."

"Yeah."

The Auxle sun was about to set. So much for progress.

12

DAYS PASSED IN DEEP CONVERSATION AND plotting with Dolpheus. We'd come up with several ideas that could plausibly resemble a plan, but none of them was foolproof enough to convince either one of us. They stood little chance of convincing someone as demanding as the King of Planet Origins.

To a large extent, our hands were bound. The King wouldn't give me additional information on Ilara's whereabouts until I offered him a solid plan for her rescue, along with secrets of my father's splicing empire. We couldn't come up with a better plan for Ilara's rescue without more information. And I knew next to nothing about my father's splicing procedures, discovering them was likely to be a perilous venture with uncertain and potentially devastating consequences.

What I really needed was to get my information straight from the source: Ilara. This thought went beyond the desires of a lover. Ilara and I were able to communicate with each other through brain waves. She was unlike the rest of Oers, most of whom relied on the crystalline amplification devices they attached to their heads during their waking hours. Those few that had to speak with the outcasts of the outer-lying regions paid to use one of the communication centers that dotted Origins. There, large, crystalline spheres magnified their brain waves enough to span the desired distances.

Ilara knew better. She was different from her subjects, beyond the royal blood that pumped through her veins. Like Dolpheus and me, she rejected limitations. Her mind remained open to possibilities, much as it was when she was first born, when it was as open as it would ever be.

She'd been able to slip into my head before I became aware of her presence. It was a game to her, to attempt to settle into my brain in such a way that I wouldn't realize she was there. I'd always catch her—although not always right away—and she'd reward me with a throaty laugh when I did.

But the stakes were different now. It wasn't a game anymore. It was a matter of life and death—hers and maybe mine. If I could reach into her thoughts, far away on some distant planet, then I might uncover a detail that could serve to our advantage in bringing her back. Perhaps there was some situation we hadn't yet accounted for, or something that had changed since she left O. It was a fishing expedition, but we were low on prospects.

Besides, there was no one else we could ask for help or

guidance. The King was apparently the only one left who knew where Ilara was. Either the King killed the person he commissioned to relocate his daughter, or the person killed himself. During the beginnings of the Andaron rule, after the bloody defeat of the Harals, loyal subjects would take their own lives when it would serve to protect the interests of the royal family. Even today, although less common than it once was, it was considered noble to end one's life in the name of the Andarons.

I didn't know if I could communicate with Ilara across the expanse of the universe, especially without knowing precisely where she was, but a chance existed. That was reason enough to try. She was attuned to my frequency. She'd recognize it right away and realize that I was trying to reach her, even if the signal that made it to her was faint or warbled.

Still, it would be undoable if I couldn't narrow down the location to which I broadcast my signal. It would take longer than my lifetime to send out a mental signal, pinging across the void, hoping to land on her by chance.

To refine her whereabouts, I needed her father to tell me where she was, or at least to give me some hint to limit the search area. No matter how many times Dolpheus and I talked through the situation, we ended up in a loop. For the King to be disposed to give me any information about Ilara's location, I needed to give him what he wanted. And right now what he wanted was something that was nearly impossible to give.

Luckily, Dolpheus and I were skilled at achieving the

nearly impossible. We were far better at it than most. My next step was to do what I wished never to have to do again: break into the most fortified facility on the entire planet and hope that my father didn't catch me doing it.

13

I WANTED TO GO TO MY FATHER'S LAB RIGHT AWAY. Three years of trying without managing to bring Ilara home had done nothing to ameliorate my characteristic impatience. We still might not have a full plan, but at least now I understood which step to take next. I wanted to do it immediately.

But Dolpheus wore me down, eventually convincing me that it was reckless to break into the lab without getting some rest. Our discussions of the last days had left little opportunity for sleep. My eyes were bleary and dry. Finally, I agreed to sleep first.

However, after awakening from sufficient sleep, Dolpheus wasn't satisfied. "You can't go yet, Tan. Be smart."

"Nothing about the plans we've come up with thus far is particularly smart."

"That's true, obviously. There's nothing safe about we intend to do. But come on, there's no need to make it more dangerous by moving too quickly."

"Too quickly? Do you think that three years is 'too quickly?'"

Dolpheus huffed. "Come on, man."

I clipped a sheath to my belt and inspected the blade of my sword.

"Your father's facility has every type of defense we can think of—or worse, that *he* can think of. Let's at least run through what we know one more time before we go."

I slid the sword into the sheath and walked to the other side of the room. I pulled open the shallowest drawer of my desk. "There is no 'we.' You're not coming with me."

"Of course I am."

"You didn't come with me last time."

"And I regret not having gone. I let you put yourself at risk alone. I shouldn't have."

"No. You should have. There's no reason for you to risk your life by going to my father's lab. It's bad enough that I have to do it."

"Tan, I'm not letting you go alone."

I concluded the examination of my choices and pulled out two knives from my collection. I tilted my eyes up at him. "I'm not asking for your permission."

"Well neither am I."

I stalked across the room and laid the knives on the table next to him. I yanked open the drawer beneath the table top. Dolpheus crossed my path and went over to my desk and pulled open the drawer I'd just shut.

"What are you doing?"

"What I choose to do. With the bees up your butt right now, I don't have time to go to my quarters to get my own weaponry. You'd be gone before I returned. So I'm going to use yours."

I stared at him, letting a full beat pass. He stared back, ran a hand through his dark hair. "Look. You've had my back all my life. Since we were boys. And I've done my best to have yours. I have no desire to abandon you now, just when it's about to get tricky. We're as close as brothers. Brothers don't let each other go into the midst of hell without support."

I continued to look but said nothing.

"I'm not letting you go in there alone." Dolpheus paused. "You'd do the same for me."

Finally, I nodded. "Grab the pearl-handled one and the Vikus-viper skin one. I sharpened them just the other day. And they throw well."

Dolpheus smiled a smile that he usually reserved for disarming the ladies. A dimple formed on one cheek, near bright, straight teeth. "Now that you've come to your senses and agreed to my company, tell me again, how exactly are we going to get by your father's security measures?"

I strapped the sheaths that fit my knives to my belt and tossed Dolpheus the ones meant for the knives he carried, one in each hand. He tried to catch the sheaths by sliding the knives meant for them inside in mid-air. He managed to do so with one; the other bounced off the metal tip.

"You're losing your touch," I called.

He grinned while bending to pick up the fallen sheath. "What's the first defense we'll encounter?"

"A force field that encircles the property, about a hundred feet away from the building."

"And I presume that we can't transport within the force field?"

Invalidating the transportation process was tricky, which was why transporting was possible everywhere, except within the palace walls and my father's facility. There might have been other places into which transport wasn't possible, but we hadn't encountered them. Invalidating transport involved reconfiguring the matrix of reality. One had to reweave the threads of the fabric that composed the unseen to forbid the possibility of transporting.

As I understood it, this reconfiguration excluded the creation of new energy within this altered matrix.

There was no one I knew to be capable of redefining the matrix's capabilities in this way and thus limiting the possibilities within it. However, there had to be at least two people on O able to do it. One to forbid transporting for the palace, and another for my father's facility, as I doubted that the King and my father were into sharing talent.

In my father's case, I suspected the one responsible for this craft was Aletox. As faithful to my father as Dolpheus was to me, Aletox had been around since before I was a boy. I'd never understood what Aletox saw in my father that inspired so much loyalty. My father didn't inspire loyalty in me, and I was his son. Yet Aletox had known my father for a lot longer than I had. I didn't know exactly how far back they went, but at least before the time that my father met my mother. Maybe Aletox remembered the man my father used to be better than I did, and that was all it was.

"I tried to transport within the force field," I said, "just in case it was actually possible, and the rumors that one couldn't were nothing more than rumors. It's quite difficult to forbid it, as you know. I figured it was worth a try."

"It didn't work, though."

"It didn't. When I attempted to transport, all that happened was that I moved as close to the force field as possible, on the trajectory to my ultimate destination, which was the inner lab area."

"Aletox."

"I think so."

"It's definitely not your father."

"I don't think so either. Although, as you reminded me earlier, it's best not to underestimate him."

"I know. But still. Reworking the matrix to forbid transporting takes a considerable amount of imagination. Your father simply doesn't have it. He lives by rules too much."

"Yeah. His own."

"For sure. But rules nonetheless. His life is too structured. If his mind works in a fixed way, I don't see how he could access the fabric of the matrix. The matrix is alive and constantly in flux. There are no real rules that govern it."

"I agree. But either way, it makes no difference. Aletox won't help us."

"No. He won't. He would hand us over to your father and offer to kill us for him for our betrayal."

A corner of my mouth lifted. "That sounds exactly like what Aletox would do. I don't know what I did to make him dislike me as much as he does."

"I don't think it has anything to do with you. He can tell you don't like your father, and Aletox doesn't tolerate anyone who doesn't worship your father as he does. Why he does, now that's something I'd pay to find out."

I smiled. "Well, if Aletox can manipulate the matrix, maybe one of us can do it too. If we're able to get Ilara back, maybe it'd be a good idea for us to forbid transporting into our quarters as well."

Dolpheus shrugged. "Yeah. Maybe. Although there aren't many Oers who can transport like we can. It's become a lost art. When the Andaron line first took over, they say almost everyone could transport. Now look at the oafs. Your father's the main threat to Ilara, and he can't transport."

"Still. Maybe we should anyway. To cover all possibilities."

"Let's worry about that later. Right now, how do we get into your father's lab? How'd you get in last time? When you snuck away without me?"

I knew I didn't have reason to feel guilty for sneaking away as I had. I'd only been trying to protect him from my father's wrath, which was as scary as any mowab we'd ever come up against. Still, the guilt was there.

"That's the thing. I'm not exactly sure."

"You're not sure how you got past a force field and into your father's lab?"

"As far as I can tell, I got past a force field, and a breath scanner and eye scanner."

Dolpheus whistled and went to the window that looked out over the valley below my quarters; it felt as if one were floating, with no other structure in sight. The valley eventually climbed into a ridge that hid everything behind it. It was my slice of private paradise where even my father left me alone.

"An eye scanner too? As if a breath scanner weren't impossible enough to beat."

"Yeah. At least, I think so. That's what father has let 'leak.' But it could be worse."

"It could be better."

"But it's probably not," we said at the same time, and Dolpheus laughed at his place next to the wall of glass. That panel cost as much as every "priceless" item contained within this room. It was one of the few advantages of being the son of a splicing empire, even though I benefited from a small fraction of what I could if father and I were on better terms. I compromised myself to secure the panel of glass; it was worth it. I'd planned a nice visit with father before asking for the funds that were well beyond what he allotted me per solar cycle. The visit didn't turn out to be as nice as I'd predetermined, but it had, apparently, been nice enough. Father must have known it was the glass that I wanted and not time with him, yet he agreed nonetheless, surprisingly congenial.

Dolpheus swiveled to look at me again. "So? How did you do it? How'd you slip by ridiculously insurmountable defenses? I mean, how'd you get past the breath and eye scanners? The breath and eye are fully unique to each incarnation. I have no idea how you could have done it."

I squirmed, which I never did, and Dolpheus' eyes grew rapt, ravenous for the tale to follow. "Come on, man. Why won't you tell me? You tell me everything. I can't imagine how you did it. I'm all ready to be impressed."

"That's just the thing, Olph. You won't be impressed. I have no good explanation for what happened, so my experience is almost completely useless."

"No way. That can't be. You got past the defenses, didn't you?"

"Yeah. I did. Somehow. But I have no idea how."

"How can you have no idea how you did something?"

"Because I was right next to the force field. I'd already tried to transport, with no success. I was standing there, thinking, when one of father's employees arrived, atop one of those bulky flying mobiles that hardly anyone uses anymore. I was just wondering whether I could force him to give me entry. But no, I couldn't. Not without having to kill him or father finding out. And I preferred not to kill him. Then I wondered if maybe I could trail him as he gained access through the breath scanner, but then I'd have to be invisible, and how would I become invisible? Maybe I could dematerialize like I did when we transport, but I'd never tried it before. I didn't know if I could break myself apart and put myself together on command when I was also trying to follow a specific linear path and had to do so before the force field closed behind the employee again.

"I was wondering all these things, if it was worth the risk of trying to break myself up without knowing if I could put myself back together again. As you know, it's a challenging process, especially if one aims to get every single piece back in the right place."

"Yeah. I wouldn't try it. Too risky. You didn't, did you?"

"In the end, I didn't."

"So how did you get in? Come on, Tan. You're the one

who's in such a hurry to get this done. Stop dragging it out."

"I fell asleep."

"You fell asleep?"

"I did. And when I came to again, I was in the inner lab, just where I needed to be."

"You're serious."

"Regrettably."

"And how did you get out?"

"Well, that part was easier. It seems that father believes no one can bypass his system to get in the facility, so he has no security on the way out, unlike with the royal palace where the guards check that all visitors conform to their records every time they stop to breathe. I found an unused sterile uniform and put it on. It has a face mask and everything, so no one could see me. I don't imagine anyone else was leaving work with a sterile suit on, but I didn't know what else to do. Wait till I fell asleep again and hope that I magically woke up on the other side of the force field?"

"Did you know for sure that Brachius didn't have any exiting security measures in place?"

"No. I didn't. I didn't know anything for sure. But I figured—and hoped—that I could count on his arrogance to get me out. Thankfully, I turned out to be right."

"And fucking lucky as shit. Lord Tanus, whose valiant heroics are already the stuff of legends, entering the most secure premises on the planet by, what you ask? By falling asleep. No way, you say ladies and gentlemen, no one breaks into a secure facility by simply falling asleep. But yes, I say to you. Lord Tanus does. Lord Tanus, who is unlike anyone else, does."

I chuckled without mirth. "I know. Pathetic. And obviously of no help to us whatsoever right now."

"Well, maybe not. But maybe. If you did it once, perhaps we can figure the way for you—and me—to do it again."

"Our plans are getting worse by the minute."

"Without a doubt."

I joined Dolpheus. A minute of silence passed as we both looked out the window. The beasts in the treetops were at their liveliest at this time of day. Dark, scaly wings stretched nearly as wide as any tree canopy.

"Are you ready to go?" he asked me.

Without any real understanding as to how we would accomplish what we were setting out to do, we both knew my answer before it came. "Yes."

Dolpheus grabbed a sword. We prepared to transport to the outer edge of my father's facility, beyond the force field, where I'd slumbered my way through it the time before.

14

It had been just days since I was last here, to break into the facility the first time. Nothing had changed since then. Mature trees surrounded the sprawling building, their full canopies nearly obscuring the structure from afar. One had to know what he was looking for to find the place.

I knew exactly. Finding it wasn't the problem. All the rest was.

"So this is it, huh? Your father's grand facility." Dolpheus looked around, but there was nothing to see but trees and a few single-unit hover crafts. "I see that your father's employees don't have enough imagination to transport." He shook his head, lamenting. "What kind of scientists is your father hiring?"

"The very best, no doubt."

Dolpheus continued to shake his head. "It truly saddens me, you know? What's happened to people? Why are they so willing to believe they're more limited than they are?"

I came up to my friend's side, indulging his reflection. "I

agree. It isn't right." I put my hand on his shoulder. "But at least *we* can transport." I smiled, trying to imbue lightness into his sudden sobriety. "And we're quite good at it."

Dolpheus continued to glare at the hover units as if they were humanity's ultimate downfall.

"Come on, Olph. Let's go see what we can do about getting into this place."

He gave regret one more second, then shook it off. "All right. So what do you propose? Should I sing you lullabies?" His grin was impish.

I wasn't really in the mood for laughing, but I laughed anyway. His look was perfectly naughty, and I hadn't seen mischief like this in his eyes in quite a while. "Maybe."

"What are we going to do?" Dolpheus' grin was gone. My father's security measures were no joke. If we got caught, the repercussions of our actions would be severe. There could be no doubt about that. My father was punctilious in maintaining the integrity of his splicing advancements, even if no one really understood what the true science of splicing was.

"I was actually just considering that maybe we should try to take down the force field. Or maybe even better, make an exception to it that allows us to enter."

"You can't be serious, Tan."

"I am. We can't try to replicate my falling asleep to get in. That would be ridiculous. It was a fluke. I don't know what happened or how it managed to get me inside, but I have an idea. I'm thinking that within sleep, where there are even fewer defining and limiting constructs than when I'm awake, I was able to manipulate the matrix. I think I managed to alter the profile of the force field so that it no longer excluded me. Certainly, the force field must have allowances for all the employees to cross it. I must have included myself as one of the allowable exceptions. Or something like that."

Dolpheus' hands came to his waist while he stared intently at the force field. It revealed itself as a shimmer in the air ahead of us. "Okay. Let's try it. Although I do wish we had a chance to practice before taking this on with so much at stake."

"I don't think there'll be any fail safes in place that would prevent modification of the force field. There are so few capable of setting one up in the first place. I don't think father would have anticipated this contingency."

"We didn't anticipate this contingency," Dolpheus muttered. But he didn't fool me. There was a spark in his eyes that hadn't been there moments before. He liked a good challenge as much as I did. "So what should we do? How should we start?"

"I imagine we should do it separately, and each try to set up both of us as exceptions to the force field. That way, all it'll take is one to achieve success for both of us to be able to get in."

"Okay. I like it. It'll double our chances of getting it done."

"Exactly." At least figuring out this part was easy.

"And as to getting it done, we just do our best to figure it out, something we've never been taught to do, nor ever really thought of doing before."

"Precisely."

"Mmmhmm."

Now we both stared ahead at the force field. I would have thought its magical shimmers beautiful if not for the obstacle it presented. It was keeping me from drawing one step nearer to Ilara.

"I'm thinking that we might begin just as we do when we transport," I said. "By closing our eyes, calling in stillness, pushing away anything outside of ourselves. Then, when the moment arrives when we barely recognize ourselves as separate from that which surrounds us, then we try to access the force field."

"At that point when our physical borders begin to fade and merge with everything that surrounds us, we reach for the force field. Before we allow ourselves to disintegrate as we do for transporting, we access it. When we feel most like everything else, it's possible that the force field won't reject us as something outside of itself. Then we can make changes from within its structure," Dolpheus added.

"I think it might work."

"At the very least, our plan's starting to sound more sophisticated. Although I'm still pretty glad there's no one here to overhear us."

"No kidding." I stared at the force field for another full minute before saying, "Ready?"

"As ready as I'll ever be to attempt to take down a force field."

"Good. I'm ready too."

There was no more to say. We'd both transported together enough that we knew when to leave each other alone to do what we had to do. Even if neither one of us had ever hacked a force field before, it was similar enough to transporting to realize how important it was to proceed without disruption. Just as with transporting, when we tore apart the fabric of our beings, the task would require our complete focus.

Hidden from sight from any employee that might come or go, standing amid the trees that lined one whole side of the force field, Dolpheus and I settled into our bones. Our legs were shoulder width apart; our weight sunk into them. Our eyes began to lose track of the details before them. When we closed them, we were one step closer to the force field, even though neither one of us had moved.

15

I HAD NO NOTION OF HOW MUCH TIME HAD PASSED since Dolpheus and I began this experiment, but it must have been a good while. One of my calf muscles was beginning to cramp from lack of movement.

Yet I'd made progress. I'd reached out to the force field, to the threads that joined to make it what it was. It seemed receptive to my interference. It would allow me to merge with it as I needed to, I was sure of it now, or at least as sure as I could be of something that I didn't fully understand.

Still, I needed a break before persisting. I'd identified the force field's particular energetic signature. Next time, I'd be able to attempt the manipulation.

The flesh of my forehead was tense from effort. I wouldn't be able to achieve what I needed with finesse if I couldn't relax any more than this. It wouldn't work. There was no way to compel what naturally resisted aggression. The force field would respond more readily, more gracefully, to a gentle manipulation that more closely approximated its own energy.

Coercion had its place. It could accomplish much. However, force ripped and tore. It destroyed. What we wanted was a gentle adjustment, a plucking of sorts, where one thread was moved this way, another that, while leaving the weaving of the force field's fabric otherwise intact.

Slowly, I began to disengage. Pulling away too quickly could cause tears in my consciousness. This was another reason why so few attempted transporting. Not only was there the risk that your body wouldn't reconfigure properly, but also that your mind might not reassemble the way it used to be, that you might leave a fragment of what you identified as yourself behind, to merge with the energy of something—or someone—else.

I pulled away bit by bit. I allowed myself to begin having identifiable thoughts again. With each thought that formed in my mind, another piece of my consciousness returned. I let go of my connection to the force field. Easy, I reminded myself when I realized I was going too quickly—drop by drop, hazy fragment by hazy fragment—until I felt myself completely separate from it.

When I experienced myself almost whole, fully within myself again, I opened my eyes. That's when I really settled back into my roots. I saw the force field's shimmer right in front of me—separate from me once more.

It was safe now to disengage all the way. I looked to Dolpheus to my left. He was reaching out to the force field. The outlines of his body were blurred, blending with the energy of the space that contained him. He was still there, unlike with transporting, where he totally disappeared, but he was only partially within his body. His physical shell didn't fully encapsulate his consciousness yet.

Disturbing him now was extremely dangerous. He could fracture, both at the mental and physical levels.

I stepped back with nearly silent footsteps. I watched where and how each boot would land among the wild grasses. When I was far enough away from Dolpheus that I didn't think sitting would affect him, I sat. I spread my legs out in front of me, rubbed my hand across my face, and suppressed a mildly disappointed sigh. I put my hands behind me and leaned into them, tilting my head to the sky. We must have been at it for longer than I thought: The Suxle Sun was high above, more than halfway through its eighteen-hour trajectory from horizon to horizon.

I was content to watch the leaves sing and dance above me while I allowed my brain the break it needed. I wasn't yet fully recovered when the edges of Dolpheus' body began to assume greater definition.

When he was himself again, he turned, looking for me. He came over to join me, plopping to the grass with unusual commotion. He landed with a loud exhale. Sword and knives clanked in their sheaths, even though there was little for them to clank against. His boots clonked out in front of him. He laid back, extending himself fully, arms out to the sides, legs spread wide. He sighed. "Well that was intense."

"It was."

"Were you able to do it?"

"No. You?"

"No. But I think I got close," he said.

"I was close, too. I'm pretty certain I'll be able to do it."

"Yeah. I feel the same. I got close enough to the force field that it let me pet it."

I smiled, still looking up at the sky. That was exactly what it felt like. A wild animal that had finally accepted me enough to allow me to touch it. If I approached it in just the right way, so that it didn't feel threatened by me, it might let me mount it, like the wild horses that roamed outside the royal city.

"It was taking a lot out of me," I said. "I couldn't tell how much more effort it would take to manipulate the fabric of the force field. I decided I could use a rest before continuing."

"Good idea. I don't know if I would've stopped if I hadn't sensed you stopping too. But now that we have, I'm glad for it. I'm exhausted."

We watched clouds, which had formed after we honed into the force field, cross our slice of sky. They were tinged red and gray against a rapidly darkening horizon.

"A storm's coming," I said.

Storms on O brewed speedily and ferociously. A clear sky could shift in what seemed like only minutes. The sky was blackening, almost to the point of obscuring the Suxle Sun, the brightest of O's two suns.

"It looks like it might hit this area," Dolpheus said. "I don't know if we'll have time to get this done before the sky breaks open and lets loose its reserves."

"I don't know if we will either, but I don't want to leave. I'm so close, I'm going to get back to it."

"Uuuuh. I'm still super tired. I don't think I can do it just yet. I might take a nap first. I don't mind a little rain."

Neither one of us minded a little rain. But O's storms usually brought quite a lot more than that.

"Take a nap then. Who knows? Maybe you'll wake up in the inner lab as I did last time."

Dolpheus yawned but didn't change position. Like a stunted star, he was ready for sleep. "Yeah. Maybe, huh?"

"If you get in that way before I do, just wait for me there. I hope to be able to get in too. But if it seems like you're waiting too long, start snooping without me. The longer we remain inside, the greater the risk of being discovered. Remember, we're looking for anything that will intrigue the King. I imagine my father won't just leave the secrets to his splicing empire lying around in plain sight."

"But he also won't expect intruders in his lab." Dolpheus studied me. "Why don't you sleep too? You look as worn out as I feel."

"I'm sure I do. But I want to take this head-on. I'm so close to being able to manipulate the force field mindfully. I want to see if I can do it. It's time for me to understand more of my capacities."

Dolpheus yawned again. "If you insist, man. I like the napping idea much better right now."

I reached over and brought a palm down on his arm with a slapping sound while I moved to stand. "And if I can't do it, hopefully you can. At least we know napping worked once before. Maybe set the intention of penetrating the force field as you drift off."

"I'm already on it, Tan. I'm already floating away into the

dream world, passing through the force field and through the lab's walls. I'll see you inside there. Or I'll see you back out here if you don't make it in."

I liked his confidence. Never one to doubt himself, there seemed no reason to begin now. Our good-natured competitiveness had long given us the edge to push forward when we might have fallen back.

I covered the few steps that brought me back to where I'd been, within inches of the force field's shimmer. I looked at the sky. Even more dark and foreboding now.

I settled back into my wide-legged stance. Brought my gaze ahead. Without another thought as to what I might or might not accomplish, I let my eyes lose focus until they barely noticed what they saw.

Then, I closed them and brought myself fully within, where nearly anything was possible.

16

As it often did when I abandoned any definition of myself, time became difficult, if not impossible, to measure. It might have taken me hours to get to the point where I now found myself. Or perhaps it had only been minutes.

I'd known that I needed to arrive here if I hoped to make any progress at infiltrating the force field. Still, once I did, it caught me by surprise, so much so that I'd almost forgotten what I was attempting to do, and nearly didn't recognize my cue to begin exploring the threads of the force field's matrix.

It was when I was fully content to be in the hazy space of nothingness and at once everything that I could proceed. Only then, I lacked the desire to do anything. Being was sufficient to satisfy my soul. My usual conceptions of reality were absent, and solidity vanished to reveal itself as it, in truth, was: fully malleable. Existence was a great gift, wholly independent from what one chose to do with that gift.

It took a great surge of will to move forward from the

contentment of being one with everything on planet O. Still, Ilara was motivation enough. There was little I wouldn't do for the woman. I'd fallen under her enchantment when I met her and was able to look into those remarkable eyes up close. She'd remained a constant part of me since that first encounter. I had to continue if I wanted her ever to be a concrete part of me again.

Exhilaration bubbled within. I must have smiled though I wasn't sure whether my mouth moved or not. I observed the exhilaration flow through me, mindful not to climb aboard its wave. Too much emotion might distract me from the serenity I needed to continue.

When stillness returned, along with the sensation that I didn't particularly care whether I succeeded, I reached out with intangible tentacles that extended from my personal energetic field. They made contact with the force field, or rather, with its components. I thrummed the threads. They responded pleasantly. So I ran my palm along the tight weave that composed the force field.

It was an artful manifestation of intelligence. I caressed it again. My own energy continued to extend toward it, admiringly. Then, I plucked one string, as if the harp wasn't my instrument, but another's.

Like a timid lover, I touched in entreaty. The thread softened and yielded at my touch, becoming supple and warm. The matrix was ready for me.

I dove in. Nothing went as I'd thought it might. Instead, it went the way it was supposed to.

I forgot all about my plan to create an exception to the force field that included Dolpheus and myself. I probably even forgot about Ilara for moments at a time. I gave myself to the sensuality of the matrix, to its ability to be almost anything. To perhaps be what I understood as the essence of life itself.

I synced myself with its rhythm. I could have stayed there, within its folds, all day.

But then, from a faraway place in my brain, in floated a prompt. The inner lab. As if in a fog, I chose to go there. I plunged farther into the soft yielding of the matrix, only to discover that I could push right through it.

Beyond the force field, all it took was a drifting, lazy thought of the inner lab, and I transported there. I was already in the midst of the mind frame necessary for effective transportation.

In the next instant I found myself no longer assaulted by the whipping winds of the gathering storm. The energy of the forces of nature was replaced by a different kind of energy. It was cool, but a different kind of cold than the one that brought out bumps across your skin and made your nipples erect. A sterile chill engulfed me, along with a silence that was far too quiet to be the product of nature.

My body reacted, realizing that its environment had changed, and that this wasn't one with which it was naturally comfortable. The sudden body awareness began to call me from the somewhere place I'd had to go to touch something outside of myself. Gradually, I grew aware of the perception of my senses. The sound. An artificial hum, soft. Still, I didn't like it. The smell. Aseptic. Of some place too clean. The taste. The air, tangy. The smell of metal.

I blinked my eyes open experimentally as if I'd been

asleep for a very long time. I noticed Dolpheus on the other side of the room, blinking as I was, disorientation written across his features.

I looked around. Blank, white walls where metal shelves weren't covering them. A wide, long bed, also metal, hovering in the air just as the King's glass bed had. Bigger than necessary for the body of any human.

I heard movement across the room. Dolpheus was standing, wobbly like a newborn mowab, much before it became as fierce as its mother. Our eyes met across thirty-or-so feet of immaculate tile. Dolpheus covered the distance between us with loud footfalls. I turned to the table, imagining the people who lay there, giving their will to my father. Dolpheus joined me. Still, neither of us said anything, not even about what had allowed us both inside this forbidden room.

Before either of us was ready for it, the sound of footfalls far down a corridor echoed somewhere, near enough to be heard. Each moment, closer.

My body resisted purposeful movement, yet I moved. Dolpheus moved. We swiveled and scanned the room, searching for a place to hide. There were no good ones. We moved to take bad ones.

I pulled a large metal drawer open. Dolpheus did the same beside me. Inside mine, there was a body. His was empty. He climbed inside his and I closed mine, without even wondering who the naked man draped in a sheet was. I yanked the one next to it open. Full. This one was a woman. Her breasts tinted blue. I slammed this drawer shut too.

I reached for the one above the woman's. This one was

empty though an awkward climb. The footsteps were nearer, loud now, several people.

I shut Dolpheus' drawer the final inch he hadn't and pulled the woman's drawer partially open again. I used it as a step to reach the one above hers. I shut hers, mindful not to look at the features of her face. It was disturbing to see bodies meant for life lying here, lifeless.

I braced my hands above my head and slid the drawer shut with me in it, careful not to cut myself on the bare metal slides and braces. The last couple of inches were the hardest to close, but I managed.

My drawer snapped shut just as the door to the room clicked open.

17

IF I'D ANTICIPATED THAT BOTH DOLPHEUS AND I would be able to breach the force field and gain access to the inner lair of my father's splicing empire, I might have planned past the initial steps. I might have allotted more effort than I had toward elaborating a sensible, all-encompassing plan.

However, it looked as if by sheer luck we found ourselves in an ideal position: hidden from sight, able to overhear whatever conversation was held within the lab.

There were no papers lying around on any of the lab's immaculate surfaces. There was no sign announcing, in big bold letters, whichever of my father's secrets would endear me to the King. There was a blank wall that hid the programming unit that controlled the many aspects of splicing. I determined this the last time I was here. It was where I had, by chance, found a trace of Ilara's transfer off planet. It was only because whomever the King had commanded to move Ilara off O wasn't as savvy with processing units as father or Aletox were.

The trace that I found was faint, nearly unrecognizable for what it was. The King's servant, or whoever he was, hadn't been entirely devoid of skill. He'd done a competent job at covering his steps. But as soon as I saw the glitch, the piece of code that wasn't supposed to be there, I knew it was about Ilara in the same way that I'd known that she was alive before I received any external confirmation of the fact. When it came to Ilara, I just knew things. There was no good explanation for the knowing, it just was.

With the confirmation that she lived, my desperation to find her had intensified. I'd try anything. I would scour my father's system, looking for anything that might interest the King, even though I suspected I'd encounter exactly what I had last time: string after string of zeros and ones that looked like nothing meaningful unless you knew what you were looking at.

I was cold, near the point of shivering already, in a frigid metal drawer intended to contain the dead, or the near dead which to me was somehow worse. I was surrounded by bodies that appeared lifeless. My dearest friend lay in another drawer, likely wondering why he'd insisted on joining me on this mission.

Still, I couldn't help but ponder whether our circumstances were unexpectedly fortuitous. Before hearing the footsteps along the hallway and jumping into this drawer, I'd had no idea how we'd procure what the King wanted. Perhaps this was our chance. If we didn't freeze before we got out of these drawers and if, within these metal boxes, we could actually hear anything that was said.

Already, the people in the lab were in conversation, yet all I could hear were faint mumblings. I couldn't even make out the timbre of my father's voice as recognizable as it was, with its forceful undercurrents that imposed themselves upon you even when he communicated in whispers.

I lay there, shivering, with my hand clamped in a death grip against my sword to keep its sheath from clanging against the metal of the drawer. Was there any way that I could open my drawer enough for the voices to waft in? But no, how could I? They would hear the drawer's click as it opened, and they would see the drawer ajar. Lifeless bodies in lifeless drawers weren't supposed to move them.

My eyeballs grew cold. I shut my eyes; perhaps my eyelids would keep my eyeballs warm, I thought, with hopeful delusion. It was dark in there, anyway.

I began to wonder if my choices would kill my best friend. He deserved the death of a hero, not death by drawer. I hoped the same could be said of me, but of that I was less certain. I remembered many of the thoughts I'd had and the actions I'd chosen, even if I wanted to forget them. I hadn't always chosen the honorable path. If anyone had to perish from death by drawer, it was me. Not him.

I decided right then, in the moment immediately before my eyelids froze, that I would push open the drawer and draw all the attention in the room to myself—this part would be easy. I would do something so that everyone would need to be involved in subduing me and—I hoped—dragging me off to another room. This would give Dolpheus the opportunity to slip out of his drawer—if he could hear enough to realize what I was doing, if he wasn't frozen to death by then, and if he (and I) could open the drawers from the inside. There were a lot more *ifs* where those came from.

It was a crappy plan with a low chance of things going the way I needed them to, but it was all I had. It was what I would do if I had to.

I waited, listening to unintelligible murmurs and counting long, freezing breaths to keep my mind from panicking. My nose hairs were frozen. Each breath tickled. It was a good thing I was too cold to sneeze.

It was time. I had to move now. The cold was slowing my brain. I'd already forgotten the conditions I set for myself to mark the moment that demanded action, but I was certain they must have been met. I steeled myself as much as I could, while I tried to reduce the shivering enough to get my muscles to work. I wriggled like a worm toward the back half of the drawer, and planted the soles of my boots firmly against the drawer's back.

I pushed off. The soles of my boots deflected off the metal and the sides of my knees slammed against either side of the drawer. Hard. I knew a blow like that should hurt, but I was too frozen to feel anything.

I hadn't even managed to push against the top of the drawer with my hands as I'd intended. I'd have to do much better next time. If not, both Dolpheus and I were likely to die in here.

I prepared myself again, and took extra time to steel myself and draw in the strength that the cold had robbed me of. This might be my final chance.

I drew in a breath that clanged around in my chest like a death rattle. My eyes shot wide open. Obviously, my eyelids weren't yet frozen shut. Still, things were worse than I thought. I planted my boots firmly, willing them not to slip again. I gripped the metal above my head with fingers that could no longer bend.

I didn't let myself think anymore. I pushed with all I had.

Nothing happened.

The drawer didn't budge. I slid around awkwardly inside it, banging joints, making more noise than I should have. My muscles just weren't working the way they were supposed to, the way they usually did.

I'd waited too long.

18

HERE'S A THING I'VE LEARNED ABOUT assumptions and plans: They never turn out to be exactly the way I imagined them. In fact, they often turn out to be the complete opposite. Thankfully, this happened to be one of those instances.

As I let my legs fall to the sides in an expression of frozen defeat, a sound that had never sounded like hope before rang out, echoing through my metal prison, like the songs of the Devoteds, promising salvation. There was a click, unmistakable in its meaning. Then there was a second one. And a third.

My drawer remained closed, yet light, sound, and ambient air traveled through the common chamber that contained all the drawers to reach my own slice of frozen torment. The air that flowed into my drawer wasn't enough to warm it, but it was sufficient to keep the freezing process from advancing.

The dim light that circumnavigated twists and turns to

reach me was just enough to highlight the corners of my cage, prompting thoughts—or delusions—that I might survive to die another day.

Finally, too, I was able to hear my father's voice. He was there. I couldn't make out all of the words being spoken, but I could make out enough. I abandoned concern for Dolpheus (assuming that he wouldn't continue to freeze, and that his drawer wasn't one of those opened since there were no sounds of surprise or alarm) and trained my sluggish mind on what was being said. Even half-dead as I was, I remembered: Ilara was out there. I would do whatever it took to bring her back where she belonged, with me.

Right away, my mind began to avoid the task I assigned it. I imposed my will upon it, with all the might that I could gather, forced it to listen and, more importantly, to remember.

The voices came to me as if from a faraway distance. A bit garbled and a bit pointless, they reached me in fragments. I exerted what effort I had left to piece them together into something useful.

"The temperature's set too low." Yeah, no shit, I thought. "It's a degree too low." This was my father, the perfectionist, who didn't realize that the temperature was much too low by many, many degrees, and that there, right next to him, he was slowly killing his only son and heir. He might not have cared, but I like to think that he would have, that the father I loved as a child was still in there, somewhere, and that I (and Dolpheus as a favor to me) would have been spared.

"Fix it." Again, father was stern. The ring of his voice

came through clearer than the almost-indistinguishable voices of the two—or three?—people accompanying him.

"Is everything set to proceed with the splicing?" Father again. Deferential mumblings followed. "Were the protocols set to my specifications, exactly?"

Even though I couldn't make out the timid response that followed, I could guess it. I understood the fear of the person speaking. I'd experienced this same fear, of disappointing my father and receiving his unforgiving judgment countless times as an adolescent, until I outgrew it. I eventually found my own strength. I'd had to or risk withering in the man's shadow. I chose to step into the sun. I never knew where the strength to do this came from, but I was grateful for it nearly every day of my life.

"And what made you think you should vary my specifications?" My father's voice was harder than the metal I lay on.

"If you had a good reason for it, what made you think that you shouldn't have asked me before doing it? I don't care if I was unavailable. You should have waited." I knew the double edge to this story. Father's assistant would have gotten into the same amount of trouble for disturbing him when he said he was unavailable, or for delaying until he could be reached. There was little winning with father, except for Aletox, who was an exception to most of my father's rigid rules.

"Thanks to your actions, we can't proceed with these three right now. And that's a very significant problem. The time frame in which we can extract the eternality and reinsert it without damage to the person is brief." Father's voice took on a lecturing tone. I was certain that the employees in the room had heard what he was about to say many times before. I, however, set my ears alert and willed them to register every sound that wound around the metal bends.

"After we've lowered the heartbeat, the body temperature, and the brain waves down to the necessary rates, we have only three days to pull out the eternality and reinsert it before permanent damage is done to the client. If we don't proceed precisely during this time period, the mind will register that the eternality has been removed from the body. It will believe the person dead, or at the very least fractured, and that's never good. We have but one opportunity to do it. It becomes more dangerous each time we interfere with the body's normal functions. Each time we slow clients down, there's an increased likelihood that we won't be able to speed them back up again, that the body will resist our meddling. This is one of the reasons why it's so important that you follow my directions precisely, and this is why your error in judgment is a very big problem. This is why I haven't hired you to make decisions. I've hired you to follow my orders."

Some apologetic mumblings before, "No, what we will do is what I say, and only that, understood?"

More frightened mutterings. I found myself empathizing with whichever poor fools were doing the unsuccessful backpedalling and wondering whether Aletox was there with them. But no, I hadn't heard his voice, always clear and unmistakable. I didn't think it would fade into indistinct mumbles as did the voices responding to my father.

"What we'll do now is go to the dining room and enjoy a nice, steaming pot of hakusha. We'll go over every specification together so that you'll be exact in the preparation for the splices. You'll do as I require of you. Or you'll find yourselves relieved of your duties."

Only father would enjoy the steaming pot of hakusha, its bitter leaves an exotic, acquired taste. His employees would be too afraid to enjoy much. But they would do as he said. Precisely.

The drawers about us clinked shut with crisp clicks. I strained my ears to hear what I knew would come. It took much longer to arrive than it should have, but when it finally did, the sound of the door to the room opening, ringing out our freedom, I'd never before in my life been more grateful for my father's daily indulgence in the hakusha plant. He'd once, in a moment of rare candor, attributed much of his brilliance to the hakusha. The plant, he said, allowed him to access an entirely different world than the one of which we were normally aware. From this alternate perspective, he could bring back its ideas.

I didn't care if he traveled to the wild deserts of all the worlds and back. All I cared about was that he'd just traveled out of this room.

I gathered strength from places unknown and thrust my drawer open a second after Dolpheus did the same.

19

THE TRIUMPH OF BYPASSING THE FORCE FIELD WAS gone, vanished, evaporated on the clouds of our cold breaths. Dolpheus and I sat on the hard floor and leaned against the metal drawers. We'd managed only to tumble out of the drawers that contained us and to close them. We collapsed just beneath them, dazed, huddled together for warmth. We rattled against each other, shivering, teeth chattering, swords and knives clinking.

"I feel," Dolpheus began, "as if... I'll never... be warm again."

I agreed with him fully but couldn't get my lips to form the words to respond.

I uncurled my legs with difficulty and flopped them out before me. They seemed like big, unwieldy blocks of ice. I might have wondered if they still worked if not for the pain their warming was causing. I sunk back against the drawer fronts, without leaving whatever warmth I could gain from my friend. My head lolled to the unsupported side before I snapped it back upright.

That got my attention. Just because we were out of the freezer drawers didn't mean we were safe. So long as we were inside my father's lair, we were never safe. I had to pull myself together, and I had to do it now, even if my body wanted no part in the idea.

Dolpheus spoke for me. "We need to get out… of here."

I managed to nod my agreement. Even if my father said they were all going to enjoy a pot of hakusha, and I knew about how long this daily ritual of his took—at least an hour—there were no guarantees. Someone could walk into this room for any number of reasons, at any time. We were exposed and vulnerable, and both of those conditions had to change right away.

After our success in crossing the force field to gain entry, I thought there was a decent chance that we could also exit by manipulating the force field. If we had our normal faculties in place. If we could guarantee uninterrupted time so that we could focus to get out of here that way.

But we couldn't meet any of these requirements. We'd have to find a way that was easy and simple, because that's all we could handle right now. If my usual humor and ability to reflect hadn't still been thawing, I might have found it funny that I'd taken on battle-proven opponents of great skill, and lived to tell the tales. Now, a refrigerated metal drawer had proven my equal, and had come uncomfortably close to winning my final battle.

"Where did you find that sterile suit last time?"

Dolpheus' back was against my side, his arms around his shins.

I'd thought it pretty reckless to don a sterile suit and walk straight out of the lab and the building the last time. I'd gotten lucky, very lucky. I'd encountered no one on my way out, no one to question the irregularity of my actions.

I didn't think concealing ourselves within sterile suits a good plan for escape this time either. However, I was desperate enough to try almost anything. "It was hanging on the wall right there." My tongue felt as thick as a log and equally limber. Dolpheus only understood what I said because we knew each other as well as we did, or perhaps because his brain was thawing at the same rate as my tongue.

Our heads swiveled in the direction I'd indicated. The mountings for a sterile suit were there, bare. Of course, I hadn't returned the suit I took, and there had only been one. Surely a facility such as this must have others, but not within the splicing lab.

"At least I know the way out of here now." Last time, it had taken a few wrong turns before I discovered the direct route out of the building.

A sound from far away, down one of the hallways, reached us through the closed door of the lab. Dolpheus and I stood right away, with an appalling lack of grace. Plan or no plan, we couldn't just huddle here until we were discovered. It wasn't a question of whether someone would find us, rather, it was a question of when.

I walked to the door while Dolpheus swept his head back and forth across the room, searching for any solution to our immediate problem. I peered out of the miniscule resin window that was set within the door at eye level, but could only see the blank wall across the hall. So I flattened my ear against the window.

Dolpheus joined me when we heard another sound. An indistinct metal ping followed by a silence that pounded in my head with alarm.

"We can't wait, Tan," Dolpheus whispered with appropriate urgency.

"I know." My voice was heavy with resignation. Resentment toward the King and my father was growing with each passing moment. The King was a bully for forcing me to put myself in this kind of danger (and consequently for putting Dolpheus in danger). My father was an asshole for making it unsafe for a son to be in his father's building, for erecting an empire of secrets between him and me, an impenetrable edifice that kept me from the relationship a son might have with an ordinary father.

There were no more sounds that I could hear. I pressed my face against the resin window, straining to see a few feet to either side of the door. It appeared to be all clear, but Dolpheus and I were well aware that we were taking a big risk by walking out into the hallway. In battle, risks as high as these could be fatal. I hoped they would be less within the supposed civility of a building of science.

I pulled in a breath, leaned one hand flat against the door, and began to turn the door handle with the other. Dolpheus was right behind me, his hand at his waist, next to the hilt of his sword. I got the door handle all the way down without an audible click. I pulled it toward me and stopped. I peered through the gap. At least in this direction, the hallway was clear. Slowly, I pulled the door all the way open and peeked out in the other direction. Clear.

I exchanged a quick glance with Dolpheus, then slipped out into the hallway. A few seconds later, I heard him pull the door closed behind us, almost without sound.

We were tall men of strong build, and we moved quickly, our steps little more than a muffled pattering against the tiled floor. I led the way, Dolpheus half a step behind. At each intersection with another hallway, I stopped and peered around the corner first. But once I stepped onto the new course, I carried my head with confidence. The secret to carrying out any deceit was to behave as if it were no deceit at all. I walked as if I belonged here, hoping we wouldn't be stopped, but if we were, that the leaping pulse at my throat wouldn't give us away.

We wound the last of the corners. The exit door was up ahead, at the end of this long hall. We traversed half the hallway before I wondered if father had designed the facility this way intentionally. If this labyrinthine layout were a defense since I'd seen no monitoring devices anywhere.

We were thirty feet, forty at most, away from the door. I had to tamp my urge to break into a run. One purposeful stride after another, soft and confident. Twenty feet. I wanted to sigh in relief—that I'd done the impossible, twice, and survived my own recklessness—but I knew better than to celebrate prematurely. There was nothing more likely to jinx things.

Ten feet. My eyes were fixed on the door up ahead, on our liberation. I saw nothing but that.

BAM. I was hit from the side. I reeled, off balance, caught by surprise. Dolpheus' hand shot out to catch me before I could fall.

Then we both turned to see what had thwarted our getaway when we were so close to surviving our impudence with no more to recover from than lingering cold.

20

A NERVOUS MOMENT SLUNK BY IN RELATIVE silence. The woman that ran into me so unbearably close to the lab's exit sat on the floor, hands behind her, legs sprawled out in opposing angles. The crash stunned her as it had me.

But now her eyes came into focus to land on me. Chances were high that she was about to scream.

Dolpheus moved first, but I was only a fraction of a second behind him. He reached for her mouth, the most dangerous part of her. He clamped his big hand around it.

That's when the shock wore off. Her eyes bulged. She thrashed against Dolpheus' hand, doing what she could to yank her head away from him. But by then I was behind her, crouched in a squat. I wrapped my arms around her torso, pinning her arms to her sides.

This wasn't our first rodeo. Dolpheus and I knew what would come next. In a second, she'd realize she couldn't get free of my hold, and that the hand clamped across her mouth wasn't going anywhere. She'd do two things. She'd attempt to bite Dolpheus' hand (with no success, he'd tighten his hand around her face so she couldn't move her jaw) and begin to buck against me. She'd try to head butt my face, pulling her legs in to gather some leverage to topple me over.

She wouldn't manage any of this, of course. But she'd try.

We didn't waste a moment on signaling each other. We knew what to do. I gathered strength in my legs and then exploded upward, taking the woman with me. She thrashed her head back, trying to make contact with my face, shoulder-length brown hair loose and wild, tickling my nose. But she didn't make any contact that was to her advantage. My face was turned to the side, out of the range of impact. She hit my collarbone once, and I think it hurt her as much as it did me.

I was taller than her by at least a foot. Her feet dangled at my shins where she attempted to kick them with the back of her shoes. If she'd hoped that would work, she shouldn't have worn soft slipper-like shoes.

"Let's get her out of here," Dolpheus whispered, with as much urgency as his suggestion deserved. I nodded curtly and began moving toward the door. We had no choice but to take her with us. I didn't want the complication, but leaving her behind would be far worse. If we left her in the lab, dead or alive, we'd be found out, immediately or eventually. Our break-in needed to remain secret. My father could never know that I—or anyone else—had been able to break into his facility. If he found out, he'd alter the building's security to make it truly impossible to bypass. And I had to be able to break in one more time. Once I received knowledge of Ilara's exact whereabouts, I'd need my father's equipment to bring her back where she belonged.

Dolpheus looked to each side of the hallway to make sure that no one else had spotted us. Then he slid the door to the outside open. Three bodies moved together as one: Dolpheus shadowed my movements to retain a firm grip on the woman's mouth, I carried her out in front of me, pressed against my body. Awkwardly, yet efficiently, we shuffled out the door. Then I backed up so that Dolpheus could reach to close the door.

Once free of the building, we walked as quickly as we could, Dolpheus with his hand pressed to the woman's face while I focused on maintaining our momentum forward despite the woman's resistance. We cut a direct line to the place where Dolpheus and I first began this expedition: the thick copse of trees that hid us from sight of any comings and goings of the lab. The foliage would be enough to hide our captive, even if it could do nothing to keep her scream from reaching the building.

When we walked through the force field, a surge of energy shocked my system, but it wasn't enough to disrupt it. We'd made it in and out of my father's lab. And we'd have been free of any suspicion if not for the complication that wriggled most uncomfortably in my arms. Ordinarily her struggling, even continuous over the distance we'd covered, wouldn't have been difficult to resist. But the cold of those lifeless drawers had drained me of much of my strength. After the several hundred feet I'd walked with her in tow, my biceps and shoulders ached, and I wished I could just fling her to the ground where she could thrash all she wanted.

Once we reached the copse of trees and walked into their cover, I said to Dolpheus, tersely, "I need to put her down."

"Over there." He pointed with his free hand, farther into the density of green. The arm he clamped around her mouth was tired too.

When we reached "over there" Dolpheus and I sidled over to a tree. We maneuvered ourselves so that I was able to slide out from behind the woman, replacing my body with the tree. With her back flat against the tree trunk, I pushed my hands, with all my weight behind them, into her upper arms.

"Grab something to bind her mouth," I panted to Dolpheus. If he could let go of her mouth, then he could better help me subdue her.

He looked to either side of us and seemed to come up with nothing. So I looked too. The foliage and the ground covering here were thick. Big, gnarled roots spanned the ground in intricate networks of connectedness. Vines hung from the trees. Leaves were everywhere, hanging from the trees and rotting atop the ground. But nowhere was there anything that would be helpful in gagging our captive.

I leaned in toward Dolpheus. "Tear my shirt. It should rip at the bottom hem."

My friend looked down over his shoulder. "You're right. It should."

The problem was that neither one of us could let go of

the woman to tear it. She realized the predicament we were in and rewarded us with a burst of wild bucking.

Now, Dolpheus and I were more than competent soldiers. There were a many number of things we could do to still and silence our captive. But neither one of us wanted to hurt her. We fought when we had to, but there was little pleasure in hurting a woman, especially one that had no particular fault. She showed up in the wrong place at the wrong time. I didn't want to punish her for that.

Dolpheus attempted to grab at the hem of my shirt with his free hand. But every time he came close to doing it, the woman tore her mouth free of his other, distracted hand.

When the grunt of frustration came from Dolpheus, I knew the woman had gone too far. She'd managed to bite him, not seriously, but enough. This time, instead of reaching for my shirt, he pulled out his knife. The woman had time only to widen her eyes in alarm before he moved the knife toward her.

I would have interfered if I thought he meant to kill her. However, I knew my friend too well. There were many ways to silence a person that didn't involve killing.

He brought the knife overhead and pointed the hilt toward her. Then she did exactly what he wanted her to do. To protect her face, she tilted it downward, bringing her chin to meet her collarbone. As soon as the back of her head was exposed, Dolpheus hit the base of her skull with the hilt of the knife.

Her head slumped all the way forward.

21

THE STORM THAT BREWED SO OMINOUSLY BEFORE we made it through the force field had cleared completely. The Suxle Sun shone brightly while inching its way toward the horizon that would soon shield it from view.

"I never imagined the sunshine could feel so glorious," I said. It wasn't particularly hot, just warm. I sat, leaning back against my hands, watching our unconscious captive. I slid my jacket off, and unbuttoned my shirt and took it off too. I folded my clothes into a rough pillow and lay back on them.

"That looks like a good idea right there," Dolpheus said, and proceeded to do the same. Once he was laying down in close imitation of me, he said, "The sun feels incredible."

"It's almost enough to make you forget that we almost just froze to death."

Dolpheus sighed pleasantly. "Yeah. Almost. But not quite."

"I thought we might both die in there."

"Me too."

"Death by freezer drawer? Can you imagine that? After all we've been through together?"

He chuckled. He could find humor in almost anything. He'd probably live forever because of this ability. "Death by freezer drawer? Really?"

"I kept thinking it, stuck inside that damn drawer. What an epitaph that would make. Not: They led soldiers in the battle to quash the Great Fifth Rebellion. Not: They fought mowabs barehanded. Do you remember that?"

"I don't see how I could forget. There's something truly unforgettable about staring into the red eyes of doom and death of a mowab. They make you feel as small and weak as a child, and just as foolish for wanting to take them on."

"That they do. Our epitaphs could have also read: They faced down the red eyes of doom and death to victory. Or even, if things start going well at some point: They rescued Princess Ilara of the Andaron Dynasty and brought her back to her rightful rule on Planet O."

"Do you think Ilara will rule if we manage to get her back here?"

I paused to think about my answer, even though it wasn't the first time I'd considered the question. Finally, I arrived at the same conclusion I had previously. "I don't know."

"King Oderon isn't in the best of shape to rule right now. I've never seen him weak as we saw him the other day."

"That's because we aren't in the habit of sharing time with the King. Besides, I'm sure he doesn't make public appearances whenever he's unwell. Father doesn't leave the house if he has even a slight illness. He doesn't want anyone to suspect him weak."

"I remember."

Of course he would. His father had served my father for many hundreds of years. One morning, Dolpheus' father, a man much kinder than my own, hadn't risen from his bed. Before his unexpected death, my father had only trusted two men. Afterward, he trusted only Aletox.

It had been many years since Dolpheus' father died, when we were adolescents, but memories of him could still cast a shadow across Dolpheus' features. I hastened to move on. "What are we going to do about her, Olph?"

Neither Dolpheus nor I were looking at our captive, still slumped into her fastenings around the tree. Our eyes were closed, our faces tilted toward the bright sunlight. But there could be no doubt of whom I was speaking.

Dolpheus groaned. "Man. We were so close to being free without complication."

"I know." I sighed. "It would have been incredibly nice if we could've left the facility without problems. But now we most definitely have a problem."

"A big one."

I rose to one elbow and shaded my eyes with my hand. "She doesn't look that threatening right now."

Dolpheus shaded his eyes to look at her as well. "No, she doesn't. She almost looks pretty, with her mouth closed, not trying to scream and bite me all at the same time."

"I guess she is kind of pretty, if you like your girls plain."

I'd expected Dolpheus to laugh at that. Instead he said,

"Not every woman can be like Ilara. You got lucky with her, my friend."

Dolpheus' brooding came on suddenly. I tried to lighten the mood, mostly because I didn't understand why it had shifted. "Well, there can't be two Ilaras on this planet, or any other. I don't think the universe could handle it." I added a half-hearted chuckle when he didn't laugh.

"No. I don't think it could," he continued in the same pensive tone.

"So what are we going to do with your pretty girl? The same thing you like to do with all your pretty girls?" I smiled, still trying to earn a smile back.

Dolpheus lay back down. "What do you think we should do with her?"

"I don't know. It's a bad situation. She's innocent, with no fault in any of this. She's a victim of circumstance."

"Victim or not, you know we still have to do something with her."

I let more time pass than a courtier would think permissible in polite conversation before answering. "I know we do." I didn't like it, but it was still the case.

"We can't just let her loose. She'll expose us. If your father were to find out that we, of all people, broke into his lab, I can't imagine what kind of fury he'd direct at us."

It would be ugly. Of that we could be certain.

"And even if she doesn't know who we are now, she's likely to figure it out in the future and tell on us then. But even if she doesn't figure out who we are, if she just tells your father that two men broke in, forget any chances of getting back into the lab to secure Ilara's return," he said.

"She'd tell on us whether or not she knows who we are. Why wouldn't she? She owes us no loyalty."

"Is there something we could say or do that would convince her to keep our secret? Because that's the only thing I can think of that would work at this point. If not, we can't return her to the lab until you've been able to bring Ilara back. And even after, who'd want to deal with your father's wrath? It'll become suspicious at work if she just disappears without reason and never returns. And it'd be equally suspicious if she were to die of unexplained circumstances. You know your father, no one is as paranoid. Even if we were to stage her death in such a way that no normal person would suspect our meddling, that doesn't guarantee that your father wouldn't."

"I don't want to have to kill her." The truth of it was that I *really* didn't want to kill her. I'd killed many people and creatures. It was a necessity of our way of life. We were soldiers. Soldiers killed for good—and sometimes bad—causes. It was how it had always been. But I remembered every single death.

"I don't want to kill her either," Dolpheus said.

"So how can we persuade her that it's a good idea to keep quiet?"

"We have to convince her that it's her own idea to keep quiet. If not, she could be swayed once she's out of sight. It has to be something that she wants to do on her own."

"All right then, renowned ladies' man. How can we make her want to share in our secret? Should you work your magic on her?"

I got a smile from him with that, although it was only a

half one and it lacked its usual depth of sincerity. "As if you didn't have your own reputation as a ladies' man. Just because you swore off all other women after you came together with Ilara doesn't mean that you're not equally capable of wooing our captive."

I could argue with him, but what would be the point? He was taking all the fun out of our usual banter. "And if we tell her the truth to start and see how she takes it?"

"We could do that. I don't know that we've ever begun with the truth in situations like these. Perhaps it could work just because it's different."

"Should we try to get her away from here before she wakes?" I asked. "Or just wait?"

"I don't think we have any choice but to wait. Anything else is too dangerous. Given her behavior from earlier, which we can't blame her for, I don't think we can rely on calm composure from her if she wakes in the middle of transporting with the same two strangers that knocked her out and tied her up to a tree."

"We could travel as the rest of Oers do, without transporting." I let the thought hang out there, waiting to see if one of us would think it a good one.

"We could," Dolpheus said in a voice that made it clear that we shouldn't. The bulky flying machines were so much less convenient than transporting. They were far too visible and far too slow to suit us. Besides, they all had to be registered with the Royal Mobility Office before they could tap into the power they needed to fly. Even if we were to borrow someone else's flying machine, it would still be tracked.

"So we wait," I said.

"We wait."

I was finally warm again. I didn't mind waiting, sprawled out on the grass in the sunshine.

I'd overheard enough information about splicing from my father that I might be able to interest the King. But what my father had spoken was far from a complete picture.

The woman tied to the tree, however, would know quite a bit more about splicing than we did. Maybe she was as much a blessing as a complication. A guy could hope.

22

WE HAD TO WAIT FOR OUR CAPTIVE TO ROUSE FOR quite a long time. Dolpheus hit her on the head squarely, in the exact spot necessary to achieve the result he was after.

We lay in much the same positions as we had before, sprawled atop the wild grasses. When the Suxle Sun began to dip, I put my shirt back on to ward off the chill of oncoming darkness, but I didn't bother with my jacket. The darkness wouldn't last long. Within the hour, the Auxle Sun would rise. It wasn't as bright as the Suxle Sun (which was why most citizens of O chose to sleep during the reign of the Auxle Sun), but it was warm enough.

The Suxle Sun was setting with its predictable splash of fluorescence. The colors were never precisely the same—my favorites were the purples and reds, which made the sky look as if it were afire—but I could always rely on the fact that the display that washed across the sky would be stunning. There were some things that were no less arresting because of their frequency. I didn't imagine I would ever think the sunset anything less than miraculous, and I wasn't one to believe in miracles.

When the wild oranges and reds pulled me away from my worries, and I'd nearly forgotten about my father's splicing empire, the King's unreasonable requests, and a captive for whom we had no good solution, Dolpheus spoke. He sounded so much farther away than he was, laying a few feet away from me. "What if we found a way to erase the woman's memories of encountering us?"

I didn't answer right away. It was another thing we'd never tried before. We wouldn't even consider it under different circumstances. It was a day for new things. But I wasn't sure it was the day for this new thing.

"It must be possible," Dolpheus added.

"I imagine it must. But just because something is possible doesn't mean we should do it."

"It would solve our problem. And we wouldn't have to hurt the woman that neither of us wants to hurt."

"It might solve our problem, true. But we might turn the woman's brain to mush. You're suggesting that we extend ourselves into her brain so we can modify it, as we attempted to do with the force field, right?"

"Yeah. Something like that."

"And if we mess up? Which is very possible since we have no certain idea how to achieve an erasure of just a few memories. It'd be dangerous for her, and possibly for us as well. If our minds were to link with hers? Or if our minds were to become confused, intertwined with the thoughts and patterns of another?"

"I don't know what would happen. I've never heard of anyone doing it before."

"Exactly. There must be a reason for that. I imagine that someone like the King, or my father, wouldn't be burdened by scruples to keep them from modifying the minds of others, but even they don't do it."

"That we know of," Dolpheus said, and I couldn't argue his point. We'd navigated the world of the powerful and elite enough to understand that someone somewhere was willing to try it—whatever it might be—as long as it was forbidden, dangerous, and descended the winding path from morality into immorality. If wealth and power were bartered effectively, there was always a willing party.

One of the character traits I admired most about Ilara was her desire to do things differently than other royals. She was one of them, the wealthy and powerful. She was at the pinnacle of the pyramid of the elite. She could do almost whatever she wanted with complete impunity. Yet she didn't. She had a clear sense of right and wrong, and she was mindful to make decisions that aligned her with the ethical side of that dividing line.

The sudden rousing of our captive distracted us from further analyzing Dolpheus' desperate and dangerous proposal.

I'd heard groans like hers many times before. No matter who the person was, they all emitted a similar sound when first waking to discover that an aching, throbbing pain overwhelmed their bodies. There was a particular tone to the groan, a lament that the pain was such as it was.

"Here we go," Dolpheus muttered under his breath as he

prepared to rise. I sighed audibly and moved my legs under me to stand. I wasn't any happier about the situation than he was. To think we'd almost escaped without any problems, and now, this.

We watched her as we approached, and observed her transformation: from confused to alarmed. First her features registered the throbbing pain at the back of her head, then she realized she was tied to a tree with her mouth gagged and no hope of breaking free of either restraint, and finally, that her captors were two armed strangers, confident and strong. Her eyes were wide and her breathing heavy, waiting for whatever would come, knowing she had no real control. I could imagine some of the thoughts that were running through her mind.

"It's all right," I said when we reached her. "We have no desire to hurt you." I spoke in soothing tones much like the ones I used when I approached wild horses. I had a perfect record of breaking wild horses. With enough persistence, most things broke, eventually.

"I'm sorry I had to knock you out," Dolpheus said. Her eyes revealed that she didn't trust us. "But we really mean you no harm."

"We'd like to talk with you and explain our situation. Perhaps you'll understand why we've done what we have," I said.

Her jaw hardened, even around the gag. Her nostrils flared.

"Look, we don't want you tied up and gagged. But we have to be certain that you won't expose us if we unbind your mouth," I said.

So much for the effect we'd hoped to have over the woman. She didn't seem persuaded by us. Women usually reacted to us better than this. But they also weren't bound.

"All right then. It's your choice," I said. "Whatever you choose, you'll still have to hear us out. If at any time you decide that you'd prefer to continue listening in greater comfort, just let us know. If you don't scream, we'll untie your mouth. If you don't run, we'll untie you from the tree." For some reason I couldn't explain, I felt the strong urge to continue. *If you believe us, we'll set you free. If you want to join us, you can. If you want to help us, we'll accept the help.*

The woman didn't seem one bit open-minded, but we began anyway. I didn't feel good about overruling her will, but there was no other way.

I didn't know what we should say to her. We hadn't bothered to strategize about the best explanation to sway her to our side. There were some things that weren't helped by premeditation. When interrogating a war prisoner, an intruder, a rebel, or a woman that happened to work in my father's lab, the most effective path was the same. You began at a benign point in the story, and then you continued as your instincts guided you, constantly modifying your story in response to the emotional cues of your captive. Even tied and gagged as the woman was, her facial expressions and her general body tenseness would guide us as to when to continue, when to back off, and when to take a different turn entirely.

I suppose it was to her credit that, in the end, what I told her was the truth.

23

I HADN'T INTENDED TO TELL HER WHO I WAS; there was a chance she might not know. But when I did tell her, she didn't act surprised. Either she'd known, or she was far more disingenuous than we suspected.

There came a time in the storytelling to our audience of one when the impact of having taken this woman hostage hit us more fully: There was no way we could free her to do as she pleased. The only way that we could let her live was if she would keep silent. And the only way we imagined she might keep silent was if we swayed her to our way of thinking.

I was trying very hard not to think of the woman as a person that I might like, as someone that might have a nice laugh and maybe a family waiting for her at home. I think Dolpheus was doing the same. I noticed how he avoided our captive's eyes.

I didn't consider it particularly fair that we were contemplating the necessity of killing one woman to return another one to O.

On Origins, it was generally accepted that the life of a member of the royal Andaron family was worth more than that of any other. If our cause were judged, we'd be justified in taking the life of one ordinary citizen to protect the life of a royal. In the history of O, this had been the case many times, and never was blood shed as profusely in the name of the Andaron line as when it first claimed the throne, waging a war to secure its power. It was before my time, but the legends of those battles tell that there were days toward the end when justice came down swiftly and upon great numbers. Blood colored the streets around what was the house of rule then. Those streets were mostly demolished later, to make way for the construction of the royal palace that stands now. Still, there are places where, if you know where to look, you can still discover bloodstains that haven't washed away in thousands of years.

An understanding of how many might have died for the cause of royal welfare did nothing to make me feel better about the woman bound to the tree. She wasn't a soldier. She hadn't knowingly taken on the risk of her life by showing up to work today. Her eyes were those of an innocent, or else she put on a good show. Either way, she wasn't a captive of war, yet the circumstances forced us to treat her as one.

We continued with our story, both Dolpheus and I avoiding her searching eyes as much as we could, wondering if she had realized the crux of her predicament. If she had, then she would know that the only way to get us to let her go was to convince us that our secrets were safe with her. But if she knew this, then we couldn't trust what she said. And the only way to know whether someone spoke the truth was to look into her eyes.

I told her what I could, with Dolpheus chiming in to fill in the story. We told her we were on a mission to help the King while omitting that I was also on a mission to help myself. Most Oers were loyalists by their nature, taught from the beginning to revere whoever wore the crown. But this woman worked for my father. When I told her we'd been asked by King Oderon himself to break into the lab, she didn't seem as impressed as I'd hoped—and I just admitted to being a son willing to betray his father for the crown.

Dolpheus approached the woman. "I'd like to untie your mouth. As we've told you many times, we don't want to hurt you and are as unhappy with your captivity as you are. Are you willing to speak with us to attempt to find a solution to our little problem here?"

The woman hesitated, then nodded, wide-eyed, with eyes that either held or effectively impersonated innocence.

"Do you promise not to scream?" Dolpheus asked, although it was a promise he knew she might not keep. Yet we were far enough away from the lab that if she were to scream, it was unlikely to draw my father's security. The walls of the facility were thick, and all windows were closed. Knowing father, he probably never allowed them to remain open. When I was little, and he still behaved as a father should toward his son, he'd advised me never to speak of something private next to an open window. You never know who might be crouching under it, he'd said.

The woman nodded again, this time more enthusiastically.

"All right. Bend your head forward."

The woman wavered for just a second before she bowed her head to the man who'd struck her with the hilt of a knife last time she exposed the base of her skull to him. Dolpheus made quick work of it.

The woman moved her jaw, up and down at first, then side to side a few times. Surely, it was sore.

I stood next to Dolpheus. I smiled, attempting to express the appropriate measure of strength so that she'd cooperate.

"I really am sorry for this. We've never gagged and tied a woman to a tree before." I hoped she didn't realize why I specified to what she was tied. There were women who chose the path of soldiers, especially among the rebels in the wild deserts. It wasn't the first time we'd tied a woman up, nor the second. It was, however, the first time we'd done so outside of the terms of military engagement.

Her eyes didn't appear particularly forgiving. Still, she hadn't screamed.

"What's your name?" I asked.

She hesitated a moment too long. "Lila." Her voice was rough from the gag.

Dolpheus smiled at Lila (or whoever she really was), and Lila turned her gaze toward him and seemed to soften. I took a mental step back and let Dolpheus take charge of the show. A lot depended on our persuasiveness. It appeared that Lila found Dolpheus more convincing than me.

Dolpheus and I had been a team for a long time. He felt the shift in tides as easily as I. He took a step closer to Lila, leaving me a step behind. "Hello Lila." He smiled at her, a real, genuine smile. She smiled back. It was a timid smile, but it was progress.

"I'd like to untie you all the way, if you'll remain to speak with us," Dolpheus said. "We bound you only because we wanted a chance to explain our position before you reacted. We wanted you to understand that we're not bad guys"—But were we good ones? I wondered—"before you made any decisions. Would you like me to untie you?"

"Yes." Her voice was already softer, after just two words.

It didn't seem as if Lila was deceived by our casual stances. No matter whether our hands were at the ready to draw our swords or not, we looked like soldiers. I was starting to get the feeling that she was as astute as we were, I just didn't know from where the feeling was coming.

Dolpheus made the unbinding of her seem somehow sensual. I watched every one of his steps, and yet I wasn't certain what it was he was doing that made the motions of untying knots and unwinding ropes seem this way. But I sensed it, and it was obvious that she did as well.

I took another mental step back to allow Dolpheus to do his thing whether he was doing it intentionally or not.

Once he finished untying her, Dolpheus offered her a hand. She paused to consider for only a moment before taking it. He led her away from the tree, thus putting physical distance between memories of our treatment of her. He took a seat and pulled her down with him. He bent a leg so that they very nearly touched, knee to knee.

I took my seat a few feet away from them. I stretched my legs out in front of me. I was closer to them this way, but not close in any way that would interfere.

"Lila," Dolpheus began, "you've heard us speak for a while now. There's more that we could share with you if you'd like. But first, do you have any questions for us? Or is there anything that you'd like to say?" My friend's voice was soothing. It was calming even my own fraught nerves.

"Is he really Lord Brachius' son?" Though she spoke of me, she didn't spare me a look.

"Yes. He is. Although I believe it's been some time since Lord Brachius remembered that he has a son."

I cringed inwardly at the blunt truth of his statement. I was a private person. I rarely shared glimpses of my personal life. I had to trust Dolpheus now. Whatever he said would only be because he felt it necessary to secure this woman's cooperation. If it led to Ilara, I had to bear it.

Dolpheus continued, "Lord Brachius thinks more of splicing than of his son."

Lila flicked a glance toward me now. It was a fast one, too quick for me to see whether it held pity.

"Lord Brachius has shared little about his splicing with Lord Tanus, which is why we had to break into the facility to attempt to secure the information the King required of us. As you know, it's a crime to deny the King a direct request."

"And why did the King ask you to do this, if Lord Tanus wasn't in possession of the details of splicing?"

I didn't mind that they were speaking of me as if I weren't there. I was listening to every inflection of what they said. Lila was intelligent. Dolpheus would have to offer her most of the truth to convince her. She'd find the lack in logic in our story if not.

"Because he's holding something over us."

She leaned forward nearly imperceptibly. This was a believable motivator for our actions. Trade when one had something another wanted was the way things had been done for ages. Power and information were more valuable than sand.

"Blackmail?" she asked.

"No. He has something we want. Something that shouldn't be bargained with, but that he's bargaining with, nonetheless." Already, what Dolpheus had said was dangerous, not just because it led directly to the question of what —or whom—did the King have that we might want, but also because it was dangerous to speak ill of the King, and Dolpheus was coming close to doing it. The King didn't have ears here. But Dolpheus was giving Lila one more thing that could be used against us. On purpose. I waited. Dolpheus was a master at what he did.

He waited a few beats, long enough for the questions to mill around within Lila. "He has information on someone we care about deeply. We can't hope to rescue this person without the King's cooperation."

"Who is it?" Lila whispered.

Dolpheus looked to me, but it was for mostly theatrical purposes. "I'm sorry. I can't tell you yet. Perhaps I'll be able to once we're certain we can trust you. But you see, telling you would risk the person we wish to save. And it might also put you further at risk. We already lament having had to involve you at all." Another pause. "Only the two of us know of our mission." A final pause. "And the King."

"I see. And the King wants information about splicing? Is that what he desires to trade for?"

Dolpheus nodded with the calm of a man who knows what he's doing and surrenders to the inevitable results. "It is. I'm sure you must know that Lord Brachius wants the throne. That he's the one behind the assassination attempts."

She didn't bother to deny what he said although the King hadn't been able to prove it.

"If Lord Brachius were able to stage a successful coup, the courtiers would turn their favor his way. They're all, or nearly all, clients of Lord Brachius. The insurance that splicing can afford the courtiers appeals to their vanity. He holds power over the courtiers, and the King knows this."

"Does the King wish to forbid splicing? To abolish the practice?" Lila asked.

It was a question I hadn't asked myself yet. I hadn't questioned what the King wanted because what I cared about was Ilara.

"I don't know. He didn't tell us," Dolpheus said.

For the first time since Dolpheus brought Lila to sit next to him, she looked away, into the thickness of the trees. Several minutes passed while Dolpheus waited. Then, she seemed to reach some sort of decision. "If you tell me the whole truth, I may help you."

This startled Dolpheus though he hid it better than I did. But Lila wasn't looking at me. She was staring into his bright brown eyes. Even for Dolpheus, this was fast work. "Why?" he asked.

"I have my reasons. I'll share them with you if you convince me that I can trust you."

"But how do we know we can trust you?"

"You have to trust me if I'm to trust you."

He nodded. "I understand." Then he looked off into another section of the forest, coming to his own decision.

When he began, I knew it was the complete truth that he'd decided to share with her. There was no way to imitate the whole truth. A person could always tell when a story was incomplete—if she really looked, listened, and sensed what was being spoken. Dolpheus couldn't withhold the truth now. Not even a master could weave a lie or a half-truth well enough for it to resound with the solidity it required to convince an astute audience.

I hoped then that Lila would prove herself worthy of the truth, of Ilara's secret. Because if not, we'd have to kill her. We'd have no choice. I didn't know whether Lila realized this as Dolpheus began. I also hoped that whatever she had to trade would be enough to win me favor with the King and bring me one step closer to bringing Ilara home.

24

WHERE I WOULD HAVE DRAGGED OUT THE BIG truth bomb, building suspense, making Lila really want it, perhaps even wait for her to offer something concrete in return for it, Dolpheus did the opposite. My two most consequential secrets were out in the open, hovering in front of a stranger.

She looked at me, with round eyes, eyebrows arched in surprise. "The Princess lives? And you two are lovers?" It didn't sound as if she didn't believe Dolpheus. But it did seem as if she hadn't expected it, especially the second part. I did my best not to mind the tone of her voice that exposed her incredulity that Ilara and I should be lovers.

Why shouldn't we be lovers? Granted, I wasn't a descendant of one of the aristocratic bloodlines that had existed for as long as the Andaron Dynasty. But wasn't marriage of a royal within certain repetitive bloodlines a bit outdated? As much as I might question my father's splicing empire, its exorbitant wealth did buy me the prestige that might make me a worthy match to a princess, or at least as worthy as anyone else. Certainly more so than those pompous, costumed courtiers who looked like women as much as men with their makeup and wigs.

And I was handsome enough. Perhaps women didn't turn their heads to watch me pass as they did Dolpheus, although I thought the attention he received was due to more than his looks, though I hadn't yet been able to understand the complete reason for it. I could stand my own ground, even next to Dolpheus. So why was Lila so surprised?

I kept silent although she'd asked me direct questions. I figured they were rhetorical enough that I should remain quiet. I didn't trust what I might say. Now more than before, we needed to sway her to our side. Much depended on it, including her life. She would have to prove worthy of this confidence and quickly. I knew Dolpheus had the same in mind even if he concealed it well.

We waited for something to happen in relative darkness. It wouldn't last long. Soon, the Auxle Sun would rise. This sun was a reddish orange and more muted than the Suxle Sun. It transformed the plainness of the sky with spectacular shades that most missed in their beds with blackout shutters.

Nothing really happened in the end. "Well, that's something," Lila finally said.

"So do you realize now why we had to break into the lab? And why no one can find out about it?" Dolpheus asked.

"I imagine the King holds information on how to find his

daughter. But what about breaking into the lab? Is the secrecy just to prevent Lord Brachius' fury? Because surely he would be furious."

"It would be nice to prevent Lord Brachius from venting his rage upon us." Dolpheus treated Lila to a smile that invited sympathetic collaboration. "But it's more than that. Lord Brachius can't find out that we've been in the lab because if he knows, he'll make it nearly impossible for us to break in the next time."

"A next time? I thought the splicing facility was already supposed to be impossible to break into."

Another endearing smile. "Tanus and I have a different definition of impossible than most people."

"I guess so." Lila's attention had returned fully to Dolpheus. I would have to congratulate him later. He was smooth; I couldn't deny it. I wouldn't have accomplished this as quickly.

It took a moment for Lila to abandon whatever thoughts were responsible for the devilry she didn't hide. Then, "And why exactly would you want to break into the lab again?"

"Because it's the only way to bring the Princess back here."

"Why?"

"Because the King sent her off planet."

Lila looked genuinely startled, more than she had since she first ran into me. "He sent her off planet?" She spoke softly, making me realize that this was more outrageous than I'd earlier thought.

Obviously, Dolpheus was reevaluating his thoughts on Ilara's removal from Planet O as well. He was watching Lila carefully; his subtly seductive coyness was momentarily gone. "He did."

Lila whistled. "Wow. No wonder you need my help."

I hadn't thought we did. I'd thought that we only needed her silence. But if she was offering....

"Are you willing to give us your help? Because we would really appreciate it. The Princess would really appreciate it."

"Hmmm. Perhaps. Tell me more."

What choice did we have? I'd thought we were in control. Yet we kept doing what she, our captive, asked of us. Dolpheus would have to tell her everything now that she'd dangled an offer to help us.

As he continued with our story, I wondered who was playing whom and wished what I hoped was not a fruitless desire: that no one was playing anyone at all.

25

DOLPHEUS POSSESSED MY TRUST; HE'D EARNED IT a hundred times over. I let him continue alone with all the telling while I did nothing more than edge closer to the two of them. He'd already revealed the biggest of my secrets. There wasn't really that much of substance left to tell. But he would find something to share that would satisfy Lila.

"Tanus and I have been searching for the Princess for more than three years, since we first learned that she'd been supposedly murdered by Lord Brachius' assassins."

Lila didn't flinch at the implication of wrongdoing that Dolpheus attributed to my father. "And how did you know she was alive? Did she contact you? Did you see her?"

"No. Tanus felt her alive. But he received no external confirmation of this until quite recently."

Lila turned sharp eyes on me. "How did you feel her? How could you possibly know that she was alive and not dead?"

I understood from her question that she'd never loved as

I did. She'd never experienced anything like what Ilara and I shared, or she wouldn't need to ask. "I just feel her, right here." I placed a hand over my heart where the longing and aching hadn't ceased since Ilara's disappearance. "I know she's alive because I can feel her alive within me." I hadn't meant to be so sentimental. Ordinarily, I wouldn't have been with anyone except perhaps Dolpheus. I had a reputation of strength to preserve. This woman would either keep the secret of my heart or take it with her to a grave that would likely be very near to where we were now sitting.

A wistful look flickered through her eyes before it disappeared entirely. It seemed that she too had an image of herself that she wanted to preserve. But I was glad that she'd revealed this glimpse into herself, however fleeting. It gave me hope that the truth—her version of it—might be close to the surface. We would deal in truths all of us or we wouldn't deal at all. This was how the terms of circumstance had defined themselves.

Lila turned her face back toward Dolpheus, who was tracking every one of her moves and inflections. She nodded. Go on.

"We searched the palace immediately after the attack. When we found nothing there, we searched everywhere within the royal city, looking for a hint, a rumor at least, that she'd survived."

"How did you get into the palace? I heard that the security at the royal palace was at the time even more strict than usual."

"It was. But we got in. Tanus is considered a courtier, through the wealth and prestige of his father. Tanus has never sought the King's favor, but the palace guards know better than to turn away any courtier without just cause. The King relies too greatly on their contributions to risk offending any of them unnecessarily."

"But Tanus is Lord Brachius' son, and Lord Brachius had just attempted to kill the King, after already killing the Queen and the Princess."

"Nothing was ever proven. Anyone who's familiar with the political environment of Origins right now suspects that Lord Brachius did it. Even the King does. But no one's been able to prove it. Lord Brachius is a cunning man."

"That he is." Suddenly, she sounded resentful of this fact. I watched Dolpheus perk in anticipation, just as I had. If my father wasn't in Lila's favor, then our odds had just improved greatly.

"When we found nothing within the royal city to indicate that the Princess had survived, we turned outside of it. We ventured into the wilds of O, looking everywhere."

"Even in the deserts? Even among the rebels?" Lila was impressed although she seemed to be trying to hide her reaction. The wildernesses of O had earned their reputation as harsh and unforgiving places. Once the lushness of the residential areas that surrounded the royal palace faded into barrenness, either the land killed you by denying you what you needed or by giving you more than you could take of its pummeling. And if the land itself didn't do it, the rebels would. They were as hardened as the parched dirt of the outlying deserts. They had to learn to survive where no one else could. It was either a fool or a soldier ordered to go there that ventured into the wilds. Few returned.

"Even there, in the wilds," Dolpheus continued. "Yet we found nothing. Not a trace, not a whisper, not a single hint that the Princess had survived the assassination."

"Yet you continued to believe that she lived?" Again, her voice was soft, as if she realized that a deep love and the faith it engendered was worthy of awe.

"Tanus did." Dolpheus leaned farther forward, so that his face was only a short length away from hers. He was reading her cues. Her emotional response to my love for Ilara was an opening to gain her sympathy. "He didn't waver for a moment. He continued to feel her within his heart."

She didn't move or say anything, just proceeded to stare at Dolpheus, round-eyed. For a quick second, I almost felt sorry for her, our captive, that she hadn't experienced a love as fulfilling as I had. Yet she was young. She looked as if she had many more centuries ahead of her than she had behind her. Her skin was still dewy and supple with the vigor of youth.

"If the Princess wasn't anywhere within the palace, nor within the royal city, nor within its outskirts, or even as far as the wilds, then she must be off planet."

"But no one goes off planet, not hardly. Only the select few that can harvest the best sands and return them to O. And they're trained for decades before they're entrusted with these missions."

"Still, it was the only option left. Besides, it also made sense. It was strange that the Princess wouldn't have reached out to her lover after she escaped."

"How did she escape?"

"She wasn't in the palace when Lord Brachius sent the

assassins in to kill her and the rest of the royal family. But no one was aware of this but her lady servant, and the assassins killed her."

"Where was she?"

"In Tanus' bed. When she snuck back into the palace in the early morning hours, that's when she must've discovered what happened, and that's when the King must've found her. We began to suspect the King must've moved her off planet O. It was the only viable option left. Tanus and the Princess are able to speak to each other with their minds."

Another widening of those round eyes. Too few understood what we humans are capable of doing. Even someone intelligent as Lila seemed to be had apparently forfeited many of her innate abilities.

"Yet he heard nothing from her. Her arrival into the chaos of the palace, to discover that her mother was dead, with her father undoubtedly desperate to see her thinking her killed and then to discover her unharmed, was the only explanation for her silence. She would've needed calm and stillness to communicate with Tanus. She definitely wouldn't have had it."

I spoke up. "It would have been the wise thing to do, to protect her. The King couldn't have known whether there would be more attempts on her life."

"The Princess was likely whisked away in a flurry and sent off planet before she had time even to process what was happening," Dolpheus said.

"And the King would have wanted to conceal the fact that his daughter lived to keep her safe. If everyone thought her dead, no one would try to kill her. So he wouldn't have wanted to use the sand industry's off planet transport machines. Too many employees monitor their functioning. Besides, they're slow and arcane compared to Lord Brachius' technology," Lila contributed.

Lila was smart. I was glad we'd chosen to tell her the truth. She would have seen through our lies anyhow, and we would have forfeited any chance at earning her trust, which we apparently needed even if we hadn't realized it when we first took her hostage.

"Lord Brachius' facility would have been the only smart option for off planet transport. But how did the King get in? Certainly, he wouldn't have asked for Lord Brachius' help. He'd just sent assassins to the palace," she said.

"We aren't entirely sure whom the King sent to break into the splicing facility, nor how the person managed to do it. We assume that maybe this person had help, somehow. But we're not sure. All we do know is that this person no longer lives," Dolpheus said.

"The King killed him? Or her?"

"We don't know." Now Dolpheus turned to me.

"The King just said that he's the only one left who knows what planet Ilara is on."

"The King admitted that the Princess lives and is off planet?" Lila asked me.

"Yes." I didn't figure it would change our story if I mentioned that I'd broken into the lab once before to confirm this. So I reserved at least this one piece of information.

"And has he told you which planet she's on?"

"No."

"Do you know which planet she's on?"

"No. I can feel her alive, but I can't tell whence I'm feeling her. She hasn't responded to any of my prompts. I think, however, that if I knew at least which sector of the universe she's in, I could better pinpoint my mental signals and perhaps garner a response."

"Really?" Incredulity dripped from that one word. I ignored it. I didn't have patience with those who accepted limitations that existed nowhere beyond their own minds.

"To get a better idea of where she is, I need to give the King what he's asked for: information on my father's splicing procedures. If I'm able to deliver something good enough, I'll find out the name of the planet she's on, and then I'll definitely be able to communicate with her."

"And bring her back."

"Yes. Either way, I'll want to speak with her first. Perhaps she'll have something to say that will help us bring her back." I shrugged. "Any new information would be valuable at this point. I don't know what kind of life she's been forced to live all this time, away from us, from her home, from the planet she feels bound to protect."

"What kind of information has the King asked for?" A promising question from someone that might hold the treasure I could use to trade for my lover's life.

"He didn't specify. He said I'd know it when I saw it. Since no one outside of the splicing lab seems to know anything about splicing except for what its end result promises to be, I can only guess at what the King is hoping for."

"Hmmm," was all she said, and I had nothing more I

wanted to add just then. It was all out there in the open, laid out like an opulent feast in front of a stranger. Now it was her turn to choose what she'd do with my secrets.

She leaned back away from Dolpheus to think; at least, that's what it looked like she was doing. Her gaze was set on a point away from both of us, away from anything in particular.

The moments ticked away.

Finally, she spoke. "You couldn't have hoped to find much at the lab. Lord Brachius is extremely careful not to leave any trail of his methods or any records of the procedures that he's already performed. He's highly concerned that someone will steal his splicing secrets. You must have known that."

"We did," Dolpheus said. "We knew it wouldn't be easy, and that it might be a waste of effort."

"Yet you broke in anyway? Knowing you might be risking your lives for nothing?" This question was for me.

"We didn't risk our lives for nothing. We did so for love. Wouldn't you?" It was then that I thought we might have her, in that moment when she thought of what she might do for a love she hadn't yet experienced, perhaps never would.

After a pause, Dolpheus spoke. "Brachius must keep some records of his splicing methodology. All labs must to be able to progress with their work. If not, he'd have no way of knowing what precise circumstance affected the process for good or bad, especially if something unforeseen were to occur years down the line."

Lila would, of course, be familiar with the scientific method. "Is it the records that you need?" she asked.

"I don't think so," Dolpheus said. "The King asked only for something he would find useful."

Lila retreated into herself to think some more. Dolpheus and I let her.

Like a whisper of hope, or a tantalizing promise, or a tease of aid, her voice articulated the sentence we'd been hoping for.

"I possess information that the King will find useful."

26

Dolpheus and I stood before Lila, giving her our full attention. She rose from the stone she'd been sitting on to take a few steps toward us. She'd experienced the shift in power between captors and captive. She understood now that she had something we wanted. It seemed that she intended on wielding her power, and that perhaps she'd forgotten that we still posed a threat to her. Whether or not I liked it, I'd still kill her to protect Ilara if I had to. It might not be fair, but life wasn't often fair; I'd do what I had to do.

I wanted to ask her if she'd give us the information the King would find useful, but I held my tongue. I could see it all over her face, in the sudden vivaciousness of her features, the twinkling in her eyes. She planned to play a game with us. She didn't seem to realize that in the game of cat and mouse, no matter how clever the mouse was, eventually, the game arrived at an end, with the cat on top. I saw Dolpheus and myself as the cats, and we were strong ones. My sense of urgency to bring Ilara to me made my decisions more rash than usual. I was a cat looking for a reason to pounce.

Dolpheus must have been contemplating some of my same thoughts because he didn't ask the question she was waiting for us to ask of her either. He waited, and I waited. Neither one of us was particularly patient, but we knew how to play this game, now that she insisted on playing it.

She waited too. Finally, she tucked her chin toward her chest a bit, arched her eyebrows slightly, and smiled. "So, aren't you going to ask me whether I'll give you this information or not?"

I waited for Dolpheus. I wasn't in the mood for diplomacy, and gruffness probably wouldn't get us nearly as far as its opposite.

"I figured you'd tell us," he said.

She swirled her hips a bit in a flirtatious move that would have been more effective had she been wearing a dress and not a lab suit. "And do you want me to tell you?"

I looked at her, my face impassive, willing what I really thought of these childish games to remain concealed.

"I'm sure I speak for Tan in saying that yes, we'd very much like that. He's been longing for his beloved for a long time. It's important to him to return her to safety."

"Perhaps she's safer where she is than she would be here." She said this with a lightness that had the same effect on me as metal scraping against stone. I wouldn't be able to do this much longer. I'd been on edge since Ilara's disappearance. I hadn't snapped yet, and I hoped that I wouldn't, but she was pushing the wrong buttons right now, and it looked as if she had every intention of continuing without realizing how dangerous it was.

"Whether she's safer on or off of O depends greatly on where she is, which we don't know. However, it's clear that our planet would be safer with her back on it. The safety and well-being of all the citizens of Origins may depend upon her return."

"Hmmm," was all she said. She'd already shown herself intelligent enough to work out the reasons on her own. It was impossible to predict how rule under my father would be, but he was unlikely to put the needs of Oers over his own. Ilara, however, felt the need to protect Planet Origins coursing within her blood. If someone was to replace King Oderon on the throne, I'd want it to be Ilara, even if she weren't my lover. And if neither my father nor Ilara took the throne, Ilara's survival would reinforce King Oderon's rule. We'd all experienced his rule for centuries. Even though he wasn't as generous as I knew Ilara to be, he was more generous than my father. His rule had been mostly fair.

"So my helping you would be a matter of state?" She chuckled lightly and began to step back and forth.

"It would," Dolpheus said.

"What would I get in return if I decided to help you?"

I glared at her and didn't care if she noticed, which she didn't seem to. Why did people always need something in return? Why did they always think of themselves before the good of others? This seemed to be the prevalent attitude of Oers, beginning with the courtiers all the way down to the workers, although it was worse with the courtiers, those that had more than they needed. Greed and selfishness was as prevalent across O as any infectious disease. It repulsed me. There were times for looking out for oneself, and there were just as many times when that shouldn't be the priority.

I was grateful Dolpheus had insisted on joining me on this journey. I probably would have throttled the selfish look right off of Lila's pretty face by now.

"Your freedom," Dolpheus said, and by how he said it, I knew he was sharing some of my resentment.

Lila didn't like Dolpheus' answer. "What you've done here is wrong," she said. "You taking me by force was wrong. You should free me just because it's the right thing to do."

Where had her sense of absolutes been just seconds before, when she was willing to leave a princess, a woman, alone and abandoned on a planet that could be much more dangerous than our own?

"We didn't want to take you against your will. We really didn't. Our actions were forced. We've apologized for how things worked out."

Her look was suddenly petulant. I'd known enough women to understand that their moods could change quickly and unpredictably. But this woman changed faster than the weather on O.

"No, you haven't apologized."

"Oh? I thought we had," Dolpheus said. "I'm sorry, truly."

"As am I," I said. "We had no desire to hurt you in any way." I meant it, even though I didn't think apologies counted for much when we were still threatening her life. It seemed that she'd really forgotten this part. Just because our swords and knives were sheathed, we were no less dangerous. I once watched Dolpheus kill a mowab, the most ferocious of beasts, with his bare hands when they were the only weapon available to him.

She appeared convinced by the earnestness of our apologies and allowed them to appease her. "I will help you," she said a little too soon. She circled us in a languid walk. Her theatrics would have fooled only an amateur. Perhaps she was younger than I'd originally thought.

She returned from her jaunt to face us. "But you will have to allow me to return to the lab right now."

"We can't do that," Dolpheus said.

We couldn't. There was no chance that we would.

"They'll have noticed me missing by now. They'll wonder where I am and raise the alarm."

"Were you supposed to get off at the setting of the Suxle Sun?" Dolpheus asked.

Most work shifts were tailored around the paths of the two suns. The Suxle shift was eighteen hours long, three longer than the Auxle shift. Yet the Auxle shift was the less desirable one. It was shorter to make up for its lack of appeal; if not, no employees would want to work the shift that had most others sleeping.

"No. I was scheduled to work though to the setting of Auxle."

She was lying. It was reassuring to see that she wasn't all that good at it.

"So you were scheduled to work a double shift? Since we ran into you when the Suxle Sun was still up," Dolpheus said. A double shift would be nearly thirty-three hours long.

For obvious reasons, they were rare and mostly reserved for emergency situations.

"I was." She didn't meet our eyes, pretending to be interested in our surroundings.

"I see," Dolpheus said. "What will they do once they discover you gone when you're scheduled to work?"

She looked straight at him. "They'll review the security footage to see what happened to me."

She was lying again. I'd checked for the telltale signs that security recordings were underway. When a recorder was present, light reflected off its surface a bit differently than its surroundings. If you knew where and how to look, a recorder would be shinier than the surrounding wall, even if the wall itself was reflective. The surface of the recorder was made of a different material, and I could locate it, even if the differences that made it stand out were minute.

There were no recorders in the lab or the hallways. I'd made sure to check. I wasn't surprised by their absence even though most high-security places incorporated them into their basic construction. Father didn't like to leave a trail of his actions. He was more secretive than anyone in the royal family. He didn't risk the discovery of his many secrets. I knew little of them other than to know that he had them, and I was his son. There were no recorders in the splicing facility, just as there were no recorders in our house, not because he trusted others, but precisely because he didn't. He wanted no one watching him. He was assured enough in the security of his buildings to assume that no one could ever break into them. He didn't need recorders. He didn't want them.

Dolpheus knew all this as well as I did, but he didn't call her out. "Then I guess that's a risk we'll have to take. We can't send you back in there now."

"And why not?" Her tone was defensive as if she were a dear friend and we were betraying the trust essential to all good friendships.

This time, I chuckled. "Because we don't know that we can trust you." I said the obvious.

"But you can trust me!"

"How do we know that?" Dolpheus asked.

"Because I'm telling you that you can." Now she was angry.

What emotion would come next? I wondered.

"And why can we trust you? Why do you want to help us?" Dolpheus said.

"Because I want to see the splicing facility destroyed." She said this with convincing spite.

Finally, we were getting somewhere.

27

WOMEN COULD BE SOME OF THE MOST DANGEROUS of creatures—if they were the vengeful type, the kind that remembered a wrong as long as they lived. If you wronged this kind of woman, you needed to be on guard as much as if an enemy dispatched its assassins to kill you. The right type of woman—or the wrong type—would hunt you down to set right whatever she viewed as wrong. She was unrelenting in her fury.

No one told me this. I learned it on my own, from observing the dealings of angered women with others, before I'd made the mistake of offending one of these dragons myself. I could see from the fire burning behind Lila's otherwise ordinary eyes that she was one of these women. The kind with which you needed to be careful. The kind that it was easier not to befriend to avoid the risk of any misstep.

Lila hid it well. Nothing about her appeared to be extraordinary. Her face and body were modestly attractive, but I wouldn't have given her a second look if she weren't our reluctant captive. Still, even though nothing stood out about her at first glance, I was surprised my father hadn't recognized her potential for betrayal. He too was wary of women like her. Only a fool of a man wouldn't be. My father was many things, but a fool he wasn't. Perhaps he didn't know her well, an employee too far down the ladder to cross his path often. But even so, it was strange. My father didn't take unnecessary risks. It made more sense for him to personally screen every one of the employees that worked in his lab. Personality was as important a condition for employment as skill in science.

Something about Lila wasn't adding up, apart from her obvious lies. I just couldn't figure out what. I didn't know enough about my father's splicing facility to understand what within it would cause her to erupt like this. What about it was so terrible that she'd want to see my father's splicing empire crumble? We'd have to unearth what this was about, and we'd have to do so carefully now that we realized we were dealing with a dragon that would burn us as readily as she wanted to destroy my father.

"Why do you want to destroy the splicing facility?" Dolpheus asked the obvious question with admirable composure. He was cool as if he didn't care one way or the other whether she did or not.

Lila crossed her arms across her chest and pouted. It seemed that her grand statement of intent hadn't received the response from us that she wanted. "Because it's evil." She looked straight at us, defiance blazing in her eyes.

Neither Dolpheus nor I was about to contradict her, at

least not outwardly. Evil seemed like a strong word to describe my father's splicing empire. My father was a different man than he'd been when I was a child, before my mother left us in the middle of the night when I was eight, soon after my father made breakthroughs in splicing and foresaw the potential of fortune and ease for our family, something we hadn't yet had.

I have few memories of the time with my mother, some of them tinged with sorrow. I remember my mother crying, begging my father to do something which he wouldn't do. I never learned what. Still, although things hadn't been perfect between my parents, they'd been good enough from what I witnessed. I was shocked—and heartbroken—when she left us. I'd done my best to recover. But I didn't think my father ever did. After she left, he changed in a way that even, as a boy, I noticed. The change was slow and gradual at first, but then, at a point I can't define, he ceased to be the father I'd known to become the man he was now.

Still, he wasn't evil. Unsympathetic, unmerciful, and unyielding, yes. He was all of these things and more. But these characteristics weren't evil. I didn't trust in my father's ability to make good judgments, but he wouldn't create something evil.

Saying the splicing facility was evil was an accusation leveled at my father. Lila could have been considered either stupid or trusting for making this statement in front of us. My father would see her punished for it if he ever found out. Yet Lila had revealed enough of her true self already to indicate that she was neither stupid nor trusting. So what was she up to?

"Why do you think the splicing facility is evil?" Dolpheus asked. Yeah, tell us, I thought.

Lila hesitated, and I could see the reasons why scroll across her face. She wanted to tell us. A dragon woman desires to vent what she sees as her righteous anger. But Dolpheus and I outmatched Lila. If she told us what she knew, she gave up whatever leverage she had over us.

When she opened her mouth to speak, I wondered which of the two had won out: anger or prudence.

"Because of what it does to people."

Ah. So she was trying to compromise and walk the line between both.

"And what does it do to people?"

"It changes them." She looked away. She uncrossed her arms. Her shoulders relaxed. She might have chosen truth or at least some version of it.

"How does it change them?" Dolpheus asked. Was she going to make us draw it out of her question by question?

"Their personalities change."

"How?"

She looked at Dolpheus. "Lots of little changes happen, but it distills down to the person becoming meaner, less pleasant to be around, more prone to anger, more close-minded and less understanding." She shifted her eyes toward me. "I've noticed these changes in your father over the years. Haven't you?"

I nodded, slowly, hesitantly. "I have." She worked with him closely then.

"Didn't you ever wonder why he was changing?"

I wasn't prepared to talk about my father in this way. I

hadn't expected the conversation to turn in a personal direction. I wasn't embarrassed about revealing anything that showed weakness in front of Dolpheus. But I normally wouldn't in front of someone like Lila. I did anyway, and I didn't understand why. Maybe it was because we still might have to kill her.

"I thought it was because my mother left him."

"I wasn't working for him then. But I'm certain that his woman leaving isn't the reason for the person he's become. I work in statistics and record keeping, in the department that monitors all clients of the splicing lab. We monitor clients every three months. We check them out and probe from top to bottom. And I can tell you without a doubt that each time a person is spliced, a change takes place."

"A change in personality?" Dolpheus asked.

"Something like that." Lila's attitude had shifted. She now seemed earnest.

I allowed myself to believe what she was saying—for now, at least. I knew next to nothing of splicing. The information she possessed was worth sand, lots and lots of sand, if any of what she said was true. It would be enough to trade for Ilara.

"Their biorhythms are altered, although your father would deny this. Their bodily functions appear normal, but there's something different about them after they've been spliced. Nothing in the lab results will support this conclusion, but I'm sure of it. Each time we do a splice, we have to slow down the body's normal functions enough so that we can remove the eternality, which is a tricky thing to do. We can't do the splice with the eternality within the body. It doesn't work. If we split the eternality when it's still in the body, the body dies because a body can't survive without it. But if we remove the eternality, then we can split a piece of it off. When we reinsert the eternality back into the body, the body doesn't react as if a piece of it were missing. It reintegrates the eternality."

"Did my father experiment on people to figure this out?" I asked.

"Oh yeah. Lots of people died until he figured out that the eternality had to be removed for the splicing to be effective." Lila didn't seem bothered by this fact. "We experimented on rebels, so no one missed them when they died."

This didn't seem to be the part Lila considered evil. A pit of dread began to fester deep within my stomach. If experimenting on unwilling rebels and killing them didn't bother Lila at all, I didn't want to imagine how awful something would have to be for her to consider it evil. My stomach churned.

"To do a proper splice, we have to slow the body down so much that it enters a state of stasis. We lower the heart rate. We slow down the brain waves so that they're only active in maintaining the body's basic functions, those needed to keep it alive. There are no actual thoughts. We lower the respiration so that the person breathes only the minimum to maintain life. We fully express the intestinal system so it's free of any residue so that the body doesn't direct any energy toward digestion. You get the idea. We do everything necessary to slow down the body."

"Does it take long to do this?" Dolpheus asked.

"A few days. Once it's done, we have only three days to

do the splice and reinsert the eternality. Anything past that window, and the body shuts down anyway, even after we reinsert the eternality. If we miss the three day window to put the eternality back in, the client dies."

I wondered how many rebels it had taken to narrow the window of reinsertion down to three days.

"Is it complicated to do the actual splitting of the eternality once it's outside the body?" Dolpheus said.

"Oh it's very complicated. There's nothing more fragile than the eternality."

"How do you even take it out of the body?" I asked.

The look on Lila's face told me she was once again deliberating how much to tell us, even though it seemed that she'd told us enough that there was no point to withholding information any longer. "Very carefully," she said.

I wanted to hear more before she shut us out. Much of what she was saying rang true. My father had confirmed some of it with what dialogue I overheard in the lab. I prompted Dolpheus with a widening of my eyes when Lila turned her gaze away from us for a moment.

"Is the splitting of the eternality what causes the change in the person? Is that what you think?" Dolpheus cued her.

"I think so." She spoke these words as if her thoughts were far away. The words seemed ready to float off to join the rest of her, wherever she was.

"Is this splitting of the eternality evil, do you think?"

This snapped her back from wherever she'd gone. "Yes." Her eyes trained on Dolpheus. She was firm. Again, a wronged she-dragon, although I couldn't yet see how she'd been personally harmed. This sounded like a concern for humanity. But she obviously had no concern for the rebels they must have bought from bounty hunters that culled the wilds, looking for people as a miner looked for precious metal. So it couldn't be a concern for humanity unless her consideration of humanity were dependent on social class only. Yet she didn't seem to be of an upper class. Again, I realized we must be missing something. The picture she was painting was incomplete.

"Dividing the eternality, even if all we're taking from it is a minute fragment, causes harm. I don't know why exactly."

I couldn't understand how Lila didn't see why it would cause harm. Or why my father didn't either. It was obvious to me. You can't fragment what isn't meant to be fragmented. You can't split and splice an eternality that is meant to be whole, to be the source of energy that sustains a human life. Of course you can't do that. Of course it will cause harm. Of course the eternality is traumatized after that, and the person can never again be the same person as before. The eternality *is* the person. He isn't a piece of the eternality. He's the whole.

I supposed that my father must not have foreseen this eventuality because he didn't want to; he was astute enough to work through all the ramifications of any experiment. He must have overlooked this because doing so was the only way to move forward. Now, why he cared so much about splicing was a different mystery. Why did he need to extend natural life? Why did he find it necessary to do what whichever force had blown life into us had not?

Lila continued on her own. "The client is never the same

after splicing. I've seen it over and again. Although I seem to be one of the few ones at the lab that does."

"There are others that have noticed this?" Dolpheus asked.

"Yes. Although the others are too afraid to speak of it. Even I've never told anyone outside of the lab before now. Your father would crush us. He'd grind us into dust and blow us away himself if he discovered that we did anything to oppose his precious splicing. There aren't many of us who've noticed. It's mostly those of us that work in the monitoring of the clients. We see the changes in them. Most of them are courtiers so they're not particularly friendly with us to begin with. To them, we're servants, there to do a job for them, a job that they pay highly for. If they have multiple splicing procedures done, they get meaner to us each time. It's pretty obvious, especially now that we know to look for it. One of the courtiers, the one who's had it done eight times already, is nasty. I can't even do his check up. We do a drawing among the employees to see who has to deal with him each time. He's disgusting. It's awful."

"Is he evil?" Dolpheus asked. I was glad he was trying to peg why she'd insisted on that word.

She shrugged. "He might be. And there's something about his eyes that isn't right anymore. But Lord Brachius is the worst. He's spliced himself at least ten times—that I know of—and I have no idea if he did it more than that before I joined the staff."

I sighed, releasing sadness for my father I hadn't acknowledged in a long time. Why would he care about extending his life so much that he would ruin it? Was this what my mother had been begging him to stop right before she left? Had she seen what he'd been unwilling to look at?

"So why did you say the splicing facility was evil?" Dolpheus tried again.

"Because it is. It has to be. If you saw what I've seen, you'd agree. These people aren't the same they were when they began. They change. They become someone else. Maybe even something else. And whatever they become, it's evil."

28

MAYBE MY FATHER'S SPLICING FACILITY WAS EVIL. Even though Lila hadn't said it this way, there must be some consequence for altering things that aren't supposed to be altered. The eternality is so fragile, and yet so mighty as to control the source of life; it should have been guaranteed that nothing could be done to defile it.

Although I was the last one to talk of things being sacred, I believed that the eternality was something much better left alone. Already, with just what Lila had told us, I had enough to decide that the eternality wasn't intended for interference. It was perhaps the only thing within our bodies that should be left within it at all times—no exceptions.

Yet my father had found a way to remove the eternality and to extend life unnaturally through its removal, to prolong a life span that averaged a thousand years or so already. With splicing, a person could live indefinitely. A courtier could continue his relatively pointless existence as long as he wished. He could live long enough to comment on all the fashions that passed through the royal palace. He could live to wear his hair long and short, colored and plain, and hidden beneath wigs. He could make up his face in all sorts of shades to conceal the "evil" that was festering within the imbalance of his eternality.

I began to understand my father more. I began to suspect some of the reasons that might have caused him to reject his son, the only family he had left, and why after my mother took off he didn't search for her, the woman I believed he'd loved.

"You seek to destroy my father's facility?"

Lila blushed, and I found myself smiling at her, two unexpected reactions.

"Well, I hadn't thought I could do anything to destroy it myself until you both came along and kidnapped me. I knew something needed to change, but I didn't think I'd be the one to change it." Candor. "But when I realized that Lord Brachius' son had taken me, well, it occurred to me that you might be able to destroy it, with your friend. Both of your reputations are known to me. I think most of O probably knows of you and your victories. You could take down the splicing lab. You could keep this from happening anymore."

Dolpheus and I could—perhaps. However, taking on an industry that created a kind of race of immortal, evil humans hadn't been my plan this morning. I didn't know if I wanted to mess with the situation. I didn't always make noble decisions. I told you that, remember? My intentions were only to save Ilara. I wanted to save her mostly because I loved her, and it wasn't an easy thing to find the right woman to love. I wanted to share my life with her, with both of us on the same planet. Saving the rule of the Andaron Dynasty, while important, was a distant second to the real reasons I wanted to see her return. Restoring her purpose as protector of Origins was also important though I placed it on this second tier as well. Dismantling my father's empire didn't even have a tier right now. I didn't even want to think about it.

Dolpheus and I were soldiers, even if lately we'd become soldiers for hire. We weren't heroes. We had no interest in righting all the wrongs that were omnipresent all across Origins. Despite all things, my father was still the hand that fed me. I lived off of the fruits of splicing, even if I didn't know precisely what the process involved. My father might have abandoned me in the ways that mattered most to a son, but he'd always provided for my physical needs. Dolpheus and I lived on one of my father's estates, the one we'd chosen, without concern for our wants. We did mostly as we pleased.

"What you ask of us extends far beyond our mission," Dolpheus said.

"But you could still do it, couldn't you? You could stop this." Had Lila grown a conscience in the last few minutes?

"Maybe we could. But either way, we can't now. We need to find the Princess."

"You don't understand. It's worse than you think. I'm the one who looks into these people's eyes. It's not a good thing, not at all."

No, she hadn't grown a conscience that had a place for murdered rebels, I realized. It was fear that tinged her voice.

It wasn't strong, but it was there. Every good soldier knew how to detect fear.

"Have these people ever done anything?" Dolpheus asked, and I couldn't blame him for his inability to articulate the question. How did you ask if a splicing client had done anything immoral when courtiers held a general disregard for any life they considered more lowly than their own? Squashing, backstabbing, pillaging, taking what wasn't theirs, and even murdering were all part of their regular methods of operation, though they usually ordered underlings to do the more unsavory tasks.

"I don't know. They've never hurt me. But it's just not right. I'm telling you, it isn't right. It's evil."

"And you still want us to let you go back to the lab? Even after all you've told us?" I asked. Now that she'd shared some of the truth with us, there didn't seem much of a point to keeping up the ruse she was trying, not very artfully, to spin.

"If I don't go back, if I just disappear from the lab, your father will send people to look for me. And when they find me, they'll kill me."

I searched her eyes. I sought confirmation within brown irises.

"You don't know when you start there. The pay is good. We even get our bonuses in pure sand. The hours are good. No double shifts." She didn't even bother to cover the tracks of her previous lie. She must have realized that lies were pointless at this stage. "We even get vacation time. The work is interesting enough. Lord Brachius is a nightmare to deal with, but you get used to it. It takes a long while to understand what you've gotten yourself into. For me, it took years. But then, once you realize, you also see that there's no way out. You stay, or they kill you. Because the secrets we learn working there are more valuable to Lord Brachius than a human life. If his clients begin to question what he does, then splicing falls apart. They won't pay for something that makes them evil, even as greedy as they are."

Maybe. Maybe not. I knew most of the courtiers that made regular appearances at the royal palace. More than a few might think it worth the degradation to achieve immortality. Besides, I didn't think Lila realized how depraved many of the courtiers' practices were even before they began splicing themselves.

"So what's your idea?" Dolpheus asked. "You want us to send you back to the lab where you'll pretend everything is normal until we can come in and wage a battle against Lord Brachius and bring down the splicing industry?"

Lila didn't answer. She didn't have to. The fact that this had been her hope, and that she hadn't thought it very far through, was obvious from the appeal scrawled across her face.

Dolpheus turned toward me. For the first time since this all started, he really looked at me. We couldn't do what she'd asked. We both knew it. We couldn't send her back into the lab. It didn't matter that we might believe her story, at least the parts of it that rang as truth. We couldn't trust her to keep the secrets we needed kept. She was unreliable, and worse, now we realized that she was also scared. The instinct for survival forced most people to do things they wouldn't normally do, and this one had a blurry sense of right and wrong to begin with.

We didn't want to invade the lab. Maybe we'd revisit the dangers of splicing at a future time, but now we had other things to focus on.

Just looking at the resigned features on the face I knew so well, I recognized that we'd both come to the same conclusion. And it stunk. We couldn't set Lila free because her freedom posed too grave a danger to us. And matters had just gotten worse. If we couldn't let her return to the lab now, it seemed that we wouldn't be able to in the future either. We couldn't send her back in there at any point if they were going to kill her.

The information she possessed was highly valuable. Certainly, there was more of it than she'd shared with us. With a process as complicated as splicing, there had to be more details important enough to affect how Dolpheus and I would view matters and the decision it seemed we'd eventually be forced to make, one way or another.

All this boiled down to one depressing conclusion: We were stuck with her, a woman we didn't particularly like and certainly couldn't trust.

29

THANKS TO OUR UNINTENDED CAPTURE OF LILA, I had more than enough secrets of my father's splicing empire to trade King Oderon for Ilara's whereabouts. Undoubtedly, the King would be intoxicated by the discovery that my father's secrets were dirty—evil even, as Lila insisted they were. The King would relish the thought of what he could do with the information, how he could hold it over my father, just like any other bully. And what was the king if not a bully? He wielded power over his subjects by force. He wielded power over me by dangling something that I wanted right in front of me, just out of reach. This something was a someone sufficiently important to me that I could justify doing many otherwise questionable things to reach her.

Now, I had to decide how far I'd go to secure Lila's silence. "Dolpheus, will you join me in a private conversation?"

Lila looked a bit surprised that we should want to exclude her from our planning, and that amazed me. She'd surely proven that she was intelligent enough to put together facts and their ramifications to reach accurate deductions. She couldn't possibly believe that after all the instability she'd revealed to us, and just a day in our company, we'd include her as an equal partner of our team.

"You won't scream, right?" Dolpheus asked. He, too, had noticed the offended look on her face. "We're just going to discuss how we can make this work in the best way for everyone, you included. Our desire not to hurt you in any way continues. You'll wait here for us, yes? Quietly?"

Lila frowned a bit, but finally nodded her reluctant agreement. I was glad Dolpheus had said what he had. This woman appeared to be predictably unpredictable. She seemed genuine in her agreement to wait for us in silence.

Dolpheus and I walked far enough into the trees to make sure that Lila wouldn't overhear us, but not so far that we couldn't reach her if she were to decide to bolt after all. My friend and I stood side by side, eyes trained on the woman, hands on our hips.

"Phhhhh." Dolpheus blew out frustration. "That's one nutso woman."

"Right? I was wondering if you were thinking the same thing. She's all over the place."

"All over."

"We have to be careful with her. I kept thinking she was like a she-dragon. Like the wealthy women who are so petulant and horribly vengeful when they think they've been wronged."

He nodded, dark hair bouncing. "She *is* a she-dragon.

She breathes fire, and I have the feeling we've only seen a hint of what brews inside her."

"Well. Let's hope we don't have to see any more of it. I've seen enough to want to run far, far away from this lady."

"Me too. I wish we could."

I sighed heavily. "We're stuck with her. You realize that, right?"

"Of course. We're totally stuck with her. We can't send her back to the lab, no matter what she tries to convince us of."

"Agreed. No way can we send her back to the lab."

"And we can't just set her free either," Dolpheus said.

"No. She'd definitely talk at some point. Well, maybe not definitely, but it's certainly possible."

"Which leaves us two last options."

"Which are?" I asked.

"Either we kill her, or we're saddled with her."

"I don't want to kill her."

"Neither do I," Dolpheus said. "Until I think about what it's going to be like having her along with us for who-knows-how-long."

I groaned. "It's going to be miserable. And we have no idea how long we might have to keep her with us. None of the reasons for not being able to set her free are likely to change soon."

"Exactly," Dolpheus said. "Are you sure we can't just kill her and save ourselves the agony?"

I knew my friend well enough to realize he was only partly serious. We weren't the kind of people who'd kill without a thought as to what the action meant and without grave consideration of the finality of death. But neither one of us enjoyed complications that would disturb the relative comfort of our daily lives either, especially when they came in the female form. Dolpheus kept his trysts casual mostly to avoid the difficulties that inevitably came with attachment. This would be a change in lifestyle neither one of us would like.

"Think of it this way," I said. "Maybe something good will come from her continued company. We didn't anticipate that she'd be the source of the information we needed for the King when we first took her. Perhaps there's something still unforeseen in the future that'll be sufficient reason to put up with her."

Dolpheus huffed again, doing more complaining than I'd seen him do in a long while. "I hope so. Because I'm not looking forward to this."

"Hey, at least she likes you. She doesn't seem to like me much."

"I'm not sure her liking me is going to make things easier."

I chuckled. Dolpheus glared at me, which made me laugh harder. "Jerk," he said, and I tried in earnest to stop laughing. I didn't really want to upset my friend. I hadn't forgotten that he was in this mess only because of me. "So what are we going to do with her exactly?" I asked, trying to achieve seriousness.

Yet another sigh from Dolpheus, this one of resignation. "Well, we can't risk transporting with her. It's too dangerous. Even if she *is* one of the few who knows how to transport on her own, we still can't risk it. We have no way to ensure that she'll transport with us. While we're in the midst of the process, she could escape."

"Agreed. Transporting is out. And obviously we can't just set up camp here until things resolve themselves. We need to get away from here as soon as possible. The longer we stay in the vicinity of the facility, the higher our chances of being discovered."

"Where can we take her?"

"I don't want to take her to our estate. I don't want her meddling with our private lives any more than she already has."

"Okay. So where? One of the station cabins?"

"Yeah. Maybe. They're removed enough that no one'll be able to hear her if she screams, which means that we can leave her alone while we go away without having to gag her."

"We'll still need to tie her up though," he said.

"I think so too. One of the station cabins might be the place. Few people know about them."

"Your father does."

"True. But I can't imagine he's been to any of them in a long while. He doesn't take time out from the splicing to hunt anymore, at least not that I know of. And I doubt that he makes time to retreat into the forest for silence or meditation as he used to when I was a boy."

"Where do you think he goes when he tells his employees that he doesn't want to be disturbed?"

"I don't know. Home, I would guess. He has everything he needs there to ensure comfort. It's over-the-top private.

No one enters unless he wants them to. And the only person there with him is Aletox."

"And servants."

"Sure, but you know my father has no issue with ordering people to remain out of sight when that's what he wants."

"So which cabin should we go to? Which one is safest? The one in the western wilds?"

"Perhaps. That one's probably the safest. It's most removed from the trails the merchants use to trade with the rebels and wilderness dwellers. We'd have the highest chance of not being noticed by any wandering passerby."

"Then let's go there."

"Look at that," I said. "She's actually glaring at us right now." Lila's hands had come to her hips in imitation of us. She was staring straight at us.

"What do you suppose she's thinking with that she-dragon look on her face?"

"I have no idea, and that might be a good thing. Her mind seems to be an unstable and stormy place. Wait," I said. "I just remembered a station cabin that I'd nearly forgotten entirely. My father took me there only once when I was a boy. I haven't been back since, nor have I heard my father mention it. He took me fishing and we stayed there. If I remember correctly, it was pretty rudimentary. Less fixed up than the others."

"Which would make it perfect. I think your father enjoys his comforts now. He'd be less likely to go somewhere he has to rough it. At least, that's what I think."

"I hope I can find it. It was along the Gorgeene River, deep in the wilds."

"We won't be able to find it based on that. Do you remember anything more?"

I stared off into the distance, searching for the memory. Lila caught my stare and tried to hold onto it. I turned to look some place else knowing that Dolpheus wouldn't let her out of his sight. "I remember a big, flowing tree and an outcropping of rocks from which you could see far into the wilds on any side."

"That still won't help us much, Tan."

"No, Olph, I believe it will. I remember, the tree was huge. Really, really big. Bigger than normal trees."

"It might be down in the southern wilds then. The forests are thicker there, older."

"You're right. It must be there. Let's hope. We'll just have to be open to changing our plans if we can't find the station cabin."

Dolpheus nodded. A good soldier always kept an open mind, willing to shift tactics along with the tides of battle and life. Certainly, in life, there were no guarantees, not even in times of peace. Not ever.

"How will we get there?" Dolpheus said. It was a question we didn't often ask ourselves. There was no process more efficient and streamlined for any kind of travel across Origins than transporting.

"We'll have to use a flyer of some sort."

"Take one of those over there?" Dolpheus signaled with his head toward the employee parking lot that was behind the building, hidden from sight.

"That would be easiest." We could borrow it instead of steal it, and return it once we'd finished with it. "But it'd be noticed missing soon. That would raise alarms. No one should be out here that doesn't belong. The facility is too remote and its security too heightened to draw a common thief. It'd be better to take a flyer from somewhere else, closer to a main population center."

"So we walk? With her in tow?"

"I don't see any other alternative. We can't call a travel service. That would leave witnesses and all sorts of opportunities for Lila to cause trouble for us."

"Well, this ought to be fun. She's glaring at us again. She's been staring at us almost the entire time we've been over here talking," Dolpheus said. "Should we walk with her without securing her mouth?"

"You don't think she'll call out for help if we leave her as she is?"

Dolpheus deliberated. "No, I don't think so. She's too interested in the situation. Her desire to destroy your father's splicing facility isn't lacking in self-interest. I don't think it's just about her wish to rid the world of an evil, as she calls it. There's something more there. There has to be. And if she believes she might be able to persuade us to do her dirty work for her, she'll play along."

"All right. You have a good point. She doesn't seem like the generous, heroic type."

"Definitely not. She seems like the vengeful, kill-you-in-your-sleep type. That innocent face and those big eyes aren't fooling me."

"So we'll have to be alert. We can do that. And get rid of her just as soon as we can," I said.

"That very same second."

"Ready?" I asked.

"As ready as I'll be for this."

"Let's go."

We headed back toward our petite captive, dreading the upcoming travels more than any battle.

30

WE'D BEEN WALKING FOR HOURS, BUT THE HOURS seemed like days. The Auxle Sun would set at any moment, already kissing the horizon it would soon slip beneath. The sky was fluorescent. Grayish clouds stood out in contrast against its yellow, laying out a feast for the eyes. I was grateful for the distraction and the reminder that there were many things to be grateful for, even if Lila hadn't stopped talking except to draw breath since we first left the field across from the splicing facility.

If she'd been speaking of the splicing process, I might not have minded it as much; there would have been sufficient reason to bear it. But it was nonsense. She obviously didn't think so, attributing importance to seemingly anything that crossed her mind.

Dolpheus and I had traveled long distances thousands of times when the circumstances hadn't supported the efficiency of transporting. However, when he and I traveled across the land, we were mostly silent. Even with troops of soldiers under our command following immediately behind us, thousands of men didn't produce as much chatter as this one woman.

I would have blamed women in general, knowing they're more prone to talking than men. Yet not all women feel the urge to fill silence merely for the sake of filling it. Many people—both women and men—understand that silence holds value and can be an essential factor to maintaining reflection and inner calm.

Walking with Lila, half listening to her constant chatter, I wanted desperately to escape the barrage of sound, to shield myself from it; it was an assault. I wanted to hear the bird-calls and the rustling leaves of the ancient trees that spanned above us. I wanted to hear the wind.

I needed to be able to hear the calls of predators. No particular predator in this area of the forest was overly threatening to us on its own, but a pack could cause trouble. We wouldn't hear them until they were upon us. I couldn't hear my own thoughts.

"Can't we find horses to ride or something?" she was saying in a whiny voice that sparked renewed sympathy in me for parents worldwide. "My legs are tired."

"I'd imagine her mouth would be tired," Dolpheus said to me under his breath.

We didn't bother replying to her. We'd realized early on that she neither expected nor required answers from us. She'd continue whether we participated in the conversation or not.

"There must be horses around here somewhere that you can steal. Don't people ride horses anymore? They must. We should be looking for horses not just traipsing aimlessly through the woods."

Of course, we weren't traipsing aimlessly. We were cutting the most direct route we could, taking into account changes in terrain, toward the fishing cabin in the southern wilds. But we wouldn't be able to make it there on foot, not with Lila. The journey would take several days, and Dolpheus and I would either go mad from her drivel or kill her and regret it later. We were already looking for horses, or for any other kind of beast, that could carry us where we were going faster. The route we'd chosen would lead across horse ranches soon.

We weren't thieves despite Lila's casual assumptions that men of battle like us must be. We had principles of our own, and we kept to them—ordinarily. We didn't cause unnecessary destruction. And we didn't steal. Still, these were desperate times.

Finally, the Auxle Sun completed its journey below the horizon. Almost an hour of near darkness followed, when the only thing to dispel it was the purple light of the Plune Moon, dim in comparison even to the Auxle Sun, the least bright of Origins' two suns. The Plune Moon shone just enough to highlight dips and rises in the forest floor.

Dolpheus and I stalked quietly through the forest, avoiding roots and stones easily enough. Lila, however, who lacked the inner stillness necessary to flow with the forest, emitted a near constant litany of yelps, ouches, and ows. Dolpheus' soft chuckles reached my ears a few times, and I was surprised that he should enjoy someone else's misery. It wasn't like him. Lila must have pushed him to an edge he didn't often reach.

"You know," I said to her, and it wasn't the first time since we left that I made a suggestion like it, "if you just slow down and really see what's in front of you, you won't trip or hurt yourself as much."

"How do you expect me to slow down when you keep walking so fast?" she snapped.

"I don't mean for you to slow down your steps. I mean for you to slow down your mind."

"That's ridiculous. How will slowing down my mind help me see better in the dark? Ouch." She tripped, tromped loudly for a few steps, tripped again, then, "Besides, there's no way that I'd want to slow down my mind if that's what you two are doing. You're the dullest people I've ever met. You don't even talk. Haven't you ever heard of polite conversation? It's not polite to ignore people."

I was pretty sure she would change her mind about wanting us to speak if she had any idea of the effect she was having on us. For the first time since I met her, I wondered what could have made her the way she was. What was she masking inside with this outward aggression? Was it as simple as unhappiness? Did she make sure right from the start that people wouldn't like her so they wouldn't want to get close and potentially hurt her? What was it? No one was like this because they wanted to be. No one resembling her could like herself very much. Then I wondered, why would my father, a highly intolerant man, be willing to put up with her character? Perhaps her skill set was greater than we'd previously suspected. My father did everything with an ulterior motive. He'd need to have a very good reason for dealing with someone like Lila.

"There," Dolpheus said, the relief in his voice plain. I followed his outstretched arm to see where he was pointing. Finally, a horse ranch. When we neared it, Dolpheus said, "Lila, you'll need to be completely silent now."

"Why? And why do you think you can keep ordering me around? I'm not your captive anymore. We're partners. I gave you information that you'll be able to use to return the Princess. That counts for a lot."

That did count for a lot, but it certainly didn't make us partners. "Lila," I said in the unusual reversal of roles in which I had more patience than Dolpheus, "you need to be silent because we're about to take horses from that ranch, just like you wanted us to. But we'll be discovered before we can take any horse if you keep making noise the way you have been."

"You've been complaining about walking for hours. If you want to ride a horse, you can't make a sound," Dolpheus said. "Not one."

"Okay," she said. "Fine."

When we were near enough to the corral that we could make out each horse, we stopped next to a large tree that was capable of concealing Lila. I turned to her. "You'll need to stay here in absolute silence. Don't make a sound until we tell you that you can." I could almost feel the wheels turning in Dolpheus' mind, making a joke, or maybe a hopeful wish. We wouldn't tell her she could make a sound. Ever.

"Okay, I guess," she said.

"Horses spook easily," I continued, "especially when they don't know the people approaching them. If the horses spook, they'll make noise. The noise will rouse their caretakers. If the horses rouse their caretakers, we won't be able to take a horse for you. Do you understand?"

"Yes, I understand. I'll be quiet. Jeesh."

"And remain out of sight, behind the tree, just in case." I looked toward my friend. "Do you have paper?"

"No. Not even the reusable kind. I left everything I usually carry behind when we left to break into the lab."

"Damn. I don't have any either."

"Why do you need paper?" Lila asked.

"Because we aren't thieves, despite your opinions about us," Dolpheus said.

"We want to leave a note for the owners, so that they know we intend to return the horses, with compensation for their use," I said.

"Oh. Well then, I have paper. And a pencil. A good scientist is never without them." Suddenly, she was perky, the one thing she hadn't been yet, as she reached for an inside pocket of her lab coveralls. "Here."

"Thank you," I said and received a small notebook and pencil.

"You can just tear out a page."

"Great," I said. She peered over my shoulder as I wrote. I was certain she couldn't see a single word as I could barely see to write. The light of the Plune Moon was a deep and dark purple. I wrote anyway, making a point to write neatly to compensate for my nearly blind writing. I tore out the page and handed the writing implements back to her. "Thank you."

"You're welcome," she said, perfectly pleasant. Perhaps she was happy to discover that we weren't the rogue thieves she thought we were. Perhaps it was something else I couldn't fathom. Her emotions were a mystery too great to attempt to make sense of them.

"Remember, quiet and out of sight," I said.

"Yes. I remember. You only just told me, right after he'd just told me."

Dolpheus and I left her there, confident she wouldn't run while we were getting the horses; she wanted to ride so badly. And if she escaped, I suspected that neither Dolpheus nor I would mind too much, regardless of the risk that she might expose us.

Our approach was nearly silent. We'd trained as boys for eventual excellence in combat. A great part of that was being agile and light on your feet, able to take your enemy by surprise. Even in our boots, the sound of leaves and grasses being crushed was muted by the softness of our step.

When we drew close enough to the horses that they could scent us, we clung to the shadows to continue our approach. The horses were still dozing, beneath trees that had shaded them while the Auxle Sun was up. They rested during the rule of the lesser of the suns, just like humans, and hadn't yet started stirring at the upcoming day.

When the first of the horses looked up, searching for the disturbance he sensed in his surroundings, we stood from our crouch, slowly. We stepped out of the shadows. Then, we didn't move at all. We waited for the horse to find us. Once he did, we looked at him, doing everything we could to emanate calm. We're not a threat to you, I said to him in my mind, even though I didn't know if he would receive my message. You can trust us, I said.

After a long while, so long that I doubted if it would happen, the horse dipped his head to us. He did so only once, and only barely, but we got his message. We had his permission to approach.

We did so with infinite care. Our success depended on the horses' easy acceptance of us, which was a greater challenge than usual when we couldn't risk even a friendly sound from them or us. We climbed the fence to their paddock. Then we waited for them to adjust to us inside their safe zone. Once they had, we took a few steps toward them. We waited. We stepped. We waited. We stepped and waited until we were finally close enough to touch them.

I put my palm out flat for the closest one to smell me. It would have been easier if I'd had food. I didn't and had long grown used to making the most out of less-than-ideal circumstances. He sniffed me. I rubbed his nose. I ran my hand along his mane and his back. I nuzzled him with as much caring as I would a woman. He leaned into my touch.

When I turned my back and took a step away from him, he moved to follow me. I put my hand on his neck and led him to the gate and out the paddock. Dolpheus was right behind me. I wedged the note in the metal of the gate's hasp.

We walked with the two horses under the painted sky that cast everything in sight in an eerie purple. Bathed in that light, I experienced something strange that felt almost like a premonition. I was suddenly aware of the existence of other worlds, apart from O, but close enough to step right onto any of them.

We could link worlds, or we could part them. With faithum, we could accomplish nearly anything—when we believed.

Under this Plune Moon, the course of my life shifted.

All I had to do to reach another world was to step through one eerie purple reality into another.

What was coming? I wondered. Because whatever it was, it would change my life in a way that I couldn't now foresee. I knew it just as I'd known that Ilara was out there and that I'd find the way to reach her.

There are times when a certain outcome, a twist or turn of fate, finds you. And there's little you can do to hide from it.

Whatever was coming for me, I would greet it head-on.

A flurry of something—part excitement, part apprehension, part something else—fluttered through me. When I exhaled, it blew away on the purple of the night, the night that had changed something within me forever.

READ MORE BY LUCÍA ASHTA

THE WITCHING WORLD

Magic Awakens

The Five-Petal Knot

The Merqueen

The Ginger Cat

The Scarlet Dragon

Mermagic

Spirit of the Spell

MAGICAL ARTS ACADEMY

First Spell

Winged Pursuit

Unexpected Agents

Improbable Ally

Questionable Rescue

Sorcerers' Web

Ghostly Return

Transformations

Castle's Curse

Spirited Escape

Dragon's Fury

Magic Ignites

Powers Unleashed

PLANET ORIGINS

Planet Origins

Original Elements

Holographic Princess

Purple Worlds

Planet Sand

Holographic Convergence

Mowab Rider

THE LIGHT WARRIORS

Beyond Sedona

Beyond Prophecy

Beyond Amber

Beyond Arnaka

DRAGON FORCE

Invisible Born

Invisible Bound

Invisible Rider

POCKET PORTALS

The Orphan Son *

Huntress of the Unseen

A Betrayal of Time

Daughter of the Wind

The Unkillable Killer

Whispers of Pachamama

Immortalium *

(* coming soon)

For an updated list of Lucía's books, please visit her website: www.LuciaAshta.com.

ABOUT THE AUTHOR

Lucía Ashta, a former attorney and architect, is an Argentinian-American author who lives in Sedona with her beloved and three daughters. She published her first story (about an unusual Cockatoo) at the age of eight, and she's been at it ever since.

Learn about Lucía's books at LuciaAshta.com.

Printed in Poland
by Amazon Fulfillment
Poland Sp. z o.o., Wrocław